TRIGG COUNTY, KENTUCKY VETERANS

LEST WE FORGET...

TURNER PUBLISHING COMPANY

Dedication

Young men and women fight wars in the prime of their life. They set forth with courage, vision and dreams to solve world problems and to make our nation great, We sacrifice our young in international warfare, because they refuse to give up, even when facing insurmountable odds. For their service to our country and the price they pay for freedom, we honor and pay tribute to these heroes and heroines,

When the wars are over, soldiers return home and begin to rebuild their lives and make contributions to postwar America. Soon the battles, sacrifices and achievements become a distant memory.

Read this book and continue to draw inspiration from the military men and women who have inspiring stories of courage and faith. Their stories, military records and experiences will be with future generations after these soldiers are gone.

David Shore
President
Trigg County Historical and Preservation Society

Turner Publishing Company

Acknowledgments

There are many people who helped bring this book into being. All the veterans and family members who contributed deserve our thanks. The veterans' memoirs would not exist were it not for their courage and patriotism. We dedicate this book to them.

In the period of time used to gather this material, conduct interviews and collect photographs, we had invaluable assistance from all - young and old. Individuals, organization, churches, and businesses have supported this project.

From conception to completion, this book required many hours of volunteered work. We thank the following for believing in this book and for making it a reality.

Veterans Book Committee
Virginia Alexander, Betsy Carr Taylor - Co-Chairpersons
Stan White, Sandra Myers

With assistance from:
Nell Vinson, Tom Vinson, Barbara Shore, Ann McAtee, Elaine Sanders, Richard Pauze,
Mary Graham, David Shore, Larry L. Walston, American Legion Post #74,
Veterans of Foreign Wars Post #7890, Trigg County Senior Citizens Center, John L Street Library

The stories herein were written from the writers' memories. Some submissions have been edited due to space limitations. The Veterans Book Committee regrets any errors that may have occurred during the transition process.

Contents

Early Wars

PETER BATTOE, Soldier of the Revolutionary War (b. 1759), was a private in the British army and served with the King's Rangers. He was captured in the Battle of Savannah (GA). "Light Horse" Harry Lee (father of Robert E. Lee) marched the British prisoners to Ninety Six, SC. It was there that Peter swore allegiance to the American forces and enlisted in Lee's Legion on 9 Jun 1781. He served 18 months under Capt. Michael Randolph and Col. Henry Lee. He was at the siege of Ninety Six and the Battle of Eutaw Springs. Thereafter, he served under Col. Lawrence and Maj. Eggleston in several other skirmishes. On 14 Dec 1782 he marched into Charleston with Lee's Legion and evacuated the British. On Christmas, 1782, Peter Battoe was discharged at Varings, 30 miles north of Charleston.

It was not unusual for men of his time to have fought on both sides during the American Revolution. In the South there was little interest in fighting for the King, but there was little interest in fighting for the rebel government. People in South Carolina weren't paying much attention to the fighting until the British came down to their colony and invaded it to open a second front. Many men were pressed into the service of the King because they were considered British subjects. These men were not given a choice.

Peter Battoe and his wife Mary Adair, and four children came from South Carolina to Ramsey's Creek (which runs into Blue Springs Creek) about 1800. Their children were William, John, James and Sarah.

Peter's son, William, settled on Little River where he farmed, built and operated the first ferry.

The second son, John, moved to southern Illinois. John's son, James E. Battoe, remained in Trigg County. He and his third wife, Eliza Lawrence, were the parents of Ella Mae Battoe Radford. Their children grew up in Trigg County and descendants are still living in the county.

James Battoe married Elizabeth Tart. Their descendants still live in Kentucky. Among them are the children of grandson James J. Battoe and Charity Bridges.

Sarah married Meredith Outhouse, then Zachariah Cudd. They moved to Missouri.

Peter Battoe died 7 Dec 1833 in Trigg County. His name is among those Revolutionary War soldiers to whom a monument has been placed in East End Cemetery in Cadiz. *Submitted by Charles Drennan, ggggg-grandson.*

JOHN BLAKELEY SR., Revolutionary War Veteran and pioneer settler in western Christian (now northeast Trigg County, KY), was born in Pittsylvania County, VA, 29 Oct 1755, eldest of eight children of James Bleakeley Sr. (Blakeley), lived on Strawberry Creek, died in Pittsylvania County, June 1799, and his wife Rebecca. John Blakeley Sr. grew to manhood amid the growing hostility against England. On 6 Oct 1777, he joined the 3rd South Carolina Regiment of the Continental Army, commanded by William Thompson. He fought throughout the war in this regiment. On 2 Aug 1783, he married Jane Shields, also of Pittsylvania County, born 30 Jun 1766, daughter of Samuel and Jane Fulton Shields. Their first child, James Blakeley, was born in Pittsylvania County. In 1785, the young couple moved to Clarke County, GA, where they settled on a farm near the Oconee River. Here their children Samuel, Polly, John Jr., Thomas, Salley, Smith and Josiah were born.

In the spring of 1802, the family set out on the long trip to settle in Kentucky. They found suitable land upon which to settle on the waters of Horse Creek south of Buie's Knob and about three miles southeast of Cerulean Springs. John Blakeley received a grant of 200 acres there on 10 Jul 1805, and he patented another 200 acres on 22 Jan 1814. On 29 Jan 1825, he sold 133 acres off the east side of this 400 acre tract near the Christian County line to his youngest son Josiah Blakeley. This land was deeded by Josiah Blakeley to his son Josiah Richardson Blakeley, 7 Nov 1863, thence to his son, J. Lloyd Blakeley on 1 Jan 1897. J. Lloyd Blakeley sold the land in 1909, thus a part of the original John Blakeley homeplace remained in the family for over a century. Here the last two children of John and Jane Shields Blakeley, Nancy and Martha, were born.

In 1833, John Blakeley and his wife moved to Calloway County to settle near their son Smith Blakeley in the Clarks River section. John Blakeley died there in February 1836. Jane Shields Blakeley was listed in the household of her son Josiah Blakeley in Trigg County in the 1850 Census. Their burial place is not known. *Submitted by William T. Turner.*

JOEL COHOON (CALHOUN) born 9 Jul 1763 in Edgecombe County, NC, the son of John and Priscilla Flowers Cohoon. Joel served with the North Carolina Troops at two different times during the Revolutionary War. His first enlistment was in March 1781 at the Nash County Courthouse. His second was a few months later at Tarboro, the Edgecombe County seat. Both terms of service were under the overall command of Gen. Nathaniel Greene, and among officers in charge of his outfit were Col. Cain, Maj. Coffield, Maj. Scarcer and Capt. James Wilson. He was 18 years old at the time. At one time during his second enlistment the British came within six miles of his father's home in Edgecombe County.

After the Revolution, Joel returned to his father's plantation. On 4 Aug 1785, he married Naomi Futrell, daughter of Sanders Futrell of Northampton County, NC.

Joel was the oldest of five children. The others were Mary, Charity, Ava and Simon. Joel's sister Charity married Drury Bridges, and Ava married Daniel Futrell, brother of Joel's wife Naomi. In 1805, Joel, his wife, their three children: David Greene, Nathan and Archibald, along with his mother, and his brother Simon, migrated to Kentucky and settled in the Donaldson Creek Valley of what is now Trigg County, and where they spent the rest of their lives.

On 7 Sep 1833 Joel applied for a U.S. government pension (No. 8576) for his service during the Revolution and it was approved 24 December that same year. In 1835, at the age of 72, Joel died at his home in the Donaldson Creek Valley. Naomi, his widow, who outlived him by several years, was in her 80s when she died. They were originally buried in the Calhoun Family Cemetery near their home, but when Lake Barkley was formed, their graves were moved to Little River Cemetery near Cadiz.

In the passage of time, the spelling of the surname Cohoon was changed to Calhoun, but very likely most or possibly all of the Calhouns in Trigg County today are descendants of either Joel's three sons: David Greene, Nathan and Archibald, or from Ross, son of his brother Simon.

WILLIAM DAVENPORT, was likely born in Virginia. He was the son of Stephen and Mary (Slaughter) Davenport.

At the time of his enlistment, in the latter part of 1776, William was living in Halifax County, VA. He was a soldier in the Virginia line during the Revolutionary War. He enlisted for five years under Gen. George Washington. Along with his unit, he marched to Boston and New England and was there in a battle and forced to retreat. He was also at the battle of Brandywine and then marched to North Carolina and was at the battle of Guilford Court House in March 1781 under Gen. Greene. He then marched to South Carolina and was at the battle of Eutaw Springs. He left the service in the fall of 1781. Patsy (Wallis) Davenport received a pension for the service of her husband in the Revolutionary War.

Following the Revolutionary War, William moved to Chester County SC where he married Patsy, daughter of William Wallis, on 4 Jul 1793. They were the parents of the following children: Newton (b. June 1794) married Eleanor Morris; Thomas (b. 1795) married Elizabeth Wallis; Mary (Polly) (b. 1796) married Ferdinand Wallis; Permelia (b. 1797) married James Wallis; Elizabeth (Betsy) (b. 1798) married John Wallis; Frances (b. 1799); Sally (b. 1804); Cynthia (b. 1808). The last three children were born in Trigg County.

It is believed that William and his family, along with his wife's Wallis family, were members of the Methodist Class at the Young settlement on Bird's Creek which was the beginning of the Cadiz Methodist Church.

William Davenport died 22 Apr 1819/20 in Trigg County, KY where he was buried. *Submitted by Kay Wallace Sloan.*

JAMES EDERINGTON/EDRINGTON, born in 1742 at Stafford County, VA and died 4 Jun 1847, at the home of his daughter, Catherine Edrington Henderson, in Trigg County, KY His second wife was Catherine McTier/McTear. They were married at Fairfield County, SC, before 1793. His third wife was Mary Forbes. They married 24 Oct 1813, at Green County, KY No record of his 1st marriage has been found.

James Edrington was a private in the militia from Fairfield, County, SC. His services during the Revolutionary War were as follows: ...one of Militia, placed under command of Gen. Williamson and Col. Joseph Kirkland on Florida Expedition, and later stationed at Orangeburg under command of Capts. Liles, Frost and Hughes. They marched to Congaree River, placed under command of Gen. Greene at Eutaw Springs and was there in battle on 15 Sep 1781. Served at various times of about three months each, about 18 months in all as a private." For reference to his

Military Record refer to Military Pension Files, R 3230, James Ederington, Revolutionary War (RG 15 A).

The children of James and Catherine M. Edrington were George, 1st wife Elizabeth Mansfield and 2nd Mary A. Mansfield; William md. Eliza Wilson 30 Nov 1820; Robert (b. 1795) md. Martha Hudsneth; John (b. 12 Jun 1796) md. Ameila Hudsneth; Thomas md. Ann Duke; Catherine (b. 6 Jun 1802, md. Bennett Henderson; Nancy md. Wm. Flin (Flynn); Polly and Sally Edrington.

NATHAN FUTRELL,

NATHAN FUTRELL, was reputed to be the youngest drummer boy in the Revolutionary War. He was a native of Northampton County, NC. Bible records show that he was the son of William Futrell. Nathan married Charity Futrell, daughter of Thomas and Sarah Futrell, in North Carolina, before 1798.

Nathan Futrell was listed as head of household on the 1800 US Census for Northampton County, NC. He and his family moved to Western Kentucky's Donaldson Creek by 1803. Nathan first appeared on the Christian County, KY, tax rolls in 1804.

Nathan Futrell and his brothers-in-law, John Futrell and David Cahoon, enlisted as privates in Capt. Benjamin H. Reeves' Company, 6th Regt. of Kentucky Militia during the War of 1812.

Nathan and Charity Futrell joined Donaldson Creek Baptist Church in May 1814; a month after the congregation was formed. Nathan was on the first board of deacons. He and Charity lived in the Donaldson Creek Community on Beechy Fork until 1817, when they moved across the Cumberland River and settled near Ford's Creek. By 1819, he was taxed for 378 acres in the "Between the Rivers."

Nathan was a surveyor, miller and mechanic. He planted the first apple orchard in Trigg County. Governor Joseph Desha appointed him as a magistrate for Trigg County on 29 Oct 1824. He built one of the earliest gristmills in the area that stood near where Laura Furnace was later built.

Nathan and Charity Futrell are buried in a family graveyard on their farm. In 1990, TVA enclosed the cemetery with a rail fence and a DAR plaque was placed on his grave. A nearby Kentucky Historical Highway Marker pinpoints the site. Nathan and Charity Futrell were the great-grandparents of Governor Junius Marion Futrell (Democrat-Arkansas). *Submitted by Roger H. Futrell.*

JESSE GOODWIN,

JESSE GOODWIN, North Carolina patriot soldier in the Revolutionary War, was born in Virginia ca. 1760, son of Robert Goodwin.

From "The North Carolina State Colonial Records" Vol. X and XII, 1776-1778: Vol. X, page 578.

"The Congress met on Saturday, 11 May 1776, and awarded the following Jesse Goodwin, a soldier in the service of this Colony, having been dangerously wounded and rendered incapable for some time to come to get a subsistence by his labor, Resolved, that the Treasurers or either of them, pay to the said Jesse Goodwin the sum of 28 pounds and be allowed in their accounts with the Public." Jesse Goodwin received a land grant of 816 acres in District 96, Pendleton County, SC, 5 Jun 1786. He sold this land in 1803.

Robert Goodwin, Samuel and Jesse, traveled with young Andrew Jackson to Fort Nashboro in 1789. In 1792/93, Robert Goodwin and his sons made the first permanent settlement in the Cerulean Springs Community.

Jesse Goodwin and his family settled on land known as the Wake Place in 1884, near Cerulean Springs. By Survey No. 3508, he patented 200 acres on Muddy Fork Creek, Survey No. 856, 5 Apr 1804, and a final patent of 200 acres, also on Muddy Fork, Survey No. 3569, 25 Apr 1817. The No. 856 Survey (200 acres) was sold to his son John Goodwin in 1814; given to his daughter, Leah Goodwin Turner, wife of Robert Rogers "Squire Bob" Turner, in 1832; thence to her son John James "Jim" Turner, in 1869; then sold by his widow, Martha E. Atwood Turner to her son-in-law, County Judge J. Lloyd Blakeley in 1909; and finally passed out of the family in 1949 when Judge Blakeley's daughter-in-law sold the farm to C.W. and Wallace E. Davis. This farm remained in the Goodwin-Turner-Blakeley family for 145 years.

Jesse Goodwin married Susannah Howard. Their 10 children were John, Samuel, Jesse Jr., Elizabeth Parrish, Ann Hirsch, Leah Henderson, Polly Fullbright, Rebecca Ridgeway, Martha Ridgeway and Nancy Reeves.

Jesse Goodwin, his wife, and several of their children left Cerulean Springs in 1825 and moved to Weakley County, TN. He died in the spring of 1848 and is buried in the Goodwin Cemetery in Weakley County. *Submitted by William T. Turner*

ROBERT GOODWIN,

ROBERT GOODWIN, born in 1739 and married Jane Tulloch. They had a number of children born in Virginia, among them, Samuel Goodwin and Jesse Goodwin. The family settled in South Carolina after serving there during the Revolutionary War. Robert Goodwin received a grant 12 Oct 1780, for 200 acres in Cravens County. He had the survey made on 3 Apr 1782, for 200 acres on Branches of Little River and Bush River. This is present Laurens County, SC. A nearby tract surveyed in December 1784, with grant dated 5 Jun 1786, for 152 acres, was located on both sides of Durbin Creek of the Enoree River in Laurens County and was sold 23 Oct 1786. He moved to Pendleton County, SC, District 96.

Robert Goodwin settled on what was called in 1884, the Gardner farm, a short distance from Cerulean Springs. By Survey No. 3571, he patented 200 acres on Horse Creek, 17 Dec 1798, and 200 acres on Muddy Fork Creek, Survey No. 3710, 31 Dec 1798. On 24 Oct 1803, Christian County Court exempted Robert Goodwin from paying the County Levy on account of age. On 8 Sep 1807, he sold the 200 acres on Muddy Fork Creek, bought earlier from Richard Biggs. Thus he owned 400 acres upon his death in the late spring of 1809. Robert Goodwin was buried in the Military Cemetery north of Cerulean Springs (location not presently known). *Submitted by William T. Turner.*

JOHN GRASTY,

JOHN GRASTY, a Revolutionary War soldier, was born 16 Sep 1762, at Fairfax County, VA. He served in South Carolina under Capt. John Liles. He was a private with two years service. He was granted a pension #R4201 on 29 Aug 1832, Trigg County, KY. For reference for military service see Vol. 2, page 127, State Libraries History of Virginia Revolutionary Soldiers.

His first marriage was to Frances ? on 15 Nov 1785. She died 17 Nov 1786. They had one daughter, Polly Grasty (b. 21 Aug 1786).

John married Lucy Fitzpatrick on 7 Jul 1791. Lucy was born in 1773 at Newberry District, SC. She died in Trigg County, KY, on 6 Oct 1839. Their children were Sashal (Shankall), farmer and constable born 28 Nov 1795, married Lucinda Burke; John M. (b. 1806), married Cynthia McWaters; William (b. 1807), married Tabitha Hawkins; Milton married Laura Baker; Laura B. (b. 1812, d. at age 16); Harvey (b. 11 Apr 1815) married Mary Barnnwell (nee Little); and Thomas who was never married.

John Grasty died at Trigg County, KY, on 17 Nov 1833.

DAVID HAGGARD,

DAVID HAGGARD, soldier, carpenter, farmer, Baptist preacher, and a Trigg County resident between 1823 and 1836, was born near Charlottesville, Albemarle County, VA, 4 Feb 1764, the sixth son and ninth of 10 children born to Nathaniel Haggard (b. 21 Nov 1723, d. 21 Aug 1806), and Elizabeth Gentry Haggard (b. 14 Aug 1731, d. 28 July 1820). The family lived within two miles of Charlottesville when David was called into the service.

The militia served in tours of two months each and as soon as he was 16 years of age he was required to enter the service and because of the pressing need of troops he served three successive tours with only intervals at home.

Tour one started in March 1781, when he entered the service of the United States as a private in the army of the Revolutionary War and in the Virginia Militia. He joined the army at Moppen Hills, VA, in Gen. Lawson's Brigade under the command of Col. Holt Richardson.

After remaining at home two or three weeks, David was called out a second time and joined the main army at Chickahominy Swamp below Richmond and was again in the regiment of Col. Holt Richardson.

The third tour of service began when he joined the army just above Williamsburg and was attached to a small body of light infantry under Col. Sampson Matthews. David was then relieved in his service in the light infantry and joined the main army and served out his time of two months.

Two days after the Cornwallis surrender, David joined the division, three companies of militia under the command of Captain Joshua Fry of the American Army, and he was discharged about 2 Nov 1781.

Returning home to Albemarle County, David took up the carpenter's trade and worked part-time on the construction of Mr. Jefferson's Monticello between 1789 and 1793.

David Haggard married Nancy Dawson on 6 Nov 1790 and they had 10 children: Elizabeth Lander (b. 1791, d. 1835); Dawson (b. 1793,

d. 1829); Martha Routt, then Newton (b. 1795, d. 1871); John (b. 1800, d. 1847); Sallie Lander (b. 1801, d. 1843); Cinthia Babbitt (b. 1805); Melvina Rucker (b. 1808); Mahalla McCaughan (b. 1810); twins—Louisa Blakeley (b. 1813, d. 1884) and Louesa Thompson (b. 1813, d. 1838).

In 1794 the couple moved to a farm in Clark County, KY, near Winchester. In 1823, the family moved to Trigg County, KY, and settled in Cerulean Springs.

David and Nancy Haggard moved to Bloomington, McLean County, IL, in May 1836, where he died on 1 Apr 1843. Nancy Dawson Haggard died 1 Dec 1857 on Horse Creek south of Cerulean Springs, KY, and was buried in the Kenady Graveyard near Wallonia.

Source of War Record: General Services Administration, National Archives and Records Service. *Submitted by William T. Turner.*

MILES HOLLOWELL, born 4 Feb 1761 in Perquimans County (borders Atlantic Ocean), NC. He served as a US Private in the American Revolutionary War with the "North Carolina Line." He received a veteran's pension from the US Congress of $30 annually, which started for him on 18 Oct 1833. His military service and veteran's pension information are recorded on page 181 of the "Kentucky Pension Roll of 1835," the Report prepared by the US Secretary of War in obedience to Senate Resolutions of 5 and 30 Jun 1834 and 3 Mar 1835.

After the war, he married Ann (Anna) Smithwick on 27 Mar 1792 in Martin County, NC. Ann (b. 1773) was the daughter of John and Mary Smithwick of Martin County, NC.

About 1811, nine years before Trigg County became a separate county, Miles and his family came by wagon train along the Wilderness Road through the Cumberland Gap to what is now Trigg County. With them were their eight children: Whitby (b. 1793); twins Irvin and Sally (b. 4 Feb 1796); Noah, (b. 1798); Sovreign (b. 1801); Penelope (b. 1804) (married William Larkins of Bethesda Methodist Church Community); Lucretia (b. 1806); and Eliza (b. 1809).

Descendants of Penelope Hollowell and William Larkins include the Trigg County families of Brandon, Francis, Henderson, Kennedy, Larkins, Minton and Thomas (including Virginia Dare Thomas Alexander), to name a few. Samuel Larkins, son of Penelope and William, served in the State Legislature in 1863-65.

After settling in the new Trigg County area, Miles and Ann had the following four additional children: Mary (b. 1812); Adaline (b. 1814); Lott (b. 1817) married Elizabeth Kennedy; and July (or Judy) Ann (b. 1820).

Miles was a farmer and he and his sons, Irvin and Noah, acquired extensive land holdings in Trigg County and Caldwell County. The farm land included 200 acres on Little River purchased in 1824. Irvin was also a lawyer.

Miles died 6 Feb 1843 and his wife Ann died 7 Oct 1846. Miles was buried in the Larkins Cemetery overlooking Larkins Spring (Iron Post Spring) on the old stagecoach road, just above the present day P'Pool Road in northeast Trigg County. The earliest grave found in the Larkins family cemetery is that of Miles.

The cemetery is remarkable because of Noah, son of Miles and Ann (Anna) S. Larkins. When Noah died in Caldwell County in 1872, he left a will with details for the 28 foot marble monument erected in the Larkins-Hollowell-Brandon family cemetery and for the decorative iron fence surrounding it. The spectacular monument, designed by C. Zuckreigel of Owensboro, was brought in from the landing at Eddyville by several teams of oxen.

This veteran history was prepared, in part, from the pioneer history summary (with corrections) of Miles Hollowell included on page 136 of Trigg County History, the Past 100 years 1885-1985, Vol. I, published by Trigg County Historical and Preservation Society. Joan Larkins Crowe, ggg-granddaughter of Miles Hollowell also submitted information. *Submitted by the Society's first president, Kenneth Kennedy, a gggg-grandson of Miles Hollowell. J*

ABSALOM HUMPHRIES, Charles J. Humphries and America M. Humphries had seven children: John, Charles, Thomas, Absalom, James Bennett, Richard and one daughter. The first five sons served in the Revolutionary War. (See related article on Thomas Humphries).

Absalom Humphries (b. August 1760, d. 9 Dec 1834) is buried in the Humphries Cemetery located in Trigg County. On his tombstone was written "In memory of Absalom Humphries a soldier of the Revolutionary War, an honorable husband and kind father. An honest man lies here at rest."

A letter from the Veterans Administration, dated October 1939, documents the claim for pension under File W2942. "While residing in Chester County, SC, Absalom Humphries enlisted in 1780, served eight or nine months as private in Capt. Bratton's company, Col. Bratton's South Carolina regiment, was in a skirmish at Mobley's Settlement and several other skirmishes, names of which were not given. He enlisted in 1781 while living in Fairfield County, SC, served as private in Capt. Jacob Barnett's company, Col. Henry Hampton's South Carolina regiment, was in the battle of Eutaw Springs, in skirmishes at Orangeburg, Juniper Springs, Old Church, and in an engagement at Dorchester Bacon's Bridge. In December he joined Gen. Wayne in Georgia and was in an engagement with the Indians near Savannah; entire length of his service was 10 or 12 months."

Absalom married Berthenia Wall, the daughter of Jesse and Susanna Wall, on 31 Mar 1791 in South Carolina. She was a sister of Mary Wall who married Thomas Humphries. They moved to Kentucky and settled on Sinking Fork Creek, near Little River, about five or six miles east of Cadiz. Children born to this marriage according to the war pension are John (b. 15 Mar 1793); Absalom Jr. (b. 11 Jul 1797); Jesse (b. 6 Apr 1800); Polly (b. 11 Feb 1803); Charles (b. 4 Jul 1805); Thomas (b. 2 Jan 1808); Richard Bennet (b. 29 Apr 1810); James Madison (b. 10 May 1812); Susan Ship (b. 23 May 1816). Other records indicate two other children, Misarena (b. 28 Sep 1818) and William S. (b. 1821).

Ref: "The Wilford-Williford Family Treks into American by Eurie Pearl Wilford Neel, 1959.

Counties of Christian and Trigg Kentucky Historical and Biographical by William Henry Perrin, 1884. Submitted by Suellen Hendricks.

THOMAS HUMPHRIES, Charles J. Humphries and America M. Humphries had seven children: John, Charles, Thomas, Absalom, James Bennett, Richard and one daughter. The first five sons served in the Revolutionary War. (See related article on Absalom Humphries).

Captain Thomas Humphries (b. 18 Dec 1756, d. 25 Jul 1827) is buried in the Humphries Cemetery in Trigg County. He married 3 Nov 1786, Mary Wall, daughter of Jesse and Susanna Wall. She was a sister of Bartheny Wall who married Absalom Humphries.

Children of this marriage, according to a deed dated 20 Aug 1787 executed to George Blissett are Elizabeth, Susan Luck, Mary Ally, Thomas J. and Jesse.

Absalom Humphries came to Trigg County about 1804 or 1805 and was followed shortly afterward by his brother, Capt. Thomas Humphries, both of whom were prominently identified with the early history of the county. They were members of a very prominent Virginia family and achieved some distinction in the war of the Revolution, Thomas having risen to the position of captain in the army of Washington. Thomas settled on Little River in 1810. He was a Methodist preacher of some note and preached in various places throughout the county during the early years of its history.

Ref: "The Wilford-Williford Family Treks into American by Eurie Pearl Wilford Neel, 1959.

Counties of Christian and Trigg Kentucky Historical and Biographical by William Henry Perrin, 1884. Submitted by Suellen Hendricks.

CHARLES KENNEDY, whose surname is also spelled in some references as "Kennady," "Kenady" and "Kenedy," is included in the list of "Trigg County, KY Soldiers of the American Revolutionary War" and is credited with serving in Virginia. In 1832, while a resident of Trigg County, he applied for and received a veteran's pension for his military service in the American Revolution. His pension number is S13617.

Charles was born 12 Dec 1763 in New Jersey (believed to be in Hunterdon County) to the parents of John Kennedy and wife Elizabeth Kennedy. In 1779, he moved with his parents and family to Kentucky which was not yet a state; it was still part of Virginia. In 1780, the Kentucky region had only three counties: Lincoln, Fayette and Jefferson. What is now Trigg County was then a part of Lincoln County.

In that same year of 1780, Charles volunteered for military service under Peter Sturgus against the Indians and British invasions to the Piqua towns in the new state of Ohio.

On 10 Jul 1784, Charles married Jane Johnson. From the time of his marriage until the death of his parents in 1802, he, his wife and several of his brothers lived in the area of the present day Nelson County. His father was one of the 10 founding fathers of the town of Bealsburg near Bardstown. The town no longer exits. Charles was the oldest son and he has several brothers: John, Moses, Peter (who was mentioned prominently in the famous *Collins's History of Kentucky*, especially as an Indian fighter), James, Daniel, Henry, George and William. The Kennedy family had large settlements of land in the Younger Creek Area of Nelson County.

In 1806, Charles moved with his family to the Wallonia area of Trigg County. Trigg became a county in 1820. He settled with his family on land consisting of several 100 acres in the Wallonia area on Kenady Creek, located just below Kennedy Spring and the Kennedy homestead. Kenady Creek is named for Charles Kennedy as an early pioneer to the area. Somewhere along the way, he built and operated a mill on Kenady's Creek. That is mentioned in *Perrin's History of Trigg County*.

Charles and his wife both died during the cholera epidemic of 1834 which almost wiped out the entire family. He died 23 July and she died two days later. They and their family are buried in the Kennedy Family Cemetery, located at the Kennedy homestead area.

His children included Peter, Charles, Benjamin, Miles (who served as a Cadiz Postmaster), Robert, Mary, Josiah (great-great-grandfather of this writer), James and Jane.

This history was prepared by Kenneth Kennedy, son of Durward B., son of Edmond W., son of Albert Y., son of Josiah, son of Charles.

ROGER LARKINS, a Revolutionary War soldier, was born ca 1730/1735 in Hew Hanover County, NC. His wife was Susannah Portevent. They were married at North Carolina in 1784. Roger died in June 1828. No record can be found of the place of his death, but have information that he died in Trigg or Graves County, KY. Susannah Portevent Larkins died in 1830/40 at Graves County, KY.

Roger Larkins was a soldier in Wilmington District, NÇ during the American Revolution. Proof of his service is found in the *Roster of Soldiers from North Carolina in the American Revolution*, page 212, No. 378, North Carolina, Revolutionary Army Accounts Book W, No. 1, page 15, No. 378."

On 4 Nov 1808 Roger Larkins was living in New Hanover County, NC, and appointed William Bloodwrth to be his lawful attorney to collect any monies due from any person in North Carolina, and gave him power to sue in his name to recover same.

The children of Roger and Susannah were John Larkins, born in New Hanover County, NC; William Larkins, born 13 Nov 1791, at New Hanover County, NC; Roger Portevent Larkins born at New Hanover County, NC in 1798; Samuel Larkins, Margaret Larkins and Mary Larkins. Their son William married Mattie Penelope Hollowell. Her father was Miles Hollowell, a Revolutionary War soldier.

JOHN MABRY SR., born Sunday, 8 Apr 1764 in Surry County, VA and died 7 Apr 1845 in Trigg County, KY. He volunteered in July 1780 in Louisburg, Franklin County, NC being 16 years old. Served as a private with North Carolina troops under Colonels Benjamin Seawall and Tilghman Dixon. In August 1781 he was transferred to Capt. Michael Rudolph's company in Col. Henry Lee's Legion in which he served until end of the war. During his service he took part in a skirmish with the British on Roanoak River. He was at the surrender of Charleston, South Carolina and at the famous Battle of Eutaw Springs.

John Mabry Sr. a surveyor by trade, was given 640 acres of land for his service as a private. He settled in Christian County, KY, later Trigg County about 1786 with his wife and one child, Martha Nancy. His acre-

age was near Rockcastle Community on Little River. He kept a journal of his activities. From his journal dated 1833 to his death, he mentions a pension that he received twice a year, $36 each payment. In 1834 his 1,650 acres was valued at $2,186 for property taxes. He paid his taxes with four horses and 13 head of cattle. His journal contains his Last Will and Testament. It lists the following:

1) Martha Nancy (b. ca. 1786 in North Carolina) had daughter Mary Narcissa, who married Hardy Wilson Smith.

2) Margaret "Peggy" (b. ca. 1794) married Joseph Bounds 29 Sep 1810 in Christian County).

3) John Mabry Jr. (b. ca. 1800, d. 12 Nov 1849) married Ellenor Mitchell on 24 Nov 1827.

4) Polly (b. ca. 1802, d. before 1834) married Thomas S. Mitchell on 20 Feb 1826. Left two children Polly and Thomas Mitchell.

5) Elizabeth "Betsey" (b. ca. 1804, d. before 1850) married Benjamin Mitchell 21 Apr 1827.

6) Jesse Mabry (b. ca. 1810, d. 17 Mar 1834) married Susan Mitchell on 30 Jul 1832. Susan died 3 Apr 1834 and left daughter Elizabeth who married William F. Faughn.

7) Lewis B. Mabry (b. 1811, d. 1856) married Sarah Starnes on 12 Feb 1835.

8) Francis Allen Mabry (b. 1813, d. 1866 in Crittenden County, KY) married on 15 Jun 1843 to Rebecca H. Oliver.

Donald E. Collins of Bailey, CO (formerly of Milwaukee, WI) published a book "The Mabry Family descendants of Francis Maybury and Elizabeth Gilliam of Surry County, VA," Gateway Press, Inc. Baltimore, MD 1987. This book contains the ancestry of John Mabry Sr.

The Veterans Administration furnished a grave marker for John Mabry Sr. It was placed in the "Sugar Jim" Mitchell Cemetery off Reddick Pond Road by great-great-great-grandson Leo Yeateman Wilson of Hopkinsville, KY on 14 May 1994. *Submitted by Leo Y. Wilson.*

RANDOLPH JOHNSON, born in North Carolina in 1759. During the Revolutionary War he served in the North Carolina Line. Later, he and his wife Mary Holcomb, moved to Clarksville, TN, then to Canton, KY about 1831.

Randolph and Mary Johnson had several children. Their daughter Tabatha married Kenchen Battoe, grandson of Peter Battoe. Their son James J. Battoe married Charity Bridges. Many of their descendants still live in Kentucky.

Randolph died in 1846 and was buried in Canton, KY. *Submitted by Charles Drennan, gggg-grandson.*

JAMES THOMAS SR., born 1762 in Bertie County, NC. On 12 May 1781, at the age of 19, he enlisted with the North Carolina Line to fight the British in the Revolutionary War.

Young James served as a private under Gen. Nathaniel Greene in the 10th Regt. of Capt. Donoho's Company, with Col. Abraham Shepherd in command. He spent most of his time in service with Gen. Greene's army in skirmishes against the British, mostly in South Carolina. He was discharged 2 May 1782 and returned to his father's plantation in Bertie County.

On 6 Sep 1790, James married Mary Standley who lived on a neighboring plantation. They had seven children, the last of whom was born in Kentucky, where they had migrated in 1806.

On arrival at his new home, James acquired 200 acres of land in the fertile Donaldson Creek Valley and 400 acres on Bird's Creek a few miles north. His land was in an area of Christian County which in 1820 became part of Trigg County.

James and Mary's children included Cullen, Temperance, Perry, Starkie, Mary, James Jr., all born in North Carolina; and Stanley, born in Kentucky. After Trigg County was formed in 1820, each of his sons became active in the public affairs. Cullen was appointed by the governor as the first sheriff, Perry served for 21 years as tax assessor and later, as census enumerator, Starkie and James Jr., each served several terms as justice of the peace, and Stanley was elected sheriff by popular vote, and later, was elected to represent the county in the state legislature. Daughter Temperance, married and died while still in her teens. Her sister Mary married William Bridges and became progenitor of the large Bridges family, many of whom still live in Trigg County.

James Thomas Sr. died 9 Sep 1832 at the age of 70, and his grave is located about a half-mile south of his original homesite.

THOMAS WOOSLEY, born 2 Jun 1760 in Buckingham County, VA. Thomas was living in Amelia County, VA, when he joined the Revolutionary War in March 1777. He enlisted in the 1st Light Dragoons, Capt. John Hughes' Company, Virginia Continental Line commanded by Col. Anthony Walton White. He served as a private until the end of the Revolutionary War, receiving his discharge from Gen. Benjamin Lincoln in the Fall of 1783.

His father (Moses) and seven of his sons served in the Revolutionary War. Thomas and three of his brothers received war pensions: Moses, Aaron and David. Four of the brothers came to Kentucky: Joshua moved to Hart County, Samuel and David to Edmonson County, and Thomas to Christian County. Aaron moved to Giles County, TN and William to North Carolina.

Thomas Woosley married Dinah Tribble, daughter of Peter Tribble, in Halifax County, VA 18 Apr 1786. She was born in August 1762. They had four children: Thomas E., Moses, Susan (Woosley) Jones and B. (Burrell?).

Thomas was on the Christian County tax rolls in 1800. He served on the grand jury of inquest during the second term of Trigg County Circuit Court held at the residence of Robert Baker on 23 Aug 1820. He lived near Cerulean Springs which was formed into Trigg County from Christian County in 1820. In 1820 he moved from Trigg County to the Sinking Fork Community in Christian County. Thomas' older brother Moses died in Halifax County, VA. Two of Moses' sons, James T. Sr. and Samuel S. came to the Sinking Fork Community after Thomas.

Thomas' first wife, Dinah died 2 Aug 1839. Thomas then married Jane S. Covington, widow of William Covington, 28 Jan 1842 in Christian County. Thomas died 12 May 1856 and Jane died 27 Feb 1868. They had no children. Thomas is buried with his first wife Dinah, son Moses, and daughter-in-law Elizabeth (Jones) Woosley on the Moses Woosley farm.

As far as it is known, Thomas Woosley was the last Revolutionary War soldier to die in Christian County. His name is on the Revolutionary War soldiers memorial tablets in East End Cemetery, Cadiz, and Riverside Cemetery, Hopkinsville, Christian County, KY.

WILLIAM YOUNG, born in either Ireland, South Carolina or Virginia. In about 1772, he married Ellender McClerkin. She was born in Ballymena County, Ireland and immigrated to the colonies with her family just before the American Revolutionary. She was the daughter of James McKerkin, a soldier in the American Revolution.

William Young was a soldier in the South Carolina Militia during the American Revolutionary War. He is listed in the Daughters of the American Revolution "Patriot Index".

In about 1813, the Young family settled in the area of Christian County, that became Trigg County, KY. According to Herrin's History of Trigg County, an early Methodist Class was held before 1820 on Bird's Creek at the Young Settlement. Youngs and Wallis' were in attendance. This was the beginnings of the Cadiz Methodist Church.

William and Ellender (McClerkin) Young were the parents of the following children: Mary married William Gunnell Sanders, Elizabeth (Betsy) married James Minnis, Thomas Jr. married Martha Bearden, Nancy married a Mr. Wallis or Wallace, Ellender or Ellen (called Nelly) married William Wallis (the first school teacher in Trigg County), John married Elizabeth Bearden, William Jr. married Rebecca Bearden, Ann married Thomas O. Bryant, John, Sally married Jessie Langley, Susan married Mr. Wallis or Wallace, Ferdinand (Vardy) married Elizabeth Langley James, Ezekial S. married Nancy Jones.

William Young made his Will 22 Sep 1824, it was probated in Trigg County, KY on 19 Sep 1826. This Will can be found in Trigg County Will Book A, page 114-116. William was buried in Trigg County, KY. *Submitted by Kay Wallace Sloan.*

WILLIAM CUNNINGHAM SR., born 1776 in Bonnie, Scotland. His father was James Cunningham and his mother is unknown. When 15 years old, William stowed away on a boat for a six month voyage to Virginia to avoid a mandatory two years in the military. William had apprenticed to his father as a tailor and this is the occupation he assumed after arriving in America.

Alexander Hamilton's excise tax of 1791 caused much protesting and rioting among those who made whiskey, primarily located in Western Pennsylvania. This tax was viewed as unfair and an added insult to a people who felt that they were getting little support from a government they helped establish. Amidst this turmoil, Thomas Jefferson resigned from his position as Secretary of State in 1793, in protest because George Washington was agreeing too much with Hamilton and the Federalists.

President Washington requested troops from the militia in Pennsylvania, Maryland, New Jersey and Virginia to quell this insurrection. On 14 Oct 1794 Washington ordered the militia of 12,000, commanded by Governor Harry Lee of Virginia, to proceed into western Pennsylvania. A number of people were seized but actually little resistance was met. The two offenders that were convicted of treason were pardoned by Washington.

This situation is referred to as the "Whiskey Rebellion." It is important because it was the first test of the federal government's law enforcement power and the president's right to command the use of state militias.

William Cunningham Sr., from the age of 16, served two years in the U.S. Army, 1792-1794, participating primarily in the Whiskey Rebellion in western Pennsylvania. By the end of November 1794 the rebellion was subdued and the solders returned to their homes.

The next year on Christmas Eve 1795, William Cunningham married Nancy Elizabeth Carr. They lived in Albemarle County, VA until 1818 when they moved to Christian County, now Trigg County, KY. They made this journey with 10 children, the 11th child was born along the way.

William and Nancy Cunningham settled in the Rockcastle Community in an area now know as Trigg Furnace. The family grew corn and tobacco and established a mill. These are the grandparents of the vast family of Cunninghams in Trigg County. William Cunningham Sr. died in 1823 at the age of 47 and is buried in the family cemetery at Trigg Furnace.

WAR OF 1812

JESSE ADAMS, Cornstalk Militia, was commissioned ensign, 29th Regt., November 1800, Mason County Regiment.

These records are taken from the book titled *Corn Stalk Militia* by Glenn Clift, listing the commissions of officers in the organization from the beginning of statehood to the commencement of the War of 1812.

Jesse Adams enlisted 1 Sep 1812 as a private and served in the War of 1812 until 23 Dec 1812. From roll of Capt. Thomas Stokes' company, 6th Regt., Kentucky Militia and on file in Office of the Adjutant General Commonwealth of Kentucky Dept. of Military Affairs Frankfort, KY 40601.

Jesse Adams was one of three sons of Drury and Nancy "Ann" Adams. They came to Trigg County (then a part of Christian County) around 1799 and settled on Muddy Fork of Little River. Jesse was born in Virginia on 10 Jul 1785. He married Elizabeth Cooper on 30 May 1812 in Trigg County, KY. and they had 11 children: Mary Ann (Burnham), Madison, Jane "Jenny" (Ramey), Nancy (Banister), Martha Malinda (Minton), Isaac Newton, George Washington, Spotwood Wilkerson, Frances Elizabeth (Goodwin), Amanda (Cook) and Henry Clay. Jesse died on 20 Oct 1848 and is buried in the Adams Cemetery in Trigg County, KY. *Submitted by Nancy Sivills Thompson, gggg-granddaughter of Jesse Adams.*

JAMES ATWOOD, Canton farmer and veteran of the War of 1812, was born in Shenandoah County, VA, a son of John and Elizabeth Roy Atwood. He volunteered 6 Jul 1813 for service as a private in the Virginia militia, Captain Walter Hambough's Company of Riflemen, 97th Regt. He later served in Capt. James H. Sowers Company of Infantry, attached to the 4th Regt. Virginia Militia. Pvt. Atwood was discharged 10 Jan 1814, at Norfolk, VA. He was allowed 15 days pay for allowance to walk the 300 miles home to Woodstock, VA. Pay was $8 per month.

After returning home James Atwood married his first cousin, Mary "Polly" Allen on 7 Dec 1815. Following the birth of their first son William Jackson Atwood, 30 Sep 1817, James and Mary Atwood left Shenandoah County in 1818 and settled at Brush Creek, located on the Smith-Wilson County line in Tennessee. The James Atwood family moved to Dickson County about 1823. In 1839 they built several log rafts and with all their earthly goods, put into the Cumberland River and floated downstream to Canton, Trigg County, KY, where the family resided the remainder of their lives. James Atwood died 19 Mar 1850.

Mary Atwood filed papers on 3 May 1855, in Trigg County Court for 80 acres of bounty land that James Atwood was due for services rendered in the War of 1812. The grant was made 13 Oct 1856, claim number 41389.

James and Mary Allen Atwood had seven children: William Jackson, Martha, Moses Allen, Thomas Hooker, John H., James R. and Mary Jane. James and Mary Atwood are buried on the hill above Canton. *Submitted by William T. Turner.*

VINCENT GUTHRIE, son of Charles and Maria Guthrie, was born 28 Aug 1794, in Halifax County, VA. A veteran of the War of 1812, Vincent Guthrie enlisted 13 Aug 1814, and was discharged 4 Mar 1815. A private in the 7th Regt., Virginia Militia, he served under Capt. Samuel Carter in the regiment of Lt. Col. David Sauders. Both his enlistment and his discharge show that he enlisted as a substitute for Elijah Hart.

On 28 Aug 1817, he married Sarah Stowe, daughter of John and Jane Stowe in Person County, NC. Sarah was born 11 Apr 1801 and died 18 Jan 1882. The family moved to the Christian-Trigg County area in 1829 and settled on a farm in Trigg County. Vincent died 17 Feb 1872, in Trigg County, KY.

After Vincent's death, Sarah was awarded a widow's military pension of $ 8.00 per month. He and Sarah are buried in the Jeff Stewart Cemetery, Radford Road, Trigg County, KY along with seven of his 13 children. This cemetery is located on the farm purchased by John Stowe in 1830.

The 13 children of Vincent and Sarah Stowe Guthrie are:

1) Jane Guthrie (b. 26 Jul 1818, d. 4 May 1889) married John Henry Sizemore, a farmer.

2) Martha Guthrie (b. 29 Feb 1820, died young).

3) John James Guthrie (b. 27 Dec 1821, d. 21 Nov 1914, Christian County, KY), a wheelwright, married Nancy Catherine Jones.

4) Sarah Ann Guthrie (b. 11 Feb 1824, d. 3 Jan 1911) was unmarried.

5) Joel Johnson Guthrie (b. 11 Dec 1825, d. 28 Jan 1917) married Alice Miranda Sheridan, daughter of Rev. John Sheridan who was the first pastor of Burnett's Chapel Church in Graves County.

6) Asa Guthrie (b. 17 Oct 1828, d. 25 Nov 1885) married Louisa Jane Turner, daughter of R.R. Turner, Cerulean, KY

7) Patrick Henry Guthrie (b. 30 Sep 1830, d. 3 May 1879) married Lutitia Rogers. They lived in Williamson County, IL.

8) Mary Elizabeth Guthrie (b. 19 Apr 1834, d. 1 Aug 1931) married William Wortham, a farmer.

9) Drucilla Frances Guthrie b. 7 Oct 1836, d. 18 Mar 1879) married George Jefferson Stewart, for whom Jeff Stewart Cemetery is named.

10) Charles William Guthrie (b. 18 Apr 1839, d. 3 Nov 1861) was unmarried.

11) Virginia Catherine Guthrie (b. 2 Oct 1841, d. 5 Jun 1917) married Lewis Stewart, a farmer near Gracey, KY.

12) Nancy Caroline Guthrie (b. 14 Jan 1845, d. ca. 1846).

13) Thomas Jefferson Guthrie (b. 17 Apr 1846, d. 20 Oct 1848).

Descendants of this family can be found world-wide in the year 2001, as well as in Western Kentucky. *Submitted by Betty McCorkle, ggg-granddaughter of Sarah and Vincent Guthrie.*

BENNETT HENDERSON, a veteran of the War of 1812, was born 8 Dec 1795 in Virginia, the son of Richard I and Margaret "Peggy" Brockman Henderson. On 30 Jul 1814 in Albermarle County, he volunteered to serve in the Virginia Militia. He was assigned to duty as a private in Capt. Jesse B. Key's Company in a Brigade under the command of Brig. Gen. Robert Porterfield. He was discharged Feb 2, 1815.

Three years later on 18 Oct 1818, he married Catherine Edrington/Ederington in Green County, KY. She was born 22 Oct 1802, the daughter of James and Catherine McTier/McTeer Edrington, of Kentucky. Her father, James Edrington/Ederington, was a Revolutionary War veteran and was living in her home in Trigg County when he died 4 Jun 1847.

Her husband, Bennett Henderson, died 18 Mar 1865. On 12 Jun 1880, she filed application for a Service Pension Bounty Land No. 30,581, listing Trigg County as his place of residence. She died 31 Dec 1892 in Lyon County, KY, and is buried in New Bethel Cemetery near Fredonia, KY

Their children were John P. (b. 21 Jun 1821) married Susan Ann Larkins; Maranda Jane (b. 1824) married Jeptha T. Garnett; Thomas E. (b. January 1826) married Florence Gray; William T. (b. ca. 1829) married Hardenia Tandy; Mary Ann (b. ca. 1832) married J.S. Young; Robert E. (b. ca. 1834) married Mary Ann Gray; Sarah Eliza (b. ca 1836) married William P. Easley; Joshua C. (b. ca. 1838); Henry H. (b. ca. 1841) and Richard Bennett Henderson, who was killed in the Civil War.

JAMES HENRY FUQUA was born 23 Apr 1786 (date obtained from tombstone on bluff of Cumberland River at Canton, KY, transcribed by his great-great-grandson, Joseph Terry Fuqua (who erected a new stone there in 1974). The poorly legible dates were read the same way by Judith Ann Maupin in "Trigg County Cemeteries."

Buckingham County, VA, was formed from Albemarle County in 1758. The 1782-1787 tax lists show in Buckingham County only Joseph and William Fuquas (former had one slave and latter had three).

In 1810 census the only Fuquas in Buckingham County were Aaron, Moses and two Roberts (the 2nd of those listed in New Canton of that county).

James Henry Fuqua fought in War of 1812 (National Archives record), a sergeant in the company commanded by Capt. Anthony W. Woodson of artillery from Prince Edward County, VA, in the regiment of Virginia volunteers. He volunteered at Walker's Church in Prince Edward County 14 Jun 1814 and was honorably discharged at Norfolk, VA, December 1814.

He was married on 13 Feb 1812 to Judith Forbes by Baptist minister, Gabriel Walker. (National Archives).

He came to Tennessee about 1817, where he farmed and "carried on a mill."

He was elected major of state militia and served as justice of the peace "for years."

Census 1820 Robertson County, TN, gives a Jas. Fuqua w/himself in the 26-45 age bracket, three girls under 10, wife(?) 26-45, one other female over 45, and one slave.

Census 1830 that county gives Jas. Fuqua with two males under 5, two males 5-10, one 10-15, one 15-20, and three 20-30; plus two females 10-15 and one 15-20. There is a Jas. H. Fuqua in Robertson County in both 1830 and 1832 (Robertson County was created 1796 and Davidson, its parent county, in 1783).

In 1837 he came to Trigg County, KY, on the way to Missouri "but was taken sick and died after a long illness on 3 May 1837." He was buried on the bluff not far from the Lake Barkley navigation light north and slightly west of the Old Canton Hotel.

His widow settled in Trigg County. They had nine children. The widow Judith applied 5 Feb 1857 for bounty land and again on 6 May 1857. She could produce no record of her marriage or of her husband's discharge. W.D. Grace swore that he among others "sat up with the corpse" of James Henry Fuqua. Judith signed her name with an "X."

I strongly suspect but cannot prove that James Henry Fuqua was brother to William Fuqua (b. 28 Dec 1776 in Virginia, d. 1 Nov 1857 in Robertson County, TN), both are in Robertson County about 1820-1830 and were born in Virginia (Jas. H. proven by wife's affidavit). *Submitted by J. Terry Fuqua.*

JOHN HANBERRY was a soldier in the US War of 1812 and was born in Virginia on 29 May 1981 to the parents of Jabe and Phoebe Hanberry.

The Hanberry family history includes various spellings of the Hanberry name, including Hanbury and Hanbery. The part of his family which emigrated from Trigg County to Christian County in the 1800s sometimes spell their family name as "Hanbery."

Records of the War of 1812 show this same "John Hanbury" and a Thomas Hanbury as being soldiers of the Virginia Militia. The Virginia

Militia Index of the War of 1812 Pay Rolls and Muster Rolls lists them on page 459.

The publication entitled "Trigg County Death Records, 1852-1862" recorded the following: Family #1022—John Hanberry, 76, male, farmer, son of Jabe and Phoebe Hanberry, born in Virginia, Soldier of War of 1812, died 1857.

John's family emigrated from Virginia to what is now Trigg County, KY. His wife Mary was born in North Carolina about 1784.

The Hanberry family settled in the community now known as the Bethesda United Methodist Church Community, about five or six miles north of Cadiz, KY on Hwy. 139. When Bethesda Church was organized in 1845, three of the Hanberry family members, Rebecca, D.S. (Daniel) and J.W. Hanberry, were three of the 30 organizing members of the church. Source: Page 154, Perrin's History Of Trigg. Perrin also shows that Daniel Hanberry was one of the three ministers who in August 1875 established Oak Grove Baptist Church in Trigg County.

Hanberry School, a one-room school house founded in 1893, was named for the same Hanberry family. Hanberry School was located beside Bethesda Church.

Census records show John and Mary Hanberry had the three following children: Joseph J. "Ham," Lucy and Thomas W.

Joseph J. "Ham" Hanberry married Eliza B. Gardner, and they had the following children: Mary Adeline "Addie" C., a school teacher; Lucy Caroline "Pug" (Haydon); Flavious Josephus "Cephas" married Mary Conway; and Eliza Van Wick (Henderson) married Carroll Sovereign "Bud" Henderson, the great-grandparents of the author of this veteran history.

Flavious Josephus "Cephas" (b. 28 Jun 1853) and Mary Conway Hanberry had the three following children: Jack Hanberry; Maxie M. Hanberry, a Judge; and Flavious Josephus "Flave" Hanberry (b. 28 May 1888) who married Bessie Huel Williams.

Flavious Josephus "Flave" Hanberry and wife Bessie H. Williams had the following eight children: Mary Adeline; Beulah Estelle; Maxie Millard; Flavious Josephus (b. 19 Oct 1922); Sarah Maebelle; Jack Thomas Sr. who has been an employee for the Trigg County Road Department for many years. He and his wife, Betty, live west of Cadiz and have six children: Jack Jr., Scotty, Steven Wayne, Lisa, Dawn and Rebecca; John Robert; Olivia Nell.

Two of Veteran John Hanberry's relatives of local historical note include Jack T. (J.T.) Hanberry and Jack T.'s sister, Cordelia Hanberry. Jack T. served as circuit judge for Trigg and Christian Counties. His photo hangs in both the Trigg and Christian County Circuit Courtrooms. He presided over the 1911 Hopkinsville criminal trial of "Night Rider" leader, Dr. David Amoss. Reference: pp. 181-201 of Trigg Circuit Judge Bill Cunningham's book on the Night Rider Story, *On Bended Knees.*

Cordelia "Cordie" Hanberry, a young school teacher, became the third wife of Trigg Countian John Francis White on 12 Sep 1883. He owned thousands of acres of land and was a farmer, tobacco dealer, and Baptist preacher. He pastored Rocky Ridge Baptist Church many years until his death in 1898. He is the ancestor to many in the White family of Trigg County. Cordie and John Francis White had three children: daughter Anna, and two sons, Rueben Pollard and Stephen Pettus, both of whom received university degrees from Harvard - Rueben in English and Stephen Pettus in law. Stephen Pettus practiced law in Hopkinsville with his two sons, Pollard White (b. 12 Apr 1920) and Stephen P. White (b. 20 Dec 1915). Pollard still practices law in Hopkinsville. Stephen P. White later served as circuit judge for Christian and Trigg counties. He passed away 7 Sep 1981. Their sister is Sarah.

War of 1812 Veteran John Hanberry passed away 7 Apr 1857 and was buried in Hanberry Cemetery beside Bethesda Church.

This history, copyrighted in 2001, was written from the Hanberry History Book notes of his great-great-great-grandson, Kenneth Kennedy, former Trigg County Attorney and retired lieutenant colonel from US Army (Active duty and Kentucky Army National Guard), who hereby gives his permission for its publication in Trigg County Veteran's History Book.

SPANISH-AMERICAN WAR

CLARENCE BENNETT ALDRIDGE, born 16 Jun 1882, entered the US Army and served in the Philippines during Spanish-American War. He married Myrtle Lockhart and they have a son Burton R. Aldridge Sr. and four daughters: Irene Compton, Carmen Graham, Louise Wise and Pauline Muncy. He died 18 Dec 1978.

LANNES HENRY "L.H." HUGGINS, veteran of the Spanish-American War, was born at Center Furnace, Between the Rivers, Trigg County, KY, 31 Oct 1873, eldest child of 11, born to Robert Henry "Bob" and Sarah Elizabeth "Bettie" Bogard Huggins. The family moved to Christian County in 1879, where Bob Huggins operated a general store at Beverly. They lived in Hopkinsville, 1881-1883; moved to Kyle, Hays County, TX, 1884-1888, and farmed there; then returned to Christian County where Lannes farmed with his father.

L.H. enlisted at Nashville in June 1898 in Co. K, 1st Regt. Tennessee Inf. Vol. and camped at The Presidio at San Francisco for five months. He fought in the Battle of Manila, 5-6 Feb 1899, and participated in the taking of Ililio, 11 Feb 1899; Jaro, 12 Feb 1899; and LaPaz, 13 Feb 1899. He took part in the Cebu Expedition and was mustered out of service at San Francisco in the fall of 1899. In later years he was a member of Hiram P. Thomas Camp, a Spanish-American War Veteran.

After the war Sgt. Huggins worked in general stores at Bear Spring in Stewart County, at Allen's Creek and at Carlisle, all in Tennessee.

In 1909 merchant Huggins bought the general store at Caskey, Christian County, KY, five miles from Hopkinsville on the L&N R.R. He served as Caskey Postmaster from 1910, until the office was discontinued in 1933, and continued operation of the store until his death 27 Jan 1946.

Sgt. Huggins married Lydia W. Rex, of Hustinford, WI, 10 Feb 1901, and they had four children: Gladys (b&d. 1902); Robert Rex (b. 1904, d. 1947); Elizabeth (b. 1905, d. 1995); and Joe Ferguson (b. 1907, d. 1971).

Mr. Huggins was a Mason, Odd Fellow, Elk and a member of Ferrell Boys Reunion Association. The family is buried at Riverside Cemetery, Hopkinsville. *Submitted by William T. Turner.*

HARRY C. RIGGIN, born 2 Sep 1875, a son of William M. and Maggie Cartwright Riggin. He was married 23 Sep 1923 to the former Ila Earl Rogers. They had four children: Juanita, Malcolm, Dorothy and Reva Mae. He had eight grandchildren.

Mr. Riggin came to Cadiz in 1923 and began a 41 year career as a newspaperman with the *Cadiz Record.* He retired in November 1964. He began his newspaper career in the old *Madisonville Hustler,* had been employed at newspapers in Chicago and had been in a newspaper partnership in a Nome, AK weekly paper during the gold rush era when papers sold for $1.25 per copy. Anecdotes concerning Mr. Riggin scissor-sharp wit and humor are legend.

Mr. Riggin used his Cadiz Record column "East Cadiz, Nom de Plume" to state his opinions and beliefs concerning politics, the state of the nation and states he was a master of the 4-7 line blurb that could create more controversial opinions among his readers who could also laugh with him at some of the human antics he reported in his terse style. His brief paragraphs were quoted in newspapers and magazines throughout the United States.

Mr. Riggins served as chairman of the Trigg County Selective Service Local Board. Prior to his residency in Cadiz. Mr. Riggin had served in the Spanish-American War and was also a veteran of WWI. He had served in the U.S. Marine Corps, USN and U.S. Army. A world traveler, Mr. Riggin brought to Cadiz a wide range of knowledge about world conditions.

He was a member of the Cadiz United Methodist Church and faithfully supported his church until he died at age 94.

Civil War

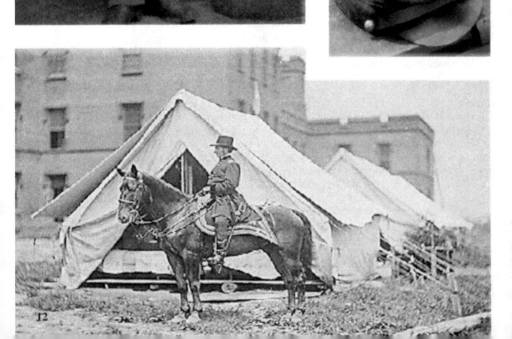

GEORGE W. AHART, Private, born 1 Jan 1839 in Tennessee and died 11 Dec 1888. Enrolled on 14 Aug 1862, mustered in 13 Sep 1862 at Henderson, KY and mustered out 23 Sep 1863 at Russellville, KY. He served with Co. L, 8th Kentucky Regt. Cav. (USA). There was a younger George W. Ahart (b. 1855, d. 1945), who lived in Trigg County during this era. He married Ann Eliza Leneave on 19 Dec 1875. They are both buried in Trigg County at the Alexander Cunningham Cemetery at Peal's Chapel.

The War for Southern Independence veteran George W. Ahart was a brother of Joseph Ahart. Joseph Ahart and a Green W. Ahart are listed in the Kentucky Adjutant General's Report as members of Co. L, 8th Kentucky Volunteer Cav. (USA). We think George W. Ahart and "Green" W. Ahart are one and the same. Other than the Kentucky Adjutant General's Report, we cannot find any reference to a "Green" W. Ahart.

His father was George Ahart (b. 27 Feb 1808 in Virginia, d. 25 Nov 1876) and his mother was Sarah (Hawkins) Ahart (b. 1810 in Tennessee, d. 4 Feb 1883). They are buried in the Long Creek Cemetery in Trigg County, KY.

G.W. Ahart married Margaret J. Baker on 14 Oct 1861 in Trigg County. His sons, William Guthrie Ahart married Tennie E. Jones on 29 Dec 1887 in Trigg County and James L. Ahart married Nevada E. Graham on 16 Jan 1890 in Trigg County; Joseph Monroe Ahart married Edna R. Graham on 14 Dec 1893 in Trigg County.

In the 1850 Trigg County Census he is listed as George W. Ahart, age 11 years and living with his father George Ahart, age 42 years; his mother Sarah (Hawkins) Ahart, age 36 years; and five siblings: Joseph, age 13 years; Martha A., age 9 years; Hannah L., age 7 years; Andrew J., age 4 years; and James, age 1 year.

George W. Ahart is buried in the Long Creek Cemetery with his wife Margaret J. (Baker) Ahart (b. 20 Jan 1841, d. 12 Jun 1899). His three daughters: George Ann (b. 24 Jun 1862 in Kentucky, d. 12 May 1881), Mary Jane (b. 8 Oct 1868, d. 8 Nov 1915) and Martha Ann (b. 22 Oct 1874, d. 23 May 1876) are all buried in the Long Creek Cemetery.

His three sons: William Guthrie (b. 11 Jul 1864 in Kentucky, d. 24 Feb 1929); James L. (b. 19 Mar 1866 in Kentucky, d. 14 Oct 1940); Joseph Monroe (b. 22 Feb 1874 in Kentucky, d. 1 Dec 1927 in Kentucky) are all buried in the Long Creek Cemetery. *Complied by Larry L. Walston.*

JOSEPH AHART, born May 28, 1837 in Smith County, TN. He is the eldest of a family of six born to George and Sarah (Hawkins) Ahart. His father was born 1808 in Virginia, died 1876 in Trigg County, KY and his mother was born in 1810 in East Tennessee, died February 1883. On coming to Trigg County they settled two miles west of Canton, KY. There our subject was reared. At age 22 he commenced farming on land given to him by his father. This was sold afterwards to his brother. In the fall of 1863 he came to the farm which he now rents, consisting of about 100 acres and where he has since resided.

He enlisted in August 1862 in Co. L, 8th Kentucky Cav. (Union) and served his enlistment. He was married in February 1859 to Nancy E. Bell (b. 12 May 1945 in Trigg County, d. 31 Aug 1883) and they had three children: Jesse M., Henry J. and Martha L.

Mr. Ahart's second marriage was to Mary E. Greham Ricks on 13 Jan 1884. She was born in Trigg County and has three children by a former marriage: George R., Leona A., Fredonia "Donie" A. Ricks.

Mr. Ahart is the agent of the Fungo Landing for all shipments for Golden Pond. He is a member of a Masonic Order.

Letter written in 1884 about Joseph and Mary Ahart. The letter was signed with a note thanking people for helping find the information for Cathy L. Cravens.

JAMES ALEXANDER, Private, born ?? and died ??. Enlisted 26 Sep 1861 for three years by Capt. J. Qualls at Camp Reeves, TN. He was last paid 30 Jun 1863 by Capt. McKinney. Served with Co. G, 8th Kentucky Regt. Inf. (CSA). Pvt. James Alexander was badly wounded at Jackson, MS on 11 Jul 1863 and was never able to return to his unit.

References: Cannot find in Vol. I, Kentucky Adjutant General's Report (CSA); cannot find in Vol. II, Kentucky Adjutant General's Re-

port (CSA); page 23, Trigg County Civil War; not found in Simmons 1850 Trigg County Census; not found in Simmons' 1860 Trigg County Census; not found in Simmons' 1870 Trigg County Census; not found in Neel's 1880 Trigg County Census; not found in Jones' 1900 Trigg County Census; National Archives Microfilm, Series 319, Reel 124. *Complied by Larry L. Walston.*

WILLIAM H.H. ALEXANDER, born 8 Mar 1841 in Kentucky, d. 22 Dec 1904. He enlisted on 15 Oct 1861 for three years by Maj. Davis at Camp Alcorn in Hopkinsville, KY and served with Co. G, 8th Kentucky Regt. Inf. (CSA). Muster Roll dated 26 Sep 1861-31 Jul 1863, absent, sick in the hospital; Muster Roll dated July and August 1863, absent, sent to hospital from Jackson, MS in July 1863; Muster Roll dated March and April 1864, sick, in hospital. He was captured at Fort Donelson on 16 Feb 1862, sick; Muster Roll dated 24 Aug 1862 at Camp Morton, IN, Prisoner of War exchanged at Vicksburg, MS September 1862.

William H.H. Alexander married Eliza Sanders on 12 Oct 1870 in Trigg County.

In the 1850 Trigg County Census he is listed as "William H.H." Alexander, age 9 years, and living with his father John Alexander, age 39 years; mother Martha (Ramey) Alexander, age 30 years; and three siblings: Sarah J., age 7 years; John J., age 5 years; and Eleanora A., age 1 year. Also living with this family is Eliza Harrell, age 21 years; Mary S. Harrell, age 2 years; and Andrew Alexander, age 20 years.

In the 1900 Trigg County Census he is listed as "William H.H." Alexander, a farmer, age 59 years and living with his wife Eliza (Sanders) Alexander, age 49 years (married 29 years); son Alvin, age 26 years; and a servant Charley Martin, age 15 years. Eliza (Sanders) Alexander has had three children, all three were still living when the census was taken.

William H.H. Alexander is buried in the Sivills Cemetery with his father John Alexander (no stone) and his mother Patsey (Ramsey) Alexander (no stone). According to cemetery records, there is no stone marking William H.H. Alexander's grave. *Compiled by Larry L. Walston.*

ZENAS ALEXANDER, born in Trigg County, KY on 8 May 1843. His parents were Thomas and Ann Mariah (Sanders) Alexander. He married Elizabeth Jones. Zenas' great-grandfather, John Ramey, died in Caldwell County, KY, was a soldier in the Revolutionary War.

Zenas joined the Confederate Army on 26 Sep 1861 at Camp Reeves, TN. He served as a private in Co. C, 8th Regt., Infantry.

Zenas was captured at the battle of Fort Donelson and was imprisoned at Camp Morton, IN. He was later exchanged and returned to his unit. Severally wounded in the battle of Jackson, MS on 11 Jul 1863, Zenas was sent to a hospital in Lauderdale, MS. It was decided that his injuries were so severe that he should not serve in his military unit. Zenas, who was very loyal, chose to serve the Confederacy by working at the Confederate hospital where he had been taken when he was wounded. *By Kay Wallace Sloan.*

WILLIAM H. ANDERSON, Private, born ca. 1839 in Kentucky, died ?. He enlisted 11 Aug 1861 at Camp Burnett, TN and served with Co. G, 4th Kentucky Regt. Infantry (CSA). Pvt. William H. Anderson was taken prisoner at Kennesaw Mountain, GA on 20 Jun 1864 and sent to Camp Morton, IN on 30 Jun 1864. Pvt. Anderson was exchanged on 15 Mar 1865.

He is listed as having voted in the 6 Aug 1860 election at Canton, KY.

In the 1850 Trigg County Census, William H. Anderson is listed as age 11 years and living with his father James Anderson, age 42 years; his mother Harriet Anderson, age 41 years; and four siblings: C.D. (male), age 20 years; Elizabeth, age 16 years; Harriet A., age 14 years; and Melton J., age 7 years.

In the 1860 Trigg County Census there is a "W.H." Anderson, age 24 years and living with his wife "J." Anderson, age 21 years, and two children, "J.R." (male), age 2 years; and "M.A." (female), age 9 months.

References: Page 174, Vol. I Kentucky Adjutant General's Report (CSA); he is not found in Maupins Trigg County Cemetery Records; page 264, Neel's Statistical Handbook of Trigg County, Trigg County Voting Records; page 25, Simmons' 1850 Trigg County Census #452; page 65, Simmons' 1860 Trigg County Census #965; not found in

Simmons' 1870 Trigg County Census; not found in Neel's 1880 Trigg County Census; Kentucky State Archives Microfilm, Drawer 528, Series 319, Reel 96. *Compiled by Larry L. Walston.*

JAMES H. ARMSTRONG, Private, born ca. 1846 in Kentucky, died ??. He enrolled 13 Aug 1863, mustered in for one year on 26 Oct 1863 in Princeton, KY and mustered out 19 Dec 1864 in Bowling Green, KY. He served with Co. F, 48th Kentucky Regt. Mounted Infantry (USA).

His father was Andrew Armstrong (b. ca. 1800 in North Carolina, d. ??) and his mother was Almira A. (McCoy) Armstrong (b. ca. 1812 in Kentucky, d. ??).

In the 1850 Trigg County Census James H. Armstrong is listed as age 4 years and living with his father Andrew Armstrong, age 50 years; his mother Almira A. (McCoy) Armstrong, age 38 years; and nine siblings: David H., age 20 years; Mildred E., age 19 years; Sarah E., age 17 years; Mary J., age 15 years; Andrew J., age 13 years; John E., age 10 years; Susan C., age 8 years; Lucy A., age 6 years; and Samuel L., age 2 years.

In the 1860 Trigg County Census James H. Armstrong is listed as age 14 years and living with his father Andrew Armstrong, age 59 years; his mother E.A. (Almira A.) (McCoy) Armstrong, age 48 years; and five siblings: M. (female), age 16 years; S.L. (Samuel L.), age 11 years; M.E. (female), age 7 years; G.W. (female), age 5 years; and F.P. (female), age 3 years.

In the 1870 Trigg County Census James H. Armstrong is listed as age 23 years and living with the Sarah A. Clark (age 32 years) family in this census.

His unnamed brother died on 1 Nov 1852 at the age of one day. The parents were A. (Andrew) Armstrong and E. (Almira) Armstrong of Trigg County.

REUBIN T. ATKINS, born 27 Aug 1827 in the Blue Ridge Mountains of Patrick County, VA. He came to Trigg County about 1840, without his parents and spent the rest of his life.

According to his descendants, he was a soldier in the Civil War but uncertain as to whether it was for the North or the South. He was among a group who assembled at Canton, KY on 9 Apr 1861 to muster for the Kentucky Militia. Five days later the Confederates captured Fort Sumter.

Loyalties of the people in Trigg County were divided. Many of the men who mustered at the Indian Spring at Canton, soon enlisted to serve with the Confederacy; others joined the Federal Army.

For them the war became a reality with the Battle of Fort Donelson in February 1862 just across the Tennessee line from Trigg County. Many Trigg Countains were involved in this battle which the Confederacy lost. Many escaped during the surrender and made their way across the Cumberland River back to their Trigg County homes.

According to family legend Reuben fought at Fort Donelson along with a friend, Steven Edmunds, who enlisted in the Federal Army.

Was Reubin a Rebel or a Yankee? Some think he may have been both. Was he one of those who escaped or was he among the 12,000 Confederates taken to Camp Douglas army prison after the battle and later paroled by signing an oath of allegiance to the United States? Perhaps he re-enlisted later.

Among his possessions was an oath of allegiance he signed 28 May 1863 swearing to uphold the US Constitution, and of Kentucky and loyalty to the US government. The breach of his solemn oath would be death or any other punishment inflicted upon him by the judgment of a court-martial or military commission.

He was the father of 13 children, seven by his first wife Nancy Wilson, whom he married 24 Sep 1846 and six by his second wife, Martha Boren, whom he married 25 Nov 1866. He was a farmer in civilian life and a faithful member of Dry Creek Primitive Baptist Church. He died 11 Dec 1898 and was buried in Atkins Cemetery, Trigg County. *Submitted by Margie T. Darnall.*

JAMES R. ATWOOD, Private, born 23 Oct 1832 in Tennessee, died 16 Jan 1866. He enrolled 14 Aug 1862, mustered in for one year on 13 Sep 1862 at Henderson, KY and mustered out 23 Sep 1863 at Russellville, KY. He served with Co. L, 8th Kentucky Regt. Cav. (USA). Mustered in 4 Aug 1864 at Paducah, KY, mustered out 12 Feb 1965 at Paducah, KY and served with Co. B, 1st Regt. Kentucky Capital Guards, Paducah Battalion (USA). James Atwood was a farrier in the Union Army.

James Atwood's brother John Atwood and his sister Mary Atwood were both born in Tennessee. His mother was Mary Atwood (b. ca. 1795 in Virginia, d. ?).

J.R. Atwood voted in the August 1856 election at "Furgerson" Precinct. He also voted at the Ferguson Precinct in the 1 Aug 1859 election.

In the 1850 Trigg County Census there is a James Atwood, age 17 years, listed as a laborer living with his mother Mary Atwood, age 55 years, and two siblings, John, age 21 years, and Mary, age 15 years.

In the 1860 Trigg County Census there is a J.R. Atwood listed as a blacksmith, age 27 years and living with his wife A.J. Atwood, age 28 years, and two children, M.H. and M.M. There is also a Wilson Atwood, age 18 years, and J.B. Dix, age 25 years and living with the family in this census.

He is buried in the Atwood Cemetery. There is only one other grave in the Atwood Cemetery and it is unidentified. This cemetery is located on the Long Creek Road in Trigg County.

WILSON ALLEN ATWOOD, First Sergeant, born 28 Nov 1841 in Kentucky, d. 3 Nov 1904. He enlisted 14 Sep 1861 at Camp Burnett, TN, Co. G, 4th Kentucky Regt. Inf. (CSA). He was promoted from private to third corporal 10 Jan 1863; from third corporal to first sergeant 18 Apr 1864 when 1st Sgt. W.T. Battoe was reduced in rank. 1st Sgt. Atwood was captured at Washington, GA 6 May 1865 and took the Oath of Allegiance at Washington, GA 21 May 1865. He is listed in the Kentucky Adjutant General's Report as W.A. Attwood.

His father was William Jackson Atwood (b. 30 Sep 1817, d. 24 Nov 1887) who married Louisa Woodson Franklin on 14 Jan 1841. William Jackson Atwood is buried in the Long Creek Cemetery in Trigg County. His mother Louisa Woodson (Franklin) Atwood (b. 1820, d. 22 Jun 1907) (wife of W.J.) is buried in the Turner or Cerulean Cemetery in Trigg County.

Wilson A. Atwood failed to muster with Capt. Alfred Thomas' company at Cadiz, KY on Saturday, 7 Apr 1861. He did muster, however, at Indian Springs with the battalion on Saturday, 7 Sep 1861.

Wilson A. Atwood married Donna Littlejohn on 2 Aug 1866. In later life they may have moved to Marshall County, KY. We can find no record of their being married in Trigg County.

In the 1850 Trigg County Census Wilson Allen Atwood is listed as age 8 years and living with his father William J. Atwood, age 32 years; his mother Louisa W. (Franklin) Atwood, age 30 years; and three siblings: William G., age 7 years; Mary J., age 5 years; and Martha A., age 9 months.

In the 1870 Trigg County Census Wilson Allen Atwood and his wife Donna (Littlejohn) Atwood are not found in this census. However, his father William J. Atwood, age 52 years, and his mother Louisa (Franklin) Atwood, age 49 years, are listed with their two sons Benjamin F., age 18 years, and Thomas R., age 16 years.

In the 1880 and 1900 Trigg County Census none of this family is found.

His infant daughter (daughter of W.A. and Dorina Atwood) (b&d. 21 May 1867) is also buried in the Turner or Cerulean Cemetery. *Compiled by Larry L. Walston.*

BENJAMIN F. BACON, Private, born ca. 1833 in Kentucky, died ??. He enlisted 12 Feb 1863 in Columbia, TN, Co. A (Woodward's) 15th Kentucky Regt. Cav. Benjamin Bacon's father Edmund Bacon (b. 28 Mar 1785, d. 19 Jan 1866) and his mother Nancy (Smith) Bacon (b. 6 Jan 1786, d. 1 Jun 1868) are both buried in the Edmund Bacon Cemetery in Trigg County.

In the 1850 Trigg County Census his father Edmund Bacon, age 65 years; his mother Nancy Bacon, age 65 years; and a brother Edmund Jr., age 21 years, are listed. Benjamin F. Bacon is not listed.

In the 1860 Trigg County Census "Ben" Bacon is listed as age 27 years and living with "W.J." (male) Bacon, age 28 years; a Robert Hill, age 31 years; Martha S. Hill, age 26 years; and their son Samuel Hill, age 2 years.

His father is listed as "E." (Edmund) Bacon, age 75 years and living with his mother, "Nancey" Bacon, age 74 years, and a Sally Henry, age 16 years.

In the 1870 Trigg County Census Benjamin Bacon is listed as age 35 years and living with his wife Gabriella Bacon, age 26 years, and their three children: Maggie, age 6 years; Willie (male) age 3 years, and Lilly, age 1 year.

Ben Bacon is listed as a farmer, age 47 years and living with his wife "Gabe" Bacon, age 37 years, and their six children: Maggie, age 15 years; William, age 13 years; Lila, age 10 years; Ella, age 8 years; Malcolm, age 6 years; and Edmond, age 4 years.

None of this family is found in the 1900 Trigg County Census.

Benjamin Bacon's brother W.J. Bacon (b. 16 Sep 1832 in Salem, KY, d. 22 Jun 1898) is also buried in the Edmund Bacon Cemetery.

CHARLES D. BAKER, Private, born in February 1837 in Trigg County, KY and died ??. First enlistment was in October 1861 in 1st Kentucky Cav. (CSA) and served with Co. B, 1st Kentucky (Helm's) Regt. Cav. (CSA) with Col. Helm, Capt. Billie Caldwell, 1st Lt. Bill Elliott and 2nd Lt. Bill Poindexter. His second was in Spring 1863 in 11th Alabama Regt. Cav. (CSA).

Charles D. Baker's father was Alexander Baker (b. ca. 1794 in Virginia, d. ??) and his mother was Catherine T. Baker (b. 17 Feb 1802 in Virginia, d. 5 Oct 1878). Catherine T. Baker is buried in the East End Cemetery.

Charles D. Baker married Miss Laura M. Barbour on 8 Aug 1859 in Trigg County. In Trigg County Court Records, an Affidavit of Mrs. Laura J. Withers states that C.D. (Charles D.) Baker, J.E. (James Edgar) Baker and Miss Lucy E. Baker are only heirs of Alexander Baker.

His sister Lucy Ellen Baker married Thomas W. Saffarans (b. 25 Jun 1843, d. 15 Oct 1876) on 27 Oct 1874 in Trigg County. He is buried in the East End Cemetery with their infant daughter Katie T. (b&d. 14 Aug 1873). In Neel's book his name is spelled "Laffarans." Lucy Ellen (Baker) Saffarans (b. 1841, d. 1930) married second, Thomas K. Torian (b. 1843, d. 1928) on 4 Oct 1886 in Trigg County.

According to his pension application date 6 May 1912, he was discharged from the 1st Kentucky Cav. July/August 1862 and re-enlisted in the 11th Alabama Cav. in the Spring of 1863. He stayed with the 11th Alabama until 17 May 1865, when he was paroled at Pond Springs, AL. He took the Oath, but was arrested as soon as he returned home to Trigg County after being paroled. At the time of his pension application, he was engaged in farming. No wife.

In the 1900 Trigg County Census he is listed as age 63 years and living with his son Charlie A., age 31 years; son Oscar B., age 25, and brother James E. Baker, age 61 years. Charles D. Baker is listed as a widower and as a livery man.

FRANCIS M. BAKER, 2nd Lieutenant, born 17 Oct 1837 in Kentucky, died 20 Nov 1874. He enlisted 13 Sep 1861 at Camp Burnett, TN and served with Co. G, 4th Kentucky Regt. Inf. (CSA).

There was another Francis M. Baker (b. ca. 1852) who lived in Trigg County in this era. He was the son of Thomas L. Baker and Melinda J. Baker.

This Francis M. Baker appears as being 8 years old on page 53 #976-447 of Simmons' 1850 Trigg County Census.

Francis M. Baker married Mary Ann Bryant on 29 Dec 1859 in Trigg County, KY.

In the 1850 Trigg County Census he is listed as age 12 years living with his father Peter Baker, age 45 years; his mother Rhoda Baker, age 43 years; and six siblings: Docia, age 14 years; Charles W., age 10 years; James M., age 9 years; Robert A., age 7 years; Fielding W., age 6 years; and Thomas W., age 2 years.

In the 1860 Trigg County Census he is listed as age 22 years and living with his wife Mary A. (Bryant) Baker, age 21 years, no children. They have been married within the year of when the census was taken.

In the 1870 Trigg County Census Francis M. Baker is not found in this census, but his father Peter Baker is listed as age 65 years old and living with his sons Robert A., age 27 years, and Thomas W., age 21 years.

Francis M. Baker is buried in the Bryant Cemetery in Trigg County with two of his daughters. Margaret Louisa (Lulu) Baker (b. 5 Aug 1862 in Kentucky, d. 9 July 1896) is buried in the Bryant Cemetery; and Frankie Baker, daughter of F.M. and M.A. Baker (b. 4 Jun 1875 in Kentucky, d. 2 Sep 1880, age 5 years), is also buried in the Bryant Cemetery in Trigg County.

GERMAN BAKER, Private, born ca. 1842 in Kentucky, died 30 Nov 1861 in Hopkinsville, KY. He enlisted 13 Oct 1861 in Hopkinsville, KY, Co. C, 8th Kentucky Regt. Inf. (CSA). He is buried in row #1 in Riverside Cemetery in Hopkinsville, KY.

In the 1850 Trigg County Census he is listed as age 8 years and living with the Peyton S. Nance family.

In the 1860 Trigg County Census German Baker does not appear.

References: Page 386, Vol. I, Kentucky Adjutant General's Report (CSA); *Kentucky New Era*, Saturday, 4 Mar 1899, article "Dead Soldiers Names, Brought to Light after 37 Years, Mr. Gant's Discovery" gives the death date and unit of Pvt. German Baker; page 36, Simmons' 1850 Trigg County Census #655; not found in Simmons' 1860 Trigg County Census; Kentucky State Archives Microfilm, Series 319, Reel 124.

HAZZARD PERRY BAKER, 1st Lieutenant, born 2 Jan 1835 in Trigg County, KY, son of Blake Baker II and wife Edna (Gresham) Baker.

On 9 Jul 1861 Baker enlisted in the Confederate Army and served for 12 months in the Oak Grove Rangers, 1st Kentucky Cav. commanded by Col. Ben Hardin Helm. Baker was instrumental in organizing Woodward's 2nd Kentucky Cav. He served as a 1st lieutenant in Co. D, 2nd Kentucky Cav. from September 1862 to the end of the war. He fought at Fort Donelson, Shiloh, Stone River, Tullahoma, Jackson (MS), Chickamauga, Chattanooga and the siege of Atlanta.

At the close of the war when the Confederate Government was forced to leave the Capitol at Richmond, VA, President Jefferson Davis and his family, along with his cabinet members, proceeded to travel South. The 2nd Kentucky Cav. fell in with President Davis and his party at Charlotte, NC. Following the last meeting of the Confederate Cabinet, President Davis was concerned that the large number of soldiers with his party would attract the attention of any Union Soldiers in the area. At that time, Davis asked Capt. Given Campbell of the 2nd Kentucky Cav. to select 10 good soldiers to act as his personal escort for the remainder of the trip. The 10 men chosen, all members of the 2nd Kentucky were: Capt. Given Campbell, 1st Lt. Hazzard Perry Baker, 3rd Cpl. Minus C. Parsley, F.P. Ingram, 1st Cpl. W.A. Howard and Harrison Smith all of whom were from Trigg County, KY. The other members of the escort were: James T. Halbert of McCracken County, KY; Thomas S. McSwain of Henry County, TN; and W.L. Heath of Corbin, KY.

On the afternoon of 9 May 1865 the Davis party and their escort pitched camp for the night at a location just south of Washington, GA about one-mile from Irwinville on the road leading to Ableville.

On the morning of 10 May, Capt. Campbell and three other members left the camp to obtain food and provisions for the party. During their absence two detachments of the Union Army descended upon the camp and arrested President Davis, the Confederate Officials and members of the escort.

Lt. Hazzard Perry Baker, the ranking officer of the escort, officially surrendered President Jefferson Davis, his sword and flag to the Union Soldiers.

Following his release, Hazzard Perry Baker returned to his Trigg County, KY home. On 24 Nov 1867 he married Sue Canon. To the union were born two daughters, Molly and Lilly, and a son Hugh. Baker was married a second time on 12 Nov 1877 to Henrietta Wallace. They were the parents of a son Paul and a daughter Eddy. Baker may have married a third time, name of wife is unknown and probably there were not children born to this marriage. *Submitted by Kay Wallace Sloan.*

JOHN FREEMAN BAKER SR., Captain, born December 1824 (no dates on tombstone), son of Blake and Edna, died ?? (no dates on tombstone). He enlisted 18 Sep 1861 at Camp Burnett, TN and served with Co. G, 4th Kentucky Regt. Inf. (CSA). He was elected 3rd sergeant 14 Aug 1861; 2nd lieutenant 15 Sep 1861 and captain 20 July 1863.

John F. Baker Sr. was a brother to Hazard P. Baker. His parents were Blake Baker (b. ca. 1804 in North Carolina, d. 29 Aug 1852) and Edna (Gresham) Baker (b. 1806 in Virginia, d. ??). They were married on 2 July 1822.

He was married to Martha Ann Creekmur (b. 1854, d. 4 Jun 1938), she later married a Malone. We cannot find her burial place.

In the 1850 Trigg County Census there is a John F. Baker, age 26 years and living with his father Blake Baker, age 45 years; his mother

Edna (Creekmur) Baker, age 45 years; and eight siblings in this census: Christian F., age 19 years; Laurinda, age 17 years; Hazard P., age 15 years; Blake, age 13 years; Thomas K., age 11 years; Helen E., age 9 years; Luin B., age 6 years; and Mary E., age 2 months.

In the 1870 Trigg County Census he is listed as John F. Baker, age 45 years and living with George and Henry Grasty near Edna Baker, age 60 years. His mother Edna (Creekmur) Baker is listed as a widow, age 60 years, and living alone in this census.

In the 1880 Trigg County Census he is listed as John Baker, age 56 years living with his wife M.A. (Creekmur) Baker, age 26 years, and two daughters, Minnie, age 4 years, and Birdie, age 2 years.

In the 1900 Trigg County Census he is listed as John F. Baker, age 75 years, a farmer and living with his wife Martha Ann (Creekmur) Baker (married 12 years), age 49 years; a son "Louis," age 19 years, and a daughter Fleety, age 17 years.

Martha A. (Creekmur) Baker has had four children all still living when this census was taken.

There is a John F. Baker, Co. G, 4th Kentucky Regt. Inf. buried in the Blue Springs or Mount Pleasant Cemetery.

JOHN F. BAKER JR., Lieutenant, born ca. 1834 (Thomas and Malinda's son), died ??. He enlisted 14 Aug 1861 at Camp Burnett, TN and served with Co. G, 4th Kentucky Regt. Inf. (CSA). Pvt. Baker was promoted from private to 3rd sergeant on 1 May 1863 and 3rd to 4th sergeant on 12 Oct 1863. He was demoted from 4th sergeant to private on 20 Jan 1864. He may have been promoted to 2nd lieutenant at one time. He was succeeded in command by Lieutenant Robert W. Major.

John Baker died of congestive fever in St. Helena Parish, LA on 5 Aug 1862.

He was the son of Thomas L. Baker (b. 3 Apr 1801, d. 17 Jan 1870) and Malinda Elizabeth (Cunningham) Baker (b. 30 Nov 1802, d. 29 Jan 1871). Thomas L. Baker and Malinda Elizabeth Cunningham were married on 19 Aug 1821. John F. Baker Jr. is found in Maupin's Trigg County Cemetery Records. His parents are listed as being buried in the Thomas L. Baker Cemetery. They are also listed as being buried in the Blue Springs or Mount Pleasant Cemetery.

In the 1850 Trigg County Census there is a John F. Baker, age 16 years and living with his father Thomas L. Baker, age 49 years; his mother Malinda Baker, age 48 years; and seven siblings: Caroline B., age 21 years; Blake, age 18 years; Alexander, age 15 years; Thomas L., age 12 years; Anne, age 10 years; and Francis M. (male) age 8 years.

In the 1860 Trigg County Census there is an "F" Baker, male, age 23 and living with "T.L." (Thomas L.) Baker, age 59 years; a "M" to Windal Baker, age 57 years; and one sibling A.D. Baker (Ann), age 19 years in this census.

In the 1870 Trigg County Census there is a John F. Baker listed as living alone and age 27 years, but we don't feel this is our Lt. Baker.

MARION E. BAREFIELD, born December 1845 in Georgia, died ??. He enlisted ?? and was one of the last Confederates living in Trigg County.

M.E. Barefield age 22 years of Trigg County (born in Campbell County, GA) married Mary E. (Ladd) of Trigg County, age 20 years, on 23 Jan 1868. It was the first marriage of both bride and groom.

In the 1900 Trigg County Census he is listed as Marion E. Barefield a farmer, age 54 years and living with his wife Mary E. (Ladd) Barefield (married 38 years) age 52 years; Carey M. Barefield, an apprentice age 13 years; and mother-in-law Jemima Ladd, age 73 years. Mary E. (Ladd) Barefield has had two children, both of whom were still living when this census was taken.

In the 1920 Trigg County Census Marion "Barifield" is listed as a farmer age 74 years and living with his wife Mary E. (Ladd) "Barifield," age 72 years; son Wesley, age 48 years; daughter-in-law Mamie, age 46 years; and four grandsons: Virgil, age 24 years; John W., age 22 years; Walter E., age 17 years and Lander H., age 12 years. Marion Barefield's son Sam Barefield is listed as Sam "Barifield" a farmer, age 46 years and living with his wife Mary M. "Barifield," and three children: Herman B., age 16 years; Aubrey H., age 14 years; and Tera J., age 8 years.

M.E. Barefield (b. 1845, d. 1903??) is buried in the Lander Cemetery in Christian County near the Trigg County-Christian County line with his wife Mary E. (Ladd) Barefield (b. 1847, d. 14 June 1922) at age 74 years. (We question Mr. Barefield's death date on his tombstone. It may have been closer to 1933 rather than 1903).

Affidavit of Sam Barefield states that J.W. Barefield and Sam Barefield were the sons of Marion E. Barefield and that Marion E. Barefield was the husband of Mrs. Mary E. Barefield. Dated 19 Jul 1922.

GIDEON W. BARNES, born ca. 1845 in Kentucky, died ??. He enlisted 24 Oct 1861 at Camp Alcorn in Hopkinsville, KY and served with Co. B, 8th Kentucky Regt. Inf. (CSA). Pvt. Gideon W. Barnes was wounded at Fort Donelson on 15 Feb 1862.

His father was Cader F. Barnes (b. Ca. 1789, d. ca. 1846) and his mother was Arlena E. (Dunning) Barnes (b. 8 Mar 1828, d. 20 Jan 1875). Cader F. Barnes voted in the election at Cadiz, KY on 3 Aug 1842. Cader Barnes was married to Winifred Beal on 15 Aug 1809. They were married by Fielding Wolf in Christian County.

Arlena E. Dunning married first, Cader F. Barnes in July 1842 and married second, Alexander Dunning on 31 Jul 1847.

Gideon W. Barnes, age 24 years of Trigg County, married Susan C. Faulkner, age 18 years, of Montgomery County, TN on 15 Sep 1869. It was the first marriage for both bride and groom.

K.E. (King E.) Dunning married Aurora A. Curney on 4 Apr 1871 in Trigg County.

In the 1850 Trigg County Census a Gideon W. Barnes is listed as age 5 years old and living with his step-father Alexander Dunning, age 25 years; his mother Arrena E. (or Arlena. E.) (Dunning) (Barnes) Dunning, age 22 years; a step-brother King Dunning, age 1 year; a step-sister Maranda E. Dunning, age 3 months; and a Martha Dunning, age 11 years.

In the 1860 Trigg County Census Gideon W. Barnes is not found, but his mother is listed as "Irene" E. (Dunning) (Barnes) Dunning, a widow, age 43 years and living with her children: Maranda, age 20 years; Malissa, age 17 years; Martha, age 15 years; and Ebb, age 8 years.

In the 1870 Trigg County Census Gideon W. Barnes' step-brother King E. Dunning is listed as age 21 years living with a black farm hand Draper Dunning, age 20 years.

Gideon W. Barnes is buried in the Dunning Cemetery in Trigg County, but according to cemetery records, there is no stone at his grave. He is the only person with the surname of Barnes buried there.

WILLIAM BARNES, Private, born October 1836, died ??. He enlisted ? and served with Co. F, 50th Tennessee Regt. Inf. (CSA). His unit is given on his tombstone. We cannot be sure that any of the following men were the Pvt. William Barnes of the 50th Tennessee Regt. Inf. (CSA).

William Barnes married first, Elizabeth Johnson on 2 Oct 1863 in Trigg County and married second, "Mitt" Lawrence on 30 Oct 1889 in Trigg County.

In the 1850 Trigg County Census there is a William Barnes, age 17 years and living with the James and Margaret Thomas family.

In the 1860 Trigg County Census there is a W.O. Barnes listed as a "cooper," age 26 years and living with his mother "M. Barnes," age 49 years, and two siblings, J.S. (male), age 19 years, and A.B. (male), age 28 years.

In the 1870 Trigg County Census there is a William A. Barnes, age 35 years and living with his wife Elizabeth (Johnson) Barnes, age 22 years and two children, a daughter Margaret, age 4 years and a son William G., age 2 years.

In the 1900 Trigg County Census there is a William Barnes listed as a farmer, age 63 years and living with his wife Armenta Barnes (married 8 years), age 33 years; a son Albert J., age 3 months; a step-son Jesse L. Futrell, age 14 years, and a step-daughter Lucy W. Futrell, age 11 years. Armenta (Lawrence) Barnes has had five children, three of whom were still living when this census was taken.

In the 1920 Trigg County Census "Mit" Barnes is listed as a widow, age 53 years and living with her son Albert J., age 19 years. They lived on the Linton Road in this census.

William Barnes is buried in the Skinner Cemetery with an "R. Mitty" (Armenta?) Barnes (b. 18 Aug 1870, d. 23 Feb 1939). The 1900 Trigg County Census seems to confirm that Armenta Barnes and "Mitt" Barnes were the same person.

WILLIAM L. BARNETT, Private, born ca. 1832 in Kentucky, died ??. He enlisted ?? and served with Co. B, Woodward's 2nd/15th Kentucky Cav. Regt. (CSA).

His step-mother may have been Martha Newby who married Nathan Barnett on 24 Jun 1837. William L. Barnett does not appear in any Trigg County Cemetery Records.

In the 1850 Trigg County Census William L. Barnett is listed as age 18 years and living with his father Nathan Barnett, age 45 years and seven siblings: Delia, age 16 years; Isaac, age 14 years; James J., age 13 years; Josiah, age 11 years; Nathan L., age 9 years; John F., age 7 years, and Lucy A., age 6 years. All members of the above Barnett family in the 1850 Census were born in Kentucky.

In the 1860 Trigg County Census all members of both Barnett families listed were born in Tennessee.

JAMES B. OR E. BATTOE, 1st Corporal, born January 1827 in Illinois, died 2 Aug 1906. He enlisted 11 Sep 1861 at Camp Burnett, TN and served with Co. G, 4th Kentucky Regt. Inf. (CSA). The Kentucky Adjutant General's Report gives his name as James B. Battoe.

James Battoe Jr., married three times: first, Elizabeth D. Linn on 6 Nov 1850 in Trigg County. James Battoe, age 38, married second, Nancy Jane Martin, age 21, born in Trigg County, KY on 20 Mar 1865. At age 40 years he married third, Eliza Lawrence of Trigg County, age 22 years, on 12 May 1869. It was the first marriage for the bride and the third marriage for the groom.

James' and Eliza's daughter Ella May Battoe married Lorenzo D. Radford on 27 Nov 1900.

In the 1850 Trigg County Census he is listed as "James Battoe Jr.," age 24 years, born in Illinois and living with the Kinchen Battoe, a surveyor, age 32 years; a Tabitha (Johnson) Battoe, age 32 years; and their children: Mary A., age 13 years; James J., age 12 years; Teresa E., age 11 years; John K., age 9 years; Alpha E., age 8 years, and William F., age 6 years.

James E. Battoe is buried with his third wife Eliza (Lawrence) Battoe (no stone) in the Lawrence Cemetery.

James Battoe's second wife, Nancy Jane (Martin) Battoe (b. 22 Jan 1843, d. 30 Dec 1868) is buried in the Pete Light Cemetery. (Maupin's reference is incorrect in giving her death date as 30 Dec 1863. Neel's reference is correct in that it gives her correct death date as 30 Dec 1868).

WILLIAM T. BATTOE, Private, born ca. 1844 in Kentucky, died ??. He enlisted 11 Aug 1861 at Camp Burnett, TN and served with Co. G, 4th Kentucky Regt. Inf. (CSA). Pvt. Battoe was a teamster. He was promoted from private to first corporal 10 Jan 1863 and then to first sergeant 12 Oct 1863. He was demoted from first sergeant to private 18 Apr 1864. He was wounded in the left knee at Resaca, GA on 14 May 1864. Pvt. William T. Battoe was captured at Washington, GA on 6 May 1865 and took the Oath of Allegiance on 18 May 1865.

His father was Kinchen Battoe (b. ca. 1818 in Kentucky, d. ??) and his mother was Tabitha (Johnson) Battoe (b. ca. 1818 in Tennessee, d. ??).

William Battoe's sister Mary A. Battoe married William C. Cheatham on 23 Oct 1858 in Trigg County.

William Battoe's brother James J. Battoe married Charity Bridges on 15 Oct 1859 in Trigg County. (Charity (Bridges) Battoe's brother, Cullen Bridges was a Confederate soldier.)

In the 1850 Trigg County Census William T. Battoe is listed as "William F. Battoe," age 6 years and living with his father Kinchen Battoe, age 32 years; his mother Tabitha (Johnson) Battoe; age 32 years, and six siblings: Mary A., age 13 years; James J., age 12 years; Teresa E., age 11 years; John K., age 9 years; and Alpha E., age 8 years. A James Battoe Jr. (born in Illinois), age 24 years, is living with the family in this census.

In the 1860 Trigg County Census William T. Battoe is not listed.

JAMES T. BATTS, 2nd Corporal, born ca. 1841 in Kentucky, died ??. He enlisted 18 Oct 1861 at Bowling Green, KY and served with Co. G, 4th Kentucky Regt. Inf. (CSA). He was promoted to 2nd corporal on 8 Jul 1863. He was taken prisoner at Intrenchment Creek, GA on 5 Aug 1864 and sent to Camp Chase, OH. He was released from Camp Chase on 8 May 1865 and took the Oath on 15 May 1865.

An I.T. Batts (J.T. Batts) voted in the 3 Nov 1868 election at Cadiz, KY.

In the 1870 Trigg County Census James T. Batts is listed as age 28 years and living with his wife Elizabeth J. Batts, age 28 years, and their two children, William F., age 3 years, and Keziah J., age 1 year.

In the 1880 Trigg County Census William Batts, age 13 years, born in Kentucky (his parents were both born in Kentucky), works on a farm and is living with the Perry Thomas and Aorla Thomas family. Also living with Perry and Aorla Thomas are Henry Kennady, age 22 years; Eliza Guier, age 20 years; and Mary Kasey, age 17 years.

RICHARD A. BATTS, Private, born ca. 1842 in Kentucky, died ??. He enlisted 14 Sep 1861 at Camp Burnett, TN and served with Co. G, 4th Kentucky Regt. Inf. (CSA). Pvt. Richard A. Batts was taken prisoner at Jonesboro, GA on 1 Sep 1864.

In the 1860 Trigg County Census Richard A. Batts is listed as age 18 years and living with his father William Batts, age 50 years; his mother Jane Batts, age 38 years; and seven siblings: Thomas, age 19 years; S.C. (female), age 14 years; W.G. (male), age 12 years; M.E. (female), age 10 years; M.F.(female), age 8 years; G.W. (male), age 4 years; and H.R. (female), age 2 years.

THOMAS BATTS, Private, born ca. 1841, died ??. He enlisted 18 Oct 1861 at Bowling Green, KY and served with Co. G, 4th Kentucky Regt. Inf. (CSA). He was promoted to first sergeant then reduced in ranks. Pvt. Thomas Batts was taken prisoner at Jonesboro, GA on 1 Sep 1864.

In the 1860 Trigg County Census Thomas Batts is listed as age 19 years and living with his father William Batts, age 50; his mother Jane Batts, age 38 years; and seven siblings: R.A. (Richard), age 18 years; S.C. (female), age 14 years; W.G. (male), age 12 years; M.E. (female), age 10 years; M.F. (female), age 8 years, G.W. (male), age 4 years; and H.R. (female), age 2 years.

JOHN W. BELL, Private, born ca. 1845 in Tennessee, died ??. He enlisted 11 Aug 1861 at Camp Burnett, TN and served with Co. G, 4th Kentucky Regt. Inf. (CSA). He was taken prisoner at Kennesaw Mountain, GA on 20 Jun 1864 and sent to Camp Morton, IN, 1 Jul 1864. Pvt. John W. Bell was exchanged on 15 Mar 1865. He surrendered on 3 May 1865 at Greensboro, NC and took the Oath at Greensboro on 21 May 1865.

In the 1850 Trigg County Census all of the family were born in Tennessee except for Emily A. Bell and Monroe T. Bell who were born in Kentucky.

John Bell's father was George Bell (b. ca. 1817 in Tennessee, d. ??) and his mother was Lavina (Hamilton) Bell (b. ca. 1821 in Tennessee, d. ??).

In the 1850 Trigg County Census he is listed as John W. Bell, age 5 years and living with his father George Bell, age 33 years; his mother Lavina (Hamilton) Bell, age 29 years; and four siblings: Robert A., age 9 years; Elender C., age 8 years; Emily A., age 2 years; and Monroe, age 1 month.

In the 1860 he is listed as "J.W." Bell, age 15 years and living with his father George Bell, age 43 years; his stepmother Mary E. (Cochran) Bell, age 20 years; and five siblings: Emily A., age 12 years; Monroe T., age 9 years; Benjamin F., age 8 years; and Emanuel, age 5 years; and a half-sister Viola, age 1 year.

In the 1870 Trigg County Census John Bell is not found.

LYNN B. BELL, born 1 Apr 1827 in Kentucky, died 1 Feb 1869. Lynn B. Bell was a brother of Richard Bell. His mother was Elizabeth Bell (b. ca. 1806 in South Carolina, d. ??). His sister Mary Ann married James Sumner on 25 Oct 1843; sister Nancy E. married Joseph Ahart on 31 Jan 1859; brother Richard married Pernice Downs on 6 Jan 1878; brother Benjamin, age 26 years, married first, Josephine Harrell, age 16 years, from Trigg County on 25 Oct 1865 and married second, Francis E. Williams on 9 Jan 1873. All were married in Trigg County.

In the 1850 Trigg County Census Lynn B. Bell is listed as age 23 years and living with his brother-in-law James Sumner, age 26 years; James' wife Elizabeth A. (Bell) Sumner, age 25, and their children. Also living with the family are Lynn B. Bell's sisters, Lucy Ann, age 21 years, and Maudann, age 19 years. Lynn B. Bell's mother Elizabeth Bell, age 44 years, is listed as living nearby. Elizabeth is living with her children: Nancy E., age 15 years; Richard, age 13 years; James, age 11 years; and Benjamin, age 9 years.

Lynn B. Bell is buried in the Long Creek Cemetery in Trigg County, KY. He is the only person with the surname Bell buried in the cemetery. His niece Orphia Elizabeth Bell, daughter of Richard and Permelia Bell (b. 1897, d. 1920), is buried in Kuttawa, Lyon County, KY. His brother Richard Bell (b. 2 May 1836 in Kentucky, d. 19 Feb 1898) is buried in the Cumberland Missionary Baptist Church Cemetery in Trigg County.

RICHARD BELL, Private, born 2 May 1836 in Kentucky, died 19 Feb 1898. He mustered in 13 Sep 1862 at Henderson, KY and mustered out 23 Sep 1863 at Russellville, KY. He served with Co. L, 8th Kentucky Regt. Cav. (USA). He mustered in 4 Aug 1864 at Paducah, KY and mustered out 12 Feb 1865 at Paducah, KY and served with Co. B, 1st Kentucky Regt. Capital Guards, Paducah Battalion (USA).

Richard Bell was a brother of Lynn B. Bell. His mother was Elizabeth Bell ca. 1806 in South Carolina, d. ??). Richard Bell married Penuce Downs on 6 Jan 1878 in Trigg County. His sister Mary Ann married James Sumner on 25 Oct 1843 in Trigg County and sister Nancy E. married Joseph Ahart on 31 Jan 1859 in Trigg County. (Joseph Ahart was a Civil War veteran from the Union Army.)

Richard Bell's brother Benjamin, age 26 years from Trigg County, married Josephine Harrell, age 16 years from Trigg County, on 25 Oct 1865; he married second, Francis E. Williams on 9 Jan 1873 in Trigg County.

In the 1900 Trigg County Census Richard Bell's widow Pumecia C. (Downs) Bell is listed as age 43 years (b. September 1856) and living with her nine children: Robert H. (Hosi), a railroad tiemaker, age 21 years; Hattie G., age 19 years; John S., age 17 years; Benjamin B., age 15 years; Linn B., age 13 years; James F., age 11 years; Ruth E., age 9 years; Richard L., age 6 years; and Ophie E., age 3 years.

Richard Bell was initially buried in the Cumberland Baptist Church Cemetery. With the formation of Lake Barkley his body was moved to Kuttawa in Lyon, County, KY.

JACKSON T. BERKLEY, 1st Lieutenant, born 25 Sep 1835 in Kentucky, died 1 Oct 1893. He enrolled 4 Aug 1864; mustered in 4 Aug 1864 at Paducah, KY for six months and mustered out 12 Feb 1865 at Paducah, KY. He served with Co. B, 1st Regt. Capital Guards, Paducah Battalion.

Jackson T. Berkley's mother may have been Mary Berkley (b. ca. 1776 in Virginia, d. ??). Jackson T. Berkley married Martha Futrell on 2 Nov 1857 in Trigg County and married second, Beershela (Colson) Futrell on 27 Oct 1877 in Trigg County.

"Bashba" Coalson married William Futrell on 1 Jun 1849 in Trigg County.

J.T. Berkley voted in the May 1867 election at Futrell's Precinct.

In the 1850 Trigg County Census Jackson "Burkley" is listed as age 14 years and living with a Mary ("Burkley") Casey, age 35 years; a James C. Casey age 2 years; and a Mary "Burkley," age 74 years (b. in Virginia).

In the 1870 Trigg County Census Jackson Berkley is listed as age 34 years living with his wife Martha J. (Futrell) Berkley, age 33 years and five children: George L.J., age 12 years; Mary M., age 9 years; James G., age 6 years; Clarrisa J.E., age 3 years; and Minesota (b. November 1869), age 7 months. Jackson Berkley's first wife Bathsheba (Colson) Futrell is listed as age 39 years and living with her husband William Futrell, age 53 years, and two sons Henry B., age 17 years and Thomas N., age 15 years.

In the 1880 Trigg County Census he is listed as "John T. Buckley," age 44 years and living with his wife Bashaba (Colson) (Futrell) "Buckley," age 49 years.

Jackson T. Berkely is buried in the Pleasant Hill Church Cemetery in Trigg County, KY.

SEABORN BERKLEY, born 1 Jan 1820 in Kentucky, died 1 Jul 1888. S. "Burkley" is listed with the enrolled militia on parade in Trigg County on Saturday, 6 Apr 1861.

Martha (Frizzell) Berkely, Reuben Frizzell and Jessy Frizzell were all born in Tennessee.

Seaborn Berkley's daughter Mary A. listed as Mary Ann "Buckley" married W.J. Noles on 24 May 1860; daughter Susan H. (b. May 1846, d. ??) married John H. Gorden (b. April 1843, d. ??) on 20 November 1866; daughter Etmni (Etna) (b. ca. 1856, d. ca. 1890) married DeWitt Clinton Luton (b. August 1850, d. 1935) on 28 Feb 1876; and daughter Nannie A. (H.) married Lyman H. Eggner on 4 Nov 1879. All were married in Trigg County.

Seaborn Berkley's son Benjamin R. married Mary J. Fuller on 23 Oct 1874 and son James W. married Della Ladd on 10 Oct 1880, both in Trigg County.

Seaborn Berkley is buried in the Indian Springs Cemetery in Trigg County, KY with his wife Martha (Frizzell) Berkely (b. 13 Oct 1819 in Tennessee, d. 9 Dec 1896). They are the only Berkleys listed as being buried in the Indian Springs Cemetery.

His daughter's husband DeWitt Clinton Luton (b. August 1850, d. 1935) is buried in the Matheny Cemetery, near Golden Pond. He was moved from the Cumberland Baptist Church Cemetery when Lake Barkley was impounded.

JABEZ BINGHAM, Major, born 27 Feb 1827 in Athens County, OH, died 13 Oct 1884. He enlisted 24 Oct 1861 at Camp Alcorn in Hopkinsville, KY and served with Co. B, 8th Kentucky Regt. Inf. (CSA). He was elected captain of Co. B on 24 Oct 1861, then promoted to major 25 Sep 1862 only to resign and leave the service in 1864.

Jabez Bingham's father was born in Virginia and his mother was born in Rhode Island.

He is listed in the Wallonia Poll Book as having voted in the 4 Aug 1856 election.

Jabez Bingham married Sarah Virginia Daniel (b. 1 Feb 1834, d. 18 Nov 1867) on 23 Nov 1850 in Trigg County. At age 42 he married second, Susan B. (Norris) Hopson (born in Tennessee), age 31 years, of Trigg County, on 24 Jun 1868. It was the second marriage for both bride and groom.

In the 1860 Trigg County Census he is listed as "J." Bingham, age 33 years and living with his wife S.V. (Sarah V.) (Daniel) Bingham, age 27 years, and two children, W.C. (William C.), age 9 years, and G.B. (George B.), age 5 years.

Susan Bingham was born Susan Norris on 31 Jan 1835 in Dixon County, TN. She was married to Jabez Bingham by Rev. J.C. Peters of the M.E. Church South. His company surrendered at Columbus, MS in 1865. She has no property and no family except for a daughter-in-law. Her son Samuel V. Hopson had died in 1908. The pension application is dated 24 Jun 1912.

He is buried in the Wall Cemetery near his wife Susan (Norris) Bingham (b. 1835 in Tennessee, d. 1913). According to Maupin's records, her tombstone reads that her maiden name was "Morris". Her Confederate widow's pension application relates that her maiden name was "Norris."

His first wife Sarah Virginia (Daniel) Bingham is buried in the Wall Cemetery. An infant son (b. 12 Dec 1856, d. 14 Dec 1856) and a daughter (b. 12 Feb 1856, d. 14 Nov 1859), "children of J. and S.V. Bingham" are both buried in the Wall Cemetery.

ALEXANDER CLEMENCE BLANE M.D., Second Sergeant, born 18 Dec 1841 in Kentucky, died 29 Nov 1898. He enlisted 18 May 1861 at Dover, TN and served with Co. E, 14th Tennessee Regt. Inf. (CSA). Second Sgt. Alexander Blane was wounded in the knee and shoulder at the Battle of Chancellorsville, VA on 3 May 1863 and was discharged from service at Orange Court House, VA on 12 Sep 1863.

There is an Alexander Blane listed in the 1850 Trigg County Census (page 7, #131), but this man was born ca. 1810 in Tennessee).

Alexander Blane was a brother to Henry Blane. His father was Johnnie Blane and his mother was Sallie (Tillotson) Blane. They were married on 2 Dec 1829, in Mackington County, VA.

He married Mary Cornelia Jones on 12 Feb 1879. His daughter Birdie B. (b. 18 Dec 1879, d. 8 May 1968) married Luther A. Tucker (b. 14 Jul 1882, d. 27 May 1963) on 29 Dec 1903. They are buried in the East End Cemetery.

In the 1870 Trigg County Census he is listed as "A.C." Blane, age 23 years, listed as living alone and as a medical student.

Second Sgt. Alexander C. Blane is buried in the East End Cemetery. Mary Cornelia (Jones) Blane (b. 9 Oct 1860, d. 31 Mar 1927) "wife of Dr. A.C. Blane" is buried in the Nunn Cemetery in Trigg County. Alex R. Blane (b. 30 Jun 1894, d. 10 Dec 1924) "son of Dr. A.C. and Mary C. Blane" is buried in the Nunn Cemetery.

HENRY BLANE M.D., Private, born 27 Sep 1837 in Virginia, died 1908. He served with Co. E, 14th Tennessee Regt. Inf.

Henry Blane was a brother of Alexander Blane. His son Plomer Blane's middle name may be Alexander or Ambrose. Trigg County History gives his name as "Ambrose." His father was John (Johnnie) Blane and his mother was Sallie (Tillotson) Blane of Mackington County, VA. They were married on 2 Dec 1829.

His first wife is unknown. His sons Robert L. and Aurelius L. were by her. There is an Alpha Griffin Blane who died on 25 Dec 1868, and is buried in the East End Cemetery. This lady could possibly have been Henry Blane's first wife.

Henry Blane married second, Lucy Boyd Dyer on 21 Dec 1871 in Trigg County. His children Homer, Plomer A., Verna, John and Henry were by her. Henry Blane married third, Eliza H. (Hooks) ca. 1888. We can find no record of their marriage in Trigg County.

In the 1870 Trigg County Census Henry Blane is listed as a physician, age 32 years and living with his two sons Robert L., age 5 years, and Aurelius L., age 3 years. He has as two housekeepers, Elizabeth Futrell, age 28 years, and Matilda Futrell, age 22 years.

In the 1880 Trigg County Census he is listed as Henry Blane a physician, age 42 years and living with his wife L.B. (Lucy Boyd) (Dyer) Blane, age 27 years, and five children: R. Lee, age 15 years; A.L. (Amelius L.), age 13 years; T.V., age ?; Homer, age 5 years; and Plomer, age 1 year.

In the 1900 Trigg County Census he is listed as Henry "Blain," age 62 years, a physician and living with his wife Eliza (Dyer) (Hooks) "Blain" (married 12 years) age 45; daughter Verna, age 17 years; son John, age 14 years; son Boyd, age 13 years; and their cook Bettie Wooldridge, age 22 years. Eliza (Dyer) (Hooks) Blane has had three children, none of whom were still living when the census was taken.

Dr. Blane is buried in the East End Cemetery with his second wife Lucy Boyd (Dyer) (b. 1850, d. 8 Mar 1888).

WILLIAM A. BLANKS, born January 1845 in Kentucky, died 1925. His sister Martha J. Blanks married Nathan C. Foster on 22 Apr 1859 in Trigg County.

In the 1850 Trigg County Census he is listed as William A. Blanks, age 6 years and living with his father William Blanks, age 41 years; his mother Dolly Blanks, age 40 years; and four siblings: Martha J., age 14 years; Eliza E., age 12 years; John W., age 7 years; and Sarah E., age 4 Years.

In the 1860 Trigg County Census he is listed as William A. Blanks, age 15 years and living with his father William Blanks, age 51 years; his mother Dolly Blanks, age 54 years; two siblings, John W., age 19 years, and Sarah E., age 13 years. Also living with the family in this census is William Blanks' brother-in-law, N.C. Foster, age 26 years, a farm laborer, and William A.'s sister Martha J. (Blanks) Foster, age 26 years.

In the 1880 Trigg County Census he is listed as William A. Blanks Jr., age 35 years and living with his father William A. Blanks Sr.; sister Sarah E., age 33 years; sister Eliza E., age 14 years; wife Sarah, age 24 years; and their son Robert Lee, age 3 years. Evander Ladd, age 60 years, is living with the family.

In the 1900 Trigg County Census he is listed as William A. Blanks, a farmer, age 55 years and living with his wife Sarah, age 44 years, and their five children: Minus, age 19 years; John F., age 15 years; Rosella, age 13 years; William H., age 11 years; and Otho (son), age 6 years. Sarah Blanks has had seven children, only five of whom were still living when this census was taken.

William A. Blanks (b. January 1845, d. 1925) is buried with his wife Sarah Blanks (b. January 1856, d. 1937) in the Turner or Cerulean Cemetery in Trigg County. Her tombstone states she was born in 1855. The 1880 Census states Sarah Blanks was born in 1856.

JOHN THOMAS BLOODWORTH, born 10 Aug 1847 in Kentucky, died 1 Dec 1895. He enlisted ??. Both Maupin and Neel indicated J.T. Bloodworth as a Civil War veteran.

In the 1880 Census he states that he was born in Kentucky, but he does not state where his parents were born.

John T. Bloodworth, age 23 years, a farmer from Trigg County, married A.E.C. Mitchuson, age 17 years, a young lady from Trigg County on 19 Sep 1872. It was the first marriage for both bride and groom.

In the marriage records John states his father was born in Kentucky and his mother was born in Tennessee. Ailcey, his wife, states that both of her parents were born in Tennessee.

In the 1880 Trigg County Census John T. Bloodworth is listed as age 29 years living with his wife Ailcey E. (Mitchuson) Bloodworth, age 22 years, and their three children: William T., age 6 years; Ben A., age 3 years; and Fadie B. (Phoeba B.), age 5 months.

In the 1920 Trigg County Census John T. Bloodworth's son William T. is listed as a farmer, age 46 years and living with his wife Leona (Rowland) Bloodworth, age 41 years; and their two sons, R. Thomas, age 14 years, and William T., age 10 years. John T. Bloodworth's son Ben is listed as a farmer, age 42 years and living with his wife Emma (Taylor) Bloodworth, age 43 years, and their six children: Agnes I. (B.), age 21 years; Barnie (Ernie) B., age 18 years; Vivian (Uyvan) H., age 15 years; Mary, age 12 years; Elsie, age 11 years; and Joe, age 8 years. The surnames Boatright or Boatwright do not appear in Blue & Sellers' 1920 Trigg County Census.

J.T. Bloodworth is buried in the Hematite Cemetery in Trigg County with his wife Cebella (Mitchusson) Bloodworth (b. 10 Oct 1855, d. 12 Nov 1931). J.T. Bloodworth was moved from the Savells Cemetery to the Hematite Cemetery (or Center Furnace Cemetery).

ELIAS BOATWRIGHT, born ca. 1828 in Kentucky, died ??. He enlisted ??. He is listed on the enrolled militia on parade in Trigg County on Saturday, 6 Apr 1861.

His mother Susan Boatwright was born ca. 1810 in Louisiana. One of Elias Boatright's sons was John H., son-in-law of John Thomas Bloodworth, a Civil War veteran.

Elias Boatright married Mrs. Mary Taylor (b. ca. 1824 in Tennessee, d. ??) on 5 Jan 1860 in Trigg County.

In the 1850 Trigg County Census he is listed as Elias Boatwright, age 22 years and living with his mother Susan Boatwright, age 40 years; brother Major S., age 12 years and brother Claiborne L., age 8 years.

In the 1870 Trigg County Census he is listed as "Elias" Boatwright, age 44 years and living with his wife Mary Ann (Taylor) Boatwright, age 35 years, and their six children: Eliza A., age 16 years; James C., age 9 years; John H., age 7 years; Susan Ann, age 5 years; Elias S., age 3 years; and Benjamin, age 1 year.

He is buried in the Matheny-Ferguson Springs Cemetery in Trigg County, but there is no stone at his grave. His daughter Susan (Boatright) Colson (b. 1866, d. 1902), "wife of Dewey Colson" is buried in the Colson or Pleasant Valley Cemetery.

JOHN N. BOATRIGHT, Private, enlisted 3 Oct 1861 at Camp Reeves, TN and served with Co. G, 8th Kentucky Regt. Inf. (CSA).

References: Page 396, Vol. I, Kentucky Adjutant General Report (CSA); not in Simmons' 1850 Trigg County Census; not in Simmons' 1860 Trigg County Census; not in Simmons' 1870 Trigg County Census; not in Neel's 1880 Trigg County Census; not found in Jones' 1900 Trigg County Census; not found in Blue & Sellers' 1920 Trigg County Census; Kentucky State Archives Microfilm, Compiled Service Records, Drawer 528, Series 319, Reel 124.

JOHN DANIEL BOGARD, Trigg County native, Confederate veteran and Arkansas farmer was born near Fungo (late Golden Pond) Oct. 19, 1840, eldest child of seven born to Charles Columbus Bogard (b. 29 Jan 1814, d. 16 Aug 1854) and Elitha Griffin Bogard (b. 27 Feb 1819, d. 8 Apr 1890).

Late in 1860 in self-defense John committed an act that would have brought great distress upon his widowed mother and family to have appeared in court. He relocated to the home of his father's brother, Zachariah Bogard in Independence City, AR.

Late in July 1861, he was induced to join the Rebel Service, Co. B, 8th Arkansas Inf. as a private to serve one year from 10 Sep 1861. He was discharged 11 Dec 1861.

He was induced to commence business with a relative at Indian Mound, TN, 30 miles from home. About the last of March 1862, he returned home for a five-day visit. His mother's home was Union headquarters. His mother was paid 50 cents per week for cooking for the Union soldiers.

On his return to Indian Mound, John was captured seven miles from Golden Pond by Lt. Neely, USA and sent to a Union prison at Alton, IL.

In late June 1862, John's mother, Elitha Griffin Bogard wrote a stirring letter to Gen. Hallock on 2 July urging that her son be released from prison and to be allowed to go home with her to die. Letters from Col. Olney of Paducah and Gen. Strong of Cairo to General Scholfield in St. Louis were obtained for influence.

The Provost Marshall General ruled that no charges stood against this prisoner and he was released. John came home with his mother in July 1862 and on 29 Oct 1863 married Sarah Jane Ryan.

John died or was killed in Bridgeport, TX 14 Jun 1882. He was buried near Heber, Cleburne County, AR.

On 30 Jan 1884, Sarah J. Bogard married S. Morris, age 47. In October 1885 she went to Kentucky for a visit and died near Golden Pond 14 Jan 1886.

The children of John D. and Sarah Jane Bogard were: Charles (b. 1865, d. 1902); William Joseph (b. 1867, d. ??); Martha (b. 1869, d. 1872); Elitha (b. 1871, d. 1872); Mary (b&d 1873); Tenna (b. 1874, d. 1875); C.C. (b. 1876, d. 1939); and Simon (b. 1879, d. 1882). *Submitted by William T. Turner*

JOSEPH BAZZELL OR BEZELL BOGARD, born 23 Jun 1844 in Kentucky, died 22 Jun 1864 in Trigg County, KY. According to Bogard family history, this man was murdered by guerrillas near Canton in Trigg County on the day before his 20th birthday. I don't know if they were Confederate or Union guerrillas. Both Maupin's and Neel's references list him as a Civil War soldier, but we can't find him in any Civil War regiment, Confederate or Union.

His father was Charles Columbus Bogard (b. 29 Jan 1814 in Tennessee, d. 16 Aug 1854) and his mother was Elitha (Griffin) Bogard (b. 1819 in North Carolina, d. 1890). His sister Hester A., age 18 years, from Trigg County married W.T. Crass, age 24 years, from Henry County, TN on 7 Feb 1865; brother William A. married Emeline Gordon on 20 Nov 1866; and brother Zach T., age 21 years, from Trigg County married Georgia W. Luten, age 20 years, also from Trigg County on 24 Feb 1870. It was the first marriage for both bride and groom. Z.T. married second Ollie Futrell on 29 Jan 1890. All were married in Trigg County.

In the 1860 Trigg County Census he is listed as "J." (Joseph) Bogard, age 15 years and living with his mother "E" (Elitha) Bogard a widow, age 40 years; and seven siblings: "J.D." (John D.), age 19 years; "W.A." (William Arthur), age 16 years, "H.A." (Hester A.), age 12 years; "Z.T." (Zackariah T.), age 10 years; "S.E." (Sarah E.), age 9 years' and "M.A." (Mary A.), age 6 years.

He is buried near his father in the Bogard Cemetery in Trigg County. His sister Hester Ann (Bogard) Crass (b. 25 Jun 1846, d. 21 Mar 1905) is buried in the Bogard Cemetery with her daughter Elitha Crass (b. 24 Mar 1878, d. 14 Sep 1887). His brother Zachary Taylor (b. 24 Oct 1848, d. 1923) is buried with his first wife Georgia A. (Luten) Bogard (b. 18 Aug 1850, d. 18 Oct 1887) in the Bogard Cemetery.

WILLIAM ARTHUR BOGARD, Trigg County farmer, Golden Pond merchant, and a Union soldier, was born in Trigg County 25 Jun 1842; the second son of Charles Columbus Bogard (b. 1814, d. 1854) and Elitha Griffin Bogard (b. 1819, d. 1890).

William was mustered into service as a private in Co. L, 8th Kentucky Regt. Cav. (USA) at Henderson, KY 13 Sep 1862. He was mustered out on 23 Sep 1863 at Russellville, KY.

He married Emeline Gordon (b. 12 Dec 1845, d. 16 Jul 1901) on 20 Nov 1866. Their 11 children were: Elitha (b. 1868, d. 1876); John (b. 1869, d. 1937); Ada Miller (b. 1871, d. 1954); Sarah Etta (b. 1873, d. 1876); Charles C. (b. 1875, d. 1878); Mary Alice (b. 1876, d. 1896); Carl (b. 1879, d. 1949); Dolly Baber (b. 1881, d. 1925); Willie (b. 1883, d. 1900); George (b. 1886, d. 1936); and Kitty Fooshee (b. 1893, d. 1971).

Union soldier William Bogard, with a brother in the Confederate service, owned a general merchandise store at Golden Pond and lived on a farm near "The Elbow" on Cumberland River, upstream from Canton, KY. Family members are buried in the Bogard graveyard on the hill above Golden Pond. William A. Bogard died 10 Feb 1906. *Submitted by William T. Turner.*

BENJAMIN WINFREY BOND, Private, born 25 Nov 1814 in Virginia, died 2 May 1876. He enlisted 1 Dec 1861 at Camp Alcorn in Hopkinsville, KY and served with Co. B, 8th Kentucky Regt. Inf. (CSA).

He is listed as "Winfrey" Bond in the Kentucky Adjutant General's Report.

His wife was Frances R. (Wadlington) Bond (b. 2 Aug 1815, d. 10 Jan 1878). Their daughter Miriam married Thomas J. Powell on 3 Oct 1860 in Trigg County and daughter Eliza married W.S. Bond on 3 Sep 1861 in Trigg County. Son Thomas W., age 24 years, from Trigg County

married first Susan A. Forth, age 20 years, from Christian County on 16 Feb 1865. Then Thomas, age 30 years, a farmer from Trigg County married second Sarah E. Ross, age 18 years, a young lady also from Trigg County. It was the first marriage for the bride.

In the 1860 Trigg County Census Benjamin W. Bond is listed as age 45 years and living with his wife Frances R. (Wadlington) Bond, age 44 years, and seven children: Thomas, age 20 years; Miriam, age 17 years; Elizabeth, age 15 years; Eliza, age 13 years; B. (Benjamin F.), age 8 years; J. (male), age 5 years; and R. (female), age 4 years.

He is buried with his wife Frances R. (Wadlington) Bond in the Bethel Methodist Cemetery.

FRANCIS M. BOUNDS, Private, born ca. 1836 in Kentucky, died 20 Dec 1861 in Bowling Green, KY of disease. He enlisted 14 Sep 1861 at Camp Burnett, TN and served with Co. G, 4th Kentucky Regt. Inf. (CSA).

There is no record of his death in Bowling Green found in the Compiled Service Records on microfilm in the Kentucky State Archives.

His sister Martha Bounds married Parmetas Boyd on 21 Sep 1854 in Trigg County. Parmetus Boyd's son William T. Boyd was a Confederate soldier.

Parmetas Boyd married Milly Stallings on 17 Aug 1842 in Trigg County.

His brother Starling Bounds married Julia Ann M. Vinson on 18 Dec 1856 in Trigg County.

In the 1860 Trigg County Census Francis M. Bounds is listed as age 23 years and is living with his father Joel (Joseph) Bounds, age 74 years.

Also living with Joseph, the father, and Francis, the son, is Francis' brother-in-law W. Ballentine, his wife Ellen (Elender) (Bounds) Ballentine and their three children: Alvira, age 6 years; Elbert, age 4 years; and Dudley, age 1 year.

WILLIAM THOMAS BOURLAND, Private, born ca. 1844 in Kentucky or Tennessee, died in the fall of 1861 of measles in Hopkinsville, KY. He enlisted 3 Oct 1861 at Camp Reeves, TN and served with Co. G, 8th Kentucky Regt. Inf. (CSA).

We believe W.T. Bourland and Thomas Bourland are the same person. It is possible this man took the surname of "Bourland" upon entering Confederate service in the Fall of 1861. Up until the war, he had been known as William Thomas "Took" or "Tuck." Compiled Service Records state that "He is listed absent, sick, whereabouts unknown, left camp about 1 Nov 1861." (He left Camp Alcorn in Hopkinsville on about the 1 Nov 1861, sick with measles and we have no record as to whether he made it home to Trigg County or died along the way).

His guardians were Andrew K. Bourland (b. ca. 1805 in Kentucky, d. ??) and Medis Bourland (b. ca. 1807 in Tennessee, d. ??).

Samuel Bourland married Martha Ann Harris on 17 Jan 1855 in Trigg County. Martha Ann (Harris) Bourland married Robert C. Kennedy on 29 Dec 1892 in Trigg County.

In the 1850 Trigg County Census he is listed as a Thomas "Took," age 6 years and living with Andrew K. Bourland, age 45 years; Medis Bourland, age 43 years; and their three children: Sarah, age 20 years; Rebecca F., age 19 years; and Samuel, age 21 years.

In the 1860 Trigg County Census he is listed as Thomas "Turk," age 16 years and living with "A.G. Bowland" (born in Kentucky), age 55 years and living with his wife "B. Bowland" (born in Tennessee), age 53 years.

Samuel Bourland, age 32 years and a carpenter, is listed as living with his wife Martha Ann (Harris) Bourland, age 22 years, no children.

In the 1870 Trigg County Census William Thomas Bourland nor William Thomas Took or Tuck are not found.

LYNN BOYD, Private, born ca. 1837, died ??. He enlisted 11 Aug 1861 at Camp Burnett, TN, Co. G, 4th Kentucky Regt. Inf. (CSA).

In the 1850 Trigg County Census a Linn Boyd, age 13 years (born in Kentucky), is mentioned on page 1, #19 as living with the Quintus and Emily Tyler family. Quintus Tyler is a teacher and Lynn Boyd is his pupil.

Linn Boyd, age 49 years (born in Tennessee), is mentioned on page 20, #367 as living with his wife Ann L. Boyd, age 31 years, and one child, Butler, age 5 years. George R. Boyd, age 40 (born in Kentucky), is living with the family.

Linn Boyd, age 10 years (born in Kentucky), is mentioned on page 52, #955 as living with his father Robert Boyd, age 45 years; his mother Jane Boyd, age 39 years; and six siblings: Maria, age 19 years; James J., age 17 years; Alexander, age 15 years; Francis M. (male), age 12 years; Robert, age 7 years, and his twin Maranda, also age 7 years.

In the 1860 Trigg County Census the only Linn Boyd mentioned is listed as a farm laborer, age 19 years (born in Kentucky) and living with the J.J. Boyd, age 28 years; and the A.E. Boyd (female), age 21 years; family in this census. (According to records, however, his parents were Sam W. Boyd and Ellen Boyd).

WILLIAM T. BOYD, Private, born 1843 in Kentucky, died 1 Jul 1864. He enlisted 14 Sep 1861 at Camp Burnett, TN and served with Co. G, 4th Kentucky Regt. Inf. (CSA).

He was mortally wounded on 28 May 1864 at Battle of Dallas, Georgia. Pvt. William T. Boyd died in Atlanta, GA on 1 Jul 1864.

His father was Permetus Boyd (b. Jun 1820 in Kentucky, d. 1901) and his mother was Milly (Stallings/Stallons) Boyd (b. ca. 1824 in Kentucky, d. ca. 1852). They were married 17 Aug 1842 in Trigg County, KY. His father Parmetas Boyd married second, Martha Bounds, on 21 Sep 1854 in Trigg County. Her brother Francis M. Bounds was a Confederate soldier. Permetus Boyd married third, Elizabeth C. Brewer, on 11 Oct 1877 in Trigg County.

In the 1850 Trigg County Census he is listed as "William" Boyd, age 7 years, and living with his father "Parmetus" Boyd, age 28 years; mother Milly (Stallons) Boyd, age 26 years; and four siblings: Franklin, age 6 years; Arena, age 3 years; Malissa A., age 2 years; and Rufus K. age 3 months.

In the 1860 Trigg County Census he is listed as "W.T. Boyd," age 18 years and living with his father Parmelus Boyd, age 40 years; stepmother Martha (Bounds) Boyd, age 26 years; and seven siblings: A. (Arena), age 14 years; M.A. (Malissa A.), age 12 years; R.K. (Rufus K.), age 9 years; Thomas, age 7 years; Ellen, age 5 years; George, age 3 years; and C. (female), age 9 months.

William T. Boyd is buried in the Confederate Cemetery in Atlanta, GA.

General Benjamin Hardin Helm, brother-in-law of Abraham Lincoln, was the first soldier buried in this cemetery. General Helm was reinterred to the Helm family cemetery in Bardstown, KY in 1884.

WILLIAM H. BRABOY, born 1843 in Trigg County. His enlistment date of record is 14 Sep 1861, private, Co. G, 4th Regt. Kentucky Inf. Per Perrin's 1884 history, a group of 75 young men (including William, age 18) met at Canton 1 Jul 1861 under Dr. J.L. Price, captain and John Cunningham, 1st lieutenant. On 2 Jul they went to Camp Burnett, TN; 15 Aug they were mustered and assigned to 4th Regt. Kentucky Inf., Co. G, Confederate Army; with other regiments that were brigaded under Gen. Simon Bolivar Buckner.

On 16 Nov Brig. Gen. John C. Breckenridge took command. Their first battle was Shiloh, where William, wounded, was saved from death by close friend, J.T. Lancaster. This brigade went to Corinth, Tupelo, Vicksburg, Port Hudson, then to Jackson, MS. Under orders of Confederate President Davis, the 4th and other brigades, were to overcome Bragg in Kentucky. They moved to the Gap, but after Bragg's retreat, returned to Knoxville, thence Murfreesboro, then Nashville.

On 28 Dec, Bragg moved to the crossing of Stone River. The Kentucky brigade took command position on the river, front line. Two days later Lt. Major was ordered to take men and dislodge the enemy from a house near the river. Taking H.D. Wallace and William Braboy with him, he crept along under the bank to near the house, then at a given signal he and comrades rushed the house. The 6th took the front. The enemy driven out, Major set fire to it. Their objective accomplished, the company returned to the line through a hail of bullets. The brigade was paroled at Washington, GA on 7 May 1865. Only 37 of 75 men remained to be paroled; all had from one to five wounds.'

William was the son of John and Edey Starnes Braboy. Following the war, he married Matilda Hendricks in 1870. They had four sons: Richard, Robert, Stan, and Ellis. Edey died in 1879.

William married Ellen (Graham) Hendricks in 1880. They had six children: Hugh, Jessie, Homer, Matilda, Hilda and Cornelia. In 1891, they moved to Bonham, TX settling on land owned by John Cunningham, William's commanding officer. William died 25 Mar 1892 of pneumonia; buried at Bonham, TX, Ellen and children returned to Trigg County. She applied for Widow's Confederate Pension in 1912; died in 1923.

CULLEN THOMAS BRIDGES, a veteran of the Civil War was born 12 Aug 1844 the son of William and Mary Thomas Bridges of the Maple Grove Community, Trigg County. In 1862, less than two months before his 18th birthday, he volunteered for service with the Confederate Army in the Civil War.

He was assigned to Co. D, 2nd Cav. Regt. under the command of Col. T.E. Woodward at Hopkinsville, KY. Four months later, young Cullen's cavalry unit had temporarily joined with Morgan's Raiders and were playing havoc with the railroads in the vicinity. That unit is now recognized as part of The first Kentucky "Orphan Brigade." In Feb 1863, Co. D. was assigned to BGen. N. B. Forrest and participated in a number of his campaigns in western Tennessee.

Cullen was honorably discharged at Columbia, TN 10 Aug 1863 in order to return home to care for his ill and widowed mother. Kentucky was then under control of the Northern Army and Cullen was immediately arrested and placed in prison. "I reluctantly agreed to take the Oath of Allegiance to the North so I could get out of prison," he explained.

On 9 Nov 1863, Cullen married Virginia Ann Thomas, daughter of Peyton and Sarah Ethridge Thomas who lived in the Donaldson Creek Valley. In 1868 they went to live with Cullen's mother in the Maple Grove Community where they spent the rest of their lives. In 1873, he was appointed postmaster at Maple Grove, a position he held for 40 years.

Cullen and Virginia were the parents of 10 children; three died young. The seven who grew to adulthood were: Ghent A., Ora A. (Mrs. R.H.) Thomas, Mark Dale, John T., Rose L. (Mrs. Ell) Cunningham, Mollie M. (Mrs. Ben T.) Grigsby, and Jesse C.

Cullen's wife, Virginia, died 30 Aug 1911 and Cullen died 15 Apr 1913. Surviving were seven children and 39 grandchildren. He was so proud of his service with the Confederate Army that he had his record listed on his gravestone. *Submitted by Edison Thomas.*

DREWRY W. BRIDGES, Private, born 20 Jan 1827 in Kentucky, died 4 Jul 1916. He enlisted 9 Dec 1862 at Williamsport, TN and served with Co. B, Woodward's 2nd/15th Kentucky Regt. Cav.

He was a brother to Cullen Thomas Bridges and William Bridges, both Confederate soldiers.

He married first, Peachy Ann Tart (b. ca. 1833 in Kentucky, died ??) on 23 Oct 1849 in Trigg County. She is buried in the Drewry Bridges Cemetery, but there is no stone to her grave. He married second, Nancy A. Gresham (b. Dec 1856 in Kentucky, d. ??) on 13 Jun 1887 in Trigg County.

In the 1870 Trigg County Census Drewry W. Bridges is listed as "Drewry" Bridges, age 43 years and living with his wife Peachy Ann (Tart) Bridges, age 37 years, and their eight children: Henrietta G., age 17 years; Louisa, age 14 years; James F., age 12 years; William H., age 10 years; John R., age 8 years; David S., age 5 years; Martha E., age 2 years; and Drewry, age 1 month (born in April 1869).

In the 1880 Trigg County Census he is listed as "Drury" Bridges, a farmer, age 53 years and living with his wife Peachy A. (Tart) Bridges, age 47 years; and their six children: William A., age 20 years; John R., age 18 years; Stanley, age 14 years; Martha E., age 12 years; Peachy E., age 6 years; and Edda, age 4 years. His daughter Henrietta G. (Bridges) Sumner, age 27 years, is listed as living with her husband Benjamin Sumner, a farm worker, age 30 years; and their four children: Julia, age 7 years; Emma E., age 5 years; John C., age 2 years; and William H., age 2 months.

Drewry Bridges is buried on the hill of the Drewry Bridges Cemetery in Trigg County. His wife Nancy A. (Gresham) Bridges (b. 22 Dec 1854, d. 7 Jul 1901) is buried in the garden of the Drewry Bridges Cemetery.

WILLIAM BRIDGES, born Oct 3, 1834 in the Maple Grove Community of Trigg County, Kentucky, the seventh child of William and Mary Thomas Bridges. He grew up on his father's farm and attended Maple Grove School.

With the coming of the Civil War, William and 73 other Trigg County men, enlisted as privates in the Confederate Army Jul 1, 1861 at Canton, KY. He was 26 years old and single. The Company was organized by Dr. J.L. Trice, the captain. Other members of the command were Dr John Cunningham, 1st lieutenant; John F. Baker, 2nd lieutenant, and Francis M. Baker, 3rd lieutenant.

William and the group marched some 60 miles to Camp Burnett near Clarksville, TN where, on Nov 14, 1861, they were inducted into the Confederate Army for a period of three years. William was assigned as a member of the Regimental Band. In December he was transferred to Bowling Green, KY, and assigned to duty with Co. G, Fourth Regt., first Kentucky Brigade, later to become known as "The Orphan Brigade."

The Confederate Army abandoned Bowling Green in February 1862 and William and the Kentucky Brigade headed for Nashville, TN. In March the Brigade was ordered to Corinth, MS where, on Apr 6-7, 1862 it experienced the horrors of war in the Battle of Shiloh.

Shortly after that battle, William, along with many others of his brigade, was stricken with malaria. All the sick and injured were shipped by train to Castillian Springs, near Durant, MS, where the Confederacy had converted a resort hotel into a hospital. William died there Apr 22, 1862 and is buried in an unmarked grave in the Westley Church Cemetery in Castillian Springs. In 1989, through efforts by a family member, a commemorative marker was placed in the cemetery in his honor. *Submitted by Edison Thomas.*

JOHN A. BROWN, Private, born circa 1846, died ??. Enlisted in November 1861 at Camp Alcorn in Hopkinsville, KY and served with Co. B, 8th Kentucky Regt. Inf. (CSA).

His Compiled Service Records state that "John A. Brown is listed as "missing" after the Battle of Harrisburg, MS on Jul 14, 1864. This was the last entry in his records.

His father was "J.H." Brown, a carpenter (b. circa 1800 in Kentucky, d. ??) and his mother was "S." (Sarah) Brown (b. circa 1798 in Virginia, d. ??)

His sister Nancy E. married A.J. (Andrew Jackson) Choat on 18 Dec 1860; sister Cary Ann Lawson married P.J. Bryant on 13 Jul 1862; sister Annis C. married W. Bryant on 15 Oct 1863; sister Eliza Ellen, age 17 years, married William B. Gentry, age 20 years, on 24 Dec 1868 (first marriage for both bride and groom). All were married in Trigg County Census

In the 1860 Trigg County Census he is listed as J.A. Brown, age 14 years and living with his father J.H. Brown, age 50 years; his mother S. (Sarah) Brown, age 52 years; and five sisters: C.A. (Cary Ann), age 21 years; N.E. (Nancy E.), age 19 years; A.C. (Annis C.), age 17 years; S.C. (listed as a female), age 12 years; and E.E. (Eliza Ellen), age 9 years.

HENRY H. BRYANT, Private, born: 9 Feb 1843 in Kentucky, died Saturday, 25 Nov 1899 at White River, AR. Enlisted 24 Oct 1861 at Camp Alcorn, Hopkinsville, KY and served with Co. B, 8th Kentucky Regt. Inf. (CSA).

Private Bryant was discharged from Confederate service on account of disability on 21 Jan 1862. In April 1899 he moved from Gracey, KY to Clarksville, TN.

He died on 25 Nov 1899 while on a hunting trip to White River, AR. While cleaning their rifles in preparation for going home, he was accidentally shot in the side by one of his hunting companions, Mr. J.P. Watson. The complete details of his death are given in the Monday, 27 Nov 1899 issue of the *Kentucky New Era*. Private Henry H. Bryant was a brother-in-law of Francis M. Baker of Co. G, of the 4th Kentucky Regt. Inf. (CSA).

Henry H. Bryant's father was Lawrence Bryant (b. 24 Jan 1809 in Virginia, d. 23 Jan 1879) and his mother was Margaret or Margarette Bryant (b. 25 Jul 1810 in Kentucky, d. 9 Feb 1879). They are buried in the Bryant Cemetery in Trigg County

He married first, Blanche Farmer (b. 27 Dec 1847, d. 3 Aug 1891), the daughter of Capt. John S. Farmer of Logan County, KY, and married second, Miss Mary Guthrie, the daughter of John Guthrie of Nelson County, KY.

In the 1880 Trigg County Census he is listed as Henry Bryant, a farmer, age 37 years and living with his wife Blanch (Farmer) Bryant, age 23 years, and one daughter Pearl Bryant, age 2 years. John W. Blankenship, age 46 years and manager of the farm, is living with the family in this census. Marion Farmer, a niece, is also living with the family in this census.

Henry is buried in Greenwood Cemetery in Clarksville, TN. His first wife Blanch (Farmer) Bryant is buried in the Bryant Cemetery in Trigg County, KY.

HENRY CORNELIUS BURNETT, Colonel, born 5 Oct 1825 in Virginia, died 28 Sep 1866. He enlisted 11 Nov 1861 at Camp Alcorn in Hopkinsville, KY and served as Staff Officer, 8th Kentucky Regt. Inf. (CSA)

Notes: He was a member of the Confederate States Senate from Kentucky. He was appointed Colonel on 24 Dec 1861, but resigned his Colonelcy on 3 Feb 1862. He was present at the Battle of Fort Donelson, but escaped the surrender with General John B. Floyd.

He was a brother of Robert A. and James M. Burnett. His father was Isaac Burnett Sr. (b. circa 1801 in Virginia, d. ??) and his mother was Martha F. Burnett (b. circa 1805 in Virginia, d. ??). His sister Mary Virginia Burnett married William H. Dupuy on 8 Jan 1853 and sister Martha F. (Fannie) Burnett married Dr. James Allison on 23 Sep 1858. Both married in Trigg County.

He married Mary A. Terry (b. 30 Mar 1830 in Virginia, d. 16 Aug 1925) on 13 Apr 1847. His father-in-law was Abner R. Terry (b. 10 Feb 1807 in Virginia, d. 29 Nov 1847) and his mother-in-law was Eleanor (Dyer) Terry (b. 6 Feb 1805 in Virginia, d. 9 Dec 1892). They are buried in the Old Cadiz Cemetery.

In the 1860 Trigg County Census he is listed as H.C. Burnett, a lawyer and M.C., age 32 years and living with his wife Mary A (Terry) Burnett, age 28 years, and one child, Harry (Henry), age 10 years. John R. Burnett, age 26 years, and Emeline Burnett, age 24 years, are living with the family in this census. All the above people are living with Mary's mother Eleanor (Dyer) Terry, age 54 years, and her three children: Martha Terry, age 19 years; George Terry, age 16 years; and Lucy Terry, age 13 years.

Henry C. Burnett is buried in the East End Cemetery (moved from Old Cadiz Cemetery) with his wife Mary A (Terry) Burnett. This couple's son Terry Burnett (b. 15 Jul 1851, d. 30 Jul 1851) is buried in the East End Cemetery with his parents.

JAMES E. BURNETT, birth and death dates unknown. There is the inscription "C.S.A." on his tombstone. He is buried in the Old Cadiz Cemetery.

References: Cannot find in the Kentucky Adjutant General's Report; page 25, Maupin's Trigg County Cemetery Records; not found in Simmons' 1850, 1860 or 1870 Trigg County Census Reports.

JAMES M. BURNETT, Private, born circa 1828, died 11 Aug 1862. Enlisted 24 Aug 1861 at Camp Burnett, TN and served with Co. E, 4th Kentucky Regt. Inf. (CSA). According to family history, he died at the Battle of Shiloh in April of 1862.

According to Trigg County Civil War notes, he is listed as a brother of Robert Burnett and Henry Burnett and was mortally wounded at the Battle of Shiloh in April 1862. According to microfilm of his compiled service records in the Kentucky State Archives, he died of disease at the Comite River, LA, on 11 Aug 1862.

There is no record of a James M. Burnett ever being married in Trigg County.

In the 1850 Trigg County Census James M. Burnett is listed as age 22 years, a medical student living with his father Isaac Burnett who was a physician, age 49 years and his mother Martha F. Burnett, age 45 years, and three siblings: Mary Virginia Burnett, age 14 years; Isaac Burnett Jr., age 12 years; and Fanny Burnett, age 8 years.

In the 1860 Trigg County Census James M. Burnett is listed as age 30 years, a lawyer and living with his father Isaac Burnett Sr., age 59 years; his mother Martha F. Burnett, age 55 years; one sibling Ike (Isaac Jr.) Burnett, age 22 years; R.A. Burnett, a circuit clerk age 27 years, and his sons: George, age 5 years; James, age 4 years: and Robert, age 2 years, are living with this family in this census.

JOHN J. BURNETT, Private, born circa 1841, died: ??. Enrolled 25 Aug 1863; mustered in 26 Oct 1863 at Princeton, KY and mustered out:19 Dec 1864 at Bowling Green, KY. He served with Co. F, 48th Kentucky Regt. Mounted Inf. (USA).

His father was Cornelius S. Burnett (b. circa 1820 in Virginia, d. ??) and his mother was Nancy A. (Wallis) Burnett (b. circa 1824 in Kentucky, d. ??).

In the 1850 Trigg County Census John J. Burnett is listed as age 9 years and living with his father Cornelius Burnett, age 30 years; his mother Nancy A. (Wallis) Burnett, age 26 years; and five siblings: William H., age 7 years; Mary J., age 6 years; Rufus M., age 5 years; Sarah H., age 4 years; and Elizabeth N,. age 2 years.

In the 1860 Trigg County Census he is listed as John J. Burnett, age 18 years and living with his father Cornelius Burnett and 10 siblings: William H., age 16 years; Mary J., age 14 years; Rufus M., age 12 years; Sarah M., age 11 years; Elizabeth N., age 10 years; G.A. (female), age 8 years; V. (female), age 6 years; L. (female), age 4 years; C.R. (male), age 2 years; and C.T. (male), age 1 year.

JAMES R. BURNHAM, Private, and born circa 1829 in North Carolina, died ??. Enlisted 9 Dec 1862 at Williamsport, TN and served with Co. B, Woodwards 2nd/15th Kentucky Regt. Cav.

In Simmons' 1850 Trigg County Census all family members were born in North Carolina. In Simmons' 1860 Trigg County Census James' mother-in-law Sarah Holly was born in North Carolina.

His father was Wilson Burnham (b. circa 1798 in North Carolina, d. ??) and his mother was Elizabeth Burnham (b. circa 1810, d. ?? in North Carolina).

James R. Burnman (Burnham) married three times: (1st) Sarah J. Holley on 4 Feb 1851 in Trigg County; (2nd) Lucy A.E. Heydon, age 22 years (he was 36), on 4 Jul 1865 in Trigg County; (3rd) Mrs. Bettie Hill on 23 Jul 1885 in Trigg County.

In the 1850 Trigg County Census James R. Burnham is listed as age 21 years, born in North Carolina and living with his father Wilson Burnham, age 52 years; his mother Elizabeth Burnham, age 40 years; and one sister Parmela Burnham, age 15 years.

In the 1860 Trigg County Census "J.R." Burnham is listed as age 39 years, born in North Carolina and living with his wife S.J. (Sarah J.) (Holley) Burnham, age 32 years; and three children: H.R. (Haywood R.), age 7 years; Ira, age 5 years; Delia, age 3 years; and his mother-in-law, Sarah Holley, age 72 years. James R. Burnham's father Wilson Burnham is listed as "W." Burnham, age 65 years, a widower and living alone. He was born in North Carolina.

In the 1880 Trigg County Census James R. Burnham is listed as a farmer, age 53 years and living with his second wife Lucy Ann (Heydon) Burnham, age 37 years, and four children: Haywood K., age 27 years; Ira McP., age 25 years; William E., age 13 years; and Minnie, age 4 years. An Amanda Ladd, age 22 years, is living with the Burnham family in this census.

James' third wife and William's step-mother, Bettie J. (Hill) Burnham, a widow age 55 years, is living with the family in this census. Bettie (Hill) Burnham has had one child by the 1900 census, but it is listed as deceased.

W.H. BURNHAM, (possibly Wilson Burnham of Trigg County), born circa 1830 in Kentucky, died ??. He enlisted on 13 Sep 1862 at Clarksville, TN and served with Co. B, Woodwards 2nd/15th Kentucky Cav. Regt. (CSA). There were three Wilson Burnhams who lived in Trigg County during the 1850s. Only two of these would have been of age to serve in the WSI.

In the 1850 Trigg County Census a Wilson Burnham is listed as age 15 years and living with his father Isaac Burnham, age 51 years; his mother Elizabeth (Rolston) Burnham, age 36 years; and six siblings: Benjamin, age 17 years; Celia, age 13 years; Catherine, age 8 years; Isaac, age 6 years; Jane, age 3 years; and Samuel, age 2 years. M. Vanlandingham (male), age 81 years, is living with the family in this census. A second Wilson Burnham is listed as age 20 years and living with an Elizabeth Burnham, age 50 years and a Minerva Burnham, age 14 years, born in Kentucky.

In the 1860 Trigg County Census Isaac Burnham is listed as age 59 years and living with his wife E.A. (Elizabeth) (Rolston) Burnham, age 40 years and their four children: "C." (Catherine), age 17 years; Isaac, age 16 years; Jane, age 13 years; and David, age 8 years. Isaac Burnham's son Wilson Burnham is not listed in the 1860 Trigg County Census. Elizabeth Burnham's son Wilson Burnham is not listed in the 1860 Trigg County Census. No Wilson Burnhams that would be of age to serve in the war appear in the 1860 Trigg County Census.

In the 1870 Trigg County Census Wilson Burnham, age 28 years, is listed as living with his wife Jane Burnham, age 28 years, and four children: Mink (female), age 12 years; John, age 10 years; Edmund, age 4 years; and Kneely (female), age 1 year. We think this Wilson Burnham is the son of Isaac Burnham only because he is listed as #642 in the 1870 census and Isaac Burnham is listed as #641. Isaac is listed as age 70 years and living with his wife Mary Burnham, age 57 years, and their two sons, David C., age 19 years, and William Isaac, age 25 years.

WILLIAM I. BUSH, Sergeant, born circa 1841 in Kentucky, died 13 Feb 1905. He served with Co. A, 9th Texas Regt. Inf. (CSA). His unit is given on his tombstone.

William I. Bush, age 27 years of Trigg County, married Lucy Ann Grasty, age 23 years of Trigg County, on 21 Nov 1865.

In the 1870 Trigg County Census William I. Bush is listed as a farmer, age 29 years and living with his wife Lucy (Grasty) Bush, age 27 years, and one son Edmund, age 1 year.

He is the only person with the surname of Bush buried in Baker Cemetery on the Trigg County-Lyon County line.

PATRICK HENRY CAIN, 2nd Corporal, born 28 Oct 1838 in Calloway County, KY, died: 21 Mar 1914. Enlisted 26 Apr 1861 at Murray, KY and served with Co. F, 1st Kentucky Regt. Inf. (CSA). When he enlisted, he was under the command of Col. Blanton Duncan, Capt. Kirk Bowman and 1st Lt. Elias Hopkins. He was appointed 2nd corporal 28 Apr 1862, at the reorganization of the regiment. He was honorably discharged from Confederate service with his entire regiment at Richmond, VA in the summer of 1862. He was captured in 1863 by federal troops, taken to Paducah, KY, and there made to take the oath of allegiance.

He was a resident of Cadiz, Trigg County, KY. Maupin's Trigg County Cemetery record and his Veteran's Pension application gives his birthday as 28 Oct 1838, but the 1900 census gives his birthday as October 1846. He was first buried in Allen Cemetery in Trigg County, then moved to the Bush Cemetery in Trigg County.

Patrick Henry Cain and Nancy Jane Allen were married 23 Dec 1875 by Rev. John F. White. His father-in-law was Robert H. Allen (b. 1821 in Tennessee, d. 1898) and his mother-in-law was Harriett Elizabeth (Turner) Allen (b. 1825 in Tennessee, d. 1893).

John W. Kelley was his attorney, free of charge, at the time of his application for a pension. Elias Robertson and J.G. Churchill were his witnesses for his veteran's pension application. Nancy Jane (Allen) Cain applied for her widow's pension on 21 Mar 1914. Her witness was Charles A. Chappell. They were first buried in the Allen Cemetery, but were moved when Lake Barkley was impounded.

In the 1900 Trigg County Census he is listed as Patrick Cain, a farmer age 53 years, and living with his wife Nancy J. (Allen) Cain (married 24 years), age 51 years, and five children: William C. (Christopher), age 21 years; Festus, age 17 years; Annie L., age 16 years; Altis S., age 12 years; and Odie M. (daughter), age 8 years. George Cherry, a boarder age 17 years, is living with the family in this census.

He is buried in the Bush Cemetery with his wife Nancy Jane (Allen) Cain (b. 10 Jun 1849, d. 28 May 1929). They were first buried in the Allen Cemetery, but were later moved to the Bush Cemetery when Lake Barkley was impounded.

JOHN H. CALDWELL, Ordinance Sergeant, born 22 Aug 1842, died ??. Enlisted 22 Sep 1861 at Russellville, KY and served with Co. A, originally the 5th Kentucky Regt. and later the 9th Kentucky Regt. Inf. (CSA)

His tombstone lists him as being in the 9th Kentucky Cav., CSA. We found him listed in the 9th Kentucky Inf. He was in the 1st Kentucky Brigade, Breckinridge's Div., Hardees Corps, Army of Tennessee. He was promoted to 3rd sergeant on 14 May 1862. He was promoted to ordinance sergeant for the regiment on 30 Jan 1864. Sgt. Caldwell was paroled out of the Army on 6 May 1865, at Washington, GA. He took the oath of allegiance on 2 May 1865. He was a brother of Pvt. Joseph W. Caldwell and Pvt. Thomas B. Caldwell. He became a resident of Cadiz, Trigg County, KY, on 1 Jun 1865.

His parents may have been John H. Caldwell (b. 6 Jun 1817 in Virginia, d. 27 Sep 1848) and Martha (Barksdale) Caldwell (b. 11 Jun 1821 in Virginia, d. 18 Jul 1846). They are both buried in the Boyd Cemetery in Trigg County.

J.H. Caldwell, age 26 years of Trigg County, married C.F. (Cornelia Frances) Boyd, age 20 years of Trigg County, on 16 Dec 1868. It was the first marriage for both bride and groom.

He applied for his veteran's pension on 14 Aug 1912. John W. Kelly was his attorney. Sergeant Caldwell's wife was deceased when he applied for his pension. R.B. Chastain and R.M. Hogan were witnesses for his pension application.

In the 1880 Trigg County Census he is listed as J.H. Caldwell, a teacher age 38 years and living with his wife Fannie (Boyd) Caldwell, age 31 years; and four children: Willie (daughter), age 10 years; John, age 7 years; Wister, age 5 years; and Fanney, age 11 months.

He is buried with his wife Cornelia Frances (Boyd) Caldwell (b. 21 Jul 1845, d. 6 Sep 1881) in the Boyd Cemetery in Trigg County. His daughter Miss Willie Caldwell (b. 17 Nov 1869, d. 3 Dec 1957) is buried in the East End Cemetery.

His son Joseph Wistar Caldwell (b. 22 Nov 1874, d. 28 Oct 1958) is buried with his wife Ella (Nabb) Caldwell (b. 13 Sep 1879, d. 11 Dec 1937) in the East End Cemetery.

JOSEPH W. CALDWELL, M.D., Private, born ca. 1846, died ??. Enlisted 9 Dec 1862 at Williamsport, TN and served with Co. A, Woodwards 2nd Kentucky Regt. Cav. (CSA). He was a brother of Sgt. John H. Caldwell and Pvt. Thomas B. Caldwell.

Page 1, Simmons' 1850 Trigg County Census #19, he is listed as "Joseph W." Caldwell age 4 years and living with his two brothers, John H. age 8 years and Thomas age 6 years, these orphans were living with the Quintus and Emily Tyler family in this census.

THOMAS B. CALDWELL, Private, born ca. 1844, died 6 Apr 1862. Enlisted 22 Sep 1861 at Russellville, KY and served with Co. A, 9th Kentucky Regt. Inf. (CSA). He was a brother of Sgt. John H. Caldwell and Pvt. Joseph W. Caldwell. Pvt. Thomas B. Caldwell was killed in action at the Battle of Shiloh on 6 Apr 1862.

On page 1, Simmons' 1850 Trigg County Census #19, he is listed as "Thomas" Caldwell, age 6 years and living with his two brothers, John H., age 8 years, and Joseph W., age 6 years—these three orphans are living with the Quintus and Emily Tyler family in this census.

GEORGE M. CALHOUN, Private, born ca. 1841, died ??. Enlisted 14 Sep 1861 at Camp Burnett, TN and served with Co. G, 4th Kentucky Regt. Inf. (CSA). He mustered in on 6 Jul 1861 in Trigg County. The last record of his Confederate service was the 31 Dec 1861 roll.

His father was Archibald Calhoun (b. ca. 1799 in North Carolina, d. ??) and his mother was Charity (Cohoon) Calhoun (b. ca. 1809 in Kentucky, d. ??). Archibald and Charity married on 25 Oct 1825 in Trigg County. They are both buried in the Griff Calhoun Cemetery in Trigg County. Archibald Cohoon voted in the August 1862 Election in the Cadiz Precinct.

Mildred Calhoun married Thomas W. Milam on 10 Jan 1878 in Trigg County.

In the 1860 Trigg County Census he is listed as "G.M." Calhoun, age 19 years and living with his father "A.B." (Archibald) Calhoun, age 61 years; his mother "C" (Charity) Calhoun, age 51; and one sibling, N.L. Calhoun (female), age 17 years.

In the 1870 Trigg County Census George M. Calhoun is not listed in this census, but his mother is listed as Charity "Cahoon," age 61 and living with a Mildred Cahoon, age 18. Mildred (b. 1859, d. ??) is buried with her husband Thomas W. Milam (b. 16 Mar 1852, d. 1 May 1935) in the Milam Cemetery.

ROBERT CALHOUN, Private, born ca. 1850 in Kentucky, died of disease at Atlanta, GA on 10 Feb 1862. Enlisted 14 Sep 1861 at Camp Burnett, TN and served with Co. G, 4th Kentucky Regt. Inf. (CSA).

In the 1860 Trigg County Census the only Robert Calhoun listed in the 1860 Trigg County Census is 10-year-old Robert, son of Henry Calhoun.

SULAUNT WOODFORD "WOOD" CALHOUN, born 1837 in Kentucky, died 11 May 1897 at about age 60 years. Enlisted June 1861 and served with Co. D, 14th Tennessee Inf., CSA.

He is buried in the Pleasant Hill Baptist Church Cemetery with his wife Julia A. Calhoun (b. 21 Jun 1841, d. 31 Oct 1909). Jones' 1900 Trigg County Census gives her birth month and year as April 1835, and born in Kentucky.

In the 1900 Trigg County Census Woodford Calhoun's wife Julia A. Calhoun is listed as a widow, age 65 years and living with her nephew Gus Jones, age 24 years, his wife Sopha Jones, age 25 years, and their two children, Dixie, age 3 years, and Jasper, age 9 months. There is no record of Julia A. Calhoun ever having any children.

JAMES H. CAMERON, Private, born ca. 1842 in Kentucky, died ??. Enrolled 14 Aug 1862, mustered in 13 Sep 1862 in Henderson, KY and mustered out 23 Sep 1863 at Russellville, KY. He served with Co. L, 8th Kentucky Regt. Cav. (USA). He was a brother of Pvt. James H. Cameron, a Union soldier, also of Co. L, 8th Kentucky Cav. (USA).

His father was John Cameron (b. ca. 1805 in Tennessee, d. ??) and his mother was Frances Cameron (b. ca. 1817 in Kentucky, d.??)

In the 1850 Trigg County Census he is listed as Thomas Cameron, age 8 years and living with his father John Cameron, a gunsmith and a silversmith, age 45 years; his mother Frances (Daniel) Cameron; and five siblings: Catherine, age 15 years; Susan, age 13 years; Sarah, age 11 years; James, age 8 years; and Martha, age 5 years.

In the 1860 Trigg County Census James Cameron is not found.

THOMAS J. CAMERON, Private, born ca. 1842 in Kentucky, died ??. Enrolled 14 Aug 1862, mustered in 13 Sep 1862 in Henderson, KY; mustered out 23 Sep 1863 at Russellville, KY; served with Co. L, 8th Kentucky Regt. Cav. (USA). He was a brother of Pvt. James H. Cameron, a Union soldier, also of Co. L, 8th Kentucky Cav. (USA).

His father was John Cameron (b. ca. 1805 in Tennessee, d. ??) and his mother was Frances Cameron (b. ca. 1817 in Kentucky, d. ??).

In the 1850 Trigg County Census he is listed as Thomas Cameron, age 8 years living with his father John Cameron, a gunsmith and a silversmith, age 45 years; his mother Frances (Daniel) Cameron; and five siblings: Catherine, age 15 years; Susan, age 13 years; Sarah, age 11 years; James, age 8 years; and Martha, age 5 years.

Thomas Cameron is not found in the 1870 Trigg County Census, but his father is listed as John Cameron, a gunsmith, age 65 years living with his wife Frances Cameron, age 53 years, and two siblings, Dora, age 17 years, and Irene, age 14 years.

WILLIAM M. CAMPBELL, Private, born 3 Oct 1842 in Kentucky, died: 28 Sep 1896. Enlisted first on 10 Sep 1861 at Williamsport, TN and served with Co. B, Capt. T.G. Woodward's 2nd/15th Kentucky Regt. Cav. CSA. Co. B of Woodward's Cav. later became Companies A and B of the 1st Kentucky Cav. under Gen. Ben Hardin Helm. His second enlistment was 9 Dec 1862 at Williamsport, TN with Co. A. Co. A, Helm's 1st Kentucky Regt. Cav. CSA.

His father was William Campbell (b. 26 Oct 1897 in Kentucky, d. 1885) and his mother was Sarah J. (Sally) (Baker) Campbell (b. ca. 2 Apr 1806 in Kentucky, d. 7 Apr 1854). They married 1 Dec 1827 in Trigg County. They were first buried in the Campbell Cemetery, but were later moved to the Little River Relocation Cemetery.

In the 1880 Trigg County Census William M. Campbell is listed as age 37 years, a farmer living with his wife Rebecca C. (Holland) Campbell, age 34 years, and seven children: Minerva J., age 13 years; John S., age 12 years; David Wall, age 10 years; William M. Jr., age 8 years; Sarah E., age 6 years; Richard B., age 4 years; and an infant son not yet named, age 10 days (this would have been Albert Holland Campbell born on 20 Mar 1880).

DOUGLAS CANNON, Private, born ca. 1835 in Kentucky, died 13 Aug 1862 at Baton Rouge, LA. Enlisted 11 Sep 1861 at Camp Burnett, TN and served with Co. G, 4th Kentucky Regt. Inf. Douglas Cannon and his brother Walter Cannon failed to muster with the men of Trigg County on 6 Jul 1861.

Douglas Cannon's sister Susan Cannon was the first wife of Hazard P. Baker, a Confederate soldier. According to Confederate records, he was "shot in the calf of the leg" on 5 Aug 1862 and died on 13 Aug 1862.

His father was John J. Cannon (b. 5 Sep 1794 in Virginia, d. 4 Jan 1850) who married Elizabeth Holland (b. ca. 1807 in North Carolina, d. ??) on 2 Feb 1825. His sisters: Elizabeth married Richard M. Smith on 25 Aug 1850; Emily married Robert M. Rogers on 25 Sep 1858 in Trigg County; and Sue (Susan) married Hazard P. Baker on 24 Nov 1867 in Trigg County. His brother Walter W., age 27 years of Trigg County, married Christina C. Wadlington, age 21 years, also of Trigg County, on 10 Sep 1869. It was the first marriage for both bride and groom.

His father John J. Cannon; sister Ellen (Cannon) Rogers (b. 1850, d 1916), wife of John H. Rogers (b. 1847, d. ??); and sister Susan (Cannon) Baker (b. 22 Feb 1840, d. 30 Jan 1877), wife of H.P. Baker, are all buried in the Rogers Cemetery, Trigg County.

In the 1850 Trigg County Census Douglas Cannon is listed as age 15 years and living with his mother Elizabeth Cannon, age 45 years, and eight siblings: Lucinda, age 23 years; Elizabeth, age 21 years; Emily, age 13 years; Susan, age 11 years; Walter, age 9 years; Martha, age 7 years; Ellen, age 4 years; and Sarah, age 1 year. A Richard M. Smith, age 25 years, is living with the family in this census.

JOHN GREEN CARR, born ca. 1841 in Kentucky, died ??. mustered in 25 Jun 1864 at Paducah, KY; mustered out (information not given); served with Co. K, 8th US Colored Artillery (Heavy) (USA).

John Green Carr is listed as being buried in the Carr Cemetery. There is also a John Green Carr buried in the Scott-Futrell Cemetery, but we feel this second John G. Carr man may be a white person.

Page 187, Simmons 1870 Trigg County Census #2200. He is listed as John G. Carr (black) age 29 and living with his wife Katherine Carr, age 27 years, and their three children: Mary B., age 6 years; Cater L., age 2 years; and Samuel A., age 1 year.

PEYTON C. CARR, Private, born 10 May 1842 in Kentucky, died 22 Oct 1925. Enrolled 13 Aug 1863, mustered in 26 Oct 1863 at Princeton, KY and mustered out 19 Dec 1864 at Bowling Green, KY. He served with Co. F, 48th Kentucky Regt. Mounted Inf. (USA).

Peyton C. Carr's father was John R. Carr (b. ca. 1814 in Kentucky, d ??) and his mother was Julia A. Carr (b. ca. 1825 in Kentucky, d ??).

There is a John R. Carr (b. 1814, d. 1862) buried in the Scott-Futrell Cemetery.

According to Neel's records, Peyton C. Carr married Elizabeth Sholar on 12 Dec 1866, in Trigg County, KY. His tombstone, however, gives the wedding date as 12 Dec 1865.

In the 1900 Trigg County Census he is listed as "Payton" C. Carr, age 58 years, a farmer living with his wife Elizabeth A. (Sholar) Carr (married 33 years), age 57 years, and their five children: Pinkney V., age 24 years; Ovie A., age 22 years; Charley D., age 19 years; Banson J., age 19 years; and Tabitha, age 17 years. Elizabeth has had five children, all five of whom were still living when this census was taken.

He is the only person with the surname of Carr recorded as buried in the Coleman Cemetery in Trigg County. His wife Elizabeth (Sholar) Carr (b. 17 Jan 1843, d. 10 Feb 1918) is buried in the Sholar Cemetery in Trigg County, KY.

WILLIAM E. CARR, Private, born ca. 1836 in Tennessee, died ??. mustered in 4 Aug 1864 at Paducah, KY, mustered out 12 Feb 1865 at Paducah, KY and served with Co. B, 1st Kentucky Regt. Capital Guards, Paducah Battalion (USA).

His father was T.J. Carr (b. ca. 1822 in Missouri, d. ??) and his mother was Elizabeth Carr (b. ca. 1826 in Kentucky, d ??).

In the 1860 Trigg County Census there is a William Carr whose true age is 14 years living with his father T.J. Carr, age 38 years; his mother Elizabeth Carr, age 34 years; and two brothers, Perry, age 12 years, and Charles, age 10 years.

William E. is buried in the Newton Cemetery in Trigg County.

JAMES W. CHAPPELL, Private, Enlisted 24 Oct 1861 at Camp Alcorn in Hopkinsville, KY and served with Co. B, 8th Kentucky Regt. Inf. (CSA). Pvt. James W. Chappell died on 4 Mar 1862 from wounds he had received at the Battle of Fort Donelson in February 1862.

GEORGE W. CHESTNUT, Private, born ca. 1834 in Kentucky, died ??. Enrolled 29 Jul 1863, mustered in 26 Oct 1863 at Princeton, KY and mustered out 19 Dec 1864 at Bowling Green, KY. He served with Co. F, 48th Kentucky Regt. Mounted Inf. (USA).

A George W. "Chenutt" is mentioned in the Roaring Spring Precinct Poll Book for the 6 Aug 1860 and 1861 elections.

In the 1860 Trigg County Census a George W. Chestnut is listed as a barkeeper, age 26 years, and living with a hotelkeeper, T. Powell and his wife Mrs. M.J. Powell.

JAMES C. CHOATE, Private, born ca. 1832 in Kentucky, died ??. Enlisted 15 Oct 1861 at Camp Alcorn, Hopkinsville, KY and served with Co. G, 8th KY Regt. Inf. (CSA). Pvt. James C. Choate was captured at Fort Donelson and took the Oath at Camp Morton, IN.

A James Choate voted in the 5 Aug 1867 election in the Cadiz Precinct.

In the 1860 Trigg County Census James C. Choate is listed as age 28 years and living with William Choate, age 38, and Julia Choate, age 27 years.

James C. Choate is not found in the 1900 Trigg County Census; however, William Choate and Julia Choate are found in this census. William Choate is listed as William "Choat," age 76 years and living with his wife Julia "Choat" (married 48 years), age 67 years. There is no record that this couple ever had any children.

RICHARD M. CHOATE, Corporal, born 18 Nov 1804 in Kentucky, died 7 Jan 1871. Enrolled 4 Aug 1862, mustered in 4 Aug 1864 at Paducah, KY and mustered out 12 Feb 1865 at Paducah, KY. He served with Co. B, 1st Kentucky Regt. Capital Guards, Paducah Battalion (USA).

He was married to Christian Choate (b. 20 Dec 1808, d. 24 Jul 1871). His wife and all of his children were born in Tennessee except for Julia, the youngest. His sons-in-law, Moses McWaters and William G. Gordon, were also War for Southern Independence veterans. He was great-great-grandfather of WWII Army veteran John Douglas Williams.

In the 1860 Trigg County Census Richard M. Choate is listed as R.M. Choate, age 54 years and living with his eight children: Margaret, age 24 years; E.J. (female), age 18 years; Samuel, age 17 years; C.C. (female), age 15 years; M.E. (Martha A.), 14 years; N.F. (Nancy F.), age 12 years; S.E. (Sarah Elizabeth), age 10 years; and Julia, age 8 years. Richard Choate's wife "C." (Christian) Choate, age 47 years, is listed as living nearby with "D.P." Austin, a farmer, age 38 years; his wife "F." Austin, age 27 years; and five children: Mary, age 11 years; "W." (male), age 7 years; John C., age 6 years; D.E. (female), age 2 years; and "W.E." (male), age 6 months.

Richard M. Choate and his wife Christian are buried in the Long Creek Cemetery near Devil's Elbow in the west side of Lake Barkely.

WILLIAM CLAXTON, Private, Enlisted 1 Nov 1861 at Camp Alcorn in Hopkinsville, KY and served with Co. B, 8th Kentucky Regt. Inf. He was wounded at Fort Donelson and taken to the hospital in Clarksville TN. Confederate records state he was from Tan Yard in Trigg County, KY.

J. WILLIAM COCHRAN, Private, born ca. 1825 in Kentucky, died 8 Jan 1862. Enlisted 26 Sep 1861 at Camp Reeves, TN and served with Co. G, 8th Kentucky Regt. Inf. (CSA).

He died of disease in the hospital at Clarksville, TN. Pvt. Cochran is buried in the Riverview Cemetery in Clarksville, TN.

In the 1860 Trigg County Census he is listed as age 35 years, a wheelwright and living alone in this census.

JAMES M. COLEMAN, Private, born ca. 1830 in Kentucky, died ??. Enlisted: 21 Jul 1861 at Camp Boone, TN and served with Cobb's Kentucky Battery of Field Artillery.

In the 1850 Trigg County Census there is a James Coleman listed as age 20 years and living his wife Rebecca Coleman, age 25 years, and one child Mary Coleman, age 7 months.

JOHN P. COLEMAN, Private, born ca. 1842 in Kentucky, died ??. Enlisted 26 Jul 1861 at Camp Boone, TN and served with Cobb's Kentucky Battery of Field Artillery.

His father was William Coleman (b. ca. 1800 in Kentucky, d ??) and his mother was Susan (Crane) Coleman (b. ca. 1803, d ??"). William Coleman married Susan Crane on 16 Nov 1822 in Trigg County.

In the 1850 Trigg County Census he is listed as age 8 years and living with his father William Coleman, age 50 years; his mother Susan (Crane) Coleman, age 47 years; and seven siblings: William T, age 22 years; Jemima, age 17 years; Mary A., 15 years; Caroline, age 13 years; Martha, age 11 years; and Lessenby (male), age 5 years.

JOHN T. COLLINS, Private, born ca. 1844 in Kentucky, died ??. Enlisted 22 Aug 1861 at Camp Boone, TN and served with Co. K, 2nd Kentucky Regt. Inf. (CSA). This John T. Collins of Co. K, 2nd Kentucky Regt. Inf. is the only man of this name found in the report. According to the Kentucky Adjutant General's Report he was killed while trying to escape from prison at Camp Morton, IN.

His father was George W. Collins (b. ca. 1807 in Tennessee, d. ??) and his mother was Mildred Collins (b. ca. 1812 in Virginia, d. ??).

John's father George W. Collins voted in the May 1850 referendum on the New Constitution at Cadiz, KY.

In the 1850 Trigg County Census John Collins is listed as age 8 years and living with his father George W. Collins, age 43 years; his mother Mildred Collins, age 38 years; and eight siblings: Martha, age 19 years; William T., age 17 years; July A., age 15 years; Sarah J., age 13 years; Daniel, age 11 years; Mary, age 8 years; Elizabeth, age 4 years; and James E., age 1 year.

LEWIS/LOUIS COLSON, Private, born 22 Mar 1836 in Kentucky, died 4 Mar 1912. Enrolled 4 Aug 1864, mustered in 4 Aug 1864 at Paducah, KY for six months and mustered out 12 Feb 1865 at Paducah, KY. He served with Co. B, 1st Kentucky Regt. Capital Guards, Paducah Battalion (USA).

His parents were Joel Colson (b. ca. 1797 in North Carolina) and Margaret (Griffin) Colson (b. ca. 1798 in North Carolina). They married on 16 Feb 1826 in Trigg County, KY.

In the 1880 Trigg County Census he is listed as Louis Colson, a farmer age 44 years and living with his wife Harriett (Futrell) Colson, age 36 years, and their four children: Charley O. Colson, age 14 years; James E., age 13 years; Lithy, age 9 years; and Bailey, age 2 years.

Lewis Colson is buried in the Colson or Pleasant Valley Cemetery with his wife Harriett (Futrell) Colson (b. 16 May 1842, d. 17 Jan 1911).

STARKIE COLSON, Private, born 1846 in Kentucky, died ??. Enrolled 4 Aug 1864, mustered in 4 Aug 1864 at Paducah, KY and mustered out 12 Feb 1865 at Paducah. He served with Co. B, 1st Kentucky Regt. Capital Guards, Paducah Battalion (USA)

Starkie's parents were Sanders Colson (b. ca. 1828 in Kentucky, d ??) and Mary (Cohoon) Colson (b. ca. 1829 in Kentucky, d. ??).

Starkie Colston, age 21 years of Trigg County, married Sara Jane Ahart, age 18 years also of Trigg County, on 28 Nov 1867. It was the first marriage for both bride and groom.

In the 1880 Trigg County Census he is listed as Starkie "Colston," a laborer age 40 years and living with his wife Anna E. "Colston," age 24 years, and their four children: William, age 12 years; James M., age 10 years; Joseph L., age 6 years; and Ann, age 4 years.

In the 1880 Trigg County Census his father Sanders Colson is listed as a farmer age 50 years and living with his son Bithael, age 25 years; daughter Dixie, age 23 years, son Needom J., age 10 years and daughter Martha A., age 8 years.

Starkie Colson is buried in the Long Creek Cemetery with his father "Sanders" Colson (b. 1828), no stone, and his stepmother Martha Ann (Ahart) Colson (b. 1841 in Tennessee, d ??). There is no stone at her grave either.

GIPSON COMPTON, Private, born 10 Oct 1838 in Tennessee, died 23 Aug 1915. He mustered in 13 Sep 1862 at Henderson, KY and mustered out 23 Sep 1863 at Russellville, KY. He served with Co. L, 8th Kentucky Regt. Cav. (USA).

Gipson Compton was a brother of Issac D. and John V., both Union soldiers. His father was William T. Compton (b. 26 Sep 1817 in Virginia, d. 27 Oct 1879) and his mother was Rachel Amanda (Nunn) Compton (b. 2 Oct 1819 in Virginia, d. 22 Dec 1896). William and Rachel are buried in the Long Creek Cemetery.

Gipson Compton, a farmer age 31 years, married Ruth E. Garner, age 26 years, in Trigg County on 4 Nov 1869. It was the first marriage for both bride and groom. According to Maupin's Trigg County Cemetery Records, Ruth E. (Garner) Compton is buried in the Wenger Cemetery in Trigg County, but there is no stone at her grave.

Gipson married second, Victoria F. Jones (b. 4 Feb 1854, d. 16 Oct 1909).

In the 1870 Trigg County Census he is listed as "Gipton" Compton, age 31 years and living with his wife Ruth (Garner) Compton, age 26 years, and three children: Robert G., age 10 years; Emily, age 8 years; and Hennrietta, age 2 years. We think Henrietta Compton was visiting her grandparents on the day the census was taken and Hennrietta was listed twice in the 1870 Trigg County Census.

In the 1880 Trigg County Census he is listed as Gipson Compton, a farmer age 38 years and living with his second wife Victoria F. (Jones) Compton, age 27 years, and their four children: William M., age 6 years; Ader F., age 5 years; Wadkins (daughter), age 2 years; and Mary Ann, age 5 months.

He is buried in the Compton Cemetery with his second wife Victoria F. (Jones) Compton.

ISAAC COMPTON, Private, born 28 Oct 1843 in Tennessee, died 15 Oct 1919. He served with Co. L, 8th Kentucky Regt. Cav. (USA).

All Compton family members older than John were born in Tennessee. Isaac Compton was a brother of Gipson Compton and John Compton.

Isaac married Mahala Evelyn Solomon (b. 7 Feb 1845, d. 2 Mar 1909) and both are buried in the Compton Cemetery. Their daughter Rebecca (b. 1 Mar 1877, d. 6 Sep 1878) and son I.P. Compton (b. 27 Jun 1884, d. 3 Feb 1886) are also buried in the Compton Cemetery.

JOHN COMPTON, Private, born ca. 1846 in Kentucky, died ??. He mustered in 4 Aug 1864 at Paducah, KY, mustered out 12 Feb 1865 at Paducah and served with Co. B, 1st Kentucky Regt. Capital Guards, Paducah Battalion (USA).

John Compton was a brother to Gipson and Isaac Compton.

JOHN B. CRAIN/CRANE, Private, born 1841 in Trigg County, KY, died ??. He enlisted in September 1861 and served with Co. D, 6th Tennessee Regt. Inf. (CSA). He enlisted in Col. Suggs' Regiment and Capt. Sam Greyhouse's Company. He was wounded at Fort Donelson a few days before the battle and sent to the hospital in Nashville on furlough in February 1862. Private Crain was captured at Nashville, took the oath of allegiance in October 1862 as he was in ill health and was unable to return to his command.

He was a resident of Salinburg, Trigg County, KY. His father was Sam Crane (b. ??, d. ca. 1848) and his mother was Nancy (Mason) Crane (b. ca. 1821 in Tennessee, d. ??). They married on 26 May 1840 in Trigg County. Nancy married second, Philip Heyers on 28 Nov 1860. John B. married Parthenia Crain.

ALSEY BROOKS CRAWLEY, came to Trigg County shortly before the Civil War broke out. He was born on 14 Mar 1836 in Charlotte County, VA to Lindsey J. and Coley (High) Crawley. His parents died when he was just a child and thereafter he was reared by his grandparents, William and Sarah (Davis) Crawley, in Charlotte County, VA.

Mr. Crawley enlisted in the Confederate Army according to military records on 21 Sep 1861 in Hopkinsville, KY as a member of Co. G, 8th Regt. Kentucky Inf. where he was taken prisoner at Fort Donelson on 16 Feb 1862, sent to Camp Morton, IN and from there to Vicksburg, MS to be exchanged. He was on the muster roll for Co. D, 8th Regt. Kentucky Inf. from 31 July to 31 Oct 1862 where he was promoted to the rank of corporal on 22 Sep 1862. On 5 Dec 1862 he was wounded in action near Coffeeville, MS while in Co. B, 8th Regt. Kentucky Inf. Military records show in March and April 1864 Corporal Crawley was "on duty with Provost Guard. Government horse."

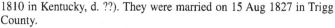

According to his obituary, he was in a number of battles throughout Kentucky, Tennessee, Mississippi, Louisiana and other states, and was one of only five of his company who returned home to Trigg County after the war without having been seriously wounded.

Following the war, he returned to the home of his birth to marry his childhood sweetheart, Sarah "Sallie" Witt Roberts, daughter of Robert and Eliza (Smithson) Roberts, and brought her back to Trigg County where they lived the rest of their life. Nine children were born to this union: John Robert Lindsey, Ella Mae, James L., Colie Lee, Virginia "Jenny," Epha Della, Thomas W.B., Alsey R. Witt and Katie Felton Crawley.

Alsey Crawley died of dropsy, 7 Aug 1907, age of 71, and is buried in East End Cemetery, Cadiz.

ALSBROOK B. CRAWLEY, 2nd Corporal, born March 1836 in Virginia (1900 census), died 1907. He enlisted 24 Oct 1861 at Camp Alcorn in Hopkinsville, KY and served with Co. G, 8th Kentucky Regt. Inf. (CSA). Private Crawley was captured with his unit at the Battle for Fort Donelson and imprisoned at Camp Morton, IN. He was exchanged late 1862, only to be wounded at Coffeeville, MS, 5 Dec 1862. He surrendered 15 May 1865, and was paroled at Columbus, MS on 19 May 1865.

His daughter Colie Lee married Whitson Mitchell on 10 Nov 1890 in Trigg County; son Lindsay R. married Leah Mitchell (b. 1869, d. 1895) on 7 Mar 1891 in Trigg County. Leah is buried in the Sivills Cemetery in Trigg County. Lindsay married second, Mattie McCargo on 27 Oct 1897 in Trigg County.

Alsbrook is buried in East End Cemetery with his wife Sarah W. (b. 1842 in Virginia, d. 1909). Their daughter Epfa D. (or Epha) (b. 23 Feb 1878 in Kentucky, d. 29 Apr 1878); daughter Ella E. Crawley (b. 1870 in Kentucky, d. 1946); and son James L. (b. 13 Nov 1871 in Kentucky, d. 19 Jul 1877), are all buried in the East End Cemetery.

HENRY E. CRUTE, born 1840 in Virginia, died 1894. Both of his parents were born in Virginia. Henry E. married Nancy Elizabeth Hayden (b. 1846 in Kentucky, d. 1894) on 10 Dec 1863 in Trigg County. He is buried in the Cumberland Baptist Church Cemetery with his wife Nancy Elizabeth (Hayden) Crute.

His son Samuel B. married Lillie Gillihan on 7 Nov 1896, in Trigg County. Samuel B. (b. 2 Oct 1872 in Kentucky, d. 2 Oct 1909) was initially buried in the Cumberland Baptist Church Cemetery with his wife Lillie (Gillihan) Crute (b. 4 Oct 1873 in Kentucky, d. 14 Dec 1894) and later they were moved to the re-interment location at the Matheny Cemetery. Their son Henry D. (b. 1906, d. 1926), daughter Fannie (b. 1898, d. 1903) and an infant (b&d. 1903) are buried there as well. (According to Jones' 1900 Census Fannie was born in June of 1899).

ALEXANDER "ZAN" CUNNINGHAM, born 22 Jan 1845 in Kentucky (January 1846, 1900 Census), died in Evansville, IN. He served with Co. D, Woodward's 2nd/15th Kentucky Regt. Cav.

His father was Alexander Cunningham (b. 1812/13 in Virginia, d. ??) and his mother was Jacyntha (Wallace) Cunningham (b. 1822/23 in Tennessee, d. ??). They married on 1 Sep 1839 in Trigg County and are buried in the Alexander Cunningham or Peal's Chapel Cemetery in Trigg County.

According to Neel's records, Alexander Cunningham, age 22 years of Trigg County, married Maud H. Shryer, age 14 years of Trigg County, on 3 Feb 1869. It was the first marriage for both bride and groom.

Zan is thought to be buried in Evansville, IN.

DAVID D. CUNNINGHAM, born August 1837 (according to the 1900 Census) and in *The Cunningham Family* by Bertie Gingles, David D. Cunningham is listed as a Confederate WSI veteran.

He was a brother to Elias Alexander, William Thomas and Mickens Carr Cunningham Jr. Their father was William Cunningham (b. ca. 1898 in Virginia, d. ??) and mother was Jane (Mitchell) Cunningham (b. ca.

1810 in Kentucky, d. ??). They were married on 15 Aug 1827 in Trigg County.

David married Mary Ellen Atwood (b. 8 Aug 1849) on 29 Jun 1877 in Trigg County. From Gingles Records this couple had the following children: Mary Virginia (b. 25 May 1878); William Thomas (b. 9 Aug 1880); Maggie Lena (b. 23 Feb 1884); Minnie Lundy (b. 1884, died age 1 year).

ELIAS "ELSE/ALEX" ALEXANDER CUNNINGHAM, Private, born 12 May 1844 in Kentucky, died 22 Mar 1921. He enlisted 14 Sep 1861, at Camp Burnett, TN and served with Co. G, 4th Kentucky Regt. Inf. (CSA). Private Elias A. Cunningham enlisted under Col. Trabue and Capt. John B. Trice. His last colonel was Col. Albert P. Thompson. He was promoted from private to 4th corporal on 10 Jan 1863 and demoted from 4th corporal to private on 7 Jun 1863. He was a member of the famous "Orphan Brigade" and participated in the battles of Batan Rouge, Chickamauga, Dalton, GA and many others. He was wounded in the knee at the Battle of Chickamauga, 20 Sep 1863. Pvt. Cunningham surrendered on 6 May 1865 in Washington, GA, and was paroled there on 7 May 1865. He took the oath of allegiance on 21 May 1865.

He applied for his Pension on 9 Aug 1920. Perrin's History of Trigg County and his Confederate Veterans Pension Application give his birth date as 12 May 1843 and Trigg County History gives his birth date as 30 May 1843.

His father was William Cunningham (b. ca. 1798 in Virginia, d. ??) and his mother was Jane (Mitchell) Cunningham (b. ca. 1810, d. ??).

Elias Alexander was a brother to David, William Thomas and M.C. Cunningham Jr. He was a resident of LaFayette, Trigg County, KY.

He married first, Margaret E. Hendricks (b. ca. 1846, d. January 1877), daughter of George and Jane (Boyd) Hendricks, on 19 Nov 1866 in Trigg County; he married second, Elizabeth "Betty" Stallons (b. ca. 1859, d. February 1881), daughter of Reuben Stallons, on 12 Feb 1877 in Trigg County; and married third, Susan F. Robinson (b. 14 Feb 1864, d. 4 Nov 1901), daughter of Charles Robinson, on 2 Apr 1881 in Trigg County.

Children of E. Alexander Cunningham (from Gingles Records) by Margaret E. (Hendricks) Cunningham: David Davidson (b. 1867); George Harvey (b. 25 Feb 1869); James William (b. 15 Nov 1871); Dabney C. b. 4 Sep 1874.

Children by Betty (Stallons) Cunningham: Janie and Maggie.

Children by Susan F. (Robenson) Cunningham: Vangie (b. 1882); Eula (b. 4 May 1885); Mamie; Emma (b. 25 Feb 1894(?)); Albert (b. 19 Apr 1889); Charles Josh (b. 19 May 1896); Lola Cunningham (b. ??).

Elias is buried with his third wife Susan F. Robinson Cunningham in the William Thomas "Tom" Cunningham Cemetery.

JAMES GREEN CUNNINGHAM, Private, born 3 Oct 1840, died 5 Feb 1909 in Mayfield, KY. He served with Co. G, 4th Kentucky Regt. Inf. (CSA). According to the Confederate records, he was "absent in Trigg County on sick furlough" on the 30 Nov to 31 December 1861 rolls. He may be listed As "G.G." Cunningham in the Adjutant General's Report.

The James Green Cunningham family moved to Calloway County, KY in November 1886. His parents were Andrew and Nancy (P'Pool) Cunningham.

James Green married Amanda Ophelia Harris (b. 22 Nov 1852) on 26 Nov 1871. She died when she fell from a horse. He married second, Martha E. "Dollie" Pugh (b. 24 Mar 1862) on 13 Oct 1878. According to Gingles Records their children were Mary (b. 18 Apr 1880); Daisy Hope (b. 10 Sep 1882); Effie (b. 17 Sep 1884); Lola (b. 16 Mar 1887); Toy (b. 4 Mar 1889); Ethel (b. 3 Jun 1891).

DR. JOHN CUNNINGHAM, lst Lieutenant (Surgeon), born in Trigg County, KY, on 21 Sep 1836. His parents were John and Mary "Polly" (Gresham) Cunningham. His father, a colonel in the Kentucky Militia, also was magistrate. Three of John's grandfathers, Moza Gresham, James Boyd and Gideon Carr, served in the continental forces during the Revolutionary War. His father William Cunningham came to America in 1795 from Scotland.

John Cunningham obtained his literary training in common schools of Kentucky and at Bethel College, Russellville, KY He attended St. Louis Medical College and Galveston, TX, Medical College, where he received his second medical diploma.

He practiced medicine in Trigg County until the breaking out of the War Between the State. He married Ann O. Patterson, daughter of George W. and Margaret (Carloss) Patterson. They were parents of one son, Byron Blair. Ann Cunningham died shortly following the birth of the child.

Enlisting in the Confederate Army, Co. G, 4th Kentucky Inf., John Cunningham was elected a 1st lieutenant. His unit fought for two days in the battle of Shiloh, the regiment went into battle with 900 men and came out with 450. Later he was Gen. Wheeler's surgeon. He then, with Gen. Bragg's invasion of Kentucky, helped to organize a cavalry company of which he was elected 2nd lieutenant and later elected captain. He was captured at Paris, TN and imprisoned at Nashville, TN, and Camp Chase, OH, and Fortress Monroe, VA.

Following the war, John settled in Revenna, Fannin County, TX and opened a medical practice. He owned several large ranches and a mercantile store in Fannin County.

He married a second time to Fannie Agnew, daughter of Allen Agnew. They were the parents of three children: Henry Allen (who later became a judge in Fanning County), Annie Laurie and William Murray.

Dr. John Cunningham was elected to five terms in the Texas Legislature and was the last Confederate Soldier serving in the Texas Government. His picture hangs on the walls at the Texas Capital in Austin.

John Cunningham died 6 Feb 1924 and was buried on his Sandy Ranch in Fannin County, TX. A large Confederate Monument on the west side of the square in Bonham, Fannin County, TX lists the committee who obtained the monument, John Cunningham is the first name listed. *Submitted by Kay Wallace Sloan.*

MICKENS CARR "MICK" CUNNINGHAM Jr.,

Private, born 26 May 1839 in Trigg County, KY, died 26 May 1910 in Trigg County, KY. He enlisted 14 Sep 1861, at Camp Burnett, TN and served with Co. G, 4th Kentucky Regt. Inf. (CSA). According to his Confederate Veteran's Pension Application, he enlisted on 22 Aug 1861. Wounded on his face (near his ear) at the Battle of Shiloh in April 1862 and discharged on 25 Jul 1862. He returned to his home where he recovered. He re-enlisted at Beech Grove, TB on 14 Apr 1863, into his old company, Co. G, 4th Kentucky Regt. Inf., and served until the end of the war.

He surrendered at Washington, GA on 6/7 May 1865 and took the oath of allegiance on 21 May 1865.

His parents were William (b. 1800 in Virginia, d. 1879) and Jane "Jennie" (Mitchell) Cunningham (b. 1811 in Kentucky, d. 1878).

Mickens, age 25 years, married Laura J. Hendricks (b. 19 Sep 1848, d. ??), age 18 years on 30 Dec 1865. They were married at Laura's father's home in Trigg County by Rev. Thomas Baker. Children of this marriage (from Gingles Records): Sarah Jane (b. 23 Oct 1866); Lee Annie (b. 21 Aug 1868); John William (b. 27 Dec 1869); Eliza (b. 28 Jun 1872); N.A. (b. 29 Jul 1877, d. in infancy).

Mickens is buried with his wife Laura Jane (Hendricks) Cunningham (b. 19 Sep 1846, 22 Apr 1928) in the William "Buck" Cunningham Cemetery.

MICKENS CARR CUNNINGHAM SR.,

Private, born ca. 1833 in Dickson County, TN, died ??. He enlisted 14 Sep 1861 at Camp Burnett, TN and served with Co. G, 4th Kentucky Regt. Inf. (CSA). M.C. was slightly wounded in the scalp at Mill Creek Gap near Resaca, GA, on 9 May 1864. He surrendered at Washington, GA on 6 May 1865 and took the oath of allegiance on 21 May 1865.

His father was Gideon Carr Cunningham and his mother was Harriett (Tidwell) Cunningham.

Mickens Carl Cunningham Sr., age 31 years, married Mrs. Penelope Cunningham Gray, age 28 years, on 21 Aug 1865. Penelope was the widow of William Gray and is buried with William Gray in the James Cunningham Cemetery. Penelope married William Gray on 9 Jan 1853, in Trigg County. Children from this marriage: Warren (b. 22 Jun 1866); Nellie Bly (b. 21 Feb 1868); Daniel Webster (b. ca. 1870), single; Alphy (b. December 1871); Zilphy Porter (b. 1 Nov 1875).

Mickens Carr Cunningham Sr. is buried in the Mt. Pleasant or Blue Springs Cemetery.

On page 87, Simmons' 1870 Trigg County Census #1008, he is listed as Mickins C. Cunningham Sr., age 36 years, living with his wife Penelope (Cunningham) (Gray) Cunningham, age 32 years; step-son James G. Gray, age 15 years; step-son Isaac Gray, age 13 years; step-son Levi Gray, age 13 years; step-daughter Sarah Gray, age 9 years; son Warren Cunningham, age 4 years; daughter Millie Cunningham, age 2 years; and Sally Cunningham, a black 16-year-old servant). (Penelope's children: James G., Isaac, Levi and Sarah are by William Gray.)

WILLIAM THOMAS "TOM" CUNNINGHAM,

born 20 Mar 1938 in Trigg County, KY, died 1915. He enlisted September 1861 at Fort Donelson, TN and served with Co. A, 1st Tennessee (Forrest's) Regiment Cavalry under Captain May. Co. A of the lst Tennessee Regt. of Cavalry would later become Co. C, 3rd (Forrest's Old) Tennessee Cav. Regt. William Thomas Cunningham was captured at Gallatin, TN, and sent to Camp Chase, OH. He was exchanged in August 1862 and went back into the Confederate Army. He was honorably discharged at Murfreesboro, TN in November 1862.

His father was William Cunningham (b. ca. 1798 in Virginia, d. ??) and his mother was Jane (Mitchell) Cunningham (b. ca. 1810 in Kentucky, d. ??).

Tom married Martha Jane "Mat" Cameron (b. 30 Aug 1844 in Kentucky, d. 1912) on 12 Mar 1868. Children of this marriage: Nettie (b. 12 Aug 1869; George (b. 4 Aug 1871, d. at age 21 years), single; Ell (b. 19 Oct 1874); Susie Francis (b. 29 Mar 1878); Eliza (b. 30 Jun 1880); Cleveland (b. 12 Mar 1885).

He is buried in the William Thomas "Tom" Cunningham Cemetery with his wife Martha Jane "Mat" (Cameron) Cunningham (b. 30 Aug 1844, d. 1912).

BENJAMIN FRANKLIN DALTON,

Private, born 25 Oct 1835 in Louise County, VA, died 17 Jul 1876, in Trigg County, KY. He enlisted in March 1862, in Buckingham County, VA and served with Co. K, 6th Virginia Cav. (CSA). His unit surrendered at Appomattox Courthouse, Appomattox County, VA, with Robert E. Lee. Private Benjamin F. Dalton and his wife Ann (McCary) Dalton moved from Virginia to the Herndon area of Trigg County, arriving in 1865. His widow applied for a Confederate pension on 21 May 1912.

His daughter Benjamin F. Dalton was born in Virginia and his son Robert T. Dalton was born in Kentucky.

Benjamin married Ann McGary (b. 8 Jun 1833 in Buckingham County, VA, d. ??) They were married in Buckingham County, VA by John C. Hawkins.

His daughter Burnie F. (Benjamin F.) Dalton married L.A. (Stephen) Ledford on 24 Dec 1884 in Trigg County.

He is listed in the Roaring Spring Poll Book as of November 1868.

JESSE LINN BOYD "NUCK" DARNALL,

born 16 Feb 1842 in Marshall County, KY. At age 19 when war broke out between the states, he volunteered for the Confederacy. He enlisted 3 Aug 1861 at Camp Boone, KY as a private in Co. G, 3rd Kentucky Inf. (mounted) Regt. His officers were Capt. Crit Edwards, John Morgan, 1st Lt. Mose Riley, 2nd Lt. Col. Tilmond, Lt. Albert Thomas and Maj. Aderson.

During the Civil War, he fought in many hard battles and escaped without a wound. In the heated Battle of Shiloh he was seen jumping a rail fence as a cannon ball shot the fence from under him. His comrades said "They got "Nuck." When the smoke cleared he miraculously showed up unhurt He and his company were captured and surrendered. He took the oath of allegiance voluntarily to the US Government at Paducah, KY under

Col. Meredith. "I knew I had it to do" he stated on his pension application. He was discharged 4 Aug 1864 at Tupelo, MS.

After the war he was a farmer. He married Miranda Edwards of Marshall County (b. 9 Jun 1859, d. ??) and they had 12 children.

In 1885 he was ordained a Baptist minister. Soon after, he came to Trigg County to Dry Creek Primitive Baptist Church. He pastored there from 1888 to 1915. He was moderator of the Little River Baptist Association for 18 years.

On 29 Sep 1888, he married Martha Ann Atkins of Trigg County. An article in the *Hopkinsville Kentuckian*, 13 Feb 1908, stated he was the father of 24 children (17 by his first wife and nine by his second wife). Only seven lived from the second marriage. His wife and four of their children died during the week of 9-12 Nov 1918 in the flu epidemic. Only two children, Althea Darnall Skinner and Elder J.N. Darnall, and Jesse Linn Boyd Darnall II, child of his son Perkins, were left to carry on his Trigg County legacy.

During the tobacco war 1905-11, with his livelihood still coming from farming, the night riders came to his house because he sold some tobacco. They called him out of the house but for some unknown reason, let him go free.

He lived in Trigg County for over 27 years, a leading citizen of the Linton Community where he died 7 Feb 1915 with burial in Atkins Cemetery, Trigg County. *Submitted by Mrs. Joe L. Darnall.*

WILLIAM N. DAVIS, Private, born circa 1842 in Illinois, died ??. He enlisted 24 Oct 1862 at Camp Alcorn in Hopkinsville, KY and served with

Co. B, 8th Kentucky Regt. Inf. (CSA).

According to the 1860 Trigg County Census, the father "F." Davis was born in Tennessee; Alfred A. and William N. Davis were born in Illinois; Mary A. Davis was born in Kentucky; and Samuel C. and George B. Davis were born in Tennessee.

William N. Davis' wife Minerva Jane (Faulkner) Davis and Samuel C. Davis' second wife Susan C. Faulkner (Barnes) Davis were sisters. They were the sisters of Confederate veteran Benjamin Faulkner. (See Benjamin Faulkner).

W.N. Davis of Trigg County, born in Jefferson County, IL, was a farmer, age 27 years, married Minerva Jane Faulkner, age 29 years (b. December 1839, d. ??) of Trigg County, on 18 Feb 1869. It was the first marriage for both bride and groom.

His daughter Kitty Davis (b. circa 1872, d. ??) married Andrew J. P'Pool on 17 Oct 1891 in Trigg County.

His brother Samuel C. Davis, a farmer from Trigg County, age 22 years (born in Smith County, Tennessee), married first Virginia Kenady, age 18 years of Trigg County, on 13 May 1869. It was the first marriage for both bride and groom. Samuel C. (b. October 1847, d. ??) married second, Mrs. Susan C. (Faulkner) Barnes (b. December 1850, d. ??) on 27 Jan 1886 in Trigg County.

William's nephew William Lee Davis (b. 1870, d. 1944) is buried with his wife Frances B. Broadbent Davis (b. 1880, d. 1936) in the Wall Cemetery in Trigg County. Numerous infant children of this couple are buried in the Wall Cemetery with the parents.

EDGECOMB LEWIS DAWSON, born circa 1846 in Kentucky, d. ??. Both Maupin and Neel list him as a War for Southern Independence veteran.

His father was Joseph A. Dawson (b. circa 1824 in Kentucky, d. ??) and his mother was Mary A. (Lewis) Dawson (b. circa 1824 in Kentucky, d. ??). They were married on 3 Aug 1846.

His brother Thomas V. Dawson married Sallie E. Stapp on 1 Nov 1882 in Trigg County.

Edgecomb Lewis is buried in the Dawson Cemetery in Trigg County, KY, but has no stone at his grave.

CALVIN POINDEXTER DEARING, Captain, born 29 Oct 1842 in Bedford County, VA, died 26 Aug 1929. He enlisted 27 Apr or 1 May 1861 in Virginia and served with Co. G, 28th Virginia Regt. Inf. (CSA). Mr. Dearing served under Capt. Penter, Lt. T.C. Holland and Col. Preston. He was taken prisoner at the Battle of Gettysburg and held as a prisoner at Fort Delaware for two years. He took the oath of allegiance on 15 May 1865, then was released from prison on 18 May 1865.

His farm was eight miles south of Cadiz in the Maggie Community.

Calvin Poindexter Dearing married Susan Jeanette Frances Creasy (b. 2 Aug 1850 in Bedford County, VA, d. November 1937) on 21 Mar 1866 in Bedford County, VA. The bride was age 18 years and the groom, a farmer, age 23 years. The bride's parents were Samuel H. and C. Creasey and the groom's parents were J. and Nancy Dearing.

This couples' daughters: Lizzie, Nannie and Mary Ann were born in Virginia. Lelia and Abyth and all daughters thereafter were born in Kentucky.

Daughters: Margaret Elizabeth "Lizzie" married Anderson Pinkney "Pink" Russell on 12 Mar 1891 in Trigg County; Nancy Bell "Nannie" married William Henry Sholar on 26 Dec 1898 in Trigg County, KY; Mary Ann married Benjamin Franklin Davis; Virginia Catherine and Mattie Olivia died young; Lelia Thomas married L. "Isaac" Burnett Porter on 17 Jan 1898 in Trigg County, KY; Rubena Alma married Henry Mitchell; Sudell Nellie married Howard Edgar Maddux; Sallie Ida married Ed Hite; Birdie Ethyl married Terry Freman; Maggie Lucretia married Henry David Sholar; Emma Cynthia married Hillary A. Tuggle.

Calvin applied for a Confederate Veteran's Pension Application on 10 Jun 1912. His widow Susan Francis (Creasy) Dearing had been a resident of Trigg County since 1870, and had moved from Bedford County, VA and applied for the pension on 16 Sep 1929. Her statement was verified by Robert Crenshaw of Cadiz, KY.

He is buried in East End Cemetery with his wife Susan (Creasy) Dearing (b. 1848 in Virginia, d. 1929). Mattie O. Dearing "daughter of C.P. and S.E." Dearing (b. 11 Oct 1874 in Kentucky, d. 28 Jul 1876) is buried in the Dearing Cemetery in Trigg County, KY.

WILLIAM DELAWSON, Private, born 1842 in Kentucky, died 1862 at Louisville, KY. He enlisted 14 Oct 1861 at Camp Alcorn in Hopkinsville, KY and served with Co. G, 8th Kentucky Regt. Inf. (CSA). Private Delawson was captured at Fort Donelson on 16 Feb 1862 and died in prison at Louisville, KY

His father was John Delawson (b. circa 1815 in Connecticut, d. ??) and his mother was Nancy Delawson (b. circa 1816 in Kentucky, d. ??).

William's brother Joseph Delawson married "E." ?? circa 1858 when he was about 19 years of age. Joseph Delawson, age 29 years of Trigg County, married Sarah Braboy, age 24 years also of Trigg County, on 25 Feb 1868. It was the first marriage for the bride and the second marriage for the groom.

William's brother Francis M. Delawson (b. December 1845, d. ??) married Mary Mitchell on 20 Nov 1862, in Trigg County when he was about 16 years of age. Francis M. married second, Frances E. "Fannie" Bush (b. June 1848, d. ??) on 5 Nov 1879, in Trigg County.

His brother John Henry Delawson (b. September 1849, d. ??), age 20 years and a farmer from Trigg County, married Lucy B. Bush (b. May 1855, d. ??) age 16 years, also from Trigg County, on 29 Mar 1870. It was the first marriage for both bride and groom.

Henry C. Delawson (b. 1890, d. 1937) and his wife Christa V. Delawson (b. 1886, d. 1956) are buried in the Cherry or Siloam Church Cemetery in Trigg County.

JAMES ELBERT DENSON, born 13 Oct 1835 in Kentucky, died 19 Apr 1888. Both Maupin and Neel list James as a WSI veteran.

An Elizabeth Denson married William W. Martin on 4 Aug 1858 in Trigg County.

James' father, James Denson (b. circa 1809 in Tennessee, d. 1 Feb 1853 in Trigg County), and his mother, Permelia (Brown) Denson (b. 1818 in Kentucky, d. ??), were married on 16 Apr 1831 in Trigg County. The records show that James Denson's parents were John and Esther Denson. Maupin's Trigg County Cemetery records show that James Denson is buried in the Pinnegar Cemetery.

James Elbert Denson and a Thomas Denson (b. 1828, d. 10 Mar 1892) are buried in the Pinnegar Cemetery in Trigg County, KY.

ROBERT WICKLIFFE DEW, 1st Corporal, born November 1841 in Trigg County, KY, died 29 Jan 1918 in Canton, KY. He enlisted 14 Sep 1861 at Camp Burnett, TN and served with Co. G, 4th Kentucky Regt.

Inf. (CSA). He was under the command of Capt. Trice, lst Lt. John Cavanaugh, 2nd Lt. Freen Baker, and 3rd Lt. Francis Baker. He was wounded in the thigh at Resaca, GA on 14 May 1864. His military unit is given on his tombstone. Robert Dew mustered with the Canton Company of volunteers at Indian Springs on 7 Sep 1861.

He was mustered out of the Confederate Army in 1865 at Washington, GA, and was paroled. He had to take the oath of allegiance in Nashville, TN, before the Federal authorities would allow him to return home to the state of Kentucky. He applied for a pension on 10 Jun 1912, with W.W. Ryan and E.A. Cunningham as his witnesses.

Robert W. Dew, a resident of Canton, KY, is a brother of William F. and Wilson W. Their father was John J. Dew (b. circa 1807 in Virginia, d. ??) and mother was Nancy Edwards Dew (b. circa 1817 in Kentucky, d. ??). They married on 10 Oct 1836 in Trigg County, KY.

Robert Wickliffe Dew married Martha Cathern Brien on 19 Dec 1858, in Benton, KY. James A.B. Dew married Mary A. Stone (b. April 1865 in Tennessee, d. ??) on 13 Oct 1881 in Trigg County. Martha Cathern (Brien) Dew was born in Marshall County, KY.

Robert is buried with his wife Martha Cathern (Brien) Dew (b. June 1843 in Kentucky, d. ??) in the Dew Cemetery. There is no stone at Martha's grave. A Tabby Adair (b. 1801 in North Carolina, d. ??) is buried in the Dew Cemetery also. There is no stone at her grave either. (Note: Both of Martha Dew's parents were born in Kentucky, so Tabby Adair cannot be her mother.)

WILLIAM F. DEW, Private, born 16 Mar 1843 in Trigg County, died 4 Mar 1920 at Cadiz, KY. William, along with Dr. John L. Trice, R.W. Dew, R.W. Major, Freeman Baker, Frances Baker, E.A. Cunningham, Dr. John Cunningham, David Cunningham, Mickers Cunningham, William Braboy, D. Wallace and others joined the Southern Army as a member of the 4th Kentucky Inf. He was a charter member of Floyd Tilghman Camp Confederate Veterans of Trigg County. He enlisted 14 Sep 1861, at Camp Burnett, TN and served with Co. G, 4th Kentucky Regt. Inf. (CSA).

Private Dew was wounded, then captured at the Battle of Atlanta on 22 Aug 1864, but escaped after five or six days. His unit surrendered at Greensboro, NC on 26 Apr 1865, where he was paroled. The Federal officers would not let him return home until he took the oath of allegiance.

William F. Dew, brother of Robert W. and Wilson W. Dew, was a resident of Canton, KY. He was later "disabled because of great pain in his breast owing to the fact that he was shot in battle, the ball entering his chest, passing in through the lower wall of the breast bone. The ball has never been extracted and when he works, it gives him great trouble and he is also very much debilitated."

His father was John J. Dew (b. circa 1807 in Virginia, d. ??) and mother was Nancy Edwards Dew (b. circa 1817 in Kentucky, d. ??). They married on 10 Oct 1836, in Trigg County, KY.

William F. Dew, age 22 years of Trigg County, married Frances "Fannie" Curley (b. 6 Jun 1845, d. 20 Sep 1896) of Graves County on 28 Oct 1865. W.F. Dew married second, Mrs. Zerilda F. (Reese) Cayce (b. September 1859 in Kentucky, d. 1951) on 3 or 4 Apr 1897 in Trigg County. Zerilda (Reese) (Cayce) Dew was born on 30 Sep 1861 in Hopkins County, KY. Zerilda was the widow of William H. Cayce whom she married on 13 Nov 1879 in Trigg County. In the marriage records she is listed as "Gerilda F. Rees."

William F. served in Capt. Trice's Company under the command of lst Lt. John Cunningham, 2nd Lt. Freen Baker and 3rd Lt. Francis Baker.

Zerilda applied for a Widow's Pension in July 1932. This application was witnessed by Mr. H.D. Wallace. Her family at the time of application consisted of two daughters, Mrs. Nannie Wallace and Mrs. Willie Wallis. In the Confederate Veteran's Widow's Pension Application, Zerilda's maiden name is spelled "Roos."

William F. Dew is buried with his first wife Frances (Curley) Dew in the Mt. Pleasant or Blue Springs Cemetery in Trigg County.

WILSON W. DEW, 5th Sergeant, born circa 1835, died ??. He enlisted 2 Sep 1861 at Camp Burnett, TN and served with Co. G, 4th Kentucky Regt. Inf. (CSA). He was promoted from 3rd corporal to 5th sergeant 10 Jan 1863. Pvt. Wilson W. Dew surrendered at Washington, GA 6 May 1865, and took the Oath on 21 May 1865.

Wilson W. Dew is a brother of Robert W. Dew and William F. Dew. Their father was John J. Dew (b. circa 1807 in Virginia, d. ??) and mother was Nancy Edwards Dew (b. circa 1817 in Kentucky, d. ??).

Wilson Dew, age 35 years of Trigg County, married Emeline Eidson, age 25 years also of Trigg County, on 23 Dec 1869. It was the first marriage for bride and groom.

Emeline Eidson Dew's brother William B. Eidson was a Confederate soldier who was killed at Griffin, GA, in 1864. (See William B. Eidson.)

ROBERT DUDLEY, 4th Corporal, born circa 1844 in Kentucky, died ??. He enlisted 16 Jul 1861, at Camp Boone, TN and served with Cobb's Kentucky Battery of Field Artillery. He was a transfer from Co. B, 4th Kentucky Regt. Inf. We have no proof that the Robert Dudley of Cobb's Battery is the same Robert Dudley as lived in Trigg County in the 1850 Trigg County Census.

His father was John A. Dudley (b. circa 1820 in Kentucky, d. ??) and mother was Catherine (Hayden) Dudley (b. circa 1828 in Kentucky, d. ??).

DAVID A. DUNN, Private, born circa 1843 in Kentucky, died ??. He enrolled 17 Aug 1863, mustered in 26 Oct 1863 at Princeton, KY and served with Co. F, 48th Kentucky Regt. Inf. (USA). He mustered out 19 Dec 1864 at Bowling Green, KY

His father was William Dunn (b. circa 1812 in Tennessee, d. 2 Sep 1852 in Trigg County) and his mother was Margaret Dunn (b. circa 1818 in Kentucky, d. ??).

David married Martha in 1861.

JAMES DUNN, Private, born circa 1839 in Kentucky, died ??. Enrolled 13 Aug 1863, mustered in 26 Oct 1863 and served with Co. F, 48th Kentucky Regt. Inf. (USA). He mustered out 19 Dec 1864.

His father was Jackson L. Dunn (b. circa 1810 in Tennessee, d. ??) and his mother was Sarah (Stow) Dunn (b. 1811 in Kentucky, d. ??).

JOHN JAMES DUNN, born 14 May 1843 in Trigg County, KY, was the son of John and Sarah A. Dunn of Trigg County. He enlisted in the Union Army during the Civil War on 25 Oct 1863 and served in Co. F 48th Volunteer Mounted Inf. Regt. The regiment was distributed along the line of the Louisville & Nashville Railroad and were later transferred to Fort Donelson, TN and Mufreesboro, TN

Dunn was severely wounded in the hip and walked with an ornate walking cane. The cane was especially made for veterans wounded in battle. After his service he returned home to Trigg County near Roaring Springs where he farmed and raised a family. He had three sons: Richard Aubrey, Hugh Darnall and Erwood Terry. Aubrey and Hugh later served in the military during WWI. Dunn has five living granddaughters: Jewell Simmons and Ethelene Wallis of Trigg County; Eunice Carr of Memphis, TN; Dorothy Darnall of Beaumont, TX; and Ruth Nunn of Sellersburg, IN, and two deceased grandchildren: Johnnie Dunn Meredith and Terry Lee Dunn.

Dunn died 6 Dec 1918 and is buried in the Darnall Family Cemetary near Roaring Springs. *Submitted by Jewell Simmons (granddaughter).*

JOHN J. DUNN, Private, born 13 May 1846 in Kentucky, died 6 Dec 1918. Both Maupin and Neel list John J. Dunn as a veteran from the War for Southern Independence.

There is a John Dunn who lists his age as 21 years (born 1853) when he was married in 1874, but both his parents are listed as being born in Tennessee. There is a Josiah J. Dunn who married Elizabeth J. Dunn on 20 Mar 1848, in Trigg County. This couple is listed in Simmons' 1850 Trigg County Census, Page 35, #638-102. They have a daughter Sarah J. Dunn, age 1 year.

John J.'s father John Dunn (b. circa 1823 in Tennessee, d. ??) and his mother was Sarah A. (Taylor) (Skinner) Dunn (b. circa 1816 in North Carolina, d. ??).

His mother Sarah Ann first married Ross Skinner on 17 Aug 1838 in Trigg County and they had a son Jonathan Skinner (b. circa 1840, d. ??) and a daughter Frances A. Skinner (b. circa 1843, d. ?).

John J. married Mrs. Nellie T. (Dyer) (b. 11 Jun 1859, d. 2 Jul 1922) on 12 Nov 1892 in Trigg County.

PINKNEY DUNN, Private, born circa 1844 in Kentucky, died ??. He enrolled 13 Aug 1863, mustered in 26 Oct 1863 at Princeton, KY and served with Co. F, 48th Kentucky Regt. Inf. (USA). He mustered out 19 Dec 1864 at Bowling Green, KY. We have assumed this Pinkney Dunn of the 48th Kentucky is the Levi Pinkney Dunn of Trigg County.

His father was William Dunn (b. circa 1812 in Tennessee, d. 2 Sep 1852 in Trigg County, KY) and his mother was Margaret Dunn (b. circa 1818 in Kentucky, d. ??).

JOHN DUNNING, his parents are not identified. He enlisted as a private, 24 Oct 1861 at Hopkinsville, KY, under Maj. Hewett for three years. He was assigned to Co. B, 8th Kentucky Inf. and appears on the company muster roll for 24 Oct 1861 to 31 Jul 1862, but never paid. John Dunning died 19 Nov 1861 at Hopkinsville, KY. *Submitted by Joyce Britt Dunning.*

JOHN WILLIAM DUNNING, born 28 Dec 1843 near Wallonia, Trigg County, KY, son of Shadrach and Elizabeth Poole Kenady Dunning. He enlisted as a private 24 Oct 1861 at Hopkinsville, KY under Maj. Hewett for three years. He was assigned to Co. B, 8th Regt., Kentucky Inf. John William was captured at Fort Donelson 16 Feb 1862 and sent to Camp Morton, IN. Later he was sent as a POW to Vicksburg, MS to be exchanged, 10 Nov 1862, then served to the end of the war.

John moved to Henry County, MO, where he married his cousin Sarah Isabel Dunning on 13 Mar 1870. After living in Texas for a while, they returned to Henry County where they lived at Deepwater, MO. John died 11 Dec 1900 in Deepwater. He and Sarah are buried in Englewood Cemetery, Clinton, MO. *Submitted by Joyce Britt Dunning.*

JOSEPH TANNER DUNNING, Private, born circa 1842. He enlisted 24 Oct 1861 at Camp Alcorn in Hopkinsville, KY and served with Co. B, 8th Kentucky Regt. Inf. (CSA). He was a brother to Pvt. Levi S. Dunning and 2nd Lt. William L. Dunning. According to Kentucky State Archives, he was discharged from Confederate service on 19 Feb 1863. There is another Joseph Dunning (Page 227, Jones' 1900 Trigg County Census #381-381), but he was born in December 1850. We can find no record of Pvt. Joseph T. Dunning in Trigg County after the 1860 Trigg County Census.

His father was Levi Dunning (b. 3 Oct 1797 in North Carolina, d. 16 Apr 1853) and mother was Jennet M. (Carney) Dunning (b. 24 Nov 1803 in North Carolina, d. 3 Apr 1877). They are buried together in the Dunning Cemetery.

Joseph married Frances J. McConnell on 23 Dec 1863 at Cobb, KY. He died 24 Mar 1892 and is buried in the Pollard Cemetery, Caldwell County, KY.

His sister Jennett A. married James M. Earley on 29 Jun 1861, in Trigg County. Jennett (b. 4 Jan 1844, d. 26 Apr 1863) is buried in the Dunning Cemetery with her parents.

His sister "F.E." (Fare Ellendar) married A.J. Martin on 8 Apr 1861 in Trigg County. Fare Ellendar (b. 1836, d. 4 Nov 1933) is buried in the Dunning Cemetery with her husband Andrew Martin (b. 1830, d. 1886)

His brother Wiley W. (M.) Dunning married Cynthia Ann Wimberly on 26 May 1853 in Trigg County.

His brother Carney F. (b. 15 Mar 1826, d. 14 Jun 1872) is buried in the Dunning Cemetery.

Brother William L. (b. 24 Dec 1834, d. 17 Jan 1908) is buried in the Dunning Cemetery.

His brother Levi S. (b. 25 Nov 1832, d. ??) is buried in the Dunning Cemetery with his wife Henrie S. (Shelton) Dunning (b. 30 Jun 1850, d. 6 Apr 1918).

LEVI SHOULDERS DUNNING, 1st Sergeant, born 25 Nov 1832 or 1839 in Kentucky, died (illegible on tombstone). He enlisted 24 Oct

1861 at Hopkinsville, KY and served with Co. B, 8th Kentucky Regt. Inf. (CSA). He was a brother to Pvt. Joseph T. Dunning and 2nd Lt. William L. Dunning. Levi was elected 1st sergeant at the reorganization of the regiment in September 1862.

Perrin's History states that he was born on 25 Dec 1832. His father was Levi Dunning (b. 3 Oct 1797 in North Carolina, d. 16 Apr 1853) and mother was Jennet M. (Carney) Dunning (b. 24 Nov 1803 in North Carolina, d. 3 Apr 1877). They are buried together in the Dunning Cemetery.

According to Trigg County Records "S.S." (Levi S.) Dunning, a farmer age 30 years from Trigg County, married "S. Heun" (Henrie S.) Shelton, age 21 years from Paducah, KY, on 3 Sep 1871. It was the first marriage for both bride and groom. Levi is buried with his wife Henrie S. (b. 30 Jun 1850, d. 6 Apr 1918) in the Dunning Cemetery.

This couple's daughter Addie Lee (b. 11 Mar 1880, d. 12 Aug 1899); son Virgil Wilton (b. 5 Sep 1875, d. 21 Jun 1876); and son Clyde Vernon Dunning (b. 25 Apr 1882, d. 16 September 1899) are all buried in the Dunning Cemetery.

Levi's sister Jennett A. Dunning married James M. Earley on 29 Jun 1861 in Trigg County. Jennett (b. 4 Jan 1844, d. 26 Apr 1863) is buried in the Dunning Cemetery with her parents. She is listed as the wife of James M. Early and the daughter of Levi S. Dunning and Jinnett Dunning. Jennett A. (Dunning) Early died during her 19th year of her life.

His sister "F.E." (Fare Ellendar) married A.J. Martin on 8 Apr 1861, in Trigg County. Fare Ellendar (b. 1836, d. 4 Nov 1933) is buried in the Dunning Cemetery with her husband Andrew J. Martin (b. 1830, d. 1886).

His brother Wiley W. (M.) Dunning married Cynthia Ann Wimberly on 26 May 1853 in Trigg County.

His brother Carney F. (b. 15 Mar 1826, d. 14 Jun 1872) is buried in the Dunning Cemetery.

His brother William L. (b. 24 Dec 1834, d. 17 Jan 1908) is buried in the Dunning Cemetery. Maupin's records state that William L. was a member of Co. B, 8th Kentucky Regt. Inf., CSA. There is no tombstone at his grave, however.

WILEY MOORE DUNNING, born 2 May 1828 near Wallonia, Trigg County, KY, the fourth son of Levi and Jennet Dunning. He served in the Civil War in Texas. On 5 Jul 1862 Wiley, age 34, enlisted for three years at Sherman, TX. He was a 4th sergeant assigned to Co. B, 5th Regt., Martin's Regt., Texas Partisan Rangers, later changed to Martin's Regt., Texas Cavalry, CSA.

Records show he traveled 15 miles to Camp Reeves for rendezvous on 5 Jul 1862. His horse was valued at $200 and his equipment at $40. According to family legend he engaged in battle in eastern Oklahoma. Martin's Regt. Texas Cavalry was dismounted Feb 17, 1865.

After marrying Cynthia Ann Wimberly, daughter of Gilford and Margaret Alexander Wimberly, they moved to Grayson County, TX and spent their lives on a farm near Pottsboro, TX. They are buried in Wimberly Cemetery, Pottsboro. *Submitted by Joyce Britt Dunning.*

SHADRACH DUNNING, born 1815 in Kentucky. His son John W. Dunning was in Co. B, 8th Kentucky Regt. Inf. (CSA). According to Maupin's records, Shadrack Dunning was a WSI veteran.

Shadrack Dunning married Elizabeth Kenady on 28 Jan 1841 in Trigg County.

According to Maupin, Shadrach Dunning is buried in the Dunning Cemetery. There seems to be no evidence of any of the rest of his family being buried there, however.

WILLIAM LEANDER DUNNING, born 22 Dec 1834 near Wallonia, Trigg County, KY, son of Levi and Jennet Moore Dunning. He was 27 when he enlisted 24 Oct 1861 at Hopkinsville, KY in the Confederate Army. He was a 2nd sergeant in Co. B., 8th Regt., Kentucky Inf., CSA and was appointed 1st sergeant 23 Dec 1861 and 2nd lieutenant 2 Feb 1862.

After four months of training, his regiment marched to Clarksville, TN, then took steamboats to Fort Donelson, where they engaged in three days fighting with heavy losses. He was one of 15,000 Confederate troops captured by General Grant, 16 Feb 1862. From Fort Donelson he was sent to Camp Chase, OH, 1 March.

On 9 Apr 1862, Lt. Dunning was sent to Johnson's Island, Sandusky, OH, then to Vicksburg, MS on 1 Sep 1862. His name appears on a roll of prisoners of war, 1104 in number, arriving Vicksburg aboard the steamer *John H. Done,* 20 Sep 1862. He was exchanged at Aikens Landing, 10 Nov 1862. One document states that he drew $560 for the time spent as a prisoner.

He rejoined from a "recruiting expedition in Kentucky" 10 Dec 1862. Lt. W.L. Dunning was on a roster of his regiment at Tupelo, MS, 12 May 1864. The 1863 and early 1864 records show him present in his regiment, then his name appears on muster rolls and on a list of quartermasters in Maj. Gen. Forrest's Cavalry Corps, 1 Aug 1864, Tibbee, MS.

William served until the close of the war, then married Laura Coy and moved to Texas. He later moved to Pottawatomie County, OK. William died 17 Jan 1908 and is buried in Mars Hill Cemetery, Marvin, OK. *Submitted by Joyce Britt Dunning.*

WILLIAM L. DURRETT, 3rd Corporal, born circa 1844. He enlisted 14 Sep 1861 at Camp Burnett, TN and served with Co. G, 4th Kentucky Regt. Inf. (CSA) He was wounded and captured at Shiloh 6 Apr 1862, and later died at Paducah, KY.

WILLIAM C. DYER, who often signed his name W. Covington Dyer, was listed as 7 years old in the 1850 census. He was the eldest child of John J. and Mirah Haydon Dyer. The family lived on a farm about four miles west of Cadiz off US 68. He was a school teacher prior to the Civil War.

Letters written to his family are the source of the following information: He joined the Confederate Army at the beginning of the war and was assigned to the First Tennessee Inf. Regt. On 30 Jan 1862, his father received a letter from him from Camp Recovery near Bowling Green, KY. The next letter to his family was dated 11 May 1862 from Corinth, MS, soon after the Battle of Shiloh. He described the two day battle as he experienced it, "I was at the fight at Shiloh a description of which I can never give as I felt. I can say one thing sure there never was, I believe, a man that knew his feelings on a battlefield before he is on one."

It is believed that he was wounded at this battle but he does not mention it. A friend of the family named Treadwell wrote John Dyer from the US Military prison at Camp Chase, OH, dated 16 Jan 1865, stating that he had received a letter from W.C. written in June 1864 from Alabama. He was in fine health and had recovered from his wound but not sufficiently to return to active service. That was the last correspondence preserved from W.C. Dyer until after the war. The 1st Tennessee was a famous Confederate unit. It's history is recorded in a book written by Sam R. Watkins, Pvt., CSA, titled *Co Aytch.*

After the war W.C. came home a sick man. The family was financially bankrupt. The names of his wife and children are not known. He first moved to Graves County about 1866 and taught school. His health continued to deteriorate as indicated in letters to his father and brother. In March 1875 he moved to Spencer, TN, where his wife's family lived. A post card to his brother Rufus Dyer dated 29 Jul 1875, in which he stated that he was suffering considerably with fever, was the last correspondence.

STEPHEN EDMONDS, Private, born 18 Dec 1832 in Kentucky died 28 Jul 1925. He enrolled 5 Aug 1863, mustered in 26 Oct 1863 at Princeton, KY and mustered out 19 Dec 1864 at Bowling Green, KY. He served with Co. F, 48th Kentucky Regt. Inf. (USA).

We cannot find any record of the Edmonds children buried in Trigg County.

Stephen Edmonds married Nancy A. Boren on 20 Sep 1855 in Trigg County. He is buried with his wife Nancy (Boren) Edmonds (b. 21 Feb 1836, d. 28 Nov 1906) in the Cox Cemetery in Trigg County.

His daughter Julia R. married James H. Beaver on 11 Jun 1894 in Trigg County, and daughter Sarah E. married John B. Clark on 12 Jul 1893 in Trigg County.

CHARLES B. EDWARDS, Private, born 1841 in Kentucky, died 21 Mar 1862, at Camp Morton, IN. He enlisted 19 Oct 1861 at Camp Alcorn in Hopkinsville, KY and served with Co. G, 8th Kentucky Regt. Inf. (CSA).

Private Edwards was captured at Fort Donelson on 16 Feb 1862, and died of typhoid fever in prison at Camp Morton, IN on 21 Mar 1862. According to Kentucky State Archives, he is buried in the Greenlawn Cemetery near Indianapolis, IN.

His father was John Edwards (b. ca. 1898 in Virginia, d. 30 Sep 1868 (at about age 70 years) and his mother was Nancy T. (Shelton) Edwards "wife of John Edward" (b. 24 Dec 1810 in Virginia, d. 6 Dec 1886). According to Neel, they are buried in the Edward Cemetery on the Cameron Farm in Trigg County. Also according to Neel, Nancy was born on 29 Dec 1810, not 24 Dec 1810 as are found in Maupin's records.

His brother Robertson Edwards (b. 1845 in Kentucky) is buried in the Edwards Cemetery in Trigg County.

His sister Eliza Ann Edwards married William A. Robertson on 12 Dec 1853 in Trigg County. Eliza (b. 26 Nov 1835, d. 11 Feb 1875) is buried with her husband William A. Robertson (b. 8 Mar 1822, d. 8 Jan 1879) in the Edwards Cemetery. She is also listed as being buried in the Robertson Cemetery.

His sister Sallie A. (Sarah A.), age 22 years, married I.W. (Irvin W.) Wallis, age 30 years on 8 Feb 1865 in Trigg County. Sarah (b. 3 Apr 1842, d. 11 Mar 1910) is buried with her husband Irvin W. Wallis (b. 4 Aug 1834, d. 12 Oct 1910) in the Wallis Cemetery in Trigg County.

His brother John H. married Eudora Minton on 22 Jan 1880 in Trigg County. John H. (b. Jun 1849, d. 1936) is buried with his wife Eudora (Minton) Edwards (b. 2 Oct 1854, d. 2 Oct 1935) in the Minton Cemetery in Trigg County.

WILLIAM B. EIDSON, 3rd Sergeant, born ca. 1841 in Kentucky, died 12 Sep 1864, at Griffin, GA. He enlisted 10 Aug 1861 at Camp Burnett, TN and served with Co. G, 4th Kentucky Regt. Inf. (CSA).

He was promoted from private to first corporal 10 Jan 1863, then to third sergeant, 20 Jan 1864. He was wounded near Atlanta, GA on 21 Aug 1864 and died at Griffin, GA, 12 Sep 1864.

His father was Hardy Eidson (b. ca. 1818 in Tennessee, d. ??) and his mother was Arena Eidson (b. ca. 1818 in Kentucky, d. ??). They married on 6 Oct 1841, in Trigg County.

His sister Emeline Eidson, age 25 years of Trigg County, married Wilson Dew, a farmer, age 35 years, of Trigg County, on 23 Dec 1869. It was the first marriage for both bride and groom. Wilson Dew was a Confederate soldier. (See Wilson Dew).

His sister Adaline Eidson, age 17 years of Trigg County, married Lynn Boyd, age 24 years of Trigg County, on 6 Feb 1868. (Not found in Simmons' 1870 Trigg County Census.)

His sister Adaline Eidson married Thomas Stallons on 24 Dec 1889, in Trigg County. (Not found in Jones' 1900 Trigg County Census.)

His niece Eleanor Eidson (listed as Elnora) married W.A. Hall on 5 Mar 1885 in Trigg County. (Not found in Jones' 1900 Trigg County Census.)

J.J. (John) Eidson married Edna Delawson on 19 May 1888 in Trigg County. (Not found in Jones' 1900 Trigg County Census.)

RICHARD ELLIS, Corporal, born 10 Nov 1844 in Kentucky, died 13 Feb 1913. He enrolled 14 Aug 1862, mustered in 13 Sep 1862 at Henderson, KY and mustered out 23 Sep 1863 at Russellville, KY. He served with Co. L, 8th Kentucky Regt. Cav. (USA).

There is a Richard "S." Ellis listed as a corporal in the 8th Kentucky Regt. Cav. (USA). In census records and cemetery records, however, he is always listed as Richard "T." Ellis. His uncle was John D. Tyler, also a WSI veteran.

His father was Ira Ellis and mother was Elizabeth K. (Tyler) Ellis. They were married on 21 Nov 1843, in Trigg County, KY.

Richard T. Ellis, age 23 years of Trigg County, married Miranda Ellen Humphries, age 18 years, on 25 Feb 1868. It was the first marriage for both bride and groom. He is buried in the Redd Cemetery with his wife Miranda E. (b. 17 Jun 1850, 13 Jul 1930).

His grandfather Richard K. Tyler (b. 1804, d. 24 Oct 1878) and his grandmother Minerva Tyler (b. 13 Nov 1813, d. 27 Dec 1879) are also buried in the Redd Cemetery.

Daughter Helen Mary Ellis married Orrin H. Malone on 15 Apr 1891. Helen Mary (b. (b. 19 Dec 1872, d. 1 Feb 1892) is buried with her husband "O.H." (Orrin H.) Malone (b. 22 Nov 1866, d. 5 Jun 1924) in the East End Cemetery. This couple's daughter Helen Malone (b. 8 Oct 1892, d. 11 Sep 1896) is buried near them. Orrin H. married second, Pearl Smith on 23 Jun 1897.

Richard Tyler Ellis II (b. 4 Jul 1871, d. 1939) married "Martin" (Elizabeth) Averitt on 16 Mar 1892. Richard Tyler is listed as "Tyler" Ellis and is buried in the East End Cemetery with his wife "Martha" Elizabeth (Averitt) Ellis (b. 1874, d. 1939).

G.M./GILLIAM M. EZELL, 2nd Lieutenant, born ca. 1829 in Kentucky, died ??. He enlisted 14 Sep 1861 at Camp Burnett, TN and served with Co. G, 4th Kentucky Regt. Inf. (CSA). Gilliam M. Ezell was promoted from Private to Brevet 2nd Lieutenant on 5 May 1863. He then resigned his commission on 8 Aug 1863.

There seems to be a Gillum Ezell, born in Tennessee, and a Gilliam M. Ezell, born in Kentucky, living in Trigg County in the middle of the 19th century. The Gillum Ezell of the 1850 Census was listed as being born in Tennessee, but the Gilliam M. Ezell of the 1860 Census and all other references thereafter is listed as being born in Kentucky. There was a Pvt. Gillium Ezell of Co. D of the 17th Kentucky Regt. Inf. (USA) who died on 17 Jun 1862, in Trigg County, KY. He was a private in Co. F of the 25th Kentucky Regt. Inf. (USA) before consolidation.

Gilliam M. Ezell married Sarah Ellen Campbell on 11 Mar 1851 in Trigg County. Neither Maupin nor Neel list Gilliam M. Ezell nor Sarah Ellen (Campbell) Ezell as being buried in Trigg County.

His daughter Sallie (Sarah J.) married William C. Major on 31 Jan 1878, in Trigg County. Sallie E. (Sarah J.) (Ezell) Major (b. 31 Jan 1857, d. 16 Feb 1935) is buried near her son Fred G. Major in the East End Cemetery.

His granddaughter Carry Anna Major (b. 31 Mar 1881, d. 27 Aug 1886) "daughter of S.J. and W.C. Major" is buried in the Yates Cemetery in Trigg County.

Grandson Seldon T. Major (b. 2 Dec 1885, d. 12 Apr 1969) is buried with his wife Mary C. Major (b. 10 Nov 1897, d. ??) in the East End Cemetery.

Fred G. Major (b. 2 Nov 1892, d. 16 Oct 1972) "KY, PFC, WWI" is buried near his mother in the East End Cemetery.

JOHN F. FARLEY, Private, born ca. 1843 in Tennessee, died ??. Enlisted 5 Oct 1861 at Camp Reeves, TN and served with Co. G, 8th Kentucky Regt. Inf. (CSA).

According to the Kentucky Adjutant General's Report, he died of disease in Trigg County, KY, date unknown.

John and his siblings, Henry S. and Edward R., were born in Tennessee. All the rest were born in Kentucky.

His father was Richard E. Farley (b. ca. 1815 in Virginia, d. ??) and his mother was Susannah A.E. (Farley) Farley (b. 24 Dec 1820 in Virginia, d. 24 Feb 1860). Susannah A.E. is buried in the Humphries Cemetery in Trigg County.

WILLIAM FARMER, Private, born ca. 1839 in Kentucky, died ??. He enrolled 23 Jul 1863, mustered in 26 Oct 1863 at Princeton, KY and mustered out 19 Dec 1864 at Bowling Green, KY. He served with Co. F, 48th Kentucky Regt. Mounted Inf. (USA). In the Kentucky Adjutant General's Report on Union soldiers, he is listed as "absent, wounded, at muster out of company."

His siblings: Lucinda C., John, James, Margaret J. and Thomas, were all born in Tennessee. The others were born in Kentucky.

His father was Jeremiah Farmer (b. ca. 1800 in North Carolina, d. ??) and his mother was Jinsey Farmer (b. ca. 1810 in Tennessee).

William Farmer, age 31 years of Trigg County, married Mrs. Eliza J. (Pitts) (McCauley), age 26 years also of Trigg County, on 10 Mar 1870. Eliza Farmer was born in Kentucky. Eliza's first husband was John M. McCauley (b. 5 Jun 1838, d. 8 Apr 1866) and is buried in the Pitts Cemetery in Trigg County. J.M. and Eliza were married on 25 Dec 1860 in Trigg County.

JOHN HENRY "DURGAN" FAUGHN, enlisted at Hopkinsville, KY on 15 Oct 1861 into the 1st Kentucky Cav. CSA, commanded by Col. Helm for a period of one year. He was enlisted by General Tilghman as a private and was a member of Co. G., Capt. Morrison Wilcox commanding, and Capt. Ben D. Terry at that time 1st lieutenant. Records show that he was wounded at Saratoga, KY, 26 Oct 1861 and served 13 months.

He served in the Confederacy close to and in the county of his home in Kentucky. He was captured at Fort Donelson, KY 16 Feb 1862 and

listed on the roll of Prisoners of War at Camp Morton, IN, June 1862. He was taken by boxcar to Vicksburg, MS, 24 Aug 1862 to be exchanged.

John (b. Mar 4, 1836 in Trigg County, KY) was the son of James Faughn (b. 1780 in North Carolina) and Elizabeth Adams (b. 1799 in South Carolina). He was one of four known children: William R., Mary Elizabeth and Thomas L. Faughn.

He married first, Mary Jane Stovall, daughter of David and Eliza Stovall, who died in childbirth. To this marriage was born one child Mary Jane "Mollie" Faughn (b. 8 Feb 1867) who married William Jackson Sherbut on 12 Apr 1884. He married second, Mildred "Millie" Litchfield in 1870 in Golconda, IL. Her widow's pension applications states they ran away on horseback. Millie Litchfield (b. 1853, Trigg County, KY, d. 1917) was the daughter of William "Billie" Litchfield and Eliza E. Oliver. Their children were Ben, Terry, Martha Ann, James M. and Josephine Faughn.

He was a Baptist by faith and held his membership at Hurricane Baptist Church.

After his death on 31 Oct 1912 in Trigg County, KY, his wife Millie received a Widow's Confederate Pension of $6.00 per month until her death in 1917. They are both buried at the Piercy-Oliver Cemetery. *Submitted by a great granddaughter, Betty Sellers.*

BENJAMIN FAULKNER, Private, born ca. 1844 in either Tennessee or Kentucky, died ??. Enlisted 9 Dec 1862 at Williamsport, TN and served with Co. B, Woodward's 2nd/15th Kentucky Regt. Cav. (CSA).

His father was Hutchens B. Faulkner (b. ca. 1815 in Tennessee, d. ??) and his mother was Elizabeth (Gray) Faulkner (b. ca. 1816 in Tennessee, d. ??. They married on 18 Dec 1838 in Trigg County.

His sister Minerva Jane, age 29 years of Trigg County, married W.N. Davis, age 27 years, also of Trigg County, on 18 Feb 1869. He was born in Jefferson County, IL and was a Confederate veteran. It was the first marriage for both bride and groom. Minerva lists that she was born in Tennessee.

His sister Mary F. Faulkner married Robert Boyd on 24 Dec 1866, in Trigg County.

His sister Susan C. Faulkner, age 18 years of Trigg County, married Gideon W. Barnes, age 24 years of Trigg County, on 15 Sep 1869. It was the first marriage for both bride and groom. Susan lists that she was born in Montgomery County, TN. Mrs. Susan C. (Faulkner) Barnes married second, Samuel C. Davis on 27 Jan 1886 in Trigg County.

His brothers: Richard W. married Eliza J. Ladd on 15 Mar 1877 in Trigg County and Wilson Lee married Emma Blanks on 20 Jun 1891 in Trigg County. Wilson L. (b. 1863, d. 1944) is buried with his wife Emma B. (b. 1868, d. 1854) in the Wall Cemetery in Trigg County.

Benjamin's niece Kitty Davis (b. ca. 1872, d. ??) married Andrew J. P'Pool on 17 Oct 1891 in Trigg County.

CHARLES B. FAULKNER, Private born ca. 1837 in Kentucky died ??. Enlisted on 10 Nov 1861 at Hopkinsville, KY and served with Co. G, 8th Kentucky Regt. Inf. (CSA). Charles B. Faulkner was reported missing at Fort Donelson and not heard from again.

Charles' father was John Faulkner and his mother was Elizabeth. His brother John J. married Lucicy A. (Louisa) Baker on 24 Jan 1849 in Trigg County. John J. died 25 Jun 1852 in Trigg County at age 25 years. His sister-in-law Louisa A. married Newton Payne on 13 Jul 1853 in Trigg County.

LYNN BOYD FERGUSON, Private, born ca. 1844 died ????? He enrolled 7 Sep 1863, mustered in 26 Oct 1863 at Princeton, KY and mustered out 19 Dec 1864 in Bowling Green, KY. He served with Co. F, 48th Kentucky Regt. Inf. (USA).

His father was John E. Ferguson (b. ca. 1810 in Kentucky, d. ??) and his mother was Fruzy Ferguson (b. ca. 1813 in Kentucky, d. ??).

Lynn Boyd Ferguson, a farmer, age 24 years from Trigg County, married Hannah E. Jones, age 16 years, also from Trigg County on 12 May 1869. It was the first marriage for both bride and groom.

Lynn's sister Delinda married Hyram N. Cherry on 20 Nov 1892 in Trigg County, and his brother Reuben J. married Frances Oakley on 24 Jan 1878 in Trigg County.

FRANCIS MARION FORGASON, Private, born ca. 1843 in Kentucky (1850 Census), Tennessee (1860), died 14 May 1864 at Resaca,

GA. Enlisted 14 Sep 1861 at Camp Burnett, TN and served with Co. A, 4th Kentucky Regt. Inf. (CSA). Private Francis Marion Forgason was killed at the Battle of Resaca, GA, on 14 May 1864. He was a brother of John D. Forgason, also a Confederate soldier.

His father was Robert Forgason (b. ca. 1801 in North Carolina, d. ??) and his mother was Nancy Forgason (b. ca. 1808 in Virginia, d. ??).

His brother Andrew J. Forguson married Mary Susan Fort on 20 Dec 1859 in Trigg County.

His sister Eliza Ferguson (Forgason) died in December 1853, at the age of 22 years. Her parents were listed as Robert and Nancy Ferguson.

JOHN D. FORGASON, Private, born ca. 1844 in Kentucky, died 7 Apr 1862 at Battle of Shiloh, TN. Enlisted 14 Sep 1861 at Camp Burnett, TN and served with Co. I, 4th Kentucky Regt. Inf. (CSA), then transferred to Co. G, 4th Kentucky Regt. Inf. (CSA). He was mortally wounded and captured at the Battle of Shiloh on 7 Apr 1862. He may also be listed in the census records as John Ferguson or John Forguson. Neel's reference gives John's middle initial as "D."

His father was Robert Forgason (b. ca. 1801 in North Carolina, d. ??) and his mother was Nancy Forgason (b. ca. 1808 in Virginia, d. ??).

His brother William Forgason was born in Tennessee. All other siblings are listed as being born in Kentucky.

John Forgason was a brother of Francis Marion Forgason.

His brother Andrew J. Forgason married Mary Susan Fort on 20 Dec 1859 in Trigg County.

His sister Eliza Ferguson (Forgason) died in December 1853 at the age of 22 years. Her parents were listed as Robert and Nancy Ferguson.

His nephew William H. Forgeson (son of Andrew J. Forgason) (b. 27 Apr 1861, d. 18 Feb 1929) is buried in the Long Creek Cemetery with his wife Adelia A. (Nunn) Forgeson (b. 9 Apr 1873, d. 12 Apr 1928).

His nephew F.L. (Francis L.) Forguson (b. 1863, d. 1948) is buried in the Cumberland Baptist Church Cemetery with his wife Llewellyn (Williams) Forguson (b. 1867, d. 21 Mar 1937).

JAMES M. FORGUSON, Private, born ca. 1844 in Kentucky died ??. Enlisted 14 Sep 1861 at Camp Burnett, TN and served with Co. G, 4th Kentucky Regt. Inf. (CSA).

His father was James D. Ferguson (b. ca. 1815 in Kentucky, d. ??) and his mother was Mary (McWaters) Ferguson (b. circa 1818 in Kentucky, d. ??). They were married on 16 Feb 1836 in Trigg County.

His father James D. Ferguson married second, Mrs. Elizabeth Ann (McQuade) Huggins on 21 Nov 1857 in Trigg County. (Neel's record gives her married name as "Huggins" rather than Higgins.) Her first husband, Josiah Huggins, died on 5 Feb 1853 at age 35 years in Trigg County. His parents were Robert and Jane Huggins.

James M.'s brother William H. married Miss Mary Baker on 14 Mar 1860 in Trigg County. His step-brother James Huggins married Ellen Robertson on 20 Jan 1876 in Trigg County.

DAVID O. FREEMAN, enlisted in the Union Army at Indianapolis, IN on 4 Sep 1863 as a private in Co. "F," 7th Reg. IN Volunteer Cav. at the age of 14-1/2 years old. He was mustered out Feb 18, 1866 at Austin, TX.

David was born 11 Jan 1849 in Howard County, IN, the son of Joshua and Elizabeth Lytle Freeman. His brother Lindsay Howard Freeman also served in the Union Army. His father, Joshua Freeman, living in that area when the war broke out, and not withstanding he was considerably past the meridian of life, he offered his services to his county, and his name was enrolled as a member of the 26th Indiana Inf., Co. C. The hardships

of a soldier's life proved too much for him to bear, and he was taken sick and sent home, only to die a short time after his arrival in Howard County in February 1862. Thus was a courageous and patriotic spirit sacrificed on the altar of our country

On 26 Jan 1868 in Kokomo, Grant County, IN, he married Nancy Larowe (b. 1847, d. 1906), the daughter of Wilson Larowe and Matilda Armstrong. David and Nancy had seven children, all but one being born in Kokomo, Howard County, IN. Their children were Mary Elizabeth (b. 1868, d. 1924); John Lindsay (b. 1870, d. 1913); Janie May (b. 1873, d. 1947); William Otto (b. 1876, d. 1951); Sarahan Rosietille (b. 1878, d. 1946); Errea Myrtle (b. 1882, d. 1906); and Edward Wilford (b. 1886, d. 1949).

In 1884 he and his family moved from Indiana to Trigg County, KY where he farmed and worked in a sawmill. He was an avid fisherman. He was also a wood craftsman and for Janie May's wedding gift he presented her with a hand carved box which is still in the family.

David married second, Mahala Mildred Allen (b. 1861, d. 1927) on 24 May 1908 in Cadiz, KY. They had no children.

He filed for pension 7 Feb 1890 and his original application was rejected on account of his inability to produce the evidence then called for. His file was reopened 8 Apr 1904 and again on 1 Jun 1912 which he was granted. Upon his death his widow Mahala M. Freeman also applied and received a widow's pension. He is buried in the East End Cemetery at Cadiz, KY.

He also had two grandsons, Samuel Wilford Freeman, who served in WWI, and William Thomas Freeman, who served during peacetime before WWII. *Submitted by his great-granddaughter, Betty Freeman Sellers*

L. SHADRACH FUTRELL, born 1831, died 1906, was both a Confederate cavalryman and artilleryman. He initially enlisted as a private with Co. D, 2nd. Regt. Kentucky Cav. under Captain E.A. Slaughter's command. Co. D was composed primarily of Trigg County, KY men who formed the unit in Christian County at the Summer farm on the road between Cadiz and Hopkinsville. The old Summer home is still standing and is known as the John O. Hill place. The farm is five miles west of Hopkinsville on US-68 and adjoins Green-Hill Memorial Gardens. It is currently owned by Mrs. Linda (Hill) Arnold.

When Co. D disbanded, its members scattered out into other commands. L.S. Futrell joined Capt. James L. Parris' Battery (Clark Artillery), Missouri Light Artillery. His service record indicates he enlisted 1 Apr 1862 at Cumberland Furnace, TN under Lt. Johnston's command.

Capt. Farris' Battery surrendered with the Confederate forces of Alabama and Mississippi at Citronelle, AL on 4 May 1865 four weeks after General Lee's surrender at Appomattox Court House. Futrell was paroled at Gainesville, AL on 10 May 1865. The parole indicates he was a resident of Canton, KY.

Futrell was a native of Rushing Creek in Stewart County, TN. He moved to nearby Trigg County, KY when he married Miss Charity Futrell on 3 Jan 1856. L.S. and Charity lived in the Laura Furnace Community where he farmed and worked as a cabinetmaker. They were members of Pleasant Hill Baptist Church and had five children: James Madison, Mary Caroline, Isaac Rix, Andrew Jackson, and Mastin Cook Futrell.

L.S. Futrell was awarded the Confederate Veterans "Cross-of-Honor" in 1906. In his letter of application for the medal he named Sam Sumner, Sam Lancaster, Bob Thompson, C.T. Bridges, Dr. John Cunningham and Zan Cunningham as other Trigg Countians who were originally members of Co. D, 2nd. Regt. Kentucky Cav.

Futrell was an early family historian. He wrote the Futrell Family Record in 1905 while visiting in Garland, TX. L.S. Futrell died at Rockwall, TX in 1906 and was buried in the town's municipal cemetery.

WYATT GAINES, served with Co. C, 13th US Colored Artillery (Heavy). Mustered in 1 Feb 1865 at Paducah, KY. He is buried in the New Rocky Ridge Negro Cemetery. There is no stone at his grave.

NATHANIEL "NATHAN/NAT" GAITHER, Private, born 26 Nov. 1844 in Trigg County, KY, died 15 Jan 1918 in Christian County, KY. Enlisted 10 Nov 1862 at Murfreesboro, TN and served with Co. H, 6th Kentucky Regiment Cavalry. Nat was attending school in Columbia, KY, where his grandfather Dr. Nathan Gaither lived, when he enlisted in Capt. Bowling E. Roberts' company of Confederate Cavalry. This company was the personal escort for Gen. Roger Hanson.

After the death of Gen. Hanson, the company was transferred to Capt. J. Warren Grisby's Co. H, 6th Kentucky Cavalry (CSA).

He moved to Hopkinsville in 1866. Private Gaither became a salesman for Forbes Manufacturing Company after the war. He also helped found the Ned Meriwether Camp #241, United Confederate Veterans in Hopkinsville.

He first married Miss Zollikoffer, daughter of Gen. Felix Zollikoffer in 1869. She died in 1871. They had one child Felix Gaither, who later moved to Fort Worth, TX. Nat married second, Miss Rebecca Gant, daughter of Mr. J.K. Gant, in 1875. Their children were Dr. J. Gant Gaither of Hopkinsville; Nick Gaither of Texas; Mrs. Robert W. Green of Mayfield, KY; and Miss Rebecca Gaither of Hopkinsville.

Nat is buried with his wife Rebecca (Gant) Gaither just north of the Confederate monument in Riverside Cemetery in Hopkinsville, KY.

JAMES GARDNER, mustered in 16 Oct 1864 at Bowling Green, KY and served with Co. "A.," 13th US Colored Artillery (Heavy). He is buried in the Cadiz Negro Cemetery, but there is no stone to his grave.

WILLIAM H. GARNETT, Private, born ca. 1836 in Kentucky died ??. He enrolled 4 Aug 1863, mustered in 26 Oct 1863 at Princeton, KY and mustered out 19 Dec 1864 at Bowling Green, KY. He served with Co. F, 48th Kentucky Regt. Inf. (USA).

His father was James G, Garnett (b. ca. 1812 in Kentucky, d. ??) and his mother was Elizabeth (Hardy) Garnett. They were married on 29 Jul 1830 in Trigg County. Elizabeth (Hardy) Garnett died in the middle 1840s. James G. Garnett married second, Rebecca A. Golladay (b. ca. 1827 in Kentucky, d. ??) on 1 Jun 1850 in Trigg County. Sister's Marriage:

William's sister Nancy Garnett married Thomas A. Wilson on 14 Dec 1855, in Trigg County.

His half-sister Susan Garnett married William H. Smith on 23 Oct 1866, in Trigg County. (In Neel's Statistical Handbook of Trigg County Marriage Records, Neel erroneously gives the page number on which this marriage is found as page 366. It is actually given on page 336).

His half-sister Julia Ann Garnett married Damascus Burnett on 11 Mar 1874, in Trigg County.

His half-sister Mary Ella Garnett married Walter A. Ladd on 21 Nov 1892, in Trigg County, KY.

His half-brother Lewis S. Garnett married Zena Redd on 8 Nov 1893, in Trigg County.

The only member of this family found in Trigg County Cemetery Records is Arthur Cressie Burnett, son of Julia Ann (Garnett) Burnett, (b. 23 May 1875, d. 18 Jul 1960) and his wife Lucy (Spiceland) Burnett (b. 28 Jun 1875, d. 23 Jan 1850). They are buried in the East End Cemetery.

JEFFERSON F. GENTRY, Colonel, born 10 Sep 1819 in Tennessee, died 21 Mar 1887 and is buried in East End Cemetery. He enlisted 20 Aug 1861 in Danville, KY and served with Co. I, 7th Kentucky Regiment Cavalry (CSA). According to Kentucky State Archives, he was a 2nd lieutenant in the 7th Kentucky Regiment Cavalry CSA.

Jefferson F.'s wife Sarah was born in Virginia and their three oldest children were born in Tennessee while Blanche and Sarah (or Sue) were born in Kentucky.

His daughter Blanche (b. 1863, d. 1926) md. Harry H. Garton (b. 1859, d. 1930) on 21 Oct 1880 in Trigg County. Blanche is buried in the East End Cemetery with her husband.

His daughter Mary L. "Mollie" married R.L. Waller on 26 Oct 1882, in Trigg County (Page 359).

His daughter Sarah (Lou or Sue) (b. 25 May 1865, d. 4 Jan 1844) married Albert Jefferson Jr.(b. 25 Jul 1869, d. 14 Feb 1933) on 26 Oct 1891 in Trigg County. Both are buried in the Jefferson Cemetery in Trigg County.

His son Robert H. (b. 1851 in Kentucky, d. 1904) married Lillie H. Jefferson (b. 1862, d. 1945) on 25 Dec 1883. Both are buried in the Malone Cemetery in Trigg County. Kentucky Grandsons' Burials:

JAMES R. GILFOY, 2nd Lieutenant, born ca. 1839, died ??. He enlisted 24 Oct 1861, at Camp Alcorn in Hopkinsville, KY and served with Co. B, 8th Kentucky Regt. Inf. (CSA). He enlisted as a private and was promoted to 1st corporal on 3 Oct 1862, to 2nd lieutenant on 23 Oct 1862 and served until the summer of 1863, when he was assigned to the Con-

script Bureau. He was sent on conscript duty and never returned to his company. This is the last record we have of 2nd Lt. Gilfoy.

His father was James Gilfoy (b. ca. 1804 in Pennsylvania, d. ??) and his mother was Elmira (Goodwin) Gilfoy (b. ca. 1815 in Kentucky, d. ??). They married 26 Nov 1835 in Trigg County. James voted in the 3 Aug 1842 election at Cadiz, KY. He is also listed in the Wallonia Poll Book dated 4 Aug 1856.

GRANDERSON GRIFFITH "G.G." GOODWIN, Private, born 23 Sep 1815, died 12 Aug 1880 at Cerulean, KY. He enlisted on 9 Dec 1862 at Williamsport, TN and served with Co. A, 2nd/15th Kentucky Regt. Cav., (CSA). Listed as a private in the Kentucky Adjutant General's Report (CSA).

G.G. married Martha Dawson on 1 Dec 1847 in Trigg County. He is buried with his wife Martha (b. 1 Sep 1828 at Roaring Spring, KY, d. 23 Dec 1885 at Cerulean, KY) in the Goodwin Cemetery, in Trigg County.

His daughter Ann Eliza, age 19 years of Trigg County, married James T. Greer, age 27 years, also Trigg County, on 28 Nov 1867. It was the first marriage for both bride and groom.

His daughter Virginia E., age 20 years of Trigg County, married William R. Read, age 21 years of Christian County, on 15 Nov 1870. It was the first marriage for both bride and groom. W. Read (b. 30 Jun 1849, d. 7 Aug 1884) is buried in the Goodwin Cemetery. Virginia later married Elihu R. Smith on 1 Feb 1888 in Trigg County.

His daughter Alice B. married Wiley A. P'Pool in Trigg County, KY, on 23 Dec 1874.

His daughter Lelia married James E. Pool on 4 Jan 1888 in Trigg County. They sold land to M.F. Hopson on 22 Nov 1897 in Trigg County.

His son J.H. (b. 1856, d. 1924) is buried in the Robertson Cemetery with his wife Frances Elizabeth "Fannie" (Hartigan) Goodwin (b. 1863, d. 1934).

His son Oscar (b. 1868, d. 1956) is buried with his wife Lula Goodwin (b. 1871, d. 1949) in the Turner or Cerulean Cemetery.

WILLIAM C. GOODWIN, Private, born ca. 1829 and died ??. He enlisted 9 Dec 1862 at Williamsport, TN and served with Co. B, Woodward's 2nd/15th Kentucky Cav. Regt. (CSA).

In the 1850 Trigg County Census #189, he is listed as William C. Goodwin, age 31 years, living with Henry C. Calhoun, age 41 years and Emily G. Calhoun, age 34 years, family in this census.

GEORGE E. GRACE, Private, born ca. 1844 in Kentucky and was killed in action at Jackson, MS on 9 Aug 1863. He enlisted 14 Sep 1861 at Camp Burnett, TN and served with Co. G, 4th Kentucky Regt. Inf. (CSA). According to Kentucky State Archives, dated September-October 1862, "He had been left sick in Nashville, TN in a helpless condition on 17 Feb 1862, and has since rejoined the regiment in good faith."

"He was sick in the hospital at Jackson, MS, since 20 Jun 1863."

His father was Elliot Grace (b. ca. 1815 in Kentucky, d. ??) and his mother was Mary A. (Meredith) Grace (b. ca. 1821 in Hopkins County, KY, d. 17 Feb 1853, in Trigg County, KY). Mary Ann (Meredith) Grace was the daughter of Samuel and Milly Meredith. Mary Ann and Elliot married on 21 May 1836 in Trigg County. They are both buried in the Grace Cemetery (no stone). Elliott Grace married second, Jane Waddell on 12 Dec 1853 in Trigg County.

George was a brother to Pvt. Richard J. "R.J." Grace, who at age 24 years married Emma G. Waddell, age 26 years of Todd County, on 8 Nov 1865.

WILLIAM L. GREEN, first child of Collin Green and Winnie (Hogan) Green was born 22 Aug 1835 in Stewart County, TN near Dover. He married Endora Marshall on 2 May 1860 in Stewart County.

William was a veteran of the War Between the North and South. As a Confederate soldier serving in the Confederate Army, he fought through the entire four years of the conflict. He served in Co. H, 8th Arkansas Inf. CSA. In 1864, while engaged in the Battle of Franklin, TN, he was wounded, taken prisoner and sent to Camp Chase, OH. He was then transferred to a prison hospital at Lookout, MD. He was held prisoner for two years, then returned home on 7 Jun 1867. Dot Loveday, his granddaughter, still has the ball he was wounded with.

He moved from Stewart County to Trigg County, KY, near the close of the war and resided in the Between the Rivers area until he died on 26

Jul 1927. He is buried at the old Ricks Futrell Cemetery in the Laura Furnace Community in Land Between the Lakes.

He is survived locally by his granddaughter Dot Loveday, great-granddaughter Connie Board, great-great-grandson Jimmy Woody, great-great- granddaughter Gloria Rosencrans, great-great-great granddaughter Crystal Woody, great-great-greatgrandson Jamie Woody and great-great-great-great-grandson Cody Shane Woody, all of Trigg County.

At the time of his death, there were only seven men living in Trigg County, that were soldiers in the Confederate Army during the Civil War. They were: M.E. Barefield of Cerulean, Zennas Alexander of Caledonia, C.P. Dearing of Maggie, Samuel Lancaster of Donaldson Community, Joe H. Mitchell, three miles south of Cadiz and Cas Futrell of Golden Pond.

Samuel Davis Green, William Green's younger brother, fought for the North during the Civil War. He was discharged at Sioux City, IA. He died 16 Aug 1918 in Trigg County near Golden Pond.

Another younger brother, John Green, enlisted in the CSA at the age of 15. His mother tried to have him returned home due to his youth, but he would not. He was killed at the Battle of Nashville and buried at Nashville, TN.

Parts of this information were taken from the Ross, Green, Futrell and Futrell family history book and obituary columns.

WILLIAM HOWARD GREENWOOD, Private, born 1826 in Tennessee and died in 1896. He enlisted 23 Jul 1861 at Camp Boone, TN and served with Co. E, 3rd Kentucky Regt. Inf. (CSA). The company was under the command of Capt. J.M. Emerson. At the death of Capt. Emerson at the Battle of Shiloh, command of the company was assumed by Capt. S. Payne Ridgeway.

There may have been two Charles H. Robertsons living in Trigg County during this era. The Charles H. Robertson who married Virginia Greenwood, William's sister, was born in Kentucky around 1834 and was a brick mason. The other Charles H. Robertson was born in Virginia around 1824 and was married to Casendiana S. Robertson and was a farmer.

William's father was James C. Greenwood (b. ca. 1800 in Virginia, d. ??) and his mother was Mary W. Greenwood (b. ca. 1803 in Virginia, d. ??).

William's daughters: Almira married R.L. Delawson on 3 Dec 1873, in Trigg County; Anna Belle married Drewry F. Son on 23 Dec 1879; and Ella M. married Sidney I. Kirby on 3 Dec 1890 in Trigg County.

William Howard Greenwood is buried in the Bush Cemetery with his wife Martha Jane (McCraw) Greenwood (b. 1826 in Virginia, d. 1905).

MOSE GRESHAM, born in Calloway County on 16 Aug 1836. He enlisted in the Army of the Confederate States at Camp Burnett in Montgomery County, TN on 3 Sep 1861. He was enlisted by Capt. John L. Trice of the 1st Kentucky Brigade, the 4th Regt., Co. G., to serve three years.

He was wounded at the Battle of Shiloh on 7 Apr 1862 where he lost his left index finger and left thumb immobil. He was captured at Caldwell County, KY on 5 Dec 1862 and imprisoned at Camp Chase. On 28 Mar 1863 he was transferred to City Point, VA for exchange, by order of Col. Wm. Hoffman, Commanding General of Prisons, in charge of Capt. J.C. Moon, Co. B, Gov. Guards.

Mose married Sarah Francis Martin of Trigg County, KY on 20 Jun 1967. She was born 19 Sep 1846. Mose was a farmer at the time of enlistment. He and Sarah are buried at Pete Light Farm Cemetery in Trigg County, KY.

RICHARD GRACE, Private, born ca. 1841 in Kentucky, died ??. Enlisted 14 Sep 1861 at Camp Burnett, TN and served with Co. G, 4th Kentucky Regt. Inf. (CSA). Kentucky Adjutant General's Report states "discharged from service 6 Dec 1861, at Bowling Green, KY, reason not given." He was a brother of Pvt. George E. Grace.

His parents were Elliot Grace (b. ca. 1815, d. ??) and Mary A. (Meredith) Grace (b. ca. 1821, d. 17 Feb 1853). They were married on 21 May 1836.

R.J. Grace, age 25 years of Trigg County, married Emma G. Waddell, age 26 years of Todd County, on 8 Nov 1865.

GORDON W. GRASTY, Private born ca. 1844 in Kentucky, died ??. Enlisted 10 Dec 1862 at Williamsport, TN and served with Co. B, Woodward's 2nd/15th Kentucky Regt. Cavalry (CSA). Gordon is buried in the Baker Cemetery, but there is no stone, no dates.

His father John M. Grasty (b. ca. 1801 in Kentucky, d. ??) married his mother Cynthia McWaters (b. December 1816 in Kentucky, d. ??) on 3 Aug 1835 in Trigg County.

His sister Elizabeth J. Grasty married Blake Baker on 24 Jan 1859 in Trigg County. Elizabeth (b. 22 Oct 1839, d. 10 Oct 1901) is buried in the Baker Cemetery with three of her sons: I.J. (b. 25 May 1866, d. 11 Feb 1889); J.W. (b. 16 Oct 1868, d. 1 Oct 1884) and M.S. Baker (b. 25 Aug 1874, d. 23 Feb 1897).

Gordon's sister Lucy Ann, age 23 years of Trigg County, married William I. Bush, age 27 years, also of Trigg County, on 21 Nov 1865. William served with Co. C, 9th Texas Inf., CSA. He died 13 Feb 1905 and is buried in the Baker Cemetery.

His sister Isora Grasty married James Osborne on 14 Feb 1872 in Trigg County. Isora married second, D.F. Rogers on 18 Nov 1884 in Trigg County.

Gordon's brother James W. married Ambie Creekmur on 31 Mar 1881 in Trigg County.

His brother Samuel married Ida Mitchell on 4 Mar 1886 in Trigg County. Samuel (b. 5 Jan 1858, d. 2 Jun 1938) is buried with his wife Ida (b. 25 Aug 1862, d. 21 Jun 1943) in the Baker Cemetery.

SAMUEL D. GREEN, born 27 Oct 1844 in Tennessee, died 16 Aug 1918. His father was Collin Green and his mother was Winney (Hogan) Green (b. ca. 1818, d. d. 9 Aug 1879. Winney (b. ca. 1818,. d. 9 Aug 1879) "wife of Collin Green and mother of S.D. Green" is buried in the Dixon Cemetery.

Samuel D. Green married Mary J. Futrell circa 1868, according to Jones' 1900 Trigg County Census. He is buried in the Dixon Cemetery with his wife Mary Josephine (b. 13 Oct 1850, d. 30 Aug 1928). His tombstone reads "a good comrade soldier, served three years and two days." He had three daughters: Elizabeth Pinkie, Mary Winnie and Nannie E.

Elizabeth Pinkie Lee Green (b. 29 Apr 1874, d. 26 Oct 1915) married William B. Shaw on 1 Jan 1890 in Trigg County. Elizabeth and William (b. 18 Apr 1866, d. 17 Dec 1916) are buried at the Colson or Pleasant Valley Cemetery. Many of their children are also buried in this cemetery.

Mary Winnie R. Green married Robert L. Ross on 4 Oct 1892, in Trigg County. Mary W.R. (12 Oct 1875, d. 19 Apr 1956) and Robert (b. 24 May 1871, d. 5 Jun 1914) are buried at the Dixon Cemetery.

Nannie E. Green married Benjamin F. Hicks on 9 Nov 1897 in Trigg County. Nannie E. (b. 4 Jan 1877, d. 12 Jun 1949) is buried with her husband Benjamin (b. 9 May 1867, d. 11 Jul 1941) in the Dixon Cemetery.

WILLIAM L. GREEN, born 22 Aug 1839 in Tennessee, died 26 Jul 1927. He served with Co. H, 8th Arkansas Regt. Inf. (CSA). William L. Green is buried with his wife Eudora (Marshall) Green (b. 24 Feb 1838, d. 15 Feb 1915) at the Futrell or Laura Furnace Cemetery.

There is a Green family missing #130-132, page 250 in Jones' 1900 Trigg County Census.

In the 1880 Trigg County Census all of the Green children of this family were born in Tennessee except Tissie.

There were two Isaac Comptons who lived in Trigg County during this era. The Isaac Wilson Compton who married Sarah L. Green was the son of Mary Compton and was born ca. 1858 in TN. The Isaac Compton who married Mahala Evelyn Solomon was born on 28 Oct 1843, and was a WSI veteran.

William's daughter Sarah L. Green married Isaac Wilson Compton on 27 Jun 1880 in Trigg County. Sarah died soon after her marriage. Sarah L. (b. ca. 1862 in Tennessee, d. ??) is buried with her infant in the Futrell or Laura Furnace Cemetery (no stone).

William's daughter Mary Letitia "Tissie" (Green) Jones (b. 21 Mar 1880, d. 24 Sep 1978) is buried with her husband Markus Evan Jones (b. 23 Feb 1876, d. 6 Apr 1943) at the Futrell or Laura Furnace Cemetery.

HENRY GREENWADE, Private, born ca. 1835 in Kentucky, died ??. He mustered in 19 Aug 1864 at Paducah, KY and served with Eighth US Colored Artillery (Heavy).

Both Neel and Maupin indicate he is a WSI veteran.

Private Henry Greenwade is buried in the Corinth Negro Cemetery, but there is no stone to his grave.

Page 185, Simmons' 1870 Trigg County Census #264. He is listed as Henry Greenwade, a farmer, age 35 years, living with his wife Sally Greenwade, age 30 years, and three daughters: Bettie, age 14 years; Ida, age 3 years; and Eliza (born in October) age 7 months.

JOSEPH GREENWADE, Private, mustered in 25 Jun 1864 at Paducah, KY and served with Co. K, Eighth US Colored Artillery (Heavy) Both Neel and Maupin indicate he is a WSI veteran. Pvt. Joseph Greenwade is buried in the Corinth Negro Cemetery, but there is no stone to his grave. Corinth Cemetery is at the Malcolm Hardy Farm at Casey Creek.

STEWART GREENWADE, Corporal, born ca. 1831 in Kentucky, died ??. He mustered in 25 Jun 1864 at Paducah, KY and served with Co. K, Eighth US Colored Artillery (Heavy). Both Neel and Maupin indicate he is a WSI veteran. Cpl. Stewart Greenwade is buried in the Corinth Negro Cemetery, but there is no stone to his grave. Corinth Cemetery is at the Malcolm Hardy Farm at Casey Creek.

Page 185, Simmons' 1870 Trigg County Census #2165. He is listed as "Steward" Greenwade, a farm worker, age 39 years, living with his father Charley Greenwade, age 80 years; his mother Pleasant Greenwade, age 75 years; his brother Merrett Greenwade, age 30 years; and Milly Greenwade, age 47 years.

WASHINGTON "WASH" GREENWADE, Private, born ca. 1830 in Kentucky, died ??. He mustered in 25 Jun 1864 at Paducah, KY and served with Co. K, Eighth US Colored Artillery (Heavy).

Page 170, Simmons' 1870 Trigg County Census #2007. He is listed as Washington Greenwade, a farmer age 40, living with his wife Martha Greenwade, age 31 years, and five children: Elvarage (son), age 12 years; Fanny, age 7 years; Nancy, age 6 years; Sherman, age 2 years; and Washington Jr. (born in December), age 5 months.

HENRY A. GRIGSBY, Private, born 11 Jan 1841 in Kentucky, died 13 Feb 1905. He enrolled 4 Aug 1863, was mustered in 26 Oct 1863 at Princeton, KY and mustered out 19 Dec 1864 at Bowling Green, KY. He served with Co. F, 48th Kentucky Regt. Mounted Inf. (USA). Henry A. Grigsby was an older brother to John F. Grigsby a Union soldier. He is buried in the Grigsby Cemetery with his parents and siblings.

His parents were Jesse Grigsby (b. 22 Jul 1807 in Virginia, d. 8 Jan 1864) and Mary M. (Mosely) Grigsby (b. 4 Mar 1812 in Kentucky, d. 7 Mar 1897). They are buried in the Grigsby Cemetery with many of their children.

His sisters:

Susannah M. (Grigsby) Alexander (b. 2 Mar 1837, d. 14 Sep 1911) is buried in the Grigsby Cemetery.

Martha A. Grigsby married Thomas H. Carloss on 18 Jul 1855 in Trigg County.

Sophoronia J. married James M. Champion on 16 Dec 1861 in Trigg County.

Susan A. married John P. Freeman on 25 Nov 1875 in Trigg County.

Francis Elizabeth Grigsby married Peter T. Light on 3 Sep 1876 in Trigg County. Frances E. (b. 1850, d. 1921) is buried in the Pete Light Cemetery with her husband Peter (b. 25 Feb 1840, d. 14 Feb 1918) and his first wife Mary Josephine (Martin) Light (b. 8 Mar 1849, d. 20 Aug 1876).

Olin Grigsby married Drewry Sholar on 25 Nov 1886 in Trigg County.

Brothers: Robert J. Grigsby married Tabitha L. Rogers on 8 Sep 1866 in Trigg County. Robert (b. 1843, d. 1928) is buried with his wife Tabitha (b. 1843, d. 1917) in the Grigsby Cemetery.

John F. Grigsby married Mary Josephine Lawrence on 1 Apr 1876 in Trigg County.

JOHN F. GRIGSBY, Private, born 22 Jul 1846 in Kentucky, died 20 Mar 1888. He enrolled 15 Aug 1863, mustered in 26 Oct 1863 at Princeton, KY and mustered out 19 Dec 1864 at Bowling Green, KY. He served with Co. F, 48th Kentucky Regt. Mounted Inf. (USA). John F. was a younger brother of Henry A. Grigsby, a Union soldier.

His parents were Jesse Grigsby (b. 22 Jul 1807 in Virginia, d. 8 Jan 1864) and Mary M. (Mosely) Grigsby (b. 4 Mar 1812 in Kentucky, d. 7 Mar 1897). They are buried in the Grigsby Cemetery with many of their children.

John F. married Mary Josephine Lawrence on 11 Apr 1876 in Trigg County. He is buried in the Grigsby Cemetery with his wife Mary Josephine (b. 19 Mar 1849, d. 5 Feb 1913).

Sisters of John F.:

Martha A. Grigsby married Thomas H. Carloss on 18 Jul 1855 in Trigg County.

Sophoronia J. Grigsby married James M. Champion on 16 Dec 1861 in Trigg County.

Susan A. Grigsby married John P. Freeman on 25 Nov 1875 in Trigg County.

Frances Elizabeth Grigsby married Peter T. Light on 3 Sep 1876, in Trigg County. Frances (b. 1850, d. 1921) is listed as buried in the Pete Light Cemetery with her husband Peter T. Light (b. 25 Feb 1840. d. 14 Feb 1918) and his first wife Mary Josephine (Martin) Light (b. 8 Mar 1849, d. 20 Aug 1876).

Olin Grigsby married Drewry Sholar on 25 Nov 1886, in Trigg County.

Susannah M. (Grigsby) Alexander (b. 2 Mar 1837, d. 14 Sep 1911) is buried in the Grigsby Cemetery.

His brother Robert J. Grigsby married Tabitha L. Rogers on 8 Sep 1866 in Trigg County. Robert J. (b. 1843, d. 1928) is buried in the Grigsby Cemetery with his wife Tabitha L. (b. 1843, 1917).

KAD GROOMS, both Neel and Maupin indicate that Kad Grooms was a WSI soldier. He is buried in the Kerby Negro Cemetery.

DAVID H. HALE, Private, born ca. 1835 in Tennessee, died ?? He enlisted 14 Sep 1861 at Camp Burnett, TN and served with Co. G, 4th Kentucky Regt. Inf. (CSA).

According to the Kentucky State Archives, he was absent, sick in the hospital in Bowling Green, KY, November to December 1861 Roster. He was left sick in the hospital in Nashville, TN, when the Confederates evacuated Nashville in the Spring of 1862. He was dropped from the rolls on 1 Sep 1862.

In the 1860 Census he and all of his family are listed as having been born in Tennessee.

On page 264, Neel's Statistical Handbook of Trigg County, Trigg County Voting Records, he is listed as D.H. Hale on the Canton Poll Book, 6 Aug 1860.

In Simmons' 1860 Trigg County Census #558. He is listed as David Hale, age 25 years, living with his wife Tempe, age 24 years and two children: Wilson, age 4 years, and J.B., age 3 years.

JAMES H. HAMILTON, born 17 Aug 1822 in Tennessee, died 27 Sep 1908. He is listed as a member of the enrolled militia on parade on 6 Apr 1861, G.M. Ezell Captain. He is listed in Roaring Spring Poll Book, 6 Aug 1860. He is buried in the Hamilton Cemetery with his wife Nancy A. Hamilton (b. 22 Aug 1831 in Kentucky, d. 7 Aug 1904).

His son-in-law, Thomas W. Bond was the son of Ben Winfrey Bond, a Confederate soldier (see Ben Winfrey Bond). Thomas W., age 24, married a Susan A. Forth, age 20 years of Christian County, on 16 Feb 1865. We believe Susan A. Hamilton and Susan A. Forth are somehow the same person.

James' former son-in-law Thomas W. Bond, a farmer age 30 years of Trigg County, married Sarah E. Ross, age 18 years and also of Trigg County, on 17 Dec 1870. It was the second marriage for the groom and the first marriage for the bride.

Children of James H. Hamilton:

Thomas A. married Sallie Jane Sholar on 17 Feb 1891 in Trigg County.

Susan A. (Hamilton) Bond (b. 5 May 1844, d. 28 Oct 1869) is buried in the Hamilton Cemetery in Trigg County with the following list of brothers and sisters: Sarah L. (b. 12 Nov 1849, d. 7 Dec 1872); Martha L. Hamilton (b. 31 Jul 1851, d. 7 Sep 1874); Nancy Jane Hamilton (b. 3 Dec 1856, d. 10 Jun 1888); James E. (b. 24 Oct 1854, d. 11 Oct 1887) drowned in the Hillsboro River in Dade County, FL; John W. (b. 11 Mar 1860, d. 23 Dec 1862); Henry G. (b. 1 Jun 1865, d. 1 Jun 1865); Francis W. (b. 1 Jun 1865, d. 9 Oct 1890); Finis R. (b. 3 Jun 1868, d. 10 Apr 1925).

On page 78, Simmons' 1860 Trigg County Census #1156, he is listed as "J.H." (James H.) Hamilton, age 38 years living with his wife "N.A." (Nancy A.) Hamilton, age 29 years and eight children: "S." (Susan A.), age 16 years; "S.L." (Sarah L.), age 18 years (?); "M.A." (Martha L.), age 8 years; "W.M." (William N.), age 7 years; "J.E." (James E.), age 5 years; "N.J." (Nancy Jane), age 3 years; "T.A." (Thomas A.) (male), age 2 years; "J.W." (John W.), age 3 months.

JAMES H. HANCOCK, Private, born 15 May 1843 or 1844 in Kentucky, died 12 Nov 1923. He enrolled 7 Aug 1863, mustered in 26 Oct 1863 at Princeton, KY and mustered out 19 Dec 1864 at Bowling Green, KY. He served with Co. F, 48th Kentucky Regiment Mounted Infantry (USA).

James H. Hancock of Trigg County, age 24 years, married Minerva J. McCain, age 20 years of Trigg County, on 19 Dec 1867. It was the first marriage for both bride and groom.

He is buried in the Flat Creek Cemetery with his first wife Minerva J. (McCain) Hancock (b. 24 Apr 1847, d. 3 Nov 1907) and his second wife Cornelia Hancock (b. 8 Sep 1874, 1 Aug 1918).

References: Page 40, Simmons' 1850 Trigg County Census #739. He is listed as age 8 years and living with has father James Hancock, age 50 years; his mother Jane Hancock, age 46 years; and six siblings: Josiah, age 23 years; Jesse W., age 20 years; Sarah E., age 18 years; Richard J., age 15 years; Joseph J., age 13 years; and William T., age 10 years.

Page 175, Simmons' 1870 Trigg County Census #2055. He is listed as age 27 years and living with his wife Minerva J. (McCain) Hancock, age 23 years, and one daughter Jane, age 1 year.

Page 205, Neel's Statistical Handbook of Trigg County, 1880 Trigg County Census, middle of page. He is listed as James Hancock, a farmer age 37 years, living with his wife Jane Hancock, age 33 years, and five children: Jennie, age 11 years; Minnie, age 9 years; Lealer (daughter), age 7 years; Henry, age 4 years; and Mary, age 1 month.

PINKNEY B. HARRELL, son of Harrison and Elizabeth (Taylor) Harrell, was born in the Dry Creek area of Trigg County on 10 Aug 1835.

The youngest of a very large family, he moved with his parents to the area of Donaldson Creek shortly after his birth. After the death of his father when he was about 8 years old, his mother married Mr. Robert Jones.

In early manhood, Pinkney was employed in the lumber business in Canton, but soon thereafter engaged in farming where he remained the rest of his life. When the War Between the States broke out, he enlisted on 9 Apr 1861 in General Tilghman's Division of Co. F, 50th Tennessee Volunteers. He helped build the fort and fought at the Battle of Fort Donelson in February 1862, and was taken prisoner to Camp Douglas, IL. He was kept in prison for several months and was later taken to Vicksburg, MS and exchanged for other prisoners. Pinkney re-enlisted in the war at Jackson, MS and was at Port Hudson, LA. He came home on a furlough in September 1862 but returned to his command later and was in the Battle of Missionary Ridge and saw the Battle of Lookout Mountain.

While on furlough again in 1863, the US soldiers began to harass him causing him to go to Fort Donelson and take the oath of allegiance to keep him from being put in prison again. He declared, "This is the only question that I dislike to answer" while applying for a pension.

On 21 Dec 1865, he married Matilda Adeline Dixon, daughter of John and Matilda (Lawrence) Dixon. To this union 12 children were born: Mary Tyler "Mollie," Sarah Quiantly, John Amett, Peachey Matilda, Pinkie Elizabeth, Nannie Cordelia, Willie Adeline, Sidney Dixon, Oscar Turner, Hattie Chappell and Olga Major Harrell.

After his marriage, he bought land and farmed, living three miles west of Cadiz. He was a very popular gentleman, read a great deal, and delighted in the discussion of public matters while being a member of the Democratic Party. Pinkney died on 5 Nov 1923 and was buried in Lawrence Cemetery, Trigg County. *Submitted by Jeannie Lancaster.*

RILEY HARRELL, Private, born ca. 1833 in Tennessee, died 5 Aug 1862. He enlisted 14 Sep 1861 at Camp Burnett, TN and served with Co. G, 4th Kentucky Regt. Inf. (CSA). According to Kentucky State Archives and the Kentucky Adjutant General's Report, Pvt. Harrell died at Amite City, LA, on 5 Aug 1862.

On page 87, Simmons' 1860 Trigg County Census #1278 there is an "R.T. Herrell" listed as a carpenter, age 27 years, and living with the William G. Hester, age 43 years, and Henrietta M. (Sammons) Hester, age 50 years, family in this census.

B.F./F.B. HARRIS, Major, born on a farm in Trigg County, KY and at an early age lost his father. When the War Between the States began, young Harris stole away from his mother and entered the Confederate Army. He enlisted at Cadiz under Col. Thomas Woodward. This was Woodward's Battalion, 2nd Kentucky Cav.

In February 1863, he was with fighting Joe Wheeler when he made the attack on Fort Donelson. He was in the Battle of Chickamauga and was with Gen. Wheeler until the close of the war. He was in the Atlanta Campaign when Sherman marched to Savannah and fought with Wheeler through Georgia and the Carolinas. When General Lee surrendered and President Davis and his cabinet came through the Carolinas, he was one of Davis' escorts to Washington, GA.

After the war Maj. Harris was a successful merchant at Rock Castle, Canton and Paducah. For 21 years he was employed by the St. Bernard Coal Co. and held the position as superintendent of the South Diamond Mines at Morton's Gap.

He was a member of Madisonville, KY, Camp UCV and was a delegate to the Confederate Veteran's Association held in New Orleans. He was a member of Col. Bennett H. Young's staff, appointed assistant pay master and major. His name has three listings: B.F., F.B. and Frankens.

JOHN T. HARRIS, 3rd Corporal, born ca. 1835 in Kentucky, died ??. He enlisted 24 Oct 1861 at Camp Alcorn in Hopkinsville, KY and served with Co. B, 8th Kentucky Regt. Inf. (CSA). According to the Kentucky Adjutant General's Report, he was discharged from service on 19 Dec 1861 in Hopkinsville, KY (reason not given).

His mother was Malinda (Franklin) Harris (b. ca. 1819 in Kentucky, d. ??).

J.T. Harris is listed in the 6 Aug 1860 and 5 Aug 1861 Bethesda Poll Book.

John T. Harris of Trigg County (born in Lyon County), a farmer age 22 years, married Mary I. (J.) Byram of Trigg County, age 19 years, on 21 Sep 1871. It was the first marriage for both the bride and groom.

His sister Martha A. married Samuel Bourland on 17 Jan 1855 in Trigg County; brother Joseph T. married Susan A. Means on 31 May 1861, in Trigg County; and brother Achilles C., a commercial merchant, age 26 years of Trigg County, married Kate C. Dawson, age 20 years of Trigg County, on 22 Jul 1873. It was the first marriage for both bride and groom.

On page 24, Simmons 1860 Trigg County Census #254. He is listed as "J.T." Harris, age 25 years(?), living with his mother "M." (Melinda) Harris, a merchant, age 42 years, and three siblings, "J.G." (Joseph), age 19 years(?); "F.B." (Frankens), age 15 years; and "A.C." (Achilles C.), age 13 years. "K. (King) F." Baker is listed as a merchant, age 39 years, born in Kentucky and living close by.

JOSEPH "JOE" T. HART, Private, born ca. 1835 in North Carolina, died ??. He enlisted 24 Oct 1861 at Camp Alcorn, Hopkinsville, KY and served with Co. B, 8th Kentucky Regt. Inf. (CSA). According to the Kentucky Adjutant General's Report he was discharged on account of physical disability on 2 Dec 1862 (1861?) at Hopkinsville, KY.

In the 1850 Trigg County Census, only the children, Elizabeth and Thomas, were born in Kentucky. All other family members were born in North Carolina. His father was Joseph Hart Sr. (b. ca. 1793 in North Carolina, d. ??) and his mother was Nancy Hart (b. ca. 1802 in North Carolina, d. ??).

His father Joseph Hart Sr. is listed on the Wallonia Poll Book, dated 1 Aug 1856.

His brother John Hart married Mildred Ann Coy on 10 Nov 1851 in Trigg County.

On page 323, Neel's Statistical Handbook of Trigg County, Trigg County Marriage Records.

Page 272, Neel's Statistical Handbook of Trigg County, Poll Book Records of Trigg County

On page 7, Simmons' 1850 Trigg County Census #115. He is listed as Joseph, age 15 years, living with his father Joseph Sr., age 57 years; his mother Nancy, age 48 years; and four siblings: John, age 21 years; Willis, age 12 years; Elizabeth, age 8 years; and Thomas, age 6 years.

REUBEN H. HAYDEN, Private, born ca. 1843 in Kentucky, died ??. He enlisted 20 Nov 1861 at Camp Alcorn in Hopkinsville, KY and served with Co. B, 8th Kentucky Regt. Inf. (CSA).

He was captured at Lebanon, TN on 5 May 1862, taken to Camp Chase, OH and then exchanged on 25 Aug 1862. He was wounded 11 Jul 1863 at Jackson, MS.

There was a William Clinton Haydon (b. 12 Apr 1826, d. 22 Dec 1896) and his wife Eliza Ann (Robertson) Haydon (b. 1 Oct. 1836, d. 2 Dec. 1907) who lived in the Trigg County area at this same time. However, they usually spelled their name "Haydon."

Reuben's father was Samuel Hayden (b. 14 Mar 1814 in Kentucky, d. 25 Aug 1869) and his mother was Martha (Dyer) Hayden (b. ca. 1826 in Kentucky, d. ??). They were married on 3 Oct 1842 in Trigg County. Samuel Hayden is buried in the Wall Cemetery in Trigg County.

Reuben's brothers: Luther married Melissa A. Dunning on 23 Aug 1874 in Trigg County; Leslie married Lucy C. Hanberry on 14 Feb 1875 in Trigg County; Jefferson (b. 26 Apr 1863, d. 6 Dec 1863) is buried in the Wall Cemetery in Trigg County; and Robert (b. 1 Jul 1867, d. 1 Dec 1867) is buried in the Wall Cemetery.

On page 30, Simmons' 1860 Trigg County Census #443. He is listed as "R.H.," age 17 years, and living with his father "S." (Samuel) Hayden, age 46 years, and his mother "M." (Martha) Hayden, age 36 years, and three siblings: "L." (Leslie), age 13 years; Luther, age 8 years; and "L.E." (Samuel E.), age 6 years.

JAMES W. HENDERSON, Private, born ca. 1838 in Kentucky, died 3 Dec 1863 at Princeton, KY. He enrolled 13 Aug 1863, mustered in 26 Oct 1863 at Princeton, KY and served with Co. F, 48th Kentucky Regiment Mounted Infantry (USA).

His guardians were Fountain Crane (b. ca. 1805 in Tennessee, d. ??) and Nancy Henderson (b. ca. 1806 in South Carolina, d. ??). They married 26 Sep 1826. Fountain Crain is listed as voting at the Burnett's Precinct on 5 Aug 1829, and he is listed on the Roaring Spring Poll Book dated 1 Aug 1842.

On page 44, Simmons' 1850 Trigg County Census #808-269. He is listed as James W. Henderson, age 12 years, living with Fountain Crane, age 45 years, and Nancy (Henderson) Crane, age 44 years, no children.

LEE HENDRICKS, 5th Sergeant, born ca. 1843 in Kentucky, died February 1862. He enlisted 26 Sep 1861 at Camp Reeves, TN and served with Co. G, 8th Kentucky Regt. Inf. (CSA). He died of disease near Cadiz, KY in February 1862. Sergeant Lee Hendricks was a brother of Pvt. Thomas C. (Charles) Hendricks.

His parents were Thomas Hendricks (b. ca. 1806 in Virginia, d. ??) and Nancy (Cameron) Hendricks (b. ca. 1804 in Kentucky, d. ??). They were married on 22 Nov 1836 in Trigg County.

His sister Mary Elizabeth Hendricks married Alexander Baker Jr. on 14 Jun 1856 in Trigg County. Mary Elizabeth is buried with her husband Alexander Baker and their son Thomas L. Baker in the Thomas L. Baker Cemetery. There are no stones to any of their graves.

A Sarah A. Hendricks married Evander Ladd in 1874 in Trigg County. (Either Sarah A. Hendricks did not marry Evander Ladd or she died soon after the marriage for he is living with his parents in the 1880 Trigg County Census.

His brother George D. (b. 25 Oct 1845, d. 30 Sep 1897) is buried with his wife Missouri A. Cunningham Hendricks (b. 13 Sep 1846, d. 13 Dec 1920) in the Hendricks Cemetery with their son Charles T. Hendricks (b. 1869, d. 1892). Later they were all moved to the Little River Relocation Cemetery at the flooding of Lake Barkley..

His brother Thomas Charles Hendrick (b. 11 Apr 1837, d. 17 Jul 1905) is buried with his wife Eliza Hendrick (b. 15 Sep 1837, d. ??) in the Hall Cemetery in Trigg County with their son George D. Hendricks (b. 1 Dec 1871, d. 28 Aug 1887).

On page 28, Simmons' 1850 Trigg County Census #513. He is listed as "Leony" Hendricks, age 7 years, living with his father Thomas Hendricks, age 32 years, his mother Nancy (Cameron) Hendricks, age 38 years and five siblings: Elizabeth, age 11 years; Thomas, age 9 years; Sarah A., age 5 years; George, age 4 years; and Mariah E., age 1 year.

HENRY HENSON, Private, born ca. 1840 in Kentucky, died ??. He enrolled 14 Aug 1863, mustered in 26 Oct 1863 in Princeton, KY and mustered out 19 Dec 1864 in Bowling Green, KY. He served with Co. F, 48th Kentucky Regiment Mounted Infantry (USA).

William Henson and Ailcey Henson may be Henry Henson's grandparents rather than his parents. William Henson was born ca. 1785 in South Carolina and Ailcey Henson was born ca. 1789 also in South Carolina.

His brother Martin V. Henson married Martha Frances on 23 Dec 1859 in Trigg County.

On page 42, Simmons' 1850 Trigg County Census #780, he is listed as age 10 years and living with his father (or grandfather) William Henson, a farmer age 65 years, his mother (or grandmother) Ailcey Henson, age 61 years, and seven siblings: John, age 37 years; Wiley, age 25 years; Sarah, age 28 years; Sarah, age 26 years; Jessy, age 5 years; Martin V., age 13 years; and Wiley, age 4 years. It is difficult to tell just from the census exactly how these folks are related to each other.

ALFRED "DOCK" HICKS, born 2 Jan 1845 in Kentucky, died 27 Nov 1923. His father was Garland Hicks (b. ca. 1818 in Tennessee, d. ??) and his mother was Rebecca (Futrell) Hicks (b. 5 Apr 1818 in Kentucky, d. 26 Aug 1886), buried in the Pleasant Hill Church Cemetery.

Alfred Hicks married Sarah Elizabeth Finlay (b. 1 Apr 1852, d. 20 Oct 1908). They are both buried in the Hicks Cemetery in Trigg County. Their daughter Eliza Jane (Hicks) Berkley (b. 2 Apr 1871, d. 28 Apr 1931), the wife of Charles Alonzo Berkley (b. 29 Jan 1870, d. 25 Feb 1958) is also buried in the Hicks Cemetery.

Alfred's sister Malinda Elizabeth Hicks, age 20 years of Trigg County, married Rufus W. Vinson, age 20 years of Stewart County, TN, on 26 Dec 1867. It was the first marriage for both bride and groom.

His sister Mary J. (Hicks) Downs (b. 1840, d. 1906), wife of Alfred Downs (b. 7 Jun 1834, d. 16 Jan 1911) are both buried in the Alfred Downs Cemetery near Bethlehem Baptist Church.

On page 60, Simmons' 1850 Trigg County Census #1096. He is listed as Alfred, age 6 years, living with his father Garland Hicks, age 32 years; his mother Rebecca (Futrell) Hicks, age 31 years; and four siblings: Pernecia A., age 8 years; Mary J., age 10 years; Elizabeth M. (Elizabeth Melinda), age 4 years; and Thomas A., age 1 year. Lemuel Outland, age 28 years, is living with this family in the 1850 Census.

On page 234, Neel's Statistical Handbook of Trigg County, 1880 Trigg County Census, middle of page. He is listed as Alfred Hicks, a farmer age 34 years, living with his wife Sarah E. (Finlay) Hicks, age 28 years, and six daughters: Sarah E. age 14 years; Panera H., age 12 years; Luella, age 10; Eliza J., age 8 years; Rosita, age 6 years; and Cora, age 2 years.

OTTAWA C. HICKS, Private, born ca. 1832 in Virginia, died ??. He enlisted 15 Oct 1861 at Camp Alcorn, Hopkinsville, KY and served with Co. G, 6th Kentucky Regt. Inf. (CSA). He was discharged in Hopkinsville, KY in the fall of 1861 due to rheumatism.

His father was "E." Hicks (b. ca. 1811 in Virginia, d. ??) and his mother was Ardenia Hicks (b. ca. 1821 in Virginia, d. ??).

On page 34, Simmons' 1860 Trigg County Census #508. He is listed as "Otway" Hicks, age 18 years, and the only child of "E." Hicks, age 49 years, and Adenia Hicks, age 39 years.

W.W HIGGINS, born ca. 1819 in Tennessee. According to Maupin's records, he was a WSI veteran, is buried in Higgins Cemetery in Trigg County, but has no stone to his grave. Neel also describes W.W. Higgins as a WSI veteran.

W.W. Higgins is listed in the Poll Book for Furgerson Precinct in August 1856.

On page 462, Neel's Statistical Handbook of Trigg County, List of Trigg County Civil War Veterans.

On page 3, Simmons' 1860 Trigg County Census #36. He is listed as "W.W.," age 31 years living with his wife Margaret, age 25 years (born in Illinois), no children.

Cannot find in Simmons' 1870 or in Jones' 1900 Trigg County Census.

GUSTAVIUS "GUSS" HILLMAN, Private, mustered in 25 Jun 1864 in Paducah, KY and served with Co. K, Eighth US Colored Artillery (Heavy)

Both Neel and Maupin list Guss Hillman as a WSI veteran. He is buried in the Bayliss Negro Cemetery, but there is no stone to his grave.

References: Page 148, Vol. II, Kentucky Adjutant General's Report (USA).

Page 10, Maupin's Trigg County Cemetery Records.

JOHN W. HODGE, Private, born ca. 1843 in Tennessee. He enrolled 12 Jul 1863 and mustered in 26 Oct 1863 at Princeton, KY. He transferred to the 3rd Kentucky Cavalry (USA) on 1 Apr 1864 and served with Co. F, 48th Kentucky Regiment Mounted Infantry (USA).

J.W. Hodge married Jamima Stewart on 13 Feb 1866 in Trigg County.

His mother Eliza (Pollard) Hodge married Thomas Joyce on 7 Jan 1854, in Trigg County.

His sister Sarah E., age 16 years of Trigg County, married M.M. Ruckett, age 18 years of Christian County, on 14 Aug 1865 in Trigg County.

His brother James E. married Mrs. Mary E. Hodge on 1 Jul 1874, in Trigg County and his brother Aaron F. married Sarah Lamkin on 6 Apr 1876 in Trigg County.

His brother Samuel H. is listed as voting in the Canton Precinct in August 1856 and in the Futrell Precinct on 1 Aug 1859.

On page 59, Simmons' 1850 Trigg County Census #1079. He is listed as John W. Hodge, age 7 years, living with his father James C. Hodge, age 39 years; his mother Eliza (Pollard) Hodge, age 36 years; and seven siblings: Samuel H., age 18 years; Jessey, age 16 years; James E., age 12 years; Isaac E., age 9 years; George A., age 3 years; Aaron F., age 3 years; and Sarah E., age 2 months.

On page 131, Simmons' 1870 Trigg County Census #1566. He is listed as John W. Hodge, age 25 years, living with his wife Jemima (Stewart) Hodge, age 17 years, and a daughter Sarah F. age 1 year.

There is no Hodge family in Jones' 1900 Trigg County Census.

JAMES E./W. HOLLAND, born ca. 1829. He served with Co. D, 14th Tennessee Inf. (CSA). In *Tennesseans in the Civil War*, there is a James M. Holland listed as being in Co. D of the 14th Tennessee.

In Simmons' 1850 Trigg County Census, his middle initial is given as "E." In Neel's 1850 Trigg County Census his middle initial is given as "W."

The W.J. Fuqua who married Cinthia Holland was a grocer born in Tennessee about 1830. William J. Fuqua, the dry goods merchant in the 1860 Trigg County Census, was married to Caroline Virginia Cash and was also born in Tennessee about 1830.

James Holland's father was A.W. Holland (b. ca. 1803 in Tennessee).

On page 3, Simmons' 1850 Trigg County Census #53, he is listed as James E. Holland, age 21 years, living with his father A.W. Holland, age 47 years; his brother William C., age 23 years; and his sister Cynthia A., age 20 years.

There is no evidence of this family after the 1870 Trigg County Census.

ENNIS OR "EUIS," HOPSON, born ca. 1829 in Kentucky. He is buried in the Bayliss Negro Cemetery, but there is no stone to his grave. Maupin indicates he is a WSI veteran.

"Innes" Hopson is listed on the Poll Book, Canton Precinct, election on Saturday, 6 Sep 1890.

On page 77, Simmons' 1870 Trigg County Census #904, he is listed as Ennis Hopson, a farmer age 41 years, living with his wife Martha, age 30 years, and seven children: John, age 16 years; Lilley, age 14 years; Edward, age 12 years; George, age 10 years; James L., 6 years; William, age 4 years; and Henry, age 17 years. Also living with this family during this census are Sarah J. Harper, age 18 years; Mary T. Harper, age 12 years; and Martha R., age 9 years.

Cannot find in Neel's Statistical Handbook of Trigg County, 1880 Trigg County Census or in Jones' 1900 Trigg County Census.

RICHMOND/RICHARD HOPSON, born ca. 1825 in Kentucky. He is buried in the Bayliss Negro Cemetery, but there is no stone to his grave. Maupin indicates he is a WSI veteran.

He is listed on the Poll Book, Canton Precinct, election of Saturday, 6 Sep 1890.

On page 77, Simmons' 1870 Trigg County Census #905, he is listed as Richmond Hopson, age 45 years and living with his wife Jane Hopson, age 35 years, and six children: Syntha, age 16 years; Margaret, age 14 years; Nathaniel, age 12 years; Leetha (female), age 4 years; and Vinity, 4 months.

JOHN B. HOWARD, Private, born ca. 1835. He enrolled 25 Jul 1863 mustered in 26 Oct 1863 at Princeton, KY, mustered out 19 Dec 1864 at Bowling Green, KY and served with Co. F, 48th Kentucky Mounted Regt. Inf. (USA).

His mother was Sarah Howard, born ca. 1808 in Tennessee. Sister's Marriage:

On page 45, Simmons' 1850 Trigg County Census #823, he is listed as "John B." Howard, age 15 years, living with his mother Sarah Howard, age 42 years, and four siblings: Mary W., age 20 years; Martha J., age 19 years; Richard H., age 17 years; and Susan A., age 13 years.

On page 86, Simmons' 1860 Trigg County Census #1266, he is listed as "J.B." Howard, age 25 years and living with his wife "M." (Mary) Howard, age 23 years, and three daughters: "L." (Louisa), age 4 years; "A." (Alabama), age 2 years; and "N." (Nancy), age one month.

LEROY (LEE) S. HUDDLESTON, Private, born 11 May 1839 in Brooshaw County, NC, died 29 Jan 1927, age 97 years. He enlisted in September 1861 and served with Co. D, 50th Tennessee Regt. Inf. (CSA).

He was captured first at the surrender of Fort Donelson, sent to prison, exchanged and captured again at Kennesaw Mountain, GA. He was sent to Camp Douglas, IL both times for imprisonment.

Private Huddleston did not take the Oath of Allegiance, but was mustered into Federal service at the close of the war and sent to Dakota Territory to fight Indians.

He resided in Canton, Trigg County from 1866 until the end of his life.

Private Huddleston applied for his Confederate pension on 14 Aug 1912.

Leroy S. Huddleston married three times: (1) Temperance Brown, age 22, born in Stewart County, TN on 30 Jun 1867, in Trigg County; (2) Mrs. Courtney Strawbridge on 24 Oct 1875, in Trigg County; and (3) Melinda Jane __ ca. 1883.

He is buried in the McIntosh Cemetery in Trigg County, KY, with his third wife Melinda Jane Huddleston (b. 1865, d. 1933).

His son Jesse Lee Huddleston (b. 16 Jun 1868, d. 26 Jan 1848) is buried in the Milam. Cemetery with his wife Lizzie Milam Huddleston (b. 12 Jul 1879, d. 25 Aug 1911).

On page 157, 1870 Simmons' Trigg County Census #1864 (He is listed as Lee S. Huddleston, a farmer age 32 years, living with wife Temperance (Brown) Huddleston age 26 years, and three children: Benjamin F., age 4 years; Jesse L., age 2 years; and Henrietta C., age 6 months.

On page 151, Jones' 1900 Trigg County Census #213-216, he is listed as "Lee S." Huddleston, a farmer (born in North Carolina), age 61 years, living with his wife Melinda Jane Huddleston (married 17 years), born in Tennessee, age 37 years, and five children: Jesse L. (son), age 28 years; Henrietta C., age 26 years; Samuel J., age 15 years; Mary J., age 7 years; and Alvin G., age 1 year. Melinda has had seven children, only three of whom were still living when this census was taken.

HAMPTON "HAM" MASON HUGHES, Corporal CSA, born in Graves County, KY on 4 Mar 1842, one of six children, to Joseph and Elizabeth (Mason) Hughes. At age 18, he  moved to Trigg County to join his brother, Thompson Zem Hughes, where the Southern cause was quickly gaining support. The two Hughes brothers joined the Confederate Infantry Company being formed by Lt. John Cunningham. On 13 Sep 1861, they took the Oath of Enlistment at Camp Burnett, TN. Lt. Cunningham's company officially became Co. G, 4th Kentucky Inf. Regt. (CSA). In October 1861, the 4th Inf. Regt., along with eight other CSA KY Regiments departed Camp Burnett to become the nucleus of the 1st Kentucky Brigade, CSA (later to be known as the famous" Orphan Brigade).

Ham fought in the following major battles or campaigns: Shiloh, Vicksburg, Baton Rouge, Murfreesboro/Stones River Battle, Jackson, MS, Chickamauga and Missionary Ridge, Atlanta Campaign (7 May-2 Sep 1864), where Ham was wounded on 22 Jul 1864. Next it was on to Utoy Creek, then to Jonesboro, the last Battle of the Atlanta Campaign.

The Orphans were converted to Mounted Infantry and ordered to Griffin and Barnesville, GA. From the Fall of 1864 through late Dec, the Mounted Infantry attempted to impede Sherman's "March to the Sea" Campaign through Georgia, on to the South Carolina Campaign into North Carolina before the war ended.

The 4th Kentucky Inf. Regt., and Cpl. Hampton "Ham" Hughes continued "the Fight for the Confederacy" for nearly three weeks after Gen. Robert E. Lee surrendered at Appomattox. On 29 Apr 1865, an order was received, announcing the Confederacy's surrender, and asking him "to recall these old Veterans from their familiar work, and lead them to Washington, GA, to part with their friends (as they called their trusty Enfield rifles) for the last time."

Ham Hughes was paroled on 7 May 1865 at Washington, GA. Returning to Trigg County, Ham Hughes settled west of Cadiz and took up farming as his vocation. Six years after the war, he married Mary Della Guier, 20 years old and the daughter of Richard Tart Guier and Elizabeth Ann Cunningham on 12 Sep 1871. Nine children were born: Joseph Richard (Joe), Luther Lee (Luke), Elizabeth Ellen (Bessie), Mason Ham, George Err, Ida Martin, Verna Della, Lela Margaret and John Harvey.

Ham Hughes died at age 66 on 16 Jan 1909. Mary Della Guier died 16 Apr 1929. Both are buried in the Lawrence Cemetery. *Compiled and written by Kim Fortner, great-great-granddaughter; John R Edwards, Col USAF Ret, great-grandson; and Paul Evans Fourshee, great-grandson.*

ZEM HUGHES, lst Sergeant, born ca. 1840 in Kentucky in Graves County, KY. He enlisted 14 Sep 1861 at Camp Burnett, TN and served with Co. G, 4th Kentucky Regt. Inf. (CSA). According to Kentucky State Archives, the Company Roster from 30 Nov to 31 Dec 1861, he was listed as "sick on furlough."

Pvt. Hughes was promoted to lst sergeant 17 Sep 1861. He was taken prisoner at Kennesaw Mountain, GA, 20 Jun 1864, arrived in Nashville, TN 25 Jun 1864, in Louisville, KY 27 Jun 1864 and arrived in Camp Morton, IN on 30 Jun 1864. lst Sgt. Hughes was released from Camp Morton, IN on 3 Feb 1865.

Zem Hughes, age 25 years of Graves County, married Helen Cunningham, age 19 years of Trigg County, KY, on 17 Nov 1865. He married second, Sue Pitts on 19 Jul 1881 in Trigg County.

On page 61, Simmons' 1870 Trigg County Census #702, he is listed as age 29 years and living with his wife Helen M. (Cunningham) Hughes, age 23 years and one child, Guthrie age 1 year.

On page 178, Neel's Statistical Handbook of Trigg County, 1880 Trigg County Census, toward top of page, Sue Pitts is listed as "does housework" age 19 years (born in Georgia) and boarding with the town jailer, J.G. Shoemaker and his family.

ABSALOM J. HUMPHRIES, born 24 Aug 1831 in Kentucky, died 26 Apr 1899. His father was John Humphries (b. 15 Mar 1793 in Georgia, d. 13 Jul 1869) and his mother was Elizabeth (Husk) Humphries (b. 21 Dec 1797 in Hopkinsville, KY, d. 4 Jun 1852 in Trigg County, KY). John and Elizabeth Humphries are buried in the Humphries Cemetery in Trigg County.

There was an Absalom W. Humphries (b. ca. 1838), son of Charles Humphries and Mary (Wimberly) Humphries, living in Trigg County during this era. Both Charles and Mary Humphries were born in Kentucky. At this same time there was an Absalom J. Humphries (b. ca. 1831), son of John and Elizabeth Humphries, living in Trigg County. John Humphries was born in Georgia and Elizabeth Humphries was born in Kentucky. Absalom J. may have been a cousin or an uncle of Absalom W., Calhoun and of John L. Humphries.

Absalom J. Humphries was a WSI veteran. There is no record of Absalom W. Humphries being a veteran.

A.J. Humphries first married Susanarh (Susan) __ Humphries ca. 1854. There is no record of this marriage in Trigg County records. At age 38 years he married (Lou) Saraina Malvina Tompkins, age 18 years of Trigg County, on 3 Aug 1869.

He is buried near his first wife Susanarh Humphries (b. 19 Apr 1836, d. 10 Mar 1869) in the Humphries Cemetery in Trigg County. Also buried close by is his second wife Lou Saraina Malvena Tompkins Humphries (b. 1851, d. 1932).

In Simmons' 1850 Trigg County Census #147, he is listed as Absalom J. Humphries, a farmer age 18 years and living with his father John Humphries, a farmer (born in Georgia), age 57 years; his mother Elizabeth, age 53 years (born in Kentucky) and one brother Thomas J., a farmer age 17 years.

On page 45, Simmons' 1860 Trigg County Census #663, he is listed as A.J. Humphries, age 29 years, living with his wife Susan, age 20 years and two children: John H., age 5 years and Frances F. (female), age 3 years.

On page 35 Simmons' 1870 Trigg County Census #389 he is listed as Abner J. Humphries, a farmer, age 38 years living with his wife Lorana J. (Saraina) (Tompkins), age 18 years and a John Humphries, age 14 years. Charles McCaughan, a tinner, age 50, is living with the family in this census.

CALHOUN HUMPHRIES, Private, born ca. 1842 in Kentucky. He enlisted 26 Sep 1861 at Camp Reeves, TN and served with Co. G, 8th Kentucky Regt. Inf. (CSA). He was severely wounded at Fort Donelson on 15 Feb 1862 and made his way home to Trigg County. The Confederate Army did not hear from him again. He was a brother of Pvt. John L. Humphries.

His father Charles Humphries and his mother Mary Wimberly were married on 13 May 1835, in Trigg County. Charles (b. 4 Jul 1805, d. 21 Jun 1878) and Mary (b. 8 Jun 1811, d. 20 Feb 1850) are buried in the Humphries Cemetery in Trigg County.

Charles Humphries married second, Frances Ann (Garnett) (Carloss), widow of William Carloss Jr., on 11 Sep 1854. Frances Ann was first married to William Carloss Jr. on 10 Oct 1839 in Trigg County.

John Calhoun Humphries (listed as J.C. Humphries) married Mattie Hardy on 17 May 1874 in Trigg County. Their son, John Locke Humphries (b. 1875, d. 1952) is buried in the East End Cemetery.

On page 17, Simmons' 1850 Trigg County Census #312, he is listed as age 8 years, living with his father Charles Humphries age 44 years and seven siblings: Absalom W., age 12 years; John L., age 11 years; Andrew J., age 9 years; Charles, age 6 years; Richard, age 2 years; Mary C., age 4 years; and Sally A., age 6 months. Calhoun's mother Mary had just died the previous February 20, 1850.

On page 55, Simmons' 1860 Trigg County Census #807, Calhoun is listed as age 18 years and living with his father Charles Humphries, age 55; his stepmother Francis A., age 38 years; and five siblings: A.W., age 22 years; John L., age 20; Andrew J., age 19 years; Charles, age 17 years; and Richard J., age 13 years. Susan Carloss, age 8 years, is living with the family in this census. Susan is the daughter of Frances Ann by her first husband. The older Carloss children are living with either their Garnett grandparents or Garnett aunts and uncles.

JOHN L. HUMPHRIES, born ca. 1839 in Kentucky. He enlisted 25 Jan 1863, in Charlotte, TN and served with Co. B, Woodward's 2nd/15th Kentucky Cav. Regt. (CSA).

He was a brother of John Calhoun Humphries. Their parents, Charles Humphries and Mary (Wimberly) married on 13 May 1835, in Trigg County. Charles Humphries (b. 4 Jul 1805, d. 21 Jun 1878) is buried with his wife Mary Wimberly Humphries (b. 8 Jun 1811, d. 20 Feb 1850) in the Humphries Cemetery.

On page 17, Simmons' 1850 Trigg County Census #312, he is listed as John L. Humphries, age 11 years and living with his father Charles Humphries, age 44 years, and seven siblings: Absalom W., age 12 years; Andrew J., age 11 years; Calhoun, age 8 years; Charles, age 6 years; Richard, age 2 years; Mary C., age 4 years; and Sally A., age 6 months. John L.'s mother Mary had just died the previous 20 Feb 1850.

On page 55, Simmons' 1860 Trigg County Census #807, he is listed as John L. Humphries, age 20 years, living with his father Charles Humphries, age 55 years; his stepmother Frances Ann (Garnett) (Carloss) Humphries, age 38 years, and five siblings: "A.W" (Absalom W.), age 22 years; Andrew J., age 19 years; Calhoun, age 18 years; Charles, age 17 years; and Richard J., age 13 years. Susan Carloss (Frances' daughter by William Carloss Jr.), age 8 years is living with this family in this census.

RUFUS B. HUTTS, Private, born ca. 1839 in Kentucky, died 1861. He served with Co. D, 14th Regt. Tennessee Inf. (CSA). He was actually the first soldier from Trigg County killed in the war, but he served in a Tennessee Regiment.

His parents, Cornelius N. Hutts (b. ca. 1811 in Virginia, d. 1850s) and his mother Nancy Burnett (born probably in Virginia, died ca. 1844), married 30 Aug 1830 in Trigg County, KY.

His father married second, Sally (Sarah) Wilson (b. ca. 1818 in one of the Carolinas) on 23 Mar 1846 in Trigg County, KY. After the death of their father, the Hutts children were farmed out to whomever would take them in.

Cornelius N. Hutts and Nancy Burnett were married on 30 Aug 1830 in Trigg County, KY. His father C.N. Hutts married second, Sally (Sarah) Wilson (b. ca. 1818 in South or North Carolina) on 23 Mar 1846, in Trigg County, KY.

On page 65 Simmons' 1860 Trigg County Census #967, he is listed as "R.B." Hutts, age 21 years, living with his sister Susan M., age 18 years; brother-in-law William B. Sholar, age 40 years; his sister Mary E., age 28 years; a niece Gemima, age 8 years; nephew Cornelius, age 7 years; nephew Drewery, age 5 years.

On page 20, Simmons' 1870 Trigg County Census #225, Rufus Hutts' mother Sarah is listed as a cook, age 60 years, living with the John Wilson (possibly her brother), age 68 and Margaret A. Wilson, age 44 years, and their family in this census.

FRANCIS P. INGRAM, Private, born ca. 1845 in Kentucky. He enlisted 14 Sep 1861 at Camp Burnett, TN and served with Co. G, 4th Kentucky Regt. Inf. (CSA). According to Kentucky State Archives, he was left in the hospital in Nashville, TN, when the Confederates evacuated that city in the spring of 1862. This is according to the 1 Jan-1 May 1862 Roster. He was dropped from the rolls on 1 Sep 1862.

There were two "F." Ingrams who lived in Trigg County during this period. One was Franklin Ingram, who was usually listed in the census records as a merchant born ca. 1813 in Tennessee. The other "F." Ingram was Francis P. Ingram of Co. G of the 8th Kentucky (CSA), born ca. 1845 in Kentucky, always listed as a farmer and was married to Permelia Elizabeth (Bettie) Ingram.

His father was possibly Thomas N. Ingram (b. ca. 1815 in Tennessee, d ??) and his mother was possibly Nancy J. (martin) Ingram (b. ca. 1819 in Kentucky, d. ??).

Willis R. Thomas states that the only living heir to F.P. Ingram is his son Harlan T. Thomas as his son Lloyd Ray (b. 26 Jul 1889, d. 28 Dec 1904) and daughter Mary Jane (Ingram) Thomas (died intestate on 14 Apr 1906), leaving Harlan as his only surviving heir and W.R. Thomas as the surviving husband.

On page 57, Simmons' 1850 Trigg County Census #1049, he is listed as Francis P., age 5 years, living with his father Thomas N. Ingram, age 35 years; his mother Nancy J. (Martin) Ingram, age 31 years, and four siblings: James F., age 11; Sarah E., age 9; Martha W., age 7; and Eudora P., age 1 years.

On page 211, Neel's Statistical Handbook of Trigg County, 1880 Trigg County Census, toward bottom of page, he is listed as Francis Ingram, a farmer, age 35 years, living with his wife, Parmelia E. Ingram, age 26 years, and a sister Catherine, age 15 years. Also living with the family are Ingram orphans: Willie, age 18 years; Nancy J., age 16; Fannie V., age 14; Joan, age 12 years; George, age 10 years; and Samuel, age 7.

WILLIAM H. JACKSON, Private, born ca. 1849 in Arkansas. He enlisted 24 Oct 1861 at Camp Alcorn in Hopkinsville, KY and served with Co. B, 8th Kentucky Regt. Inf. (CSA). The Kentucky Adjutant's Report states that he was wounded at Jackson, MS on 11 Jul 1863 and sent to the hospital. He was then placed on detached service after 22 Sep 1863.

William H. Jackson may have been a nephew of William Wilson Jackson. There is no information on whom William H. Jackson's parents were, but it is possible both were born in North Carolina. His guardians, William Wilson Jackson and Mary Jane Foutch married on 3 Jul 1853 in Trigg County. Their children were: Thomas Levi Jackson (b. ca. 1854, d. 28 Oct 1906), buried in the Stewart Cemetery with his wife Alice Jackson (no dates) and Peter Jackson (b. 13 Feb 1872, d. 30 Mar 1939), who is buried with his wife Katherine (Thomas) Jackson (b. 20 Jun 1871, d. 1 Oct 1951) in the Starkie Thomas Cemetery.

On page 38, Simmons' 1860 Trigg County Census #559, William H. Jackson is listed as age 10 years, born in Arkansas and living with his guardians William Wilson Jackson, age 37 years, and (Mary) Jane (Foutch) Jackson, age 28 years. Other children living with the family are (Thomas) Levi Jackson, age 6 years, and John J. Jackson, age 1 year. (William H. Jackson was listed at the end of the list of children which leads us to believe he was not a child of William Wilson Jackson).

WILLIAM WILSON JACKSON, Private, born ca. 1827 in North Carolina. William Wilson Jackson may have been an uncle of William H. Jackson. He enlisted 14 Sep 1861 at Camp Burnett, TN and served with Co. G, 4th Kentucky Regt. Inf. (CSA). According to Kentucky State Archives, Private William Wilson Jackson was left in the hospital when the Confederates evacuated Nashville, TN, in February 1862. He was dropped from Confederate rolls 1 Sep 1862.

William Wilson married Mary Jane Foutch on 3 Jul 1853 in Trigg County, KY. Their children: Sallie F. married Albun A. Rutland on 19 Jan 1879; Bettie M. married Jasper F. Guier on 18 Oct 1883; John J. married (1st) Norah Harris on 14 Sep 1881 and (2nd) Annie Cunningham on 16 Oct 1884; David married Lizzie Jefferson on 24 Dec 1892; Thomas Levi married Alice Jackson; and Peter married Katherine Thomas.

On page 38, Simmons 1860 Trigg County Census #559, he is listed as age 37 years, living with wife Jane (Foutch), age 28 years, and two children: Levi, age 6 years, and John J., age 1 year. William H. Jackson, age 10 years, is also living with the family in this census, but at the very end of the listing of the children.

Mary Jane (Foutch) Jackson (b. ca. 1832 in Tennessee, d. 26 Sep 1906) is buried in the Mount Pleasant, Blue Springs Cemetery.

RICHARD E. JAMES, Private, born ca. 1824 in Tennessee, died ??. He enlisted 14 Sep 1861 at Camp Burnett, TN and served with Co. G, 4th Kentucky Regt. Inf. (CSA). Richard E. failed to muster with the local militia at Indian Springs on 6 Jul 1861.

According to Kentucky State Archives, R.E. James was listed on the November-December 1861 rolls as "Absent in Trigg or Todd Counties without leave. He left on a 4-day furlough and was sick when he left."

According to the Kentucky Adjutant General's Report, Richard E. James was discharged for disability on 25 Jun 1862.

Also, according to Kentucky State Archives, he was captured by Federal authorities in Trigg County on 14 Sep 1863. He enlisted in the US Army and was mustered into the 5th Kentucky Battery.

He is listed in the Cadiz Poll Books dated August 1856, 5 Aug 1867 and 3 Nov 1868.

On page 90, Simmons 1870 Trigg County Census #90, he is listed as age 46 years, living with his wife Margaret, age 33 years, and six children: Isabella, age 17 years; Elizabeth, age 14 years; William, age 11 years; Quintilla, age 9 years; Morgan, age 6 years; and Felix, age 3 years. This is the last Trigg County record we have of this family.

SAMUEL A. JEFFERSON, born ca. 1824 in Tennessee. He enlisted at Camp Burnett on 14 Sep 1861 and served with Co. G, 4th Kentucky Regt. Inf. (CSA). According to the Kentucky Adjutant's Report, he was captured at Jonesboro, GA, on 1 Sep 1864.

There is no information on whom his parents actually were. Albert G. Jefferson may have been Samuel's brother or uncle.

His guardians were Albert G. Jefferson (b. ca. 1810 in Tennessee, d. ??) and Elizabeth Jefferson (b. ca. 1816 in Tennessee, d. ??).

Samuel A. Jefferson is listed in the Canton Precinct Poll book for the August election of 1856 and is listed in the Cadiz Poll Book dated 1 Aug 1859.

On page 176, Vol. I, Kentucky Adjutant General's Report (CSA), Samuel's date of capture at Jonesboro, GA, on 1 Sep 1864, is the last record we have found of this soldier.

On page 54, Simmons' 1850 Trigg County Census #996, he is listed as age 26 years, living with an Albert G. Jefferson, age 40 years, born in Tennessee, Elizabeth Jefferson, age 34 years, and their six children: Peterfield, age 18 years; John J., age 12 years; Virginia E., age 6 years; Sarah C., age 8 years; and Martha M., age 3 years.

Samuel A. Jefferson is not found in Simmons' 1860 Trigg County Census.

HENRY JOHNSON, served with Co. B, 13th US Colored Artillery (Heavy). Both Neel and Maupin indicate that he is a WSI veteran.

He is buried in the Cadiz Negro Cemetery, but there is no stone to his grave.

On page 138, Simmons' 1870 Trigg County Census #1643, Henry Johnson is listed as a black woodchopper, age 25 years, and living with the Joseph Headspeth, age 25 years, and Julie Headspeth, age 20 years, family in this census.

LEROY JOHNSON, born 15 Oct 1840 in Kentucky, died 27 Apr 1923. He enrolled 7 Aug 1863, mustered in 26 Oct 1863 at Princeton, KY and mustered out 19 Dec 1864 at Bowling Green, KY. He served with Co. F, 48th Kentucky Regiment Mounted Infantry (USA).

The 1900 Census has his birthdate listed as being in October 1838.

His mother may have been Martha Johnson (b. ca. 1822 in Virginia, d. ??)

L.R. Johnson, age 24 years of Trigg County, married Nancy C. Skinner, age 17 years also of Trigg County, on 1 Jan 1868. It was the first marriage for both bride and groom.

Nancy C.'s parents, Edwin Skinner and Elizabeth Pitts, married on 10 Feb 1841 in Trigg County, KY. Edwin (b. ca. 1807 in Kentucky, d. ??) and Elizabeth (b. ca. 1808 in Tennessee, d. ??).

Leroy's daughters: Jennie Lee married Powell H. Hester and Lula A. married Thomas N. Hester on 19 Dec 1899 in Trigg County, KY.

Leroy is buried in the Skinner Cemetery with his wife Nancy C. Skinner Johnson (b. 20 Jun 1850 in Kentucky, d. 31 Oct 1931). They had nine children.

On page 154, Simmons' 1880 Trigg County Census #1835, Leroy is listed as age 27 years, living with his wife Nancy, age 20 years, and one son Charles, age 1 year.

On page 176, Blue & Sellers' Trigg County Census #2422, Leroy is listed as a farmer, age 78 years, living with his wife Nancy, age 67 years; and three children: Frank, a widower, age 46 years; Truman, single, age 38 years; and Minnie, single, age 27 years. Also living with him are two grandchildren: Ray Johnson, age 13 years, and Maurine Johnson, age 17 years.

NATHANIEL "NATHAN" MARION JOINER, Private, born ca. 1844 in Kentucky. He enrolled 25 Aug 1863, mustered in 26 Oct 1863 at Princeton, KY and mustered out 19 Dec 1864 at Bowling Green, KY. He served with Co. F, 48th Kentucky Regiment Mounted Infantry (USA).

His father was Nathan Joiner (b. ca. 1818 in Kentucky, d. ??) and his mother was Nancy Joiner (b. ca. 1822 in Kentucky, d. ??).

On page 200, Neel's Statistical Handbook of Trigg County, 1880 Trigg County Census, middle of page, he is listed as Nathan Joiner, a farmer age 36 years, living with his wife Malissa, age 30 years, and five children: Cassius, age 11 years; Adelia, age 9 years; Nancy, age 8 years; Mary, age 6 years; and Richard, age 10 months.

On page 223, Neel's Statistical Handbook of Trigg County, 1880 Trigg County Census, middle of page, his father is listed as Nathan Joiner, a farmer age 62 years, living with his wife Nancy, age 58 years, and three children: Thomas, age 25 years; Bettie E., age 20 years; and Joseph N., age 27 years.

JOHN J. JONES, Private, born 15 Dec 1839 in Kentucky, died 25 Dec 1862. He enlisted 26 Sep 1861 at Camp Reeves, TN and served with Co. G, 8th Kentucky Regt. Inf. (CSA).

According to the Kentucky Adjutant's Report, Pvt. Jones was severely wounded at Fort Donelson on 15 Feb 1862 and died at his home in Trigg County, KY.

His father Mark Jones (b. 20 Sep 1818 in Tennessee, d. 30 Jul 1896) and mother Elizabeth (P'Pool) Jones (b. 5 Jan 1814 in Virginia, 26 Dec 1875) were married ca. 1838, but there is no record of their marriage in Trigg County. Mark Jones married second, Mrs. Susan S. Wallis, widow of William R. Wallis, on 17 Dec 1876 in Trigg County.

On page 52, Simmons' 1860 Trigg County Census #764, he is listed as age 20 years and living with his father Mark Jones, age 42 years; his mother Elizabeth, age 46 years; and five siblings: Charles C., age 17 years; Addison W., age 15 years; Elizabeth, age 10 years; Martha, age 8 years; and Mark S., age 2 years.

John J. Jones is buried in Trigg County, KY, in the Mark Jones Cemetery with his parents, Mark and Elizabeth (P'Pool) Jones.

THOMAS BENTON JONES, Private, born 6 Aug 1840 in Kentucky, died 27 Apr 1926. He served with Co. F, 50th Tennessee Regt. Inf. (CSA).

His parents Solomon Jones (b. 15 Dec 1810, d. 1845) and Clarissa (Cohoon) (Jones) Futrell (b. ca. 1822, d. ??) married on 2 Nov 1835 in Trigg County. Clarissa later married Joel C. Futrell in Trigg County on 17 May 1847.

Thomas Benton Jones married (1st) Susan Frances Allen on 22 Nov 1859; (2nd) Rhoda (Mayes) ca. 1869; (3rd) Ada Foutch on 25 Aug 1887 in Trigg County.

Page 58, Simmons' 1850 Trigg County Census #1072-543, Thomas Benton Jones is listed as Thomas B. Futrell, age 9 years, living with his mother Clarissa (Cohoon) (Jones) Futrell, age 38 years; his stepfather Joel C. Futrell a farmer age 25 years; three siblings: Malachia Jones, age 11 years; David Jones, age 7 years; Amanda Jones, age 5 years; and a half-sister Mary Futrell, age 2 years.

Page 118, Simmons' 1870 Trigg County Census #1384, he is listed as age 26 years and living with his wife Rhoda (Mayes) Jones (born in Tennessee), age 23 years and four children: Elizabeth, age 5 years; Stape (Stapleton), age 4 years; Rufus, age 3 years; and Rebecca, 7 months.

Page 105, Jones' 1900 Trigg County Census #342-342, he is listed as "Thomas B.," age 59 years living with his wife Ada (Foutch) Jones (married 12 years), age 42 years, and seven children: Henry, age 16 years; Beulah, age 16 years; Beuk (?) (daughter), age 16 years; Francis H. (son), age 9 years; Lillie, age 8 years; Flossie E., age 6 years; and Burnett, age 2 years. Sullivan Jones, age 12 years, is listed as a stepson. Thomas is listed as a farmer. Ada (Foutch) Jones is his third wife.

Thomas Benton Jones is buried in the Pleasant Hill Church Cemetery in Trigg County.

WILLIAM W. JONES, Private, born ca. 1827 in Kentucky. He enrolled 2 Feb 1865, mustered in 1 Mar 1865 at Louisville, KY and mustered out 20 Sep 1865, at Louisville, KY. He served with Co. D, 17th Kentucky Regt. Cav. (USA).

On page 32, Simmons' 1860 Trigg County Census #471, W.W. Jones is listed as age 33 years and living with his wife C.A. Jones, age 30 years and four children: "C.E." (Charles E.) age 12 years; "L.C." (Levi C.), age 9 years; "E.J." (Elizabeth J.), age 6 years; and "W.W." (William W.), age 4 years.

On page 226, Simmons' 1870 Trigg County Census #2676, Clarissa A. Jones is listed as age 36 years (born in Kentucky), living with four children: Levi C., age 17 years; Elizabeth, age 14 years; William W., age 12 years; and Charles E. age 22 years.

William W. Jones is buried in the Cunningham or Trigg Furnace Cemetery with his wife Matilda Caroline Jones (b. 1847, d. 1922).

ALEXANDER JOYCE, Sergeant, born 2 Jul 1837 in Tennessee (on tombstone), died 25 Feb 1917. He enrolled 14 Aug 1862, mustered in 13 Sep 1862, at Henderson, KY and mustered out 23 Sep 1863, at Russellville, KY. He served with Co. L, 8th Kentucky Regt. Cav. (USA).

Enrolled a second time on 4 Aug 1864, mustered in 4 Aug 1864 at Paducah, KY and mustered out 12 Feb 1865 at Paducah, KY. He served with Co. B, First Regiment Capital Guards, Paducah, KY.

According to Jones' 1900 Trigg County Census, his birthdate was in July 1836. Alexander Joyce was a brother of J.P. Joyce and Martin Joyce.

Page 61, Simmons' 1850 Trigg County Census #1118, he is listed as Alexander Joyce, age 12 years, living with his father Thomas Joyce, age 44 years; his mother Elizabeth Joyce, age 42 years; and five siblings: James, age 18 years; Mark L., age 16 years; Martin, age 14 years; Henry, age 10 years; and Nancy, age 8 years.

Page 5, Simmons' 1860 Trigg County Census #66, he is listed as age 22 years and living with his wife Mary Jane (Lowery) Joyce, age 20 years, no children.

He married Mary Jane Lowery on 17 Feb 1859 in Trigg County, KY.

He is buried in the Jenny Ridge Cemetery with his wife Mary Jane (Lowery) Joyce (b. 20 Jun 1839, d. 15 Mar 1904).

MARTIN VAN BUREN JOYCE, Private US Army, was the son of Thomas Patrick Joyce and Elizabeth Colson Joyce. He was born in Grainger County, TN, 12 Sep 1835 and came to Trigg County in the mid-1840s with his parents. They settled in the Golden Pond area of the Land Between the Rivers.

At age 27 he was mustered into service with Co. L, 8th Regt. Kentucky Cav., US Army for a period of one year. The whole regiment numbered 1,248 men, was recruited and organized within the space of three weeks from the time authority was issued for same, and was composed of the very best material in the state. The line officers were competent and gallant soldiers, and, from the day of organization their respective commands were well disciplined and under perfect control.

Martin Van Buren Joyce mustered out with the regiment on 23 Sep 1862 at Russellville, KY. At which time he returned home to Golden Pond, KY, married in December 1863 and reared a family of 14 children: Charles T., Nancy Jane, Harriet Heneritta, Alexander Martin, William Robert, James Lacy, John Allen, Sarah Ann Pricilla, Mary Jane, George Patrick, Tandy Joyce, Cora Catherine, Carrie Washington, and Bailey Ulysses.

Martin Van Buren Joyce died on 31 Dec 1904 and is buried in Jenny Ridge Cemetery in LBL along with his wife Sarah Catherine Lowery Joyce and several of his children and other family members.

NELSON JOYCE, born ca. 1841 in Tennessee. Enrolled 8 Aug 1862, mustered in 6 Oct 1862 at Paducah, KY, mustered out 6 Oct 1863 at Paducah, KY and served with Co. D, 15th Kentucky Regiment Cavalry

According to Simmons' 1850 Trigg County Census all of his siblings were born in Tennessee except for Martha and Mary who were born in Kentucky.

His father John Joyce and mother Nancy (Mayes) Joyce (b. ca. 1820 in Tennessee) were married in Grainger County, TN on 27 Dec 1836. Nancy married William Miller Sr. on 11 Aug 1853 in Trigg County. William Miller Sr., however, seems to have died before the 1860 Trigg County Census.

Nelson Joyce, age 24 years of Grainger County, TN, married Mary Cross, age 17 years of Trigg County, on 7 Jun 1865.

On page 61, Simmons' 1850 Trigg County Census #1120-591, he is listed as Nelson Joyce, age 9 years, living with his mother Nancy Joyce, age 30 years and five siblings: Wilson, age 12 years; Mahala, age 7 years; Elizabeth, age 6 years; Martha, age 2 years; and Mary, age 5 months.

On page 121, Simmons' 1870 Trigg County Census #1428, he is listed as Nelson Joyce, age 30 years, living with his wife Mary, age 21, and two daughters: Penny, age 4 years, and Julia, 11 months.

Nelson Joyce is buried in the Turkey Creek Cemetery in Trigg County, Kentucky, but has no stone to his grave.

WILLIAM JOYCE, Private, born ca. 1845 in Tennessee, died 2 Jan 1864 in Trigg County KY. He enrolled 10 Sep 1863, mustered in 26 Oct 1863 in Princeton, KY and served with Co. F, 48th Kentucky Regt. Mounted Inf. (USA)

His father was James Joyce (b. ca. 1802 in North Carolina) and his mother was Nancy Joyce (b. ca. 1814 in Tennessee).

On page 60, Simmons' 1850 Trigg County Census #1106, William Joyce is listed as age 5 years and living with his father James Joyce, age 48 years; his mother Nancy Joyce, age 36 years; and five siblings: Orlena, age 21 years; Elizabeth, age 18 years; John H., age 16 years; Susannah, age 12 years; and Robert, age 10 years.

On page 230, Neel's Statistical Handbook of Trigg County, 1880 Trigg County Census, middle of page, his brother John H. Joyce is listed as a farmer, age 46 years, living with his wife Elizabeth A. Joyce, age 46 years (born in Kentucky) and eight children: Ellen, age 24 years; Samuel, age 22 years; Mary, age 20 years; Jane, age 18 years; William, age 16 years; Nack (Mack), age 14 years; Luisa, age 12 years; and July Dean, age 5 years.

JOHN EDWARD KELLY, 2nd Sergeant, born 1839 (according to his tombstone) in Kentucky, died 1904. Enlisted 25 Oct 1861 at Camp Alcorn in Hopkinsville, KY and served with Co. B, 8th KY Regt. Inf. (CSA). According to the Kentucky Adjutant's Report, he was on parole since 17 Jul 1863.

His parents John W. Kelly (b. 11 Jun 1796 in Virginia, d. August 1840) and Ann T. Kelly (b. 13 Oct 1810 in Virginia, d. 3 Dec 1874 are buried in the Kelly Cemetery in Trigg County.

John Edward was married to Elizabeth (Baker) Kelly (b. 1842 in Kentucky, d. 1876). They are both buried in the Kelly Cemetery in Trigg County, KY.

On page 66, Simmons' 1870 Trigg County Census #765, he is listed as John E. Kelly, a lawyer age 30 years and living with his wife Sarah E., age 27 years, and four children: Lela M., age 9 years; Edward A., age 7 years; Tecia, age 4 years; and Benjamin B. (born in September) age nine months.

JAMES HENRY KNIGHT, Private, born ca. 1842 in Kentucky. Enrolled 7 Aug 1863, mustered in 26 Oct 1863 at Princeton, KY, transferred to 26th Kentucky Regt. Inf. on 11 Aug 1864 and served with Co. F, 48th Kentucky Regt. Mounted Inf. (USA).

According to the 1880 Census, his father was born in Kentucky and his mother was born in Tennessee.

The James Knight in the 1900 Census lists both parents as being born in Tennessee. His father was Richard Knight (b. ca. 1815 in North Carolina) and his mother was Martha (Woodward) Knight (b. ca. 1824 in Tennessee).

James H. Knight married Martha A. Dunn on 16 Mar 1863 in Trigg County.

On page 42, Simmons' 1850 Trigg County Census #778, he is listed as age 8 years, living with his father Richard Knight, age 35; his mother Martha Woodward Knight, age 26; and four siblings: William K., age 11 years; George Washington, age 6 years; Mary A., age 5 years; and Jessey L. (male), age 1 year.

On page 204, Neel's Statistical Handbook of Trigg County, 1880 Trigg County Census, middle of page, he is listed as "Henry" Knight, a farmer, age 35 years, living with his wife Martha A. (Dunn) Knight, age 32 years; four children: Gustie (daughter), age 12 years; Sidney, age 9 years; Synthie, age 6 years; and Richard, age 5 years. A niece Mary Knight, age 17 years, is also living with the family.

JOHN KNIGHT, Private, born ca. 1825. Enrolled 7 Aug 1863, mustered in 26 Oct 1863 at Princeton, KY and mustered out 19 Dec 1864 at Bowling Green, KY. He served with Co. F, 48th Kentucky Regt. Mounted Inf. (USA).

On page 161, Simmons' 1870 Trigg County Census #1902, he is listed as John Knight, age 35 years, living with his wife Nancy Knight, age 32 years, and six children: John R., age 15 years; William A., age 12 years; Joseph M., age 8 years; Emily, age 5 years; Quint, age 3 years; and Levi, age 3 months.

His son John R. Knight (b. 1854, d. 1925) married Louella G. Smith (b. 1856, d. 1935). Both are buried in the Nunn Cemetery on Crockett Creek in Trigg County.

JOHN H. LADD, Private, born ca. 1843 in Kentucky, died 1 Mar 1862 at Camp Morton, IN. He enlisted 24 Oct 1861 at Camp Alcorn in Hopkinsville, KY and served with Co. B, 8th Kentucky Regt. Inf. (CSA). Private Ladd died of pneumonia as a prisoner of war at Camp Morton, IN, 1 Mar 1862.

On page 11, Simmons' 1850 Trigg County Census #210 (possible), he is listed as John H. Ladd, age 7 years and living with his father Samuel C. Ladd, age 31 years; his mother Sarah A. (Ladd) Ladd, age 26 years, and four siblings: William A., age 9 years; Susan E., age 6 years; Dock S., age 4 years; and Joseph P., age 1 year.

SAMUEL C. LADD, Private, born ca. 1819 in Kentucky. Enlisted 24 Oct 1861 at Camp Alcorn in Hopkinsville, KY and served with Co. B, 8th Kentucky Regt. Inf. (CSA). His son John H. Ladd also served in Co. B of the 8th Kentucky Regt. Inf. (CSA).

Kentucky Adjutant General's Report states that he deserted and took the oath of allegiance to US on 20 Aug 1862.

Samuel C. Ladd married Sarah A. Ladd on 28 Oct 1837. On page 11, Simmons' 1850 Trigg County Census #210 a Samuel C. Ladd is listed as a laborer, age 31 years and living with his wife Sarah A., age 26 years, and five children: John H., age 7 years; William A., age 9 years; Susan E., age 6 years; Dock S., age 4 years; and Joseph P., age 1 year.

THOMAS J. LADD, born ca. 1834 in Kentucky. He served with Co. B, lst Kentucky (Helm's) Cav. Regt. CSA.

His father was John C. Ladd Jr. (b. 1793 in South Carolina, d. 1863) and his mother was Mary J. (Jones) Ladd (b. 1787 in South Carolina, d. 10 Dec 1880). They are both buried in the Ladd Cemetery.

Thomas J. Ladd married Martha A. Pursley on 24 Mar 1855 in Trigg County. Thomas and Martha (b. 29 Jan 1838 in Kentucky, d. 8 Jun 1900) are both buried in the Ladd Cemetery.

On page 11, Simmons' 1850 Trigg County Census #207, he is listed as the only child left at home, age 17 years, and living with John C. Ladd Jr., age 56 years and Mary J. Ladd, age 62 years.

On page 219, Simmons' 1870 Trigg County Census #2593, he is listed as age 37 years and living with his wife Martha A. (Pursley) Ladd, age 32 years, and seven children: Mary V., age 13 years; Susan A., age 12 years; Benjamin F., age 9 years; John J., age 8 years; Mildred E., age 6 years; Finis E., age 3 years; and Analiza age 1 year.

On page 251, Jones' 1900 Trigg County Census #139-142, he is listed as Thomas J., age 67, living with his wife Martha A., age 62 years (married 45 years), and two children: Susan A., age 42 years, and William A., age 28 years.

SAMUEL LANCASTER, son of William Dorsey and Mary (Colson) Lancaster, was born in the Donaldson Creek area of Trigg County on 29 Jul 1843. Samuel enlisted in October 1860, in the Confederate army, at Stewart County, TN as a member of Co. F, 50th Tennessee Regt. Inf. This regiment was taken at once to Fort Donelson and assisted in the erection of the fort and fought through the battle at Fort Donelson in February 1862. The regiment was captured at the fall of the fort but Samuel was able to escape capture and returned home. His company was later exchanged for other prisoners at Vicksburg on 29 Sep 1862, and later reorganized at Sweetwater, MS.

Samuel rejoined his original company, but did re-enlist in the Confederate army in Woodward's 2nd Kentucky Cav. Regt. during August 1862, which was prior to the reorganization of his old company. He served in this company until his capture by the Federals and was confined in a Federal prison at Hopkinsville. According to an application for a Confederate pension, Samuel discloses the fact that he was confined to the prison in March 1863, but was released the same month when the Federal prisoners at that place were to be moved. He was sick at the time and unable to travel, but was told that if he took the oath of allegiance to the US Government he would be allowed to go home. Samuel took this oath during that same month and was allowed to return home.

He married the following year on 11 Jan 1864 to Parthenia Lawrence, daughter of Humphrey and Harriett (Mitchell) Lawrence. They had four children: Sarah "Sadie," Samuel Henry, James Monroe, and Daisy Ader Lee Lancaster. Following Parthenia's death on 14 Jul 1915, he married on 5 Sep 1915 to Maggie Hutcherson. Samuel Lancaster died 18 May 1933 in Trigg County and is buried in the Allen Cemetery, Trigg County.

JOHN TYLER LANCASTER, Private, born 17 May 1841 in Kentucky, died 17 Nov 1880. He enlisted 14 Sep 1861 at Camp Burnett, TN and served with Co. G, 4th Kentucky Regt. Inf. (CSA).

He was wounded and captured on 7 Apr 1862 at the Battle of Shiloh and taken on the USA Hospital Steamer "Empress" to the USA General Hospital in Keokuk, IA. His medical service record states he suffered gunshot wounds in the arm, shoulder and knee.

When released, he was sent to Alton Military Prison in Alton, IL. He was exchanged on 23 Sep 1862 at Vicksburg, MS. He re-enlisted into his old company, Co. G, 4th Kentucky Inf., and served until the end of the war. He was surrendered on 7 May 1865 in Washington, GA.

His father, Wiley Lancaster, married his mother, Nancy Craig, on 23 Oct 1824 in Trigg County. Wiley (b. 11 Nov 1803 in North Carolina, d. 1 Aug 1863) and Nancy (b. 1806 in Kentucky, d. 17 Aug 1869) are buried in the Dixon-Lancaster Cemetery.

John Tyler Lancaster, age 27 years, married Malissa Cunningham, age 21 years, on 28 Mar 1869. Both are from Trigg County. John is buried in the Dixon-Lancaster Cemetery.

On page 50, Simmons' 1850 Trigg County Census, #920, he is listed as John Tyler Lancaster, age 9 years and living with his father Wiley Lancaster age 46 years, his mother Nancy (Craig) Lancaster, age 50 years, and three siblings: Levi, age 15 years; Barbery (Basherly), age 13 years; and William H.H., age 11 years.

On page 222, Neel's Statistical Handbook of Trigg County, 1880 Trigg County Census, bottom of page, he is listed as John T. Lancaster, a farmer age 38 years and living with his wife Malissa (Cunningham) Lancaster, age 39 years, and six children: Basheba, age 10 years; Watford, age 8 years; Wilford, age 7 years; Rosaline, age 5 years; S.B. (daughter), age 3 years; James W., age 3 months; and a niece Nancy Lancaster, age 15 years; and a nephew Robert L., age 12 years.

JAMES LESTER, 4th Corporal, born ca. 1836 in Kentucky. He enlisted 26 Sep 1861 at Camp Reeves, TN and served with Co. G, 8th Ky. Regt. Inf. (CSA).

He was captured at Fort Donelson and sent to Camp Morton, IN and exchanged on 1 Sep 1862. He was appointed 4th corporal at reorganization of the regiment on 22 Sep 1862, but deserted in the retreat from the Hatchie River on 4 Dec 1862. He was captured by Union troops in Trigg County on 15 Aug 1863 and sent to the Union prison camp in Louisville, KY. He was then sent to Camp Chase, OH, and arrived there on 2 Sep 1863, then sent to the Rock Island, IL prison, arriving there 24 Jan 1864. He enlisted in the USN at the Navy Barracks at Rock Island on 5 Feb 1864.

4th Corporal James Lester was a brother of Private John Lester and Private Samuel Lester. Private Samuel Lester also joined the USN at Rock Island, IL.

His father William Lester Sr. (b. ca. 1801 in Tennessee) and mother Jane (Fowler) Lester (b. ca. 1812) were married 26 Feb 1840 in Trigg County.

On page 22, Simmons' 1850 Trigg County Census #397, he is listed as age 14 years and living with his father William Lester, age 49 years; his mother Jane (Fowler) Lester, age 38 years; and 10 siblings: William, age 17 years; Samuel, age 13 years; Teresa, age 21 years; Matilda, age 19 years; John, age 9 years; Joseph, age 8 years; Enos, age 6 years; Martha, age 5 years; Lizetta (or Lizella), age 2 years; and Armistead, age 2 months.

On page 30, Simmons' 1860 Trigg County Census #437, he is listed as age 22 years and living with his father William Lester, age 59 years; his mother Jane Lester, age 50 years; and eight siblings: William, age 25 years; Matilda, age 22 years; Samuel, age 21 years; John, age 18 years; Enos, age 17 years; Martha, age 15 years; Lizetta, age 13 years; and Armistead, age 8 years.

JAMES B.R. (RICHARD) LESTER, Private, born in March 1843 in Missouri and died in 1906. He enlisted 2 Oct 1861, at Camp Reeves, TN and served with Co. G, 8th Kentucky Regt. Inf. (CSA).

Captured at Fort Donelson and imprisoned at Camp Morton, IN, after which he was paroled and exchanged on 1 Sep 1863. According to the Kentucky Adjutant General's Report he was captured, returned to duty and gallantly fought to the very end of the war.

His father James Lester Sr. (b. ca. 1811 in Kentucky) and mother Delila (Savills) Lester (b. ca. 1814 in Kentucky) were married 9 Jan 1837 in Trigg County.

J.B.R. Lester married George Ann Mitchell on 18 May 1866, in Trigg County.

His guardian, George W. Lester, married three times: (1st) Lucinda Lester ca. 1840; (2nd) Sara M. Adams on 29 Dec 1859 in Trigg County; (3rd) C.A.T. Adams on 2 Aug 1866 in Trigg County.

J.B.R. is the only Lester buried in the East End Cemetery. His guardian, George W. Lester (b. 24 Jan 1830, d. April 1909) is buried in Adams-Lester Cemetery in Trigg County with his third wife Clarisa A.T. (Adams), daughter of Wesley Adams Lester (b. 17 Apr 1842, d. March 1901).

On page 23, Simmons' 1850 Trigg County Census #430, James Lester is listed as age 7 years, living with his father James Lester, age 36 years, and four siblings: Miles, age 10 years; Gabriella, age 5 years; Demascus L., age 2 years and Mary E., also age 2 years.

On page 10, Jones' 1900 Trigg County Census #88-91, he is listed as a postmaster, age 57 years (born in Missouri in March 1843) and living with his wife Dona (Hammond) Lester (born in Kentucky in June 1865), age 35 years (married 12 years); two sons, Duk, age 11 years (born in Kentucky), and Mark, age 7 years (born in Missouri); and his mother-in-law, Martha Hammond, age 70 years). Dona Hammond Lester is listed as a deputy post-master.

JOHN LESTER, Private, born ca. 1841 in Kentucky. He enlisted 26 Sep 1861 at Camp Reeves, TN and served with Co. G, 8th Kentucky Regt. Inf. (CSA). Private John Lester was a brother of 4th Corporal James Lester and Private Samuel Lester.

According to the Kentucky Adjutant General's Report, he deserted his command on 1 Dec 1862 in the retreat from the Hatchie River.

On page 22, Simmons' 1850 Trigg County Census #397, he is listed as age 9 years and living with his father William Lester, age 49 years; his mother Jane (Fowler) Lester, age 38 years; and siblings: William, age 17 years; James, age 14 years; Samuel, age 13 years; Teresa, age 21 years; Matilda, age 19 years; John, age 9 years; Joseph, age 8 years; Enos, age 6 years; Martha, age 5 years; Lizetta, age 2 years; and Armistead, 2 months.

On page 30, Simmons' 1860 Trigg County Census #437, he is listed as age 18 years and living with his father William Lester, age 59 years; his mother Jane Lester, age 50 years; and siblings: William, age 25 years; James, age 22 years; Matilda, age 24 years; Samuel, age 21 years; Enos, age 17 years; Martha, age 15 years; Lizetta, age 13 years; and Armistead, age 8 years.

SAMUEL LESTER, Private, born ca. 1839 in Kentucky. He enlisted 26 Sep 1861 at Camp Reeves, TN and served with Co. G, 8th Kentucky Regt. Inf. (CSA). He was captured at the surrender of Vicksburg on 4 Jul 1863 and was paroled on 4 Jul 1863. He was captured in Trigg County, KY, on 15 Aug 1863, and sent to Camp Chase, OH, arriving there on 2 Sep 1863. He was then sent to Rock Island, IL, prison, arriving there on 25 Jan 1864. He subsequently enlisted in the USN at Rock Island Navy Barracks on 5 Feb 1864.

He was a brother of 4th Corporal James Lester and Private John Lester.

On page 22, Simmons' 1850 Trigg County Census #397, he is listed as age 13 years and living with his father William Lester, age 49 years, and his mother Jane (Fowler) Lester, age 38 years, and siblings: William, age 17 years; James, age 15 years; Teresa, age 21 years; Matilda, age 19 years; John, age 9 years; Joseph, age 8 years; Enos, age 6 years; Martha, age 5 years; Lizetta, age 2 years; and Armistead, age 2 months.

On page 30, Simmons' 1860 Trigg County Census #437, he is listed as age 21 and living with his father William Lester, age 59 years, and his mother Jane Lester, age 50 years, and siblings: William, age 25 years; James, age 22 years; Matilda, age 24 years; John, age 18 years; Enos, age 17 years; Martha, age 15 years; Lizetta, age 13 years and Armistead, age 8 years.

R.M. LINDSAY, Private, born ca. 1833 in Kentucky. He enlisted 9 Dec 1862 in Newman, TN and served with Co. B, Woodward's 2nd/15th Kentucky Cav. Regt. (CSA). Pvt. R.M. Lindsay was a brother of Private William N. Lindsay.

His father was Sackfield S. Lindsay (b. ca. 1801 in North Carolina) and his mother was Mary (Northington) Lindsay (b. ca. 1806 in North Carolina).

Remolous Lindsey was registered on the Roaring Spring Poll Book dated 6 Aug 1860. S.S. Lindsey and William N. Lindsey are also listed in this record.

On page 44, Simmons' 1850 Trigg County Census #807, a "Romulus" Lindsay is listed as age 17 years and living with his father S.S. Lindsay, age 49 years; his mother Mary Northington Lindsay, age 44 years; and three siblings: Albert G., age 21 years; William N., age 19 years; and James, age 15 years.

On page 72, Simmons' 1860 Trigg County Census #1062, a "R." Lindsay is listed as a merchant, age 25 years, and living with has father S.S. Lindsay, age 61 years, and brother W.N. Lindsay (a physician), age 29 years.

WILLIAM N. LINDSAY, Private, born ca. 1831 in Kentucky. He enlisted 9 Dec 1862 in Newman, TN and served with Co. B, Woodward's 2nd/15th Kentucky Cav. Regt. (CSA). Pvt. William N. Lindsay was a brother of Pvt. R.M. Lindsay.

His father was Sackfield S. Lindsay (b. ca. 1801 in North Carolina) and his mother was Mary (Northington) Lindsay (b. ca. 1806 in North Carolina).

A William N. Lindsey married Mary E. Rascoe on 18 Aug 1860 in Trigg County.

On page 44, Simmons' 1850 Trigg County Census #807, a William N. Lindsay is listed as age 19 years and living with his father S.S. Lindsay, age 49 years; his mother Mary (Northington) Lindsay, age 44 years; and three siblings: Albert G., age 21 years; Romelus, age 17 years; and James, age 15 years.

On page 72 Simmons' 1860 Trigg County Census #1062, a W.N. Lindsay is listed as a physician, age 29 years and living with his father S.S. Lindsay, age 61 years, and his brother R. Lindsay, age 25 years, is listed as a merchant.

WILLIAM T. LITCHFIELD was born in 1844. He resided in the area known as Rock Castle all his life. He was a farmer and operated a sawmill. He introduced one of the first wheat thrashing machines to this part of the country. William was a Confederate States of America veteran of the Civil War.  He married Sarah Hall in 1864 and had eight children: Lillie, Bell, Adilia, Fadia, Jimmie, Waymon, Ollie and Josephine. He later married Azzie (Azza) Wimberly and they had 10 children: Willie, Floyd, Demp, Corbie, Harvey, Garnie, Robert, Nellie, Luther and a son who died as an infant. William died in 1929 at the age of 84. He is buried in the Marvin Oliver Cemetery in Trigg County. He is survived by one son Robert (Bob) Litchfield who still resides in Trigg County. *Submitted by gg-granddaughter Barbara Tyler.*

JOHN C. LOWERY, Private, born ca. 1832 in Kentucky. He enrolled 14 Aug 1983, mustered in 13 Sep 1862 at Henderson, KY, mustered out 23 Sep 1863, at Russellville, KY and served with Co. L, 8th Kentucky Regt. Cav. (USA). Pvt. John Lowery was a brother of Pvt. James B. Lowery and Thomas Lowery.

His father William Lowery (b. 1810 in Kentucky, d. 1860) and his mother Harriet Lowery (b. 1812 in Virginia, d. 1862) are buried in the Lowery Cemetery with their son Thomas Lowery. The accuracy of their death dates are questionable because both parents are found in the 1870 Trigg County Census.

There is a John Lowery (b. 4 Jul 1840(?), d. 1890) buried in the Ross-Turner Cemetery in Trigg County, KY.

On page 12, Simmons' 1860 Trigg County Census #167, he is listed as John Lowery, age 18, living with his father William Lowery, age 43 years; his mother Harriett Lowery, age 43 years; and three siblings: Thomas Lowery, age 17 years; J.B. (James B.) Lowery, age 15 years; and S.C. (Sarah C.) Lowery, age 14 years.

On page 124, Simmons' 1870 Trigg County Census #1459, he is listed as John C. Lowery, age 29 years, living with his wife Rowena, age 33 years, and two children: William, age 4 years, and Melcena (female) age 2 years.

On page 237, Neel's Statistical Handbook of Trigg County, 1880 Trigg County Census, middle of page, he is listed as John C. Lowery, a farmer, age 38 years, living with his wife Rolaney Lowery, age 36 years, and five children: Meelaney (daughter) age 11 years; __ (daughter), age 9 years; Sanford, age 6 years; Ardell (son), age 5 years; and Becky A., age 2 years.

THOMAS LOWERY, born ca. 1833. There was a Thomas Lowry in Co. F of the llth Kentucky Cavalry (USA) that mustered in Louisville, KY, and a Thomas Lowery in Co. G of the 53rd Kentucky Mounted Inf. (USA) that mustered in Lexington, KY.

Thomas Lowery was a brother of James B. Lowery and John C. Lowery. Their father was William Lowery (b. 1810 in Kentucky, d. 1860) and mother was Harriet Lowery (b. 1812 in Virginia, d. 1862). The accuracy of their death dates are questionable because both parents are found in the 1870 Trigg County Census.

Thomas Lowery is buried in the Lowery Cemetery with his parents and there is no stone to his grave.

On page 12, Simmons' 1860 Trigg County Census #167, he is listed as Thomas Lowery, age 17 years, living with his father William Lowery, age 43 years; his mother Harriett Lowery, age 43 years; and three siblings: John, age 18 years; J.B. (James B.), age 15 years; and S.C. (Sarah C.), age 14 years.

HENRY E. LUTON, Captain, born 22 Feb 1822 in Tennessee, died 31 May 1890. He enrolled and was mustered in 4 Aug 1864 at Paducah, KY, mustered out 12 Feb 1865 at Paducah, KY and served with Co. B, lst Regiment Capital Guards, Paducah Battalion

He was married to America J. Luton (b. 1828 in Tennessee, d. 1916). Henry E. Luton with wife America and Benjamin F. Luton with wife Martha sold land on Crooked Creek in Trigg County to Q.A. Luton on 23 May 1856.

He is buried with his wife America in the Colson or Pleasant Valley Cemetery in Trigg County, KY.

On page 128, Simmons' 1870 Trigg County Census #1532, he is listed as Henry "Luten," age 48 years, living with his wife America J. "Luten," age 41 years, and six children: Dewitt, age 19 years; Pinckney age 14 years; Corintha, age 11 years; Corlene, age 7 years; Shearman, age 5 years; and Milton, age 1 year.

On page 21, Blue & Sellers' 1920 Trigg County Census #252, his son Dewitt C. Luton is listed as age 69 years, living with his daughter Gertie (Luton) Wallace, age 32 years; her husband Arthur Wallace, a farmer, age 37 years; and their six children: Maurice C., age 10 years; Clyde F., age 8 years; Liew C., age 6 years; Howard L., age 4 years; Joe L., age 4 years; and Etna D., age 1 year.

RICHARD MABREY, Private, born ca. 1841 in Kentucky, died 6 Apr 1862 at the Battle of Shiloh. He enlisted 14 Sep 1861 at Camp Burnett, TN and served with Co. G, 4th Kentucky Regt. Inf. He was killed at the Battle of Shiloh 6 Apr 1862.

His father was Lewis B. Mabrey (b. ca. 1811 in Kentucky) and his mother was Sarah (Starnes) Mabrey (b. ca. 1810 in Tennessee). According to Simmons' 1850 Census his father was a blacksmith and married Sarah Starnes on 12 Feb 1835, and according to Simmons' 1860 Census, Sarah lists her age as still 40 years, but now born in Kentucky.

On page 20, Simmons' 1850 Trigg County Census #360. He is listed as Richard "Mabry," age 10 years, living with his father Lewis B. "Mabry," age 39 years; his mother Sarah (Starnes) "Mabry," age 40 years and two siblings: Wayman C., age 14 years, and Lucy L., age 12 years.

YEATMAN STACKER MABRY, His army discharge dated 6 Sep 1865 states that he was 19 years of age when he left his unit in Louisville, KY. He was a private of Capt. James B. Rogers' Co. D, Sixth Regt. of Kentucky Vet Cavalry Volunteers. He was enrolled 2 Mar 1864 to serve three years or during the war. The discharge paper describes him as 5'9" high, dark complexion, gray eyes, dark hair and by occupation a farmer. Y.S. Mabry applied for a pension on 12 Jan 1899. A receipt dated 28 May 1912 shows that he received a pension.

Yeatman Stacker Mabry was the grandson of John Mabry Sr., a Revolutionary War veteran who lived in Trigg County from about 1786 to his death 1845. Y.S. was the son of Rebecca Oliver and Francis Allen Mabry of Trigg and Crittenden counties, KY. He was born 23 Sep 1845 in Trigg County and died 15 Apr 1916 in Webster County, KY. He is buried in New Harmony Baptist Church Cemetery, Wheatcroft, KY. His grave is marked with an old style military marker.

He married A. Elizabeth Farmer on 31 Jan 1869. They had four sons and two daughters. For more information on his ancestors and descendants see Trigg County History Book I and II, pages 376-377 and pages 547-548. Also pages 136-137 in Vol. II. *Submitted by Leo Yeateman Wilson.*

ROBERT WADE MAJOR, 1st Lieutenant, born 13 Jan 1842 in Kentucky, died 19 Oct 1891. He enlisted 2 Sep 1861 at Camp Burnett, TN and served with Co. G, 4th Kentucky Regt. Inf. (CSA). He was promoted to lst lieutenant on 10 Jul 1863, then badly wounded at Resaca, GA 14 May 1864. He was taken prisoner at Jonesboro, GA on 1 Sep 1864.

Trigg County Genealogical Society History gives his death date as 29 Oct 1891, but his tombstone gives his death date as 19 Oct 1891.

His father Charles Humphrey Major (b. 17 Sep 1817 in Virginia, d. 5 Feb 1906) and mother Mary J. (Clark) Major (b. 21 Aug 1826 in Kentucky, d. 28 Jul 1903) are both buried in the Yates Cemetery in Trigg County.

R.W. Major married Emma F. Chappell on 16 Oct 1873. He is buried in the East End Cemetery in Cadiz, KY, with his wife Emma (b. 30 Jan 1848 in Kentucky, d. 8 Oct 1913). According to the 1880 census, Emma's father was born in Kentucky and her mother was born in Tennessee.

On page 88, Simmons' 1870 Trigg County Census #1016, he is listed as age 28 years and living with his father Charles H. Major, age 52 years; mother Mary J. (Clark) Major, age 43 years; and 10 siblings: Charles H., age 30 years; Joshua, age 26 years; William C., age 20 years; Eleanor J., age 18 years; Thomas P., age 16 years; Mollie H., age 15 years; Seldon Y., age 11 years; Henry H., age 5 years; Mattie B., age 7 years; and Edwin F., age 2 years.

On page 179, Neel's Statistical Handbook of Trigg County, 1880 Trigg County Census, toward top of page, he is listed as R.W. Major, a clerk in a dry good store, age 38 years and living with his wife Emma (Chappell) Major, age 32 years, and two children: Charley D., age 2 years, and Bessy M., age 1 year.

On page 2, Jones' 1900 Trigg County Census #12-12, his wife Emma C. (Chappell) Major, age 52 years, is listed as a widow living with her three children: Bessie M., age 21 years; John W., age 16 years; and Winnie D., age 12 years. According to the 1900 census, Emma was married for 32 years and has had eight children, only three of which are still living when this census was taken.

ALEXANDER MALONE, Private, born ca. 1842 in Kentucky. He enlisted 3 Oct 1861, at Camp Reeves, TN and served with Co. G, 8th Kentucky Regt. Inf. (CSA). On a muster roll on the Kentucky Adjutant's Report dated 31 Jul 1861 to 2 Sep 1862, he is listed as "Absent without leave in Kentucky."

His father was Moses Malone (b. ca. 1818 in Kentucky) and his mother was Rebecca (Randolph) Malone (b. ca. 1820 in Kentucky).

On page 19, Simmons' 1860 Trigg County Census #287, he is listed as age 17 years and living with his father Moses Malone, age 43 years; Rebecca (Randolph) Malone, age 40 years; and six siblings: "T.D." (Thomas), age 19 years; William, age 15 years; "J.K.P." (James K.P.), age 13 years; Caroline, age 9 years; John R., age 5 years; and "N.J." (Nancy), age 3 years.

On page 199, Simmons' 1870 Trigg County Census #2335, he is not found in this census, but his father is listed as Moses Malone, age 53 years, living with his wife Rebecca Malone, age 50 years; and seven children: Caroline, age 20 years; John, age 16 years; Nancy, age 13 years; Davis, age 9 years; Lee, age 5 years; William, age 24 years; and Polk (James K. Polk), age 22 years. None of this family is found in Neel's 1880 Trigg County Census.

THOMAS D. MALONE, Private, born ca. 1840. He enlisted 3 Oct 1861 at Camp Reeves, TN and served with Co. G, 8th Kentucky Regt. Inf. (CSA). On a muster roll in the Kentucky Adjutant's Report dated 31 Jul 1861 to 22 Sep 1862, he is listed as "Absent without leave in Kentucky."

His father was Moses Malone (b. ca. 1818 in Kentucky) and his mother was Rebecca Randolph Malone (b. ca. 1820 in Kentucky).

On page 19, Simmons, 1860 Trigg County Census #287, he is listed as age 19 years, living with his father Moses Malone, age 43 years; Rebecca Randolph Malone, age 40 years; and six siblings: "Alex" (Alexander) age 17 years, William age 15 years, "J.K.P." (James K.P.), age 13 years; Caroline, age 9 years; John R., age 5 years; "N.J." (female), age 3 years.

WILLIAM MALONE, Private, born ca. 1845. He enlisted 26 Sep 1861 at Camp Reeves, TN and served with Co. G, 8th Kentucky Regt.

Inf. (CSA). According to the Kentucky Adjutant's Report, he deserted his command on 26 Oct 1861.

His father was Moses Malone (b. ca. 1818 in Kentucky) and his mother was Rebecca Randolph Malone (b. ca. 1820 in Kentucky).

On pages 19 and 20, Simmons' 1860 Trigg County Census #287, he is listed as age 15 years, living with his father "M." (Moses), age 43 years; his mother "R." (Rebecca) Malone, age 40 years; and six siblings: "T.D." (Thomas), age 19 years; "Alex" (Alexander), age 17 years; J.K.P. (James K.P.), age 13 years; Caroline, age 9 years; John R., age 9 years; and "N.J." (female), age 3 years,

On page 199, Simmons' 1870 Trigg County Census #2335, he is listed as age 24 years and living with his father Moses Malone, age 53 years; his mother Rebecca Malone, age 50 years; and six siblings: Caroline, age 20 years; John, age 16 years; Nancy, age 13 years; Davis, age 9 years; Lee, age 3 years; and Polk (James K. Polk Malone), age 22 years. None of this family is found in Neel's 1880 Trigg County Census.

JAMES M. MANNING, Private, born ca. 1838 in Tennessee, died 1 Feb 1862 at Camp Alcorn in Hopkinsville, KY. He enlisted 26 Sep 1861 at Camp Reeves, TN and served with Co. G, 8th Kentucky Regt. Inf. (CSA).

Cornelius, N.H. and John W. Manning are listed in the Cadiz Poll Book - 1 Aug 1853.

James' father Cornelius B. Manning (b. ca. 1785 in Virginia) is buried in the Manning Cemetery in Trigg County (stone missing). Maupin incorrectly lists his birthdate as 1820. According to Neel, there is a broken tombstone in the Manning Cemetery that reads "Nancy, wife of..." which could be the wife of Cornelius Manning.

On page 31, Simmons' 1850 Trigg County Census #564-28, he is listed as James M. Manning, age 12 years, living with his father Cornelius Manning, age 65 years; his mother Nancy Manning, age 61 years; and five siblings: Nathanial H., age 35 years; Harriett A., age 38 years; John W., age 27 years; George W., age 11 years; and Elizabeth N., age 7 years. The following Roberts children are living with the family in this census: John C., age 9 years; James O., age 7 years; William T., age 5 years; and Minerva A., age 2 years.

Page 182, Neel's Statistical Handbook of Trigg County, 1880 Trigg County Census, toward top of page, James is not found in this census, but his brother N.H. (Nathanial H.) Manning is listed as a farmer, age 67 years and living with his wife Ellen B. Manning, age 31 years, and five children: Mary, age 13 years; Clarence N., age 9 years; Claudius, age 7 years; Daisie, age 4 years; and Nancy E., age 2 years. John W. Manning is listed as his brother and a farmer living with the family in this census.

JOHN MARTIN, born ca. 1842. He enrolled 14 Aug 1862, mustered in 13 Sep 1862 at Henderson, KY and mustered out 23 Sep 1863 at Russellville, KY. He served with Co. L, 8th Kentucky Regt. Cav. (USA).

His father was William Martin (b. ca. 1812 in Maryland) and his real mother died ca. 1846. His father married his stepmother, Amanda M. Johns on 1 Sep 1847 in Trigg County. She was born ca. 1826 in Virginia.

On page 50, Simmons' 1860 Trigg County Census #734, he is listed as age 18 years and living with his father William H. Martin, age 47 years; his mother Amanda (Johns) Martin, age 32 years; and four siblings: Theodore, age 16 years; William, age 11 years; Ann, age 8 years; and Watson, age 6 years.

DAVID MAYES, born 6 Nov 1826 in Tennessee, died 17 Mar 1886. He served with Co. I, 50th Tennessee Regt. Inf. (CSA).

According to Neel's 1880 Trigg County Census, David Mayes was born ca. 1817 in Tennessee while his father was born in Virginia and his mother in Tennessee.

His wife was Catherine Mayes (b. ca. 1824 in Kentucky) and both her parents were born in North Carolina.

He is buried in the Turkey Creek Cemetery near his daughter Rebecca (Mayes) Flynn (b. 11 Oct 1862, d. 26 Aug 1941)

On page 13, Simmons' 1860 Trigg County Census #189, he is listed as age 33 years and living with his wife Catherine, age 23 years, and four children: Elizabeth, age 6 years; Caroline, age 4 years; Nancy J., age 3 years; and Josephine (Josephus), age 3 months.

On page 125, Simmons' 1870 Trigg County Census #1498, he is listed as age 44 years, living with his wife Catherine, age 30 years, and seven children: Faith, age 16 years; Caroline, age 14 years; Nancy J., age

12 years; Josephus, age 10 years; Rebecca, age 8 years; John D., age 6 years; and Rufus, 6 months.

JORDAN MCGEE, served with the 101 USC Inf. Co. H during the Civil War. In civilian life, he was a farmer. Jordan is the great-grandson of James Ray McGee.

FREDRICK H. MEREDITH, born ca. 1840 in Kentucky. He enrolled 4 Aug 1864, mustered in 4 Aug 1864 at Paducah, KY and mustered out 12 Feb 1864 at Paducah, KY. He served with Co. B, First Regt. Capital Guards, Paducah, KY.

His father was Fredrick Meredith (b. ca. 1803 in South Carolina) and his mother was Susan Meredith (b. ca. 1806 in Kentucky).

F.H. Merideth, age 23 years of Trigg County, married Eliza A. Freeman, age 22 years of Tennessee, on 6 Jul 1865.

There is an F.H. Meredith (b. 1830(?), d. 1926) buried with his wife Liza Ann Meredith (b. 1842, d. ??) in the Mark Jones Cemetery. Fredrick H. Meredith's son Fillmore Meredith (b. 15 Dec 1880 in Kentucky, d. 8 Jan 1925) is buried in the Faulkner Cemetery in Trigg County, KY.

On page 11, Simmons' 1860 Trigg County Census #148, he is listed as "F.H." Meredith, age 20 years and living with his father Fredrick Meredith, age 55 years; his mother Susan Meredith, age 50 years; and nine siblings: "H." (Robert H.(?), age 23 years; Robin H., age 25 years; "D." (Elizabeth D.(?), age 30 years; "M.S" (female), age 16 years; "M." (female), age 13 years; Thomas, age 10 years; "F." (female), age 6 years; William, age 5 years; and "S.A." (female), age 6 years.

Page 183, Neel's Statistical Handbook of Trigg County, 1880 Trigg County Census, bottom of page, he is listed as F.H. Meredith, a farmer, age 41 years, living with his wife Eliza Freeman Meredith, age 32 years, and six sons: James H., age 13 years; William, age 11 years; Richard E., age 10 years; Robert Lee, age 5 years; Fillmore, age 3 years; and Thomas, age 5 months.

WILLIAM MEREDITH, 4th Sergeant, born ca. 1832, died 11 Sep 1864. He enlisted 10 Sep 1861 at Camp Burnett, TN and served with Co. G, 4th Kentucky Regt. Inf. (CSA). Private Meredith was promoted to 4th sergeant on 20 Jan 1864. He was mortally wounded at Jonesboro, GA on 7 Sep 1864 and died on 11 Sep 1864.

On page 6, Simmons' 1860 Trigg County Census #89, he is listed as age 28 years and as a woodcutter. He is living with R.J. Grace, age 19 years, also a woodcutter.

LEWIS L. MERSHON, 3rd Corporal, born ca. 1837 in Kentucky, died 11 Jul 1863. He enlisted 26 Sep 1861 at Camp Reeves, TN and served with Co. G, 8th Kentucky Regt. Inf. (CSA). He was listed as Absent Without Leave on a C.S. Army muster roll dated 26 Sep 1861 to 31 Jul 1862. He rejoined his unit on 24 Dec 1862 and was reduced in rank from corporal to private. Pvt. Mershon was killed at the Battle of Jackson, MS on 11 Jul 1863.

His father was Eli T. Mershon (b. ca. 1812 in Kentucky) and his mother was Margaret Mershon (b. ca. 1813 in Kentucky).

On page 19, Simmons' 1860 Trigg County Census #279, he is listed as age 19 years and living with his father E.T. (Eli T.) Mershon, age 50 years; his mother Margaret Mershon, age 48 years; and seven siblings: W.J. (James Wallace), age 22 years; Mary B., age 17 years; Gabriella, age 16 years; Louisa, age 14 years; M.N. (Marshall N.), age 9 years; H.H. (Hellen), age 5 years; and A.D. (Alford), age 3 years.

GREGORY H. MICHERSON, Private, born ca. 1842. He enrolled 14 Aug 1862, mustered in 13 Sep 1862 at Henderson, KY and mustered out 23 Sep 1863 at Russellville, KY. He served with Co. L, 8th Kentucky Regt. Cavalry (USA).

His father was Z.F. Mitcherson (b. 1807 in Kentucky) and his mother was Nancy (Johnson) Mitcherson (b. 1818 in Tennessee). Z.E.F. Mitchuson married Nancy M. Johnson on 19 Mar 1833 in Trigg County.

G.H. Mitchuson (age not given) married Charity M. Flynn (age 18 years from Christian County) on 1 May 1865 in Trigg County.

On page 3, Simmons' 1860 Trigg County Census #48, he is listed as "H.G. Mitchesson," age 17 years, living with his father "Z. Mitchesson," age 51 years; his mother Nancy Johnson "Mitchesson," age 43 years; and five siblings: William A., age 20 years; "Z.D." (male), age 15 years; Ben, age 7 years; Eveline, age 2 years; and Huston, age 2 years.

Gregory H. Mitcherson is not listed in Simmons' 1870 Trigg County Census.

ELIJAH MITCHELL, Private, born ??, died February or March 1862. He served with Co. G, 8th Kentucky Regt. Inf. (CSA). He was mortally wounded at Fort Donelson and taken to the hospital in Clarksville, TN.

According to the Kentucky Adjutant General's Report, he died at his home in Kentucky. He is listed in the *Confederate Veteran Magazine* article as "E. Mitchell," Eighth Kentucky, Cadiz, KY. (Page 66, Volume 9, Confederate Veteran Magazine, Kentucky State Archives.)

Elijah W. Mitchell married Kessey Jane Gore on 21 Aug 1844 in Trigg County. He is listed in the Bethesda Poll Book 6 Aug 1860.

JOSEPH "JOE" H. MITCHELL, lst Sergeant, born 17 May 1842, died 19 Feb 1932. His father was David D. Mitchell (b. ca. 1807 in Tennessee, d. 4 Jul 1853) and his mother was Celia (Holley) Mitchell (b. ca. 1815 in Alabama).

He enlisted 26 Sep 1861 at Camp Reeves, TN and served with Co. G, 8th Kentucky Regt. Inf. (CSA). Promoted to lst sergeant at reorganization of regiment on 22 Sep 1862. He was discharged from service in July 1863 at Carrollton, MS.

Sergeant Mitchell was wounded at Jackson, MS on 11 Jul 1863 and sent to a hospital at Lauderdale, MS. Another soldier had died and was buried by mistake as Joe H. Mitchell. When Joseph was released from hospital he walked back to Trigg County and on the way saw a grave stone with his name on it.

On page 182 Neel's Statistical Handbook of Trigg County, 1880 Trigg County Census, top of page, he is listed as J.H. Mitchell, age 37 years and living with his wife Sarah J. Mitchell, age 36 and six children: William C., age 14 years; Oscar B., age 11 years; Ira N., age 9 years; Arthur, age 5 years; Naomi, age 4 years; and Osawood (a son), age 1 year.

On page 32, Jones' 1900 Trigg County Census #259-266, he is listed as Joseph Mitchell a farmer age 58 years, living with his wife Sarah J. Mitchell (married 35 years) age 57 years, and five children: Cortez, age 34 years; Arthur, age 25 years; Naomi, age 23 years; Ocie (a daughter), age 21 years; and Gertrude, age 14 years. (Sarah has had eight children, six of which were still living when this census was taken.)

NATHAN B. MITCHELL, Private, born ca. 1844, died 16 Nov 1861. He enlisted 16 Jul 1861 and served with Cobb's Battery of Field Artillery. He is listed in the Kentucky Adjutant General's Report as "N." Mitchell.

His father was David D. Mitchell (b. ca. 1807 in Tennessee, d. 4 Jul 1853 at age 50 years) and his mother was Celia (Holley) Mitchell (b. ca. 1815 in Alabama).

On page 28, Simmons' 1850 Trigg County Census #524, there is a "Nathan" Mitchell, age 6 years living with his father David D. Mitchell, age 43 years; his mother Celia (Holley) Mitchell, age 35 years; and eight siblings: David D., age 16 years; James M., age 15 years; Blake B., age 13 years; Sally A., age 12 years; Fury(?) (a female) age 10 years; Josiah H., age 8 years; George W., age 3 years; and Mary A., age 1 year.

RILEY MITCHELL, Private, born 22 Jul 1827, in Trigg County, KY, died 6 Jun 1866 in Trigg County, KY of consumption. He enlisted in the spring of 1861 at Eddyville, KY and served with Cobb's Kentucky Battery of Field Artillery.

When Capt. H.B. Lyon and Capt. R.H. Cobb of Eddyville were forming the battery that afterwards took the name of "Cobbs" Battery, to go to Fort Donelson, they had no experienced men to handle the guns and to teach others. Riley Mitchell had been in the artillery service in the Mexican War and was an expert in the business. He was past military age, married, had seven children and was living near the homes of John F. White and Wm. Wharton. In order to obtain his experience in teaching men to shoot cannon, Mr. Wharton and Mr. White agreed to take care of his family while he was in the army.

He was placed in charge of this battery at Fort Donelson and after training the young men was placed in active service of shooting what was called "Long Tom" and unusually long cannon that would sink boats several miles down the river. That cannon is now standing on end in the cemetery at Dover.

After the surrender at Dover, Mitchell was exchanged and placed in charge of artillery at Vicksburg. He had under his personal supervision a large cannon known as "Whistling Dick" because the ball made a whistling noise when fired. This cannon was used to sink Federal gun boats that tried to pass the fort at Vicksburg and succeeded in doing so. One particularly large boat known as the *"Queen of the West"* was sunk by Mitchell during the siege of Vicksburg. "Whistling Dick" is still on the bluff at Vicksburg battle field.

In July 1863 Mr. Mitchell was broken in health and came home. He died in 1866 of consumption contracted in the army.

His wife Elizabeth (Adams) survived him by many years and was about 97 years old when she died. After the death of Riley she married Robert Ramey and after his death she remained a widow. She had nine children by Riley Mitchell and none by second husband, Robert Ramey.

WILLIAM YOUNG MITCHELL, Private, born 1842 in Kentucky, died 1891. He served with Co. G, 8th Kentucky Regt. Inf. (CSA).

William Young Mitchell was registered in the Bethesda Precinct Poll Book dated 4 May 1867. He is listed as "Young" Mitchell.

He married Melinda ?? ca. 1867, but we cannot find a record of this marriage in Trigg County.

On page 143, Neel's Statistical Handbook of Trigg County, 1850 Trigg County Census, top of page, a Young Mitchell is listed as age 7 years living with his father William Y. Mitchell, age 25 years; Cassandra (Fowler) Mitchell, age 21 years; Nancy J. Mitchell, age 3 years; and Joseph K. Mitchell, age 6 months. The family is living with the Mordicai Fowler, age 72 years and Jane V. Fowler, age 67 years in this census.

On page 57, Simmons' 1870 Trigg County Census #654, there is a William Y. Mitchell, age 26 years living with his wife Malinda M. Mitchell, age 34 years, and a daughter, Lucy E. Mitchell, age 2 years.

On page 221, Neel's Statistical Handbook of Trigg County 1880 Census of Trigg County, bottom of page, he is listed as "W.Y." Mitchell, age 37 years living with his wife Malinda Mitchell, age 42 years, and three children: Lucy E., age 12 years; William G., age 7 years; and Henry C., age 3 years.

He is buried in the Curling Cemetery with his wife Malinda M. Mitchell (b. 1836, d. 1891). We cannot find any of their children buried in Trigg County.

JOSHUA EDWARD MIZE, Private, born 1 Jul 1843 in North Carolina, died 17 Feb 1906. During the Civil War he answered the call to arms 9 Sep 1861 at Fort Donalson, TN, mustered in 25 Dec 1861 and was a member of Co. B, 50th Tennessee Regt. Inf. (CSA). During his four years of service (1861-65) he was imprisoned twice and wounded three times and lost his left hand at the wrist.

The Joshua E. Mize family moved from Stewart County, TN, to Trigg County, KY, around 1889. All the Mize children were born in Stewart County, TN.

J.E. (Joshua E.) Mize married M.E. (Mary E.) Colley on 28 Feb 1872 in Trigg County. J.E. is buried in the Yates Cemetery with his wife Mary E. (b. 10 Aug 1850 in Kentucky, d. 18 Jan 1933).

Both of Joshua E. Mize's parents were born in North Carolina. Mary E. Mize's father was born in Virginia and her mother was born in Tennessee.

Page 121, Jones' 1900 Trigg County Census #1-1, he is listed as a farmer, age 46 years living with his wife Mary E. (married 28 years), age 49 years, and seven children: Harry H., age 25 years; Eddie G., age 21 years; William D., age 19 years; John R., age 16 years; Mattie M., age 15 years; Raymond R., age 12 years; and Adelia T., age 8 years. Mary has had nine children, all of whom are still living in the 1900 Census.

CHARLES CHRISTOPHER COLUMBUS MOOREFIELD, born 2 Aug 1822 in Virginia, died 25 Jun 1910. He served with CSA Army of northern Virginia.

Notes: According to the Trigg County Family History Book, he married Phoebe Ann Chaffin (b. 1839). His sons Otis Morris and William "Will" were for many years involved in the blacksmithing business in Trigg County, and his son Custis H. was a veterinarian.

Charles Christopher is buried in the East End Cemetery in Cadiz, KY.

ROBERT H. NEWTON, born 10 Jun 1845 in Virginia was the son of Godfrey Marion and Frances Newton. Robert "Bob" served in the Civil War. At the age of 21 years, 4 Aug 1864 he enlisted as a private in Co. B with duties listed as Kentucky Capital Guard. After serving six months he was discharged 2 Feb 1865.

He is the father of Robert "Ben" and the grandfather of Lillian Newton Calston.

JOHN NICHOLS, Private, born ca. 1844 in Kentucky. He enlisted 15 Oct 1861 at Camp Alcorn in Hopkinsville, KY and served with Co. G, 8th Kentucky Regt. Inf. (CSA). John Nichols "escaped capture at Fort Donelson and was discharged in 1862 on account of sickness." We cannot find any reference to John Nichols after his discharge from the Confederate Army in 1862.

His father was Maxey (possibly Maxwell) Nichols (b. ca. 1805 in Virginia and his mother was Martha (Hughes) Nichols (b. ca. 1808 in Kentucky)

According to Maupin's records, there is a John Nichols buried in the Curling Cemetery in Trigg County, but there is no stone to his grave.

On page 25, Simmons' 1850 Trigg County Census #450, John is listed as age 6 years and living with his father Maxey Nichols, age 45 years and his mother Martha, age 42 years, and six siblings: Thomas, age 21 years; William, age 19 years; Sarah A., age 14 years; Emily, age 12 years; Martha, age 4 years; and an unnamed female child (Eliza), 2 years.

Page 34, Simmons' 1860 Trigg County Census #500, John is listed as age 14 years and living with his father "M." (Maxey) Nichols, age 50 years; his mother Martha Nichols, age 45 years; and four siblings: Sarah A., age 18 years; Martha, age 13 years; Eliza, age 12 years; and Ellen, age 7 years.

FRANCIS MARION OAKLEY, Corporal, born 23 Jun 1835 in Tennessee, died 4 Jun 1906. He enrolled 14 Aug 1862, mustered in 13 Sep 1862 at Henderson, KY and mustered out 23 Sep 1863 at Russellville, KY. He served with Co. L, 8th Kentucky Regt. Cavalry (USA).

His father was George Oakley (b. ca. 1787 in Virginia) and his mother was Sarah Oakley (b. ca. 1801 in North Carolina, d. 10 Aug 1853).

On page 61, Simmons' 1850 Trigg County Census #1130-601, he is listed as age 15 years living with his father George Oakley, age 63 years, and his mother Sarah Oakley, age 49 years.

On page 119, Simmons' 1870 Trigg County Census #1400, he is listed as a farmer, age 34 years living with his wife Nancy (Bass) Oakley, age 24 years, and three children: Francis T. (Kansis T.), age 10 years; Margarett F., age 4 years; and Hulda N. (Hugh N.), age 2 years.

On page 228, Neel's Statistical Handbook of Trigg County, 1880 Trigg County Census, middle of page, he is listed as an attorney at law, age 49 years, living with his wife Nancy Oakley, age 36 years, and seven children: Margaret, age 15 years; Hugh N., age 12 years; Moses, age 10 years; Nannie J., age 6 years; Sallie, age 4 years; Daisy, age 1 year; and Kansis (a son), age 21 years.

Page 68, Jones' 1900 Trigg County Census #73-73, he is listed as a farmer, age 63 years living with his wife Nancy C. Oakley (married 42 years), age 56 years, and two children: Daisy, age 21 years, and Henry B., age 17 years. (Nancy C. Oakley has had eight children, five of whom were still living when this census was taken.)

EPHIRAM D. OSBORN, born 4 May 1844, died 5 Sep 1913. He served with Co. B, 8th Kentucky Regt. Inf. (CSA). Perrin's History of Trigg County gives his birth as 4 May 1842; Trigg County Cemetery Records gives his birth date as 4 May 1844 and Jones' 1900 Trigg County Census has his birth month and year as May 1844.

His father Miles "Osborne" married Margaret Sanders on 28 Oct 1833 in Trigg County. Miles Osborn was born ca. 1814 in either Mississippi or Louisiana and Margaret Ann Sanders Osborn was born ca. 1815 in Kentucky. They are buried in the Yates Cemetery in Trigg County, but there are no stones to their grave.

Ephiram is buried with his wife Sarah Elizabeth Luttrell Osborn (b. 27 Jan 1847 in Tennessee, d. 27 Nov 1903) in the Yates Cemetery.

On page 22, Simmons' 1860 Trigg County Census #315, he is listed as age 14 years and living with his father "M" (Miles) Osborn, age 49

years; his mother "M.A." (Margaret Ann) Osborn, age 44 years, and seven siblings: Thomas, age 17 years; Jesse, age 17 years; Sarah, age 12 years; C. (male), age 10 years; John, age 9 years; James, age 5 years; and P. (male), age 2 years.

On page 140, Jones' 1900 Trigg County Census #133, he is listed as Ephriam D., a farmer, age 56 years, living with his wife Sarah E. Osborn (married 31 years), age 53 years, and seven children: Emma G., age 24 years; Jesse A., age 21 years; Henry N., age 19 years; John S., age 17 years; Seldon, age 14 years; Mary A., age 11 years; and Rhean H. (male), age 9 years. Sarah E. Osborn has had 12 children, eight of whom were still living when this census was taken. Jesse A. Osborn is listed as a school teacher in this census.

ANDREW J. PARSLEY, 3rd Corporal, born ca. 1845 in Kentucky. He enlisted 24 Oct 1861 at Camp Alcorn Hopkinsville, KY and served with Co. B, 8th Kentucky Regt. Inf. (CSA). He was promoted to 3rd corporal and served as a courier for Col. Ed Crossland after consolidation. He was promoted to 5th corporal on 23 Dec 1861. He was captured at Fort Donelson and sent to Camp Morton, IN. Andrew J. was a brother to John F. and Minus C., both Confederate soldiers.

A.J.'s father was Jesse S. Parsley (b. ca. 1793 in Virginia) and his stepmother was Sarah A. (Burchett) Parsley who married Jesse Parsley on 6 Feb 1855 in Trigg County, KY.

A.J. at age 22 married H.A.G. Faulkner, age 19 years on 11 Jul 1867, in Trigg County. This was the first marriage for both. Both bride and groom were born in Trigg County, KY.

According to Simmons' 1860 Trigg County Census, Page 41, #607, Henrietta A.G. Faulkner (b. ca. 1849 in Kentucky) was the daughter of D.D. Faulkner and Nancy Faulkner.

On page 18, Simmons' 1850 Trigg County Census #336, he is listed as age 6 and living with father Jesse S. Parsely, age 57 years, and six siblings: James J., age 17 years; John F., age 15 years; Minus C., age 12 years; Nancy A., age 10 years; Sarah J., age 8 years; Susan C., age 3 months.

On page 189, Neel's Statistical Handbook of Trigg County, 1880 Trigg County Census, toward bottom of page, he is listed as "A.J. Pursley" a blacksmith, age 36 years, living with his wife Henrietta "Pursley," age 30 years, and five children: James, age 12 years; Zula, age 9 years; Frances (daughter) age 8 years; Linnie (daughter), age 5 years; and Willie (daughter), age 2 years.

JOHN F. PARSLEY, Private, born ca. 1831 in Tennessee. He enlisted 24 Oct 1861 at Camp Alcorn in Hopkinsville, KY and served with Co. B, 8th Kentucky Regt. Inf. (CSA). He is listed as AWOL at home in Kentucky in a C.S. Army roll dated 24 Oct 1861 - 31 Jul 1862. He was captured by Union troops in Trigg County then sent to Vicksburg via Cairo, IL, 24 Dec 1862. John F. Parsley was a brother to Andrew J. and Minus C., both Confederate soldiers.

John F. married "Rabecca" W. Jennings on 26 Oct 1857 in Trigg County.

On page 18 Simmons' 1850 Trigg County Census #336, he is listed as age 15 years and living with his father Jesse S. Parsley, age 57 years and six siblings: James J., age 17 years; Minus C., age 12 years; Nancy A., age 10 years; Sarah J., age 8 years; Andrew J., age 6 years; and Susan C., age 3 months.

On page 41, Simmons' 1860 Trigg County Census #599, he is listed as age 29 years and living with his wife Rebecca (Jennings), age 23 years on the farm of Elizabeth Jennings, his mother-in-law, age 64 years.

MINUS C. PARSLEY, 3rd Sergeant, born ca. 1838 in Tennessee. He enlisted 9 Dec 1862 at Williamsport, TN and served with Co. A, 15th (Woodward's) Kentucky Cav. Regt. and Co. B, 2/15th (Woodward's) Kentucky Cav. Regt.

Sgt. Parsley was one of 10 Confederate soldiers who made up the last escort of President Jefferson Davis. Minus C. Parsley was a brother to Andrew J. and John F. Parsley, both Confederate soldiers.

On page 18, Simmons' 1850 Trigg County Census #336, he is listed as age 12 years and living with his father Jesse S. Parsley, age 57 years, and six siblings: James J., age 17 years; John F., age 15 years; Nancy A., age 10 years; Sarah J., age 8 years; Andrew J., age 6 years; and Susan C., age 3 months.

JAMES W. PENDLETON, Private, born ca. 1843 in Kentucky. He enlisted 10 Dec 1862 at Williamsport, TN and served with Co. A, Woodward's 15th Kentucky Regt. Cav. He was captured on 24 Dec 1863, but the place is not known.

He is listed on the Roaring Spring Poll Book November 1868 as J.W. Pendleton.

J.W. Pendleton, age 23 years of Christian County, was married to Isabel V. Wilson, age 31(?) years from Trigg County, on 28 Jan 1867.

He is buried in the Wilson-Raldolph Cemetery (no stone) with his wife Isabella (b. 9 Sep 1852, d. 15 May 1888).

On page 17, Simmons' 1870 Trigg County Census #180, he is listed as "James W. Penelton," age 26 years, living with his wife E. Isabel (Wilson) "Penleton," age 18 years, no children.

Page 175, Neel's Statistical Handbook of Trigg County, 1880 Trigg County Census, toward bottom of page, he is listed as "James Pendleton" a farmer, age 37 years, living with his wife Belle, age 28 years, and four children: Graves, age 9 years; James, age 7 years; Oscar, age 4 years; and Iva (a daughter), age 10 months.

CARROLL B. PEPPER, Private, born ca. 1824 in Tennessee. He served with Co. D, 17th Kentucky Regt. Inf. (USA). Enrolled 12 Nov 1861, mustered in 1 Jan 1862 at Calhoun, KY and discharged April 1862 at, Shiloh TN. His second unit was Co. L, 17th Kentucky Regt. Cav. (USA). He enrolled 23 Jan 1865 at Louisville, KY, mustered in 13 Mar 1865 at Louisville, KY and mustered out 20 Sep 1865 at Louisville, KY.

Neel lists him as War Veterans, Page 460. He is listed as a Civil War Veteran. According to Page 594, Vol. I, of the Kentucky Adjutant General's Report, Pvt. Pepper was discharged at Shiloh, TN in April 1862. He was a private in Co. F, 25th Kentucky Infantry prior to consolidation.

He is the only Pepper buried in the Skinner Cemetery (no stone). None of Carrol Pepper's immediate family is found buried in Trigg County, KY.

On page 153, Simmons' 1870 Trigg County Census #1825, he is listed as "Carel B. Peppers," a farmer age 46 years, living with his wife Harriet S. "Peppers," age 43 years, and five children: William M. (Moses), age 16 years; George W., age 13 years; Thomas F., age 11 years; Nancy C., age 7 years; and Carel J., age 4 years.

RICHARD POGUE, Private, born ca. 1842 in Tennessee. He enlisted 14 Sep 1861 at Camp Burnett, TN and served with Co. G, 4th Kentucky Regt. Inf. (CSA).

According to the Adjutant General's Report, he was missing 30 Sep 1862 and was discharged on account of disability 20 Jul 1863.

All of the members of his family were born in Tennessee except for his youngest sister, Susan Pogue.

James and William Pogue are mentioned as being registered in the Ferguson Spring Poll Book - 1 Aug 1859. John Pogue is listed on the Poll Book for the Forgerson precinct in August 1859.

His father John A. Pogue, age 50 years, born in Jefferson County, TN, married Mary A. Wimms, age 34 years of Trigg County, KY, on 16 May 1867. It was the second marriage for both bride and groom.

According to Neel's Statistical Handbook of Trigg County, War Veterans, Page 463, Richard Pogue is a Civil War Veteran and is buried at Fort Henry, TN.

Page 7, Simmons' 1860 Trigg County Census #93, he is listed as age 18 years and living with father John Pogue, age 52 years; his mother Martha Pogue, age 40 years; and seven siblings: William, age 29 years; James, age 22 years; Martha, age 24 years; Sophia, age 18 years; Francis (male), age 14 years; Thomas, age 12 years; and Susan, age 6 years.

ALEXANDER B. POSTON, Private, born ca. 1845 in Kentucky, died 15 Feb 1862 at the Battle of Fort Donelson. He enlisted 26 Sep 1861 at Camp Reeves, TN and served with Co. G, 8th Kentucky Regt. Inf. (CSA). He was the first Confederate in a Kentucky Regiment from Trigg County to be killed on the field of battle in the Civil War. Actually, Rufus Hutts of Trigg County, a private in the 14th Tennessee Regt. Inf. had been killed in 1861.

His father was Alexander H. Poston (b. born ca. 1815 in Tennessee) and his stepmother was Mary D. (Carson) Poston (b. ca. 1822 in Kentucky). They were married on 24 Oct 1848, when Alexander was about 3 years of age.

Private Alexander B. Poston is buried in a common grave at Fort Donelson, TN.

On page 94, Simmons' 1860 Trigg County Census #1385, he is listed as age 15 years and livinq with father Alexander H. Poston, age 46 years, his stepmother Mary D. (Carson) Poston, age 36 years, and three siblings: John H., age 20 years; Mary A., age 11 years; and Betty A., age 7 years.

JOEL F. PRICHARD, 1st Corporal, born ca. 1839 in Kentucky. He enlisted 10 Sep 1861 at Camp Burnett, TN and served with Co. G, 4th Kentucky Regt. Inf. (CSA). He was wounded at Dallas, GA on 25 May 1864. The name is often spelled "Pritchard."

There were two Cynthia Harrells living in Trigg County during this era and both seemed to be married to a J.M. Harrell. We believe Joel's sister was Cynthia A. Harrell and the other lady was Cynthia H. Harrell.

His father William Prichard (b. ca. 1811 in North Carolina) and mother were married ca. 1832. William married second, Elizabeth Tally (b. ca. 1804 in South Carolina) on 19 Feb 1847 in Trigg County, KY; he married third, Rebecca Harris on 18 Jan 1855 in Trigg County and at age 57 married his fourth wife, Mrs. Julia Atwood, age 45 years, on 2 Jun 1869.

On page 48, Simmons' 1850 Trigg County Census #873, he is listed as age 11 years and living with his father William Prichard, age 39 years; his first stepmother Elizabeth (Talley) Prichard, age 46 years; and three siblings: Cintha A., age 15 years; Eliza (Joel's twin), age 11 years; and Mary A., age 5 years.

On page 58, Simmons' 1860 Trigg County Census #861, he is listed as age "J.F." Prichard, age 18 years, living with his father William Prichard, age 47 years, and his second stepmother "R." (Rebecca) (Harris) Prichard, age 43 years, and his sister Mary A., age 15 years.

Page 211, Neel's Statistical Handbook of Trigg County, 1880 Trigg County Census, middle of page, (Joseph or Joel) Prichard is listed as a farmer, age 38 years and living with his wife Sophia J. Prichard, age 33 years, and six daughters: Annie Lee, age 12 years; Mary E., age 11 years; Minnie M., age 9 years; Lilly M., age 8 years; Iva Dell, age 4 years; and Edda H., age 6 months. His father William Prichard is listed as a house carpenter, age 68 years living with the family in this census.

JOSEPH P. PRYOR, Private, born 2 Mar 1843 in Kentucky, died 16 Mar 1917. Enrolled 20 Jul 1863, mustered in 26 Oct 1863 in Princeton, KY and mustered out 19 Dec 1864 in Bowling Green, KY. He served with Co. F, 48th Kentucky Regiment Mounted Infantry (USA).

His father was William Pryor (b. ca. 1804 in Kentucky) and his mother was Mary Pryor (b. ca. 1808 in Virginia).

J.P. (Joseph P.) Pryor married Elizabeth E. McCain (b. 26 Jan 1854, d. 9 Jul 1902) on 29 Feb 1872 in Trigg County, KY. He is buried in the Pryor Cemetery with his wife.

On page 41, Simmons' 1850 Trigg County Census #753, he is listed as age 7 years and living with his father William Pryor, age 46 years; his mother Mary Pryor, age 42 years; and six siblings: Adeline, age 22 years; Delila C., age 17 years; Jonathan E., age 15 years; James R., age 13 years; William L., age 10 years; and Lucy A., age 3 years.

On page 84, Simmons' 1860 Trigg County census #1228, he is listed as age 18 years and living with his father William Pryor, age 58 years; his mother Mary Pryor, age 50 years; and three siblings: James R., age 23 years; William L., age 20 years; and Lucy A., age 14 years.

Page 208, Neel's Statistical Handbook of Trigg County, 1880 Trigg County Census, middle of the page, he is listed as "Joe" Pryor, a farmer age 36 years, living with his wife "Emilie" Pryor, age 26 years; and three children: Ozella (daughter), age 7 years; Albie (daughter), age 5 years; and Oscar, age 3 years..

MATTHEW M. PUCKETT, Private, born ca. 1843 in Kentucky. He enrolled on 14 Aug 1862, mustered in 13 Sep 1862, at Henderson, KY and mustered out 23 Sep 1863 at Russellville, KY. He served with Co. L, 8th Kentucky Regt. Cav. (USA).

John T. Puckett was the only sibling of Matthew born in Virginia. All the others were born in Kentucky.

His father was Isaac Puckett (b. ca. 1811 in Virginia) and his mother was Elizabeth (Rickman) Puckett (b. ca. 1817 in Virginia).

On page 35, Simmons' 1850 Trigg County Census #631-94, he is listed as Matthew M. Puckett, age 7 years and living with his father Isaac Puckett, age 39 years; his mother Elizabeth Rickman Puckett, age 33 years; and five siblings: John T., age 18 years; "Permelia" A., age 12 years; Mary J., age 10 years; Nancy M., age 5 years; and Elizabeth H., age 3 years.

On page 9, Simmons' 1860 Trigg County Census #126, he is listed as "M.M." Puckett, age 14 years and living with his father "J." (Isaac) Puckett, age 45 years; his mother "E." (Elizabeth) Rickman Puckett, age 40 years; and seven siblings: "J.T." (John T.) age 27 years; "R.A." (Pamelia A.) age 18 years; "M.J." (Mary J.) age 16 years; "N.M." (Nancy M.) age 12 years; "E.H." (Elizabeth H.), age 11 years; "G.W." (George W.), age 9 years; and "S.A." (Susan A.), age 5 years.

ASPASIA E. REESE, 3rd Sergeant, born ca. 1840 in Kentucky. He enlisted 26 Sep 1861 at Camp Reeves, TN and served with Co. G, 8th Kentucky Regt. Inf. (CSA). He was severely wounded at Fort Donelson on 15 Feb 1862, taken prisoner and sent to Camp Morton, IN. He was not able to be exchanged with his regiment at Vicksburg the following September and was permanently disabled from further military service and finally took a non-combatant's oath to return to his home.

Aspasia's father Joseph Reese is listed in the Roaring Spring Poll Book, April 1841, and the Roaring Spring Poll Book, August 1861.

On page 18, Simmons' 1850 Trigg County Census #325, he is listed as Aspasia E. Reese, age 10 years, living with his father Joseph B. Reese, age 50 years, and two sisters: Marian C., age 18 years, and Zoria A., age 12 years.

On page 53, Simmons' 1860 Trigg County Census #781, he is listed as Aspasia Reese, age 19 years living with his father J.B. (Joseph B.) Reese, age 68 years.

FRANK REYNOLDS, Private, born ca. 1839. Enrolled 30 Jul 1863, mustered in 26 Oct 1863 in Princeton, KY and mustered out 19 Dec 1864 at Bowling Green, KY. He served with Co. F, 48th Kentucky Regiment Mounted Infantry (USA). Frank B. Reynolds is listed as "absent sick" when the company was mustered out of service.

According to the 1850 Census all of the children in the family were born in Tennessee except for Abigail, Mary and Charles.

Ben or B. Reynolds is listed in Roaring Springs Poll Book - 6 Aug 1860. Ben or B. Reynolds is listed in Roaring Spring Poll Book - Aug 1861 Election. Ben or B. Reynolds is listed in Roaring Spring Poll Book - Nov 1868.

Frank's father was Benjamin Reynolds (b. ca. 1796 in South Carolina) and his mother was Susan Reynolds (b. ca. 1805 in South Carolina).

In the McGraw Cemetery in Trigg County, there is buried a Lula Reynolds "wife of Frank," but there are no dates or other information.

On page 36, Simmons' 1850 Trigg County Census #667, he is listed as age 11 years, living with his father Benajah Reynolds, age 54 years; his mother Susan Reynolds age 45 years; and eight siblings: William E., age 24 years; Hester A., age 20 years; John, age 18 years; Joseph, age 15 years; James, age 13 years; Abigail, age 9 years; Mary, age 7 years; and Charles C., age 4 years.

On page 82, Simmons' 1860 Trigg County Census #1202, he is listed as age 21 years, living with his wife "N." Reynolds, age 19 years, no children.

THOMAS W. RHODES, born ca. 1846 in Kentucky. He enrolled 4 Aug 1964, mustered in 4 Aug 1864 at Paducah, KY and mustered out 12 Feb 1865 at Paducah, KY. He was a member of Co. B, 1st Regiment Capital Guards, Paducah Battalion (USA).

His father Ephiram Rhodes married Jane Mitchell on 2 Mar 1844, in Trigg County.

T.W. Rhoades is listed as being buried in the Rhoades Cemetery in Trigg County, KY. There is no stone at his grave, however.

On page 2, Simmons' 1860 Trigg County Census #33, a Thomas W. "Rhoades" is listed as age 13 years, living with his father "E." (Ephriam) "Rhoades," age 38 years; his mother Jane "Rhoades," age 27 years(?); and two siblings: Josephine, age 9 years, and "A." (Ander King Killas), age 2 years.

On page 101, Simmons' 1870 Trigg County Census #1173, a Thomas Willie Rhodes is listed as age 22 years, living with his father Ephriam Rhodes, age 49 years; his mother Jane Rhodes, age 48 years; and two siblings: Ephriam W., age 14 years, and Anking K. (Ander King Killas) 20 years(?).

On page 235, Neel's Statistical Handbook of Trigg County, 1800 Trigg County Census, toward bottom of page, he is listed as Thomas W. "Rhoads," a farmer age 33 years, living with his wife "Sousan Rhoads," age 22 years, and one son Euen, age 2 months.

WILLIAM HENRY RHODES, born ca. 1848 in Kentucky. He enrolled 4 Aug 1864, mustered in 4 Aug 1864 at Paducah, KY and mustered out 12 Feb 1865 at Paducah, KY. He served with Co. B, 1st Regiment Capital Guards, Paducah Battalion (USA). (If this man served in the War for Southern Independence, he was a very young soldier.)

His father was Robert Rhodes (b. ca. 1818 in Kentucky). We believe his mother was Eliza J. (Nicey) (Higgins) Rhodes (b. ca. 10 Jan 1821 in Kentucky, d. 11 Dec 1855). They were married in Trigg County, KY, on 30 Sep 1840. We believe his mother is buried in the Salem Church Cemetery along with her son Robert W. Rhodes (b. ca. 1849 in Kentucky, d. 18 Jan 1853) There is no stone to Robert's grave.

His wife was Lurana or Lurane Rhodes (b. 1848 in Kentucky, d. 1880). She is buried in the Savells Cemetery.

On page 63, Simmons' 1850 Trigg County Census #1162-633, he is listed as William H. Rhodes, age 2 years living with his father Robert Rhodes, age 32 years; his mother Eliza Jane (Higgins) Rhodes, age 27 years; and four siblings: Thomas G., age 7 years; Mary A., age 5 years; Jane D., age 3 years; and Robert W., age 5 months.

On page 103, Simmons' 1870 Trigg County Census #1191, he is listed as Henry Rhodes, age 23 years living with his wife Lurane Rhodes, age 21 years, and two children: Mary J., age 3, and George T., age 1 year.

On page 236, Neel's Statistical Handbook of Trigg County, 1880 Trigg County Census, top of page, he is listed as a farmer, age 33 years, living with his wife Laurana, age 32 years, and five children: Mary F., age 12 years; George T., age 10 years; Alpha D., age 8 years; John R., age 6 years; and Evie A., age 1 year.

On page 89, Jones' 1900 Trigg County Census #224-224, he is listed as a farmer, age 50 years living with his wife Cora Rhodes, age 24 years, and three daughters: Curva R., age 7 years; Hollie, age 6 years; and Myrtie, age 2 years.

GEORGE RIDDLES, Private, mustered in 17 Feb 1865 at Covington, KY and served with the only George Riddle we can find from Kentucky. He was in Co. M of the 13th US Colored Artillery (Heavy) (USA). According to Neel's Record, George Riddles is a War for Southern Independence veteran buried at Canton, KY.

According to Maupin's reference, a George Riddles is a War for Southern Independence veteran and is buried in the Yates Cemetery in Trigg County, KY.

THOMAS RILEY, Private, born ca. 1827 in Tennessee, died 4 May 1862 in Camp Morton, IN. He enlisted 24 Oct 1861 at Camp Alcorn in Hopkinsville, KY and served with Co. B, 8th Kentucky Regt. Inf. (CSA). He was captured at Fort Donelson on 16 Feb 1862, and sent to Camp Morton, IN, where he died on 4 May 1862.

On page 6, Simmons' 1860 Trigg County Census #86, he is listed as Thomas Riley, a woodcutter age 33 years and living with the Sam McWaters family in this census.

JORDAN B. ROACH, born Jan 1840 in Kentucky, died 1910. In the 1850 Census he was born in Kentucky while his mother Mary J. Roach was also born in Kentucky, but his brothers, Oliver and Marshal, were born in Tennessee.

J.B. Roach married Rebecca Rushing on 18 Aug 1880 in Trigg County. According to Maupin, Jordan and Rebecca had a son Porter and perhaps a daughter Ida.

On page 61, Simmons' 1850 Trigg County Census #1115-586, he is listed as Jordan B. Roach, age 10 years, living with his mother Mary J. Roach, age 40 years, and two brothers: Oliver D., age 17 years, and Marshal A. (Ney), age 13 years)

On page 125, Simmons' 1870 Trigg County Census #1497, he is listed as a farmer, age 29 years, living with his mother Mary J. Roach, age 65 years.

On page 229, Neel's Statistical Handbook of Trigg County, 1880 Trigg County Census, middle of page, he is listed as age 39 years and living alone in this Census), but very near Marshall N. Roach, his brother.

On page 83, Jones' 1900 Trigg County Census #182-182, he is listed as a farmer, age 60 years, living with his wife Rebecca J. Roach (married 19 years), age 39 years, and six children: Sarah A., age 16 years; Jordan O., age 13 years; Beulah, age 1 year; James P., age 9 years; Mathew, age 7 years; and Cloid, age 3 years. Rebecca J. Rushing Roach has had eight children, seven of whom were still living when this census was taken.

MARSHAL NEY ROACH, born 10 Jun 1837 in Hardin County, TN, died 28 Feb 1917. He enlisted in 1861 near Bloomfield, MO and served with Co. C, 4th Missouri Regt. Cav. (CSA).

In the 1850 Census his mother Mary J. was born in Kentucky while his brother Oliver D. was born in Tennessee and his brother Jordan B. was born in Kentucky.

According to Confederate Pension Applications, only the daughters, Mary M. (Roach) McQuithey and Bettie Roach were living in 1917.

He was married to Romanza B. Sholar on 17 Jan 1869 in Trigg County, KY.

Marshal Ney is buried in the Pinnegar Cemetery with his wife Romanza Bell Vadra (Sholar) Roach (b. 31 Aug 1852, d. 16 Jan 1939)

Page 61, Simmons' 1850 Trigg County Census #1115-586, he is listed as "Marshall A." Roach, age 13 years, living with his mother Mary J. Roach, age 40 years, and two brothers: Oliver D., age 17 years, and Jordan B., age 10 years.

On page 13, Simmons' 1860 Trigg County Census #194, he is listed as "M." Roach, a farm laborer, age 22 years living with his mother Mary J. Roach, age 48 years, and two brothers: Jordan Roach, age 22 years, and Oliver Roach, age 26 years.

On page 128, Simmons' 1870 Trigg County Census #1526, he is listed as age 32 years, living with his wife Romanza (Sholar) Roach, age 16 years, and one child Mary M., 2 months.

On page 229, Neel's Statistical Handbook of Trigg County, 1880 Trigg County Census, he is listed as Marshal "A." Roach, age 42 years and living with his wife Romanza (Sholar) Roach, age 29 years, and five children: Mary M., age 10 years; Pennyetta, age 8 years; Ferlisa J. (Phelisa Jane), age 6 years; Alley L., age 4 years; and James W., age 1 year.

On page 88, Jones' 1900 Trigg County Census #214-214, he is listed as Marshall N. Roach, a farmer age 62 years, living with his wife Romanza (Sholar) Roach (married 30 years), age 40 years, and five children: Mary M., age 30 years; James, age 21 years; Bettie, age 17 years; Marcella (female), age 15 years; and Saul T., age 10 years. Romanza Roach has had nine children, eight of whom are still living in this census.

ROBERT W. ROACH, Lieutenant, born 8 Jul 1841 in Trigg County, KY. He served with 1st Kentucky Regt. Cav. (CSA) and Co. A, Woodward's 15th KY Regt. Cav. (CSA). He was discharged at Chattanooga, TN, in August 1862. He never took the oath of allegiance.

His parents were Cuthbert W. Roach (b. 10 Jun 1801 in Virginia, d. 14 Sep 1875) and Francis A. Roach (b. March 1813 in Virginia, d. July 1850). They are buried in the Roach Cemetery in Trigg County. All of the Roach children mentioned in the 1850 census were born in Virginia except for Martha J., Robert W., Mary E. and Joseph J. who were all born in Kentucky.

R.W. Roach, age 26 years of Trigg County, married Mary Virginia Watkins, age 24 years (b. ca. 1843 in Kentucky), on 18 Dec 1867 in Trigg County.

On page 2, Simmons' 1850 Trigg County Census #22, he is listed as Robert W. Roach, age 9 years, living with his father C.W. Roach, listed as a merchant, age 48 years; his mother Francis A. Roach, age 36 years; and seven siblings: John J., age 25 years; Camella, age 18 years; E.C., age 18 years; Virginia W. age 14 years; Martha J., age 12 years; Mary E., age 6 years; and Joseph J., age 2 years.

On page 94, Simmons' 1860 Trigg County Census #1378, he is listed as a merchant/clerk, age 20 years living with his brother John J. Roach, age 34 years; his sister-in-law C.P. Roach, age 25 years, no children.

On page 187, Neel's Statistical Handbook of Trigg County, 1880 Trigg County Census, toward bottom of page, he is listed as a farmer, age 58 years, living with his wife Mary Roach, age 58 years, and five children: Lula, age 18 years; Maud, age 18 years; Cuttie, age 10 years; and Garnett, age 5 years.

On page 132, Blue & Sellers' 1920 Trigg County Census #1846, he is listed as Robert W. Roach a farmer, age 78 years living with his wife Mary V. Roach, age 76 years, and a married daughter Catherine, age 46, living with them in this census.

JAMES O. ROBERTS, Private, born ca. 1843 in Kentucky, died 7 Nov 1861 in Hopkinsville, KY. He enlisted 26 Sep 1861 at Camp Reeves, TN and served with Co. G, 8th Kentucky Regt. Inf. (CSA). He died of disease in Hopkinsville, KY, on 7 Nov 1861.

His parents may have been Robert B. Roberts (b. ??, d. prior to 1850) and Minerva Adeline (Manning) Roberts (b. 9 Feb 1815, d. April 1848). They were married on 20 Aug 1838 in Trigg County, KY.

According to Maupin, he is buried in the Manning Cemetery, but there is no stone to his grave. His mother Minerva Adaline (Manning) Roberts is also buried in the Manning Cemetery.

On page 31, Simmons' 1850 Trigg County Census #564, he is listed as age 7 years living with his maternal grandparents, Cornelius and Nancy Manning and family and three siblings: John C., age 9 years; William T., age 5 years; and Minerva A., age 2 years.

On page 70, Simmons' 1860 Trigg County Census #1026, he is listed as "J.O." Roberts, age 18 years, living with "N.M." (Nathaniel H.) Manning, age 47 years; "J.W." (John W.) Manning, age 37 years; and "H.J." (Harriett I.) Manning, age 42 years; and siblings John C. Roberts, age 20 years, and Minerva A. Roberts, age 12 years.

JOHN C. ROBERTS, Private, born ca. 1841 in Kentucky, died 9 Nov 1861 in Hopkinsville, KY. He enlisted 26 Dec 1861, at Camp Reeves, TN and served with Co. G, 8th Kentucky Regt. Inf. (CSA). He died of disease at Hopkinsville, KY, on 9 Nov 1861.

His parents may have been Robert B. Roberts (b. ??, d. prior to 1850) and Minerva Adaline (Manning) Roberts (b. 9 Feb 1815, d. Apr 1848). They were married 20 Aug 1838 in Trigg County, KY.

According to Maupin, he is buried in the Manning Cemetery, but there is no stone to his grave. His mother Minerva Adeline (Manning) Roberts is also buried in the Manning Cemetery.

On page 31, Simmons' 1850 Trigg Co. Census #564, he is listed as age 9 years and living with his maternal grandparents, Cornelius and Nancy Manning and family, and three siblings: John O. Roberts, age 7 years; William T. Roberts, age 5 years; and Minerva A. Roberts, age 2 years.

On page 70, Simmons' 1860 Trigg County Census #1026, he is listed as "J.C." Roberts, age 20 years and living with "N.H." (Nathaniel) Manning, age 47 years, "J.W." (John W.) Manning, age 37 years, and "H.J." (Harriett I.) Manning, age 42 years, and two siblings, "J.O." (James O.) Roberts, age 18 years, and Minerva A. Roberts, age 12 years.

JAMES P. ROBERTSON, Private, born ca. 1845 in Kentucky. He enrolled 7 Aug 1863, mustered in 26 Oct 1863 at Princeton, KY and mustered out 19 Dec 1864 at Bowling Green, KY. He served with Co. F, 48th Kentucky Regiment Mounted Infantry (USA).

His father was Samuel Robertson (b. ca. 1800 in South Carolina) and his mother was Nancy Robertson (b. ca. 1802 in South Carolina).

On page 41, Simmons' 1850 Trigg County Census #750, he is listed as age 5 years living with his father Samuel Robertson, age 50 years; his mother Nancy Robertson, age 48 years; and four siblings: Joel, age 23 years; Amanda E., age 14 years; Malinda C., age 11 years; Thomas, age 8 years; and James P., age 5 years.

On page 84, Simmons' 1860 Trigg County Census #1238, he is listed as "J.P." age 15 years, living with his mother "N." (Nancy) Robertson, age 58 years, and an "R.T." Robertson (male), age 18 years, and born in Tennessee.

On page 192, Simmons' 1870 Trigg County Census #2257, he is listed as a farmer, age 25 years, living with his wife Manizey Roberts, age 21 years, on the farm of his mother Nancy Robertson, age 64 years. James P. Robertson and his wife have no children.

JOSIAH ROBERTSON, Private, born ca. 1828 in South Carolina, died 16 Nov 1863 at Princeton, KY. He enrolled 23 Jul 1863, mustered in 26 Oct 1863 at Princeton, KY and died before being mustered out. He served with Co. F, 48th Kentucky Regiment Mounted Infantry.

We believe his father was Samuel Robertson (b. ca. 1800 in South Carolina, d. ??) and his mother was Nancy Robertson (b. ca. 1802 in South Carolina)

Josiah Robertson's name is mentioned in the Roaring Spring Poll Books for August 1860 and August 1861 elections.

He married Rhoda (b. 25 Oct 1829 d. 10 Dec 1910). She is buried in the Flat Lick Cemetery.

On page 41, Simmons' 1850 Trigg County Census #751, he is listed as living with his wife Rhoda J., age 21 years, no children.

On page 86, Simmons' 1860 Trigg County Census #1267, he is listed as age 31 years and living with his wife Rhoda, age 30 years, and three children: "W.P." (male), age 9 years; "M.A." (female), age 7 years; "J.J." (male), age 3 years.

On page 294, Jones' 1900 Trigg County Census #71-71. Rhoda J. Robertson is listed as a widow age 30 years, living with her son Tom Robertson, a farmer, age 37 years (born November 1862), his wife Almer L. Robertson (married nine years), age 33 years, and six grandchildren: Volar M., age 8 years; Minie L., age 7 years; Gracie W., age 5 years; Freeman, age 4 years; Raymon, age 4 years; and William P., age 1 year. Rhoda Robertson has had seven children, five of whom are still living at this census.

JOHN JAMES ROGERS,

JOHN JAMES ROGERS, born 16 Oct 1846 in Trigg County, enrolled in the US Army 1 Aug 1863. Corporal Rogers was mustered in 26 Oct 1863 at Princeton, KY for one year. He served as a Union soldier with Co. F, 48th Kentucky Volunteer Mounted Infantry and died of smallpox, 9 Dec 1864. at Bowling Green, KY.

The 48th Regt. Mounted Inf. was organized at Princeton, KY 26 Oct 1863; attached to District of Southwest Kentucky, 1st Division, 23rd Army Corps, Dept. of Ohio, to April 1864; 1st Brigade, 2nd Division, District of Kentucky, 5th Division, 23rd Army Corps, Dept. of Ohio to December 1864.

Duty at Princeton, KY until 1 Dec 1863. Moved to Russellville 1 December and duty there (Cos. B, F, G and H) and at Bowling Green, KY (Cos. A, D, I and K) until 6 Apr 1864. Guard duty on line of Louisville & Nashville Railroad from Cave City to Louisville, KY. Co. A at Elizabethtown, Companies B, F and H and headquarters at Munfordsville; Companies C and K at Fort Boyle, Colesburg: Co. D at Cave City; Co. E at Shepherdsville; Co. I at Louisville; and Co. G at Smithland until 8 Jul 1864. Action at Salem 8 August (Detachments from Companies B and C), regiment relieved and mounted. Moved to Calhoun 13-19 August and joined Hobson's operations against Adam Johnson 19-24 August, Canton, KY; 24 August, moved to Cadiz, thence to Princeton, KY, and operating against guerrillas in counties bordering on the Cumberland River until 1 December. Skirmish in Union County, 31 August (Detachment), Weston 14 September. Action with Lyon's forces 6 November (Detachment Cos. F and K). Eddyville 17 October. Providence 21 November. Mustered out 19 Dec 1864.

Regiment lost during service—seven enlisted men killed and mortally wounded and one officer and 96 enlisted men by disease. Total 104.

Rogers was the eldest son of William Scott and Matilda Tart Rogers. In addition to his parent, he was survived by brothers and sisters: Joseph Green, William Henry, Cyrus Wayne, Mary Ellen, Franklin Hardin, Treeman Tart and Ira Byron Rogers.

Trigg County descendants of John Rogers include grandnephew, James William Rogers, and grandniece, Ruth Janelle Rogers Simmons.

J.W. ROSS,

J.W. ROSS, Private, born May 1827 in Tennessee. He mustered in 13 Sep 1862 in Henderson, KY and was discharged 3 Mar 1863 in Russellville, KY. He served with Co. L, 8th Kentucky Regt. Cav. (USA).

James W. Ross died between 1900 and 1905. We believe James Ross' father was Johathan Ross (b. ca. 1811 in Kentucky) and his mother was Narcissa Ross (b. ca. 1810 in Tennessee)

James Ross married Anna (Gordon) Rich (b. ca. 1814 in Tennessee) on 17 Sep 1848 in Trigg County, KY. James W. Ross married Mrs. Frances L. (Cothran) Duncan on 1 Feb 1889 in Trigg County, KY. Mrs. Duncan was the widow of J.G.W. Duncan whom she married on 24 Sep 1882 in Trigg County, KY.

There is a J.W. Ross, designated as a WSI veteran buried in the Ross Cemetery, but there is no stone to his grave.

Mrs. Martie (Martha) Ann (Ross) Ahart, wife of James Ahart, is certified as the only child and the only heir of James W. Ross on 4 Sep 1905.

On page 59, Simmons' 1850 Trigg County Census #1080, James Ross is listed as a laborer, age 21 years, living with his wife Anna (Gordon) (Rich) Ross, age 36 years, and three stepchildren: Jasper (or Joseph) Rich, age 15 years; Marion F. Rich (male), age 13 years; and Louisa Rich, age 10 years.

On page 118, Simmons' 1870 Trigg County Census #1383, James W. Ross is listed as a farmer, age 40 years, living with his wife Mary Ann Ross, age 50 years, and a daughter Martha Ann, age 14 years.

On page 115, Jones' 1900 Trigg County Census #419-419, he is listed as a farmer, age 73 years, living with his wife Frances L. (Cothran) (Duncan) Ross, age 55 years, no children.

AMOS P. RUTLEDGE,

AMOS P. RUTLEDGE, Private, is listed as mustering with a group of men in Trigg County on 6 Jul 1861. He is also in a list of men who mustered with Capt. Alfred Thomas at the Trigg County Courthouse in Cadiz, KY on 7 Apr 1861. He may have served in a Tennessee Unit.

Amos P. married Elizabeth H. Dixon on 23 Jun 1857 in Trigg County, KY. Elizabeth H. (b. 10 May 1838 in Kentucky, d. 21 Jan 1859) is buried in the Lancaster-Dixon Cemetery in Trigg County, KY with her father John Dixon (b. 13 Feb 1807 in Kentucky, d. 30 Sep 1880) and her mother Matilda Lawrence Dixon (b. 25 Aug 1812 in Kentucky, d. 26 May 1894).

On page 328, Neel's Statistical Handbook of Trigg County, Trigg County Marriages.

On pages 485 and 486, Neel's Statistical Handbook of Trigg County, Lists of Enrolled Militia.

On page 63, Simmons' 1860 Trigg County Census #937. "M.J." Rutledge (female), age 1 year, is living with her maternal grandfather John Dixon, age 53 years, and her maternal grandfather Matilda (Lawrence) Dixon, age 49 years, and their children: "M.A." (Matilda A.), age 14 years, and "P.A." (Peachy A.), age 12 years.

WILLIAM WALLACE RYAN,

WILLIAM WALLACE RYAN, 3rd Sergeant, born 29 Oct 1840 in Missouri, died 29 Mar 1916. He enlisted 11 Aug 1861 at Camp Burnett, TN and served with Co. G, 4th Kentucky Regt. Inf. (CSA). He was promoted to 3rd sergeant on 10 Jan 1863. His tombstone reads as follows: "A Confederate soldier, faithful to every duty; a member of Co. G, 2nd Kentucky Regiment".

He married first, Nancy E. (Nannie) Yarborough (b. 30 Oct 1845 in Kentucky, d. 10 May 1876) ca. 1868 and married second, Marguerite (Maggie) Hayes Smith on 6 Jun 1878, in Trigg County, KY,

He is buried with his wife Marguerite (b. 14 Apr 1859, d. 24 Apr 1923) in the Matheny Cemetery. His first wife Nancy E. (Nannie) Yarborough Ryan is also buried in the Matheny Cemetery.

On page 65, Simmons' 1850 Trigg County Census #1199, he is listed as William Ryan, age 10 years (born in Missouri) and living with the Benjamin F. Luten and Martha (Hamilton) Luten family in this census.

On page 99, Jones' 1900 Trigg County Census #298-298, he is listed as William W. Ryan a farmer, age 59 years and living with his wife Margaret A. Ryan (married 21 years), age 41 years, and five children: Emmet, age 21 years; Willie, age 17 years; Gertie, age 16 years; Cecil, age 13 years; and Conley, age 3 years. Margaret Ryan has had 11 children, five of whom are still living at this census.

JAMES T. SAVILLS,

JAMES T. SAVILLS, Private, born ca. 1843 in Kentucky, died 26 Feb 1862 at Camp Morton, IN. He enlisted 26 Sep 1861 at Camp Reeves, TN and served with Co. G, 8th Kentucky Regt. Inf. (CSA).

According to the Kentucky Adjutant General's Report, he was taken prisoner at Fort Donelson and died in prison at Camp Morton, IN, on 26 Feb 1862.

His father was Thomas W. Savills Jr. and his mother was Elizabeth S. (Goodwin) Savills. They were married on 1 Apr 1840 in Trigg County, KY.

On page 27, Simmons' 1860 Trigg County Census #403, he is listed as age 17 years, living with his father "T.W." (Thomas W.) Savills Jr., age 42 years; his mother "E.S." (Elizabeth S.) (Goodwin) Savills, age 40 years; and eight siblings: "S.W." (Samuel W.), age 19 years' "A.E." (Ann E.), age 15 years; "M.E." (Mary E.), age 13 years; "W.D." (William B.), age 11 years; "S.A." (female), age 6 years; "P.C." (female), age 4 years; "S.A." (female), age 4 years; and "M.C." (female), 1 year.

MONROE SEARS, Private, born ca. 1834 in Montgomery County, TN, died 27 May 1864 at Dallas, GA. He enlisted 14 Sep 1861 at Camp Burnett, TN and served with Co. G, 4th Kentucky Regt. Inf. (CSA). He died at Dallas, GA on 27 May 1864.

Monroe Sears, age 21 years, (b. ca. 1834 in Montgomery County, TN) married Rosey Jane Bell, age 22 years (b. ca. 1835 in Logan County, KY) on 19 or 20 Sep 1855 in Trigg County, KY.

According to Maupin, Monroe Sears is buried in the Matheny-Cumberland Cemetery (no tombstone).

On page 7, Simmons' 1860 Trigg County Census #102, he is listed as "M." (Monroe) Sears, a coach driver, age 25 years and living with his wife Rosey Jane (Bell) Sears, age 20 years, and one son Thomas Sears, age 3 years.

On page 110, Simmons' 1870 Trigg County Census #1287, Monroe and Jane Sears' sons are listed as William T., age 12 years, and Jefferson D., age 8 years, living with an aunt and uncle, A.J. Cherry and Eveline Cherry in this census.

STEPHEN W. SHELTON, Captain, born 18 Nov 1839, died 14 Nov 1861. He served with Buckner's Company, 2nd Kentucky Cav. Stephen W.'s unit is given on his tombstone.

His father Henry Shelton (b. ca. 1801 in Virginia) and mother Susan A. Shelton (b. ca. 1815 in Virginia) are buried in the Edwards Cemetery (no tombstones).

Stephen is buried with his brothers Henry T. (b. 18 Nov 1836, d. 14 Nov 1861) and William O.B. Shelton (b. 1 Jan 1847, d. 27 Sep 1864) in the Edwards Cemetery.

John N. Shelton was the only sibling of Stephen W. that was born in Virginia. All others were born in Kentucky.

On page 13, Simmons' 1850 Trigg County Census #229, he is listed as Stephen W. Shelton, age 10 years, living with his father Henry N. Shelton, age 49 years; his mother, Susan A. Shelton, age 35 years; and six siblings: John N., age 18 years; Henry T., age 14 years; Susan A., age 12 years; Keziah F., age 8 years; Sally H., age 5 years; and William O.B., age 3 years.

ALBERT WAYNE SHOLAR, Private US Army, born 2 Jan 1845 and died Jul 31, 1902 in Trigg County, KY. He enlisted in the Union Army and served in Co. F 48th Regt. Inf. which was organized and mustered into service in Princeton, KY by Capt. Charles H. Fletcher of the 13th US Inf. on 26 Oct 1863 for a period of one year.

He served two years under Capt. C.K. Vanpelt, Col. Hartwell T. Burger, Lt. Col. William W Hester and Maj. William H. Hoyt commanded the 48th Regt. This was a mounted infantry regiment that enlisted principally from the counties of Trigg, Lyon, Livingston, Crittenden, Union, Christian, Caldwell, Muhlenberg, Breckinridge and Grayson counties. *The above information was taken from the Union Army, Vol. 4, page 342 and submitted by James G. Sholar, 2nd great-grandnephew. The following is from another source.*

Albert W. was the oldest son of James A. Sholar (b. ca. 1814 in Kentucky) and Telitha Jane (Rogers) Sholar (b. ca. 1821 in Kentucky). They were married 12 Sep 1840 in Trigg County, KY.

A.W. Sholar married Sarah Josephine Rogers on 14 Jan 1867 in Trigg County, KY. He is buried in the Sholar Cemetery and Sarah is buried in the Sholar-Rogers Cemetery.

On page 44, Simmons' 1850 Trigg County Census #817, he is listed as age 5 years and living with his father James A. Sholar, age 36 years; his mother Jane E., age 29 years; and four siblings: Martha, age 8 years; Elizabeth, age 7 years; Julia A., age 2 years; and James P., age 6 months.

On page 216, Neel's Statistical Handbook of Trigg County, he is listed as "Abner" W. Sholar, age 35 years, living with his wife S.J. (Sarah), age 35 years, and four children: B. Frank, age 12 years; Mollie, age 10 years; Jennie, age 7 years; and J.E. (James E.), age 1 year.

HENRY WASHINGTON SHOLAR, Private, born 28 Oct 1828 in Trigg County, KY. He is the son of Penelope Sholar. His occupation prior to hostilities was a schoolteacher in the Golden Pond area of Trigg County.

As it turns out, Henry Washington Sholar served in the CSA, Army and Union Army. He was first in Co D, 5th Arkansas Inf. His enlistment was on 13 Jun 1861 at Wittsburg, AR for one year in state service. This unit was soon transferred to confederate service on 27 Jul 1861.

He was also in Capt. Joel Andersons's Company, which became a part of Co. "E" Cockses, Arkansas Inf. Regt. This regiment was formed during the summer of 1862 and Mr. Sholar shows an enlistment date of 17 Jun 1862 and his resignation being accepted 30 Oct 1862 due to disabilities. There is a later enlistment shown in the same unit as 18 Apr 1863 at Little Rock, AR. The muster roll dated 31 Aug 1863 lists him as deserted.

On 15 May 1863 Henry W. Sholar enrolled in the 2nd Missouri State Militia, the 14th Missouri Volunteer Cav. at Cape Giradeau, MO for a period of three years. He requested a transfer to the regular Army, USA, and was enrolled 8 Oct 1864 for a period of three years.

He became ill and was admitted to the Post Hospital, Burton Barracks, MO, Hospital #1441, Ward 2. He was returned to duty but was readmitted to the Post Hospital on 30 Dec 1864. Henry Washington Sholar was diagnosed with smallpox and transferred to the Smallpox Hospital at St. Louis, MO where he died 11 Jan 1865. He and other smallpox victims were buried on Arsenal Island, MS. His remains along with 470 other soldiers were disinterred and their remains were then re-interred as a group burial at Jefferson Barracks National Cemetery, 101 Memorial Drive, St. Louis, MO.

Mary (Polly) Vinson Sholar, widow of Henry W. Sholar, applied for a Widow's Pension on 11 Dec 1865. The pension was granted and with the money she received she was able to raise her four children. *Submitted by Katye G. Shelton, great-granddaughter.*

JAMES A. SILLS, Private, born ca. 1830 in Tennessee. He enlisted 20 Dec 1861 at Camp Alcorn in Hopkinsville, KY and served with Co. G, 8th Kentucky Regt. Inf. (CSA). According to the Kentucky Adjutant General's Report, he was captured at Fort Donelson, but escaped from a transport steamer en route to prison.

On page 67, Simmons' 1850 Trigg County Census #1239, he is listed as a farmer, age 21 years, married ca. 1849 and living with his wife Elander Sills, age 20 years, no children in this census.

On page 38, Simmons' 1860 Trigg County Census #560, he is listed as age 26 years and living with his wife M.E. (Elander), age 24 years and three children: Mary E. age 9 years; James, age 3 years; and Viola T., 1 year.

JACK SIMMONS, Private, enlisted 2 Jul 1861 at Camp Burnett, TN and served with Co. M, 3rd Kentucky Regt. Mounted Inf. (CSA). This was the only Jack Simmons from the Trigg County area we could find in a Kentucky Regt. Maupin lists him as a War for Southern Independence Veteran. He is the only Simmons buried in the Roaring Springs Community Cemetery (no tombstone).

JAMES H. SIMPSON, Private, born ca. 1838 in Kentucky. He enrolled 18 Aug 1863, mustered in 26 Oct 1863 at Princeton, KY and mustered out 19 Dec 1864 at Bowling Green, KY. He served with Co. F, 48th Kentucky Regt. Mounted Inf. (USA).

Ruth A. (Cox) Simpson's father was William Cox (b. 1813 in Kentucky) and Rebecca (Shelton) Cox (b. 1814 in Kentucky). They are both buried in the Cox Cemetery in Trigg County, KY.

He married Ruth Ann Cox (b. ca. 1831 in Kentucky) on 3 Feb 1857 in Trigg County, KY.

He is listed in the Roaring Spring Poll Book dated for the August 1861 election.

On page 73, Simmons' 1860 Trigg County Census #1078 (He is listed as "J.H." (James H.) Simpson, age 22 years and living with his wife "R.A." (Ruth Ann) (Cox) Simpson and one daughter "M.J.," age 1 year.

WARREN SIVELLS, grandfather of Lamont Sivills, was born in Gallatin County, IL about 1836. He migrated to Stewart County, TN sometime before 1858, the year he married Susan C. Armstrong, from Trigg County, KY. They were married on 25 Oct 1858 in Trigg County.

Warren enlisted in the Union Army during the Civil War in his home county, Gallatin County, IL. His residence at the time of enlistment was Golconda, IL. He was 24 years old and left behind not only his young wife, but two young sons, Andrew Jackson (father of Lamont) and Buckner in Trigg County. He was mustered into service on 15 Oct 1861. He was assigned to the 6th Illinois US Cav., Co. L, with the rank of private.

Little else is known of Warren's military service. He re-enlisted as a veteran when his first term was up, but never returned from the war. His wife, Susan, not being able to confirm his death, went to a fortune teller to learn of his fate. The fortune teller "saw" him being robbed and beaten, and his body being thrown into a river.

Susan eventually filed for a Civil War veteran widow's pension. On 17 May 1867, she married again to William Henry Harrison Simmons in Dover, TN. They subsequently had seven children: Sephus Mansfield, William Samuel, Cora, Emma, Elizabeth, Thomas Frank and Flavous Eugene before her death in 1890/3 in Graves County, KY. *Submitted by Nancy Sivills Thompson, gg-granddaughter of Warren Sivells.*

ANDERSON SIZEMORE, born 29 Oct 1794, was a private in the 4th Regt. 2nd Bde. of the Virginia State Militia commanded by Capt. William Leigh.

He was drafted at Halifax County, VA Courthouse for the War of 1812 with Great Britain and discharged December 1814 near Richmond, VA with the rank of private. Anderson received two land grants, 80 acres each, for his service.

Moved to Christian (now Trigg) County, KY in 1818 and settled near Cerulean Springs. He was a farmer and a member of Muddy Fork Primitive Baptist Church.

Married 23 Apr 1811 to Sarah Goode, and they had 11 known children: George G., John H., William J., Daniel Campbell, Lucinda Cavaness, Nancy G. Henry G., Charles Jones, Elizabeth Ann, Martha Susan and Rebecca Jane.

Married second, Martha Gregory Rogers and had twins, Franklin A. and Mary Ellen. Anderson divorced Martha when the children were about a year old.

He married third, Cynthia Nolen Dunning and had daughter, Teletha.

Married fourth, Margaret McElhaney and had four children: James Thomas, Jesse Brown, Lewis Jefferson and Margaret D.

Anderson died 18 Apr 1869 near Cerulean, KY and is buried in the Stewart/Guthrie Cemetery.

RUSSELL P. SKINNER, Private, born ca. 1845 in Kentucky, died 12 Dec 1863 at Russellville, KY. He enrolled 23 Jul 1863, mustered in 26 Oct 1863 at Princeton, KY and served with Co. F, 48th Kentucky Regt. Mounted Inf. (USA). (Page 643, Union Regiments of Kentucky.)

On page 45, Simmons' 1850 Trigg County Census #830, he is listed as 5 years old and living with his father Edwin R. Skinner, age 33 years; his mother Elizabeth (Pitts) Skinner, age 31 years, and four siblings: William R., age 8 years; Callum, age 6 years; Peyton D., age 3 years; and Augusts L., age 1 year.

On page 90, Simmons' 1860 Trigg County Census #1320, he is listed as "R.T." Skinner, age 15 years and living with his father Edwin R. Skinner, age 43 years; his mother Elizabeth, age 42 years; and nine siblings: Callum, age 17 years; Peyton D., age 13 years; Augustus L., age 11 years; N.C. (Nancy C.), age 9 years; A.A. (Annie A.), age 8 years; L.B. (Lynn B.), age 6 years; J.R. (James R.), age 3 years; R.H. (male), age 2 years and P.R. (Pinkney R.), age 3 months.

WILLIAM ROSS SKINNER, Private, born ca. 1842 in Kentucky, died 13 Dec 1863 in Trigg County, KY. He enrolled 20 Aug 1863, mustered in 26 Oct 1863 at Princeton, KY and died before he was mustered out. He served with Co. F, 48th Kentucky Regt. Mounted Inf. (USA).

He is listed as W.R. "Skiner" who married Matilda Cox on 22 Aug 1860 in Trigg County, KY.

According to Maupin's record, he is buried in the Skinner Cemetery (no stone).

On page 45, Simmons' 1850 Trigg County Census #830, he is listed as age 8 years and living with his father Edwin R. Skinner, age 33 years; his mother Elizabeth (Pitts) Skinner, age 31 years; and four siblings: Callum, age 6 years; Russell P., age 5 years; Peyton D., age 3 years; and Augustus L., age 1 year.

On page 74, Simmons' 1860 Trigg County Census #1090, he is listed as age 18 years and living with his wife "R.M." (Matilda) (Cox) Skinner, age 16, and no children in this census.

ALPHONSO E. SLAUGHTER, Private, born ca. 1827 in Kentucky. He served with Co. A, Woodward's 15th Kentucky Cav. Regt. Some records have him as E. Alphonso Slaughter and other have him as Alphonso E. Slaughter. Captain E.A. Slaughter is mentioned in Trigg County Civil War Records page 28 as being in Col. Woodward's Cav. which operated in southwest Kentucky and middle Tennessee.

E. Alphonso Slaughter married Caroline Lindsay on 26 Jan 1859 in Trigg County, KY. (Page 330, Neel's Statistical Handbook of Trigg County, Trigg County Marriages.)

On page 256 and 258 Neel's Statistical Handbook of Trigg County, Trigg County Poll Books.

On page 3, Simmons' 1850 Trigg County Census #56, Alphonso Slaughter is listed as age 12 years and living with Lurana Savills, age 70 years; Lurana Savills, age 27 years; and Susan Savills, age 24 years.

On page 94, Simmons' 1860 Trigg County Census #1386, he is listed as a druggist, age 23 years and living with his wife Caroline Lindsay Slaughter, age 22 years, and one son E.L. Slaughter, age 3 months.

HOWARD M. SLAUGHTER, Private, born May 1834 in Tennessee. Maupin lists him as a WSI veteran in her Trigg County

Howard M. Slaughter, age 21 years, married Mary F. Alexander, age 20 years, on 30 Aug 1865 in Trigg County, KY. There is a Howard Slaughter buried in the County Poor Farm Cemetery.

On page 432, Simmons' 1870 Trigg County Census #483, a Howard Slaughter is listed as a carpenter, age 30 years and living with his wife Mary F. Alexander Slaughter, age 26 years, no children.

On page 243, Neel's Statistical Handbook of Trigg County, 1880 Trigg County Census, toward top of page, he is listed as a mechanic, age 45 years and living with his wife Mary F. Alexander Slaughter, age 35 years, and a daughter Emma, age 3 years.

ALEXANDER C. SMITH, Private, born ca. 1820 in Tennessee. He enlisted 14 Sep 1861 at Camp Burnett, TN and served with Co. G, 4th Kentucky Regt. Inf. (CSA). Pvt. Alexander C. Smith was awarded the Medal of Honor. He was wounded at Kennesaw Mountain, GA on 25 Jun 1864.

There is an Alexander Smith Jr. listed in the Canton Poll Book dated 6 Aug 1860.

Alexander Smith married Sarah Hixon on 9 Oct 1854 in Trigg County, KY.

On page 60, Simmons' 1860 Trigg County Census #883 (possible), there is an "A. Smith," age 40 years, listed as a farmer living with "S." Smith, a 55-year-old female who was born in Tennessee.

FERMAN (OR FIRMAN) A. SMITH, Private (husband of Pernecia), born 13 Jun 1834 in Kentucky, died 16 Feb 1918. He enlisted 26 Sep 1861 at Camp Reeves, TN and served with Co. G, 8th Kentucky Regt. Inf. (CSA). According to the Kentucky Adjutant General's Report and the Kentucky State Archives, he deserted his command on 1 Dec 1862, in the retreat from the Hatchie River.

There were two Ferman A. Smiths who lived in Trigg County during this era. This one was a farmer married to Pernecia Smith. The other Firman Smith was a wheelwright/farmer and married to Sarah F. (Peal) Smith. We are not sure which Ferman Smith was in Co. G, of the 8th Kentucky Regt. Inf.

In every census record Pernecia U. Smith gives her father as being born in England and her mother being born in Georgia.

Firman A. Smith is buried in the Oakley Cemetery with his wife Pernecia Smith (b. 16 Jan 1842 in Kentucky, d. 18 Mar 1908).

On page 206, Simmons' 1870 Trigg County Census #2420, he is listed as Firman A. Smith a farmer, age 35 years and living with his wife Pernecia E., age 28 years, and three children: William R., age 5 years; Charles E., age 3 years; and Emma A., age 1 year.

On page 238, Neel's Statistical Handbook of Trigg County, 1880 Trigg County Census, 2nd paragraph, he is listed as Ferman A. Smith, a farmer, age 46 years and living with his wife Pernecia Smith, age 38 years, and six children: William R., age 15 years; Charles W., age 13 years; Emma A., age 11 years; Ella, age 9 years; Lindsey Ann age 5 years; and Mary E., age 2 years.

FERMAN (OR FIRMAN) A. SMITH, Private (husband of Sarah), born ca. 1843 in Kentucky. He enlisted 26 Sep 1861 at Camp Reeves, TN and served with Co. G, 8th Kentucky Regt. Inf. (CSA).

There were two Ferman A. Smiths living in Trigg County during this era. One was the husband of Pernecia Smith and the other was the husband of Sarah F. (Peal) Smith. We are not sure which Ferman Smith was in Co. G, 8th Kentucky Regt. Inf.

Ferman A. Smith, age 26 years, a wheelwright from Trigg County, married Sarah F. Peal, age 27 years of Trigg County, on 23 Nov 1869. It was the first marriage for both bride and groom.

On page 208, Simmons' 1870 Trigg County Census #2451, he is listed as "Ferman A." Smith, a wheelwright, age 29 years and living with his wife Sarah F. (Peal) Smith, age 28 years, and no children in this census.

On page 227, Neel's Statistical Handbook of Trigg County, 1880 Trigg County Census, bottom of page, he is listed as "F.A." Smith, a farmer age 37 years and living with his wife Sarah F. (Peal) Smith, age 38 years, and four children: Joseph N., age 9 years; Ora E., age 7 years; Harvey G., age 5 years; and Mary B., age 2 years.

HARRISON SMITH, born ca. 1847 in Caldwell County, KY. He served with Co. B, Woodward's 2nd/15th Kentucky Cav. Regt. (CSA).

In the obituary of Hazard Perry Baker it is mentioned that Private Harrison Smith was one of the six Confederate soldiers who made up President Jefferson Davis' last escort.

On page 115, Jones' 1850 Caldwell County Census, Part I, #867, he is listed as Harrison Smith, age 3 and living with his father William J. Smith, age 21 years; his mother Jane (Davenport) Smith, age 26 years; and a brother William D. Smith, age 1 year.

On page 81, Jones' 1860 Lyon County Census #633, he is listed as Elias H. Smith, age 12 years and living with his father William J. Smith, age 31 years, and his mother Jane (Davenport) Smith, age 35 years, and five siblings: William D., age 10 years; Lucinda J., age 9 years; Esther E., age 5 years; Susan, age 2 years; and Reuben, age 6 months.

On page 105, Simmons' 1870 Trigg County Census #1232, he is listed as "Harrison" Smith, age 23 years whose occupation is "engineer" and living alone.

J.E. SMITH, Private, born ca. 1833 in Tennessee. He enlisted at Camp Alcorn in Hopkinsville, KY, on 24 Oct 1861 and served with Co. B, 8th Kentucky Regt. Inf. (CSA).

On page 1, Simmons' 1860 Trigg County Census #13 (possible), he is listed as age 27 years and living with wife Sarah J., age 22 years, and three children: Mary F., age 5 years; Henry B., age 4 years; and Thomas J., age 1 year.

WILLIAM M. SMITH, Private, born ca. 1841 in Kentucky, died 11 Nov 1861. He enlisted 26 Sep 1861 at Camp Reeves, TN and served with Co. G, 8th Kentucky Regt. Inf. (CSA). According to the Kentucky Adjutant General's Report, he died of pneumonia and measles while in training at Hopkinsville, KY on 11 Nov 1861.

His father Hardy W. Smith (b. ca. 1812 in Kentucky) married Elizabeth Creekmur (b. ??, died early 1840s) on 20 Feb 1840 in Trigg County, KY. Hardy married second, Mary Narcessa Mabry (b. ca. 1810) on 27 Mar 1845 in Trigg County, KY.

On page 8, Simmons' 1850 Trigg County Census #140, he is listed as age 9 years and living with his father "H.W." (Hardy W.) Smith, age 27 years; his step-mother Mary N. (Mabry) Smith, age 34 years; and three siblings: Martha E., age 5 years; Leander (male), age 3 years; and Mary L., age 4 months.

On page 23, Simmons' 1860 Trigg County Census #338, he is listed as age 19 years and living with his father "H.W." (Hardy W.) Smith, age 38 years; his step-mother "M.N." (Mary Narcissa) (Mabry) Smith, age 40 years, and six siblings: "M.E." (Martha E.), age 13 years; "M.L." (Mary L.), age 10 years; Leander, age 12 years; "C.F." (female), age 8 years; "M.S.W." (Margaret S.W.), age 6 years; and "S.A." (Sarah Ann) age 3 years.

WILLIAM D. SOLOMON, Private (husband of Mary A.), born ca. 1839 in Tennessee. He enrolled 4 Aug 1864, mustered in 4 Aug 1864 at Paducah, KY and mustered out 12 Feb 1865 at Paducah, KY. He served with Co. B, 1st Kentucky Regt. Capital Guards, Paducah, Battalion.

There are about three men of the name William Solomon who lived in the Trigg County area during the WSI era.

He is buried in the Turkey Creek Cemetery (no stone). References: On page 124, Simmons' 1870 Trigg County Census #1466, he is listed as William D. Solomon, a shoemaker age 31 years and living with

his wife Mary A. Solomon, age 30 years, and three children: Sarah C., age 10 years; James R., age 7 years; and John W., 1 month.

WILLIAM D. SOLOMON, Private (son of Hardy and Mary Solomon), born ca. 1847 in Kentucky. He mustered in 4 Aug 1864 at Paducah, KY and mustered out 12 Feb 1865 at Paducah, KY. He served with Co. B, 1st Kentucky Regt. Capital Guards, Paducah, KY.

There were about three men of the name William Solomon who lived in Trigg County during the WSI era.

His father was Hardy Solomon (b. ca. 1825 in Virginia d. ??) and his mother was Mary Solomon (b. ca. 1830, d. ??) in Kentucky. He is buried in the Turkey Creek Cemetery in Trigg County, KY.

On page 11, Simmons' 1850 Trigg County Census #202, he is listed as William D. Solomon, age 2 years and living with his father Hardy Solomon, age 25 years, and his mother Mary Solomon, age 20 years.

On page 32, Simmons' 1860 Trigg County Census #474, he is listed as William Solomon, age 13 years and living with his father "H." (Hardy) Solomon, age 34 years; his mother "M.E." (Mary) Solomon, age 29 years; and two siblings, "S.E." (female), age 10 years; and "M.J." (female), age 6 years.

On page 212, Simmons' 1870 Trigg County Census #2502, he is listed as an "Apprentice Blacksmith," age 22 years and living with the Jesse S. Pursely and Sarah A. Pursely family in this census.

On page 238, Neel's Statistical Handbook of Trigg County, 1880 Trigg County Census, there is a William Solomon, a farmer age 31 years and living with his wife Tisdan E. Solomon, age 27 years, and five children: Charley, age 11 years; "L." (female), age 7 years; Luba J. (female), age 5 years; Beckey C., age 3 years; and Samuel E., age 1 year.

EDWARD C. SPICELAND, 2nd Lieutenant, born ca. 1826 in Tennessee. He enrolled 14 Aug 1862, mustered in 13 Sep 1862 at Henderson, KY and mustered out 9 Jun 1863 - Promoted to Reg. Commission. He served with Co. L, 8th Kentucky Regt. Cav. (USA). He is on a list of the Canton Company (C.S. Army) who failed to muster at Indian Springs under J.W. Shoemaker and Riley Vinson on Saturday, 7 Sep 1861.

He married first, Martha J. Ross (b. 23 Apr 1823 in Tennessee, d. 1 May 1866) on 20 Oct 1848 in Trigg County, KY. He married second, Martha Bartee on 28 Mar 1872 in Trigg County, KY.

His wife Martha J. (b. 23 Apr 1823 in Tennessee, d. 1 May 1866) is buried in the Matheny Cemetery

On page 1, Simmons' 1850 Trigg County Census #7, he is listed as E.C. Spiceland, a merchant clerk, age 24 years and living with his wife Martha J. Spiceland, age 26 years, and a son Sandford J. age 10 months.

On page 38, Simmons' 1860 Trigg County Census #568, he is listed as E.C. Spiceland, a merchant, age 34 years and living with his wife Martha J., age 37 years, and two children, Sandford J., age 10 years, and Mary A., age 2 years.

On page 215, Neel's Statistical Handbook of Trigg County, 1880 Trigg County Census, top of page, he is listed as "Ed C. Spiceland," a dry goods merchant, age 53 years and living with his wife Martha Spiceland, age 27 years, and four children: "N.W." (Netta W.), age 19 years; "H.T." (Helen T.), age 7 years; Harlan, age 4 years; and M.O. (Minnie O.), age 1 year.

JAMES F. STALLONS, Private, born ca. 1846, died Nov 1861. He enlisted 26 Sep 1861, at Camp Reeves, TN and served with Co. G, 8th Kentucky Regt. Inf. (CSA).

Private James Stallons died of pneumonia and measles in Hopkinsville, KY, in November 1861. He was a brother of John W. and Joseph A. Stallons, both Confederate soldiers.

His father William Stallons (b. ca. 1818 in Kentucky) and mother Mary (Barnes) Stallons (b. ca. 1817 in Kentucky, d. 1 Jun 1852) were married on 4 Jan 1837, in Trigg County, KY.

William B. Stallons married second, Mary Bonds on 26 May 1853, in Trigg County, KY.

On page 52, Simmons' 1850 Trigg County Census #950, he is listed as age 4 years and living with his father William Stallons, age 32 years; his mother Mary (Barnes) Stallons (born in Kentucky), age 36 years; and three brothers: John W., age 12 years; Cater, age 10 years; and Joseph A., age 7 years.

On page 23, Simmons' 1860 Trigg County Census #336, he is listed as age 14 years and living with his father "B." (Barnes) Stallons, age 45 years; his stepmother Mary E. (Bonds) Stallons, age 33 years, and four siblings: John, age 23 years; Joseph, age 17 years; M. (male), age 6 years; and Nancy, age 4 years.

Page 171, Neel's Statistical Handbook of Trigg County, 1880 Trigg County Census, toward top of page, James' father is listed as Barnes "Stallions," a laborer age 63 years and living with his wife Mary E. (Bonds) "Stallions," age 54 years; a daughter Lourna B., age 33 years; a daughter Bettie, age 9 years; and a grandson Barnes Pollard, age 2 years.

JOHN W. STALLONS, Private, born ca. 1837, died 22 May 1863. He enlisted 14 Sep 1861 at Camp Burnett, TN and served with Co. G, 4th Kentucky Regt. Inf. (CSA). Pvt. John W. Stallons was a brother of James F. and Joseph A. Stallons, both Confederate soldiers. He died of disease at Beech Grove, TN on 22 May 1863.

His father William Stallons (b. ca. 1818 in Kentucky) and mother Mary (Barnes) Stallons (b. ca. 1817 in Kentucky, d. 1 Jun 1852) were married on 4 Jan 1837 in Trigg County, KY.

William B. Stallons married second, Mary Bonds on 26 May 1853, in Trigg County, KY.

On page 52, Simmons' 1850 Trigg County Census #950, he is listed as age 12 years and living with his father William Stallons, age 32 years; his mother Mary (Barnes) Stallons, age 36 years; and three brothers: Cater, age 10 years; Joseph A., age 7 years; and James F., age 4 years.

On page 23, Simmons' 1860 Trigg County Census #336, he is listed as age 23 years and living with his father B. (Barnes) Stallons, age 45 years; his stepmother Mary E. (Bonds) Stallons, age 33 years; and four siblings: Joseph, age 17 years; James, age 14 years; M. (male), age 6 years; and Nancy, age 4 years.

On page 171, Neel's Statistical Handbook of Trigg County, 1880 Trigg County Census, toward top of page, John's father is listed as Barnes "Stallions," a laborer age 63 years and living with his wife Mary E. (Bonds) "Stallions," age 54 years; a daughter Lourna B., age 33 years; a daughter Bettie, age 9 years; and a grandson Barnes Pollard, age 2 years.

JOSEPH A. STALLONS, Private, born ca. 1843, died Nov 1861. He enlisted 26 Sep 1861 at Camp Reeves, TN and served with Co. G, 8th Kentucky Regt. Inf. (CSA). Pvt. Joseph Stallons died of pneumonia and measles at Hopkinsville, KY, in November 1861.

Pvt. Joseph Stallons was a brother of John W. and James F. Stallons, both Confederate soldiers.

His father William Stallons (b. 1818 in Kentucky) and mother Mary (Barnes) Stallons (b. ca. 1817 in Kentucky, d. 1 Jun 1852) were married on 4 Jan 1837 in Trigg County, KY.

William B. Stallons married second, Mary Bonds on 26 May 1853 in Trigg County, KY.

On page 52, Simmons' 1850 Trigg County Census #950, he is listed as age 7 years and living with his father William Stallons, age 32 years; his mother Mary (Barnes) Stallons, age 36 years, and three brothers: John W., age 12 years; Cater, age 10 years; and James F., age 4 years.

On page 23, Simmons' 1860 Trigg County Census #336, he is listed as Jos., age 17 years and living with his father B. (Barnes) Stallons, age 45 years; his stepmother Mary E. (Bonds) Stallons, age 33 years; and four siblings: John W., age 23 years; James, age 14 years; M. (male), age 6 years; and Nancy, age 4 years.

On page 171, Neel's Statistical Handbook of Trigg County, 1880 Trigg County Census, Joseph's father is listed as Barnes "Stallions," a laborer age 63 years and living with his wife Mary E. (Bonds) "Stallions," age 54 years; a daughter Lourna B., age 33 years; a daughter Bettie, age 9 years; and a grandson Barnes Pollard, age 2 years.

REUBEN STALLONS, son of Aaron and Elizabeth (Barnes) Stallons, was born in Trigg County around 1830, the youngest of four children. His father died when he was about 11 years old.

Reuben enlisted as a private in Company D, Eighth Regt. Inf. in the Confederate States Army at Camp Reeves, TN on 26 Sep 1861. This unit camped and drilled at Hopkinsville, KY during the fall of 1861 just before the Battle of Fort Donelson. On 16 Feb 1862, this company was among those that surrendered and were captured at Fort Donelson. They were held prisoner of war at Camp Morton, IN. After being exchanged, they returned to duty at Vicksburg, MS on 24 Aug 1862 under Gen. Forrest's command. At the reorganization of the company at Jackson, MS in September 1862, the unit became Co. "G," as it was known for the

remainder of the war. Reuben took part in many battles throughout Alabama, Tennessee and Mississippi, during which time he was well known as an expert marksman and sharpshooter. In March 1865, after a three-day battle near Corinth, MS, nearly half of the 8th Regt. were killed, wounded or captured. After hearing of the surrender of Gen. Lee in Virginia, the remainder of the 8th Regt. surrendered on 16 May 1865. Reuben was one of the few Trigg County men that remained in the unit at the time of surrender.

Through deed transaction records, it is apparent that Reuben lived on Little River, possibly in the Mershon's Bridge Community. On 14 Oct 1847, Reuben married Sarah Boyd. To this union six children were born: Leander W., James Wylie, Joseph M., Reuben A., Joshua and Elizabeth Stallons. Sarah died on 2 Jun 1859 in Trigg County. Her burial place is unknown.

On 10 Jan 1866, Reuben married Ann Eliza Boyd, daughter of Archibald and Elizabeth (Noel) Boyd. To this marriage three children were born: John Morgan, William Barnes and Archie Thomas Stallons.

The exact death dates are not known for either Reuben or Ann Eliza. Reuben was removed from the tax lists on 6 Dec 1894 because of death. Ann Eliza died between 1880 and 1900. Their burial places are also unknown. *Submitted by Kim Fortner.*

WILEY T. STEWART, a farmer and the husband of Mary Stewart, born September 1835 or 1836 in Kentucky.

There were two Wiley Stewarts living in Trigg County after the War for Southern Independence. One was a farmer and the husband of Mary. The other was a carpenter and the husband of Elizabeth or Bettie. This is the Wiley T. Stewart indicated by Maupin as being the War for Southern Independence Veteran.

His father was James Stewart (b. 1 Oct 1799 in Virginia, d. 2 Feb 1872) and his mother was Jemima Stewart (b. 2 Jan 1800 in Virginia, d. 4 Oct 1876). They are buried in the Robertson Cemetery in Trigg County, KY.

Wiley Stewart married Mary Stewart (born in Georgia) on 11 Jan 1860.

On page 13, Simmons' 1850 Trigg County Census #243, he is listed as Wiley Stewart, age 13 years and living with his father James Stewart, age 49 years; his mother Jemima Stewart, age 49 years; and eight siblings: Wilson Jr., age 20 years; Elizabeth, age 17 years; Cassandra, age 23 years; John, age 18 years; Fielding, age 16 years; Anderson, age 13 years; and James M., age 11 years.

Page 243, Neel's Statistical Handbook of Trigg County, 1880 Trigg County Census, bottom of page, he is listed as Wiley Stewart, a farmer age 43 years and living with his wife Mary A. (Stewart) Stewart (born in Georgia), age 43 years, and three children: Armena, age 13 years; Sarah C., age 11 years; and Larra (son), age 9 years.

On page 31, Jones' 1900 Trigg County Census #256-263, he is listed as "W.T." Stewart, a farmer age 63 years (b. September 1836) and living with his wife Mary A. (Stewart) Stewart, age 65 years (married 38 years) and one daughter, Sarah C. Stewart (born December 1869), age 30 years. Mary A. Stewart has had six children, five of whom were still living when the census was taken.

WILLIAM H.H. STOKES, Private, born ca. 1842 in Kentucky. He enlisted 19 Oct 1861 at Camp Alcorn in Hopkinsville, KY and served with Co. G, 8th Kentucky Regt. Inf. (CSA).

According to the Kentucky Adjutant General's Report, he was missing at Fort Donelson and not heard from again.

He is listed as "William H.H. Stokes" in this reference. There is a "Henry Stokes" listed in Neel's 1880 Census, but he is listed as being born in Tennessee.

His mother Nancy Stokes was born ca. 1813 in South Carolina.

On page 30, Simmons' 1850 Trigg County Census #548, he is listed as "W.H.H." Stokes, age 8 years and living with his mother Nancy H. Stokes, age 37 years, and five siblings: Nancy C. (Stokes) Wallis, age 19 years; Frances (female), age 15 years; Jackson A., age 12 years; Mary J., age 10 years; and Zachariah T., age 3 years.

On page 52, Simmons' 1860 Trigg County Census #754, he is listed as "H.H." Stokes a farm laborer, age 19 years and living with W.R. Thomas, age 33 years; his wife Elizabeth Thomas, age 32 years; and their four children: William C., age 10 years; Thomas, age 7 years; Ann E., age 5 years; and Emily O., age 3 years.

On page 17, Simmons' 1860 Trigg County Census #244, a W.H. Wallis is listed as a coaling manager, age 33 years (born in Ohio) and living alone in this census.

JOHN LILBURN STORM, Private, born 6 Mar 1842 in Kentucky, died 17 Feb 1923 in Cobb, KY. He enlisted 24 Oct 1861 at Camp Alcorn, Hopkinsville, KY and served with Co. B, 8th Kentucky Regt. Inf. (CSA).

His father was Andrew J. Storm (b. ca. 1810 in Indiana) and his mother was Harriett Storm (b. ca. 1810, d. 1876). His mother may be the "Haret Storn" who died in 1876 and is buried in the Dunning Cemetery in Trigg County, KY.

John L. is buried in the Rogers Cemetery in Christian County,

On page 48, Simmons' 1860 Trigg County Census #485, he is listed as age 18 years and living with his father Andrew J. Storm, age 49 years; his mother Harriett Storm, age 49 years; and three siblings: H.D. (male), age 14 years; William A., age 12 years; and M.J. (female), age 11 years.

Page 226, Simmons' 1870 Trigg County Census #2668, he is listed as age 28 years and living with wife Jane, age 19 years, and one child Andrew J., age 8 months.

SAMUEL SUMNER, born 27 May 1845 in Kentucky, died 7 Jun 1920. He served with Capt. Slaughter's Company, Col. Woodward's Regt. (CSA).

The child born on 31 Jul 1869 may be either Carlin or Caroline. The 1870 Census record names it Caroline, and the tombstone names it Carlin. Carlin would seem more correct.

His father was Joel Sumner (b. ca. 1801 in North Carolina) and his mother was Catherine (Miles) Sumner (b. ca. 1803 in Kentucky). They married on 18 May 1822 in Trigg County, KY.

Samuel Sumner, age 21 years from Trigg County, married Lucy E. Rogers, age 17 years from Trigg County, on 20 Nov 1865. Samuel married second, Jane Futrell in Trigg County, KY, on 27 Jan 1897. He is buried in the Delmont Church Cemetery with his wife Lucy L. (Rogers) Sumner (b. 13 Jul 1849 in Kentucky, d. 23 Apr 1896). His second wife Martha Jane Futrell (b. 31 Mar 1865, d. 27 Oct 1905) is also buried in the Delmont Church Cemetery.

On page 48, Simmons' 1850 Trigg County Census #876, he is listed as Samuel, age 5 years and living with his father Joel Sumner, age 49 years; his mother Catherine (Miles) Sumner, age 47 years; and seven siblings: Joseph G., age 20 years; Dudley A., age 18 years; Isaac N., age 16 years; Sarah S., age 15 years; Martha E., age 13 years; Mary E., age 11 years; and Benjamin age 8 years.

On page 60, Simmons' 1860 Trigg County Census #886, he is listed as "S.," age 15 years and living with his mother C. (Catherine) (Miles) Sumner, age 55 years; his brother Benjamin, age 17 years; and his paternal Grandmother "E." Sumner, age 75 years and his maternal grandmother "E" Miles, age 79 years.

On page 148, Simmons' 1870 Trigg County Census #1763, he is listed as age 24 years and living with wife Lucyell D. (Rogers) Sumner, age 20 years, and two daughters: Catherine (Kitty), age 3 years, and Caroline N., age 10 months.

ALFRED LEROY SUMNER (The War Between the States), was the son of North Carolina natives, Joel and Catherine Miles Sumner, He was born in Trigg County, KY, in 1825. On 29 Mar 1848, he was married to Martha Lancaster in Trigg County, KY. She was the daughter of Edmond and Elizabeth Outland Lancaster.

Their children were Benjamin Miles who married Henretta Gabrella Bridges; Elizabeth Catherine (Bet) married Cullen Futrell; James Edmond married (1) Mary Louisa Bridges and (2) Sally Thomas; Faithy married Joel Lee Ricks; Sarah Ann (Sally) married John Davenport; Julia Ella married John F. Davis; William L. (Bill) married Mary Jane Thomas; and Joel Calvin (Cal) married (1) Nannie Carr and (2) Martha Nora Thomas.

Alfred, Martha and their children lived in the Donaldson Creek Community in an area known as Sumners' Ford. He was a member of Donaldson Creek Baptist Church. Later the family moved to the Oak Grove Community.

He mustered into the Confederate Militia on 6 Jul 1861, under Capt. Alfred Thomas and served as a wagoner.

Alfred died in May 1887 and is thought to have been buried near the intersection of the Maple Grove and Donaldson Creek Roads in an un-marked grave per the late Bayliss Sumner, who was Sumner historian along with the late E. Raymond Sumner. Martha died in 1903 and is buried in the Edmond Lancaster Cemetery on the farm of Louise Sumner Thomas on the Floyd Sumner Road.

Alfred's brother, Samuel Sumner, served in Capt. Slaughter's Company, Col. Woodward's Regt. He was captured by the Union Army, confined in Louisville, KY, and later released. *Submitted by Joyce Davis Banister, great-granddaughter of Alfred Sumner.*

WILLIAM B. TANKERSLEY, born 1822 in Tennessee, died 1898. Both Maupin's Records and Neel's Records acknowledge William B. Tankersley as a WSI veteran.

He was married to Ann Vaden Tankersley (b. 1836, d. 1894). Their son (?) Madison F. Tankersley married Bettie Magraw on 18 May 1898 in Trigg County, KY. William and his wife Ann are both buried in the Colson or Pleasant Valley Cemetery.

References: Can be found on page 38, Maupin's Trigg County Cemetery Records, on page 372, Neel's Statistical Handbook of Trigg County Marriages. On page 161, Jones' 1900 Trigg County Census #292-296, Madison F. Tankersley is listed as a hotel keeper, age 51 years and living with his wife Bettie (Magraw) (married two years), age 39 years, no children. Bettie (Magraw) Tankersley has had no children as of the 1900 Trigg County Census. Madison Tankersley was born in Tennessee in August 1848. Bettie (Magraw) Tankersley was born in Kentucky in March 1861.

G. WASHINGTON TAYLOR, Private, born ca. 1824 in Kentucky. He enlisted 14 Sep 1861 at Camp Burnett, TN and served with Co. G, 4th Kentucky. Regt. Inf. (CSA).

His first wife was Margaret Henderson. George Washington Taylor of Trigg County married Sarah Harrell of Christian County in Trigg County, KY, on 1 Sep 1874. It was both the bride's and the groom's second marriage. He was listed as being 50 years and she was listed as being 45 years of age.

He is listed as "G.W." Taylor in the Roaring Springs Poll Book, August 1861 election.

On page 37, Simmons' 1850 Trigg County Census #673, he is listed as age 26 years and living with his wife Margaret (Henderson) Taylor, age 20 years, and two children, Elizabeth, age 4 years, and Mary, age 3 years. G. Washington Taylor and his family are living with the I.G. Foster and Elizabeth Foster family in this census.

On page 90, Simmons' 1860 Trigg County Census #1318, he is listed as G.W. Taylor, age 36 years, living with his wife M. Taylor, age 32 years, and six daughters: "E.J." (Elizabeth J.), age 14 years; "M.A." (Mary A.), age 12 years; "M.A." (Martha A.), age 10 years; "T.E." (Thomas E.), age 8 years; "J.P." (Julia P.), age 6 years; and "E." (Margaret E.), age 1 year.

On page 186, Simmons' 1870 Trigg County Census #2182, he is listed as age 50 years and living with his wife Margaret C. (Henderson) Taylor, age 40 years, and four daughters: Martha A., age 19 years; Thomas E. (female), age 17 years; Julia P., age 14 years; and Margaret E., age 11 years.

BENJAMIN DYER TERRY, Captain, of Cadiz first served with the Kentucky Cavalry, company of the Confederate army. The company was first stationed at Hopkinsville and first saw service at the battle of Fort Donaldson where the entire company was captured and sent to prison at Johnson's Island in February 1862. In September 1862 he was released in a prisoner exchange and rejoined his company which was later transferred to Morgan's command. He was in the battle of Chickamauga in 1863 and several smaller engagements up to the battle at Cynthiana, KY. Here his battalion was thrown out as a rear guard to cover the army's retreat where he was again captured with most of his command and sent back to Johnson's Island prison. He was paroled in June 1865 and returned to Cadiz.

When the Confederate Home was established at Pewee Valley, Capt. Terry was appointed by Gov. Beckham as one of the commissioners, and at the time of his death was serving his second term.

He died in 1906 and is buried in the old Cadiz cemetery. He was survived by two brothers, Capt. Felix G. Terry, who served in the Confederate Army, and Rear Admiral Silas W. Terry of the USN, and a sister, Mrs. W.C. White of Cadiz.

BEN DYER TERRY, Captain, born 23 Dec 1831 in Kentucky, died 29 May 1906. He enlisted 15 Oct 1861 at Camp Alcorn in Hopkinsville, KY and served with Co. G, 1st Kentucky Cav. He was promoted to captain 28 Sep 1862. He took the place of Capt. Morrison D. Wilcox when Capt. Wilcox transferred to the 8th Kentucky Regt. Inf. "Morgan's Cav." is the unit given on his tombstone.

He was a brother to Felix G. Terry of Co. G, 8th Kentucky Regt. Inf. and a brother-in-law to Col. Henry C. Burnett. Sisters' Marriages:

He is buried in the Old Cadiz Cemetery with his parents, Abner R. Terry (b. 10 Feb 1797 in North Carolina, d. 29 Nov 1847) and Eleanor (Dyer) Terry (b. 6 Feb 1805 in Virginia, d. 9 Dec 1892).

On page 176, Neel's Statistical Handbook of Trigg County, 1880 Trigg County Census, bottom of page, Ben D. Terry is listed as "B.D." Terry, age 50 years and living with his mother "E." (Eleanor) Terry, age 74 years; his brother "G.A." (George A.) Terry, a confectioner, age 35 years; his sister Mark (Martha A.) McCarty, age 35 years; a niece Elizabeth McCarty, age 15 years, and a nephew Eddie McCarty, age 17 years.

On page 12, Jones' 1900 Trigg County Census #104-107, he is listed as Ben D. Terry, single, an insurance agent, age 68 years and living with a John H. Neel, a boarder, single, a hardware salesman, age 25 years. According to this census record, Ben D. Terry was born in December 1831 in Kentucky. His father was born in North Carolina and his mother was born in Virginia.

FELIX GRUNDY TERRY, Captain, of Cadiz and attended the Naval School at Annapolis, but when the Civil War broke out, he returned to Cadiz and joined CSA, Co. G, 8th Kentucky Mounted Inf. under Maj. Gen. Breckinridge at Vicksburg, MS as a lieutenant.

He was at the battle of Vicksburg in September 1863 when his company had to fire on gunboats on the Mississippi River including one commanded by his brother, Ensign Silas Terry of the USN. He was later listed as Capt. F.G. Terry, acting assistant inspector-general, with Brig. Gen. Buford, 2nd Div., Forrest's Cav. in and around Tupelo, MS, 22 Jul 1864. He was paroled with his company in May 1865 and returned to Cadiz and opened a drug store.

He married in the Reform Church in Cadiz 1 Dec 1868, the same time and church (but different ministers), that his sister Lucy married W.C. White. He died in Cadiz, 6 Mar 1926 and is buried in the Cadiz cemetery.

SILAS W. TERRY, Rear Admiral, of Cadiz, KY, entered the Naval Academy at the age of 16 as an acting midshipman. At the outbreak of the Civil War and before completing his course, he was ordered to active sea duty.

From June 1861 to September 1862 he served on the *Dale* in the Atlantic Coast blockade. He was promoted to ensign and made an aid on the staff of Rear Admiral Lee until July 1863 when he was transferred to the Black Hawk of the Mississippi Squadron.

He took part in the Red River Expedition, and because of his bravery was placed in command of the transport *Benifit* to carry dispatches and supplies for Admiral Porter. For this work he was commended by the Admiral in an official report to the Secretary of the Navy, and was advanced five numbers in grade of lieutenant for gallantry by President Lincoln.

Admiral Porter appointed him a detail officer on his staff, retaining him in that capacity to the end of the war. He was present at the fall of Richmond, and attended President Lincoln when he entered that city.

In January 1882 while commanding the *Marion*, he rescued the crew of the bark *Trinity* which had been wrecked in October 1880 on Heard Island, Indian Ocean. In February 1882 while in Cape Town, he hauled the British ship *Paoonah* off the beach, saving her from total loss, for which he received the thanks of the governments of Cape Colony and England.

He was Commandant of the Navy Yard at Washington from 1900-1903 and at the Naval Station in Honolulu from 1903 until his retirement in December 1904. He died in Washington, DC 11 Nov 1911 and was survived by a sister, Mrs. W.C. White, of Cadiz, and a brother, Capt. F.G. Terry, CSA, of Cadiz.

DR. ALBERT THOMAS, born 8 Apr 1822 in Kentucky and died 25 Nov 1914. He was an assistant surgeon in Union Army for two years. He is buried in the Perry Thomas Cemetery.

On page 47, Simmons 1850 Trigg County Census #850, he is listed as a physician, age 26 years and living in what we assume was a hotel.

On page 133, Simmons' 1870 Trigg County Census #1590, he is listed as Albert Thomas, a physician, age 48 years and living with his wife Mary Jane Thomas, age 39 years, and one son James Thomas, age 17 years, who works on the farm.

On page 234, Neel's Statistical Handbook of Trigg County 1880 Trigg County Census, bottom of page, he is listed as Albert Thomas, age 58 years, a physician, living with his wife Mary Jane Thomas, age 50 years, and granddaughter Olive Futrell, age 9 years.

ALBERT D. THOMAS, born 4 Mar 1844 in the Donaldson Creek Community of Trigg County, KY. He was the second son of Peyton and Sallie Ethridge Thomas. His grandparents were Cullen and Elizabeth Futrell Thomas and David T. and Penina Skinner Ethridge.

Albert acquired the nickname of "Bud" during his childhood, and it stuck with him all his life. His father, Peyton Thomas, operated a farm, general store and blacksmith shop at the intersection of the Dover and Donaldson Creek roads, and during his youth, Albert was kept busy helping at one or the other of them.

When the Civil War began, Albert was only 17 years old. His brother Alfred, who at 19, marched off one hot July day in 1861 along with a number of other Trigg Countians to fight for the Confederacy. Not to be outdone, Albert went to Hopkinsville and volunteered to serve as a water boy with the Second Kentucky Cav. which had been organized under the command of Col. Thomas Woodward. On 4 Mar 1862, on his 18th birthday, Albert was sworn in as a regular in the 2nd Kentucky and with that outfit saw considerable action against the Yankees in Southern Kentucky and West Tennessee.

He later left the army, and in 1864 married Mary Jonathan Vinson, daughter of Edmund J. and Jacqueline Wimberly Vinson of Stewart County, TN. Their eight children were Lena, who married first, Thomas Cable and second, Dill Stalely; Enola C. married Dr. J.M. Skaggs; Lucy D. married Charles W. Roper; Sally married Frank Cook; James Maston married Flora Seawright; Fruzzie married Clete Griffin; Bertie never married; and John P. died when he was 8.

Albert raised his family on a farm in Stewart County, TN, and died there 1 Apr 1921, at the age of 77. He is buried in the Peyton Thomas Cemetery in the Donaldson Creek Valley near where he was born. His wife Mary, who outlived him by eight years, died 10 May 1929 and is buried in the Hendon Cemetery in Stewart County, TN.

ALFRED THOMAS, Captain, born 29 Apr 1836 and died 26 Jul 1906. He served with Capt. Alfred Thomas' Co. F, 50th Tennessee Regt. Inf.

His father was Starkie Thomas (b. 29 Jun 1799 in North Carolina, d. 15 Sep 1881) and his mother was Mary (Bridges) Thomas (b. 25 Jul 1807 in Kentucky, d. 7 Oct 1890). They were married on 19 Mar 1825 in Trigg County, KY.

Alfred Thomas was married to Eliza A. Martin (b. 1 Oct 1841, d. 30 Jul 1902) on 27 Mar 1863 Trigg County, KY. They are buried in the Alfred Thomas Cemetery in Trigg County, KY.

On page 50, Simmons' 1850 Trigg County Census #923-384, he is listed as Alfred Thomas, age 15 years and living with his father Starkey Thomas, age 50 years, his mother Mary (Bridges) Thomas, age 42 years, and six siblings: James J., age 17 years; Francis M., age 10 years; Bluford H., age 9 years; Perry, age 7 years; Starkey A., age 5 years; and Mary J., age 3 years.

On page 7, Simmons' 1870 Trigg County Census #77, he is listed as "Alford" Thomas, age 35 years, living with his wife Eliza A. (Martin) Thomas, age 28 years, and two daughters, Ida, age 6 years, and Ines, age 3 years.

On page 183, Neel's Statistical Handbook of Trigg County, 1880 Trigg County Census, bottom of page, he is listed as Alfred Thomas, a farmer, age 45 years, living with his wife Eliza (Martin) Thomas, age 38 years, and four children: Ida, age 16 years; Inez, age 16 years; Thomas M., age 5 years; and Gracie, age 3 years.

ALFRED CULLEN THOMAS, was born 11 Nov 1842, the oldest child of Ethridge Thomas in the Donaldson Creek Community of Trigg County. He grew up on his father's farm, and attended the Donaldson School.

On 1 Jul 1861, at age 19, he walked nine miles from his home to Canton, KY, to volunteer for service in the Confederate Army. The next day, he and over 70 other young men from Trigg County, marched to Camp Burnett, TN. They were assigned to Co. G. Fourth Regt. as privates and transferred to Bowling Green, KY, as part of Kentucky's "Orphan Brigade." Little did Alfred know at the time, but he would live and fight with this brigade for the next four years before he would return to his home in Trigg County. The brigade got its first taste of war 5-6 Apr 1862 in Tennessee during the Battle of Shiloh. From there, Alfred's military career took him through some of the bloodiest battles of the Civil War, including action at Vicksburg, Baton Rouge, Stones River, Chickamauga, Missionary Ridge, Rocky Face, Kennesaw Mountain, Atlanta and Jonesboro.

At wars' end, Alfred, with the rank of sergeant, was discharged 7 May 1865, at Washington, GA, and he along with 23 other Trigg County men headed for home. When he arrived, he had grown a beard and was so gaunt that his family did not recognize him.

Alfred married Nancy Ann Vinson 28 Sep 1871 and settled on a farm in Calloway County, KY, where he also operated a general store near the Tennessee River. They had 10 children: James C., Amanda (Mrs. John) George, Peyton, Sally J. (Mrs. Marion) Futrell, Lillie D. (Mrs. Robert W. McCage, Permelia (Mrs. John) Kelley, Julia Maude (Mrs. George C.) Bell, Edmond C., Albert Carnell and Beatrice (Mrs. Erie D.) Cunningham.

Alfred's wife Nancy died in 1915 and he died in 1932 at the age of 90. Both are buried in the Thomas-Lassiter Cemetery near Hamlin in Calloway County, KY.

BLUFORD M. THOMAS, born 28 Feb 1841, died 3 Jun 1923 He was a brother to James J., Stanley and Alfred Thomas. His father was Starkie Thomas (b. 29 Jun 1799 in North Carolina, d. 15 Sep 1881) and his mother was Mary (Bridges) Thomas (b. 25 Jul 1807 in Kentucky, d. 7 Oct 1890). They were married on 19 Mar 1825 in Trigg County, KY.

B.M. Thomas, age 28 years of Trigg County, married Peachy Ann Martin, age 20 years also of Trigg County on 2 Dec 1869. It was the first marriage for both bride and groom.

He is buried with his wife Peachy Ann (Martin) Thomas (b. 1849, d. 1928) in the Starkey Thomas Cemetery in Trigg County, KY.

On page 50, Simmons' 1850 Trigg County Census #923-384, he is listed as age 9 years and living with his father Starkey Thomas, age 50 years; his mother Mary Thomas, age 42 years, and six siblings: James J., age 17 years; Alfred, age 15 years; Francis M., age 10 years; Perry, age 7 years; Starkey A., age 5 years; and Mary J., age 3 years.

On page 63, Simmons' 1860 Trigg County Census #931, he is listed as "B.M." (Bluford M.) living with his father "S." Sr. (Starkey Sr.), his mother "M." (Mary) (Bridges) Thomas, age 52 years, and four siblings: "F.W." (Francis M.), age 20 years; "P.C." (Perry C.), age 17 years; "S.A." (Starkey A.), age 15 years; and "M.J." (Mary J.), age 12 years).

Page 80, Simmons' 1870 Trigg County Census #935, he is listed as Bluford Thomas, a farmer, age 29 years and living with his wife Peachy Ann (Martin) Thomas, age 21 years, and a Drewry Major, age 23 years, also a farmer.

On page 140, Jones' 1900 Trigg County Census #137-140, he is listed as a farmer, age 59 years and living with his wife Peachy A. (Martin) Thomas (married 29 years), age 51 years, and two children, Mollie, age 26 years, and Johnnie E. (female), age 19 years. Peachy A. Thomas has had four children, three of whom were still living when this census was taken.

GREEN THOMAS, Private, born ca. 1840 in Kentucky, died 1 May 1912 at the age of 82 years. He mustered in 25 Jun 1864, at Paducah, KY and served with Co. K, 8th US Colored Artillery (Heavy).

He is buried in the Old Pleasant Hill Negro Cemetery with his wife Malinda Thomas (b. 31 May 1840, d. 6 Mar 1920).

Page 83, Simmons' 1870 Trigg County Census #957, he is listed as a farmer, age 30 years and living with his wife Malinda, age 28 years, and four children: Addison, age 11 years; Benjamin, age 10 years; John, age 5 years; and Nancy age 3 years.

On page 41, Jones' 1900 Trigg County Census #328-338, he is listed as Green Thomas, a farmer, age 69 years and living with his wife Malinda Thomas (married 40 years), age 60 years, a son Edmond H. Thomas, age 26 years, and daughter-in-law Mary S. Thomas, age 14 years. Malinda Thomas has had seven children, six of whom were still living when the census was taken. Mary S. Thomas had no children when the census was taken.

JAMES JASPER THOMAS, the son of Starkie and Mary Bridges Thomas, was born 19 Mar 1833 in Trigg County, KY. Starkie was a native of Bertie County, NC, while Mary was born in Trigg County. He was married to Mary "Polly" Cunningham (b. Dec 4, 1838, Trigg County), the daughter of John and Mary "Polly" Gresham Cunningham, on 6 Jul 1856.

Their children were Seldon Trimble (md. Martha Elizabeth "Betty" Bridges); John Cullen (md. Onia F. Thomas); James Jasper Jr. (md. Lulu Crews); Ophelia (md. Charles Pursley); Starkie William (md. Julia Louise Sumner); Ella Mae (md. Clarence Winston Wilson); John Spurlin (md. Hattie Lee Ricks); Cicero Berta (md. Edward Scamore Spurlock); and Clyde Edgar, single.

James J., Mary and their children lived on the Old Dover Road in the Oak Grove Community. They were charter members of the Oak Grove Baptist Church when it was organized in 1875.

He mustered into the Confederate militia on 6 Jul 1861, along with his brothers William B., Stanley, Bluford M., Francis M., Perry C. and Alfred M., under the command of Captain A.C. Thomas. A family story is that while James J. was serving the Confederacy at Fort Donelson, TN, a short distance from his home, he was granted a leave. As he rode his horse home, Union soldiers trailed him. Upon his arrival, he hid in the cellar, which had its only opening inside the house. Mary placed a rug and a bed over the cellar door, then laid in the bed pretending to be ill. The Yankee soldiers did not locate the cellar door or James J. They did steal horses and provisions.

James J. died 23 Jan 1903 and was buried in the Starkie Thomas Cemetery near his home. Mary died 12 Nov 1911 and was buried beside her husband. *Submitted by a great-granddaughter, Joyce Davis Banister.*

JOHN W. THOMAS, Private, born ca. 1843 in Kentucky. He enlisted 3 Oct 1861 at Camp Reeves, TN and served with Co. G, 8th Kentucky Regt. Inf. (CSA). According to the Kentucky Adjutant General's Report, he died of disease, date unknown.

His father Wimberly Thomas (b. ca. 1812 in Kentucky) and mother Sarah (Savills) Thomas (b. ca. 1809 in Virginia) md. 13 Aug 1832 in Trigg County, KY.

On page 29, Simmons' 1860 Trigg County Census #419, he is listed as age 17 years and living with his father "W." (Wimberly) Thomas, age 48 years; his mother Sarah (Savills) Thomas, age 51 years; and three brothers: James, age 22 years; T.J. (Thomas J.), age 9 years; and Seth, age 6 years).

ROBERT B. THOMAS, 3rd Sergeant, born 4 May 1845 in Kentucky, died 12 May 1913. He enlisted 9 Oct 1861 at Camp Alcorn in Hopkinsville, KY and served with Co. A, 8th Kentucky. Regt. Inf. (CSA).

He is the only Robert Thomas we can find in listed in Co. A of the 8th Kentucky Regt. Inf. and he is listed as "Robert" in the Kentucky Adjutant General's Report.

His father Stanley Thomas (b. 6 Nov 1805 in Kentucky, d. 11 Apr 1858) and mother Sarah B. (Thompson) (Rothrock) Thomas (b. 15 Nov 1815 in Kentucky, d. 11 Apr 1853) were married on 6 Feb 1844 in Trigg County, KY. Sarah was previously married to Noah W. Rothrock on 26 Feb 1833, in Trigg County, KY. Sarah and Stanley are buried in the East End Cemetery.

Robert is buried in the East End Cemetery with his half-sister Emily J. (Jane) (Rothrock) Smith (b. 1835, d. 24 Jun 1860); his half-brother Jack (John) James Rothrock (b. 1837, d. December 1861); and his parents.

On page 3, Simmons' 1850 Trigg County Census #51, Robert B. Thomas, age 5 years is living with his father Stanley Thomas, age 42 years, and his mother Sarah B. (Rothrock) Thomas, a half-brother John H. Rothrock, age 14 years, a half-sister Emily J. (Jane) Rothrock, age 16 years, and a brother Henry C. Thomas in a tavern/hotel with many guests. Thomas H. Grinter, age 26 years (born in Kentucky), was a merchant staying at their hotel in this census.

On page 93, Simmons' 1860 Trigg County Census #1371, Robert B. Thomas, age 15 years and his brother Henry C. Thomas, age 13 years, are living with the Thomas H. Grinter and Mary Ann Grinter family in this census.

On page 76, Simmons' 1870 Trigg County Census #893, Robert is listed as a grocer, age 24 years and living with Jerry T. Hillman listed as a clerk, age 20 years.

WILLIAM BRIDGES THOMAS, born 20 Dec 1825 in Kentucky, died 9 Jul 1901. He enlisted 7 Jul 1861 and served with Capt. A.C. Thomas' Company, 50th Tennessee Reg. Inf. CSA.

William Thomas married Nancy Jane Rogers on 15 Oct 1847, in Trigg County, KY. He married second to Sarah E. Light on 8 Mar 1877, in Trigg County, KY. He is buried in the Starkey Thomas Cemetery with his first wife Nancy J. (Rogers) Thomas (b. 23 Apr 1831, d. 19 Mar 1875) and his second wife Sarah E. (Light) Thomas (b. 1 Dec 1850, d. 27 Aug 1919).

On page 50, Simmons' 1850 Trigg County Census #919, he is listed as age 24 years and living with his wife Nancy Jane (Rogers) Thomas, age 19 years, and one child Peachy A., 1 year)

On page 59, Simmons' 1860 Trigg County Census #877, he is listed as age 34 years and living with his wife Nancy Jane (Rogers) Thomas, age 29 years, and five children: Peachy A., age 11 years; S.J. (Sarah J.), age 9 years; J.S. (Jonathan S.), age 7 years; M.E. (Martha E.), age 2 years; and W.M. (William M.), age 5 months.

On page 81, Simmons' 1870 Trigg County Census #941, he is listed as age 44 years and living with his wife Nancy Jane (Rogers) Thomas, age 38 years, and seven children: Peachy A., age 21 years; Sarah J., age 18 years; Jonathan, age 17 years; Martha E., age 12 years; William M., age 10 years; Mary E., age 8 years; Bluford, age 3 years; and Jane age 11 years.

H.H. THOMPSON, Private, served with Co. B, 8th Kentucky. Regt. Inf. (CSA). His name may have been Henry Hiram Thompson who is mentioned in the Cadiz Poll Book-26, 27, 28 Apr 1841. Hiram Thompson is mentioned in the Poll Book of the Vote of the New Constitution at Cadiz, May 1850. Henry H. Thompson is mentioned in the Wallonia Poll Book, 4 May 1867. H.H. Thompson is mentioned in the Wallonia Poll Book, November 1868.

On page 1, Simmons' 1850 Trigg County Census #16, Hiram Thompson is listed as a farmer, age 40 years, living with his wife Ursula P. Thompson, age 34 years, and two children, Alexander B., age 14 years, and Charles W., age 12 years.

JAMES THOMPSON, born April 1836 in Kentucky, was mustered in 7 Dec 1864 at Paducah, KY. There was a James Thompson who mustered into Co. B of the 119th US Colored Inf. at Paducah, KY on 7 Dec 1864. There are many James Thompsons in the record, however.

He is buried in the Old Pleasant Hill Negro Cemetery in Trigg County, KY.

On page 44, Jones' 1900 Trigg County Census #347-357, he is listed as James Thompson, a farmer, age 64 years and living with his wife Susan Thompson (married 10 years), age 32 years, and three children: Emma, age 26 years, Jasuh (son), age 12 years, and Thomas, age 9 years.

ROBERT B. THOMPSON, Private, born March 1841 in Kentucky. He enlisted 8 Nov 1861 in Todd County, KY and served with Co. D, 2nd/15th Kentucky Regt. Cav. (CSA). He served under Capt. E.A. Slaughter and J. Woodward. He was home sick on furlough and was captured by Union forces under Col. Stanley on 24 Nov 1863. He was sent to prison in Louisville, KY, where he took the oath in prison in 1864. He applied for a pension on 10 Jun 1912.

His father Moses S. Thompson (b. 4 Apr 1807 in Kentucky, d. 16 Mar 1884) and mother was Clarissa H. (Smith) Thompson (b. 17 Apr 1813 in Culpepper County, VA, d. 29 Dec 1886) were married in Trigg County, KY, on 29 Mar 1831.

Robert B. Thompson is buried in the East End Cemetery, but there are no dates on his tombstone, only CSA.

On page 54, Simmons' 1850 Trigg County Census #993, "Robert" Thompson is listed as age 9 years and living with his father M.S. (Moses S.) Thompson, age 43 years, his mother Clarissa H. Thompson, age 36 years and six siblings: James P., age 15 years; Louisa C., age 13 years; Mary, age 11 years; William F., age 7 years; Harriet B., age 3 years; and Moses, age 1 year)

On page 68, Simmons' 1860 Trigg County Census #997, "R.B." (Robert B.) Thompson, age 18 years is living with his father "M." (Moses B.) Thompson, age 53 years; his mother "C.H." (Clarissa H.) Thompson, age 47 years, and three siblings: "W.F." (William F.), age 16 years; "H.B." (Harriet B.), age 13 years; and "M." (Moses,) Jr., age 9 years.

On page 183, Neel's Statistical Handbook of Trigg County 1880 Trigg County Census, toward bottom of page, he is listed as Robert B. Thompson, age 36 years and living with his father Moses Thompson, a farmer, age 76 years, and his mother Clarissa Thompson, age 66 years.

On page 22, Jones' 1900 Trigg County Census #192-198, he is listed as Robert B. Thompson, a veterinary surgeon, age 59 years, single and living alone (born in March 1841). His mother was born in Virginia and his father was born in Kentucky.

SAMUEL TINSLEY, Private, born ca. October 1845 in Kentucky. He mustered in on 25 Jun 1864 at Paducah, KY. He served with Co. K, 8th US Colored Artillery (Heavy). There is no stone to his grave.
The 1900 Census gives his birth month and year as October 1852. Both Neel's and Maupin's records list him as a WSI veteran.

He is the only Tinsley listed as being buried in the Roaring Springs Community Cemetery in Trigg County, KY.

He is listed as Samuel Tinsley, a farmer, age 25 years and living with his wife Leah B., age 28 years, and two daughters, Mary E., age 3 years, and Telitha A. (born in July 1869) age 10 months

On page 326, Jones' 1900 Trigg County Census #330-331, he is listed as Sam "Tinzley," a farmer, age 47 years and living with his wife Liza A. Tinsley (married 11 years), age 40 years, and two daughters: Laura A., age 16 years, and Jane D., age 9 years.

JOHN T. TODD, Private, born ca. 1843 in Tennessee. He enlisted 14 Sep 1861 at Camp Burnett, TN and served with Co. G, 4th Kentucky. Regt. Inf. (CSA).

The 1880 Trigg County Census is the only record we can find of anyone by the name of Todd ever living in Trigg County.

On page 202, Neel's Statistical Handbook of Trigg County, 1880 Trigg County Census, he is listed as John T. Todd, a farmer, age 27 years and living with his brother William Todd, a farmer, age 38 years, his wife Elizabeth Todd, age 36 years, and two nephews: Richard Todd, age 14 years, and William F. Todd, age 12 years. All the members of this family were born in Tennessee.

JOHN L. TRICE (M.D.), Captain, born 18 May 1831 in Kentucky, died 19 Jun 1890. He enlisted 15 Sep 1861 and served with Co. G, 4th Kentucky Regt. Mounted Inf. (CSA).

He was wounded and captured at the Battle of Shiloh on 6 Apr 1862. He was exchanged and later restored to his command of Co. G on 14 Dec 1862. At the Battle of Murfreesboro he was again wounded and was finally discharged from service because of blindness caused by the wound he received at the Battle of Shiloh. On 20 Jul 1863 he resigned from the army to return home to Trigg County, KY.

His father was Tandy H. Trice (b. 1808) and his mother was Mary Jane (Galbraith) Trice (b. 1814).

Dr. John L. Trice married Julia A. Billings (b. 11 Dec 1838 in Tennessee, d. 23 May 1920) on 7 Jun 1856 in Trigg County, KY. Children: Tandy H. (b. 1859), James B. (b. 1868), George, Ella (b. June 1877) and Fannie (b. Dec 1882).

He is buried in East End Cemetery.

On page 71, Simmons' 1870 Trigg County Census #832, he is listed as a physician, age 40 years and living with his wife Julia A. Trice, age 33 years, and two children, Tandy H. (male), age 11 years, and James B., age 2 years.

On page 12, Jones' 1900 Trigg County Census #105-108, his widow Julia A. (Billings) Trice is listed as a widow, age 68 years and living with her daughters Ella, age 22 years, and Fannie, age 17 years. Both Ella and Fannie are listed as dress-makers in the 1900 census. Julia A. (Billings) Trice has had six children, five of whom were still living when this census was taken.

CHARLES E. TUCKER, Private, born 27 Feb 1844 in Virginia, died 20 Jul 1924. There is a Charles E. Tucker listed in the 2nd Tennessee Regt. Cav.

Charles Tucker's son William C. Tucker was born in Tennessee and William's mother was born in Virginia.

C.E. Tucker, age 21 of Bedford County, TN, married Martha Margaret Mathis (b. ca. 1848 in Kentucky) on 20 Nov 1865 in Trigg County, KY. Martha is listed as being from Christian County, KY.

Charles E. Tucker is buried in the House Cemetery in Trigg County, KY.

On page 154, Simmons' 1870 Trigg County Census #1830, he is listed as Charles E. Tucker, a farmer age 27 years, living with his wife Margaret Tucker, age 22 years, and four children: William C., age 11 years; Lula J., age 3 years; Silas M., age 2 years; and James W., age five months.

Charles E. Tucker is listed as a widower and a farmer, age 56 years, living with five children: Laura B. Tucker (?), his daughter and a widow, age 28 years; Joe W., age 20 years; Luther A., age 17 years; Berthie G., age 14 years; and John F., age 11 years.

JOHN TUCKER, Private, born ca. 1817 in Tennessee. He enlisted 14 Sep 1861 at Camp Burnett, TN and served with Co. G, 4th Kentucky. Regt. Inf. (CSA).

In the 1850 Trigg County Census, all members of the family were born in Tennessee, except the youngest, William Tucker.

DAVID RANDALL "DAVE" TURNER, born 12 Jan 1846 in Trigg County, KY, died 14 Oct 1935. He enlisted 24 Oct 1861 at Camp Alcorn in Hopkinsville, KY and served with Co. B, 8th Kentucky Regt. Inf. (CSA).

David R. Turner was a brother of John James Turner and Robert B. Turner. He enlisted in the Confederate Army, served for seven months then was discharged for physical disability.

His father was Robert Rogers Turner (b. 8 Feb 1812 in Kentucky, d. 9 Aug 1884) and his mother was Lear (Goodwin) Turner (b. 30 Dec 1809 in Kentucky, d. 12 Nov 1887).

He is buried in the Turner or Cerulean Cemetery with his wife Susan Ann Turner (b. 1844 in Georgia, d. 1915).

Page 10, Simmons' 1850 Trigg County Census #186, he is listed as age 4 years and living with his father Robert R. Turner, age 37 years, his mother Lear (Goodwin) Turner, age 40 years, and four siblings: Louisa J., age 15 years; Sarah A., age 13 years; Robert P., age 9 years; and John J., age 7 years.

On page 234, Simmons' 1870 Trigg County Census #2773, he is listed as age 24 years, living with his wife Susan A. Turner, age 26 years, and one daughter Minnie L., age 1 year. Both the mother and daughter are listed as having been born in Georgia.

On page 243, Jones' 1900 Trigg County Census #68-69, he is listed as a preacher, age 54 years, living with his wife Susan A. Turner, age 56 years, and one child, Minnie L. (Turner) Pursley, age 31 years, and a son-in-law Robert R. Pursley, age 29 years, and a grandson Louis Pursley, age 8 months. According to the 1900 census, Susan A. Turner has had one child and that child was still living when the census was taken. Minnie L. (Turner) Pursley has had one child and that child was still living when the census was taken.

JOHN JAMES "JIM" TURNER, Cerulean Springs farmer and Confederate Veteran, was born 15 Aug 1843 on the farm of his great-grandfather Jesse Goodwin (b. 1760, d. 1848) near Cerulean Springs, Trigg County, KY. He was the fifth of nine children of "Squire" Robert Rogers "Bob" Turner (b. 1812, d. 1884) and Leah Goodwin Turner (b. 1809, d. 1887).

Jim Turner was mustered into Co. "B," 8th Kentucky. Inf., CSA, at Hopkinsville, KY, 24 Oct 1861. He marched to Fort Donelson near Dover, TN, arriving on 11 Feb 1862. The 8th Kentucky Inf. was assigned to Col. Thomas J. Davidson's Brigade in Brig. Gen. Bushrod R. Johnson's Division. They fought the Yankees south of Dover along Forge Road, and surrendered on 16 February. Jim Turner was taken prisoner until exchanged at Vicksburg, MS 13 Sep 1862.

He re-entered 24 Aug 1862, was shot in the leg, recovered, captured again on 4 Jul 1863 and paroled 12 days later.

He was again wounded, in the Battle of Harrisburg, MS, 13-15 Jul 1864, then assigned to the 2nd Div. of Forest's Cav.

Promoted to corporal in the 8th Kentucky. Cav. CS Army, he was paroled at Columbus, MS 16 May 1865.

Returning home after the war, Jim Turner farmed and raised livestock. He bought the old Jesse Goodwin farm and additional acquisitions near Cerulean Springs.

On 29 May 1867, Jim Turner married Martha Elvira "Mat" Atwood, born on Crooked Creek, "Between the Rivers," 23 Oct 1849, daughter of William Jackson Atwood (b. 1817, d. 1887), a blacksmith at Canton, and Louisa Woodson Franklin Atwood (b. 1820, d. 1907). Jim and Mat Turner had nine children: Will (b. 1868, d. 1919); Lou Ella, (b. 1870, d. 1871); Tom (b. 1872, d. 1955); Leah Warren (b. 1874, d. 1936); Mattie Blakeley (b. 1876, d. 1958); Dalton (b. 1878, d. 1918); Ben (b. 1881, d. 1950); Minos (b. 1884, d. 1949); and Woodson Stewart (b. 1888, d. 1966).

Jim and Mat Turner and their son Tom were members of the Muddy Fork Primitive Baptist Church. Jim was church clerk, 1890-1892; Tom was clerk, 1893-1919. Jim Turner died 5 Apr 1893. On 18 Nov 1915, Mat married her late husband's brother, David Randall Turner (b. 1846, d. 1935). She died on 5 Jun 1920, and is buried in the Turner Graveyard, Cerulean, KY. *Submitted by William T. Turner.*

LEE TURNER, 2nd Lieutenant, born 10 Apr 1826 in Tennessee, died 6 Aug 1907. He enlisted 26 Sep 1861 at Camp Reeves, TN and served with Co. G, 8th Kentucky. Regt. Inf. (CSA). Promoted to captain 22 Sep 1862, at Jackson, MS and served with 8th Kentucky Mounted Inf. until consolidation with 12th Kentucky Cav. in 1865.

Lee Turner's father was William Turner (b. ca. 1778 in Maryland) and his mother was Nancy Turner (b. ca. 1790 in Virginia or North Carolina).

Lee Turner married Christine Francis Baker on 10 Nov 1853, in Trigg County, KY. He married second, Mrs. Virginia Radford (b. ca. 1841 in Virginia) on 8 Nov 1899, in Trigg County, KY. Virginia was the widow of W.R. Radford, a blacksmith.

He is buried in the Payton Thomas Cemetery with his first wife Christine Frances (Baker) Turner (b. 7 Mar 1831, d. 25 Jan 1899).

Page 47, Simmons' 1850 Trigg County Census #861-332, we believe he is listed as Green L. Turner, age 23 years, living with his father William Turner, age 72 years (born in Maryland) and his mother Nancy Turner, age 60 years (born in North Carolina).

On page 34, Simmons' 1860 Trigg County Census #499, Lee Turner is listed as "G.L.W." Turner, a miller, age 32 years, living with his wife C.F." (Christian F. Baker Turner), age 28 years, and three children: "W.K." (William K.), age 5 years; "M.W." (Matthew W.), age 4 years; and "L.E." (Laura E.), age 1 year.

Page 207, Simmons' 1870 Trigg County Census #2434, he is listed as age 43 years and living with his wife Christian F. (Baker) Turner, age 38 years, and six children: William K., age 14 years; Matthew W., age 12 years; Laura L., age 10 years; Thomas H., age 7 years; Robert L., age 4 years; and Joseph H., age 2 years.

On page 37, Jones' 1900 Trigg County Census #299-308, Lee Turner is listed as a farmer, age 74 years and living with his wife Virginia (Radford) Turner, age 59 years, no children.

ROBERT PAYTON "PATE" TURNER, Private, born 6 May 1841, died 27 Nov 1861 in Hopkinsville, KY. He enlisted 24 Oct 1861 at Camp Alcorn, KY and served with Co. B, 8th Kentucky. Regt. Inf. He died of disease in the camp hospital (the Christian Church) in Hopkinsville, KY. He is buried in the Turner or Cerulean Cemetery.

Robert P. Turner was a brother of John James Turner and David R. Turner.

On page 10, Simmons' 1850 Trigg County Census #186, he is listed as age 9 years and living with his father Robert R. Turner, age 47 years, his mother Lear (Goodwin) Turner, age 40 years, and four siblings: Louisa J., age 15 years; Sarah A., age 13 years; John J., age 7 years; and David R., age 4 years.

On page 48, Simmons' 1860 Trigg County Census #707, he is listed as age 19 years and living with his father Robert Rogers Turner, age 47 years, his mother Lear (Goodwin) Turner, age 49 years, and four siblings: John J., age 17 years; David R., age 15 years; Mary, age 7 years; and Martha age 7 years.

THOMAS J. TURNER, Private, born 16 Sep 1845 in Stewart County, TN. He was in Colonel Woodward's and Major Tom Lewis' command in the Confederate States Army. He went home when Col. Woodward was killed and his unit disbanded. He never took the Oath of Allegiance.

Thomas G.(?) Turner age 34 years, born in Tennessee, married Mary D. Turner, age 25 years, born in Trigg County, on 3 May 1880. It was the groom's second marriage and the bride's first.

He was a resident of Golden Pond, KY, and had been a resident of Kentucky for forty-two years prior to his Confederate pension application.

He is buried in the Colson or Pleasant Valley Cemetery with his wife Mary D. (Turner) Turner (b. 1 Jun 1855, d. 19 Oct 1919)

On page 79, Jones' 1900 Trigg County Census #146-146, Thomas J. Turner is listed as a farmer, age 54 years and living with his wife Mary D. Turner, age 44 years, and two children: Minnie B. (listed as a teacher), age 18 years, and Johnnie (son), age 15 years (listed as a farm laborer). Mary D. Turner has had three children, two of whom still living when the census was taken.

JAMES E. TUTT, Private, born Jan 1837, in Todd County, KY. He enlisted in 1861 and served with Cobb's Kentucky Battery (CSA). He was attached to Gen. Helm's Brigade and Breckenridge's lst Kentucky Division. He left the army when he was cut off from his command near Nashville, TN, in 1864. He took the oath of allegiance when he surrendered at Hopkinsville, KY, and had no chance of escape. This was in December 1864.

Private Tutt made his application for a pension on 15 Apr 1912. According to his pension application, his wife was Margaret Tutt.

According to the 1880 Census, James E. Tutt's father was born in Virginia and his mother was born in Kentucky.

According to the 1900 Census, both his father and mother were born in Virginia.

According to both the 1880 and 1900 Census, Margaret (Powell) Tutt's father was born in North Carolina and her mother was born in Virginia.

James E. Tutt, born in Todd County, age 25, married Lucy M. Powell, born in Christian County, age 21, on 23 Dec 1864.

The 4 May 1867, Cadiz Poll Book lists a James Tutt as having voted there. He is also listed in the Cadiz Poll Book dated 3 Nov 1868. He is buried by himself in the East End Cemetery. There are no dates on his tombstone.

On page 25, Simmons' 1870 Trigg, he is listed as James E. Tutt, a cistern plasterer, age 30 years, and living with his wife Lucy M. Tutt, age 25, no children.

On page 172, Neel's Statistical Handbook of Trigg County, 1880 Trigg County Census, top of page, he is listed as James Tutt, age 41 years and living with his wife Margaret, age 36 years, and a daughter Lena (is really their son Leonard), age 9 years, and a son Floyd, age 4 years.

Page 8, Jones' 1900 Trigg County Census #79-82, he is listed as James E. Tutt, a roof-hand, age 63 years living with his wife Margaret (Powell) Tutt (married 35 years), age 56 years, and two sons: Lenard, age 29 years, and Floyd, age 24 years. Margaret Tutt has had six children, only two of whom are living when this census was taken. Margaret Tutt is listed in this census as a seamstress and both Leonard and Floyd Tutt are listed as paper hangers.

HENRY TYLER, Private, born ca. 1842 in Kentucky. He enlisted 26 Sep 1861 at Camp Reeves, TN and served with Co. G, 8th Kentucky. Regt. Inf. (CSA). He was discharged from service in January 1862, cause unknown. References:

On page 27, Simmons' 1860 Trigg County Census #389, he is listed as age 18 years and is living with his brother George W. Tyler, age 16 years on the George Crump and Mary Crump farm in this census).

On page 226, Neel's Statistical Handbook of Trigg County, 1880 Trigg County census, bottom of page, Henry is not found in this census, but his brother is listed as G.W. Tyler, a farmer, age 35 years and living with his wife Nancy J. Tyler, age 30 years, and five children: M.E. (daughter), age 12 years; Alice, age 11 years; Lilly, age 9 years; Ida L., age 6 years; and James J., age 3 years.

JOHN D. TYLER, born ca. 1827 in Tennessee. According to the 1870 Census, he was a merchant in the town of Canton, KY. John Tyler's nephew Richard T. Ellis was a Union WSI veteran in Co. L, 8th Kentucky. Regt. Cav. (USA).

His father was Richard K. Tyler (b. ca. 1804 in Virginia, d. 24 Oct 1878) and his mother was Minerva R. Tyler (b. 13 Nov 1813 in Kentucky, d. 27 Dec 1879). They are both buried in the Redd Cemetery in Trigg County, KY.

His first wife, Hellen M. Tyler (b. 1 Jun 1829 in Kentucky, d. 1 Sep 1870) is buried in the East End Cemetery in Trigg County. He is buried in the Bristoe Lancaster Cemetery, but there is no stone to his grave.

On page 17, Simmons' 1850 Trigg County Census #211, John D. Tyler is listed as age 23 years and living with his wife Hellen M. Tyler, age 21 years, no children.

On page 57, Simmons' 1860 Trigg County Census #844, John D. Tyler is listed as "J.D.," a farmer, age 32 years and living with his wife Helen Tyler, age 29 years, no children.

Page 92, Simmons' 1870 Trigg County Census #1065, John D. Tyler is listed as a merchant, age 42 years and living with his wife Hellen M. Tyler, age 38 years, no children.

On page 214, Neel's Statistical Handbook of Trigg County, 1880 Trigg County Census, middle of page, he is listed as John D. Tyler a farmer, age 53 years and living with his wife S. Lizza M. Tyler (born in Alabama), age 38 years and two children: Mary M., age 6 years, and Richard K., age 4 years.

HENRY CULLEN VINSON, son of Allison and Emeline Thomas Vinson, was born in Trigg County, KY, 10 Apr 1847. He enlisted in the Confederate Army, Co. D, 2nd Kentucky Cavalry commanded by Thomas G. Woodward. This company was organized in September 1862 on the Sumner farm between Cadiz and Hopkinsville (Perrin's History of Trigg Cognty).

The records of this unit have been lost, but it is known that the 2nd Kentucky Cavalry fought with Gen. Forrest in the western Tennessee campaign and later assigned to Gen. Joseph Wheeler's Cavalry corp. They fought from Murfreesboro, TN through Georgia and South Carolina to the ocean in front of Gen. Sherman. Capt. F.G. Terry of Cadiz reported in the November 1926 issue of the *Confederate Veteran* that Henry Vinson enlisted in Capt. Slaughter's company of Col. Tom Woodward's regiment of cavalry when quite young and served in Kentucky. He was captured and held in prison until too late to experience much service.

After the close of hostilities, he resumed work on his father's farm and became one of the more prominent men of his county, "loved and honored by all."

Soon after the war he married Mary Catherine Sumner, daughter of John and Terece Coleman Sumner. They were the parents of Thomas Alford, Lula, Jesse Monroe, John Robert and Clyde Herman. Mary Catherine died 26 Jan 1920 and Henry died 15 Jul 1925. They are buried in the Vinson Cemetery located near the homeplace presently owned by his great-grandson, Tom Vinson, who lives in the house that Henry and his sons built. The confederate uniform that he probably wore in parades and his bayonet are still in the possession of his family.

FELIX M. WADLINGTON, Private, born ca. 1834 in Kentucky. He enlisted on 16 Jul 1861 at Camp Boone, TN and served with Cobb's Kentucky Battery of Field Artillery.

Felix Wadlington does not appear in any Trigg County Record after the 1850 Trigg County Census. In the 1850 Census there were three Thomas Wadlingtons in Trigg County. Thomas Sr. was age 68, born in North Carolina and the husband of Rhoda. His son was Thomas Jr., age 30, born in Kentucky and the husband of Phoebe. Felix's father was age 52 years, born in Kentucky and the husband of Frewry Wadlington.

His father was Thomas Wadlington (b. ca. 1798 in Kentucky, d. in Trigg County, KY, on 16 Apr 1853) and his mother was Frewry (Baker) Wadlington (b. ca. 1811 in Kentucky).

Page 29, Simmons' 1850 Trigg County Census #525, he is listed as Felix Wadlington, age 16 years and living with his father Thomas Wadlington, age 52 years, his mother Frewy (Baker) Wadlington, age 39 years, and five siblings: Celia, age 15 years; Wayman, age 10 years; Ann, age 8 years; Mark, age 6 years; and Lee B., age 1 year

On page 20, Simmons' 1860 Trigg County Census #296, his mother is listed as "F." Wadlington, a farmer, age 48 years and living with her son "M.H." (Mark), age 16 years; "C.C." (Christina C.), age 13 years; "B." (Lee B.), age 9 years; and May T., age 8 years.

HAMPTON WADE, 4th Corporal, born ca. 1820 in Tennessee, died between 1880 and 1900. He enlisted 24 Oct 1861 at Camp Alcorn in Hopkinsville, KY and served with Co. B, 8th Kentucky. Regt. Inf. (CSA). Discharged from service due to disability on 10 Dec 1862.

All of his known siblings were born in Tennessee except for William and Polly who were born in Virginia, and Virginia Wade who was born in Kentucky.

His father was Peter Wade Sr. (b. ca. 1788 in Virginia, d. November 1860) and his mother was Elizabeth (Wortham) Wade (b. 1788 in Virginia, d. 29 Mar 1866). They are both buried in the Wade Cemetery in Trigg County, KY.

Hampton Wade, age 48 years, married Mrs. Dianah H. (Faulkner) Brandon (b. September 1841), age 27 years, on 12 Jan 1869 in Trigg County, KY.

On page 11, Simmons 1850 Trigg County Census #206, he is listed as "Hampton" Wade, a farmer, age 30 years and living with his father Peter Wade, age 67 years, his mother Elizabeth (Wortham) Wade, age 63 years, and six siblings: William, age 40 years; Polly, age 34 years; Robert, age 25 years; Diana, age 24 years; Peter Jr., age 20 years; and Virginia, age 18 years.

Page 222, Simmons' 1870 Trigg County Census #2621, he is listed as age 49 years and living with his wife Dinah H. (Faulkner) (Brandon) Wade, age 29 years, and one child William S., age 6 months.

On page 190, Neel's Statistical Handbook of Trigg County, 1880 Trigg County Census, toward bottom of page, he is listed as Hampton Wade, a farmer, age 60 years, living with his wife Dianna (Faulkner) (Brandon) Wade, age 38 years, and a son William age 10 years; a daughter Susan, age 4 years; and a stepdaughter Bertie Brandon, age 18 years.

On page 367, Jones' 1900 Trigg County Census #26-28, Hampton Wade's widow Dianna is listed as "Dianna Waid," age 58.

JOHN SAMUEL WALL, 1st. Lieutenant, born 25 Jan 1840 in Tennessee, died 18 Jan 1862. He enlisted on 24 Oct 1861 at Camp Alcorn, Hopkinsville, KY and served with Co. B, 8th Kentucky. Regt. Inf. (CSA). He was elected 1st lieutenant at the organization of the regiment on 24 Oct 1861. 1st Lt. Wall died of disease in Hopkinsville, KY on 18 Jan 1862.

His father David D. Wall (b. 24 Aug 1810 in Virginia, d. 16 Mar 1885) and his mother Mary Elizabeth Wall (b. 3 Oct 1818 in Virginia, d. 29 Oct 1876) are buried in the Wall Cemetery in Trigg County.

He married Letitia L. Baker ca. 1858. John Samuel is buried in the Wall Cemetery with his wife Letitia L. (b. 1841, d. 1923).

On page 6, Simmons' 1850 Trigg County Census #103, he is listed as an only child, age 10 years and living with his father D.D. Wall, age 39 years, and his mother Elizabeth A. Wall, age 31 years.

On page 41, Simmons' 1860 Trigg County Census #609, he is listed as age 20 years and living with father D.D. Wall, age 49 years, his mother E.A.L. Wall, age 41 years, his wife Letitia L. (Baker) Wall, age 17 years, and a daughter Lula Wall age 10 months. (

On page 217, Simmons' 1870 Trigg County Census #2564, his widow Letitia (Baker) Wall, age 28 years, is living with her children Lula 10 and Susan B. age 8 years.

On page 194, Neel's Statistical Handbook of Trigg County, 1880 Trigg County Census, toward bottom of page, his father is listed as D.D. Wall, a farmer, age 67 and living with his wife Elizabeth Wall, age 58 years; daughter-in-law Tisha (Baker) Wall, age 38 years; granddaughter Fannie Wall, age 17 years; and a boarder at school, Joseph Standrod, age 17 years.

ABITHAL WALLACE, born 18 Mar 1839 in Tennessee, died 22 Feb 1903. He served with Co. D, Col. Woodward's Second Regt. of Kentucky Cav.

In the 1850 Trigg County Census only Munroe S. Wallace was born in Kentucky. All others in the family were born in Tennessee.

Abithal's father was James Wallace (b. ca. 1817 in Tennessee) and his mother was Martha Wallace (b. ca. 1820 in Tennessee).

He married Mary D. Cameron on 7 Feb 1861 in Trigg County, KY. Abithal Wallace is buried in the Goodwin Cemetery near Cerulean, KY, with his wife Mary D. (Cameron) Wallace (b. 18 May 1833 in Kentucky, d. 24 Feb 1917).

On page 22, Simmons' 1860 Trigg County Census #322, he is listed "A. Wallis," a carpenter, age 22 years and living with his father James Wallis, age 43 years, his mother Martha Wallis, age 40 years and five siblings: J.W. (male), age 16 years; George W., age 14 years; Thomas H.W., age 12 years; Caroline J., age 10 years; and Munroe S., age 2 years.

On page 215, Simmons' 1870 Trigg County Census #2541, he is listed as age 31 years and living with his wife Mary D. (Cameron) Wallis, age 36 years, and three children: Moses A., age 6 years; James D., age 4 years; and Josiah W., age 1 month.

On page 194, Neel's Statistical Handbook of Trigg County, 1880 Trigg County Census, toward bottom of page, he is listed as a carpenter, age 41 years, living with his wife Mary D. (Cameron) Wallace, age 40 years, and two sons: Alex, age 16 years, and James, age 15 years.

ALEXANDER WALLACE, 2nd Lieutenant, born ca. 1840 in Kentucky, died 24 May 1864, at Dallas, GA. He enlisted at Camp Burnett on 14 Sep 1861 and served with Co. G, 4th Kentucky Regt. Inf. (CSA). He was promoted from 1st sergeant to 2nd lieutenant on 30 Sep 1863. He was killed in battle on 24 May 1864 at Dallas, GA.

He was the son of Axum G. Wallace and Elizabeth Ross Wallace. He lived between the rivers in Trigg County. He was ggg-uncle of Army veteran John Douglas Williams and gg-uncle of Navy veteran Jesse C. Gordon.

On page 68, Simmons' 1850 Trigg County Census #1263-734, he is listed as age 9 years and living with Alfred R. Wallace and his wife Sophia Wallace and their two children: Green F. Wallace, age 5 years, and Margaret Wallace, age 2 years.

Alexander's siblings in this census seem to be Ann E. Wallace, age 16 years; Hugh D. Wallace, age 13 years; and Mary Wallace, age 8 years.

HUGH D. WALLACE, 2nd Sergeant, born ca. 1836 in Tennessee. He enlisted at Camp Burnett on 14 Aug 1861 and served with Co. G, 4th Kentucky Regt. Inf. (CSA). He was promoted from 3rd sergeant to 2nd sergeant on 12 Oct 1863, was wounded and captured at Jonesboro, GA, on 1 Sep 1864.

He was a brother to Alexander Wallace

There was a Hugh D. Wallace born in Trigg County around 1873 and another Hugh D. Wallace born in 1884. The Hugh D. Wallace born in 1873 is buried in the Mount Pleasant-Blue Springs Cemetery. The Hugh D. Wallace born in 1884 was moved from the Cumberland Baptist Church Cemetery to Paducah when Lake Barkley was impounded.

We do not know who Hugh D. Wallace's parents were, but we feel he and his siblings were adopted by Alfred R. and Sophia (Dew) Wallace when these siblings became orphans ca. 1846.

Alfred R. Wallace (b. 15 May 1820, d. 8 Sep 1872) married Sophia Dew (b. 15 Apr 1826, d. 4 May 1868) on 29 Jun 1842 in Trigg County, KY. Both are buried in the Matheny-Cumberland Church Cemetery.

On page 68, Simmons' 1850 Trigg County Census #1263-734, he is listed as age 13 years, living with Alfred R. Wallace and his wife Sophia (Dew) Wallace and their two children: Green F. Wallace, age 5 years, and Margaret Wallace, age 2 years.

On page 7, Simmons' 1860 Trigg County Census #96, Hugh D. Wallace is listed as age 24 years, living with Alfred R. Wallace, age 40 years; Sophia (Dew) Wallace, age 33 years; "G.T." (Green T.) Wallace, age 14 years; Margaret Wallace, age 12 years; "E.M." (male) Wallace, age 9 years; and a "W.W." (male) Wallace, age 7 years.

On page 132, Simmons' 1870 Trigg County Census #1581, Hugh D. Wallace is not found in this census.

TAYLOR WALLACE, Private, born 1847 in Kentucky. He enlisted on 14 Sep 1861, at Camp Burnett, TN and served with Co. G, 4th Kentucky. Regt. Inf. (CSA). He was discharged for disability on 25 Dec 1861.

The following man is the only Taylor Wallace of record found in Trigg County. His father William K. Wallace (b. ca. 1813 in South Carolina) and mother Elizabeth M. (Phillips) Wallace (b. ca. 1814 in North Carolina) were married in Trigg County on 14 Dec 1832. On page 56, Simmons' 1850 Trigg County Census #1029, his father is listed as William K. "Wallis," age 37 years, living with his wife Elizabeth M. (Phillips) Wallis, age 35 years, and six children: James B., age 16 years; Isaac P., age 13 years; Zachens L., age 10 years; Edward T., age 7 years; Betty A., age 4 years; and Crittenden T., age 1 year.

Page 37, Simmons' 1860 Trigg County Census #552, he is listed as "Z. Taylor" Wallis age 13 years, living with his father "W.K." (William K.) Wallis, age 48 years, and his mother "E.M." (Elizabeth M.) Wallis, age 46 years, and four children: Elizabeth, age 14 years; Edward T., age 16 years; and Fernando age 6 years.

We can find none of this family in any Trigg County records after the early 1870s.

WILLIAM K. WALLACE, Private, born ca. 1813 in South Carolina. He enlisted on 14 Sep 1861 at Camp Burnett and served with Co. G, 4th Kentucky. Regt. Inf. (CSA). He was discharged for disability, the date not given.

This man is the only William K. Wallace we could find in Trigg County Records of this era.

He married Elizabeth Matilda Phillips (b. ca. 1814 in North Carolina) on 14 Dec 1832 in Trigg County, KY.

On page 56, Simmons' 1850 Trigg County Census #1029, he is listed as William K. "Wallis," age 37 years, living with his wife Elizabeth M. (Phillips) Wallis, age 35 years and six children: James B., age 16 years; Isaac P., age 13 years; Zachens L., age 10 years; Edward T., age 7 years; Betty A., age 4 years; and Crittenden T., age 1 year.

Page 37, Simmons' 1860 Trigg County Census #552, he is listed as "W.K." Wallis age 48 years, living with his wife "E.M." (Elizabeth) Wallis, age 46 years, and four children: Elizabeth, age 14 years; Edward T., age 16 years; Z. Taylor, age 13 years; and Fernando, age 6 years.

JOHN J. WALLIS, Private, born ca. 1840 in Kentucky, died 14 Dec 1864 in Bowling Green, KY. Enrolled 15 Aug 1863, mustered in 26 Oct 1863 in Princeton, KY and died before he was mustered out. He served with Co. F, 48th Kentucky Regt. Inf. (USA).

His father was John Wallis (b. ca. 1807 in South Carolina) and his mother was Elizabeth Wallis (b. ca. 1809 in South Carolina). According to the 1850 Census, all of their children were born in Kentucky.

John J. Wallis married Martha Guier on 25 Nov 1869 in Trigg County, KY.

On page 30, Simmons' 1850 Trigg County Census #556, he is listed as age 10 years and living with his father John Wallis, age 43, his mother Elizabeth Wallis, age 41 years, and seven siblings: Lucy A., age 16 years; W.B. (male), age 15 years; Permelia E., age 12 years; Iredell H. (male), age 8 years; Cynthia A., age 5 years; and infant Nancy E.

On page 61, Simmons' 1870 Trigg County Census #699, John J. Wallis' parents are listed as John Wallis, age 63 years, living with his mother Elizabeth Wallis, age 61 years, and three children: Nancy E., age 19 years; George R., age 17 years; and Iradell H., age 26 years.

WILLIAM WALLIS, Sergeant, born ca. 1835 in Kentucky. Enrolled 15 Aug 1863, mustered in 26 Oct 1863 at Princeton, KY and mustered out 19 Dec 1864 in Bowling Green, KY. He served with Co. F, 48th Kentucky Regt. Mounted Inf. (USA).

His father was John Wallis (b. ca. 1807 in South Carolina) and his mother was Elizabeth M. (Phillips) Wallis (b. ca. 1809 in North Carolina).

References: Page 642, Union Regiments of Kentucky.

On page 30, Simmons' 1850 Trigg County Census #556-20, he is listed as "W.B." Wallis, age 15 years, living with his father John Wallis,

age 43 years, his mother Elizabeth, age 41 years, and six siblings: Lucy A., age 16 years; Parmelia E., age 12 years; John J., age 10 years; Iredell H. (male), age 8 years; Cynthia A., age 5 years; and infant Nancy E.

On page 68, Simmons' 1860 Trigg County Census #998, he is listed as "W.B." Wallis, age 25 years, living with his father "J." (John) Wallis, age 53 years, his mother "E." (Elizabeth) Wallis, age 52 years, and six siblings: "P.E." (Parmelia E.), age 21 years; "J.J." (John J.), age 19 years; "I.H." (Iredell H.), age 16 years; "C.A." (Cynthia A.), age 12 years, "N.E." (Nancy E.), age 10 years and "G.R." (George R.), age 8 years.

WILLIAM HENRY HARRISON WARREN, born 12 Oct 1833(?), died 27 Jan 1893 in Trigg County, KY. His tombstone states he was born in 1833, but all the census records state he was born around 1840. In 1833, his father would have been about 15 years of age and his mother would have been around 13 years of age. He enlisted in Christian County, KY and served with Co. B, 1st Kentucky Regt. Cav. (CSA).

His father was William H. Warren (b. 13 Jan 1818 in Virginia, d. 14 Jan 1864) and his mother was Nancy (Stuart) Warren (b. 14 Feb 1820 in Virginia, d. 6 Apr 1904). They were married on 25 Dec 1838 in Trigg County, KY.

W.H.H. Warren married Sarah E. Pursley (b. 7 Sep 1847 in Kentucky, d. 8 Aug 1877) in Trigg County, KY on 10 Oct 1865. He married second, Virginia Forest Elliott (b. 11 Mar 1862 in Kentucky, d. 14 Jun 1939) on 1 May 1879 in Trigg County, KY.

He is buried with both his wives and his parents in the Cerulean or Turner Cemetery in Trigg County, KY.

On pages 15 and 16, Simmons' 1850 Trigg County Census #264, he is listed as William H. Warren, age 10 years, living with his father William H. Warren, age 35 years; his mother Nancy (Stuart) Warren, age 30 years, and three siblings: George W. age 8 years; Mannin (male), age 6 years; and Francis A. (female), age 2 years;

On page 232, Simmons' 1870 Trigg County Census #2750, he is listed as William H. Warren, a farmer, age 30 years, living with his wife Sarah E. (Pursley) Warren, age 22 years, and two children, William N. Warren, age 2 years, and Robert F. (Franklin) Warren, age 1 year.

Page 240, Jones' 1900 Trigg County Census #44-45. His widow, Virginia F. (Elliott) Warren is listed as a widow, age 38 years.

AARON WATKINS, Private, born ca. 1840 in Kentucky, mustered in 20 Jan 1865 at Paducah, KY and served with Co. B, 13th US Colored Artillery (Heavy).

He is buried in the Old Rocky Ridge Cemetery in Trigg County, KY, but there is no stone to his grave. References:

On page 222, Simmons' 1870 Trigg County Census #2625, he and his family are living with Smith L. Brandon, age 19 years, and Nancy E. Brandon, age 18 years, in this census. He is listed as a black farmer, age 30 years, living with his wife Mandy, age 32 years; a son Dick, age 13 years; a son Caswell, age 11 years; a son John, age 8 years; a daughter Bell, age 6 years; and a son Aaron F., age 5 years.

On page 373, Jones' 1900 Trigg County Census #70-72, he is listed as a farmer, age 65 years, living with his wife Mandy Watkins (married 44 years) age 60 years, and one son, Frank Watkins (b. March 1879), age 21 years. Mandy Watkins has had 14 children, only six of whom were still living when the census was taken.

FRANCIS MARION WATKINS, 2nd Sergeant, born ca. 1842 in Kentucky, died 2 Nov 1862 in Coldwater, MS. He enlisted 24 Oct 1861 at Camp Alcorn, Hopkinsville, KY and served with Co. B, 8th Kentucky. Regt. Inf. (CSA). He died of disease (fever) at Coldwater, MS on 2 Nov 1862.

Francis M. Watkins is a brother to George W. and William L. Their father was Hezekiah B. Watkins (b. 1 Nov 1806 in Tennessee, d. 27 Nov 1874) and his mother was Dianah (Wade) Watkins (b. 15 Nov 1806 in Kentucky, d. 14 Nov 1874). They are buried in the Wade Cemetery in Trigg County.

On page 8, Simmons' 1850 Trigg County Census #150, he is listed as age 8 years and living with his father Hezekiah B. Watkins, age 44 years, his mother Dianah Watkins, age 43 years, and 12 siblings: Samuel J., age 21 years; Euphemia E., age 18 years; Judy Ann, age 16 years; Martha J., age 15 years; Hezekiah T., age 15 years; Charles J., age 13 years; Catherine, age 11 years; William L., age 11 years; George W., age 9 years; Susan, age 7 years; Jesse M., age 5 years; and Sarah C., age 2 years.

On page 43, Simmons' 1860 Trigg County Census #631, he is listed as "Marion" Watkins, age 18 years, living with his father Hezekiah B. Watkins, age 53 years, and nine siblings: J.R. (male) (?), age 32 years; Martha, age 26 years; Charles, age 23 years; William L., age 20 years; George W., age 18 years; Susan, age 16 years; Jesse, age 13 years; Sarah, age 11 years; and Ellen, age 9 years.

GEORGE WASHINGTON WATKINS, Private, born ca. 1842 in Kentucky. He enlisted 24 Oct 1861 at Camp Alcorn in Hopkinsville, KY and served with Co. B, 8th Kentucky. Regt. Inf. (CSA).

George Washington Watkins is a brother to Francis Marion Watkins and William L. Watkins. Their father was Hezekiah B. Watkins (b. 1 Nov 1806 in Tennessee, d. 27 Nov 1874) and his mother was Dianah (Wade) Watkins (b. 15 Nov 1806 in Kentucky, d. 14 Nov 1874). They are buried in the Wade Cemetery in Trigg County.

On page 8, Simmons' 1850 Trigg County Census #150, he is listed as age 8 years and living with his father Hezekiah B. Watkins, age 44 years, his mother Dianah Watkins, age 43 years, and 12 siblings: Samuel J., age 21 years; Euphemia E., age 18 years; Judy Ann, age 16 years; Martha J., age 15 years; Hezekiah T., age 15 years; Charles J., age 13 years; Catherine, age 11 years; William L., age 9 years; Francis, age 8 years; Susan, age 7 years; Jesse M., age 5 years; and Sarah C., age 2 years.

On page 236, Simmons' 1870 Trigg County Census #2789, he is listed as age 27 years and living with his wife Lucretia, age 21 years and no children.

WILLIAM L. WATKINS, Private, born 5 Jun 1840 in Kentucky, died 21 Dec 1861 in Hopkinsville, KY. He enlisted 24 Oct 1861 at Camp Alcorn in Hopkinsville, KY and served with Co. B, 8th Kentucky. Regt. Inf. (CSA). Private William L. Watkins died of disease in Hopkinsville, KY.

William L. Watkins is a brother to George W. Watkins and Francis M. Watkins. Their father was Hezekiah B. Watkins (b. 1 Nov 1806 in Tennessee, d. 27 Nov 1874) and his mother was Dinah (Wade) Watkins (b. 15 Nov 1806 in Kentucky, d. 14 Nov 1874). They are buried in the Wade Cemetery in Trigg County.

William L. Watkins (b. 5 Jun 1840, d. 21 Dec 1861) is buried in the Wade Cemetery.

On page 8, Simmons' 1850 Trigg County Census #150, he is listed as age 9 years and living with his father Hezekiah B. Watkins, age 44 years, his mother Dianah Watkins, age 43 years, and 12 siblings: Samuel J., age 21 years; Euphemia E., age 18 years; Judy Ann, age 16 years; Martha J., age 15 years; Hezekiah T., age 15 years; Charles J., age 13 years; Catherine, age 11 years; George W., age 8 years; Francis, age 8 years; Susan, age 7 years; Jesse M., age 5 years; and Sarah C., age 2 years.

Page 43, Simmons' 1860 Trigg County Census #631, he is listed as age 20 years and living with his father Hezekiah B. Watkins, age 53 years, and nine siblings.

DAVID N. WATWOOD, Private, born ca. 1843. He enlisted 3 Oct 1861 at Camp Alcorn in Hopkinsville, KY and served with Co. G, 8th Kentucky. Regt. Inf. (CSA). He was captured at Fort Donelson in February 1862, exchanged in September 1862 and finally deserted his command at Mayfield, KY on 27 Mar 1864. He is listed with a group of men of the enrolled militia on parade in Trigg County on Saturday, 6 Apr 1861.

His father was William S. Watwood (b. ca. 1816 in Tennessee) and his stepmother was Eliza A. (Smith) Watwood (b. ca. 1833 in Kentucky). His father William S. Watwood (b. 1816) is buried in the Atwood-McNichols Cemetery in Trigg County, but there is no stone to his grave. He is the only person with the surname Watwood buried in Trigg County.

On page 36, Simmons' 1850 Trigg County Census #650, he is listed as age 6 years and living with his father William S. Watwood, age 34 years, his stepmother Eliza A. (Smith) Watwood, age 17 years, and one brother James Watwood, age 1 month.

On page 71, Simmons' 1860 Trigg County Census #1041, he is listed as D.N Watwood, age 17 years and living with his father William S. Watwood, age 44 years, his stepmother Eliza A. (Smith) Watwood, age 30 years, and one sister, M.E. (Elizabeth) Watwood, age 5 years.

David N. Watwood is not found in this census. None of this family is found in Neel's 1880 Trigg County Census.

JOHN WEAVER, Private, born ca. 1832 in Alabama. He enlisted 13 Oct 1861 at Camp Alcorn in Hopkinsville, KY and served with Co. G, 8th Kentucky Regt. Inf. (CSA).

On page 17, Simmons' 1860 Trigg County Census #246, he is listed as a woodcutter, age 28 years and living with the Sam Pattengill family.

WILLIAM E. WELLS, Private, born 19 Mar 1839 in Kentucky, died 20 Jul 1915. Enrolled 21 Jul 1863, mustered in 26 Oct 1863 at Princeton, KY and mustered out 18 Dec 1864 at Bowling Green, KY. He served with Co. G, 48th Kentucky Regt. Mounted Inf. (USA).

His tombstone states he was in Co. E, but records show he was in Co. G of the 48th Kentucky. Most of the members of the 48th Kentucky Mounted Inf. from Trigg County were in Co. F.

His father was born in North Carolina and his mother was born in Alabama. Both of Barbara E. Wells' parents were born in Virginia.

He is buried in the Jenny Ridge Cemetery.

Page 229, Neel's Statistical Handbook of Trigg County, 1880 Trigg County Census, top of page, there is a William C. Wells, age 41 years, living with his wife Barbara E. Wells, age 41 years, and seven children: Sarah M., age 18 years; James C., age 16 years; Martha A., age 13 years; Barbara E., age 11 years; William D., age 9 years; Laura L., age 6 years; and Lillie F., age 3 months.

On page 95, Jones' 1900 Trigg County Census #270, he is listed as William C. Wells, a farmer, age 61 years and living with his wife Barbara Wells (married 39 years), age 61 years, and five children: Sarah, age 38 years; James C., age 36 years; Elizabeth, age 31 years; William D., age 29 years; and Louisa, age 26 years. Barbara Wells has had 11 children, only seven of whom were still living when this census was taken.

WILLIAM WHARTON, born at the old Wharton homestead on 5 Jan 1822. He was a Union man during the War Between the States, but conservative in his views.

William was prominent in the county from his early manhood. Politically in early life he was an intense Whig and cast his first vote for Henry Clay for President in 1844.

He was married in early manhood to Miss Sarah Carloss, daughter of William Carloss and his wife Olivia. There were four daughters and one son: George T. Wharton, Mrs. Charles Jackson, Mrs. I.G. Sallee, Mrs. Alex Grace and Miss Mildred Wharton

GEORGE H. WILFORD, 1st Lieutenant, born 1836, died 8 Mar 1863. He enlisted 26 Sep 1861 at Camp Reeves, TN and served with Co. G, 8th Kentucky Regt. Inf. (CSA). He was elected 2nd lieutenant on 10 Feb 1862 and promoted to 1st lieutenant 22 Sep 1862. 1st Lt. Wilford died of disease on 8 Mar 1863.

His tombstone states that he died on 15 Jun 1862 and that he was in Co. D of the 8th Kentucky. George H. Wilford is buried in the Wilford Cemetery.

His father was Bennett Wilford (b. 6 Jun 1802 in North Carolina, d. 8 Jun 1860) and his mother was Sarah Wilford (b. 27 Sep 1804 in North Carolina, d. 22 Oct 1867).

Page 17, Simmons' 1850 Trigg County Census #317, he is listed as age 11 years and living with his father Bennet Wilford, age 48 years; his mother Sarah (Raldolph) Wilford, age 46 years; and four siblings: Merrel (male), age 21 years; Minerva, age 14 years; Sarah J., age 7 years; and Doctor B., age 5 years.

On page 55, Simmons' 1860 Trigg County Census #803, his father Bennett Wilford, age 58 years; his mother Sarah Wilford, age 53 years, and four siblings: Meret(?), age 28 years; Sarah, age 17 years; Burnett, age 12 years; and Betty, age 9 years; are mentioned in this census. George Wilford is not listed in this census.

JOE (JOSEPH) WILLIAMS, Private, born ca. 1837 in Kentucky. There was a Private Joseph Williams in Co. G, 14th Tennessee Inf.

He was a brother to Joel Williams. Their father was Shadrack Williams (b. ca. 1799 in North Carolina) and mother was Elizabeth (Sumner) Williams (b. ca. 1805 in North Carolina). They were married in Trigg County on 15 Apr 1825.

He married Mahala Ann Armstrong on 11 Apr 1869 in Trigg County. It was his first marriage and her second. She was born in Dixon County, TN. Joseph was age 32 years and Mahala was 40 years of age.

His second marriage was to Martha E. Herndon on 15 Sep 1881 in Trigg County. He is buried in the Wilson-Redd Cemetery in Trigg County, KY.

On page 50 and 51, Simmons' 1850 Trigg County Census #925-386, he is listed as Joseph Williams, age 13 years, living with his father Shadrack Williams, age 51 years, his mother Elizabeth (Sumner) Williams, age 45 years, and three siblings: Aquilla (female), age 19 years; Temperance, age 14 years; and Joel, age 12 years.

On page 61, Simmons' 1860 Trigg County Census #906, he is listed as a "J." Williams, a farm laborer, age 24 years and living with the "M." (Mahala A.) Armstrong, age 39 years (female born in Tennessee), family in this census).

On page 89, Simmons' 1870 Trigg County Census #1034, he is listed as Joseph Williams, age 33 years, living with his wife Mahala (Armstrong) Williams, age 48 years, no children.

JOEL WILLIAMS, born ca. 1836 in Kentucky. He served with Co. F, 50th Tennessee Regt. Inf. (CSA). His tombstone gives his unit.

His father was Shadrack Williams (b. ca. 1799 in North Caroline) and his mother was Elizabeth (Sumner) Williams (b. ca. 1805 in North Carolina). They were married in Trigg County on 15 Apr 1825.

Joel Williams married Lucretia Lancaster on 19 Aug 1862 in Trigg County. He is buried in the Dixon-Lancaster Cemetery. There is no record of any of his wives being buried near him.

Page 50 and 51, Simmons' 1850 Trigg County Census #925-386, he is listed as Joel Williams, age 12 years, living with his father Shadrack Williams, age 51 years; his mother Elizabeth (Sumner) Williams, age 45 years; and three siblings: Aquilla, age 19 years; Temperance, age 14 years; and Joseph, age 13 years.

Page 64, Simmons' 1860 Trigg County Census #938, he is listed as "J." (Joel) Williams, age 21 years, living with his father "S." (Shadrack) Williams, age 60 years; his mother "E." (Elizabeth) Williams, age 55 years; and two siblings, "Q." (Aquilla), age 28 years, and "T." (Temperance), age 24 years.

Page 142, Simmons' 1870 Trigg County Census #1694B (Joel is not found in Simmons' 1870 Trigg County Census.

HENRY C. WILLIAMS, born 1824 in Tennessee, died ca. 1865. He is listed as "The Enrolled Militia on Parade on Saturday, 6 Apr 1861 in Trigg County." According to Trigg County history, he died of drowning when returning from the War for Southern Independence.

His father was William Williams (b. ca. 1794 in Kentucky) and his mother was Arametta Williams (b. ca. 1804 in Tennessee).

Page 485, Neel's Statistical Handbook of Trigg County, List of Militia on Parade on Saturday, 6 Apr 1861 in Trigg County.

Page 67, Simmons' 1850 Trigg County Census #1240-711, he is listed as age 26 years, living with his father William Williams, age 56 years; his mother Arametta Williams, age 46 years; and six siblings: William S., age 22 years; Elizabeth P., age 20 years; James F., age 18 years; Melvina M., age 11 years; and Edgar L., age 5 years.

Pages 7 and 8, Simmons' 1860 Trigg County Census #104, he is listed as age 36 years, living with his mother "A.D." (Armetta) Williams, age 56 years and four siblings: "W.S." (William S.), age 32 years; "M." (Melvina), age 21 years; "M." (Marcus M.), age 18 years; and Edgar Williams, age 14 years.

MELVILLE MARCUS WILLIAMS, Private, born 24 Feb 1842 in Tennessee or Kentucky, died 22 Feb 1923. He enlisted 14 Sep 1861 and served with Co. G., 4th Kentucky Regt. Inf. (CSA). He is listed as "Men Enrolled in Militia on Parade on Saturday, 6 Apr 1861 in Trigg County." He is listed as "M.M." Williams in the Kentucky Adjutant's Report.

Marcus M. Williams, age 26 years, married Mary Jane (Jennie) Huggins, age 16 years, on 19 Apr 1868 in Trigg County. It was the first marriage for both bride and groom.

He is buried with his wife Jennie Williams (b. 18 Apr 1852, d. 20 Feb 1904) in the Matheny Cemetery in Trigg County.

Page 485, Neel's Statistical Handbook of Trigg County, Men Listed as Enrolled in Militia on Parade on Saturday, 6 Apr 1861 in Trigg County.

Page 67, Simmons' 1850 Trigg County Census #1240, he is listed as age 8 years and living with his father William Williams, age 56 years; his mother Armetta Williams, age 46 years; and six siblings: Henry C.,

age 26 years; William S., age 22 years; Elizabeth P., age 20 years; James F., age 18 years; Melvina M., age 11 years; and Edgar L., age 5 years.

Page 109, Simmons' 1870 Trigg County Census #1278, he is listed as age 28 years and living with his wife Mary Jane (Jennie) Williams, age 18 years and daughter Armetta, 4 months.

Page 237, Neel's Statistical Handbook of Trigg County, 1880 Trigg County Census, middle of page, he is listed as Marcus Williams, age 38 years, living with his wife Mary J. Williams, age 28 years, and four daughters: Armenta, age 10 years; Eler L., age 8 years; Flor__ C., age 4 years; and Iva D., age 2 years.

WILLIAM S. WILLIAMS, Private, born ca. 1828 in Tennessee, died ca. 1878. He enlisted 14 Sep 1861 and served with Co. G, 4th Kentucky Regt. Inf. (CSA). He is listed on a list of "Men Enrolled in the Militia on Parade, Saturday, 6 Apr 1861 in Trigg County.

His brother Marcus M. Williams, age 26 years, married Mary Jane (Jennie) Huggins, age 16 years on 19 Apr 1868 in Trigg County. It was the first marriage for both bride and groom.

On page 67, Simmons' 1850 Trigg County Census #1240-711, he is listed as age 22 years, living with his father William Williams, age 56 years; his mother Arametta Williams, age 46 years; and six siblings: Henry C., age 26 years; Elizabeth P., age 20 years; James F., age 18 years; Melvina M., age 11 years; Marcus M., age 8 years; and Edgar L., age 5 years.

On page 133, Simmons' 1870 Trigg County Census #1587, he is listed as age 42 years (born in Tennessee) living with his wife Sarah Williams, age 24 years, and two children: Effie D., age 2 years, and Luellen, age 1 year.

W.T. WILSON, 5th Sergeant, born ca. 1842 in Kentucky. He enlisted at Camp Reeves, TN, on 26 Sep 1861 and served with Co. G, 8th Kentucky. Regt. Inf. (CSA). He was promoted to 5th sergeant on 22 Sep 1862. He was wounded, but the time and place were not stated.

On page 19, Simmons' 1850 Trigg County Census #246, he is listed as William T. Wilson, age 8 years, living with his widowed mother Myresena (or Myrenne) Wilson, age 31 years; and three siblings: Edwin B., age 6 years; John P., age 4 years; and Susan B., age 2 years.

BENJAMIN F. WIMBERLY, 4th Sergeant, born ca. 1838 in Kentucky, died 18 Nov 1861. He enlisted 24 Oct 1861 at Camp Alcorn in Hopkinsville, KY and served with Co. B, 8th Kentucky Regt. Inf. (CSA). He died of disease 18 Nov 1861 at Hopkinsville, KY.

His father was Alfred Wimberly (b. ca. 1800 in North Carolina, d. ca. 1873) and his mother was Mariah H. (Savills) Wimberly (b. ca. 1806 in Virginia d. ca. 1885). They are listed as being buried in the Sivills Cemetery in Trigg County, but there are no stones marking their graves.

Benjamin F. is buried in the Wimberly Cemetery in Trigg County. He is listed as "B.F." There is a marker at his grave.

Page 30, Simmons' 1850 Trigg County Census #547, he is listed as Benjamin, age 11 years, living with his father Alfred Wimberly, age 50 years; his mother Mariah H. (Savills) Wimberly, age 44 years; and five siblings: Gabrilla, age 14 years; Margaret, age 9 years; Edward, age 7 years; Richard, age 4 years; and Alfred T., age 2 years.

On page 41, Simmons' 1860 Trigg County Census #604 (Benjamin Wimberly is listed as age 22 years and living with the W.S. Coy and Virginia Coy family in this census.

CLABORN B. WOLFE/WOOLFE, 2nd Sergeant, born ca. 1827 in Kentucky. He enlisted 24 Oct 1861 at Camp Alcorn, Hopkinsville, KY and served with Co. B, 8th Kentucky. Regt. Inf. (CSA). He was promoted to 2nd sergeant from private. Sgt. Woolfe was discharged from service 30 Sep 1863. The place and reason for his discharge are not stated

His father was George Wolfe (b. ca. 1805 in Kentucky) and his mother was Saleta (Dodson) Wolfe (b. ca. 1813 in Virginia). They were married on 9 Dec 1834 in Trigg County.

On page 7, Simmons' 1850 Trigg County Census #128, he is listed as age 10 years and living with father George Wolfe, age 45 years; his mother Saleta Wolfe, age 37 years; and one sister, Levina A. (J.) Wolfe, age 13 years.

On page 33, Simmons' 1860 Trigg County Census #482, he is listed as age 20 years and living with his father George Wolfe, age 55 years;

his mother Saleta Wolfe, age 48 years; and one sister S.D. Wolfe, age 4 years.

On page 227, Simmons' 1870 Trigg County Census #2686. His father George Wolfe, age 65 years; his mother Saletta Wolfe, age 59 years; and his sister Saletta D. Wolfe, age 13 years are listed in this census. We cannot find Claborn B. Wolfe in this census.

WILLIAM R. WRIGHT, Private, born ca. 1824 in Kentucky. Enrolled 20 Jul 1863, mustered in 26 Oct 1863 at Princeton, KY and mustered out 19 Dec 1863 at Bowling Green, KY. He served with Co. F, 48th Kentucky. Regt. Inf. (USA).

William R. Wright married Elizabeth France (b. ca. 1835 in Kentucky) on 27 Feb 1854 in Trigg County.

His son W. Henry Wright (b. 1861, d. 1923) is buried with his wife Mary R. Wright (b. 1877, d. 1909) in the Carr Cemetery.

On page 42, Simmons' 1850 Trigg County Census #779-240, William R. Wright is not found in this census, but his future wife Elizabeth France is listed as Elizabeth "Francis," age 16 years, living with her father Levi "Francis," age 57 years; her mother Jane "Francis," age 37 years; and three siblings: Nancy, age 11 years; Luvenia T., age 10 years; and Mary A., age 8 years.

On page 84, Simmons' 1860 Trigg County Census #1234, William is listed as age 26 years and living with his wife Elizabeth (France) Wright, age 25 years, and two children: "F." "Knight" (Wright??) (female), age 8 years, and "V." Wright (female), age 4 years.

Cannot find any of this family in Jones' 1900 Trigg County Census or in Blue & Sellers' 1920 Trigg County Census.

SAMUEL A. YARBOROUGH, Private, born ca. 1840 in Kentucky, died 1 Jul 1862 of disease. He enlisted 14 Sep 1861 at Camp Burnett, TN and served with Co. G, 4th Kentucky. Regt. Inf. (CSA).

His father was Asa Yarborough (b. 1810 in Stewart County, TN, d. 1871) and his mother was Temperance Yarborough (b. 1819 in Stewart County, TN). They are buried in the Matheny-Cumberland Cemetery.

Samuel Yarborough is buried in Matheny-Cumberland Cemetery (no stone) References:

On page 4, Simmons 1860 Trigg County Census #57, he is listed as age 20 years, living with his father Asa Yarborough, age 41 years; his mother Tempy (Temperance) Yarborough, age 41 years; and six siblings: Lucy, age 23 years; Nancy, age 16 years; Mary, age 14 years; George, age 8 years; L. (Florence), age 7 years; and A. (Alabama), age 4 years.

On page 237, Neel's Statistical Handbook of Trigg County, 1880 Trigg County Census, middle of page, his mother Temperance Yarborough is listed as age 61 years, living with her daughter Alabama F. Yarborough, age 25 years.

On page 230, Neel's Statistical Handbook of Trigg County, 1880 Trigg County Census, bottom of page, his brother Henry P. Yarborough is listed as a physician, age 28 years, living with his wife Sarah H. Yarborough, age 23 years, no children.

World War I

JOSEPH FRANCIS AHART, Private, the following is verbatim:
Dear Great Uncle Joe,

This letter is a thank you for your willingness to serve our great United States of America in the capacity of a United States soldier during World War I.

My dad, Jesse Oakley, has talked about you, as his mother Alpha was your sister. He (Jesse) was but a child when you came to visit Alpha and her family the day before you left Golden Pond, KY, to be inducted in the army at Cadiz, KY, on 2 Oct 1917. He told us you were on crutches that cool fall day but he never knew why.

Your sister, Daisy, was my favorite great aunt and she talked of you affectionately as she remembered your kindness. Your brothers, Prentice and Willie, spoke of your often.

James Monroe and Margaret Evelyn must have been so happy and proud at the birth of their son Joseph Francis Ahart on 14 Jan 1890. James must have been just as sad when your mother died and just heartbroken when he was notified of the death of his young son on 5 Jan 1918.

We know you were assigned with 81 Co. 21 Bn. 159 Dep Brig and Hq Co. 336 Inf. as a private until your death as a result of empyema. Our family visits and maintains Long Creek Cemetery in Land Between the Lakes. The marker with your name is in a neat row with many of our family members.

Again, Uncle Joe, we say thank you.
With deepest gratitude, Vickey Oakley Lane

CHARLES BAKER SR., born 20 May 1894 and served in the U.S. Army as a private during WWI. He married Tee Sholar (deceased) and they had the following children: Clyde, Flora (deceased), Lydia (deceased) and Charles Baker Jr. (deceased). Grandchildren: Linda Kaye (deceased), Laura LaVern, Kenneth Earl, Kent Allan and Herman Stanley Baker. Charles Baker Sr. died 5 Jan 1980.

JESSEE FREEMAN BAKER, born 8 Oct 1895 in Trigg County, the son of Hedwick and Julie Atkins Baker. He was drafted into the Army in 1917 and stationed at Fort Benjamin Harrison, IN. He received an honorable medical discharge for back injury in 1918.

He and his wife are both deceased. They had two children, Merle and June, and three grandchildren.

JOHNNY COWARD BAKER, Private, born 11 Sep 1896 and died 27 Feb 1968. He was a private in the U.S. Army and served in WWI. Although his children have little information on his military history, they are aware that he served and was instrumental in the construction of Fort Knox, KY. The date of his enlistment is not known. He returned to his hometown of Cadiz, KY and worked as a farmer.

He was married to Rosetta Wilford, and the four children from this marriage were Mosetta, Alvin, J.C. and Norris. He later married Levi Rogers in 1939. From this union there were eight children: Johnny J., Tommie, Jimmie, Robert, Catherine Zellner, Emma Webb, Suszie Martin and Rotressa Yelling. Presently, there are 38 grandchildren.

Mr. Baker died in 1968, and his wife, Levi, died in February 2000. *Submitted by Suszie Baker Martin.*

AUDIE BALENTINE, Corporal, born 11 Jan 1895 in Rock Castle, KY in Trigg County. He enlisted in the U.S. Army 28 Jul 1917. Balentine sailed the 3rd day of October 1917 on the SS *Cedric* bound for France. The trip lasted 40 days under unusual hardships, cramped and overcrowded quarters and illness. Several men died on the ship and were buried at sea.

After arrival in France he was assigned to Vinass Base Hospital #88 Lackfrom, France. While there he cared for wounded soldiers as they were brought into the tent that was being used for the hospital. Balentine gave shots, dressed wounds, bathed and cared for the soldiers that were there. He spoke of soldiers that were very badly wounded, but lived to return home. Balentine served his time in the Vinass Medical Base Hospital until 6 Aug 1919 when he was Honorably Discharged from the U.S. Army.

Balentine re-enlisted in the U.S. Army 25 Sep 1919 at Jefferson Barracks, MO, where he was assigned to the Medical Dept., Fitzsimons General Hospital, Denver, CO. While at Fitzsimons he was appointed corporal of the Medical Dept. on 12 Jun 1920. Balentine was honorably discharged from the U.S. Army on 24 Sep 1920.

On 27 Dec 1920 he married Florence Askew of Trigg County, KY; at this time they moved to Between the Rivers, Golden Pond, KY. Ten children were born at Golden Pond and two in Cadiz. The children are Ralph, Flora Mae, Dorothy, Tommy, Helen, Velie, David, William, Elijah, Alice, Margie Nell and Jerry. The couple has 25 grandchildren.

Balentine was a farmer his entire live; however, the last 40 years he was also a minister at Jenny Ridge Pentecostal Church. He died at 78 years of age on 23 May 1973.

Audie Balentine was proud of his years in the Army and serving his country.

ETHELL MOORE BLACKFORD, a veteran of WWI, was born 22 Oct 1895, Montgomery County, TN. When he entered service his address was listed as Linton, Trigg County, KY. His name is listed in the Military Records and Research Branch, Frankfort, KY, but no information was available.

Ethell was the son of Joseph Randolph Blackford, M.D., and Izora Thomas Weakley Blackford, who moved to Linton, KY early in 1900. Dr. Blackford and his family were very active members of the Methodist Church at Linton. Ethell had one brother, Thomas, and four sisters: Carmen Ercel, Winnie Aline, Rebecca Mariah and Leona Lurline Blackford.

He was a merchant and postmaster at Linton, KY, and retired as an employee of Farmers Home Administration, a government agency, of Hopkinsville, KY.

On 11 Feb 1919, he married Ella M. Thomas, daughter of Richard E. and Nannie Hendricks Thomas. They had a son, Ethell M. Blackford Jr., who died 3 Oct 1975, and an adopted daughter, Rosemary, who is deceased.

Ethell died 8 Dec 1972, at Hopkinsville, KY. His wife, Ella Thomas Blackford, died 14 Feb 1988, at Hopkinsville, where the family had resided for several years. Both are buried in East End Cemetery, Cadiz, KY.

JOSEPH WILEY BOREN, born 25 Mar 1889 in Tobacco Port, TN. When WWI came, he enlisted 2 Oct 1917 at Cadiz, KY. He entered a private 1st class unassigned in the U.S. Army. Due to the nature of his assignment and world conditions, he was not to know his destination when he left the U.S. 18 Mar 1918. In a letter written to his brother,

Fraud Boren, he said he could not reveal where he was going. These letters are still in possession of the family today.

He was last assigned to 117th Field S__ Battalion. He returned 27 Apr 1919. He actually served in England, by coincidence, the exact same place his son was sent in WWII over 40 years later. He was honorably discharged 7 May 1919 by convenience of the government at I So. 137 Hwy., Camp Zachary Taylor, KY and returned to farming in Trigg County.

His physical condition was good, and he had no wounds in service. It states he was single and of excellent character, signed by 1st Lt. C.A. Williams, FA USA Casual Des., 1st Battalion 159th DOB. He was entitled to a railroad ticket from Louisville, KY to Cadiz, KY and a bonus of $60. This was signed by Capt. F.L. St. Claire OMC USA, Camp Zachary Taylor, KY and 1st Lt. W.E. Smith, Infantry, USA, personnel adjutant 159th D.B.

His discharge papers stated he was a farmer, 28 years and 7 months of age, and five feet nine inches tall. It also stated he had blue eyes, black hair and a ruddy complexion.

His civilian jobs included working as a janitor for the American Legion Club house, working for the Kentucky State Department of Transportation as well as farming. He retired as a farmer.

He was a member of Union Hill Freewill Baptist Church. Fishing and bird hunting were his hobbies. His marriage to Bessie Bland took place 13 Jul 1919. They had five children: Prenta Mae, Lacy, Marvin Green, Hazel and Carolyn, and 11 grandchildren. He died 17 Dec 1955 with burial at Union Hill Cemetery, Trigg County. *Submitted by Hazel Boren Ford.*

ALBERT CLAUD BRIDGES, Private, born 26 May 1895 in the Maple Grove Community of Trigg County. His parents were Alfred Franklin and Minnie Lancaster Bridges. Alfred's first wife was Ella Turner and they had three children: Charlottie "Lottie," John Madison "Matt" and Annie. On Jan. 28, 1899 he married second, Minnie Lancaster and they had five children: William H. "Willie," Bluford C., Albert Claud, Amby Lois and Denny Lee.

Alfred F. was shot and killed on 8 Mar 1902; therefore, Minnie was left with her five children and three stepchildren to rear.

In WWI Albert Claud was a private in the Army in Co. M, 323rd Inf. After his discharge he went to Bowling Green, KY and enrolled in vocational training. During this time he married Ethelene Bonner of Mont Community in the between the rivers section of Trigg County. They were married by Judge C.J. Gresham at the courthouse in Eddyville, KY on 17 Apr 1922. Ethelene's parents were Oscar and Beulah Bonner from Mont Community.

After returning from Bowling Green they lived in Lyon County and finally in Eddyville. There were four children born to them: Margaret Virginia (b. 5 Jan 1923, died 4 Jan 1933); Mildred Imogene (b. 27 Feb 1926); Albert Claud Jr. (b. 27 Jan, 1935); and Billy Franklin (b. 15 Jan 1937).

Claud was a rural mail carrier between the rivers for many years. He died 21 Dec 1964 and was buried at Woodson Chapel Cemetery in LBL.

PERCY DILLARD BRIDGES, In March 1902, Percy D. Bridges and several other young men were inducted into the U.S. Navy at Louisville, KY. A couple of the others were Thomas Wilson Marlow and Jesse

Roy Ladd. While at the U.S. Naval Training Station, Gulfport, MS, he wrote of Jesse Ricks visiting him.

From his barracks windows he could look out and see the Gulf of Mexico. The climate was very warm and the mosquitoes nearly "worry you to death." Wilson Marlow was with him at the time he wrote this.

He served on the battleship *Florida* and spent time in the southern waters off the coast of Brazil. After serving 18 months in the Navy, he returned to Trigg County. On Oct. 18, 1921, he was married to Edna Pearl Thomas, a native of Trigg County and daughter of Stark W. and Julia Thomas. They had one daughter Mallie Louise (b. 13 Jul 1922).

Percy farmed for a few years on one of his father's farms in the Maple Grove Community and in the 30s started following the carpenter trade.

He was the son of Mark Dale and Mallie M. Lancaster Bridges and born to them at Maple Grove, KY on 17 Apr 1902, where he attended school at the Maple Grove Graded School.

During WWII in March 1942, Percy was drafted into the Army, 62nd Inf. Div. and was sent to Ft. Jackson, SC for his basic training. It was there that some problems with his health showed up and after a few months he was given an honorable discharge.

He continued his carpenter work in various places including Birmingham, AL, where his daughter Mallie met and married H.R. Franks. They soon settled in Memphis, TN, and had two sons, Larry and Danny.

In the mid-40s, Percy and Edna came back to Trigg County, bought some land and built a home in the Maple Grove Community. Percy was a member of the Canton Masonic Lodge No. 242 and at the time of his death on 12 Apr 1967 was employed as a correctional officer at the Kentucky State Penitentiary. He died from heart problems and is buried at East End Cemetery in Cadiz, KY. There were four grandchildren (two are deceased) in the family

GEORGE BRISON, born in Trigg County, Cadiz, KY. He enlisted in the U.S. Army in 1917 and fought in WWI. The account of his military service has him listed in Germany where he died in action and was buried in Germany.

George Brison's name is engraved on the monument at Trigg County Courthouse honoring the county's war dead. The plaque reads: "At war they died and paid for peace that we might live in freedom and enjoy peace. It is our duty to preserve it."

Each year these soldiers are honored on Memorial Day. George Brison was the son of George Brison and Nancy Froman Brison. Nancy was the sister of Ira Froman. Descendants of this family are Vick Crump and Robert Smith Mayes.

George Brison had six brothers: Johnny, Ben, Caudia, Jesse, Jiles Lee, Viceroy; and four sisters: Emmie Fox, Mary Grant, Nancy Brison and Hollie Wilson. *Submitted by Emily Wilkerson.*

CLARENCE L. "BUGGS" BRUCE, Private, born 12 Aug 1896 at Eddyville, KY, the son of W.F. and Carrie Holloway Bruce. He was a resident of Cadiz, KY in 1918 when he was inducted into the U.S. Army on 27 Aug 1918 during WWI. He was assigned to 12th Co., 3rd Bn., 159th Depot Brigade at Camp Zachary Taylor, KY.

He was never in combat and never served in Europe. His military record states that his service was honest and faithful. He received an honorable discharge 8 Dec 1918 with the rank of private.

After leaving service he returned to Cadiz and served as a clerk in the county offices and later ran a dry cleaning business with his brother Frank, who also served in WWI. Buggs was very popular with the young people and especially his popcorn machine outside the cleaners where a bag of popcorn cost 5 cents with refills thrown in. He later operated a restaurant and pool room on Main Street.

Clarence had two other brothers, Hershel and D., who served one term as Trigg County Court Clerk.

Clarence and his brother D. were living at Cadiz Hotel at the time of his death on 12, Jan 1979. He was buried in East End Cemetery at Cadiz.

FRANK J. BRUCE, Sergeant, born April 1894 in Eddyville, KY, the son of W.F. and Carrie Holloway Bruce. He was a resident of Cadiz, KY in 1917 when he was inducted into the U.S. Army on 2 Oct 1917 during WWI. He was assigned to Co. C, HQ Bn., GHQ - AEF and served overseas in France, but was not in combat.

His service record stated that he was honest and faithful with no absences. He was entitled to wear two Gold Chevrons. Frank was honorably discharged 24 Jun 1919 with the rank of sergeant. His occupation was clerk.

He and a brother, Clarence L. "Buggs" Bruce, composed the firm of Bruce Brothers of Cadiz. They were owners of Bruce Brothers Cleaners on the corner of Marion and Main Streets (now [2001]location of Cadiz City Hall)

He had three brothers: Clarence L. (served in WWI); Hershel (lived in Berkley, CA) and D. (who served a term as Trigg County Court Clerk and retired as bookkeeper for Burke-Thomas County.

Frank Bruce married and became a resident of the state of Tennessee.

WILLIAM AMOS BUSH, born Dec. 22, 1889 in Trigg County. He served in the U.S. Army during WWI and received a medical discharge. As a civilian he was a farmer, woodcrafter and worked for TVA. Married Irene Louise Bulloch 22 Sep 1928 and they had five children: Lola Lane, Annie Huddleston, Don Gary Bush, Caroline Bush Rogers and Jo Hazel Cunningham. Grandchildren are Larry Huddleston; Bonnie Pool; Connie and Sheila Hampton; Lori Ann Rogers; Steven Gary Bush; Michael Dean, Gary and Anthony Lane; Frank Sylvester Jr.; and Anna Allen. William passed away 13 Sep 1970.

JAMES ORBIT CAMPBELL, Corporal, born 1 Oct 1893 in Trigg County. Inducted into Regular Army 2 Oct 1917, at Cadiz, KY and assigned to 159 Den Brigade to 27 Dec 1917; Headquarters Company, 336th Inf. to March 1918; Co. G, 168th Inf. to May 10, 1918. He served in combat in France with Co. G, 23rd Inf. Regt. from 9 Apr 1918 to 3 Aug 1919.
Promoted to PFC 16 Feb 1919 and corporal 2 Jun 1919. He was honorably discharged 3 Aug 1919.

Married Irene Pryor 2 Apr 1922 and they had six children: Beuton C. Towler, Leonard Campbell, Susie C. Towler, Marvin Campbell (Deceased 1 Jun 1996),

Thomas Campbell and Jo Ann Campbell Wilson. Grandchildren: Patricia Towler Lockwood (Deceased 21 Jul 1993), Jimmy Towler, Gwen Campbell, Marsha Campbell, Donna Wilson, Deborah Wilson Anderson and Charles Jones Campbell.

James was employed at Fort Campbell, KY, working in restricted area known as the "Bird Cage" where Atomic Bomb was said to be stored (until disabled in 1952). He passed away 12 Aug 1960.

ARCHIE VERNON "JACK" CARNEY, born 7 Aug 1895 in Sturgis, KY, moved to Trigg County when he was a young boy and was a farmer growing up.

He was inducted in the Army from Trigg County on 24 May 1918. His assignment was Btry. A, 327th FA until he was discharged. He served 8 Sep 1918 until 4 Feb 1919 in France.

After his honorable discharge, he became a farmer. He married Maggie Phillips and they had one son, Edward Carney, who served in WWII. After Maggie died he married Virginia Forbes in Hopkinsville. They moved to Evansville, IN and had two daughters, Nancy and Marlyn.

When WWII started he began working in the ship yard. Archie Vernon died in February 1960 and was buried in Evansville.

ARTHUR CARPENTER, Private, born 28 Jan 1893 in Trigg County, KY. He enlisted in 1917, was stationed at Camp Taylor, then in France during WWI where he was killed on 10 Oct 1918. He is buried in the Sivills Cemetery in Trigg County, KY.

Before the military, he lived on the family farm in Trigg County. He was married to Kathleen Collins (also of Trigg County) and they had one son Arthur Duvall Carpenter (b. 13 Apr 1918, d. 19 Jun 1999), whose dad only got to see him once when he was 3 months old. Arthur Duvall married Audrey Brown in September 1947.

Arthur Duvall's daughter, Kathy Carpenter, married Michel Eugene Martin Nov. 22, 1980 and they have two children, Andrew Michial (b. 6 Mar 1982) and Matthew Ryme (b. 6 Jun 1985).

His daughter-in-law, granddaughter and her family all live in Lakeland, FL.

LUCIAN MITCHELL CARR, Private, born 11 Jan 1889 in the community known as Lock E which was near Canton, KY. He was drafted in the U.S. Army 2 Oct 1917 at Camp Taylor, KY. He served overseas in England, France, Belgium and Germany. He was discharged May 29, 1919 from Co. K, 126th Inf. at Camp Taylor, Louisville, KY.

Returned home and lived with his mother until he married Emma Calhoun 15 Jun 1921. There were two sons born to this couple, Lacy Darvin (b. 18 Jul 1922) and Edgar Mitchell (b. 1 Jul 1926, d. 9 Nov 1926). Lucian had a hard fight for life after he returned as he suffered from TB and spent most of his time in the hospital.

Lucian was laid to rest in the Carr Cemetery near Lock E on 11 May 1946.

ALBERT CASSITY SR., Private, born 20 Jul 1895 at Golden Pond, KY, d. 1976). Enlisted 1917 at Cadiz, KY and served with 30th Div., 120th Inf. "Old Hickory" Div. (named after Andrew Jackson).

Accomplishments include when 27th and 30th American Corps and XIXth British Corps were first to enter Belgium; cracked the Hindenburg Line, going "over the top." Comments by a high Australian officer after his observations at an inspection of the battlefield showed that in every instance a dead American soldier lay in a position indicating that he died facing the enemy.

After his discharge he was a farmer, elected justice of the peace, magistrate of First District of Trigg County for 16 years. Married Wavel Higgins Jan. 1, 1919 and had eight children: Mildred (deceased), George, Anthony, Albert, Barbara, Hayden, Bobby and James.

VERNON C. COLEMAN, born 5 Nov 1886 in Trigg County, KY. He enlisted in the U.S. Army on 13 Dec 1917 in Paducah, KY and assigned to Troop G, 15 Cav. On 2 Oct 1918, his troop left the U.S. for France, and upon their arrival there learned of the signing of the Armistice. He returned to the U.S 19 Jun 1919 and received an honorable discharge 25 Jun 1919.

Following his discharge from the service he went to South Dakota and acquired work in wheat harvest for a season before returning to Calloway County as a share cropper. It was there he met Ruby Grugett and they were married in August 1920. They moved to St. Louis, MO where he was employed by Fisher Body Car Mfg.

In February 1936 they returned to Calloway County to live on a 100 acre farm they had purchased. He was elected to serve as magistrate in Calloway County in November 1953. In this particular election Mr. Coleman received 195 votes and his opponent received one vote.

He and his wife had two daughters, Nora Mae and Clara Nell. Nora married Eugene C. Ferguson and Clara Nell married George O. Lathram. The Colemans had four grandchildren: Carol Jean Ferguson, Nancy Lee Ferguson (deceased), Ginger Kaye Lathram and Scott Coleman Lathram.

In 1964 Vernon and Ruby moved to Benton, KY where their younger daughter lived and in 1970 celebrated their 50th wedding anniversary. V.C. Coleman passed away 20 Jan 1976 in Marshall County, KY.

GENTRY COLSON, born 13 Dec 1895 the parents were Joel and Sarah Oakley Colson. Gentry was inducted into the Army 24 May 1918 at Camp Zachary Taylor, KY and on 4 Feb 1919, he received his honorable discharge papers for reason of dependent relative.

Gentry never married and always lived with his sister Fannie Colson, where they resided at Energy, KY. Gentry help to build the Ferguson Spring Baptist Church, where he was a member until his death in December 1972. He is buried at Oakley Cemetery.

LONNIE COLSTON, born 8 Feb 1895, the son of Tandy and Charlotte Savels Colston, Trigg County. Lonnie was a private of Med. Detachment, 55th Artillery. He was inducted on 24 Jun 1918, Eddyville, KY to serve for the period of emergency.

On 21 Oct 1918, Lonnie sailed from the U.S. to France and returned to the port of the U.S. on 1 Feb 1919. He received an honorable discharge 20 Feb 1919. Lonnie, Gentry Colson, Herbert Cothran, Willy Fennell and Finus Futrell all left Golden Pond about the same time for WWI.

Lonnie and Lillian Newton Colston were married 28 Dec 1936, and they resided at Energy, KY. Lonnie help build the Ferguson Springs Baptist Church, where he was a member. On 14 Jun 1944, Lonnie passed away was buried in the Oakley Cemetery at Energy, KY.

ELVIS COMPTON, born 7 Dec 1894 and died 1 Jan 1983. He was married to Jessie Jones. They had two sons, James Compton and William Compton, and one daughter, Dorothy Compton Gamboe. He served in WWI in the 9th Bn. 159th Depot Brigade. He was a farmer and blacksmith.

ARLENE COSSEY, Private, born 14 Mar 1897, Trigg County, the son of John and Tinney Wood Cossey. He was drafted 21 Aug 1918 and discharged 11 Dec 1918. Arlene died 2 Sep 1923 and was buried at Hematite or Center Furnace Cemetery, "Land Between the Lakes."

CHARLES COSSEY, Private, born 29 Feb 1888, the son of John and Tinney Wood Cossey. He was drafted 21 Jul 1918 and was discharged 21 Dec 1918. He died 20 Aug 1934 and was buried at Hematite or Center Furnace Cemetery, "Land Between the Lakes."

GENTRY COTHRAN, Private First Class, born 16 Dec 1894, Golden Pond, KY. During WWI he served in 30 RCT Co. Gen. Svc. Inf. He married Minerva Bannister and they had four children: Sherman, Willie, John and Agnas Paschal. Gentry passed away 16 Jan 1960 and is buried at Lawrence Cemetery, Trigg County. *Submitted by Retta Balentine.*

HERBERT PUTNAM COTHRAN, born 3 Apr 1894 in the Energy Community, between the rivers. He was the son of Daniel Hanberry and Alice Puckett Cothran. He was inducted into the U.S. Army 7 May 1918 and after basic training was shipped overseas. He was placed on the front lines of the Muese-Argonne Forest, 29 Oct 1918 until the war ceased 11 Nov 1918. His last assignment was with Co. B, 603rd Engrs. He arrived back in the U.S. 20 Jun 1919 at Camp Zachary Taylor, KY. Herbert died 21 Jan 1970 and was buried in Long Creek Cemetery, Land Between the Lakes. *Written by his daughter, Dora Lee Cothran Roberts.*

JOHN COTHRAN, born 17 Nov 1893, Golden Pond, KY. He enlisted 25 Feb 1918 and served with the 32nd Co. 8th BN 159th Depot Brigade, 25 Feb 1918 to 23 Mar 1918; Co. D 1st Sio Inf., 24 Mar 1918 to 1 Sep 1918; Salvage Co., 2 Sep 1918 until the date of discharge on 24 Feb 1919 at Spartanburg, SC, where he had served as the Salvage Co. camp supply officer at Camp Wadsworth, SC.

He married Josie Higgins 22 Feb 1920 and they had three children: Dorothy Cothran Baker, Juanita Cothran Jones and Lawrence Cothran. John Cothran passed away 16 Mar 1940 and is buried at Cassity Cemetery, Golden Pond. *Submitted by Retta Balentine.*

THOMAS TERRY CUNNINGHAM, born 1 Feb 1895 in Trigg Furnace, KY, son of George Lee and Emaline Hopper Cunningham. The family of seven children included Lucien Andrew and Hopper Cunningham who also served in WWI. Thomas, at age 17, was a ticket agent at Illinois-Tennessee Central Railroad, Hopkinsville, KY, when called to military service. He served in France, training men to use bayonets.

After an honorable discharge in 1920 he found his job waiting for him at Hopkinsville and worked there in the office for 47 years before retiring to farm life.

He married Mildred Mae Rich in Louisville, KY on 3 Apr 1923 and they had one daughter, Patricia Ellen (md. Harmon Bach); and three grandchildren: Mildred Ellen Bach Taylor, Carol Lynn Bach Spurr and Judson Harmon Bach.

Thomas and friend, Bentlyey Major, are remembered for bringing big dance bands into Blue Springs-Cerulean area. Thomas passed away on Father's Day, 17 Jun 1974 and was buried in Riverside Cemetery, Hopkinsville, KY. Mildred passed away 10 Feb 1975.

ROBERT GUY DAVIS, born 21 Apr 1897, was the oldest son of John F. and Julia Ella Sumner Davis. In the summer of 1918 he enlisted in the U.S. Navy and was sent to the Naval Training Station at Great Lakes, IL. He remained there until his discharge in January 1919. He contracted a form of fever from which he never fully recovered.

After his discharge he returned to his profession of farming. He was living with Felon and Earl Wilkins Vowell on the Jim Guier farm on the Maple Grove Road in Trigg County. He became ill of pneumonia on 15 April and died on 19 Apr 1919.

He was a member of the Oak Grove Baptist Church. Funeral services were conducted at the graveside in the Lawrence Cemetery in Trigg County by Rev. E.L. Andrews, pastor of the Cadiz Baptist Church.

Guy was preceded in death by his mother, Julia Ella Sumner Davis, 18 Aug 1916. He was survived by his father, John F. Davis; four older sisters: Iva Cunningham, Myrt Bridges, Lola Light and Johnnie Boyd, all of Trigg County; three younger brothers: Alfred Leroy "Bill," Julius Dabney "Gobe" and Wade Davis, all of the home. *Submitted by a niece, Joyce Davis Banister.*

JOHN MCKINLEY DOWNS, Fireman 1/c, born 23 Feb 1897, near Canton, KY, the son of John B. and Etta Sumner Downs. During WWI he enlisted in the U.S. Navy for a term of four years beginning 20 Jun 1918. He was honorably discharged from the USS *Maddox* on 24 Feb 1920 with the rank of fireman first class.

Soon after the war was over, John married Flora Rosevelt Williams. They are the parents of James B. and Madolen R.

Johnny was a crane operator by trade and moved with his young family around the country as an employee of numerous construction companies. Later in life, they purchased a home in Trigg County near Dyer Chapel Church where they remained until his death in January 1970. John and Flora are buried in the Lawrence Cemetery near their former home.

HUGH DARNALL DUNN, born in Trigg County near Roaring Springs. He vas the son of John James Dunn, a Civil War veteran, and Nellie T. Dunn. Hugh trained at Camp Zachory Taylor (near Louisville, KY) and was honorably discharged a short time later with a back injury.

After returning home from service he married Gertrude "Gertie" Futrell and they reared two daughters, Ruth Mae Nunn and Johnnie Elizabeth Meredith. Later, he studied agriculture at Bowling Green Teacher's College. He then farmed and operated H.D. Dunn Grocery store in Trigg County.

He died 9 Jan 1980 and is buried in East End Cemetery. His wife Gertie passed away 20 Aug 1976 and is also buried in East End Cemetery, Cadiz, KY. *Submitted by his niece, Jewell Simmons.*

RICHARD AUBREY DUNN, Private, born in Trigg County near Roaring Springs. He was a son of John James Dunn, a Civil War veteran, and Nellie T. Darnall. Aubrey did his basic training at Camp Zachary Taylor, KY, near Louisville and later was stationed at a U.S. Army post near St. Augustine, FL. He was a private in the 11th Co. 3rd Bn. 159th Brigade.

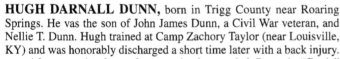

While training, Dunn contracted the flu, which killed millions around the world and the U.S. during the early 1900s. He also suffered from tuberculosis and was hospitalized in St. Louis before being discharged from the Army 22 Dec 1918 at Ft. Zachary Taylor, KY.

After returning home from service, he married Dorothy Myrtle Choate, daughter of Gideon Choate and Emmie

Jackson on 1 Aug 1920. A life-long Trigg County native, he raised a family of four daughters: Jewell Simmons, Eunice Carr, Dorothy Darnall and Ethelene Wallis. Dunn owned and operated R.A. Dunn Grocery Store on the South Road for 55 years. The store was a poplar place for many years and served as a meeting place for many of the locals.

He was a proud member of the American Legion and attended meetings regularly. Richard passed away 13 Sep 1974 and Myrtle on 13 Feb 1985; both died in Trigg County and are buried in the Green Hill Memorial Gardens Cemetery in Christian County. *Submitted by daughter Jewell Simmons.*

HARVEY EVLIS EZELL, born 12 Jan 1896, was one of a group of the first 10 men to leave Trigg County for WWI. They were notified on Monday that they were to leave on Wednesday 18 Sep 1917. Seldom, if ever, in the history of Trigg County has there been such an outpouring of people and enthusiastic demonstration as was manifested as the 10 were escorted to the depot in Cadiz.

Everyone having an automobile was called on to participate in the "send off." The 10 young men were ushered into three of the largest autos in front of the courthouse, and when they arrived at the depot the marchers formed a line on each side of the street and the "called boys" came down between the lines to the steps of the special coach prepared to carry them away.

Having a few minutes before train time, Hon. John T. King in a brief and eloquent address expressed the thoughts in every heart, closing his talk by presenting each of the 10 with a copy of the New Testament.

The train pulled out amid the sobs of loved ones and the smiling faces of the boys, peering from the pullman windows. The thoughtfulness of Mr. Dale Bridges in bringing with him a "call bugle," was appreciated. The soft dirge he blew as the cars moved quietly off was very impressive and the crowd returned to their homes impressed with the thought, "We are really at war," and this is our first offering.

The special coach carrying the young men was part of a special train starting from Wickliffe at 6:30 was joined to the special train at Princeton and was to reach Louisville at 5:30 in the afternoon. The boys were to be carried directly to Camp Zachary Taylor, near Louisville where they were to begin their training.

After completing their training the unit was preparing to be shipped overseas. Ezell was taken ill with measles and was not shipped out. After a short time he was given an honorable medical discharge and sent home (he registered, was drafted and discharged all in the same year).

He married the former Viva Mae Hunter on 29 Dec 1920 and they had five children: Eugene, Pauline, Frank, Glen and Shirley, and four grandchildren. He passed away 24 Nov 1970.

ADOLPHUS FRANKLIN FAUGHN Wagoner, was inducted into the U.S. Army 2 Oct 1917 at Cadiz, KY during WWI and served in France. He was a member of 159th Dep. Brig. to 27 Dec 1917; He was a member of HQ Co. 336th Inf. to 21 Mar 1918; Co Taylor Apr Repl Draft to 1 May 1918; HQ Tr 1 Dep Division to 27 Dec 1918; HQ Tr 41 Div to honorable discharge on 6 Mar 1919. His grade was Wagoner with no disabilities and no engagements.

Adolphus was the oldest of 14 children born to James Benjamin "Ben" and Martha Ann "Annie" Faughn of the Bethesda Community of Trigg County. Siblings: Mattie, Ada, Mary, Francis, Eliza, Letha, Alpha Lou, Alfred, Robert, Zan, Hazel, Mamie Evelyn and an unnamed infant. His younger brother Alfred also served in WWII and his maternal grandfather, John H. Faughn, in the CSA during the Civil War.

Adolphus returned home to Trigg County and worked in a saw mill and farmed. He was a country boy with little education, unable to read or write, but he served his country in a foreign land in the time of WWI. After returning from service his youngest sister Mamie Evelyn died of typhoid fever. He was the brother who ran with all of his heart for the doctor to save his little sister.

His mother told the story of the fresh oranges that he rolled onto the hearth at Christmas for his little brothers and sisters. She also laughed about his "famous mule trading" and coming home once with his harness on his back. No hunting party was complete in the Bethesda Community without Adolphus Faughn.

On the 21 Nov 1931 he married Beulah Lois Mitchell, the daughter of Thomas Jefferson "Tinker" Mitchell and Charlotte Bell "Lottie" Stegers. They were married by Rev. Luther Sanders. Witnesses thereof were L.F. Faughn and G.T. Stone. Adolphus and Beulah had no children.

Adolphus purchased a farm in the Bethesda Community adjoining the farm of his father. Upon this farm also was the Sivell's Cemetery where he and his wife Beulah are now buried. Beulah died 11 Mar 1967 and Adolphus died 22 Sep 1974. *Submitted by his niece, Betty Sellers.*

BURNETT FINLEY, born 6 Dec 1890, son of William and Alphy Cunningham Finley, in the Mount Pleasant Blue Spring Community. He enlisted in the U.S. Army 2 Oct 1917, and left Cadiz with a large number of men from Trigg County. They traveled by train for Camp Taylor, KY, for basic training. He immediately formed a companionship with Jim Campbell from Lafayette. They were together every day until he was wounded. During basic training a deadly flu epidemic took many lives. After training they went to New Port News, VA where they shipped out overseas on a steam ship USS *Antigon*.

They arrived in France 29 Apr 1918, after a month at sea. They marched many miles to the front lines, fighting battles at Belo Wood, Oregon Forest and Chareau Thierry. After the battle at Chareau Thierry they took a large number of German prisoners. When marching the prisoners across a large field the Germans started shelling them and more prisoners were killed than the small number of American guards. Burnett was hit and seriously wounded with shrapnel and artillery shell that hit close enough to lift him several feet in the air landing on his neck and shoulders rendering him unconscious. His buddy Jim Campbell witnessed it all and immediately went to him, turned him over and believing he was dead, joined the march; when they reached their destination they reported him killed in action. Burnett regained consciousness at sunset, the main wound was in his left thigh with steel shrapnel about 1x2 inches up the thigh. He crawled across the field, down into a valley where he was found by a Frenchman who carried him to his unit and field hospital. Surgeons operated on him and he returned to a French hospital. After a few weeks he recovered and was put on the next ship to the USA.

When he reached Cadiz he was on crutches and started walking home to Mount Pleasant when a man in a buggy picked him up and carried him home. He was awarded six medals, among them the Purple Heart. He married Myrtie Cunningham on 15 Jun 1919 and they had six children. One son survives.

JOHN ROY FORD, E-5, born 24 Apr 1896, the sixth child and fourth son, to Albert Samuel and Martha Gordon Ford. He was born in the southern part of Trigg County.

He served in WWI from 12 Jul 1918 to 3 Dec 1918. He served in France with the 159 Dep Brig at Hospital #117. He was then transferred to Base Hospital #49 where he served until 21 Jun 1919. On 1 Jun 1919 he was promoted to private 1st class, and then again promoted to E5 on 18 Jul 1919. He became ill and was admitted to Base Hospital #33 until he was honorably discharged on 4 Nov 1919.

He married Pansy Turner and one son, John Lacy, was born 9 Jun 1924. He and his family were members of the Boyd Hill Baptist Church.

His health continued to deteriorate and he was later hospitalized at the TB Hospital at Dawson Springs, KY. He was dismissed from the hospital and died at his home on 28 Apr 1942 with interrment at the Fuller Cemetery near the Boyd Hill Church Community.

I never knew Uncle Roy as he passed away four years before I was born. At Lacy's death, my Aunt Merle Downs received the memorial book from Uncle Roy's funeral. The book contains the names of the Legionaires who served as pallbearers. Their names are Clifford Thomas, Clarence Bruce, Lee Gordon, Marvin Joiner, Maynard Williams (my maternal grandfather) and Clarence Calhoun. All these men had served their country honorably and were members of the American Legion Post #74. *Respectfully submitted by Carolyn Ford Bland, great niece.*

THOMAS DUDLEY FORD, PFC, born 21 Sep 1887 near Linton in Trigg County. He was the second of eight children born to Albert Samuel and Martha Gordon Ford. Tom entered the U.S. Army on 25 Feb 1918. He served with Co. B, 335th Inf. from then to 6 October 1918 when he was transferred to Co. D, 347th MGBN. He stayed in that company until his discharge as PFC 1 Dec 1918.

He served on the front lines supplying ammunition to our troops. He had a mule and cart. The mule was shot and killed during one of the battles he served in.

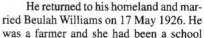

He returned to his homeland and married Beulah Williams on 17 May 1926. He was a farmer and she had been a school teacher until her marriage. They had no children of their own but adored their nieces and nephews. They resided in the Williams Hollow and children were at their house night and day. Everyone loved Tom, especially his nieces and nephews. He would just decide out the clear blue sky to invite them to spend the night and he would take them to Cadiz to "the picture show." Tom was a farmer and later operated a sawmill.

One story that come to mind: He was eating dinner at the home of Ira Dixon. The host said now if there is anything you want or can't reach, let me know, and we'll get it and pass it. Tom, with his wit, had spied a quart of home canned peaches sitting in a high cabinet, pointed and said, "Well, I'd sure like some of those peaches."

He was a gentle giant to all who knew and loved him. He had a rather high pitched loud voice, the kind that would draw a child to him.

They left the Williams Hollow and built a frame home on US 68 near the old rock quarry. He mowed the grass with an old push type mower (not gas powered) and on 23 May 1960 he suffered a heart attack and died in his yard. I (great-niece Carolyn) was an 8th grade student at Linton Grade School. Our exams were that day and that night we were having 8th grade graduation. The teachers: Mrs. Lillian Lawrence, Mrs. Jewell T. Futtrell, Aunt Mavis (Ford) Wolfe, and Mrs. Christine S. Dawson had received a call about Uncle Tom's death, but decided it best not to tell me and my siblings, Gail and Tony, until after our exams. Needless to say, my graduation was dampened by the loss of Uncle Tom.

Brother D.W. Billington officiated at Uncle Tom's funeral, and I'll always remember his first words, "Tom Ford never had thousands of friends, Tom Ford never knew thousands of people. What a wonderful way to sum one's life. He was a friend to all and was dearly loved by family and friends."

Uncle Tom and Aunt Beulah are buried in Lawrence Cemetery, US 68 West of Cadiz. *Submitted by Carolyn Ford Bland, great-niece.*

LUKE GARNETT FRANKLIN, born 7 May 1896 in Trigg County, was the first WWI Trigg County soldier to pay the supreme sacrifice on the field of battle in France. His mother, Sallie Oakley Franklin of near Golden Pond, received a telegram from the War Department at Washington announcing his death on 7 July. According to a letter received from his nurse he was wounded on 6 June.

He was 22 years of age and was the son of James Franklin and Sallie Oakley Franklin. His father died 17 Aug 1907 and his mother died 9 Apr 1963. He spent most of his life with his grandfather, A.J. Franklin, of the Energy community, between the rivers. He registered under the draft law and left Trigg County for Camp Taylor on 2 Oct 19_.

Luke married Audra Crump about 1921 and they had 10 children: Thomas R., Mattie, Dorothy Mae, Luke C., Blenard R., Phillip, Beth, Jane, Ramie and Ruth.

SAMUEL DELL FREEMAN (b. 19 Aug 1895 in Bethel area, d. 27 Aug 1973 in Trigg County) was the son of Sam Fox Freeman and Margaret Aldridge Freeman. He enlisted in the military 25 Feb 1918 at Cadiz, KY and served in France, Belgium and Germany from 9 Jul 1918 to 7 Jul 1919. He was in combat, but never spoke of his war experience.

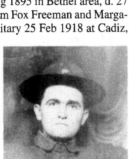

As a civilian he was a farmer in Trigg and Christian counties, was Farm Bureau Insurance agent and served on the ASCS Committee in Christian County.

On 30 Aug 1922 he married Tyline Mitchell and they have two children, Dell Jr. and Barbara Ann; and three grandchildren: Carla, Dell III and Smith T. Freeman.

SAM WILFORD FREEMAN was born in 1894 in Trigg County, KY the son of John Lindsay and Claude Wallis Freeman. He had one sister Lucy Lu Freeman Ladd (b. 1900, d. 1926) and two half brothers, Robert David "Robbie" and William Thomas Freeman.

Cadiz Record 1917 - Trigg county boy was one of soldiers to help fire first shot of war - Sam W. Freeman, a Trigg County soldier, was one of the crew of the merchant ship *Mongolia* who sank a German submarine in British waters on 19 April. This was the first gun fired in the war with Germany.

The fact was made public last Thursday and according to the statement of Captain Rice of the steamer's crew, the German submarine was about to attack the great liner. It is stated that the gunners made a clean hit at 1,000 yards completely shattering the periscope of the enemy vessel, when it disappeared.

Young Freeman enlisted in the Navy in October 1913, at Evansville, IN. He was given his first assignment on the *New York* and has been promoted several times for his splendid marksmanship and handling of guns. He was assigned to the *Mongolia* about a month ago, and his people here had a letter from him before he sailed, in which he told them if they never heard from him again they could rest assured that he "had a good time before he went down." He is a native of Cadiz, and a son of John Lindsay Freeman, who died about four years ago. He is a grandson of Mr. David O. Freeman, of this place, a Union veteran of the Civil War. Sam is about 22 years of age, about six feet tall and would weight, when last here, about 160 pounds.

On the 21 Oct 1917 he was honorably discharged from the USS *New York* and from the Naval Service of the United States. He married Grace Marie Page on 28 Nov 1917 in Evansville, IN.

Sam and Grace had seven children: Ursel, Aubrey, Jacquetta, John, Donald, Robert and Sam. They resided in Evansville, IN and Sam was employed as an engineer for the L&NRR. They were members of the Christian Church. Grace and Sam died in July 1975 and are buried at the Tupman Cemetery in Vanderburgh County, IN. *Submitted by his niece, Betty Freeman Sellers.*

JOE J. FUTRELL, born 23 Nov 1892, d. 17 Feb 1977, was inducted into the U.S. Army 24 May 1918. He was stationed at Camp Taylor, KY (now Fort Knox) and discharged 18 Dec 1918.

Joe Futrell and Lucille Vinson (b. 11 Oct 1899, d. 9 Jun 1971) married on 7 Sep 1919. They went to live on their 525 acre New Hope Road farm which Tom Armstrong, Lucille's grandfather, bought in 1892. They lived there the rest of their life. Their four children were born there: Tom J. (b. 18 Nov 1920, d. 20 Mar 1978); J.W. Futrell (b. 26 Jan 1922); Henry Scott Futrell (b. 1923, d. 25 Jul 1924); and Jane (Futrell) Wright (b. 29 Aug 1925).

Jane married Carl M. Wright 29 Sep 1944 and to their union was born C.M. Wright Jr. (b. 31 Jul 1950, 11 Oct 1998). At the time of C.M.'s death, he was the fifth generation to operate the Futrell farm. Joe Futrell Wright (b. 25 Jul 1955) married Cathy Morris on 23 Jun 1979. To their union was born Laura E. Wright (b. 2 Jul 1987) and Sam Thomas Wright (b. 24 Aug 1990). They live in Louisville, KY where Joe is an attorney for "Truequote" and Cathy teaches history at UK Community College. Joe, Lucille, Tom, Carl and C.M. are buried in the Futrell-Wright Cemetery located on the Futrell farm.

ELIAS AND JOHN FUTRELL, twin sons of John Bluford and Omega Nunn Futrell, were born 25 Jan 1899 on the family farm near Linton in Trigg County. During WWI the twins left high school to enlist in the U.S. Army. They were assigned to officers' training school at Ogden College on the Western Kentucky State Normal School campus in Bowling Green. Once during their training a sergeant checked John at the head of a column of marchers and thought he saw him again at the end of the line. He said something, the brothers laughed and were immediately put on KP.

At war's end, the Futrell twins continued their education with their final degrees being from the University of Louisville Medical School. In 1942, at the beginning of World War II, both doctors volunteered for service in the U.S. Army.

John was accepted into the Medical Corps as a captain. He spent 3-1/2 years in uniform, first serving at a Camp Breckinridge, KY, hospital, and then following the combat through North Africa, Sicily and Italy. On his return to the United States he was stationed at Fort Story, VA and was discharged from Fort Knox, KY in March 1946.

Elias was declared medically ineligible in 1942. Later, when his ailment became acceptable he was ruled essential to the area and told to remain in Trigg County where there was a shortage of practicing physicians. Herschel Caudle, an employee of the Futrell twins, was deferred to drive Elias as he made far-reaching house calls.

After World War II ended, John returned to Cadiz and the twins continued their medical practice at the Futrell Clinic on Main Street. A long time dream was realized for the Futrells when Trigg County Hospital was built through the efforts of many Trigg County citizens. Later, Elias and John built, owned and operated Shady Lane Nursing Home.

In 1974, after a short illness, John died at Vanderbilt Hospital in Nashville, TN. John's wife, the former Mary Frances DeBaun preceded him in death. Their three daughters: Barbara F. Wombwell, Mary F. Eggers, Patsy F. Dallas, and 11 grandchildren survived him.

Elias retired in 1975 and after a long illness died at Trigg County Hospital in 1979. His wife, the former Anna Duncan McBride; their two daughters, Ann F. Rankin and Margaret F. Whitehouse; and four grandchildren survived him.

CLARENCE P. GENTRY, born in Trigg County 7 Mar 1901. His parents were Robert H. and Lillie Jefferson Gentry. At an early age he left Trigg County with friends: Gobe Davis, Jesse Bridges and Homer Stephens, and went to Michigan to seek employment as jobs were scarce in Trigg County. The date and place of his enlistment in the service is not known.

At the time of his death in the early 1970s he was retired from Chrysler Corporation and was living in the Los Angeles, CA, area.

His brothers and sisters were John "Colonel" Gentry, Robert "Doc" Gentry, Thomas P. Gentry, Mary Gentry Cunningham, Nancy Gentry Gray, Lillie Gentry Roberts, Pocohontas Gentry Wilkins, Irene Gentry Burgess, and James Gentry.

THOMAS P. GENTRY, born 5 May 1894 in Trigg County, KY was inducted into the U.S. Army 25 Feb 1918. He served in Co. D, 1st Pioneer Inf. from start to discharge.

He went to Camp Zachary Taylor, Louisville, KY and served in France and Germany. He was stationed on the Rhine River and was there when the Armistice was signed on 11 Nov 1918. He served overseas from 9 Jul 1918 to 7 Jul 1919.

After receiving an honorable discharge with the rank of corporal, he returned to Trigg County and married Eliza Dell Hughes. He engaged in farming on the farm they bought from Eliza's parents and remained there the rest of their lives. They were the parents of five children: Thomas Hughes, Lillian Pearl (died at birth), Rachel Louise, Clara Dell and Mary Jo. They also have six grandchildren: Scott and Jeffrey Erath, Pamela Sharples, Kim Parasky, Clara Beth Hyde and Patrick Whitmer. Thomas P. Gentry was buried in the Lawrence Cemetery.

ALVIN G. GOODWIN, born 15 Apr 1895 at Cerulean Springs, KY. Inducted at Cadiz, Trigg County, KY 2 Oct 1917. Served in HQ Co. 336th Inf. to Nov. 6, 1918; Provisional Tr Regt 83 Div to Dec. 5, 1918; Co. F 311th Inf to discharge 25 Jul 1918.

Served overseas from 9 Sep 1918 to 30 May 1919 and was honorably discharged 5 Jun 1919.

As a civilian he worked for the railroad. He married Lucy Edith Nichols in 1919. He has two children, E.F. and Effice Grace Goodwin Higdon. E.F lost his life in

WWII and the body was returned and buried in the Cerulean Cemetery, Cerulean, KY.

ARTHUR KELLAR GOODWIN, PFC, born 27 Sep 1892 in Cerulean, KY, was the son of Oscar and Lula Ladd Goodwin. On 14 Mar 1918, he married Ida Baker.

Mr. Goodwin was inducted in the U.S. Army 19 May 1918 at Hopkinsville, KY. He was assigned to 154th Dept. Brigade Detachment, Provost Guard Co. at Camp Meade, MD. He was a private first class receiving his honorable discharge 13 Feb 1919.

After his military service, he and his wife Ida moved to Chillicothe, OH near his only brother Carl Ray Goodwin. There he taught WWI veterans in a trade school. He later entered Worsham College of Mortuary Science in Des Plaines, IL to become a licensed mortician. After completion of his schooling in 1937, they moved home to Trigg County and purchased the family farm in the Montgomery Community. Mr. Goodwin opened the A.K. Goodwin Undertaking Company in downtown Cadiz.

In addition to operating his business, he became chairman of the Trigg County Ration Board during WWII. After the close of WWII he became a charter member of American Legion Post No. 74, Cadiz, and served as service officer for many years, assisting Trigg County Veterans.

In 1946 Mr. Goodwin envisioned providing improved and additional services through his funeral business for all those he served. With determination to provide a professional funeral home, he purchased The Wilford Home (a family residence), 138 Main Street, Cadiz, from Julian Atwood. The first funeral in the new Goodwin Funeral Home was held in June 1946. Goodwin Funeral Home still operates under the same name.

Mr. Goodwin was a member of the Cadiz United Methodist Church. He was also a member of the Cadiz Masonic Lodge, No. 121 and a 32nd degree Mason. Following a three-month illness, Mr. Goodwin died 26 Sep 1962. He was remembered for his generosity and kindness of spirit to people in every walk of life, and for his philanthropy to the churches and civic organizations throughout the county. He was buried in East End Cemetery.

JESSE COLUMBUS GORDON, born 3 Aug 1888 at Golden Pond, son of William Jasper "Bill" Gordon and Mattie Wallace Gordon. He attended college at Bowling Green, KY and taught one-room schools in Trigg County (one of which was Woodville School, Between the Rivers). He enlisted 1 Jul 1918 at Louisville with assignment as hospital apprentice, 2nd class, USN, pharmacist, proficiency in rating 3.2.

He graduated from Max Morris School of Pharmacy in Macon, GA. He lived in Cadiz, KY and retired as a pharmacist from Blane's Drug Store, then for a few years he owned and operated Gordon's Pharmacy in Cadiz. He retired in 1953 when he sold the pharmacy. He married Mamie Mae Atwood, no children. He was a member of Cadiz Baptist Church and American Legion Post No. 74. He is buried at East End Cemetery.

CLAUDE GRASTY, born March 1890 in Trigg County and died March 1930. He served in the military air service during WWI. He was the son of Sam and Ida Mitchell Grasty and an uncle of Elizabeth Grasty Finley, Phil Grasty and Ray Grasty. Claude is buried in Baker's Cemetery at Rockcastle.

ARRICE GRAY, PFC, Co. G, 4th Inf., 3rd Div., son of James and Bettie Hall Gray was born Aug. 28, 1897 in Trigg County, KY. He volunteered and enlisted in the Army at Jeffersonville, IN in June 1917. Assignment Co. L, 2nd Inf. Ind. to Co. L 132nd Inf.

He was sent from Jeffersonville to Camp Shelby, MS, and remained there until he was sent overseas to France. He had not been heard from by his parents after reaching France until the War Department in Washington sent a brief message that the young hero had been killed in battle on 29 Jul 1918. There was an article of his death and also a letter of sympathy from a fellow soldier to the family printed in *The Cadiz Record*, 1918

His parents were to learn later he had been severely wounded at the battle of Chateau Thierry in France, 29 Jul 1918, but still alive. He was transferred from a hospital in France to a hospital in the States 9 Oct 1918, He was honorably discharged from the Army 5 Feb 1919.

His brother, Schuyler Gray, also serving in the Army, lost his life from wounds received in battle 31 Aug 1918 and was buried in Anise, France.

Arrice was married to Eva Baker and they were parents of four children. Two of the children died while young. Their daughter, Nina Gray Prescott and their son, James Thomas Gray, reside in Trigg County. *Submitted by grandson, Bobby Prescott.*

HERBERT ARTHUR GRAY, son of Walter and Lula Hancock Gray, was born in Trigg County, 28 Aug 1895. He was a WWI veteran, inducted at Cadiz, KY, 15 Apr 1918, and honorably discharged 19 Jul 1919.

Organizations served in, with dates of assignments: Training Det., Indianapolis, IN to 7 Jun 1918; Mec Rep Shop, 305th QMC to 5 Sep 1918; Rep Unit 308 MT_ to discharge. He served overseas from 15 Sep 1918 to 11 Jul 1919.

He was married to Lillian Earl Ricks (b. 20 Oct 1912 in Trigg County) and their children were Herbert Earl Gray, Anita Joyce Gray Duvall, Ann Gray Piza and Wanda Gray Prosser. Herbert also had a stepson, Arthur Eugene Williams.

Herbert was employed for 27 years with the State Highway Dept. in Trigg County and at the time of retirement was a surveyor employed by Preston H. Thomas of Trigg County. Herbert died 15 Feb 1988 and his wife died 19 Jan 1993. Both are buried in East End Cemetery, Cadiz, KY.

LAWNS HOLLIS "DOCK" GRAY, PFC, born 14 Aug 1890 at Wallonia, KY. In 1918 he enlisted in the U.S. Army and was private first class in Co. B, 603rd Engrs. He was at Fort Benjamin Harrison, IN; Camp Merritt, Weehawken, NJ and finally in France during WWI.

In his diary (now in possession of his daughter) he describes his participation in the Battle of Argonne-Forest: "5 November - We stayed at the front under heavy shell fire. Was in Meuse-Argonne Battle. On the night of 10 November we built a pontoon bridge over the Meuse River. Before it was hardly completed, it was blown out by heavy shell fire. We then lashed boats together ferrying the boys across. We then took the town of Pauls. The morning of 11 November we had German prisoners carrying our wounded men on boards. as there were no more stretchers, We received word at 11:00 a.m. 11 November that the war was over."

After the war was over, Dock returned to civilian life and became the owner and captain of towboats, operating them on the Cumberland

River. On one of his landings at Rockcastle, he met and fell in love with Launa Jefferson, a teacher at Rockcastle School. They were married 10 Nov 1923. At that time they purchased the N.T. Gray Store and the Hendricks Hotel nearby. They ran a successful business at Rockcastle for many years. The hotel became their home.

They were the parents of a daughter, Virginia, who married Carl C. Davis in 1948 and accompanied him to assignments throughout the U.S., Newfoundland and Japan during his 20-year military career. Their children are Jeannie, Janis and Rick (grandchildren whom Dock never knew).

Lawns Hollis Gray was born 14 Aug 1890 to Joe N. and Docia Cook Gray at Wallonia, KY. He was named for the doctor who delivered him, thus the nickname Dock.

He was a member of the Cadiz Masonic Lodge and American Legion; also a member of Trinity Baptist Church of Paducah. He was a Trigg County magistrate for several years.

As an astute business man and a friendly, out-going person, Dock seemed to never meet a stranger. He died 7 Feb 1947 at the age of 56 with an instant heart attack while listening to the radio in his store. His wife died 9 May 1969 and both are buried at East End Cemetery, Cadiz.

SCHUYLER GRAY, Private, born January 1893, the son of James and Bettie Hall Gray, Trigg County, KY. He entered the U.S. Army 2 Oct 1917 and served in 81st Co., 21st Bn., 159th Depot Bde. to 27 Dec 1917; transferred to HQ Co., 336th Inf. Regt., Camp Taylor, KY.

Assigned overseas 16 Mar 1918; transferred to Co. K, 126th Inf. Regt. 18 Apr 1918. He died 31 Aug 1918 of wounds received in action in France and was buried in Military Cemetery, Block D, Row 35, Grave No. 21 at Anise, France.

A memorial has been placed in Mount Pleasant Church Cemetery, Trigg County, KY in his honor.

AMOS IRA GUIER, Seaman 2/c, born 17 Jun 1894 in Trigg County, the second child of Nathan Stanley and Emma Sumner Guier. He was a member of the 3rd Inf. of the Kentucky Brigade at Camp Stewart, El Paso, TX in 1916. This Kentucky unit was part of the U.S. forces commanded by Gen. John Pershing in Mexico in an effort to capture Poncho Villa and his gorilla army.

Later records show that he enrolled in the U.S. Navy on 13 Apr 1918 at Louisville, KY during WWI. He was honorable discharged 11 Sep 1919 at the Navy Demobilization Station, Pittsburgh, PA with the rating of seaman second class.

After returning from military service he married Lois Bridges, the daughter of Alfred and Minnie Lancaster Bridges. Seven children were born to this union.

Amos was a carpenter and farmer. They lived on the farm that had been in Lee's family for four generations in the Oak Grove Community. During the 1930s Lee traveled with construction crews building dams for TVA. He later formed his own construction business. Amos died 3 Jan 1962 and is buried with his wife and six of his children in the Lawrence Cemetery.

PINK HARRELL GUIER, Private, born 23 May 1893 in the Oak Grove Community of Trigg County. His parents were Edwin and Mollie Harrell Guier. He was inducted into the Army 24 May 1918 at Cadiz, KY during WWI. He was stationed at Camp Zachary Taylor, KY and assigned to the 4th Co., 1st Bn., 159th Dep. his occupation was farming. He did not serve overseas. He suffered from the measles, mumps and typhoid fever in addition to other diseases that he contracted while in service. The diseases left him with a crippled left arm and he received a disability discharge 8 Jun 1919 with the rank of private.

After the war Pink returned to the family farm in Trigg County. He married Alma Williams 24 Jul 1920 and they were the parents of two sons, Lacy and Pink Jr. He and Alma built their home near his parents home on U.S. 68 and lived there the remainder of their lives. Pink died 27 Apr 1967 and Alma died in March. They are buried in the Green Hill Memorial Gardens near Hopkinsville, KY.

LANNICE WILSON GRIFFIN, Corporal, born 20 Apr 1891 at Energy, KY, Trigg County in what is now Land Between the Lakes. He was the son of James W. and Susan Pogue Griffin.

Enlisted in U.S. Army; his occupation is listed as farmer. He was a member of 2nd Inf., Co. G, 1 Mar 1915 to 4 Jun 1919 at Camp Dodge, IA; sergeant (NCO 4 Jun 1919), sup. sergeant 15 Sep 1919; sergeant 2 May 1920; marksman 29 May 1919. He did some service in territory of Hawaii (between November 1916 and February 1918 he was a guard for the last queen).

No battles, no engagements, no wounds, single, good character, he re-enlisted in state of Kentucky when he was 28-1/2 years old and stationed at Camp Sherman, OH to date of honorable discharge 20 Sep 1920. He was a member of Co. G, 2nd Inf. and attained the rank of corporal.

He married 14 Oct 1922 in Red Oak, IA, Cass County to Gladys Olive Myers. They had three children: Shirley Margaret (b. 10 May 1924), Gwendolyn Gladys (b. 26 May 1934) and Charlotte Laniece (b. 8 Apr 1937). The family resided in Lewis, IA.

Lannice died 17 Mar 1948 and is buried Oakwood Cemetery, Lewis, IA. *Information from his service records and submitted by his niece Gladys Fennell Wallace. She was born 7 Nov 1919, shortly after his last visit to Kentucky and named for his friend whom he later married.*

MOSCO F. GUIER, born 26 Jun 1887, son of Bettie Foutch and George E. Guier, was born in Trigg County in the community of Blue Spring near Mt. Pleasant Church. A farm boy he was inducted into service at the age of 30 on 2 Oct 1917 at Camp Zachary Taylor, KY. Sent to France with Co. F, 23rd Inf. AEF. During that time in battle, his mother and daddy received word from the War Dept. that he was missing in action. It was weeks before they heard from him. He told when he came home how long he lay on the battlefield before he was picked up and how he played dead to keep the enemy from finishing him off. Wounded in his left leg only, he was discharged from Camp Zachary Taylor 25 Aug 1919.

Masco settled down with his farming and caring for his mother as his daddy died 21 Jan 1920. On 29 Apr 1933 h e married Ercel Blackford Bogard, a teacher at Blue Spring School. They had no children but had a foster son Kenneth Akeman.

In later years he bought a house on the hill across from Mt. Pleasant Church and there he owned a little country store at the crossroads. His customers were mostly school kids as the school was just above the store. I suppose he gave away more candy then he ever sold. He was laid to rest 27 Feb 1972 and his wife Ercel in 12 Jan 2000 in the Mt. Pleasant Cemetery. *Submitted by Myra Dean Guier Carr.*

CLAUDE H. HALL SR. First Lieutenant, enlisted in the U.S. Army in May 1917, and was discharged a first lieutenant on 28 Nov 1918. A native of Kuttawa, KY, he came to Cadiz after his discharge. He served as Cadiz postmaster for several years before resigning in 1932 to join the Cadiz Milling Co. as sales manager, a position he held for 30 years. He was a leader in the Republican Party and served in numerous campaigns for state and national leaders.

He was a member of Trigg County Post No. 74 of the American Legion, and served as Cadiz Police Judge for 35 years, the longest anyone had served in that position in the state of Kentucky. He died 7 Mar 1972 and was survived by a son, Claude H. Hall Jr. (Col., USA, Ret.) of Enterprise, OR, a former Cadiz native and WWII veteran.

CLAUDE H. HALL, born 21 Oct 1894, son of James H. and Mollie Hildreth Hall. A WWI Veteran was a native of Kuttawa, KY. He was married 4 Nov 1917 to Mayme Isabel Williams. She preceded him in death 19 Oct 1970.

He was Cadiz City Judge for 35 years and was serving as judge at the time of his death. Judge Hall was active in Trigg County Post No. 74 of the American Legion and a leader in the local Republican Party. He was a member of Cadiz Baptist Church and had taught a Sunday School Class. He had been a salesman for Cadiz Milling Co. since 1933.

Judge Hall and his wife had one son, Judge Claude H. Hall Jr. (Col. USA, Ret'd) of Enterprize, OR; a grandson Ron Hall of Enterprise; a granddaughter Mrs. Steve Barber, Paris Landing, TN and a great-granddaughter. He died at St. Thomas Hospital, Nashville, TN and was buried at East End Cemetery, Cadiz, KY.

MACK M. HOPSON, born 18 Sep 1895 in the Cerulean Springs Community of Trigg County, KY, was the son and sixth child of Mack Forest and Lucy Jane Gray Hopson. He entered the service in April 1917 and served as an aviator in France during WWI. A letter written by him and dated 13 Nov 1918 states he "was in Nantes when the fighting on the front stopped." He wrote about the "rejoicing" and the French people's appreciation of the American soldiers.

In his civilian life Mack Hopson was a man of varied interest. After his discharge from the Air Corps he returned to Trigg County and began to buy worn out farm land which he slowly restored. Eventually the land supported both cattle and sheep grazing with some areas being cultivated. He also operated a stone and gravel company and had a construction company that built roads and bridges in Kentucky and Tennessee. In the middle 1940s he developed land, including building an airstrip for small planes, where U.S. 68 crossed the newly flooded Kentucky lake.

For health reasons, in approximately 1945, Mack and his wife Georgia Alexander Hopson built and moved into a home on Main Street in Cadiz. In September 1946, Georgia preceded him in death. Mack died 11 Nov 1949.

ERNEST SMITH JOHNSTON SR., born in 1894 and died in 1923, the son of John Smith Johnston and Mary Eugenia Hayes (b. 1869, d. 1943). To John Smith's second marriage, five children were born: Henry Loyd, Ernest Smith, Raymond, Shirlie and Beulah. They made their home in Trigg County.

Ernest Smith Johnston Sr. served in WWI. His military training was at Camp McClellen, AL. After WWI, he married Georgia Humphries (b. 1897, d. 1977). They were married at Cadiz Baptist Church in 1920. They made their home in the Caledonia Community. One son was born, Ernest Smith Johnston Jr. Ernest Smith Sr. died when his son was 9 months old.

Ernest Smith Jr. married Willie Mae Goode in 1949. To this marriage two children were born, Suellen Johnston (b. 1952) and Jerry Johnston (b. April 1957, died in infancy).

Ernest Smith Johnston Sr. was buried in Humphries Cemetery in Trigg County. A marker has been placed at Jones Cemetery beside his wife, Georgia Humphries Johnston.

IRA RAYMOND JOHNSTON, Raymond Johnston was the third son of John and Mary E. Hayes Johnston. He was born 12 Nov 1898 and died 23 Jun 1980 and buried in Flagler Memorial Park Cemetery in Miami, FL.

The following article was printed in the local newspaper on 13 Dec 1917. "Ira R. Johnston, a Trigg County boy who enlisted in the Navy last April, was in training at Norfolk, VA, two months, and from there was sent to Charleston, SC where he remained several months. The rest of his training was on board the USS *Bridge*, stationed at New York. He writes his mother, Mrs. J.H. Johnston-Faulkner of near Caledonia, that he has just returned from across the waters. They stopped for a short while at Breast, France and Queenstown, Ireland. He says that it was a little exciting going through the war zone. All the boys had on their life preservers, as they did not know what minute they might be called on to do a little swimming stunt. They were in three storms, but came through all okay. Although they were 500 miles from land on Thanksgiving, they were furnished with a fine dinner of turkey with oyster dressing and asparagus, olives, apple pie, cakes and ice cream. It is a sight, he says in his letter, to see the crew when the mail comes in. Each one is so eager to hear from home and friends. They have changed my rating from seaman to that of hospital corps. You can imagine "Dr. Johnston" giving hot toddies to the sick, and, of course, sampling each to be sure it's just right. It was a treat for us boys to get back to New York. We felt somewhat safer there than in the European waters. Will be here only a few days. Then we will sail again. We are not allowed to tell when and where we are going."

He was a veteran of WWI and II and served as a x-ray and lab technician. He was also a member of the Biscayne Bay Masonic Lodge 124 and Mahi Shrine Temple. He attended Miami Community Shores Community Church.

While living in Trigg County, he married Sadie Wallis. Sadie was the daughter of Nay and Lula Wallis. No children were born to this marriage.

FRANCIS HAYWOOD JONES, born 6 Jan 1891, d. 4 Feb 1975, was the son of Ada Baker Jones (b. 21 Oct 1857, d. 15 Jan 1918) and Thomas B. Jones of Route 1, Golden Pond, KY. He enlisted in the U.S. Army at Camp Zachary Taylor as a private.

Francis Jones fought in France during WWI, was wounded there and lost his right leg. He was returned to the USA and transferred to Camp Taylor where he recuperated. His discharge was from Camp Taylor on 8 Feb 1919. He was awarded the Purple Heart.

On 11 Feb 1918 he married Ola Mae Puckett. There was one son, Thomas Reed Jones of Cadiz; two daughters, Robbie Crutcher of Murray and the late Jessie Compton of Herndon; 10 grandchildren and two great-grandchildren.

Francis and family lived in Golden Pond until they were relocated, then moved to the South Road, Cadiz, KY. He was an avid coon hunter. When Gerald R. Ford was President of the U.S., the family received a certificate stating "The United States of America honors the memory of Francis H. Jones..." *Submitted by Thomas R. Jones.*

JOLLY B. JONES, born 13 Oct 1896, Henatite Community of Trigg County, KY. He enlisted in the service in 1918 in Ohio, but got the flu so never saw active service.

Male children born in Land Between the Rivers in Jones days were not given first names until they grew up then selected their own names. When Jones went into the Army and the sergeant asked him his name, Jones answered "Ghost Jones." The sergeant said "That's a nickname."

Jones answered "It's the only name I ever had. The name was because he had a grey mule he rode hanging onto the mule's neck. When the sergeant wouldn't accept the nickname, Jones told the sergeant, "My daddy always called me his little Jolly Boy." The sergeant said "Good, now you are Jolly Boyce Jones for military purposes." And thus he was named.

After military he got a job with the Kentucky New Era as a typesetter, a job he continued at the *Cadiz Record* until his retirement.

Married Pearl Routen and they have children: Charline, Jolly, Wallis, John, Julia and Edna; and 15 grandchildren. Jolly passed away 3 Oct 1958.

PINKNEY LOYS LANCASTER, while serving in the Marine Corps, World War I broke out, but Pinkney Loys Lancaster was never shipped to Europe to fight the enemy, as were many of his Trigg County buddies. However, while in the Marine Corps, his duty to his country was nevertheless important.

Loys, as he was known, was born 6 Nov 1896 in Trigg County, son of Ezekiel "Zeke" and Peachie Matilda (Harrell) Lancaster. His mother died several months before his 8th birthday. He was a farmer by trade, but his favorite past time was spent hunting where he was well known for his hunting skills. When he was 18 years old, he traveled to Peoria, IL and enlisted in the

U.S. Marine Corps, on 14 Sep 1915, where he served with the expeditionary force of marines that landed in Haiti for the protection of America's interest. While in the service he was treated for malaria in 1916 and 1917. From 6 Apr 1917 to 13 Sep 1919 he served in Cuba, Charleston, South Carolina and New Orleans, LA.

While in the service, Loys qualified as a sharpshooter as reported by Headquarters, U.S. Marine Corps in Washington, DC. The Marine Corps officials considered his performances in gunnery as fantastic, and they expected him to break many marksmanship records before his enlistment expired. He was honorably discharged on 13 Sep 1919 and returned to his home in Trigg County.

On 14 Feb 1922, he married Virginia T. Mitchell, daughter of Whitson and Colie Lee (Crawley) Mitchell. They had seven children: Thomas Loys, Dorothy Lee, Matilda June, Curtis Allen, Joe Boyce and Wendell Lancaster. The family moved to Christian County, KY around 1926. At the age of 43, with his body weakened by diseases he contracted while in the service, he developed pneumonia and died at Jennie Stuart Memorial Hospital on 27 May 1938 in Hopkinsville. He is buried in Lawrence Cemetery, Trigg County.

Loys had two sons, Thomas and Curtis, to serve in the U.S. Army while his youngest son, Wendell, served in the U.S. Marine Corps.

CLAUDE WASHINGTON LANE, born 4 Apr 1895 in Golden Pond, KY. He entered the U.S. Army 2 Oct 1917 at Cadiz, KY, was a member of Co. H, 162nd Inf. and stationed in France. He received an honorable discharge 3 Jun 1919 at Camp Zachary Taylor, KY.

Married Pearl Mae Baccus in December 1916 and they had three children: Frank Sylvester, Frank Ray and Charlene Lane Allen, and seven grandchildren: Mike, Tony,

Frankie and Gary Lane; Bobby Lane, Jerry Lane and Anna Lane Ellen. Claude passed away in April 1951.

MIKE EARL LANE, born in Trigg County. He entered the service in 1918 and was stationed at Camp Taylor, KY. He took the flu and was sent home to recover and while there the war ended and he was discharged.

As a civilian he was a car salesman, investigator, then worked for L&N Railroad until retirement in 1955. He married Martha Grief and second Lula Ahart Hollis. No children. Mike Earl Lane is deceased.

LONNIE S. LAWRENCE, born 27 Feb 1890, in Trigg County, KY. His parents, Edmund and Molly Heath Lawrence, lived in the Warrenton Community, Trigg County. He served in the U.S. Army during WWI from June 1917 to February 1919. Part of his time was spent in France with the American Expeditionary Force under command of Gen. John J. Pershing.

He was a compositor by profession and early in his career worked for his cousins Henry and George Lawrence, publishers of *The Cadiz Record*. He later went with the Hopkinsville, KY, *New Era*, where he was employed until retirement.

Lonnie married Ruby Morris of Christian County. They had one daughter, Jane Claire (b. 15 Oct 1925). He died 17 Jul 1950, and is buried in Riverside Cemetery, Hopkinsville, KY.

OSCAR RUFUS LAWRENCE enlisted in the U.S. Navy in 1917, at Omaha, NE. He was 21 years of age. Oscar left his home in Trigg County at an early age and went West seeking employment.

He was the son of Edmund and Molly Heath Lawrence. Oscar was the youngest of three children: Lonnie who married Ruby Morris, and Pearl who married Eura Thomas. Oscar was never married. His best friend was George Roberts who was a WWI veteran.

Oscar died in the Naval Hospital, Great Lakes, IL, 10 Sep 1918. Cause meningitis. He is buried in the Lawrence Cemetery, Trigg County, KY.

IRA LITTLEJOHN, PFC, born 13 Aug 1887 at Hematite, KY near Golden Pond. He was never married. What time he lived in Kentucky he lived with his brother Harvey Littlejohn and their mother Bell Calhoun Littlejohn.

He worked at Center Furnace for the Hillman Land and Iron Co. After the closing of Center Furnace he continued working for Hillman Land Co. for a while then he was drafted into the Army 7 Oct 1917 and assigned to the 73rd Co., 19th Bn., 189th Depot Brigade at Camp Zachary Taylor, KY.

He departed from the U.S. 16 Mar 1918 for France and returned to the States in 1919 and received an honorable discharge 3 Jun 1919 with the rank of PFC.

After returning home he worked as a blacksmith for Hillman Land Co. for awhile then moved to Saint Louis and operated a gun shop for John Mayo and did gunsmith work for him also. Later on in years, he worked in Evansville, IN then moved to Fort Knox. After retiring he moved to Louisville and lived there until he passed away 14 Sep 1974. He is buried at Hematite Cemetery in Land Between the Lakes.

BURBON DEWARD McCAIN, PFC, born 26 May 1895 in the Sabine Creek area of Trigg County. He was the son of John Flavious and Cornelia Cassandra Carr McCain.

Burbon served in WWI as a PFC with HQ Co. 120th Inf. He wrote from France on 13 Oct 1918, "We advanced 1,000 yards ahead of the infantry in a trench and they shot all over and around us. Three of them tried to capture us, but I had my eyes open and got six shots out of my 45 first." He also wrote of the boys in service who drank water from horses tracks, because the enemy had poisoned the water supply.

Burbon married Clyde Harrell who died 23 Apr 1956. She is buried in Cerulean, KY. Burbon married Edmonia Randolph Rye 14 Feb 1957. He was a farmer in the Cerulean Community. Burbon and Edmonia lived on Nunn Boulevard in Cadiz. He died 9 Jan 1969. They are buried in East End Cemetery. *Submitted by Etha Lurline Hancock.*

HARLON PRENTICE McCAIN, Private, born 2 Apr 1897 in the Sabine Creek area of Trigg County. He was the son of John Flavious and Cornelia Cassandra Carr McCain.

Harlon served in WWI as a private in the U.S. Army. His time in service was 1917-1918. He did not talk of the war and the time he was away.

Harlon married Nancy L. Campbell and they had one son Harlon Winfield McCain. Harlon died 25 Sep 1978 and Nancy in 1953. They are both buried in Cerulean, KY. *Submitted by Etha Lurline Hancock.*

OVID McCAWLEY, Private, born 2 Feb 1894 in Hematite, KY, the son of Frank and Lucy (Turner) McCawley. He enlisted in the service 2 Oct 1917 at Cadiz, KY and was discharged with the rank of private 13 Dec 1917.

He married Josie Aline Calhoun on 3 Dec 1929; no children. Ovid passed away 13 Aug 1972 and is buried in the Lawrence Cemetery.

BENJAMIN OWEN McGEE, Private, born 6 Mar 1895 in Benettstown, KY. He enlisted 25 Feb 1918 in Trigg County, KY and was stationed at Camp Zachary Taylor, Louisville, KY and Camp Sevier, SC.

On 9 Jul 1918 he left for France and participated in the Battle of the Marne and Aisne Marne Offensive. He was a member of Co. 2, 319th Inf. and was discharged 11 Jun 1919 with the rank of private.

He married Mary Bertha Banister 21 Dec 1920 and they had two children, Monroe and Lois, and one grandchild, Anthony McGee. Benjamin was a farmer and passed away 18 Oct 1971 and is buried East End Cemetery, Cadiz, KY.

LUCIAN McGEE, born 21 Jan 1892 in Bennettstown, KY. He enlisted in January 1918 in Trigg County and was stationed at Camp Zachary Taylor, Louisville, KY and Camp Sevier, SC.

He was sent overseas to France in July 1918 and was discharged in June 1919.

Lucian married Della Faulkner on 17 Dec 1921, no children. He passed away 13 Aug 1990 and is buried East End Cemetery, Cadiz, KY.

SIDNEY SIMS McKINNEY, Lieutenant, born 30 Jan 1896 in Cadiz, KY. Coming from families of professional men on both his father's and mother's side, he chose the profession of law for his life's career. He was a student at Washington and Lee University when World War I came and he volunteered his services to the Army, entering officers' training school. He was commissioned with the rank of lieutenant. He served in six major campaigns: the Marne, Chateau Thiery, Soissons, Belleau Wood the Argonne and St. Mihiel.

After the close of WWI he re-entered Washington and Lee continued his collegiate course. After graduating from this institution, he studied law at Harvard.

He came home, began his law work and served three years as city attorney, four years as county attorney, and eight years as master commissioner. In 1939 he married Clarice Carfield of Hammond, LA. Sidney was the son of Henry Bowden and Roberta Sims McKinney, and the grandson of Honorable Fenton Sims and Sidney Redd Sims.

He was a member of Cadiz Methodist Church, member of the Kappa Sigma Fraternity and American Legion Post #74. He served during WWII on the war ration and gas board and the ration board of Trigg County, also on Trigg County Draft Board.

He died 4 Nov 1946, at Outwood Sanitarium. Funeral services were held at his home in Cadiz. As according to his request military rites were accorded at East End Cemetery by the American Legion Post #74, assisted by a firing squad from Camp Campbell.

RAYMOND EVERETT MAGRAW, was one of the first boys drafted in Christian County, KY in September 1917 at the beginning of WWI. He died of pneumonia at Camp Zachary Taylor, Louisville, KY, in the year of 1918, at age 22.

Raymond was born in 1896 at Roaring Springs, Trigg County, KY. His parents, Dr. Norris C. and Letitia Hayes Magraw, moved to Christian County when he was a lad. The family moved to Cadiz where his father opened an office for the practice of medicine on 1 Jan 1918.

He had twin brothers who died in infancy; one sister, Norene Magraw Humprhies; and three brothers: Cottrell, Ralph and Paul Magraw.

Raymond was single and is buried in East End Cemetery, Cadiz, KY.

ROBERT ELLIOTT MALONE, youngest child of Edmund Pendleton and Teresa Elizabeth Lawrence Malone, was born in Trigg County on 5 Jan 1896. His siblings were Ida, Schuyler, Ethel, Annie, Henry and Janie.

Elliott was drafted into the U.S. Army in July 1918 and received his basic training at Camp Taylor, KY. He was assigned to Co. D, lst Pioneer

Infantry, and served in the Occupation Army in France until his discharge on 7 Jul 1919.

Elliott returned to Trigg County where he worked with his father and his brother, Henry, on the family farm about three miles west of Cadiz. He married Annie Lucille Williams, second child of Thomas Green and Johnie Vara Thomas Williams, on 11 Oct 1922.

Elliott and Annie lived on the family farm the remainder of their lives. Their children are Martha Nell Smith, Edmund Pendleton III (deceased), Celena Ann Mejia, Betty Sue Hayes, Vara Jo Powell and Robert Jr.

Elliott died on 15 Aug 1964, and Annie on 5 Jul 1982. They are buried in the Lawrence Cemetery.

CYRIL MILLER, born in Cadiz, KY, the son of Hugh and Ada Bogard Miller. From 1 Feb 1907 to 31 Jan 1910 he served with Co. K, 18th Inf. His second enlistment was 1 Jun 1917 at Eddyville, KY. He was a member of Co. A, 17th Engrs. and served in France.

Cyril Miller married Minnie Collins and they had four children: Gordon, Mary Bell, Cyril Jr. and Hugh.

FORREST CRENSHAW MILLER, Seaman 2/c, born 22 Jun 1891 near Roaring Springs, Trigg County, KY. He was operating the family farm when WWI started. In 1917 Congress passed a Selective Service Act for all men 21 to 30 to register. Forrest preferred the Navy, so 29 May 1918 he enrolled at the Navy Recruiting Station in Louisville, KY. He was sent to the Great Lakes area to a training station, the Naval Rifle Range and Cape May Naval Base in New Jersey. He took pride in becoming an expert in rifle shooting. As a "sharpshooter" he was assigned to train others. He would take a group out on the lakes where they practiced shooting at targets 600 yards away.

He was on a ship in New York harbor ready to leave for Europe when the war ended abruptly. Thus he never went overseas. He was discharged 28 Aug 1919 as a seaman 2/c. He received the Victory Medal without clasp. He remained in the Naval Reserve Force until a lack of funding caused a drastic cut in the Reserves, then he was released 30 Sep 1921.

After service he returned home and married Ruby Larue Hamilton on 29 Dec 1920 and they lived near Roaring Springs, KY. They had two daughters, Sarah Frances and Mary Crenshaw. The family moved from Trigg County in 1937 to a farm near Pembroke, KY. The girls graduated from Pembroke High School and both graduated from Western Kentucky Teachers College. Sarah Frances also attended a Bible and Mission School. In 1946 she went to northeast Brazil where she served as a missionary for 43 years. She retired in 1989 and lived in Franklin, KY. She died suddenly in 1997.

In 1944 Mary Crenshaw married Claud T. Johnson from Warren County, KY. She taught school for 32 years. They had three sons: Claud Miller, Johnny Mac and Thomas Lee.

In 1951, Forrest moved to a larger farm in south Christian County, KY. He retired in 1972, then he and Ruby moved to Donna Drive in Hopkinsville, KY. He was a Christian gentleman in all aspects of his life. His priorities were church, his family and education. He loved to talk to everyone, especially about his grandsons. He liked to read and enjoyed walking in his neighborhood. He died 11 Dec 1983. Ruby moved to Franklin to be near her daughter and she died 5 Jun 1985.

THOMAS MITCHELL, born 13 Dec 1888, the son of Andrew "Buck" Mitchell and Aurora Cunningham Mitchell. He enlisted in the U.S. Army 19 Sep 1918 and was honorably discharged 13 Dec 1918.

Thomas married Flora Belle Crute, daughter of John R. Crute and Elizabeth Miller Crute, on 27 Dec 1911. They had two children, Thomas C. Mitchell and John C. Mitchell.

JACK MIZE, born 3 Mar 1896 in Trigg County, KY, the oldest son of J. Lewis and Kitty Boyd Mize. He enlisted 19 Sep 1917 and was honorably discharged 21 Oct 1919. His last duty assignment was HQ Casual Det, Camp Zachary Taylor, KY.

After his discharge, Jack returned to Trigg County to resume his life. He married Lillian Ethel Blakeley on 28 Aug 1922 and they had two sons, Harold and Jack Jr.

Jack was working for Adkins Dairy of Hopkinsville when he was killed in an automobile accident on 26 May 1951. He is buried in a cemetery at Ceruleon Springs, KY.

TROY MORRISON, born in Trigg County, KY, on 29 Jun 1894. He died in Calloway County, KY, on 14 Jul 1945. He was inducted into the Army 25 Feb 1918 and was discharged 21 Jan 1919. While in the Army he served with the American Expeditionary Forces in Germany.

After his discharge he married Fannie Stalls Morrison and they had two children: J.D. Morrison who served in the U.S. Navy in WWII and Iva Lee Morrison Higgins. Both were born in Trigg County, KY.

After, Fannie's death in 1938, Troy was married to Lelia Cothran Morrison. They also had two children: Peggy Jean Morrison Thompson and Joe Clarence Morrison.

Troy and his wives, Fannie and Lelia, are buried at the Matheney Cemetery in "The Land Between the Rivers," in Trigg County, KY.

OSIE DIX NEWTON, Private, born 9 Oct 1889 in Golden Pond, KY, the son of James Reed and Francis Dix Newton.

He was a veteran of WWI as a member of the 159 Depot Brigade, Armed Forces of the U.S. National Army. He served from 30 Aug 1918 until 7 Jan 1919, when he received an honorable discharge with the rank of private.

He taught school in Trigg County, KY before moving to Todd County, KY in 1945 where he became a very prominent farmer. In 1946 he married Lorene Fennell and had one step-daughter Annette McClain Bailey. He was a member and deacon of the Bethel Baptist Church, Fairview, KY. He died 3 Feb 1969 and is buried in Green Hills Memorial Garden.

HUGH D. PALMER, born 26 Mar 1895 in Cerulean, KY, son of William Henry and Frances Kirby Palmer. He was drafted into the U.S. Army 1 Apr 1918 and served during WWI.

After his discharge he married Alberta Wallace on 20 Nov 1920 and they had 11 children. In 1928 he united with Cane Spring Baptist Church and under the pastorage of Rev. R.H. Pendleton, he was ordained as a deacon in 1950.

He worked on the farm and for I.C. Railroad for 42 years and passed away 10 Jun 1992. His wife and seven children preceded him in death. He is survived by four children: Annie Hughes, Jessie Watkins, Irene McGown, Edna Boyd, 25 grandchildren, 46 great-grandchildren and 20 great-great-grandchildren.

BENTLEY PIERCY, First Sergeant, born 11 Jan 1883 in Caldwell, KY. He was discharged from the military in 1919 with the rank of first sergeant.

Bentley was the first commander of American Legion Post 74 in Cadiz, KY.

He married Ruth Cunningham on 23 Nov 1921 and they had two children, Dean D. and Robert B., and five grandchildren: Katherine Ford, J. Bentley, Mickens D., Matthew and Susann Piercy. He passed away 14 Feb 1930.

ROBERT PORTER PIERCY, Corporal, "Columbia gives to her son the accolade of the new chivalry of humanity. Robert P. Piercy (b. 1895, d. 1970), Corporal, Co. H, 28th Infantry, served with honor in the World War and was wounded in action." Woodrow Wilson

Porter Piercy served his country, community and his church. He was associated with Trigg County Farmers Bank for over 50 years, serving as president and as chairman of the board of directors. He served as mayor for a number of years. As a member of Cadiz Baptist Church, he served as deacon and as a Sunday School teacher for numerous years. He served on the board of

directors of the Trigg County Hospital and as treasurer of the Trigg County Board of Education. He was married to the former Alice Jackson.

PETE POGUE, born 10 May 1884 in Bleidt, KY (Cumberland area, Trigg County), a vocation farmer, he was drafted 25 Feb 1918 at Cadiz, KY. Pete's Army combat unit was the First Pioneer Infantry, USA. Pete was inducted into the Army at Camp Zachary Taylor, KY. The birthplace of the First Pioneer Infantry USA was Camp Wadsworth, SC. His commander was Col. James S. Boyer.

"What is a Pioneer?" The Personnel Bureau of the War Department, in its directions for selecting soldiers for the various services, laid down the following suggestions: Men experienced in life in the open, skilled in woodcraft and simple carpentry, substitute occupation, rancher, prospector, hunter, scout.

After being uniformed with "some" training most of Pete's regiment entrained for Hoboken, NJ and embarked on the transport *Mount Vernon,* arriving in France 18 Jul 1918. The unit chaplain, Harrison W. Forman, said of these men: Many of these men who came to us were only embryonic soldiers. They were diamonds but were still in the rough. Some could neither read nor write. May the name, First Pioneer Infantry, come to be known for what it actually represented, a necessary, vital force in the saving of the world in 1918.

Pete returned to the States on 7 Jul 1919, but many in the regiment did not. Pete participated in combat offensives Marne-Aisne, 25 July-6 Aug 1918; Oise-Aisne 18 Aug-10 Sep 1918 and Meuse-Argonne 26 Sep-11 Nov 1918.

Pete received an honorable discharge 16 Jul 1919 at Camp Zachary Taylor, KY. Last unit of assignment listed as Co. D, 1st Pioneer Infantry. Others from Trigg County that were in Pete's outfit included Williams

Maynard, Robert E. Malone, Dell Freeman, Lee Shelton and Thomas Gentry. Pete made his living as a farmer and making moonshine whiskey (only when times got bad).

Pete married Array Hoskins in 1942, a widow with six children: Dorothy, Virgie, Martha, Willie, Argene and Billy. Pete and Array had three children: Donnie, Frank and Dixie. Pete died 25 May 1971 and is buried at the Cumberland Cemetery, Land Between the Lakes, Golden Pond, KY.

CLAUDE VINSON POINDEXTER, Private, born 28 Jul 1891, in Christian County, KY, the eldest son of William Crittenden and Margaret Smith Poindexter. He had three sisters: Ozie, Grace and Nora, and three brothers: Leslie, Perry and William. The family lived in the Otter Pond and Wallonia communities of Caldwell County during his early years.

Claude was drafted into the Army 2 Oct 1917 at Cadiz, KY. He was sent to Camp Taylor in Louisville, KY for training and from there to Gravesend, England and then to Calais France in March 1918. He often told the story of going for 28 days without a change of clothes but rarely spoke of the hard times he endured.

After being discharged 25 Apr 1919 as a private, he returned to Trigg County where he continued to be a barber, a trade he acquired in the service. On 7 Nov 1921 he married Lena Mae Marlow, the daughter of Orrin Rascoe Marlow, a former Trigg County jailer, and his wife Maggie Maddox Marlow. Two children were born to Claude and Lena: daughter Eleanor (b. 17 Oct 1923, Trigg County) and Mary Anne (b. 25 Sep 1931, Hopkinsville). They had three grandchildren: Edward Douglas Atkins Jr., Judith Anne Atkins and Patricia Jean Atkins.

Claude worked at several barber shops in Hopkinsville, finally opening his own shop at 8th and Virginia Streets in 1940 and operating it until his retirement in 1965. After the opening of Camp Campbell in 1942, he would often bring home a young soldier boy for a home-cooked meal. He would say "This is the least I can do for these young men." He was a member of the DAV for a number of years

Upon retiring he spent his time fishing, gardening and enjoying his grandchildren until his death 24 Mar 1974. He is buried in East End Cemetery, Cadiz, KY.

OTIS E. "HOP" P'POOL, PFC, born 14 Mar 1891 in Trigg County, the son of Richard and Margaret Lester P'Pool. He was in WWI with Co. B, 116 TN Ho & MP and received the rank of PFC.

After the war, Hop worked as a hospital attendant and worked at Outwood Hospital in Dawson Springs, KY for 20 years from which he retired.

He remained a bachelor and was a member of Blue Springs Baptist Church. In his later years he became a patient at Shady Lawn Nursing Home where he died on 27 Jan 1971. He is buried in Wall Cemetery near Wallonia in Trigg County, KY.

WALTER CLYDE RAMEY, born 4 Mar 1894 in Trigg County. He was inducted into U.S. Army 56 Dep Brig on 4 Sep 1918 and received an honorable discharge on 21 Nov 1918 due to disability. He married Jettie

Ladd in 1921. They were the parents of two daughters, Millowdean Wynn and Magdalene Gray. Walter was a farmer until 1944 when he moved to Princeton, KY. He worked in a factory, for the state highway department, and was employed by the city of Princeton at the time of his retirement in 1964. Walter died 7 Nov 1977.

HOMER CLAY RANDOLPH, Musician 3/c, born 31 Jul 1895 in Trigg County, KY, was inducted into WWI, 2 Oct 1917 at Camp Zachary Taylor, 325th Field Artillery. Discharged 3 Mar 1919 at Camp Zachary Taylor from the 325th, Field Artillery, Musician third class, HQ Co.

He was married to Bessie Mae Skaggs, daughter of Dr. James Monroe Skaggs and Enola Skaggs of Donaldson Creek, KY, on Apr. 1, 1916. They had four children: Dorothy, Earl Maurice, Robert and Homer Louis (Boots). From this line there are now five grandchildren, seven great-grandchildren and four great-great-grandchildren.

During Homer's service in France he was assigned to the Army Band and played second trumpet. At that time he became friends with the first trumpet man who was French and whose name was Maurice (Mar-reece). Maurice was an accomplished musician and helped Homer who had no formal musical training but had a special talent of hearing a tune one time and being able to play it through. So during all the army music, marches, formal tunes, etc. Homer was right there playing his part. When Homer's first son was born in 1923 he was named Earl Maurice in honor of this good friend.

After returning from the war Homer farmed in Trigg County, worked in the oil fields in Louisiana, Illinois Central Railroad shops in Paducah and the Shipyards in Evansville, IN. During WWII, two sons went into service and Homer moved to Evansville and was employed by the Evansville Shipyards building LSTs for the war.

All these years he continued to play music having his own band, lots of community entertainment and winning many Accolades and prizes at the Old Fiddler's contests. At one time he was known as "Mr Music" of Trigg County.

He passed away 2 May 1965 and he and Bessie (d. 25 Aug 1968) are buried in the Peyton Thomas Cemetery.

MILUS McKENZIE RANDOLPH, born 18 May 1890. He was inducted 24 May 1918 and served with 38 Co., 10 Trn. Bn. to 16 Jun 1918; Btry. D, 327th FA to 13 Jul 1918; and 2nd Co. Dev Bn. to discharge on 8 Nov 1918 with 10% disability.

He married Lucy Beatrice Guthrie. Milus passed away 19 Jan 1963.

WILLIAM HINKLE RAWLS, Sergeant, enlisted in 1917 and served with Co. E, 12th Ammo Train, Camp McClellan, AL. He attained the rank of sergeant and was discharged in 1918.

He returned to Cerulean then to Cadiz to work at the Chappell and Cowherd Grocery. He was first commander of American Legion Post 74 and led in getting first legion club house and swimming pool in Cadiz.

William married Olive Larkins in 1918 and they had two children, Jane and William Jr., and several grandchildren. After Olive's death he married Alta Meador. William Hinkle Rawls is deceased.

DR. DURWARD B. ROACH, Captain, born 18 Sep 1883 in Roaring Springs, Trigg County, KY. He was educated in Major Ferrell's School, Hopkinsville, KY and graduated from the University of Louisville Medical College in 1906. He returned to Roaring Springs and started his practice until his enlistment date.

He enlisted 13 Jun 1918 in the U.S. Army in Nashville, TN and was assigned to the Medical Corps with the rank of captain. Assignments were Rockerfellow Inst. Army Medical School, Washington, DC and Fort Snelling, MN.

Durward participated in WWI until his discharge 6 Sep 1920 at Jefferson Barracks, MO. He was discharged to accept an appointment in the U.S. Regular Army 7 Sep 1920. Dr. Roach left the States on 5 May 1921 to serve duty in the Philippines. He returned to the States 18 May 1922 and was discharged from active duty the next day with the rank of captain.

Returned to Roaring Springs and practiced medicine until 1925 when he moved his practice to LaFayette, KY. He married Sara Horn Brandon in 1928 and they had three children: Durward, Irene and Robert, and nine grandchildren. Sara had three sons from her first marriage: Charles, Wesley and Richard.

Durward also practiced in Hopkinsville, KY from 1942-49, then moved to Pembroke, KY and practiced until his death 22 Nov 1949. He and his wife are buried in Rosedale Cemetery, Pembroke, KY.

GEORGE LEE ROBERTS, Seaman 2/c, born 8 Sep 1894, in Trigg County and died 20 Jan 1975. He enlisted 13 Apr 1918 at Louisville, KY and was stationed at Camp Logan, IL, 13 May 1918 to 31 May 1918; Annapolis, MD, 1 Jun 1918 to 25 Jan 1919; Philadelphia, PA, 25 Jan 1919 until discharge 27 Feb 1919 with the rank seaman second class.

After discharge he was a mail carrier for 48 years in Trigg County. He was a charter member and served as Commander of American Legion Post 74, 1931 and 1939.

He married Katherleen Barber 15 Jan 1930 and they had three children: Ann Barber Roberts (md. Mike Brito); George L. Jr. and John Stanley, who both died in infancy. Grandchildren are Michael, Joseph and Angela Brito.

JULIAN STANLEY ROBERTS, Seaman 2/c, Fireman 3/c, born 1890 in Trigg County. Enlisted in the U.S. Navy 26 Jun 1918 in Louisville, KY and was stationed at Naval Training Station, Great Lakes, IL. He attained the rank of seaman second class and fireman third class. He was discharged 3 Dec 1920.

As a civilian he was a partner in J.W. Cowherd & Co. Grocery. He was a charter member of American Legion Post 74 and served as adjutant in 1926 and 1937.

Late in life he married Audrey Hale, no children. He passed away in 1973.

HOMER REDDICK, born 16 Mar 1893 in Trigg County, the son of Robert Dennis and Maude Shryer Reddick. A WWI veteran, he was inducted into the U.S. Army 2 Oct 1917. He served in Camp Sevier, SC in the U.S. Infantry and was honorably discharged on 11 Dec 1918.

He was a former resident of Princeton where he served as a police officer for a number of years, then later moved to Cadiz where he served as a police officer from February 1950 to March 1963. He retired as a corrections officer at Eddyville Penitentiary.

Homer and Artha Barnett Reddick celebrated their 66th wedding anniversary in July 1984. One daughter, Mildred Inus, died at age 14 months. Their daughter Kathleen married Bryan Stanley Hall, and they had two daughters, Elizabeth Diane Hall Oakley and Patricia Elaine Hall. His great-granddaughters: Robin, Heather and Whitney, were quite

special to him. He had a picture of them on the mantle in his bedroom. Every night (after he wound the clock) he would look at the picture and say, "Goodnight, Dumps."

Homer enjoyed mowing his yard and stripping tobacco until he was 89 years old. His favorite job in his later years was working at the Robert Bush farm and teasing "the Bush boys" as he called twins, Bob and Bill Bush.

He was a member of the Cadiz Baptist Church and a member of American Legion Post No. 74. Attending his Sunday School class, going to "legion meetings, and watching *Bonanza* were activities he especially enjoyed up until his health failed him at age 90. He passed away on 18 Oct 1984 at the age of 91.

BOGARD ROGERS, born 17 Jul 1893 in Trigg County, KY. He served in WWI and was assigned to the 801st Pioneer Inf. and fought in France.

A farmer, he was married to Elizabeth Malone and they had five children: Marjorie, Laura Mae, Bogard Jr., Eugene and Haywood, and 21 grandchildren. He passed away 12 Dec 1946.

The above information was submitted by his grandson Joe E. Rogers of Cadiz, KY, who never knew him but often wondered what kind of man he was. One day Joe came home from work and his wife approached him with a gift, not recognizing what it was at first he was slow to react, then after careful examination was elated. It was his grandfather's dog tag. He went to the graveyard where before he had unsuccessfully looked for his grave, but this time seemed to have some direction and walked right to his military headstone. I thanked him for what he had done and how truly proud I am to be his grandson.

DON CARLOSS RYAN, a native of Cadiz, Trigg County, KY, was inducted in the U.S. Army at Lexington, VA, 2 Oct 1918. He received an honorable discharge on 15 Dec 1918. His parents were G.W. and Eunice Haden Ryan. They moved from the Golden Pond Community in Trigg County, to Cadiz in 1909. Don's father was an attorney and served two terms as county judge, elected in 1921. Don Carloss had three brothers: George, Phil and Haden.

CLARENCE HERBERT RYE, Private, born 4 Jan 1896, the son of Edward Elijah and Blanche Eveline Batson Rye. Herbert served as a private in the U.S. Army in WWI. He enlisted 4 Jun 1918 in Clarksville, TN, serving in France from 1 Aug 1918 to 24 Mar 1919. He served as an interpreter of French. He was in the battle of Verdun, France, from 6-11 Nov 1918, when the Armistice ending WWI was signed.

He was married to Edmonia Gaines Randolph 29 Sep 1922. Their children were Van Layton (b. 5 Oct 1925) and Marian Louise Rye (b. 28 May 1928).

Van, who served in the U.S. Navy in WWII, married Ann Callender of New Orleans, LA, in 1945. One son Jerry (b. 26 Dec 1947) married Doris Ann Thomas, Atlanta, GA and they are the parents of a daughter Tracey. Jerry is employed by Delta Airlines in Atlanta.

Marian was married to Carey T. Davis, a Trigg Countian on 21 Aug 1946. Their two sons are M. Thomas Davis and John Timothy (J.T.) Davis.

In 1952 Van married Betty Lou Spencer of Erin, TN. Their children are Randy and Kim.

After his discharge on 24 May 1919, Clarence Herbert served as a teacher in Trigg County. He was a project foreman for WPA at the time of his death in an automobile accident on 1 Oct 1938. He was buried in East End Cemetery in Cadiz with the Trigg County Post American Legion serving as pallbearers.

His brothers and sisters were Charley Edward, Thomas Batson, Robert Hill, Mattie Malinda, Grace Elizabeth (Gordon), William Hartwell and Annie Maude. *Submitted by his daughter, Marian Rye Davis, Columbia, SC.*

ROBERT HILL RYE, born 3 Jul 1893 in Tennessee. Enlisted in the U.S. Army in 1918. His service record is unknown. He married Nellie Mary Isabelle Johnson (b. 31 Oct 1901) on 30 Dec 1922. They were the parents of three children:

1) Lena Mae Rye (b. 26 Jan 1924) who married Lemuel James Banister Jr. (b. 24 Jun 1924) on 8 Dec 1945. Two children were born to this marriage, Carey David Banister (b. 12 Feb 1947) and Charles Ray Banister (b. 9 Sep 1948). Charles died with muscular dystrophy on 13 Feb 1973.

2-3) Robert Ray (b. 15 Mar 1926, d. 1 Mar 1955) and Charles Riley (b. 7 Nov 1927, d. 19 Mar 1960). Both had muscular dystrophy since birth.

Robert also had two great-grandchildren: Dr. Jason D. Banister and Carrie Diane Banister; and two great-great-grandchildren, Sarah Brooke Banister and David William Banister.

Robert Hill Rye worked as a construction foreman, building roads, schools, bridges, etc. He retired from Federal Service from Fort Campbell, KY. His hobby was fishing. He died 10 Sep 1963. Isabelle died 25 May 1981. They are buried along with their sons in East End Cemetery in Cadiz, KY.

LEWIS J. SHERBUT, Private, enlisted in the U.S. Army, 27 Aug 1918 at Cadiz, KY. Lewis completed his basic training at Camp Knox, KY and was enlisted as a private to the Battery L, 69th Field Artillery. He was given an honorable discharge from the U.S. Army on 17 Dec 1918 due to the ending of WWI.

He was married to Hallie Turner and they had five children: E. Louise Sherbut Joyce, Gilbert Sherbut, E. Flossie Sherbut Cotton Mitchell, Lonnie Sherbut and Inez Sherbut. Grandchildren include Danny Joyce, J. Carol Joyce Gray Colley, Johnny Joyce, Charlie Joyce, Jackie Cotton, Johnny Sherbut, Jimmy Sherbut, Brenda Sherbut Noonjin and Linda Sherbut Pote.

He is laid to rest in the Hematite Cemetery in the Land Between the Lakes, Golden Pond, KY.

LAMONT SIVILLS, Private, born 21 Jan 1896, in Trigg County, KY, began his WWI military service in the U.S. Army in September 1917. He was assigned to Camp Zachary Taylor in Louisville, KY for his basic training. He served in Co. F of the 30th Infantry and was one of the few Trigg Countians sent to France, where he fought bravely on the front lines. He was honorably discharged in August 1919 with the rank of private.

After WWI ended Sivills married Lila Beatrice Wyatt on 20 Jun 1920, in Trigg County. They had two children: Calvert Wallace, who served in the Army during WWII, and Dorothy Jewell (Smith).

Lamont was a farmer and timber mill owner and operator. He and his wife were charter members of South Road Baptist Church. They had five grandchildren: Linda Susan Smith, Calvert "Buddy" Sivills, Scott Sivills, Nancy Sivills Thompson and Jani Sivills.

Lamont was a life-long resident of the "South Road" area of Trigg County until his death on 9 Aug 1956.

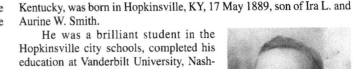

IRA D. SMITH, former circuit judge of the Third Judicial District of Kentucky, was born in Hopkinsville, KY, 17 May 1889, son of Ira L. and Aurine W. Smith.

He was a brilliant student in the Hopkinsville city schools, completed his education at Vanderbilt University, Nashville, TN, and entered upon the practice of law in 1910. In 1911 he was elected county attorney on the Democratic ticket for the term 1914 to 1918.

In 1918 he volunteered for service in WWI and served as an ensign in the USN, RF. Returning from war he was elected state representative from Christian County, in the General Assembly of 1922, and in 1927 was nominated for circuit judge, in the Democratic primary, beginning in January 1928. He was elected for six more terms, without opposition, and served a total of 42 years, a state record for circuit judges and believed to be a national record.

In 1928 the counties of Trigg, Lyon, Calloway and Christian comprised the Third Judicial District. The district was later changed and he served the counties of Trigg, Christian and Lyon.

Over the 42 years neither sickness nor sorrow nor adversity ever prevented Judge Smith from performing his judicial duties at every one of the 126 terms of his tenure.

After an outstanding career, Judge Ira D. Smith retired from the bench on 31 Dec 1969.

Judge Smith married Miss Carrie Harrison in 1924 and they had three children: Dan (md. Anne Hammond); Molly (md. Jules Morris); and Caroline (md. Jake Rudolph). Carrie Smith died 18 May 1969, and Judge Ira D. Smith died 13 Aug 1988. Interment was made in Riverside Cemetery, Hopkinsville, KY.

BINGHAM STEPHENS, a WWI veteran, was born 30 Nov 1894, in the Southern Academy Community in Trigg County. At the time of his induction into the Army his residence was RR #1, Cadiz, KY. He was inducted 24 May 1918. He was a private and assignments and transfers were 38 Co. 10 Tng BN 159 Dep Brig to 17 Jun 1918; Co. W 153 Inf to 13 Sep 1918; Co. D 126 Inf to discharge. He served overseas from 6 Aug 1918 to 20 Jan 1919. He was slightly wounded on 4 Oct 1918. Bingham was honorably discharged on 18 Mar 1919.

A native of Trigg County, Bingham was born one of nine children of William Lowery and Nannie Milton Mitchell Stephens. He was united in marriage to the former Ruby Stahl on 25 Nov 1920. To this union was born one son Ray. Ray was a graduate of Trigg County High School and attended Murray State College. He volunteered for service in the U.S. Marine Corp, 8 Dec 1941 and served 18 months overseas. He participated in the Guadalcanal Campaign and other battles in the South Pacific.

Bingham had led an active business career and at one time managed the Legion Theatre in Cadiz. He owned and operated the Stephens Dry Cleaning business for a number of years and later he and Ruby owned and operated Ruby's Dress Shop in Cadiz.

In 1953 he moved to Paducah, KY where he and Ruby owned a dress shop for two years. Moving to Daytona Beach, FL in 1955, he was a manager of a service station for four years. They moved back to Cadiz in 1959 when Bingham was forced to retire because of ill-health.

He was a veteran of WWI and was a charter member of Trigg County American Legion Post No. 74. He died 4 Oct 1961 and is buried in East End Cemetery, Cadiz, KY. His wife Ruby died 26 Dec 1998 and is also buried in East End. One grandson, Tommy Stephens, of Cody Wyoming survived her.

IRVIN JEFFERSON STEVENS (Dude or Big Man), born 9 Jun 1895 in Lyon County, KY and later moved to Trigg County, Cerulean, KY. From Trigg County, he enlisted into the U.S. Army, 24 May 1918. After training was completed, Irvin was assigned as a private with HQ. Co. 128 Infantry. He served throughout the war with this company until his honorable discharge, 17 May 1919.

Returning to civilian life, Irvin returned to the farms where he worked before the War. In 1926-56, he worked for Cerulean Stone Co. His work was as a blacksmith and with tempered steel; he shod the mules, which pulled the rock to be crushed. In 1929, trucks changed his work position; his job then was to feed the crusher and change belts. He was injured when struck by a truck at work, both arm were broken and he was never able to work again.

Irvin was the son of Robert Stevens and Prudence Gray Stevens. In 1921 he married Mamye Lois McAlister, daughter of Alex McAlister and Alice Forguson. There were 11 children: Edith Noel, Allene Blanks, Nancy Clark, Durwood Stevens, Jay Stevens, Elizabeth Oliver, Homer Stevens and Virginia Dawson. Two children died in infancy. There are 28 grandchildren, 50 great-grandchildren and 14 great-great-grandchildren.

Irvin's hobbies were hunting and training Bird dogs, pointers and setters; he trained dogs for other people. Daughter Allene says, "I would go hunting with him and carry the birds for him. I loved to watch the dogs; there is nothing prettier than a pointer and a setter."

Irvin's parents died when he was only 2 years old. He lived with his grandmother and two older sisters until he moved to Trigg County, Cerulean, KY. There he lived with Earl and Mamie Harris and worked the Broadbent farms until he went to the Army.

Irvin Jefferson Stevens died August 1965 and is buried in Cerulean Cemetery. *Submitted by Allene Stevens Blanks.*

JOHN L. STREET SR.

JOHN L. STREET SR., First Lieutenant, born 12 Oct 1888 in Cadiz, KY. He enlisted 4 Oct 1917 in Trigg's second contribution to the country's WWI. He attained the rank of first lieutenant.

He was president of Trigg County Farmers Bank for over 50 years; was leader in the fund raising for the Trigg County Hospital; a member of Cadiz Christian Church and a dedicated worker as chairman of the board, treasurer and Sunday school teacher for many years. The public library is named for him, John L. Street Library.

He married Margaret Atkinson on 12 Oct 1916 and had one son John L. Street Jr.

JOHN WILLIAM STEWART

JOHN WILLIAM STEWART, PFC, WWI, the events of 24 May 1918 were not those originally planned for John William Stewart. Instead of giving the valedictorian's speech to the graduating class of Cadiz High School as scheduled, he was inducted into the U.S. Army at Cadiz, KY. He was stationed at Camp Beauregard, Alexandria, LA, where he trained as a forward observer for Battery D of the 141st Field Artillery, 64th FA Brigade, 39th Division of the federalized U.S. National Guard.

On 26 Aug 1918, he left with Battery D from Hoboken, NJ (having been transferred to Camp Mills, NY) for Brest, France, on the USS *Agamemnon*. He recalled wondering if he would ever see the Statue of Liberty again, a question which became valid even before his arrival in France as his transport ship was narrowly missed by a German torpedo during the crossing.

On 9 Sep 1918, six days after their arrival, the 141st was moved from Brest to Guipry, and on 24 Sep 1918, they were transferred to the Artillery Center at Camp Coetquidan, an AEF base about 30 miles west of Rennes, for further training. William remained there until 19 Mar 1919, when he left for the AEF University in Beaune to study civil engineering, his intended career. He left Beaune 19 Apr 1919, when he and other AEF students sailed as a detachment of the 141st FA from Brest to Newport News, VA on the USS *Koningin der Nederlanden*. From there he moved through Camps Morrison and Hill, VA, to Camp Zachary Taylor, Louisville, KY, where he was honorably discharged as a PFC on 19 May 1919.

He returned to Trigg County planning to continue his civil engineering degree, but again events altered his plans. Family members had been ill with flu, and work on the family farm was badly behind schedule. As a result, William decided to stay and help during that season/year. He never left.

On 14 Dec 1927, he married Mary Catherine Thomas, a local girl, and the two began farming their own farm near Gracey, KY on US Highway 68, a career and location that lasted until his death on 22 Nov 1972. He changed careers only once when, during The Depression, he traveled three years as a bridge detective for the state of Kentucky.

William and Catherine had one daughter, Billie Clifford Stewart Strunk, and one grandson, William Stewart Strunk.

JOHN BOB SUMNER

JOHN BOB SUMNER, Private, born 16 Dec 1892, Trigg County. He enlisted 3 Oct 1917 at Cadiz, KY and was stationed at Camp Zachary Taylor, KY and overseas in Germany. He was a member of HQ Troop 3rd Army Corps A and F.

He married Willie Lucille Allen in April 1933 and they were parents of three children: John Douglas Sumner, Helen Joyce Sumner Dixon and Julius Van Sumner. They had 11 grandchildren. John Bob passed away 21 Jul 1964.

ELLIS LAMONT TERRELL

ELLIS LAMONT TERRELL, Private, born 5 Oct 1896 and died on 11 Jan 1955. He is the son of Joe and Mollie Vowell Terrell. He had two brothers, Henry and Lewis Terrell, and one sister, Alma Terrell Cunningham.

He served as a private in the 9th Bn 159 Depot Brigade, WWI and was discharged 18 Nov 1918.

He married Gladys Plimpton and they had one daughter, Frances Earle Terrell Baker. His second marriage was to Lois Taylor and they had three sons: Billy, Joe Lee and Gayle Terrell, and one daughter, Betty Terrell Hancock.

HENRY GARRNET TERRELL

HENRY GARRNET TERRELL, Sergeant, born 1 May 1889, Trigg County, KY. Enlisted 21 Jul 1918, was assigned to Co B CAN Co-1 AM.TM. He was discharged 3 Oct 1918 with 40% disability.

He farmed until the mid-30s then ran a produce business until retirement. He married Ophia Lawrence 2 Feb 1918, no children. Henry passed away 1 Apr 1974 and Ophia 2 Mar 1973.

ALFRED CULLEN THOMAS

ALFRED CULLEN THOMAS, born 27 Dec 1889 in Trigg County, KY. He was drafted into the U.S. Army Infantry Div. at Camp Zachary Taylor, Louisville, KY. After a few months of training he was given a medical discharge.

He returned to Trigg County and married Nellie Stewart on 15 Jun 1918. They were parents of two children, Harvey Dayton (died at age 2) and Nella Evelyn. Thomas Alfred passed away 6 Jan 1977.

CLIFFORD W. THOMAS, Apprentice Seaman, born 26 Oct 1896, Trigg County, the son of Bluford Ira Thomas and Alice Luella Vinson. He enlisted 3 Jun 1918 at Louisville, KY and was discharged 30 Sep 1921. He retired from the U.S. Postal Service in 1970 and passed away 2 May 1975. He never married.

HOWARD R. THOMAS, Seaman 2/c, born 6 Sep 1896 in the Bethel neighborhood of Trigg County, KY, died 18 Dec 1964 and is buried in the Bethel Cemetery. Married 6 Sep 1920 to Ruth Breeding Hulse (b. 6 Feb 1900, d. 21 Jan 1985).

Howard "Honk" Thomas served in the Navy during WWI from 13 Apr 1918 to 1 May 1919. Service was on the following ships: USS *Charleston, William F. Greene,* and *Halcyon II* His overseas service was 25 May 1918 to 9 Jan 1919 and 20 Jan 1919 to 24 Apr 1919. He received a War Service Chevron for having served during the war.

He later worked in the postal service  as a mail carrier and clerk in the Cadiz Post Office for many years and was the postmaster at one time. He ran his mother's farm for many years and during WWII he returned to clerking in the post office and later returned to farming when he purchased the family farm from his sister Mrs. Lloyd Sumner. He and his wife, Miss Ruth, a country school teacher, had two sons who served during WWII, one, Howard Jr., served from 24 Oct 1940 to 31 May 1945 and Robert E. served from 21 Jun 1945 to 5 Jul 1948 and also during the Korean War from 11 Sept 1950 to 25 Sep 1951.

JAMES GARNETT THOMAS, born 9 Dec 1895 in Trigg County, the son of Seldon Trimble and Martha Elizabeth "Bettie" Bridges Thomas. He was inducted in the U.S. Army in February 1918. An article in *The Cadiz Record* of 28 Feb 1918, carried the headline "Fourteen More," with a sub-heading "Of Our Boys Go To Soldiers' Training Camp." Showing the patriotism of the inductees and their families and friends, the next heading reads, "Young men leave in good spirits and large crowd go to station to see them off."

FOURTEEN PATRIOTS: Maynard Williams, Charley Nathan Ezell, Herbert Farmer, James Garnett Thomas, Lee Shelton, John Cothran, Thomas Dudley Ford, Pete Pogue, Benjamin Owen McGee, Robert Elliott Malone, Troy Morrison, Walter Elmer Wood, Thomas Perry Gentry and Dell Freeman.

Garnett first went to Camp Taylor in Kentucky, then, to Camp Sevier, SC. He was sent to France early in July and had not gotten to the front when the war ended. In a letter received by his family on 24 Dec 1918, he stated that the war was over and hoped to get home in the early spring. However, that was not to be.

On 1 Jan 1919, he and others were visiting Ehrenbreitstein, Germany, and while crossing the street was struck by an automobile. His ribs were fractured, puncturing his lungs, and he died in the hospital about 11:00 p.m.

He was buried with military honors in the city of Ehrenbreitstein. His family received many condolences from officers and fellow soldiers. One letter from his commanding officer of Co. E, First Pioneer Infantry, stated "He was known to be a good Christian, honest, trustworthy, strictly obedient and seemed always to take pride in his military duties."

Later his parents returned the body to Trigg County. The body arrived at the parents' home; family and friends accompanied the body to the Oak Grove Baptist Church. The Oak Grove Community prepared a meal at the home of Mr. and Mrs. Mason Hughes. Following the funeral service at the church, the body was moved to the Starkie Thomas graveyard. Full military rites were conducted with the local American Legion Post in charge.

Maynard Williams, who had left Cadiz at the same time in February 1918, and belonged to the same regiment, attended both the funeral and burial in Germany and in Trigg County. They were distant cousins.

He was survived by four brothers: Erwin, Carlisle, Bluford and Cecil Thomas; two sisters, Mrs. James E. (Lola) Rogers and Miss Lou Belle Thomas (Davis). Relatives living in Trigg County today include nephews, Edward Rogers, Rev. Bill Clark Thomas, Seldon Earl Thomas and Ned Davis, and a niece, Beverly Cannon. *Submitted by a niece, Joyce Davis Banister.*

LUTHER THOMAS, PFC, a WWI veteran, was inducted into the Army at Cadiz, KY, 8 Oct 1917. When inducted his address was Route 2, Cadiz, Trigg County, KY.

Luther served in HQ Co. 336 Inf. to 28 Apr 1918, and on 1 Oct 1918 he was promoted to PFC. He was transferred to 17 Sery Co. SC to discharge. During the time he was in service he served at Camp Taylor and later transferred to Fort Thomas until receiving a discharge 23 Jan 1919.

Luther was the son of Tom Thomas, born in 1894. He died 22 Dec 1921, at the home of his sister, Mrs. Floyd Bush. He was married to a Ms. Jones and they had four children. After his death his wife and children returned to Cincinnati, where Mrs. Thomas lived before marriage.

At the time of his death survivors were Mrs. Floyd Bush, Mrs. Will Bush, Mrs. Floyd Noel, Miss Alphia Thomas and Mrs. Turner Hauge. He was survived by one brother, Lewis Thomas. Luther was buried at East End Cemetery in Cadiz, KY.

PERRY AMOS THOMAS, born 10 Oct 1896, son of Walton and Jennie Thomas. He was drafted shortly before WWI ended and is believed to have served less than a year. Perry married Hattie Adams (both are now deceased). They had one child, Jewel, and one grandchild, Tim. *Submitted by Jane Thomas Braboy.*

PERRY S. THOMAS, Private, born 10 Mar 1900 in the Bethel neighborhood of Trigg County, KY. His parents were John Q. and Catherine (Bruff) Thomas. John Q. Thomas was a well known farmer in that area and Catherine (Miss Cattie) was a school teacher in the country schools, Bethel Graded School, being one that she taught. Perry worked on the farm owned by his father and went to school at Bethel, where he finished his schooling. His father John Q. died 8 Apr 1915.

On 9 Apr 1918 Perry, without his mother's permission, left home and joined the Army. He was sent to New York. When Miss Cattie found out where he was stationed she persuaded her brother-in-law, George Prentice Thomas, who was a prominent Cadiz lawyer, to go to New York and bring her wayward son home. His service was from 9 Apr 1918 to 16 Jan 1919 as a private. During this time he had been sent to France and was in Battery F, 73rd Artillery Regt., CAC, American EF, France.

The story from Uncle "Billy" Thomas on how Perry rejoined the Army is Howell M. "Uncle Billy" Thomas, at the time about 13 years old, and Perry Thomas were hoeing tobacco on a 10 acre tract of land for their mother above the Little River in June 1919 and Perry all at once threw down his hoe and told Billy "If you'll hitch up the team to the buggy and take me to town (Cadiz) I'll go see my girl in Louisville." This Billy did and that was the last that any of the family saw Perry Thomas.

It was learned that he joined the Army again and this time sent to Hawaii He re-entered service on 17 Jun 1919 at Ft. Thomas, KY and served as a private in Co. A, 3rd Engineers and was honorably discharged on 18 Aug 1922 in Letterman General Hospital, San Francisco, CA. He married a Jessie M. Ware on 21 Feb 1923 in San Francisco and died 30 Jul 1923 in Veterans Administration Hospital No. 4, San Mateo, CA of General Paralysis, Cerebal Type. He is buried in the cemetery at Bethel Church near his parents home.

R. PEYTON "PATE" THOMAS, Private, born 12 Nov 1889 in the Donaldson Creek Valley of Trigg County, KY, the son of Robert H. and Lillie Belle Thomas. On 15 Apr 1918 he was inducted as a private in the U.S. Army at Cadiz, KY, for service in WWI. He was 29 years old at the time.

He received basic training at Fort Benjamin Harrison, IN, and later was assigned to duty in the Ordnance Depot at Camp Hancock, GA. In September 1918, his company was shipped overseas, and landed in Brest, France, 11 Sep 1918 as part of the American Expeditionary Forces (AEF) under the overall command of Gen. John J. Pershing. He served in the repair shop of the Ordnance

Department near Verdun, France, through to the Armistice 11 Nov 1918. He returned to the States and was honorably discharged 29 Jul 1919.

On 23 Aug 1919, he married Birdie Lee Gordon, daughter of Jack and Olia Porter Gordon. He set up a woodworking and cabinet shop and eventually established a successful business. He pursued this line of work until ill health forced him to retire in the late 1950s. He had a great sense of humor and enjoyed repeating tales of his Army life in France. He also loved to fish and hunt, and was an individual who enjoyed a very independent life.

He and his wife had one child, Lonnie Jackson "Jack" Thomas, who married Martha Evelyn Sumner; one grandchild, Kimberley Denise, who married Raybon Crump Jr., and one great-grandchild, Brittney Nicole.

Peyton died 28 Apr 1961 adjacent to the place where he was born 71 years before, and his wife died 12 Jul 1992 at age 90, outliving him by 31 years. They are buried in the cemetery named for Peyton Thomas, his maternal grandfather.

FELIX C. WADLINGTON, Seaman 2/c, born 11 Nov 1894 in Trigg County, KY, the son of Ben C. Wadlington and Mattie Cooper Wadlington.

He rode a train from Hopkinsville to Louisville where he was inducted into the U.S. Navy 28 Feb 1918 for the duration of the war. He was stationed in Boston, MA during WWI and was discharged 23 Jul 1919 with the rank of S2/c, with very good conduct rating.

Felix married Ruby Mitchell and they had eight children. He was a farmer in Trigg County until his death in 1956.

CALVERT WALLACE, Sergeant, born in the Cumberland Community of the Land Between the Rivers on 22 May 1877, the son of Green T. and Mary Hooks Wallace.

As a young man he taught school at several schools in Trigg County. In 1913 he was appointed as County Superintendent of Trigg County Schools. At the end of his term, he went to Frankfort, KY and was employed by the State Department of Education.

In January 1918, he volunteered for service in the Army, but being above the draft age he was not accepted. The people at the induction center gave him information of the National War Work Council of which the International Committee of Young Men's Christian Association was affiliated.

On 22 May 1918, he joined this association and was immediately sent to Paris, France. He was assigned to units in France until after 11 Nov 1918. His unit worked with soldiers who were sick, wounded, gassed or needed assistance getting communication with family in the United States. They provided support to those who were in need of their services. He mentioned the battle of Chateau-Thierry where many soldiers were lost there.

The last American troops separated from Germany in 1923. Some of these soldiers were transferred to London, England to await passage back to the states. Wallace was sent to England to work with the troops there. His work was finished in 1925 and he returned to the United States.

In 1927 he married Carrie Lee Lane of the Ferguson Springs Community of the Land Between the Rivers. They were parents of four children: Calvert C. Wallace, Betty Wallace Cassity, Hugh Ann Wallace and Rebecca Wallace.

In later years, Calvert Wallace worked in the area of Adult Education for the State of Kentucky.

Wallace died in 1956 at Golden Pond, KY and is buried at Hematite Cemetery in the Land Between the Rivers.

ALLEN GRADY WALLIS, born 28 Nov 1889 in Lyon County, son of Irvin J. and Isabelle Wallis. The parents and seven children moved into the Rockcastle Community in Trigg County before 1900. Allen Grady attended school in Rockcastle, finishing 8th grade. He worked on family farm several years and then attended State Normal School in Bowling Green, did his high school work and graduated from college majoring in commercial subjects.

He was drafted into the Army in WWI and spent time in States. He was in the cavalry division.

After the war was over he married Sarah Katherine Leneave, daughter of Dillard

and Metoka Leneave, on 9 Nov 1920. They moved to Gastonia, NC where he taught school. They were active members of 1st Baptist Church in Gastonia where he was deacon and church secretary. He died at age 58 with heart failure.

Trigg County survivors are a niece, Frances Cunningham, and nephew, Carl Gray.

HENRY STANLEY WHITE SR., First Lieutenant, born 18 Nov 1889 in Cadiz, KY. A member of the Officers Reserve Corps of the U.S. Army, he entered active duty on the 15 Aug 1917 as a second lieutenant in the Infantry. He was a member of the 4th Company of the 9th Division Training Regiment at Ft. Benjamin Harrison. He was later assigned to the 159th Brigade, Camp Zachary Taylor at Louisville, KY. On 11 July he was promoted to first lieutenant and assigned to the 18th Battalion, a training battalion.

He was discharged at the end of the war, returned to Cadiz and went into the tobacco business with his father, W.C. White. In 1932 he leased the Cadiz Milling

Co., a flour mill, from the Ky-Tenn. Light and Power Co. and began expanding its operation to serve western Kentucky and west Tennessee with flour brand names of "Sunbeam," "Premo" and others, also manufacturing corn meal and wholesaling coffee. He bought the mill in 1943. The Cadiz Mill at one time had 22 employees including salesmen in Cadiz, KY and Nashville and Paris, TN, shipping its products by truck to six counties in Kentucky and three counties in Tennessee, and rail carloads to bakeries in Nashville.

In 1922 he married Gladys Hosler of Ordway, CO. He died 14 Feb 1964 and is buried in Cadiz. He is survived by three daughters and a son: Mrs. Jean Montgomery of St. Louis; Mrs. Mary Jobe of Corsicana, TX; Mrs. Carol Gray of Panama City, FL; and H. Stanley White Jr. of Cadiz, KY, a WWII Navy veteran.

JOHN F. WHITE, Private, born 13 Dec 1898, was inducted into the Army at Cadiz, KY on 2 Oct 1918. He served in the Students Army Tng. C. of Washington and Lee University, Lexington, VA. He served there as a private until his honorable discharge 11 Dec 1919.

Civilian occupation was merchant. He married Ellen Hopson and they had two children, Ben Terry White II and John Frances White (daughter), and three grandchildren: Terry Gilchrist White, Ellen Payne Wright and Virginia Faxon Payne. John White is deceased.

MAYNARD WILLIAMS, Corporal, born 20 May 1895 in Trigg County in Williams Hollow located between Linton and Boyd's Hill Church Community. His parents were Bob and Lucy Adams Williams. He attended Graham School and was an avid baseball player and was renown for his softball pitching ability.

He entered the U.S. Army on 25 Feb 1918 and served in France from July 1918 until his discharge in July 1919. He served in the Co. E 1st Pioneer Inf., fighting against the Germans. Upon his discharge he had been promoted to corporal.

Another Trigg countian and good friend, James Garnett Thomas, left Cadiz at the same time as Maynard and they belonged to the same regiment. James was killed while over there and Maynard attended both the funeral and burial in Germany and when the body was later returned to Trigg County, he attended the service for his fellow comrade as a civilian.

Maynard married Kitty Dorothy Mize on 10 Nov 1919 and they named their first son Garnett in memory of his friend. He was the father of seven children: Geneva and Norma Jean died in infancy, Garnett, Eulala (Sumner), Maxine (Ford), Carl and Glenda (Hancock). He also had 17 grandchildren.

Maynard was a farmer and school bus driver for the Trigg County School System. He left Williams Hollow in the early 1950s and purchased a home on U.S. 68 across from Sam Downs Road. He died in May 1975 and is buried at the Fuller Cemetery.

HENRY H. WILLS, Corporal, was inducted into the U.S. Army in 1916. He received his basic training at Camp Taylor, KY and from there was shipped to France. He was a military policeman and discharged in the last part of 1918 with the rank of corporal.

He married the former Alice Burks and they had four children: Richard Lane Wills, Eunice Wills Francis, Ora Wills Burke, Charles Wesley Wills and an adopted son, Charles Thomas Wills.

Both of his natural sons were serving their country at the same time. Hill Wills died 4 Oct 1967 and is buried in the Joiner's Chapel Cemetery.

ROBERT ESTILL WILSON, Sergeant, spent most of his life in the Cerulean Springs area of Trigg County. He was born 10 Apr 1889 in

Morrison, Warren County, TN. The Wilson family came to Kentucky in 1895 and resided in the Morganfield area. In 1915 he moved to Cerulean Springs and was employed by the Illinois Central Railroad as Section Foreman. The workmen called him "Captain" or "Mr. Bob."

He was drafted into the U.S. Army on 2 Oct 1917 and was stationed at Camp Taylor, Louisville, KY, in the Quartermaster Corps. He had the rank of sergeant when he was discharged on 12 Apr 1919.

He returned to work with the railroad in Cerulean and worked for them more than 40 years. He married Verdya Marie Shanks on 5 Jul 1919 and they were parents of three children: Leo Yeateman Wilson, Agnes Wilson Hillyard and Wilburn Martin "Willie" Wilson of Cadiz. "Mr. Bob" was very proud of his children as they served in the military. Leo served in the Navy in WWII and Korean War; Wilburn served in the Navy during the 1950s; and Agnes was in the Army Nurses Corps.

Robert E. Wilson passed away 12 Nov 1973 and is buried in the cemetery at New Harmony Baptist Church, Wheatcroft, KY. His grave is marked with a brass plate issued by the Veterans Administration. *Submitted by Leo Y. Wilson.*

BYRON AUBREY "NICK" WOODRUFF, born 9 Mar 1890 in Christian County, the son of Willis Byron Woodruff and Natha Etta Lafoon Woodruff.

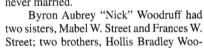

He enlisted in the U.S. Army at Ft. Thomas, KY, 17 Jun 1917 and served at MD Infirmary, 46 Inf. He did not serve overseas and received an honorable discharge on 28 Nov 1918. Following his discharge he returned to Cadiz and was manager of his father's retail lumber yard in Cadiz. He never married.

Byron Aubrey "Nick" Woodruff had two sisters, Mabel W. Street and Frances W. Street; two brothers, Hollis Bradley Woodruff and John Grant Woodruff. John Grant also served in WWI.

JOHN GRANT WOODRUFF, 2nd Lieutenant, born 9 Mar 1898, Cadiz, KY, son of Willis Byron Woodruff and Natha Etta Lafoon Woodruff.

In the spring of 1918 he enlisted in the U.S Army at Camp Grant, IL, and was appointed 2nd lieutenant Infantry 17 Sep 1918, Fr. CL; assigned Stud A Thg Sch to honorable discharge on 2 Jan 1919. He did not serve overseas.

John had two brothers, Byron Aubrey "Nick" Woodruff, who served in WWI and discharged 28 Nov 1918, and Hollis Bradley Woodruff; two sisters, Mabel W. Street and Frances W. Street.

He spent his boyhood in Cadiz and in 1916 completed his secondary school education. During his college years he remained in the region, first at the University of Kentucky in Lexington, then at Vanderbilt University in Nashville where he earned a BS degree in chemistry. His teaching began as a high school principal in Hardinsburg, KY (1920-21) and next in Vermilion, IL (1921-22).

His interest in geology had been kindled in Kentucky and John spent a year in graduate study in geology first at the University of Chicago, then at Syracuse University in New York. In 1929 he became an instructor in geology at Colgate University in Hamilton, NY. After a few years, he resumed graduate work in geology and earned a doctorate from the University of Michigan in 1936 and returned to Colgate to teach.

He married Laura Hodgson of Homer, NY in 1935 and they reared two sons, Robert D. of Hamilton, NY and James N. of Washington, DC.

In 1966 he retired after 37 years as a professor of geology at Colgate. Dr. Woodruff died in Leesburg, FL 20 Jan 1971. He was returned to Hamilton, NY for burial on a quiet wooded hill in the Colgate University Cemetery.

WILLIAM THOMAS FREEMAN, Sergeant, enlisted in the U.S. Army at the age of 15-1/2 years on 26 Dec 1925. He served two continuous enlistments in the Territory of Hawaii. He served as corporal from 10 Mar 1930, as sergeant from 27 Jun 1931 to 4 Apr 1933. He saw no combat. He was discharged both enlistment's with character "Excellent."

At an earlier age he enlisted into the USN and was sent home as underage. However in 1925 he was accepted.

"Thomas," my daddy, was born 6 Feb 1910 in Cadiz, KY. He was the son of John Lindsay Freeman and Sara Florence (Allen) Boyd. Thomas had one brother Robert David "Robie" Freeman (b. 1908, d. 1969). Thomas became an orphan at the age of 7. He also had three half brothers and two half sisters: John and Clarence G. Boyd, Hattie (Boyd) Weller, Lucy Lu (Freeman) Ladd and Sam Wilford Freeman.

Thomas made his home mainly with his uncle and aunt, Wm. O. and Minnie Freeman of Cadiz. At an early age he joined the Cadiz Baptist Church. She taught my daddy the values and manners of a gentleman.

Thomas married Hazel Lurline Faughn of the Bethesda Community of Trigg County and the daughter of Ben and Annie Faughn on 15 Sep 1935. Hazel and Thomas began their early married life in a small house on the outskirts of Cadiz located on the property of Garland Cunningham who operated the Gulf Oil Co. where Thomas worked. In 1937 their only child Betty Jane was born. They moved to Evansville in 1940.

His half brother Sam W. Freeman served in the USN during WWI and was a native of Trigg County. His grandfather, David Freeman, a resident of Trigg County after the Civil War, served with the Union Army. Daddy was a peace-time soldier who was there to do his part for his country.

He was a welder at International Steel Co. of Evansville, IN until his death of a sudden heart attack 5 May 1963. He also was a member of the First Christian Church. His greatest joy was to schedule his vacation

to be able to return "home" to hunt and fish with his family and friends in Trigg County.

He and my mother are buried at the Oak Hill Cemetery Evansville, IN. She dying 28 May 1970. *Submitted by his daughter Betty.*

CORBIT FOX, born in Trigg County on 15 Mar 1910, the son of Edd and Ada Merrick Fox. He joined the Army on 16 Jul 1927 and was sent to help guard the Panama Canal as a member of the U.S. Army Coast Guard Artillery and was discharged 15 Jul 1930.

He married Ethel Snyder of Trigg County on 11 Feb 1931. Corbit found himself with a wife and child on the way and no work as it was during the Depression. He left his wife at his father's home and traveled looking for work. His travels led him to Danville, IL where he was hired to work in the laundry at the Old Soldiers Home (now the VA) since he was a veteran. He sent for his wife to join him in Danville. He earned $12 every three days on the WPA job. He began working at Saint Elizabeth Hospital the other three days to help pay a bill for his son's broken leg. The hospital soon offered him a job six days a week for $12 plus hospital benefits. He worked there for twelve years and had six sons. With his growing family he left the hospital and went to work for General Motors, where he made in one hour what he made in one day at the hospital. He worked at General Motors for 23 years and then retired.

Corbit and Ethel recently celebrated their 70th wedding anniversary. They haven't forgotten their Trigg County roots and travel back to Kentucky to attend the Merrick Family Reunion when possible. They currently live in Rossville, IL.

HERBERT JONES, Corporal, born 5 Jun 1905, the son of Gus and Sophia Hendon Jones. He joined the Army in 1927. He served in the Territory of Hawaii as a corporal under Capt. Edgar H. Underwood. In December 1927, Cpl. Jones was with Btry. B, 15th Coast Artillery at Fort Kamekameha, HI. After discharge he returned to Kentucky.

Herbert used his military experience and training as he worked in civilian life for the Corps of Engineers as a lock operator or lockman. He worked as a lockman at Lock E on the Cumberland River. After retirement from the Corps of Engineers, he worked as a carpenter.

Herbert married Eula Irvin 27 Dec 1929 and they had a son Leslie Jones, four grandchildren, nine great-grandchildren and three gg-grandchildren.

Trigg Memory Acres (located at an exit off the 68 bypass) in Cadiz, KY, is where Herbert Jones is buried with his wife Eula Irvin Jones.

World War II

AUDREY LACY ADAMS, Seaman 1/c, born in Cadiz, KY, 14 Feb 1926, the son of Jagoe Adams and Lois Barnes Adams. He enlisted into the USN 30 May 1944, was assigned to Great Lakes, IL for basic training, then to Norfolk, VA. From Norfolk he left for New Orleans, LA, and to the LST 783. They sailed to the Hawaiian Islands, then to the Far Eastern Theater of War, where he served in the Philippine Islands and participated in the Philippine Islands Liberation. He also went to Okinawa.

Lacy received an honorable discharge at the USN PerSepCen, Unit 4, Great Lakes, IL, 17 Jun 1946, with the rank of seaman first class. His awards and medals received were Philippine Liberation Ribbon w/star, WWII Victory Ribbon, American Area Ribbon, Asiatic-Pacific Ribbon w/2 stars.

His memorable experience was when land mines exploded and knocked a hole in the ship.

Returning to civilian life, Lacy participated in many activities. He enjoyed boxing, swimming and baseball. His work was with the Whirlpool Corporation of Evansville, IN until his retirement 15 May 1976.

In June 1949 Lacy married Joan Fox and they had four children: Glenda Adams Boaz, Reba Adams Miller, Pamela "Pam" Adams Ingram and Michael "Mike" Adams. There are eight grandchildren: Jennifer, Shanna, Dusty, Gentry, Jon, Michael, Ashley, Terrance and Kyle. The four great-grandchildren are Kelsie, John-David, Warren and Lori.

Lacy enjoys his hobbies of fishing and gardening at his home in Wallonia, KY. *Submitted by Audrey Lacy Adams and Glenda Adams Boaz.*

BILLY RAY ADAMS, Corporal, born 5 Oct 1926. He enlisted 10 Nov 1943 at Louisville, KY and served as mortar crewman in the Asiatic-Pacific area. From 23 Sep 1945 to 13 Jul 1946 he participated in occupation of Japan. Cpl. Adams received an honorable discharge 18 Jul 1946.

Bill Ray and Christine Skinner were married 25 Feb 1947 and reared two children, Jerry Ray Adams (deceased) and Janet Adams Stone. Grandchildren are Amber Adams, Nicholas Adams and Adam Stone. Billy Ray retired from Wasco Inc. 7 Dec 1991 and passed away 8 Mar 1994.

CHARLES C. ADAMS, PFC, born 2 Jul 1920 in Trigg County and completed the 8th grade at Bethesda, a one-room school north of Cadiz. He dropped out of school and began farming and logging with his father until joining the Army in November 1942.

Pfc. Adams did his basic training at Fort Sill, OK as an artillery crewman. He attended Antiaircraft School at Seattle, WA then returned to Camp Phillips, KS for infantry training. He was assigned to the 106th Inf. Div. and moved to Boston, MA, where the unit loaded on ships headed for Liverpool, England in August 1944.

They crossed the English Channel, landed in Calais, France, moved by truck convoy toward Belgium and went into combat in October 1944. He was captured by the Germans during the Battle of the Bulge on 17 December. He along with several other hundred POWs were loaded in boxcars, then housed in 3-story building that became an Allied bombing target. He was on the third floor when the bomb hit the center of the building and collapsed. He came to in the basement covered up with bricks, but alive. He was then marched to Stalag 12A for another 100 days of captivity. Charles' weight dropped from 150 to 80 and many POWs starved to death. On Easter Eve 1945 an American tank smashed the fences and freed the prisoners.

Charles returned home for 30 days before boarding a train for Miami, FL, where he and other Ex-POWs received the best R&R possible. Before returning to active duty the war ended and he was honorable discharged 1 Nov 1945. He received the POW Medal and Purple Heart.

Charles moved to Louisville and worked several years before returning to Cadiz and working for TVA. He retired from the city of Cadiz in 1962. He married Louina Noel in 1952 and had two children, Bonnie Thomas of Cadiz and Rita Burcham of Hopkinsville. Charles Adams passed away 21 Apr 1997.

FRANK WALDEN ADAMS, PFC, born 27 Oct 1926 near Adams Mill, the son of Ben F. and Nell Robertson Adams. He was inducted into the military at Camp Atterbury, IN, 23 Jan 1945. He received his basic training at Fort McClellan, AL, followed by Camp Rucker, AL; Fort Meade, MD; Camp Ord, CA; Camp Anzia, CA; then to Long Beach, CA, where he boarded the USS *Sumter* for overseas.

Assigned to 5th Repl. Dep. at Manila 19 Aug 1945. The war was over but there were still skirmishes with renegade Japanese. After a brief stay in the Philippines with Co. B, 3rd Engrs., 24th Inf. Div., where he was detailed to guard Japanese prisoners at Davoa City, he was transferred to Japan 26 Oct 1945 where he stayed as a crane operator until his return to the States.

Pfc. Adams was discharged at Fort Sheridan, IL 24 Nov 1946. His medals include the Victory Medal (Japan), Asiatic-Pacific Theater Ribbon w/battlestar, Good Conduct Medal, Army of Occupation Medal and Expert Rifle Medal.

He returned to Trigg County where he continued to farm. He married Dorthy Nell Carraway, daughter of Lee and Lula Miller Carraway, on 28 Jun 1974. After the 52 drought, he accepted a job with Del Monte Foods. He continues to live at his ancestral home that has been in the family for many generations.

JIMMIE ADAMS, on 29 Jan 1945, the largest group, at that time, of Trigg County men (167) left Cadiz for Louisville to take the pre-induction Selective Service examination. James Elliott "Jimmie" Adams was among that group. Following the exam, Jimmie was drafted into the US Army on 19 Nov 1945.

Jimmie spent three months in basic training at Fort Belvoir, VA. While there, he attended the Topo Drafting School, then traveled to California and shipped out to Luzon Island in the Philippines. There he was assigned to the 29th Topo Battalion, 1st Platoon, 2nd Squad.

Drafting maps from aerial photographs was among the duties assigned to Jimmie in the Philippines. He was also unofficially put in charge of a coffee house. Several soldiers were interested in having a coffee shop at their base. Jimmie volunteered to build the shop and run it. He constructed a small bar area where the men could relax and drink their coffee.

In March 1947, Jimmie was discharged from the military. On his return to California, Jimmie spent a few days visiting with his uncle, Ellis Adams, and his family. While he enjoyed the opportunity to see California and his family, he was ready to return to Kentucky.

The son of Maurice and Georgia Cook Adams, Jimmie was born 25 Sep 1926, in Trigg County. He has spent all his life here with the exception of his military travels. He is married to Opal Vanzant Adams. They have two children, James Adams Jr. and Debbie Killebrew. They also have three grandchildren: Sarah Adams, James Adams III and J.P. Proffitt. Jimmie has spent most of his adult life in the construction business, primarily building and remodeling farm buildings. His family often jokes that he got his training in the military with the coffee house project. Jimmie continues to work part time in construction. He also owns over 500 acres of farmland in Trigg County where he raises cattle and tobacco with his son. In his spare time, Jimmie enjoys fishing in the ponds on his farm.

PAUL J. ADAMS, born 23 Nov 1913 to Fanny and Maxie Adams. He attended the old Hanberry School. A school photo shows him in overalls, with an uncharacteristically serious expression. He was known for his impish sense of humor, often teasing with his brothers and other family members - even as a grown-up.

After leaving Trigg County, he worked for a road construction company in Louisville. He operated a spreader box, which filtered small rocks and gravel through a screen to smooth the surface for laying asphalt and concrete.

He was 28 when he entered the US Army on 23 Aug 1942. His three brothers: James, Charles and Billy Ray, also served during WWII.

Three months later, Paul was in training at the Army Air Base in Birmingham, AL. Despite being on KP and awaiting dental work, he wrote his sister Edna an upbeat letter.

"I have me a red-headed girl in town and she is really good looking," he wrote in pencil, signing "Paul" with a flourish.

He became a military photo technician, developing aerial reconnaissance photographs. He served 22 months in the Pacific Theater, notably in India, with the 7th Photo Technical Squadron.

Paul worked with cameras. Celebrities and cameras have a way of finding each other. In the Army, Paul met entertainers Gene Autry and Bob Hope.

Paul rose to the rank of staff sergeant. According to family lore, Paul was at home in Cadiz, at his ease, and lost a stripe for failing to salute an officer. He was discharged 17 Jan 1946 at Fort Knox.

After the war, he returned to Cadiz and worked as a construction laborer.

The fate of the red-haired woman in Alabama is not known; as for Paul, he was a lifelong bachelor.

He worked to smooth the road for others, but his own road was not so smooth. He was in ill health many years and spent the last part of his life in a nursing home. He died in the spring of 1987, at age 73. *Written by his nephew, C. Ray Hall.*

THOMAS ODELL ADAMS, born 23 Oct 1906, son of John and Adline Williams Adams. He was a member of the Ohio National Guard 37th Div., 145th Inf. Regt. and mustered into service in October 1940 with maneuvers in Louisiana, Texas and Mississippi, then trained in the jungles of the Fiji Islands.

He saw action on the Solomon Islands, Bougainville, New Georgia, Guadalcanal, Fiji and New Zealand in the South Pacific. Because of their exceptional fighting ability the regiment was nicknamed the Barracuda Regiment.

In July 1943 on New Georgia, they took part in a three month battle. They landed on Japanese occupied territory at Rice, anchorage under a canopy of shells and were bombed for 23 days and nights in succession before claiming victory.

In April 1944 he was in the battle at Empress Augusta Bay Bougainville where an estimated 8,000 out of 12-15,000 Japanese were killed. For each American soldier killed, the Japanese lost 30. Thomas was wounded by shrapnel and released from the service in 1945. He carried pieces of shrapnel in his body for the remainder of his life.

Decorations include Purple Heart, Bronze Star, Asiatic-Pacific Theater Ribbon, Combat Infantry Badge, four Overseas Bars, Rifle Marksman Badge and Good Conduct Medal.

Thomas died in Trigg County and is buried at Lawrence Cemetery. He had one daughter Barbara and four grandchildren: Alice, Mike, Connie and Chris. *Submitted by Jane Thomas Braboy, Barbara Hale and June Adams.*

CONLEY HALE AHART, born 26 Mar 1928 in Trigg County, KY, the youngest of four brothers to serve during WWII. He was drafted 10 May 1946 into the US Army and took basic training at Fort Bliss, TX, then on to paratrooper training at Fort Benning, GA. He was then assigned to the 82nd Abn. at Fort Bragg, NC. The first five times he went up in airplane, he jumped out.

In March 1947 he met a Trigg County girl, Dixie Irene Stallons, and after his discharge they were married in Hopkinsville 24 Dec 1947. They made their home in Peoria, IL where both were employed by Caterpillar Tractor Co. until 1950 when the 403rd Engrs. Reserve (which Conley had joined) was activated for two years.

He was sent to Fort Leonard Wood, MO for training. While there Conley was awarded the Expert Medal for Marksmanship by Col. Tom Logan. Dixie quit her job at Cat and went along. They bought a new mobile home and lived on the post at Fort Leonard Wood until September 1951 when the 403rd was sent to Germany. Dixie returned to Kentucky where daughter Linda Louise was born 16 Dec 1951 at Fort Campbell. Conley served in Germany eight months and was discharged at Camp Breckinridge, KY in May 1952. He first saw his daughter when she was 5 months old. He served as driver of staff car for officers of the 403rd while in Germany so got to see a lot of the countryside and also the ruins left from WWII. Once he got to ski in the Alps on a trip to Garmish, Germany.

After his discharge he worked at several jobs in Kentucky, took GI Bill training for meat cutter with Maurice Thurman as his teacher at the new Master Market east of Cadiz in 1952-53. He also drove a Bunny Bread truck in Paducah, KY before returning to Peoria in 1955. Dixie returned to Cat Tractor Co. and worked 32 years before retiring. Conley opened his own meat market and retired in 1985 to the 50 acres and new home they had built five years earlier where the Canadian geese and wild deer are a daily sight.

Daughter Linda and her husband and two children, David and Diana, moved to Texas in Fall of 1983, but both grandkids spent their entire summers from 1985-92 at their grandparents home, who took them home in time for school.

Life's journey has many bends in the road and we've had our joys as well as sorrows, but we have been truly blessed and hope to live out our days in peace and, God willing, good health. Conley had his workshop and John Deere tractor and never enough time to do all he'd like to do. Dixie has her flowers and loves to cook.

Through the years many trips have been made back to Kentucky to visit loved ones and friends. Barkley Lodge always a must place to eat. Many of our loved ones now gone, but the dearest memories will always be there to greet our future trips to Trigg County.

ELDON REED AHART, PFC, born 7 Apr 1925 in Golden Pond, KY. He enlisted 26 Aug 1943 with assignments at Fort Benjamin Harrison, IN; Camp Van Dorn, MS; Camp Breckinridge, KY and overseas in England and France.

Pfc. Ahart was wounded 12 Jul 1944, returned to duty on 14 Aug 1944 and killed 30 Sep 1944 in Luxembourg. He is buried in Andilly, France and was later returned to East End Cemetery in Cadiz, KY for final burial.

Awards include the Silver Star on 10 Jul 1944, Gold Star on 15 Dec 1944 and Purple Heart in November 1944. He was survived by his mother, Myrtle Jones Ahart-Carr; step-father L.A. Carr; brothers, Henry and Jean; and half-brothers: Earl, Cecil and Jimmie Carr.

HENRY EDMOND AHART, PFC, born 24 Dec 1922 in Golden Pond, KY. He enlisted 24 Feb 1943 with assignments at Camp Swift, TX; Camp Livingston, LA; Fort Leonard Wood, MO and Fort Mead, MD.

Overseas assignment in the European-African-Middle-Eastern Theater of War, Italy, Rome Arno and Northern Apennines Campaigns. He was wounded in England in July 1944; seriously wounded in Italy on 21 Oct 1944 and transferred to Halloran General Hospital in New York. He spent almost two years in various military hospitals until he was discharged on 5 Feb 1947.

PFC Ahart was discharged as a 100% disabled veteran. Because of the seriousness of his injuries, he was given a new car by the Veterans Administration upon his discharge from the hospital.

Medals include the EAME Theater Ribbon w/2 Bronze Service Stars, Combat Infantry Badge, Purple Heart, American Theater Ribbon and WWII Victory Medal.

Married Gladys Hall whom he met at the military hospital. They have two children, David Ahart and Dianne Ahart Null, and four grandchildren: Candace and Michael Ahart and Avril and Bryce Null.

Henry died 27 Sep 1991 at age 68. He suffered through numerous illnesses relating to his battle injuries. He was buried by his brother Eldon Reed Ahart in East End Cemetery in Cadiz, KY.

He was survived by his son and daughter; mother Myrtle Carr; brother Jean; halfbrothers, Earl, Cecil and Jimmie Carr; and a sister June Hensley. Henry was a member of the American Legion Post 74, DAV and Bethesda United Methodist Church.

T. JEAN AHART, Chief Engineer, born 25 Jun 1930 in Golden Pond, KY. He joined the Merchant Marines at age 17 and through self-study and training offered in service, he reached the rank of chief engineer.

Jean served as chief engineer on first ships that carried ammunition to Vietnam. He was on a ship that was hauling ammunition in 1966 and was struck by another while in Tokyo Bay and was very close to blowing up. He served on ships that broke the ice in order to lay the Alaska oil pipe line and served as engineer on several cruise line ships. He served as chief engineer on the world's largest ship, the SS *Manhattan*. This ship

made stops all over the world. He was drafted in the Army in 1955 and served until 1962.

In civilian life Jean served as consultant to shipping lines in the Mobile, AL area and retired from this job in 1995.

He married Eloise Mayo in 1983. Children: Allen Ahart, Hugh Ahart, Holly Ahart Lowery; stepchildren: Don Reilly, Randy Mosley, Charles Yeomans; grandchildren: Sasha Ahart, Hayden Ahart, Noah Lowery; and step-grandchild MacKenzie Yeomans

His hobbies are gardening and fishing. He is a brother to Eldon Reed Ahart and Henry E. Ahart.

JOHN "JOHNNIE" MCKINLEY AHART, born 26 Jan 1926 in Golden Pond, the son of William M. and Myrtle Ahart. He was drafted into the Army 26 Mar 1944 at Fort Benjamin Harrison, IN.

After 16 weeks of basic training at Camp Wolters, TX, he was assigned to the 100th Inf. Div. at Fort Bragg, NC. The 100th landed in Southern France in October 1944. The division became a part of the 7th Army and fought through Southern France, across the Vosges Mountains and after fierce fighting at the Maginot and Seigfried lines entered Germany and fought across the southern part of that country.

John was in a town named Geislingen when Germany surrendered. His division was preparing to go to the Pacific Theater when the Atom bomb was dropped on Japan resulting in that nation's surrender. The order for the 100th was canceled and the division was deactivated. Those who had insufficient points to return home were assigned to other occupational units in Germany. John was assigned to the 553rd Military Police Escort Guard Company and got to do a lot of traveling all over Europe.

John was discharged 29 May 1946. He married Gladys Murl Noel of Cadiz and they moved to Peoria, IL. John was a member of the 403rd Engineer Base Depot Reserve Unit which was activated during the Korean War and sent to Germany. John was finally discharged 13 Nov 1952.

John's awards were EAME Theater Ribbon w/2 Bronze Stars, Good Conduct Medal, WWII Victory Medal, Army of Occupation Medal for Germany w/OLC and the Combat Infantry Badge.

John and Murl had three children: Lavana Fay, Johnnie Steven and Beverly Selene. They have five grandchildren and two great-grandchildren.

John entered the Gospel Ministry and pastored seven churches before retiring in 1998. He is currently serving the Hurricane Baptist Church in Trigg County as Interim-Pastor. He has earned a bachelor of arts, a bachelor of theology and master of ministry degrees He also earned a degree in electronics.

John and Murl have been on two missions trips: one to Brazil and one to Russia. They have also been to Israel to study at the Jerusalem University.

MATTHEW DELLWOOD AHART, PFC, born 26 Feb 1918 in Trigg County. He was the oldest child of three children of Margary Pruitt Ahart and Ralph Ahart. He had a sister Juanita and a brother Edison.

Matthew was a farmer who voluntarily enlisted in the US Army 12 Sep 1941. While in the service he was not involved in combat. He served in the military police and received the Marksman Rifle Badge, American Theater Medal, Good Conduct Medal and WWII Victory Medal.

Pfc. Ahart was stationed for most of his service time in the Aleutian Islands. He received an honorable discharge 10 Dec 1945 at the Separation Center in Camp Fannin, TX.

He moved back to Trigg County and went to work at Fort Campbell, KY for the next 37 years. During those years he worked in the medical supply unit at the hospital and for the transportation department. He retired in August 1966 due to health problems.

Married the former Eunice E. Noel (who lived at Canton, KY) and they were parents of two sons, Don and Rick, who live in Hopkinsville. There are four grandchildren and three great-grandchildren. Matthew passed away 27 May 1983.

WILLIAM EDSEL AHART, Fireman 1/c, born 20 May 1927, Golden Pond, Trigg County, KY. He enlisted in the USN 1 Aug 1944 at Paducah, KY and served as fireman 1/c at NAS NORVA; USS *Barber* (APD-47); USS *Loy* (APD-56).

Received an honorable discharge 4 Jun 1946, honorable discharge button, USNR honorable discharge button and honorable service lapel button.

Civilian employment was as taxi driver and construction supervisor. He married first Adeline Holland and had one son William Edsel Ahart Jr. (deceased). Married second Doris and had five stepchildren: Jim, Robert and Richard Dovicsak; Debi Cunningham and Doris "Sam" Taylor; and 10 step-grandchildren. William passed away 26 Jun 1993.

BURTON R. ALDRIDGE SR., 2nd Lieutenant, born 26 Jan 1908, the son of Clarence and Myrtle Aldridge. He entered the US Army on 14 Jul 1942 with basic training at Fort Benning, GA and attended Infantry Officer Candidate School. Attained the rank of 2nd lieutenant and received a medical discharge in 1943.

Burton was county attorney in Trigg County for 24 years. He married Eldora Chamberlian and they had two children, Burton Jr. and Portia Aldridge Ezell, and two grandchildren, Stacy Lynn Ezell and William Burton Ezell.

THOMAS CHAPPELL ALDRIDGE, Major, born 24 Jun 1922 in Trigg County. He graduated from Trigg County High in 1940, went on Western State University where he joined ROTC. He and the other members of the "Pershing Rifles" at Western enlisted in the Army. After training and being commissioned 2nd lieutenant, he was section leader in Co. H, 2nd Bn., Rainbow Division-Infantry.

Dispatched to Europe in November 1944, with "Task Force Linden," the divisions fought across Germany and into Austria until the unconditional surrender of the Germans on 7 May 1945. Lt. Aldridge had two Bronze Stars from the European conflict and other medals including service in Korea but he was always proudest of the Combat Infantryman's Badge. He likes to say that the goal was not to kill the enemy but to "impose our will upon him," and thus defeat him.

Chappell recounted the last few days of WWII when he and some of the troops had to go up the steep road in jeeps to the "Eagle's Nest" in Berchtesgaden. They were very scared that it had been fortified for a "last stand" against the Americans but were happy to find an "Empty Nest" after all. They also enjoyed visiting and photographing the homes of Hitler, Goering and the other Nazi elite. Their homes had been damaged but not destroyed by the bombings.

Major Aldridge retired from the Army in 1964. He then worked as a nuclear effects engineer for the Navy in Alexandria, VA, until retirement in June 1988. Chappell died in August 1991. He is survived by his wife of 44 years, Martha Morrison Aldridge; a son, T. Chappell Aldridge Esq.; a daughter, Mrs. Eileen Aldridge Shropshire; and two grandsons. Chappell will be remembered by family and friends as a person who was always optimistic and witty, and who never forgot where he came from and all those who helped him along the way.

DEWEY CLIFTON ALEXANDER, born 23 May 1915 to the late Hulett and Harriet Alexander. Dewey was drafted in the US Army, on 18 Nov 1942 in Evansville, IN and sent to Fort Benjamin Harrison, IN on 1 Dec 1942 for training. His unit, Co. E, 125th Inf., were in Gilroy, CA; Camp Maxey, TX; and San Francisco, CA. They were sent overseas from Camp Stoneman, CA on 4 Apr 1944 for Honolulu, HI, where he was sent to a hospital in the Philippine Island until 24 Apr 1944, then to the Pacific Theater. There was 254 people sent with him overseas and all except him and one more went to the front lines. On 22 Jan 1946, Dewey was discharged at Camp Beale, CA.

Over the years he was a farmer. Then he moved to Dexter, MO where he worked in a packing house. He lived there for many years, then returned to Trigg County and worked at Western State Hospital until his retirement in 1975.

Dewey lived in Christian County until 1980 where he had several heart surgeries and strokes. His health failed and on 15 Sep 1987 he passed away. His wife Jennie passed away in July 1980. Dewey had a son who preceded him in death in February 1949 and another son Joey is still living. Dewey's brother is Layton Alexander and sisters are Eleanor Wood in Trigg County and Martha Dixon in Caldwell County.

JAMES ALEXANDER, PFC, born 25 Feb 1924, Trigg County. He was drafted 19 Nov 1945 at Camp Atterbury, IN with basic training at Camp Robertson, AR and airborne training at Fort Benning, GA. After three jumps he quit the airborne and 3 Aug 1946, he was sent to MTO as a light truck driver in Italy.

Pfc. Alexander was discharged 24 Mar 1947 at Fort Dix, NJ. He made expert on M1 rifle and received the Good Conduct Medal.

He worked 30 years for Bell South Telephone Co., retiring 28 Nov 1981. Married Opal L. Choate 3 May 1947 in Akron, OH and reared three children: Kenneth, Sandra and Kathy. They also have four grandchildren: David, Barry, Brandon and Sara.

PRENTICE DOUGLAS ALEXANDER, Sergeant, born 6 Aug 1916 in Cadiz, KY. He was drafted into the US Army, 10 Dec 1942 and after training at Fort Benjamin Harrison, IN, his unit, the Med Dep 367th FA BN departed to the Asiatic-Pacific Theater. While serving on various Allied occupied islands in the Pacific, Douglas qualified as a driver/mech.

and gained the rank of Surgical Tech 861 Sergeant. Some of his duty was in areas containing captured Japanese prisoners held by US troops.

Decorations and citations awarded to him included the American Theater Ribbon, Asiatic-Pacific Theater Ribbon, Good Conduct Ribbon and the Victory Medal. Douglas was honorably discharged on 31 Jan 1946 at Center Camp Atterbury, IN.

He married Gladys Carloss of Christian County who taught school in Trigg and Christian counties. Douglas and Gladys had two children, Leslie Douglas Alexander and Mildred Diane Brumfield and three grand-children.

Douglas owned and operated Alexander-Carloss Jewelry in Hopkinsville for 23 years until his retirement. Gladys preceded him in death February 1986. Douglas passed away August 1995.

RUMSEY HOLT "PETE" ALEXANDER, born 13 Mar 1915, Cadiz, KY, was drafted in the U.S Army 2 May 1942. He was No. 31 on the draft board roll and the first to be drafted in Trigg County as the 30 before had volunteered.

He entered service at Evansville, IN and served with Co. C, 315th Engr. Combat BN, 90th Division. His military qualification and date were "Expert Sub Mg Cal 45 1943-Marksman M-1 Rifle 43."

He departed for European-African-Middle-Eastern Theater on 23 Mar 1944, and returned to the USA on 4 Nov 1945. His battles and campaigns were Normandy, Northern France, Rhineland, Ardennes and Central Europe. Pfc. Rumsey received the EAME Theater Medal w/Silver Star and one Bronze Arrow Head, Good Conduct Medal, American Theater and Victory Medals, WD Circular 326 1945.

Rumsey was the son of Raymond and Rhea Noel Alexander. He had one sister, Elizabeth Hopson Turner.

He was a graduate of the 1934 class of Cadiz HS. During his high school career he was active in sports and in 1929 was shortstop on the high school baseball team while still in the 8th grade. That year, the team played in the state tournament in Bowling Green, KY.

Prior to WWII he and his mother operated a restaurant, Pete's Cafe, in Cadiz, corner of Marion and Main Streets.

He owned and operated Pete's Service Station, Court and Main Streets, in Cadiz, an enterprise he started 4 Feb 1951 and continued until retirement 4 Feb 1991.

Rumsey and his wife Virginia were active members of Dyers Chapel United Methodist Church. He was a 50-year member of the Cadiz Masonic Lodge #121 and a member of the Veterans of Foreign Wars #7980 in Cadiz.

Rumsey became ill 24 Jun 2001, and passed away 18 Jul 2001. Interment was made in East End Cemetery, Cadiz, KY. *Submitted by Virginia Alexander.*

WALTER LOCKE ALEXANDER, Staff Sergeant, born 22 May 1919, Trigg County, KY. He was drafted, 8 Jan 1942, arrived Fort Sam Houston, TX, and attached to 602nd Tank Destroyer Battalion.

He took specialized training and field exercise at Camp Bullis and Camp Hood, TX; maneuvers in Louisiana; winter warfare training, Camp McCoy, WI; and maneuvers at Camp Forrest, TN.

Left New Jersey aboard SS *Bergensfjard* to Glasgow, Scotland and by rail to England, attached to Gen. Patton's Third US Army Co. A. From 24 Aug 1944 to 9 May 1945 Third Army was attached to 18 different units and five separate task forces, one time (with exception of one day) Third Army spent 131 days on the line without rest or relief. He was with Third Army for all but the last few weeks of the war. On 8 Dec 1944, he was wounded but asked to stay on duty and 4 Apr 1945, was wounded again and did not return to duty as V-E Day was 9 May 1945. He recalled the hard bitter months spent for the cause of freedom but relieved and thankful. He thought of those comrades who gave their life.

Four Battle Stars were received for Battle of France, Battle of the Ardennes, Battle of the Rhineland and Battle of Germany. Service in the Army was three years, nine months and 23 days. Basic duty as private for two months; heavy truck driver as T-5 for two years; tank commander as sergeant for one year and anti-tank, NCO S/Sgt., nine months. Received six ribbons, EAME Theater Ribbon, w/4 Bronze Stars, Good Conduct Ribbon, Purple Heart w/cluster, Bronze Star Medal and American Theater Ribbon. Received honorable discharge 30 Oct 1945.

Married Lurline Aldridge 15 Nov 1945, moved to Gracey, KY, 31 Dec 1946 and resided there until his death 27 Oct 1990. He is buried in Jones Cemetery Highway 272, Trigg County; a daughter still born 25 Sep 1954. As a civilian he farmed, owned and operated a fleet of trucks and was a cattle buyer for several livestock companies. Retired in January 1984. He was a life-long member of Locust Grove Baptist Church, Trigg County.

Quotes from Col. US Army Retired, Peter J. Kopcsak "on behalf of all members of the 602nd Tank Destroyer Battalion May I express our heartfelt condolence to you in your loss of a truly remarkable husband. In A Company Walter was always exposed to vigorous enemy fire and took part in large tank battles. Walter always demonstrated utmost bravery in these battles. We are thankful to him for his contribution to the success of the battalion, you can be proud that his spirit will continue to be respected by all of us and we beg you to stay in touch with our association."

WILLIAM F. ALEXANDER, Boatswain's Mate 2/c, born 4 Feb 1922. He volunteered and joined the USN, along with Alfered Reddeck, Herman Mitchell and Willard Henderson. They took basic training at Great Lakes, IL.

All four of them stayed together and left Great Lakes for the Pacific to New Calodonia Island where they stayed for two years. Also served aboard the USS *Fairfield* for one year.

Received honorable discharge 1 Feb 1946. Awards include the American Area, Good Conduct Medal, WWII Victory Medal, Philippine Liberation and Asiatic-Pacific.

Returned home and farmed with his father, then Mid-American Truck Line, Louisville, KY until retiring 1 Nov 1979. Married Norma Dean Wyatt 25 Oct 1947 and reared two children, William "Mike" and Antoinett "Toni." They also had three grandchildren: Michael Christopher and Casey Lyn Alexander, and Jade Nicole Green.

He enjoys working in garden and raising chickens at his home in Cadiz, KY.

JAMES ROBERT ALLDRIDGE,

born on 4 Apr 1908, in Trigg County. He was saved and baptized at Cadiz Baptist Church. He graduated from Cadiz HS and attended business college. A memorable experience for him was attending the World's Fair in Chicago.

Robert was drafted to serve in WWII, but was unable to serve overseas because of poor eyesight. He was assigned as a clerk-typist and was stationed at Jasper, IN, Miami Beach, FL and Grenada, MS. For years afterward he would tell exactly how many years, months, days and minutes he was in the Army! He collected WWII postcards.

Robert was a member of the Lion's Club in Cadiz. For a time he worked at the Alldridge-Hughes Grocery Store on Main Street in Cadiz, of which he was co-owner. He also worked for the Nunn Brothers Lumber Co. and Hopkinsville Pallet Co., and was sent to Hazlehurst, MS, to open a pallet company there. He later worked for Grenada Industries in Grenada, MS, from which he retired.

Robert married Willie Mae Beckwith of Carrollton, MS on 29 Aug 1954. They had two children, Jim Alldridge of Houston, TX, and Rose Alldridge Bear of Terre Haute, IN. He was always ready with a joke, a pun, or a tall tale to share. He was interested in coin collecting, magic tricks, inventing and carpentry. Robert died 13 Sep 1982 and is buried in the Evergreen Cemetery in Carrollton, MS. *Prepared by Rose Alldridge Bear.*

CECIL E. ALLEN,

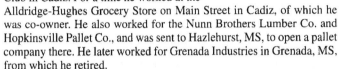

born 15 Mar 1918 in Cadiz, KY, the son of Bob and Ruth Mitchell Allen. He married Margarine Mize on 29 Oct 1946; there were no children born to this union. Mr. Allen passed away on 8 Jan 1991.

Due to an illness, his wife Marge was unable to contribute to this article, therefore, it is submitted by his nieces and nephews who unfortunately do not have a lot of information regarding the time he spent in service for his country.

We do know he went into active service with the Army on 26 Jul 1944 and was discharged 19 Aug 1946. He served with the 1st Bn., 381st Regt., 96th Div. in the Ryukyus Campaign during WWII and his troop was called upon to replace troops fighting on Okinawa.

Allen and a fellow survivor of WWII, Jim Algrin from Bellview, WA with whom he served, were featured in a newspaper article which appeared in *The Cadiz Record* several years ago. The article told of the reunion between the two soldiers, at Allen's home in Cadiz.

At the time the article was published, the men had not seen each other since they left the island of Luzon in the Philippines some 39 years before. As the men recounted their story, they told how that first day on the island as being the most difficult, with artillery blasts and bullets flying everywhere. They were among the mere 21 who survived out of 186 in their regiment. Quoted as saying "We were both very thankful to come out of the war without a scratch, even though there were times when bullets hit our helmets." The article read how the men developed a close relationship as they had a lot in common having both been raised on farms and how they shared their faith in God to get them through.

According to discharge papers, Allen was presented the Victory Medal, Asiatic-Pacific Theater; Ribbon w/Bronze Battle Star, Philippine Liberation Ribbon w/3 Overseas Service Bars and Good Conduct Medal.

J.D. ALLEN,

T-5, born 17 Feb 1926 in Trigg County, KY. He was drafted into the US Army 15 Nov 1945, although WWII was over draftees were still being called to serve their country. He was sent to Louisville, KY and on to Camp Atterbury, IN. He completed his basic training at Fort Belvoir, VA then was assigned to Camp Beale, CA in March 1946 for overseas assignment.

While at Camp Beale he was selected for duty with the Transportation Corps of the Army, transferred to Fort Eustis, VA and assigned to the Amphibian Unit. He was a member of the 460th Amphibian Truck Co., stationed at the Transportation Corps Center at Fort Eustis, VA.

T-5 Allen drove one of the famous Transportation Corps DUKWs in the Army Day Parade in Washington DC and also participated in "open house" at Bolling Field and in the Cherry Blossom Festival in Washington DC, dressed in uniform, white gloves and scarf. This was quite an experience and honor for a 20-year-old who had never been away from home and knew nothing but farm life.

In May 1947, he proudly came home with an honorable discharge of honest and faithful service to his country. He married his sweetheart of two years, Grace Wood, daughter of Smiley and Ruby Wood, on 24 Dec 1947. He farmed for five years but decided he had to find a better income to raise a family. He went to work at Trigg Knit Hosiery Mill and after 35 years service retired as head mechanic and plant manager. He had three sons: Jerry, Michael and Barry Allen and four grandchildren: Darla, Jessica, Chelsey and Austin Allen. J.D. passed away 14 Nov 2000, leaving his wife of almost 53 years who proudly placed at the foot of his grave a marker showing off his loyalty to his country.

JAMES GARNETT ALLEN,

Sergeant, born 23 Apr 1918 at Cadiz, KY. He was inducted into service 28 Aug 1942 at Fort Benjamin Harrison, IN at age 24.

Basic training was at St. Petersburg, FL, then to Gulfport, MS for AM School and advanced training at AAB, Pyote, TX. Supercharges training on B-17 and appointed to crew chief on a B-17. Sgt. Allen was discharged 30 Jan 1944.

He farmed for a while in Trigg County, then moved to Paducah and operated an auto parts store until retirement in December 1981. Married to Audra Cunningham since 19 Jan 1942, they like to travel, go boating and fishing.

Pete, as he is known, belongs to the Masonic Lodge #127 where he has been an active member since 1950. Both he and Audra are active members of the East Baptist Church in Paducah, KY.

LACY EDWARD ALLEN,

born 9 Aug 1921, in Cadiz, KY, died 18 Feb 1999, in West Point, MS. He was the son of Rebea Earl and Lillie Cunningham Allen of Trigg County. Lacy attended the Trigg County schools, where he was active in class life and playing football with the Trigg County Wildcats. He graduated with the Class of 1941.

Following graduation from high school, he ventured off to Mississippi following his older brother Ragon and his sister Monaco. After living in Tupelo, MS, Lacy met and married Bonnie Ballard, 2 Apr 1942. He enlisted in the USN on 11 Jul 1942, completing his training in Oxnard, CA. He later was assigned to the naval depot in New York, where he took his ultimate assignment, at the Arlington National Cemetery, where he was assigned for the remaining four years in service. Lacy was assigned to the Honor Guard, with the task of burying so many of his fellow naval men, as well as the other branches of the United States Armed Forces.

As I recall, the recount my dad shared with me on many occasions over my lifetime of the days that he spent with the Naval Honor Guard, earlier in high school his ambition was to become a "mortician" and with this in mind and the happen chance to be chosen to serve in this "Honor Guard" ultimately led to his civilian occupation of being a funeral director. Dad also spoke of the morning that, in the height of WWII, he, with the rest of the unit he was serving with, were called to attention and the commanding officer called him and two others out of formation with special assignment to Washington, DC with no idea of where he was going or what he was going to do. He wound up at Arlington National Cemetery in Washington, DC. While stationed in Washington, DC, he moonlighted with a mortuary/funeral home, which gave him more desire to seek a job as an "undertaker" which, by the way, was the vocation that was listed on his DD-214 as a civilian occupation.

Over his life following his 44 months in the Navy, Lacy worked with Cockrell Banana Co. in Tupelo, MS, then, later opening and operating Grenada Produce Co. In November 1955, he moved to West Point, MS, where he worked for National Life & Accident Insurance Co. as a salesman. That is where he came to know David R. Calvert of Calvert Funeral Home. Working with Mr. Calvert for five years, at Mr. Calvert's retirement, he assumed the management and ownership of the Calvert Funeral Home until his death 18 Feb 1999. He and his wife Bonnie had three children: Priscilla, Susanne and Scotty, and six grandchildren.

WILLIAM RAGON ALLEN, Seaman 1/c, born on 16 Nov 1908 as the first son of Rebea and Lillie Cunningham Allen of Trigg County, KY.

He enlisted in the USN on 15 Sep 1942. During his tenure, he received training and was a fireman at the USNTC at Millington, TN. He was later reassigned and shipped with the 7th Fleet to the Philippine Islands. While on the Philippines he was with the Seabees and operated a "cherry picker." His letters home discussed many of the hardships that all of our troops were enduring such as the intense heat, rain and the poor quality and quantity of food. He mentioned that he would often pass the time by thinking of his childhood on the family farm that was located on the banks of the Cumberland River.

His son, William Ragon Allen Jr., was born in August 1945 while he was overseas, causing his attention to be turned to getting home for that first glimpse of his legacy. In late October 1945 his lottery number was chosen to be on the next available ship back to the United States. After several days waiting, he departed on what he described as a small ship. His description of that trip home was everything but good. While en route, they encountered severe weather and he described the small ship as tossing and turning with even the dishes not being able to stay on the table during mess. He described the walls of water, as being so high that it appeared the ship would go under at any moment. However, they did make it and he was honorably discharged as a Seaman First Class on 2 Dec 1945.

Several years before the war he moved to Mississippi and upon discharge returned there to be with his wife Lanette Sargent Allen and his newly born son. Ragon returned to work as warehouse manager for Cockrell Banana Co. in Tupelo, MS where he had worked before the war. A daughter Anna was born to Lanette and Ragon in 1948. He retired at the age of 65 in 1973 with more than 40 years of total service with Cockrell Banana Co. After his retirement he would look forward to his return trips to Kentucky to attend family reunions and visit friends and relatives. He always enjoyed returning to the origin of his "roots" in Trigg County, KY. His wife preceded him in death and he died, just after his 89th birthday on 8 Dec 1997.

THOMAS T. ALLEN, born 27 May 1926 in Trigg County, son of Taylor Allen and Doanie Johnson. He went into the USN in 1944 and served until 1946. He left the Navy and enlisted in the US Army.

Allen spent a number of years overseas. He was in Germany for eight years, one tour of duty in France, Korea during the war and two tours of duty in Vietnam. During his time in Vietnam and until his retirement at Fort Campbell, KY, he served as a medic.

Thomas Allen married Gearldine Compton of Trigg County and reared five daughters and a son: Sandra Zeigel, Linda Sowell, Bobbie Henson, Judy Mabry, Bonnie Allen and Steve Allen. There are eight grandchildren.

He lived in Hopkinsville, KY until his death 13 Dec 1996.

ALMER BACON, served in WWII. He is buried in New Corinth Cemetery.

CLYDE BAKER, Tech 4, born 15 Sep 1921 in Cadiz, KY. He was drafted into the US Army, 1 Dec 1942 and served 18 months in the European Theater of Operations.

After basic training in Camp Robinson, AR, he was attached to Co. A, 370th Inf., 92nd Div. as a basic infantry rifleman. He spent 18 months in the US and was then sent to Italy where he fought in WWII. It was there when he was wounded in action, and Baker vividly remembers that day, "I was moving forward on the battlefield as the BR man. The Germans threw a hand grenade. While jumping into the foxhole I was hit by shattering fragments from the hand grenade. I was immediately taken to medical, patched up, and sent right back out on the front line." He received the Purple Heart on 26 Feb 1945.

After receiving enough qualifying points he left the battlefield and was appointed as a cook. Serving as a cook he supervised the work of eight men. He was responsible for three meals per day for military personnel consisting of meats, vegetables and deserts.

In addition to his Purple Heart he received the EAME Theater Ribbon w/3 Bronze Service Stars, American Theater Ribbon, Good Conduct Medal and WWII Victory Medal.

When he got out of the service he held the position of technician 4th grade. He was honorably discharged at Fort Knox, KY on 2 Dec 1945.

After his discharge he returned to Cadiz, KY and in 1946 went to work as a truck driver for the next 19 years in Fort Campbell, KY. After 19 years he was moved to forestry as a machine operator until he retired in 1988.

In October 1948, he married Lillie Mae Street and together they raised three sons: Kenneth Earl, Kent Allen and Herman Stanley. Lillie Mae died 10 Jun 1987.

Today at 79 years, Clyde is still enjoying his retirement residing at his home on Line Street in Cadiz. He serves as a Deacon at Pleasant Hill Baptist Church, where he also helps with janitorial services. He provides transportation to and from the doctor for older people who do not drive, and utilizing his cooking expertise from his military experience, he will whip up a good meal for his grandkids when they visit during the holidays.

JAMES M. BAKER SR., born 13 Feb 1925 in Cadiz, KY, the son of Samuel Lee and Evelyn C. Baker. He was drafted into the Army in May 1945 and sent to Camp Stewart, GA for basic training, then to Munich,

Germany where he remained until November 1946. He received an honorable discharge in February 1947.

When he returned home he went back to school and received his high school diploma in 1948. He married Lyla Morrison, a teacher at the Cadiz Grade School, in August 1947 and they reared three sons: Tommy, Jim Jr. and Randy. They also had five grandchildren.

In January 1950 Jimmy and Lyla moved to Nashville, TN and Jimmy enrolled at Nashville Diesel College, attending nights and working days at Avco Aerostructures Corp. In January 1951, a machine he was working on double tripped, coming down on his right hand mangling it so badly, he lost one finger, half of his thumb and partial use of his hand. He had to drop out of school, but continued working at Aerostructures until his retirement in February 1988.

Jimmy was always very involved in all the boys activities and worked with the Boy Scouts for 18 years. He was so proud that all three of his boys and his only grandson all made Eagle Scout.

When the boys were grown Jimmy and Lyla took western square dance lessons and joined the Nashville Squares dance club. They really enjoyed traveling and dancing for 25 years until Jimmy's health wouldn't permit it anymore. He was diagnosed with terminal lung cancer December 1994 and with many prayers and a very strong will to live, he made it until July 1997. Lyla, his sons and families still reside in the Nashville area.

NORRIS C. BAKER, Tech 5, born 25 Dec 1919 in Trigg County. He joined the military 6 Apr 1942 at Indianapolis, IN and served with 32nd Transportation Truck Co., Fort Eustis, VA.

Received honorable discharge 24 Aug 1951. Awards include Marksman Rifle M-1, EAME Ribbon w/2 Bronze Service Stars, American Theater Ribbon, Asiatic-Pacific Ribbon, Good Conduct Medal and WWII Victory Medal.

He graduated from Kentucky State University with BS in mathematics; taught school at Dunbar High, McUpton and Trigg County School; and was principal at Dunbar HS. After 31 years he retired from teaching at Trigg County.

Married Alma Crump on 27 Aug 1949 and reared 12 children (11 living): Nathaniel, Vivian Hood, Sheneda Little, Norris Jr., Betty Wharton, Houston, Gwendol, Alvin, Almeria, Tanisha Kabithe and Celeste. Norris is widowed and lives with his daughter and son-in-law, Betty and Robert Wharton on Kings Chapel Road, Cadiz.

LACY ADAMS BANISTER, Corpsman, born 27 May 1928 at Cadiz, KY, the son of Arthur T. Banister and Mary Adams Banister. He enlisted in the USN at Louisville, KY in 1946 at the age of 17.

Lacy received his naval training at the naval base in Great Lakes, IL. He was assigned to the Navy Hospital School at Portsmouth, VA,

receiving the rank of corpsman. Assignments for duty were spent in various naval hospitals in and around the Continental United States. Lacy received his discharge in 1948 at Norfolk, VA.

As a civilian he held various jobs including South Central Bell Telephone Co. in 1952 and retired from that in 1988 at LaFollette, TN.

Lacy was married 15 Apr 1950 in LaFollette, TN to Joyce Pickle. Their children are Donald Lee Banister and Janet Banister Lowe. Donald is an employee of NASA in Houston, TX and Janet is a lab technician with MEDIC in Knoxville, TN. Lacy and Joyce have four grandchildren. Lacy is an ardent fisherman and has spent a lot of enjoyable times fishing in the lakes and streams of East Tennessee.

He is a member of West LaFollette Baptist Church, where he has served as song leader, Sunday School teacher for 20 years and worked with the youth in the church. He and his wife reside in LaFollette and enjoy their grandchildren.

LEMUEL JAMES BANISTER JR., PFC, born 25 Jun 1924 on a farm near Muddy Fork Creek in the Siloam Community. I was drafted into the US Army 12 Apr 1943 at Fort Benjamin Harrison in Evansville, IN. Basic training was with 535th Armored Inf. Bn. at Camp Polk, LA and training as medical technician at Camp Polk and Harmon General Hospital, Longview, TX.

Transferred to South Pacific, 21 Sep 1944 on USS *Monterey* and stationed briefly at Hollandia, New Guinea. Traveled to Leyte, Philippines by way of HMS *Mannora* arriving 25 Oct 1944. Served on DS with 36th EVAC Hospital (MASH) and 126th General Hospital. Returned as a patient to Letterman General Hospital, San Francisco on HMS *Samuel G. Langfit* hospital ship on 11 Jun 1945. Transferred to Wakeman Convalescent Hospital at Camp Atterbury, IN.

Discharged on 18 Aug 1945 as private first class, I served two years, four months and eight days. Medals include Good Conduct, Asiatic-Pacific w/3 Battle Stars, Philippine Liberation w/Battle Star, New Guinea Campaign, Victory and probably others.

My basic duties were medical technician. I saw two of the boys that raised the flag on Iwo Jima, ate lunch by the movie star, Lew Ayres. I saw many dead and wounded and was shot at and bombed.

I married Lena Mae Rye (b. 26 Jan 1924) on 8 Dec 1945. We had two sons, Carey David Banister (b. 12 Feb 1947) and Charles Ray Banister (b. 9 Sep 1948). Carey David has one son, Dr. Jason David Banister (b. 17 Aug 1968). Jason's mother is Karon Faye Kaler of Symsonia, KY. Carey David is married to Barbara Diane Knight Banister (b. 5 Jan 1957). They have a daughter, Carrie Diane Banister (b. 19 Feb 1984). They presently reside in Lenoir, NC.

Charles Ray Banister had muscular dystrophy since birth and was confined to a wheelchair most of his life. He died 13 Feb 1973.

As a civilian, I have been part owner with Delbert Stagner in a taxicab business, custodian of the American Legion, operated Banister Standard Service Center, parts man at Island Motor Co. and with Department of the Army, Fort Campbell, KY. I retired 28 Feb 1980 as Chief Plans and Operations, DIO, Fort Campbell, at age 55.

Since retirement I have fished, raised many gardens and truly enjoyed harassing folks. My wife Lena and I have resided on Hammond Lake Road for the past 41 years.

I know this book is about military veterans, also we should remember folks that provided the food, weapons, equipment, transportation necessary to fight these wars. Don't forget the people at home that kept our country running, tears that were shed and the prayers that were said. I believe that we were all veterans and could not have been victorious without everyone's help. Let's remember the main veteran, God Almighty, who through his forgiveness, love and grace allowed us these victories. Lest we forget.

JOHN TURNER BANISTER, Chief Gunners Mate, born 23 Aug 1919 in the Siloam Community of Trigg County to Arthur Turner and Mary Adams Banister. He attended grade school in Cadiz and Cadiz HS through his junior year. In the fall of 1938, high school students from Cadiz and Trigg County attended the consolidated Trigg County HS. John, a senior, was graduated in 1939 with the second class to graduate from Trigg County High.

On 13 Sep 1939, he left Trigg County as a volunteer for the USN with a friend, Charles E. Gray, the son of Ben H. and Lula Cherry Gray. The boys received their basic training at Great Lakes Naval Station, Great Lakes, IL, after which they went their separate ways.

The vessels and stations John served on included NTS, Norfolk, VA; USS *Pyro*; USS *Louisville* (4 years), SCTC Miami, FL; USS *Micko Del 76*; USS *Albemarle*; USS *San Marcus* and ATB, Coronado, CA. On 5 Oct 1945, in Minneapolis, MN, after serving six years and 23 days, John was honorably discharged with the rank of chief gunners' mate.

In mid-November 1941, John's ship was docked at Pearl Harbor, HI. They were sent to the Philippine Islands, missing the Japanese attack on Pearl Harbor by three weeks. His crew was involved in battles in the Philippines and Midway. They were on patrol in the Bering Sea around the Aleutian Islands for many months. In jest he made the statement, "I've crossed the equator seven times."

When the war ended in August 1945, John was home on leave. He and his younger brother, Lacy, were fishing in a pond on the Ed Mize farm off the Jackson Road. A passerby yelled to them that the war was over. In a moment of jubilance John threw Lacy in the pond. Later Lacy joined the Navy for a tour of duty.

Their older brother, Percy Blane, also served in the Navy, enlisting from his home in Thompson Falls, MT. Percy and John were able to hook up for a visit in California. They were delighted to see each other and talked about the visit when they met through the years. In 1984 Percy and John, with their wives, met in Honolulu for a vacation. They toured the memorial at the sight where the USS *Arizona* was sunk and silently read the names of those lost confirming that some of John's friends from basic training were lost as he had feared. They talked of how happy they had been to see each other in California and how happy they were to have the time together in Honolulu, which was to be their last earthly visit.

John was employed by Pennyrile Rural Electric in February 1947, and retired as district manager on 31 Jan 1981. On 25 Dec 1947, he was married to Joyce Davis. Their two daughters are Dr. Suzanne Banister, an associate professor of music at Western Washington University in Bellingham, WA, and Betsy Scroggins, R.N., a nursing supervisor at Marshall County Hospital in Benton, KY. Betsy's daughter, Casey Elizabeth Linn, is a student at Murray State University.

John died on 17 Aug 1985, and was buried in East End Cemetery in Cadiz. His widow, Joyce, resides in Aurora with Betsy, Steve, and Casey. *Submitted by his wife, Joyce D. Banister.*

PERCY BLANE BANISTER, born 14 Jan 1914 in Trigg County, the son of Arthur Turner and Mary Adams Banister. He attended school

in Cadiz and was a member of the class of 1933 of Cadiz HS. He was a printer's devil for *The Cadiz Record* and a clerk at Cowherd and Company grocery.

In the fall of 1936 he went to Paradise, MT, as a member of the CCC (Civilian Conservation Corps). Soon after his term with the CCC, he returned to Thompson Falls, MT, to make his home. On 30 Aug 1939, he was married to Alice Saint of Thompson Falls.

A year later he joined the staff of First State Bank as a bookkeeper. From that position Percy advanced to the position of teller and assistant cashier before entering the USN in October 1942, for what was to be a three-year stint, He spent two of his three years in the Navy in the South Pacific and received his discharge at Williamsburg, VA, in October 1945.

He returned to Thompson Falls and his position at the bank where he advanced to cashier, vice-president and cashier, and executive vice-president. In 1975 he was elected the third president in the life of the bank. He served on many local, regional and state banking committees. He served two terms on the Thompson Falls City Council, the school board and as Master of the Thompson Falls Lodge of Free and Accepted Masons. He was a member of the Scottish Rite in Missoula and of the Algeria Temple of the Shrine in Helena.

He retired from the bank in 1977 as president and chief operating officer.

Percy and Alice were the parents of one son, Larry Saint Banister, who was born 24 Dec 1945. He was in ROTC while at the University of Montana in Missoula and upon his graduation with a degree in business administration, was commissioned a 2nd lieutenant in the USAF. His marriage to Elizabeth Kuebler of Bozeman, MT took place on 19 Dec 1966.

Larry served at Lawyer AFB, MI at Goodfellow AFB, San Angelo, TX, and in Brindisi, Italy. They are the parents of two sons, Ben Saint Banister, a graduate of the University of Montana and an employee of the US Forest Service and James Banister, also a graduate of the University of Montana. He is a registered nurse in a Missoula Hospital. Both Ben and James are married and each has two children.

In 1983 Percy and Alice moved from Thompson Falls to Missoula to be near Larry and his family. On 29 May 1996, Percy passed away in Missoula. *Submitted by his sister, Mary B. Graham.*

HENRY EARL "BUD" BARNES, born 1923, son of Manzie Hargrove Barnes and Lee Barnes. The children in this family were Henry Earl "Bud", Homer F. "Tick," Plomer "Muck" Barnes, Floy Barnes, Dorothy Barnes Noel, Mary Barnes Thomas. All of them are deceased but Mary Barnes Thomas who resides in Cadiz, KY.

Henry Earl served with the US Marines during WWII in the South Pacific. Henry, his wife, a son and his sister Floy were killed in a wreck in 1966. He is survived by one son Danny Barnes. *Submitted by Mary Barnes Thomas.*

HOMER F. "TICK" BARNES, born on 20 Oct 1915 in Trigg County. He entered the armed force's on 30 Jan 1942. He was first stationed at Camp Wheeler, GA. On 16 Sep 1942 he earned his corporal's rating and on 7 Oct 1943 he was advanced to the rank of sergeant. He was sent overseas in June 1944 and arrived in England on 23 July and two days later he was shipped to France. On 9 August he was wounded slightly and 15 days later was back on the front line duty. On 11 September he was again wounded and died on the 13th. He was buried in France.

Homer's parents were Manzie Hargrove Barnes and Lee Barnes. The children in this family were Homer F. "Tick," Henry Earl "Bud," Plomer "Muck" Barnes, Floy Barnes, Dorothy Barnes Noel, Mary Barnes Thomas. All of them are deceased but Mary Barnes Thomas who resides in Cadiz, KY. *Submitted by Mary Barnes Thomas.*

JOE BASTIN, Staff Sergeant, born 24 Oct 1925, Clarksburg, WV, where my father was in the manufacturing of window glass. The glass company had factories in West Virginia and Vincennes, IN. My family moved back to Vincennes when I was a 1 year old. I went to grade school and high school in Vincennes.

In 1943 as a senior at Vincennes HS, I joined the USAAC as a cadet. I took the allegiance at Evansville, IN and sent to Miami, FL for basic training and several other air fields in Florida for gunnery. Most of my training was on B-17 bombers, but our crew training was with B-24 bombers.

As a crew we picked up a new B-24 at Mitchell Field, NY and flew to North Africa via Newfoundland and Azor Islands in mid-Atlantic Ocean. From Tunis, North Africa we were sent to southern Italy where the US engineers were building air fields. The US 5th Army was still fighting the Germans and Italians near Rome.

I was credited for flying 32 missions as a flight engineer and top turret gunner and received the Air Medal w/2 OLCs, two Presidential Unit Citations, six Battle Stars (Rome Arno, Po Valley, Air Combat Balkans, Air Combat France, Austria and Germany). We encountered the first jet airplanes ME-262 (which were German) on our way to bomb the Munich airdrome.

Some of the most heavily fortified targets, 200-300 antiaircraft guns, 88s and 105s, were the oil refineries at Ploesti, Romania and Blechammer, Germany. At our very early morning briefings when we were told that we were going to these targets there would be complete silence, a sinking spell, each man with his own thoughts as we knew we would lose 25 to 30% of our aircraft. This is when we made our promise to God for our safe return.

After the war I attended Indiana University for undergraduate work and Northern Illinois College of Optometry. I married Phyllis Armstrong in 1947 who died of cancer in 1988.

I practiced optometry in Hopkinsville, KY from 1950 and still do part time. I had a branch office in Cadiz, KY from 1950-1955. My son Dr. Bob Bastin is in partnership with me and my son Joey Bastin, an optician, works with us. Two daughters, Bonnie Haney and Lisa Smith, live in Hopkinsville. I also have 10 grandchildren.

I've had farms in south Christian and Trigg counties. I have lived the past 18 years in Trigg County on Lake Barkley. I married Mary Elizabeth Glover (who was my girlfriend in the first grade) in 1997.

JACK F. BELFORD, Colonel, born 12 Apr 1921 in Okmulgee, OK and died 7 Apr 1999 in Cadiz, KY. He served in the US Army as an infantry officer from 1943 to 1973 and retired as a full colonel.

He was an officer in WWII and Korea and was in the Philippines waiting the invasion of Japan when the atomic bomb was dropped on Hiroshima, Japan. He served in WWII and the Korean War and received the Bronze Star.

Other stations include the Philippines; Fort Benning, GA; Fort Campbell, KY; Fort Bragg, NC; Fort Leavenworth, KS; Guam, Camp Chickamugee, Japan; the Pentagon; V Corps in Frankfurt, Germany; and Mainz, Germany.

He was a member of the 187th Regimental Combat Team, Airborne Association (Rakkasans), The Retired Army Officers Association, Sierra Club, Airborne Static Line Association, Donald F. Pratt Museum, Nature Conservatory, Kentucky Chapter and the Infantry Officers Hall of Fame, Fort Benning, GA.

His survivors include his wife Pauline; two sons, Matthew and Mark; three daughters: Janice, Kathleen and Patricia; 12 grandchildren; one great-grandson; and two sisters, Bobbie Allen and Audine Brondes.

GEORGE ROBERT BEORN, Staff Sergeant, born 17 Jan 1918. On 7 Dec 1941 George and a friend were riding around town listening to the radio when the announcement came on that Pearl Harbor, HI had been bombed by the Japanese. Then President Roosevelt announced the US was declaring war on Japan.

George was sworn into the US Army 13 Jan 1942 and sent by train to Fort Benjamin Harris, IN. He was there for 30 days then sent to Camp Wolters, TX, where he took three months basic training in the Infantry.

In June he was transferred to New Orleans, LA where he was loaded, with many other recruits, onto a boat headed for Trinidad. The boat traveled cautiously through waters known to be seeded with mines. Finally the boat docked at Jamaica, West Indies. George and 13 other soldiers were told they would be joining and assigned to the 89th Bn., Co. A, 590th. They were being stationed there to guard the US against possible invasion from the Japanese. George spent 20 months on that island.

In December 1943 he was sent back to the States and stationed at Camp Wheeler, GA. He was promoted to staff sergeant and was assigned to a platoon of new recruits to train.

On his first weekend pass, he caught a bus to Akron, OH to visit his parents and a childhood sweetheart he had been writing to, Dorothy Thomas. After several weekend passes and long hectic bus trips, he and Dorothy were married on 17 Mar 1945 in Akron. After a weekend honeymoon, they moved to Macon, GA near camp. On 5 Nov 1945 George was discharged and they returned to Akron.

In January 1946, with daughter Dixie, they moved to Phoenix, AZ. George was in the termite business for awhile. In November 1947 he was hired as a carrier for the Phoenix Post Office. Two boys were born in Phoenix, Randy in 1948 and Rusty in 1958. In 1962 George was transferred to Medina, OH Post Office. He retired in January 1978 with 31 years of service, and he and Dorothy moved back to Cadiz.

For awhile he drove a school bus, and in 1982 he was hired as custodian at the Cadiz Baptist Church where he, Dorothy and Rusty are members. After 13 years he retired for the second time. They have five grandchildren: Kelly, Christopher, Randy Michael, Jacob and Tina Marie, and three great-grandchildren: Alex, Emily and Jamie. George and Dorothy reside with their son Rusty in Cadiz where they have lived for 22 years.

EDMOND R. BERKLEY, Corporal, born 1 Jan 1923 in Golden Pond, KY. He entered active service 26 Jan 1943 at Evansville, IN. Service schools attended include Automotive Mechanic School Automobile Mechanic, Biak Islands, Shouaten Islands Group for five months.

Assigned to Btry. A, 745th Anti-Aircraft Artillery Gun Bn. and participated in action in Southern Philippines (Liberation) Luzon.

He was discharged 17 Jan 1946 at Fort Knox, KY. His awards include the American Theater, Asiatic-Pacific Theater w/2 Bronze Service Stars and Bronze Arrowhead, Philippine Liberation Medal, Good Conduct and WWII Victory Medal.

In 1948 he started training to be an upholster under the GI Bill. He did upholstery, designed and made cornices for a number of furniture stores and retired from Sears Roebuck with 20 years in 1989.

Married Jacqueline Dixon 22 Feb 1947 at Hopkinsville, KY and they have three children: Sue Carol Patroff, Sylvia Joy Badgerow and Vicki Denice Jones, and five grandchildren: John Patroff; Mandi and Megan Badgerow; Tara and Mathew Jones.

Ray and his wife belonged to a camping club for 25 years where they did community services and used their motor home for Special Olympics. They drove for several years for the Law Enforcement Torch Run with the proceeds going to the Special Olympics. They also supported other organizations. Ray's favorite place to travel and visit was Kentucky, the place he always called home. He died 29 Nov 1995 of congestive heart failure.

NOBLE L. BIRDSONG, Sergeant, born 17 Sep 1921, in Golden Pond, KY. He joined the service 17 Oct 1939 and was stationed at Fort Knox. His specialty was automotive mechanic and he participated in European-African-Middle East Campaign.

Sgt. Birdsong was discharged 22 Nov 1945. His awards include the Middle Eastern Theater Ribbon, American Defense Ribbon, American Theater Ribbon, Good Conduct Medal and WWII Victory Medal.

HARVEY WILLIAM BLANKS, Staff Sergeant, born 9 Aug 1920 in Cerulean, KY. He was inducted into the US Army, 18 Nov 1942 at Evansville, IN.

Harvey was a Technician Fourth Class, Btry. C, 537th FA-BN. His military occupational specialty was Clerk General 055. In 1942, he was located in Muskogee, OK; Seattle, WA; and Missouri. Most of his time was in bivouac where he set up camp and trained truck drivers.

The war was over, and there was no overseas trip. He was discharged at Separation Center, Jefferson Barracks, MO, 14 Feb 1946; his rank was Staff Sergeant (Tec 4).

Harvey received marksmanship badges in 2nd Class Gunner (AR); Rifle SS., 10 Dec 1943; medals and ribbons include Good Conduct Medal, American Theater Campaign Ribbon and WWII Victory Ribbon.

When he returned to civilian life, it was to the farm and work at the post office. He was a substitute mail carrier and letter carrier for 34 years, and continued to work on the farm until he retired four years ago; at that time he turned the farm over to the boys. In 1976, Harvey received the Conservation Award for his outstanding accomplishments in resource conservation in Trigg County. He continues to live on the farm in his retirement years.

Harvey's parents were William Henry Blanks and Mary Nannie Pollard Blanks. The Blanks family was one of the earliest group of settlers of Wallonia, and they came from North Carolina and Virginia. In 1955, Harvey Blanks married Allene Stevens. There are two children, Terry Edwards Stevens and Harvey Kent Blanks; two grandchildren, Darin Mitchell Stevens and Margaret Denise Stevens Alexander, and three great-grandchildren. *Submitted by Allene Stevens Blanks.*

RAY E. BOYCE, PFC, born 23 Dec 1914 in Bloomfield, MO. He enlisted 26 Sep 1942 at Jefferson City, MO and was inducted into the US Army, 10 Oct 1942.

Ray's training was at Jefferson City, MO, and his assignment was the ETO. His position was a combat infantryman. He was a rifle (sharpshooter) and his occupational specialty was Ammunition Carrier 504. He departed with Co. M, 16th Inf. on 2 Nov 1943 and arrived there 9 Nov 1943; time was spent in England before going into France. He participated in the Normandy Campaign (Battle Star) and was wounded in action 6 Jun 1944 in Normandy, France. After he was shot, he remained on the beach for 2-1/2 days.

Ray returned to the USA, 13 Oct 1944 and returned to Wakeman General Hospital at Camp Atterbury, IN, where he remained in a cast for six months. He was discharged from Wakeman General Hospital at Camp Atterbury, IN, 6 Sep 1945. He was honorably discharged 8 Sep 1945 as a PFC.

Awards and Medals received were EAME Ribbon, Good Conduct Ribbon, Purple Heart and Distinguished Unit Badge. His markmanship honors were Rifle (SS) 23 Mar 1943, Combat Infantryman 13 Oct 1944. A Lexington paper did refer to him recently, "Ray Boyce 83, a Purple Heart recipient who took seven bullets in his right hip on a D-Day beach in 1944."

Returning to civilian activity, Ray was owner and operator of a grocery store and service station in Trigg and Christian counties. After retirement, he enjoyed gardening, fishing, travel, and continuing to operate a service station.

In 1967, Ray and Belva Boyce were married. They have a son, Jim Boyce, and two grandchildren, Pamela and Richard Boyce. Ray has a sister Virginia Nesbitt who lives on Canton Road, Cadiz.

Ray E. Boyce is a resident of Thomson-Hood Veterans Center, Wilmore, KY.

ADRIAN CLAYTON BOYD, GM2/c, born 19 Mar 1925 in Trigg County. He enlisted 26 Jul 1944 NRS Louisville, KY and saw action in the China Sea. His stations included NTC Great Lakes, IL; ATB, Solomons, MD; USS LCS(L)(3) 127; USS LCI(G) 514; LCI(L) FLOT-37.

He was discharged 7 Jun 1946. His medals include the Asiatic-Pacific Ribbon, American Area Ribbon and WWII Victory Medal.

Went to college on GI Bill and graduated in 1952 with BS in geology, Washington State University. Worked in oil fields, Halliburton Oil Well and Cementing Co. logging department, 1955-went to work as geologist with Western Kentucky Gas Co. and developed and discovered Greenville, KY, gas field. Retired from West KY Gas in June 1962.

Married Bette Lee Hewins 27 Nov 1952 and they reared two children, Adrian Jr. and Cheryl Anne McCrystal. They have four grandchildren: Sara Elizabeth and Stephen Boyd McCrystal and Nicholas and Kathryn Boyd. Adrian Boyd passed away 16 Feb 2000.

BYRON PRESLEY BOYD JR., Seaman 1/c, born 14 Jan 1926 in Graves County, KY, enlisted in the Navy as seaman apprentice on 23 Oct 1943. He reported for active duty to the Navy V-12 Unit in Bowling Green, OH on 1 Mar 1944. His next station was NTS in Great Lakes, IL followed by AGC in Brooklyn, NY. He was then assigned to the SS *Benjamin Holt* and later to the USS *Grimes* (APA-172).

He attended the Armed Guard School in Norfolk, VA and was honorably discharged from USN Personnel Separation Center, Great Lakes, IL on 18 Jul 1946 as seaman 1/c. His awards included the American Area Campaign Medal, Victory Medal, Asiatic-Pacific Area Campaign Medal, EAME Area Campaign Medal and the Philippine Liberation Ribbon.

After attending Murray State for a short time, Boyd entered the US Maritime Service and for two years traveled and worked major seaports of the world. In 1949 he re-entered Murray State where he earned a degree in physical fitness and agriculture. He and Sally Ann Humphries were married on 27 Jan 1951.

Following graduation they moved to Mayfield where Boyd first worked at Union Carbide, then managed the J.B. Humphries Tobacco Floor, and later became a salesman for Dairyman's, Inc. He served on the Mayfield City Council and was Moderator for First Baptist Church. Their sons are Stephen McKelvey, Thomas Michael and John Byron. Their two grandchildren are Roxanne Marie and Heather Amanda. His long service with the 321st Military Intelligence Detachment of the Army Reserve started in Paducah in 1959.

In 1972 the family moved to their lake home at Barkley Shores near Cadiz, and he continued with the USAR until his retirement 14 Jan 1986 as WO4, transferring to Retired Reserve the same month. He was awarded the Army Achievement Medal in 1984, and served several summers as quartermaster for a Reserve Training Camp in Michigan.

Boyd was instrumental in the establishment of the VFW Post in Cadiz and was active in all phases of the Post from construction to Quartermaster to Commander. He loved being a part of the Post and their Cadiz activities. The VFW District became part of his agenda, as well.

Physical fitness was an ongoing lifestyle throughout his life and the Fitness Center at Barkley Lodge was a favorite of his.

Following the death of his wife on 15 Mar 2001, he was diagnosed with a brain tumor resulting in his death on 11 Apr 2001. He was buried at Highland Park Cemetery in Mayfield. The VFW Post in Cadiz held a memorial service at the post on Sunday, 3 May 2001, for Byron and Sally Boyd.

HERMAN J. BOYD, Tech Sergeant, born 11 Jul 1911 in Trigg County, KY. He enlisted 29 May 1942 at Cadiz, KY and was stationed at Fort Benjamin Harrison, IN; Keesler Field, MS; and Kingman, AZ.

He was assigned to 431st Bomb Sqdn. and participated in battles and campaigns: Air Offensive Japan, Eastern Mandates and Western Pacific. He flew 40 combat missions as flight engineer in B-24.

Sgt. Boyd was discharged 7 Nov 1945. His awards include the American Theater Medal, Asiatic-Pacific Theater Medal w/3 Bronze Stars, Air Medal w/Silver Star and two Bronze Stars, Good Conduct Medal and WWII Victory Medal.

Herman was postmaster at Cadiz Post Office and retired in 1977. He passed away in 16 Dec 1997. Married Louise Thomas 11 Jun 1946, there are no children.

WILLIAM HAYDON BOYD, PFC, born 30 Aug 1927 in Wallonia, KY. He was drafted into the Army 17 Jan 1946 and after basic training at Camp Robertson, AR was sent to Camp Carson, CO for further training.

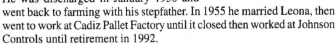

He was sent to Japan as part of the occupation forces and guarded military installations, broke up riots and helped keep a military presence in Japan after the war.

One of the things he will never forget is traveling through Hiroshima and Nagasaki by troop train after the Atomic Bomb was dropped on the two cities.

His awards include the Occupation Medal, Good Conduct and Victory Medal. He was discharged in January 1950 and went back to farming with his stepfather. In 1955 he married Leona, then went to work at Cadiz Pallet Factory until it closed then worked at Johnson Controls until retirement in 1992.

He had three children: Deborah (lives in Cadiz, KY), Daniel (lives in Lexington, KY) and David (deceased); also five grandchildren: Luke, Aaron, Mary Katherine, Matthew and Will.

J. ROBERT "BOB" BRAME, Sergeant, born 3 Nov 1911 in Christian County, KY. He was inducted in service at Camp Atterbury, IN in October 1943 and was stationed at Hollandia, New Guinea, Finchhaven, Leyte, Lingayen Gulf, Luzon, Tac Loban, Subic Bay, Manetta, Botangus, Tokyo, Atsugi Air Force Base, and Yokohoma. Sgt. Brame served in the HQ 8th Army and also with the 11th Airborne and was discharged in February 1946.

He does not like to recall his service experiences, they are still too vivid and awesome.

His civic activities include being a Mason, Shriner, Jester, Charter Member of the Trigg, Hopkins, and Christian County Board of Realtors

He was married to the late Atwood Davenport Brame in June 1939, and to Helen Davenport Sanderson Brame in June 1974. He has one son, J. Robert Brame III and five grandchildren: Rob, Blake, Virginia, John and Thomas.

He retired in June 1972 from the Post Office, farming and from being a real estate broker and appraiser. He resides with his wife in Cadiz, KY.

ALFRED JAMES BRIDGES, born in Canton, KY, was the son of Sam Bridges and Georgia Tandy Bridges. He served in the USN from 1941-47 during WWII.

After his discharge he returned to civilian life in Newark, NJ. He worked many years in the US Post Office and also worked for Amtrak. He lived, worked and married in New Jersey. He remained there in retirement and is buried there.

His two brothers also served in the USN: Sam Jr., 1954-58 and Jack, 1956-58. *Submitted by his sister Juanita Trail, who lives in Detroit, MI.*

CLIFFORD E. "PETE" BRIDGES, PFC, born 11 Apr 1917, son of the late John T. and Maggie Cunningham Bridges, who lived in the Maple Grove Community of Trigg County, KY. He grew up on his father's farm and attended Maple Grove School along with many of his Bridges cousins who lived in the neighborhood.

Pete's WWII service began when he was inducted in the US Army 24 Jun 1942, at Evansville, IN. He spent almost three and a half years in service, over two years of which were spent in the Pacific Theater of Operations with Co. E, 593rd Engr. Boat and Shore Regiment.

His outfit saw action among several islands of the Bismarck Archipelago in the South Pacific, including New Guinea, and was with Gen. Douglas MacArthur's troops when he made his spectacular island hopping drive on his return to the Philippines. He participated in battle for Manila, and continued into northern Luzon to complete forcing the Japanese from the islands. He was there when the atomic bomb was dropped on Hiroshima which ended the war.

His military decorations include American Theater Ribbon, Asiatic-Pacific Theater Ribbon w/3 Bronze Stars, Philippine Liberation Ribbon, Good Conduct Ribbon, Bronze Arrow, and WWII Victory Medal.

Pete received an honorable discharge as a private first class, 16 Dec 1945 at Camp Atterbury, IN. He married Lillie Frances Smith of Princeton, KY, 14 Feb 1942. They have no children. Returning to civilian life Pete worked in the building industry much of which time was spent as a carpenter and as an electrician. He has been retired for several years, and he and his wife Frances presently live in Princeton, KY.

CLYDE TAYLOR BRIDGES, Private, born 3 Nov 1920 in Cadiz, KY. He enlisted into the US Army 8 Oct 1942 at Fort Benjamin Harrison, IN. He was stationed at Camp Barkeley, TX with the occupational specialty - machine operator. He was given a medical discharge 7 Jan 1944.

Clyde was a retired electrician and passed away 10 Feb 1998. He is buried at Drury Bridges Cemetery, Cadiz, KY. He married first Willa Lee Sharp 14 Dec 1941 and second Dorothy Wadlington 26 Mar 1973. He and Willa had three children: Florence Mayfield, Clyde T. Jr. and Carolyn Lee Williams; also, six grandchildren: Bobby, Lauren and Steven Mayfield; Angela and Jeffery Bridges; and Donald Scott Williams.

DAVID STANLEY "D.S." BRIDGES, born 25 Sep 1921 in Maple Grove Community of Trigg County, KY. He enlisted in the US Army in June 1940 and was assigned to 13th Armored Cav. at Fort Knox, KY.

In July 1940 the 1st Armd. Div. was organized with Maj. Gen. Adna R. Chaffee as commander. D.S. was now a member of 13th Cav. 1st Armd. Div. In the early part of January 1941, D.S. was assigned to the 4th Armd. Div. Later a cadre was formed at Watertown, NY and a part of the 13th Cav. was transferred to Camp Bowie, TX.

In the autumn of 1943, D.S. was involved in a jeep accident, injuring a foot and a hand, subsequently ending his military service with a disabled discharge.

D.S. remained in Texas, married and raised two daughters. He died 9 Jan 1998 and his wife died 18 Feb 1999, both are buried in Waco, TX. *Submitted by Gilbert and Hilda Bridges.*

G.D. BRIDGES JR., Lieutenant Colonel, born 22 Jul 1924 in Trigg County, the son of Garland D. and Annie Thomas Bridges. G.D. was inducted into the Army Air Corps as an aviation cadet on 25 Jan 1944. His flight, 200 cadets, was eliminated from pilot training 19 Feb 1944. The next assignment was to Radar Repair School as a private. He completed B-29 Radar Repair School in May 1945 and was discharged in May 1946 as a corporal in the Air Corps Reserves.

He went to Texas, married Johnnye F. Buth and enrolled at Texas Tech University in Lubbock. In September 1946, G.D. received a BS in education and a USAF Commission in the Reserves in 1949 plus a masters of education in 1950. In June 1951, G.D. was recalled for the Korean War and stayed for an Air Force Career.

In September 1964, he became Director of Personnel at Wheelus AB, Tripoli, Libya, while there, the Arab/Israeli Six Day War occurred. Home made bombs were thrown over the air base fence. Russian fighter planes appeared in the area. His first job was to get all military families and other Americans in the Tripoli area to Wheelus AB. The next task was to evacuate some 6,000, mostly women and children, out of Libya by air. All this urgent activity took place in less than 10 days.

In May 1972, G.D. arrived at Da Nang Air Field, Vietnam as Director of Personnel. Da Nang was known as "Rocket City" as Russian rockets frequently rained down upon the base. He was there for 10 months (until the war was over). Lt. Col. Bridges retired from the USAF 30 Jun 1975 with 31+ years service, WWII, Korea and Vietnam. He served eight years overseas. His decorations included two Meritorious Service Medals and a Bronze Star.

After retirement, the family moved to Austin, TX. G.D.'s second career was as a life insurance salesman for 15 years. Since 1990, he and Johnnye have enjoyed traveling, playing golf and working with senior citizens. A Life Time Member of the Thomas-Bridges Association, G.D. has missed only two of the annual reunions in Trigg County since the first one in 1972.

He has two sons, Gary L. and Alan W., and three grandchildren all in Texas. G.D. is a member of the American Legion, Veterans of Foreign Wars and Sons of the American Revolution. He now resides in a retirement community in Temple, TX.

GILBERT N. BRIDGES, born 20 Oct 1915, Maple Grove Community, Trigg County, KY. He registered for military service 13 Oct 1940, volunteered the same day and was inducted into the US Army 28 Nov 1940 at Fort Knox, KY. He was assigned to 6th Armd. Inf., 1st Armd. Div. On 3 Feb 1941 he was promoted to specialist 4th class and assigned as company armorer and artificer.

Left 4 Sep 1941 for maneuvers in Louisiana and South Carolina for combat training. He returned to Fort Knox on 6 Dec 1941 and was scheduled for discharge on the 8th, but the Japanese canceled that on 7 Dec 1941.

Gilbert departed the States 30 May 1942, destination unknown. They arrived in north Ireland 12 June. While in Scotland he was assigned to British navy. On a British Coast Guard vessel, laden with military personnel and ammunition, they sailed through the Strait of Gibraltar to North Africa. They landed in Oran Harbor 8 Nov 1942 and the enemy forces lay-in-waiting and "all hell broke loose." There were 354 American military personnel lost - 11 of the 42 survivors were not injured (including Gilbert).

He was engaged in combat throughout the African Campaign; held prisoner five days by the French navy and Vichy police; engaged in combat in Italian Campaign; and made staff sergeant in November 1943.

He arrived home in Cadiz, KY 30 Jan 1945, married Hilda Williams on 4 February and honeymooned in Miami Beach, FL. Returned to Fort Knox to service in the Armored Center. He was honorably discharged 23 Jun 1945 at Camp Atterbury, IN.

Next employment was with Department of the Army, US Corps Engineers, Lock and Dam Division, retiring in August 1974. Gilbert and Hilda reside in Trigg County, KY. They have one son, Gillis A. Bridges, who lives in Murray, KY.

IRA CLIFTON BRIDGES JR., born on 17 Apr 1923 in the Maple Grove Community of Trigg County, was the third child and second son of Ira Clifton and Flo Templeton (Bridges) Bridges. He was the grandson of Mark Dale and Malle Lancaster Bridges and D. Stanley and Jane "Jennie" Thomas Bridges. Junior attended grade school at Maple Grove and one year at Hamburg, TN. Three years of high school were completed at Trigg County High and he graduated from Calvert City HS in Marshall County in 1942. The family had moved to Calvert City to be near Kentucky Dam where Ira Sr. was working as a carpenter.

After graduating Ira Jr. went to Murray College and enrolled in a job training program, and when completed he went to Connecticut and worked for a while at Mystic, CT. It was while there that WWII was declared and rather than being drafted into the armed forces, he chose to join the Merchant Marines and attended the Merchant Marine Academy at King's Point, Long Island, NY.

Junior served on several escort ships to convoys that carried arms and supplies to the European war zones during WWII. The escort ships were not allowed to be armed and some of the sister ships in this convoy were sunk during their voyages.

After WWII he continued his career as a civilian merchant seaman and sailed as deep sea engineer for many years (1945-1970). He shipped out of New York, Galveston, Houston, Panama City, New Orleans, and other Atlantic seaports.

For several years he lived in New Orleans, LA in the French quarters, where he met and married his wife, Frances. They were married on 18 Dec 1952, at Gulfport, MS. She had served in the Women's Army Corps in WWII. Ira Jr. sailed to many sea ports all over the world, including Korea, during the Korean Conflict and also to Vietnam during the Vietnam conflict. While there he visited with a nephew, Lanny Bridges, who was in the Army and on duty there.

In 1961 he purchased a house in Cadiz and that became his home until his death on 5 Feb 1970. He had just returned from an intercoastal voyage from Morrisville, NJ to California when he was stricken with a fatal heart attack driving his automobile on the New Jersey Turnpike, near Edison, NJ. His body was returned to Trigg County for burial. He was member of the Canton Masonic Lodge No. 242, a 32nd degree Mason and a Shriner. He also belonged to the Seafarer's International Union.

Frances died on 26 Jun 1980 and they are both buried at the Bridges Family Cemetery at Maple Grove along with many of the Bridges ancestors.

LACY WADE BRIDGES, PFC, born 11 Jul 1921 in Canton, Trigg County. He was drafted into the US Army 12 Aug 1942. After six weeks training in Camp Wolters, TX, he was sent to Camp Stone in California, and after two or three days was shipped to Alaska. He stayed there over three years, was put into another company and came home on furlough before going overseas. He was half-way out in the ocean when the war

ended. They went to Pearl Harbor and he returned home in November 1945 and stayed in the reserves for three years.

Lacy married a Trigg County girl, Martha Bryant, on 7 Dec 1946 and they had three children: Dannie and Deanne (twins) and Kathy. Dannie died in infancy. Grandchildren are Chad and Greyson. They lived in Illinois for several years and he worked for Lock & Dam, Operator #53 for Corp of Engineers. He was injured in 1972, retired and moved to Cadiz, KY in 1974.

RICHIE SMITH BRIDGES, born 11 Sep 1920 in Trigg County, Cadiz, KY. He was drafted into the US Army on 29 Sep 1942 in Evansville, IN. He was then transferred to Fort Benjamin Harrison, IN, completing his basic training at Fort Leonard Wood, MO.

He was sent to the 16th Forward Observation Battalion as a Technician Fifth Grade Flash Ranger, where he surveyed and tested the accuracy of heavy artillery units. The unit was attached to Gen. George S. Patton's Third Army in the European Theater.

His tour of duty included travels through Indiana, Texas, Wisconsin and New York. He also traveled overseas into Germany, England, France, Belgium, Wales and Holland.

He recalls Hitler's army bombing England with V-1 and V-2 Buzz Bombs that were 10 or 12 feet long. He experienced many close calls during the Battle of Central Europe, Northern France, Rhineland and the Ardennes.

Richie and thousands of others were thrown into one of the most horrendous, battles in Europe, the Battle of the Bulge. They endured almost 200 straight days of combat without reinforcements from October 1944 until May 1945, reportedly more consecutive days of combat than any other in the European Theater of Operations.

Richie recalls the Battle of the Bulge taking place in the winter. His units worked only at night, miles ahead of their main units. They were alone in the cold and snow and were constantly under enemy fire.

He received the Good Conduct Medal, the American Campaign Service Medal, the EAME Campaign Medal w/4 Bronze Stars and the WWII Victory Medal.

Richie was treated in tent hospitals for battle fatigue and shell shock. He contracted rheumatic fever in 1944 and was hospitalized in Germany, France and England. He was released and sent to Wales for his recuperation period.

Upon the arrival of V-E Day, he began processing for the invasion of Japan. Before processing was complete, the troops were notified of V-J Day. He received an honorable discharge on 30 Nov 1945 at Fort Knox, KY.

A charter member of Maple Grove Baptist Church, he married Willie Mae Dixon in Christian County, KY on 22 Jun 1946. They have four children: Richie Dale, Ronnie Gale, Linda Diane and Bruce Wayne; nine grandchildren and one great-grandchild.

Richie worked as a building inspector, a union carpenter and retired form Eddyville State Penitentiary as a licensed stationary engineer in 1985.

He is currently owner of Richie's Odds and Ends. He is a master mason of Local Lodge #121. He resides outside of Cadiz, KY, with his wife and continues to attend Maple Grove Baptist Church.

ROBERT CHAPPELL BRIDGES, born 4 Oct 1913, in the Maple Grove Community of Cadiz, KY, was drafted into the USN from Cadiz in March 1944. He was the second son of Jesse C. and Myrtress (Davis) Bridges.

After boot camp at Great Lakes, IL, he was stationed at the Amphibious Training Base at Fort Pierce, FL, holding the rank of carpenter's mate 2/c. His unit repaired various kinds of landing craft, including LCVPs and LCMs, which were being used in the training of troops, and were damaged daily by the seamen in the learning process.

Following his service in Florida, he was stationed briefly at Camp Perry, VA, then was sent to Port Hueneme, CA, where as a member of Logistics Support Company 70, he shipped out for Japan in September 1945.

"If the war hadn't ended, our ship would have been in grave danger," he relates. "We were headed for Sasebo Bay, Japan, which had to be entered through a narrow channel, each side of which were catacombed and fortified. As occupational forces, we went into these tunnels, which were being used to build, on an assembly line, one-man submarines. We hauled many of these out to sea and sunk them, as we did with disarmed bombs and artillery.

"I was fortunate not to have seen combat. I thanked God every day for that and prayed for those thousands of men who did!"

He married Virginia Mize on 9 Oct 1937, and they had one daughter, Faye Lynn, when they moved to Granite City, IL, in 1942. A son, Robert Dwain, was born following WWII. They have three grandchildren: Amy, Emily and Kyle, all of whom reside in Granite City.

He worked most of his life as a carpenter and retired from the Carpenter's Union, Local 633, Granite City, IL, in November 1978.

He and his wife now reside in Hot Springs Village, AR, where they live near their daughter. They both enjoy watching the many birds and squirrels that inhabit their back yard. They attend the Barcelona Road Baptist Church in the Village.

THOMAS EDISON BRIDGES, Lieutenant Commander, was born 19 Feb 1918 in Trigg County, son of Garland D. and Annie Thomas Bridges. He enlisted in the Navy in 1934 and served in the battleship USS *Mississippi* for two years.

Soon after discharge, Edison joined the Merchant Marines and served on commercial ships. He started work as a wiper in the engine room and

rapidly advanced to chief engineer. Edison traveled far and wide. During WWII he wore the naval officer's uniform. His highest rank was lieutenant commander. His ships, frequently in convoy, made the very dangerous shipping route to Murmansk, Russia. Edison described one typical attack, "For days we were under constant aerial bombardment, sighting many submarines and our sister ships sinking. No clean clothes, regular meals or real sleep for weeks! We just snatched what sleep and food we could while standing our posts. Finally my ship was hit and sank. We had to jump into the oily, flaming, arctic sea. The force of the sinking ship was sucking us under. We were at death's door but somehow escaped and were rescued." He survived three shipwrecks, three times rescued from the icy seas off Russia's northern most seaport, Murmansk. He suffered extreme exposure and acute frost bite!

After the war he married Dolly Armstrong. They had a daughter Gretchen. Edison and Dolly divorced in 1950. He continued sailing the oceans as chief engineer on commercial ships until his retirement in 1971. He settled in Norfolk, VA and married Carole Horned in 1973. He adopted Carole's daughter, Ann. Edison worked five years, part time, on inport US ships as port engineer and as local part time representative of the Marine Engineers Benefit Association. Edison became an avid golfer and he and Carole traveled extensively, his favorite place to visit was back to his roots, Trigg County. A life time member of the Thomas-Bridges Association, he rarely missed the annual reunion and became affectionately known as "our kissing cousin." Edison died 7 Jan 1993 from cancer. He was buried in Trigg County beside his parents.

TROY HUGHIE BRIDGES, son of Garland D. and Annie Thomas Bridges, was born 11 Oct 1910 in Trigg County. He enlisted in the Navy in 1927 and served on the battleship USS *Mississippi* for 10 years Soon after discharge from the Navy in 1937 he joined the Merchant Marines and served on commercial ships until 1948.

Troy started work as a wiper and oiler in the engine room. In 1939, he became a pumpsman on oil tankers. It was in this position that he made his greatest contribution to WWII. His job was to load and unload the vital crude oil rapidly without spillage. Because of his outstanding skills in this work he was affectionately known as "Mr. Pumps." His actions expedited a fast turn around for our critical oil tankers. The ship's owner paid Troy's railroad fare from tanker loading in the south USA to unloading in north USA and back to the south etc. In this way, Troy would load the tanker, travel by railroad to the north arriving before the tanker and be ready to unload. The submarine threat to our tankers in the coastal shipping routes and Troy's scarce expertise as pumpsman made his rail travel to and fro by railroad absolutely necessary.

He left the Merchant Marines in 1948. Troy moved to Louisville, KY and begin a successful sales career. He married Dorothy Kerr of Louisville. They had no children.

Troy was an active Mason. He served as master of his lodge, a Shriner and Grand Royal Patron of the Kentucky Order of Amaranth. He was also a charter and lifetime member of the Thomas-Bridges Association. Troy served as president and on the board of directors. He had traveled widely but his favorite trip was back to his roots, Trigg County. Troy was a regular attendee at the Thomas-Bridges family reunion.

Troy died 21 Jun 1979 and was buried in Louisville, KY.

WILLIAM BURLEY BROADBENT JR., PFC, served in the US Army in WWII from December 1942 until October 1945. He was in D Co. of the 351st Engineers and served 28 months overseas in the European Theater of Operations.

During the Battle of the Bulge in December 1944, his unit was called to the front lines. One night they were attacked by German rockets and one fell close to William's machine gun emplacement causing the foxhole to cave in on him. As a result of this action, he suffered a partial loss of hearing and the total loss of smell.

William was all over Europe during his tour of duty and helped to build airfields for the B-17 bombers while in England. He saw the battle damaged shot-up planes limp back to base daily "on a wing and a prayer." He, his fellow American troops and the English home folks endured the bombing raids of the German Luftwaffe.

His unit crossed the English Channel to Normandy a few days after D-Day. The destruction and death of battle was still very much evident. His unit fought and built its way across France to Paris and then into Belgium and Luxembourg. It was in this area while the Battle of the Bulge raged that the rocket attack took place.

One action he spoke of often was of a German sniper who was a crack-shot. He hit each of his victims in the same spot on the head. The Americans couldn't figure out from where the fatal shots came. Finally, the church steeple became the suspected sniper's nest. A tank was called in to shoot it down. The body of the German soldier was found in the debris.

William married Dorothy Mae Sholar on 28 Aug 1946. A son William Vernon was born 6 Jan 1952 and he had a daughter Emma Jean by a previous marriage. William was a self-employed carpenter and many houses and barns he built can still be seen in Trigg County and surrounding areas. William passed away 13 Jun 1996 and is buried in Trigg Memory Acres.

LINDSAY BURKE, Sergeant, was born and reared in the now Fort Campbell area near Roaring Springs, KY. They moved to Christian County in 1942 and shortly after, Lindsay was drafted from Trigg County.

He received his basic training at Fort Benning, GA and was a sergeant with the 540th Engineers all the time he was in service. He was sent overseas and served in Sicily, Africa and Naples. He was proud to serve his country and received several decorations and citation. He was discharged 5 Nov 1945 in Fort Belvoir, VA.

He married the former Ora Wills and they have one daughter Linda Burke Vier. Lindsay passed away 19 Mar 1984 and is buried in Green Hill Cemetery.

HORACE RAY BUSH, Sergeant, born 28 Aug 1910 in Trigg County. He enlisted 24 Jun 1942 at Camp Atterbury, IN and participated in action in Central Europe with the Army Postal Unit.

Sgt. Bush was discharged 10 Sep 1945. Awards include the EAME Theater Ribbon w/Bronze Star and Good Conduct Medal.

Civilian activity as US Postal Service and rural carrier. Married Kathleen Browning and they had two children, Jamie Bush Pfeiffer and Ray Browning Bush; and four grandchildren: Douglas and Michael Pfeiffer and Kevin and Angela Bush. Horace Ray Bush is deceased.

BILL CALHOUN, Tech 5, born 18 Oct 1920 in Cadiz, KY, was drafted into the US Army 13 Oct 1942. After two months of basic training at Camp White, OR, his unit 459th Engrs. Depot Co. was sent to Camp Young, Desert, CA for more training.

On 4 Sep 1943 their unit left New York for the ETO and arrived 22 Sep 1943 in England. They participated in battle campaigns in France, Germany and Belgium (Battle of the Bulge) with the 3rd Div. Under Gen. Patton. Bill broke his foot at the Rhine River and was sent back to a Army hospital in Germany.

He was placed in a replacement pool to be sent to Japan, but the war ended in Germany so he was sent back to Thayer General Hospital in Nashville, TN where he stayed from July-October 1945.

His awards include the ETO Ribbon w/5 Bronze Stars and Good Conduct Medal. Highest grade was T-5.

After his discharge, he returned to Cadiz, KY and to the girl he had married on 24 Apr 1943. They lived in Michigan for a while then he worked for the Nashville Corps of Engineers, Lock and Dam at Lock E near Canton, KY on the Cumberland River until it was flooded. Transferred to Watts Bar, TN until 1964; moved to Kentucky Dam until 1973; followed by Lake Barkley Dam until his retirement in 1977.

Bill and Magdalene have five children, grandchildren and great-grandchildren. They live on the lake at Canton, KY on Lake Barkley and go to church at Cadiz Baptist Church.

CLARENCE DABNEY CALHOUN, PFC, born 15 Feb 1916 at Canton, KY, son of William Joseph and Willie (Carr) Calhoun. He was inducted into the infantry division of the US Army 4 Jun 1941 at Fort Thomas, KY and departed for the Asiatic-Pacific area.

Participated in battles in New Guinea and Luzon and received the following citations: Asiatic-Pacific Ribbon w/2 Bronze Stars, Good Conduct Ribbon, Victory Medal, American Defense Medal, American Theater Ribbon, Bronze Arrowhead and Philippine Liberation Ribbon w/ Bronze Star.

Pfc. Calhoun served with Co. D, 20th Inf., 6th Div. and was honorably discharged 11 Dec 1945 at Camp Atterbury, IN.

In June 1950 he received a BS degree from Murray State University and later received a master's degree from Murray State. In August 1950 he married Glenn Edna Campbell and in September 1950 began teaching in Paducah Public Schools where he later served as Director of Pupil Personnel for 23 years. In July 1976, he retired as principal of Cooper-Whiteside Elementary School.

Clarence passed away 8 Sep 1998 and is buried in East End Cemetery in Cadiz. He was a member of Maxon Christian Church where he served as a member of the church choir al long as his health permitted.

HERSHEL TAYLOR CALHOUN, served in the Pacific arena during the most intense fighting of the entire war with the Japanese. During the summer of 1943, American troops were engaged in fierce combat in an effort to secure the Solomon Islands, New Guinea and other strategically located Pacific Islands. The Japanese were "dug in deep" so that advance bombing raids were rather ineffective. The troops had the difficult task of storming the beaches and literally "rooting out" the Japanese troops. The loss of Americans was quite heavy as were the injured.

Hershel's story was best told by himself to his fellow residents of Friendship House in Hopkinsville, KY near the end of his life. Although he seldom spoke of the war events, this short autobiography gave those that knew him an unusual glance at his life in the military. Only two or three years before his death, he penned the following:

"I was born on 6 Jul 1915, the seventh in a family of 12 children. My parents were Henry Lee and Donie Ricks Calhoun. We lived on a farm in the southern part of Trigg County, KY. My schooling took place in a one-room school called Ross School.

I lived and worked on the farm until 1941, when the US entrance into WWII drew me into military service. On New Georgia Island, on 12 Jul 1943, I was wounded in action. I was carried back to the landing beach, where there was a makeshift hospital. The next day, under a canvas stretched beneath a big tree, my leg was amputated at the ankle. The "recovery room" where I awoke was in a dugout, with an air raid going on overhead.

Infection developed in my leg, and two days later, in a hospital on Guadalcanal, a second amputation removed my leg a few inches below the hip joint. I spent six or eight weeks in Fiji hospital, and in October 1943, I was back in San Francisco. After a few weeks in a hospital there, I was sent to McCloskey Hospital in Temple, TX. My stay there lasted until 23 Jun 1944, when I was discharged from the hospital and also given an honorable discharge from the armed forces."

He married Margaret Boaz in June 1952 and lived many years in Detroit, MI. After Margaret's death in 1980, Hershel moved back to Kentucky where he remained until his death in 1994.

JAMES LACY CALHOUN, Senior Master Sergeant, born 17 Jan 1927, son of James Jefferson and Ruth Calhoun. Entered military service 28 Feb 1945 and served overseas in the following countries: Philippine Islands, Korea, Puerto Rico, Trinidad, BWI, Japan, England, France, Spain, Guam, Vietnam, Thailand and Saipan.

Assignments were in Indiana, Georgia, Alabama, Oregon, South Carolina, Colorado, Texas, New Mexico, Ohio, Maine and New York. He served in both the US Army and USAF.

His decorations include the Bronze Star Medal, AF Commendation Medal, US Presidential Citation, Philippine Presidential Citation, Korea Presidential Citation, AF Outstanding Award, Army Good Conduct, AF Good Conduct, American Defense, American Campaign, Asiatic-Pacific Campaign, WWII Victory Medal, Army of Occupation Medal, National Defense Medal, Korean Service Medal, Vietnam Service Medal, AF Longevity Award, Small Arm Expert Ribbon, Philippine Defense Ribbon, Philippine Liberation Ribbon, UN Medal and Vietnam Campaign Medal.

After 30 years and four days of service, he retired from the USAF 1 Mar 1973

James and his wife Louise live in Sherman, TX and have two daughter, Belinda and Janet, and two grandchildren.

J.W. CAMERON, Corporal, born 5 Feb 1924, in Cerulean, KY, the son of Will J. and Grace Dunning Cameron. He was inducted into the U.S Marine Corps on 4 Jul 1943.

After finishing "boot camp" at the Naval Training Station, San Diego, CA, he was sent for training in Oklahoma. On 18 Mar 1944 he completed training courses from the Aviation Ordnance School, Norman, OK, and the Naval Air Gunners School, Purcell, OK. His final phase of training was at the Naval Air Station in Jacksonville, FL where he received the Wings of a Marine Aircrewman.

Until March 1945 he was stationed at the Marine Corps Air Station in El Centro, CA. He then served in the Pacific area (Guam) as a small arms mechanic until June 1946, a period of one year, two months and six days. On 6 Jun 1946 he was discharged with the rank of corporal at Camp Lejeune, NC.

J.W. returned to Cadiz where in 1943 he married a Trigg County girl, Edith Earl Stewart. They built a home on their farm located south of Cadiz where he continued to farm. J.W. died on 21 May 1973, from injuries sustained when a tractor overturned while he was mowing the shoulder of a road in front of the farm. He was 49 years of age.

KENNETH EDWARD CAMERON, Lieutenant, born 7 Dec 1922 in Cadiz, KY, son of John Gordon and Roby Litchfield Cameron. He had two sisters, Mary Grace Teague of Ledbetter, KY and Martha Jean Miller Brown of Dawson Springs. He was an Eagle Scout, an avid swimmer and had a passion for roller skating. He lived close to Little River and

spent many hours there row boating with John L. Street Jr. He attended Cadiz Grade School and graduated from Trigg County High with honors in extemporaneous speaking and debating. He debated with John D. Minton and eventually Ned Breathitt after entering University of Kentucky in 1941.

He joined the US Army at Fort Gordon, GA in 1943 and served until 1946 with the 10th Armd. Div. in the Adjutant Generals Dept. Lt. Cameron was overseas in Germany, 1944-46. His awards include the Bronze Star.

Re-entered the University of Kentucky, Beta Gamma Sigma, and graduated in August 1947 with BS - BA degree with distinction. Entered MBA program Northwestern University, Evanston, IL, 1948. He was selected by Kemper Ins. Co. as outstanding student and joined them to become assistant personnel manager in home office in Chicago. In 1953 he joined Industrial Nucleonic Corp. in Columbus, OH as personnel manager and remained with them through 1967 as assistant to president and corporate secretary.

In 1964 he married his secretary, Natalie Klingler of Columbus and son John Kenneth was born 18 Jan 1966. Kenneth established the Kenneth E. Cameron Co. in 1967 which purchased Dynametrics Inc. He founded or co-founded six other corporations in the computer and electronics field and served as director or officer of each. Home offices were located in Ohio and California.

His wife Natalie passed away in 1970. Ken and his son moved to the Kentucky Lake area and commuted to Ohio and California until he merged and sold interest in companies (1970-72). In 1976 he became executive director of Marshall County, Senior Citizens Inc. Comprehensive Education Training Program, Benton, KY. He is also a member of Four Rivers Boy Scout Executive Board, Marshall County.

Ken passed away of cancer 23 Oct 1980. His son John Kenneth graduated from Castle Heights Military Academy, Lebanon, TN in 1984. He joined the US Army with basic training at Fort Jackson, Columbia, SC; permanent duty station at Fort Hood, TX. Received AIT at Fort Gordon, GA; April 1990 to Fort Benning, GA, then overseas to Baumholder, Germany. He was discharged in 1992.

John married Jennifer Gunn of Columbus, GA in 1994. Both are working at Callaway Gardens, Columbus in office management while working on their college degrees.

FAY D. COSSEY, PFC, born 1920 and died in 1945 crossing the Rhine River. He is buried at Elm Grove Cemetery, Calloway County. He is survived by his parents, Will and Sarah (Young) Cossey; brother Ander Elvis and sister Leonia.

ROBERT GLENN CAMERON, Master Sergeant, born 1 Feb 1918 in Trigg County, KY, son of Will J. and Grace Dunning Cameron. Robert served in the US Army for over 26 years and attained the rank of master sergeant. He held a wide variety of important staff positions.

During his military career, Robert served with the Third Armored Division, Fort Knox, KY; HQ Fort Benjamin Harrison, IN; US Army Logistical Command, Japan; HQ RYUKYUS Command, Okinawa; 101st Abn. Div., Fort Campbell, KY; HQ USAREUR, Germany; US Army Combat Development Command, Fort Ord, CA; HQ 2nd Inf. Div., Korea; HQ Fort Baker, CA; and 1st Air Cav. Div., Vietnam.

His medals and commendations include Army of Occupation of Germany,

Army of Occupation of Japan, National Defense Service Medal, Korean Service Medal, Armed Forces Expeditionary Medal, Vietnam Service Medal, Good Conduct Medal (7th Award), Purple Heart, Rifle Sharp Shooter, Army Commendation Medal, 1st Oak Leaf Cluster in 1966, 2nd Oak Leaf Cluster in 1969, Bronze Star Medal, Republic of Vietnam, Meritorious Service Medal and Certificate of Appreciation.

He married Elizabeth Davis from Christian County, KY on 9 November 1940. They had three sons: Billy Rowe, Donald Glenn and Philip Rodney Cameron, and four grandchildren.

Robert and Elizabeth retired from the Army in 1973 and moved first to Long Island, NY, then to Punta Gorda, FL. Robert died 10 Feb 1992 and is buried at Riverside Cemetery in Hopkinsville, KY.

CLARENCE J. CARR, Corporal, born 18 Feb 1918 in Stewart County, TN and died 28 Dec 1981 in Trigg County KY. He was the ninth child of Thomas Jefferson (b. 1875, d. 1956)

and Daisy Sumner Carr (b. 1875, d. 1944). Clarence was a direct descendant of several early pioneers of Trigg County who came mostly from North Carolina, that include William Carr, William Turner, Isacc Sumner, Drewry Bridges, James Thomas and Nathan Tart.

Clarence grew up in a household with older sisters, and visiting nieces and nephews, some, not much younger than he. His sisters and brother were as follows: Louise (b. 1896, d. 1992) who married Edison Feltner; Molly (b. 1899, d. 1968) married Perkins Carr; William Amos (b. 1901, d. 1904); Jennie (b. 1903, d. 1984) married Gilbert Clark; Elna (b. 1906, d. 1991) married Bernice Rogers; Tommie Blanche (b. 1909, d. 1917); Annie Pearl (b. 1911, d. 1991) married James Carroll Kingins; and Dorothy (b. 1914, d. 1979) married Paul Kingins.

When Clarence was about 10, his father moved the family from "the hill" in Stewart County to across Saline creek to the general store and its attached house (that he had bought) in Trigg County. Clarence helped his father with some farming duties and clerking in the store until he entered service 29 May 1942. He took his basic training in Greenville, MS.

Back at home his parents had to close their store and move because their home had become a part of Camp Campbell Military Reserve.

Clarence spent three years, seven months and 20 days in service; three years, 27 days in continental service; and six months 23 days in foreign service. His military occupational specialty was supply clerk, while stationed at bases in Alaska and the Aleutian Islands. He was awarded the Asiatic-Pacific Theater, American Theater, Good Conduct and WWII Victory Medal. Cpl. Carr was separated from the Army Air Force at Fort Knox, KY, 18 Jan 1946.

A few years after service, Clarence became a civilian employee at Fort Campbell as a supply clerk where he worked for 20 years. He lived with his father, helping him run another rather small general store on Cadiz south road. After his father died, Clarence bought a farm where he lived until his health began to decline. He then lived with his sister Jennie until his death.

Clarence liked to foxhunt and from his youth kept hunting dogs. The writer remembers his fox horn hanging on the porch. He also liked to play the harmonica, especially when his father was picking the mandolin. *Submitted by Patsy Kingins Myers, niece of Clarence J. Carr.*

CLELAND F. CARR, Radioman 1/c, born 5 Jan 1921 in Christopher, IL. He moved to Trigg County when a baby with his grandparents. Cleland joined the USN in May 1942 and served until October 1945. He trained at Great Lakes, IL and was sent to Radio School at Northwestern University in Evanston, IL.

He began his service on the destroyer USS *Rodman* and participated in the Normandy invasion and invasion of southern France. Later his ship was converted to a mine sweeper and sent to the Pacific. The *Rodman* was in the longest kamikaze battle (off Okinawa) of the war. He was discharged in October 1945.

After service he was with the J.C. Penney Co. for 40 years. He was store manager in four different stores. He moved to Memphis, TN in 1972.

Cleland married Eunice Dunn 31 Aug 1942 and they have two daughters, Irma Carr Idell and Marilyn Carr Elledge, and one grandson Andrew David Idell. Cleland died 7 Nov 1994.

HOLLIS WADE CARR, Supply Sergeant, son of Eva Lena Calhoun and Fay Carr, was born 22 Jul 1919 in the Lock E Community. He was drafted in the US Army 31 Jan 1942 at Fort Benjamin Harrison, IN and after 13 weeks training at Camp Wheeler, GA, he departed with 111th Inf., Co. B for the Coastal Artillery Dist., MA and Chesapeake Bay, VA sector where they patrolled the eastern shoreline.

The 111th (part of the 28th Div.) was re-organized into a combat team and arrived 12 Nov 1943 at Schofield Barracks, HI in the Pacific Theater of Operations. Th 7th Inf. Div. Cav. and Co. B, 111th Inf. Participated in action in the Marshall Islands; captured the island of Cecil and Carter; secured the Cecil Pass into the Kwajalein lagoon; and assaulted the islands of Carlos and Carlson.

Battleships and heavy cruisers joined the pre-invasion bombardment and the Army Air Force added six B-24 bombers to the effort, dropping 15 bombs, 1,000 and 2,000 pounds, on Kwajalein. The collective power of Army, Navy and Air Force was overwhelming; all beach defenses were completely destroyed. The following days were mop-up, rebuilding and guard duty.

They returned to Schofield Barracks 6 Oct 1944 for a rest until 17 Jan 1945 when they arrived on Pula in Palau Island and assumed tactical duties of the 321st Inf. RCT, 81st Inf. Div. The 111th Inf. Received heavy casualties during mopping up operations on Peletier Island.

The war in the Pacific ended in September 1945 and Hollis returned home and was discharged 10 Dec 1945 at Fort Knox, KY. His awards include the Marksman, Combat Infantry Badge, Eastern Mandates Western Pacific, WWII Victory Medal, American Theater Ribbon, Good Conduct Medal w/clasp and the Asiatic-Pacific Theater Ribbon w/2 Bronze Service Stars.

A few months after discharge he was employed with Lasalle Steel Mill, Hammond, IN. He married a Trigg County girl, Myra Dean Guier, on 3 Dec 1946. In 1947 they bought a farm in Kentucky from Myra's grandfather, but farm life was short as he took a position with the US Corp of Engineers in November 1947 as a lockman at Lock D, Dover, TN.

In 1965 the impoundment of Barkley Dam, Lake City, KY submerged Lock C, D and E and he was transferred to Barkley Reservoir as construction maintenance supervisor. He was given the honor of Kentucky Colonel 27 Apr 1971 with Louie B. Nunn, Governor. After 36-1/2 years of service, he retired 31 Dec 1978.

Hollis and Myra have one son Jeffrey, born 16 Sep 1959, daughter-in-law Christi, and two grandchildren, John Parker and William Joseph. They enjoy traveling, being with their grandchildren and are active in community and church affairs. They live in Cadiz, KY. He thanks God for being so good to him and he is proud to be a veteran of the good ole USA.

PRUITT CARR, Corporal, born 19 Dec 1910, Trigg County, to Milton and Mary Futrell Carr. His sisters are Kathleen Askew and Myrtie Jane Kreutzer. His niece, Ann Askew Major, currently resides in Trigg County. Pruitt married Doris Evans 8 Jan 1938, in Colorado. Their daughter Ellen Carr Harris was born 21 Jul 1943. Grandchildren are William Harris and Karla Araneda and great-grandchildren are Brittany Harris and Jayme and Kassandra Araneda. Pruitt loved horses and managed a horse ranch.

He enlisted in the Army and was assigned to the 358th Regt., 90th Div. which was reactivated at Camp Barkeley, TX 25 Mar 1942. Participated in the Normandy invasion, landing on Utah Beach. He was awarded the Bronze Star for heroic achievement 11 Jun 1944. From a news clipping: "...Cpl. Carr, despite intense enemy fire, patrolled the flank of the 358th Combat team and established needed liaison between the 357th and 358th regiments...."

They advanced toward Germany through the summer and early fall. Reached Thionville on the Mozelle River just a few miles from the German border on 12 September. Days of rain turned the river into a raging torrent, 1.5 miles wide and it became the "other" enemy. Ground troops crossed 9 November. Engineers were unable to establish a bridge to enable armor and vehicles to cross and support the ground troops. German artillery shelled the crossing sites with deadly accuracy from observation posts across the river.

"...Cpl. Carr, a squad leader and acting platoon sergeant, voluntarily and at risk of his own life..." carried a wounded comrade over 60 yards of open ground to safety. He then charged the enemy gun position with a bazooka. Although Cpl. Carr was fatally wounded in this action, the fearless courage with which he attacked the enemy emplacement diverted their attention and enabled a comrade advancing from another direction to destroy it..." He was awarded a Silver Star and a Purple Heart for his actions.

His legacy is an important part of his family's history. *Submitted by Ellen Harris and Ann Major.*

ROBERT PERKINS CARR, PFC, born 26 Oct 1921 in Trigg County, KY. His parents were Mollie and Perkins Carr. He was a graduate of Trigg County HS and enlisted into the US Army 23 Oct 1945. His entry into service was at Camp Atterbury, IN; organization was Co. B, 504th MP BN. He served in Germany as a military policeman #677 until 1947.

Decoration, citations and badges earned include the Army Occupation Medal, WWII Victory Medal, M-1 Rifle (145) MKM, Robert Perkins was honorably discharged from the military service at the Separation Center, Fort Dix, NJ on 16 Feb 1947.

In civilian life he returned to Linton, KY and made his home there. He clerked in a grocery store owned by his father. Robert passed away in 1985. *Submitted by Thomas Carr.*

WILLIAM HULETTE CARR, son of Mr. and Mrs. G.H. Carr, left Trigg County, KY for duty in the US Army 9 Sep 1942. Hulette Carr was over the draft age but felt it was his duty to join the fight.

He was assigned to foreign service in January 1943 and participated in the invasion of North Africa, the Sicilian Campaign and the Salerno Campaign. He was a chief rigger on the supply ship.

William was wounded on 17 Jul 1943 when the troops were loading supplies onto barges for the Sicilian invasion and died shortly after. He is buried in East End Cemetery, Trigg County, KY. Awards include the Purple Heart and the European Theater Ribbon. *Information from Mrs. Litchfield's scrapbook.*

LLOYD J. "BOURBON" CHEWNING, Master Sergeant, born 4 Nov 1916 near Cadiz, Trigg County, KY, son of Jack and Emma Chewning. He attended grade school at Crossroads and Rogers HS at Linton, KY (GED 1961). They were farmers and he remained on the farm until his enlistment in the US Army 8 Nov 1937.

Lloyd received his military training at Fort Benjamin Harrison, IN and went on to many places such as Fort Custer, MI; Fort McClellan, AL; Fort Knox, KY; South Carolina and Iceland.

He retired as master sergeant 1 Apr 1966 at Fort Knox, KY after having served 27 plus years in the States and overseas as platoon sergeant, Co. G, 27th Inf., Japan; Tank Co., 110th Inf., Germany; instructor, Weapons Department, US Armor School, Fort Knox, KY; Co. L, Student Regt., US Armor School, Fort Knox, KY. At the time of his retirement he was an instructor, Committee Group, US Army Training Center, Armor, Fort Knox, KY (basic rifle marksmanship).

MSgt. Chewning received the Bronze Star, Purple Heart, Good Conduct w/silver clasp and two loops, American Defense Service Medal, American Campaign, Asiatic-Pacific Campaign, WWII Victory, Army of Occupation (Japan and Germany), National Defense Service, Korean Service, UN Service, Philippine Liberation Ribbon, Philippine PUC, ROK PUC, Combat Infantry Badge, many Good Conduct Awards and numerous medals for pistol competitions.

He was injured from a flamethrower (severe burns) and hospitalized in Osaka, Japan; suffered a broken ankle in a fall from a balcony; and witnessed the explosion of the Atom Bomb in Nevada.

In 1948 he married Missoula Sue McKinney, daughter of Alvie and Maudie McKinney of Cadiz. They returned to Japan where their son Eddie Earl was born. After returning to Fort Knox, KY, they purchased a home at Valley Station, KY.

After retirement from the service in 1966 he had a second career of 16 years with the University of Louisville Speed School as a shop maintenance instructor.

Lloyd's son Eddie is now a retired AF master sergeant and Eddie's son Brian is a loadmaster with the USAF. Eddie's daughter Keli is continuing a college education. Missoula passed away in 1985. Lloyd married Ruth in 1988 and they reside in Pleasure Ridge Park, KY, a suburb of Louisville, KY. *Submitted by Ruth Chewning.*

WILLIAM R. CHILDRESS, Sergeant, born 9 Nov 1920. He joined the service 15 Jan 1940 at Nashville, TN and was assigned to the 6th Cav., Fort Oglethorpe, GA, 15 Jan 1940 to 1 Feb 1942.

Stationed at Camp Blanding, FL; Fort Jackson, SC, Ireland, England and France. He participated in the Battle of the Bulge 9 Jan 1945 to 29 Apr 1945.

Sgt. Childress was discharged 25 Sep 1948. His awards include the American Defense, American Theater, POW Medal, WWII Victory Medal, ETO and Good Conduct.

Employed with Linen Supply Co., Chicago, IL from 1948 to 1983 and retired from Means Services. He is single and lives in Cadiz, KY.

JAMES CLAYTON CHOATE, Tech 5, born 6 Feb 1924. He was drafted 10 Mar 1943 and left Cadiz 17 Mar 1943 for active duty. He went to Fort Benjamin Harrison, IN and Fort Lawton, Seattle, WA. He took basic training, Infantry 521 and longshoreman and truck driving.

Left Seattle 25 Sep 1943 for Africa, loaded equipment on ship and left for India. They unloaded ship at Calcutta and sent supplies to Burma and China. They had a lot of air raids but were never hit.

James was discharged 19 Feb 1946 as tech 5. His awards include the american

Theater Ribbon, Asiatic-Pacific Theater Ribbon, Good Conduct and Victory Medal.

He worked at Firestone Tire and Rubber Co., Akron, OH, until retirement on 1 Jan 1982. Married Clara Wicks in 1948 and their sons are William, John L., Michael, Norman, James, John Martin (adopted); two grandchildren; and Jeffery Allen Stone (foster child).

AL CLINARD, Captain, born 27 Jun 1923, Carlsbad, TX. He graduated from Lake View High in June 1939 and enlisted in Hq&Hq Btry., 15th FA, 2nd Inf. Div., 16 Jul 1939 at Fort Sam Houston, San Antonio, TX.

Shipped overseas in October 1942, landing in Belfast, northern Ireland. He became a forward observer, directing artillery fire while working with the 9th Inf. Combat Team. From Ireland, South Wales to Portmouth, England to Normandy, France on 6 Jun 1944, D-Day, Omaha Blue Beach. He participated in Belgium Bulge in the winter of 1944, crossed the Rhine River on the Remagen Bridge before it fell in and met the Russians at the Elbe River, then to Czechoslovakia until the war ended 8 May 1945.

Discharged 23 Jun 1945, took a few days leave then enlisted in the Signal Corps with assignments in Okinawa, Guam, Fort Bragg (1951), France (1953-56), Fort Campbell (1956-59), Korea (1959-60). Returned to Fort Campbell as post signal officer until his retirement 1 Nov 1961.

Medals include the Bronze Star w/valor, EAME Campaign Medal w/5 Bronze Stars, Good Conduct, American Defense Service Medal, Occupation Medal (Japan), Korean Service Medal and Army Commendation Medal w/5 OLCs.

Married Jane 30 Dec 1942 and they have four children: Harry, Tom, Richard and Rosa; eight grandchildren and six great-grandchildren. Resides in Cadiz, KY; chaplain, VFW 1913; Masonic Post 121, Cadiz; 33rd degree Scotish Rites, Madisonville.

JANE A. CLINARD, born 21 Sep 1921. Served in the Army Nurse Corps from May 1941 through 1942. She was assigned to Brooke Army Medical Center, Fort Sam Houston, TX. As a second lieutenant in 1941, she met her husband Al Clinard while he was in the US Army and assigned to Fort Sam Houston during treatment of yellow jaundice. He was in the hospital for three months, and during that time they fell in love and were married on 30 Dec 1942.

She was promoted in 1942 to first lieutenant and subsequently received orders to England; however, it was discovered she was pregnant and was taken off orders and Army regulations forcing her to resign from the military.

She entered civil service as a nurse and served at Vancouver Barracks, Washington State until 1945 when her husband returned from WWII. In 1945, she earned her master's degree in nursing from St. Mary's University, TX. She spoke fluent French, Spanish and Italian and as she accompanied her military, career husband around the world, she was always involved with health care. Whatever country she and her officer husband were stationed, she conducted "Mother and Baby Care" courses.

They settled down in Trigg County where she served as Trigg County Public Nurse for eight years. She provided home health care for 12 to 15 military veterans that were dialysis patients from Lyon, Trigg, and Caldwell counties,

Always proud of the fact that though not a doctor, she was a doctor's helper. More than once when she came upon a scene of an accident she was ready to help. Family and friends remember "Janie" Clinard, as someone who did whatever she had to do to help others. She was above all a caring nurse, a devoted wife, mother and most certainly a courageous individual. She was always proud of the fact that she had served as an Army nurse during WWII.

She and husband Al Clinard have four children: Rosa Ann, Thomas David, Richard Joe and Harry Louis and seven grandchildren. In 1981, Jane's health began to fail and in 1994 she passed away.

GEORGE D. COLBERT, Sergeant, enlisted in the service 27 Oct 1942 at Chicago, IL. He participated in action in Leyte, Samar, Mindoro in Philippines and Okinawa.

Assignments included squad leader, comm. chief, cook, rifleman, provost sergeant and others. Sgt. Colbert was discharged 4 Jan 1946. He received the Purple Heart (2) Bronze Star and others.

Civilian employment as farmer, factory worker, cannery worker, law officer, auto mechanic, meat cutter, storekeeper, security guard and steel mill.

Married Helen in 1968 and they have five children: David, Cynthia, Patricia, Todd and George Jr.; and seven grandchildren: Amy, David, Michael, Kimberly, Zackary, Victoria and Allen.

George's three brothers served in the Navy during WWII; four brothers-in-law served in the Air Force; two sons and two grandsons served in the Marines.

JAMES R. CLARK, born Aug. 8, 1920 at Milford, IL. He enlisted in the USMC in 1941, but was allowed to finish his senior year of college at Western Illinois University. He graduated on 8 August (my birthday) and left at 7:00 a.m. 9 August by bus, for basic training at Paris Island, SC.

After basic, he went to Officers Training at Quantico, VA and graduated with Plt. 633. After a brief leave, it was on to Camp Elliott, CA. Basic and officers training was tough, but what he soon encountered was tougher. Rank was insignificant in conflicts.

Setting sail for New Caledonia in the Russell Islands was not without either seasickness or homesickness. They were a battalion of amphibious tanks and attached to the 1st Marine Division headed to Peleliu, one of the bloodiest battles of the South Pacific.

They returned to Russell Island, regrouped for assignments in Okinawa, Guam, Saipan, and lastly for him, Nagasaki, where the 2nd Atomic Bomb was dropped, for the occupation of Japan. After three years, he was among the fortunate to return home. He was a recipient of the Purple Heart, Battle Stars and scars as many others did.

He still prays for all wars to end.

HARRY CLINTON COLEMAN, Aviation Machinist's Mate 3/c, born 11 Apr 1918 at Cadiz, KY. He was drafted into the USN 31 Jan 1942 with training at Naval Training Station, Great Lakes, IL; NAV Training School, Navy Pier, Chicago, IL; Lion No. 1; AV Rep. And Overhaul Unit, Espiritu; NAS Treasure Island, CA.

After training in Chicago, Harry was given a 10-day leave before reporting to Moffett Field, CA. In school he completed training for an aviation machinist. From California he boarded the SS *Mormacport*, crossed the Equator 6 May 1943 bound for the Fiji Islands, and crossed the 180th Meridian 13 May 1943. They were part of the Far Eastern Theater of War. From the Fiji Island they went to the New Hebrides.

Returned to California where he was discharged as aviation machinist's mate 3/c, USNR at San Pedro, 10 Nov 1945. Awards include WWII Victory Medal, Good Conduct and Asiatic-Pacific Theater.

Harry recalls "the rains came and torpedoes were launched all around us."

Returning to civilian life, he began work at Henry White's Chevrolet then at Fort Campbell from where he retired in January 1970.

Harry is the son of Johnnie Pearl Bridges Coleman and Herman Coleman. He married Irene Fourshee they live in Cadiz, KY. He is a member of Canton Baptist Church.

ELMO HODGE COLSON, born 31 Jul 1921 in the community of Ferguson Spring, Golden Pond, KY, the son of James Hardy and Irene Fennell Colson. He was drafted into the Army in 1943, assigned to Co. 369 MPEGC and was killed in a jeep accident 3 Dec 1945 in Leavenworth, KS. He was brought back home and buried at Ferguson Spring Cemetery. *Submitted by Mary Grace Anderson.*

HOMER B. COLSON, Corporal, born 2 Mar 1916 at Golden Pond, KY. He enlisted in the service 10 Jul 1941 at Louisville, KY. Cpl. Colson was discharged 27 Sep 1945. His awards include the American Defense Ribbon.

Homer married Lorene Shelton 9 Nov 1951 and they have one daughter Peggy and two grandchildren, Kaci Lane and Halee Shay Greer. Homer was employed with TVA and passed away 6 Sep 1984.

LACY W. COMPTON, Sergeant, born 7 Jul 1916 in Trigg County, KY. He was drafted into the US Army 17 Feb 1943. After basic training at Fort McClellan, AL, he was sent to Fort Prebble Army Base, ME. After further training he planted mines off the Atlantic Coast.

When the opportunity arose he joined the Army Air Corps and went to Fort Benning, GA for paratrooper training. On the eve before shipping out to France, they made their last practice jump and his parachute came down through a pine tree. He injured his eyes, along with other injuries, so was left behind. Unable to jump again, he trained to be a radioman and served two years in the American Theater as radioman and inspector.

Sgt. Compton received his separation papers 28 Feb 1946 at 13th Div, USAAC, Camp Atterbury, IN. He received the American Theater Ribbon, Good Conduct Medal and WWII Victory Medal.

After discharge he went to Detroit, MI where he retired from General Motors Co. He later moved to Clair, MI where he worked with Auxiliary Police. In later years he volunteered his time working with youth offenders.

He married Helen Clark in 1939 and they had one son. They divorced and he later married Maxine Brogdon and they had a son. There are three grandsons from his first marriage. Lacy passed away 16 Oct 1993 and is buried in Clair, MI.

LOYD CLAYTON COMPTON, PFC, born 6 May 1922 in Trigg County, KY. He married Thelma Choate 22 Nov 1941 and was drafted into the US Army 26 Dec 1942 at Fort Benjamin Harrison, IN. He was attached to 176th Inf. in Anacosta, DC where they lived in tents near the Potomic River.

He took basic training at Fort Myers, VA and A.P. Hill, VA. One night as they maneuvered over rough terrain, he fell and injured his right

wrist. After basic training they were transferred to Fort Benning, GA in 1943. His wrist was getting worse and when he was sent to the hospital for surgery, they discovered he had a cracked bone. Because of this he was transferred out of the 176th as PFC to Co. B Academic Regt. Inf. School where he remained until his honorable discharge 8 Dec 1945.

His awards include the American Theater Ribbon, Good Conduct Medal and WWII Victory Medal.

After discharge he returned to Cadiz, KY and worked in the timber industry. In 1948 he moved to Hopkinsville, KY and worked with civil services at Fort Campbell, KY until retirement 2 Aug 1986. He enjoys gardening and hunting. He and his wife are members of Parkway Baptist Church.

GROVER DOUGLAS "BUBBY" CREAMER, born in Trigg County on 21 Jun 1912 to Tom and Hester Creamer. He was inducted into the Army on 29 Jul 1942 at Evansville, IN. After completing training on the Pacific Coast, Bubby was sent to the Pacific arena for combat. Bubby received distinction as rifle marksman and bayonet expert.

Bubby was attached to Co. D 800th MP Bn. He served in Australia, the Philippines, and occupation of Japan after its surrender. Bubby drove army trucks up to 5-ton capacity to transport supplies, equipment, and personnel. His separation qualification record states that he drove under blackout conditions, over all types of terrain and in convoys.

Bubby was awarded the Asiatic-Pacific Theater Ribbon w/Bronze Star, the Philippine Liberation Ribbon, Good Conduct Medal, and WWII Victory Medal. Bubby was honorably discharged 12 Jan 1946 from Camp Atterbury, IN. Two days later, he married his Trigg County sweetheart, Ell Maurine Cunningham. Maurine's father, Elsworth Cunningham, was sitting on the front porch the first day Bubby walked up. El had been blinded for a number of years, but he recognized Bubby's footstep and started calling for "Reen" to come quick because Bubby was home.

Bubby and Maurine had two children, Thomas Elmer and Donna Jane (Carter) before Maurine's death on 21 Nov 1950 after a battle with breast cancer. Bubby was left to raise two preschoolers. He never once entertained the idea of not having his children at his side always.

Although Bubby married twice after Maurine's death, his heart remained true to Maurine. In June 1973 Bubby was diagnosed with pancreatic cancer. About two weeks before his death, Bubby's final act of devotion was to send roses to Maurine's gravesite. On 21 Oct 1973, he joined her in their final resting place in Allen Cemetery on Floyd Sumner Road. They currently reside at Streets of Gold, Heaven. Their landlord is Jesus.

HENRY PETER CROCETTI, Chief Clerk, born 29 May 1926 in Gifford, IL. He enlisted as an aviation cadet in the USAAF in April 1944 at Chanute Field, Rantoul, IL, then to Fort Sheridan Induction Center. Took his basic training at Keesler Field, MS, and stayed there for B-32 Specialist School, Airplane and Engine Repair Tech School, then on to Kelly Field, TX for B-32 flight engineer training.

On the way to Kelly Field V-E Day occurred and B-32 was declared obsolete and the school closed. He was shipped to Tinker Field, OK for redeployment. While at Tinker he re-enlisted for one year and was sent to Europe as part of the Army of Occupation.

He was assigned to the 632nd Air Material Sqdn. in the European Air Transport Service in Bovington, England and later in Bremen, Germany, where he was chief clerk, at the time of his discharge in December 1946. He enlisted in the USAAFR and was discharged in December 1949.

He married Marguerite Terry from Hornbeak, TN on 13 Jul 1952. They have three children: Mitchell, Cynthia, Jeffrey; and five grandchildren: Adam, Mitchell, Jordan, Jane and Jessica. He retired after 31 years service from the Teletype Corp. where he was an instructor in the Teletype Technical Training Center. They moved to Trigg County, Cadiz, KY in April 1982.

ALVIN HALE CRUMP, PFC, born 5 May 1922 in Lyon County. He enlisted in November 1942 at Cadiz and participated in all European Campaigns and in England during WWII. Pfc. Crump was discharged 25 Oct 1945.

Married Leenora Higgins 21 Dec 1946 and they live in Cadiz, KY. He has three stepchildren: Pauline Crump, Donald Jones, Retta J. Balentine; and four grandchildren: Paula C. Flood, Raybon Crump Jr., Stephen Jones and Lori Lee Jones. Alvin retired in 1988 from Howard K. Bell Consulting Eng.

ALBERT DALE CUNNINGHAM, PFC, was the second child and son of George Clyde Cunningham and Robbie (Bridges) Cunningham. He was born 30 Aug 1925 and grew up on Beechy Fork Creek in the Maple Grove Community. He attended Lower Donaldson School and Maple Grove School.

On 15 Nov 1943, at the age of 18, he entered the US Army and received his basic training at Camp Blanding, FL. He was given furlough 28 Mar 1944-7 Apr 1944, then left for Fort Meade, MD where he was shipped overseas in May 1944. On 18 May he landed in Naples, Italy as part of Co. G, 143rd Inf. Regt., 36th Inf. Div., which was part of the 5th Army under the command of Gen. Mark Clark. The 36th was the Texas Division and the troops were known as the "T-Patchers" due to their insignia being made up of an arrowhead with a capital T in the middle. He was assistant gunner on an 81mm mortar.

Starting in May 1944 he fought in various locations across Italy and Southern France. On 28 Nov 1944, Pfc. Cunningham was killed in action during heavy fighting as the remainder of the German 19th Army threw everything it had at the 36th in an effort to hold the Vosges Mountain passes. For the first time in history the St. Marie Pass had been successfully taken by an attacking army.

Albert was buried at Epinal France. His body was returned to the States in April 1948 and he was buried in the Allen-Cunningham Cemetery with full Military Honors.

He was a member of the Maple Grove Baptist Church, a devout Christian and a good soldier. He is survived by his mother, Robbie Bell Bridges Cunningham; two brothers, Aubry and Alfred; three sisters: Dollie May Stokes, Martha Quarles and Mava Brown.

Albert's mother dreamed in detail about his death the night he died. Ten years later Clarence Malone of Trigg County came to Albert's dad and told him he was with Albert (both on the mortar gun) the night he died and told him in detail what happened and it was exactly as Albert's mom had dreamed he died.

GUY TERRY CUNNINGHAM, PFC, born 12 Oct 1902, at Canton, Trigg County, KY. His parents were Charles B. and Beulah C. Cunningham. He had two brothers, Arvin Lois and Carl Treavor, and three sisters: Edna Lilian, Thelma Ion and Juanita Rose.

He was inducted 26 Aug 1942, at Evansville, IN. He was 39 years of age and his occupation was listed as a truck driver, light. Guy received an honorable discharge from the Army of the United States Enlisted Reserve Corps 25 Sep 1944, at Fort Hayes, Columbus, OH. His rank was private first class.

Guy, who was called "Fatty" by his friends, was a friendly individual and active in Trigg County politics. He retired as a truck driver with the Kentucky Highway Department in Trigg County.

Guy Terry Cunningham died 10 Jul 1964. He was buried in the family plot, East End Cemetery, Cadiz, KY.

JAMES ARVIN CUNNINGHAM, Ship's Cook 2/c, born 18 Feb 1926 in the Canton area of Trigg County, the oldest child of Olive and Roberta Cunningham. He was drafted into the Navy 30 May 1944; took boot training at Great Lakes, IL and amphibious training at Little Creek, VA.

Transferred to Charleston, SC on 11 Dec 1944 and went aboard USS LSN 200 for commission ceremony. The LSM 200 was a flotilla flag ship for Flotilla 11. They served as training ship until preparation for invasion of Japan. In summer of 1945 they loaded pontoons at Providence, RI and headed for Japan.

While going through the Panama Canal, the Atomic Bomb was dropped and they continued on to Pearl Harbor and transported Marines and equipment to smaller islands in the Pacific. After serving in both the Atlantic and Pacific, the 200 returned to Green Cove Springs, FL where the ship was decommissioned in June 1946. He was discharged 4 Jun 1946 as ship cook 2/c.

Married Betty Jo Bridges in February 1948 and they have three daughters: Shearon Outland, Karen Baker, Patti Heaton, and son David. They also have nine grandchildren and two great-granddaughters. They reside in Cadiz and are members of Maple Grove Baptist Church.

James is a graduate of Trigg County HS and Tennessee Automotive Trade School in Nashville. In 1960 he entered into a partnership business, East Cadiz Garage, and worked as an auto body repairman. He retired in December 1987.

He joined the National LSM Association in 1992 and attends reunions each year. In August 2000 they attended the reunion in Omaha, NE and toured the LSM 45 which was given to the Association by Greece and has been restored by the Association and is on display at Freedom Park, a naval museum in Omaha.

RAYMON HAYDEN CUNNINGHAM, Tech 4, born 3 Mar 1920 in Rockcastle Community, Trigg County, son of Waymon and Velno Cunningham. He was drafted into active service of US Army 9 Sep 1942. He was assigned to HQ&HQ Sqdn., 14th Air Force, Sioux City, IA.

He received training at San Antonio, TX, California and Arizona; completed course study in Air Craft Torpedo School, Keyport, WA, May 1943; and course study in Naval Mine Warfare School, Aerial Mines, Yorktown, VA, August 1943.

One furlough was all he had before he went overseas. His last day in Trigg County was 15 Mar 1944. His ship sailed from Virginia 22 Apr 1944, destination NATO, and arrived in CBI 10 Aug 1944. He served in the Pacific Theater as ammunition worker, stored, issued, loaded, unloaded or destructed all types from supply points, performing duties under Japanese plane attacks in China.

Returned to the States and received honorable discharge 13 Jan 1946 at Camp Atterbury, IN with the rank Tech 4. His awards include the American Theater Ribbon, Asiatic-Pacific Theater Ribbon w/2 Bronze Stars, EAME Theater Ribbon, Good Conduct and WWII Victory Medal.

Married Frances Gray in February 1946 and they lived and worked on a farm. Their children are Rebecca Knight, Sarah Neighborgall, David, Eunice Stone; and three grandchildren: Jason and Melanie Knight and Mackenzie Stone. Raymon passed away in 1995 and is buried in Hurricane Cemetery. Frances still lives on the farm.

SHIRLEY ALLEN CUNNINGHAM, Corporal, born 26 Nov 1916. He joined the US Army in 1941 with basic training at North Carolina.

He laid communication lines in Austraila, North and Southern New Guinea and Canada. He was proud of his service and that he worked along with his men helping them even though he was corporal-in-charge. He left active duty in 1945.

As a civilian he farmed, worked for Cadiz Housing Authority, University of Kentucky Farm Cooperative Coordinator, and was an active member in the Cadiz VFW.

Married Marie Curlin in October 1953 and had three children: Shirley Jr., Henry and Molley Sue (deceased); also six grandchildren: Christopher, Brandon, Shirley III, Thomas, Ricardo and James. Shirley Allen passed away 24 Mar 2000.

THOMAS ELWOOD "TOMMY" CUNNINGHAM, 2nd Lieutenant, born 23 Nov 1927 near Canton in Trigg County. He was drafted into the US Army on 10 Mar 1946 at Camp Atterbury, IN. He was transferred to Fort Lewis, WA and assigned to the 2914th Engineer Base Equipment Co. as a heavy truck driver. His last assignment was Fort Belvoir, VA. He was discharged 9 Sep 1947 as a Tech 5.

Tommy graduated from Trigg County HS in 1945 and from Western Kentucky University with his BS and MA degrees and Rank I Certifica-

tion. He completed ROTC and was a 2nd lieutenant in the USAFR and was discharged 3 Apr 1959.

He retired in 1985 from a career in education which included positions as teacher, coach, Federal Program Coordinator, Director Of Pupil Personnel and principal. During his career he and his family lived in a number of Kentucky communities including Cadiz where he was a teacher and assistant basketball coach from 1959-63. He retired as principal of Clarkson Elementary School in Grayson County, KY and later moved to Columbia, KY.

Tommy was the son of Olive James and Roberta Williams Cunningham. He married Frances Lucille Wesley 16 Aug 1950. They have two daughters, Debora Fran (md. Thomas Hayse Jr.) and Tomi Renae (md. Walter H. Miller); four grandchildren and two great-grandchildren. Tommy passed away 29 Jun 1990 and is buried in Haven Hill Cemetery, Columbia, KY.

BOYCE W. CURRY, Sergeant, born in Trigg County, son of Thomas and Nanny Curry. He entered the US Army in 1942 and served in WWII as a radioman with the Signal Corps in the South Pacific.

While on active duty, Boyce was killed by a sniper 23 Jun 1945 on Luzon Island. He is buried there in the US Military Cemetery. His brother is Sam Curry.

CURTIS CURLIN, was stationed at Fort Bragg, NC and served in WWII. He was not at Pearl Harbor when the attack was made and the bombing occurred when his ship was late for its destination.

JESSE BOYD DARNELL, Staff Sergeant, born 12 Aug 1918 in Trigg County, KY. He was drafted into the US Army 23 Jan 1941 and left Cadiz along with seven other Trigg County boys and were sworn in at Louisville, KY.

From Fort Thomas, KY they were sent to Fort Crockett, TX and re-manned an old Coast Artillery fort, which had been under caretakers since WWI, with 10 and 12 inch Coast Artillery guns. He was ready to come home when Pearl Harbor was bombed, so there went his discharge. He was a gun commander on the 12-inch guns and began training recruits for combat. He stayed there throughout the war, guarding the raw chemical plants, the Houston ship channel and the Texas City Refinery.

In 1943 he married a Trigg County girl, Eleanor Moore and they have four children: Larry, Virginia, John and Marcha; seven grandsons and nine great-grandchildren. Larry served in the Navy in the Cuban blockade and John was wounded in Vietnam.

As a civilian he worked in construction in Chicago, IL. After retirement he moved back to Cadiz in 1980. They are members of East Cadiz Baptist Church. Of the eight boys who left Trigg in 1941, he is the only one still living.

JESSE THOMAS FENTRESS DARNELL, Major, born 24 Sep 1918 in Trigg County, KY and entered the US Army 19 Sep 1940. He went to Fort Knox where he met his brother Johnnie C.

Neither had known the other was volunteering for service. After basic he went to Fort Bragg, NC as a private. His brother went another direction.

At Fort Bragg, he met Mary Lou McNeill, Fayetteville NC and they married 21 Aug 1941. He went to Camp Gruber, OK and Fort Benning, GA. He left Georgia in November 1943 for North Africa staging area after Rommell's defeat. His troop-train passed through Fayetteville, NC where he said it was hard to resist jumping off the train.

In 1944 he made tech sergeant and after battle training he went by boat to Italy with the 350th Inf. Regt. Battles began from the toe of the boot of Italy all the way to Austria. During battle, with his leaderless company under heavy attack, he took command. He saved his company by going into enemy territory and directing his comrades where to fire, unceasingly if his radio went silent, knowing he would likely be killed.

For meritorious service, splendid courage and bravery in battle, he was given a Battlefield Commission making him 2nd lieutenant and awarded the Bronze Star, 2 Apr 1945 by Commanding Gen. J.C. Frye. One month later he was promoted to 1st lieutenant.

He was discharged from active duty 21 Oct 1945 and re-entered the Army with duties as gunnery officer and ordinance shop officer. Served as commanding officer in south Korea in June 1950, made motor officer 3 Aug 1951, and as dock ordinance officer went to Japan 26 Mar 1952. His wife joined him there shortly and later his brother Elias arrived in the same port.

In March 1953 he was transferred to Michigan as Ordinance Tank and Automotive Commander; April 1957, sent to France as Post Ordinance Officer; December 1957, made company commander. Maj. Darnell retired from the Army in July 1965 at Fort Bragg. His awards include Service Medals, WWII Victory, Good Conduct Medals, Bronze and Silver Stars and OSS Bars.

He retired in 1980 as general manager of an automobile dealership. He was of Christian faith and passed away 28 Nov 1990 with interment in Fayetteville, NC. He left his wife Mary Lou, two children, Jamie and Susan Elaine, and granddaughter Shelby Darnell.

CAREY THOMAS "SONNY" DAVIS, born 23 Oct 1923 in Trigg County, KY, the son of Alfred L. "Bill" and Lou Belle Thomas Davis. He lived with his parents in Detroit, MI, from 1925 until the Great Depression came in late 1929. His parents returned to Trigg County, sold their shiny new Model A Ford, bought a wagon and a team of mules and in 1930 resumed life as farmers.

Sonny and his baby sister, Joyce, adapted to the changes rapidly. He had started school at Oak Grove, later attending Lower Donaldson, Warrenton and again Oak Grove. In May 1938, a baby brother Carl Gary "Ned" joined the family.

When the United States became engaged in WWII, he attempted to join the USN, however, he did not pass the physical. In December 1943, he joined the US Merchant Marines in Memphis, TN, as a merchant seaman. He received his basic training in St. Petersburg, FL. In October 1944 he was promoted to 2nd asst. engineer. On May 18, 1945, he was promoted to the rank of first asst. engineer, while he was serving in the Army Transportation Service in LeHavre, France.

A highlight of his basic training was to represent Kentucky on a nationwide CBS radio program *To Man the Victory Fleet."* The program pointed out the needs and advantages of the Merchant Marine Service.

On 15 Aug 1945, not knowing the war was ending, he wrote to his parents from Southampton, England, stating "I'm being sent where I can't write to you and you can't write to me, but don't worry."

Soon after the war ended he returned to Trigg County where he was connected with the Island Motor Co., owned by M.W. "Chuck" Thomas and H.P. Hooks, later purchasing the interest of Mr. Hooks.

On 21 Aug 1946, he was married to Marian Louise Rye. Their children are Col. (Ret.) M. Thomas Davis, born July 6, 1950 and J.T. Davis, who was born 2 Feb 1957, in Saudi Arabia.

In 1951 Sonny began a career in oil exploration, first in Saudi Arabia with Aramco. Later he was with Exxon where the family lived in Benghazi, Libya. He worked with Texaco in Colombia and Ecuador. In 1978 while in Quito, Ecuador, a heart condition became evident. He was retired from Texaco and returned to Columbia, SC, where he and Marian had built a home. On 1 Feb 1979, a final heart attack took his life. His body was returned to Cadiz where interment was in East End Cemetery. *Submitted by his sister, Joyce Davis Banister.*

WILEY AMOS DELAWSON, PFC, born 23 Mar 1927 in Trigg County, KY, the son of Wade and Ethel Oliver Delawson. He grew up in the Wallonia Community and was drafted in the US Army 19 Jul 1945. Training was at Camp Atterbury, IN; Keesler Field, MS; and Rigger School in Spokane, WA. Then to Camp Stoneman, CA and in April 1946 shipped to South Pacific, Guam.

He served in the 20th Army Air Force and was assigned to 315th Bomber Wing, 75th Air Service Group in communications. January 1947 shipped to Saipan for processing to return to States. Arrived in San Francisco, CA and, by train, sent to Fort Sheridan, IL. Pfc. Delawson was discharged 5 Mar 1947.

He married Martha Ann Simpson from Princeton, KY on 23 Aug 1947. They have four daughters: Paula Ann, Sandra Lynn, Shirley Kay and Susan Jane. They have six grandchildren and five great-grandchildren. They were married 49-1/2 years when Martha Ann died 4 Mar 1997.

After several jobs, he began trucking in 1951 with Arnold Ligon Truck Line. Also worked for Noel Concrete, John Woodruff Construction and after 41 years of trucking, retired from Smith Coal 24 Apr 1992.

Today he enjoys good health and lives in Princeton, KY. His hobbies include hunting, fishing and part-time farming. He is a member of Masonic Lodge, American Legion, VFW and attends Wallonia Christian Church.

CARMINE "JOHNNY" DENAME, Staff Sergeant, born 23 Dec 1919, in Brooklyn, NY and was drafted into the US Army 11 Sep 1942, at Fort Dix, NJ. He served his country honorably from 11 Sep 1942 through 22 Oct 1945, then re-enlisted from 22 Oct 1945 to the regular Army for one year and discharged 7 Dec 1946, with the rank of staff sergeant.

DeName was assigned to Fort Jay, NY, as an escort guard to pick up AWOL soldiers and return them to their camps. His next assignment was in a combat engineer unit at Camp Ellis, IL. He was then transferred to Fort Sheridan, IL, waiting for another assignment. While there, he operated the rifle range and became an expert with the sub-machine gun, 45 cal., 1917 Springfield rifle, and the anti-aircraft gun, Marksman.

DeName then transferred to Fort Custer, MI, as an escort guard riding the railroad and seeing a lot of the United States. His next assignment was Camp Breckinridge, KY, where he attended classes on Prisoners of War and how to train and handle them to work on local farms. He then came to what was then Camp Campbell, KY, as an assistant compound commander in charge of guarding German prisoners of war.

It was at Camp Campbell, he met and married the love of his life, Frances Thomas, who was his dancing partner for 49 years and 10 months. His fondest memories of Camp Campbell were dancing in Army shows, making the All-Star softball team and breaking up a two-man prison break, which earned him a Letter of Commendation and a three-day pass. He received the Victory Medal and Marksmanship Medals.

Johnny and Frances have three children: Tony DeName, Vicki Godwin and Cindy Long; and four grandchildren: Jacob Long, Clinton Long, Shea Godwin Harper and Bridger DeName. Johnny is retired and enjoys singing in the choir at the Cadiz United Methodist Church

CHARLES E. DIXON, Sergeant, born 24 Aug 1924, at Golden Pond, Trigg County, KY and was drafted into the US Army 12 Apr 1943 at Fort Custer, MI.

On 28 Dec 1943, after training at Army Air Force Separation Base in Drew Field, FL, Baton Rouge, LA, and six weeks of engineer fire fighting training in New Orleans, he and his unit, Sqdn. A, 301st AAF Base Unit, traveled by ship to England on 12 Jan 1944. Charles was an Auto Equipment Operator 345.

At the base where he was stationed during the Normandy Invasion, he drove a fire truck, operated the pumper and was trained to extinguish fires from fighter planes, helicopters and bombers that were returning to the base from fighting elsewhere. He was one of seven who comprised a "crew." Three crews worked 24 hour shifts. These C-46 planes were loaded with five gallon cans of gasoline plus the gas carried in the plane's tank. The fire fighters never knew when the planes were going to explode. They didn't have radar then so a biplane was sent out to locate the downed plane if it didn't crash close to the runway. They used water and chemicals (foam) to extinguish the fires.

Charles remembers the surviving Germans and Americans being brought to the medic barracks. They had an air raid shelter in England and guns were set up on base for their protection, but he never heard one go off while he was there.

Gliders were used to transport men, guns, ammunition, gas and jeeps to locations where they were needed. These gliders were both American made and English made. He remembers engineers traveling to these lo-

cations and in eight hours constructing a makeshift runway for the planes to land. When Charles left England, he spent a short time in France and then to Belgium where he was shipped back to the Drew Field Base in Florida on 21 Aug 1945.

Charles was honorably discharged on 10 Dec 1945, as a sergeant. He received the American and EAME Theater Ribbons, Good Conduct Medal and Victory Medal.

He married Edna Ross on 11 Feb 1948. They have one daughter, three grandchildren and five great-grandchildren. Over the years Charles has worked as a farmer and as a car salesman in Michigan Today, at 76 he and Edna reside in Murray, KY. He enjoys gardening and hunting with his beagle dogs.

HAE B. DIXON, Tech 5, born 23 Feb 1914, Golden Pond, KY. He enlisted in the service 24 Jan 1945 and assigned to Co. I, 149th Inf. He was discharged 15 Nov 1946. Awards include the Asiatic-Pacific Theater Ribbon, WWII Victory Medal and Army of Occupation Medal.

Married Mae White and they have one son Timothy Neal and two grandchildren, David and Tammy. Hae was a farmer and also operated a service station in Golden Pond, KY. He passed away 3 Dec 1987.

HOMER DIXON, Tech 5, born 23 Aug 1916, Golden Pond, KY. He entered the US Army 22 Apr 1941 at Louisville, KY and was assigned to Co. I, 149th Inf.

He fought in battles and campaigns in the Southern Philippines, Luzon and New Guinea. His MOS was light truck driver.

Discharged 6 Nov 1945, his awards include the Philippine Liberation Ribbon w/Bronze Star, Good Conduct Ribbon, Asiatic-Pacific Theater Ribbon w/3 Bronze Stars, Good Conduct, American Theater Ribbon and American Defense Service Medal.

Married Hettie Hall in April 1941 and had two children, Paula Cripe and Larry; and three grandchildren: Nicole Sivertson, Kimberlee Cripe Costanzo and Danielle Crowder. Homer retired in 1978 from Caterpillar, East Peoria, IL. He passed away 24 Dec 1998.

JOHN THOMAS "TOPPY" EDWARDS, Corporal, born 1 Sep 1917 in Cadiz, KY, the son of John E. Edwards (b. 1874, d. 1918) and Lillian Prescott Edwards (b. 1884, d. 1980). He was educated in Cadiz schools and in his teenage years worked in drug stores, the "White Eagle" Restaurant in Cadiz and as a shoe salesman in Hopkinsville, KY. He then worked in Cunningham's Service Station and later became owner of the business as "Toppy's Service Station."

He was drafted and inducted into service on 26 Aug 1942, and received his basic training at bases in Ogden, UT; Edwards Air Force, CA; Sioux City, IA; and Pendleton, OR. When told he could have a furlough home, he said he would have to wait until pay-day. By then he had been assigned to the 554th AAF and was in New York ready to ship out overseas, so no furlough!

He served 28 months as a T/5 with the 379th Bomb Group, B-17 planes, 8th Air Force stationed at Kimbolton, England. He met several Trigg County boys on leave in London: Tommy Draper, James Smoot, Calvert P'Pool, Horrace Bush and Charles White. The worst action he saw was while visiting London with Charles White and a "buzz-bomb" hit their hotel. "Toppy" just lost his cap but Charles required several stitches in his head.

He was then transferred as an auto repairman with the Air Transport Command in North Africa with rank of corporal. This tour was for eight months. Cpl. Edwards was given an honorable discharge with the American Theater Ribbon, Good Conduct Medal, Distinguished Unit Badge w/

Bronze Cluster and the WWII Victory Medal. He was discharged at the Separation Base, Patterson Field, OH on 14 Nov 1945. His separation papers and travel-pay being made out to Cadiz, OH. When told it would take several days to get the error corrected for more travel-pay, he took what they had and hitchhiked home to Cadiz, KY.

He returned to the operation of "Toppy's Service Station." He married Huel Thomas, 8 Dec 1946 and has son John Thomas Edwards Jr. (b. 14 Nov 1948), son (b. 23 Dec 1952, died at birth), a daughter-in-law Sue Thomas Edwards; and one granddaughter, Ellen Edwards.

On 19 Jan 1948 he became agent for Standard Oil Company in Trigg County which he continued for 29 years. After selling out to Jack Pedley, Chevron Agent in Princeton, KY, he continued with Chevron until retirement in 1989.

He has served as commander of the American Legion Post #74, also as treasurer of Cadiz Rotary Club and Cadiz Chamber of Commerce. He is a member of Cadiz Baptist Church. He is retired and lives on Nunn Blvd. in Cadiz and at this writing is 83 years of age.

MARY REDD MAJOR EMBRY, Seaman 2/c, born 30 Sep 1923, Gracey, Trigg County, KY. She was the daughter of Rodman Jackson and Edna Sholar Redd and had a brother James Rodman Redd.

Mary enlisted as an apprentice seaman in the USN on 17 Mar 1944 at Cincinnati, OH. She served at USN Training Station (Women's Reserve), Bronx, NY; USN Barracks, Washington, DC; and USN Hospital, Bethesda, MD.

She served from May-August 1944 and received an honorable discharge by R.R. Payne, ENS (HC)USN by T.E. Murphy, CTC USN. She attained the rank of seaman second class V-10.

Mary married Joel Robinson Embry Jr. on 27 Jan 1947 and they had one son Joel Robinson Embry III (b. 3 May 1950). Mary died 12 Feb 1999 and is buried at Riverside Cemetery, Hopkinsville, KY.

JESSIE FLOYD EZELL, born a twin on 11 Feb 1916 at Trigg County, KY, and was drafted in the US Army in 1942. Ezell traveled to Fort Benning, GA for basic training as an infantryman.

He was sent to Europe and killed in action 5 Oct 1945 in France. Pfc. Ezell was the last of the war dead to be returned to Trigg County for burial in the Bristoe-Lancaster Cemetery, 12 Jan 1949.

FRANK BOYD EZELL, twin brother of Jessie Floyd Ezell, was also drafted in the US Army. He was inducted on 18 Nov 1942 and entered active service at Evansville, IN on 1 Dec 1942.

After training as a light mortar crewman, Ezell was assigned to Troop B, 107th Cavalry Reconnaissance Squad. Ezell sailed for Europe 3 Jan 1945, arrived 16 Jan 1945 and served in northern France, Rhineland and Central Europe, where he earned the EAME Theater Ribbon with three Bronze Stars. Pfc. Ezell sailed from Europe 11 Aug 1945 and arrived in the United States 21 Aug 1945. He was discharged 15 Oct 1945 at Camp Atterbury, IN.

Upon discharge Frank returned to Trigg County to join his wife, Mattie Elizabeth Whitman Ezell, They were the parents of nine children: Billy Wayne, Judy Elizabeth Sumner, Waymon Dale, Frank Glenn, Jesse Floyd, Ronald Lee, Freddie Joe, Sharon Dianne Wolfe and Rose Rene Sholar.

Ezell worked as a timber man at sawmills, in construction at Fort

Campbell, KY, at Albert Wallace Furniture and later retired as a custodian from the Trigg County Court House. He served many years as the men's Sunday School teacher at South Road Missionary Baptist Church.

Frank died 7 Jul 1990 and was laid to rest near his twin brother in the Bristoe-Lancaster Cemetery.

LACEY FRANK EZELL, PFC, born 22 Jan 1925, the son of Harvey E. and Viva Mae Hunter Ezell. He was drafted into service in WWII on 26 May 1944, received training in Fort Hood, TX, then sent to Germany.

He spent more than 100 days on the front line in Gen. Patton's 385th Inf. He told of standing behind trees and bullets knocking the bark off. He saw many of his buddies falling all around him. He was one of the lucky ones and returned home unharmed on 4 Sep 1945.

The following is from a letter written 23 Jul 1945 by Chaplain Vern A. Slater to his parents: "It gives me great pleasure to write you about your son, Pfc. Lacey Frank Ezell of Co. F, 385th Inf. Lacey was at a chapel service that I held for the men at their guard post yesterday. Only a few present, but the Lord was with us and that made it a great service. I spoke from II Timothy 2-1-15, using the thoughts – the Christian is a son, a soldier and a student.

"Lacey, as many of our soldiers, has found his Christian experience much more precious to him during combat experience and long days of separation from home and loved ones than ever. It brought joy to my heart to hear him say he wanted his life to be a blessing to others and he anticipates taking more active part in the work of the church when he returns.

"I was interested to discover after all these weeks that your son and Ellis Futrell were from the same church. I had talked with Futrell several times, but had never talked with Lacey before about his home church. They are in different companies.

"I was a Baptist pastor in civilian life and naturally am happy to find our Baptist men faithful in chapel attendance. With best of wishes and praying the Lord's blessing upon you and your family." Sincerely Vern A. Slater After being discharged and returning home, Lacey Frank was married to Louise Ricks. They had two children, Patricia Ann, Jerry Wayne and two grandchildren. Lacey passed away 17 Dec 1988.

ALFRED FAUGHN, PFC, born 5 Jul 1910 in Trigg County, KY, son of James Benjamin "Ben" and Martha Ann "Annie" Faughn of the Bethesda Community of Trigg County. He was one of 14 children: Adolphus, Mattie, Ada, Mary, Francis, Eliza, Letha, Alpha Lou, Robert and his twin Zan, Hazel, Mamie Evelyn and an unnamed infant.

Alfred joined the US Army 26 Aug 1942 and started service on 9 Sep 1942 in Evansville, IN. His brother Adolphus also served in WWI and his maternal grandfather, John H. Faughn, in the Civil War. Alfred received his basic training in Texas and was also stationed at Camp Rucker, AL.

He married Beulah Wood Oliver, a young widow of Trigg County, 14 Jun 1943. Beulah was the young mother of two children, Aleen (Mrs. Floyd Ashley) and Dorris Owen Oliver.

On 24 Dec 1943 while at Camp Rucker, he was called home to attend the funeral of his brother Francis.

Rumors were they soon would be shipping overseas. He desperately wanted to see his mother, daddy and wife. His best friend Kelly from northern Indiana agreed to go AWOL for the purpose of seeing their families "one more time."

The young AWOL soldiers walked almost all the way from Camp Rucker, AL arriving in Cadiz. Word was sent to his sister he was in town and was hiding until dark. After eating, Kelly went to Indiana hoping to see his daughter. He returned to Camp Rucker and his record shows he lost 65 days under AW 107.

PFC Alfred Faughn arrived overseas 12 May 1944 a part of Co. G, 320th Inf. He received the Combat Infantry Badge on 11 Jul 1944 while serving in the European African Middle Eastern Theater. He and Kelly served in the Campaign of France. During the Normandy invasion, Alfred was wounded and Kelly was killed.

Alfred returned to the States 22 Oct 1944. An article printed in the *Cadiz Record* 2 Nov 1944 states:

"Pfc. Alfred Faughn is back in the States. He is now in Thayer Hospital, Nashville, TN, and is doing fine. Among those who visited him from Cadiz last Wednesday were his wife, Mrs. Alfred Faughn; parents, Mr. and Mrs. J.B. Faughn; sister Mrs. Lloyd Allen; brother Zan Faughn; and Mr. Clarence Wood.

Alfred received a certificate of disability for discharge. He received the Combat Infantry Badge, Good Conduct Medal and the Purple Heart. He returned to Trigg County after months of recuperation and began to farm.

Bonnie Carolyn Faughn, the daughter of Alfred and Beulah Faughn, was born 12 Sep 1947 in Trigg County. Bonnie, Aleen and Dorris were raised on the family farm. The family was active members of the Hurricane Baptist Church. "Carolyn" became the wife of Rev. Jimmy Gibbs (b. 1946, d. 1992) of Trigg County and the mother of three children: Dwaine, Neil and April Gibbs. In September 1992 she became the wife of Jerry Loyd "Bud" Cannon.

Beulah died 6 Oct 1979 and Alfred died 8 Mar 2000 in Kuttawa. They are buried in the Hurricane Baptist Church Cemetery. *Submitted by Betty Sellers at the request of Carolyn Cannon.*

EDISON LEE FELTNER, PFC, born 13 July 1924 in Trigg County, KY, the son of Mr. and Mrs. Ben E. Feltner. He was drafted in the Army on 10 March 1943, and after basic training was sent to North Africa where he served as an infantry rifleman with the 3rd Inf. Div. of the 7th Army.

During the invasion of Italy in 1944, Feltner was disabled/wounded on Anzio where he was in some of the most intense fighting that occurred during WWII. After a period of time in a Rome hospital, he was returned to Stark General Hospital in South Carolina, then flown to Kennedy General Hospital in Memphis, TN. Later, he was transferred to Wakeman General and Convalescent Hospital at Camp Atterbury, IN.

He received a Certificate of Disability at Wakeman Hospital on 29 April 1945, and an honorable discharge on 2 May 1945. Awards include the European-African-Middle-Eastern Theater Ribbon and a Battle Star for his participation in the Italian Campaign and the American Legion Silver Star Certificate which states in part, "For devoted service to our country which resulted in wound or disablement in the line of duty during WWII."

His death occurred on 28 Jul 1986 and burial was in the Fort Donelson National Military Cemetery, Dover, TN. A US Army Honor Guard participated at his funeral. He was never married. *Submitted by his brother, Bill D. Feltner.*

CORD S. FENNELL, Sergeant, born Nov. 5, 1905, Golden Pond, KY. He enlisted in the military 3 Mar 1942 at Cadiz, KY, took basic training at Camp Wallace, TX. He served as construction foreman with 286th Combat Engineers Battalion and they removed mines, road blocks and worked on roads and bridges.

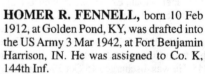

He participated in battles/campaigns in France, Germany, Rhineland and Central Europe. Sgt. Fennell was discharged 2 Dec 1945. His awards include the American Theater Ribbon, EAME Theater Ribbon w/2 Bronze Stars, Good Conduct and WWII Victory Medal.

As a civilian he farmed and worked for TVA in LBL until retirement in November 1975. He was single. Fennel passed away 11 May 1996 and is buried in Eastend Cemetery, Cadiz, KY.

EDWIN "TED" FENNELL, PFC, born 8 Oct 1912 in the Ferguson Springs Community, Trigg County, KY, son and sixth child of George and Clara Griffin. He was drafted in the US Army about 1943-44, trained in Co. C 778th Tank Bn., Camp Barkeley, TX and Camp Howze, TX.

Sent to Europe where he was injured in December 1944 in the Battle of the Bulge. Returned to 163rd US General Hospital in England where he died 14 Jan 1945. Edwin was buried in Cambridge American Cemetery, Plot F, Row 4, Grave 110, Cambridge, England. *Submitted by his sister Gladys F. Wallace.*

ELLIS "PETE" FENNELL, born on 14 Jun 1919, at Golden Pond, KY. He was inducted into the US Army on 26 Jan 1944, at Evansville, IN. Following completion of basic training and eight months continental service, he was assigned to the 3139th Signal Service Company and was shipped overseas to participate in the Ardennes and Rhineland Campaigns.

While serving he received the European-African-Middle-Eastern Theater Service Ribbon w/2 Bronze Stars, Good Conduct Medal and WWII Victory Medal. He was discharged following one year two months foreign service on 27 Dec 1945, at Fort Knox, KY.

He returned to Trigg County and moved to Christian County with his wife, the former Etna Dean Wallace, whom he married in 1939. He worked as a tenant farmer for two years, then purchased his own farm and operated it until his death in November 1991.

He and his wife had three children: Frank, Hal, Judy; 11 grandchildren and eight great-grandchildren. *Submitted by Hal Fennell.*

ELMER R. "BUDDY" FENNELL, Staff Sergeant, born 3 May 1909 in Trigg County near Golden Pond. He entered the US Army on 22 April 1941, and reported to Camp Shelby, MS for basic training. He was assigned to Co. I, 149th Inf.

Following completion of basic, he was transferred to enlisted Reserve on 5 Dec 1941, and was recalled to active duty 15 Jan 1942, at Fort Thomas, KY. He completed two years of continental service, one year, nine and one-half months of foreign service, and participated in the campaigns in the Southern Philippines, Luzon and New Guinea. He was awarded the Asiatic-Pacific Theater Ribbon w/Bronze Star, American Theater Ribbon, and WWII Victory Medal. He was discharged with the rank of staff sergeant on 6 Nov 1945, at Camp Atterbury, IN.

He returned to Trigg County and continued to live on the family farm until it was purchased by TVA as part of the Land Between the Lakes project. He and his brother then purchased a farm located north of Cadiz on the Princeton Road. He continued to live here until health problems forced him into the nursing home. He died 29 Jan 2001, the last member of a family of 12 brothers and sisters. *Submitted by Hal Fennell.*

HOMER R. FENNELL, born 10 Feb 1912, at Golden Pond, KY, was drafted into the US Army 3 Mar 1942, at Fort Benjamin Harrison, IN. He was assigned to Co. K, 144th Inf.

He left the States on 28 May 1942 and served in Puerto Rico until 30 Nov 1943. He returned to the States 5 Dec 1943, and was discharged at Fort George Meade, MD, on 28 Sep 1944.

Upon being discharged, he returned to

the family farm located in the Land between the rivers and lived there with his family until the property was purchased by TVA for the Land between the Lakes project in 1965. He and his brother Elmer purchased a farm north of Cadiz on the Princeton Road. He lived here until declining health forced him into a nursing home. He died 4 Feb 1989. *Submitted by Hal Fennell.*

EULAS BELTRON "JACK" FENNELL JR., Corporal, born 30 Apr 1922 at Ferguson Spring, near Golden Pond, in Trigg County KY. Jack is the son of Eulas Beltron and Winnie Maud Fennell. He was drafted into the US Army from Trigg County, KY 3 Nov 1942 along with 14 other Trigg County men. They were sent to Fort Polk, LA for basic training, then went on war maneuvers in Louisiana and Texas. Five Trigg County men were drowned when they ran a tank into a bayou in Louisiana. At Camp Barkley, TX he was part of the 11th Armd. Div.

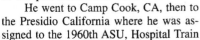

He went to Camp Cook, CA, then to the Presidio California where he was assigned to the 1960th ASU, Hospital Train Unit. They transported wounded and sick soldiers to their homes throughout the US. During this time he was promoted to corporal. He traveled to all 48 states several times during his tour of duty.

He was discharged from the military 15 Feb 1946 at Camp Atterbury, IN. He then went to Calloway County, married Treva Billington and they lived in Almo, KY. He worked at the Tappan Stove factory for 32 years and now works for a security company. He and Treva have two children, EB and Marie, and four grandchildren. *Submitted by Bill Fennell.*

THOMAS C. FITZGIBBONS, 1st Lieutenant, was drafted and entered the Army on 14 Feb 1942 at Camp Upton, Long Island, NY. Following basic training at Camp Forrest, TN, he was assigned to Co. A, 131st Inf. Regt. until 8 Oct 1942, at which time he applied for and was accepted into Officer Candidate School at Aberdeen Proving Grounds, MD.

After being commissioned 2nd lieutenant as an Ordnance Officer, he was assigned as cadre to the 641st Ordnance Ammunition Company, an all black unit at Camp Gruber, OK.

After training until January 1944, the 641st embarked for England where they prepared for the invasion of France. Tom served with the 641st from their landing on Utah Beach in June 1944 until April 1945. During that interval he served as ammunition supply officer, depot supply officer and executive officer.

In April 1945 he was assigned as the commander of the 597th Ammunition Company, serving in that capacity until May 1945 when the war ended in Europe. Tom participated in all the major campaigns in Europe. Orders were then received to return to the US for reassignment. Tom chose to accept assignment as 1st lieutenant in the Army Reserve in lieu of further active duty.

WILLIE C. FORT, a World War II veteran, born 18 Jun 1915, Wallonia, Trigg County, KY, was the son of Will Thomas and Ambie Adams Fort. He had one brother Wilton Fort.

Willie was drafted and inducted 29 Jun 1942, entering service at Evansville, IN. He served in 194th Field Arty. Bn.; battles and campaigns were Naples-Foggia; Rome-Arno; North Apennines, Rhineland and Central Europe.

Decorations and citations include the EAME Theatre Ribbon w/5 Bronze Stars and Good Conduct Ribbon. He was overseas 29 months and received an honorable discharge 18 Oct 1945 at Separation Center, Camp Atterbury, IN.

At age 12 Willie took his first job working at his uncle's restaurant in Cadiz for $3 a week; later clerking at a local grocery for $9 a week. After returning from the war he re-entered the grocery business, spending 60 years working at stores throughout Western Kentucky. He and brother Wilton purchased a store in Cadiz from Rudolph Thurman and named it "Economy Food Store." They owned the business for 15 years.

In 1949 he married Nell Calhoun. She passed away in 1998, just short of their 50th wedding anniversary. They owned and operated Goodnight Motel in Cadiz for 15 years.

Willie and Nell had one son Bill, pastor of a 1300 member Baptist Church in Richmond, KY. Bill and wife Patience have two sons and a daughter. Willie has been a member of American Legion for over 50 years, member of Veterans of Foreign Wars, and member of Cadiz Baptist Church. *Submitted by Willie Fort.*

WILTON BLANE FORT, Staff Sergeant, born 16 Jul 1913 in Trigg, County, Cadiz, KY, the son of Will Fort and Amby Adams Fort. He was drafted into the USAF 12 Aug 1941. Assignments and locations were Wichita Falls, TX, Amarillo Fields and Fort Logan, CO. The next stop was New Orleans, LA, for overseas.

Over seas duty was to the South Pacific area, Far Eastern Theatre of War. He served in the Philippines to the Netherlands Indies, Malaysia, New Guinea and Okinawa. Wilton served in this area for four years. His discharge with rank of staff sergeant was 22 Oct 1945. He was awarded various medals and ribbons.

Returning to civilian life, Wilton went to Murray to operate a grocery store. From Murray, he went to Cadiz and joined his brother Willie to form a partnership in a grocery store. After many years, Wilton bought the Cadiz Restaurant and operated it until retirement. Willie also bought into another business.

He married Hattie M. Bridges on 20 Dec 1943. They have one son, Carl Blane Fort (b. 12 Jul 1952) who lives and works in Florida.

Wilton Blane Fort died 24 Sep 1997 and is buried in the Adam Cemetery, located off the Princeton Road in Trigg County.

THOMAS CLAY FOURSHEE, Tech 5, born 22 Nov 1920 in Trigg County to parents Riley Isaac and Edna Carr Fourshee. He was raised in the Lock "E" Community. Following graduation from Trigg County HS, Tommy was inducted into the US Army, 29 Sep 1942.

After training at Fort Leonard Wood, MO, with HQ Battery of the 16th Field Observation Battalion, he traveled with the unit to Texas and Louisiana for maneuvers, then was stationed at Fort Bragg, NC.

On 22 Jun 1944, the battalion left Camp Shanks, NY for Liverpool, England. After the arrival of their equipment, they departed Southampton on 16 Aug 1944, and landed on Utah Beach, Normandy, France on 17 August. The HQ Battery was assigned to survey and position the enemy.

After Normandy the Battery was in Brest, France then Luxembourg and Belgium and was caught up in the Battle of the Bulge; crossed the Rhine and moved across Germany with Patton's 3rd Army. His unit was in Prague, Czechoslovakia when victory was declared.

Tommy transferred 7 Jul 1945 to the Service Battalion 955th Field Artillery and began training for service in the Pacific. After Japan surrendered in August, he was stationed at Camp Lucky Strike in France. While waiting to return home he volunteered as a truck driver to transport American GIs on furlough to Paris.

On 27 Dec 1945, Tommy was discharged at Fort Knox, KY as tech 5. Throughout his tour of duty he fought in four battles: Northern France, Ardennes, Rhineland and Central Europe. He received the American Theater Ribbon, European-African-Middle-Eastern Theater Ribbon w/4 Bronze Stars, Good Conduct Medal and WWII Victory Medal.

Tommy returned to Cadiz and in 1946 married Geneva Nell Mize. They had three sons: Anthony, John, Paul; and three grandchildren: Edye, Amy and John Matt. After Nell's death in 1975, Tommy married Edith Stewart Cameron 11 Sep 1976.

He worked several years in construction at Fort Campbell, KY before starting his own business. In 1953 he formed Fourshee Building Contractor. Tommy retired in 1991. Fortunate to have good health, he now enjoys volunteering with the Cadiz Baptist Church and the local chapter of the VFW and working on small construction projects throughout the county.

He and Edith travel and especially enjoy army "buddies" reunion held in their various states.

JOE B. FOWLER JR., Seaman 2/c, born 24 Jul 1926 in Trigg County, KY. He joined the USN 22 Nov 1944 and sent to the Asiatic-Pacific, Samar Leyte and Leyte Gulf. He served on clean-up of islands in Philippines and PT Boat Base 17, Samar Island.

His memorable experience was seeing all the devastation caused by war on the many islands in the Pacific. Discharged 6 Apr 1946 and received the Good Conduct and Marksmanship.

In 1949 he married Sara Major, no children. He retired in 1978 from the Indiana Farm Bureau Coop Inc.

GARNETT EDWARD FRANCIS, EM1/c, born 5 May 1920 in the Maple Grove Community of Trigg County, the son of Homer E. and Lola Frances Francis. He grew up on his father's farm, attended Maple Grover School and graduated from Trigg County HS where he excelled as a member of the basketball team.

Edward enlisted in the USN 8 Apr 1942 at Hopkinsville, KY. After completing boot camp at the Naval Training Station in San Diego, CA, he was assigned to duty aboard the heavy cruiser, USS *Northampton*. One of its first assignments after Edward arrived on board was to escort the aircraft carrier, USS *Hornet* to within flying distance of Japan so its planes could bomb Tokyo for the first time. Other missions involving the *Northampton* included the Battle of Santa Cruz, New Georgia, Solomon and Russell Islands and Sainte Isabel.

Ed's most terrifying experience was on the night of 30 Nov 1943 during the Battle of Guadalcanal, when the *Northampton* was fatally torpedoed by the Japanese and the crew was ordered to abandon ship. About 50 men lost their lives, but Edward was one of some 500 men rescued from the murky waters and taken to the island of New Caledonia.

After some shore duty, Edward was assigned to the USS *Jicarilla* and returned to the Asiatic-Pacific Theater in the South China Sea. His ship was in the Philippines at war's end.

Edward was honorably discharged as electrician's mate first class, 8 Nov 1945, at Great Lakes, IL. Service decorations include American Theater Ribbon, Asiatic-Pacific Ribbon w/6 stars, Philippine Liberation Ribbon w/2 stars, Good Conduct Medal, WWII Victory Medal and 3rd and 5th Fleet ribbons.

He returned to civilian life as an electrical engineer, and was living in Trigg County when he died 24 Apr 1993 at age 73. He is survived by his wife the former Eunice Wills, an adopted son David Edward Francis by his first wife, the former Mabel Tuggle.

LACY REX FRANCIS, born 10 Mar 1927, the son of Homer E. and Fannie Bridges Francis of the Maple Grove Community of Trigg County.

He was inducted into the US Army 19 Jul 1945 at Louisville, KY. He was 18 years old and a junior at Trigg County HS at the time.

After basic training in the United States, he was assigned to the 296th Military Police Company and transferred to Germany where he served almost a year with the Army of Occupation. Going on duty for the first time as an MP, he was told not to worry about the Germans, just "beware of the Russians."

His military decorations and citations included Army of Occupation Medal and WWII Victory Medal. He was honorably discharged from service 30 Dec 1946 at Fort Dix, NJ.

After he returned home, he re-entered high school and graduated two years behind his original class. He topped off his education at the Coyne Electrical School in Chicago, and followed a career as an electrician.

On 6 Jun 1948, Rex married Eva Marie Kennedy. They have five children: Larry Brent (md. Dawnelle Kraick), Deborah Lynn (md. Larry F. Harris), Randall Kent (md. Yuson Cho), Rhonda Faye (md. first Juan A. Garcia and second Charlie Owen Stout); and Gregory Trent. They also have eight grandchildren.

Rex has been retired several years and he and his wife, along with their youngest son Gregory Trent, live in Cadiz.

THOMAS REED FRANKLIN, SM2/c, born 21 Jan 1925 in Golden Pond, KY. He joined the service 24 Nov 1943 and served in the South Pacific. He participated in the battle of Philippine Sea, Invasion of Leyte, Okinawa and others.

He was discharged 15 Jan 1946. His awards include the WWII Victory Medal, American Theater, Asiatic-Pacific and Philippine Liberation.

Married Kathleen Forguson 30 Aug 1947 and they have three chidlren: Kenneth, David and Darrell; and seven grandchildren: Brandon, Carrie, Laura, Sara, Jeremiah, Katie and Karlie.

Retired from Whirlpool Corp. in 1984 and now enjoys playing clabber (cards) and pool.

RICHARD SHERMAN FREEMAN, Sergeant, born 26 Oct 1908, in Cadiz, Trigg County, KY, the son of William Allen Freeman (b. 16 Aug 1866, d. 25 Jan 1916) and Bertie W. Hammond Freeman Bogard (b. 26 Apr 1888, d. 5 Sep 1968). He graduated from Cadiz HS where he was active on the baseball team and he later played league baseball in Hopkinsville.

Freeman moved to Clarksville, TN in 1929, where he opened and operated Freeman's Cafe on Commerce Street until his retirement in 1980. He now resides at Clarksville Residential Care Center.

In 1942 Freeman joined the Army Air Corps and was stationed at Charleston Army Air Corps Field, SC. He attained the rank of sergeant and served for 42 months as a troop train cook. During his military absence, his brother Lacy Freeman, operated the cafe.

The WWII veteran married Elizabeth Huggins 13 Dec 1947. She was born at Allen's Creek, Stewart County, TN, 12 Dec 1905 and died in Clarksville, 27 Feb 1995. She worked as a secretary at the Camp Campbell Army Hospital during the war. Freeman, an avid bird hunter, is a member of Madison Street Methodist Church, Clarksville. *Submitted by William T. Turner*

RAYMOND EWING FULLER, son of Charles Fenton and Amble Hall Fuller, was born 27 Oct 1906. He married Louise Vanzant 23 Feb 1935, and they had two sons, Raymond Earl and James Harold.

He was inducted into the US Army 14 Jan 1944, at Evansville, IN. Raymond was in Co. A, 28th Bn., Engineers and stationed at Fort Leonard Wood, MO. He got real sick and was in the Hospital at Fort Leonard Wood with pneumonia complicated by asthma. After an extended stay in the hospital, he was discharged 27 May 1944.

He returned to Trigg County, his family and his job in 1944. After returning to his job at Pennyrile Rural Electric he later became manager in which he served several years. He was also Superintendent of Cadiz Water Works for 17 years, and Superintendent of Barkley Water District from 1966 until 1976, when he retired.

Raymond had five grandchildren: Keith Fuller, Tracy Fuller Taylor, John Fuller, Jim Fuller and Jamie Fuller. He died 17 Nov 1981 and is buried at Siloam Cemetery.

AMOS A. FUTRELL, born 10 Sep 1919, the son of Wiley A. and Nannie Dixon Futrell of Trigg County, Cadiz, KY. Amos was part of the first group from Trigg County to be drafted into the US Army. On 12 Sep 1941 he entered into service for his country in Louisville, KY and was sent to Galveston, TX for basic training.

On 27 Dec 1941 (20 days after the Japanese attacked Pearl Harbor) Amos was sent to Hawaii where he served as a telephone switchboard operator at a lookout station atop Diamond Head. He was also trained as a cannoneer and rifle marksman.

In October 1944 Amos was sent to the Mariana Islands in the South Pacific for nine months. In July 1945, he obtained a 30-day leave to return to the States and while on leave the war ended.

On 4 Sep 1945 (after having served three years, 11 months and 20 days) he received an honorable discharge from the US Army at Camp Atterbury, IN. His military decorations and citations included Asiatic-Pacific Theater Ribbon, American Defense Service Medal, Bronze Star and the Good Conduct Ribbon.

On 8 Sep 1945 Amos made his way to Akron, OH where his fiancée, Marie Sumner (a Trigg County girl) lived. They were married 13 Oct 1945 and remained in Akron the duration of their time together. Due to severe radiation burns from aggressive cancer treatments, Amos had to take a disability retirement from the Goodyear Tire & Rubber Company after 36 years of service.

The next 16 years were spent in much pain and suffering until he passed away on 18 Oct 1997. He left behind a wife of 52 years and three sons: Victor, Mark and Ray, and seven grandchildren: Kirk, Tara, Jennifer, Aaron, Clayton, Melissa, and Brandon. *Submitted by Marie Sumner Futrell.*

BERLIE PRENTICE FUTRELL, Chief Radio Electrician W-2, actively served in the USN from 18 Sep 1925 until 16 Mar 1946. His total service was 30 years ending 2 Dec 1955.

At age 21, Berlie left his home in Golden Pond, KY (unbeknownst to his parents) to enlist in Fleet Reserves in Nashville, TN. A recruiter had passed through Golden Pond and Berlie became interested in what the man said about serving our nation. He saw the hardships that his family and many others experienced. His goal was to one day retire and farm the land his great-grandfather, Pioneer Nathan Futrell, had once owned. By enlisting in the USN he had the privilege to serve his country and as a career naval warrant officer he would learn about life outside of Kentucky.

During his career with the Navy he served mainly in radio technology. His last ranking was chief radio electrician (CRM) W-2. He served in Naval Training School, Hampton, VA. From there he served in the USS *Vireo;* USS *Antares;* Guantanamo Bay, Cuba (Naval Station); USS *Bobolink;* Naval Research Lab, Bellevue, DC; USS *Utah;* USS *Ontario;* USS *Richmond;* USS *Upshur;* USS *Woolsey* (during WWII), USS *Walke;* USS Navy Yard, Portsmouth, NH; USS *Trenton;* Mare Island Naval Shipyard in California. During WWII Berlie served on the USS *Woolsey* as chief radioman. He was regarded as being very conscientious and diligent in his service to the USN.

During his service at the Naval Radio Station 8th Naval District in Norfolk, VA, he met Zola Marie Mansfield. She worked as a waitress at a restaurant Berlie frequented. They fell in love and married 7 Dec 1940. He was 36 years old and she was 26 when they married. Their first child, Barbara Jeanette, was born 17 Dec 1941. One year after her birth, Berlie saw his daughter for the first time due to being detained at sea during WWII. On 26 Aug 1945 his son, Carl Prentice, was born. The following year the Futrell family moved to Berlie's childhood home in Golden Pond, KY. He joined the Fleet Reserves, Class F-5. During the next several years, he owned and operated a farm in Golden Pond until 1969. At this time, he moved to Hurricane Mills, TN after TVA purchased his land.

Sadly, on 12 Mar 1994 he passed away due to a sudden heart attack and is buried in Kingston Springs, TN at the Middle Tennessee Veterans Cemetery. He was 89 years old.

CHARLES H. FUTRELL, Sergeant, born 12 Oct 1911 in Trigg County. He was the son of Lamont Futrell and Roberta Thomas Futrell. A Rogers HS graduate, he sold insurance in various south central Kentucky towns, including Columbia and Albany, in the 1930s. He was drafted at the commencement of WWII.

Futrell served in an Engineering Section of the 12th Army Air Force B-26 Marauder Bomber Group in the Mediterranean Theater from 1942 until the conclusion of the war. His unit was cited by French Gen. Charles DeGaulle for outstanding achievement in important missions over Italy and other European locations. He attained the rank of sergeant.

After the war was over, Futrell returned to Trigg County. On his arrival in Cadiz, he went to the Main Street Medical Clinic of his uncles, Drs. Elias and John Futrell. Dr. Elias called his wife, Anna Duncan Futrell, and daughter, Ann, and they drove Sgt. Futrell to the Cumberland River home of his parents at Linton in Trigg County.

Thereafter, Futrell returned to Albany in Clinton County and married his pre-war sweetheart, Kathleen Perkins. Subsequently, he earned BS and MA degrees in agriculture from the University of Kentucky. His wife died in 1958 and he remained a widower for the balance of his life. He was a high school agriculture teacher in Clinton County from the 1950s to 1970s and a cattle farmer in Clinton County until his death in 1991.

DILLARD ELAS FUTRELL, PFC, born 28 Nov 1923. He entered the service 30 Apr 1944 at Fort Benjamin Harrison, IN. Basic training was completed at Fort McClellan, AL, then to Camp Miles Standish, MA. From there he boarded a ship to England and landed in France.

They went up through Luxemburg and crossed the Sauer River into Germany. Assignments were Ardennes, Rhineland and Central Europe. Dillard served as a combat infantry soldier with Co. I, 385th Regt. of the 76th Inf. Div. He was a platoon runner with Co. I and carried messages and binoculars between three squads. Co. I was constantly out in front taking it and giving it, but always giving more than they took.

When the 76th disbanded, he served with the Military Police Battalion 796th at military stockades guarding American prisoners in Belgium and France.

Discharged May 22, 1946 as PFC at Camp Atterbury, IN. His awards include the EAME Theater Ribbon w/3 Bronze Stars, Good Conduct, WWII Victory Medal (Germany), Combat Infantry Badge and Rifle SS.

Returning to civilian life he worked briefly at a shoe factory, Ragland Potter Wholesale Grocery, as a deck hand, placed Kentucky State tax stickers on cigarettes and retired from Thomas Industries.

Dillard is the son of Wiley Futrell and Nancy Jane Dixon Futrell. He married Vivian Rose Burcham 3 Jan 1948. Their children are Jimmy, Betty Ann Thomas, Robert, Elwanda Adams, Angelia Ladd and Lanita Cox. Grandchildren are Kelvin, Bill, Josh, Brent and Zack Futrell; Teresa Joiner; Cody and Logan Adams; Amanda, Emily and Hunter Ladd; Kimberly, Kelsie and Kalli Jo Cox.

He is a member of Rocky Ridge Baptist Church where he serves as a deacon and Sunday school teacher. His memory of WWII was an answer for an exam at college where his report was on the action of the 76th Inf. Div. His final statement was, "It was a million dollar trip, but I wouldn't give you a dime for another."

JAMES PLOMER FUTRELL, Private, born 5 Jun 1920, the son of James Soloman and Daisy McCoy Futrell. He was drafted into the military 17 Dec 1942 and served in the Infantry at Camp Wolters, TX.

Pvt. Futrell was discharged 12 Mar 1943. Awards include Rifle Marksman.

As a civilian he worked at several jobs, but was disability retired in 1969 from Thomas Industries after 13-1/2 years.

Married Mintie Herndon in April 1942 and had two children, Shirley Clark and Shelia Shelton-Ohler; five grandchildren: Thomas and Kevin Shelton; Johanna Lee; Jeff and John Clark; and two great-grandchildren, Breanna Shelton and Katelyn Clark. James Futrell passed away at VA Hospital in Nashville 3 May 1994 and is buried at House Cemetery, Linton, KY. *Submitted by Mintie Futrell.*

MAURICE CHILTON FUTRELL, Staff Sergeant, born 28 Jan 1923 near Linton, KY. Enlisted in the army 25 Jun 1942 in Bowling Green, KY and served in the Army ROTC at Western State College until 9 Apr 1943. Basic training was at Fort Harrison, IN and mechanical training at Camp Wolters, TX. He was placed in HQ Co. 2nd Bn. 127th Inf. Regt. 32nd Div.

Arrived in Australia 10 Nov 1943 and with Gen. Douglas MacArthur's men went to Port Moresby, New Guinea. He was assigned to intelligence 22 Apr 1944; made amphibious landing at Aitape, New Guinea and invasion of the Philippines in the Leyte Gulf, 19 Oct 1944. March 1944 began the battle for Luzon, which included 125 days of fighting through the Villa Verde Trail.

Futrell repeatedly patrolled behind enemy lines, observing and reporting accurately enemy activity. He won the respect and confidence of his comrades by his ability to move silently in the face of known danger and gain information.

On one occasion, Futrell led a patrol into enemy territory and after completing their mission the Yanks began the return trip. Suddenly they were subjected to machine gun and rifle fire. Directing his men to take cover, the Kentuckian crawled forward alone to locate the enemy weapons.

After spotting the enemy position, Futrell returned to his men and led them safely to a friendly defense perimeter. Contacting a mortar section he then directed effectively fire against the Japanese machine gun. The citation reads in part:…Pvt. Futrell's courage and initiative made possible the destruction of a formidable enemy threat." Since this action he was promoted to sergeant tech.

In early August he was promoted to staff sergeant for combat in the hills north of Baguio. On 14 Oct 1945 he went to Sasebo, Japan in the army of occupation.

He was discharged 23 Dec 1945 at Fort Knox, KY as staff sergeant. Awards include Asiatic-Pacific Theater Ribbon w/3 Bronze Stars, Philippine Liberation Ribbon w/Bronze Star, Good Conduct Medal, Bronze Star Medal and the WWII Victory Medal.

Graduated from Western KY State College with a BS in agriculture, MS from University of Wisconsin in 1949, and Ph.D. in plant pathology and agronomy, 1952. He began his career in 1952 at College Station, TX, he determined the distribution of races of rust diseases of cereal crops and aided in the development of resistant varieties. During this period he was a member of the faculty at Texas A&M University.

In 1964 he was stationed at Ahmadu Bello University, Samaru-Zaria, Nigeria, where to increase food production in West Africa, he identified sorghum, millet and corn varieties with resistance to diseases including downy mildew, ergot and sooty stripe disease.

Returned to the States in 1966 and spent the remainder of his career at Mississippi State University as a member of a research team developing disease and insect resistance in corn and was a faculty member. Here, he was instrumental in both identifying the seriousness of the southern corn leaf blight epiphytotic in 1970 and in formulating the recommendation for control of the disease, which was later adopted by the entire USA Corn Belt. Over his career, Dr. Futrell published more than 90 scientific articles and was associated with eight professional and honorary societies. His professional accomplishments are recognized widely. In 1967, he was awarded the honorary Ph.D. from the University of Coahuila, Mexico. In 1971 he was the recipient of the Gamma Sigma Delta Research Award for outstanding contributions to Mississippi agriculture. In view of Dr. Futrell's contributions to world agriculture, the Agriculture Research Service is deeply indebted and offers this Citation in sincere appreciation."

In 1975 he received a Certificate of Merit from the US Dept. of Agriculture which read "For his contributions towards reducing crop losses caused by plant pathogens over a period of 23 years while a research scientist of the Agriculture Research Service, US Dept. of Agriculture."

His concern for mankind and his Christian service was well depicted by his efforts in the formation in 1970 of the Agricultural Mission Foundation and for his efforts on behalf of Cuna Indians of the San Bas Islands. While in Nigeria he was awarded a Certificate of Honor by the Foreign Mission Board of the Southern Baptist Association for his efforts in caring out a student ministry during the Civil War. He was a member and Deacon of First Baptist Church, Starkville, MS. Every year his vacation was spent on a mission trip.

He married Mary Dean Feltner in 1947 and their children are Edison Leon, John Maurice, and Lula Dean. Grandchildren are Lauren Elizabeth, Jonathan Simmons, Richard Landy Jones, Michael Dean, and Cathryn Grace.

Maurice died 31 Aug 1975 and in 1976 his wife and sons founded a school in Bangalore, India in honor of him. This is the 25th anniversary of the school, and there is now an orphanage with 40 boys at the school, in honor of John's son Michael Dean.

PAUL GARDNER JR., Tech 5, born 7 Jan 1920 in Cerulean, KY, the son of Paul Gardner Sr. and Laurel Burgess Gardner. He graduated in the first graduating class of Trigg County HS in 1938 and received BA and MA degrees from Western Kentucky University.

Inducted 6 Jun 1944 in Louisville, KY, he was sent to Camp Atterbury, IN, then to Fort Knox for basic training. Attended Armored School then to the clerical department. His MOS was clerk typist 405. He received orders for overseas but they were cancelled overnight.

He remained in the States to work officer's basic at the Fort Knox Post, then transferred as a clerk at the discharge section, Fort Benning, GA, where he was discharged 6 Dec 1945 with the rank T-5. He was awarded the Victory Medal.

Before entering the service Paul taught school at Cerulean, 1940-42; Golden Pond, 1942-43; deferred to teach at Hopkinsville High, 1943-44. When he entered the service in Christian County, it was with students he had taught at Hopkinsville High.

After the service he returned to Hopkinsville HS and taught nine more years, then he came to Trigg County Junior HS and taught until his retirement in 1971. He then drove a school bus for 10 years. Paul was a charter member of Cadiz Civitan Club. He was awarded Eagle Scout rank and Silver Beaver Medal. Paul attended World Scout Jamboree in Moisson, France in 1947.

Today he is active in the Cadiz Civitan Club, Trigg County Historical Society and Retired Teachers.

MALCOLM REX GARLAND, Corporal, born 4 Jun 1925 near Golden Pond in Trigg County, KY. His parents are Roy Finley and Myrtle Ross Garland. He attended Trigg County Schools and graduated from Trigg County HS in Many 1944.

On 29 Nov 1944 he entered the US Army with basic training at Fort Sills, OK. On 10 Jun 1945 his unit departed from California and arrived in the Philippines 2 Jul 1945. He was a gun crewman in light artillery, 82nd FABN and participated in the Battle of Luzon and Philippine Liberation.

Cpl. Garland was discharged 19 Nov 1946 at Fort Sheridan, IL. His awards include the Philippine Liberation Ribbon w/Bronze Battle Star, Asiatic-Pacific Theater Ribbon w/Bronze Battle Star, Army of Occupation Medal (Japan), Victory Medal, Good Conduct Medal, Lapel Button and two Overseas Bars.

He returned to Trigg County and engaged in farming. He married Ardoth Pendleton 14 Aug 1949 and in 1950 they moved to Hammond, IN. He was employed with Ford Motor Co., Marbon/Borg Warner and Keil Chemical/Ferro Corp. from where he retired in July 1990.

He and Ardoth purchased a new truck and travel trailer and spent most of their time traveling the USA. They have two children, Malcolm Paul and Sarah Virginia "Jenny," and grandchildren: Kimberly, Michael, Shannon, Anthony and Benjamin. They also belong to the Calumet Gem & Mineral Club (past president) and he enjoys showing his large collection of gem stones and using his computer.

ROBERT M. GARLAND, war and the rumor of the possibility of the United States' entry into the 1940's fury already raging in Europe, was enough for a young Robert Garland to go down to the local Marine recruitment office to enlist. However, Robert's mother soon disclosed that the Marine's newest recruit was only 16 years old. Thus, his career as a Marine was cut short by the fact he was underage.

The story was different, however, on that day that still lives in infamy, the bombing of Pearl Harbor; because by 1941, Robert had reached his 18th birthday. Nothing prevented him now from joining in service to his country and he shortly began his duty in the USN.

Following training Robert was shipped out on a destroyer assigned to convoy duty across the South Pacific. On watch one night, Robert collapsed with a ruptured appendix. One of the ships in the convoy, fortunately, had five flight surgeons on board. The doctors were brought to the destroyer, and using the mess hall table as their operating station, successfully removed Robert's appendix. Since the destroyer had no facility or personnel for postoperative care, Bob was put ashore at Brisbane, Queensland Australia for hospitalization. His ship was to sail south around Australia to Fremantle where there was a USN Base. After his recuperation and discharge from the hospital in Brisbane, Bob was sent by Trans Australian Railway across country to Fremantle where he was to rendezvous with his ship. Robert arrived safely but his ship was not as fortunate. For somewhere in transit it lost all hands, probably sunk by a Japanese submarine which were reported to be in that area. Had his appendix not saved him, Bob too would have suffered the same fate as his comrades aboard the destroyer.

Bob remained on duty in Fremantle and was put in charge of a Supply Depot at the naval base. Later, he was sent north to Exmouth Gulf. When his service there had been completed he was again returned to the base at Fremantle. During his time in Fremantle, he met a young Australian girl from the nearby city of Perth and was welcomed by her family and friends. He accepted their welcoming ways, grateful for their warm hospitality to a young serviceman stationed halfway around the world from his home in Illinois.

With the signing of the armistice with Japan, US servicemen were shipped back to the States. Following the completion of his service, Bob was mustered out at Great Lakes, IL. He planned to continue his education, which had been interrupted by years of war. In 1948 he decided to return to Perth, Western Australia to marry his Australian sweetheart, Jean Steel.

In 1952 at the urging of Bob's mother, the young couple decided to visit his family in Illinois. They sailed by way of England to New York. There the long trip continued by train to Illinois. Bob found work in construction as an ironworker. Plans to return to Australia were changed with the birth of their daughter, Tracey. Her arrival into the family was followed some years later by another daughter, Darcy, and son, Robert William.

Bob enrolled in Logan College of Chiropractic in St. Louis, MO where he successfully completed his Doctor of Chiropractic degree. After his graduation he moved to Kentucky to begin his practice of chiropractic medicine. He opened an office in Cadiz and later took over the practice of Dr. Lindley in Hopkinsville, KY, following Dr. Lindley's death.

Bob practiced in Hopkinsville until his retirement in November 1997. On the day of his retirement, however, he suffered a cerebellar infarction. Although he recovered from this stroke, his health, affected by the onset of diabetes, forced many of his retirement plans to be put on hold. On 4 Jul 2000 Bob suffered a massive stroke. Although his attempts at physical therapy and recovery were valiant, there was simply too much damage for him to overcome. After a strong fight and great courage Robert Garland's life ended at his home under the care of his family and hospice on 14 Dec 2000.

THOMAS HUGHES GENTRY, PFC, born 12 Oct 1925 in Trigg County, KY and was drafted in the 6th Air Force, ATO, USAAC on 15 Nov 1945 at Camp Atterbury, IN.

He served as supply clerk in Attkinson Field, British Guiana. Pfc. Gentry was discharged 13 Dec 1946.

Returned to Trigg County and married Nella Thomas 11 May 1947. He farmed, was a car salesman, worked for Elk Brand Manufacturing and for the US Postal Service in Cadiz, KY from where he retired in 1990. He is a member and past master of the Cadiz Masonic Lodge #121, York Rite Mason, Knight Templer, 32 Degree Scottish Rite Mason and member of Legion Post 74.

Tom and Nella have two God children, Kim Robin Erath and Mary Scott Roberts. They still live on the farm and have cattle.

PRESTON GOODE, was the fourth son of William M. and Julia Grace Goodwin Goode. He was born in Trigg County on 8 Oct 1912 and died 21 Feb 1955 and is buried in Painesville, OH.

Preston served in the Navy during WWII and was stationed in Iceland.

He was a member of Methodist Church in Painesville, OH. Preston had three sisters: Lucile Martin Goode (b. 1906, d. 1920); Mary Davis Goode Brame (b. 1919, d. 1994); and Willie Mae Goode Johnston (b. 1926-). He also had two brothers, Eddie Lee Goode (b. 1903, d. 1981) and Buster Cullom Goode (b. 1908, d. 1920).

Preston married Dorothy Patterson from Painesville, OH. No children were born to this marriage.

EDWARD F. GOODWIN, Staff Sergeant, enlisted in the USAAF 10 Feb 1943. Sgt. Goodwin was a radio operator and gunner in the Air Corps. Before being shipped out of the States, he was stationed in Boise, ID.

Overseas he was stationed in Italy and flying out from there with a B-24 bomber when he was killed in action 23 Apr 1944. His foreign service was from 17 Feb 1943 to 23 Apr 1944.

Following is an excerpt from a letter received by his mother, Mrs. Lucy E. Goodwin, from HQ USAAF, Washington and signed by Brig. Gen. Leon W. Johnson: "Staff Sergeant Edward F. Goodwin was killed

in action 23 Apr 1944. The B-17 (Flying Fortress) bomber on which he was serving was downed two miles southwest of Ternitz, Austria while on a bombardment mission to Wiener Neustadt, Austria."

The body of SSgt. E.F. Goodwin was returned to Hopkinsville, KY, 16 Dec 1949. The last rites were held at Cerulean Baptist Church with interment in the Cerulean Cemetery. Pallbearers were J.E. Broadbent, Marvin Broadbent Jr., Garnett Hayes, Howard Hopson and J.W. Cameron.

Edward F. Goodwin was the son of Alvin G. Goodwin and Mrs. Lucy E. Goodwin. He had one sister, Effie Grace Higdon. He was a graduate of Cerulean Grade School and Trigg County HS. On his last furlough home he had made application to join the Masonic Lodge.

WILLIAM CURTIS GORDON, PFC, born 15 Jul 1918 in Trigg County. He joined the military 20 Dec 1942 in Trigg County, trained at Fort Benning, GA, and assigned to Co. B, 39th Inf. as light machine gun and runner. He participated in the European Theater, Battle of the Bulge and all over Europe.

He was wounded 30 Dec 1944 in Belgium and again 22 Mar 1945 in Germany and had shrapnel in his leg the rest of his life. Pfc. Gordon was discharged 31 Dec 1945. His awards include the American Theater Ribbon, EAME Theater Ribbon w/2 Bronze Stars, Good Conduct, Purple Heart and WWII Victory Medal.

He married Rebecca L. Futrell 1 Oct 1938 and had one daughter Helen. He retired in 1988 from civil service, post engineer, Fort Campbell, KY. William passed away 20 Aug 1998 at Clarksville, TN.

JOE W. GRAHAM, Staff Sergeant, born 16 Apr 1922 in Trigg County, KY, the son of Grover and Rebecca Tishel Graham. He was drafted in the US Army in Chicago, IL on 9 Mar 1943, received his basic training at Fort Jackson, SC where he was assigned to the 106th Div., Co. D, 424th Inf.

After maneuvers in Tennessee, he was stationed at Camp Atterbury, IN. In October 1944, he left New York with his division for duty in the European Theater of War. Arriving in England, advancement was made to France where the 106th participated in the Battle of northern France and Ardennes, Rhineland, in the Battle of the Bulge.

On 17 Dec 1944 near St. Vith, France, the fighting was fierce with the Germans, and many of Joe's Infantry, the 424th of the 106th were taken as POWs and Joe was listed as MIA. His wife was telegramed later that he was wounded and in the hospital in France. Joe received the Purple Heart for being wounded in action. When he recovered he was sent to Belgium for duty with the Motor Pool.

Joe's decorations and citations were American Theater Ribbon, EAME Theater w/3 Bronze Stars, Good Conduct Medal, Purple Heart and WWII Victory Medal. Qualifications were Expert Infantryman, Combat Infantryman, Carbine Marksman and Heavy Mortar Crewman. SSgt. Graham received his discharge 28 Nov 1945 at Fort Knox, KY.

Joe and his wife Mary Banister Graham, both Trigg County residents, after their marriage on 15 Feb 1942 lived in Chicago, IL where he was employed a short time before being drafted. They were the parents of Joe H. (b. 3 Jan 1943) and John W. (b. 18 Sep 1946). Joe and Mary have six grandchildren.

At the war's conclusion, Joe and his family lived on his Dad's farm awhile, later moving to Cadiz, KY where Joe was employed as a contract mail carrier and rural mail carrier; he retired in 1983 from the Cadiz Post Office.

Joe was a member of the Cadiz United Methodist Church, where he had served as financial secretary, and on the Board of Stewards. He was a member of Disabled American Veterans and the Cadiz Golf Club. He was a fan of baseball, basketball and football games, sports he participated in in his Trigg County HS days where he graduated in 1941. Joe was also an avid hunter.

Joe W. Graham died of a heart attack at the age of 64 in Jacksonville Beach, FL on 8 Feb 1987. He and Mary were visiting their son John and his family, who were Florida residents at the time. Joe is buried in the East End Cemetery in Cadiz, KY.

NORRIS GRANT, born 2 Feb 1922 in Trigg County, Cadiz, KY, the son of Bessie Mae Gresham Grant and Jack Grant. He was drafted into the US Army, 17 Dec 1942. Since it was so close to Christmas, the draftees were given nine days to report to active duty, Norris reported on 26 Dec 1942 at Evansville, IN.

From Evansville to Camp Hood, TX (now Fort Hood), Norris went to join the 809th TD-BN, which he served with throughout the War. Basic training was completed at Camp Hood and other training was completed at different locations.

Assigned for overseas, destination ETO, arrival was 8 Dec 1944. In January 1945, his unit left England for France. The battles and campaigns were Central Europe and Rhineland, where he was wounded 7 Mar 1945.

The return to the States was 10 Jul 1945; all were given a 30 day leave. It was on their return journey to Camp Bowie, TX, when the news was heard that Japan had surrendered and Norris's unit was discharged. Norris received the Good Conduct Medal, EAME Ribbon, Purple Heart Medal and Marksman and Badges: Carbine (MM), Rifle M1 (SS), Gun 76m (EXP).

Returning to civilian life, Norris worked in Granite City, IL at the International Lead Plant until the economy became unstable. Then he worked at General Mills 2-1/2 years. From 1950-65, Norris worked for The *Kentucky New Era,* Hopkinsville. From 1965 to retirement in 1981, he worked at Pulitzer Publishing Company, St. Louis, *The St. Louis Post Dispatch.*

Today, Norris talks of his hobbies: hunting rabbits, running his Beagles, garden and work around the house. He married Pansy Geneva Taylor on 8 Mar 1941. There are three children: Jeannette M. Joiner, Norise D. Nichols, and Ronald G. Grant. Two other children, Brookfie Ann and Zandra Leith, died as infants. There are also 10 grand children and 10 great-grandchildren. Geneva Taylor Grant died 12 Jul 1994.

WILLIAM JACKSON GRANT, Corporal, born 20 Apr 1918, in Trigg County, KY. He was drafted into the US Army during WWII on 2 May 1942 and began his tour of duty with basic training at Fort Dix, NJ.

He was first assigned to the 7th Army but was transferred to the 3rd Army as a lineman for the 28th Signal Corp.

He was sent to England, Africa, Sicily, France and Germany. He received the Bronze Medal, European Theater Medal, and the Good Conduct Medal. Cpl. Grant was discharged in October 1945.

He first married Mary Charlene Dixon and they had two children, Willie Ray and Jimmy Douglas. They divorced and he married Ruby Flynn on 2 Sep 1963. Willie and

Ruby lived in Princeton until the late 60s, when they moved to Hopkinsville. They have five grandchildren: Kevin, Kelley, Amy, Dana and Crystal. They also have one great-grandchild Brice Whittington. Willie still works part-time and enjoys yard work and gardening. They reside in Hopkinsville.

CHARLES ADAMS GRAY, Corporal T-5, born 25 Jul 1920. He volunteered and was inducted into service 12 Aug 1942 at Evansville, IN. Sent to Camp Wolters, TX for basic training then on to Camp Stoneman and Camp Knight, both in California.

They boarded a British ship, went to Bombay, India; Khorramshahr, Iran. He was in the Persian Gulf Command 338 Port BN Co. A. His position was stevedore working on the Euphrates River. They unloaded supplies going to Russia and transported them to the Russian border. While there the temperature was 140° so they had to work at night. One night he fell around 40 feet and broke his ankle.

After 18 months at Khorramshahr, he was shipped to Marseilles, France and placed in the Military Police. Next move would have been the South Pacific, but the atomic bomb changed that plan. The doctor said he should go home so he was placed on the hospital ship, Algonquin, and landed Staten Island, NY, where he was glad to see the Statue of Liberty. He was discharged 19 Nov 1945 from a hospital in Louisville, KY.

Returned to Cadiz, KY, met and married Hodgelene Stallons 25 Nov 1947. They had two sons, Ronnie (b. 15 Jun 1950) and the late Barry Gray (b. 20 Jun 1964). There are five grandchildren and one great-grandson. Charles retired from the Dept. of Transportation after 28 years.

Charles' uncle, Schuyler Gray fought in WWI with Co. K 126th Inf. and is buried in Oise-Aisne American Cemetery in France. He also had three brothers who served in WWII: Herbert Gray (b. 1912, d. 1972), served in the Army; James Gray (b. 1918, d. 1982), served in the Air Force; and Schuyler Gray (b. 1923, d. 1999) served in the Army.

CHARLES E. GRAY, Chief Turret Captain, Gunner's Mate, born 24 Jul 1919 in Trigg County. He entered the military in 1939 at Louisville, KY and participated in the Pacific Theater. Assignments include the USS *Texas*, USN Norfolk, VA and USS *Alaska*.

Charles was discharged in November 1945 to care for his ill father and to run the family farm. His awards include the Good Conduct Medal, Atlantic Theater Medal and Victory Medal.

He married Marie Ryan 18 May 1944 and they have 10 children: Dan, Peggy, Brent, Cherry, Joe, Eddie, Eileen, Theresa, David and Tim; also 16 grandchildren. Charles passed away in 1981.

GEORGE MANLEY GRAY, Seaman 1/c, born 24 Jan 1924 in Trigg County, KY where Lake Barkley is now located, the son of Andrew and Lola Bridges Gray. He enlisted in the Navy 28 Mar 1945 at USNRS Louisville, KY and went to boot camp at USNTS Sampson, NY, located on Lake Seneca.

After a short leave home, he rode a troop train across country to USN base at Oakland, CA. A few days later he rode a troop ship under the Golden Gate Bridge going west – first stop Leyte Anchorage, Philippines. He was assigned to a floating hotel (APL-11) Service Div. 101 as seaman on a LCMP with the duty to keep this craft ready to hit the beaches.

On a hot dark night the latter part of August, a sailor came in and said, "We are under attack, the big ship across the bay has her search lights on." Everyone wanted to look; ships in all parts of the bay had their lights on and were shooting flares, then a voice came over the PA system, "The war is over."

Left the Philippines 1 December on a small ship, crossed the China Sea to Shanghai, landed at the Navy Pier and was assigned to a yard freighter. In mid-May he boarded a troop ship for home. They went by way of Japan to pick-up personnel and word was passed around if the weather was clear in the morning to look west. It was awesome to view Mt. Fuji at sunrise from Tokyo Bay.

Most welcome sight was the Golden Gate Bridge from the west on the way to the naval base in San Francisco. He was discharged 6 Jun 1946. His awards include the WWII Victory Medal, American Area and Asiatic-Pacific.

Married Marily Miller Clark 6 Jul 1951 and they have two children, Deborah (md. Billy Stobaugh) and David (md. Patricia Chalea); and three grandchildren: Ashley, Robert and David.

HERSHEL EARL GRAY, PFC, son of Willie C. and Emma Gray, Canton, KY. He entered the US Army 31 Jan 1942 at Fort Benjamin Harrison, IN and served with Co. M, 111th Inf., 3rd Bn. with duty as truck driver.

He participated in battles in Eastern Mandates, Western and Central Pacific. Pfc. Gray was discharged 10 Dec 1945 at Fort Knox, KY. His awards include the Combat Infantry Badge, Asiatic-Pacific Theater Ribbon w/2 Bronze Stars, Good Conduct Medal and WWII Victory Medal.

During the war Hershel was married to Beulah and they had one daughter Ann Gray Carr.

JAMES T. GRAY, Private, born 23 Sep 1925. He was drafted in November 1943 at Trigg County, KY. He served with the 1st Marine Div. at San Diego, CA; Okinawa and China. He was discharged 30 May 1946.

James T. married Garvie Malone 9 Nov 1946 and they have two children, Jeannie (b. 1949) and John Thomas (b. 1953); and three grandchildren: Jennifer (b. 1976), Jonathan (b. 1978) and Josh (b. 1984).

A contractor in Trigg County, He retired in 1988 and lives in Cadiz, KY.

JESSE JAMES GRAY, Seaman 1/c, born 21 Feb 1909 in Trigg County, the son of William Henry and Nancy Gentry Gray. He enlisted

22 Mar 1944 and served in the USN until 11 Nov 1945 when he was discharged as seaman first class.

He was married to Lacy Crisp 16 Jun 1934 and they have one daughter Sondra Gray Cossey and one grandchild, Al Cossey Jr.

Jesse was a member of the Cadiz Masonic Lodge 121 and was a retired supervisor of the butcher department at Fort Campbell, KY, where he retired in 1971. Jesse passed away 7 Feb 1981.

JOHN ELMER GRAY, Platoon Sergeant, born 28 Oct 1920 at Lamasco, KY, son of John D. and Julia Cunningham Gray. His sisters are Nellie G. Ramey, Anna Lee Oliver, Zelma Stallons, Imogene Faughn; and brothers are George Garland and Lawrence Gray.

John worked as a truck driver for a lumber company at Middletown, OH when he was inducted into service 20 Jul 1942 with date of entry into active service 2 Aug 1942, at Cincinnati, OH.

Participated in battles and campaigns in Southern Philippines, Bismarck Archipelago and Luzon. He was a platoon sergeant in charge of 24 men and served in the central Pacific 38-1/2 months.

Received an honorable discharge 24 Nov 1945 at Separation Center, Camp Atterbury, IN. His awards include the Bronze Arrow Head, three Bronze Stars, Asiatic-Pacific Theater Ribbon and Philippine Liberation Ribbon.

John returned to Lamasco, KY and farmed a few years, later worked with the state building bridges then worked 18 years with TVA.

In 1947 he married Dorothy Alene Boyd. They had three children: Linda G. Sumner, Virginia G. Routen and Eliott Gray. They moved to Trigg County in 1958. Dorothy Alene died in December 1965. John married Sarah Earlene Baker in 1967 and they reside on Cerulean Road and are members of Liberty Point Baptist Church.

He has been a member of Union Carpenter since 1945 and retired in 1982 from construction work at Blanch Memorial Hospital, Fort Campbell, KY.

WALLIS DUDLEY GRAY, son of Hurley and Jean Gray of Rockcastle, was born 16 May 1922 and entered the Army 18 Nov 1942. He served in the 104th (Timberwolf) Inf. Div. as they pushed through France, Belgium, and into Germany. Pfc. Gray was awarded the American Campaign Medal, EAME Campaign Medal, Good Conduct Medal and Bronze Star Medal. He received an Honorable Discharge 6 Nov 1945.

He married Magdalene Ramey on 11 Jun 1947 and in 1950 received a bachelor's degree in agriculture from Murray State College. Also in 1950, their only child, Joseph Dudley Gray, was born on 8 February.

Wallis taught in the Veterans Program from 1950-51 in Lyon and Christian counties and then taught vocational agriculture at Symsonia HS (1952-54) and Caldwell County HS (1954-1965). From 1966 until his retirement in 1980 he taught general science and biology in Caldwell County.

In 1959 he surrendered to the Gospel Ministry and served as pastor of the following churches: Lamasco Baptist Church, 1961-73; Beulah Hill Baptist Church, 1973-84; Cedar Bluff Baptist Church, 1984-87. He retired from pastoring due to health problems but continued to do supply and interim preaching assignments until his death in January 1995.

On 1 Sep 1943 his parents gave him a small Bible to carry into combat in Europe. As the infantry moved through Europe he held onto his gun but somewhere in the ruins of Germany he lost his Bible. He doesn't remember exactly when he lost it nor where. Years later in the 1960s, Jacques M. Dublin, an attorney from Chicago, was travelling in Cologne, Germany and was befriended by a German couple, Mr. and Mrs. Willi Mock. They gave the attorney a Bible that Mr. Mock had found in Weisweiller, Germany in April 1945 and asked him to trace PFC Gray and return the Bible. After contacting the National Personnel Records Center, Mr. Dublin received Wallis's address as of 1945. The Bible was returned to Wallis in 1970, 25 years after it was lost in Germany. In the back of the Bible there was a dated notation indicating that he had the Bible in his possession on 14 Jan 1945. He recalled that he and other GIs frequently took shelter in basements of destroyed buildings and that he may have lost the Bible in a basement or ruins of a building in Weisweiler, Germany.

Today Magdalene resides in Princeton, KY and son Joe lives in Chattanooga, TN with his wife and two daughters.

JOHN GARTON GRIGSBY, Tech 5, born 28 Dec 1921, in Trigg County, the son of John Garton and Georgia McAtee Grigsby. He joined the service 19 Jan 1943 at Fort Benjamin Harrison, IN with duty as light truck driver.

He was stationed at Camp Breckinridge, KY; Camp Carson, CO and overseas at Okinawa. He was discharged 14 Mar 1946, Tech 5, QM Railhead Bn. His awards include the American Theater, Asiatic-Pacific Theater, Good Conduct, WWII Victory Medal and Rifle Marksman (with only one good eye).

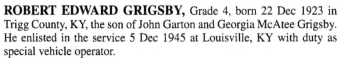

John Garton passed away 16 Sep 1999. As a civilian he farmed and did construction work. He married Notra Dane Johnson 13 Aug 1948 and had two children, John Garton Jr. and Deborah Dane Catron.

ROBERT EDWARD GRIGSBY, Grade 4, born 22 Dec 1923 in Trigg County, KY, the son of John Garton and Georgia McAtee Grigsby. He enlisted in the service 5 Dec 1945 at Louisville, KY with duty as special vehicle operator.

He saw action in the ETO and Germany. Discharged 10 Dec 1948. Awards include the WWII Victory Medal, Army of Occupation Medal, Lapel Button and Qualified Carbine, M-2.

Robert farmed and worked for Baker Bread Co. in Peoria, IL. He married Marianne Boesl while in Germany and had two children, Robert Grigsby and Christine (Grigsby) Watts, and one grandchild Sean Watts. Robert passed away 25 Aug 1992.

JAMES R. GUESS JR., Corporal, born 26 Oct 1926 in Paducah, KY, son of Rev. and Mrs. J.R. Guess. He moved with his family to Trigg County in January 1942 when his father was called as pastor of Mt. Pleasant Baptist Church. James graduated from Trigg County HS in 1944. He took a test given nationwide by the Army Specialized Training Reserve Program given to high school senior boys, then was sent to Purdue University for two semesters college.

After Purdue he was sent to Camp Livingston, LA in 1945 for basic training, then assigned to the Army Finance Office in the Officer's Pay section. Transferred to Camp Atterbury, IN, followed by Camp Pickett, VA and Camp Kilmer, NJ, where he was put on a ship in New York bound for Le Havre, France to be in the Army of Occupation in Germany. He ended up near Berlin and joined the 82nd Abn. Div., 508th Prcht. Inf. Regt. as a paratrooper and sent to Frankfurt, Germany for jump training.

Left Europe in December 1946 and was honorably discharged 17 Jan 1947. His awards include the Good Conduct and ETO.

After returning home, he worked as an insurance agent then for Luther Thomas Co. until 1950 when he went back to Lincoln Ins. Co. In 1960 he bought the local Western Auto Store and operated it for 25 years before retiring in 1985.

Married Naomi Peal 14 Nov 1947 and they live in Cadiz, KY. They have two children, Stanley Guess and Lana Weaver Thompson, and four grandchildren: Jeff and Jason Weaver and Adam and Rene Guess.

LACY E. GUIER, Corporal, born 7 Mar 1921, in Trigg County, Cadiz, KY, the son of Pink H. Guier Sr. and Alma Williams Guier. He was inducted into the US Army 30 Jul 1942 in Trigg County. After training for many months, Lacy attended service school at Amarillo Fld., TX, where he studied airplane mechanic courses. He was then assigned a departure date, 9 Aug 1944 to the destination of ETO, where he arrived 21 Aug 1944.

Battles and campaigns in which Lacy participated: Rome-Arno, North Apennines, Rhineland, Southern France, and Central Europe.

When Lacy received his next departure date, 1 Sep 1945, the destination was to the USA. He arrived in the USA 12 Sep 1945 and was discharged at Separation Center, Camp Atterbury, IN, 13 Nov 1945. He was a corporal with the 83rd Abn. Sqdn. His awards include the EAME Theater Ribbon w/5 Bronze Stars, Good Conduct Ribbon, WWII Victory Medal and Distinguished Unit Citation.

Returned to the family farm in Trigg County and married a Trigg County girl, Juanita Stone, on 27 Jul 1950. There are two children, Vicki Lynn Guier Hammond and Russell Wayne Guier. The grandchildren are Christopher Wayne Guier and Sarah Elizabeth Guier. Lacy passed away 26 Sep 1991 and is buried at Green Hills Memorial Gardens. *Submitted by Junita Guier.*

BRYAN STANLEY HALL, Staff Sergeant, born 7 Feb 1916, in Wallonia, KY. His parents were Robert and Bessie Murphy Hall. After graduation from Cobb HS, Stanley moved to Washington, DC, where he worked at St. Elizabeth's Hospital.

He enlisted in the US Army on 18 Jun 1941, in Baltimore. He wanted to become a pilot. He was on his way until the last test showed that he was color blind. Instead of fighting WWII in the sky, he fought it on the ground, with Troop B of the 6th Cavalry.

During the war, Stanley's mother had not heard from him in a long time. One day she received a postcard. Excited, she turned it over to find he had written only one word - "Stanley." In later years, he would show people that card and laugh. He explained that his troop had left so hurriedly that there was time for him to write only his name. He wanted his mother to know he was safe. All of Bessie's sons who served in the war: Stanley, Kenneth and Reginald, returned home safely, and so did her grandson, Dempsey.

Stanley talked little about the war. When he did, it was about the extremes: the peace and beauty he found during a visit to Switzerland; the privations of weeks in the field, without once changing clothes. The worst memory, apparently, was this: As he and other soldiers opened their presents from home one Christmas Eve, their shelter was bombed and many soldiers were killed.

He served in Northern and Central Europe, the Ardennes and, ultimately, Germany. His decorations included five Bronze Battle Stars.

Once in Germany, he heard someone yell, "Stanley Hall!" He turned to see an acquaintance from Princeton, KY. The man said he didn't have to see Stanley's face, he knew Stanley by his ears.

Stanley was discharged as a staff sergeant on Oct. 28, 1945. He and Kathleen Reddick married in December 1945 and moved to Washington, DC, where Stanley attended Strayer's Business College and worked at St. Elizabeth's Hospital.

They returned to Cadiz in 1953. Stanley worked at the Economy grocery store with the Fort brothers. He and Kathleen ran Hall's Cafe on the Princeton Road for a few years. They served pit barbecue and homemade pies made from scratch by Kathleen's mother, Artha.

Stanley liked to hunt, fish, garden, travel, go to auctions and read. He enjoyed attending the Sixth Cavalry reunions in Chattanooga, TN. He kept war mementos - including photos of Gen. George Patton, but he rarely spoke of the war. He didn't watch war movies and he disliked the TV series *Hogan's Heroes*, a light-hearted portrayal of a Nazi prison camp.

Stanley eventually became assistant manager of the commissary at Fort Campbell, retiring in 1973 because of declining health.

He and Kathleen had two daughters, Diane and Pat; three granddaughters: Robin, Heather and Whitney; and seven great-grandchildren. He lived in Cadiz until his death in May, 1993.

CLAUDE H. HALL JR., Colonel, son of WWII veteran Judge Claude H. Hall Sr. and Mamye Hall was born in Cadiz in 1920 and graduated from Cadiz HS in 1938. He attended the University of Kentucky and was in the ROTC program when called to active duty as a 2nd lieutenant in the Army. He served in the Pacific Theater and was in the battle of the Philippine on Luzon Island. He retired from the Army as a colonel and became a county judge in Washington State.

PAUL EVERETT HALL, Tech 5, born 29 Jan 1921, Lyon County, KY. He enlisted at Fort Knox, KY 29 Aug 1940 and served with Btry. A, 27th FA.

Assignments: Fort Knox, KY, 18 months and Fort Dix, NJ, one month. He left to go overseas from New York City on the ship *The Queen Mary* to Belfast, Ireland on 10 May 1942. He traveled through Scotland by train to Manchester, England where he was loaded onto another ship at Liverpool, England. From Liverpool, he landed on Oran Beach in Africa on 8 Nov 1942.

After a few months, he was shipped from Africa to Italy where he landed on Salerno Beach. He went from Cassino, Italy around to Anzio Beachhead, then traveled through Rome, Italy to Lake Comeo. At that point, the war in Europe was over.

While overseas he was under the command of two generals. His general in Africa was General George S. Patton of the 5th Armored Division, and while in Italy his commanding general was General Mark Clark.

Major Campaigns and Battles: North Apennines, Algeria- French Morocco; Tunisia; Po Valley, Naples Foggia and Rome Arno. His most memorable battle was Anzio Beach Head.

He worked out of the motor pool as a tank wrecker driver. Discharged 3 Aug 1945, Separation Center, Camp Atterbury, IN with the rank T5. His awards and decorations include the EAME Theater Ribbon, six Bronze Stars, American Defense Service Medal and Good Conduct Medal.

He worked as a farmer from 1945 to 1965 then started working at the Kentucky State Highway Department in Trigg County. He retired in 1988.

Married Dorthy Emogene (King) Hall 9 Nov 1945 and they have two children, Dennis Everett Hall (deceased) and Janice Paulette (Hall) Finley who married to Paul Finley. They have two grandchildren, Kendell Lynn and Lanny Everett Finley.

ROBERT HENRY HALL, Seaman 2/c, born 9 Feb 1922, in Trigg County, KY, son of Henry C. Hall and Buelah Faulkner Hall, with siblings Hugh Hall, Earl Hall and Mary Grace Hall Poe. Robert Hall is the grandson of James Johnson Hall and Betty Young Hall and Wiley Pollard Faulkner and Dora Smith Faulkner. The Hall family has resided in Trigg County since the mid-1700s when Peter Hall moved to Kentucky from Virginia.

Robert Hall married Mildred Hunter Hall on 19 Sep 1945. They lived in Hopkinsville, KY and their family includes two daughters, Freida Utley and Judy Hall; three grandchildren: Todd Hancock, Kelly Lile and Amanda Hayes; and four great-grandchildren.

Robert Hall, at age 20, enlisted in the USN as AS-V6 on 11 Sep 1942 at Louisville, KY. He was stationed at the USN Training Station, Great Lakes, IL, on the USS *Louisville*, at the USN Air Station, Adak, Alaska, the US Navel Hospital, PSNY, Washington, and Receiving Station, PSNY, Bremerton, WA.

On 29 Jan 1943, after the battle of Rennell Island, while cruisers and destroyers covering the movement of transport forces to Guadalcanal, the USS *Chicago*, a heavy cruiser was damaged. The USS *Louisville*, a heavy cruiser is credited with a "masterful piece of seamanship" by taking her sister ship in tow to safety in complete darkness.

While serving on the USS *Louisville*, Robert Hall was injured in the line of duty and partially disabled while the USS *Louisville* was operating in the Aleutians. Robert Hall received an Honorable Medical Discharge on 27 Nov 1943 from the USN Hospital, PSNY, Bremerton, WA. At the time of his discharge Robert Hall was rated S2C (seaman 2nd class) USNR.

Robert Henry Hall died on 10 Mar 1995 and is buried in Green Hill Memorial Gardens, Hopkinsville, KY. His burial included a military Honor Guard presentation of the US flag and a grave marker attesting his proud service for his country.

WILLIAM PERRY HAMMONDS, better known as "Bill," was born 7 Mar 1920 in Cadiz, KY. He was drafted into the US Army in February 1942. His first three months of training was at Camp Wheeler, GA. He was also stationed at Maryland, Hawaii, Virginia and other states.

While William was in the Army he had six first cousins who enlisted in the service: John Mason, James Mason, McKinney Mason, John Sizemore, Charles Sizemore and Harvey Sizemore. When William was stationed in Hawaii he had a chance meeting with his cousin, Charles Sizemore, also from Cadiz. They were only together a few days. Bill was stationed in the Pacific for about two years and served guard duty, but was never on the front lines.

Bill left for the Army the same day that James Larkin and Harry Coleman left Cadiz. James died while serving in the Army. Bill was discharged in November 1945 and returned to Cadiz to do carpenter work.

On 4 Mar 1951, Bill married Sarah Ruth Smith of Shelbyville, KY. She was employed by the Dept. of Human Resources in Hopkinsville where they had met. They were parents of three children: Perry Neel, Louis Smith and Ruth Ann.

Bill and Sarah traveled extensively with pre-load construction before settling down in Frankfort, KY, where he stripped, refinished and sold antique furniture for many years until his death on 23 Oct 1990. He had just returned home to Frankfort that night after visiting with his sister, Susie Hughes and her family.

Although he had been gone from Trigg County for over 40 years, he never forgot his roots. He had visited Trigg County four times the year he died because he was so proud of his great nephew, Jordan Bostick, who was born that year.

FLAVIOUS J. "F.J." HANBERRY, Tech 5, born in October 1922 in Trigg County, Cadiz, KY, the son of Bessie Williams Hanberry and F.J. Hanberry. He enlisted in the US Army 17 Dec 1942. To complete training, F.J. went to Fort Bend, IN; Camp Wolters, TX and Vancouver Barracks in Vancouver, WA, where he was in the Quartermaster School. F.J. served with the 346 QM Supply Co. His position in army life was supply clerk 835.

F.J. traveled to Fort Ord, CA and was delayed there until he went to New York, NY to be shipped out, 16 Jul 1943. The trip to Scotland/England took 11 days; they arrived 27 Jul 1943. His assignments were in England, France and Germany. He participated in battles in Normandy, northern France and Central Europe.

Some of the towns that F.J. and his company worked supplies were Portmouth, England and Newbury, England (when the invasion started on 29 Jul 1943). Other towns where they were located (6 Jul 1944 until 27 Apr 1945) were Omaha Beach, France; Cherbourg, France; Munchan Gluback, Germany; Munster, Germany; Herford, Germany; and Nürnberg, Germany. F.J. and his company traveled through Ochenfurt and into France where the company left 28 Nov 1945 to return to the USA. They arrived in the States 10 Dec 1945.

F.J. was discharged from 346 QM Supply Co. and Co. K 315th Inf. Regt. at Camp Atterbury, IN, 15 Dec 1945. His rank was tech 5. His awards include the EAME Ribbon w/3 Bronze Stars, Good Conduct Medal and Victory Medal.

Returning to civilian life he went to work at Wilbur Boggess Chevrolet Co. until retirement in August 1985. Today in retirement, he enjoys working around home, fishing and enjoying life. His home is on Canton Road, Cadiz. *Submitted by Flavious J. "F.J." Hanberry.*

HERSHEL LINDSEY HARGROVE, Staff Sergeant, born 5 Jul 1918 to John Henry Hargrove and Dora Ellen Battoe Hargrove in Trigg County, KY. When he registered into the US Army, 12 Aug 1944, his home of record was Route #1, Repton, KY.

Place of entry into service was Louisville, KY, with the Co. C, 12th Inf. Regt. where he served as a staff sergeant. His MOS was squad leader 745, where he held the Combat Infantry Badge. He served in four campaigns: Normandy, Central Europe, Northern France and Rhineland.

He was hospitalized with frost bite in Germany where a nurse named Zonda, who Dad said was so nice to him that he would like to name one of his children after her. Mother said she was jealous of this nurse named Zonda, so told him "Why don't we name the new baby girl, Wanda," which they did, but Dad said "If we ever have another girl her name will be Zonda." Two and one-half years later came Zonda.

He married Mary Elizabeth Baker Hargrove and they had seven married daughters: Patricia Jean Bush, Brenda Lois Bush, Joyce Kaye Schweitzer, Wanda Ellen Thomas, Zonda Lee Gregory, Vicky Lou Glunt, April Lindsey Washer. Grandchildren are Tina Lynn Bush Birdsong, Tonya Elizabeth Bush Allen, Dianne Bush McNichols, Hershel Givens Bush, Vicky Denise Bush Bland, Gary Michael Bush, Mareth Schweitzer, Ken Allen Thomas, Brian Lindsey Thomas, Amanda Beth McCormick, Sara Lacy Starling, Joshua Benjamin Glunt, Paige Aubrey Glunt, Hilary Louise Washer and Donovan Warren Washer. Ten great-grandchildren are also treasured members of the family.

Hershel lost his hand in a gun accident shortly after his return home from the War. After several months of recovery he had a difficult time finding work, yet he never felt he was handicapped. He worked most of his life as a Civil Service employee at Camp Breckinridge and Fort Campbell, KY. He also operated a family owned trucking business and a small country restaurant in the Wallonia Community. He had a great love of family. Fishing and hunting were his favorite past time activities. He died of a heart attack on Christmas Day morning, 1964. *Submitted by Wanda H. Thomas.*

HOWELL EVERETT HARGROVE, born 28 Sep 1926 in Golden Pond, KY. He entered the US Army 1 May 1945 at Louisville, KY, went through basic training at Camp Blanding, FL, then was stationed at Fort Riley, KS.

Departed the US on 13 Oct 1945 with PTO as his destination, arriving 1 Nov 1945. His division, Co. A, 340th Engr. Cons. Bn. was stationed along the 38th Parallel in South Korea.

Arrived back in the States 18 Nov 1946 and was discharged 3 Jan 1947. His awards include the Victory Medal, Asiatic-Pacific Theater Ribbon, Meritorious Unit Award and Army of Occupation Medal (Japan).

Returning to civilian activity, Howell worked in Hammond, IN, 1947-50, before returning home and entering school at Murray State University. He taught school for 30 years in the Trigg County school system until his retirement in 1986 from Trigg County Middle School,

Howell married Edna Birdsong Hargrove 29 May 1959 and had two sons, Douglas and David. Howell passed away 20 Mar 1988 and is buried in East End Cemetery.

WILLIAM RICHARD HARPER, Engineer 1/c, born 21 Aug 1921, Montgomery County, TN. He joined the service 13 Aug 1942 at Great Lakes.

Assignments: Great Lakes; USN Group, China; Naval Liaison, Calcutta; USN Dry Dock.

William was discharged 4 Aug 1948 as engineer first class. His awards include the WWII Medal, Asiatic-Pacific Campaign Medal w/star, Good Conduct Medal, American Theater Medal and China Service Medal.

As a civilian he was a farmer, businessman and retired from the soil conservation service. He married Margaret D'Mello and

they had nine children: Richard Jr., Wayne, Bobby, Dennis, Mike, Sidney, Terry, Darrell and Bryan. William is deceased.

RICHARD M. HART, Staff Sergeant, born 5 May 1921. He enlisted 27 Oct 1942 at Detroit, MI with MOS of cook and rifleman. He participated in action in the southern Philippines.

SSgt. Hart was discharged 20 Feb 1946. His awards include the American Theater Ribbon, Asiatic-Pacific Ribbon w/ Bronze Star, Philippine Liberation Ribbon w/Bronze Star and Good Conduct Medal.

Returned home and to his career of farming. Richard and Birtie Robertson were married 29 Jun 1946 and have four children: Richard, Sidney, Jimmy and Dianne, and seven grandchildren: Kevin, Brett, Darrell, Austin and Garrett Hart, and Stephen and Stephanie Wallace. Richard passed away 2 Mar 1997.

CARROLL HENDERSON, Seaman 2/c, born 9 Feb 1925 in Trigg County, KY. He entered the USN at Louisville, KY on 24 Jan 1943. After basic training he left for active duty in WWII. Carroll received several honors and awards for his accomplishments in the Navy and attained the rank of AS, S2/c.

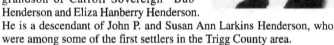

Returning to civilian life in Kentucky he married Linda Futrell. They had one daughter Carolyn Rustin. Carroll passed away 8 Nov 1998 and is buried in the Caldwell Blue Springs Cemetery.

Carroll was the son of Irl Henderson and Columbia Carpenter Henderson and the grandson of Carroll Sovereign "Bub" Henderson and Eliza Hanberry Henderson. He is a descendant of John P. and Susan Ann Larkins Henderson, who were among some of the first settlers in the Trigg County area.

FRED CLARK HENDERSON, Apprentice Seaman, born Jan. 1, 1919 in Hopkinsville, the son of Fulton Henderson and Forrest Major Henderson of Cadiz, KY. He served in the USN from June 1937 to October 1963 and was the only man from Trigg County who served aboard a submarine throughout WWII.

Fred Clark Henderson enlisted as apprentice seaman 5 Oct 1937 at Louisville, KY for four years. Vessels and stations served include USNRS, Louisville, KY; USNTS, Great Lakes, IL; USS *Hollands*; USS *Perch*; USNH, Canacao, P.I.; and US Receiving Ship at San Francisco.

Henderson, an electrician's mate third class was honorably discharged from the US Receiving Ship at San Francisco, CA, on 30 Oct 1941.

Fred Clark Henderson married Muriel Grace 5 Jan 1951. There are two children, Donna and Michael Charles of Salem, MA. Fred Clark passed away 13 Aug 1973 in a Salem hospital following surgery.

CHARLES RAY HENDERSON, born 13 Dec 1923 in Rockport, KY. He graduated from Trigg County HS in 1943 and was drafted in the USMC 26 Apr 1944. He was based in San Diego, CA and was honorably discharged 13 Jun 1944 because of medical problems.

At the age of 30 months Charles was taken from the Kentucky Children's Home by Ebb and Mary Henerson to rear. His mother, Bertha

Tate, died at the age of 35, and his father, Sam Tate was left with four children to raise. He was owner and operator of his restaurant in Evansville, IN, so he put the two younger children in the children's home. The Henderson's took Charles and reared him as their own. Charles went by Henderson all through school. He was legally adopted when he went into the military. Ebb and Mary Henderson were wonderful parents and he had a great life.

After Charles was discharged from the military, he went to Evansville, IN to work at the Servall Co. In 1947 his father Ebb had a heart attack and Charles returned to Trigg County to run the family farm.

Charles married Mary Grace Peal on 8 May 1948 in Trigg County. They had two children, Carolyn Sue and Charles Ray Jr. (who died 2 Nov 1992 of lung cancer). They also have three grandchildren: Tara Dray, Andrea Dale and Tasha Rachel.

Charles and Gracie loved to travel, one of their most memorable trips was to the Holy Land. One of his hobbies was a ham radio operator. He loved talking to people around the world. Charles served as deacon, treasurer, brotherhood president, and teacher at Blue Spring Baptist Church. He died 22 Jun 1985 of a farming accident at the age of 61.

CHARLES TRIMBLE HENDERSON, Pharmacist Mate 1/c, born 27 Apr 1916 in Trigg County, KY. He was the son of Fulton Henderson and Forrest Major Henderson. A veteran of WWII and the Korean Conflict, Charles Trimble served with the USN.

He has a certificate that states, "This is to certify that Charles Trimble Henderson, a pharmacist's mate first class, USNR, is honorably discharged from the USN Personnel Separation Center, Boston, MA and from the naval service of the United States this 7th day of October 1945. This certificate is awarded as testimonial of fidelity and obedience." and is signed by J.C. McCutchen, Captain, USN, Commanding.

In civilian life, Charles was an art teacher and had taught in several colleges and high schools. At the time he became ill, he was teaching in Douglas, GA. He was admitted to the Nashville Hospital 27 January and died Monday, 1 Feb 1965 at Veterans Hospital in Nashville. Funeral services were conducted by his pastor, the Rev. J. Norman Ellis, Dr. R.W. Niles, Mrs. Tom Magraw and Mrs. Karle Glenn, organist, had charge of the music service. Burial was in East End Cemetery, Cadiz, KY.

SUE HILLMAN HENDERSON, born 20 Feb 1914 in Trigg County, KY, entered the USMC 25 Mar 1943. She had enlisted for Officer Training at Hunter College New York; however, the Marine Corps had overfilled the class and she was sent to Camp Lejeune, NC for basic training.

After completing basic she was temporarily assigned to Personnel Dept. at Camp Lejeune. While there she became sick and had surgery for a ruptured appendix. While recuperating from surgery the next Officer Training Class was filed so she was given an honorable discharge on 27 Oct 1943.

She married Edward C. Henderson of Trigg County, KY on 20 Mar 1938. Sue retired from the federal government after more than 30 years service on 30 Jun 1972. She still owns property in Trigg County. Since retirement her favorite pastime is traveling throughout the US, Canada and Europe. She is also an avid bird watcher.

DUDLEY IDELL HENDRICKS, born 18 Aug 1921 in Cadiz, KY, the son of Dennis Hendricks and Blanche Cunningham Hendricks Carr and stepson of J. Pink Carr. Idell was born at the Trigg County Jail, as his grandfather, Mr. Lee Hendricks, was the jailer. When Idell started to school, his first grade teacher asked him where he was born, and he said "I was born in the jail." He grew up in Cadiz and attended the Cadiz Schools.

Some months before WWII began, Hendricks enlisted in the Army where he served six years in the European Theatre. During this time, he was wounded three times. He was discharged from the Army in September 1945.

On 17 Oct 1940, he united in marriage to Miss Mae Shannon of Burkesville, KY. They made their home in Cadiz where Hendricks started the Skyline Taxi Company. In early April 1947, the family moved to Burkesville.

On 16 Apr 1946, Idell Hendricks was drowned in the Cumberland River near Burkesville, KY, when the gasoline motor boat from which he and two others were fishing capsized and sank. His body was returned to Cadiz for the funeral and burial was in East End Cemetery.

JAMES W. HENDRICKS, Corporal, born 27 Sep 1927 in Cadiz, KY, the eldest of eight children born to Clifton E. and Nancy L. Hendricks. In 1945 he registered for the draft and was called for his physical 13 October. He got his greetings 17 Dec 1945 at Fort Harrison, KY, then returned home until 17 Jan 1946 when he reported for duty at Camp Atterbury, IN. Two days later he signed up for two years of service with the US Army. He received $21 a month salary as a private an average of .70 per day. His insurance was $10.40 a month and laundry $3.00 a month, leaving his gross salary at $7.40 per month.

James stayed at Camp Atterbury for six months, then was transferred to Fort McCullen, AL for basic training. After basic he reported for duty at Camp Stoneman, CA. He received orders for Korea but had less than 18 months to serve so he did not have to go. He was then transferred to Letterman General Hospital in San Francisco, CA where he worked in medical supply as a clerk. He was a corporal at the time of discharge with a net salary of $90 per month.

On 11 Jun 1946, he married Katherine Thomas and they have three children: Willard Dale, James Maxfield and Rosemary Hendricks. They also have three grandchildren: Lee, Jeremy, Jamie, and two great-grandchildren, Dalton and Aubree.

James has been a member of Calvary Missionary Baptist Church since December 1954 and has served as church clerk for 46 years, taught young boys Sunday School for 30 years and served as Sunday School Superintendent for several years. He served the city of Cadiz as a councilman for 16 years and was a member of the Cadiz Fire Department for 38 years, retiring as a lieutenant.

He was co-owner of East Cadiz Garage for 28 years where he was an auto, truck and tractor mechanic. In 1988 he went to work at Lake Barkley State Resort Park at the Boots Randolph Golf Course. He presently still works and loves every minute of it.

On 2 Jun 1996 Katherine and James celebrated their 50th wedding anniversary with a reception hosted by their children at Lake Barkley State Resort Park. In December 1996 they were chosen to be the Grand Marshall's for the Cadiz Christmas Parade.

Most of all he wants to thank God for his health, for taking care of his family and all of the blessings that He has bestowed upon them.

LEO HENDRICKS, Major, born 24 Sep 1919 in Cadiz, KY, the son of Dennis Hendricks and Blanche Cunningham Hendricks Carr and stepson of J. Pink Carr. He was the husband of Gwendoline "Peg" Hendricks.

Hendricks enlisted in the Marine Corps 20 Feb 1939 in New Orleans, LA. He served his country for 25 years then retired with the rank of major on 1 Jul 1963.

Leo Hendricks was stationed in Pearl Harbor and was on his way to breakfast when the attack on Pearl Harbor occurred on 7 Dec 1941. He was very lucky, his only injury was a very small cut on his finger.

He was in many battles during his career, including Pearl Harbor, Saipan, Tinian, Iwo Jima, Guadalcanal, Okinawa, and Korea.

While stationed in New Zealand, he met and married a registered nurse in Masterton, Gwendoline "Peg" Mitchell, who survives him. Upon retirement, they made their home in Carlsbad, CA. They are the parents of a daughter, Anne Hendricks Jewell, and two sons, Christopher and Craig Hendricks. They have five grandchildren and two great-grandchildren.

On retirement from the Marine Corps, Leo owned and operated several Chevron stations in the Oceanside, CA, area before retiring for good and pursuing his favorite sport (trout fishing) and loved going to his favorite "fishing hole" at Lake Tauho in New Zealand. This suited Peg just fine and getting together with her family was great fun—the men would fish and the women would shop!

Hendricks received many citations over the years from the Marine Corps. He was a member of the Retired Officers Association, 3rd and 4th Defense Bn., 2nd Armored Amphibian Bn. Association and others. Leo Hendricks died on 2 Dec 2000.

JOHN R. HENWOOD, born 18 Jan 1926 at Philipsburg, PA, the son of Lulu Irene and John Henwood. He has one sister Betty who lives in Clearfield, PA. John attended elementary school at Clearfield and high school at Robertsdale, PA. He is a graduate of the University of Oklahoma.

Shortly after graduation from high school, he enlisted at the age of 17 in the Army Aviation Cadet Program. Between the time of enlistment and reporting for duty, he was required to train with a Civil Air Patrol Squadron at Niagara Falls, NY. During that time, John also worked at Bell Aircraft Corp. as an aircraft assembler on the Bell P-63 aircraft and, also worked as a modification mechanic on the P-63 and other aircraft. His WWII service consisted of "on-the-line" training while awaiting openings to pre-flight training.

His tour of duty included Camp Upton, NY; Keesler Field, MS; Greenwood AAB, MS; Hendricks Field, FL; and Scott Field, IL. While at Scott Field the Japanese surrendered and shortly thereafter, John, along with many other aviation cadets, were given the choice to separate from the military or sign over to regular Air Force. John opted to separate with 26 Nov 1945 as date of separation.

After being out of service for almost five years, attending aircraft and engine mechanics school at Roosevelt Field, Mineola, NY and working at various airports as a licensed A&E mechanic, he joined the 28th Inf. Div. of the National Guard as an aircraft mechanic. When the US became involved in the Korean Conflict, the 28th Div. while on summer encampment at Indian Town Gap, PA, was placed on active duty status and ordered to Camp Atterbury, IN.

After training personnel for combat ready service, the division was sent to Germany in November 1951 for occupational duty. While in Germany, John was the "line chief" of the infantry light aviation section and responsible for maintenance of six to eight liaison aircraft. He returned from Germany in 1952 and was discharged at Fort George Meade, MD.

After 34 years of federal civil service, John, his wife Doris Jean and their poodle retired to Trigg County, KY which they adopted as their home. The Henwoods now reside on the Christian Church Campus, Hopkinsville, KY.

CLARENCE WOODROW HERNDON SR., Aviation Chief Radioman, born 2 Sep 1917 in Trigg County near Canton. He enlisted in the USN 16 Nov 1937 and received basic training as apprentice seaman at Great Lakes, IL then sent to San Diego, CA for trade school.

He was first assigned to the USS *Wright* Patrol SQD11 (Flag); and USS *Memphis* (Flag). Later he served on the aircraft carrier *Ranger* and

Yorktown. Most of these years were spent patrolling the Atlantic and Pacific oceans. He was honorably discharged as aviation radioman first class on 3 Nov 1941.

Less than a month later, 7 Dec 1941, Pearl Harbor was bombed. He was immediately called to appear for service and re-enlisted in the Navy 19 Mar 1942. He reported to the Naval Air Station at Corpus Christi, TX where flight training was being taught. Here he went into communications, also navigation and flying assignments were included (called hazardous duty) for about two years.

During this time he was married to Katee Dawson, his fiance from Trigg County, at Corpus Christi on 3 Jun 1942. Their first son, Clarence Woodrow Jr., was born the next year not long before he was sent overseas.

He crossed the Equator several times and the International Date Line, went to Okinawa and others. His ship was hit by a Japanese kamikaze and their records burned, so no there is no proof of medals. After over nine years he received his last honorable discharge from the Navy in March 1946.

Went to college on the GI Bill and graduated in 1949. He worked at Murray University for two years as instructor, then 29 years at Union Carbide.

He and Kate have four children: Clarence Jr., Robert Michael, Nancy Carol and Elizabeth Ann; four grandchildren, three step-grandchildren, and three great-grandchildren. One grandson is deceased due to an airplane crash at West Point during training.

ROBERT VERNON HERNDON, Master Sergeant, son of Nicodemus "Nick" Herndon and Maggie Lee Dawson Herndon, was born July 30, 1914, in Linton, KY. He was known to his family and friends as Vernon. After graduation from Rogers HS in Linton in 1933, he joined the Civilian Conservation Corps and was stationed near Glendale, CA. Following a suggestion by his sister, Winnie, he began correspondence with Mary Frances Sholar which lasted for about a year. They married on 12 Jun 1935.

During the Depression, Robert worked for the WPA, and on riverboats operating out of Paducah. In October 1942, he joined the Army Air Corps and was sent to the reception center at Fort Benjamin Harrison, IN, then went through basic training at Camp Luna near Las Vegas, New Mexico. He was stationed at Gravelly Point, Washington (DC), then at New Castle Army Air Base at Wilmington, DE, 1943-44, after which he served overseas for 16 months (July 1944 to November 1945) in Ceylon. His unit was attached to Lord Louis Mountbatten's command in the China-Burma-India Theater.

After the war, Robert was stationed in Alaska for 14 months (December 1946 to February 1948), then at Wright-Patterson AFB in Dayton, OH. He was next stationed at Victorville AFB in southern California

(1948), then at Kelly AFB, San Antonio, TX. At Kelly, he was a Military Policeman. On 15 Apr 1952, he received a Letter of Commendation from the base's commanding general calling his performance of his investigative duties "outstanding." At the time, Robert was only a tech sergeant, but his devotion to duty and effective performance was noted by Major General Clements McMullen, who wrote, "I am pleased and proud that you are a member of my command."

Education and self-improvement were very important to Robert. Family members recall his writing poems and an unpublished novel called *Sonny Boy*. In Texas, he spent his discretionary time obtaining a college education. In 1954, at the age of 40, he graduated from Trinity University with a bachelor's degree in sociology and English.

Robert's military papers state that the medals and campaign ribbons awarded or authorized for him to wear included American Theater Ribbon, Asiatic-Pacific Theater Ribbon, Good Conduct Medal, Distinguished Unit Badge; Good Conduct Medal w/clasp; National Defense Service Medal, American Campaign Medal, WWII Victory Medal, Good Conduct Medal (Br w/3 lps). He achieved the rank of master sergeant (October 1952) and held that rank for the three years prior to his final discharge.

Robert's final stint was served at Travis AFB, Fairfield, CA. In July 1955, he received an honorable discharge and returned to civilian life in San Antonio, TX. He enrolled at Trinity University and St. Mary's University to earn remaining credits needed for a teaching certificate and that fall he began teaching English at Southcross Junior HS. He also earned a master's degree in sociology and education from Trinity in 1959. In 1962, he moved his family back to Kentucky, where he became guidance counselor at Trigg County HS in Cadiz, where he worked until he took early retirement and began farming full-time.

Robert's favorite pastimes included genealogy, political history and writing newspaper editorial letters on preserving the freedoms of our country. Robert and Mary had eight children: Robert "Billy," Jerry, Kay, Donald, Sandra, James, Joy and Nick; 24 grandchildren; and 17 great-grandchildren. He died on 29 Jun 1986 and is buried in the Fuller Cemetery on the Linton/Canton Road.

ROBERT GLENN "BOB" HINSON, EM1/c, born 19 Aug 1922 in the Boyd's Hill Community of Trigg County, KY, the son of Johnie J. and Ruby Thomas Hinson. He grew up in Trigg County and attended Upper Donaldson School and Trigg County HS.

On 7 Jul 1942, Bob enlisted with the USN at Louisville, KY, and received "boot camp" training at Great Lakes Naval Training Station. On 27 Aug 1942 he was assigned duty aboard the heavy cruiser, USS *Wichita* at Brooklyn, NY. In November, the *Wichita* was among a large convoy of ships headed across the Atlantic Ocean. On 8 Nov 1942 his ship faced its first enemy fire during the landing of troops at Casablanca in North Africa.

By January 1943, his ship was in the South Pacific, where, beginning at New Caledonia, it participated in every major battle including Guadalcanal, and the Solomons. After a trip to the Aleutians, his ship backed up the army of General Douglas MacArthur during his island hopping return to the Philippines. The *Wichita* withstood numerous kamikaze attacks around Okinawa, landed at Nagasaki, Japan, after the first atomic bomb was dropped, and was at Tokyo Bay on 3 Sep 1945 when the peace treaty with Japan was signed aboard the battleship *Missouri*.

Bob was honorably discharged 11 Nov 1945 as electrician's mate first class after traveling an estimated 300,000 miles with stops at every USN base between Portland, ME and Attu, Alaska. His decorations included service medals from all three theaters of operation, each with several Gold and Bronze Stars. He returned to civilian life as an electrician in Akron, OH, where on July 18, 1948, he married Donna Fouts.

He was recalled to active duty 7 Oct 1950 and assigned to the San Diego Navy Yard to oversee the electrical re-commissioning of destroyers during the Korean War. Discharged in 1952 Bob joined a Los Angeles electronics firm. He retired in 1985 and he and his wife settled in Bishop, CA. She died 3 Jun 1994. Their family includes two children, Wilbert J. "Bill" Hinson, Glenna Hinson Cadmus, and two grandsons, Russ and Shaun.

ROBERT WHITSON "WHIT" HITE, CPO, born 8 Nov 1922 and in December 1943, Whit enlisted in the USN. After basic training at Great Lakes Training Center and advanced diesel engine training in Chicago, Seaman Hite reported to San Diego. He was next transported to the South Pacific aboard a former French vessel, which had been confiscated by the US and renamed the *Rochambeau*.

Supporting the Allied campaigns on Guadalcanal and in the sea approaches to New Guinea, Hite's unit first stopped on New Caledonia, then traveled to Tulagi and Gavutu in the Solomon Islands.

As the Allied forces moved beyond Tulagi, Hite's command was temporarily left behind without enough food or other supplies. They were eventually relieved by another vessel in the area and taken to Guadalcanal. Hite's mechanical skills soon earned him a shipboard assignment, which included preparing landing craft engines.

Initially a motor machinist's mate third class, Hite's careful monitoring of the ship's engine soon earned him a promotion to "motor mac one." On the last of two voyages transporting troops and supplies to the Philippines and Okinawa, Hite's ship encountered the notorious late-1945 typhoon which damaged or sank several of the fleet's vessels. After a 30-day leave home, Hite headed back to California for re-assignment.

Hite left San Francisco on the "shakedown" cruise of the destroyer, USS *Thompson*. A delay in orders put him aboard a new ship, the USS *Bexar*, an amphibious transport which set sail from Portland, OR. During the first voyage of the *Bexar*, Hite received word that his younger sister, Juanita, had died from an accident. Unable to secure leave, he continued on the voyage to Japan, which returned approximately 600 troops of the Sixth Army back to the States. From San Francisco, Hite traveled by train back to Great Lakes Training Center for discharge in February 1946.

Recalled from civilian life during the Korean War, Hite served at Norfolk. At first transporting recruits by bus, Hite later served as a chief petty officer on the seagoing tugboat, USS *Catawba* (code name Maw John Peter, 365). Throughout the Chesapeake Bay area, this vessel towed disabled ships to safety, maneuvered oil lines in fueling operations, and aided larger vessels in docking procedures.

Hite was discharged in 1952 and settled back in Trigg County with his wife, Deane Cunningham Hite, and his children, Danny (b. 2 Feb 1949) and Jan (b. 2 Mar 1953) on the family farm in the Montgomery Community.

FRED W. HOLLAND, born 3 Oct 1910 to William "Bill" and Eurla Holland at Energy, KY. Fred entered the service 15 Oct 1940 (the same day he enlisted) at East St. Louis, IL. He entered as a private first class with the Co. A, 10th Inf. as a rifleman 745.

Fred was sent to Normandy, Northern France and Rhineland. Arrived in ETO 16 Sep 1941 and returned to the States 12 Jul 1945. His decorations include the Combat Infantry Badge, EAME Theater Ribbon w/3 Bronze Stars, American Defense Service Medal and Good Conduct Medal w/Bronze Star.

He married a lady from Illinois where they were living at the time of his death. Fred had one brother Douglas Holland who also served in WWII. Doug and his wife Betty live around Alton, IL and have two children, Cathy and Doug.

JOE HOLLAND, PFC, born 31 Jul 1924 in Golden Pond, KY. He was the son of William S. and Eula Oakley Holland. He entered active service in the US Army at Scott Field, IL on 29 Apr 1943.

He trained at Fort McClelland, AL and Fort Meade, MD. His military occupation specialty was automatic rifleman with the 3rd Inf. Div. On 4 Oct 1943, he left the States and arrived in Africa on 21 Oct 1943.

He was taken as a prisoner of war by the Germans in southern Italy in the late winter of 1943. The US prisoners were forced to march to a POW camp in Germany, passing through the Swiss Alps. During the march, Joe's feet became frozen, causing permanent circulatory damage to his feet and legs that left him partially disabled.

The conditions at the POW camp were harsh, with the prisoners' diets consisting mostly of boiled potatoes. Joe's weight dropped to less than 100 lbs. He spent 14 months in the camp, which was eventually liberated by the Russians.

Pfc. Holland's military service totaled two years and eight months. His decorations and citations included the EAME Theater Ribbon w/2 Bronze Stars, Good Conduct Ribbon, and a Victory Medal. His separation date from the Army was 14 Dec 1945 at Separation Center, Camp Atterbury IN.

Joe married Maxine Colson, also a native of Golden Pond, on 19 Dec 1947. They had two children, Donnie (b. 1949) and Jennifer (b. 1965). He worked for Ford Motor Co. in Louisville for a few years, was a farmer, and eventually became a guard at the Western Kentucky Correctional Institution in Eddyville, KY. Three grandchildren: Darla Holland Thomas, John Holland and Amanda Baker, were born after his death. He died from a heart attack following surgery in Memphis, TN on 16 May 1971. *Submitted by Maxine Sumner.*

CHARLES ROBERTS HOOKS, Sergeant, born 31 May 1921 in Trigg County. He enlisted in the service 17 Jan 1942 with assignments in Guadalcanal, Hiroshima and Bougainville with the 3rd Special Weapons Bn. 3/44.

He always remembered how frightening it was to be on guard during the night when the battles were raging. He was discharged 10 Sep 1945. His awards include the Good Conduct, Occupation, Purple Heart and Bronze Star.

Employed in civil service with industrial operations, Maintenance Division at Fort Campbell until retirement 13 Mar 1972.

Charles married Martha Gray 29 Jun 1951 and they had two children, Charles Elliot and Paul Anthony, and four grandchildren: Jessica, Perry, Catherine and Taylor. Charles Roberts Hook passed away 23 Jan 1977.

MALCOLM T. "DOODLE" HOPSON, born 10 Sep 1923 in Trigg County, the son of the late Archie and Bertha Lloyd Childress Hopson. He is a 1941 graduate of Trigg County HS.

After graduation he enlisted in the Navy and on 21 May 1941 was at the Great Lakes Naval Training Center to receive basic training. He then attended Aviation Maritime School in Chicago, IL and was assigned to Fleet Air Wing 16, Squadron VP31, which covered most of the northern Atlantic Ocean searching for German submarines. The squadron operated out of Puerto Rico, Trinidad and Natal Brazil. The squadron was then ordered to follow a convoy to Africa.

Three years later he was sent back to the States to learn how to maintain aircraft carriers (F4Us) fighter planes. He was then sent to Roosevelt Rhodes Naval base in Puerto Rico where he was stationed until receiving his discharge 12 Nov 1946.

After returning to the States he went to Michigan and was employed by the CSX Railroad for 32 years, retiring in 1981. He now resides in Flint, MI with his wife Ardeth. They have two children and four grandchildren.

A brother, Archie Jr., was also born in Trigg County and drafted in 1941. He took his basic training at Fort Bragg; was assigned to the Americal Inf. Div. and sent to Guadalcanal where he was injured. He was sent to the Figi Island for medical treatment where he contracted malaria. After receiving a medical discharge from the Army, he returned to the States and settled in Louisville, KY. He passed away in 1959 from complications due to war injuries.

An older brother, Elmer, enlisted in the Army in 1939 and was assigned to the 7th Signal Corps at Fort Ord, CA where he was injured in a tank accident. After receiving a medical discharge, he went to work as an electrician in the space program at Moffett Field, CA. He died in 1977.

Malcolm's two sisters, Mildred and Virginia Ann, both served their country during the war by working for the War Dept. in Washington DC. Mildred died in February 2000 and Virginia Ann and her husband reside in Louisville, KY.

W.J. HOPSON, Corporal, born 20 Jul 1925 and enlisted in the service 26 Oct 1943. Boot camp was at Camp Pendleton, CA, then overseas to Oahu, HI, 14 Jan 1944.

He was attached to 6th Field Depot whose work was to supply mostly ammunitions but also other supplies to Marine divisions in the South Pacific. He was an acting sergeant in charge of a group loading ammunition in caves and other warehouses. Being stationed in Hawaii was an advantage in that he was able to see many from Trigg County who came through there. He was discharged 30 Mar 1946 with the rank of corporal.

W.J. went to college and graduated with an AB degree in agriculture from Murray State University in 1949. He taught veterans in Missouri for several years, moved back to Cadiz in 1956 to sell insurance. He is a member of the Cadiz Baptist Church and a former deacon. He has served as a councilman or as mayor for 20 years; served on the PADD board for 16 years and is a former chairman; and he is a charter member and still active in the Rotary Club.

He married Marynell Hardin in 1947 and they had three children: Leanne Futrell, Shara Hardy and Madelyn Retersdorf. Grandchildren are Margaret Futrell; Scot, Brian and Mary Hardy; Jennifer Arenth; Henry, Ben and Will Retersdorf; and three great-grandchildren.

WINTHROP HOWELL HOPSON II, PFC, born 1 Dec 1926 and enlisted 11 Aug 1944 at Louisville, KY. He was stationed at Parris Island, Camp Lejeune, Camp Pendleton and Maui, HI. Pfc. Hopson was discharged 16 Feb 1946.

As a civilian he farmed; attended Murray State College and graduated from University of Kentucky, College of Agriculture; and a member of Cadiz Christian Church.

Married Celia Moore 23 Dec 1949 and they had one child, W. Howell Hopson III, and two grandchildren, Eli W. Hopson and Shawn Perry.

JACKSON HOWELL, Tech 4, born 21 Jul 1919 in Trigg, County, KY. He enlisted in the Army on 29 Jun 1939 and was sent to Fort Benjamin Harrison, IN for basic training. Following which the 5th Div. held their field training at Fort McClellan, AL from the fall of 1939 to May 1940. This was the largest peacetime maneuvers in the history of the United States, with over 70,000 troops participating.

Jackson was then stationed at Fort Custer, MI where he started preparing to go overseas. In January 1942 he sailed to Iceland where he stayed for 18 months. They left Iceland and went to England, Scotland and Ireland to prepare for the French invasion. They landed on Normandy Beach in France 1 Jul 1944. It was horrible with the bombings and people being killed all around them. He thanks the Lord for protecting him.

They had some very hard battles as they moved across France pushing back the German Forces. Took shrapnel in the arm near Metz, France and taken to the army hospital where he remained for several months until he was well enough to return to battle. Following his recovery he spent 43 months in the European Theater Operation. At the wars end he left France and arrived in Miami, FL, then on to Camp Atterbury, IN, where he was discharged on 11 Aug 1945 as Tec-4.

While in Europe Jackson was stationed at Iceland, England, Ireland, France, Luxembourg, Belgium, Germany, Austria and Czechoslovakia. Awards include the Combat Infantryman Badge, Rifle Sharpshooter, EAME Theater Ribbon w/5 Bronze Stars, Purple Heart for being wounded in battle and the American Service Defense Medal.

Following the war Jackson settled in Evansville, IN where he met his wife, Hettie Eckert. They were married on 15 Nov 1945 and had three daughters: Peggy, Darline and Jacqueline. Jackson and his family moved to Illinois in 1956 where he worked as a stationary engineer until his retirement. At which time he returned to his boyhood home in Trigg County, KY. His youngest daughter Jacqueline met and married a native of Hopkinsville, Dave Gossett, and they have two children, Angela and Jonathon.

In April 1994 Jackson's wife Hettie passed away after 48 years of marriage. Jackson now resides in Hopkinsville, KY.

RAYMOND EDSEL HOWELL, PFC, born 20 Jun 1926 in Trigg County, KY, in the Cross Roads Community near the Tennessee State Line. When he was 17 he went to Detroit, MI and worked in a defense plant until he was 18. At that time he was drafted in the Army 26 Oct 1944 and sent to Camp Blanding, FL for his basic training.

Shipped to Germany where he joined the 14th Armd. Div. as a machine gunner on a half-trac until the war ended and the 14th Armd. Div. was dissolved. At this time he was placed in the 45th Inf. Div. (15,000

strong) and put on a ship headed for the Japanese war. When that war ended (thanks to the Atomic Bomb) they came back to Camp Swift, TX where he was placed in the 2nd Inf. Div. until discharge.

Discharged 20 Mar 1946. His awards include the Victory Medal, EAME Theater, Overseas Bar, Good Conduct Medal and Combat Infantry Badge. He is proud to have served his country.

He returned to Detroit and worked in Construction and the Marathon Oil Co. for 33 years. He married Margaret Coleman and they had three children: Pamela, Rebecca and Keith. After Margaret passed away he married Clara Turner and they reside in the same area where he was born.

DAVID LAYTON HUDSON, PFC, born 7 Aug 1925. He enlisted in service in 1942 and fought in hand-to-hand combat in the Alps Mountains in the European Campaign. His job was to seek and destroy Hitler's intelligence officers.

Discharged in January 1946, his decorations include the Good Conduct Medal, Bronze Medal, WWII Victory Medal and the Bronze Star.

After the war he went to work for the Fish and Wildlife Dept., from where he retired in 1982. He married Thelma Lorine Dunn 28 Jan 1950 and they had one son, Roger Dale, and two grandchildren, Layton Dale and Lisa Marie Hudson Frost. David passed away at Calloway County Hospital in Murray, KY in 1986 and was buried at Cumberland Cemetery, Land Between the Lakes. His widow lives in Murray, KY.

ROSS HUDSON, Tech 4, born 2 May 1919 at Canatoy, MO. He enlisted in the service 18 Nov 1942 and served with Btry. C, 929th Field Arty. Bn. in Northern France and Central Europe. He was discharged as Tech-4 on 10 Oct 1945. His awards include the Bronze Star, EAME Service Medal and Good Conduct Medal.

Married first Margrot Drennan and second Mae Dixon. He has two children, Hershel and Michael, and one grandchild, Vada. Ross retired from Hoover Manufacturing in 1985 and passed away 11 Dec 1987.

WILLIAM E. HUNTER, Corporal, born 7 Feb 1925 in Linton, KY. He enlisted in the service 30 Apr 1944 at Trigg County and served with the Military Police in Puerto Rico, where he assisted in enforcement of military regulations; was maintainer of maintenance control of military private sectors; seen that the military did no trouble; and guarded the gate to general's house.

Cpl. Hunter was discharged 19 Dec 1945. His awards include the American Theater Ribbon, Good Conduct Medal and WWII Victory Medal.

As a civilian he did farm work and retired from Caterpillar Tractor Co., Peoria, IL, 24 Mar 1975. Married Martha Calhoun 26 Jan 1948 and they had two children, Lonnie Gene and Debra Hunter Lee, and three grandchildren: Lorie Yoder, Jennifer Gibbs and Shauna Lee. William passed away 29 Jul 1983.

CLIFFORD THOMAS JEFFERSON, MML2, born 14 Jan 1925 in Trigg County, KY. He was drafted into the USN 30 Jan 1943 and earned the rank of machinist mate second class. His assignments were at NSMRS Evansville, IN; NTS Great Lakes, IL; and with the USS *Birmingham*.

His awards include the Philippine Liberation w/Bronze Star (America area), Asiatic-Pacific w/5 Bronze Stars and WWII Victory Medal. He was discharged in April 1946.

Began his civilian life by enrolling at Murray State University. The day of graduation he received the call to return to the Navy, 11 Jun 1951, to the USS *Hubert J. Thomas* (DDR-833). His awards include the Korean Service w/star, United Nations and Japanese Occupation. He was discharged in April 1952 with the rate MML2.

Returning to civilian life, Clifford was employed by REA in 1959. He worked with the electric company as a customers' service representative until retirement.

Woodworking and travel were hobbies enjoyed by Clifford; he excelled in woodworking and many items were sold in this area. Clifford is deceased. He was the son of Lena Jones Jefferson and John P. Jefferson Sr. *Submitted by Clifford's brother, John P. Jefferson Jr.*

THOMAS F. JOHNSON, PFC, Born 6 Sep 1919 in Linton, KY. He was inducted into WWII 24 Jan 1941 at Fort Thomas, KY. He was then sent to a temporary camp outside of Galveston, TX for basic training and served time there. This was a temporary camp set up to guard against invasion of shipping harbors out of Houston.

TF as he was known in service, was sent to the Philippine Islands in 1943. He served in the 737 Anti-aircraft Division firing weapons at enemy ground troops and aircraft. Memorable experience was dealing with the natives.

TF was discharged from the military in December 1945 with numerous medals and ribbons including the American Defense Service Medal, American Theater Ribbon, Asiatic-Pacific Ribbon w/2 Bronze Stars, Philippine Liberation Ribbon, Good Conduct Medal and WWII Victory Medal.

Upon completion of that tour, TF was recalled from the active reserve list in 1951 and served six months in the Korean War. As well as most of the people growing up in that time of the century, daddy's education was very limited, as a matter of fact he could not read or write. He learned the soldier creed by listening to the other soldiers reciting it as they lay in bed at night.

TF married Stella Hendricks 13 Aug 1942 while still in service and together they had seven children: Tommy, Janie, David, Diane, J.L. "Corky." Karen and Jackie. They also had 12 grandchildren and four great-grandchildren. TF worked in general construction until retirement in 1984.

Our knowledge of daddy's war days is very limited due to the fact that dad never talked about his days in service. The only knowledge we have is what others told us at different times. TF, William Stanley Boren and William "Hooks" Page were in the first group drafted out of Trigg County. TF and Stanley served most of the war together and became best friends even after their war days. Since dad could not read or write, we found out that Mr. Boren wrote all of dad's love letters that mom received, and when mom wrote back, he read the letters to dad. Mr. Boren told us children that in their war days they made a deal that when the first one died, the one left behind was to place a rose in the hand of the dead. After many years, Boren kept that promise and placed a rose in dad's hand on 25 Apr 1991.

DOYLE THORPE JOHNSTON, Corporal T-5, born 13 Apr 1925 in Lamasco, KY, the son of John and Naomi Thorpe Johnston. He has one brother Murl and two sisters, Ileen J. Oliver and Opal J. Boyd. Doyle graduated from Trigg County HS.

He enlisted in the service 13 Jan 1945 and served with 293rd Joint Asslt. Signal Co. (JASCO) in Luzon, P.I. and with 318th Fighter Control, 7th Air Force in Hiawa. He was discharged with the rank of corporal 29 Aug 1946. His awards include the Infantry Badge, Exp. Rifleman, Asiatic-Pacific and Good Conduct.

Married Lala Gray 9 Jun 1945 and they have three children: Vance Eugene, Debra Kay and Steven Ray. Grandchildren are Lance Curt Derington, Megan Johnston, Eric Ramsey Johnston and Amy Elizabeth Johnston; great-grandson is Wade Thomas Derington.

Doyle worked 36 years for B.F. Goodrich Chemical Co. and retired in October 1988. He lives in Benton, KY.

ERNEST S. "IKE" JOHNSTON JR., born 6 Oct 1922 in Caledonia Community to Ernest Smith Johnston Sr. and Georgia Humphries Johnston. After the death of his father at 9 months of age, his mother moved to her homeplace on sinking Fork Creek.

After graduation from Trigg County High in 1939, he attended Western at Bowling Green, received BS degree in agriculture in 1943. One night while standing in front of old Cadiz Hardware, Mr. Preston Atwood, chairman of the draft board in Cadiz said "Since you are not married, I'm sorry to tell you but your number came up at the board meeting tonight." After being inducted, he was sent to Camp McClellan, AL for basic training.

At the end of the month, they lined up for pay. Everyone's name was called except his. He walked up to the desk and reported Pvt. Johnston, 35836898. Looking at his records he said "Pvt. Johnston, you owe the government money." Being inducted the last day of the previous month, they took out two months of allotments to his mother and also life insurance. This exceeded his pay. Immediately he fell in love with the Army.

After basic, he was assigned to the 76th Inf. Div., 385th Regt., 3rd Bn., M. Co. at Camp McCoy, WI. The division was moved to Camp Miles Standish, MA. On Thanksgiving Day 1944, they had turkey dinner on land and again on ship the same day. After a month in England, they crossed the English Channel into France, Belgium and Luxembourg into Germany where he was wounded by a mortar shell.

While returning to M Co. from the hospital in a 40-8 boxcar, 7 May, they learned the war in Germany was over. On Memorial Day 1945, the 7th Div. was represented by color guards from M Company at American Military Cemetery in Eisenach, Germany. He was one of the four color guards at this service. Each cross on that hillside was in memory of someone who gave his life for the freedom they have today. Several from their squad were either there or in another cemetery.

Members of the 76th Div. were in combat 110 days, 433 were killed in action, 1,811 wounded and 90 died from wounds.

Ike received three Battle Stars (Rineland, Battle of Bulge and Central Europe). In addition, he was awarded Combat Infantry Badge and the Purple Heart.

He was on a ship returning to the States for training for CRI service when war with Japan ended and he was discharged after 22 months of service.

In 1947-1951 he was the instructor of veterans on farm training. He married Willie Mae Goode in 1949. One daughter Suellen Johnston Hendricks (b. 1952) and Jerry who was born in April 1957 and died in infancy. Ike retired from USDA Soil Conservation Service in 1987. *Submitted by Suellen Hendricks.*

HUBERT JONES, born 22 Nov 1901, entered the US Army and served in WWII. When basic training was completed, he was assigned to a training division for engineers and his assignment was that of a US Army engineer.

When he was discharged from the military, he returned to Kentucky. In civilian life he went to Detroit, MI and worked in the steel mills. It was in Michigan that he remained during his working years until he retired from the steel mills.

Retirement years were enjoyed as he worked in his garden and at his yard work. Hubert D. Jones is buried in Pleasant Hill Cemetery, Land Between the Lakes, in Golden Pond, KY. Hubert Jones was the son of Gus and Sophia Hendon Jones.

JOHN KAY JONES, PFC, born 26 Apr 1927 in Hopkinsville, KY. He enlisted 19 Jul 1945 and served with the 78th Div., 101st Abn. in the European Theater of Operations. He served in Berlin, Germany where his outfit was assigned to clean-up of war devastation. Pfc. Jones was discharged 29 Dec 1946.

He married Mae Melton and they had two children, Diana and Brenda, and four grandchildren. When he retired, John was working in Norton, OH as a press machinist molding auto parts.

MORRIS "C.T." JONES, Buck Sergeant, born 28 Jan 1925, Between the Rivers in the Golden Pond area of Trigg County. His family moved to Lyon County when he was 4 years old.

Morris was drafted into the Army 2 Aug 1945 and sent to Camp Lee, VA for basic training, then to Aberdeen, MD for training in pontoon bridge building. He was then stationed at Fort Belvoir, VA at HQ Company. Upon completion of six weeks military police training with the 7071st, he was assigned to the 71st Military Police at Fort Belvoir. As part of his duties, he made monthly trips accompanying an armored vehicle to either Washington DC or Alexandria, VA to pick up the monthly three and one half million dollar payroll for Fort Belvoir. He was discharged in the spring of 1947 as a buck sergeant.

Morris applied to the Maryland State Troopers and passed all their exams but did not meet their height requirement. He returned to Lyon County and began farming with his family. In 1948, he and his family returned to Trigg County. On 15 Sep 1951, he married Myrtle McCracken from Lyon County. They have four living children: Delpha Jones Bailey, Donna Jones McNichols, Randall Jones and Ricky Jones. They also have eight grandchildren: Jimmy McNichols, Tatum McNichols, Joshua Bailey, Todd Bailey, Mathew Jones, Kayla Gray, Kimberly Jones and Caitlin Jones.

Morris farmed until 1963 when he worked as a school bus driver/maintenance worker for the Trigg County School system. From 1963-66, he worked for Henderson Moorefield Lumber Co. in Hopkinsville, KY. In 1966 he went to work for Hoover (Johnson Controls) where he retired in 1990.

Morris currently lives in Cadiz with his wife. In September 2001, they will celebrate 50 years of marriage. His farm roots run deep and he still enjoys gardening.

WILLIS WHITE "BILL" JONES, born 11 May 1921, in Canton, KY at the Old Canton Hotel. He was the only child of Leonard Adolphus and Helen Futrell Jones; the third generation of his family to be born there, and he was a direct descendant of Perry Thomas, a son of James Thomas. He graduated from Trigg County HS and lived in Canton until 1941 when he went to St. Charles, MO, to work at the Wellston Springs Ordinance Plant, a government project.

He registered for the Army in St. Charles. Because of his job he was allowed two deferments from the Army. He was transferred to the same type of project in Kings Port, TN, the Holston Valley Ordinance Works. His second deferment came to an end, and he was inducted into the US Army at Jefferson Barracks, MO.

He received his basic training at Camp Barkley, TX, near Abilene. After basic training he was sent to Camp Carson, CO. In less than a year he was sent to the South Pacific to the New Hebrides Islands. A very hot and humid climate took a great toll on men's lives. Many came back with incurable fungus and deteriorating diseases. He was given an honorable medical discharge.

On 5 Jul 1941, Bill married Mildred Helen Stewart of Gracey in St. Charles, MO. Mildred was able to live with her husband as long as he was in the United States, but when he left the States she entered nursing training in the Methodist Deconess Hospital in Louisville, KY. She later became ill, came home to live with her parents in Gracey, and taught school in Gracey for three years from 1944-47.

Bill was discharged in May 1946, they moved to Cadiz in 1947, where she taught school for five years. She then went to Fort Campbell, KY, teaching there for 32 years, retired in June 1984.

Mildred and Bill had one child, Shawn Hiler Jones (b. 9 Oct 1954). Hiler married James Rodman Redd Jr. They had three children, James R. Redd III, Leigh Piercy and Kathryn Wiley.

After he returned from the war, Bill graduated from Murray State University. Bill and Mildred operated Mildred's Flowers in Cadiz, KY. Bill became a teacher and taught history at Trigg County HS until his death of a heart attack on 13 Mar 1983. He was elected "Teacher of the

Month" and "Teacher of the Year." Bill and Mildred were members of the Cadiz United Methodist Church. Mildred died on 26 Dec 1998.

Bill was a Mason, Shriner and Jester. He belonged to the Rizpah Temple of the American Legion, Veterans of Foreign Wars, was a Kentucky Colonel, and a disabled American veteran.

LEONARD LEE "RED" JOYCE, Chief Machinist Mate, born 7 Sep 1919, son of Mr. and Mrs. Bailey U. Joyce. He enlisted in the USN 8 Dec 1941. Red was stationed aboard the USS *Makin Island* as a chief machinist mate.

The USS *Makin Island* departed San Diego 19 Jun 1944 to ferry aircraft and men to Pearl Harbor, Majuro and Kwajalein, returning to San Diego 24 Jul 1944. The escort carrier then trained and prepared for combat until 16 Oct 1944. She then sailed for Ulithi arriving Nov. 5, 1944.

On 10 Nov 1944, the ship left for Leyte, protecting convoys in transit. On 22 November they sailed to Manus for the invasion of Luzon.

While at the Lingayen Gulf (3 Jan 1945) the carrier was subjected to air attack with no damage reported. For 11 days she remained flying air support for the amphibious operation.

The USS *Makin Island* was active during the invasion of Iwo Jima. Her planes made pre-invasion strikes and provided aerial fire support until March 8. During this time the carrier group came under heavy Japanese suicide attacks, but *Makin Island* was not hit. Replenished at Ulithi, she sailed for Okinawa as the flagship.

Arriving at Okinawa 25 March, she remained on station for 67 days, flying fire support and reconnaissance missions for the ground forces. The ship's aircraft flew 2,258 combat sorties, 8,000 hours of flying time. Relieved 1 Jun 1945, the carrier sailed for Guam.

Again on 11 July she provided air cover for ships conducting minesweeping and raiding operations in the East China Sea. She provided air cover for the evacuation of Allied prisoners of war.

Makin Island was decommissioned 19 April 1946 at Puget Sound and sold 1 Jan 1947. While in battle the *Makin Island* received five Battle Stars for WWII service.

"Red" took part in the invasion of Leyte and Lingayen Gulf in the Philippines, the conquest of Iwo Jima and the 77-day battle for Okinawa. "Red" returned home Sunday, 18 Nov 1945 after completing 47 months of service.

On 22 Dec 1945 he married E. Louise Sherbut, they had four children: Charlie Joyce, Danny Joyce, J. Carol Joyce Gray Colley and Johnny Joyce. Grandchildren include Scotty Gray, Billy Colley, Melisa Joyce, Kimberly Joyce Harper, Michael Joyce and Danielle Joyce.

"Red" was awarded eight service ribbons with five Battle Stars. He was also awarded the Bronze Star Medal.

On 13 Jan 1964 Leonard Lee "Red" Joyce died of a brain tumor. He was laid to rest in the Trigg Furnace Cemetery, Trigg County, KY.

THELBERT H. JOYCE, born 30 Jul 1918. He enlisted in the USN 20 Apr 1944 in Trigg County and served in the USS *Reno*.

Participated in Iogema strikes and invasion of Philippine Islands. Memorable experience was when the *Reno* was hit by a 22 foot torpedo and suicide plane. Discharged in December 1945. Awards include five Battle Stars.

Married Elise Higgins 31 Dec 1937 and they ran a grocery store at LBL for 10 years then moved to Marshall County. They have three children: Ella Mae Crump, Katherine Balentine and Tony Joyce; also, three grand-children: Spencer Balentine and Troy and Tracy Joyce. They reside on Hwy. 80 in Marshall County.

EDMOND "LUCIAN" KENNEDY, born 6 Jun 1925, in Trigg County, KY, the son of Durward and Clarice Kennedy. Lucian was the second child of 11 children and drafted into the US Army at age 20 on 9 Nov 1945. He began active duty 19 Nov 1945.

He entered the service at Camp Atterbury, IN, as a rifleman 745 - rifle MKM. He did his basic training at Fort McClellan, AL. Lucian was a PFC, Co. G, 31st Inf. Regt. In May 1946, Lucian received orders for reassignment for duty in Seoul, Korea.

He left Fort McClellan by train to Camp Stoleman in Pittsburg, CA. He remained there for three weeks before boarding the SS *Marine Devil Ship*. The trip to Korea took 21 days through high seas and storms. Most aboard became violently sick. Edmond told how awful it was with everyone being seasick. He was one of the 500 aboard who did not experience the sickness and says it was because he ate crackers and slept in the top bunk.

He served in Seoul, Korea as a military police in the unit of Co. G, 31st Inf. from 13 Jun 1946 until 5 Apr 1947. Once he pulled MP duty for 15 days without sleep. He was asked to re-enlist but said, "No." He wanted to return home to marry his love, Ethel Carlene Calhoun.

At age 22, only five days after being discharged, he married Carlene on 5 Jul 1947. They had four children: Patricia Ann Kennedy Williams, Jimmy Dale Kennedy (md. Shelia), Wanda Faye Kennedy Birdsong and Trudy Carol Kennedy (md. Robert S. Allen). He has three granddaughters: Lisa Williams Otejen, Kendal Leigh Birdsong, and Heather Michelle Allen; one step-granddaughter, Meagan Watts; and one step-grandson, Jason Clark. He also has two great-grandchildren, Landon Kyle Otejen and Kaci Allison Otejen, children of Lisa and Kelly Otejen.

Lucian received a WWII Victory Medal. He was honorably discharged 1 May 1947, at Separation Center, Fort Lawton, WA. Lucian was presented a plaque and medal for serving in the Korean War from Gen. Norman Schwarztkoff by daughter and son-in-law, Patricia and James Lloyd Williams. He was always proud to show it to everyone. Having served during the time of 1 Dec 1941 through 31 Dec 1946, he officially became a WWII Veteran.

He was saved and became a member of Caldwell Blue Spring Missionary Baptist Church in April 1951. He loved his church, was a faithful member, and provided transportation there for many. He also surrendered to preach and became a licensed Baptist minister. He was an electrician at International Shoe Co. and Phelps Dodge, Hopkinsville, KY, and retired in 1989.

His greatest battle began 12 Feb 1988, when he thought he had the flu but learned later he had lung cancer. After surgery proved unsuccessful, he began chemotherapy and radiation treatments. He also developed throat cancer in 1989. He fought with all he had, body and soul, and always said that he would beat this. He survived 12 years after his first diagnosis and participated in three Relays for Life for which he was so proud of his medals.

He would often visit many cancer patients and tell them that they would make it and not to ever give up. On 25 Aug 2000, he lost his last battle. Never before has his daughter Wanda ever witnessed the strength, faith and courage her father possessed. He was a true soldier. With full military rites, he was buried in Caldwell Blue Spring Cemetery. *Respectfully submitted by his daughter, Wanda K. Birdsong.*

BONELL EDWARD KEY, SC3/c, born 5 Apr 1926 in Hazel, Calloway County, KY. He entered the USN 23 May 1944 at Louisville, KY. He was sent to USN Training Center in Great Lakes, IL followed by amphibious training, Chesapeake Bay, MD.

Left for the Pacific Theater (the Philippines and Manila). Their task was to clear the harbor for supply ships to pass through. Japan sunk Japanese ships to form a blockade to prevent supplies from getting through. The USN raised the ships and cleared the harbor. Japan also dumped their silver money into the waters. US divers gathered the silver and returned it to the Philippines.

Bonell's locations and service were LCT(5) FLOTILLA TWO; USS LCT 1239; LST 640; LCT(6) 1239; LCT(6) 1240; USS LCT 1240; LCT(6) Group E1 FLOTILLA #27.

He left the States 16 Oct 1944 and returned 5 Apr 1946. His ranks were AS, S2/c, S1/c and SC3/c. His awards and medals include the Victory Medal, Asiatic-Pacific Area Campaign Medal, American Area Campaign Medal, Philippine Liberation Ribbon and Navy Unit Commendation Ribbon.

After returning to the States, he was at the USN Separation Center in Great Lakes, IL where he received an honorable discharge 18 Apr 1946.

Returning to civilian life, Bonell returned to 611 Broad Street, Murray, KY. He worked for Tappan Stove Co., factory work and later surrendered to preach. He studied at Clear Creek School, Murray State University and Bethel College. He graduated from Bethel College, Hopkinsville, KY. He served as a pastor in Calloway, Marshall and Muhlenburg counties; went to Pike County then returned to Murray to pastor at Canton Baptist. While working at Trigg Supply he was pastor at Hurricane and Rock Front. Irene Coleman and Bonell Key bought Trigg Supply and worked there until retirement.

Bonell is the son of Albert and Queenie Baker Key. He married Evelyn King in 1944 and there were four children: Lloyd (deceased), David (pastor at Mayfield), Jimmy (works at Flynn Enterprise), Ricky (works in Cadiz).

Today Bonell is retired from his business, but continues to work for Cadiz and Trigg County as he serves on the Planning Commission as chairman. He lives at 101 W. End Street in Cadiz, KY.

JOHN GARRETT LADD, born 29 Feb 1920 Cerulean Community. During a Saturday night of fun at the Old Legion Hut, John and John R. Thomas decided to enlist in the Navy. The following Monday they hitched a ride to Nashville and enlisted in the USN 12 Dec 1939. They went through Boot Camp at Norfolk. John's training was interrupted because of an appendectomy.

Thomas was assigned to the Pacific Fleet, and Ladd to the Atlantic. Ladd's first ship was an old WWI four stack destroyer USS *Babbitt*. Mid-1941 they began convoy duty in the North Atlantic by route of Halifax Nova Scotia, Greenland, Iceland usually to Londonderry, Ireland, at this time none of their ships were equipped with radar or sonar, so sometimes they couldn't even see the convoy. This is some of the roughest waters in the world. They had to lash their bunks with 1/2 inch line and crawl into their bunk from the end. They were constantly taking 50 to 65 degree rolls.

They usually made a convoy trip about every four weeks. Each time they arrived back stateside, a lot of them talked of going AWOL, just talk. After a couple of liberties they were broke and ready to sail again.

Ladd did convoy duty in the North Atlantic until January 1943 when he was transferred to a new destroyer, USS *Spence*, at Boston. They got underway for Guantanamo Bay, Cuba for two weeks of underway training, then exited the Panama Canal for San Francisco, then to the South Pacific for 13 months deployment. Arrived at Solomon Islands September 1943, was assigned to Captain Arleigh Burkes Little Beaver Destroyer Squadron. Their operating base was Tulagi, across the strait from Guadalcanal.

From September 1943 to February 1944 they made those 31 knot runs up the Solomon Island slot, up to Bouganville, shooting up the supply ships, the Japanese were using to supply their troops, back to Tulagi the next morning refuel, back up again that night. Their destroyer squadron was engaged in two major sea battles during this operation. Battle of Empress Augusta Bay and Cape St. George.

Admiral Burkes Destroyer Squadron was the only entire destroyer squadron to receive the Presidential Unit Citation. The squadron earned eight Campaign Stars. Ladd is authorized to wear the following ribbons or medals: American Area Campaign, Asiatic-Pacific w/8 stars, Victory Medal, European-African-Middle Eastern Area, American Defense w/ Bronze A, Naval Reserve Medal, Good Conduct Medal and Presidential Unit Citation.

John was on occupation duty in Japan when the war ended in August 1945 until 10 December. John's six year enlistment ended 12 Dec 1945 and he was discharged 26 Dec 1945 at Long Beach, CA. Re-enlisted in the Navy and retired with 26 years of service from the Naval Reserve.

John married a California girl and they have lived in Garden Grove for 57 years. John and Virginia have three children, nine grandchildren, and 16 great-grandchildren (including boy triplets).

MALCOM FAY LADD, Tech 5, born 8 Apr 1926 in Trigg County, KY. He enlisted in the US Army in Louisville, KY on 25 Jun 1946. He was sent to Camp Atterbury, IN for processing, then to Aberdeen Proving Grounds for basic training. After completing basic, Malcom was sent to Connley, GA to Ordnance School then transferred to Camp Kilmer, NJ.

On 23 Dec 1946 after more processing, he was sent to Leghorn, Italy for a time period of nine months. His duties included guarding German prisoners of war and guarding ordnance supplies.

He returned to the States on 27 Nov 1947 with the rank of T/5 and went back to Camp Kilmer, NJ for further processing. From there he was sent to Fort Bragg, NC where he was assigned to the 82nd Division for approximately six months. Next he was sent to Fort Jackson, SC for six months. After that he was sent to Camp Chaffee, AR where he trained new recruits.

He was discharged from the Army on 24 Jun 1949. He returned to Trigg County, KY and married Betty Miller on 15 Sep 1950. Malcom farmed for a few years then worked at Thomas Industries for 17 years. He has been working as a self-employed builder for the last 29 years. He continues to live in Trigg County on North Montgomery Road. He is a member and attends Buffalo Lick Baptist Church where he serves as a trustee and Sunday school secretary.

JOE LACY LANCASTER, Pvt, born 27 Sep 1922 in Trigg County, KY, was inducted into the US Army 27 Mar 1945. He served stateside during WWII as a private at Camp Atterbury, IN.

He married Martha Gertrude Ezell on 15 May 1947. She died on 4 Apr 1968. Their children are Peggy Lancaster Smith and Joe Lacy Lancaster Jr. He married Lucy Lancaster on 11 Dec 1970. She has two children, Connie Parker Allen and Terry Lynn Parker. Joe Lacy has five grandchildren (two are deceased), six step-grandchildren and one step-great-grandchild.

Joe and Lucy reside on the homeplace south of Cadiz. He is a retired farmer, building contractor and used car dealer.

FRANK BONNER LANE, Corporal, born on 23 Jun 1923 to B.P. and Nida Lane. He was the oldest of six children (four boys and two girls). Three of the four brothers served in the military.

Our nation was at war with Japan, Pearl Harbor was still on the minds of the people. Frank was a junior in high school when he was drafted into the USMC on 22 Mar 1944. He went to Louisville KY, where he was assigned to the 1st Recruit Bn. Rec Depot in San Diego, CA. He received his basic training, then was transferred to 6th Replacement Draft Training Command at Camp Pendelton CA. In July 1944, he was transferred to the 2nd Bn. 25th Marines, Fourth Marine Division. He left Camp Pendelton and arrived at Maui, Hawaii. He received training there for an amphibious landing on the island of Iwo Jima.

On 16 Jan 1945 he left Maui and arrived on Iwo Jima on 19 Feb 1945. This island was important to the US because of the air bases. They were losing planes and pilots at sea because of no place to land. Taking the island would allow our B-29s the ability to take-off to Japan and it would allow our crippled aircraft a place to land. The island was heavily fortified. From 9 Aug 1944 until 19 Feb 1945, six months and 10 days the island was bombed heavily. On 19 Feb 1945, the 3rd, 4th, and 5th Marine Divisions began their beach landing. For 26 days they fought, only moving 100 yards a day, getting up the next morning, counting their losses and doing it again. On 23 February the American flag was raised on Mt. Suribachi, but the fighting continued, there were other strategic areas to capture: Hill 382, the Amphitheater, Turkey Knob and Menarmi Village, were the nerve centers of the island. Finally on 17 Mar 1945 the island was declared secured and mopping operations began. The battle was over, the island now belonged to us. The cost was tremendous.

Frank returned to the States on 23 May 1946 and at Camp Lejeune NC, was discharged with the rank of corporal. He returned home and everyone was glad. They all knew he had seen and been through a lot.

He went to Indiana and got a job. He met Mary Messer, who was a Kentucky girl, and they married on 25 Apr 1951. They had four children: Donald, Debra, Daniel and Dwayne. Frank and his family moved back to Trigg County where he raised his family.

He worked for Penwalt Corp. in Calvert City. The TVA forced him and his family to move to Marshall County where they presently live. He worked for 23 years before retiring because of health problems. On 16 Nov 1983, Frank B. Lane died with cancer at the age of 60 years, leaving a wife, four children, and five grandchildren. There are now eight grandchildren and two great-grandchildren.

FRANK SYLVESTER LANE, PFC, born 15 Dec 1926 at Golden Pond, KY, served in the USMC from 20 Jul 1945 to 25 Aug 1946. His rank upon discharge was private first class.

He retired from Airco Carbide of Calvert City in December 1982 and permanently resided in Cadiz. He spent the rest of his life working on cars and fishing with his friends.

He married Lola Mae Bush on 3 Mar 1950 and they had five children: Michael Lane, Anthony Lane, Anna Lane Allen, Frank S. Lane Jr. and Gary Lane. He had nine grandchildren: Rhonda Allen Shiro, Rita Allen Gallogly, Trisha Allen Short, Kenny Allen, Mikey Lane, Jennifer Lane Parsons, Nicole Lane, Matt Lane and Amy Lane. He was a member of Siloam Methodist Church and went on missionary work to Jamaica. He passed away on 19 Jan 1998.

JAMES MARION LARKINS, born on 12 Jan 1920. He was the tenth child born to George W. and Zona (Sanders) Larkins. After graduating from Cadiz HS in 1940, he married Ann Alexander on 8 Jan 1942. Ann Alexander was the daughter of James Otis and Lexie (Atwood) Alexander.

James, "Jim" as he was called, entered the service while working for a business firm in Louisville, KY. He entered the US Army on 31 Jan 1942. His Army Service Number (ASN) was 35254511.

He was sent to Fort Benjamin Harrison, IN, for training as a private in Co. D RC. He took out VA insurance in the amount of $8,000 in March 1942 and another $2,000 in July of the same year. By 1 Dec 1942, he was in Co. L, 101st at Fort Meade, MD.

Jim's only child, James Marion Larkins Jr., was born on 25 Feb 1944. Jim was able to be at home one last time in August 1944 for 24 hours before shipping out to France.

On 11 Oct 1944, a chaplain at Camp Shanks, NY, wrote a note to Jim's wife, Ann, saying that while attending chapel, Jim had made a personal commitment to Christ and his Church.

At the time of his death, Jim was serving in the 26th Inf. Div. under Major General W.S. Paul. He was killed by a German grenade near Moyenvic, France, on 9 Nov 1944.

On 22 Nov 1944, the Larkins family received a telegram saying that Jim had been killed in action. On 23 Nov 1944, the Adjutant's office sent a letter confirming the earlier telegram. Ann also received additional information from Cook, one of Jim's closest friends.

After two previous interments, Jim was laid to rest on 29 Apr 1949 in Plot J, Row 14, Grave 6 of the Saint-Avoid American Cemetery in Saint-Avoid, France. Upon his wife Ann's death in 1993, a stone was placed in the Cadiz cemetery commemorating both Ann and Jim's lives and deaths.

GEORGE STROTHER LAWRENCE JR., Lieutenant, born 11 Feb 1919 in Trigg County, Cadiz, KY. He attended school in Trigg County, Columbia Military Academy in Columbia, TN and the University of Kentucky. He was graduated as a first lieutenant and entered the US Army in June 1941.

George was in the 1st Armd. Div. and left for overseas on 31 May 1942. He served with the 6th Armd. Inf. in North Ireland and Scotland. He was killed aboard the ship HMS *Walney*, while entering harbor at Oran, North Africa on 8 Nov 1942.

The national weekly, *Colliers*, printed a story, *Oran Overture*, by Leo S. "Bill"

Disher. In his account of the invasion he mentioned George S. Lawrence Jr. Mr. Disher's article opened: "... There was this kid from Kentucky, Lt. George Lawrence of Cadiz, stretched out in a armchair in the officers lounge, swaying with the roll of an old American Coast Guard cutter that pushed southward toward the African coast. He took off his tin hat and let strong fingers drum against its rounded dome. Absently he said 'Onward sailed the six hundred.' Then he looked up and grinned sheepishly. The old cutter, now known as the HMS *Walney*, flying the British flag - pitched through the blackness."

Lt. Lawrence with 600 others were patrolling ahead of the invasion armada for submarines. The men were ordered to break the boom in Oran harbor, land commando, American troops and naval ratings, capture the fort and board the warships. Mr. Disher explains the gun fire, fire below deck, the bitter battle and the terrific explosions of the *Walney*. We learned from his story that Lt. Lawrence was machine gunned to death in the water. The mission was a success and opened the way for the landing of the invasion troops at Oran. Bill Disher, a fearless correspondent, fought side by side with the soldiers. He was decorated for extraordinary heroism during this engagement.

Lt. Lawrence is buried in Plot H, Row 3, Grave 12 in an American military cemetery, Tunis (Carthage) in North Africa. A bronze memorial marker is placed on his parents lot in East End Cemetery in Cadiz, KY. Lt. Lawrence was the first casualty from Trigg County in WWII

HERCHEL L. LENEAVE, MSgt, born 28 May 1927 and joined the service 14 Jul 1945 in Cadiz, KY. Assignments include Fort Lewis, WA; Camp Kilmer, NJ and numerous other bases in the states; France; Germany, 4th Armd.; two tours in Korea, 1951-52 and 1953-54 with the 25th Inf. Div.; New Foundland, England, Australia, Bermuda, Azores, Hawaii, Africa, Morraco, Japan, Guam, Midway and Wake Island.

MSgt. Leneave retired at Eglin AFB, FL in November 1967. His awards include the Good Conduct, two Bronze Stars, five Battle Stars, ETO Ribbon, two Korean War Medals and from President of Korea, Syngman Rhee Medal.

Married Diane McCutcheon on 10 Jul 1954 and they live in Crestview, FL. They have three children: Herchel Ray, Dale A. and Audrey, and seven grandchildren: Kalie, Kari and Adam Calhoun; Jennifer Jessica, Jane, Herchel and Daniel Leneave.

MACK WILLIS LENEAVE, Private, born 20 Apr 1925. He was drafted 7 Jul 1943 and served in Germany and France. He drove jeep, 3/4 ton and 1-1/2 ton trucks in an antitank outfit in the European Theater. They transported military personnel, supplies and equipment, hauled ammunition, rations, clothing, etc. and made minor truck repairs. They drove at night, during black-out conditions, and over all types of terrain.

Discharged 22 Oct 1945 at Camp Blanding, FL with the rank of staff sergeant. On the same day he re-enlisted in Reserve Corps until 12 Dec 1946 when discharged at Fort Campbell, KY.

Married Cordie Herndon 9 Mar 1946 and has five children: Roger, Jimmie, Shelia, Larry and Kathy; nine grandchildren: Tracy, Christy, Andrea, Ray, Andy, Shane, Jeremy, Jackie and Jody.

Worked in civil service at Fort Campbell as crane operator until retirement 25 Nov 1977. He lived 40 years in Hopkinsville, KY until his death 14 May 1985.

VANCE BOGARD LENEAVE, Metalsmith 1/c, born 25 Aug 1920 to Homer and June Bogard Leneave in the Golden Pond Community of Trigg County. Soon after graduating from high school he enlisted in the USN and received training at Great Lakes, IL as a metalsmith.

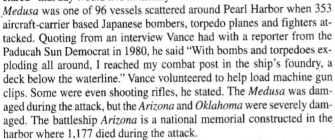

He was assigned to the repair ship *Medusa* and sent to the South Pacific. The ship was not a fighter, but was armed and during the Japanese attack it shot down two Japanese planes and sank one Japanese two-man submarines.

WWII began for Vance on 7 Dec 1941 when President Franklin D. Roosevelt declared "that day would live in infamy." The *Medusa* was one of 96 vessels scattered around Pearl Harbor when 353 aircraft-carrier based Japanese bombers, torpedo planes and fighters attacked. Quoting from an interview Vance had with a reporter from the Paducah Sun Democrat in 1980, he said "With bombs and torpedoes exploding all around, I reached my combat post in the ship's foundry, a deck below the waterline." Vance volunteered to help load machine gun clips. Some were even shooting rifles, he stated. The *Medusa* was damaged during the attack, but the *Arizona* and *Oklahoma* were severely damaged. The battleship *Arizona* is a national memorial constructed in the harbor where 1,177 died during the attack.

Vance served on several ships during his tour of seven years in the Navy. He was discharged 1 Oct 1945 and returned to Golden Pond. As a civilian he was in the general merchandise business, a rural mail carrier, farmer, one of the first directors of Bank of Cadiz and was chairman of the board at his death on 19 Sep 1993. He was a member and past commander of the Trigg County Post 74 of the American Legion, a member and past president of Kentucky Chapter of Pearl Harbor Survivors Association. National Conventions are held in Honolulu every five years and he attended four of them.

Married Nell Upton 10 Nov 1946 and had two children, Pamela Ladd and John Blane. Grandchildren are Ashlea Parks, Alison Ladd, Kyle and Lana Leneave. *Submitted by Nell Leneave.*

WILLARD WILSON LESTER, Cheif Yeoman, born in Lyon County, KY, near Confederate on 18 Jul 1918. He entered the USN on 18 Dec 1942 and took basic training in Norfork, VA.

Lester was attached to the 80th USN Construction Bn. and later the 24th Special Naval Construction Bn. He was stationed in Trinidad during 1943 for one year and in California during 1944. In November 1944, he was shipped to the Philippines and served there until the end of the war.

After the war, Chief Yeoman Lester returned to the States and was discharged in St. Louis, MO, on 10 Nov 1945. He returned to Cadiz to manage Cunningham's Gulf Oil. He later owned and ran this business until his retirement.

Willard and his wife, Mary "Cotton" have two girls, Penny and Mimi, and five grandchildren. They continue to live in Cadiz on East Main Street.

CORBIE A. LITCHFIELD, born 27 Sep 1904 in Cadiz, KY, was the son of W.T. (Tom) and Azza Wimberly Litchfield. Corbie was inducted into the Army on 29 Jul 1942 at Evansville, IN. He entered Army training 12 Aug 1942 and was stationed at an Army Air Base in Columbia, SC. Corbie, a member of the 96th Base Headquarters and Air Base Sqdn. served with the QM Corps. Transferred to ERC on 2 Jun 1943 and discharged 2 Oct 1944 at Fort Hayes, OH.

A newspaper clipping from Azza Litchfield's scrapbook reads: "Pvt. Corbie A. Litchfield honorably served in active federal service..." The discharge continued to read that "...his character was excellent and that he had been transferred to the Enlisted Reserve Corps. Pvt. Litchfield will operate his 140 acre farm, 10 miles north of Cadiz. He states that during his service in the US Army, that he served in six different camps."

Before entering the Army, Corbie worked as a farmer, carpenter and logger (cutting and hauling logs and cross ties). When he returned to

civilian life, he again worked as a farmer and carpenter. He lived and worked most of life in sight of where he was born and buried.

Corbie married a schoolteacher, Rebecca Kilgore, in March 1948. There were four children: Jim, Tommy, Gary and Nancy. Corbie was a strong, hard-working man with good character and many friends. He died 5 May 1992 and is buried in a cemetery near the home and farm in Lyon County, KY. He was a brother of Harvey J. Litchfield. The two brothers are two of the four sons of W.T. and Azza Litchfield. Their mother compiled two large scrapbooks which contain records of soldiers and their pictures during the war years. The clippings are from area newspapers published in several near counties during WWII.

HART S. LITCHFIELD, the son of Mason and Hettie Adams Litchfield, was born in Trigg County, KY, 14 Apr 1921.

Hart joined the US Navy in early 1940, and was discharged in June 1942. In November 1942, he entered the US Army. He saw duty in North Africa and in the European Theater of War. He was in battles in Sicily, Italy and France. He was wounded twice, once in Cassino on 18 Mar 1944 and once at Bruze, France. He received the Purple Heart with Oak Leaf Cluster. He was discharged from the Army, 23 Jun 1945.

Hart and the former Jean Gill, daughter of Rev. and Mrs. Everett Gill, were married 10 Feb 1945. They made their home in Huntsville, AL. Hart and Jean were both employed with US Army Missile Command and they retired from there.

Hart passed away 26 Jul 1998 and Jean died 25 Jul 2000, they are both buried in the East End Cemetery in Cadiz, KY. They had no children.

HARVEY J. "BOOT" LITCHFIELD, born 20 Aug 1907 in Lyon County, KY, was the son of W.T. (Tom) and Azza Wimberly Litchfield. Harvey entered service 10 Feb 1942 and was stationed at Fort Bliss, TX. He was then assigned overseas duty.

A newspaper clipping from Azza Litchfield's scrapbook states: "Arrives Safely Overseas—Mrs. Azza Litchfield has received word that her son Pfc. Harvey Litchfield has arrived safely in North Africa. He entered the service 10 Feb 1942. His address is Pfc. Harvey J. Litchfield, Co. A, 3rd Bn., APO 3929, Care Postmaster, New York, NY."

Harvey's assignments and locations overseas were North Africa, Sicily, Italy, France and Belgium. His date of separation from the Army was 5 Sep 1945. He returned home uninjured. His awards include four Battle Stars which he received as an infantry soldier.

Returning to civilian activity, Harvey attended school as a veteran, worked as a carpenter, farmed and lived on his farm in Caldwell County, Black Hawk Community.

He married Nellie Oliver Gray in 1955. Harvey is known for his hard work and getting out early. He is a member of the Blue Spring Baptist Church. He is a brother of Corbie Litchfield. The two brothers are two of the four sons of W.T. and Azza Litchfield. Their mother compiled two large scrapbooks which contain records of soldiers and their pictures during the war years. The clippings are from area newspapers published in several near counties during WWII.

MALCOLM AVERITT LITCHFIELD, Corporal, born 14 Aug 1925 in Trigg County, the son of Demp and Fannie E. Cunningham Litchfield.

He joined the service in 1945 and served with the 172 Military Police in Alaska. He attained the rank of corporal.

Married Mary Jeanette McVey in August 1949. No children. He passed away 22 Jun 1972.

ROBERT J. "BOOTLE" LITCHFIELD, Master Sergeant, born 29 Jan 1928 in Trigg County, KY, the son of Lewis and Sarah Belle P'Poole Litchfield. He joined the Navy with Lacy Banister in 1946. After four years in the Navy, he got out and started to college in or around Terre Haute, IN. After six weeks of college he quit school and went back into military service. This time he joined the Army for three years and completed his tour of duty in various parts of the world.

After the Army, he joined the Air Force where he completed 14 more years of service and retired as an E-9 master sergeant. The remaining three years in the Air Force he went to college at night and some during the day as he was granted this privilege by the military. He majored in business administration and was first in his class in all of the business administration subjects. He received his degree from the University of Dayton in Ohio. His duty station the last few years in the Air Force was Wright/Patterson AFB, Dayton, OH.

Robert Litchfield was working as a computer programmer for the Air Force Academy in Colorado Springs, CO as a civilian when he was killed in a car-train wreck on Saturday while going to work, in November 1972. His body was returned to Christian County, KY and he is buried in the Green Hill Memorial Gardens near Hopkinsville, KY.

JAMES E. LITTLEJOHN, Tech 4, born 10 Apr 1921 in Trigg County. Joined the service 31 Sep 1942 and took his basic training at Fort Belvoir, VA; advanced training in New York and Detroit, MI. He served in the States with the 486 Engineers Heavy Shop Co. and with the 1669 Engineers Utility Detachment in Europe.

Landed in England, crossed the Channel and served throughout France, Belgium, Holland, Luxembourg and Germany. His unit helped prepare for the Potsdam Conference after the war ended. He was discharged 13 Feb 1946 as tech 4.

Married Mary Oakley 18 May 1946 and they have three children: Sandra Littlejohn Hall, Linda Littlejohn and Harold Littlejohn. Grandchildren are Bradley, William, Ashley, Meredith, Christina and Jeremy. He retired from Air Products 1 Apr 1985 and now farms, hunts, travels and fishes.

OVID F. LITTLEJOHN, PFC, born 13 Mar 1919, Hemitite, Trigg County, KY, the son of Calvin and Annie Lane Littlejohn. He was drafted into Army 238 Combat Engineer Batallion on 15 Oct 1942.

After three months training at Fort Lewis, WA and Camp White, OR, he was shipped out to England for more advanced training. Shipped out to Cherbourg, France, traveled until contacted USSR forces at Mulde River.

Battles/Campaigns: Utah Beach, Cherbourg Campaign, Battle of the Bulge, Roer River, Rhine and Rose Pocket. Pfc. Littlejohn was discharged 11 Nov 1945. Awards include the Good Conduct, European Theater and others.

Married Ruth Downing 14 Dec 1940 and they have two children, Shirley Hargrove and Dorothy Sullivan. Grandchildren are Kimberly and Craig Sullivan-Matthew and Amanda Hargrove. Ovid retired from General Tire 30 Jun 1983 and now enjoys fishing and hunting.

PAUL HAYES MAGRAW, PFC, born 13 Aug 1912 in Christian County. He entered the service 2 May 1942 at Evansville, IN and served with SEC BG 4103rd AAF Base Unit during WWII.

Pfc. Magraw was discharged 2 Feb 1945 at Camp Chaffee, AR. His awards include the Good Conduct Ribbon and Police Sharpshooter.

Paul was bookkeeper for Street's Dept. Store. He married three times: Kathleen Bush, Martha Malone, Catherine Street; had two stepchildren, Ray Bush and Jamie Bush Pfeiffer; and four step-grandchildren. Paul is deceased.

THOMAS HOPPER "TOM" MAGRAW, Master Sergeant, born in Cadiz KY on 25 Jan 1915 to Richard ""Dick" Alphonso Magraw and Lucy Hopper Magraw. He was a graduate of Cadiz HS and the University of Kentucky. He married Marie Schaeffer King on 1 Jan 1937. They had one daughter, Diane King Magraw, born 27 Mar 1938.

He majored in criminology at the University of Kentucky and upon graduation enrolled in the FBI academy. He was employed as a special agent for the Federal Bureau of Investigation in Washington DC from 1938 until induction into the US Army in June 1944.

He was attached to the 117th Counter Intelligence Corp. Detachment MID, Washington, DC. He served on both the east and west coasts of the United States in the capacity of CIC Special Agent. He received an honorable discharge in 1946 with the rank of master sergeant. He was a member of the US Army Ready Reserve (active status) from September 1949 until honorably discharged in January 1953. He was awarded the Meritorious Service Unit Plaque, WWII Victory Medal, American Campaign Medal and Good Conduct Medal.

Tom and family moved to St. Matthews, KY at the end of the war and he was employed with Reynolds Metals Company in their security division. The family settled permanently in Cadiz in 1948 and Tom worked for the Trigg County Insurance Agency until he retired in the late 1980s.

He was a devout Christian and a very active member of the Cadiz Baptist Church. He served as mayor of Cadiz, briefly as police chief, was involved in the creation of the Cadiz Water Department facility, was a member of the American Legion, the Lions Club, Society of Former Agents of the FBI, and Gideons International.

Tom was dedicated to helping others and did so quietly and unassumingly. Until his death he was passionate about the law and was avid about his responsibility to uphold it.

He and Marie were married 61 years. She was 81 at the time of her death in 1998. He was 84 when he passed away in 1999.

GEORGE C. MAJOR, born 23 Feb 1919. Enlisted ROTC, 2nd lieutenant, June 1941. Assigned to 5th Div., Fort Dix, NJ and participated in the Battle of Victorville in France.

Wounded, taken prisoner, stayed in hospital for two weeks then re-captured by US forces. He served in Europe, Asia and Iceland. Retired in June 1962. He received the Purple Heart. Single, he resides in Cadiz, KY.

LESTER DALTON MAJOR, Staff Sergeant, born Nov. 7, 1923 in Stewart County, TN. He enlisted 24 Jun 1943 and served in Avon Park, FL; Fort Myers, FL; Craig Field, Selma, AL and overseas in England as tail gunners mate.

After his discharge on 13 Feb 1946, he was a teacher at Clarksville HS, Clarksville, TN and an agent for Volunteer State Life Ins. Co.

Married Lois McGee 15 Mar 1947, no children. Lester passed away 2 Aug 1958.

WARD MAJOR, born in Canton, KY, the son of Levi Major and Rosa Bridges Major. Ward was a cousin of Jack Bridges, Alfred James Bridges and Sam Bridges Jr. These four men, all born in Canton, KY, knew each other well and all served in the USN.

Ward enlisted in 1939 and served during WWII. After his discharge from the USN, he returned to civilian life in San Diego, CA. He lived and worked there all of his life.

ROY CLAYTON MARQUESS, Tech Sergeant, a veteran of WWII, was born 7 May 1921, at Trigg County, KY. He was the son of Johnnie and Addie Pope Marquess. He had four sisters: Willie Maud, Mary, Hattie and Thelma; three brothers: Lindsey, Odell and Thomas. Roy attended Oak Grove School in Trigg County.

Roy was inducted into the service 28 Aug 1942 and entered active service 11 Sep 1942, at Fort Benjamin Harrison, IN. He was a tech sergeant in the Infantry, Co. H, 32nd Inf. 7th Div. He was a heavy mortar crewman 1607. His military qualifications were Combat Infantryman Badge, Sharp Shooter Pistol. Battles and campaigns: Southern Philippines, Eastern Mandates, Ryukus and Aleutian Islands.

Decorations and citations include Asiatic-Pacific Theater Ribbon w/4 Bronze Stars; Philippine Liberation Ribbon w/2 Bronze Stars; Good Conduct Ribbon; WWII Victory Medal. Roy was separated from service with a honorable discharge 27 Nov 1945, at Camp Atterbury, IN.

Roy and Lois Light were married in 1947. She was the daughter of Elzie and Peachie Light. They had one son, Roy Clayton Marquess Jr. Roy and Lois had three grandchildren: Brian Clayton Marquess, Rachel Ann England and Kevin Dwight Marquess; also two great-grandchildren.

In 1949 Roy went into the ministry. His first churches were Pleasant Hill Baptist Church in Lyon County and New Hope Church in Trigg County. He became full time minister of New Hope. Other churches pastored were Allegrie Baptist in Todd County, KY; Bible Baptist in Christian County; Liberty Point Baptist in Trigg County; Liberty Baptist in Muhlenberg County; and Bumpus Mills Baptist, Bumpus Mills, TN, where he retired in 1973. His son, Roy Clayton Marquess Jr., is also a Baptist minister pastoring Parkview Baptist Church in Christian County, KY.

Roy passed away 1 May 1982, and is interred at Peyton Thomas Cemetery, Donaldson Creek, Trigg County, KY.

JOHN B. MASON JR., born 25 Apr 1924 in Cadiz, KY, was drafted into the US Army 23 Jun 1943. Inducted in the Army at Fort Benjamin Harrison, IN; basic training at Camp Croft, SC; December 1943, amphibious training at Fort Ord, CA; January 1944 was sent to Fort McDowell, or Angel Island at San Francisco, CA; February 1944 went to Treasure Island for 20 millimeter training.

In February 1944 was placed on a merchant marine Liberty ship, the *William D. Boyce.* Thirteen of them acted as armed guard on the ships crossing. In March 1944, they landed at Sydney, Australia, and on 17 Mar 1944 they landed in Milne Bay, New Guinea. After two weeks in the replacement depot they went to Maffin Bay, Wakde Island area to join the 6th Inf. Div.

He was transferred to the 158th Regimental Combat Team for the landing at Noemfoor. After a few days at Noemfoor went back to Maffin Bay, then placed in the Pioneer and Defense Platoon of Division Headquarters.

Their division made a landing 30 Jul 1944 at Sansapor, New Guinea. On New Years Day 1945, the 6th Division left for Luzon, Philippines. The division landed at Lingayen Gulf, Luzon on D-Day, 9 Jan 1945. While on Luzon a 6th Division officer captured a nip lieutenant and suddenly recognized him as a fellow member of the Oxford University baseball team where they had played on the same team before the war.

The war ended in August 1945 and their division was sent to Korea in September 1945. The division landed at Inchon, Korea, headquarters was set up at Chonju. In Korea he was transferred to the 706 Ordnance Company. Left Korea in December 1945, landed at Vancover Barracks, Vancover, WA on 27 Dec 1945, went by train to Fort Knox, KY where he was discharged on 11 Jan 1946.

Received the following decorations and citations: Philippines Liberation Ribbon w/Bronze Star, Asiatic-Pacific Theater Ribbon w/2 Bronze Service Stars, Bronze Arrowhead, Korean Occupational Medal, WWII Victory Medal and Good Conduct Medal. He achieved the rank of corporal.

Married Ann Parrent of Cadiz, 29 Aug 1946. Enrolled at Bowling Green Business University in September 1946, graduated in January 1949. Worked for Pennyrile RECC from January 1949 to 1 May 1986, 37 years. Lived in Fort Myers, FL for eight years, then to Hopkinsville, KY, where they live today. Ann and John have one son who lives in Cincinnati, OH. Their son John Thomas is with Cinergy. He and his wife have two sons, David and Daniel. David is with Fidelity Investments and Daniel still in college at Arizona State, Tempe, AZ. They belong to the First Baptist Church in Hopkinsville.

CHASTINE VANCE MAXFIELD, Corporal, born 7 Mar 1926 in the rural community of Frances, Crittenden County KY, the son of Isaac Newton and Ina Ialeen Adams Maxfield. He received his elementary edu-

cation at Owen School, a one-room school near their home, and his high school education from the Frances HS.

When he reached the age of 18 years, he volunteered to serve in the USMC on 24 Jun 1944. He received his basic training at the Marine Corps Base, San Diego, CA. During this time, he was able to see his brother Vernon who was serving in the US Army and stationed at Riverside. He received a 10-day leave at the end of basic and was warned that was not enough time for him to attempt to visit his homes. However, he felt compelled to take the opportunity to visit his parents, as this was the first time he had been away. It took 4-1/2 days of travel by bus, car, foot and taxicab before arriving at his parent's house in the middle of the night to awaken them to pay the cab driver. He had barely enough time to enjoy one of his mother's home cooked meals, before he had to begin the trip back to California to continue his training. He received amphibious and advance infantry training at Camp Pendleton, Ocean Side, CA. Their unit embarked by ship to the South Pacific Islands 12 Nov 1944, reaching Guam they were the 28th Replacement Regiment and later joined the 3rd Marine Div., 9th Marines. They received further training and intricate details of combating heavily fortified positions.

We loaded and boarded a ship with unknown destinations. After two days at sea, they were shown maps, and told they would be landing on Iwo Jima, a volcano island. The island was eight square miles and very important to the United States for the use of landing and reinforcement of B-29 bomber aircraft. After seeing our men fight to defend their country, giving their all, sharing the fear, being surrounded by injured and dying, did he realize that he was no longer a naive boy, but was suddenly a man who had witnessed the worst of war, and time would never be able to erase those memories. The courage and indomitable will of every man there won the battle of Iwo Jima.

The US dropped the powerful atomic bomb on Hiroshima 6 Aug 1945, the second bomb was dropped on Nagasaki 9 Aug 1945. This was a turning point for our marines. Instead of additional combat duties, they were now training for duty in an occupied country. Chastine's assignment was China from 5 Jan 1946 to 12 Jul 1946. The Great Wall of China and their culture so different from ours overwhelmed him, as well as the people overpowered by government that would never know the freedom that so many in the United States take for granted. He now proudly wears his Marine dress uniform with his medals: USMC, M1 Rifle, Browning Automatic Rifleman in Combat, Sharp Shooter, Asiatic-Pacific War and Iwo Jima Battle Star.

He returned to the Marine Corps Base, San Diego, CA with the rank of corporal and received his honorable discharge on 3 Nov 1946. On his journey home, he reflected on his past experiences, not the turbulence, but the good, and all the men who touched his life. He shall never forget his 19th birthday, 7 Mar 1945, when their commanding officer, 2nd Lt. John H. Leims, rescued casualties under machine gun fire, for the third time. He was awarded the Medal of Honor for his heroic actions. His fellow marines came from all walks, rural, inter-city, educated, non-educated and all those men who gave the ultimate sacrifice. His heart was full of thanksgiving for life, the freedom we cherish, and the honorable feeling for the privilege of serving his country. It was evident his life would be changed forever and he felt the need to serve his fellow man in all walks of life.

He arrived home and took many jobs to earn his keep, including working in a fluor spar mine. Next he traveled to Detroit, MI and begin work in a steel mill, later as an insurance salesman, and finally with strong determination reached for his dream. He sought the help of the GI Bill to complete his education and receive training to become a licensed mortician. He served his profession for 41 years, beginning February 1951 with Goodwin Funeral Home in Cadiz, KY and continued until he retired in January 1992. During those years, his desires were fulfilled, working and serving his community. It was with pride that he became service officer for American Legion Post No. 74, Cadiz, serving for 28 years. He also participated in other civic, fraternal, and business organizations. He married Iva Martha Doom on 28 Sep 1947; they have lived, and worked together for 53 years. They are members of the Cadiz Baptist Church. Their daughter Judith Catherine Maxfield Bilyeu and her husband Steve live in Nashville, TN.

He continues to have special respect and deep personal feeling for our military. Should he be asked, "What has been your greatest achievement?" I would have to reply "Having the privilege of serv-

ing my country in the USMC." His Marine Corps experience gave him wisdom, courage and motivation to work and serve others, a true American Dream.

ROBERT LEE MEADOWS, Tech 4, born 2 Jul 1919, in Cynthiana, IN. He enlisted in the U.S Army on 14 Jul 1942, in Madisonville, KY. He attended the Signal Corps Radio School in Lexington, KY for nine months, and entered active service on 23 Apr 1943. He was sent to Blanford, England, serving as a pharmacist in the DML-ERC from 24 Jul 1944 to 19 Jul 1945.

Discharge was received at Camp Sebert, AL on 24 Oct 1945, with a tech 4 ranking, and having received a Good Conduct Medal AR 600-68 EAMETO-MED.

Robert married Roberta Huddleston on 2 Jan 1942. They have two children, Connie Lee Meadows Thomas and John Robert Meadows. There are four grandchildren: Tracie Lee Thomas Atwood, Marcellus John Thomas Jr., John Peyton Meadows and Lee Whitney Meadows. There are four great-grandchildren.

"Bob" owned and operated Meadows Pharmacy in Cadiz, KY for 24 years. He was a deacon and former Sunday school teacher at Cadiz Christian Church, and was a member of Cadiz Masonic Lodge #121. He was a former member of the Trigg County Board of Education and the Cadiz Water Commission. He was one of the founders of Radio Station WKDZ, and a former partner in Trig County Manor.

Robert Meadows died 2 Apr 1999 at Trigg County Hospital.

WILLIE R. MEREDITH, Sergeant, born 20 Oct 1919 in Stewart County, TN, the son of Jim and Maggie Meredith.

Willie met his future wife, Georgia McGehee, in the summer of 1940 when he was visiting his uncle in Granite City, IL. He enlisted in the US Army 7 Oct 1941 and completed basic training at Camp Croft, SC. He then served in the last cavalry unit in Fort Bliss, TX. Since he grew up on a farm in Tennessee, he was given the job of grooming and caring for the horses. He participated in several parades in and around El Paso. His highest rank was sergeant. He was a sharpshooter with an M-1 rifle and a marksman with a .45 automatic pistol.

While on leave he married Georgia on 25 Oct 1942 in St. Louis, MO. They lived in El Paso, TX, where Willie was stationed at Fort Bliss. They would often walk across the bridge over the Rio Grande River to Juarez, Mexico. They loved to go in all the shops and listen to music in the clubs.

Willie was honorably discharged from the Army on 27 Sep 1943. After the service, he worked with his brother, Hoyt, in the shipyards in Evansville, IN, building LST landing craft. He continued working as a pipefitter and welder. He and Georgia moved several times before making their permanent home in Trigg County in the 1950s.

They built a home on the South Road in 1962. Willie was a member of Linton Methodist Church. He was a member of the Plumbers and Pipefitters Union for over 25 years before his retirement in 1981.

Their children are David Meredith, Janice Pickard and Eddie Meredith. Grandchildren are David Alan Meredith, Scott Meredith, Gina Rogers, Ken Wallace, Ashley Meredith and Adam Meredith.

Willie and Georgia moved to Lafayette Street in Cadiz in 1991, where he died of cancer in 1995.

ANDREW MERRICK, Sergeant, born 10 Dec 1909 in Caldwell County, KY. He joined the USMC 30 Jul 1930 at Parris Island, SC. He was also stationed at San Diego, CA and Honolulu, HI. Andrew served sea time in the USS *Arizona*, USS *West Virginia*, USS *New Orleans* as a gun pointer.

Andrew was appointed PFC in August 1932, corporal in May 1937 and sergeant in September 1938. His weapons qualifications were pistol marksman, October 1934; Pistol Expert, October 1937; Sharpshooter on M20, August 1939. Awards included the Good Conduct Medal. Sgt. Merrick was honorably discharged 23 Jul 1940.

He married Gertrude Alton of Clarksburg, WV on 30 Jul 1940. They returned to Trigg County, KY to farm on the family farm, raising corn, tobacco, cows, sheep and hogs. They had three children: a daughter who died in infancy; two sons, William Roger and Leroy Dale; and four grandchildren.

Andrew semi-retired in 1971 but continued to work on the farm repairing fences and buildings. He passed away 24 Jul 2000. He was a member and deacon of Blue Springs Baptist Church.

HUELL B. MERRICK, PFC, born in Trigg County, KY, the son of Fred and Ella Merrick. He volunteered for the Army on 11 July 1941 in Louisville, KY. He took his basic training for 14 weeks at Camp Wheeler, GA. He then went with the 36th Armd. Div. Co. G to Camp Polk, LA. He qualified for the Combat Infantry Badge and Sharpshooter 29 Aug 1941.

Huell served in the European Theater from 16 Sep 1943 to 23 Oct 1945 in France and England and saw campaigns in Normandy. A total of 61 men out of Co. G were killed in WWII, Huell was wounded in France 4 Oct 1944 and spent two months in a French hospital. He was assigned to the 397th Military Police Battalion Co. C that transported American AWOLs back to their units in Germany.

His decorations and citations include the American Defense Ribbon, American Theater Ribbon, European-African-Middle Eastern Ribbon w/Bronze Star, Good Conduct Medal, WWII Victory Medal and the Purple Heart. Huell was honorably discharged as a PFC 16 Nov 1945.

After the war, he worked at Rumsey Taylor Lumber Co., Outwood

Hospital for 14-1/2 years until it closed, and retired from the VA Hopsital in Nashville, TN. He married Frances Wilson and has one son, Dennis and two grandchildren, Cara and Brandon. He currently lives in Princeton. Huell also owns a farm in Trigg County that he purchased several years ago so that his elderly parents would have a home. Though his health is poor, Huell still goes to the farm each week.

ROBERT A. MERRICK, Tech 4, born in Trigg County, KY, the son of Fred and Ella Merrick. He was inducted into the Army at Fort Knox, KY on 6 Aug 1940. He was with the 29th Signal Co. and helped to lay wire and install telephone equipment for a signal construction unit in a combat area. He saw action in Normandy, Northern France and Rhineland. He was also a heavy truck driver and medium tank driver. On one occasion, Robert had to swim across a river in Germany with telephone wire in his mouth to help re-establish telephone communications for the Allied Forces after the German's had blown up the bridge and cut the wires. While Robert was in France and on his way to a battle, he spotted his brother Huell B. Merrick on his way to a battle. The brothers only had time to say "hi" and "bye" to each other.

Robert received the EAME Theater Ribbon w/3 Bronze Stars, American Defense Medal, Good Conduct Ribbon and the Bronze Star Medal. He was honorably discharged at Camp Atterbury, IN 25 Jun 1945 as a Tech 4. He spent a total of two years, five months and 17 days foreign service and two years five months and three days in the United States.

After Robert's departure from the Army, he worked several jobs including police work in Hopkinsville; as a security guard; and a distillery worker in Owensboro. He also worked at Fort Campbell, KY for several years. Robert married and has one daughter, Ella Ann. He died of cancer 25 Oct 1992 and is buried in Merrick Cemetery in Caldwell County, KY.

JOHN DEAN MINTON, Lieutenant (SG), born in Trigg County 29 Jul 1921, son of John Ernest and Daisy Wilson Minton. Graduated from Trigg County HS in 1940 and entered the University of Kentucky that year. Enlisted in the Navy 30 Apr 1942. Appointed to USN Reserve Midshipmen School, Northwestern University, Chicago, IL, September 1943 and was commissioned ensign December 1943. He was ordered to Amphibious Training Base, San Diego, CA. Transferred to Oceanside, CA, where he trained as a small boat operator and served as a division officer in a standard landing craft unit. Minton served overseas in the Southwest Pacific from 1 Apr 1944 to November 1945. He was promoted to lieutenant (JG) April 1945 and was released from active duty June 1946. He remained in the Naval Reserve and was promoted to lieutenant (SG) in January 1949.

During the first months overseas, he trained with various units on Guadacanal, the Florida Islands at Tulagi, and with the 1st Marine Division on Pavuvu in the Russell Islands. The duty on Pavuvu was in preparation for the invasion of Peleliu. His landing craft unit was assigned to the 1st Marine Division for that invasion. Peleliu was a Coral Island approximately six miles long and three miles wide. It had a terrible terrain, jungle covered coral cliffs with large ridges and deep, wide caves. Its afternoon temperatures would reach 110 to 120 degrees.

The invasion began 15 Sep 1944, and continued for 73 days in spite of the fact the Marine General in charge had stated that it would be rough but short, two to three days. On 20 October, after suffering heavy casualties, the 1st Marine Division was relieved by the 81st Wildcat Division of the Army which had invaded Anquar, a nearby island. That unit finished the Peleliu campaign. On 25 Nov 1945, the commanding Japanese General announced it was finished on Peleliu and he and his assistant committed suicide.

Peleliu was a costly venture. The 1st Marine Division posted 6,526 casualties, which included 1,252 killed, with 73 missing. The 81st Infantry Division lost 1,393, including 208 killed. It is estimated that 10,900 Japanese died in the conquest with slightly over 300 captured.

Minton remained on Peleliu for a total of 14 months following the invasion. His unit remained on the island to bring ashore fuel for the planes on the airstrip and food supplies for the island.

After returning to the States in late November 1945, Minton's final naval assignment was as a curriculum writer in the Standards and Curriculum section of the Bureau of Naval Personnel, Washington, DC. He served there until released from active duty at Great Lakes, IL, on 16 Jun 1946. He received the Victory Ribbon for WWII, American Theater Ribbon and Asiatic-Pacific Ribbon w/star.

After the Navy, he followed an education profession, returning to the University of Kentucky where he completed a master's degree and from there to Vanderbilt where he completed a Ph.D.

In 1947, he married Betty Redick of Trigg County, and they have two sons, John Jr. and James Ernest, and five grandchildren: Page, John Dean III, Dustin Cole, James Zachary and Christina Maria.

He taught at the University of Miami and at Fort Lauderdale HS in Florida. He returned to Trigg County in 1954 to become principal of Trigg County HS where he served until 1958.

In 1958, he joined the faculty at Western Kentucky University. At Western, he served as professor of history, dean of the Graduate School, vice president for Student Affairs, and as fifth president. He retired in 1986. He and Betty continue to reside in Bowling Green.

Two good accounts of the invasion of Peleliu from which some of the specific details have been taken are:

The Devil's Anvil - The Assault on Peleliu, James H. Hallas, Praegar, Westport, CT, 1994 and *Peleliu: Tragic Triumph: The Untold Story of the Pacific War's Forgotten Battle,* Bill D. Ross, Random House, New York, 1991.

LAYTON WILSON MINTON, Carpenter's Mate 1/c, born 23 Sep 1914, served in the USN Construction Battalion (Seabees) as carpenter's mate first class during WWII. He served from 18 Apr 1943 to 18 Jan 1946.

He was in boot camp at Great Lakes Training Center, in Providence, RI and Williamsburg, VA for a time, then to Port Hueneme, San Francisco, CA, where he shipped out to the Pacific Area. He was assigned to the 99th Construction Battalion and was on Canton Island, Guam and the Philippines, helping to build roads and airstrips.

Layton received the American Theatre Medal, Asiatic-Pacific Medal, Philippine Liberation Medal, Victory Medal and the Good Conduct Medal.

Before entering the service he had worked with the Kentucky Highway Department in 1932-35. Then he had worked with Tennessee Valley Authority at Kentucky Dam. After discharge, he continued with TVA at various locations in Kentucky, Tennessee and Alabama. He retired from Brown's Ferry Nuclear Plant in Athens, AL in 1976 as a civil engineer.

He married Retta Eaves from Fulton, KY on 21 Sep 1947, who also worked with TVA at Kentucky Dam until they married.

They were blessed with two sons, Jack Eaves and William Layton. Jack, who graduated from Auburn University in 1971, worked for TVA for nine years. He then received a degree in nursing from Western Kentucky University in 1988. He has worked in an emergency room since that time.

Bill graduated from Auburn University in 1974 with a degree in pharmacy. He has worked as a pharmacist since then.

Bill married Lesa Newby in 1985. Jack married Sophie Barcroft in 1991. Later arrived two grandsons, Layton Wilson II and Robert Carson, and one step-granddaughter Leslie.

Layton was active in the Baptist Church, becoming deacon and a Sunday school teacher. On New Year's Day 1977, Layton and Retta moved to Trigg County to retire on small farm in the Caledonia area. He had always wanted a farm, but that was not to be. After six and 1/2 months into retirement, he suffered a massive heart attack and was in and out of hospitals for the next five years. Coming out of Vanderbilt Hospital in 1980, they moved to Bowling Green, KY. On 29 Dec 1982 he went to be with the Lord and was buried on East End Cemetery in Cadiz, KY. He did not live to see his sons marry or to see his grandchildren. He had looked forward to this very much.

Layton loved Cadiz and Trigg County and went back as often as he could. Layton's wife, Retta, his son Jack and wife Sophie, and stepdaughter Leslie live in Bowling Green, KY. His son, Bill, wife Lesa, and grandsons, Will and Carson, live in Decatur, AL.

We are all very proud of his service for his country and for the person he was.

JAMES D. "J.D." MITCHELL, Sergeant, born 12 Oct 1922 at Cadiz, KY, the son of Mr. and Mrs. M.X. Mitchell. There was one sister, Mildred Mitchell. He was graduated from Trigg County HS. He attended Murray State Teacher's College and was employed by Pratt and Whitney Aircraft Co., Hartford, CT.

He entered the AAF in February 1943, attended basic training then sent to Scott Field, IL where he completed radio operator and mechanics course.

After further training in the States he was sent overseas in July 1944. He moved from Hawaiian Island to Palau Islands and on to Okinawa.

Technical Sergeant James D. Mitchell, radio operator and gunner with the 7th AAF, member of 494th Group, 865th Sqdn., was reported missing in action on 17 Jul 1945. On that day he was one of those who flew in the greatest mass air attack of the war on Shanghi, China. His plane was hit by flak over the target and two of the engines were put out of use. Crew members worked faithfully trying to make it back to their base at Okinawa. When a third engine failed they had to bail out about 140 miles out in the China Sea. Five of the men were never seen again.

In November 1943, he was married to Madeline Miller of Tiffin, OH. They have one daughter Kathleen Marie.

JOHN C. MITCHELL, born 5 Mar 1927, the son of Thomas Mitchell and Flora Belle Crute Mitchell. He served with the Army of Occupation in Germany. John passed away 25 Dec 1971. No other information is available

LACY MITCHELL, Tech 4, born 25 Oct 1912 in Trigg County, KY, the son of Rufus and Myrtle Reddick Mitchell.

Lacy was inducted into the US Army on 21 Apr 1942 in Evansville, IN. He was assigned to the 64th General Hospital as a medical technician. He spent two years, two months and nine days in foreign service. His battles or campaigns included Rome/Arno/North Apennines. He received the EAME Theater Ribbon w/2 Bronze Stars; American Theater Ribbon and the Good Conduct Ribbon. He received an honorable discharge as a Tech 4 on 3 Nov 1945 at Camp Atterbury, IN.

After the war, Lacy went back to work at Western State Hospital and retired from there. He made his home in Christian County. He has one son, Edward Lacy Mitchell, from his first marriage and two grandchildren, Edward Jr. and Leanne.

Lacy died 14 Dec 1998 and is buried at Green Hills Memorial Gardens in Christian County, KY.

VICTOR ROBERT MITCHELL, Corporal, born 6 Jan 1925 in Chicago, IL. Enlisted in the USMC 9 Apr 1943 at Chicago and served in Guam, Mariana Islands and Occupation of China during WWII. Discharged 9 Mar 1946. His awards include the Good Conduct, HS and HD Buttons.

Married Donna Bruin on 4 Dec 1948 and had five children: Kathi Steele, Vicky P'Pool, Debra Bynum, Sharon Oliver and Pattie Coleman; grandchildren are Jim Steele; Jenny Ivy; Kim Henley; Mike P'Pool; Rob Bynum; Greg, Chris and Brian Oliver; Tina Chivalier; Amanda, Carla and Victor Coleman; and 10 great-grandchildren.

Victor retired from Johnson Controls in Cadiz in April 1990. He passed away 6 Mar 2000.

THOMAS C. MITCHELL, born 20 Feb 1919, son of Thomas Mitchell and Flora Belle Crute Mitchell. Inducted into the Army Air Force on 10 Jul 1941 and served overseas in England and France.

Citations include American Defense Ribbon, American Theater Ribbon, EAME Ribbon and Good Conduct Medal. He was honorably discharged 1 Nov 1945.

Married Pauline E. Deese of Union County, NC on 16 Aug 1953. They have three children: Rev. John Thomas Mitchell and Terry Paul Mitchell of Cadiz and Timothy James Mitchell of Whitesville, KY. Grandchildren are Ashley Mae Mitchell, Jason James Mitchell, Nathan Paul Mitchell and Yevonna Carol Mitchell. Thomas passed away 23 Oct 1988.

CLIFTON MEADE MIZE, Staff Sergeant, born 14 Jan 1919 in Tonasket, WA. He joined the US Army 6 Mar 1941. After 18 months in the States which included basic training at Fort Snelling, MN, he was shipped out and spent the next three years in Bermuda, the Philippine Islands, Ryukyus Islands (Okinawa) to name a few.

Before, and during his time as a squad leader, he was wounded in battle. SSgt. Mize was discharged 19 Sep 1945, after four years, five months and four days of service to his country. His awards include the Asiatic-Pacific Theater Ribbon w/3 Bronze Stars, American Theater Ribbon, American Defense Medal, Philippine Liberation Ribbon w/Bronze Star, Good Conduct and Purple Heart.

Married Bessie Lancaster on 18 Jul 1948 and they have five children: David Meade, Stephen Reed (deceased 1970), Randall Vance, Michael Kevin, Karen Lynn; and four grandchildren: Rhiannan, Randall Blake, Fletcher Thomas and Cheyenne Marie.

Clifton retired from Thomas Industries in Hopkinsville, KY 30 May 1980. He lives in eastern Trigg County, Cadiz, KY where he does farming and gardening.

HAROLD H. MIZE, Staff Sergeant, born 28 Nov 1923 to Jack and Ethel Blakeley Mize in Cerulean Springs, KY. Harold attended Cerulean

Grade School and graduated from Trigg County HS in 1941. After graduation, Harold worked for Dollar Bros. in Hopkinsville, KY.

He was inducted in the USAAC 16 Jun 1943 and entered active duty 30 Jun 1943 at Fort Benjamin Harrison, IN. He attended Aerial Gunnery School at Laredo, TX in 1944.

Left for overseas duty in the South Pacific on 22 May 1944. He was assigned to the 400th Sqdn., 90th Bomb Group (Heavy), 5th Army Air Corps. While in the South Pacific he flew 48 combat missions as a tail gunner aboard a B-24.

Returned to the States 3 Apr 1945 and attended Aerial Gunnery Instructor School, Laredo, TX for six weeks. SSgt. Mize was honorably discharged 26 Oct 1945. His awards include the Good Conduct Ribbon, Asiatic-Pacific Ribbon and Philippine Liberation Ribbon.

Harold returned to civilian life worked with Dollar Bros. Shoes in Bowling Green and Winchester, KY. He married Mary Ruby Holmes on 12 Jun 1943. They moved to Beaver Dam, KY and Harold went to work at F.K. Casebier's, a retail clothing store. In November 1953 Harold and family moved to Cadiz, KY where he became a partner in F.B. Wilkinsons and eventually became full owner until his death 23 Nov 1993. He was buried in the East End Cemetery in Cadiz, KY.

KING JOSH MIZE, Ensign, born 31 Oct 1909 in the area of Canton, KY, the son of J. Lewis and Kitty Boyd Mize. Josh worked on the family farm until the spring of 1932 when he entered the Civilian Conservation Corps and worked two years in California and Idaho.

He returned to Trigg County in the fall of 1934. In 1939 he became involved in the insurance business in Christian County. He married Wynonna on 13 Apr 1941.

Josh enlisted in the USN and entered active service 13 Mar 1942 as a yeoman and was honorably discharged 27 Jan 1945 as ensign.

He returned to Christian County (where he still resides) and formed K. Josh Mize Insurance Agency. He sold out in 1969.

WAYMON TAYLOR MIZE, Seaman 1/c, born 31 Mar 1915, the youngest son of Lewis and Kitty Boyd Mize of Canton, KY. He was inducted in the USN 11 Apr 1945 and achieved the rank of seaman first class. He was honorably discharged 3 Mar 1946.

After his discharge Waymon returned to Hopkinsville and resumed his trade as a carpenter. He was killed in an auto accident 10 Nov 1967 and is buried in the Mize Cemetery in Canton, KY.

JOHN FRANKLIN MOORE, Staff Sergeant, born 5 Mar 1922 in Cadiz, KY. He was inducted into the Army 20 Oct 1942 and assigned to 3rd Army, 55th Armd. Inf., 11th Armd. Div. He served in the Ardennes, Rhineland and Central Europe.

SSgt. Moore was discharged 8 Jan 1946. His awards include the Good Conduct Medal, American Theater Ribbon, WWII Victory Medal, EAME Theater Ribbon w/3 Bronze Service Stars.

At age 17 he was in CC Camp and worked as a farm hand before the war. After service he worked in construction until 1959 then started work at Goodrich in Calvert City, KY, until retirement 5 Mar 1987.

Married Ovilee Colson Moore 24 Mar 1944; four children: Shelby Dianne Moore Driskill, Daniel Franklin Moore, Ricky Alan Moore and Ginger Kay Moore Jones; seven grandchildren: Dedria

Driskill Moore, Elizabeth Moore Dunnigan, Joseph Peck; and Dale, Ryan, Amy and Eric Moore.

Johnny passed away 10 Oct 1998 in Marshall County, KY. He is buried at Memory Gardens in Marshall County. Ovilee resides at 522 Vicksburg Est. Road, Benton, KY.

JAMES OSCAR MOORE, was born 27 Mar 1910 in Cadiz, KY. He entered the US Army as a private at Fort Benjamin Harrison, IN. He received his basic training at H. McClellan, AL as an infantry combat engineer. He served at Beauregard, LA 18th, 25th Service Cmd. 1299.

He was appointed as a military policeman (MP) while at Camp Bowie in Brownwood, TX. As a MP, he rode the troop trains and guarded prisoners. He once guarded President Roosevelt and even walked his dog. James received a medical discharge on 19 Dec 1944 at Camp Atterbury, IN.

He married Elsie Florine Mitchell on 16 Sep 1944 in Longview, TX. They lived in East Texas and then Baytown, TX with their four children: Jackie, Don, John and Carolyn. He had 10 grandchildren and 10 great-grandchildren. He retired to Longview and spent many hours gardening. His favorite past times were fishing and squirrel hunting. He died 24 Jul 1989 in Longview, TX.

AMOS R. MORRIS, born 26 Nov 1922 in Trigg County, KY, son of Oscar and Bessie Wyatt Morris. His brother was Prentice Morris and sister, Geneva M. Payne.

Inducted into service 8 Feb 1943 and entered active service 15 Feb 1943, at Fort Custer, MI. His MOS was switchboard operator 650. Battles and campaigns include Bismarck Archipelago and Southern Philippines (Luzon).

Separated from service 18 Dec 1945 at Fort Sheridan, IL. His decorations and citations include the WWII Victory Medal, Asiatic-Pacific Theater Ribbon w/3 Bronze Battle Stars, Philippine Liberation Ribbon w/Bronze Battle Star, five Overseas Service Bars and Good Conduct Medal and clasp.

Returned to Detroit, MI after being discharged and worked for General Motors for two years, then returned to Hopkinsville, KY. He went into the service station business from where he retired in 2000.

His two children, Bruce Morris and Donna Rae Bostick, live in Nashville, TN. They also have five grandchildren. Bruce is a hair dresser and Donna is an RN at the VA Hospital. They are members of Church of Christ and live at 209 Milbrooke Drive, Hopkinsville, KY.

JAMES PRENTICE MORRIS, Corporal, born 21 Sep 1921 and entered the service 12 Aug 1942 at Evansville, IN. He served with the 4126th Army Air Force.

James received an honorable discharge 28 Jan 1946. His awards include the Good Conduct Medal, WWII Victory Medal and American Theater Ribbon.

James passed away 7 Jul 1997 and is survived by his wife, one son and two granddaughters.

JAMES JOSEPH MCALEER, Sergeant, born 22 Mar 1921 in Philadelphia, PA. He enlisted in the service 23 July 1941 and was stationed at Fort Campbell, KY. Discharged 22 Jan 1953.

James is deceased. His children are Teresa Bailey and Jim L. Thomas There are also four grandchildren: Shannon and Shane Knight, Erin and Rachel Thomas.

FRANK THOMAS MCATEE, Tech 5, On the Ben White farm north of Cadiz, on 27 Jan 1927, Frank Thomas McAtee was born the sixth child of Clarence and Janie Malone McAtee. He began school at the early age of 5 and graduated from Trigg County HS in 1944.

Upon graduation, Frank joined the Army, getting two years' college credit from the University of Kentucky through the Army Specialized Training Reserve. His classes were in basic engineering. Frank entered basic training at Fort Riley, KS, then was shipped out to Italy for active duty. His job was that of a construction machine operator, operating bulldozers and road graders in the construction and maintenance of roads and post areas of Headquarters Company, 10th Port of Embarkation, Leghorn, Italy.

For his service, Tech 5 Frank T. McAtee received an Army Occupation Medal (Germany) and a WWII victory ribbon. He received an honorable discharge on 26 Nov 1946 and mustered out of the Army at Fort Meade, MD.

Frank returned home to the Roaring Springs area of Trigg County to farm with his father. He married Freda Redd on 20 Jan 1951 and they raised four children: Teresa, Tommy, Jimmy and Jo Alyce in this area of the county.

Frank was active in the Cadiz United Methodist Church in the Sunday School department and as Chairman of the Board of the church for many years. He also coached several Little League and Youth baseball teams; was active in Farm Bureau and 4-H Council as president and in other capacities; and served on the Trigg County Hospital Board for almost 20 years.

Frank died on 14 Feb 1998 just after celebrating his 71st birthday from complications of emphysema. Presently his son Jimmy is the third generation farmer of the family farm.

ROBERT H. MCATEE, Tech 4, born 21 Aug 1920. He was drafted 12 Aug 1942 at Camp Atterbury, IN and sent to Camp Wolters, TX for basic training. From there to Camp Stoneman, CA then to New York, arriving 28 Apr 1943.

Overseas duty was in Sicily, Italy and Africa. Memorable experience was visiting Florence and the ruins of Pompei in Italy. Elliot Hooks from Cadiz, KY was also in Taranto, Italy when Robert was there.

Robert was discharged in February 1946. His awards include the Good Conduct and European Theater w/3 stars.

He married Martha Martin 8 Jan 1955 and they have two children, Paula Maddox and Mary Jane Stewart, and four grandchildren: Robert and Sarah Maddox, Marisa and Andrew Stewart. Robert is semi-retired from farming and lives on 4770 Hardy Road, Cadiz, KY.

WILLIAM EUGENE MCBRIDE, Private, born 21 Feb 1922, the oldest child of William Carl and Ollie Lois Atkins McBride. There were six other children plus Carl had two children with his first wife. The family lived on Dry Creek near Linton, KY and later moved to Cadiz. During the late 30s, Carl operated a service store in Cadiz, where Eugene was employed. When he was nearly 19 years old he and some other young men about town decided they would join the Army. Two of the others were Idell Hendricks and Marcelleous Ricks. The date of enlistment was 28 Oct 1939. They were sent to Fort Knox, KY, where Eugene trained as a radio operator at the Armored Force School. Later he was sent on maneuvers in Louisiana.

Overseas duty was in the South Pacific and he was stationed in the Fuji Islands. While there, he was infected with malaria and returned to the States 14 Jul 1943 to Bushnell General Hospital in Brigham, UT. After nearly five years, Pvt. McBride received an honorable discharge on 5 Oct 1943. Awards include the Asiatic-Pacific Theater and American Defense Ribbon.

Eugene married Barbara Bridges on 29 Dec 1949 and they moved to Orleans, IN, where he worked in the TV manufacturing industry and later in the TV repair business. After their two daughters, Lois (b. 1950) and Leah (b. 1951), were grown, Eugene and Barbara moved to Greenville, KY in 1978, where once again Eugene worked as a TV repairman. Eugene passed away 21 Jan 1988 and was buried in the Drewry Bridges Cemetery, Maple Grove, Trigg County, KY. Barbara now lives in Orleans, IN near her daughters and two grandchildren Leah Linnea and Joseph Brady Morgan.

JOHN LYNDSAY MCCAIN, born 24 Apr 1921 in the Saline Creek area of Trigg County. He was the son of John Flavious and Cornelia Cassandra Carr McCain.

John served with the US Army in WWII and one of his locations was Kodiak, AK. He was injured when loading a ship when the load shifted and the fell on him, bruising a kidney and making removal of it necessary.

John married Annie Louise Gardner and they had three children: John Wayne, Paulia and Linda (Mrs. Feldman). Annie passed away 7 Jun 1998 and is buried in Cerulean, KY. John lives in Tuson, AZ. *Submitted by Etha Lurline Hancock.*

A.T. MCCARLEY, Commander, born in Ettawa, TN. Graduated from USN College, Newport, RI in August 1960. Retired 1 Aug 1960 after 30 years of active duty in the USN. Cmdr. McCarley received many commendations including the Atlantic, Asiatic and Pacific service medals.

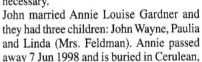

In August 1960 he accepted a position as hospital administrator of Trigg County Hospital, Cadiz, KY. He retired from active civilian service in 1973.

He married Ruth Meeker on 2 Aug 1949 at Hattiesburg, MS. Ruth is a graduate of Murray State University. They have one daughter, Sandra Loomis, of Gardiner, NY. She was born at Naval Hospital, Jacksonville, FL. Their grandchildren are Matthew Loomis, who is serving in the USAF in Korea, and Rachel Loomis, a 5th grade student. A.T. and Ruth live in Cadiz, KY.

JOHN BURWELL "MAC" MCCLURE, Lieutenant Colonel, a native of Cleveland, OH was a 2nd lieutenant in the Coast Artillery when he came to Cadiz, KY as an officer of CCC Camp 599 in 1933. He was later transferred to Ordnance and given the rank of captain.

In 1938 he left CCC and went into civilian life working for Cleveland Graphite Bronze at Cleveland, OH. In 1941 he was ordered back into service and was on active duty in 1946.

His rank was major. He retired in 1972 as lieutenant colonel with over 20 years active service, which was unusual for a reserve officer.

He was married to Mary Louise Street in February 1934. Mary Louise was the daughter of Edward R. Street Sr. and Mabel Woodruff Street. John and Mary Louise had two daughters, Mary Lou and Elizabeth Katherine.

Following retirement in Ohio, John and Mary Louise returned to Trigg County and purchased the Peal lakeside property. They moved to Fort Myers, FL, where John died 1 Jun 1985. Mary Louise resides Fort Myers.

CHARLES LESLIE MCGRAW, Major, born in Warrensburg, MO on 26 Oct 1921 and entered the Army Air Corps in February 1943.

He received pre-flight, primary, basic and advanced training at Kelly Field in San Antonio, TX and other airfields in the Midwest. Early on, he demonstrated the daring and bravado that has always been the trademark of fighter pilots.

During his training, he met a college coed from Pierre, SD. To impress her, on 7 Apr 1944 he "buzzed" her workplace by flying his P-47 Thunderbolt less than 300 feet from the ground during a gunnery mission. Nearly court marshaled, he was punished under the 104th Article of War.

That summer, he was assigned to the 351st Fighter Squadron in the 353rd Fighter Group. He was stationed in Raydon, England on 18 Aug 1944. Starting out on P-47s, he soon converted to the new P-51 Mustangs, one of the most heralded fighter aircraft in WWII.

He accompanied Eighth Army bombers on numerous raids into enemy territory. One of the most dangerous occurred in December 1944, when he lead an attack on Darmsfoot, Germany. There he dive-bombed critical oil storage units and ammunition dumps.

After another high-risk but successful mission, the *New York Times* not only recorded his heroics, but also quoted him.

For these and other performances he received the Distinguished Flying Cross, Air Medal w/7 Oak Leaf Clusters, European Theater Campaign w/4 Bronze Stars, Distinguished Unit Badge, American Theater Campaign Medal, WWII Victory Medal, and Occupation Medal (Germany).

The Oak Leaf Cluster Citation read, "For meritorious achievement as fighter pilot during an extended period of aerial combat over enemy occupied continental Europe. The courageous devotion to duty and outstanding flying ability displayed by this officer reflects great credit upon himself and the Armed Forces of the United States."

Said to be one of the youngest majors in the Army Air Corps, Charles was sent stateside in August 1945. He was eventually discharged in May 1947. During his last year of service, he met his future wife. (See Missouri Idaho McGraw.)

After living in Arizona for 20 years, Charles and his family moved to southern Trigg County. He died 9 Mar 1997. *Submitted by Tim McGraw.*

MISSOURI IDAHO "IDA" MCGRAW, 1st Lieutenant, born 24 Jan 1921 in Trigg County, served her country in Europe and Korea. Ida graduated Trigg County HS in 1940, attended Murray State Teachers College for a year, then entered the Nazareth School of Nursing in Lexington. Receiving her degree in 1944, she started nursing at St. Joseph's Hospital in Lexington.

After joining the service on 2 Jun 1944, Ida did her basic training at Billings General in Indianapolis, IN. In October 1944, she caught the *Queen Elizabeth* for Europe. Landing in Scotland, she was transported to France, where she served in various makeshift hospitals not long after the D-Day invasion. She not only cared for wounded Allied soldiers, but also for captured German soldiers.

As she would put it later in life, "I was holding boys' hands as they died while my friends were holding boys' hands on dates."

In April 1946, she was transferred back to the States and assigned to William Beaumont General Hospital in El Paso, TX. It was there she met and fell in love with one of her patients, an Army Air Corps fighter pilot.

In June 1947, Ida returned to active duty overseas, this time to the 34th General Hospital in Seoul, Korea. She served there a nearly a year before returning to the States and being discharged as a 1st lieutenant in June 1948. Two weeks prior to her separation from the Army, she married that El Paso patient, Charles McGraw, in Phoenix, AZ. (See Charles Leslie McGraw)

During her military career, Ida was awarded the European-African-Middle East Campaign Medal, American Campaign Medal, WWII Victory Medal and the Army of Occupation Medal for Germany and Japan.

She continued to nurse off and on until 1983. For 15 years she was a charge nurse at Shady Lawn Nursing Home in Cadiz.

Throughout her life, she said her years spent in the service were the most enjoyable time of her life. Missouri Idaho McGraw died at her home in southern Trigg County on 8 Mar 2000. *Submitted by Tim McGraw.*

SIDNEY EARL MCKINNEY, Seaman 1/c, born 15 Dec 1923 in Linton, KY, son of Ewin Alva McKinney and Maudie A. Shelton McKinney. Attended Cross Roads School, Trigg County High, Murray State University and graduated from Austin Peay State College in 1953 with a major in physical education.

He joined the USN 30 Jun 1943 and was stationed at NTS Great Lakes, IL; Armd. Guard School, Gulfport, MS; AGC, New Orleans, LA; ATB, Little Creek, VA; and USS LSM(R) 403. Received an honorable discharge 10 Dec 1945. Awards include the American Theater Ribbon and WWII Victory Medal. He served his country well and briefly discussed his job while at sea, telling about the huge shells they mounted and about ships being destroyed close to he ship he was on.

He was a principal and taught school at Bumpus Mills, TN, Fort Campbell, KY and at Stewart County HS, Dover, TN, from where he retired in 1986. During his teaching years he gave everyone a nickname. He loved to joke and kid with everyone and treated people like he wanted to be treated.

Married Betty June Feltner in August 1950 and they have children: Tomm, Pam and twins Ronnie and Connie. Sidney was deacon of Big Rock Baptist Church, where he served until his death on 27 Sep 1994.

ROBERT W. NILES, Staff Sergeant, born 19 Jun 1922 in Spokane, WA. He moved to Livingston, MT at age 6 where he attended grade school

and high school. After employment with Northern Pacific Railroad for two years, he was drafted into the Army at age 20. Entered active duty 5 Jan 1943 with basic training at St. Petersburg, FL.

After duty at Lincoln, NE, he was sent to Camp Howze, TX for combat infantry training, than assigned to the 9th Inf. Div., 3rd Army with duty in Germany. Sgt. Niles was discharged 21 Mar 1946 at Camp McCoy, WI. He was the recipient of American Theater Service Ribbon and the EAME Ribbon.

Decided upon a career in Optometry and completed courses in pre-optometry at Montana State University and Pacific University in Forest Grove, OR, where daughter Peggy was born. He graduated from Chicago College of Optometry in June 1954 with BS and doctor of optometry degrees. He opened a practice in Cadiz, KY in August 1956 and retired 1 Mar 1999.

Married to the former Marian Cowherd of Fairview, KY for 41 years. In addition to daughter Peggy Smith who lives in Idaho, they have a daughter Becky Cain of Paducah, KY, five granchildren and two great-grandchildren.

ARLEY H. NOEL, PFC, born 15 Apr 1914 in Canton (Kyle) KY. He was inducted 29 Sep 1942, Cadiz, KY with basic training at Fort Benjamin Harrison, IN. Combat service was in the South Pacific (New Guinea, Southern Philippines, Luzon) while assigned to the 34th Inf. Regt., 24th Inf. Div. as assistant gunner (30 cal. water cooled heavy machine gun).

Released from active duty 5 Dec 1945 at Camp Atterbury, IN. His memorable experiences include surviving without being wounded when over 90% of his original unit was killed or wounded; training and refitting unit in Australia and New Zealand; and preparing for invasion of Japan when Atomic Bomb ended the war.

His awards include the Combat Infantry Badge, Asiatic-Pacific Theater Ribbon w/3 Bronze Stars, WWII Victory Medal, Philippine Liberation Ribbon w/2 Bronze Stars, Bronze Arrowhead and Good Conduct Medal.

Civilian employment as farm worker, WPA worker, construction worker, highway department employee, factory employee and retired from Hoover (Johnson Control) in 1979. Arley and Katherine married 30 Oct 1948 and have two children, Tommy and Edward; granddaughter Angela R. Noel Miller; and great-grandson James Noel Ray Miller. Arley passed away 17 Jun 1982 and is buried in Robertson Cemetery, Montgomery, KY.

REBA O. NOEL, PFC, born 14 Sep 1921 in Trigg County, KY. Inducted 15 Dec 1943 at Evansville, IN with basic training at Fort Benjamin Harrison. He was assigned to Co. C, 121st Inf. Regt. as a rifleman for combat service in Northern France and Central Europe during WWII.

Memorable experience was being wounded in action while rescuing a wounded friend. He was hospitalized in England for a period of time then returned to action.

Discharged 10 Jan 1946 with rank private first class. His awards include the Combat Infantry Badge, EAME Ribbon w/3 Bronze Stars, Good Conduct Ribbon, Purple Heart w/Oak Leaf Cluster, Bronze Star Medal (Valor) and WWII Victory Medal.

As a civilian he worked as a farm hand, general labor, construction, block layer and factory maintenance work. He retired in the early 90s from a small factory in Gallion, OH.

Reba passed away 17 May 1995 and is buried in the Robertson Cemetery in Montgomery, KY.

CHARLES MORROW NUNN, PFC, born 15 Nov 1919, drafted from Cadiz, KY in April 1944 and processed through Fort Benjamin Harrison, IN. He was assigned to the 467 Army Air Force Base Unit.

He Trained with the grand forces of the B-29 and was sent to Kearns, UT where the *Enola Gay* and others were ready for flight when the point system came out. He, having a wife and two children, was not sent overseas. He stayed at Kearns Post and every day drove the mail truck to the Salt Lake Post Office to pick up the Post mail. The rest of the day he helped with the phones and gassed up the planes.

Discharged 11 Apr 1946 from the Separation Center, Fort Douglas, Salt Lake City, UT. Charles passed away 26 Apr 1991. *Submitted by his wife Ruth Nunn.*

MAXIE HAYWOOD OLIVER, Sergeant E-5, born 27 Feb 1921 in Cadiz, KY and was drafted into the US Army at the beginning of WWII. He served with the 654th Engineer Topographic Bn. His battalion trained at Fort Devens, MA before deploying to Europe.

They left the US from Fort Shanks NY on board the *Aquitania* for a final destination of England where the 654th spent six months at Tetbury England. While in Tetbury they constructed a detailed scale model of Omaha Beach for the upcoming invasion. The scale was one inch to 68 feet. The model covered an area on the ground of six miles long by five miles deep.

From there the 654th sailed to France across the English Channel and arrived at Omaha Beach on 3 Jul 1944. From there they moved in country to set up the business of making and producing maps. Later that month they moved into Belgium where they stayed more than six months. Before the battalion moved into Rhineland, Germany, the Germans launched a counteroffensive commonly known as the Battle of the Bulge. During this battle they stayed in Belgium. In the spring of 1945, the 654th moved into Duren, Germany where they cleared mines and built bridges. This is where Oliver and the rest of the 654th completed their mission for which they had trained - production of maps to guide the Army. Oliver obtained the rank of seargent E-5 before the end of his Army career.

After his time in the Army, Oliver returned home to Cadiz and mar-

ried a local girl from Cobb, KY, Emma Lee Oliver, on 21 May 1945. The couple had two children, Connie Jo and Jackie Odell.

Before Oliver passed away in September 1985 he had four grandchildren: Jesse Frye Jr., Marcus Frye, Jason Oliver and Carla Oliver, all still reside in Trigg County. Emma Lee passed away in June 1994.

JOHN CASEY OVERBY, born 8 Jun 1923 in Trigg County, KY, son of Mr. and Mrs. John H. Overby of Trigg County. He attended Trigg County School and worked on the family farm until WWII. In September 1941 he enlisted in the US Army.

After three months of basic training at Camp Irvin, CA, he was sent overseas and stationed on the island of Guam. Pfc. Overby was discharged from the Army in September 1944.

In June 1948 he enlisted with the USAF and served during the Korean War. He was discharged in June 1952 from Carswell AFB, Fort Worth, TX.

He moved to Hammand, IN and began employment with General Motors, Chicago, IL.

He married Mrytle Stevens of Manchester, KY in May 1954 and had four children: James, David, Randy and Rita. He retired from General Motors in 1986 with 30 years of service, then moved to his farm in Jamestown, KY. He enjoyed life on the farm until he was diagnosed with cancer and died at his home on 3 Jun 1990. His body was brought back to Trigg County and buried in the family plot of the John Fry Stewart Cemetery.

CLAUDE F. PAGE, Tech 5, born Jan. 24, 1906 in Golden Pond, KY. He was drafted into the US Army 29 Dec 1942 at Fort Benjamin Harrison, IN.

After taking six weeks basic training at Fort McClellan, AL, he and his unit 832nd AMPH Trk. Co. were shipped to Southern France. He was a truck driver and received a theater ribbon w/4 Bronze Stars, two Bronze Stars w/Arrowhead, Good Conduct Ribbon and WWII Victory Medal. Received an honorable discharge 12 Dec 1945 as tech 5.

After service he worked at several different jobs before he retired. Married Edna Futrell Hunter 29 Jan 1928. He was living on Third Street in Cadiz, KY at the time of his death 14 Feb 1979.

MANSON DUNCAN PAGE, born in Trigg County, KY on 10 Apr 1913, the second child of Lucy Mae and Jim Page. He enlisted in the US Army at the beginning of WWII. After training, he was stationed at Fort Crockett in Galveston, TX, where he remained throughout his military service. While in Galveston, he met and married Dorothy Lou Beaver 25 Dec 1942. He received a medical discharge in Temple, TX on 1 Jan 1944. After being discharged, Manson Page stayed in Texas except for a brief return to Cadiz, KY during the late 1940s. He worked for the Houston Independent School District for 25 years, retiring in 1975. After retiring, he enjoyed growing vegetables at his place in Conroe, TX and working at a nearby flower nursery.

Manson and Dorothy Page had four children before her passing in 1967. Several years later he married Lura Myers, with that marriage lasting 20 years. After a long and fruitful life he passed away on 8 Nov 2000 at the Veteran's Administration Hospital in Houston, TX.

STONNIE PARKER, BM2/c, born 30 May 1921, Trigg County, KY, the son of Green and Eula Gray Parker. He volunteered for the USN and left New York in 1941. He was on the LST ship going to North Africa and was in the invasion there; also, South France, Normandy and South Okinawa. Out of 46 ships that left New York only two survived.

Stonnie was a boatswain's mate second class (T) USNR. He was honorably discharged from the USN Personnel Separation Center, Great Lakes, IL, 27 Dec 1945. After being discharged he returned to Trigg County.

Stonnie married. Edith Marie Sumner on 6 Nov 1946. They were parents of three children: Stonnie Ray Parker born 23 Aug 1947, died 11 Aug 1973; Tonie Renia Parker, died at birth 5 Mar 1962, and Teresa Elaine Parker, born 24 Jan 1964. Teresa married Chris Burt. Their grandchildren are Madison Lashea Outland and Parker Ashton Burt.

In 1978 Stonnie retired as captain from Kentucky State Penitentiary, Eddyville, KY. He died 15 Oct 2000 at a hospital in Bowling Green, KY. He is buried in the family plot, Trigg Memory Acres, Cadiz, KY.

Stonnie and Marie had moved from their home on Princeton Road, Trigg County, to 39 Cardinal Drive, Cadiz, KY, where Marie still resides. They were members of East Cadiz Baptist Church.

He had been a member of the Masonic Lodge for over 40 years.

WILLIAM PAUL PERDUE, Staff Sergeant, born 17 Feb 1910 in Murray, KY, and volunteered for duty in the US Army Air Force. He entered active duty on 31 Oct 1942, but was ineligible for overseas duty because of knee injuries incurred while playing football at Murray State College, so served most of his years in the service as an athletic instructor at Maxwell Field AFB in Montgomery, AL. He attended physical training instruction schools in Miami Beach, FL and San Antonio, TX. He received a Good Conduct Medal in August 1945 and was honorably discharged from the service on 2 Oct 1945; his rank was staff sergeant.

Prior to entering the service, Paul had graduated from Murray State University in 1936. He then entered the teaching profession, coming to Trigg County HS in 1937 as football coach and history teacher. He also coached basketball and track. He married a Trigg County girl, Martha Mae Minton, in May 1941.

After his service career, Paul returned to Murray as head of the VA program at Murray State University. Through that program, veterans could get their college degrees. After the VA program ended, Paul opened a dry cleaning business, and during that time, earned his masters degree from Murray State.

In 1956, Paul commuted for one year to Trigg County to fulfill the position of assistant superintendent of the Trigg County School system.

In 1957, he moved his family to Trigg Country to accept the position of principal of Trigg County HS. He remained in that position until his death on 26 Oct 1961. He was a member of the Cadiz Baptist Church.

Paul Perdue dedicated many years to the Trigg County School System as an administrator, teacher and coach. He introduced the sport of football to Trigg County and was the school's first football coach. Trigg County HS's football stadium was posthumously named Perdue Field in his honor.

He and his wife, Mae Minton Perdue, had three children: William Paul "Bill" Perdue Jr., Patsy Perdue Brandon and Gary Perdue. They are five grandchildren.

EARLY H. PERRY JR., Sergeant, born 14 Nov 1925 in Caldwell County on Route 2, Cobb, KY, the first born son of Early H. Sr. and Pansy Pruitt Perry.

Perry was drafted into the US Army in November 1944 through the enlisting and processing Station in Louisville, KY. From there he was sent to Camp Atterbury, IN and assigned to a regular Army Training Post. He was shipped off to Fort McClelland, AL for basic training.

Following basic training they were shipped to Fort Mead, MD, and from there to the Philippine Islands in the Pacific Theater where they served in the Adjutant General Department assigned to General MacArthur's Headquarters for the operation of the Replacement Depots processing Troops for the front lines.

Upon the surrender of the Japanese their 18th Replacement Depot was used to process US Prisoners held in Japan by the Japanese. This was a joyful moment of his military career especially when he was united with a neighbor, Curly Thompson, from adjoining Lyon County and a survivor of the Batan Death March forced by the Japanese almost five years earlier in the surrender of the Philippines. Curly weighed 90 lbs upon arrival at their base. He never left Early's side, night or day, trying to adjust to a new life during his medical treatment on his way home. Early was the first person he had seen from near home in over five years.

In January 1946 they headed home and in February they were processed back through "ole" Camp Atterbury, IN where he was discharged with the rank of sergeant.

His great reward was arriving safely back home in Trigg County and in August 1946 he married his sweetheart, Nell Perkins, daughter of their mail carrier, Route 2, Cobb for 29 years. They have two sons, Ken and Steve, a daughter Susan Quinlan and three grandchildren: Jeff, Jennifer and Sarah.

Retired from Kentucky Farm Bureau and Community Bankers of Kentucky, since 1991 has operated a children apparel company as a vendor of University Licensed Products for Wal-Mart.

DEAN D. PIERCY, Tech 4, born 23 Aug 1924, son of Bentley and Ruth Cunningham Piercy. Inducted into the Army 19 Jan 1943 in Evansville, IN and received basic training at Camp Haan, CA. At completion of training they were shipped to the South Pacific.

Despite the small population of Cadiz, he met a friend from home on each island: Charles Hooks on Guadalcanal, Howard Thomas on Bougainville, Junior Bannister and Jodie Davis on Leyte, then John Bell Mason while awaiting discharge at Fort Knox.

After spending 30 months overseas, Dean was discharged 15 Jan 1946 with the rank of tech 4. He received the Asiatic-Pacific Theater Ribbon w/2 Bronze Service Stars, Philippine Liberation Ribbon w/Bronze Star, Good Conduct and WWII Victory Medal.

He enrolled in the Bowling Green Business University in September 1946 and graduated from the University of Denver in April 1950. He was working in Princeton, KY when he met Joan A. Berry in 1951 and they were married some three months later. From July 1954 to December 1980 he was employed by the US Treasury Dept. When he retired from that position he worked for Union Planters National Bank, Memphis, for approximately seven years.

Joan and Dean have three children: Katherine P. Ford, J. Bentley and Mickens D. Grandchildren are Merritt and Kasey Ford.

They now live in Nesbit, MS and play bridge on a regular basis. He enjoys golfing, fishing and reading. They will celebrate their 50th wedding anniversary on 15 Nov 2001.

ROBERT B. PIERCY, PFC, born 27 Jan 1927 at Cadiz, KY. Joined the service 19 Jul 1945 at Louisville, KY and was stationed at Camp Fannin, TX and Fort Benning, GA. He was discharged 18 Dec 1946 as private first class.

Civilian Activity: M.S.C. 1951, Union Carbide Corp./Martin-Marrietta, from where he retired in 1985.

Married Antoinette "Toni" 11 Jun 1955 and they live in Paducah, KY. Children are Charles Matthew and Susanne Palmer, and grandchildren are Ryan Piercy and Rachel Peircy.

ISAAC FRED PORTER SR., PFC, born 7 Nov 1918 in Trigg County, Cadiz, KY. He joined the service 26 Dec 1941 and was stationed at Arlington, VA; Fort Benning, GA and Paris, France. He served during WWII with 2nd Inf. in Brest, France as machine gunner.

Pfc. Porter was discharged in September 1945. His awards include the Bronze Star, Purple Heart, two major Battle Stars and Combat Infantry Badge.

He is a member of the Pennyroyal Mental Health-Mental Retardation Center, member of DAV (served as president and adjutant), member and deacon at First Baptist Church and 40 year member of Masonic Lodge at Canton and a former Rotarian.

Isaac was principal at Christian County HS, 1960-65; Pennyrile Allied Community Services, 1966-79; substitute teacher, 1979-89; part-time as member of general staff at Hughart-Beard Funeral Home.

Married Virginia Nunn Gardner 21 Mar 1940. Children are Teresa Dawn Porter Adams, Isaac Jr. and Virginia Lisa Porter Bruce; grandchildren are C.A. Parker III, Teresa Dawn Parker Martin, Virginia Jane Bruce and Garnette Porter Bruce. Isaac passed away 14 Nov 1991 and his widow resides at Christian Church Campus Village, Hopkinsville, KY.

STANLEY CRENSHAW PORTER, Maintenance Crew Chief, born 28 Jun 1916 in Trigg County, graduated from Cadiz HS in the late 1930s and joined the Army Air Corps in 1941. He received training in the aircraft maintenance field and then was assigned to the Caribbean for jungle warfare.

After completion of jungle warfare training he was assigned to the Pacific Theater and spent most of his active duty on Iwo Jima. He served as a maintenance crew chief for fighter aircraft assigned to the island. He was discharged in 1946 and made Boynton Beach, FL, his home.

For many years Stan operated a Standard Oil station and served as a volunteer fireman. In 1961, he became a regular firefighter and retired as a fire inspector after 22 years service.

He married Charlene Clendening and they had a daughter named Tammy. He was a member of the Lake Worth Scottish Rite, Boynton Beach Masonic Lodge, American Legion and the State Firemen's Association. Stanley passed away 11 Jul 1993, and burial was in Boynton Beach Memorial Park.

CLARENCE NOBLE P'POOL, Staff Sergeant, born 4 Jan 1911 in Trigg County, KY. He entered the service 28 Apr 1939 at Fort Knox, KY. Other stations included Fort Campbell, KY; Fort Dix, NJ and San Francisco.

SSgt. P'Pool was discharged 25 Oct 1945. His awards include the American Theater Ribbon, Good Conduct, WWII Victory Medal and Service Stripes.

Worked at US Post Office in Cadiz, KY until retirement in July 1974. He was a member of the Trigg County American Legion. He passed away 5 Feb 1982 and is buried in Adams Cemetery, Trigg County, KY.

Married Tennie Ruth Cook 13 Sep 1941 and had two children, Ronnie P'Pool and Donna Sumner. Grandchildren are Mike Sumner, Lori Lawrence, Eddie P'Pool and Sherri Downing.

E.L. P'POOL, Tech Sergeant, born 17 May 1916 in Trigg County (Princeton Road), son of Ebb Lester and Lillian Adams P'Pool. Attended grade school at Hanberry and Montgomery, graduated from Cadiz HS in May 1935, and signed up for the Army in a tent on the courthouse yard 29 Jun 1940.

Sworn into Army Air Corps 1 Jul 1940 at Fort Knox. Sent to Maxwell Field, Montgomery, AL for basic training. After basic training he went to Airplane Mechanic School, Chanute Field, Rantoul, IL.

Sent to Cochran AAB, Macon, GA and worked on flight line as a mechanic. Went to Glider Pilot School, then Liaison Pilot School. Served the rest of his time as liaison pilot in the States, Belgium, Germany and France.

Discharged 12 Oct 1945 with the rank of tech sergeant. His awards include the EAME Theater Ribbon w/2 Bronze Stars, American Theater Ribbon, Air Medal and Good Conduct Medal

Married Christene Sumner 27 May 1946 and has four children: Jerry, Ted, Smitty and Redonda. All three sons served in the military—Jerry and Smitty in the Air Force and Ted in the Army. Grandchildren are Jason, Grady, Joey, Julie, Bryan and Michael. He worked as a farmer until retirement in 1989, he now resides in Hopkinsville, KY.

JOHNNIE ROBERT P'POOL, Tech 5, born 17 Mar 1913 in Trigg County, KY. He was drafted into the US Army 26 Jun 1941 at Fort Knox,

KY and was a reconnaissance car crewman. His battles and campaigns were Algeria-French Morocco; Tunisia; Naples-Foggia; Rome-Arno; Po Valley; and North Apennines. He served under Gen. George Patton.

Received honorable discharge at Camp Atterbury, IN on 15 Jun 1945. Awards include the EAME Theater Ribbon w/6 Bronze Stars, American Defense Service Medal and the Purple Heart for wounds received in action in Italy on 18 Mar 1944.

After the war, Johnnie moved to Evansville, IN where he married and began working at the Swift Meat Packing Plant. After his retirement and the death of his first wife Mary Lou, he moved back to Trigg County and settled near Muddy Fork Creek on Hwy. 139 North where he could fish and do volunteer work at the Trigg County Recreation Complex where he served on the Board of Directors.

Johnnie married Lena 8 Jan 1983 and continued to do various volunteer jobs. He joined the local VFW and was a lifetime member of the VFW in Evansville. Lena died of cancer and Johnnie moved to Cadiz. He died of a heart attack 28 Dec 1995 and is buried in Mt. Zion Cemetery in Trigg County. He had three stepchildren and nine step-grandchildren.

FRANK WATKINS P'POOL, Tech 5, entered the US Army at Fort Benjamin Harrison, IN on 26 Aug 1939. He was a member of the 1580th SCU Medical Section serving as a meat and dairy inspector 120.

He spent a total of six years in the Army being honorably discharged on 18 Sep 1945 at Camp Atterbury, IN as tech 5. He received the American Defense Service Medal and the Good Conduct Ribbon.

After the war, Frank settled in Woodstock, IL. He married and had two children, Betty and Dickie. Frank died in 1955. He was the son of Richard and Ninnie Watkins P'Pool and the brother of John Robert P'Pool whom also served in WWII.

ALFRED C. PROFFITT, PFC, was born 14 Feb 1915, in Trigg County, KY. He volunteered for the US Army 15 Aug 1940, taking training and serving in the US to May 1942. He first landed in North Ireland and was later sent to North Africa landing in Casablanca. There he entered combat duty and was wounded 23 Mar 1943 in the Tunisian battle. He received the Purple Heart.

He was sent back to the States to a Fort Deavers, MA Hospital, later sent to Nicholas General Hospital in Louisville, then to Percy Jones Hospital in Battle Creek, MI. He was treated there from November 1943 to his death on 14 Jun 1946. He underwent an operation on 22 May and pneumonia followed causing his death.

Funeral services were conducte[ ] 17 June and burial was made in the Peyton Thomas graveyard on Do[ ]. [ ] Creek. Pallbearers were servicemen of WWII: Clarence Hargr[ ] Bill Ford, Henry Earl Barnes, Ray Tucker, Odell Taylor and Plomer [ ]trell.

He was the son of James Lee and Rosa Hargrove Proffitt. He had three sisters: Florence P. Herndon, Violet P. Atkins, Miss Lurline Proffitt and three brothers: Roy, Stanley and William Proffitt.

HAYDON LEWIS RADFORD, born 8 Jan 1923 in Trigg County. Early in 1943, he received his Army notice and was sent to Fort Lewis, WA, for training in the heavy weapon company. Next they were sent to Louisiana for 30 days of jungle training.

Overseas duty followed with fighting across France into Germany. At the Rhine River, the Germans had blown the bridge out, so they waited for the English to build a pontoon bridge. They kept moving across Germany where he was wounded three times, hospitalized, then sent back to front lines. They moved across Austria into the Alp Mountains. Around this time, the war came to an end. They were sent back to the States for jungle training to go to Japan. Luck was with them, just before landing at New York, the Japanese gave up and they were discharged at a camp in New York.

He was a squad leader while in the Army and received the Machine Gun, Rifle and Pistol Medals, Good Conduct Medal, Combat Infantry Medal, European Medal, Bronze Star, Purple Heart w/Oak Leaf Cluster. He was presented the Silver Star by Bingham Stevens from the American Legion.

One thing he will never forget is where he was when President Roosevelt died. They were in the old World War trenches out from Manheim when a German on a loud speaker told them to give up because their captain had died

Haydon returned to Trigg County and his wife, the former Lois Wyatt. They lived in Cadiz for about two years before moving out on the South Road. They bought a grocery store and operated it for 35 years. He worked for the Civil Service at Fort Campbell for 27 years before retiring. They had two children, Judy and Jerry, both married with two children each.

He lost his first wife after being married for almost 50 years. Later on, he married Myra Nell King.

EARL MAURICE RANDOLPH, Staff Sergeant, born 14 Oct 1923 in Trigg County, KY, was drafted into the US Army during WWII on 12 Jun 1943 at Evansville, IN. He was inducted into the 281st Field Artillery Battalion, Motor Pool.

After five days at Camp Atterbury, IN, they went by troop train to Camp Cook, CA. They were stationed at Camp Cook for nine months, then transferred to Fort Sill, OK for another nine months training.

The men had been issued guns but no ammunition until arriving at Fort Sill. To these country boys who had handled guns since they were 12 or younger this was too great a temptation even though they had been told, no shooting. Shots could be heard when a pesky squirrel popped up in a tree in front of Earl's tent and his gun went off and no more squirrel. Orders from Headquarters came down to find where that shot had come from. By the time the lieutenant got to Earl's tent, his gun had been cleaned and oiled so nothing came of it except some anxious moments.

From Fort Sill they were sent to the New York Embarkation Port and boarded ship. They landed in Liverpool, England and on to North Wales where they were billeted in empty private homes over Christmas and during the Battle of the Bulge. Then they crossed the English Channel and landed at LeHavre, France and on into Germany. From there on, the Motor Pool and vehicles and men moved behind the front lines and were changing positions almost every day.

War ended May 1945 in the European Theater, but for the next year this unit was stationed near Nuremburg, Germany. The motor pool's men and vehicles (60 of them) under Earl's supervision were used to haul coal for the Nuremburg Trials. During this time a club was set up for the soldiers and Earl formed a band and was active in music.

Earl returned to the USA in 1946 and was discharged 1 Apr 1946 as staff sergeant with American Theater Ribbon, EAME Ribbon w/2 Bronze Stars, Good Conduct Medal, and a WWII Victory Medal.

He was married to Frances Jones Lively for 32 years; she is now deceased. He has retired from three related companies after 40 years, Servel, Arkla and Preway. He continues to live in Evansville and is still active in music. *Written and submitted by Mrs. Dorothy R. Thomas.*

HENRY B. "H.B." RANDOLPH,
HENRY B. "H.B." RANDOLPH, Staff Sergeant, born 18 Feb 1922, son of Claud and Lillie Porter Randolph, Trigg County, KY, was inducted into the US Army 12 Apr 1943 as reserve and began active duty 19 Apr 1943 at Fort Benjamin Harris, IN, assigned to the US Air Corps.

He was sent to Seymour Johnson Field, NC for basic training and tech school, was reclassified and assigned to Radio Operators School at Truax Field, WI, followed by orders for the ETO and assignment to SAC, 8th Air Corps, 474th Sub-Depot attached to the 489th BG, servicing B-24 bombers.

Upon completing 100 or more missions, the 489th BG and the 474th Sub-Depot received orders for the Asiatic-Pacific Theater with a delay en route for transition training to B-29 bombers, 12 Dec 1944. Completing B-29 tech school at Tinker AF, OK and training at Pratt AAB, KS, the 474th Group was changed to the 369th Air Service Group, 806th Engineering Sqdn., 20th Air Corps and received orders to Fort Lawton, WA, POE for the Asiatic-Pacific Theater, 6 Aug 1945.

While en route, orders for the 369th Svc. Gp. were canceled due to the Japanese surrender. They were then directed to Harmon Field, Guam for convenience of US Govt.

Arrived back in the States 27 Dec 1945 and was honorably discharged 6 Jan 1946 at Fort Knox, KY. His medals include the Asiatic-Pacific, Good Conduct, WWII Victory Medal, EAME and American Theater.

He worked for A.M. Bowles, heating, sheetmetal and welding shop in Hopkinsville, KY and for Dept. of Army, Fort Campbell, Civil Service, Post Engineers Heating Dept. where he retired 19 Jan 1981 as foreman of heating shop.

Married Imogene Green, Trigg County native, on 26 Dec 1941. They have two children, Janice Kay and David Gary. Grandchildren are Janet Lee Toman, Susan Lynett Toman and David Scott Randolph. Henry and his wife live in Hopkinsville, KY.

HOMER LOUIS "BOOTS" RANDOLPH,
HOMER LOUIS "BOOTS" RANDOLPH, PFC, born 3 Jun 1927 in Paducah, KY to Homer Clay Randolph and Bessie Mae Skaggs Randolph. Inducted into the Army on 22 Aug 1945 in Camp Atterbury, IN, took basic training at Camp Lee, VA. Other training and schooling while there included Clerk Typing School and Band Training School for five weeks each. He then joined the 329th Army Service Forces Band for the duration of his military career.

By day, Boots played the saxophone with the military marching band, and by night played dance music at Officers NCO and USO Clubs, plus various other venues in that area.

The band was moved to Camp Kilmer, NJ in late November and their new duties were to welcome the troops coming home from overseas and also war brides coming from other countries. The band would set up on Staten Island, NY piers at 6:00 a.m. and played pop music of the day and jazz from the big band era for all the ships as they came in.

After being discharged from the service, Boots returned to Evansville, IN. Starting to play locally in Evansville, he decided to make music his career. After about a year he met and married Carolyn Dolores Baker. His musical career took off and soon he and Dee were traveling, playing clubs and lounges all over the country. They had a daughter Linda in 1948 and a son Randy in 1955. Boots and Dee settled in Decatur, IL where he played at local venues for four years.

In 1957 the family moved back to Evansville for a musical location job that lasted four more years.

In 1961 Boots and family moved to Nashville, TN where Boots started his recording career. At first he was a studio musician playing behind such famous performers as Brenda Lee, Elvis Presley, Al Hirt, Pete Fountain, Chet Atkins, Floyd Cramer, Perry Como, Roy Orbison and many more.

Boots started his recording career in 1958 at RCA Records, later with Monument Records and recorded about 40 albums including his hit song *Yakety Sax.*

He now lives on his farm close to his children and five grandchildren (Jennifer, Patrick, Kenneth and Dustin O'Neal and Tara Nicole Randolph) and does a limited amount of touring. He enjoys golf, skiing, working on the farm and spending time with the family.

The Army started his musical career.

MILUS MCKENZIE RANDOLPH JR.,
MILUS MCKENZIE RANDOLPH JR., Tech 5, born 27 Sep 1920 in Trigg County, the son of Milus McKenzie and Lucy Guthrie Randolph. He married Marie Ezell 30 Dec 1941 and entered the Army 24 Jun 1942. His first child, Donnia Ann Randolph was born 30 Sep 1943 and he did not see her until he returned home when she was 3 years old.

Inducted at Fort Benjamin Harrison, IN and left San Fransisco, for "overseas" on 3 May 1943. They went through Pacific, docked at New Zealand, to Sidney Australia, through the India Ocean to Colombo, Ceylon to Bombay, India, through the Arabian Sea to Kharramshakr, Iran, arriving 26 Jun 1943.

He was detached to an engineer corps and served as a crane operator loading and unloading military vehicles, equipment, food and supplies as a member of a port company in Persia and the Middle East. He participated in the battles and campaigns of the Rhineland and received the EAME Campaign, Fidelity Efficiency Honor, Good Conduct Ribbon, American Theater Ribbon, Victory Medal, Bronze Star and 3hree Battle Stars

He left Kharramshakr, Iran 26 Jan 1945 through Persian Gulf, Gulf of Oman, Gulf of Aden, through Red Sea and Suez Canal, Port Said, Egypt, through Mediterranean Sea, Catinia, Sicily, through Straits of Sicily to Marseilles, France. He went by land across France to Antwerp, Belgium and from there through the English Channel across the North Atlantic Ocean to Newport News, VA. He was discharged from service Nov. 23, 1945 at Camp Atterbury, IN.

He retired in 1984 from Sisk Motor Co. and lives with his wife Marie in Hopkinsville, KY. They have three children: Donnia Ann Cunningham, Marilyn Moss and Kandy Lou Waters. Grandchildren are Randy, Carroll and Shayne Cunningham; Melisa and Timothy Moss; and Heather Waters.

Their son-in-law, Don Cunningham is also retired from the Army with 23 years of service. Also, grandsons Randy Cunningham is retired from the Army with 20 years of service and Shane Cunningham is currently on Active Duty with 19 years of Army service. His other grandson, Carroll Cunningham, was in the Army for three years.

JAMES THOMAS RASCOE, Tech 5, born 21 Mar 1924 at Roaring Springs, KY, enlisted into the US Army on 30 Oct 1942. After three months of basic and tank training at Fort Knox, KY, he was transferred to Camp Campbell, KY in January 1943. In September 1943 he participated in the Tennessee Maneuvers, then transferred to Camp Barkley, TX, 1943-44.

From Camp Barkley he was sent to New Jersey for disembarkment to Marseilles, France but, due to Germany bombing the French harbor, he was rerouted to England for a months duration. Action started heating up at the Siegfried Line where the Germans had placed permanent fortifications along with miles of tunneling.

James participated in the Rhineland and Central Europe campaigns, 1944-45. During these campaigns, he won the Victory Medal, American Theater Ribbon, and the EAME Theater Ribbon while serving with the 23rd Tank Battalion of the 12th Armd. (HELLCAT) Div.

During these campaigns, the Hellcat Division killed or captured over 84,000 German soldiers, which was seven times the Hellcat Division strength. While on outpost duty, James personally captured two German soldiers who were hiding in a foxhole. Among the German soldiers possessions were a rifle, burp gun, two hand grenades and a pistol. James was part of the mystery tank division under the command of Gen. Patch where all tank identification was removed under directions of Gen. George Patton. While recovering at a field hospital, James got to see Gen. George Patton who was visiting the wounded soldiers. Upon discharge from the Army, James had attained the rank of technician 5th grade.

James married a Trigg County girl, Myra Dean Cunningham, in March 1947. They have five children, 12 grandchildren and six great-grandchildren. Over the years he has worked at several different jobs and retired from Trigg County Farmers Bank in 1989. Today at 76 years of age, he and Myra reside comfortably outside the city of Cadiz on Highway 68. They are members of Cadiz Christian Church.

WILLIAM H. RAWLS JR., Corporal, born 23 Dec 1921 and joined the service in June 1944 at Baltimore, MA. He was stationed at Camp Davis, NC, assigned to 557th Antiaircraft Bn. attached to 84th Div. and fought in the Battle of the Bulge in 1944.

The 557th Bn. Co. B was credited with shooting down the first German jet plane. The missile fired hit the bomb the pilot had just released and blew up both bomb and plane.

Operated Rawls CB Food Store, wrote for the *Cadiz Record,* and has a book that is in the process of being published. Married Charline 23 Dec 1941 and had two children, Mary Kay Cooke and Margaret Jo Shockley, and one grandchild Ann Marie. William passed away 3 Jul 2000.

CHAPPELL B. REDD, the son of D.B. and Bessie Redd, was born in Trigg County, KY on 10 Mar 1924. He graduated from Trigg County HS and enlisted in the USMC at Indianapolis, IN on 11 Mar 1943. He took basic training at San Diego, CA. After the war ended he was discharged on 22 Jun 1946.

He re-enlisted in the Marines on 28 Nov 1947. He married Vernell Johnson on June 30, 1949 and they were blessed with four children: Gerald, Ronald, Nancy and Rickie. All three of his sons were in the military in 1956. He served in Korea during that war and remained in the military until 31 Dec 1964 when he retired.

He and his family settled in Colorado Springs, CO, where he worked as a Civil Service employee at Fort Carson. Chappell died on 15 Mar 1983 in Colorado Springs. Burial ceremonies included a Marine Corps honor guard.

During his military career he was awarded various medals, including WWII Victory Medal, American Theater Medal and a Presidential Unit Citation.

JAMES RODMAN REDD, born 23 Feb 1919, in Gracey, KY. He was the first child of Rodman Jackson Redd and Edna Sholar Redd. Through his mother, he was a direct descendant of Starkey Thomas, a son of James Thomas. James graduated from Hopkinsville HS after attending grade school in Gracey. He was raised on the Redd farm on what is known as Redd Lane, or Old Hopkinsville Road, and straddles Trigg and Christian County. It is just south of Highway 68.

Much of James' military history has been obtained from his Navy friend, Harvey Hooks, of Birmingham, AL. It is last known that James was stationed at NAS Jacksonville, FL, in Squadron VN13. He had previously enlisted in the Navy and had been through training and an aviation school. James later went to flight school.

James is next known to have been stationed at Great Lakes in Michigan. From there he went to the West Coast and was stationed near San Francisco. From there he transferred to the island of Guam and was placed in a Navy station maintaining aircraft. It is believed he was on the island when the *Enola Gay* flew from there.

Upon returning from the war, James married Virginia Louise Wiley McClean of Princeton. Virginia's first husband, James McClean, had been killed after he was shot down over Europe. Virginia and James first lived in Hopkinsville, KY, and later moved back to the Redd farm and bought an adjoining farm and raised two children, James Rodman Redd Jr., born 9 Sep 1952, and Margo Edna Redd, born 30 Jun 1955. Virginia was born on 6 Dec 1922, the daughter of J.D. and Edna Wylie.

James Rodman Redd Jr. married Shawn Hiler Jones on 30 Oct 1971. They had three children: James R. Redd III, born 14 Jul 1972, Leigh Piercy Redd, born 23 Aug 1977, and Kathryn Wiley Redd, born 25 Mar 1982.

Margo Redd married John Leneave on 29 Jul 1977. They have two children, John Kyle Leneave, born 24 Mar 1983, and Lana Upton Leneave, born 26 Apr 1990.

James was a farmer his entire life and also worked for the Kentucky Burley Tobacco Growers Cooperative. James was a member of the Gracey West Union Baptist Church, and later in his life was a member of the Cadiz United Methodist Church.

James died on 11 Dec 1996, from complications of melanoma cancer.

Throughout his life James had a love for the USN and particularly airplanes. He was also a tremendous University of Kentucky basketball fan and an avid golfer.

ALFRED J. REDICK, First Class Petty Officer, born 6 Jan 1920. He enlisted 2 Oct 1942 with assignments at Great Lakes Naval Training Station, IL (4 weeks), Ship Repair Unit in South Pacific AD40, New Meuma, New Caledonia from December 1942 to August 1944. Reassigned to Fleet Oiler AO94, hauling aviation fuel from behind enemy lines to the front.

Returning from Okinawa, their ship was met by three Japanese planes, two of which were kamikaze and one a dive-bomber. The 20 millimeters got the kamikaze from each side of the ship. The 5-inch 38 got the dive bomber from the rear of the ship hitting him head on.

Alfred was honorably discharged at Great Lakes, IL on 17 Dec 1945 as first class petty officer. Received the Good Conduct Medal and Asiatic-Pacific Medal w/Battle Star.

In 1943 there were six Trigg County boys on the island of New Meuma off New Caledonia that spent the day together.

Returning home he was walking down the street and someone asked, "Where do you think you're going sailor"? Before he turned around, he knew who was calling. It was Lorene Alexander, the girl he had been writing to for 3.5 years. Neither of them knew just how serious they were, but it didn't take long. After marrying 22 Dec 1945, he farmed for five years. In 1951 they headed north to the Motor City. Where he began laying brick and then in 1957 was recommended for a job at General Motors, from where he retired from their Gear and Axle Plant as a bricklayer on 3 Mar 1982.

Alfred and Lorene have four children: John Wesley, James Harvey, Connie Sue Redick Pickett and Jeffrey Alexander. They also have 11 grandchildren: Wendy Pickett Hammond, Kimberly Pickeett Cagle, Jennifer Redick Hopkins, Melissa Redick Knapp, Travis Pickett, Jacob Redick, Kirsten Redick, Laura Redick, Adam Redick, Bridgette Redick, Austin Redick and four great-grandchildren: Devin Hammond, Michael Hammond, Ryan Cagle and Hannah Hopkins.

SAM E. REEDER, MM3, born 12 Jan 1929 in Paducah, KY. He enlisted in the USN 15 Jun 1946. After 10 weeks basic training at Bainbridge, MD, he was assigned to the destroyer USS *Hyman* (DD-732) which was dry-docked at the Charleston Naval Shipyard in Boston, MA. At that time the *Hyman* was undergoing major repairs as a result of a kamikaze attack in the South Pacific during WWII.

After repairs were completed in late 1946, the ship operated in the Atlantic Ocean, Mediterranean Sea and Adriatic Sea until April 1948. Reeder was assigned to the ship's machine shop as machinist mate.

After discharge from the regular Navy in April 1948, Reeder was on inactive duty in the Naval Reserve for eight years.

In 1987 he retired from BellSouth after 37-1/2 years service. He and his wife, the former Martha Sue Mason also from Paducah, have resided part time since 1992 at Cumberland Shores on Lake Barkley. They attend Dyers Chapel United Methodist Church.

ALVIN ETHELL RICKS, son of the late Douglas F. and Ida Pope Ricks, was born 30 Sep 1916 in the lower Donaldson Community of Trigg County, KY. He grew up on his father's farm, attended Graham Elementary School and was graduated from Rogers HS at Linton, KY with the Class of 1936.

Shortly after the bombing of Pearl Harbor by the Japanese, Alvin, who at the time was employed by the US Quartermaster Depot in Jeffersonville, IN, went to Cadiz and volunteered for service with the US

Army. Quotas were full at the time, and it wasn't until July 1942 that he was called for duty. He did his basic training at Fort Leonard Wood, MO.

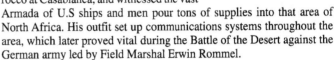

Alvin was assigned to The Army Signal Corps, sent to Fort Dix, NJ where he was given a three-day pass to visit his wife in Akron, OH. Three days later he was among several hundred other troops aboard a ship bound for North Africa.

He participated in the invasion of Morocco at Casablanca, and witnessed the vast Armada of U.S ships and men pour tons of supplies into that area of North Africa. His outfit set up communications systems throughout the area, which later proved vital during the Battle of the Desert against the German army led by Field Marshal Erwin Rommel.

At war's end, Alvin qualified for immediate discharge, and returned to the US aboard the British liner, *Queen Mary*. He arrived home in Akron, OH, in December 1945 in time for Christmas and, as a proud father, saw his daughter Bonita for the first time.

Alvin married the former Lilly James Hinson on 16 Aug 1941 in New Albany, IN. Their family consists of two daughters: Judith Aloma, who died as a baby, and Bonita Lee, who married David Madden; two granddaughters and a great-grandson. Alvin died 17 Mar 1994 at the age of 78, in El Cajon, CA, and is buried in Fort Rosecrans National Military Cemetery, at Point Loma, CA.

IVAN S. RICKS, PFC, a casualty of WWII, was born 15 Jun 1918 in Trigg County, KY. He was a private first class in the Army and killed in Belgium 12 Jan 1945. He was buried in the American Military Cemetery, Belgium.

Ivan was a graduate of Cadiz HS in the Class of 1936 and attended college in Bowling Green.

He was the son of Jesse O. and Gertrude Meador Ricks. He had one brother Billy Ricks; three sisters: Abbie Ricks, Katherine Ricks Wright and Esta Ricks Redd; nephew, Montie Redd; and a niece Arlene Tilly.

JAMES MALCOLM "GOOBER" RIGGIN, born 22 Jun 1924, the son of Mr. and Mrs. H.C. Riggin, spent all of his early life in Cadiz, KY. He received his primary education in the Cadiz Grade School and graduated from Trigg County HS.

He was an outstanding sport star, being the quarterback of the football team for three years, 1940-42 and participated in basketball. The best tribute given him was by two of his teammates who said, "Malcolm was the toughest and fastest man who had ever played on the Trigg County team, and he was never afraid to go through." There is no doubt these same characteristics were displayed in the "game" he was playing at the time of his death.

After graduation from TCHS, he entered the mechanical school conducted by the NYA at Murray and after finishing was employed for a short time in a submarine factory in the east.

He enlisted in the Marines in October 1942 and took boot training at Parris Island. The very fact that he wore the Marine Corps uniform fulfilled the greatest of this young man's ambitions, for as his father before him, he seemed born to soldiering and a place in the Corps was his fondest dream. In December 1942 he was in the South Pacific and participated in many of the engagements in the islands of that area.

His family received word 23 Dec 1943 that Malcom was killed and buried at sea. He was the recipient of the Purple Heart. He had three sisters: Juanita, Dorothy and Reva Mae. He was a member of the Cadiz United Methodist Church.

JAMES WILLIAM "JAMIE" ROGERS, Sergeant, born 1 Jul 1927 in Cadiz, Trigg County, KY. He was drafted into the US Army 19 Oct 1945. After training at Aberdeen and Edgewood Arsenal, MD, he was assigned to the 25th Mec. Cav. Recon Troop, 25th Inf. Div., Osaka, Japan. His duties were occupation and patrolling the city.

In Japan he saw first hand the destruction of the A Bomb. He returned home and was separated 24 Mar 1947. After a short time of farming, he re-enlisted in the Army 7 Sep 1949.

Assignments included Wheel and Track Maintenance School; 1st Inf. Div. "Big Red One," Aschaffenburg, Germany; Grafenwhohr, Germany; Fort Riley, KS; 4th Armd. Div., Fort Hood, TX; two tours in Germany; two tours at Fort Knox; 1957-61 with B Troop, 15th Cav., 4th Armd. Div., Schwabach, Germany; 1961-64, Fort Knox Training Center; D Co., 1st Bn., 33rd Armd., 3rd Armd. Div., Gelnhausen, Germany; back to Fort Knox; 1969, D Co., 161 Inf. Bn., 5th Inf. Div., Quang Tri, Vietnam,

Retired 18 Jul 1970 with 13 years overseas duty and 22 plus years service. Decorations include two Bronze Stars, Army Commendation Medal, Good Conduct (six times), Occupation (Japan and Germany), Vietnam Service Medal and Vietnam Campaign Medal.

After retirement he worked Civil Service, Wright Patterson AFB, OH, until retirement 29 Dec 1989 with 38 years of government service. Received two superior awards.

Married Vera on 16 Apr 1955. When Vera passed away in 1993 he moved back to Trigg County. Married Kay Birdsong 6 Apr 1996. He has one son Donald; four stepchildren: Delana, Lance, Lori and Lisa; granddaughter Katarina; seven stepgrandchildren: Miranda, Lynzie, Randi, Adrienne, Quinton, Seth and Kamryn. Kay and Jamie reside at 2823 Maple Grove Road and attend Delmont Church.

LUTHER MONROE ROGERS, Private, born 22 Oct 1925 at Layfette, KY, the ninth of 10 children (one died at birth). His father passed away when he was 5 years old, leaving his mother with nine children to care for. No one wanted a woman with nine children to work their farms, so they moved every year dividing out time between Trigg and Christian County

Luther thought there must be something better, so when he was 16 he joined the Army, putting his age at 22 Oct 1923, which made him old enough. He went to the local board, filled out the papers and was on his way the next day.

After induction at Lousville, KY, he was sent to Camp Forrest, TN where he received his basic training, later he was sent to Camp Phillips, KS where he received special training. He served with the 80th Div. 318th Inf., Co. F. in France. Being wounded he was returned to the States, going to Borden General Hospital at Chickasha, OK.

After an extended period of medical treatment he was discharged from the Army on 7 Jul 1945. He received the Purple Heart, ETO Ribbon and Expert Infantryman Badge for his service in France.

After his discharge he returned to Trigg County, just a short distance out of Cadiz, on the old Miller farm where his mother lived. He enrolled at Murray State Teachers College. He met Nellie Merl Calhoun, at the store her parents ran a short way beyond Russel Hill on Hwy. 68.

They married and started housekeeping at Murray, KY. After one year at Murray College he transferred to Wayne State Collage in Detroit, MI to complete his schooling.

They lived in the suburbs where he owned a construction business and pastored Baptist Churches until his retirement in 1988. Now he does no work except what he does for the Lord. He teaches the adult Sunday school class at the 12 Ryan Baptist Church, Warren, MI.

He and Nellie have two children: (1) Zondra, who has a daughter Monica Leah, and (2) Edward, who has a son Brandon Daniel. They reside Macomb, MI.

DUNCAN EVE ROSE, born 2 Dec 1922 and died 19 Mar 1972. He was the second son of Felix Doris and Daisy Feltner Rose. He graduated from Trigg County HS and joined the USN during WWII.

He served in South America and was an aircraft radio operator. He graduated from Western State University after the war, then served as a US Soil Conservationist in several Kentucky counties.

He was married to the former Sarah Buchanan for 25 years. They made their home in Munfordville, KY before their deaths. They had one son in Munfordville and one daughter in Knoxville, TN. They also had three grandsons.

FELIX DEWEY ROSE, born 10 Jan 1924 and died 4 Jul 1996. He was the third son of Felix Doris and Daisy Feltner Rose. He joined the US Army in 1944 during WWII where he saw action in Germany. He received the Purple Heart for injuries received in battle.

Before his retirement and death he worked for the US Government as a hospital cook at Fort Campbell, KY. He was married to the former Bonnie Hargis and lived in Bumpus Mills, TN. They have a daughter, son and two grandchildren who live in Hermitage, TN.

RAYMOND DOUGLAS ROSE, born 4 May 1920 and died 9 Jan 1982. He was the oldest child of Felix Doris Rose and Daisy Feltner Rose. He joined the US Army during WWII and served as a medic at a US hospital in Colorado. He worked in the US Government's CCC program prior to enlisting in the Army.

After the war he lived and worked in the Evansville, IN area for Swift Meat Packing Co. He was married to the former Dean Long who preceded him in death. They had three daughters, one son, eight grandchildren and six great-grandchildren who live in the Hopkinsville, KY area.

JAMES RUTLAND, born 6 Sep 1920 in Bethel Community in Trigg County. In 1942 he was 22 years old and joined the USMC in Chicago, IL. He had his boot training in San Diego, CA, then moved to Camp Elliot where he had to opportunity to spend the week-end in Los Angeles and dancing at the Hollywood Canteen.

Left by ship for the South Pacific, landed in New Caledonia, then sailed to Melbourne, Australia. After a short stay went on to Wellington, New Zealand where he joined the 2nd Marine Div. that had just left Guadalcanal. After six months training in artillery, he went to the island of Tarawa where he had his first encounter with the enemy. It was there that he asked God to let him live and he would turn his life over to him. The battle lasted three days and there were many killed and wounded. From there they were sent to Hawaii for R&R.

Moved on to island of Saipan, where many of his buddies were killed by the fierce artillery fire, and on to Tinian, where the Japanese came down the hills in a banzai attack saying Marines tonight you die, but instead they died. Went back to garrison troop at Saipan where they were bombed by Japanese every moonlit night and bullets from fighter planes flew everywhere. From there they went to Okinawa for the last battle of WWII, rested in Saipan for a few days then ordered to battle in Japan. When the atomic bomb was dropped and the war ended, orders were changed and they were sent to Nagasaki for occupation duty. This was the most devastated place he had ever seen. There was rubble everywhere and dead Japanese floating in the harbor.

He was discharged 8 Dec 1945 at Chicago, IL.

VAN LAYTON RYE, born 25 Oct 1925 in Trigg County, the son of Clarence Herbert and Edmonia Randolph Rye. He attended Trigg County schools and was graduated from Trigg County HS with the Class of 1943. He en-listed in the USN on 30 Sep 1943 in Louisville, KY. He received his basic training at Great Lakes Naval Base, Great Lakes, IL.

Van served aboard the USS *Dunlap*, USS *Ogalola* and the USS *Pronetreus*. His awards include the Asiatic-Pacific w/2 stars; American Area, Victory Medal; Philippine Liberation w/star. He was discharged 19 Mar 1946, after serving two years, five months and 20 days.

Van was married on 21 Nov 1945 to Anna Marie Callendar of New Orleans. Their son, Jerry was born on 26 Dec 1947 in Hopkinsville. Jerry received the "Best Drill Team" award in high school presented by his military science professor at Fulton HS in Atlanta. Later Jerry served his country in the military. Jerry and his wife, Doris Ann have a daughter, Tracey Diane. He is employed by Delta Air Lines in Atlanta.

In 1952 Van was married to Betty Spencer of Erin, TN. Their children are Mark Randolph "Randy" and Kimberly Rye. There are four grandchildren.

Van had a successful career as a Civil Service employee in finance and accounting in Atlanta. After retirement he and Betty moved to Tennessee Ridge, TN, near Erin, Betty's hometown. On 3 Apr 2000, Betty was critically ill in a Tennessee hospital and Van was with her. Around 2:00 a.m. on the 4th of April, Van suffered a fatal heart attack and Betty died two hours later. Their bodies were taken to Atlanta where a memorial service was held on 8 April. Interment was in Atlanta where the three children and grandchildren reside. *Submitted by Van's only sister, Marian Rye Davis, who lives in Columbia, SC.*

EURA ELVIS SANDERS, Staff Sergeant, born 23 Mar 1920 in Wallonia, KY, the son of Clarence Murl and Annie Ruth Morris Sanders, was inducted into in the US Army on 24 Jun 1942 at Fort Benjamin Harrison, IN.

After basic training at Camp Lee, VA, he attended a three month Motor Repair Shop School-Motor Maintenance training at Beltsville, MD. He was assigned to the 11th Armored Division, 491st Armored Field Artillery in the Headquarter Battery at Camp Polk, LA. Other assignments included Camp Barkley, TX, Camp Ibis, CA, Camp Cook, CA, and Camp Kilmer, NJ.

SSgt. Sanders left New York on 28 Sep 1944, aboard the British Samaria ship. He arrived in Liverpool, England, on 12 Oct 1944. He served and fought in England, France, Luxembourg, Germany, Belgium, and Austria. Sanders served with the 11th Armored Division, Field Artillery, which was attached to the 3rd Army under Gen. Patton. While in Europe, he was first under fire and battle on Dec. 30, 1944. His division

rescued the 10th Armored Division in the Battle of the Bulge on 31 Dec 1944. He was in the Battle of the Rhine (16-28 Mar 1945) and the Battle of Austria (29 Mar 1945).

Sanders received the American Theater Ribbon, WWII Victory Medal, Good Conduct Medal, Expert Marksmanship Medal, EAME Ribbon w/3 Bronze Stars (Ardennes, Rhineland and Central Europe).

Sanders left Marseilles, France aboard the USS *Hagerstown*. He arrived at Camp Miles Standish, Boston, MA on 26 Nov 1945. He was discharged at Fort Knox, KY on 30 Nov 1945. His wife, 4-year old son, and 6-month old daughter (whom he had never seen) met him in Hopkinsville, KY.

Eura Elvis Sanders was married to Elaine Baker Sanders on 14 Dec 1940. They had two children, Jack Sanders and Joyce Sanders Bozarth. They have four grandchildren: Kelly S. Haugh, Steven B. Sanders, Kendra S. Redd and Ashley S. Hunter. There are four great-grandchildren: Erica Anderson, Emily Anderson, Caroline Redd and Elizabeth Redd.

Eura Elvis Sanders lived his adult life in Wallonia, KY. He served as a rural letter carrier for 32 years. He was an avid sportsman and a farmer. Mr. Sanders died on 16 May 2000 at the age of 80.

MURL SANDERS JR., Corporal, born 19 Jul 1918, Wallonia, KY was drafted into the Army on 11 Apr 1941 at Fort Thomas, KY. His unit, 38th Div., 149th Inf. Regt., I Co. left for Hawaii in December 1943, traveling from New Orleans by ship through the Panama Canal. In June 1944 they traveled to Ova Bay, New Guinea and in December 1944 landed in Leyte Islands, Philippines. They moved to Manila in 1944 and returned to Los Angeles, CA, in September 1945 and was discharged 9 Nov 1945, Fort Benjamin Harrison, IN.

"Jr." was transferred to Third Battalion Headquarters and served as Headquarters Message Center Clerk. He was promoted from private to corporal around 1943. A wartime article in *The Cadiz Record* described some of the action Sanders saw during WWII. "While in the Zambales mountains of central Luzon, his battalion engaged in clearing out some 10,000 Japanese who had retreated into prepared positions in the mountains for a suicide stand. When some important enemy documents were captured one evening, a call went out for volunteers to take them back to headquarters. Although the trail was dangerous in the dark because of the high cliffs and also because of Japanese snipers, Pfc. Sander's volunteered for the mission and arrived safely at headquarters with the valuable papers. The information obtained help shorten the operation by several days."

"He has earned the Combat Infantry Badge, the Asiatic-Pacific and Philippine Liberation Campaign Medals w/2 Battle Stars and the Bronze Arrowhead for making an assault landing on enemy shores." He was with Gen. MacArthur when he went to shore at MacArthur's "return" to the Philippines.

The most tragic thing that happened was when his mother died in 1944. He was stationed in Hawaii and not allowed to come home.

A family member once overheard "Mutt" and "Jr." debating which one had seen "Real" action in the war. Mutt, of course, insisting he was "really" in the war in Germany at the "Battle of the Bulge" and Jr. equally adamant the "real" action was in the Pacific where he was. The discussion as far as we know was never resolved and probably continues in heaven since it was an argument they both were relishing!

Prior to entering the Army, Sanders graduated from the first graduating class of Trigg County High where he played basketball and was voted "Most Likely to Succeed." After the war, he returned home and married Marcella Wood Cobb on 1 Aug 1948. They had three children: Janice Boyd, Bruce Sanders and Cindy Laxton. Grandchildren are

Johnston Sanders Boyd, Aubree Sanders, Scott Sanders, Bryce Laxton, Colby Laxton, Joy Laxton and Isabel Laxton.

Focusing on his work at Wallonia and Cadiz IGAs, and family, for which he very successfully (as foreseen by his classmates) provided. He had such a zest for living while at the same time exhibiting a strong work ethic. His strong values as evidenced from his thoughts about war—once stating it is stupid and senseless—has always been a great influence to family and friends. He died on 7 Apr 1991 and is buried under a shade tree, as he requested, at Wall Cemetery. The character shown by my father is a wonderful legacy that is gratefully passed on to our children. *Lovingly submitted by Janice Sanders Boyd.*

OLLIE WILTON "BUSTER' SCOTT, PFC, born 30 Jun 1911 in Trigg County. He married Verna McKinney 30 Jun 1941 and was inducted at the age of 30 on 1 Oct 1942. His basic training was in Oregon and the Mojave Desert. Shoes two sizes to large and fatigues with both knees out were issued to him. He was transferred to Camp Polk, then to New Jersey for shipment on the *Queen Elizabeth* on 1 Jul 1943. They were there 11 months.

His unit, the 358th Engineer Regt., landed on Omaha Beach three days after D-Day. Devastation! the water was still red from the blood of bodies still there and the beach was strewn with many corpses. Germans located just above in bunkers were attacking so heavily, it was impossible to bury them. Many of the 358th were left there too.

The engineers constructed buildings, bridges, airports and cleared seaports of sunken vessels. In combat with Co. K, 290th Inf., they cleared mine fields for advancing troops. The German mine was underground with three two-inch wires above ground, making it impossible to detect them. If your foot touched those wires the mines detonated, killing or crippling you.

He served in Belgium, Normandy, France, Rhineland and Central Europe. He arrived home 24 Nov 1945 (his wife's birthday) and was discharged 15 Dec 1945 at Fort Knox, KY.

He returned to the farm his wife had bought in Christian County during his absence. (Fort Campbell had taken their Trigg County farm shortly before his induction, but after drafting him in Trigg.)

Pfc. Scott received the Good Conduct Medal, WWII Victory Medal, EAME Theater Ribbon w/4 Bronze Stars. "You'll never know it felt to see the Stars and Stripes raised after a hard won battle," he would say. He died 18 Mar 1996, shortly before his 85th birthday and 55th anniversary. *Written by wife Verna McKinney Scott.*

WILLIE F. SCOTT, PFC, was drafted on 5 Oct 1942 and entered active duty on 19 Oct 1942 by reporting to Fort Ben Harrison, IN. The first 16 weeks of training was at Camp Blanding, FL. He was then moved to Tullahoma, TN for nine weeks. He then went on to Camp Atterbury, IN for an additional four months. From there he went on to Camp Kilmer, NJ where they were shipped out 12 Feb 1944.

They landed at Vasco, Scotland 24 Feb 1944 where they spent two weeks. From there he was sent to Manchester, England where they stayed until 6 June. On 12 June they entered battle on a beach head of Normandy. He spent one year and 10 months and 13 days on foreign soil. After the battle he was signed to MP outfit in Lemas, France where he was guarding American prisoners until 15 Dec 1945. He was an automatic rifleman who served with the 30th Inf. Div. in the ETO for 22- 1/2 months.

He was discharged on 30 Dec 1945 at Fort Knox, KY. He remained in the Army Reserves until he was discharged on 30 Dec 1948. He married Doretta Underhill on 6 Apr 1951 and retired from TVA in July 1984. His parents were Plomer Scott and Fannie Page Scott.

His war medals include American Theater Ribbon, Good Conduct Medal, WWII Victory Medal, EAME Theater Ribbon w/2 Bronze Stars and the Combat Infantryman Badge.

HORACE W. "BILL" SEASE, Tech 4, born 31 Aug 1926 in Durango, CO. He was drafted 28 Dec 1944 and took his basic and field artillery training at Fort Sill, OK.

He was part of the occupation forces at Okinawa and among the first occupation troops to arrive in Korea, 8 Sep 1945.

Discharged 22 Nov 1946 as tech 4. His medals include the Asiatic-Pacific Campaign, WWII Victory Medal, Army of Occupation and Good Conduct.

As a civilian he worked for General Telephone in Long Beach, CA; Everett, WA; Chicago, IL; Stamford, CT; Dallas, TX; and Santa Monica, CA. After 38 years with GTE, he retired 28 Nov 1986.

Bill and his wife Virginia have two children, Steve Sease and Peggy Sease Garciduenas. Grandchildren are Stephanie Sullivan, Freddy and Raquel Garciduenas.

He lives on Lake Barkley, Cadiz, KY and enjoys gardening, stained glass windows, volunteer art center and food bank.

IRA EWING SHELTON, born 13 Jun 1926 near Cadiz, KY. He was drafted into US Army 26 Oct 1944 and was sent to Fort Knox, KY, where he took 17 weeks of tank and infantry training. He was then sent to Fort Ben Harrison, IN and went into the MPs.

His awards include the Good Conduct Ribbon and Victory Ribbon. He received his discharge 25 Jan 1946.

He met Vivian Futrell (born and reared in Trigg County) in 1951. They married 28 Mar 1953 and live in Cadiz, KY. They have two children, Sandra Davis and Don Shelton; and one grandchild, Britany Davis.

Ira worked at several jobs, but retired from Kentucky State Prison.

PAUL NELSON SHELTON, Tech Sergeant, born 4 Nov 1916 in what today is the Joiners' Chapel Community of Trigg County. He served with the 38th Div., I Co., 149th Inf., from early 1941-45.

He participated in training at Camp Shelby, MS and maneuvers and training exercises in Louisiana and Florida, before the division embarked on their campaign against the Japanese in the South Pacific.

His rank at the time of his discharge in November 1945 was technical sergeant. Awards include the Bronze Star.

He married Elnora Clayton in April 1946. They had three children: Gayle, Gary and Paula Shelton; four grandchildren: Jacob and Shelley Howe and Blake and Sara Shelton.

He retired from Sunflower Milling Company in 1982 with over 20 years with the company. They lived in Christian County, KY, until his death in December 1995. He is buried in Green Hill Memorial Gardens, Christian County, KY.

ALFRED BRANDON SHOLAR, PFC, Brandon grew up on the family farm with his brothers and sisters in southern Trigg County near Roaring Springs. He was son of Trigg County natives, James Edward Sholar and Christie Ethel Chewning Sholar. He was born 30 Oct 1918 in Trigg County.

Prior to WWII, Brandon was inducted into the US Army on 22 Apr 1941. He was a private in the Anti Tank Company, 149th Inf. After the Japanese attack on Pearl Harbor 7 Dec 1941, he was sent to the Pacific Theater of Operations. While in the service Brandon was shipped overseas to the southern Philippines. He saw action against the Japanese on Luzon and in New Guinea. He was later sent back to Honolulu, Hawaii where his division was awaiting orders for the invasion of Japan. After the atomic bombs were dropped on Hiroshima and Nagasaki the war was ended with a full unconditional surrender of the Japanese and Brandon was returned to the States.

For service to his country he received the Asiatic-Pacific Theater Ribbon w/3 Bronze Stars per War Department General Order 33/45. He also received the American Theater Ribbon, American Defense Service Medal, Philippine Liberation Ribbon w/Bronze Star per War Department General Order #33145, Good Conduct Ribbon, and the WWII Victory Medal. Brandon also received the Combat Infantryman's Badge and was a rifle marksman. His listed Military Occupational Specialty and number was Pioneer 729.

Brandon was honorably discharged as private first class 6 Nov 1945 at Camp Atterbury, IN. His honorable discharge was filed in the Trigg County Court House on 17 Nov 1945.

Brandon returned home to County and married Dorothy Gardener of Cerulean. They later moved and reared a family of two sons in Hopkinsville, KY. Brandon died 10 Sep 1985 in Hopkinsville, KY and was buried in the Green Hills Memorial Gardens, Hopkinsville, KY. He was a lifelong member of the VFW. *Submitted by James G. Sholar, nephew.*

HERSHELL KIEDEL SHOLAR, T-5, Corporal, US Army, "Kiedel" grew up on a farm in southern Trigg County. He was born on 4 Sep 1921, the son of James Sholar and Christie Chewning Sholar.

Shortly after his 21st birthday Kiedel was drafted. He was inducted into the Army on 29 Sep 1942 and received his basic training at Fort Belvoir, MD. He was in the 1st Div., Combat Engineers Battalion, Co. "B."

He acquired the nickname "Tommy" during the war because he carried a "Thompson" machine gun. He was a specialist in automatic weapons and was expert in demolition.

He saw his first action in North Africa participating in Operation Torch, which began 8 Nov 1943. He was in the invasion of Sicily July 1943 code named Operation Husky. For 38 straight days his company was in constant combat as they battled their way up the coast from the landing beach to Messina. He was nearly killed when wounded in the chest by German artillery round and was sent to a North African hospital for two months to recover.

On 6 Jun 1944, Cpl. Sholar participated in "Operation Overlord." His division went ashore on the Normandy Beach, D-Day. "Tommy" and his combat engineer company were instrumental in breaching the German defenses and allowing the American Army to break. Kiedel now was a veteran of his 3rd amphibious landing.

The 1st Division became involved in the Hurtgen Forest Campaign. When the Germans attacked allied positions around Bastogne. Kiedel was involved in the Battle of the Bulge lasting from 16 Dec 1944 to 28 Jan 1945.

In Aachen, Germany Sholar was slightly wounded by shrapnel. In February 1945, near Dern, Germany, he was seriously wounded in the right foot.

He was discharged from the Army at Fort Atterbury, IN 11 Aug 1945. At discharge, he accumulated 114 points. A total of two years and 10 months spent in service of his country.

Hershell was awarded the Purple Heart w/Oak Cluster (for being wounded twice), the Good Conduct Medal, WWII Victory Medal, Meritorious Unit Emblem, EAME Campaign Medal, several Unit Citations, Honorable Service Lapel Pin, the French Croix de Guerre, and four Bronze Stars. His rank at time of discharge was T-5, Corporal. His honorable discharge is recorded in Veterans Discharge Book No. 2, page 81 in Trigg County Clerk's Office, in Cadiz, KY, 10 Sep 1945. *Submitted by son, James G. Sholar.*

ROBERT ELTON SHOLAR, PFC, born 16 May 1914 in Trigg County. He was the oldest son born to James Edward Sholar and Christie Ethel Chewning who were both Trigg County natives. He was inducted into the Army as a private on 19 Jan 1943 at Evansville, IN. His serial number was 357231116.

He was trained as a cook and served in the 1687th Ord S&M Co. (Avu) 40th Service Group and was stationed at Avon Park, FL. Robert was not sent overseas for combat duty. His wife was hospitalized due to a work related injury. He was honorably discharged as private first class on 20 Sep 1943 by reason of Dependency, per section 5 Ar 615-360 & WD air 48, 1943, and per 2 SO 262

He returned home to Trigg County to his wife and a career as a chef. He married Mattie Marie Bryant of Trigg County on 16 Aug 1940. They had a daughter Patricia Yvonne Sholar born 15 Oct 1949.

Robert and his family would later move to Murray, KY, then to Manitou Springs, CO and again back to Murray. The family loved Colorado and would return to Manitou Springs and Colorado Springs. Robert was head chef at the Penrose Hospital there and was an accomplished cook.

Robert died 28 Jun 1983 at the Colorado State Veterans Nursing Home in Florence, CO and was buried in the Green Hills Memorial Gardens Cemetery in Hopkinsville, KY.

JOHN W. SILLS, born 28 Apr 1914 in the present Land Between the Lakes area near Linton, KY, was drafted into the US Army, 17 Dec 1942. He reported to Fort Benjamin Harrison, IN, along with 27 other fellow Trigg Countians, to be informed of a designated transferal for training.

Sills was sent to Camp Roberts in San Diego, CA for training with the 80th Inf. Then he went to Fort Rosecrans Post Artillery, also in San Diego, to guard post and help engineers put in diesel motors to pull generators in case of power outage for gun power.

When this service was completed Sills reported to the 803rd Field Artillery for instruction to go to Fort Sill, OK for full track school for approximately a month. Then his unit was sent to Camp Bowie for artillery training for several weeks. When this assignment was completed Sills was sent to Camp Stoneman near San Francisco with orders to be shipped overseas. He was sent to the Asiatic-Pacific Region, first briefly stopping at Hawaiian shores to take on necessary supplies. The ship was at voyage for about 42 days with major difficulties, including a collision with another ship, evasion of subs, and blackouts. The ship docked at Eniwetok for repairs to vessel. After a few days his ship went to the island of Leyte for approximately a month to combat invasion.

Then Sills went to Luzon Island for the same purpose until the war ended. He did not get to come home, however, but was sent to Manila in the Philippines for Shore Patrol Duty for three months. Finally, he was shipped back to the United States.

Discharged 23 Feb 1946. His awards include the Asiatic-Pacific Theater Ribbon, Philippine Liberation Ribbon, American Theater Ribbon, Good Conduct Ribbon and WWII Victory Medal.

At home, back in Trigg County in Linton, Sills rejoined his wife, Daphne Tucker Sills, whom he had married on 11 Jan 1932 before he was inducted into the Army. He continued a career of heavy construction, including self employment and working for TVA until 1982 when he retired. His wife died in 1990 and now Sills resides in Bowling Green, KY with his daughter, Donna Mize, a teacher.

THOMAS R. "TED" SILLS, born 23 Apr 1923 near Linton, KY. He lived there all his school days and went to Trigg County High from 8th grade to graduation in 1941. He entered Western State Teachers College in 1941 on football and basketball scholarships. While he was at Western, he lived in the athletic village until he registered for the draft. He remembers 7 December when the Japanese bombed Pearl Harbor, and war was declared. Knowing they weren't going to get another semester, about six of them decided to go to Bristol, CT to work in the defense plant (New Departure) ball bearing plant. They worked about six months and he got his orders to report to Fort Ogelthorp, GA.

He was there about two weeks and had his supplies issued and was told they were headed for parts unknown. The first morning on troop train they had salmon for breakfast and he made up his mind that he didn't like this. They were on the train three days and it didn't get any better.

They found their new home in Camp Cook, CA and started their basic training. About seven months later they were shipped to Camp Shanks, NY where they left for overseas duty.

They trained in England for about six or eight months and went to combat about 15 or 20 days after D-Day. They fought several skirmishes at first and were ordered to the small town of Le Cloitre to clean out machine gun nest. As they did, mortar was dropped on them and they had to take cover.

A nearby round sent shrapnel through his back, side and right arm. He applied first aid to myself and continued to treat other wounded. By the time they all arrived at the aid station, his wound had not improved. He was transferred to an evac hospital in France where his right arm was amputated above the elbow. From France he was transferred back to a military hospital in England. While in the hospital in England, he was awarded the Silver Star for "Gallantry in Action" and the Purple Heart. From England he returned to the States aboard a hospital ship, so did not get to see the Statue of Liberty.

Most of his rehabilitation came at McCloskey General Hospital in Temple, TX. After several operations and lengthy training with an artificial right arm, he came home.

CECIL RAY SIMMONS, Corporal, born 31 Jul 1918 in Trigg County. He joined the USAF 13 Oct 1942 at Trigg County, Cadiz, KY.

Served with the ground crew in northern France, Normandy, Air Offensive Europe, Rhineland and Central Europe. Discharged 11 Sep 1945 with the rank of corporal. His awards include the EAME Theater Ribbon w/6 Bronze Stars, Good Conduct and Distinguished Unit Citation.

A retired farm worker he now lives in Carrolton, TX with his wife, the former Kathleen Armstrong. Married since 14 Dec 1946, they have two children, Judy Bracy and Tanna Calhoon, and four grandchildren: Tammy, John, Joey and Greg.

EARL WAYNE SIMMONS, born 21 Apr 1915 at Trigg County, Linton, KY. He enlisted in the military service from Trigg County on 9 Sep 1942. He was inducted at Camp Atterbury, IN, then transferred to Mitchel Field, NY for basic training.

After training, he and a division of his group were transferred to a motor school in Elkins, WV. Later they rejoined their company in Leesburg, FL - the company had been transferred directly from Long Island, NY. The entire company was moved to Orlando AB, FL.

In February 1943, Earl's company formed a new company of 156 men, the 1955 Ordnance Aviators Co., and was shipped to Floria, MS for basic training. When training was completed at Mount Rainier near Tacoma, WA, they were transferred to the Pittsburgh, CA, embarking center on 7 Dec 1943, ordered to Townsville, Australia then to Darwin, Australia where the company joined the 5th Air Force.

Earl served as an ordnance depot supplier in New Guinea and the Philippine Islands until the war ended in the Pacific Theater. He was transferred to Angel Island for R&R, then shipped to Camp Atterbury, IN, where he was discharged in December 1945.

Returning to civilian life, Earl entered Mechanical School in Cincinnati, OH. After completing school he began work at Collins-Buick where he stayed until retirement.

On 27 Sep 1941 he married Geneva Williams and they have two children, Evelyn Kaye Stagner and Beverly Ann Wilson; three grandchildren and two great-grandchildren. *Submitted by Earl and Geneva Simmons.*

HUBERT DOUGLAS "BUD" SIMMONS, PFC, born 12 Jan 1926 at Linton, KY, was drafted in the US Army, 15 Jun 1945.

Simmons was inducted at Louisville, KY and traveled to Camp Blanding, Jacksonville, FL for basic training. During machine-gun qualification, a buzzard flew through the target area. All 60 gunners fired at the bird, but when cease-fire was called, it flew away without losing a single feather.

Upon completion of basic training, Simmons was assigned to Camp Blanding as a military policeman with Headquarters Detachment Section 1, 1448 SCU PW Camp, guarding German POWs. Following reassignment to Camp Bell Haven POW Camp, Miami, FL, he returned to Camp Blanding, where he was honorably discharged on 25 Mar 1946 to enlist in the Regular Army.

Simmons traveled to Camp Atterbury, IN for reassignment to Fort Lawton, Seattle, WA for advanced infantrymen training. On 5 Jul 1946 (11 months after the bombs were dropped on Hiroshima and Nagasaki) Simmons sailed on the ship, *Marine Serpent,* to Japan. During the voyage. The ship encountered a violent typhoon; sea water filled the bottom compartments and nearly capsized the ship.

After arriving in Yokohama, on 18 Jul 1946, Simmons graduated from Paratrooper School. In August 1946 he was assigned to Headquarters Company, 188 PIR, 10th Abn. Div. in Sendai, Japan. During parachute training the airplane's engine failed. Following a safe landing, the airplane reloaded with other passengers. During takeoff, it crashed killing all 23 aboard.

Completing an assignment in Fukuoka, PFC Simmons returned to Sendai as a telephone operator. The battalion consisted of six individuals: a colonel, major, captain, lieutenant, sergeant and Simmons.

He departed Japan 21 Feb 1947 and his ship once again encountered a typhoon. He sailed under the Golden Gate Bridge in San Francisco on 3 Mar 1947, After processing through Oakland Airbase, CA, he was sent to Fort Sheridan, IL for discharge on 28 Mar 1947. Awards include the Good Conduct and Occupation (Japan).

Simmons returned to Trigg County where he married Ruth Janelle Rogers on 27 Mar 1947. They have two daughters, Shirley R. Ezell and Brenda Thompson; six grandchildren and 10 great-grandchildren

After four years of farming, Simmons moved his family to Christian County where he worked as a carpenter for the Meacham family, building houses and repairing barns until his retirement 10 years ago. He and his wife currently reside on Old Major Lane in Hopkinsville. His interests include gardening, fishing and hunting.

Simmons was licensed to preach by Julien Baptist Church on 23 Dec 1956. In addition to serving as assistant-interim pastor at several churches, he has conducted services at the Brookfield Manor Nursing Home every Wednesday night since December 1967.

MAXIE SMITH SIMMONS, Machinist Mate 1/c, born 3 Mar 1922 in Trigg County, KY. He joined the USN during WWII and served on the USS *Prairie,* 11 May 1943; USS *Briareus,* 8 Dec 1943; arrived in Pearl Harbor, 25 Feb 1944, crossed Equator and had initiation, changing from Pollywag to Shellback by King Neptune on 29 Feb 1944.

Other locations include New Hebrides, Admiralty Island, Manus Harbor, Tulagi, Purvis Bay, Samar and Leyte, Okinawa, Pearl Harbor and arrived back in San Francisco on 3 Jan 1946 and discharged 9 Jan 1946.

Called back to service 5 Feb 1951 for Korean Conflict and reported to *Bon Homme Richard* (CV-31). Crossed International Date Line, dropped off extra planes and made first raid on Korea 30 Jun 1951. Joined Task Force 77 off Korea and left for Yokosuka. The USS *Essex* joined Task Force 25 Aug 1951 and made raid on north Korea. After Korea they were Flag Ship of Task Force 77.

He was discharged 23 Mar 1952. Medals include American Campaign Medal, Asiatic-Pacific Medal, WWII Victory Medal, Navy Occupation Service Medal w/Asia Clasp, Korean Service Medal, UN Medal and the Philippine Liberation Ribbon (awarded by Philippine Government).

Employed as millwright and machinist for Barber Green Heavy Equipment Mfg. in Aurora, IL, retired and moved back to Cadiz, KY.

Married Norma VanKlavern and had two children, Lynette and Joseph, and four grandchildren: Nevada, Tommy, Brian and Danny. Maxie passed away 27 Sep 1995.

CALVERT WALLACE SIVILLS, Tech 4, born 25 Mar 1921 in Trigg County, KY. He was drafted into the US Army on 29 Oct 1942.

Assigned to the 16th FOB Field Artillery Battalion at Camp Atterbury, IN, and sent to Fort Leonard Wood, MO, for basic training. After an assignment at Camp Bowie, TX, and field maneuvers in Louisiana, he was sent to Fort Bragg, NC, where be learned radio and telegraph communications.

On 29 Jun 1944, he sailed out of Camp Shanks, NY on the ship, *The Louis Pasteur,* for Liverpool, England. From there, he was assigned to Battery D of the 551st AAA AW BN, XX Corps of the Third Army as a radio operator. His unit was deployed to France, Luxembourg and Germany.

On 18 Jul 1944, Sivills and the XX Corps or "Ghost Corps" as they were called, embarked on one of the fastest sustained marches in military history from St. Jacques to Verdun, France. They traveled over 600 miles in 30 days, crossing six rivers in 15 days and liberating scores of French towns and cities. In December and January of 1944-45, Sivills and his unit fought in the Battle of the Bulge.

Sivills would later recall to his children how his unit helped liberate Buchenwald, a Jewish concentration camp near Weimar, Germany. He shot photographs of the horrors he and his comrades witnessed there, and his children and grandchildren have shared the photographs over the years with history students at Trigg County High.

Sivills was promoted to technician fourth grade on 31 May 1944. He was honorably discharged from the Army on 30 Oct 1945, at Camp Atterbury, IN.

Returning to Cadiz, he married a hometown girl, Dorothy Dean Stallons, on 10 Aug 1946 in Hopkinsville. He was an active member of Cadiz Baptist Church, the Cadiz Civitan Club, the Cadiz Masonic Lodge, American Legion Post No. 74 and the TCH "Boosters" Club. He worked for many years at Baldwin Truck and Tractor Co. in Hopkinsville, and later at Cadiz Auto Parts.

He and his wife had four children: Calvert "Buddy," Scott, Nancy (Thompson) and Jane. He died on 19 Dec 1969.

CHARLES STANLEY SIZEMORE, Sergeant, born 21 Oct 1916 near Wallonia, KY, the son of the late Jacob Lawrence and Martha Ann (Mason) Sizemore. He was drafted into the US Army 13 May 1941 from Detroit, MI.

He was sent to Camp Grant, IL, then to Camp Davis, NC where he received basic training in coast guard anti-aircraft gun battery, on the Army's 3 inch AA guns.

In December 1941 he was sent to Angel Island, Fort McDowell located in San Francisco Bay. On 27 Dec 1941 he left for Pearl Harbor, Hawaii, arriving at Honolulu 7 Jan 1942

He was assigned to Battery D 752nd AAA Gun BN near Pearl Harbor. 5.25 inch anti-aircraft guns and fire control equipment were removed from the war ships sunk in Pearl Harbor and mounted on concrete in a diamond formation. In the fall of 1944 we received the Army's 120mm AAA guns with the M-10 director and radar.

On 7 Jan 1945 the battalion was sent to Eniwetok. From there he went to Saipan for about a month. He arrived in Iwo Jima in early April 1945 after the organized Japanese resistance was beaten down by the Marines and Army. The first few days were spent at the base of Mt. Suribachi. The guns, tents and equipment were located near the airfield. The Japanese made only a token air raid, dropping a few bombs while he was there.

After the war ended he spent the month of September 1945 on Saipan. He arrived back at Camp Grant, IL and was discharged 31 Oct 1945.

When he got out of the service his rank was sergeant in charge of communication. His battles and campaigns included Eastern Mandates and Western Pacific. His decorations and citations included one Service Stripe, seven Overseas Service Bars, American Defense Ribbon, Asiatic-Pacific Theater Ribbon w/2 Bronze Battle Stars and Good Conduct Medal.

Before being sent overseas, he became engaged to Rilda Schoneman, a girl he met at Trinity Baptist Church, Detroit, MI. They were married 15 Dec 1945 and had two sons: Douglas (a professor at Covenant College in Lookout Mt., GA) and Donald (manager with Pfizer, Inc. in Ann Arbor, MI).

He served as church clerk of Wallonia Baptist Church in the 1930s. At Trinity Baptist Church he served as a deacon, secretary of deacons board and was elected deacon emeritus.

He worked at the Western Electric Co. for 37 years, retiring 5 Feb 1974. At retirement he was Dept. Chief of Personnel and Public Relations which covered about 2,000 employees working in the state of Michigan. For 10 years he and wife Rilda traveled and enjoyed doing the things they liked. In 1983, Rilda's health began to fail and on 28 Dec 1986 she died.

Today at 84 he still resides at his Livonia home and keeps busy with housework, yard work, attends Trinity Church and plays golf - 9 holes 77 times in year 2000.

HARVEY THOMAS SIZEMORE, born 3 Jun 1923 near Wallonia, Trigg County, KY. He volunteered for the Air Force 10 Nov 1942 at Nashville, TN and was inducted at Fort Hayes, Columbus, OH.

He went to San Antonio Aviation Cadet Center, San Antonio, TX for his cadet training. He became ill and received a medical discharge 16 Jun 1943.

Harvey married Jean Patterson Mitchell on 7 Aug 1943 and had five children: Harvey Thomas Jr., James Hubert, Jeanie Mitchell, William Lawrence and Charles Allison.

Owned and operated Sizemore Welding and Equipment Co., Cadiz, KY. He was an active member of Cadiz Baptist Church. Harvey passed away 8 Sep 1966 and was buried in Greenhill Memorial Gardens, Christian County, KY.

JOHN WILLIAM SIZEMORE, PVT, born 21 Aug 1918 near Wallonia, KY. He was inducted into the Army 23 June 1943 at Fort Benjamin Harrison, IN. His basic training began 7 Jul 1943 at Camp Croft, SC.

In March 1944 he was sent to Fort George Meade, MD. He left Meade 11 Apr 1944 and arrived in Italy 8 May 1944.

Sizemore was in Co. F, 349th Inf. Regt., 88th Div. (Blue Devils) of the 5th Army. He qualified as a expert rifleman and received the Combat Infantry Badge.

Sizemore precipitated in the battles of Northern Apennines, Po Valley and Rome-Arno. He received the, EAME Theater Ribbon W/3 Bronze

Stars, Good Conduct Medal and the WWII Victory Medal.

He left Italy on 12 Jan 1946 and arrived in the USA 23 Jan 19146. He was discharged at Camp Atterbury, IN, 28 January 1946 with the rank of private. He returned home to Trigg County and continued his life as a farmer.

He never married and died 29 Aug 1993 and was buried in Lander Cemetery, Christian County.

LACEY H. SKINNER, Tech 5, born 20 Feb 1922 in Trigg County, KY. He joined the service 3 Nov 1942 at Evansville, IN. His MOS was automotive mechanic (014); stations were Fort Benjamin Harrison, IN; Camp Polk, LA; Camp Cook, CA; and Camp Kilmer, NJ.

He served with the 11th Army Div. and fought in the Ardennes, Rhineland and Central Europe. Memorable experience was traveling to London, England and Paris, France.

Skinner received his discharge on 15 Jan 1946. His awards include the EAME Theater w/3 Bronze Stars, American Theater, Good Conduct, Marksman (Carbine) and WWII Victory Medal.

Married Margaret Hazel Williams on 15 Mar 1947 and has two children, Teresa Skinner Smith and Roger Terry Skinner. Grandchildren are Lacey Smith and Mathew Skinner.

Due to blindness, he retired from International Shoe Co. 25 Feb 1972. He resides in Hopkinsville and enjoys listening to sports and audio books.

WILLIAM HOWARD SKINNER, Corporal, born 26 Jun 1925 in Trigg County, KY, the son of Carnell and Gracie Askew Skinner. Drafted in January 1944 and trained in Camp Hood, TX, with 293rd Field Artillery, Obsn Bn.

After training, they were sent to Camp Shank, NY, and from there, to Le Havre, France, to Northern France Campaign, to Rhineland Campaign in Germany.

He feels it was an honor to serve his country. There were so many experiences he could write about, but the ones that stick out in his memory, are the children left there without parents, trying to survive. It made his realize this very well could be our own country. Living through this experience makes him so thankful every day for our freedom. May we never take it for granted.

He is thankful his complete company made it back safe. Through the years he has kept in touch with one of the fellows in his company. He lived in Florida, but passed away in 2000.

After serving in the US Army, three years, his rank was corporal. His awards include the EAME with 2/Bronze Stars, Good Conduct Medals, American Campaign Medal and WWII Victory Medal.

He returned to Cadiz and Trigg County, where his family resided. He married Adell Thomas Skinner on 17 Jan 1944 and they have seven children: Howard T., Anthony, Kevin, Melba Futrell, Rebecca Smith, Barbara Fowler and Karen Adams. He has 11 grandchildren and five great-grandchildren. Adell passed away in August of 1996.

William retired from Civil Service, Fort Campbell, KY in December 1980, and still reside in Cadiz, KY. He has several hobbies, loves to travel, and has a farm on Donaldson Creek, where he was born and raised. He attends Dry Creek Primitive Baptist Church.

GIRVIS R. SMITH, born 19 Oct 1919 in the Energy Community Trigg County, KY, the son of William R. and Fannie Colson Smith. He was drafted in the US Army at Louisville, KY, on 12 Aug 1941.

After his basic training, he made sergeant and was assigned to Co. 115th Infantry. His division left 2 Oct 1942 for overseas duty in the European Theater of War.

Girvis was in the Battle of St. Lo, in France, and participated in the Battle of Normandy where he was wounded in battle. He led a squad of five men into the battle, using rifles to destroy the enemy. Wounded 1 Aug 1944, he laid on the battlefield until the next morning, and his squad continued on to help capture Normandy. Girvis was hospitalized for 11 months and received his discharge, 14 Jun 1945 at Camp Atterbury, IN.

Decorations include the Purple Heart, European American Theater Ribbon w/2 Bronze Stars, Good Conduct Medal, Expert Infantryman and Rifleman.

Girvis married Lennie R. Newton 4 Sep 1947, and they were the parents of Frances Smith (b. 12 Jul 1948) and Jannie Smith (b. 20 Feb 1951). They resided in the Energy Community, where Girvis was a farmer and later a bus driver for Golden Pond School, until the Corps. of Engineers obtained their farm land.

In the late 1960s Girvis was employed with the Kentucky State Penitentiary, where he worked until the time of his death, 3 May 1973. He is buried in Trigg Memort Acres, Cadiz, KY. Girvis received his education at Ferguson Springs School, and was a member of the Ferguson Springs Baptist Church. His brothers, Jessie and Woodson, also fought in WWII.

JAMES G. SMITH, Corporal, born 1 Nov 1920 in Cadiz, KY. Enlisted in November 1943 at Fort Knox, KY and assigned to the 788th Amphibian Tractor Bn. as a tractor driver.

Participated in the Philippine landing on Leyte and the Easter Sunday assault on Okinawa. While making a landing on one of the islands, the tractor he was driving sank and they were forced to evacuate and try to swim to shore.

Memorable experience while on Okinawa was running into a good friend, Chance Francis Jr.) from Clarkesville, TN. They had both been through the Okinawa Campaign, but didn't meet until the island had been secured.

James married Virgie Rogers on 3 Sep 1941. After his discharge in the spring of 1946, they moved to Detroit, MI where he worked for the Chrysler Corp. In 1959 they moved to Florence, AL where he and good friend, Douglas Farley, bought and operated Tri-Cities Transmission Service until he retired in 1985.

James was a member of the Florence Blvd. Church of Christ and served as an elder for over 30 years. He became ill in 1992 and passed away in June 1993. He had two daughters, Glenda Young and Sara Fulton, four grandchildren and four great-grandchildren.

JESSIE DALE SMITH, PFC, son of W.R. and Fannie Oakley Smith, was born 26 Feb 1917 at Energy, KY. He was inducted into the army on 16 Oct 1941 and assigned to Co. L, 168th Inf., 34th Div. as rifleman.

Battles and Campaigns include Algeria-French Moroccan Tunisian. Shortly after he arrived at the North African shores, Jessie was taken as a prisoner of war.

Decoration and Citations were EAME Theater Ribbon w/2 Bronze Stars. His discharge was on 12 Jun 1945.

Jessie married Betty Prescot, after his return home and had one son, Ritchie Lou Smith. They were members of the Ferguson Springs Baptist Church and resided at Energy, KY. Then they moved to Calvert City, KY where he was employed at Union Carbide. Jessie was laid to rest in Murray, KY at the Calloway Memorial Gardens.

WOODSON SMITH, Corporal, son of W.R. and Fannie Oakley Smith, was born 15 Mar 1922 at Energy, KY. Prior to the service, Woodson was a truck driver. He was inducted into the Army on 18 Nov 1942 at Fort Benjamin Harrison, IN and assigned as truck master with 413th Inf. Regt.

Woodson departed for the European African Theater on 27 Aug 1944 and participated in battles and campaigns at Northern France, Rhineland and Central Europe.

He returned home 3 Jul 1945 and was discharged 9 Nov 1945. His awards include Combat Infantry Badge, American Campaign Medal, Good Conduct Medal, WWII Victory Medal, EAME Campaign Medal, Bronze Star and Distinguished Unit Badge.

Woodson and Grace Berkley married 18 Apr 1942 before he went into the Army. They have one daughter, Sherry (b. 1947), and two grandsons, Shawn and Todd. They resided around Pleasant Hill and later moved to Peoria, IL, where he was first employed at Caterpillar Plant for a number of years, than with a car dealership. Woodson passed away 16 Jun 1996.

JAMES ELLIOT SMOOT, Staff Sergeant, born 14 Oct 1919 in Graves County, KY. He taught at Trigg County HS 1939-41 and was drafted in May 1942 at Cadiz, KY. He was assigned to the US Air Corps.

After being trained as a tail gunner on B-17, he went overseas to England in November 1942. James participated in the European Theater of Operations and flew in the first US daylight mission on Germany in January 194. He was wounded on his 23rd mission in June 1943 on a raid on Bremmen, Germany.

He was discharged as a staff sergeant in September 1945. James received many awards and medals throughout his military career including the Purple Heart, Distinguished Flying Cross, Air Medal w/3 Oak Leaf Clusters, ETO w/Bronze Star, Good Conduct Medal and three Overseas Service Bars.

Special memories include a hospital visit in England from Gen. Frank Armstrong to award James the Purple Heart and a surprise hospital visit from Toppy Edwards, a friend from Cadiz. Of special note is James' survival of a mid-air collision over England in 1943.

James met and married Rosemary Touzet in New Orleans, LA in 1949. They had two children, Richard Smoot and Gene Marie Stewart. Their grandchildren are Madeline, Mark, Craig, and Melissa. Rosemary passed away in November 2000 after 51 years of marriage to James. James retired as a production supervisor for DeSoto, Inc. in October of 1981 after 23 years of service.

James' activities are limited at the present time due to his recovery from lung cancer. However, at 81, he still maintains his own household and enjoys reading about WWII and related subjects. James resides in Garland, TX

JAMES DELBERT STAGNER, Petty Officer 1/c, born 5 Jun 1919, son of Silar Marion and Mallie Wyatt Stagner who are buried in East End Cemetery in Cadiz, KY. He joined the USCG at Nashville, TN on 2 Feb 1942 and received training at Brooklyn, NY. From there he was sent to Ship Bottom, NJ to Philadelphia for training as Ship's Cook.

His next station was at Cape May, NJ for off-shore submarine patrol. Patrolling the Atlantic Coast during that period in a decoy ship was a very dangerous situation since German submarines were just off-shore all up and down the Atlantic. Delbert was stationed on the DuPont yacht since the Coast Guard used the DuPont yacht and other private yachts as decoy ships to look for submarines along with blimps overhead, which dropped depth charges on submarines. Some shore patrol, walking the beach, was also part of his duty.

From Cape May, Delbert was sent by train to California where he boarded the USS *Savage*, a Destroyer Escort, which patrolled the Pacific Ocean, the Berring Sea and the Gulf of Alaska. This duty included convoy duty and weather patrols. He was assigned to Commander "Bull" Halsey's fleet. Eventually, his ship patrolled from the Bering Straits down off the Coast of Japan. When Tokyo was bombed, he could hear the Japanese planes.

From this last assignment, he was sent back to Alaska, then to Seattle for a long train ride home. He was discharged at St. Louis, MO. He had been in the service for three years and eight months, almost all that time at sea.

In 1946, Delbert volunteered for the Navy Reserve and served two years active duty at Bainbridge, MD as emergency maintenance electrician. He was promoted to first class petty officer while at Bainbridge and was discharged in 1951.

Delbert Stagner married Ronella Morris on 28 Nov 1946 and they have three children: Jeannie, James D. Jr. "Monty" and David; and eight grandchildren: Will, Annie, Josh and Aaron Stagner; Jeanna Johnson Arfsten; Justin Johnson; Nikolas and Jennifer Bodine; and two great-grandchildren, Dana Arfsten and Caroline Johnson.

ENOCH FOREST STEPHENS, Sergeant, born 18 Aug 1906 in Trigg County, KY, son of William Robert Stephens and Etheline Sanders Stephens. Gillespie enlisted into the US Army, 5 Jul 1940.

He served 27 months with Co. M, 110th Inf., 28th Div. in the West

Indies and European Theater of Operations as a machine gunner and directed a machine gun squad as sergeant and squad leader.

Stephens was wounded in Germany on 9 Nov 1944 and discharged 18 Jul 1945. He received the EAME Theater Ribbon, Purple Heart and American Defense Service Medal w/Bronze Star.

He married Doshie Ethel Woods on 14 Dec 1942 and worked as a carpenter and farmer. They had five children: Pauletta Stephens Calhoun, James Headly, Herbert Hopson, Bobby Wade, Donnie Ray; four grandchildren: Dietta Calhoun Carr, Tammy Lynn Settles, James Nelson Calhoun and Tracy Calhoun Oakley and seven great-grandchildren.

Stephens was a charter member of Calvary Baptist Church and died 8 Aug 1992.

GENE TUNNEY STEPHENS, born 23 Jul 1927 to Arnett Melvin and Alvie Mitchell Stephens. The youngest of seven children, he was born in the Bethesda Community of Trigg County, KY. When he was approximately 5 years old his family moved to Cadiz where he attended Cadiz Grade School through the sixth grade, then Trigg County HS to the senior year. He enlisted in the USAF in the fall of 1945. He was first stationed in Mississippi for his basic training, then to Lackland AFB in San Antonio, TX for further training. He also trained at Buckley Field near Colorado Springs, CO as a military policeman. He then was transferred to McDill AFB, Tampa, FL, where he served as a member of the infantry, a military policeman and drill instructor. While he was in Florida, he was sent to Greenland for approximately three months, then returned to Florida. He was later transferred to the US Aviation Corps of Engineers. In 1948 he was discharged after serving honorably for three years.

In 1949 he married Juanita Bridges whom he had known socially during his teen years. He was employed by Preload Construction Company of Long Island, NY. He and his wife began several years of traveling throughout the United States building water tanks for cities and private industry. He interrupted his traveling career for about five years while he was employed at several different local places. He worked at Calvert City, KY for Analine Film Company, a chemical plant making detergents and other products. He then accepted a position as water plant operator for the city of Cadiz where he was employed approximately five years. He then worked as a lumber sales representative for the W.C. White Lumber Co. in Cadiz. Finding new employment at Hopkinsville in another plant, he worked for Mallory Metallurgical for a short time. Then he had the longing to go back on the road with the old company, Preload Construction.

After his return to the Preload Construction Company, he spent the next 18 or so years traveling until his retirement in 1989. He and his wife, Juanita, make their home west of Cadiz, KY.

LONNIE JACKSON SKINNER, Corporal, born 18 May 1927 in Trigg County, KY. He enlisted 19 Nov 1945 and was sent to Camp Atterbury, IN, then on to Fort Sills, OK for basic training.

After a furlough home he was sent to Fairfield Suisun AAB in California, where he was a ccok. He made corporal and was discharged 9 May 1947.

He was a farmer, never married, and passed away 28 Jun 1999. *Submitted by Mayme Stewart.*

WILLIAM JINKS STEWART, Seaman 1/c, born 22 Jul 1933 in Trigg County. He enlisted 21 Feb 1945, was sent to Bremerton, WA and served in the South Pacific.

He made nine round trips overseas on the USS *Puget Sound* before being discharged 10 Jul 1946.

Married Mayme Skinner on 24 Dec 1947 and has three children: Rita Stewart Swift, Ronnie Stewart and William Darrell Stewart (d. 18

Apr 1974). Grandchildren are Dana Swift Earheart; Holli Swift Dill; Caroline, Jonathon and Shon Stewart.

Retired from SKW in Calvert City, KY in October 1981, he resides in Trigg County and still helps farm, has a garden, reads, watches TV and go on vacations.

LLOYD ODELL STONE, AOM2/c, born 29 Jul 1922 in a log cabin four miles north of Cadiz, KY in Trigg County, the son of Bishop and Bertha Stone. Lloyd and his older brother Orbie decided to enlist in the USN and on 24 Sep 1942 were sworn in at Hopkinsville, KY.

Basic training was at Great Lakes, IL, followed by Aerial Gunnery School, Dam Neck, VA. Early in 1945 he was sent to a Bomb Disposal School in Washington, DC area for three months. From there he was assigned to a unit at Jacksonville, FL NAS where he instructed in the use of bombs and fuses.

While in Florida his sweetheart, Lillian Nell Adams from Kentucky, came to see him and they were married the next day, 20 Jun 1945. He received an honorable discharge 8 Dec 1945.

After military he worked in a factory for three years, farmed for five years, four years college, 20 years as a walking postman, 27 years prison ministry and 9-1/2 years in real estate. Retired he does volunteer rest home ministry, design and makes checker boards, and writes poetry.

Lloyd and Linda have one daughter, Lana Colleen Stone Crawford, and one granddaughter, Candice Crawford Bolivar. They reside in Newburgh, IN.

ORBIE HOPSON STONE, Aviation Machinist Mate 2/c, born 30 Jan 1918 in the Siloam Community of Trigg County, KY. He enlisted in the USN, Louisville, KY on 24 Sep 1942. He attended NTS, Great Lakes, IL, NATTC, Memphis, TN, and served on Patrol Squad-201. He was a member of Bombing Squads 111 and 105 in anti-submarine operations at the Bay of Biscay and the western approaches to the US Kingdom from 17 Aug 1943 to 25 Jun 1944.

Stone was awarded the Air Medal for meritorious conduct upon completing his fifth bombing mission and the Gold Star at the completion of his tenth bombing mission. He served as second class aviation machinists mate (hydraulics) and machine tail gunner aboard bombing missions. He was honorably discharged in Memphis, TN on 7 Oct 1945. Awards include the Air Medal and Gold Star.

Following his discharge from the Navy, he worked at several jobs in Trigg and Caldwell counties including IKT, Mitchell Implement Co. and operated Stone's General Merchandise and Filling Station at Hopson Lake. He was employed at Thomas Industries in Princeton, KY, moving to their Hopkinsville location in 1955, and retiring in May 1980 after 28 years. He died 19 Oct 1981 from complications associated with ALS (Lou Gehrig disease).

"Our father was a quite man, who raised us to believe in God and to always do the right thing." He served the Lord from an early age as a deacon, most recently at Henderson Memorial Baptist Church, Hopkinsville, KY. His wife Laverne of almost 40 years; son O. Eugene Stone, Watauga, TX; daughter Janice Sholar, Hopkinsville, KY; and five grandchildren survive him.

RAYMOND EUGENE STONE, PFC, SN, born 3 Feb 1925 in Trigg County, Cadiz, KY. He was drafted into the Army 15 Nov 1945 with basic training at Fort Sill, OK. He was assigned to 7818 SCU at Darmstadt, Germany as warehouse foreman, supervising 350 German civilians in a bakery making bread for Army consumption.

After 11-1/2 months in the ETO, he was discharged at the Separation Center, Fort Dix, NJ. On 5 May 1949 he joined the USN and after boot camp at San Diego, CA was assigned to duty on the USS *Helena* (CA-75) as a deckhand. He later transferred to the Supply Division and was in charge of the spare parts store room.

After a nine month cruise in the South Pacific he received a dependency discharge at San Diego, CA, on 19 Jun 1950; served in the USNR (inactive) for four years, then discharged 19 May 1954.

His decorations include the Army of Occupation Medal, WWII Victory Medal and China Service Medal.

Farmed in early life, was factory worker for 35 years and retired 28 Feb 1940 from Whirlpool Corp., Evansville, IN.

Married Margaret Jane on 28 Feb 1992. He has two daughters, Edythe Maria Banko and Sharon Gay Hull; and one grandson, Parker Alan Hull.

JOHN LYDDALL STREET JR., Lieutenant Colonel, born 6 Aug 1923 in Hopkinsville, KY, son of John L. Street Sr. and Margaret Atkinson Street. After Cadiz Grade School he began his military career in 1937 entering Columbia Military Academy at the age of 14. He then attended ROTC camp at Clemson, SC, qualifying for the commission as second lieutenant and entered Vanderbilt University. When Congress lowered the draft age he entered active duty 28 Nov 1942, and served as a military occupational specialist; designation: Adjutant 2110; Inspector Administrative 2121; Records Officer 2407.

In WWII John participated in the battles and campaigns of Rome-Arno, North Apennines and Southern France.

After enlisting 28 May 1942, he departed for Africa 4 Mar 1943 and landed in Casablanca, Africa 18 Mar 1943. From there he was transferred to Oran, Africa in May 1943; Leghorn, Italy 3 Dec 1944; Caserta, Italy 20 Dec 1944; I.G. HQ Italy, 1 Feb 1945; HQ 7th RD May 1945 and HQ 1st Staging Area B 2 Oct 1945. At the HQ of Mediterranean Base Section, John was a courier with "the mission of safe and speedy transmission of important official communications." He returned to the USA 11 Dec 1945 and was separated at Camp Atterbury, IN and appointed to the Officers Reserve Corp. of the US Army on 17 Dec 1945.

John transferred to the Retired Reserve 12 Nov 1963, Fort Wadsworth, Staten Island, NY. His medals and citations include EAME Service Medals WWII Victory Medal, Bronze Battle Stars for Rome-Arno Campaign, North Apennines, Southern France Campaign and Expert with US Service Pistol Cal. 45.

John returned to Vanderbilt University and graduated in 1949. He went to New York City and worked with The New York Trust

Company, Chemical Bank and Bankers Trust Co. He was a member of the Boards of Trigg County Farmers Bank, Trigg County Insurance Agency and Chairman of the Board of Trigg Bancorp, Inc.

In 1987 John returned to his hometown of Cadiz and restored his Grandmother Street's Victorian house. On returning he served as president of Trigg County Farmers Bank and chairman of its board of directors. His family had a long history with this bank as his Grandfather Street was instrumental in its formation.

John's interest in the arts was evidenced by his presence on the board of directors of the Metropolitan Opera in New York and his support of many arts organizations. Notable among them are Harkness Ballet and Ballet Met. Upon his move to Cadiz he continued his support of the arts by serving on the board of directors of the Janice Mason Art Museum and the Southern Kentucky Independent Theater.

A fascination with Africa prevailed throughout his entire life. He traveled extensively in Africa and supported the Ngare Sergoi Rhino Sanctuary and served on the board of Rhino Ark, both located in Kenya, East Africa.

John's love of literature resulted in the construction of the John L. Street Library, named in honor of his father. John served as president of the Library Board leading it through construction which more than doubled its size in 1998. Upon his death, 7 May 2000, John bequeathed his beloved Main Street home and its furnishings to the Library as a museum. John is buried beside his parents in East End Cemetery in Cadiz.

GERALD B. SUMNER, Aviation Ordnanceman, born 19 Mar 1924 in Trigg County, Cadiz, KY, the son of Chester and Stella Thomas Sumner. He graduated from Trigg County HS in 1942 and was drafted into the Marine Corps 21 Apr 1943, from Akron, OH to San Diego, CA for basic training. Transferred to Norman, OK in June 1943 for tech training to become an aviation ordnanceman for seven months.

He was transferred back to San Diego to be shipped out to the South Pacific. Landed in Bonens Island 10 Jun 1944 and was there for two months. From there to Marshal Islands for 12 months. Back to the States 26 Jun 1945, for 30 day leave. It took 30 days to arrive in San Diego, 26 Jul 1945.

End of the war. Went back to San Diego and from there to North Carolina 1 Oct 1945. Onto Bainbridge, MD for discharge 2 Feb 1946. Married 19 October 1946 to Donna Puckett; they have three children: Roy, Michael and Paula. Gerald retired from Goodyear Tire after 44-1/2 years. He now resides in Akron, OH.

LACEY DAVENPORT SUMNER, Private, HQ Co. 40th Inf. Div., born in Trigg County 2 Mar 1918, the ninth child of William L. and Mary Thomas Sumner. The family moved to Akron, OH after the death of his father in 1925.

The following information was taken from his mother's diary and letters she received. "Lacey left Akron for the Army 24 Jun 1941, he is at Fort Riley, KS."

In a letter dated 10 Aug 1941 to his mother, he tells her things are not as bad as he thought they would be. He had met lots of good men from all over and made several friends who referred to him as Kentucky.

He left the States in April 1943. During the last of 1944 he was on the front lines when he took malaria, and his buddies put him by the side of the road and covered him with their coats. He was picked up and taken to the hospital.

On 15 Feb 1945 his mother received a letter from Lacey that was written 26 January - nearly three months since he last wrote.

After his discharge 27 Nov 1945, Lacey returned home 28 Nov 1945. He started corresponding with a girl he met back home in Kentucky, Marceline Moore. They were married 25 Nov 1950 and had three children: Kenneth Ray (b. 3 Jun 1953, d. 30 May 1991), Allen Lee (b. 7 Nov 1957) and Gerald Lynn (b. 8 May 1964).

Lacey and Marceline moved back to Trigg County in the Fall of 1953 where they made their home. Marceline died 15 Nov 1974 and Lacey three months later on 18 Feb 1975. Allen and Gerald reside in Trigg County. *Submitted by his sons, Allen and Gerald Sumner.*

LAMONT SUMNER, PFC, born 7 Mar 1914 in Cadiz, KY, the son of Calvin and Nora Sumner. He was inducted into the US Army 17 Dec 1942.

He served with the 2nd Bn. 34th Inf. Div. during WWII as a rifleman and sharpshooter. Battles and campaigns he participated in include Po Valley Campaign, North Apennines Campaign, Rome-Arno Campaign.

Lamont received a certificate of disability for discharge on 30 Mar 1946 at Fort Knox, KY. His awards include the Purple Heart (Italy, 1944), Good Conduct Medal and the EAME Theater Medal w/3 Bronze Stars.

He remained single his entire life and lived in the Donaldson Creek Community in Trigg County. He died 15 Feb 1994 and is buried in the Chilton Thomas Cemetery.

JULIAN CLYDE SUMNER JR., Corporal, born 28 Feb 1922 in the Donaldson Creek area of Trigg County, KY. He was inducted into the Army on 3 Nov 1942 at Evansville, IN.

After about a year of training he received orders to report to a replacement battalion in Lehier, France for the 11th Armd. Div. Here he served under Gen. Patton of the 3rd Army, assigned to a scout patrol that consisted of three men: a driver, a gunner and Sumner as the leader. One of his accomplishments was the capturing of a German tank while on patrol with his two comrades. There were only two Germans aboard and they sent them back for interrogation.

Most memorable experience was at the Battle of the Bulge, where they fought long and hard to seize and hold while losing many comrades. Other battles include the Ardennes and Rhineland in Central Europe. They fought off and on until the spring of 1945 when the war ended.

Discharged 15 Jan 1946 at Fort Knox, KY with the rank of corporal. His awards include American Theater w/3 Bronze Service Stars, Good Conduct and WWII Victory Medal.

Returned home to Trigg County where he worked as a timber man and drove a truck until 1959 when he started work for the Kentucky State Hwy. Dept., from where he retired at age 65.

In December 1946 he married Eulala Williams and had four children: Gary (b. 1947), Carl Ray (b. 1949), Cheryl (b. 1953) and Darrell (b. 1955). Eulala died of cancer in 1973 and his daughter Cheryl in 1985 from cancer. He remarried to Hazel McCraw in 1980 who also died of cancer in 1996.

Gary served in the Navy from 1966-70 and Carl Ray in the Army, 1968-70. Gary lives in Amhurst, VA; Carl in Trigg County; and Darrell at Bumpus Mills, TN. Julian lives in Cadiz, KY and has nine grandchildren.

LUTHER T. SUMNER, PFC, born 15 Mar 1924 in Trigg County, the son of William Sumner and Molly Virginia Wilson. He was drafted in the US Army 23 Jan 1945, sent to Camp Atterbury, IN, then on to Georgia for basic training.

From Georgia to Fort Riley, KS to California then overseas 16 months in Luzon and Japan. He was a truck driver with HQ Co., 2nd Bn., 34th Inf. and drove in all kinds of weather over all types of roads. He was also a cook.

Discharged 5 Dec 1946 from Fort Sheridan, IL. After returing home he went to work for Pennyrile Rural Electric for many years. Later, he worked for himself, selling cars.

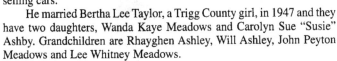

He married Bertha Lee Taylor, a Trigg County girl, in 1947 and they have two daughters, Wanda Kaye Meadows and Carolyn Sue "Susie" Ashby. Grandchildren are Rhayghen Ashley, Will Ashley, John Peyton Meadows and Lee Whitney Meadows.

THOMAS H. SUMNER, Corporal, born 6 Apr 1917 in the Oak Grove neighborhood of Trigg County. He attended Oak Grove Grade School and Cadiz HS and was a farmer.

He was drafted in service October 1942; took his basic training at Camp Polk, LA; was stationed at Camp Barkley, TX and Camp Cook, CA before being sent overseas. While at Camp Barkley, he spent four weeks-on maneuvers at Camp Ibis near Needles, CA.

He was a tank gunner with Co. B, 41st Tank Bn., 11th Armd. Div. and served in Europe from September 1944 to January 1946 when he was discharged with the rank of corporal. He served as a part of General Patton's Third Army as they moved across Europe and was wounded in Belgium in January 1945.

He was awarded the Purple Heart and received three Battle Stars (Rhineland, Ardennes and Central Europe), the American Theater Ribbon, EAME Theater Ribbon and three Bronze Stars.

He was a member of the 11th Armd. Div. Assoc. While serving in Europe in 1945, he spent two enjoyable weeks on furlough in Paris, France.

Following his discharge, he returned to Trigg County where he raised cattle and farmed. Thomas was a member of the Trigg County Post 74 of the American Legion from 1946. He served as post-commander several years; as vice commander and held other offices numerous times. Also he served as State Vice-Commander, District Vice-Commander, and as a delegate to the National Convention in Miami Beach, FL in 1974. He served as a delegate to all State and District conventions since 1956.

He was appointed to the National Law and Order Committee in 1984 and again in 1985; he has been a member of the Hopkinsville Post 1913 of the Veterans of Foreign Wars since 1946 and attended State and District meetings several times.

Thomas was a member of the Oak Grove Baptist Church, Thomas-Bridges Association, Kentucky Dark Fired Tobacco Association and the Kentucky Farm Bureau.

Following an illness of several months, Thomas passed away on 27 Dec 1998, and was buried in the family plot in the Starkie Thomas Cemetery on the Floyd Sumner farm.

HARRY EUGENE TAYLOR, Seaman 1/c, born 27 Nov 1924 in Trigg County, KY. He entered active service 28 Jul 1944 at NRS Louisville, KY.

Vessels and stations served on include Great Lakes, IL; NCTC, Camp Peary, VA; ATB, Camp Bradford, VA; ATB, Fort Pierce, FL; NAB, Little Creek, VA; NTS, Newport, RI; and USS *Taconic* (AGC-17).

Discharged 18 Mar 1946 at Separation Center, Great Lakes, IL. His awards include the American Area Ribbon, WWII Victory Ribbon, Honorable Service USNR Discharge Button and Discharge Button.

Worked as a farmer, factory work and carpenter until retirement in April 1975. Married Delois Jean 1 Aug 1954 and they have two children, John Allen and Lisa Ellen. They currently live in Cadiz, KY.

JULIAN EDWARD TAYLOR, Corporal, born 21 May 1922 in Cadiz, KY. He was drafted into the US Army 30 May 1944. After three months training at Camp Wichita Falls, TX, their company traveled to New Guinea in Asiatic-Pacific Theater.

He served in the Pacific Theater of Operation with the 1539th AAF Base Unit, Air Transport Command for 17 months. He drove semi-trailer and 2-1/2 ton truck in transporting military supplies and personnel. Drove day and night, over all types of terrain, observed military and civilian traffic regulations, convoy rules and road discipline. He made repairs, replacements and adjustments on vehicles. Also drove a 7-1/2 ton wrecker. After

the peace treaty was signed he spent one year in the restoration of Japan.

Discharged 11 Apr 1946, at Camp Atterbury, IN. His decorations include the WWII Victory Medal, Asiatic-Pacific Theater Ribbon w/ Bronze Star and Good Conduct Medal.

Civilian activity: Tube Turns, Louisville, KY. Married Mary Elizabeth Dunnagan 24 Apr 1943 and had two children and three grandchildren: Kevin Shellie and Kelly Hendricks. Julian passed away 10 Oct 1980.

GEORGE E. TERRELL, Allow me to take time to look back at history's calendar as I lead up to my entry into the military service of our country and how it changed our lives. It is important to historians, family members and the public to know the many fascinating. as well as, devastating stories. These are my experiences in WWII.

In the Fall of 1941, war was raging in Europe and I was following its progression. On 7 Dec 1941, I was in Princeton, KY on a date with my future wife (Gladys Opal Gray) when her father (Mr. Bentley M. Gray) came out on the front porch and announced that Japan had bombed Pearl Harbor in Hawaii. That hit me very hard. We were all devastated. I turned to him and said. "They will be looking for me." Later that same evening when I reached home my parents and I had a long conversation. My mother said, "Do not volunteer just yet." Reluctantly, I promised her I would not but knew, many of my friends would.

The draft had not yet been instituted, but, I knew that I had an obligation and I knew what I had to do. The next morning at breakfast there was silence. My brother Robert and I talked about the bombing of Pearl Harbor. I spoke up and said, "no use talking about it, I am going and you are staying." I had already been away from home off and on since 1939, so, I wanted no arguments.

They knew I was going to serve my country. I was drafted and reported to the county seat for a trip to Evansville, IN for a military physical. Passing without any trouble, I came home for one week, then it was time to go. The morning I was to leave I asked my mom and dad not to come see me off because I didn't want them to cry. We departed for Camp Atterbury, IN. Three (3) days later I was an official GI and on a troop train headed west. Our first stop was Tuscon, AZ where I joined up with the 8th Air Force. The next stop was the Mojave Desert in California for basic training, then onto Stockton, CA for more transition and onward to an air base at Camp Pendleton, OR.

We arrived late in the night and were assigned our barracks. Upon entering the barracks and preparing for the nights sleep. I turned down the mattress and what did I see under it, *The Cadiz Record,* my hometown newspaper with the name Mr. Toppy Edwards on it (who still resides in Cadiz, KY). That old cliche, "It's a small world" never rang more true. From Pendleton, OR we went back to Stockton, CA for more training then back to Pendleton, OR the second time for a short stay. Then from Pendleton, OR to Sioux City, IA.

Next we went to Camp Kilmer, NJ, boarded a ferry for New York Harbor and went aboard a ship late at night. Crossing the Atlantic Ocean was an experience I will never forget. There were ships of all kinds and sizes as far as the eye could see. An armada unparalleled in history en route for England with America's best resources of men, materials and determination to protect our allies, our loved ones. homeland and the very heart of freedom itself—our democracy. Ten days later we were on a train bound for Flixton Air Base, Bungay, England, Station 125, the 446th Bomb Group flying the magnificent B-24 Liberators. This was home for the duration of the ETO (European Theatre of Operations).

On this tour of duty there was lots of sweat, loss of sleep, loss of many friends, planes and many terrible accidents. The sounds of air raids, Buzz Bombs and dogfights in the night air with search lights on the action is still fresh in my memory. There were 58 aircraft lost, 410+ men killed in action, many captured and interned in camps as prisoners of war after being shot down by enemy aircraft and ground fire. Indeed-war is HELL"

To all the ground troops in every branch of service, the Army, Navy, Air Force, Marines as well as all the others who took the brunt of the war, I stand and salute each and every one of you for giving so much, your dedication, sacrificing your families, loved ones and for many, your life. It's a privilege and honor to have served by your side.

We came home in July 1945, on the ship *The Queen Mary* for a 30 day leave and were to go directly to the Pacific, but Japan surrendered. Next, I reported to Sioux Falls, SD where I awaited my discharge on points. Do you remember the point system? And who could ever forget the "Ruptured Duck?"

This is but a small part of my story of the war; so, no bragging, no lying, no trying to impress anybody. I am proud to say I am a veteran of World War from Trigg County, KY and do not regret one single day of effort I gave to preserve these great United States of America.

He is authorized to wear the following ribbons: EAME Theater, Bronze Star to ETO Ribbon, Normandy Campaign, Northern France Campaign, Ardennes-Alsace, Rhineland, Central Europe and Southern France.

DALLIE B. THOMAS JR.,

born 8 Feb 1923 in the Donaldson Creek Community. His parents were the late Dallie B. Sr. and Ollie Downs Thomas. He enlisted in the Army and served from 26 Jan 1943 to 15 Dec 1945. He spent 11 months in the northern Solomons and other South Pacific Islands.

He had an ankle injury while in the South Pacific and was returned to the States for medical treatment. His awards include the Bronze Star, Good Conduct and WWII Victory Medal.

Married Lucille Gardner in May 1945

and had three children: Michael, Sharon and Janice. He moved his family to Colorado Springs, CO in 1950. He passed away in October 1982 and was returned to Cadiz for burial at East End Cemetery.

EDISON HUGH THOMAS, born 5 Jun 1912 in the Donaldson Creek Community of Trigg County, KY, the youngest of three children of Robert H. and Ora Bridges Thomas.

He was assistant editor and business manager of *The Cadiz Record* when the Japanese bombed Pearl Harbor 7 Dec 1941. He volunteered for service in the USN 14 Apr 1942. After basic training at the USN Training Station, San Diego, CA, duty assignments included Navy Yard, Bremerton, WA; ship's company, Naval Training Station, Farragut, ID; Acorn Gropac Pool, Port Hueneme, CA, San Nicholas Island; Ulithi Atoll in the Carolines; and the islands of Palawan, Samar and Luzon in the Philippines. In Spring of 1945, he was assigned to the USN Air Base at Cavite, on Manila Bay, in preparation for the invasion of Japan.

He describes it this way: "We were bringing in tons of supplies, thousands of ships, planes and men. Preparing to invade Japan. We had never heard of the atomic bomb, but when word came that one had been dropped on Hiroshima, and the end of the war was near, there was quiet a celebration. Some people today complain that the atomic bomb should never have been dropped. I certainly don't have any regrets. Our outfit would have been among the first wave in the attempt to invade Japan, and loss of American lives would have been appalling."

Edison was honorably discharged 14 Oct 1945 and resumed work as a journalist, first with the Louisville *Courier-Journal,* then later, with the Public Relations department of the Louisville & Nashville Railroad (now part of the CSX System) from which he retired in 1977. A professional writer, he is author of three books, *The Thomas & Bridges Story, John Hunt Morgan and His Raiders,* and *A Letter to Our Children.* An ongoing project is The Thomas-Bridges Association, a family oriented group which he helped organize, and for which he has edited The *TBA Newsletter* for the past 30 years.

His wife of 45 years, the former Thelma Waits Garrett, died 8 Feb 2001. Their family includes four children, 11 grandchildren and nine great-grandchildren. He lives in Louisville, KY.

GUY C. THOMAS, F1/c, born in Cadiz, KY on 12 Sep 1924. His parents are Myrtle Green (Chewning) and John Taylor Thomas. Guy entered the USN in Akron, OH on 7 Apr 1943.

His ranks included AS, S2/c, F2/c, F2/c, F1/c. He attended Diesel School in San Diego, CA and recruit training at Great Lakes, IL. He served at NTS, Great Lakes, IL; San Diego Recruit Depot, San Diego, SRU Affirm, USS *Bushell* (USS Columbia Cl-56), USS B. Navy #128, Sub Division, 45 Relief Crew (USS *Snapper*). He was honorably discharged from the Navy and went to work in Akron, OH at the B.F. Goodrich plant. He then moved to Colorado Springs, CO and worked as a Bellhop prior to joining the USMC (USMC).

He re-enlisted at Denver, CO into the USMC and continued his service career until his retirement in San Diego, CA, on 1 Jun 1965. During his tours of duty, he participated in the Wonsan-Hungnam Chosin Campaign, and was awarded the Presidential Unit Citation for extraordinary heroism in action against armed enemy. He also served in North Korea from 28 Oct 1950 to 4 Dec 1950; participated in the capture and securing of Seoul, Korea, from 21 Sep 1950 to 7 Oct 1950. He received Good Conduct Medal period commendes 29 Nov 1950 toward 1st bar; Issued Certificate of Satisfactory Service; PEBD 11 Apr 1945.

He was married to Carleen (Kocurek) Thomas on 21 Sep 1952 and they were blessed with two daughters, Reva Yvonne Thomas and Vicki Louise Thomas. Guy Thomas passed away on 27 Jun 1966 from lung cancer.

HERSCHEL JEFFERSON THOMAS, PFC, born 7 Nov 1915 on Donaldson Creek, Trigg County, KY. He was drafted into the US Army 13 Jan 1943 at Cadiz, KY. After basic training at Camp Grant, IL, he was assigned to the 34th Field Hospital at Camp Cook, CA. Soon his unit boarded a troop train for a trans-continental trip to New York, a trip that took one week.

At New York he boarded a ship, one of many in a convoy transporting troops to the European Theater of action. While in the Mediterranean, the convoy was attacked by the Nazis. Although his ship wasn't hit, one of their supply ships was sunk.

After landing in Bizerta, Tunisia, North Africa, the US 5th Army was united with the British 8th Army and was transported to Italy. Interestingly enough, his transport craft was a LSD made in Evansville, IN. In Italy the 5th Army established headquarters in an existing building that was immediately behind the front lines of combat. Here many casualties were treated and transferred to hospital ships destined for the States. Fatalities were identified (when possible) and buried in a temporary cemetery near the compound.

As the war in Europe was winding down, there was an opportunity for R&R. It was on a trip to Rome that by chance, Thomas came into contact with famed War Correspondent, Ted Malone, who interviewed him and the radio broadcast was aired back in the States.

After two years in Italy the war in Europe ended and the 5th Army was shipped to the Pacific to join forces against the Japanese. Thomas, along with 3,000 other troops, boarded a transport for the long voyage across the Atlantic to the Pacific via the Panama Canal and on to New Guinea for supplies before landing in the Philippines. Here he recalls the most awesome display of military power that could be imagined. All units were alerted for the invasion of Japan when President Harry Truman ordered the use of the Atomic Bomb which brought the end of WWII.

Finally, he headed for the States. Thomas remembers Christmas dinner in 1945 at sea. After landing in San Francisco, he was returned to Fort Knox, KY where he was discharged as a private first class on 13 Jan 1946.

After discharge he returned to his pre-war job with Goodyear Rubber Co. in Akron, OH, where he was employed until retirement in 1978. After retiring he returned to Cadiz where he has enjoyed over 20 years of gardening, fishing and associating with old friends of long ago. His wife of 62 years, the former Sudie Ricks, passed away in October 2000.

GEORGE PRENTICE "G.P." THOMAS Jr., PFC, born 13 Oct 1914, son of George Prentice Thomas Sr. and Annie Meacheam of Cadiz and Trigg County. George Sr. was a prominent lawyer in Cadiz and was the State House Representative at one time and also a postmaster. He owned a large farm in the Bethel neighborhood.

George Jr. graduated from Cadiz HS in the Class of 1932 and attended Murray College, Murray, KY. He was a member of the Cadiz Methodist Church. He was inducted into the USAF 2 May 1942, at Fort Benjamin Harrison, IN. His military occupation is listed as Air Plane Propeller Mechanic 687, AAF Tech Badge with Airplane Mechanic Bar Carbine Marksman. His decorations and citations were American Theater Ribbon, Good Conduct Medal and WWII Victory Medal. G.P. was discharged 10 Dec 1945, at Patterson Field, OH.

George Jr. never married. He died 25 Sep 1978 and is buried in the family plot in East End Cemetery, Cadiz, KY.

HOWARD RANSON THOMAS JR., Tech Sergeant, born 3 Oct 1922 in Trigg County, KY (Bethel neighborhood on his grandmother's farm, the homeplace). His parents were Howard R. and Ruth (Hulse) Thomas. He attended grade school in Cadiz and Bethel and started high school at Trigg County High then moved to Cumberland County and finished at Burkesville HS graduating in 1940.

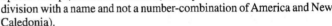

He joined the Army at Fort Knox, KY on 24 Oct 1940. After the War started in 1941 he was sent overseas to the South Pacific serving in the Philippine Islands, Guadalcanal, Northern Solomons in HQ Special Troops, Americal Division (the only division with a name and not a number-combination of America and New Caledonia).

He received the Asiatic-Pacific Theatre Ribbon w/3 Bronze Stars, American Defense Service Medal, Philippine Liberation Ribbon w/Bronze Star), Good Conduct Ribbon, and the Combat Infantryman Badge. He returned to the States 12 Apr 1945 and was discharged 31 May 1945 as a technical sergeant having served three years two months and 20 days overseas for a total of four years, seven months and eight days active service.

On 27 Jun 1945 he married his "Pen Pal" (Evelye Mae Johnson) that he had been corresponding with and they were together until his death 14 May 1996, having celebrated their 50th anniversary the previous year. They had four boys and two girls: Howard Ranson III, John Dwaine, Ruth Elaine, Richard Jay, James Robert and Mary Kay. There is a marker for Howard R. Thomas Jr. in the Bethel Church Cemetery placed by his children.

The following poem was written by (Chaplin) Maj. Arthur F. Weaver and submitted by Howard Ransom Thomas Jr. - Maj. Weaver was assigned to HQ, 37th AAA Gun Battalion in Japan and was with the 24th US Inf. Div. in Korea. This poem was printed in the 31 May 1951 issue of the Army "Stars & Stripes" newspaper.

IN MEMORIAM

Softly step, my comrades, softly
In this bivouac of the dead;
Disturb not their peaceful slumbers
With the pulse of martial tread,
These, our fathers, uncles, brothers,
Cousins, and perhaps a son—
Sleep the deep sleep of the weary
And their marching days are done.

Concord, Lexington, and West Point,
Valley Forge, and Bunker Hill
Saratoga too, and Yorktown—
Honored heroes, sleeping still!
Call the roll in gentle whisper;
Rouse them not 'till that great morn
When the battlefields, and oceans
Open up at Gabriel's horn
(This poem has six more verses)

JOHN ALEX THOMAS, Tech 5, born 20 Jun 1907 in the Oak Grove Community of Trigg County. He attended Oak Grove grade school, Cadiz HS and graduated in 1927.

He was drafted into the Army 18 Nov 1942 and served with Co. E, 351st Engineers until his discharge. He took basic training at Fort Lewis, WA before being sent overseas where he served two years in the European Theater. He received Battle Stars for Northern France, Rhineland, and Ardennes. He was discharged from the Army 20 Sep 1945 with the rank of Tech 5 at Camp Atterbury, IN. He was given $14.85 travel pay to return to Trigg County.

He was a member of the Oak Grove Baptist Church, Cadiz HS Alumni Association, Thomas-Bridges Association, Woodman of the World and the Farm Bureau.

On 13 Aug 1949 in Hopkinsville, he married the former Louise Sumner who was a teacher in the Trigg County School System for 37 years. They bought a farm where they lived and he continued to farm until his health failed. Following an illness of several months, he passed away 22 Dec 1982. He was buried in the Starkie Thomas Cemetery on the Floyd Sumner farm.

Louise, who suffered a massive stroke 13 Sep 1978, continues to live in their home.

JOHN J. THOMAS, Tech 5, born 27 Dec 1919, in Donaldson Creek Community, Trigg County, KY, son of Jim and Palestine Futrell Thomas. His brothers were Claude, Ruba, Hervey; sisters: Hazel T. Oliver, Adell T. Skinner and Meda T. Burcham; two half sisters, Lona Thomas Skinner and Ollie Thomas Taylor; one half brother, Albert Thomas.

He was inducted into military service 26 Aug 1942 and entered active service 9 Sep 1942, Evansville, IN. Assigned to 615th Ordnance Ammunition Company with MOS: Maintenance 833 artillery mechanic, antiaircraft minor. Participated in action at New Guinea and Luzon. John remembers his ship being bombed and shelled by suicide divers as they were going from New Guinea to the Philippines. He saw one ship with 150 men on board being blown up.

He was given an honorable discharge on 6 Jan 1946, Separation Center, Fort Knox, KY. Decorations and citations include Asiatic-Pacific Theater Ribbon w/2 Bronze Stars, Philippine Liberation Ribbon w/Bronze Stars, Good Conduct Medal and WWII Victory Medal.

He returned to Trigg County and worked as a laborer. John and Kathleen Burcham were married 26 Mar 1946. They have one son Paul (b. 3 Nov 1949). He is married to Bonnie Adams and they have a son, John Paul.

John retired from TVA in 1983. He is an avid hunter and was a member of Trigg County Fox Hunters Association. John and wife Kathleen live on Donaldson Creek Road, Trigg County, next door to their son and his family. They are members of Donaldson Creek Baptist Church.

JOHN R. THOMAS, Chief Boatswain's Mate, born 15 Nov 1919, raised in the Canton area of Trigg County. Graduated with the first class at Trigg County High in 1938. Entered the Navy in 1939 and was discharged as chief boatswain's mate in December 1945.

He is a survivor from the battleship USS *Oklahoma*, which was sunk at Pearl Harbor by forces of the Imperial Japanese Naval Forces, 7 Dec 1941, the "Day of Infamy." The USN suffered the greatest defeat in its history. Moral was low, but once we realized the American public rallied be-

hind us, we started looking west toward Tokyo. Victory would be many months away as we had to build a new Army and Navy. We never looked back. The attack on Pearl Harbor will never fade from our memory.

After Pearl Harbor, he was assigned temporary duty aboard the aircraft carrier USS *Enterprise*, then transferred to the South Pacific Theatre and became part of the Amphibian Invasion forces making many (12) invasions on islands that he had never heard of and unknown to most Americans. The major invasions consisted of the Solomon Islands, where nightly air raids and naval engagements from the Japanese based 300 miles to the north at Rabaul became routine. More than 90 Man-O-War ships were sunk by the forces of Japan and the United States.

The Solomon Island Campaign was one of the longest and costly operations of the Pacific Theatre. Japan's march toward Australia and New Zealand had to be stopped. This invasion was followed by Bouganville, Saipan, Guam, Leyte, Luzon, and smaller islands. His final major invasion was Iwo Jima. Their ship then loaded troops and equipment for the invasion of Okinawa. During their practice rehearsal, the ship developed major problems, the reduction gears, forcing them to unload and limp back to the States for repairs.

From his six years of service, five Christmas Days were spent overseas, and in 1941 he had no Christmas Day as the ship crossed the International Date line on the night of 24 December therefore the next day was the day after Christmas.

Like most Veterans stationed overseas, the days were long hard, cold or hot, but as he looks back today, he realizes those were the most precious days of his life. He was trying to maintain freedom for his country. His awards include the American Defense, WWII Victory Medal, Philippine Liberation, Asiatic-Pacific w/9 stars, China Theater and others.

He has not been a resident of Trigg County since 1939, but he will always call it home. May God bless America and may America remember Pearl Harbor.

LACY CLINTON THOMAS, born 15 Sep 1918, the son of Lilburn Clinton Thomas and Verna Mae (Herndon) Thomas. He entered the US Army during WWII and served with the 46th Medical Depot in the European Theater of War. He served with the unit from 1944-1946.

He married Dannie Merle (Sanders) on 24 Dec 1937. Their children are Joseph Lilburn, Lacy Leroy, Virginia Ruth Combs Stearman, and Danny Hale. Today the Thomas family resides in Hopkinsville, KY. *Submitted by Mrs. Lacy C. Thomas.*

LINDSAY D. THOMAS, GM1/c, born 25 Oct 1911 in the Pleasant Hill Community of what today is the Land Between the Lakes in Trigg County, KY. His parents were the late Edd Clark and Gustie Carr Thomas. He had two sisters, Edna Lucille (Thomas) Sumner, and Ambie Marie Thomas, who died in her teens. His parents later moved to the Donaldson Creek Community in Trigg County where he spent his formative years. He never married.

In 1942, during the early stages of WWII, Lindsay enlisted in the USN as a gunner's mate. He was assigned to the Navy Air Force and sent to the South Pacific where he was immediately involved in several major battles against the Japanese.

In 1945 Lindsay returned to the States and was assigned to the USN Air Station at Whidbey Island in Puget Sound, north of Seattle, WA. On

14 Feb 1945, during a night practice flight the plane in which he was a crew member, crashed into the side of a mountain in the Cascade Range. Lindsay and all members of the eight man crew were killed. Individual identification of each man was not possible, so all eight men were buried in four caskets (in a row with one large monument with all eight names) in the Golden Gate National Cemetery, San Bruno, CA.

Lindsay was a fun loving person, a talented guitar player and loved to sing country-western songs. He lived a very carefree life and at one time or another had been a waiter, cook, gold miner and partner in a restaurant. He was living in Cripple Creek, CO when he enlisted in the Navy. At the time of his death, he held the rank of gunner's mate first class.

A memorial marker in his honor is located in the Peyton Thomas Cemetery on Donaldson Creek Road in Trigg County near the graves of his parents.

MARGRET THOMAS, born 31 Dec 1923 in Trigg County, daughter of Albert and Owen Thomas. She served in the Army and is believed to have been a WAC in the 1940s.

In 1954 she married Harry McKeel in New York and they have two children, Myra and Thomas. *Submitted by Jane Thomas Braboy.*

ROBERT EARL THOMAS, Sergeant, born on 17 Nov 1926 in Cadiz, KY, son of Howard R. and Ruth B. (Hulse) Thomas. He attended kindergarten in Cadiz, grade schools at Bethel in Trigg County and Burkesville, KY. He attended high school at Burkesville for half the freshman year, then at Trigg County High where he graduated in May 1944.

He entered service 21 Jun 1945 and was discharged 24 Sep 1945 to re-enlist in the regular army 25 Sep 1945 (WWII was over and he enlisted to receive four years of the GI Bill). He served in the MP Unit at Camp Campbell, KY until sent overseas on 23 Mar 1946 and was stationed in Yokohama, Japan with Co. C, 519th MP Battalion 8th Army. He served in the MPs for a year and was promoted to sergeant and later transferred to the 44th CID Unit, 8th Army in Yokohama as a special agent until he returned to the States and was honorably discharged 5 Jul 1948.

He entered Western Kentucky State College in January 1949 until 11 Sep 1950 when he was recalled from the enlisted reserve for duty in Korea. He was sent overseas in December 1950 arriving in Korea in January 1951 assigned to B Co. 728th MP Battalion, 8th Army. Duties were road patrol, traffic directing on roads and one way mountain passes plus giving convoys priority to the front.

Received the WWII Victory Medal, Army of Occupation Japan Medal, Korean Service Medal w/3 Bronze Stars, one Chevron on sleeve for three years service, six overseas bars on sleeve for 36 months overseas service. He was discharged to inactive reserve on 25 Sep 1951.

Returned to college in 1952 and received a bachelor's degree in physics in 1954. In 1952 while in college he suffered an attack of malaria and was admitted to Trigg County Hospital for a week until the disease was diagnosed. He had contracted malaria while in Korea the previous year.

He was married 18 Dec 1961 to Dorris (Ellis) McAleer (died 9 Dec 1991). There were two children of Dorris's previous marriage adopted by Robert (Teresa McAleer and Jimmy Lee McAleer) and one child born to Robert and Dorris (Mitzi Deeneen Thomas). On 28 Aug 1994 Robert E. Thomas and Mrs. Virgie Louise (Jones) Webb were married and his son, Jimmie Lee Thomas, was his best man.

WILFORD ALLEN THOMAS, Corporal, born 6 Jul 1921, Trigg County, KY to Ted and Beulah Sumner Thomas. Enlisted with the US Army 26 Aug 1942 at Evansville, IN, with the military occupation of auto equipment mechanic, where he received the motor vehicle driver award.

He served in Rhineland with the rank of corporal and was decorated with the EAME Medal and Good Conduct Medal on 25 Mar 1944. He received an Honorable Discharge after serving continental service for one year, one month and 12 days, and foreign service for two years and 11 days.

After returning home he married Vonnie Lorene Wallace Thomas, 10 Aug 1947 and they have two children, Brenda Thomas Sholar and Gary Allen Thomas. Their grandchildren are Ken Allen Thomas, Brian Lindsey Thomas, Christopher Scott Sholar and Matthew Ted Sholar and great-grandchildren are Evan Allen Thomas, Joshua Larrabee and Thomas Carter Sholar.

Wilford enjoyed attending Donaldson Creek Baptist Church where he served as Sunday School Director. He also enjoyed cattle farming and gardening. He was a truck driver by trade and also operated a county store at Roaring Springs and later the Ted Thomas Grocery in the Maggie Community on State Highway 139 South. He later worked with the Kentucky Department of Transportation as a truck driver.

He died 19 Jul 1978 of an apparent heart attack.

WILLIAM HARDIN THOMAS, born 7 Jul 1907, was the son of John Q. Thomas and Catherine (Broff) Thomas. John Q. was a well-known farmer of the Bethel neighborhood and "Miss Cattie" was a school teacher in Trigg County.

During WWII, Hardin Thomas was drafted into the Navy for two years of active service, stationed at Baltimore, MD.

In civilian life, Hardin Thomas and his first wife, Geraldine Atkins, lived in a house that he and his brother Howard built at the intersection of the South Road (KY 139 and KY 272). He also built a building to work on cars as a mechanic. When he and his wife divorced, he sold the property. There were no children.

After his discharge from service Harden lived in Louisville, KY. He was married a second time to Elsa Carolyn Hoyt (b. 28 Dec 1926). There were two children, William Edwin (never married) and Perry Hardin who married Jacqueline Ruth Rich. The three grandchildren are Stacy Marie, Michael Perry and Stephanie Carolyn. Hardin was again divorced and continued to live for sometime in Louisville. He is now living in Shady Lawn Nursing Home in Cadiz, KY.

HOWARD WALLACE TINSLEY, PFC, born 10 Dec 1919 in Cadiz, KY. He was drafted into the US Army, 16 Oct 1941. After three months of training at Camp Wheeler, GA, he and his unit, the 34th Inf. 168th Regt., 3rd BN, Co. L, traveled to Bel Fast, Ireland where they received advanced amphibious infantry training.

On 8 November they made an amphibious landing on the North African shores. After 16 days of fighting, they were taken prisoner of

war. Later the Germans would transport 54 of the POWs to a camp approximately 60 miles from Berlin.

Tinsley still recalls 12 Feb 1945 when the Russian air force was bombing all around and they hid where ever they could. Before daylight the Germans lined them up in about three feet of snow and put them on a road march to keep them from being liberated.

By the time, Tinsley was marched into a town called Bitterfield and liberated, he had spent 800 days, three hours and 45 minutes as a Prisoner of War.

He remembers 26 April as if it were yesterday. "We entered the town of Bitterfield, and saw white flags hanging from every window and every building. I'll never forget my first sight of the 104th Inf. There they were, an American officer, a sergeant driving, and a gunner on the back of the jeep coming toward us."

When Tinsley went "in behind the barbed wire," he weighed 180 pounds. He weighed 95 pounds the day he was liberated. During his 800 days as a POW, he had no shoes, no socks, he hadn't had a bath or cut his hair.

He had not notified anyone in Trigg County that he was liberated or on his way home. Where Integra Bank sits now, a drug store and the bus stop were located. "I got off the bus with three duffel bags full of clothes. I started dragging them across the street, so I could get to a phone to call home."

"I heard breaks screaming I looked up, it was the sheriff, Charlie Humphries. I will never forget his 1941 Mercury convertible. He had that car when I left in '41. He jumped out, ran to me, and said, 'you know I wouldn't take ten thousand dollars for this.'

"He had told my dad when I got back he would bring me home, He drove me out there. He wouldn't even get out, he just unloaded my bags and put me out. My mother saw me through the front door and ran to the gate. About a week later they had a big barbecue on my dad's farm. I think half of the county came."

When he got out of the service his rank was private first class. He received back pay dating from November 1942 through July 1945. He also received the POW Medal and three Battle Stars for the Algerian, French Moroccan, Tanisa and Caserina Pass Campaigns.

He married a Trigg County girl, Elizabeth Grasty, on 18 May 1946. Over the years he worked at several different jobs. ultimately retiring from TVA in 1982.

Today, at 81 years he and Elizabeth reside comfortably outside the city of Cadiz on Hwy. 274. They go to Cadiz Baptist Church. Howard was named Grand Marshall of the 2000 Trigg County Veterans Day parade. He led the parade proudly, raising, the American Flag as he rode down Main Street on the back of Dale Ezell's motorcycle, thankful for the freedom for which he had fought.

ROY EDWARD TINSLEY, PFC, born 4 Dec 1921 in Cadiz, KY. He was drafted into the US Army 12 Jul 1942 and after six weeks training at Camp Wallace, TX, he and his unit, Btry. B 746th AAA Geen Bn., traveled to the Northern Solomons and Philippine Islands.

He was a gunner and part-time cook when he was stationed on Bougainville. The Japanese had their unit surrounded so they couldn't receive food to cook. Roy killed one of the native cows so they could have food. That was the wrong thing to do and he lost his corporal rank and became a private first class again.

He received the Asiatic-Pacific Theater Ribbon w/5 Bronze Stars and a Philippine Liberation Ribbon w/Bronze Star, Artillery Bar, Rifle Bar, Bayonet Bar and Good Conduct Ribbon.

Roy married Ruby Dean Sumner on 27 Jun 1945. They have one daughter Glenda Faye Doss and one grandson, Michael Roy Wagner. Glenda lives in Indianapolis, IN and Michael in Dallas, TX.

Roy and his brother Howard Tinsley returned to the States a few days apart. Their father and mother had a barbecue supper for them, and so many people attended that they had to park their cars in the pasture with the cows. It was a happy time for everyone.

Roy received his honorable discharge at Camp Atterbury, IN on 4 Oct 1945. He worked at a grocery store until 1950, then started to work for Pennyrile Rural Electric until his death in August 1983.

He was a Mason, Shriner and a member of East Cadiz Baptist Church. His widow resides on 3rd Street in Cadiz, KY.

JAMES E. "JIM" TIPPIN, PO2/c, born 24 May 1921 in Bloomville, OH, the son of James Tippin and Lydia Lucas Tippin. He enlisted in the USN at Toledo, OH, on 15 Nov 1942. Basic training began at Great Lakes, IL. After completing basic training, James attended Navy School at Great Lakes, then to Dearborn, MI for further schooling. The next location was Floating Drydock Training Center at Tiburon, CA. He left for active duty in December 1942 and was shipped out on the USS ABSD4. His assignment was the South Pacific Theater of War. For three years, James was in this area. His most memorable experience was being torpedoed by the enemy.

James was awarded four ribbons for his accomplishments in the Navy; his ranks were AS, S2/c, F2/c, Fl/c, MM3/c, MaM3/c. At the end of the war, James was returned to the USA and received an honorable discharge at the USN Separation Center, St. Louis, MO, 20 Dec 1945. His rank was petty officer 2nd class. His very happy experience was, "arriving home, 21 Dec 1945, just four days before Christmas."

Returning to civilian life, James used his GI Bill to attend Tiffin University and graduated with an associate degree in accounting. He worked briefly as an accountant, but salesmanship was what he enjoyed. His career in salesmanship continued until he retired from Sears in Greenwood, IN, 1 Jul 1983. In retirement James enjoys hunting, fishing, visiting and taking it easy at Rockcastle Road in Cadiz.

He married Buannah Reiter on 9 Mar 1941. There are two children, Daryl E. Tippin and Richard "Rick" Tippin; five grandchildren: Shane, Joshua, Jenna, Kyle and Stacey; and two great-grandchildren, Kyle and Taylor. *Submitted by James E. Tippin.*

GROVER CLEVELAND TOWLER JR., Staff Sergeant, born 30 Jun 1918 in Gracey, KY in the Montgomery Community, the son of Grover and Kate Bagby Towler. He graduated from Cadiz HS in May 1937 and went to work in the shoe dept. at J.C. Penney, Hopkinsville, KY.

He entered the US Army 4 Sep 1941 and saw action in the southern Philippines, New Guinea and Bismarck Archipelago.

SSgt. Towler received an honorable discharge 15 Dec 1944. He re-entered the Army 24 Oct 1950 at Fort Campbell, KY for the Korean Conflict. Separated the second time at Camp Breckinridge, KY, 15 Oct 1951.

His WWII and Korean War decorations include the Asiatic-Pacific Theater Ribbon w/2 Bronze Stars, American Defense Service Medal, Philippine Liberation Ribbon w/2 Bronze Stars, Purple Heart for wound received at New Guinea and the Korean Service Medal w/Bronze Star.

As a civilian he was an agent with Metropolitan Insurance. Married Beuton Campbell 18 Oct 1946 and had two children, Patricia Ann Towler Lockwood (deceased 1993) and Grover Cleveland III.

DENNIS MOORE TUGGLE, born 6 Nov 1923, son of Norris Huel and Emma Maude Randolph. He lived in the Tuggleville Community with his parents and siblings: Raymond Cress, Layton Carl and Mabel Evelyn Tuggle.

His education consisted of grade schools in Trigg County and high School at Trigg County High, Cadiz, KY.

He joined the USN in 1940 and was stationed at Corpus Christie, TX for a number of years.

After an honorable dismissal, he lived and worked in Evansville, IN, where he retired in 1988.

He and his wife Sharon continue to live in Evansville where she is retired as a high school English teacher.

LAYTON CARL TUGGLE, Lieutenant Colonel, born 19 Aug 1921 at their farm home in Tuggleville, approximately eight miles outside of Cadiz, KY. Layton had two brothers, Raymond and Dennis, and one sister Mabel Evelyn.

Before entering Trigg County HS, Layton attended New Hope Elementary for eight years and Roaring Springs HS for two years. He went to Western State Teachers College in Bowling Green, KY before entering the USAAC during WWII. He was commissioned as a navigator of a B-24 and sent to Italy. On his 9th mission his plane was shot down over Austria. Layton and his crew bailed out and all survived; however, Layton was injured due to a damaged parachute which failed to open fully.

He and his crew were taken captive by the Chetniks who gave them to the Germans. He spent 11 months as a POW at Stalag Luft III in Germany. After a lengthy, cold and dangerous march through a nearly defeated Germany, Layton the other POWs were liberated by Gen. Patton. He received a Purple Heart.

After the war Layton completed his education at the University of Kentucky where he earned a degree in electrical engineering. He worked for Shell Oil in Houston, TX for a number of years.

During the Korean War, Layton was stationed at Ellington Field, near Houston, where he served as a navigational instructor. As an active reservist, he also flew several combat missions during the Vietnam War. He retired as a lieutenant colonel.

Layton married Phyllis A. Griffin in 1944 and they had four children: Kathy, Suzanne, Carl and Mary. Layton passed away 17 Mar 2000 and is buried in the Veterans Cemetery in Houston, TX. *Submitted by Phyllis A. Tuggle.*

RAYMOND CRESS TUGGLE, Ensign, born 6 Sep 1911 in Trigg County, KY to Norris Huel and Emma Maude Randolph Tuggle. He grew up on the farm with his parents and siblings, Mabel Evelyn, Layton Carl and Dennis Moore Tuggle.

His education consisted of completing grade school in the Tuggleville Community, high school at Cadiz, KY, and earned a bachelor of arts degree at Western Teachers College, Bowling Green, KY.

He taught industrial arts in Paducah, KY, before joining the Armed Forces during WWII, serving in the USN, Hawaii, as an ensign.

After the war he worked with the Federal Bureau of Roads and lived in Washington, DC, Columbus, OH and Madison, WI.

Mildred Hopson was his wife and their two children were Donald Ray and Ann Elizabeth Tuggle, who gave them three grandchildren. They always loved Trigg County where they visited relatives and friends on every vacation they had.

Both Raymond and Mildred are deceased and buried at Madison, WI, their homeplace of many years.

ALPHIS FRANKLIN TURNER, Private, born 14 Dec 1920 in Golden Pond, KY. He was inducted into the US Army, 29 Nov 1944, as a private. After five months of training at Fort Sill, OK, he received orders to report to AGF Repl Depot No. 1 Fort George G. Meade, MD on 13 May 1945, for assignment for overseas duty.

In June he traveled by rail to California to board a ship and sailed 28 Jun 1945, destination Asiatic-Pacific Theater, arrived there 22 Jul 1945 and served as gun crewman heavy artillery with the 7th Calvary for six months and 29 days.

Returned to the States 26 Jan 1946 and was discharged 2 Feb 1946 as a private first class at Camp Atterbury, IN. He was awarded the Asiatic-Pacific Theater Ribbon, Phillippines Liberation Ribbon, Good Conduct Ribbon, and the Victory Medal.

Memorable experience was seeing the devastation done to Japan after the Atomic Bomb was dropped.

After his return from service, he returned to work at LaSalle Steel Company, Hammond, IN, as an electric bridge crane operator for 34 years, retiring in January 1983.

He was married to Rosa Therecia Hendon 20 Nov 1938. Four children were born to this union: Genievee; Jeanetta; Frank Jr. and Betty Ann. They have 12 grandchildren and 18 great-grandchildren.

After living in Hammond, IN, for 30 years, Frank purchased 10 acres of land and had a house built in St. John Township, Crown Point, IN, where they have lived since October 1972. At 80 years of age Frank still plants a huge garden and is also a bee-keeper. Frank and Rosa are members of Community Baptist Church in St. John, IN, where he serves as a deacon.

HARVEY AMOS TURNER, Sergeant, born 5 Mar 1917 in Trigg County. He joined the military 20 Jul 1942 in Cadiz, KY and served with the 1090th Signal Co. Service Group in the Pacific Theater (New Guinea and Philippine Liberation).

Sgt. Turner was discharged 26 Nov 1945. His decorations include the American Theater, Asiatic-Pacific w/2 Bronze Stars, Philippine Liberation, Good Conduct and WWII Victory Medal.

Married Mary Elizabeth Stewart on 19 Dec 1952. They had one son Harvey Amos Jr. and two grandchildren, Michael Amos and David Stewart.

Harvey was self-employed in the timberland lumber business and was a farmer and merchant. He passed away 10 Nov 1994 after a long battle with cancer and is interred at East End Cemetery in Cadiz, KY.

IRA HUBERT TUCKER, Private, born 18 Aug 1912, son of J.H. and Callie Hunter Tucker in Trigg County, KY. He grew up and worked on a farm until he was drafted into the service 29 Sep 1942.

After 13 weeks of basic training at Fort Bragg, NC, he was sent to Pearl Harbor. He was in the field artillery at this time, and later became a military policeman, serving with Co. C, 729th MP Bn.

Received an honorable discharge 3 Nov 1944 and returned home a disabled American vet. His decorations include the Good Conduct Medal.

Married to a Trigg County girl, Pauline Herndon, on 14 Jun 1941. They had two children, Sharon Laverne and Ira Earl, who both live in Hopkinsville, KY.

He went to work for Smith Broadbent Enterprises and retired from there in March 1967. He passed away in the VA Hospital in Nashville, TN after a long stay on 18 Dec 1987. *Submitted by Mrs. Pauline Tucker.*

JACK FROST TURNER, Sergeant, born 13 Jun 1920 at lower Donaldson in Trigg County, KY. Inducted in the US Army 27 Jan 1942 at Fort Lee, VA.

Basic training in the Medical Corps was at Fort Lee, VA. He remained with this unit until deactivated from the Army 18 Oct 1945 at Camp Atterbury, IN with the rank of sergeant.

Tours of duty included England, North Africa, Corsica, Southern France and Paris. He received the EAME Theater Ribbon w/3 Bronze Stars for participation in Rome-Arno, Rhineland and Southern France campaigns.

Enrolled in Murray State University in 1946 and received majors in business education, health and physical education; also, master of arts degree and a 30 hour program above master's at Murray State University. Four year letterman in baseball, member of "M" Club, Business Education and Veterans Club.

His teaching career began at Trigg County High in 1950 as business education teacher, head basketball and assistant football coach. He held various other positions (including assistant superintendent) in system until retirement in September 1980.

He held numerous educational and civic club memberships; was a post commander of American Legion Post #74; and Kentucky Colonel was presented to him by Governor Nunn in 1968. He was a member of Cadiz United Methodist Church, Sunday School Superintendent, substitute teacher, member of official board and board of trustees.

Married Elsie Jackson 17 Apr 1947 and had one daughter Brenda Lee. Jack passed away 17 Jul 1991 at age 71. He is buried at East End Cemetery.

JAMES RANDALL "SON" TURNER, Chief Petty Officer, born 1922 in Cerulean, KY, son of Randall Franklin Turner and Allene Larkins Turner. His family and friends knew James as "Son." James graduated from Cadiz HS in June 1939 and enlisted in the Navy in the fall of 1939.

His first ship was the cruiser *Boise* that participated in combat in the Philippines in December 1941. Assignments included the USS *Miami* and later the USS *Pine Island*. James Turner was in the Sea of Japan at the time of the Japanese surrender.

He was discharged in the spring of 1945 after serving six years. At the time of his discharge he was a chief petty officer. One of his more memorable experiences was the opportunity to view the devastation of the atomic bomb.

James married Rita Amica of Philadelphia on 14 Oct 1944. The Turners had four children: son Randall Franklin Turner (deceased in 1992), Janet D. Turner married to Daniel Helfgott, David Lewis Turner married to Patricia Walters, and Michael Edward Turner married to Wendy Slabough. The Turners had six grandchildren: Justin Michael, Andrea Nicole, Alyson Marie, Cara Michelle, Dylan James and Jeffrey Michael.

Mr. Turner was employed by Bell Telephone Co. of Pennsylvania and retired in 1982 after 36 years with the company. He was active in Scouting, Indian Guides and his church.

OSCAR GARLAND TURNER, 2nd Lieutenant, born 6 Apr 1922 at Golden Pond, KY, son of Grundy and Elizabeth Gardner Turner. He gradu-

ated from Golden Pond HS and after farming for a time, decided to volunteer for the Army. He reported in at Fort Knox, KY, on 2 Jul 1940, was sworn in 4 July for basic training and had an interesting career in the military service.

He transferred from Fort Knox to Pine Camp, Watertown, NY; from there he returned to Fort Knox for six weeks school. He received service school with the Armored Force, with a course in motorcycle mechanic at Fort Knox. Transferred to Camp Cook near Lumpoc, CA.

He received a commission as 2nd lieutenant in Epernay, France on 25 Feb 1945. Oscar received an honorable discharge during the Battle of the Bulge 5 Jan 1944. He re-enlisted and was sworn in as an officer. During service his battles and campaigns include Rhineland, Central Europe, Northern Frances and Ardennes.

His decorations include the EAME Service Medal and four Bronze Battle Stars for combat duty in France, Luxembourg, Belgium and Germany. He received an honorable discharge 5 Nov 1945 at Camp Atterbury, IN.

In 1947 he received a letter from the Adjutant General's Office, dated 14 Jun 1947 which reads in part: "The Secretary of War had directed me to issue a commission, in the highest rank attained, to each officer relieved from active duty after serving honorably in the Army of the United States during the recent war, who has not been issued a commission subsequent to being processed for relief from active duty."

After the war Oscar returned to his parents' home at Golden Pond and in 1946 he married Mary Emma Lane. They had two sons, Oscar Jr. and Robert, and three grandchildren. Oscar worked in Louisville, KY for Ford Motor Co. Returned to Western Kentucky and retired in 1982 after 32 years with B.F. Goodrich Chemical Co., Calvert City, KY. His wife Mary Emma died 12 Dec 1955. Oscar now lives in Murray, KY.

OVAL LEE TURNER, PFC, born 16 Dec 1918 in Golden Pond, KY. As a child he worked and lived on his uncle's farm, Bradford Turner. He enlisted 12 Apr 1941 and received his basic training at Camp Shelby, MS with further training in Hawaii.

He served with the 38th Div., 3rd Bn., Co. M, 149th Inf. After training he was sent to New Guinea, Southern Philippines, Luzon and Leyte Islands. He performed duty as a private first class heavy machine gunner.

Oval was discharged after the war on 6 Nov 1945. He received the EAME Theater Ribbon w/3 Bronze Stars, American Theater Ribbon, American Defense Ribbon, Philippine Liberation Ribbon w/Bronze Star, Good Conduct and WWII Victory Medal.

He met Fannie May Sanders and they were married 10 Jul 1951. They moved to Hammond, IN, where Oval worked for Stam-ray as a machine operator. He retired 20 Jun 1980 with 31 years of service. They now live on a small farm in Murray, KY, where he likes to garden and work. Fannie and Oval had one son, Dennis James, and two granddaughters, Anna Marie and Samantha.

THOMAS CLARENCE TYLER, born 5 Jun 1927 in Lamasco, KY, the son of William Fred and Nancy Ann Ramey Tyler. He lived, worked and played semi-pro baseball prior to being drafted into the US Army in November 1945. After completing basic training at Camp Atterbury, IN, he proceeded to Germany with the 1st Inf. Div.

He served in Germany as a rifleman from the 1 April 1946 to 12 April 1949, when he returned to the States after an accident, which resulted in the removal of his right kneecap. He was medically retired from the Army in June 1949 and returned to Cadiz, KY.

He married Mary Loradell Calhoun of Canton and reared six children: Beverly Lacy, Fredia Dunning, Connie McCloud, Rita Brown, Sandy Carneyhan and Thomas Wayne Tyler. After his return from Germany and release from the Army, he worked at several different jobs, ultimately joining TVA sometime in the 60s, where he worked until his untimely death 8 Jul 1980.

His son, Thomas Wayne Tyler, prepared this biography of his father's military service 20 years after his father's death. In preparing this, he explains his father in the following manner: "It doesn't do justice to the man it depicts. I cannot detail his military service and cover exactly where he served and what he may have seen or done. I know the last thing he would expect would be having something written about him that couldn't be verified. Most of this is done by referencing his discharge and induction papers. Though I may not be able to do justice to the military service, which he provided to the country he so dearly loved and proudly served, I can speak about the man. I can say that he was a man of great integrity, honor, courage and commitment. He, to my knowledge, never had an enemy that he made for himself, as all who were in attendance at Goodwin's Funeral home on 10 Jul 1980 can attest—he had more friends than could be counted.

"If my father were to be asked to name his greatest accomplishments and most memorable experiences, I believe he would say that he had six of them and they combined provided him with 16 more. He was a man of steadfast devotion and unconditional love for each of his children. Stern when providing discipline, yet soft and warm when needed. He was proud of all his children's accomplishments and supportive of their goals and consoling during their failures. He was our protector and provider, our father and our friend. He was taken from us way too soon and has been severely missed by us ever since. He may have never been a highly decorated war hero, but to us he was much, much more, he was Daddy."

ROBERT HALE "R.H." UPTON JR., Yeoman, born 5 Apr 1921 in the Lock E Community of Trigg County, the third child born to Rob and Melia (Downs) Upton. He had two sisters, Myrtle Rae (Upton) King and Nell (Upton) Leneave. He graduated from Trigg County HS in 1940 and Murray State College. While at Trigg County HS, he played football and actually played on the very first home football game ever played at Trigg County. The game was played on 7 Oct 1938 between Dawson Springs at 2:30 p.m. (Probably because there were no lights at the time on the field.)

R.H. entered the USN on 30 Jun 1942 and received basic training at Great Lakes, IL. He served aboard two battleships, the USS *Montpelier* and the USS *Denver*. He was a Yeoman First Class and worked in the communication department. He also received the Asiatic-Pacific award with eight stars,

American Theatre, Philippine Liberation Medal w/star, Good Conduct Medal and the Victory Medal. He visited many ports including, San Francisco, Japan and Australia before his discharge 1 Feb 1946.

He returned to Trigg County and married June Smiley of Princeton, KY on 25 Aug 1946. They had two children, Susan Upton Holmes of Cadiz, KY and Bob Upton of Franklin, TN. They also had three grandchildren: Jason Holmes and Rob and Lori Upton. R.H. was a lifelong member of Canton Baptist Church where he served as deacon. He was a member of the American Legion, a Mason and a member of the Bank of Cadiz Board of Directors at the time of his death.

R.H. loved construction work. He worked and drove trucks for Upton & King Trucking when he was younger and was always happiest when he was outside.

He worked overseas in Vietnam from 1966-1973. He said his company built the same airstrip about five times during the Vietnam War because it was constantly being blown up. He went to work in Saudia Arabia in February 1980. R.H. suffered a heart attack while in Saudia and was en route back home when he suffered a massive heart attack upon reaching the New York Airport. He died 9 Nov 1980. His wife June died 9 Sep 1998. Both are buried in East End Cemetery.

He loved Trigg County and it was always home.

ED LATTA VANZANT, born 26 Jan 1911 in Trigg County, KY, the son of Earl H. and Birtie Alexander Vanzant. He served in the US Army from 29 May 1942 to 10 May 1945. Ed Latta was inducted at Fort Benjamin Harrison, IN. He was in Europe for 16 months and was in the Service Company, 115th Infantry.

While serving in the military he was an auto mechanic. He received the EAME Theater Ribbon on 1 Apr 1943 and Good Conduct Ribbon 18 Feb 1944. His separation was from the 1st IN Headquarters Wakeman Hospital Center, Camp Atterbury, IN on 10 May 1945.

Upon his separation from the Army, he returned to help his father on the farm and also to his job of mechanic at Luther Thomas's Ford Garage. As Latta never married or had children of his own, his sister, Louise V. Fuller's two sons, Raymond Earl and James Harold, were his pride and joy. Latta died 10 Feb 1977, and is buried beside his parents at the Siloam Cemetery.

JOHN R. VINSON JR., 2nd Lieutenant, born 20 May 1912 in Trigg County, KY. He entered military service in October 1942 at Fort Hood, TX. He served with Tank Destroyer in WWII.

After spending six months in the hospital, he was discharged from his injuries as second lieutenant in May 1944.

Married Doris Peal 30 May 1941 and had three children: John R. III, Ann Wamser and Carolyn Holm. Grandchildren are John and David Bradly, Neal and Dale West, John Mark and Kelli Vinson, and Susan Carter.

John was a rural mail carrier for 35 years, retiring in 1973. He was Grand Master of the Masonic Lodge of Kentucky in 1959-60. He passed away 9 May 1975.

FELIX E. WADLINGTON, Sergeant, born 26 Feb 1923 in Trigg County, son of Felix C. and Ruby Mitchell Wadlington.

Drafted into the Army in 1943 and sent to Keesler Field, MS for basic training, then to Colorado for Diesel Mechanic School. He was the Golden Gloves Champion for state of Kentucky and also boxed while in the Army. Sgt. Wadlington was discharged in 1945.

He returned to Cadiz and drove a bus for Western Kentucky Stages Bus Co. until 1948, then was a city policeman in Cadiz for 10 years. After that, he drove a truck for Thomas Industries until he retired. He is a farmer and resides in Trigg County.

RAYMOND E. WALKER,

RAYMOND E. WALKER, born 2 Oct 1921 in Trigg County, Cerulean, KY. He entered the service 29 Jul 1942 at Evansville, IN, with duty as light truck driver in the Northern Solomons and Luzon.

His decorations include the Asiatic-Pacific Theater Ribbon w/2 Bronze Service Stars, Good Conduct Medal, Philippine Liberation Ribbon w/Bronze Service Star and WWII Victory Medal. He was discharged 26 Dec 1945 at Separation Center, Fort Knox, KY as Tech 5.

Raymond retired in December 1981 as Police Chief, Hopkinsville Police Dept. He was a member of Second Baptist Church, Masonic Lodge, KY Police Chiefs Association, KY Peace Officers Association and Kentucky Colonel.

Married Onie Shelton and had one son Michael and two grandchildren, Taylor and Alex. Raymond passed away in February 1983.

ALBERT DOUGLAS WALLACE, Captain, born in January 1918 in Cadiz, KY. He received his DDS degree from University of Louisville in 1938 and returned to Cadiz and began his practice of dentistry. He married Marie Clodfelter, a Trigg County HS home economics teacher.

Albert went into military service as a 2nd lieutenant in 1942 at Cadiz, KY. He was sent to Fort Snelling, MN to serve in the Military Dental Clinic for three years.

After WWII was over, he and his family came back to Cadiz to resume his dental practice. Later, he and his family moved to Murray, KY where he built a dental clinic with a home connected to the clinic, where his wife continues to reside. Albert passed away in 1996. There are two children, Mary Anna and Cecil, and two grandchildren.

ALBERT OWEN WALLACE, Gunner's Mate 2/c, born in Trigg County, KY, near Wallonia on 3 Dec 1921. He was the son of Mr. and Mrs. Calvin O. Wallace.

Albert enlisted in the USN on 14 Nov 1942 in Hopkinsville, KY, and took his "boot" training at Great Lakes, IL. He had spent 16 months at sea duty when his ship was torpedoed by a Nazi submarine in the Indian Ocean. He was asleep at the time and the impact of the explosion threw him out of his bunk. Dashing immediately to the deck, he aided his gun crew in opening fire on the Nazi sub, but only two shots could be fired when the order to abandon their sinking ship came.

Albert was in a life boat for 16 hours before being rescued and put ashore in East Africa. He had to leave all his personal belongings, including an expensive set of binoculars and a German camera, behind. He

returned to New Orleans, LA, before being placed aboard another supply-laden merchantman bound for foreign battle zones.

He received the American Theater Ribbon, European African Ribbon, Asiatic-Pacific Ribbon and Point System - 44. He received barber and machine shop training. Albert received an honorable discharge as a gunner's mate 2/c T at Great Lakes, IL on 8 Oct 1945.

Upon his discharge, he moved to Nashville, TN, and worked at Davis Cabinets for two years before returning to Trigg County to engage in farming. He also lived for awhile in Caldwell County before moving to Hopkinsville to work at Thomas Industries.

On 21 Dec 1949, Albert married Lillian Nell Merrick. They had two sons, Lawrence and Willard, and three granddaughters: Shellie, Samantha and Miranda.

Albert died 11 Aug 1972 of a heart attack and is buried in the Blue Spring Church Cemetery in Caldwell County, KY.

ARTHUR R. WALLACE, born 8 May 1925, in the Golden Pond area of Trigg County. He graduated from Trigg County HS in May 1943, and soon after graduation, at 18 years of age, joined the Army Air Force.

Arthur received his basic training at Amarillo, TX, and attended special school in Pyote, TX. He took additional aerial gunnery training at Kingman, AZ; Lake City, UT; and Herrington, KS. After training, Arthur was assigned to the Eighth Air Force in Europe. He arrived in Europe on 12 Jul 1944.

Stationed in England, he served as a tail-gunner on a B-17. He flew numerous bombing missions into Germany, France, Belgium, and the Netherlands. He was wounded in action over Leipzig, Germany, on 19 Sep 1944. He was hospitalized for about two months in England, then transferred back to the States on 28 Jun 1945, where he spent time in Johns Hopkins Hospital.

He was discharged at Scott Field, IL, on 26 Oct 1945. For his service, Arthur received the Air Medal, ETO Ribbon w/5 Bronze Stars and the Purple Heart. Arthur was one of five Wallace brothers who served during WWII. They were sons of Arthur and Gertie Luton Wallace.

After the war, he went to Murray State College, receiving his BS degree in 1949 and MA degree in 1950. He was a long time educator in Trigg County. He served as teacher and principal at Golden Pond, teacher and principal at Trigg County HS, and for many years served as principal of Trigg County Elementary School before his retirement in June 1982.

He was an active member of Golden Pond and Cadiz Baptist churches, serving as deacon and Sunday school teacher. Arthur married Patricia Morris in 1961. Arthur and Pat have three children: Amy, Margaret and Philip. A grandchild, Hannah Margaret Brack, was born in 2000. Arthur died on May 4, 1992.

After Arthur's death in 1992, one of his crew members wrote to the family about his memories of serving with him. He related that Arthur, whom they called "Whitey" was the youngest member of the crew and often brought smiles to the crew's faces during some tense moments on their missions. "Sometimes Whitey would imitate President Roosevelt and speak through the plane's intercom. On missions, after we had released our bombs over the target, he would call the pilot on the intercom and ask if we were going home. The pilot would usually say, 'Yes, Whitey, we are going home.' Arthur would then start singing what was then his favorite song, *I'll Take The Night Train To Memphis*. Hearing that song meant mission complete, we're going home. If everyone was as decent and kind as Whitey was, what a wonderful world we would have. The Eighth Air Force still today uses as one of it's mottoes, 'We have never been turned back from a mission.' It was the personification of bravery as exhibited by airmen such as Arthur Wallace that makes that motto the truth."

CLARENCE ALLEN WALLACE, born 13 Jan 1920 in Stewart County, TN. His parents were Samuel L. and Lydia Irene Wallace. He had two sisters, Charlene and Hazel, and three brothers: Owen, Leon and David. The Wallace family moved to Trigg County when Clarence was young.

Clarence and family were living in Detroit, MI, where he worked for Ford Motor Co., when he was drafted. They moved to Dawson Springs, KY, while he was being processed for the Navy, about a year. He worked for Dawson Daylight Coal Co. at that time. Clarence entered the Navy in 1943, took boot camp at Great Lakes, IL, amphibious training at Fort Pierce, FL, then to Norfork, VA, Navy Training Base.

He was assigned to the USS *Selinur*, a supply ship, and made seven trips across the ocean going to various islands. Two remembered are Okinawa and Marshall. The *Salinur* stopped seven miles off shore. He drove a PT boat into the island carrying 39 soldiers and their equipment. Planes flew overhead and made a smoke screen to protect them. Some struck land mines and were blown up. Some soldiers were rescued but most perished. The *Salinur* was anchored seven miles out when the atomic bomb was dropped on Hiroshima and Nagaski, Japan.

Clarence was honorably discharged in 1946. He received several medals for bravery and good conduct. He was a lst class coxin mate.

He returned to Evansville, IN, where his wife Eunice and daughter Barbara were living. They bought a 117 acre farm near Tennyson, IN, where they lived a few years. Their second daughter was born there. The farm was sold and the family moved to Boonville, IN, where his family live today.

Clarence died 23 Apr 1978 following an accident at his place of work. He was buried at Maple Grove Cemetery, Boonville, IN. Clarence and Eunice had two daughters, Barbara Ann and Charlotte Allen, five grandchildren, six great-grandchildren. President Jimmy Carter sent the Wallace family a beautiful plaque in honor of his outstanding service in the Navy.

HARRY E. WALLACE, Tech 4, born 20 Jan 1918 in Golden Pond, KY. Entered the military 13 Sep 1940 at Fort Knox, KY and served with Co. B 4th Tank Bn. as tank driver (medium). Battles and campaigns include Tunisia, Naples-Foggia and Rome-Arno.

Discharged 14 Jun 1945 at Camp Atterbury, IN. His awards include the EAME Theater Ribbon w/3 Bronze Stars, American Defense Service Medal, Good Conduct Ribbon and he qualified as Expert Gunner.

His family consists of two brothers, Hugh Blane "Dock" and Percy Lee.

HUGH BLANE WALLACE, T-3, born 16 Feb 1916 at Golden Pond, KY. He joined the military 22 Apr 1941 at Tomsville, KY and served with the 688th Engineers Base Equipment Co. as a highway construction equipment operator.

Battles and campaigns include Rome-Arno and Rhineland. He was discharged 18 Oct 1945 at tech 3. His awards include the American Defense Ribbon, EAME Theater Ribbon w/2 Bronze Stars and Good Conduct Medal.

Married Ruth Riggins in 1942 and they had one son Jerry and two grandsons. He retired from Murray State College Water Dept. Ruth passed away in the 1980s and Hugh in 1999, both are buried in Murray, KY.

JESSE D. WALLACE, was born 28 Feb 1922 in the Golden Pond area of Trigg County. He entered the Army Air Force in May 1943, and was assigned to Fresno, CA, for basic training. From there he went to Cheyenne, WY, for further training. Jesse was then assigned to Camp Kerns, near Salt Lake City, Utah.

In early December 1944, Wallace was transferred to Camp Gordon, GA, for advanced training, then sent to New York City to be shipped to Europe on the *Queen Mary*. After a five day crossing to Scotland and a train ride to the south of England, he crossed the channel into France, arriving in Germany in early February 1945. There Jesse was assigned to the 225th Engineering Battalion, Co. "C," as a replacement for men killed or wounded crossing the Ruhr River. The "Battle of the Bulge" had pushed

the Germans to the Ruhr. The assignment was to build and repair bridges, build and repair roads, and fight.

Wallace was there until the end of the war, May 10, 1945. At the war's end his battalion was "hold up" on the Elba River near Berlin.

Two weeks after the end of the war in Europe, Jesse was transferred to the 116th Light Equipment Company and went to Camp Boston near Paris, France. He became company clerk and was promoted to tech sergeant, with a pay increase to $78 a month. At Camp Boston his unit serviced and packaged equipment to be shipped to the unknown—most thought to the Pacific.

By late July 1945, he moved by train to the staging area in the south of France. The reader will recall, the first atomic bomb fell in Japan 8 Aug 1945, the second soon after. This activity brought the end of WWII.

Some of Jesse's fondest memories of his service in Europe was seeing his brothers, brothers-in-law, and others from "Between the Rivers" from time to time. He was one of five Wallace brothers to serve in WWII.

Jesse states in his memories, "Preparing this material has given me an opportunity to again express appreciation to family members for assistance: Geneva Wallace and Mary Gene Turner for support, and my mother, Gertie Luton Wallace, who regularly said prayers for each of her sons serving in WWII: Conley, Lew, Howard, Jesse, Arthur and sons-in-law Bernard Riggins and Ellis Fennell.

After the war, Jesse received his BS degree from Murray State University in 1950 and his master's degree from University of Missouri. He began a teaching career that included a tenure at California State University from 1958-1986. He retired in 1986. He lives in Chico, CA with his wife Helen. Their children, Jan, Elisha and Davis, all live near them in Chico.

MAURICE CONLEY WALLACE, Tech Sergeant, born 13 Jan 1910 in Trigg County near Golden Pond. He graduated from Golden Pond HS in 1931 and attended Murray State College. Before WWII, he taught school and was a storekeeper in Golden Pond.

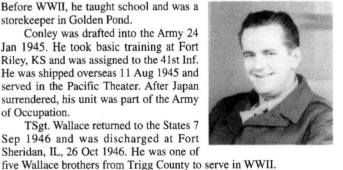

Conley was drafted into the Army 24 Jan 1945. He took basic training at Fort Riley, KS and was assigned to the 41st Inf. He was shipped overseas 11 Aug 1945 and served in the Pacific Theater. After Japan surrendered, his unit was part of the Army of Occupation.

TSgt. Wallace returned to the States 7 Sep 1946 and was discharged at Fort Sheridan, IL, 26 Oct 1946. He was one of five Wallace brothers from Trigg County to serve in WWII.

After the war, he built and ran the Sunset Inn restaurant and grocery in Golden Pond. In 1957, he went to work for the Kentucky State Department of Agriculture, retiring in 1968.

Conley married Geneva Holland on 1 Jun 1935. They have two children, Linda Wallace Dunn and Jim Wallace. Conley and Geneva lived in Golden Pond until 1967 when their home was taken by TVA during the development of the Land Between the Lakes. They then moved to Cadiz where Conley died in May 1972.

PERCY L. WALLACE, Tech 5, born 14 Dec 1912 at Golden Pond, KY. He joined the military 25 Jun 1940 at Fort Knox, KY and served with Co. C, 7th Engineer Bn. as an air compressor operator.

Battles and campaigns include Normandy, Northern France and Rhineland. He was discharged 4 Jul 1945 at Camp Atterbury, IN. His awards include the EAME Theater Ribbon w/3 Bronze Stars, American Defense Service Medal, Good Conduct Ribbon and he qualified as Rifle Sharpshooter.

Percy family consists of two brothers, Harry E. and Hugh Blane "Dock."

CLIFFORD A. WALLIS, born 9 Oct 1918 on a farm in Christian County near Cerulean, KY. He was inducted into the US Army on 25 Apr 1942 at Evansville, IN. After receiving basic training at Fort Riley, KS, he was assigned to Co. C, 727th MP Bn., Camp Forrest, TN.

On 13 Jan 1943 his company was ordered to the Persian Gulf Command to provide security for the thousands of tons of vital war supplies and equipment being sent by rail, truck and air through the Persian corridor to the armies of the Soviet Union. The Persian Gulf Command was designated a non-combat zone, so the worst enemies were malaria, dysentery, smallpox, sandfly fever, trachoma, and the ever present heat. In the southern part of the country the average summer temperature in the shade was 120 degrees from May to September.

As a result of the efficient manner in which the company performed its duty, Co. C was selected to provide security for President Franklin D. Roosevelt, Prime Minister Winston Churchill and Premier Joseph Stalin, during the Tehran conference. After more than two and half years overseas duty, he was discharged 30 Oct 1945 as Tech 4th Grade at Camp Atterbury, IN. Awards include the EAME Theater Ribbon and Good Conduct Ribbon.

In 1946 he was employed by the Veterans Administration Regional Office and after more than 29 years of service in various departments of the VA, he retired in 1975 from the Finance Department.

At present he lives in Louisville, KY, where he does volunteer work for the Walnut Street Baptist Church and Treyton Oak Towers Retirement Center.

HUGH DOUGLAS WALLIS, born 23 Jun 1924, in Siloam Community was drafted 19 Apr 1943. He reported to Fort Benjamin Harrison, IN. After basic training at Camp Polk, LA, he volunteered for Paratroopers. He completed jump training at Fort Benning, GA, in December 1943.

After a short furlough home, he headed for overseas duty via Benning; Fort Meade, MD; and Camp Patrick Henry, VA. He went by ship from Newport News to Casablanca, then by transport plane to Naples, Italy. He served in 3rd Platoon Co. H. 504th Pcht. Inf. Regt., 82nd Abn. Div., and fought at Anzio Beachhead. Wounded about two weeks later, he was evacuated to a hospital in Naples. From there, he saw Mt. Vesuvius erupt.

He returned to duty, went to England, and made the invasion of Holland in September 1944. He jumped from Plane No. 33. Shortly after they were on the ground, German jet planes appeared. To his knowledge,

this is the first time jets were used in combat. After a couple weeks, he was wounded again and evacuated to a hospital in England.

Next came the Battle of the Bulge in Belgium for three to four weeks. He froze his feet, returned to the English hospital then back to the States. He landed in New York, sent to Camp Kilmer, NJ, to Camp Buckner, NC, where he received a medical discharge 24 Aug 1945.

He married Lola Burnam in Trigg County in 1946. They moved to Louisville, where he went to trade school for radio and television service. They moved to Fort Wayne, IN, where he worked in a factory two or three years, then went into field service and was self-employed. In 1949 son James was born and in 1950 daughter Janice was born. In January 1984, Lola died and is buried in Trigg Memory Acres.

In December 1985, he married Susan Hedges. She has one daughter, Diane Lothamer. They have eight grandchildren and two great-grandchildren. He retired in July 1986 and Susan retired a year later.

They enjoy their family, traveling, bicycle riding and whitewater rafting. They are active members of First Baptist Church, where they have served on various boards 30-40 years. They live in Fort Wayne, IN.

WILLIAM DOUGLAS WALLIS, Staff Sergeant, born 11 Feb 1921 in Cadiz, KY. He joined the military 26 Aug 1942 in Trigg County and served with the 35th Transportation Corps in Bismarck Archipelago, New Guinea. Southern Philippines, Australia and Luzon.

After three years of service with no furlough, SSgt. Wallis was discharged 15 Dec 1945. His awards include the Good Conduct Medal, Philippine Liberation Ribbon and Asiatic-Pacific Ribbon w/4 Bronze Stars.

William and Ethelene were married 1 May 1947. No children. William is deceased.

JOHN N. WEEMS, born 2 Jun 1918 Southside, TN. Assignments include the Flying Cadets 30 Dec 1940 to 15 Aug 1941; Pan American Airways copilot, 15 Aug 1941 to 15 Aug 1953; USAC, 15 Aug 1943 to 30 Jun 1960.

He participated in the European Theater of Operations with 7th Air Depot Sqdn., Northern England and 86th Air Transport Sqdn., London, England and Paris, France. They transported equipment, personnel, gasoline for Patton's tanks, POWs, wounded personnel from the front line and anything else that would go into a C-47 aircraft.

John was discharged 30 Jun 1963 at Minot AFB, ND. He received the Air Medal.

As a civilian he was Director, Association for Retarded Children, Auburn, NY for eight years. He married Elizbeth Doust on 29 Jun 1950 and they now live 126 Russell Cave Road, Georgetown, KY. They have three children: Philip N., George H. and Rebecca E., and three grandchildren: Ben, Zeke and Hannah.

THOMAS N. "BOOTIE" WEEMS JR., Lieutenant Colonel, born Southside, TN. He taught school from 1937-1944 and served during WWII in the Midway, Guadalcanal and Korea.

He remained in the Reserves and attained the rank of lieutenant colonel. Awards include the Distinguished Service Cross and Air Medal.

Married Marjorie Milne 28 Apr 1943, no children. He was a dentist in Las Cruces, NM until retirement in November 1987.

BEN TERRY WHITE II, Major, born 1924 in Cadiz, KY, the son of WWII veteran John F. and Ellen Hopson White. He graduated from Trigg County High in 1940. In ROTC at the University of Kentucky, he was called to active duty in 1943 as a 2nd lieutenant in the Army. He was discharged as a major in 1945 after serving in the European Theater.

After the war he finished medical school at Duke University and practiced cardiology in Port Arthur, TX. He retired from medical practice in San Francisco and died at his home in Indian Wells,

CA in March 1993, and is buried in Carmel Valley, CA. He is survived by a daughter, Gilchrist White of Houston, TX, and a sister Francis Payne, of Nashville, TN.

H. STANLEY WHITE JR., PO2/c, born 22 May 1924 in Cadiz, KY and entered the USN 23 Jun 1943, where he was assigned to the Seabees.

After two weeks of boot camp at Camp Peary, VA, he was assigned to the 112th Seabee Battalion which was sent to Eastport, ME, to build a rest camp for wounded Navy personnel. In the fall of 1943 the 112th was sent to Port Hueneme, CA for embarkation to the Pacific Theater.

After several months in Hawaii, building landing strips, the battalion was shipped to other islands in the Pacific to build landing strips. Among them was the landing strip on Tinian, in the Marianas, from which the B-12s flew that dropped the first atomic bombs. The strips were built while under sniper fire as Japanese were holed up in caves in the hills. The 112th had several casualties from this fire.

In May 1945, the 112th was shipped to Okinawa for the invasion of that island, more casualties occurred when two of the landing craft were hit by Japanese suicide bombers. When the war ended Stan was sent home for a 30 day leave and discharge, but because of a shortage of Navy engineering ratings to run the ships he was transferred to the Pacific Fleet as a petty officer second class. He served three months aboard the USS *Fallon* (APA-18) a troop carrier.

He was discharged 20 Mar 1946, then enlisted in the Active Naval Reserve for four years, attached to the Surface Unit at Lexington, KY, while attending the University of Kentucky. While in the reserves he shipped out of New Orleans during the summer of 1947 and 1948 on destroyers on patrol duty in the Caribbean Ocean.

After graduation from UK in 1949, he returned to Cadiz to work for the Cadiz Railroad. He became one of the incorporators of the Cadiz Milling Co. with his father and Porter Piercy. In 1952 Stan was appointed superintendent of the Cadiz Railroad and in 1965 succeeded his cousin, W.C. White, as president and general manager. After his father's death in 1964 he was elected president of the Cadiz Milling Company, and held both positions until his retirement on 31 Dec 1985.

During his business career he was a charter member and president of the Cadiz-Trigg County Chamber of Commerce; served on the Industrial Committee; a charter member and a past president of the Cadiz Rotary Club. He served as chairman of the Southern Short Line Railroad Conference in Atlanta, GA and as a director of the American Short Line Railroad Association in Washington, DC.

He and his wife, the former Gayle Ice of Evansville, IN, reside in Cadiz where both are members of the USCG Auxiliary, Flotilla 87, on Barkley Lake.

FRANK H. WILCOX, Colonel, born 14 Apr 1918 in Paris, KY, son of Frank Hurst Wilcox Sr. and Mary Chisholm Wilcox, was the first distinguished ROTC graduate and first cadet lieutenant colonel of the ROTC at Eastern Kentucky University.

He married Dorothy Helen Dorris 28 Sep 1940 in Richmond, KY and they had three children: Dorris W. McCarthy, Idaho Falls, ID; Frances W. Chenoweth, Saluda, VA; and Donald Pierce Wilcox, Austin, TX. He also had a brother Charles Eugene Wilcox, Holiday Island, AR; six grandchildren and one great-grandchild.

Col. Wilcox was field artillery instructor at Fort Sill, OK; a Doolittle lead pilot in B-17s, 8th AF, WWII; legislative legal counsel for AF Secretary Symington; Commander, 12th Air Rescue Group, Europe and Africa; Chief of Safety MATS; National War College 1961; Commander Navigator Training School, Waco, TX; Commander Tan Son Nhut AB, Saigon; Chief AF War Plans Division; Joint Staff, Strategic Plans and Policy, Joint Chiefs of Staff.

In 1964 and 1965 Col. Wilcox investigated and aided in prosecution of drug traffic in Southeast Asia, in addition to flying regular missions, commanding Tan Son Nhut AB, Saigon, and acting as single manager of all flying activities, military and civilian when the air base became the busiest in the world. In the summer of 1964 he investigated and initiated action to stop the smuggling of gold from Communist China through Hong Kong in exchange for smaller piaster notes, which could be used by the Viet Cong in Vietnam, helping to finance the conflict. A $50,000 price was placed on his head by the Viet Cong.

After his Vietnam service he served as Chief of the Air Force War Plans Division and later on the Joint Chief's of Staff. Colonel Wilcox was most proud of his leadership as Director of a group of senior officers who prepared the five year plan to turn the Vietnam war over to the Vietnamese and bring our troops home. He wrote the scenario of the plan, which was approved by President Johnson and carried out without change in the Nixon administration. In 1970 he retired from the Air Force with combat disability from Vietnam.

His decorations include the Legion of Merit, Distinguished Flying Cross, Bronze Star, both Air Force and Army Commendation Medals, Air Force Air Medal w/9 clusters, European Theater Medal w/Battle Stars of the Rhineland, Ardennes, Central Europe and Battle of Germany, WWII Victory Medal, the Antarctic Service Citation, Vietnam Service and Victory Medals, and the Joint Chief of Staff Medallion.

In 1970 Col. Wilcox moved to Trigg County, KY where he built a home on Lake Barkley near Cadiz. There he practiced law and was later appointed Master Commissioner in 1992 and served until he became ill. He was dedicated to the community, active in the Christian Church, singing in the choir and serving on the Board of the Christian Church.

Frank Hurst Wilcox died at home 26 Jul 1999, after a long illness with cancer. On 29 September his ashes were interred with full honors in the Columbarium at Arlington National Cemetery.

GARNETT WADE WILLIAMS, Seaman 2/c, born 19 Feb 1923 in Cadiz, KY, was the oldest son of Maynard and Dorothy Mize Williams. Garnett was named after James Garnett Thomas, a close friend of his father (see Maynard Williams history). Garnett acquired the nickname of "Cotton" at a very early age due to the color of his hair. This nickname has remained with him all these years.

The families living in the Williams Hollow were farmers. Cotton worked along side his dad in the Cumberland River Bottoms raising their crops. He enjoyed playing baseball and fishing as a young man. He attended Graham, Rogers (Linton) and Trigg County HS.

He enlisted in the USN 26 Apr 1944 and received his basic training at the Naval Training Center, Great Lakes, IL. He was later stationed at USNH Mare Island, CA assigned to the USS *Pellias*. The day before he was to be shipped out for active sea duty, he was stricken with pneumonia and admitted to the Naval Base Hospital where he remained for three months. He remained at Mare Island until his honorable discharge 15 Dec 1944. He was ranked seaman 2nd class at the time of his discharge.

Cotton returned to his home in Trigg County and continued to farm with his dad. In 1949, he moved to Granite City, IL and worked in the steel mill and remained employed there for 31 years.

On 14 Sep 1951 he married Margaret Ann Thomas (no relation to the Trigg County Thomas). They became the proud parents of five daughters: Shirley, Kathy, Rita, Karen and Linda. These daughters have blessed them with 21 grandchildren.

Cotton and Marge still reside in Granite City but maintain a home on the South Road (KY 139). The couple also maintains two gardens to supply vegetables for their family and neighbors. Most of his leisure time is spent teaching his grandchildren to fish and bowl.

JOHN B. WILLIAMS, Tech 5, born 27 Jun 1921 in Trigg County, KY. He joined the US Army in August 1942 at Fort Wayne, IN and took his training at Camp Wolters, TX.

He was assigned to the 374th Regt. 4th Bn. and was stationed in the Aleutian Islands and Alaska. Discharged in November 1945 as tech 5.

He married Teen Noel 7 Dec 1946 and has two children, Jerry Wayne and Rexie Dale, two grandchildren and one step-grandchild, Melissa and Laura Williams and Michele Webb.

Retired since 1983 and lives in Benton, KY.

JOHN DOUGLAS WILLIAMS, Corporal, born 21 Jan 1918 at Golden Pond, KY, son of Perry Douglas and Mary Eliza Gordon Williams. He moved with family to Murray, Calloway County, KY in December 1935.

He enlisted in the US Army 12 Jun 1941 at Murray and assigned to the 2082nd 2M Trucking Co. as a cook. His training was in Wyoming, Texas and California.

Sent overseas in November 1943 to China-Burma-India and returned in November 1945. Went to Alaska in February 1947, returning in December 1948. Left for Germany in April 1950, returning in October 1950 to Walter Reed Hospital in Washington where he was honorably discharged with a permanent disability (rheumatic heart disease and hearing loss) on 31 Jan 1951.

Cpl. Williams received the American Campaign Medal, WWII Victory Medal, Good Conduct Medal, American Defense Medal, Army of Occupation Medal (Germany) and Asiatic-Pacific Campaign Medal w/2 Bronze Stars.

Retired as a maintenance worker at Calloway County HS in 1982. John passed away 16 Sep 1996.

JOHN WILSON WILLIAMS, born 4 Jun 1913 in Trigg County, Golden Pond, KY, son of Albert Sidney and Ollie (Wallace) Williams. He joined the US Army 4 Mar 1941 and died in active duty 24 Jan 1944 during WWII. He is buried at Matheny-Cumberland Cemetery, Between the Rivers. He had a brother Felix, a sister Lucy, and was a first cousin of Army veteran John Douglas Williams.

LOYS LAMONT WILLIAMS, born 22 Nov 1910 in Trigg County, son of Thomas and Vara (Thomas) Williams. He was a member of the Civilian Conservation Corporation and was stationed at Mount Shasta, CA.

Loys served four years and five months in the Army. He was stationed near Corpus Christi, TX. During his second enlistment, he served in the 106th Anti-Aircraft Bn., serving overseas in Ireland, North Africa, Sicily, Italy, Southern France, Austria and Germany. He was a T/5 Driver

and transported personnel, supplies and ammunition to points on front lines. He also drove for the battalion commander.

After his discharge 8 Aug 1945, he made his home in Hopkinsville, KY. He was self-employed for a time and later worked with the US Department of Agriculture as a livestock inspector until retirement.

On 16 Sep 1945, he married Mary Leta Boyd born 21 Dec 1914, in South Christian, KY, daughter of John Richard and Gabe (Littlefield) Boyd. Loys and Mary Leta lived in Hopkinsville. They were members of the First Baptist Church where he was a Deacon and she was a member of the Women's Missionary Union.

Loys was a member of the Veterans of Foreign Wars and the Elks Lodge where he served as Exalted Ruler. Mary Leta was a volunteer in the Hospital Auxiliary and both were members of the National Association of Retired Federal Employees.

Loys died 28 Jan 1978, and Mary Leta died 26 Jul 1985. They are buried in Green Hill Memorial Gardens in Christian County.

Loys and Mary Leta's daughter Lucretia (b. 19 Mar 1947) married Robert Louis Moran (b. 3 Sep 1945) on 5 Aug 1967. They have two daughters, Stacie Lynn (b. 5 Apr 1971) and Leslie Ann (b. 8 Mar 1974). Stacie married William Todd Watkins (b. 19 Mar 1970) on 21 May 1994. They have one daughter Morgan Shae (b. 31 Mar 1998). Leslie is a student at Austin Peay State University in Clarksville, TN, majoring in Elementary Education. She plans to graduate in May 2002. The Morans and Watkins live in Hopkinsville and are members of First United Methodist Church.

WAFFLE CONROY WILLIAMS, PFC, born 9 Oct 1924 in Trigg County, KY. He joined the military in August 1943 in Evansville, IN and served with the 57th Air Service Group, 7th Army Air Force in Saipan, Penyan, Guam and Okinawa.

Pfc. Williams was discharged in February 1946. His awards and medals include three combat area missions and Gold Star.

Married Violet Bond 8 Jul 1950 and they have four children: Roy David, Cynthia Ann, Ruth Ellen, John Bond Williams, and six grandchildren: Danelle and Richard Williams, Sam Fremen, Ben Peschke, Sara and Laura Lynerup. Waffle retired 14 Jun 1989 from A&P Grocery and resides in Trenton, MI.

RICHARD LANE WILLS, son of Mr. and Mrs. Henry H. Wills. Richard attended Trigg County HS until volunteering for the US Army in Christian County, KY in 1944. He received his basic training at Fort McClellan, AL and Fort Knox, KY. He spent most of the 12 years in Germany. Most of that time he was with an engineers company. He received his high school diploma after entering the military and was working toward a college degree when he was killed in a car accident in 1956. He is buried in the National Cemetery in Nashville, TN.

CALVERT WALLACE WILSON, born 3 Jan 1919 in Trigg County, Cadiz, KY, son of Arthur Paul Wilson and Gertrude Katherine Savells. Enlisted in the Air Force 3 Oct 1940 at Chanute Field, IL and left on the *Queen Mary* for overseas duty 27 Sep 1942.

Battles and Campaigns include Northern France – Rhineland; Tunisia Sicily – Naples-Foggia; Rome-Arno; Southern France Air Offensive; and Europe Air Combat Balkans.

His decorations and citations include the EAME Campaign Medal w/9 Bronze Stars, Good Conduct Medal, American Defense Service Medal and the Distinguished Unit Badge w/2 Oak Leaf Clusters.

Returned to the States 8 Jun 1945. Re-enlisted 17 Jun 1947 and stations at Chanute Field, IL; Long Beach, CA; Bolling Field, Washington DC; Langley Field, Newport News, VA; Reese AFB, Lubbock, TX; Tachikawa AFB, Tachikawa, Japan, 1956-1959; and Altus AFB, Altus, OK, where he retired 1 Nov 1962 with 20 years service.

In 1963 he began work in civil service at Tinker AFB, Oklahoma City, OK, until retirement in June 1974. Lived in Shell Knob, MO, 1974 until his death 23 Aug 1996. He is buried in Steele, MO.

He married Mary Kathleen Northern on 28 Jun 1945 in Steele, MO, and had two children, Jan Grey Wilson (b. 13 Feb 1947) and Deborah June Wilson (b. 9 May 1949). *Information was provided by his daughter June Cromling and submitted by his sister Marion Donaldson.*

JAMES EDWARD WILSON, Private, born 10 Apr 1927 in Louisville, KY. He enlisted 22 Dec 1945 at Camp Atterbury, IN and served as truck driver (light). He received the Victory Medal.

Civilian jobs include laborer, Nunn Lumber Co.; civil service, Fort Campbell; bus driver, Trigg County Schools; maintenance, Lake Barkley Lodge; upholsterer, Murray St. University.

Married first, Mattie L. Sholar and second, Lena Bacon. He had two children, Lonnie and Bernice, and four grandchildren. He lived in Cadiz, KY until 1988 when he moved to Louisville. He passed away 20 Apr 1993 and is buried in Crownhill Cemetery.

JAMES GARNET WILSON, Staff Sergeant, born 13 Jun 1919. He enlisted in the USAF 20 Aug 1941 and was stationed in Mississippi, Florida and North Carolina then shipped to Cairo, Egypt in 1945.

SSgt. Wilson was discharged in 1946. His decorations include the WWII Victory Medal, Defense Medal, ATO Medal, EMETO Medal and Good Conduct Medal.

Memorable experiences include visiting the Egyptian Museum, Statue of Rames II, tombs of sacred bulls, Pyramid of Gizih and Sphiny of Alexander, tombs of the catacombs.

In 1946 he managed a cattle ranch in Florida; 1948, worked with US Fish and Wildlife Service for 10-1/2 years; then worked with the US Postal Service 16-1/2 years to retirement in 1975.

Married Edith Bevis in 1943 and they had five children: James Jr., Carolyn, Betsy, Robert and Ronny, and eight grandchildren. James Garnet passed away 26 Oct 1993 and Edith in 1976, both are buried in Ocala, FL.

LACY EDWARD WILSON, born 7 Feb 1910. He joined the USAF in 1942 at Owensboro, KY and was assigned to the Air Transport Command. He served as a cryptographer in a communication squadron. Discharged in 1945.

Married Elinor Cary in 1941 and they had two children, Julian Edward and Ree Cary. He was a principal at Sorgho Elementary School in 1950 and assistant superintendent of Davis County Schools until retirement in 1975. Lacy Edward taught a Bible class for 40 years. He passed away 25 Sep 1995.

LEO YEATMAN WILSON, Chief Electronics Tech, born 31 Jul 1920 in Sullivan, KY, Union County. At six weeks of age, he came to Cerulean, KY, Trigg County. He attended school in Cerulean until his senior year and was a member of the first graduating class of the new high school in 1938. Leo went to Los Angeles, CA and enrolled in a Radio-TV Trade School for two years, then was hired by Radio Station WHOP in Hopkinsville when they went on the air 8 Jan 1940.

Leo volunteered for the USN soon after Pearl Harbor and was called to active duty 3 Jan 1942 and sent to Boot Camp at Great Lakes, IL. He was given the rank of radioman 2nd class. He was in the first group to attend Radar School in Chicago. There were about 100 men in that group. After school, he was sent to Treasure Island, CA for advanced radar training.

In September 1942 he was assigned to the Navy Dry Dock in San Juan, Puerto Rico. In December 1942 he was promoted to radioman first class. He came home on leave and was married 16 Nov 1943 to Mary Gladys Morris of Hopkinsville.

He returned to the Caribbean area and was promoted to chief petty officer and reassigned to Curacao in the Netherlands West Indies. The island of Aruba was part of the repair facility. They worked on radar and sonar equipment on the submarine chasers.

When the submarine activity waned and the war in Europe was closing down, Leo was sent to the Anti-Submarine Warfare School in Charleston, SC as an instructor. Then in late 1944 he requested a transfer to new construction and was assigned to the heavy cruiser, *Los Angeles* (CA-135), being built in the Philadelphia Navy Yard. He spent three months at the Naval Research Labs in Washington, DC to become familiar with the new sector scan search radar that was being installed on the Los Angeles's 20 and 40mm and main battery guns. He left Washington on 13 Apr 1945, the day that President Franklin D. Roosevelt died.

The USS *Los Angeles* was commissioned in late July 1945. The ship went on "shakedown" cruise about the time the first atomic bomb was dropped. A few days later the second bomb was dropped and the war was ending for Leo. He received his discharge 5 Sep 1945.

He returned to work for Radio Station WHOP. He was chief engineer, play by play sportscaster, and co-host of the early morning program with Drury "Dink" Embry.

With the start of the Korean Conflict, Leo was recalled to active duty 5 Sep 1950, exactly five years to the day of his discharge from WWII. He reported to Norfolk, VA and was assigned to the repair ship USS *Delta* (AR-9). His wife Mary and daughter Molly Marie joined him on 1 December. In February 1951 the Delta was sent to San Diego, CA by way of the Panama Canal. Mary and Molly Marie returned to Hopkinsville, then flew to San Diego early in March. Leo's term of enlistment was finished in February 1952.

The family returned to Hopkinsville in a 1938 Chevrolet automobile they had purchased with their savings. Leo's pay as a chief electronics tech was $138 per month and Mary received an allotment of $50 per month.

For more information on Leo Y. Wilson and family see Trigg County History Book 1986, Vol. I, pages 547 and 548. *Submitted by Leo Y. Wilson.*

ROY VERNON WITTY, Master Sergeant, son of Roy Albert Witty and Ruth Vernon (Wood) Witty, was born 26 Feb 1913 in Cerulean, KY. He was inducted into the US Army to active service 29 May 1942 at Fort Harrison, IN and separated 19 Nov 1945 from Camp Bowie, TX with an honorable discharge.

His unit was 193rd Sig Rep Co. His occupation was radio repairman, FM installer repairman 097. He was involved in battles and campaigns in Rhineland and Central Europe. He received the Good Conduct Medal, American Theater Ribbon and WWII Victory Ribbon.

He participated in the Battle of the Bulge and was in a water tower with two buddies, sent to repair radio transmitters when radio silence was declared. A snow fell during the night, and they had to be very still and quiet in order not to call attention to their situation. They had food rations and cheese to eat. They obeyed orders and stayed for about three days, watching the battle of tanks clash below in the snow covered grounds. Their biggest fear was being shot at by their allied troops celebrating victory over the enemy.

He was later put on a ship in Europe heading towards the Pacific but was turned back. After the Japanese surrendered, he arrived back in USA on 1 Sep 1945 and was separated back to civilian life. He returned as a tech sergeant.

He stated that if he ever got back to Trigg County after the war was over he would always make it his home, and he did. He married a local Trigg County girl, Edith Lucille Francis, and they had two children, Roy Winfield Witty and Millie Maeve Witty Robison, along with four grandchildren: Tiffany, Jacob, Jordan and Chance.

He went into private business repairing radios, and later selling and repairing television sets in Trigg and Christian Counties. Prior to entering Army service he had graduated from Coyne Electrical School in Chicago, IL. He later enlisted in the USAFR and served until just three years short of retirement benefits with a medical discharge. He received several awards and was promoted to the rank of master sergeant. He also worked for several years at Fort Campbell and retired as a civil servant with benefits.

He and his wife were fortunate to live next door to Howard and Elizabeth Tinsley, two wonderful neighbors, until his death on 13 Aug 1991.

ROBERT HARMON WOOD, Private, entered the Armed Services from Trigg County on 31 Jan 1942. He was a member of Co. E 111th Inf. Regt. His military occupational specialty was Rifleman 745 and he qualified for the Combat Infantryman Badge.

"Bud," as he was known to his family and friends, served two years and 14 days in campaigns and battles in the Western Pacific. He also served one year and 14 days in the Continental US

He received the following decorations and citations: Asiatic-Pacific Theater Ribbon w/Bronze Star, American Theater Ribbon, Good Conduct Ribbon, and the WWII Victory Medal. Pfc. Wood returned to civilian life in Trigg County 28 Nov 1945.

After his stint in the Army, he became a carpenter by trade. He worked with Jimmie Adams for many years building barns. In the mid-1970s he traveled with his brother and nephew to Washington, DC to help build a barn for the Bicentennial Celebration.

Bud married Aline Merrick Mitchell in 1979. He died in 1985 and is buried in the Caldwell Blue Spring Cemetery.

AUBREY LAYTON WOODRUFF, Seaman 1/c, born 12 Feb 1920 in Cadiz, KY. He joined the USN 16 Oct 1941 and received his Naval Training Corps Certification 30 Apr 1942. His final scores were outstanding.

Aubrey was assigned to the USS *Idaho* as a seaman first class. Primarily he worked as a radar technician, and his ship was involved in numerous major battles during WWII.

He was discharged in 1945 and returned to Cadiz to make his home. He married Ruth Fern Swickard 27 Dec 1945

and they had three children: Nick, Layton and Susan, and five grandchildren: Nickolas, Aubrey, Katie, Lee and Landee.

After returning from the war, Aubrey worked and co-owned Woodruff Lumber Co. He then worked as maintenance supervisor for the Kentucky Park System. He died in February 1977.

HOLLIS BYRON WOODRUFF, Carpenter's First Mate, enlisted in the USN 28 Jan 1942 at Louisville, KY, and served in Hawaii until 1945 as a carpenter's first mate. He received an honorable discharge 18 Sep 1945.

Hollis was born in Trigg County 29 Apr 1916, the eldest son of Francis Ellis and Hollis Bradley Woodruff. He had two brothers, John Ellis and Aubrey Layton, and one sister, Margaret Woodruff Griffin. He grew up in Trigg County and graduated in 1933 from Cadiz HS. After high school he worked for several years with his family on projects around Trigg County, Louisville and Evansville areas.

In Louisville he met Isabelle Theresa Schaeffer, whom he married after WWII and returned to Cadiz to work in the family business. Woodruff Lumber Co. was one of two lumber companies of its kind in Cadiz from the 1940s to 1960s. The company specialized in building homes, remodeling and selling home building supplies. The business operated a fleet of trucks, employed carpenters, plumbers, masons, electricians and painters from Cadiz and surrounding community.

When WWII ended Hollis' sons, Hollis Byron, Aubrey Layton and John Ellis, all married, and returned to Cadiz. They made their home in the W.B. Woodruff residence and helped operate Woodruff Lumber Co. Aubrey and John purchased homes and moved from the Woodruff residence on Main Street. Byron stayed in his grandfather's home and raised his family there. In time, Byron became the sole proprietor of Woodruff Lumber Co. until his retirement in 1971.

Hollis Byron and Isabelle had one son, Byron Lee, born in 1946. He graduated from Trigg County High in 1964. He earned degrees from Austin Peay State University and completed a doctorate from the College of William & Mary in Virginia.

In 1966 Lee married Helen Beth Gresham of Cerulean. They have two children, Jennifer Lee Woodruff Amos of Farmville, VA and Clay Britton Woodruff. They have three grandchildren. Beth worked with the Commonwealth of Virginia and served as an adjunct professor of sociology at Richard Bland College.

Byron Woodruff was a member of Cadiz Christian Church, Cadiz Masonic Lodge No. 121, and Rizpah Shrine Temple.

Byron's wife Isabelle died from natural causes in 1970. He later married Martha Ladd Cox from Lexington who is now deceased.

Byron Woodruff died 5 Dec 1984 and is buried in East End Cemetery, Cadiz, KY.

BENJAMIN RILEY WOODS, PFC, was born 29 Apr 1924, at West Dale, LA and grew up around Mansfield, LA. He was inducted in the Air Force 25 Jun 1943, volunteered for the Infantry in January 1944 and joined the 65th Div. at Camp Shelby.

Shipped out for overseas in 1944, landed at LeHavre, France; was in combat through France, Germany and Austria. While overseas he served with the 3rd Army under Gen. Patton. At the end of the war his regiment occupied Linz, Austria. He returned to USA 10 June for 30 days leave. After his leave he was to report to Fort Mead, MD to ship out to Japan, but the war ended while he was on leave. He went to Fort Benning, GA and from there was sent to Camp Campbell, KY to join the 5th Div. There he met Jean Blakeley and they married 24 Dec 1945.

He was discharged at Camp Campbell in December 1946. His decorations include the Combat Infantry Badge, Bronze Star, six Battle Stars, Victory in Europe and Good Conduct.

After leaving the Army he attended Nashville Technical College in Refrigeration, graduating in 1949. He lived in Cerulean, Trigg County from 1946-1949 then moved to Hopkinsville where he was employed with Cayce Yost Co.; returned to Cerulean in 1982 and lived there until 1999 when he returned to Hopkinsville. He retired in May 1986 from Montgomery Ward.

Benjamin and Jean have three children: Connie Lorene Joiner, Kay Harrison, Rickie, and eight grandchildren.

WILFORD EUGENE WYATT, Corporal, born 27 May 1921 in Trigg County, KY, son of Mr. and Mrs. Sherman Wyatt, Cadiz, KY. He was drafted into the US Army, 12 Nov 1942 in Michigan.

He received his basic training at Camp Swift, TX, left for overseas duty in 1944, where he was stationed in France, Holland, Belgium and Germany. He served with the 102nd Inf. Div. of the US 9th Army as a Full Tract Driver pulling a 155 Howitzer Gun until the war was over, then in Occupational until discharged 7 Apr 1947.

When he was discharged from the service his rank was corporal. He received a Conduct Medal, Battle Star, and Certificate of Merit in recognition for outstanding honor in service in Germany from 24 Nov 1944 to 8 May 1945.

He married Juanita Baker, also from Trigg County, 8 Feb 1947. They have four sons: Amos, James, David and Tommy. They also have 11 grandchildren.

He became a Baptist minister in 1950, and has lived in several different towns. He and Juanita now reside in Princeton, KY.

GEORGE L. YOAKUM, 1st Lieutenant, born 9 Feb 1921 in LaFollette, TN. He left college to join the Army Air Corps on 16 May 1942 and qualified for aircraft pilot training after going through the Classification Center at Berry Field Nashville, TN. After completing Pre-Flight School at Maxwell Field, flight training at Albany, GA, Newport, AR, and Dothan, AL, he was promoted to second lieutenant as single engine pilot in August 1943.

Yoakum checked out in the P-47 fighter plane and went by troop ship to England in January 1944 where he was assigned to the 356th Fighter Group. He flew 83 combat missions (285 combat hours) to engage enemy aircraft attacking Allied bombers over occupied Europe, dive bomb German convoys coming into the invasion front, strafe railroad locomotives and marshalling yards, and drop bombs on enemy airfields and strafe aircraft on enemy airfields.

He completed his tour of duty in September 1944 and was awarded the Air Medal w/3 clusters and the Distinguished Flying Cross w/cluster. The stateside assignment as flight instructor became boring, and he vol-

unteered for training as Weather Observer out of Marianna Islands over Japan and report weather conditions to determine the feasibility of sending out the B-29s for bombing over Japan. Victory in Japan stopped Yoakum in California before going to the assignment in the Marianna Islands.

After the war Yoakum moved to Hopkinsville, KY where he engaged in farming for about 15 years, then went to work with the Federal Government as an ammunition inspector on both conventional and special weapons munitions. He retired at Fort Campbell in 1983.

After his wife died with cancer, Yoakum married a Cadiz widow whose husband had also died with cancer. Yoakum has one daughter, Lea Ann, in Ohio and two grandchildren, Shawna and Jimmy Cornell.

His most memorable experience was 20 March "I flew 2.5 hours on what was supposed to be an escort mission. I was flying on Capt. Bailey's wing when we went into a solid overcast at 5,000 feet and one hour later turned back at 30,000 feet without seeing the top of the overcast.

After turning back, after several minutes, we came out in the clear at 5,000. We began to receive very close and very accurate flak. I was scared and called Bailey on the radio and suggested that we go down to the deck (ground level). Anticraft artillery could not get line-of-sight on low flying aircraft. We began to enjoy the scenery. I had turned my gun switch to "camera only" and got some beautiful 16mm. Suddenly, a cross country electric transmission line came into view and too late. A huge ball of fire or illumination resulted from my contact with the wires. I realized that contact with the ground was inevitable, so I called Bailey on the radio, told him that I had hit those wires, 'I think I've had it.' It suddenly came to me as if by some divine inspiration that a seldom used trim tab on the elevator (for stabilizing the plane on take-off and landing) when cranked in all the way, I was able to fly back home with 15 to 25 feet of cable hanging on the plane. Someone hung the wire overhead in the "ready room" and wrote a comment in the *Stars And Stripes* about "the lights going out in Berlin.

There are guardian angels.

WILLIAM F. YOUNG JR., PFC, born 1 Mar 1919 in Evansville, IN. He joined the service 25 Mar 1944 and was stationed at Fort Benjamin Harrison, IN; Camp Wolters, TX and left for overseas from Camp Shanks, NY.

William served with HQ Co., 2nd Bn., 289th Inf. Regt., 75th Div. He participated in the Battle of the Bulge and fought across France, Belgium, Holland and Germany. Discharged 3 Dec 1945, his awards include the Bronze Star and three Battle Stars.

Married Clara Frances 25 Jul 1939 and they have five children: William III, Larry, Michael, Steven and Francile, 12 grandchildren and 15 great-grandchildren.

Memorable Experience: On a cold day in January 1945 we were ordered into battle and as a wireman I started with a reel of wire on my back. I was smoking a cigar as I reached the crest of the hill, the cold wind blew the cigar smoke back in my face and I passed out. When I came to, my reel of wire was gone and I was alone. The Germans started shelling again. There was a building nearby and I ran for it. The shelling was getting heavier and I dove down a coal chute into the basement. In the light of my flashlight, I found a can of Campbell beans on a shelf, so I ate them. When the shelling stopped, I came out of the basement. An elderly German man came up and asked if I had cigarettes. I gave him five K-ration packs of cigarettes. On returning to my outfit, I discovered that two soldiers had found me passed out, took my reel of wire, and told my sergeant that I had been killed in action and gave him my wire. I was told to let the sergeant know I wasn't dead then go back and string my wire.

Korean War

BENNIE GENE ADAMS, born 20 Jan 1930 in Akron, OH to Jim F. Adams and Maggie Belle Hargrove Adams. They returned to Trigg County when Bennie was a young child. He attended Upper Donaldson, Oakland, Chestnut Grove and Cadiz Grade Schools. In the fall of 1942 the family moved back to Akron so Jim could work at The Goodyear Tire and Rubber Company during WWII. Bennie attended Lincoln Grade School and South High School in Akron.

In February 1947 the family bought a farm on the South Road and returned to Trigg County. Ben enrolled at Trigg County HS where he joined the football team. He was quarterback and captain his senior year. He graduated in May 1949.

In January 1951 Bennie and Harry Thomas enlisted in the Air Force. He took his basic training at Lackland AFB, TX. He served for 2-1/2 years in Japan from July 1951 until December 1953. When he returned to the States, he was assigned to Bolling Field in Washington DC until his discharge in December of 1954.

After Ben's discharge he enrolled at Penn State University where he received his degree in 1959. He taught and coached football in high schools in Pennsylvania, New Jersey and also at Grove City College in Pennsylvania. He retired from teaching in 1996.

In 1954 Ben married Joan Thomas of State College, Pennsylvania. They have a son Steve, daughter Robin and three granddaughters. Ben and Joan live in Grove City, PA. In his retirement he enjoys golfing, fishing and traveling. *Submitted by Norma Adams Swank.*

BOBBY JAMES ADAMS, born 1 Oct 1936 in Donaldson Creek, the son of Jim F. Adams and Maggie Belle Hargrove Adams. He attended grade school at Lincoln Grade School in Akron, OH and Cadiz Grade School. He attended High School at Trigg County High until the family moved back to Akron where he attended South High School and graduated from there in June 1955.

Bobby enlisted in the Air Force on 25 Jun 1955 and served until 25 Jun 1959. He took his basic training at Sampson AFB in New York. In May 1956 he went to Korea where he was stationed at Kimpo for one year.

When he returned to the USA, he was stationed at McGuire AFB in Wrightown, NJ for the next two years. He met the girl he was to marry, Patricia Stover at McGuire. She was in the Women's Air Force. After Bobby was discharged they moved back to Ohio. Bobby worked at the Lawsons/Schwebel Baking Company for the next 36 years.

Bobby and Pat have a daughter Bobbie J.; two sons, Keith and Eric; and five grandchildren. They live in Kent, OH. He now spends his time with his grandchildren and delivering Meals-on-Wheels five days a week.

DECATOR ADAMS, PFC, born 3 Feb 1929 in Trigg County, KY. Enlisted in the service 4 Jan 1951. Assignments: 393 FA BN, Camp Polk,

LA, 424 FA A Btry. After nine months training, he was sent to Korea and fought from November 1951 to November 1952.

He was discharged as private first class, 3 Jan 1953, at Camp Breckinridge, KY. His awards include the United Nations Service Medal and Korean Service Medal.

He worked for Chrysler for five years, Johnson Controls for 27 years and retired in 1993. He retired from farming in 1999. He lives in Hopkinsville, KY and stays busy mowing yards and cemeteries.

He married Betty Sue Logan 30 Nov 1957. They have two children, James Decator and Kathy Sue, and four grandchildren: Jason, Jasmine and Jade Adams and Susan Harris.

DEXTER EARL ADAMS, Chief Master Sergeant (E-9), born 24 Dec 1930. He enlisted in the USAF 27 Dec 1950 at Princeton, KY, and participated in both Korean and Vietnam wars.

Assignments: Basic training at Lackland AFB, TX; Medical Technician School, Brooke Army Medical Center, Fort Sam Houston, TX; USAF Hospital, Keesler AFB, MS, unit supervisor; USAF Hospital, Lackland AFB; USAF Hospital, Wright Patterson AFB, OH; Gunter AFB, AL; physician assistant school for independent duty; French Morocco, North Africa; West Palm Beach, FL; USAF Hospital, Travis AFB, CA; Air Evacuation School, Brook's AFB, TX; 1370th Hiran and Photo Operations, Albany, GA (special assignment); South America; Lima, Peru; South America; Bogota, Columbia; Port Moresby, New Guinea; USAF Command Hospital; Air Force Academy, Colorado Springs, CO; West Coast Air Evacuation Center, Travis AFB, CA; Camron Bay, Vietnam; Tactical Air Command, MacDill AFB, Tampa, FL, superintendent of hospital services and nursing services.

Discharged 1 May 1976 as chief master sergeant. His awards include the AF Commendation Medal, AF Outstanding Unit Award, AF Good Conduct Medal, Good Conduct Medal Joint Services, American Defense Service Medal, National Defense Service Medal, Korean Service Medal, Vietnam Service Medal, AF Overseas Longevity Ribbon, AF Longevity Service, UN Medal and RVN Campaign Medal.

Two of his many memorable experiences are (1) the large number of casualties they received from Vietnam when he was with the West Coast Air Evacuation Unit; (2) being able to help care for victims of the earthquakes which devastated the capitol city of Managua Nicaragua.

Civilian Activity: two years Hillsboro Community College, Tampa, FL, and seven years with Hillsboro County Schools. He married Phyllis Amy Smith on 13 Nov 1951, and they live in Cadiz, KY. They have three children: Karen Sue, Rodney Lee, Kathy Lynn and three grandchildren: Jessica, Harry and Kattie.

WALTER A. ADAMS, Sergeant, born 21 Oct 1931 in Trigg County, KY. The Korean Conflict was going on when he graduated from Trigg

County HS, and the draft was awaiting. As his older brother, D.C., was already in Korea serving in the Army as heavy artilleryman, Walter decided to enlist in the USMC. He was sent to San Diego, CA for boot camp, then to Joseph H. Pendleton, Oceanside, CA, for advanced infantry training, followed by orders to Korea.

In June 1952 he boarded the *General Meigs* troopship and three weeks later landed at Incheon, Korea, where they boarded a train with cattle cars and went up to the front lines. Two weeks later he was engaged in the Battle of Bunker Hill.

Returned to the States in June 1953, landing at the San Francisco Bay near the Golden Gate Bridge and Treasury Island Naval Base. From there to Cherry Point, NC, VMJ-2 Air Squadron, where he worked as a jet mechanic for the last 18 months active duty of his military career. He was then given obligated inactive reserve until 28 Dec 1959 when he was discharged.

Sgt. Adams' medals include the Korean Presidential Unit Citation, Good Conduct, Korean Service Ribbon w/2 stars, UN Ribbon and National Defense Service Medal.

Walter and Barbara were married in August 1957 and live in Trigg County. They have two sons, Walter Scott and Robert Milton, and four grandchildren: Jason, Candace, Amanda and Aaron.

Walter worked 33 years for TVA Cumberland Steam Plant and retired in 1998. Hunting and fishing are his hobbies.

WILLIAM ROBERT "BUNK" ADAMS, Specialist 3/c, born 27 May 1934 in Trigg County. Joined the U.S. Army 22 Mar 1955 with basic training at Fort Chaffee, AR. Other assignments included Fort Hood, TX, Exercise Sage Brush, four months of maneuvers at Fort Polk, LA. He served with 1st Armd. Div., 702nd Armd. Inf.

Discharged 21 Mar 1957 as specialist third class. Awards include the Expert Infantry Badge.

Memorable experience was being deployed to Suez Canal in 1956, but then deployment was canceled before leaving the States. Also memorable was witnessing 4,000 paratroopers drop during Exercise Sage Brush.

He married Carolyn Sue Baker 27 Nov 1958 and they live in Hopkinsville, KY. They have one daughter Sonya Gay Dillingham. William retired from Nations Bank in 1998. He started Bill Adams Appraisal Service and is a SRA member of Appraisal Institute. Also leads Bible study at Christian County Jail and raises roses.

ORMAN DUVELL ALLEN, Corporal, born 30 Apr 1932 in Trigg County. Joined USAR and entered active service 21 Aug 1952 at Owensboro, KY. Served with Co. A, 803rd Engr. Avn. Bn. November 1952 to January 1953, attended TSUTC, Fort Eustis, VA, Heavy Vehicle Driver Course.

Separated 7 Aug 1954 at Fort Knox, KY, and stayed in Reserves until 1960. Awards include the National Defense Service Medal and Good Conduct Medal.

He married Lula Mae Vowell 16 Jan 1952 and they live in Cadiz, KY. They have 10 children: Gary Eugene, Robert Steven, Patricia Lynn, Michael Anthony, John Neal, Penny Denise, Kerry Reed, Carl Brent, Jeffery Lane, Donna Jo; nine grandchildren: Heather, Kisha, Chad, Andrea, Anthony, Patti, Amber, Christopher, Amy; and two great-grandchildren, Hunter and Josh. Orman is retired and enjoys hunting and fishing.

DORSIE LYN BAILEY, PFC, born 25 Mar 1934 at Reagan, TN. He attended the University of Tennessee, Martin Branch, serving two years in Reserve Officers Training Corps, 1954-55. In 1955 he served as executive officer of Co. B, Cadet Battalion.

Electing not to go into advance training due to school transfer, he was later drafted in February 1957 and assigned to U.S. Army Training Center, Fort Chaffee, AR, Btry. D, 2nd Bn., 1st Regt., 25 Feb-19 Apr 1957.

After basic training he attended The U.S. Army Specialist School Command. Upon completion of this training, he was assigned to HQ Co., U.S. Infantry, Fort Chaffee, AR, where he worked in military personnel until his discharge as a private first class.

In the service he met and married Jane Loo Little, Fort Smith, AR. They had two sons, Dorsie Green and Newell Lynn, and five grandchildren. Jane passed away in April 1991. He is now married to Teresa Thomas, mother of two sons, Shannon Knight and Shane Knight, and grandmother of three.

Lynn was founder and owner of Bailey Lumber Co. He sold the business and retired in 1998. That year he was elected and is presently serving as mayor of Cadiz, KY. Lyn and Teresa reside at 143 Nunn Blvd.

CHARLES ALLEN BAKER JR., Staff Sergeant, born 9 Apr 1931 in Gracey, KY, enlisted in the U.S. Army on 8 Jun 1951 and was attached to Co. A, 40th Inf. Div., 160th Regt., 1st Bn., 8th Army in Japan, Korea.

Most of his enlisted service was war time, so he never talked much about it. He was always proud of having served in the U.S. military and wore his uniform with pride, dignity and distinction. He held the rank of staff sergeant at the time of his Honorable Discharge on 23 Mar 1956.

During his military career he received three Battle Stars, Korean Citation, Republic of Korea Presidential Unit Citation, Army Commendation Medal, Good Conduct Medal, Army of Occupation Medal, National Defense Service Medal, Korean Service Medal, and UN Service Medal.

After returning home from the military; he married Terry Jane Wilson on 2 Apr 1956. They made their home in Cadiz, KY, raising two daughters, Linda Kaye, and Laura LaVern. Linda died in September 1976. For a few years he had several different jobs before going to work in Civil Service at Fort Campbell, KY. He worked with Civil Service for 37 years before retiring in 1993. He stayed busy after retirement helping others farm and doing other odd jobs chores around the house.

He would be remembered today as an easygoing, calm, quiet and dependable person. He was faithful to his church and at home. He enjoyed laughter and was always willing to lend a helping hand.

On 19 Aug 1998 he was diagnosed with liver cancer, and died 23 Sep 1998.

FRANK E. "BEN" BENSHOFF , SFC-E7, born 11 Dec 1932 at Bellecenter, OH. He enlisted 21 May 1951 and took his basic training at Fort Campbell, KY, C Btry., 457th Arty., 11th Abn. Div., then Jump School at Fort Benning, GA., Demolition School at Fort Leonard Wood, MO.

In March 1953 he transferred to 10th SFG, Fort Bragg, NC. In November the group sailed to Europe, arrived in Bad Toelz, Germany. After two years he was assigned to 18th Engr. Bn. at Wuertzburg, Germany. There he met and married Hilde Fries. The children were Brigitti Gutierrez, Benny Ray, Bobby Lynn and B.J. One granddaughter, Kaleigh Renie, and a step-grandson Lonnie Wright.

In January 1957 he was discharged in New York, and re-enlisted in January 1959 at Denver, CO, assigned to 326th Engr. Bn. 101st Abn., Fort Campbell, KY.

In September 1965, with the 8th Engr. Bn., 1st Cav. Div., he sailed to RVN. After one jump he was all over RVN, helping to build airfields. After one year he was re-assigned to HHC 326th Engr. Bn. at Fort Campbell, KY. In 1969 he returned to RVN with the 173rd Abn. Bgde. as secretary custodian of the club system at English Air Base. In December 1970 he returned to 327th Engr. Bn. 82nd Abn. Div., Fort Bragg, NC.

One year later he voluntarily transferred to HHC 2/503nd Inf. at 101st Fort Campbell, KY until he retired in May 1973 as SFC-E7. Received the Master Parachute Badge, Good Conduct Medal (3rd award), Vietnam Service Medal w/7 Campaign Stars and Bronze Star Medal.

Since his retirement Hilde and Ben were divorced in 1987. He re-married in 1989 to Pat Adams of Trigg County, which lasted five years. Ben has two grandchildren in Tennessee.

Ben's life has been full, from a truck driver to a Mobile Home Park owner and working on the Transalaska Pipeline, hunting and fishing all over the USA. He still resides in Trigg County.

BOYCE W. BIRDSONG, Corporal, born 25 May 1929. He was drafted 6 Mar 1951 and served with 123 Medica Co., 3rd Army, Fort Benning, GA as a medic. He transferred to the Army Reserve 5 Mar 1953 and was honorably discharged 30 Aug 1956.

He worked at several jobs until he went to work for TVA in 1965 and from where he retired in September 1989.

He married Louise Littlejohn 17 Dec 1950 and they live in Cadiz, KY. They have two children, Ted and Nancy, and four grandchildren: Kendel, Matthew, Emaly and Sabastion. Boyce and Louise attend South Union Baptist Church, Canton, KY. Boyce enjoys wood working, fishin and caring for his lawn and garden.

LAWRENCE WADE BRABOY, Airman 1/c, born 14 Nov 1933 in Cadiz, KY. He was the son of Lacy Wade and Coella Baker Braboy. He enlisted in the USAF on 20 Aug 1953 in Owensboro, KY. He took his basic training at Sampson AFB in Geneva, NY. On completion of basic training he was sent to Chanute AFB in Rantoul, IL for schooling with the 3345th Technical Training Wing.

In March 1954 he left for Clark AFB in the Philippine Islands, where he served with the 581st Air Re-Supply Squadron for eight months. In November 1954 the squadron moved to Kadina AFB in Okinawa. While stationed in the Philippine Islands and Okinawa he was an engine airplane mechanic I and crew chief on B-29 aircraft. He was in 15 foreign countries including England where he had the opportunity to witness the changing of the guards at Buckingham Palace. In October 1955 he boarded the USS *Walker* for 21 days to return home.

On 15 Nov 1955, he married Carrie Elizabeth Samsil from Howell, KY. By late November, Hunter AFB in Savannah, GA became home. He was with the 308th Bombardment Wing-M-(SAC). He was also crew chief on KC-97 Refueler Tanker and refueled B-52 bombers in mid-air. On 2 Jan 1956 he left for Ben Guerir AFB, French Morocco, North Africa where he was stationed for three months. In preparing for departure from North Africa, he was ordered back to the barracks for his dog tags. Upon returning to the airfield, the airplane he was to have boarded had taken off without him and he witnessed it crashing into the side of the mountain. There were no survivors. In August 1956 he returned to North Africa to the Sidi Slimane Air Base. On 7 Apr 1957 he went to Kindley AFB in Bermuda for one month. While serving his country he received the following medals: National Defense Service Medal, Korean Service Medal and UN Service Medal.

He received an honorable discharge on 19 Aug 1957. At the time of discharge, he held the rank of airman first class. He surrendered to the ministry on 30 Oct 1962. In March 1966 he enrolled in Baptist Bible College, Springfield, MO. He graduated with a theology degree in May 1969. During his years in the ministry he was the pastor of Baptist churches in Ava, MO; Springfield, IL; and Hopkinsville, KY. He took a medical retirement in August 1990.

He and Elizabeth have four children: Deborah Lyon, Donna Walker, Denise Smith and Donald Braboy. They have seven grandchildren: Casey, Jordan, Jaime and Heather Lyon; Hannah, Allison and Zoe Braboy. After a battle with cancer Lawrence went home to be with the Lord, 2 Apr 1997.

RICHARD H. BRABOY, Airman 1/c, born 17 Dec 1930 in Trigg County, the son of Lacy and Coella Baker Braboy. On 13 Oct 1952 he joined the USAF with assignments at Owensboro; Lackland AFB, TX; Sioux City, IA; Seoul, Korea; and Maxwell AFB, Montgomery, AL.

Discharged 12 Oct 1956 and stayed in the Reserves until 12 Oct 1960. Awards include the National Defense Medal, Korean Service Medal, UN Service Medal and Good Conduct Medal.

Richard married Jane Thomas 17 Nov 1994. He retired from Tennessee Valley in 1994. Richard has three children: Karen (deceased), Barry and David, and three grandchildren: Shannon, Brandi and Heather.

EARL BARNEY BRAME, PFC, born 12 Apr 1933 in Stewart County, TN. Joined the Army 26 May 1953 and served with the Co. I, 85th Inf. Regt. as a truck driver during the Korean War. He was discharged 26 Apr 1955.

Married Jean Herndon 3 Nov 1955 and has three children: Connie, Tim and Jenny, and two grandchildren, Beth and Michael Bruce.

He was a truck driver until retirement in June 1992 and passed away 27 Apr 2000.

BILL GORDON BRIDGES, Staff Sergeant, Bill Gordon Bridges, born 20 Feb 1931, in Trigg County, Beechy Fork Creek, volunteered for the USAF in February 1951 during the Korean Conflict. At induction, he and Blanford Bridges left Hopkinsville on a Greyhound Bus bound for Owensboro, KY. After three months of basic training at Lackland AFB, San Antonio, TX, he was assigned to Pennsylvania State College for additional training. After this training, he was assigned to Tyndall AFB, Panama City, FL, where he spent the remainder of his four year tour of duty as a junior administrator in the training school for crew pilots. He reached the rank of staff sergeant.

After discharge in January 1955, he entered Murray State University, then transferred to the University of Kentucky, College of Engineering from where he graduated in 1959 with a degree in civil engineering. Upon graduation, he began work with the Division of Engineering, Commonwealth of Kentucky, Frankfort where he continues to be employed.

While a student at the University of Kentucky, he met and married June Scott, a native of Clark County, KY. They have two children: son Scott, a physician specializing in neurology and practicing in Knoxville, TN and daughter Susan, a physician specializing in obstetrics and gynecology and practicing in Martinez, GA. Susan and her husband, Hossain Alavi, M.D., have a daughter, Sara June.

Today, June and Bill live in Lexington, KY, where they intend to retire. He enjoys watching UK sports and the dynamics of state government. His military career was educational and he feels it gave him the inspiration to finish his education. His parents were Gordon and Ernestine Bridges. He still maintain ties to Trigg County as his sister Betty Cunningham and his brother Bob Bridges have kept the farm on Beechy Fork Creek, where they grew up.

BOBBY STANLEY BRIDGES, Staff Sergeant, born 3 Jun 1934 in the Maple Grove Community of Trigg County, KY, son of Gordon and Ernestine Bridges. After high school graduation he worked at J.W. Cowherd's grocery before joining the Air Force 2 Sep 1953 in Louisville, KY.

After basic training at Sampson AFB, NY he was sent to Keesler AFB, MS for flight simulator tech training, then assigned to McGhee-Tyson AFB in Knoxville, TN.

After his discharge 1 Sep 1957, he enrolled at the University of Tennessee and joined the TN ANG with duty as airborne radio repairman. In 1961 Russia built the Berlin Wall and was trying to keep aircraft out of the Berlin air corridors.

On 1 Nov 1961 President Kennedy activated the TNANG of Knoxville, TN and they were sent to Ramstein AFB, Germany with the duty to send F-104 Starfighters up the Berlin Corridor to remind the Russians we had some fast aircraft. They returned to McGhee-Tyson AFB in July 1962. Their squadron was discharged from service 15 Aug 1962 and returned to ANG status. Bobby was discharged as staff sergeant.

He went to work with the Federal Aviation Administration and retired from the FAA 2 May 1994 after 41 years of government service as manager, Air Traffic Control.

Bobby married Patsy Cook of Alcoa, TN on 16 Jul 1955. They have two children, Timothy Bridges and Rebecca Cokkinias, and two grandchildren, Kyle and Jake Cokkinias. Bobby and Patsy have lived in Crossville, TN, since 1967 and belong to the Crossville Methodist Church.

CARL T. "BUNNY" BRIDGES, Aerographer Mate, born 1 Feb 1934 in Trigg County. In the fall of 1955, the U.S. government drafted personnel for the USN, the first time since WWII and several from Trigg County besides him were drafted.

Entered the service 21 Nov 1955 with assignments at Great Lakes Naval Center Boot Camp and USNAAS Brown Field, Chula Vista, CA. He was a land loving sailor and had shore duty the length of his enlistment. Received honorable discharge 21 Nov 1961.

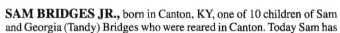

Divorced, he has two children, Richard and David, and four grandchildren: Bridget, Colten, Kyle and Zackary. He retired from Rogers Group, Inc. in 1996 and lives in Cadiz, KY. He enjoys his grandchildren, fishing and travel.

SAM BRIDGES JR., born in Canton, KY, one of 10 children of Sam and Georgia (Tandy) Bridges who were reared in Canton. Today Sam has three brothers and five sisters (still living) employed in different states. His grandparents are Jack and Emma Hopson Bridges and maternal grandparents Major and Sally Bryant Tandy.

Sam entered the USN and was on active duty 1954-58. He served during the Korean Conflict. Two of his brothers, Jack and Alfred, also served in the Navy. After his discharge, he entered civilian life in Michigan, where he worked, married, retired and is buried there.

BILLY BRYANT, born 9 Feb 1932 in Trigg County between the rivers, the ninth child of Jim and Mintie Lee (Downs) Bryant. He was drafted into the U.S. Army 7 Jan 1953 and took his basic training at Fort Bragg, NC. He was in the 42nd Engineers where he learned to operate bulldozers and road grader equipment.

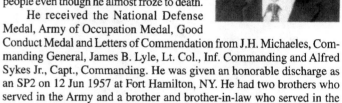

Then he was sent to Seattle, WA where he caught a ship and 18 days later landed in Seoul, Korea. He was sent to Uijongbu on the 38th Parallel where he spent 24 months cleaning up after the war. They slept in tents with dirt floors and had a potbelly stove for heat. They had to take cold showers outside. It snowed and rained a lot there.

Returned to the States to Huntsville, AL to Redstone Arsenal for three months and learned a lot about missiles. Sent to Fort Sill, OK, where he was a supply clerk and was discharged on 10 May 1956 as Specialty 4. He also entered the Army Reserves on 6 Jan 1961 and was discharged on 31 Jul 1966.

On 13 May 1956, he met his wife-to-be Wandine Fowler. They were married 13 Oct 1956 and have three children: Lisa Cunningham, Jeff and Jimmy Bryant, and six grandchildren: Jessica Bryant Williams; Matthew and Ryan Cunningham; Taylor, Jennifer and Victoria Bryant.

He worked 23 years as a diesel mechanic and seven years as a truck driver and retired from Bond Trucking in 1995. He still drives part time for McCraw Lumber Company.

Billy and Wandine have lived at 2202 New Hope Road in Cadiz for 26 years and attend Liberty Point Baptist Church. He enjoys spending time with his grandchildren, doing some hunting every now and then and working in his garden. His favorite place to travel is to Gatlinburg, TN for a few days of leisure time.

GILMAR DOUGLAS BURGESS, Corporal, born 8 Mar 1926 in Cerulean, KY to Charlie W. and Irene Gentry Burgess. He was drafted into the Army 9 Aug 1951 and took his basic training at Camp Breckinridge, KY.

Transferred to Kileen Base, TX and served as a MP with the Atomic Energy Commission. Transferred to Army Reserve 9 Aug 1953 and was honorably discharged 27 Aug 1959.

Married Janette Mitchell 1 Aug 1951 and their only child, Dorris Elaine, was born in 1953. In March 1955 Gilmar was employed as a rural letter carrier out of the Cerulean Post Office.

He was active in Cerulean Baptist Church, the Cadiz Rotary Club and in many community projects. He was instrumental in the beginning stages of bringing county water to the Cerulean Community. He was also actively involved in establishing the Cerulean Volunteer Fire Dept. It was in the service of this fire department that he lost his life. On the way to a fire on 19 Aug 1971, a drunk driver ran a stop sign, striking his car and killing him instantly.

Gilmar was killed 13 days following the marriage of his daughter to Mike McGill. He would have been the proud grandfather of three: Janay, Jody and Justin, and great-grandfather of four: Audrey and Graham Futrell and Andrew and Jacob Terrell.

EDWARD EULANE BURKEEN, SP2, born on 3 Jan 1936 at Almo, KY, the son of Joe and Addie Burkeen. He joined the Army 29 Jun 1954

at Fort Knox and was assigned to the Third Armored Division, 532nd Engineering Company, Southern European Task Force which was deployed to the Alps Mts. to construct Site 2 where he worked for 24 months in deep snow and frigid conditions constructing underground sites for Armed Service use. He said he enjoyed the experience and learning the language of native people even though he almost froze to death.

He received the National Defense Medal, Army of Occupation Medal, Good Conduct Medal and Letters of Commendation from J.H. Michaeles, Commanding General, James B. Lyle, Lt. Col., Inf. Commanding and Alfred Sykes Jr., Capt., Commanding. He was given an honorable discharge as an SP2 on 12 Jun 1957 at Fort Hamilton, NY. He had two brothers who served in the Army and a brother and brother-in-law who served in the Navy.

He married a Trigg County girl, Ben Helen Joyce on 27 Jun 1959. They have three children, Ben Hale, Anne Kay and Matthew Lane; and three grandchildren: Kandice, Jack and Will.

Edward was a graduate of Murray State University having received BS, MA degrees and Rank 1. He worked in educational administrative positions for 30 years, retiring from the Kentucky Dept. of Education in 1988.

He was active for many years in church and community activities, having served as President of Trigg County Shrine Club, Lions Club and Golf Club, Worthy Patron of Eastern Star and Sunday School Supt. of Cadiz United Methodist Church where he was a member. He was a Kentucky Colonel, an "Outstanding Educator," a sports enthusiast, and an avid golfer. He died 13 Jun 1995.

LINDY E. BURROW, Corporal, served in the Korean War from 1951-1954 He was born 26 Mar 1929 in Prentiss, MS, one of five children. He attended Jeff Davis County schools, then worked on the family farm with his dad and older brother where they grew cotton.

In 1950 he went to Lorain, OH where he got a job in the steel mill He worked there for about a year as a lorry car operator.

He enlisted in the Army 5 Jan 1951 in Cleveland, OH and was sent to Ft Knox, KY for basic training. After finishing training, he was sent to Korea where he was in combat, and served there 11 months and four days with the 27th Arty. Bn.

Awards he was given were the Korean Service Medal w/Bronze Service Star, Combat Infantry Badge, Good Conduct Medal, United Nations Service Medal and National Defense Medal.

His most significant duty assignment was with B Co. 27th Engr. Bn. (C) Fort Campbell, KY where he was stationed after returning from Korea. As a corporal he took part in a variety of duties while there including working in the motor pool and training at AP Hill, VA.

He met Virginia Ann Thomas of Trigg County in 1952. They were married in 1953 and made their home in Cadiz, KY.

On 4 Jan 1954 he received an honorable discharge from the military service and returned to Lorain, OH to his job in the steel mill as a motor inspector. He established a home there and reared four children: Janet, Kathryn, Samuel and John. There are six grandchildren.

An avid fisherman he spent many vacations fishing Kentucky lakes. He retired from the steel mill in October 1984 after 35 years of service. In January 1986 he and his wife moved back to Prentiss, MS to live. He died there 17 Jun 1987 and is buried in the Tyrone Cemetery.

CARLTON G. BUSH, PFC, was drafted into the Army on 13 Apr 1954 and took basic training at Fort Knox, KY. He was transferred to Fort Hood, TX in September 1954 and assigned to the 1st Armored Division into a tank battalion. On 5 Feb 1955, he was in a tank cleaning, when an explosion went through the tank resulting in his being burned over 60% of his body. He spent the next 10 months in the hospital at Fort Hood, TX, where he went through several skin grafts and had to learn to walk again.

He received an honorable discharge on 30 Apr 1956 with the rank of PFC. Carl Cain drove all the way to Texas to bring him home to Kentucky.

Carlton married Dixie Davis Adams on 16 Sep 1961. They have two children, Randy Glenn Bush and Carla Gwen Bush Jones. He also has two stepdaughters, Judy Adams Rennison and Patsy Adams Dougherty; six grandsons, one granddaughter and one step-granddaughter.

He is a 1950 graduate of Trigg County HS and has retired from Kentucky State Penitentiary after 27 years of work. His parents are Carlos and Martha Childress Bush.

They currently live at 307 Eddyville Road in Trigg County in the Blackhawk Community. Although he has retired, he helps his son Randy do a little farming. He also enjoys watching his grandson T.C. play in sports and going to UK ballgames.

WILLIAM D. BUTLER, E-5, born 4 Oct 1933. Served in the Army from November 1955 to November 1957, spending 18 months in Washington DC as staff car driver.

Married Sheila on 25 Nov 1971. William retired 1 Jun 1993 from Whirlpool Corp. in Evansville, IN. They now live in Cadiz, KY, where he owns an antique shop. They have three sons: Jeff, Ronald and Phillip, and eight grandchildren: Jennifer, Jamie, Joey, Eric, Ben, Caleb, Will and Jarrod.

WILLIAM GARY CALHOUN, E-5, born 28 Jan 1933 in Trigg County, KY. His parents were Arelus and Estelle Calhoun. After graduating from Trigg County HS in 1952, he was engaged in farming until he was drafted into the U.S. Army.

Entered the Army 30 Apr 1953 at Owensboro, KY and completed basic training at Camp Breckinridge, KY. His most significant duty assignment was with Co. D, 67th Tank Co. with whom he served overseas. The unit wore a triangular arm patch with the inscription "Hell on Wheels" at the base of the triangle. With the 67th he was assigned duty in Ger-

many where he was part of the constant duty guard force whose mission was to protect West Germany.

Returned to Fort Knox, KY and discharged 14 Apr 1955. He was held in AD, transferred to Army Reserve and retired in 1961. He received all the usual medals and campaign ribbons.

Gary farmed for a short time, then entered the grocery business. After operating his own company for many years, he sold the business and went to work for Johnson Control until retirement. He was a member of Trigg County American Legion and served as Commander in 1964 of Post 74.

William Gary died 10 Jul 1996 and is buried in East End Cemetery, Cadiz. His children are Gary Craig, Hermitage, TN; William Carey, Tiptonville, TN; and three granddaughters in Tiptonville, TN: Brandy Blackburn, Amber Marie and Anna Elizabeth Calhoun.

GLEN M. CAMERON, SP-3, born 2 Aug 1928 in West Palm Beach, FL. Enlisted in the Army 19 Nov 1953 at West Palm Beach and took his basic training at Fort Knox, KY.

Sent overseas to Korea and assigned as a truck driver in Service Battery, 75th FA BN. Wars/Battles: Korean Peace Keeping Force. Memorable was driving in Korea and seeing a war shattered landscape.

Discharged 25 Oct 1955. His awards and medals are unknown due to most Korean War Veterans records were lost due to a fire at St. Louis, MO Records Center.

Civilian employment as farm worker, truck driver, factory worker and seasonal employee for Kentucky State Forestry. He lives in Cadiz, KY and enjoys wood-working.

JAMES STANLEY CAMERON, Airman 1/c, born on 14 Apr 1934 in Cerulean, Trigg County, KY. He graduated from Trigg County HS then followed in his older brother's footsteps by joining the USAF on 9 Mar 1955. James took his basic training at Samson AFB, Geneva, NY. He then went to Air Traffic Control School at Keesler AFB, Biloxi, MS. After Biloxi, he was shipped to Palm Beach AFB in Florida where he was in Radar School.

While stationed at Thule AFB in Greenland, he was an air traffic ground control specialist. He was also stationed at Perrin AFB, Dennison, TX where he was an air traffic specialist. James was discharged on 1 Dec 1958 with the rank of airman first class.

He moved to Atlanta, GA where he was employed as a Federal Aviation Agency, Air Traffic Controller for 30 years. James retired in August 1989 from the Atlanta Air Traffic Control Center, Hampton, GA.

He married Helen Baker in December 1960. They have two children, Janis Carole Cameron and James Andrew Cameron. They also have five grandchildren: Jake Livingston, Chase, Brandt, Addison Cameron and Sage Livingston (deceased).

James is now enjoying his church work, grandchildren and doing some traveling. He and Helen are at home at 170 North Drive, Hampton, GA 30228.

LEONARD LEE CAMERON, Staff Sergeant, born 3 Jun 1930 on Clarence Broodbent farm in the Wallonia, Trigg County, KY, area. In December 1946 his father moved to Bill Cunduff Farm. He attended Trigg County HS and graduated in 1949. He worked on the Cunduff farm until volunteering for the USAF 20 February.

Sworn in at Louisville, KY the next day, took a train to St. Louis, MO, then traveled to San Antonio, TX for basic training. Transferred to Tyndall AFB, FL to start Basic Air Police School. After completion he was assigned as air police patrol first at Tyndall then transferred in May 1952 to Pinecastle AFB, Panama City, FL. In June 1953 he moved into the office of Provost Marshall as assistant clerk, promoted to chief clerk in May 1954, and discharged 20 Jan 1955.

He entered University of Kentucky in Lexington, KY, where he studied agriculture and graduated in January 1958. He married Annalu Baker on 26 Feb 1958, moved to Hopkinsville and began work with USDA milk inspection for Western Kentucky, then for the Department of Revenue. In 1965 he farmed with his father-in-law until 1982 when he worked at UK Research and Education until retirement May 31, 1999.

Leonard and Annalu reside in Wallonia, Trigg County. They have one daughter, Anna Elizabeth Johnson, and one grandchild, Morgan Kendall Johnson.

WALTER DURWOOD CAMERON, SP3, born 21 Jul 1925. Between July 1943 and 1950, he was called for examination for military service five times and turned down each time. In June of 1954, he was called again and this time passed the examination.

He received his basic and advanced training at Fort Knox, KY, beginning 27 Jul 1954 and was transferred to Fort Dix, NJ. From Fort Dix, he was sent to New York Harbor and boarded a ship for Bremerhaven, Germany. In January 1955, he was first assigned to H&S Co. of the 61st Tank Battalion at Liepiem, Germany, then assigned to replace the Reproduction Specialist at H&S.

About three months after he arrived, he was made the driver of the CP truck. Whenever they were on training maneuvers he was always at the head of the line and had an officer riding with him at all times.

After serving 18 months at Liepiem, he was sent back to Fort Knox, KY for military discharge and discharged 19 Jun 1956 with a rank of SP3. He lives at Barkley Manor Apts., Cadiz, KY and has attended Mount Zion United Methodist Church since birth and been a member since July 1937. He has served as Sunday School superintendent since July 1986.

WILLIAM HAYDON CAMERON, Staff Sergeant, born in Trigg County on 5 Mar 1927. He volunteered for the Air Force in Hopkinsville 9 Jul 1950 during the Korean War.

After six weeks of basic training at Lackland AFB in San Antonio, TX, he was sent to Radar Mechanic School at Kessler AFB in Biloxi, MS. After finishing nine months of school, he was sent to the 36th Ftr. Bomb Wing in Furstenfeldbruck, Germany for a 3-year tour of duty.

On arriving at Furstenfeldbruck, he was transferred to aircraft maintenance and assigned as assistant crew chief on an F84 single seat jet fighter bomber. This plane was one of the "Skyblazer's" aerobatic planes, a group which was created by then " Major" Harry K. Evans and "Lieutenants" C.A. (Bill) and Charles C. (Buck) Patillo. The Sky Blazer's performed all over Europe at air shows. Maj. Evans created the "Thunderbirds" when he was rotated back to the States. Haydon was later assigned as crew chief on an F86 fighter.

At the time he didn't enjoy his time in service but looking back later, he realized that he was able to do things and see places he wouldn't have otherwise. He visited North Africa, Paris, France, Luxembourg, Belgium, and was at the "Tulip Festival" in Amsterdam, Holland.

He came back to the States in April 1954 and on 10 Jul 1954, he discharged at Bangor AFB in Maine with the rank of staff sergeant.

He worked on the farm for a while, then went to work for Mason Hanger-Silas Mason at the "Birdcage" on Clarksville Naval Base. In 1965 he moved his family to Amarillo, TX for a year but returned home to work at the Hoover Plant (later Johnson Controls) and in 1992 retired after 26 years as quality control supervisor for 22 years.

He has been a member of Mount Zion United Methodist for 60 years and has taught Sunday School for over 50 years.

He married Yvonne Cameron in 1957. They have three children: Dolores Hampton, Keith Cameron, and Linda Brashears; also, three grandchildren: Elizabeth Hampton, Kimberly Cameron and Cody Brashears.

Haydon and Yvonne live quite comfortably near Gracey in Christian County, KY.

HARVEY C. CARR, PFC, born 21 Aug 1932 in Canton, KY, son of Herbert and Vera Carr. Enlisted in the Army 12 Feb 1953 with assignment at Fort Carson, CO as x-ray Tech.

Discharged 11 Feb 1955 as private first class. Awards include the Good Conduct Medal and Sharp Shooter Medal.

Retired from sales, 30 Sep 2000, Action Ford, Lincoln, Mercury, Springfield, TN. He is divorced, no children.

THOMAS J. CARR, SP3, born 21 Jul 1926 in Trigg County, KY. Joined the Army in July 1954 at Cadiz, KY with assignment as clerk-typist, Silver Spring, MD. Discharged as SP3 at Fort Meade, MD in June 1956.

Married Mary Baker 29 May 1948 and they live in Clarksville, TN. They have two children, Karen Slate and Thomas J. Jr.; also, two grandchildren, Jason and Mary Dailey. Thomas retired in April 1985 as an accountant, Civil Service, Fort Campbell, KY.

ALBERT CASSITY JR., PFC, born 31 Oct 1928, Golden Pond, KY. Drafted 4 Jan 1951 at Cadiz, KY. Assignments included Engineering School, Fort Belvoir, VA and 6th Armd. Div., Fort Leonard Wood, MO. He was discharged 18 Dec 1952 as private first class.

Married Betty Wallace on 8 Aug 1952 and they live in Murray, KY. They have one daughter, Norita Ann Youngblood and two grandchildren, Ryan and Laura Youngblood. Albert retired from TVA in October 1986. He enjoys his family, travel and cattle farm.

HYRUM F. CHAMBERS, Corporal, born 6 Feb 1933, in Golden Pond, KY. He was drafted into the U.S. Army on 18 Mar 1953 and took basic training in Fort Jackson, SC. It consisted of 16 weeks of training in infantry and heavy equipment. He spent three weeks at Camp Breckinridge, KY and went from there to Aberdeen Proving Grounds in Aberdeen, MD. He was assigned to the motor pool at this base.

In February 1954, he was sent to Bordeaux, France, with the 82nd Engineering Co. where he served until his discharge at Fort Knox, KY, in March 1955, as a corporal.

He married Margaret Anne Baccus on 19 Aug 1953. She was from Lyon County, Between the Rivers in the Woodson Chapel Community. They are the parents of one son, Barry F., and a daughter, Kesha Sullivan. They have two grandchildren, Lynley Anne and Hogan Gray Sullivan.

Hyrum is a retiree from General Electric in Louisville, KY. He resides in Eddyville, KY with his wife, Margaret and enjoys golfing and working with the Between the Rivers, Inc. cemetery volunteers assisting with preserving the history of Between the Rivers and caring for and locating old cemeteries there.

AUSTIN "JACK" CLAWSON, AM3, born 24 May 1929 in Chicago, IL. He enlisted in the USN 24 May 1947 and trained as an aviation metalsmith. He was stationed in Washington DC at Anacostia Naval Air Station where he was classified as an instructor.

While at Anacostia he dated a WAVE for a while and was invited to a Christmas party at her house where she lived with three other girls. He got there early and one of the other girls let him in. On 25 Apr 1953 he married Jane McAtee, the girl who let him in at the party.

Discharged from the Navy 17 Jun 1955. They lived in northern Virginia until Jane retired from the Navy Dept. September 1980 they moved to Cadiz, KY. They have three sons: John Allen, James Austin and Robert Clarence and six grandchildren: Austin, Jane, Joshua, Brittany, Shawn and Julia. Jane passed away 11 Jan 1998.

Civilian Activity: Sales and management Bond Cloths, owner/operator Hallmark store, church choir, barbershop chorus and quartet. He retired in May 1992 from Cayce Yost, Hopkinsville, KY.

ESPER CRUMP JR., PFC, born 24 Jan 1933 in Cadiz, KY, the son of Esper Sr. and Addie Crump. He enlisted in the U.S. Army in 1953 at Louisville, KY and took basic training at Aberdeen Proving Ground, MD. He then transferred to Atlanta General Depot, Atlanta, GA for additional training.

PFC Crump then headed to Park AFB, Oakland, CA, where he was shipped from San Francisco to Japan. He flew from Japan to Tegu, Korea, where he served for the next 12 months.

He returned to the States (Colorado) and was honorably discharged at the rank of PFC in St Louis, MO, 12 Jan 1955. He returned to his hometown of Cadiz, KY.

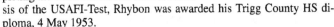

He married Dorthea Irvin on 21 Jan 1957. She passed in 1996. They had eight children: Eddie Irvin, Marjorie C. Edwards, Esper Crump III, Amelia Crump, Maryetta C. Anderson, Vernon Crump (veteran), Nathan Crump and Debbie Crump. There are seven grandchildren.

Esper was employed with several lumber companies, and later became employed with Johnson Control (formerly Hoover) 19 Jun 1967. He retired with 30 years of service in March 1998.

He is a lifelong member of Bloomfield Missionary Baptist Church, Cadiz. He serves on the Deacon Board, is a Sunday School teacher, and is the president of the Male Chorus. His hobbies are fishing, hunting heavily and spending time with his family and friends.

RHYBON CRUMP, Sergeant, born 19 Jan 1930 in Golden Pond, KY, enlisted into the U.S. Army, 21 Sep 1951 at Owensboro, KY. After training was completed, Rhybon entered the AUS ENGR branch.

His assignment was with Co. A 430th ECB, Korea. For his two years service in Korea, he was awarded the following decorations and citations: Korean Service Medal w/3 BSS, National Defense Service Medal, UN Service Medal and Meritorious Unit Citation.

Rhybon was discharged at Transfer Center, 101st Abn. Div. Camp Breckinridge, KY, 23 Sep 1953 as SGT (T). After completing the course of studies and on the basis of the USAFI-Test, Rhybon was awarded his Trigg County HS diploma, 4 May 1953.

Although Rhybon returned to civilian life, he remained in the Army Reserve 23 Sep 1953 to 23 Sep 1959. His civilian activity has been as a patrolman and an engineering aid with Waste Water of TVA/LBL. After 24 years, he retired from TVA/LBL. Today, he works as an Engineering Aid with the Kentucky Department of Transportation.

Rhybon is the son of James Monroe Crump and Beatrice McCloud Crump. He married Pauline Jones; there are two children, Paula Rhea Crump Flood and Raybon Crump Jr., and one grandchild, Brittany Nicole Crump. *Submitted by Paula Crump Flood.*

CUNNINGHAM BROTHERS, Earl Wayne and Lois Velma "Page" Cunningham, formally of Trigg County, are proud to have had six sons (five born in Trigg County, KY and one in Detroit, MI) who served in the Armed Forces.

1) Earl Eugene, E-5, was drafted in the U.S. Army and served two years at Fort Carson, CO.

2) Darryl Page joined the USN in 1957 and was stationed at U.S. Naval Hospital as X-ray tech. He was assigned to USS *McGoffin,* transferred to USS *Eldorado* (AGC-11) Amphibious Force Command Ship, transferred to Amphib. Construction Bn. I, Seabees, Coronado, CA and discharged in 1962. He joined the USARNG in 1973, HHC 1/123 Armor, Paducah, KY and had the honor of earning Emergency Field Expert Badge (was one of five to first receive this coveted award in reserve forces). Joined 100th Div. USA Reserve, Princeton, KY, C Co. and served as tank commander. Retired in 1999.

3) R. Keith, SP-5, joined the U.S. Army and served in space programs at Cape Canaveral, FL.

4) Jerald Cunningham, Lieutenant Colonel, was commissioned via AF ROTC. He completed undergraduate navigator training and navigator bombardier training at Mather AFB, CA. His first assignment was as a B-52D navigator, Pease AFB, NH. While there he deployed to Okinawa, Guam and Thailand and flew ARCLIGHT combat missions from each location.

Reassigned in 1969 to B-52H unit at Kincheloe, AFB, CA and completed second ARCLIGHT combat tour in Thailand. In 1971 selected to attend F-4 Fighter Replacement Training at George AFB, CA. He was assigned as F-4 Weapons System Operator at Seymour Johnson AFB, NC. Returned to SEA to support Linebacker II operations flying the F-4 from Thailand.

Returned from SEA in 1972 with over 90 combat missions into North

Vietnam and 22 to Hanoi. He accumulated a total of 225 combat missions with over 900 combat hours in SEA.

In 1974 he completed a MS degree in aeronautical engineering and assigned to Wright-Patterson AFB, OH as aeronautical engineer for flight test for the F5E/F program. In 1978 he returned to Asia as an F-4D flight commander for the 80th Tactical Ftr. Sqdn. At Kunsan, Korea. He received a follow-on transfer to Torrejon AB, Spain as an F-4D WSO instructor.

Served as chief of current operation, 16th AF in charge of deployment exercises throughout the Mediterranean area in 1981. Assigned in 1983 to HQ USAF in Europe, Ramstein, Germany as chief of MAJCOM Ground Launched Missile Mission Planning Branch. By the end of 1983 he completed Squadron Officers School, Air Command and Staff College and Air War College.

In 1985 he was selected as commander of the GLCM Theater Mission Planning Center at High Wycombe AS, England. Returned Stateside as the director of the USAF High Speed Rocket Sled Test Track at Holloman AFB, NM. Subsequently selected as Commander and Professor of Aerospace Studies, AFROTC Det. 643, Wright State University, Dayton, OH where he served until retirement in 1990. He received numerous military decorations.

5) Larry Lewis, enrolled in ROTC while in college at Ypsilanti where he received a degree in education. He enlisted in the U.S. Army for two years and was stationed in Vietnam at the same time his brother Jerry was flying there. He married Sandra Roose in 1969 and they have two children Kathleen and Jason.

6) Jeffrey Clark, born in Detroit, MI, was the only one of the six sons not born in Trigg County. He enrolled in ROTC while at Henry Ford College in Dearborn, MI. He was stationed at Fort Campbell, KY in 1985 as military intelligence officer in the 101st Abn. Div. and served in Desert Storm. Jeffrey married Sheri Amici 27 Apr 1985. They are parents of two, Jeremiah and Amanda.

MACK BLANE CUNNINGHAM,

Private, born 6 Jun 1932. He enlisted in the service in September 1955 with assignments at Fort Leonard Wood, MO; Fort Riley, KS; Fort Smith, AR. He was discharged in January 1956.

Married Lillie Maye Peters on 10 Apr 1953 and they live in Cadiz, KY. They have two children Linda DiAnne Tribble and Roger Dale, and two grandchildren, Brandon Fowler and Andrea Fowler Hampton.

Mack is still self-employed as a heating and cooling contractor. His hobbies are watching UK play ball and wood working projects.

WILLIAM HERBERT "BILL" CUNNINGHAM, SK1, born 17
Jan 1930 in Cadiz, KY. He graduated from Trigg County HS in 1948. He joined the Navy 3 Aug 1948 and went through basic training at Great Lakes, IL then attended Storekeeper School in Bayonne, NJ. He served aboard the USS *Salisbury Sound* (AV-13) from 1949-52 during the Korean War and made three cruises to the Orient. He was stationed at the Millington Naval Air Station outside of Memphis, TN from 1952-55.

Bill was discharged 15 Apr 1955 as SKI. He received the Good Conduct Medal, China Service Medal, UN Service Medal, Navy Occupation Medal w/Asia Clasp, Korean Service Medal and National Defense Service Medal.

In May, 1955, Bill started work for E.I. DuPont Co., Memphis Plant. He attended classes at the University of Tennessee, Memphis State University and graduated from The William R. Moore School of Technology in Memphis.

Bill married Shirley Strickland on 18 Jun 1953. They have four children: Pamela Stein, William Jr., Michael and Chris Cunningham. They have one granddaughter and four grandsons. Bill retired from DuPont in May 1985 as an engineering designer after 30 years of service. He was a regular attendee of his ship's reunions held in various parts of the country. Bill died 6 Dec 2000.

WALLACE RAY CURLING, Staff Sergeant, born 9 Nov 1932.
Joined the USAF 14 Mar 1952 at Hopkinsville, KY with assignments at Lackland AFB, San Antonio, TX; Amarillo, TX and 20 months in Japan as jet engine mechanic. Memorable experience was when his outfit flew to Korea on combat missions. Discharged 22 May 1956 and received the Good Conduct and UN Service Medals.

Wallace worked 32 years for General Motors in Michigan, retiring in March 1991. Divorced twice, he now lives in Cadiz, KY. He has three children: Wallace Jr., Debra Ann and Ann Marie, and seven grandchildren. Hobbies are fishing and gardening.

GAYLE HOPSON CURTIS, Petty Officer 3/c, born 26 Nov 1936 in
Trigg County, KY, son of Mr. And Mrs. Frank Curtis of Trigg County. He attended Trigg County Schools and in 6 Jan 1955 he enlisted in the USN.

Seaman Recruit Curtis went to boot camp at Recruit Training Center, Great Lakes, IL. After Boot Camp he went to Key West, FL for training in supplies and store keeping.

In October 1956 he was assigned to serve on the USS *Ticonderoga* (CVA-14) and was promoted to the rank of Petty Officer 3/c. He received his discharge in San Francisco, CA on 6 Jan 1959. He earned the Good Conduct Medal and other personal awards.

He moved to Hammond, IN, and was employed with S.G. Taylor Chain Co. for 24 years. He moved back to Trigg County in 1991. He has five children: Phillip, Patrick, Ricki Lynn, Samantha and Gregory. He is presently employed with Jennie Stuart Hospital, Hopkinsville, KY and resides in Trigg County, Ky.

JOHN "JACKIE" CURTIS, born 8 Jul 1938 in Trigg County, KY,
son of Clifton and Jastine Overby Curtis. He attended Trigg County Schools, but in February 1955 he left school and at the age of 16, and with permission from his parents, he enlisted with the U.S. Army.

After three months basic training at Fort Knox, KY, his infantry unit was sent to Greenland for advanced training. After 18 months he returned to the States where he was based at Fort Irvin, CA. While stationed at Ft. Irvin he received his discharge in February 1958.

Shortly after his discharge he moved to Hammond, IN and began working at LaSalle Steel.

On 10 Dec 1960 he married Patricia Griese, a native of Indiana. They have two sons Donald Ray and Michael Todd, and four granddaughters: Bailey, Brittany, Ashley and Tiffinay.

He retired from LaSalle Steel in 1991 with 26 years of service. His health began to fail and following complication from lung surgery he died 16 Feb 1997 in Chicago, IL. He was returned to Trigg County and buried in the family plot of the John Fry Stewart Cemetery.

BLUFORD ELIAS DARNALL, born 24 July 1933 in Trigg County. He enlisted in the U.S. Army 11 Oct. 1951. As a private 1, he did eight weeks of basic training at Camp Gordon, GA,

In March 1952 he had orders for Japan. His oldest brother was already in Japan and learning Elias was being shipped to Japan, consulted ship passenger lists until he found what ship he would be arriving on and the date. He arranged to be in the boarding party to meet this ship a few hours out from shore thinking he could surprise his younger brother and spend some time with him. When he was put aboard the news went out for Elias an officer was looking for him. Thinking he was going to be given a task he did not want to do, he hid out. He knew his bunk had already been checked so he just went to it and stayed until they were ready to dock. Thus missing this wonderful reunion with his brother. He did get to see him but only for a short time. Later he was able to visit in his brother's home as they both were in Yokahama for a year. While in Japan he made private 2, 14 Feb 1953. He re-enlisted for another three years 3 Mar 1953. On 22 Dec 1953 he made Corporal Spec 3.

He had three years foreign service. The most significant duty assignment was 504th MP Co., Fort Eustis, VA. He was in service four years, four months and 22 days.

He was discharged from Fort Eustis, 2 Mar 1956 as Corporal Spec 3, single, and transferred into the Army Reserve for eight years. Awards include National Service Medal, Good Conduct Medal and Mt. Fuji Medal.

All his brothers: Jesse, John, Irvin, Eugene and Elwood, were in the armed forces except Joe who was handicapped and did not pass the physical. Their parents had one or more children in service, continuously for over 25 years. He holds membership in Maple Grove Baptist Church. He has two sons and three grandchildren. Carpentry was his occupation before retirement.

He and his wife, the former Betty Coleman, have a home on the Dover Road, where they enjoy fishing, boating and gardening. He drives a bus for the Trigg County School System to keep active and, as he puts it, "have a reason to get up everyday." *Submitted by Margie T. Darnall.*

IRVIN C. DARNALL, born 25 Apr 1928. He entered the U.S. Army on 30 Mar 1948, as a 19-year-old boy. He received his basic training at Fort Knox, KY, then was assigned to the Asiatic-Pacific Theater, Tokyo, Japan. Here, he served with the First Calvary Division at Camp Drake, Alaska, Japan until 3 Aug 1948. From there he was assigned to "F" Troop, 8th Cav. Inf. Regt. at Camp Roponga, just outside of Tokyo. At the time he joined "F" Troop there were only 10-12 men in this company.

He received the Occupation Medal with Japan Clasp and the Carbine Expert Badge in February 1949 and the M-1 Rifle Sharpshooters Badge in August 1949.

Occupational duties are much different from that of wartime or regular army. Most of our duties were guard duty. He served as guard at The Bank of New York, Tokyo, Japan and also guarded the Japanese War Prisoners while transporting them from Sagami Prison to Yokohama, Japan where they were being tried for War crimes.

He was a 30 Cal. Machine Gunner for "F" Troop, 8th Cav. Regt. while on maneuvers at Mt. Fuji, Japan October 1948 and November 1949. He has many fond memories of the time he served in Japan.

After returning home to Cadiz, he married Geneva Carr on 25 Feb 1950. They have four children and eight grandchildren,

He is now retired, having served as a Baptist pastor with 47 years of service in the Little River Association. He also worked as a carpenter serving an apprenticeship with the Carpenters Local 442 of Hopkinsville, KY

Sometimes he suffers survival guilt as most of his Army buddies lost their lives in Korea. Once, he bumped into a Major Murphy, who at the time was a captain with the 8th Cavalry in Japan. He shared with Irvin how many of his buddies were killed in their sleep by the Koreans. It seems that his whole outfit was wiped out just six months after he returned home. Often he looks at some of the pictures of his Army buddies and wonders who was killed or who survived. Each day he thanks God that he escaped the Korea War.

Geneva and Irvin live at 1589 South Road Cadiz, KY. They enjoy every minute of their lives visiting with their children and grandchildren.

ROY EUGENE DARNALL, DC-3, born 10 Sep 1930 in Trigg County, KY. He was inducted into active duty in the USN at Louisville, KY, 7 Dec 1955 with rank of SR. He went to Great Lakes Naval Training Center for his "boot" training.

His last duty assignment and major duty command was the USS *Wm. Seiverling* (DE-441) and homeport San Diego. He went to Japan and other places during his tour of duty. He had one year four months and 16 days of foreign and sea service.

He was honorably discharged with the rank of DC3 on 20 Aug 1957 from the USN Receiving Station San Diego. He transferred into the U.S. Naval Reserve COM5, Norfolk, VA for stand-by duty until 6 Dec 1961.

He was the father of seven children: Carolyn, Sharron and Johnnie by his first wife, the late Mary Lou Adams, whom he married 5 Nov 1949. He and his late wife Debra Colleen Parker married 14 Oct 1957 and had four children: Rebecca, Jesse, Terri and Roy Eugene Jr. Gene had 13 grandchildren and four great-grandchildren.

His oldest son John Joseph Darnall and second son Jesse L.B. III, both Trigg Countians by birth, served in the military. John was in the Marines, October 1972-October 1975 and Jesse was in the Army in late 70s or early 80s.

Gene attended Trigg County Schools. In civilian life in Trigg County, he was a plumber and electrician by trade. He moved to Eddyville, KY and was an electrician at the Kentucky State Prison. Later he worked for Peabody Coal and moved to Marissa, IL.

He joined New Hope Baptist Church in his early married life. He was stricken with ill health and retiring at an early age, he returned to Kentucky. This illness led to his death 3 Sep 1991, Paducah, KY. He is buried in the Atkins Cemetery in Trigg County. *Submitted by Margie Darnall.*

ORBIE LEWIS DELAWSON, PFC, born on 25 Apr 1929, son of Wade and Ethel Delawson, and reared in Wallonia, KY. He was inducted into the U.S. Army on 6 Mar 1951 and was a part of the ER52 082 5799 QMC-USAR, ready reserve.

He served tours that included Europe and Germany before he became Stateside on 1 Mar 1953. After becoming stateside he became part of the Reserves for three years and was honorably discharged on 9 Jul 1956.

Orbie married Minnie May Rustin. He than began a career at McDonald and Douglas Aircraft Company. This career spanned 25 years after which he moved to Princeton, KY. On 4 Feb 1997 he proceeded both parents in death. He is survived by his wife, son Lewis Delawson, and two grandchildren, Jared and Amber.

JAMES M. DETHRIDGE, Private, born 17 Feb 1934 in Warren County. Joined the Army 13 Mar 1951 with assignments at Louisville, KY and Fort Meade, MD. Pvt. Dethridge was discharged 17 Sep 1954.

Married Ima on 12 Feb 1987 and they live in Cadiz, KY. James is employed with Holley Performance Product, BG, KY. They had four children: Pamlia, Joey, Stephanie and one deceased. Grandchildren are Christifer and Travis Carter, Tommy Dethridge and Brittany. James enjoys travel and music (gospel, country and bluegrass).

EURA W. "DOC" DIXON, Corporal, the son of Roscoe and Dewey Dixon, was born 25 Mar 1927 at Golden Pond, Trigg County, KY, and was drafted into the U.S. Army 19 Oct 1950. Doc was living in Hammond, IN, at the time he entered the Army.

Cpl. Dixon was a first gunner with the 27th Inf. Regt., Co. D. He was a heavy weapons infantryman on the front lines fighting in the Korean Conflict for 11 months.

Doc was also a member of the Colorful 27th Inf. Div. known as the "Wolfhounds." The Wolfhounds for 24 months collected monies for the Holy Family Orphanage in Osaka, Japan. In February 1952, they delivered $5,392 to the Orphanage.

Doc was also a veteran of the 25th Unit in the Korean War. The 25th Unit was engaged in patrol action near the 38th Parallel.

He was placed in the ERC 19 Jul 1952 and was honorably discharged on 6 Sep 1956. Doc received the Infantryman Badge, symbol of the frontline fighting man, the Korean Service Medal, Combat Infantryman Badge w/BSS and O/S Bar decorations and metals.

He had two older brothers who were also in service: Charles Dixon who was in the USAF, and James Dixon who was in the U.S. Army. Doc met his older brother, James, in Korea. Both were surprised to find each other in the midst of the war.

Doc married a Trigg County girl, Betty Whitney on 13 Dec 1952. They had three daughters. After living a short time at Golden Pond, KY, they moved back to Hammond, IN, where Doc remained a resident for 45 years. Doc retired from the Laborer's Union Hammond Local #41. He died 6 Mar 1988 in Hammond.

JAMES AHART DIXON, PFC, born 25 Nov 1925, at Golden Pond, Trigg County, KY, was drafted into the U.S. Army 30 De 1948.

On 8 Apr 1948, after three months of training at Camp Breckinridge, KY, he and his unit, Co. I, 29th Inf. Regt., traveled by ship to Okinawa, Japan. James was a 745 Primary Rifleman. He remembers guarding the equipment and also the severe storms that hit while he was there. He remembers the mess hall getting blown away and the soldiers having to stack poles at each end of the Quonset huts to keep the ends from being blown out.

After eight months in Okinawa, James returned to the States to Camp Stoneman, CA, on 29 Dec 1949. He traveled by train from California to Camp Breckinridge, was discharged and placed in the Ready Reserves

(active status). On 18 Oct 1950 he went to Camp Campbell (now Fort Campbell), then to Section 101st Abn. Div. at Camp Breckinridge, then to Ford Meade, MD. He was released on leave from Ford Meade. After returning to Fort Meade, James was shipped out to Korea. He was a trackman in transportation in charge of keeping the communication lines open to the front line. He remembers the train tracks being used by buses as well as trains.

James met his brother, Eura "Dock" Dixon in Korea while Eura was on rest from fighting.

James did not do any fighting in Korea. He returned by ship to Fort Meade and was honorably discharged on 8 Oct 1953, as a private first class. He received the Korean Service Metal w/3 Bronze Stars and the Army of Occupation Medal in Japan.

He married a Trigg County girl, Evelyn Jones, on 29 Dec 1951. They have two children and two grandchildren.

Over the years James has worked as a farmer, truck driver for Pennyrile Rural Electric and Paschall Truck Lines. Today, at 75 he and Evelyn reside in Murray, KY. He enjoys gardening and playing with his dog, Allie.

MARVIN GLEN DIXON, Corporal (T-16), born 11 Sep 1932 in Cadiz, KY. He entered the Armed Forces 8 Feb 1951 at Owensboro, KY. Assignment was with Tank Co. 1st Bn., 3rd Armd. Cav. Regt. He served three years at this assignment and also worked as a truck and tank mechanic for the unit.

Glen was honorably discharged 7 Feb 1954 at Camp Pickett, VA. Medals include the National Defense Service Medal and Good Conduct Medal.

Returning to civilian life, he worked on the farm with his father and brother the first year, then went to Chicago Heights, IL and worked in the steel mills for nine years. Returning to Trigg County, he went to work at the Cumberland Steam Plant for eight years and later retired from Averitt Lumber Co. in March 1989.

He married Helen Joyce Sumner on 12 May 1952. They have four children: Shelia Carol Faughn, Sandra Joy Knight, Marvin Glen Jr. and Myra Lee Teague. Grandchildren are Alison Faughn Littlefield, Heather Carol Faughn Calcido, Daniel Gregory Knight, Jeremy Keith Lipham; also, one great-grandchild, Kelsie Nicole Littlefield.

Glen and Joyce lived in Chicago Heights while he worked there. They built their home in the Linton area and lived there most of their life. Glen was born and reared in the Linton/Donaldson Creek area. His parents were Marvin Delbert and Elva Mae McCoy Dixon. In his last years, Glen was stricken with cancer. He died 7 Feb 1991 at Veterans Hospital in Nashville, TN. He is buried in Fuller Cemetery, Hwy. 164, between Linton and Donaldson Creek. Joyce resides in Cadiz, KY.

GRAHAM EGERTON, Airman 1/c, born 22 Aug 1932, Washington DC. He entered the service in December 1951 at Owensboro, KY. Assignments were at Wichita Falls, TX; Denver, CO; Tachikawa, Japan and Mobile, AL. He was discharged in September 1955.

Returning to civilian life, he made a career in insurance, real estate and was a stockbroker. He retired from PSA Financial Center, Baltimore, MD in January 1999.

He married Anne B. Redfern 10 Jan 1981 and they live in Cazenovia, NY. They have five children: Hardin, Judith, Douglas, Rowland and John. Grandchildren are Andrea, Michelle, Cory, Jessica and Casey.

JOHN WALDEN EGERTON, Specialist 3/c, born in Atlanta, GA on 14 Jun 1935, and spent all the years of his childhood and youth in Cadiz and Trigg County. He entered the U.S. Army from Cadiz on 31 Aug 1954, and was honorably discharged on 2 Jun 1956. He took basic training at Fort Knox, served 17 months as a specialist third class in Headquarters Co., 14th Armd. Cav., in Fulda, West Germany, and was discharged on his return to the States.

He subsequently graduated from the University of Kentucky, married Ann Bleidt of Golden Pond, KY, and has lived since 1965 in Nashville, TN.

BILL D. FELTNER, Specialist 3, born 25 Dec. 1933, Trigg County, KY, the third son of Mr. and Mrs. Ben E. Feltner, now deceased. His father also served in the military. He was drafted in the U.S. Army on 26 Oct 1954. After basic training at Fort Knox, KY, Feltner was sent to Fort Monmouth, NJ, which was the Signal Corp Center at that time. He was assigned to Headquarters Company and worked in the Post's Adjutant General's Office. Except for a few weeks of TDY assignment to the Army Security Agency near Warrenton, VA, he was stationed at Fort Monmouth until his Honorable Discharge 25 Oct 1956.

Feltner returned to the University of Tennessee, Knoxville where he ultimately earned three degrees including the doctoral degree in August 1963. He took time out from full-time graduate study to serve for three years as principal of Bearden Elementary and Junior High School in Knoxville. He loved the position, but wanted to be a professor at a university. Although he taught graduate courses at UT while still working toward his doctorate, he began his full-time university teaching career at age 29 as a professor at Rutgers, The State University in New Brunswick, NJ in September 1963. After teaching four years at Rutgers, Feltner was recruited by the University of Georgia, Athens, GA in 1967. For the next 25 years, in addition to his other responsibilities at Georgia, he taught graduate courses in the areas of organization, governance, management and finance of higher education. After a teaching career of more than 30 years, Feltner retired from the University of Georgia in 1992. He continues to be active as a consultant to Colleges and Universities.

Feltner was named captain and MVP of the Trigg County Wildcats basketball team after the 1951-52 season. "One of the biggest thrills of his life was to play basketball at Trigg County High. And, of course, one of his greatest disappointments was that bronchial pneumonia prevented him playing in the District Tournament during his senior year. He still has fond memories of many teachers, students and friends."

He has two children, Debi and Rodney. Debi and Paul have two daughters, Kacie and Kara. Rodney and Allison have two daughters, Hannah and Abby. Feltner resides near Atlanta in Lilburn, GA. *Submitted by Bill D. Feltner.*

MARSHALL G. FELTNER, Sergeant, born 16 Jun 1932 in Trigg County, KY, the son of Mr. and Mrs. Ben E. Feltner, now deceased. After intensive Marine Corps training at Parris Island, SC, Marshall was sent to Korea 11 Jun 1951.

He served in combat during the Korean War and ultimately was promoted to sergeant. He received the Korean Service Medal w/star and the UN Ribbon. Sgt. Feltner was shipped back from Korea to San Diego where he was honorably discharged 2 Jun 1952.

Marshall returned to Paducah, KY after his discharge. During his civilian career, he worked in the automobile related industry, including the ownership of a garage and service station.

He retired in February 1997. Soon thereafter, he became ill and died on 26 Jul 1997. He is survived by three children: Michael, Kim and Marsha. His wife Emma Lovett Feltner still resides in Paducah. *Submitted by his brother Bill D. Feltner.*

BILLIE LEE FENNELL, Sergeant E-5, born 14 Nov 1931 in the Ferguson Spring Community of Trigg County, near Golden Pond, KY, the son of Eulas Beltron and Winnie Maud Fennell. He enlisted into the U.S. Army 27 Feb 1951 at St. Louis, MO and was sent to Camp Breckinridge, KY, for 12 weeks training. He was assigned to the 101st Abn. Div. After basic he went to Fort Lewis, WA for shipment to Japan, then to Korea.

There he was assigned to the Fourth Finance Dispersing Section in Pusan, Korea, and then to a Prisoner of War holding camp on Koji-do Island, south of Pusan. There he was assigned to the HQ Co., Finance Section, 8137th Army Service Unit. He remained there until June 1953. During this period he was promoted from private to sergeant-5.

In June 1953 Bill shipped out to Japan and spent two weeks on a troopship going to Fort Lawton, WA, then home for a leave, then to Camp Crowder MO, then to Fort Riley, KS where he was assigned to the HQ, 5021 ASU and served as night dispatcher at the post motor pool.

He was honorably discharged from the military 26 Feb 1954 and returned to Alton, IL to work at Laclede Steel Co., Shell Oil Co., and construction as an electrician.

He married Mary Marquess Bridges and they had three children: William Lee, Debra Anne (who died at birth), and Malinda Gaye. Wil lives and teaches in Japan and is married to Kayo, a Japanese lady; Malinda is married to Dennis Strasen, lives in Bethalto, IL, and has three boys: Jordan William, Christian Tyler and Mica Alexander. Bill has three step-children: Karen, Michael and Gary Bridges.

Bill retired in December 1993 to enjoy the good life. He and Mary moved back to Trigg County, near Cadiz, KY where they enjoy living. He likes fishing, boating, birding, genealogy, and working in their yard. He and Mary attend East Cadiz Baptist Church.

GEORGE C. FENNELL, A1/c, born 8 Mar 1933, Golden Pond, KY. He joined the USAF 14 Mar 1952 at Owensboro, KY. Assignments include Lackland AFB, TX; Kirtland AFB, NM; Eglin AFB, FL and overseas duty in Korea.

Discharged 13 Mar 1956. Awards include the Korean Service Medal, UN Service Medal, National Defense Service Medal, Good Conduct Medal and Korean War Medal.

Retired 1 Apr 1995 from International Union of Operating Engineers, Peoria, IL. Divorced, he lives in Cadiz, KY and has two children, Carla Koenig and Karen Fennell, and two grandchildren, Jonatha and Jackie Wall. His hobby is looking this country over and lacks only the New England States.

RANDEL RAY FINLEY, Sergeant, born 29 Apr 1929, Collinsville County, IL. Before entering the service he was an inspector for International Shoe Co., Hopkinsville, KY, 1948-50.

He joined the service 11 Aug 1950, Owensboro, KY and served in the Army with Co. G, 110th Inf. Regt. and 54th, 3rd Armd. Div., 2nd Plt. He also attended 110th Inf. NCO Academy in 1953 majoring in leadership.

He received an honorable discharge 22 Jul 1954. His awards include the Good Conduct, Infantry Badge, Koreans Service Medal w/2 BSS, UN Service Medal and National Defense Service Medal.

After the service he became a Baptist minister. He married Gail Alexander 12 Nov 1954 and they had three children: Barron Ray, Sandra and Jill (Cunningham). He was pastor at Hurricane Baptist Church, Cadiz, KY at the time of his death 8 Apr 1978.

DARWIN BLANE FLOOD, PFC, born 21 Apr 1930 in Trigg County near Golden Pond, KY, He entered the service, January 14, 1953, at Owensboro, KY, the youngest son of Thomas E. Flood and Pearl Dixon Flood. His brother is Robert Flood and two sisters are Opal Flood Ahart and Lucy Flood Colson.

Darwin was drafted into the Army 15 Jan 1953 and reported to Camp Gordon, GA. He was trained for 16 weeks at the Military Police Replacement Training Center to become a member of the elite Military Police Corps. He was later stationed at Camp Stoneman, CA.

He participated in the Korean Conflict and was in foreign service for one year, four months and 16 days. Pfc. Flood was discharge 17 Dec 1954 at Fort Knox, KY. He was awarded the Korean Service Medal, UN Service Medal, National Defense Service Medal, ROK and Presidential Unit Citation.

Returning to civilian life, Darwin made his home in East Peoria, IL. He was employed as a carman with the Toledo/Peoria and Western Railroad Co. He enjoyed membership in the Woodmen of the World.

Darwin Blane Flood, age 29, died, 2 Sep 1959, at St. Francis Hospital in East Peoria, IL. He is buried in Dixon Cemetery near Golden Pond. *Information submitted by Jack and Betty Hanberry and by June Ezell.*

WALTER HOWARD FLOOD, Staff Sergeant, born June 12, 1931 at Golden Pond, KY, to Walter and Annie Flood. He entered the USAF 23 Jul 1953 in Michigan.

During his service he was stationed at New York, Kansas, England, Japan, Michigan and California. His chief duty was crash and structural firefighter. He departed the service 16 Jul 1965 with the rank of staff sergeant.

He was married to Evelyn Schmidt 16 Oct 1954 and they have five daughters: Gerry, Beverly, Vickey, Sue and Tina; eight grandchildren and three great-grandchildren.

After his departure from the service in 1965 he worked at the Detroit Metro Air Port Fire Department, until his retirement in 1978.

He and his wife moved to Brooksville, FL in 1979 where they reside today. They have recently purchased land in Michigan where they plan to build a home in the near future and once again be near most of the girls and their families.

JOE LEE FOOSHEE, E-3, born 30 Apr 1939 in Trigg County in the Linton Community as the second son of Guy Edward and Martha Margaret Nunn Fooshee.

After being drafted into the Army 2 Nov 1961, he took his basic training in Fort Chaffee, AR, then transferred to Fort Sill, OK for 14 weeks advanced artillery training.

Assigned to the first Target Acquisition Battalion, 26th Arty. In Aschaffenburg, Germany. On 27 Jul 1963 he was in an accident and taken to 97th General Hospital in Frankfort, Germany then 15 months at Walter Reed Hospital in Washington DC. He was on temporary disability until 30 Sep 1968 when he was retired with a physical disability.

His first marriage ended in divorce with two children, Sidney Guy and Sandra Lee. He married Alpha Fay Robertson in 1980 and has a stepdaughter, Wendy Carol Hargrove. He made a career of farming, timber and the sawmill business and lives in Cadiz, KY.

JOHN LACY FORD, born 9 Jun 1924 in the southern part of Trigg County near Linton, the only child born to John Roy and Pansy Turner Ford.

(photos)

Lacy, as he was called, attended school in Linton and graduated from Trigg County HS in 1943. He was a member of the Boyd Hill Baptist Church. After his dad's death in 1942, he and Aunt Pansy moved to Hopkinsville, KY and he worked at the International Shoe Company until he entered the Army on 1 Jun 1949.

He received basic training at Fort Meade, MD and served with Co. A 714th Hwy Opn. Bn. He was later transferred to Fort Eustis, VA where he remained until his discharge 7 Dec 1951.

Lacy returned to his home in Hopkinsville and moved his church membership to Second Baptist Church where he was a member until his death. He later became employed with the civil service at Fort Campbell, KY where he installed telephone lines. He received many commendations while working there. At age 68, Lacy had a heart attack on 14 Jul 1992 and died at the Jennie Stuart Hospital. He is buried at the Green Hill Memorial Gardens in Christian County, KY. *Respectfully written by his second cousin, Carolyn Ford Bland.*

ROBERT EARL FOWLER, Private, born 31 Jan 1933 in Lamasco, KY. He served in the U.S. Army from 18 Aug 1953 until 1 Jun 1955. He did his training at Fort Knox, KY and after boot camp went to QM School at Fort Lee, VA.

Served eight months at Paris, France, returned to the States and discharged 1 Jun 1955 at Fort Knox.

He is the son of Robert Cline and Blue Belle Tyler Fowler. He married Thelma Lucille Kirby and they live in Cadiz, KY where he still farms. They have two sons, Robert Craig and Kerry Lynn, and two granddaughters, Lauren Brooke and Amanda Nicole Fowler. Golf is his hobby.

RICHARD M. FRANCIS, Corporal, born 26 Nov 1933 in Trigg County. Enlisted in the Army 26 Aug 1953 at Owensboro, KY. Trained at Camp Atterbury, IN then served in Germany with the Hvy. Mtr. Co., 18th Inf. Regt. He was discharged 11 May 1955 at Fort Knox, KY.

He married Cynthia Alice Williams 17 Oct 1953 and they moved to Crete, IL 7 Jul 1955. They have four children: Vanessa Koselke, Tamara Hale, Trena Pheroff and Gina Dement. Grandchildren are Anthony and Ashley Koselke; Melissa, Bryan and Jason Hale; Allason and Ethan Pheroff; Madeline and Elisabell Dement.

Richard passed away 9 Sep 1987 and is buried at Skyline Memorial, Monee, IL.

BLENARD R. FRANKLIN, Corporal, born 24 Dec 1932, Golden Pond, KY, son of Luke Garrett and Audra Elizabeth Crump Franklin. His father served in WWI. Enlisted 10 Apr 1951 and trained at Indian Town Gap, PA.

Shipped overseas and assignments include 4th Mobile Army Surg. Hosp. at Zuffenhausen, Germany; Med. Tech School; Med NCO School; Mash Tech in Stuttgart, Germany; ambulance driver in the 95th Med. Amb. Co. in Wertheim, Germany.

Discharged 9 Apr 1955 at Fort Sam Houston, TX. Awards include the Occupational and Good Conduct (3 awards).

Married Herta Franklin 25 May 1954. She passed away in 1996. He retired from M&M, Chicago, IL in 1992. He resides in Melrose Park, IL. He enjoys traveling with his Maltese dog. Traveling to Texas and California is made possible by his two nephews.

CHARLES EDWARD FREEMAN, Corporal, born 3 Jul 1931 in Trigg County, KY. Joined the service 2 Feb 1954 in Trigg County with assignments at Fort Knox, KY; Fort Leonard Wood, MO and 19 months in Germany.

He participated in the Korean Conflict and was discharged 17 Jan 1956. Cpl. Freeman received the Good Conduct, National Defense Service Medal and OCC MED GER.

A self-employed electrician and plumber until retirement in July 1996, he now does cattle farming. Married Thelma Futrell 11 Apr 1954 and they live in Cadiz, KY. They have two children, Cathy Freeman and Debra Long and one grandchild, Brian Cayce Long.

SAMUEL DELL FREEMAN JR., Sergeant, Dell Freeman Jr., son of Samuel Dell and Tyline Mitchell Freeman, was born in rural Christian County near Gracey, KY on 30 Jan 1931. He attended Julien Grade School and graduated from South Christian High School.

Dell was drafted for two years into the Army in May 1953. His basic training was at Fort Rucker, AL, where he was assigned to an infantry unit. He spent the entire two years in the same unit with assignments at Fort Rucker, AL; Fort Hood, TX and Fort Benning, GA. Sgt. Freeman was honorably discharged in May 1955.

In 1959, Dell was married to Rose Bridges (Maxwell). Their children were Carla, Dell III, Smith T. and Brenda Susan Maxwell, stepdaughter. Dell always loved children, and the grandchildren have been truly "grand." Soon after his marriage, Dell moved his church membership from Locust Grove Baptist Church (where he taught Sunday School) to Oak Grove Baptist Church. There he served as Sunday School teacher and Deacon.

At age 22, Dell became a member of Cadiz Masonic Lodge 121, serving as Master and Secretary. He was Past Paton of Ophelia Chapter 55, O.E.S., Cadiz, and a member of Rizpah Shrine Temple, Madisonville, KY.

An auctioneer and real estate broker since 1958, Dell was also a partner in Kentucky-Tennessee Livestock Market from which business he retired in 1995. Now residing on Hospital Street, Cadiz, he never misses an opportunity to indulge the grandchildren.

BILLY RAY FUTRELL, Specialist 5, born 29 Aug 1931 in Cadiz, KY. He was drafted into the Army 15 Mar 1954. After eight weeks of basic training at Fort Knox, KY, he and his unit, went to Headquarters, 82nd Abn., Fort Bragg, NC.

From Fort Bragg, he went to Fort Polk, LA for three months of combat training, then was transferred back to Fort Bragg until his discharge 14 Mar 1956. He received the Good Conduct Medal.

While in the service, he drove the ration truck that delivered food to the A, B, and C companies.

Today, at 69 years old, he and his wife, Martha Jo, reside at 3100 Donaldson Creek Road, Cadiz, KY and are members of Donaldson Creek Baptist Church. He is still actively engaged in farming.

His children are David, Patricia Gilbert, Connie Kennedy and Debbie Parker, and grandchildren are Shad, Melissa, Lauren and Chris Mayfield; Eliza and Patrick Gilbert; Maegan and Makaela Kennedy.

HARRY WALLACE "HANK" GARLAND SR., A2/c, born on 12 Aug 1931 in Trigg County, KY, son of Mr. and Mrs. Roy Finley Garland. He graduated from Trigg County HS in May 1950. On 15 Sep 1950 he enlisted in the USAF with basic training at Shepherd AFB, Wichita Falls, TX and Tyndall AFB, Panama City, FL. He was assigned to the Strategic Air Command.

After finishing recruit training in December 1950 his unit was shipped overseas to England where he served for two years.

A2/c Garland returned to the States and was stationed at Hunter AFB, Savannah, GA where he received an honorable discharge on 15 Sep 1953.

He married a Trigg County girl, Bobbie Curtis on 10 Aug 1953 and they began married life in Hammond, IN. He was employed by Marbon/Borg Warner as a chemical operator and worked there for 16 years. In 1969 Hank, Bobbie and four sons: Harry Jr., Scott, Chris and Craig moved back to Trigg County, KY and he began his own construction business of Garland & Sons. For a number of years they built many homes in and around Trigg County. In 1984 he accepted a position with Shady Lawn Nursing Home as environmental supervisor where he continued to work until he retired in May 1997.

Since retiring he and Bobbie have spent time traveling cross country seeing the USA, and visiting their sons and two grandchildren, Kent and Melissa. He enjoys camping, fishing, and working in his garden. Today he and Bobbie reside north of Cadiz on the Princeton Road.

PHIL ROLLIE GRASTY, born 1 May 1935, the oldest son of Sadie and Thelma Sanders Grasty. He was sworn into the USN 18 Aug 1952 in Louisville, KY and shipped to USN NTC in San Diego, CA for boot camp.

Upon graduation he was sent to HTU-1 (Helicopter Training Unit), Ellyson Field NAS, Pensacola, FL in aviation mechanics. While stationed there he played half-back with the base football team (the Goshawks) and pitched for the NAS fast-pitch soft ball team. Later aboard the USS *Macon* he pitched during the Fleet Championships in Cuba and they won.

Phil also received his GED and it was signed by his cousin John Dean Minton who was than principal of Trigg County HS. In 1954 Phil went aboard the USS *Hornet* on the West Coast as a gunner's mate. After the birth of his daughter Ann, he was assigned to the USS *Macon* at Norfolk, VA in the same position.

He was released from the Navy at Norfolk in April 1956 and discharged in 1960. Awards include the National Defense Service Medal and the Good Conduct Medal.

His four children by first wife Betty Tolbert are Ann Killeen, Phil "Buddy" Jr., Sandra Blackwell, Ronnie Grasty; stepson is Gene Jones. Grandchildren are Clay and Sean Garvin; Christopher, Josh, Amy, Sara and Ruby Grasty, Michael Gee; stepgranddaughter Caitlin Jones; great grandchildren are Jacob and Alexia Garvin, and Jonathan and Christopher Grasty. Phil is now married to Mildred Wood Jones and they live in Cadiz, KY. He is retired from South Central Bell.

WILLIAM HUGH "BILL" GOLLADAY, Corporal, born 25 May 1928 in Trigg County, Roaring Springs, KY, the son of William C. and Mary Gilliam Golladay. He was drafted into the Army 2 Jan 1951 at Owensboro, KY and went to Camp Breckinridge, KY for basic and advanced infantry training.

Entered the Korean War and was assigned to 3rd Bn., HQ Co., COMO DT, 23rd Inf., 2nd Inf. Div. on 1 Jun 1951. The 23rd Army relieved the Marines at the Punch Bowl; the 9th Inf. at Bloody Ridge on 6 September and moved to Heartbreak Ridge on 13 September.

Left for the States in March 1952 and assigned to Fort Knox, KY for five months before discharge. Awards include the Combat Infantry Badge, Korean Service Medal w/3 stars and UN Service Medal.

Returning to civilian life he farmed for 14 years. In 1966 he joined W.R. Grace and Co. to sell fertilize and chemicals and became manager of the business in 1968 until retirement in 1988.

William married Mary Helen Suddeath 6 Jan 1973 and they live in Hopkinsville, KY.

WILLIAM L. GRANT, PFC, born 13 Aug 1930 in Montgomery, KY. He joined the Army 21 May 1953 at Camp Atterbury, IN. During the Korean War he served with Co. B, 88th Inf. Heavy Mortar Bn.

Pfc. Grant was discharged 23 Apr 1955. His awards include the National Defense Service Medal, Vietnam Service Medal, Korean Service Medal and Good Conduct Medal. He was discharged from the Reserves 31 May 1961.

He married Linda Boren and they live in LaFayette, KY. They have three children: Billy Don, Raymond Earl and Bryon Keith; three grandchildren and one great-grandchild. William still works as a painter.

CARL GRAY, born 15 Mar 1929 in Cadiz, KY. He was drafted into the Army in February 1951. After his induction he was sent to Fort Meade for training assignment, then sent to Aberdeen Proving Ground in Maryland for basic training. After basic training he was transferred to Atlanta, GA for Wheel Vehicle Field Maintenance School. Due to a reoccurring heart condition caused by rheumatic fever, he was not found suitable for overseas replacement for Korean causalities. Therefore, in November 1951 he was discharged.

While in the service he did serve as typist for his company. Even though most of this period was spent in the hospital, he did compete his basic training and wheel vehicle service training. The heart condition due to the Rheumatic fever has not curtailed his ability to have a successful life outside of the military.

On 16 Jul 1953 he married Maxine Henry. They have three daughters: Judy Rutter, Ruth Gray and Martha Shipley, and five granddaughters. He worked for several years for Stagner and Nunn electric and plumbing contractors. Later he returned to the family farm as a self-employed excavation contractor. Developing and selling retirement sites subsidized his farming habit. This has also given him an opportunity to get to know and develop friendships with people from other areas who chose to make their home in Trigg County. This has also helped to add to the successful growth of Trigg County. The land that was not suitable for building sites has been retained and improved for hay and cattle.

He is a charter member of the Cadiz Camp of The Gideons International. He has served on the Board of directors for the Temperance League of Kentucky. Carl is an active member of Hurricane Baptist Church.

He and his wife reside on the remainder of the family farm in Trigg County, on Barkley Lake, in the Rockcastle Community.

JOE B. GUESS, Sergeant E-5, born 22 Jan 1930 in Paducah, KY. joined the Army in July 1948 for one year active and five years reserve duty. He trained at Fort Hood, TX in the 2nd Armd. Div.

When the Korean War broke out in July 1950, he was called back to active duty in September 1950 and sent to Fort Lewis, WA for refresher course, then to Japan and assigned to 2nd Inf. Div. in Korea.

They made an amphibious landing in north Korea in 40° below zero weather and joined up with the 9th Inf. Regt. 2nd Inf. Div. who were retreating from the Chinese army. After seven months of fighting they were on the offensive and went back to north Korea.

Sgt. Guess returned to the States in August 1951 and was released to Reserves. He received a Battle Star for Wonju Offensive and May Massacre, Korean Service Medal w/star, Combat Infantry Badge and Commendation Ribbon w/pendant.

He married Louise Sons on 11 Jan 1952 and they reside in Cadiz, KY. They have one son Steven and two grandsons, Austin and Logan.

Joe retired from Thomas Industries in 1986. He and Louise are active members of Mt. Pleasant Baptist Church.

LESLIE ARTHUR GUIER, Corporal, born May 3, 1933 in Trigg County, KY. Inducted at Fort Meade, MD on 30 Apr 1953 and took basic training at Camp Breckinridge, KY. Assigned to the 101st Abn. Div., then sent to Fort Knox, KY and assigned to Svc. Co. 1st Tng. Regt. ARTC as petroleum clerk with a MOS 1485.

Cpl. Guier was discharged 29 Apr 1955. His awards include the National Defense Service Medal and Good Conduct Medal.

Civilian activity as farmer and Civil Service, Fort Campbell, KY. After a work-related injury he retired on disability in 1994. He resides in Bowling Green, KY.

Married Jane R. Herndon 7 Aug 1954 and they had five sons: Lester, Forrest Thomas (stillborn), David, Keith and Kevin. Grandchildren are Andrew, Nathan, Sam, Thomas, Nicholas, Tommy Brian, Amanda, Elizabeth and Makenzie.

He stays busy with grandchildren, church, Masonic Fraternity and Order of Eastern Star.

JACK THOMAS HANBERRY, PFC, born 8 Jul 1928 in Trigg County, KY. Joined the Army 9 Dec 1950 at Breckinridge, KY. He served with the 990th Signal Operation Co. at Camp Gordon, GA with the MOS: Light Truck Driver.

Other assignments at Fort Bragg, NC; Fort Holabird, MD; and Fort Hood, TX. Discharged in December 1952.

Returned to civilian life and continued to drive a truck for Upton Trucking, Canton, KY, then worked for the Trigg County Road Dept. until retirement in 1990.

Married Betty Lee Jones 19 Sep 1953 and they live in Cadiz, KY. They have six children: Tommy, Scotty, Stevie, Lisa, Michelle and Mrs. Rebecca Cecil. Grandchildren are Travis and Kimberly Hanberry; Allison, Erin and Brianna Cecil.

DALTON BOYD HANCOCK, A1/c, born 24 Mar 1930 in Christian County, the son of Bascom and Bessie Campbell Hancock. He attended Pembroke HS and enlisted in the USAF 30 Dec 1950 at Owensboro, KY. He received his GED while in the service.

He was stationed in Korea for three months then transferred to Nagoya, Japan for two years. While there he was assigned to special forces to play baseball, basketball and football. He was discharged 11 Jan 1954 with the rank airman first class. He was awarded the Good Conduct, National Defense, Korean Service and UN Medals.

Coming back to Hopkinsville he played baseball with the Kitty League in Hopkinsville and attended Bethel College. On 10 Jun 1950 he married Jean Petty and divorced in 1994. They had two sons, Boyd and Scott.

Retired from Thomas Industries in Hopkinsville 13 Apr 1994. He married Grace Lawrence Dawson 30 Aug 1997 and they live in Cadiz, KY. He also has stepdaughter, Pam Dawson Oliver; three stepsons: Fenton, Layton and Mont Dawson; two grandchildren, Ellery and Taylor Wade Hancock; eight step-grandchildren: Chelsea and Carly Oliver; Josh, Dillon, Lexie, Lanie, Madeline and Chase Dawson.

JAMES LOUIS HANCOCK, Corporal, born 1 Dec 1933 in Christian County, the sixth child of 16 children born to Luther and Ada Augusta Carpenter Hancock. The family moved to Trigg County to the Casey Freeman farm when he was 7 or 8 years old. He attended school at Averitt School in the Caledonia Community and worked as a farm hand until he left at age 17 for Hammond, IN, where he worked at Federal Cement and Tile Co. until he was inducted into the Army 16 Mar 1954.

His basic training was at Camp Chaffee, AR, then shipped out to Korea in March 1955 where he drove a half-track with quad 40 guns on patrols. He saw no action and was discharged 7 Mar 1956.

He returned to his old job at Federal Cement and Tile for about a year until they permanently closed. The next 10 years were at Taylor Chain Co. until 1967 when he became a member of Midwest Operating Eng. Local as a heavy equipment operator and worked for Furnace Services Inc., cleaning and repairing melting furnace and pitts in all the steel mills in the Chicago, IL and Gary, IN area. He took early retirement in 1993 and back to Trigg County.

He married Glenda Williams on 5 Mar 1958, no children. James passed away 7 Aug 1995. *Submitted by Glenda Williams Hancock.*

BRADLEY KINCAID HARGROVE, born 17 Dec 1931 in Trigg County, KY and was drafted into the Army, 12 Feb 1953 at the induction center in Owensboro, KY.

Hargrove received his basic training and was assigned to Co. B 17th Inf. Regt. and served in the Korean Conflict. He returned to the States and received his honorable discharge from active duty 26 Apr 1955 at Fort Knox, KY.

Bradley traveled home to family: his mother, Cora Louise Neeble Hargrove Creekmur; four brothers: Jack Creekmur, Calvin, Tommy and Henry Hargrove; three sisters: Eva Mae Skinner, Annette Tennant and Evelyn Bourassa. His father, William "Bill" Hargrove and a sister Edith Adams had already died.

Bradley was of Baptist faith and he worked in maintenance with local farms, private home yards, and for a number of years with Goodwin Funeral Home.

In the 1980s, his health declined and he became a resident of Trigg County Manor, a personal care home in Cadiz. This did not lesson his friendly manner and good natured personality. Bradley was known to "have never met a stranger" and was remembered as always looking for the positive things in life, no matter how much adversity he was facing. In the mid-1990s, he developed Leukemia and died 24 Nov 1996, with burial in East End Cemetery.

JOHN H. HERNDON, Staff Sergeant, born 4 Oct 1931 in the Linton Community of Trigg County. He enlisted in the USAF in November 1952 in Hopkinsville, KY. He married Louise Bridges of Cadiz on 24 Jan 1953, and on 9 Feb 1953 rode a Greyhound bus to Owensboro, KY where he was inducted the following day.

He was sent by train to Lackland AFB in San Antonio, TX for eight weeks of basic training, then to Amarillo AFB, TX for four months of jet aircraft and engine training.

At the end of his training he was assigned to the 438th Ftr. Interceptor Sqdn. at Kinross AFB, MI. He came home to visit his family before he and his wife left for Michigan, and while en route from Texas learned that the Korean War had ended. In August 1953 he and his wife arrived in Kinross, MI, just below the Canadian border. He was assigned to aircraft maintenance as a jet engine mechanic, and worked on the inspection dock as assistant crew chief in charge of pre-flight and post-flight inspections.

In 1955 his unit received orders for a tour of duty in Greenland, but at the last minute he was ordered to remain behind because of the impending birth of their first child, Debbie, who was born at Chippewa County War Memorial Hospital in Sault Ste. Marie, MI. on 6 Jul 1955. He served the remainder of his enlistment at Kinross AFB, except for temporary duties in Ohio, Georgia, and Arizona. He was honorably discharged on 9 Feb 1957 with the rank of staff sergeant.

He returned to Trigg County and after farming for himself for a few years, he began working for Smith Broadbent Jr. of Broadbent Farms in Trigg County, and was farm foreman for 30 years. He surrendered to preach in May 1962 and pastored Baptist churches in Lyon, Caldwell, and Trigg counties. He and Louise had four children: Debbie, John W., Steve and Teresa, and seven grandchildren. Louise passed away 10 Mar 2001. He currently resides in Trigg County.

ROBERT E. HIGBEE, PO2, born 28 Dec 1931 in Dawson Springs, KY, the son of Richard and Lois Higbee. He enlisted in the USN in January 1949 and after boot camp in San Diego, CA, was assigned to USS *Toledo*, a heavy cruiser in the US 7th Fleet.

President Truman authorized a round the world "Goodwill Tour" in May 1949 and he volunteered for this tour in the USS *Missouri*. The tour lasted until the Korean War was declared in 1950.

He was assigned to a combat unit at that time and was at the first invasion at Inchon, Korea and in five major combat assignments from Inchon to the 38th Parallel, at which time Gen. MacArthur was relieved of duty and brought back to the States in 1952.

Robert's enlistment was ending and he was shipped back to the States for discharge in February 1953 with the rank of second class petty officer in Seattle, WA. He has Campaign Ribbons for the Korea, five Combat Stars, Korean Presidential Unit Citation and Valor.

After discharge he married Susie E. Tharpe of Hopkinsville in August 1953. They have two children, Bruce of Cadiz, KY, and Lydia Fuller of Owensboro, KY. They also have four grandchildren.

Robert retired after 30 years as a State Farm Ins. Agent in 1995. They now live on Lake Barkley.

BRYAN CLEVELAND HUDSON, PFC, born 4 Mar 1929 in Land Between the Lakes, Golden Pond, KY. He was drafted into the Army 5 Mar 1951 and after 16 months at Fort Lee, VA was assigned to Btry. B, 13th Arty., 155 Howitzer and was sent to Inchon, Korea.

He spent seven months sleeping in a tent with seven other soldiers. Two months before returning to the States he had a appendicitis attack and was taken to a Quonset hut where he had surgery, then sent to Pusan, Korea to rest. When he returned, the tents had been replaced with bunkers for shelter.

Pfc. Hudson returned to Camp Breckinridge, KY and was discharged 4 Mar 1953. He married Myrtie Calhoun from Trigg County on 29 Dec 1953 and they now reside in Ballard County, LaCenter, KY. They have son Tony and daughter Diane Elliot, and two granddaughters, Holly and Hannah Hudson. Bryon retired after 31 years with the Dept. of Fish and Wildlife at the Ballard County Waterfowl Refuge. He enjoys yard work, gardening, building bird houses and watching the birds migrate back to Ballard County.

CLAYTON "DICK" HUDSON, Corporal, born on 1 Nov 1933 and grew up living in the Hematite/Center Furnace area of Trigg County. His parents were G.C. Hudson and Eva Mae Cossey Hudson. In 1953 he met and fell in love with Mable Taylor and they were married on 29 Dec 1953.

He was drafted into the army on 12 Jan 1954 and was stationed at Fort Knox with the 3rd Armd. Div. for basic training. While he was at Fort Knox he was selected to be a cook and sent to Food Service School. His next assignment was Port of Whittier, Alaska, where he found out he was soon to become a father. His wife went into labor early on his birthday, 1 November, and was having problems so the Army flew him home on a cargo plane. After it was determined that Mable and their new daughter, Doris Ann, were going to be fine, he was sent back to Fort Knox. He was selected to attend a special cooking school and cooked for international dignitaries at a L.O.G.X (war on paper) at Fort Lee, VA. That experience of cooking for all the high level "brass" was the highlight of his military career. He was discharged from the Army as a corporal on 12 Jan 1956.

Upon his discharge, he returned to Trigg County and managed Fisherman's One Stop bait and tackle store. Two years later he went to work for the KY Dept. of Fish and Wildlife on the National Wildlife Refuge. He trapped and transported deer and turkey to other parts of the state in an effort to restock them to areas where their populations had declined. He continued that job from 1958 to 1960.

In 1960 the family moved to Marshall County, KY and he began working for the Dept. of Fish and Wildlife at Camp John W. Currie, a youth conservation education camp, on Kentucky Lake. In 1963 his other daughter, Tammy Lynn, was born. He continued working at Camp Currie as camp superintendent until his retirement on 31 Oct 1995.

Currently Mable and Dick live at 2301 Oak Level Road, Benton, KY where he enjoys fishing, gardening and yard work. They have one granddaughter, Natalie Renee Lents.

JAMES K. HUDSON, PFC, born on 11 Feb 1927 in the Center Furnace Area, "between the rivers" in Trigg County. He was one of 11 children of G.C. "Cleve" and Eva Mae Hudson.

He was inducted into the USMC on 22 May 1952 at Owensboro, KY (selective service board No. 93, Trigg County) and served with the 5th Marine Corps Reserve and Recruitment Dis.

Pfc. Hudson was discharged 21 May 1954 at Camp Lejeune, NC. His awards include the Korean Service Medal w/2 stars, National Defense Service Ribbon and UN Service Medal.

After returning home, he was employed at Tappan Factory in Murray, KY. He married Barbara 5 Nov 1951 and they had four children: Donnie, Ronnie, Lannie and Becky and two grandchildren, Amanda and Lindsay. James passed away 22 Mar 1992.

LESLIE WADE HUNTER, Sergeant, born 13 Apr 1930 in the Linton area of Trigg County. He was drafted into the Army 21 Aug 1952. From Owensboro, he was sent to Fort George Meade, MD then to Camp Pickett, VA for basic training. In January 1953 he received orders for overseas duty at Inchon, Korea where he served with the 115th Med. Bn. 40th Div. He was discharged at Fort Knox in June 1954 with the rank of sergeant.

After serving 22 months in service, Leslie returned to Hopkinsville and his former job at International Shoe Co. He attended night classes in electronics repair and refrigeration. After graduation he went to work as an appliance serviceman for Sears. In February 1971 he opened his own business, Indian Hills TV and Appliance Service.

Leslie married Dorothy Stallons of Canton on 3 Jun 1950. A son, Roger Worth, was born 18 May 1953 at Fort Campbell Hospital and was 13 months old when he and his dad first met. Daughter Leslie Dianne was born 9 May 1956 at Jennie Stuart Hospital. Grandchildren are Jeremy Wade Hunter, Timothy Jarrod Cato and Chadwick Steger Cato. Leslie and his son Roger were co-owners of the business at the time of his death from cancer in March 1992. He is buried in Green Hill Memorial Gardens, Hopkinsville.

ROBERT E. HUNTER, Sergeant, born 11 Apr 1932, Linton, KY. He enlisted in the Army 17 Jul 1952 at Owensboro, KY and took his basic training at Fort Knox, KY. He served in Korea one year, three months and 25 days and was discharged 30 Apr 1954 with the rank of sergeant.

Married Barbara Cox 9 Oct 1954 and they moved to Steger, IL. They had three children: Sherry, Rodney and Michael, and six grandchildren: Kevin, Kyle and Chase Hunter; Kris, Lauren and Megan Cook.

Robert passed away 5 Nov 1993 and is buried Skyline Memorial Park, Monee, IL.

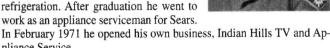

Leslie and Robert Earl Hunter.

THOMAS REED JONES, PFC, son of Mr. and Mrs. Haywood Jones,

enlisted in the Army on 13 Feb 1953 in Owensboro, KY. He was sent to Fort Belfor, VA for basic training, then to Korea where he served 15-1/2 months as a combat engineer. He was a demolition expert and was responsible for taking up land mines and demolished bridges and other structures as required.

His decorations include the UN Defense Service Medal, National Defense Service Medal, Korean Service Medal, ROK, Presidential Unit Citation and Good Conduct Medal. Thomas was discharged as a private first class 9 Dec 1954 and transferred to the Army Reserves.

WALLACE SANFORD JONES, born 25 Dec 1925 in Hopkinsville, KY. He first served in the USN from 1940-45 then joined the Army and served six years. During that hitch of duty he played platoon football and injured his shoulders.

After three years in the Veterans Hospital at Newport News, VA, he applied for overseas duty and was sent to Japan for a week then to Korea, where he was shot in both shoulders. He was re-hospitalized and later received a medical discharge.

Wallace moved to Baltimore, MD where he drove a taxicab until his friends found him dead in his room. He was cremated and the remains returned to Cadiz for burial in the family plot at East End Cemetery in 1996.

JOE B. JOYCE, Corporal, born 24 Apr 1926 in Golden Pond, KY. He was drafted into the Army 28 Jan 1949 and did his basic training at Camp Breckinridge, KY. He traveled to San Francisco, CA, boarded the USS General Walker for Yokohoma, Japan and was assigned to 229th Ordnance Base Depot, 72nd Ordnance Base Depot Co. as a parts clerk.

Returned to the States in February 1950 and discharged into the Inactive Reserves. He was recalled 24 Oct 1950 for the Korean War and reported to Fort Eustis, VA where he was assigned to the 724th Transportation Railway Operating Bn. He attended Locomotive Fireman and Locomotive Engineers School, then sent to Oakland Army Base for advanced training. Sent to Pusan, Korea and operated the rail road from Pusan to Seoul.

In November 1951 he was again placed in the Reserves and discharged in May 1953 with the rank of corporal. He received the Occupation Medal (Japan) and Korean Service Medal w/Bronze Star.

Joe married Nina Mode on 24 Mar 1953 and they live in Cadiz, KY. He retired 13 May 1981 from the Army Corps of Engineers.

They have two children, Sandra Carrion and Brenda Schymos; four grandchildren: Tracy Leity, Grady Romblad, Christine Slater, Jason Meranda; and eight great-grandchildren.

JOHN L KEATTS, PO2, born 3 Sep 1929 in Cadiz, KY. He graduated from Trigg County HS in 1947 and joined the USN 3 Jan 1951.

After nine weeks training at Great Lakes, IL he was transported by troop train, along with 19 of his fellow sailors, to San Diego, CA to board the USS *Higbee* (DDR-806), a radar pickett destroyer. He served aboard the USS *Higbee* until discharged in October 1954.

The Korean War was in full swing during the first two and one half years of service on the USS *Higbee*. The *Higbee* left the States to go to Korea in the fall of 1951 after undergoing repairs at the Mare Island Naval Shipyard in upper San Francisco Bay. The USS

Higbee operated with Task Force 77 off Korea and participated in numerous other duties and exercises during the next eight months, including a trip to Hong Kong, before returning to the States in the spring of 1952.

Upon return from Korea the *Higbee* changed its home port from San Diego to Long Beach, CA. During the next six months the *Higbee* underwent repairs at the Naval Shipyard in Long Beach, CA. The *Higbee* returned to Korea in late 1952 and was in there when the Korean War ended in 1953. The *Higbee* returned to the States in the fall of 1953. The *Higbee* once again steamed to Japan and Korea in 1954 returning to the States in the fall of 1954. All together John spent 24 months outside the States during his 46 months service in the Navy.

John served as a seaman in Division I during the first cruise to Korea. Shortly after return to the States he was sent to Disbursing Clerk School at the San Diego NTC. After graduation John became the disbursing clerk for the *Higbee*. He was discharged in October 1954 as disbursing clerk second class (PO2/c).

John located in Atlanta, GA after discharge from the Navy. He worked for General Motors for six years and then the US Postal Service for 26 years. John ended his postal service career in Tampa, FL where he now resides in retirement with his wife Louise whom he married on 13 Jun 1981. He has two stepchildren, Daniel and Kathleen Minich, that reside in the Tampa, FL area.

ALBERT MITCHEL KENNEDY, Seaman 1/c, born 31 Oct 1929 in Cadiz, KY, son of John Albert and Harvey Amos Mitchel Kennedy. He enlisted in the USN 7 May 1948 in Louisville, KY and took his basic training at San Diego, CA.

Served in USS *Dishinko* in Korea, a complement of Underwater Demolition which secured and charted all beaches prior to invasion of Korea. In addition American UDT personnel, British and Turk Commandos were also operated from the USS *Dishinko*.

First Class Seaman Kennedy received the Korean Service Medal w/ 3 stars. He was discharged from the Navy on 12 Mar 1952.

He married Ruby Grace King from Dothan, AL and they had five children: Shan, Doug (deceased), LeeRoy, Stewart and Sherrill. Albert worked as a pipe fitter for 41 years in Paducah, KY; West Palm Beach, FL; and Cumberland City, TN. He resides in Cadiz, KY.

CARROLL WOOD "MACK" KENNEDY, Corporal, born 11 May 1930 in Cadiz, KY. His parent's were Durward and Clarice Henderson Kennedy. He and his brother Robert enlisted in the USMC 31 Jul 1951 and went through basic training together at Parris Island, NC. Mack was then sent to Camp Pendleton, CA, where he worked as a stock clerk.

He married his hometown sweetheart, Betty Jean Litchfield, on 11 Jul 1952. He was discharged from the Marines 12 Dec 1952 with the rank of corporal.

The next 40 years he worked at Steel Mill S.K.W. ALLOYS as a loader operator. There were three children born to Betty and Mack: Belinda Dean Kennedy Baars, Kathy Jean Kennedy Birdsong, and Dwight Carroll Kennedy. They lived in Gilbertville, KY until 1967, then built a house in Trigg County to be close to family and friends. Mack has been an active member of Hurricane Baptist Church and was song leader for a number of years. Since retirement in 1992 Carroll has worked as maintenance worker with Lynn Waller Realtors. Grandchildren are Karen and Erin Baars; Allison Carneyhan; Jennifer and Monica Birdsong; Andrea and Matthew Kennedy; and one great-grandchild Luke Carneyhan.

ROBERT L. KENNEDY, born 15 Oct 1932 near Wallonia, KY. Soon after graduation from Trigg County HS he and his brother Carroll "Mack" volunteered for the USMC on 31 Jul 1951 and went through boot camp together at Parris Island, SC. Robert was than assigned to Marine Corps Aviation and took his basic MOS training "Aviation Airframes and Hydraulics" at Jacksonville, FL and Memphis, TN.

He was ordered to Korea via Replacement Draft #123. Having to wait approximately two months, he decided to take 30 days advanced leave and go back home. A highlight of his life was hitchhiking from El Toro, CA to St. Louis MO in just 49 hours. His route was the now famous Route 66 no longer there. It was educational and very exciting.

He served from July 1952 to June 1953 at King 6 Korea Marine AB, 1st MAW, MAG 12, VMA 212. King 6 was an old WWII Japanese Air Field with metal morris matting over the old gravel air strip. Their 24 aircraft AU-1 Corsair with inverted gull wings was the last Corsair unit to operate in combat.

After more schooling and other assignments, he returned to Japan from April 1957 through September 1958. He then served as an instructor for approximately five years in his MOS at Memphis, TN; Key West, FL; Olathe, KS and El Toro, CA.

His next duty assignment was Chu Lai, Vietnam, where his whole MAG 36 made an LST landing. The infantry had already secured the area. After nine months in Vietnam he rotated back to Japan and back to Conlus.

He was discharged at New River Marine Corps Air Facility, NC on 10 Oct 1966. Years later he joined the National Guard, 1st Div., 123rd Armor Bn., HHC. He finished his career with 29 plus years military service.

His awards include National Service Ribbon w/star, Korean Service Medal w/3 stars, Vietnam Service Medal, Korean War Medal and four National Guard medals plus two Letters of Commendation for services rendered.

Robert married Jeanne Sherbut 12 Jun 1952 before going to Korea. They have three sons, one daughter, eight grandchildren, three step-grand-children and one great-grandchild. He is a retired carpenter and they live in Paducah, KY.

ODELL C. KNIGHT, born 17 Dec 1928 in Trigg County, son of Johnny and Ada Francis Knight. He was drafted in December 1952 during the Korean War with assignments at Nashville, TN; Fort Meade, MD and Camp Polk, LA.

During basic training a silver pin in his left elbow was broken and he was given a medical discharge 4 Apr 1953.

Retired in 1996 from the Dover Sheriff Dept and passed away in 1997. He had four children: Rickie, Regina, Rhonda, Rexita (deceased); five grandchildren: Daniel, Tara, Donya, Natasha, Joanna; and two greats, Aaron and Sabryn.

ROBERT C. (BUD) KING, Lieutenant Commander, USN (Ret), son of Myrtle and Marlon King, was born in Canton in 1932. He attended Canton Grade School and graduated from Trigg County High in 1949. His maternal grandparents were Melia Downs Upton and R.H. Upton Sr. Paternal grandparents were Leona and Fred C. King of Aurora. Other family includes a sister, Louise King Calhoun, widow of James A. "Jimmy" Calhoun; an aunt, Nell Upton Leneave of Cadiz, as well as five children and eight grandchildren. Bud and his wife Shannon live in Nashville, TN.

Bud entered the Naval Aviation Cadet flight program in Pensacola, FL in 1953 during the Korean War. After 18 months' training, he received his coveted Navy Wings of Gold and was commissioned as an ensign in February 1955. Various base assignments at naval air stations during his 20 plus years included Norfolk, VA; Key West, FL; Millington, TN; Kingsville, TX; Keflavik, Iceland; and Rota, Spain.

He qualified as a naval aircraft carrier pilot during his training by completing six take offs and landings on the USS *Monterey*. Later aircraft carrier deployments were aboard the USS *Siboney* and the USS *Valley Forge*, where he flew as a fighter pilot.

He was released from active duty in June 1965, then flew in the Naval Air Reserve at Millington, TN for eight years prior to retiring. During his service as a naval officer and naval aviator, he was qualified on and flew 21 different types of aircraft, most of which were propeller and jet fighters.

Bud was among the first group of USN pilots to fly jet aircraft. His other duties included six years as an instructor pilot, and was a graduate of the U.S. Naval School of Justice (now referred to as JAG, or Judge Advocate General). His ground officer duties included court martial and other legal responsibilities.

Since retirement from the Navy and 26 years with American Airlines, he now flies for the USAF Auxiliary, known as the Civil Air Patrol, with the rank of lieutenant colonel. His duties include flying as mission pilot on search and rescue for downed or missing aircraft, as well as instructing cadets in aircraft familiarization and aerospace education.

WILFORD THOMAS LANCASTER, Corporal, born 25 Jun 1929 in Trigg County, the son of Aubrey and Julia Lancaster. He was drafted into the Army 21 Feb 1952, went to Owensboro, then to Fort Meade, MD for orientation, then to Fort Bliss, TX for basic training in light artillery.

After a month at home he went to Camp Kilmer, NJ where he was shipped overseas 8 Aug 1952. He landed in Bremerhaven, Germany and from there to Saarbrucken, Germany where he was assigned to Btry. C, AAA Light Artillery at Milenhall, England. He was assigned to a construction team building living quarters for a while, then sent to Brize Norton, England and guarded and air base with B-47 jet bombers. England was pretty good duty and Queen Elizabeth was crowned while he was there.

Left for the States 8 Jan 1954 and was discharged at Fort Knox, KY 28 Jan 1954.

He married Betty Taylor 11 Apr 1956, no children. He has worked for John Deere Implement Co. for 45 years. Now works part-time and does wood work.

HOWARD GRAY LANE SR., Corporal, born 31 Jan 1927 in Trigg County, KY. Prior to being drafted into the Army in 1952, he married Walline Chambers on 5 Aug 1950. The couple initially settled in Golden Pond, KY.

Howard enlisted at Fort Meade, MD, then transferred to Camp Breckinridge in Morganfield, KY for basic training. He was stationed there for 13 months and assigned the position of cook in the 101st Abn. Div. Cpl. Lane was then transferred to Fort Miles, DE and Camp Kilmer, NJ before being transferred back to Fort Meade, MD where he was discharged in 1954.

Howard worked construction for several years in Alabama and Georgia before permanently settling in Benton, KY. He was employed by Air Products and Chemicals, of Calvert City, KY, for 31 years. He retired from the plant in 1998. He now enjoys gardening, fishing, and spending time with family.

Howard and Walline have two children, Howard Gray Jr. and Scott Wallace. They also have three grandchildren: Leslie Lane Taylor, Christopher Gray Lane, and Cody Wallace Lane.

BERLIE R. LASSITER, Sergeant First Class, born 10 Sep 1929 in Rockport, IN. He joined the service 11 Oct 1950, Owensboro, KY. Assignments include 4th Div. 42nd FA BN A Btry., Chief of Section, Fort Benning, GA and Gelnhausen, Germany.

Discharged 10 Oct 1953 as sergeant first class. He received the Occupation Medal (Germany) and Good Conduct Medal.

Divorced, he has two children, Steven and Mary, and one grandchild Eric. He retired in 1988 from Kenosha Aviation Service. He lives in Kenosha, WI. Today, he enjoys blowing snow and mowing grass.

W.J. LAWRENCE JR., born 23 Sep 1931, son of W.J. Sr. and Madalyn Wilson Lawrence of Cadiz, KY. He graduated from high school in 1951 and farmed until 1954. He was inducted into the military in April 1954 and served until discharge in April 1956.

After discharge he attended two years college then was employed by Hopkinsville Federal Savings and Loan Assoc. on 1 Jul 1958. From 1971 to retirement in 1994 he was employed by First Federal Savings and Loan (served as president from 1983 to retirement).

Married Jean Grant Lawrence of Crofton, KY on 1 Sep 1957. They have two children, Vickie Lynn (b. 5 May 1959) and Stephen Grant (b. 25 Jun 1964).

ROBERT CLYDE LENEAVE, SP4, born 25 Nov 1934 in Cadiz, KY, son of Sidney and Katherine Hite Leneave.

Upon graduation he was sent to HTU-1 (Helicopter Training Unit), Ellyson Field NAS, Pensacola, FL in aviation mechanics. While stationed there he played half-back with the base football team (the Goshawks) and pitched for the NAS fast-pitch soft ball team. Later aboard the USS *Macon* he pitched during the Fleet Championships in Cuba and they won.

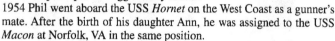

Phil also received his GED and it was signed by his cousin John Dean Minton who was than principal of Trigg County HS. In 1954 Phil went aboard the USS *Hornet* on the West Coast as a gunner's mate. After the birth of his daughter Ann, he was assigned to the USS *Macon* at Norfolk, VA in the same position.

He was released from the Navy at Norfolk in April 1956 and discharged in 1960. Awards include the National Defense Service Medal and the Good Conduct Medal.

His four children by first wife Betty Tolbert are Ann Killeen, Phil "Buddy" Jr., Sandra Blackwell, Ronnie Grasty; stepson is Gene Jones. Grandchildren are Clay and Sean Garvin; Christopher, Josh, Amy, Sara and Ruby Grasty, Michael Gee; stepgranddaughter Caitlin Jones; great grandchildren are Jacob and Alexia Garvin, and Jonathan and Christopher Grasty. Phil is now married to Mildred Wood Jones and they live in Cadiz, KY. He is retired from South Central Bell.

WILLIAM HUGH "BILL" GOLLADAY, Corporal, born 25 May 1928 in Trigg County, Roaring Springs, KY, the son of William C. and Mary Gilliam Golladay. He was drafted into the Army 2 Jan 1951 at Owensboro, KY and went to Camp Breckinridge, KY for basic and advanced infantry training.

Entered the Korean War and was assigned to 3rd Bn., HQ Co., COMO DT, 23rd Inf., 2nd Inf. Div. on 1 Jun 1951. The 23rd Army relieved the Marines at the Punch Bowl; the 9th Inf. at Bloody Ridge on 6 September and moved to Heartbreak Ridge on 13 September.

Left for the States in March 1952 and assigned to Fort Knox, KY for five months before discharge. Awards include the Combat Infantry Badge, Korean Service Medal w/3 stars and UN Service Medal.

Returning to civilian life he farmed for 14 years. In 1966 he joined W.R. Grace and Co. to sell fertilize and chemicals and became manager of the business in 1968 until retirement in 1988.

William married Mary Helen Suddeath 6 Jan 1973 and they live in Hopkinsville, KY.

WILLIAM L. GRANT, PFC, born 13 Aug 1930 in Montgomery, KY. He joined the Army 21 May 1953 at Camp Atterbury, IN. During the Korean War he served with Co. B, 88th Inf. Heavy Mortar Bn.

Pfc. Grant was discharged 23 Apr 1955. His awards include the National Defense Service Medal, Vietnam Service Medal, Korean Service Medal and Good Conduct Medal. He was discharged from the Reserves 31 May 1961.

He married Linda Boren and they live in LaFayette, KY. They have three children: Billy Don, Raymond Earl and Bryon Keith; three grandchildren and one great-grandchild. William still works as a painter.

CARL GRAY, born 15 Mar 1929 in Cadiz, KY. He was drafted into the Army in February 1951. After his induction he was sent to Fort Meade for training assignment, then sent to Aberdeen Proving Ground in Maryland for basic training. After basic training he was transferred to Atlanta, GA for Wheel Vehicle Field Maintenance School. Due to a reoccurring heart condition caused by rheumatic fever, he was not found suitable for overseas replacement for Korean casualities. Therefore, in November 1951 he was discharged.

While in the service he did serve as typist for his company. Even though most of this period was spent in the hospital, he did compete his basic training and wheel vehicle service training. The heart condition due to the Rheumatic fever has not curtailed his ability to have a successful life outside of the military.

On 16 Jul 1953 he married Maxine Henry. They have three daughters: Judy Rutter, Ruth Gray and Martha Shipley, and five granddaughters. He worked for several years for Stagner and Nunn electric and plumbing contractors. Later he returned to the family farm as a self-employed excavation contractor. Developing and selling retirement sites subsidized his farming habit. This has also given him an opportunity to get to know and develop friendships with people from other areas who chose to make their home in Trigg County. This has also helped to add to the successful growth of Trigg County. The land that was not suitable for building sites has been retained and improved for hay and cattle.

He is a charter member of the Cadiz Camp of The Gideons International. He has served on the Board of directors for the Temperance League of Kentucky. Carl is an active member of Hurricane Baptist Church.

He and his wife reside on the remainder of the family farm in Trigg County, on Barkley Lake, in the Rockcastle Community.

JOE B. GUESS, Sergeant E-5, born 22 Jan 1930 in Paducah, KY. He joined the Army in July 1948 for one year active and five years reserve duty. He trained at Fort Hood, TX in the 2nd Armd. Div.

When the Korean War broke out in July 1950, he was called back to active duty in September 1950 and sent to Fort Lewis, WA for refresher course, then to Japan and assigned to 2nd Inf. Div. in Korea.

They made an amphibious landing in north Korea in 40° below zero weather and joined up with the 9th Inf. Regt. 2nd Inf. Div. who were retreating from the Chinese army. After seven months of fighting they were on the offensive and went back to north Korea.

Sgt. Guess returned to the States in August 1951 and was released to Reserves. He received a Battle Star for Wonju Offensive and May Massacre, Korean Service Medal w/star, Combat Infantry Badge and Commendation Ribbon w/pendant.

He married Louise Sons on 11 Jan 1952 and they reside in Cadiz, KY. They have one son Steven and two grandsons, Austin and Logan.

Because of physical problems, he was discharged 7 Nov 1953. Edgar died in the Veterans Hospital in Lexington 1 Jul 1987. All other information concerning his term of service has been lost. *Submitted by his sister Verna Scott.*

ALBERT O'NEIL MEREDITH, QM3/c, born 11 Sep 1931 at Bumpus Mills, TN. He moved to Kentucky when he was a teenager. He enlisted in the USN 14 Jan 1952 and took basic training in San Diego, CA. When basic training was completed he was assigned to the USS *Curtis* (AV-4).

He was in the Navy during the Korean War and was sent to Eniwetok in the Marshall Islands, 1952-53, to experiment with the hydrogen bomb. He was discharged 9 Jan 1956 as quartermaster third class.

He re-located to Granite City, IL and was employed by Laclede Steel as a foreman. He was active in his church as a deacon and a Sunday school teacher.

Albert married the former Helen Stack from Bumpus Mills, TN on 21 Jul 1951, and they have four children: Diane, Michael, Margaret and Richard; grandchildren are Donnie, Laura, Steven, David, Amanda, Patrick, Joshua, Amy, Ian and Travis. Their son and two grandsons were also in the Navy, following in his footsteps. He became ill in March 1983 and passed away 20 Dec 1987. His family still resides in Granite City, IL. *Submitted by his widow, Helen R. Meredith.*

JACK MIZE JR., Corporal, born 11 Feb 1932, the youngest son of Jack and Ethel Blakeley Mize. He attended Cerulean Grade School and Trigg County HS. After graduation he went to work at International Shoe Co. in Hopkinsville, KY.

Jack Jr. was inducted in the US Army 21 Feb 1952 and sent to Indiantown Gap, PA for his basic and advanced infantry training. On 11 Aug 1952, he landed in Korea where he was assigned to Co. D 180th Inf. and served 11 months in combat.

Honorably discharged with the rank of corporal on 23 Nov 1953. Awards include the UN Service Medal, National Defense Service Medal, Korean Service Medal w/2 Bronze Stars and the Combat Infantry Badge.

He married Nadean Sowell 24 Jul 1954 and they resided in Cerulean where he farmed. In 1965 he went to work at Johnson Control where he was employed until his death 25 Dec 1996. He was laid to rest in Cerulean Springs Cemetery.

LLOYD MIZE, Corporal, born 30 May 1930 in Trigg County, KY. He was inducted into the Army 24 Sep 1951 at Fort Meade, MD, then sent to Camp Chaffee, AR for basic training with 5th Armd. Div.

After basic training he was sent to Oakland, CA and a month later to Korea where he maintained machine guns and barbered. Cpl. Mize was discharged 27 May 1953.

He went to Nashville Barber School, served his apprenticeship at Chaney's Barber Shop, Hopkinsville, KY, and opened his own barbershop in 1960. Semi-retired in 1992, he still barbers a day or so a week.

In 1959 he married Mary Allison Smith, a Christian County native, and they have resided in Cadiz, KY, corner of Glendale and Lafayette Street, the past 42 years. They are members of Cadiz United Methodist Church. His hobbies are gardening and fishing.

DORIS KYDELL MOORE, born 8 Apr 1928 in Trigg County, son of Jesse and Pearl Ezell Moore. Joined the service 30 Mar 1950, Owensboro, KY and served with the 523rd MP Dis Mtd. Pat and Gd Plt.

In 1951 he participated in Operation Greenhouse (testing atomic weapons) with the 516th MP Svc. Co. He was discharged 28 Feb 1953. Awards include the UN Service Medal and Korean Service Medal w/BSS.

He married Doris Dearing in 1954 and they live at 530 Moore Road, Princeton, KY. He retired from the profession of carpet installation in 1992. They have three children: Michael, Mark and Candidi.

Doris belongs to Ray-Crider-McNabb VFW Post 5595. His brother, Durwood Moore, served in the USN. His parents and brother are deceased.

GENE MOORE, born 28 Feb 1929 at Linton, KY in Trigg County. He is better known as Bill among his family and friends. He attended Linton School and later worked at the International Shoe factory in Hopkinsville. The family later moved to the Montgomery Community where he farmed on the Smith D. Broadbent Jr. farms.

He entered the Army 7 Feb 1951 and went to Fort Knox for basic training. While on leave after basic Gene married Sara Halliday 18 Jun 1951.

On 4 Jul 1951 he left Camp Kilmer, NJ for Fulda, Germany where he was a border guard and in charge of the supply truck trips for the 14th Armd. Cav.

Returned to the States on the USS *General Darby,* was discharged and returned to Trigg County 17 Jan 1953.

Gene took a job at Audas Dairy in Cadiz and continued working for different milk companies, each one selling out to another and keeping him with each buy-out. He retired in September 1990. Gene and Sara live on Hwy. 139 South Road, Cadiz. He is recovering from heart by-pass surgery and a massive stroke, 1 Apr 1997. They have two children, Billy Gene (b. 30 Jun 1955) and Debbie (b. 3 Apr 1958).

BEN T. NEWTON, E-6, born 15 Jan 1929, the son of Lillian Colston, Energy, KY. He entered the Army 21 Jul 1948 and served a tour of duty in Japan.

Ben enlisted again in 1951 and served from 1952-53 in the Korean War. After discharge he worked in Benton, KY as a police officer. In February 1962 he re-enlisted and served two years in Germany, one year in Korea, 13 months in Vietnam, three years in Alaska and his last three years at Fort Hood, TX.

He retired from the Army 1 Sep 1977. His decorations include the National Defense Medal w/3 BSS, UN Service Medal, RVN Campaign Medal, Bronze Star, Armed Forces Expeditionary Medal (Korea), Good Conduct w/clasp, Bronze 5 loops (Vietnam), Service Medal w/4 BSS, Sharpshooter, Marksman and Blacksmith Award.

After retirement he worked with the Kentucky State Highway Dept. for 15 years, then retired. Ben and his wife Emma live in Murray, KY, and are members of Ferguson Springs Baptist Church.

MARSHALL D. NOEL, SP-5, born 9 Jun 1932 in Trigg County. Joined the service 11 Jan 1953 with assignments at Fort Knox, KY (basic training); Fort Leonard Wood, MO (Engineer School); Fort Lewis, WA; Fort Ord, CA; Presidio, San Francisco. He was discharged 12 Jan 1956.

He was with the Color Guard and made Soldier of the Month twice and received the Good Conduct Medal. When he was stationed at Presidio he helped move the dignitaries about San Francisco, Oakland and other cities to meetings of the UN Summits in 1955. He was permitted to enter the meetings of concerns of the Nations of the World and was proud to meet Kruschev and dignitaries of Russia.

The 34th Engineer Group, 115 strong, accepted this honor to have new cars to move the dignitaries. They were immune from all police as long as they flew the UN flag on their cars. They were always on best behavior as they were observed by U.S. Senators, generals and U.S. dignitaries. Marshall was a sergeant over the Motor Pool for HHC 34th Engrs.

Marshall's first wife Jane is deceased. He married Bonnie 15 May 1997 and they live at 2189 Main Street, Cadiz, KY. He owned and operated his own concrete business until retiring in 1999 and is now a consultant. He has three children: Dottie Goodwyn, Doug and Bob Noel; stepson Todd Butts; grandchildren: Stephen, Stephanie, Lauren and Layton Noel, Derek and Dustin Brashears; step-grandchild Taylor Butts and one great-grandson Christopher Noel.

HIRLAM HALE NUNN, Corporal, born 12 Jun 1927 in Golden Pond, KY. He was drafted 28 Sep 1950 in the U.S. Army during the Korean Conflict.

After basic training at Fort Custer, MI, he was assigned to the 163rd MP BN. Their unit was shipped to Ludwisburg, Germany. After eight months in the police battalion, he earned the rank of corporal and was transferred to HQ&HQ 47th Ord as a personnel clerk for enlisted men.

Returned to the States to Camp Kilmer, NJ and received his honorable discharge at Indian Town Gap, PA on 10 Sep 1952.

Married Ann Williams 5 Nov 1955 and they live on Third Street in Cadiz, KY. He has been a Mason for 45 years and attends Baptist Church. He retired from A.J. Segal & Sons after 45 years.

MARTIN CHESTER "M.C." OAKLEY, entered the USN at age 17 on 1 Jun 1955, a few days after graduating from Trigg County HS. M.C. grew up in Golden Pond, KY, and attended Golden Pond Grade School and Golden Pond Baptist Church. He is the son of Jesse J. and Lila Futrell Oakley, and a brother to Ora Mae Hunter and Vickey Lane.

Three other young men and M.C. rode the Greyhound Bus from Hopkinsville, KY, to Louisville, KY, where they met a company of men and proceeded to Great Lakes Naval Training Center, Waukegan, IL, for basic training.

M.C. chose aviation for his naval career. On 29 Aug 1955, he went to Norman NTC in Norman, OK, and was there until 21 Oct 1955, for basic aviation training. On 31 October of the same year, M.C. arrived at Memphis NAS in Tennessee and was there through 17 Feb 1956. At this time he attended the Aviation Mechanics School.

After completing, M.C. went to North Island NAS in San Diego, CA, joined a new squadron and moved to Miramar NAS. The squadron, planes and equipment moved to Moffett Field NAS in northern California, where he was based until his discharge 1 Aug 1958. During this time there were training sessions in Fallon, NV, and El Centro, CA, and several months on the aircraft carrier CVA-33 *Kearsarge*.

M.C. Oakley now resides in Sun City, FL, with his wife Faye. Their children, Kathie, Rickie and Michael, and grandchildren live near by. *Submitted by his sister, Vickey Oakley Lane.*

CHARLES WILBURN OLIVER, born 24 Apr 1935 in Caldwell County, KY to Dixie Lee Oliver and Anna Lee Gray Oliver. He grew up on a farm in the Hurricane Community of Trigg and Lyon counties.

In 1951 he left high school to help out with the family farm, but following a devastating drought in 1952 he was forced north to find work, working first in Peoria, IL then for an aircraft manufacturer in Evansville, IN. He continued working in Evansville weekdays and farming with his father on weekends until mid-1953 when the company lost its aircraft contracts. He returned to Trigg County and volunteered for the draft in late 1953.

Drafted in February 1954 with basic and advanced training at Fort Knox, KY then assigned to 5th Inf. Regt. 71st Div. at Fort Lewis, WA. The 5th was a light infantry regiment and trained for speed and mobility. He served as squad leader in the Communication Squad for Fox Co. and was also a bayonet and hand-to-hand combat instructor.

After his discharge in 1956 he returned to Cadiz and shortly thereafter returned to work in Evansville. He served in reserve duty for six years, receiving an honorable discharge in 1962.

In June 1957 he married Della Baccus of the Woodson Chapel Community of Lyon County. In 1959 the couple moved back to the Blackhawk Community and he began farming full-time until 1970 when he became a full-time truck driver, a profession he continues today.

Oliver and Della live in Lyon County and have three children and three grandchildren.

Following is a letter from HQ 5th Inf. Regt. sent to his parents in 1955:

Dear Mr. and Mrs. Oliver:

For the second time within six months your son Charles has distinguished himself by being selected as the 5th Inf. Regimental "Soldier of the Week" during the period 12-17 Sep 1955.

In direct competition with his fellow soldiers of the regiment, he proved himself so outstanding when he appeared before the selection board composed of senior officers, that he was again chosen as my personal aide.

Your son is a fine soldier, both in appearance and fact. He is a great credit to you, his parents, this regiment and the military service.

Sincerely yours,
E. Rusteberg
Colonel, Infantry

GLENN EZELL OVERBY, born 4 Apr 1932, in Trigg County, KY, son of Mr. and Mrs. John H. Overby. He attended Trigg County Schools and in January 1951 entered into the Army receiving three months basic training at Fort Knox, KY, where he was assigned to the Infantry Division.

In May 1951 his unit was sent to Korea. He was discharged in January 1954 and went to work on construction. He eventually settled in Miami, FL. He married Katherine Sullivan in 1960 and has a son Eric Glenn Overby.

On 21 Mar 1971 in Hialeah, FL, he died as the result of an accident when a car hit him while he was riding his motorcycle to work. His body was flown to Cadiz, KY, where he was buried in the family plot of the John Fry Stewart Cemetery in Trigg County, KY.

BURNETT W. PORTER JR., Lieutenant Colonel, was one of five children born to Burnett and Eunice Shelton Porter and grew up on a farm in Trigg County, KY. He attended grade school at Chestnut Grove and graduated from Trigg County High in 1949. In high school, he played in the band, lettered three years in football, and was elected president of the student body during his senior year. He attended Lindsey Wilson Junior College for two years, then transferred to Western Kentucky University and graduated in June 1954, with a BA degree, a teaching certificate, and a commission in the Air Force Reserves.

Burnett entered the active Air Force in September 1954 as a 2nd lieutenant. Burnett married Joan Grace Foster while assigned to the Special Air Missions at Washington National Airport and three children: Burnett William, David Brian and Cindy Ann, were born to this union. He retired as a lieutenant colonel from the active Air Force in 1974 and was then employed by the state of Kentucky to work as a liaison between the Cabinet for Human Resources and the

District Courts in the nine counties of the Pennyrile District. He retired from the State in 1991.

Major Military Assignments: served as the Director of Transportation for a major air command (AFCS) from 1971-74; from 1970-71, served as Officer in Charge of J-4 Element, Military Assistance Command Vietnam, in the Command Post; Assistant Professor Aerospace Studies, Mississippi State University from 1967-70; squadron commander and transportation officer responsible for the operational movement of supplies and personnel to support the Department of Defense in Libya

Graduate student in transportation management at Indiana University through the Air Force Institute of Technology from 1963-64. Transportation officer responsible for movement of Militia Airlift Commands aircraft through Patrick AFB and Cape Canaveral from 1961-63. Maintained liaison with contract representatives conducting space systems tests at Cape Canaveral that required airlift support by the Air Force. Coordinated and arranged airlift of space vehicles recovered after launch on the missile range which included Col. John Glenn and Scott Carpenter's flights into space. Special air missions, Washington National, Presidential Aircraft, the Columbine.

AUDREY GARLAND P'POOL, Captain, born 31 Jan 1929 in Wallonia, Trigg County, KY. He graduated from Trigg County HS in 1947 and enlisted in the USAF in 1948. Basic training was at San Antonio, TX and Aircraft and Jet Engine Mechanic School at Chanute AFB, IL.

Assignments at Anchorage, AK; Long Beach, CA; Oxnard, CA; Moody AFB, Valdosta, GA. Accepted for Officer Candidate School, commissioned 2nd lieutenant and served another tour in Fairbanks, AK.

Sent to Suffolk County AFB, West Hampton Beach, Long Island, NY and while there attended Command and Staff School in Montgomery, AL. Made captain then sent on a tour of duty in Osan, Korea, serving as aircraft maintenance officer.

Last assignment was at Truax Field close to Madison, WI where he served as aircraft inspector. Capt. P'Pool retired 31 Jan 1968 and returned to Trigg County where he was a school bus driver for 20 plus years and a farmer for 28 years.

He was married some 50 years to Sarah Scott and had two sons, Stefan and Scott. Audrey passed away 19 Jun 2000.

JULIAN EARL RADFORD, Sergeant, born 18 Jun 1929 in Trigg County, KY. After trying his hand at several occupations he decided to enlist in the Army in 1952. He was drawn by a desire to serve his country and to see and experience other parts of the country and world.

During his 22 years of service, he completed a tour in Korea, two tours in Vietnam and nine years in Germany. Stateside he spent time at Aberdeen Proving Grounds, MD, where he completed basic and advanced

training; Fort Carson, CO; Fort Riley, KS and Fort Lewis, WA. The majority of his service was spent in field artillery units.

He retired from the Army as a first sergeant in 1974. He received a Bronze Star w/OLC for Vietnam.

On 5 Mar 1954 he married Betty Jo and they have one child, Kelly Lee. Julian worked for the Firestone Tire Co. in management and eventually retired in 1986. Betty passed away 13 Jan 2001. He lives in Hopkinsville, KY and enjoys golfing, walking and working out.

THOMAS EUGENE RANDOLPH,

COA 12th A.I. BN, 2nd Armd. Div., U.S. Army, born 1 Apr 1933, the son of Milus and Lucy Guthrie Randolph. He entered service 30 Apr 1953 at Owensboro, KY and went to Fort Meade, MD to be issued equipment.

Returned to Camp Breckinridge, KY for 16 weeks of basic training. From Camp Breckinridge he went to Camp Kilmer, NJ to New York to Worms, Germany in October 1953.

His duty in Worms, Germany was to be part of the constant duty guard force whose mission was to protect West Germany from "Little Moscow" which was across the Rhine River.

Discharged from active duty on 15 Apr 1955 and transferred to Reserve status to complete his eight years of service.

Retired from Phelps Dodge Industries and now resides in Hopkinsville, KY.

BERNARD REDD,

A1/c, was born 6 Oct 1935 in Trigg County, the son of D.B. and Bessie Redd who were residents of Canton for many years. He graduated from Trigg County HS in 1954 and shortly thereafter joined the USAF. Two of his brothers, Chappell and Billy, also served in the military. Chappell joined the Marine Corps in 1942 and retired in the mid-1960s. Billy served in the USN for four years.

Bernard served 3-1/2 years in the Air Force, where he attained the rank of A1/c. During his time on active duty he was a radar technician on jet fighter airplanes. After discharge he returned to Trigg County and entered Murray State Univ. In 1961 he graduated with a BS degree in mathematics and physics.

He accepted a position with the U.S. Food & Drug Administration following graduation and soon became involved in the investigation of the illegal trafficking in drugs. He continued in this line of work for 24 years and retired from the U.S. Drug Enforcement Administration (DEA) in 1985 as Agent in Charge of the Nashville, TN office. After leaving DEA he went to work for the Tennessee Bureau of Investigation (TBI). He was in charge of drug law enforcement for the state of Tennessee. After leaving the TBI he and two partners formed a private investigation company. Bernard sold his portion of this company in 1999 and is now semi-retired.

L-R: Gayle Clayton, Ray Noel, Billy Allen, Bernard Redd, Jack Simpson and Glyn Simpson. These six men graduated from Trigg County HS in 1954 and joined the USAF on 16 June of that year. They completed basic training at Sampson AFB in Geneva, NY. They were not together again, as a group, until this photo was taken, 40 years later, at their class reunion in 1994.

Bernard met his wife, Mary Lou, in Cincinnati, OH, and they were married in 1961. They have two sons, Jeff and Matthew, and two grand-

children. He and Mary Lou reside in Brentwood, TN, where they have lived for over 25 years.

HENRY WILLIS RICHARDSON SR.,

SFC, born 19 Jan 1928 in Fordson, MI, son of J.B. and Mary English Richardson, moved with his family back to English Hill, Trigg County in 1935. As a young boy growing up he worked in the "country store" on English Hill and also drove a truck for huckster delivery. He graduated Trigg County HS in 1946 and from Murray State Teachers College in 1950.

He was inducted into Armed Services 8 Dec 1950 and after basic training served during the Korean Conflict. He was a member of MASH unit, 101st Cav., supply sergeant in charge of distributions of uniforms and supplies to soldiers and personnel. He was also jeep driver for his commanding officer. Discharged 8 Sep 1952 as sergeant first class.

Henry married Mary Frances Weatherly 5 Sep 1954 and they have four children: Victoria (deceased as infant), Willette, Henry Jr. (Richie) and Roy. Grandchildren are Rachel and Myles Oliverio, Amber and Kelli Voorhies, Jacqueline and Will III Richardson.

The Richardsons operated Rich's Market 1972-82 in Aurora, KY; Henry operated a trucking business with partner Earl Crump; in 1982 he went to work for Invirex Demolition until retirement due to illness in 1994. They moved to Murray, KY in 1997.

JESSE M. RICKS JR.,

born 16 Feb 1929 in Trigg County, KY, the son of Lois and Jesse Ricks. As a child he lived in Canton, KY but later moved to Lock E on the Cumberland River where his father was assistant lockmaster.

Jesse attended Canton Grade School and graduated from Trigg County HS in 1947. He also attended Western Kentucky University. While working for Lea River Lines he met Lorella Kirks from Paducah, KY and they were married 29 Apr 1951.

During the Korean Conflict, Jesse was drafted into the Army and assigned to the 101st Div. at Camp Breckinridge, KY. After nine months of basic and cadre experience, he was transferred to Japan and assigned to the QM Corps. He also worked as clerks assistant to the officer in charge.

Returned to the States and was discharged in December 1952, arriving home on Christmas Eve. In the following years he worked 30 years for Southern Bell in Paducah, KY as lineman and later as marketing manager in Hopkinsville, KY. After retirement he worked for Career-Com College and Larkin Communication in Hopkinsville.

He was a Methodist lay speaker, worked with the Trail of Tears Commission, member of the Retired Marine Personnel Assoc. and Barbershop Singers of America. Jesse died of cancer in September 1997. He is survived by his wife, sons Michael and Donald, daughter Anita and five grandchildren.

HARL LLOYD ROSE,

born 4 Sep 1934, the fifth and youngest son of Felix Doris and Daisy Feltner Rose. He graduated from Trigg County HS in 1953 after which he joined the Army taking basic training at Fort Knox, KY. He was assigned to Army bases at Fort Lee, VA and Germany.

After two years of service he graduated from Austin Peay State University, Clarksville, TN.

He has been married to the former Dorothy Armstrong for 40 years. They have a daughter, son, and four grandchildren who live near them in Franklin, TN. He is retired from the Associates after working 38 years in various management positions and locations in Alabama and Tennessee.

KENNETH WALTON ROSE, born 12 Nov 1928, the fourth son of Felix Doris and Daisy Feltner Rose. He joined the Army in 1951 and took basic training at Camp Breckinridge, KY. He was assigned to a medical company and sent to Korea. He was presented the Purple Heart for injuries sustained in battle.

He presently lives in Roseville, MI with Jean, his wife of 44 years. They have three sons and three granddaughters. He is retired from General Motors after 30 years of service. He is active in church work and enjoys bowling. *Submitted by Harl Rose.*

JAMES H. "BUCK" ROWAN JR., A1/c, enlisted in the USAF 8 Jun 1951 five days after high school graduation at age 17. He received basic training at Lackland AFB, TX and Sheppard AFB, TX.

After basic training, he was assigned to Air Proving Ground Command, Eglin AFB, FL and assigned TDY (Temporary Duty) AFSC School, Fort Slocum, NY in 1952. He was discharged 10 Nov 1953 at Eglin AFB at end of Korean War. James moved to Trigg County in 1985.

RAYMOND L. ROWE, born 16 Jan 1930 in Magnet, IN. He enlisted in the Army on 20 Aug 1948 with assignments at Fort Knox, KY; Fort Lawton, WA and 388th Army Band. The band played for troop ships (arriving and departing) and service club dances. He participated in the Korean Conflict and was discharged in September 1951.

Returning to civilian life he was employed with Sears. He married Lorraine Lonske 13 Jun 1953 and they had three children: Gregory, Dana and Douglas. Grandchildren are Matthew, Daniel, Anna, Rachael, Michael, Katie, Nichole, Jennifer, Denise and Kevin. He retired 30 Jan 1992, enjoys traveling and gardening, and lives in Cadiz, KY.

DAVID WILLIAM SHORE, Corporal, born 9 Jul 1935 in Connelton, IN. He enlisted in USMC in November 1954 in Indianapolis, IN. Assignments were at San Diego, CA; Camp Pendleton, CA; Jacksonville, FL; Memphis, TN; and Opaloka, FL. Cpl. Shore was discharged in September 1957.

As a civilian he was hospital administrator, Trigg County; executive director, Pennyrile ADD, Deputy Commissioner Parks. He retired from Pennyrile Area Development District in August 1999.

Married Barbara J. Wyatt in August 1961 and they live at 122 Nunn Blvd., Cadiz, KY. They have two children, Carmen Rene Finley and Mary Jo Bryant, and two grandchildren, Taylor and Victoria Bryant. David enjoys golfing, fishing and traveling. He works part-time.

BERYL BOYD SIMMONS, Private, born 12 Mar 1928 in Trigg County. He joined the Army 8 Nov 1951 in Trigg County and was stationed at Fort Campbell, KY.

Pvt. Simmons received a medical discharge in 1952. He retired from Thomas Industries and passed away 5 Mar 1991. He was married to Janette Reason and had two children, Boyd and Ann, and four grandchildren: Megan, Bobby, Angela and Phillip.

BOBBY D. SIMMONS, SP3, born 11 Nov 1933 in Roaring Springs, Trigg County, KY, the son of Issac and Nevada Dawson Simmons. He attended Trigg County HS, worked on the farm and did odd work until 1954 when he went to work at Fuqua Funeral Home. Seven months later he entered the service.

He was sent to Fort Riley, KS for basic and advanced training for six months. On 17 Jun 1955, while on leave, he married Martha J. Clark, then was shipped to Germany for 18 months. He served with I&R Plt., attached to HHC 86th Inf. Regt. 10th Div. as jeep driver and assistant radio operator.

He left the service in 1959 went to work for Motorola Radio and TV for six years. While residing in Illinois he purchased a farm in Kentucky 1962 and moved there in 1963 and still lives there. He worked for Thomas Industries, 1963-78 and retired from US Tobacco in 1993. His wife Martha passed away 13 Nov 1986.

He married Dorothy Grace in Lake Havasu City, AZ on 29 May 1991 and they live at 8255 Pilot Rock Rd., Hopkinsville, KY. He enjoys deer, squirrel and rabbit hunting. They are members of Kelly Baptist Church and are coordinators for their Fifties Group called the Golden Oldies. He has one daughter Sandra Knight; two stepsons, Gary and Ron Grace; one grandchild; seven step-grandchildren; and three step-great-grandchildren.

EUGENE SIMMONS, PO1/c, born 8 May 1930 in Trigg County, He joined the USN in September 1951 with assignments at San Diego, Alaska and Korea. He worked on DEW Line as electrician. He was discharged

in September 1955 and received a Commendation Award for Aero Space Apollo II program.

He was an electrical engineer at the Zinc Plant in Clarksville, TN until retiring in 1986. Married Marcy 19 Oct 1959 and they live at 302 Mill Brook Drive, Hopkinsville, KY. They have three children: Steve, Denise and Michelle, and five grandchildren: Josh, Benjamin, Maggie, Christian and William. He enjoys golfing.

JOHNNY SIMMONS, born 26 Nov 1935 in Trigg County, KY. He joined the service 27 Dec 1954 and served with the Armored Division in Germany during peace time as a truck driver and dozer driver. He was discharged in December 1956.

After discharge he built roads and was a truck driver for oil wells in Elkhart, KS. Johnny and his wife Jerry had two children, Rodney and Wesley Dale, who died at age 20. Grandchildren are Jocelynn and Karalyne. Johnny was killed in truck accident in Colorado 8 May 1982.

ROBERT DAMON SMITH, born 12 Sep 1932 in Todd County, KY and sworn into the USN at the Naval Air Station, St. Louis, MO and reported for duty at NAS Pensacola, FL on 15 Oct 1954. Basic military training was conducted by the U.S. Marines. Naval orientation, pre-flight and basic aviation ground school was conducted by the USN and Marines.

At NAS Whiting, FL a new way of life and skills was begun. There Smith soloed and qualified in aerobatics, then off to NAS Saufley, FL and precise formation flying. NAS Barin, Foley, AL was the school for bombing and aerial gunnery. Then, "the best of all" was qualifying in aircraft carrier landing on the USS *Saigon*.

After that he was stationed at NAS Corpus Christi, Corpus Christi, TX studying cross-country and instrument flying.

The last assignment was with the USN CIC School at NAS Glynco, Brunswick, GA where his primary duties were keeping flight records up to date for pilots and aircraft. Glynco is now the site for law enforcement training for a number of Federal agencies.

Smith decided to transfer to inactive reserve status and return to college to prepare for a career in wildlife conservation. He returned to Western Kentucky University and completed a BS degree in agriculture and biology and entered Louisiana State University and earned a MS degree in wildlife management.

He was employed by the Tennessee Wildlife Resources Agency as a district biologist and was soon promoted to assistant chief of the Wildlife Division in Nashville. In 1965 he was hired by TVA to help guide and develop a program integrating wildlife management, forestry, recreation and environment education at Land Between the Lakes. High lights at LBL include working to successfully restore nesting Bald eagles and osprey to the region. He believes he was the first biologist ever assigned

to a national recreation area. He retired from LBL in 1988 and was selected by the University of Tennessee as a wildlife biologist/forester for the Agricultural Extension Service.

In 1996 he retired again to become a consultant in business development and natural resources management. He is a trustee and chairman of the Coalition for Recognition of Descendants of Indigenous Woodlands Peoples, Inc. He is active in the Cadiz United Methodist Church, the Lions Club, the Rocky Mountain Elk Foundation and the National Wild Turkey Federation and he is a 32nd Degree Mason. As a member of The Wildlife Society he is a Certified Wildlife Biologist and is a member of the Society of American Foresters.

In 1959 he married Mahala Jane Cline whom he met in high school at Franklin-Simpson. They reside in Trigg County and have two children MeLisa Smith Morris, Ocoee, FL and Major Eric Damon Smith, Dayton, OH, and four grandchildren: Anthony Morris Jr., Meleah Morris, Cole Damon Smith and Sabrina Smith.

Smith says, "I have enjoyed a successful career in conservation. But, sometimes I regret that I did not stay in the military longer and contribute more to my country's integrity."

EUGENE SOWELL, SP3, born 26 Oct 1931, son of Alpha and Elsie Johnson Sowell. He took basic training at Fort Knox, KY and advance training at Fort Jackson, SC.

He was sent to Wildflicken, Germany near the Russian border for 18 months. Eugene was in the service from 1954-56 and served in the 373rd Armd. Inf. Bn. 7th Army. He was discharged from Fort Dix, NJ as a specialist 3.

Eugene has owned a grocery store, feed mill, hauled lime and is now farming near Cerulean. He married Wanda Robertson 29 Dec 1961 and they have two sons.

CLARENCE LOFTON STALLONS, born 18 Feb 1933 in Trigg County, KY. He volunteered for the USN and was sworn in at Louisville, KY on 14 Jan 1952. He received basic training at the Naval Training Center in San Diego, CA.

His first duty station was aboard the USS *Curtis*, a converter sea plane tender, on loan to the Atomic Energy Commission. In the fall of 1952 they participated in one of the first A bomb experiments at the Eniwetok Proving Grounds, Marshall Islands.

He also served aboard the USS *Rendova* (CV-114), a small carrier. He also sold aboard the USS *Valley Forge* (CVE-45), a much larger carrier. He finished his tour of duty at Green Cove Springs, FL where they did maintenance on moth balled ships.

After being honorably discharged 13 Jan 1956, he spent some time working in the St. Louis area, later moving to Florida before settling down in Cadiz, KY. His Navy training as a metalsmith helped prepare him for his lifelong occupation as a welder. He retired from Averitt Lumber in 1998.

While stationed at Green Cove he met Leila J. Hampton who became his wife in December 1954. Leila died in July 1998. They had two children, Debra L. Stallons who resides in Cadiz and Terry W. Stallons who is married to the former Sandra Merrick. They also live in Cadiz with their two children, Terra J. and Matthew L.

MARSHALL W. STALLONS, born 30 Jan 1931 in Trigg County, KY. He joined the USN in May 1948 and received his basic training at the NTC in San Diego, CA. He was a Navy Air Corps machinist mate, assigned to a helicopter squadron.

He was stationed at Camp Miramar, CA most of the time but had temporary duty in Nevada where he participated in some atomic testing. He was aboard an ice breaker for a short time, breaking ice in the Bering Strait. During the Korean War, their squadron flew rescue missions off several ships that were in the area.

After being honorably discharged in May 1952, he went to work for the telephone company in Hopkinsville, KY, until his death in 1972. He was married to the former Ann Light and they had two children, Marsha and Rayetta, and one grandchild.

ROBERT A. STEPHENS SR., Master Sergeant, born May 10, 1929 in Cadiz, KY, the eldest of three children born to Stanley L. and Dellis Thomas Stephens. He volunteered with the Army on 15 Jul 1948, and completed basic training at Fort Knox, KY. He completed technical school at Aberdeen Proving Ground, MD. Assigned to the 27th Ord. Co., 1st Cav. Div. at Camp Drake, Tokyo, Japan. In July 1950 his unit was sent to South Korea where they provided support (trucks, jeeps, guns, ammo, etc.) for the combat troops.

Returned to States in June 1951 where he was assigned to an artillery battalion in New York as a battalion supply sergeant until spring of 1956, then to G4 Section, COMZ located in Orleans, France. He was sent to Lebanon from France in the summer of 1958 to form the 201st Logistical Command in support of the American Land Forces during their civil war, then he returned to France.

Returned to States in November 1959 where he was assigned to Walter Reed Army Medical Center, Washington, DC until February 1964. Then to the G4, US Army Antilles Command located at Fort Brooke, San Juan, Puerto Rico until January 1967 at which time he was reassigned to the Atlanta, GA area until January 1968.

Returned to Seoul, Korea with assignment to the G4 8th US Army in February 1968. In March 1969 he returned to Fort Campbell, KY assigned to G4 until February 1970, then sent to Vietnam assigned to the G4 Section of DMAC. In 1971 he returned to Fort Campbell where he retired 30 Jun 1971 after 23 years of service.

Special Medals received were Bronze Star, Occupation Medal of Japan, Korean Service Medal w/3 Bronze Stars, National Defense Service Medal w/OLC, Good Conduct Medal w/6 loops, Army Commendation Medal w/OLC, Armed Forces Expeditionary Medal w/Bronze Star, Vietnam Cross of Gallantry w/Bronze Star, Vietnam Service Medal w/2 Campaign Stars, Vietnam Combat Medal and the Korean War Service Medal received on the 50th Anniversary of the Korean War from the President of South Korea.

On 22 Sep 1951 he married Martha Jane Hendricks. They had four children: Tony, Robert Jr., Deborah and David Lee (died in infancy). There are 10 grandchildren: Lesley, Jennifer, Brent, Johnathon, David, Daniel, Stephanie, Benjamin, Jordan and Michael. Martha died of cancer 27 Apr 1986.

On 28 Dec 1989 he married Reba L. Goodrich; he also received a special daughter-in-law Pat and another granddaughter Valerie. Reba's son Vernon Randall died in 1976 of cancer.

Upon retirement from the Army he moved to San Antonio, TX until March 1974 when he returned to Cadiz, KY. He now resides at 250 Third Street. He is a member of Trigg County Baptist Church and the VFW Post 7890 Cadiz-Trigg County.

JOHN COWHERD STREET, a casualty of the Korean War, was born 2 Jun 1928 at Cadiz, KY, son of Edward R. Sr. and Mabel Woodruff Street.

He graduated from Columbia Military Academy and attended Western Kentucky College. He was drafted and entered the Army 7 Dec 1950. He served three months in Japan and at the time of death had served three months in Korea. He died 27 Nov 1951 from injuries sustained in a vehicle accident due to icy roads in Korea. His body was returned to the States and buried in East End Cemetery at Cadiz. He was a member of Cadiz Christian Church.

John Cowherd had one brother, E.R. Street Jr. and three sisters: Mary Louise Street McClure, Catherine Street Magraw, and Frances Street Walters.

BILLY EARL SUMNER, Corporal, born 4 Jun 1932. He was drafted in the Army 15 Jan 1953 at Owensboro, KY. Assignments were at Fort Meade, MD and Camp Gordon, GA.

After his discharge 14 Jan 1955, he worked in construction, plumbing, farming and welding.

Married June Dunn Sumner in 1958 and has one son Butch and three grandchildren: William, James and David. Still farming, he lives at 2174 South Road in Cadiz, KY.

EUGENE LEWIS SUMNER, born 10 Nov 1927 in the Oak Grove Community, son of D. Floyd and Lillie Jane Thomas Sumner. He was a life long member of Oak Grove Church and graduated from Trigg County HS in 1946.

He was drafted into the Army 2 Nov 1950 at Owensboro, KY and was among the first group of draftees from Trigg County to be inducted into the Korean War. He was sent to the newly re-opened Camp

Breckinridge, KY where he was assigned to Co. B, 53rd Abn. Inf., 101st Abn. Div. This paratrooper unit was stationed at Breckinridge at this time. Due to airborne equipment failure, he was discharged 5 Mar 1951.

He farmed for awhile then went into the electrical and plumbing business. The last few years he owned and operated Twin Lakes Electrical Co., Lake City, KY. He passed away 8 Jan 1985 and is buried at the Starkey Thomas Cemetery on the family farm.

Eugene married Frieda N. Bridges 25 May 1951 at Corinth, MS. They had three children: Elizabeth Jane (b. 11 Aug 1953), Ernest Lewis (b. 20 Jan 1956) and Eugene Christopher (b. 29 Mar 1959). At the time of his death there were four grandchildren: Anita, Thomas, Benjamin Harper and Jodi Noel Sumner.

RAYMOND P. SUMNER, Major, born in Trigg County on 20 Sep 1931. After graduating from Murray State University, he was inducted into the Army 27 Jul 1954. On 1 Oct 1954 he completed eight weeks of infantry basic training with Co. D, 36th AIB, 3rd Armd. Div., Fort Knox, KY. He attended the Adjutant General Service School, Co. C 23rd AEB Div. TN, Fort Knox, KY, 2 Oct 1954 to 13 Dec 1954. In December 1954 he was a personnel administrative specialist for the 132nd Ord. Co., Fort Meade, MD. He later served with the 555th Ord., the 330th Ord. and the 1st Ord. Bn., Fort Meade, MD. On 26 Jun 1956 he received an Honorable Discharge from active duty.

On 22 Oct 1956, he was commissioned a second lieutenant in the field artillery and guided missiles. He was assigned to the 198th FA BN, Kentucky National Guard. While serving with the 198th FA he completed the Battery Grade Officers Course. He also graduated from the U.S. Army Artillery and Missile School, Fort Sill, OK. Raymond was promoted to the rank of captain 16 May 1962. He successfully completed his educational requirements for promotion to major 29 Dec 1964. He received an Honorable Discharge as a Reserve Commissioned Officer 2 Jan 1968.

Raymond retired in 1991 after completing 35 years of service in the telephone industry. During his career he worked for four Bell Operating Companies (Southern Bell, South Central Bell, Bell South Services and Bell South Telecommunications) plus the American Telephone and Telegraph Company.

Raymond and Elgenia Bice were married 6 Oct 1957. They have three children: Sandra (b. 3 Jul 1958), Ronald (b. 31 Jul 1959) and Larry (b. 2 Mar 1964). Raymond and Elgenia live at 3019 Taralane Drive, Birmingham, AL.

WILLIAM A. SUMNER, Sergeant (E-5), born 16 May 1937 in the Oak Grove Community of Trigg County, the son of Odell and Ruby Cameron Sumner. He attended grade school at Cadiz and Blue Springs and graduated from Trigg County HS in 1956. He was a member of the high school band, safety club, and FFA. After graduation he farmed for four years.

He was drafted into the Army 1 Jul 1960 and received basic training at Fort Jackson, SC. After basic training he was sent to Fort Lewis, WA, where he was assigned to Co. B, 22nd Battle Group, 4th Inf. Div., as an automatic rifleman.

He was promoted to PFC in December 1960. In 1961 he was promoted to SP4 and became a platoon radio operator. In December 1961 he was promoted to SGT E5 and became a squad leader and a member of a firing squad for military funerals.

During the Berlin Crisis in January 1961, the Fourth Division was sent to West Germany to guard the wall. They returned to Fort Lewis, WA 28 days later. He was honorably discharged on 29 Jun 1962 with a Good Conduct Medal.

He went to work at Johnson Controls in Cadiz, KY in 1966 and worked there for 33 years, retiring in 1999. He married Maxine Colson Holland in 1973. He has two stepchildren, Donnie Holland and Jennifer Holland Baker, and three step grandchildren: Darla Holland Thomas, John Holland and Amanda Baker.

Maxine and William live on Main Street in Cadiz. They are members of Liberty Point Baptist Church, and he is a member of the American Legion Post 74.

EDWARD EARL TAYLOR, Private, born 19 Jul 1931 in Trigg County, KY. He was drafted into the Army in May 1953. He served his country during the Korean War arriving in Germany in February 1954. He received a Good Conduct Medal in Germany while serving with the 765th Field Artillery Battalion. A driver in the battalion's Battery C, he received the decoration for his exemplary behavior, efficiency and fidelity. His basic training was spent at Camp Polk, LA. He was discharged as a private in May 1955 at that time.

Earl married Margaret Harned on 1 Nov 1952 and they had three children: Margaret Ann, Donna Marie and Ronald Edward. They have six grandchildren: Chris and Jason Laster, Dana Patterson, Crystal Grant, Heather and Brent Taylor. They have three great-grandchildren. Earl made his living as a carpenter and a farmer. He moved with his family in the late 1940s to Christian County were he lived most of his adult life. Earl died at the VA Hospital in Nashville, TN at the age of 56 on 1 Dec 1987. *Submitted by Donna Grant.*

JAMES BOYD TAYLOR, Staff Sergeant, born 16 Apr 1932 in Cadiz, KY. On 3 Mar 1950 James and his cousin Doris Moore enlisted in the Army. After 16 weeks of basic training at Fort Knox, KY, he volunteered for Japan, but first was assigned to MP School in Texas.

At Camp Stoneman, CA while in line for his shots, he heard someone call "Sonny Taylor" and knew it had to be someone from home. It was Bobby Vowell. He had been overseas before and told James to eat cookies and drink whiskey and he wouldn't get seasick—it worked.

On 11 Jul 1950 he landed on Yokohoma, Japan, shipped to Camp Mowler and placed in the 7th Div., 17th RTC. Four weeks later he was shipped to Mt. Fugi where they trained South Koreans until September. Went to Korea and was in the invasion of Inchon and the battle of Seoul. His division was the only one to make it to the Yalu River.

Returned to the States in July 1951. He married Jacqueline Carr of Cadiz, KY in February 1952. James finished his tour of duty at Camp San Luis Obispo, CA and was discharged 3 Mar 1953 with the rank staff sergeant and five Battle Stars.

He lived in Chicago, IL for 20 years owning and operating a floor installation and finishing business. In 1970 he returned to Cadiz, KY and was the Sears Catalog merchant for 20 years. He lives at N. Tanyard Road. There are two children, Deborah Audas and James B. Jr., and four grandchildren.

JAMES HOWARD TAYLOR, PFC, born 3 Oct 1929 in Trigg County, Cadiz, KY. He entered the service 8 Jun 1951, trained at Camp Breckinridge, KY and participated in the Korean War, where he was wounded. Pfc. Taylor was discharged 8 Feb 1953.

James married Blondell Gibbs on 19 Dec 1953 and they had two children, Danny James and Debra Sue; three grandchildren: Melody Lynn, Samantha Jean and Danielle Nicole; and one great-grandchild, Keleb Tyler.

James worked at Johnson Control from 1965-72. He was in a car accident and paralyzed for 10 years before he passed away 23 Dec 1982 and is buried in Joiners Chapel Church Cemetery. *Submitted by Blondell Taylor.*

BOBBY GENE THOMAS, Staff Sergeant, born 31 Jul 1931. He was sworn into the USAF 27 Mar 1951 in Owensboro, KY. He was sent by train to Lackland AFB in San Antonio, TX for basic training.

After completion of basic he was sent to Oakland, CA to Aircraft and Engine School for six months, then to Mather Field AFB, CA and from there to Chanute AFB, IL for Specialized Aircraft Instrument School.

Sent to Kindley AFB in Bermuda where he spent two years working as aircraft instrument mechanic. He left Kindley in January 1954 for Sewart AB, TN, where he served the remainder of his military term.

He served during the Korean War (police action), although he saw no action.

He was discharged from the HQ 316th, TR Group, 50th Troop Carrier Sqdn. TAC at Sewart AFB on 26 Mar 1955. His awards include the National Defense Service Medal and Good Conduct Medal.

Overall he enjoyed most of his service time and thinks every young person would benefit from a tour of active duty in the Armed Forces of the U.S.

Bobby worked for Dept. of Defense at Fort Campbell, KY for 36 years from where he retired in 1986. He married Eunice E. Boyd 29 Dec 1962 and they live at 52 Wharton Road, Cadiz, KY. They have two children, Pamela Aileen and Darla Jean, and two grandchildren, Brittney Michelle and Preston Ralph Metts.

CECIL WAYNE THOMAS, Sergeant, born 20 Aug 1926 at Fredonia, KY. He moved to Canton with his parents William R. and Emma Thomas at the age of 4 and resided in Trigg County, KY until 1959 when he moved to Chattanooga, TN where he still resides.

He graduated from Trigg County HS and the University of Kentucky with a BS degree in civil engineering. He has been a life member of the UK Alumni since 1974.

Cecil joined the service 30 Apr 1953 with basic training at Breckinridge, KY. He attended Leadership School at Fort Jackson, SC, followed by NCO School at Fort Benning, GA. Upon completion he was assigned to a combat engineer battalion attached to the 13th Inf. Div. at Fort Carson, CO. Sgt. Thomas was discharged 29 Apr 1955.

On 23 Apr 1948 he married Reva Mae Riggin of Cadiz, KY. They have two children, Anita Joyce and Roger Wayne, and four grandchildren: Caitlin and Scott Heston and Megan and Lauren Thomas.

Cecil was employed by TVA from 1959-88 and was head civil engineer at time of retirement. He is a volunteer tour guide and enjoys golf, travel, UK football and basketball games.

HOWARD DOUGLAS THOMAS, PVT-2, born 2 Mar 1933 in Trigg County, KY. He was drafted into the Army and sworn in on 30 Apr 1953 at Owensboro, KY during the Korean War. He was sent to Fort Meade, MD, and after a short stay went to Camp Breckinridge, KY for basic training.

After six months of training he was transferred to Fort Ord, CA. He was with the second Army, 44th Div. with rank of Private-1. A cease fire was issued for the Korean War in 1953 not long after his induction.

His most significant assignment was at Fort Lewis WA. He served in Co. F, 123rd Inf. Regt. as a light artillery infantryman. On 24 Sep 1954 he was promoted to the rank of PVT-2 (P).

While stationed at Fort Lewis he had the unique experience of playing the role of an extra in a movie. He had the honor of meeting personally the much-decorated war hero Audie Murphy. The military news sent an article about his role in the movie to *The Cadiz Record.* Audie Murphy played the role of himself in the movie entitled *To Hell and Back.* This made Murphy a well-known film-star as well.

He was discharged from Fort Lewis on 3 May 1955. He was retained three days for the convenience of the government then released from active service to the Army Reserve Kentucky Military District under the Universal Military Training and Service Act. He was awarded the National Defense Service Medal.

In civilian life he was employed by U.S. Steel in Lorain, OH. He later worked for Kelly & Wilmore telephone contractor; for the city of Russellville, KY Water Dept.; and for Kentucky State Parks Maintence Dept in LBL.

On 14 Jan 1967, he married Norma Sue Bell. Four children were born to them but only two daughters lived to adulthood: Brenda Hays of Lyon County and Judy Moore of Trigg County. He has two grandsons, Cameron Kniaz and Noah Moore.

His hobbies are fishing, working on small engines and playing the harmonica. He is of the Baptist faith

In 1995 he retired from Lake Front Developers and at present makes his home in Lyon
Submitted by Mrs. Joe L. Darnall.

FRED THOMAS, SH1, born 19 May 1927 at Donaldson Creek, Trigg County County, son of Myrt and Taylor Thomas. He joined the Navy as soon as he turned 17 at Louisville, KY, and was sent to Great Lakes Training Station.

At Norfolk, VA he boarded the USS *Card* and from there went into the Atlantic with his air group and destroyer escorts on German submarine patrol. Also served on the USS *Boxer* (CV-21), Korean offshore air support and in Vietnam.

Other assignments include USS *Brisco* (APA-65), a target ship in the 1946 Bikini Atom Bomb tests; USS *Capps* (DD-550); USS *Orion* (AS-18); USS *President Jackson* (APA-18); Naval Air Station, Memphis, TN; USS *Searcher*; USS *Belle Grove*; LSD-2; Commisary Store, Charleston, SC; and USN Air Station, Pensacola, FL.

The most impressive part of his career came on the USS *Saratoga*. He helped put it into commission in April 1956 and served on her four years and four months. There were only nine original crew members left when he was transferred. In 1996 he had an invitation to participate in her de-commissioning in Mayport, FL when Adm. Boarda made the final decommissioning speech and the crew marched off it was like losing a family member.

Discharged 29 Mar 1965 as SH1. Awards include the Navy Occupation, Good Conduct (6), Presidential Citation, American Campaign, European-African, China Service, UN Medal and National Defense.

After service he worked in auto sales and management. Retired in 1994 and now employed part-time transferring vehicles for several dealers. His first wife Lillie (Edwards) is deceased. He married Eva Somerset in 1994. He has one daughter Sharon Thomas Atkins, four stepchildren, two grandchildren: Ryan Dillard and Katie Atkins; and nine step-grandchildren. He lives in Milton, FL.

All in all the Navy was very good to him and he has a lot of good memories. For all the old-timers "Kilroy Was Here."

GERALD DEAN THOMAS, born 30 Aug 1932, son of Odell and Leona Francis Thomas. He joined the USAF in 1952 and was sent from Owensboro to Lackland AFB in TX during Korean War.

He obtained a welding degree in 1953 at Chanute AFB, IL and served as welder during most of his duty. In 1954 he was sent to Seoul, Korea for six months then back to Tokyo, Japan for a year.

Returned to Carswell AFB, TX where he remained until his discharge in 1956. After the service he worked as a welder in St. Louis, MO and in Illinois. He has two children, Gerry Thomas and Mureka Wallace, and five grandchildren: Noah and Ethan Thomas; Cody, Autum and Seth Wallace.

HARRY CLIFFORD THOMAS, TSgt (E-7), born 6 Sep 1929 in Akron, OH. He enlisted into the Air Force on 5 Jan 1951 out of Nashville TN. After basic training at Lackland AFB, TX, he was sent to Erding AFB, Germany where he served with the 85th Veh. Rep. Sq. Erding. While at Erding he enjoyed playing football for the Erding Arrowheads in England and France.

He met his wife Ingeborg B. Gruenaug while attending the NCO Academy in Munich, Germany. They were married on 15 Mar 1954 in Erding, Germany.

Three years later he was stationed at Travis AFB, CA working with the 5th Motor Veh. Sq. In 1955 he left the military for three month returning to Cadiz, KY.

He re-enlisted and was sent to Seward AFB, TN for a brief period before leaving for Torrejon AFB, Madrid, Spain where he was attached to the 3970th Transp. Sq. Thomas was assigned to Torrejon as part of the initial group of airman to establish the base.

In 1959 he was assigned to Dow AFB, Bangor, ME with the 4060 Transp. Sq. In 1962 he was sent to Rhein Main AFB, Frank-

fort, Germany and for the next three years worked with the 370 MAT Sq. While at Rhein Main, Thomas was struck with a terminal illness.

After major surgery at Wiesbaden Medical Center, he was airvaced to Scott AFB Medical Center. After several surgeries at Walter Reed Hospital and Wilford Hall Med Center and with no hope for recovery he was discharged on 26 Nov 1970 and placed on TDRL.

Thomas was retired on 8 Apr 1974 as tech sergeant (E-7). He was awarded the Air Force Good Conduct Medal, National Defense Service Medal, Air Force Longevity Service Medal and USAF Small Arms Marksmanship Award.

Thomas and his family settled down in Trigg County. His children: Doris Susan, Robert Joseph "Sonny," and Wayne Lee graduated from Trigg County HS; his own alma mater. He remained active doing some hunting and fishing, helping to organize the Booster Club and coaching Little League Football. As of 1976, the Spirit of Trigg County, Harry C. Thomas Award is given to a deserving senior athlete during Award Ceremonies at Trigg County HS.

Thomas had five grandchildren: Nicole Leigh Thomas, Kirk Preston Thomas, Eric Brandon Jane, Rachael Lee Thomas and Cliff Nicolas Thomas. Thomas died on 18 Apr 1977 and was buried at Thomas Bridges Cemetery with military honors.

HORACE "SONNY" THOMAS, PFC, born 16 Jun 1931 in Trigg County, son of Oscar and Willie Adams Thomas. He joined the service 29 Jan 1952 with assignments at Owensboro, KY; Fort Meade, MD; Fort Dix, NJ; Tokyo, Japan; Seoul, Korea; Fort Knox, KY.

Pfc. Thomas received an honorable discharge 11 Dec 1953. He was a heavy equipment and truck driver. His awards include the Good Conduct, Korean Service Medal and Gunner Recoil Rifle Medal.

Married Mary Dell Taylor 28 Mar 1952 and they reside in Hopkinsville, KY. They have four children: Judy, Janice, Randy and Ronnie (deceased), and five grandchildren: Allyson, Brant, Jenna, Jordon and Christian. Sonny is retired from Thomas Industries.

OLEN RAY THOMAS, Hospital Corpsman 2/c, born 1 Sep 1933 in Trigg County. Being of draft age in 1953 he chose to enlist in the USN for four years to fulfill his military obligation. He enlisted at Bowling Green, KY and was shipped out to Bainbridge, MD for basic training and remained there to train to become a hospital corpsman.

He was assigned to naval hospital at Millington, TN, delivering babies of military dependants. Eventually he trained to be an operating room tech.

Other assignments include Marine Base in Parris Island, SC; Camp Pendleton, CA, in 1955 as a corpsman with the 3rd Marine Div.; Okinawa; operating room tech at Naval Hospital in Yokuska, Japan. From Japan he was able to travel many areas of the Far East including Hong Kong, Thailand, the Philippines and India.

Returned to San Diego Naval Base in 1957 and was discharged as hospital corpsman 2/c. In September 1957, he entered Western Kentucky University under the GI Bill, majoring in pre-pharmacy. Here he met his future wife, Martha Holland, who became a teacher.

After graduating Thomas located in Bowling Green for two years before moving to Mayfield, KY where he practiced pharmacy for 34 years before retiring in 1997.

The Thomases are the parents of two daughters, Dr. Dru Quarles and Holly, a physician's assistant, and one granddaughter Anabelle Quarles. Today their time is spent between Charlotte, NC, where their daughters reside, Mayfield and Donaldson Creek, KY.

BRENT D. THOMPSON, Colonel, born 4 Oct 1930 in Green County, KY. He attended public schools in Metcalfe and LaRue counties and graduated from Hodgenville HS in 1946. He then began a continuous 53 year career with military service—4 years as an AFROTC cadet; 40 years, four months, one day active duty and reserve service; nine years post retirement voluntary service as Admissions Counselor, USAF Academy.

Attending the University of Kentucky, Brent earned a BS degree in agriculture and was commissioned a second lieutenant in the USAF in 1950. Following a brief tenure as vocational agriculture teacher in Kentucky public schools, he served on Air Force active duty during the Korean War period at Scott AFB, IL and at the Air University, Maxwell AFB, AL.

Returning to civilian life, Brent continued Reserve service in training units, Recovery Squadrons and with the Air Force Academy, being promoted through officer ranks to the rank of colonel in 1974 before retirement in 1980. A highlight of his military career was that of being selected as the nations outstanding Air Force Reservist assigned to the Air Force Academy in 1974.

Following active duty, Brent earned a MS degree in education at the University of Kentucky. In 1957 he was employed by Trigg County Farmers Bank where he remained for 31 years, serving as chairman of the board, President and CEO before retirement in 1989. He then served as senior vice president for Citizens Fidelity Bank (now PNC Bank) in Hardin County for 10 years.

Brent is married to the former Dorothy Spencer and they are parents of two children—Risë, who died in an automobile accident in 1977, and Mark, Professor of Music, Northwestern State University in Louisiana, whose biography is included in this book. They have three grandchildren.

In 1999 Brent and Dot returned to Trigg County to make their retirement home at 50 Dana Drive, Cadiz, KY.

DAN DAVIS THOMPSON, Corporal, born 2 Aug 1933. He enlisted in the service 30 Apr 1951 at Owensboro, KY. He served with B Btry., 11th AAAW BN in Salzburg, Austria.

His memorable experience was skiing in the Alps and meeting all the wonderful people over there. Cpl. Thompson was discharged 14 Apr 1954. Awards include the AOM (Germany) and National Defense Service Medal.

Married Jean A. Mayes 23 Dec 1954 and they live 156 Haydon Street, Cadiz, KY. They have five children and eight grandchildren: Dion, Ladell, Richard, Elysia, Tarvia, Angela, Brian and Elisha. Dan retired from LBL TVA 30 Dec 1999.

RAYMOND L. TURNER, born 30 Jun 1931, Golden Pond, KY. He graduated from Trigg County HS in 1950 and went into the service in

1952. Assignments at Fort Knox, KY, tank commander training; Fort Hood, TX, 109th Tank Co. and Fort Sill, OK. He was discharged 1 Feb 1956.

He worked 35 years at B.F. Goodrich Chemical Co. and retired in 1994. He has lived in Murray, KY since 1963. Married Mary Gene Wallace 28 Nov 1952 and they have three children: Terry, Jane Ann and Scott, and four grandchildren: Kere, Jesse, Teffany and Taylor.

CAREY THOMAS VINSON JR., Corporal, born 5 Sep 1926, the son of Carey T. and Mallie Guier Vinson. He was a graduate of Trigg County HS and the University of Kentucky with an MA from Murray State University.

He was inducted into the armed forces 10 Apr 1951 during the Korean Conflict. He was processed at Fort Meade, MD then assigned to Co. L, 28nd Inf. Regt., 8th Inf. Div., Fort Jackson, SC for 16 weeks of basic training. After basic he attended an eight week special training school before being assigned to HHC, 28th Inf. Regt., Fort Jackson, SC. His duty assignment was classification and assignment clerk in the personnel office.

After two years of active duty he was given an honorable discharge, 9 Apr 1953 and assigned to the Reserves. At the time of his discharge he was chief of the C & A section with the rank of corporal.

Tom married Nell Petty, daughter of George and Nannie Bell Petty, on 23 Nov 1950. They lived in Columbia, SC while he was in service. Tom farmed with his father and brother Jess until 1955 when the Trigg County Board of Education employed him as their high school science teacher in September 1955. He retired as superintendent in 1984.

Tom and Nell are the parents of four sons: Carey T., Nathan W., Forest W. and James Stanley.

PRENTICE EDWARD VINSON, PVT, born 24 Feb 1936, son of John F. and Ocie Lee Vinson. He was a private in the Army and served in the Korean Conflict. He was honorably discharged 31 Oct 1962.

Mr. Vinson died 24 Oct 1973. His survivors include his wife, Mrs. Eloise Vinson; daughters: Octavia, Lamona, Shelly; stepdaughters: Marguerite Higgins and Carlotta Lander; and six grandchildren: Lavetta Street; Brian Higgins; Markita, Breanna and Audreanna Vinson; and Kendrick Radford.

LEONARD L. WADLINGTON, born 19 Oct 1930 in Cadiz, KY, son of Felix C. and Ruby Mitchell Wadlington. He joined the Navy in 1948 and took his basic training at Great Lakes, IL. He was then sent aboard the USS *Arcadia*, a mine layer tender.

In 1950 he went to Salvage School in Bayonne, NJ, then went aboard the USS *Dally* at sea. He was discharged in 1952 and returned to Cadiz.

He hired on as a deck hand on a barge boat, learned the rivers and became a pilot than a captain while employed with Mid-South Towing. He was port captain for Mid-South for several years at Paducah, KY and was responsible for the hiring and firing of personnel. His knowledge of the families of Trigg County secured good working personnel for the barge line and good paying jobs for many Trigg Countians.

Prior to his retirement, a new boat was christened the "Mary Lou," named for his wife the former Mary Lou Hunter. He resides in Draffenville, KY.

CALVERT CAMPBELL WALLACE, Sergeant, born 3 Sep 1928 in Golden Pond, KY. He joined the USMC in May 1946 at Paducah, KY and was sent to Parris Island, SC where he was put in Marine Air Command.

He was discharged in 1949, but recalled in 1950 for the Korean Crisis.

Calvert and Helen married in April 1950. They have one son Harry C. and two grandchildren, Cal and Preston. He retired from Wallace-Rush Trucking Enterprise in 1993 and now lives on a ranch in Hondo, TX.

WILLIAM LEE WALLACE, Master Sergeant, born 29 Sep 1929, at RFD #3, Cadiz, KY (Pete Light Springs), son of Morgan Hopson and Pearl Mildred (Winders) Wallace of Canton, KY. He started school in Canton in 1935, finishing the 8th grade at Gilbertsville and graduated from Benton HS, Benton, KY in 1947.

He worked on riverboats for six years, starting as a deckhand and left with a first class pilots license for the Cumberland and Ohio Rivers.

In June 1954, he married Ann Elizabeth Nall of Paducah, KY. They have four children: Susan Lee (b. 1964, IL); William Morgan (b. 1965, IL); Douglas Alan (b. 1966, IL); Angela Kay (b. 1968, TX).

In January 1955 he joined the USAF and completed basic training at Sampson AFB, NY. He was assigned to the Radiology Training School at Gunter AFB, AL. After completing training, he stayed on and taught.

In July 1957, he was assigned to Nouasseur AB, Morocco, North Africa with the 15th Air Force (SAC). In December 1958, he was honorably discharged at Charleston AFB, SC.

In January 1959, he re-enlisted in the USAF and was assigned to Orlando AFB, FL. While there, he passed his certification as a radiology technician.

In August 1959, he was reassigned to USAF Hospital Scott at Scott AFB, IL, working in radiation therapy and nuclear medicine. In 1962, he was assigned to the US Naval Hospital at Bethesda, MD, to train with the USN as a nuclear medicine technician.

In 1963, he passed the certification as a nuclear medicine technician and worked in nuclear medicine and radiation therapy.

In 1964, he passed the radiation therapy certification examination and was written up in the *Air Force Times* as the only military technician in the Dept. of Defense Medical System certified in all three fields of medicine, Radiology, Nuclear Medicine and Radiation Therapy.

In 1968, he was assigned to Wilford Hall USAF Medical Center, Lackland AFB, TX. In 1973, he was assigned to USAF Hospital, Clark AB, Philippines and while there he participated in Operation Home Coming, when the North Vietnamese released the POWs from Hanoi.

In 1975, he retired as master sergeant from the USAF at Wright-Patterson AFB, OH, and started working for the Army at Fort Knox, KY, moving to Radcliff, KY. He retired from Fort Knox in 1995.

Hobbies are genealogy and hunting. He is a member of the SAR in Louisville, KY and a Kentucky Colonel.

CARL BERNARD WILLIAMS, PFC, born 23 Jul 1929 in Williams Hollow in southern Trigg County near Linton. He was the second son and fifth child of Maynard and Dorothy Mize Williams.

Carl was a rough and tumble boy as most boys in that era were. He enjoyed playing baseball and hunting. He attended Graham School and helped his dad farm.

He was inducted into the US Army 21 Feb 1952. He had to report to Owensboro, KY. His only request before leaving Trigg County was to not get his basic training in Arkansas. He was immediately sent to Camp Chaffee, AR, serving in Co. B 10th Med Tank Bn. and remained there until being shipped to Neu Ulm, Germany. He served there for one year with Btry. 330th FABN.

After Pfc. Williams was discharged, he returned to Trigg County and found employment as a truck driver.

He remained single but dearly loved all his nieces and nephews. He earned the reputation of being the "Watermelon Man of the South Road" as he raised some of the largest melons and tomatoes in Trigg County.

In later years he became employed with the Trigg County Fiscal Court where he remained until retirement in July 1995. He was known for his short visits, never staying at any place more than 10 minutes. He enjoyed rabbit, turkey and deer hunting and was a marksman shot.

He was diagnosed with lung cancer in August 1988. The family named him "The Cat with 9 lives" as he had survived many serious accidents and health problems, but the Lord called him home on 21 Sep 1999. He is buried at the Fuller Cemetery.

WILLIAM A. WILLIAMS, Lieutenant Colonel, born 23 Nov 1929, Laurel, DE. He enlisted in the USAF in 1949 at Cambridge, MD. Served as control tower operator in Japan and Korea and navigator in Japan, Korea and Vietnam. Lt. Col. Williams was discharged 1 Jan 1972.

As a civilian he was a mechanical engineer in Saudi Arabia and Germany where he retired in 1986.

He married Charlene Brittain on 22 Jul 1953 and they have two children, David and Karen, and seven grandchildren: Joshua, Lucas, Ashlee, Sarah, Austen, Michael and Hunter. William and Charlene live at 353 Robert Mitchell Road, Cadiz, KY. He does church work, hunts and fishes.

WILBERT LESLIE "BUNK" WILLIAMS, Corporal, born 10 Aug 1930 in Cadiz, KY. He joined the Army 11 Feb 1951 at Fort Worth, OH and served in Korea with Co. C, 19th Inf.

Cpl. Williams was discharged 12 Feb 1954. His awards include the Army of Occupation Medal (Germany), UN Service Medal, National Defense, Korean Service Medal w/2 BSS, Combat Infantry Badge and Purple Heart for wound received at Heartbreak Ridge 4 Dec 1952.

He married Ann Noel 30 Jun 1956 and they lived in Cadiz KY. Wilbert passed away 4 May 1998 and is buried in Fuller Cemetery, Cadiz, KY. Children are Danita Dawn Sumner and Michael Dean Williams; grandchildren are Jody Noel and Christopher Sumner and Jamie and Christopher Williams.

CHARLES WESLEY WILLS, Sergeant, a native of Trigg County, KY, was born 4 May 1930, the son of Henry H. and Alice Burks Wills. Charles, known by his friends as Cooney, enlisted in the Army at age 17. During his enlistment he was stationed in Berlin, Germany and when the Korean conflict started, he served his country on the battlefield. Charles served in the military from June 1948 until the spring of 1955. He achieved the rank of sergeant and was honorably discharged.

After the Korean conflict Charles returned to Trigg County where he married Nancy Shumate. They made their home in Hopkinsville and had four children: Richard, Cindy Wills Carter, Brenda Wills Cansler who reside in Hopkinsville and Penny Wills Frasier who resides in Crofton, KY. Grandchildren are Amanda Knight Garrett, Tacoma, WA; Ricky and Cory Wells, Crofton, KY; Jonathan Carter, Charlie and Margo Cansler, Hopkinsville, KY.

Charles worked for Thomas Industries as a truck driver and retired after 30 years of service. He passed away on 20 Mar 1992 and is buried in Valor Gardens at Green Hill Memorial in Hopkinsville, KY.

WILBURN MARTIN "WILLIE" WILSON, First Class Electronics Technician, USN, born Cerulean, KY 13 Mar 1930. He graduated Trigg County HS in 1947, studied electronics and was announcer/engineer WPKY, Princeton, KY, 1950-51.

Enlisted in the USN 13 Feb 1951 and went to boot camp at Great Lakes, IL; Electronics Technician Seaman, Class A Electronics School, Great Lakes, 1951-1952. After graduation, promoted third class petty officer and assigned to USS *Amphion* (AR-13) Norfolk, VA, repairing electronics equipment on many ships and working part-time WTAR-TV. Also Class C school on IFF, and Fax school. Promoted to electronics technician second class petty officer late in 1953. He was at Times Square, NY when news reported Korean Conflict ended.

Transferred as leading ET to USS *Atka* (AGB-3), Boston, MA. Cleared sea lanes, Reykjavik/Keflavik, Iceland to Thule, Greenland, northward transporting scientific expedition to study ocean depths and weather.

Promoted to electronics technician petty officer first class in 1954 and transferred to USS *Dionysus* (AR-15), Newport, RI until he completed four-year enlistment 15 Feb 1955 when honorably discharged.

Returned to Princeton, WPKY Radio, hosting *"Wake Up With Willie"* morning broadcast, was news and sports director, 1955-65; 8 Apr 1966 with local Cadiz/Trigg County leaders, established first broadcast station WKDZ in Cadiz; general manager until sold 26 Jun 1986.

He married Jo Ann Campbell 23 May 1954 while serving USN Korean Conflict, 1951-55. They have twin daughters, Deborah Gay Wilson Anderson and Donna Jo Wilson. Grandchildren are John Martin Linton and twins Brandon and Bridgett Linton. Wilburn lives at 151 Sunset Circle, Cadiz, KY.

BILLIE FRANK WOLFE, CMSGT, was born in Linton, KY on 24 Sep 1932 to James Frank and Mavis Ford Wolfe, with one sister, Elizabeth Ann Wolfe Thompson and a brother, James Dwight Wolfe. They farmed in Trigg County and his mother taught school.

After graduating from Trigg County High, Billie enlisted in the Air Force on 10 Oct 1954 in Louisville, KY. After basic training in Sampson, NY, he was stationed at Chanute AFB, IL; Williams AFB, AZ; Sewart AFB, TN; Laon AFB, France; Shaw AFB, SC; Thailand, Vietnam, Sheppard AFB, TX; Osan, South Korea; Blytheville AFB, AR; and again at Sheppard AFB, TX.

Most of his military career was spent in aircraft maintenance—either working or teaching on the flightline, or teaching in the classroom. He was responsible for developing and writing training material. During his second tour at Sheppard AFB, he traveled often, negotiating F5 maintenance training package sales to Egypt, Indonesia, Kenya, Sudan, South Korea, Jordan, Brazil, Chile and Ethiopia.

While at Chanute, Billie married Robbie Dell Johnson, of Trigg County, on 10 Jun 1955 in Springfield, TN. Their first daughter, Vicki Lane, was born at Williams AFB on 16 Jun 1958. A second daughter, Linda Sue, was born at Shaw AFB, on 15 Aug 1962. They both graduated high school in Texas. Vicki went to college there and Linda went to college in Clarksville, TN. Vicki married David Patrick Lawson in Texas and they had two daughters, Ashley Lane (b. 27 Apr 1983) and Mackenzey Shae (b. 19 Apr 1987). Linda married Jeffrey Allen Gladu in Texas and they had one daughter, Annalise Nicole (b. 7 Aug 1994), sadly, she went to her heavenly home on that same day.

Billie retired at Sheppard AFB on 30 Jun 1979 proudly at the rank of CMSGT. His awards and medals include the Armed Forces Expeditionary Medal, NCO Academy Graduate Ribbon, Good Conduct Medal, Longevity Service Award Ribbon, National Defense Service Medal, Vietnam Service Medal, Meritorious Service Award in SE Asia, Meritorious Service Award in South Korea, Meritorious Service Award in Texas, Air Force Presidential Unit Citation, Air Force Outstanding Unit Award, Republic of Korea Presidential Unit Citation, Republic of Vietnam Gallantry Cross with Devices, Republic of Vietnam Campaign Medal, and Air Force Outstanding Unit Valor Medal. Also, while in the service, he accumulated 60 college hours.

After military retirement, Billie, Robbie, and Linda moved to Trigg County. They bought a small farm on Donaldson Creek Road. Billie began working Civil Service on the flightline at Fort Campbell, KY. After the first grandchild was born, they moved back to Texas where Billie continued working Civil Service at Sheppard AFB as a maintenance instructor. He retired from Civil Service in September 1994. Then he concentrated on an automobile business.

He was a member of Delmont Baptist Church, Linton Masonic Lodge, Scottish Rite Consistory in KY, Faith Masonic Lodge, Maskat Shrine Temple, Mask-at Motor Patrol, Texas Shrine Motor Patrol Association, and Red River Chapter of Harley Owner's Group.

Billie and Robbie lived outside the base in Wichita County, TX until his sudden death 11 Apr 2000. He is buried in Christian County, KY. Robbie still lives in Texas with her daughters, sons-in-law, and granddaughters nearby.

Post Korean War

ELBERT ADAMS, PFC, the son of Ben and Nell Adams of Cadiz, KY. Elbert was drafted 2 Nov 1961 and trained at Fort Chaffee, AR. From there he went to Germany for 19 months with the 51st Inf.

Pfc. Adams received an honorable discharge. His awards include a medal for Sharp Shooter.

CHARLES H. ALEXANDER, PFC, born 6 Feb 1940. He was drafted 10 Feb 1962 from Cadiz and went to Fort Gordon, GA for basic training, then spent one year overseas in Germany. He worked as a telephone installer repairman. Pfc. Alexander was discharged at Fort Hamilton, NY on 9 Sep 1964. Awards include Expert on M-1 Rifle and 45 pistol and the Good Conduct Medal.

He married Sandra Ashby O'Steen in 1966. She had three children (Michelle, Deidre and Mark) whom he adopted. Charles and Sandra's son Lee Hayden Alexander was killed in a car accident in 1988. Grandchildren are Lauren, Heath, Hayden, Jessica and Shane. Charles Alexander died 19 Jan 1983.

JAMES BAKER, 1st Sergeant, born to Johnnie C. and Levi Baker on 25 May 1941, Trigg County, Cadiz, KY. He attended and graduated from the public school systems in Cadiz and Hopkinsville, KY.

Baker volunteered for the Army in 1960. His first duty station was Fort Knox, KY where he received his first military issued clothing. He spent eight weeks of basic training at Fort Hood, TX, where a loud mouth drill sergeant met him and announced that he would be the Drill Sergeant for the next eight weeks.

After basic training he was sent to Fort Sam Houston, TX for 12 weeks at the Medical Specialist School. After Fort Sam Houston, TX he was sent to Fort Eustis, VA to McDonald Army Hospital where he worked as a medical specialist on the surgical ward. His duties consisted of observing patients, removing sutures and giving shots and other duties as assigned by the ward nurse.

His other duty stations were Dispensary NCOIC, Air Defense, Chicago, IL; Aid Station, Ankara, Turkey; Medical Specialist, Ireland Army Hospital, Fort Knox, KY; Advance Medical School, Womack Army Hospital, Fort Bragg, NC; Emergency Room Specialist, Brooke Army Hospital, Fort Sam Houston, TX; Medical Specialist, Chabanna Dispensary Nuclear Site, Okinawa, Japan; Platoon Sergeant, Fort Knox, KY; NCOIC Baumholder Army Dispensary, Baumholder, Germany; NCOIC Military Enlisted Processing Station (MEPS), Fort Jackson, SC; Medical Section NCOIC/First Sergeant, 4/7 Cav., Camp Gary Owens, Korea and last duty station First Sergeant, 498 Medical Evacuation Unit, Fort Jackson, SC.

While in the military he attended many schools, i.e., ear, nose and throat (ENT), x-ray, medical records, phlebotomy and others. He also received many commendations and awards. He received an associate of science degree in management and a BS degree in management and health care.

He and his wife, Thelma, have three children: Cassandra Palmer, Johnny Leon and Kevin Jerome. They have two grandchildren, Justin James Wright Baker and Kevin Tabor Baker.

SFC (Ret) Johnny J. Baker retired from the military on 4 Apr 1984 at Fort Jackson, SC, and is presently employed with the federal government in health care with the Military Enlistment Processing Station (MEPS), Fort Jackson, SC. He is a Mason and a member of the Veterans of Foreign Wars (VFW). He attends Fort Jackson Daniel Circle Chapel and resides in Columbia, SC.

CLAUDE E. BANISTER, Captain, born 2 Jul 1935, Cadiz, KY. He joined the U.S. Army in 1958 at Fort Bliss, TX and was discharged with the rank of captain in 1966. He was recalled to active duty during Berlin crisis.

Claude is an agent with State Farm Ins. He married Sue Wilson 30 Aug 1957 and they live in Germantown, TN. They have two children, John and Kim, and two grandchildren, John and Kay Leigh.

JACK BRIDGES, born in Canton, KY, the son of Sam Bridges and Georgia Tandy Bridges. In this family were 10 children and they grew up in Canton but are now working or retired in many different states. Jack's paternal grandparents are Jack Bridges and Emma Hopson Bridges; his maternal grandparents are Major Tandy and Sally Bryant Tandy.

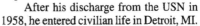

Jack entered the USN and was on active duty from 1956-58. He served during the Post-Korean Conflict. Jack's sister Juanita Trail lives in Detroit, MI. She married a Navy man who had sailed on the same ship as Jack.

After his discharge from the USN in 1958, he entered civilian life in Detroit, MI.

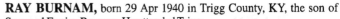

He remained in Detroit and worked there until 1982. At this time he returned to his former home in Canton. In his retirement years, he does part-time construction work and is enjoying life in Canton.

RAY BURNAM, born 29 Apr 1940 in Trigg County, KY, the son of Sam and Eunice Burnam. He attended Trigg County School and was drafted in the Army on 5 Sep 1962.

He took basic training at Fort Gordon, GA, then went to Fort Polk, LA for communication training. He later transferred to Fort Sill, OK as an instructor where he completed his tour of duty and was discharged 4 Sep 1964.

Ray lives in Cadiz, KY and works as a journeyman/wireman with an electrical union in Paducah, KY. He has one son, L. Ray Burnam II.

DONALD R. BUSH, E-4, born 12 Jan 1939 in Trigg County, son of Carloss and Martha Bush. He grew up in Lyon County and moved back to Trigg County in 1968.

He was drafted into the Army on 1 Nov 1961 and traveled to Nashville, TN where he had a physical examination. From there he was sent to Fort Chaffee, AR for basic training. After six weeks of basic training, he was sent to Fort Hood, TX and assigned to the 513th Quartermaster Company where they issued food, clothing, gas and other things.

While serving at Fort Hood, they went on 30 day training missions which included Fort Polk, LA; Fort Jackson, SC; Fort Louis, WA; and other places.

He served his country during the Cuban Crisis and was on a 72 hour alert until a resolution was reached between the United States and Cuba. He was discharged from the Army 1 Nov 1963 prior to the Vietnam War.

He is married to the former Rosella Thomas Bush. Together they have two sons, Donald Ray and Ronald; two daughters, Stephanie King and Ashley Tyler; and seven grandchildren: Donald III and Sierra Bush, Laykn Brooks, Karli Bush, Joshua and Victoria King, and Ashton Tyler. Donald and Rosella reside at 215 Herndon Circle, Cadiz, KY.

He has been actively employed for 40 plus years as a construction and heavy equipment operator, part of which was with the coal mines.

PAUL D. CANNON, Radioman 3/c, volunteered for duty in the USN in February 1958 and served four years, three months and 13 days in the Navy. He received his basic training at U.S. Naval Training Center, San Diego, CA. From there he served at Class "A" Radio School in Norfolk, VA.

He received emergency orders to Japan during the Quemoy Crisis in September 1958, and served two years at Naval Radio Station, Kami Seya, Japan and from there receive orders to the USS *Yorktown* CVS-10, homeported in Long Beach, CA.

They had several standoffs with the Russian navy during the cold war years of 1960-62, but never a shot fired; more of a harassment than anything as they tried, many times successfully, to jam our RADAR and Radio/Teletype communications.

Was also in Carrier Battle Group taking part in Christmas Islands nuclear tests. He was separated from the Navy 8 Jun 1962.

On 4 Jul 1962 he married the former Linda Anne Hire. They have two children, Christopher Dean and Deidre Anne. They presently pastor Canton Baptist Church in Canton, KY.

JAMES W. CRISP, Sergeant E-5, born 20 Nov 1935, Trigg County. Joined the service in August 1957 at Fort Knox.

Assignments include Fort Knox Armor School, November 1957-February 1958; Fort Sill, OK, battery clerk, supply sergeant, STR NCO February 1958 to November 1959; Fort Polk, LA, communications chief, November 1959-August 1960.

Recalled to active duty November 1961 to Fort Meade, MD; post signal electronics tech; TDY Camp Pickett, VA, communications chief, August 1962. Discharged in 1963 with the rank sergeant E-5.

Taught school at Trigg County HS, 1956-57; Hopkinsville HS, 1959-60; Daviess County Middle School (1961-64) and High School (1964-92); part-time English instr. 1967-92 at Brescia College, KY Wesleyan College, Owensboro Community College and Western KY University Extension in Owensboro, KY. Retired from Daviess County Public School System, Owensboro, KY, in 1992.

Married Martha on 10 Jun 1961 and they live in Owensboro, KY. They have four children: James Jr., Helen, Kathleen and John, and five grandchildren: Stephen, Matthew and Elizabeth Hardy; Philip and Mary Katherine Lanz.

ROBERT GLENN CUNNINGHAM, Machinist Mate 3/c, born 3 Dec 1937, Trigg County, KY, the youngest son of Olive James and Roberta Williams Cunningham. He was one of four brothers who all served in the Armed Forces. He enlisted in the USN with four classmates from the 1956 graduating class at Trigg County HS.

Boot camp was at Bainbridge, MD. On 15 Sep 1956 he reported aboard the USS *Yosemite* (AD-19) for TDY; 2 Nov 1956 reported aboard the USS *Glennon* for permanent duty. They made a six month Mediterranean cruise in 1957, stopping in seven foreign countries; patrolled the

coast of Lebanon during the Lebanon Crisis; and made a three month northern Europe cruise in 1960.

After being released from active duty in June 1960, he returned to Cadiz and married Linda Faye Pepper. They have one son Robert Glenn Jr. Robert Sr. worked at different jobs before starting a career with civil service at Fort Campbell, KY where he retired in 1996 with 33-1/2 years service.

Recently he has been working at the Trigg County Jail as a deputy jailer. In April 2001 he was appointed to complete the unexpired term of jailer of Trigg County. He and his wife reside on a small family farm west of Cadiz, KY where he was born and raised.

JAMES ELWOOD DARNELL, born 26 Oct 1943 in Cadiz, KY, volunteered for and was inducted into the U.S. Army on 2 Nov 1961. He is one of eight children of Joseph Nuck and Lou Ella Darnall, of which five served in the U.S. Army: Jessie Fentress, John Clayton, Irvin Chester and Bluford Elias, and Roy Eugene in the USN. A brother, Joseph Lamont, who lives in Trigg County, Cadiz KY, was left handicapped from polio was not able to serve. He also has a sister, Addie Harris, who lives in Hopkinsville, KY.

James completed basic training (A-12-4) and his advanced individual training at Fort Knox, KY. In April 1962 he was assigned to the 504th Military Police Company, Fort Eustis, VA. (An older Brother, Bluford Elias, had served in this same company from March 1955 until April 1956.) In October 1962, he was reassigned to the 52lst MP Co., Fort Belvoir, VA. He served out his enlistment there and was discharged 29 Oct 1964.

He established residency in northern Virginia, where he met Patricia Ann Morrow. They were married 24 Feb 1968 and have one son, Stephen Wayne Darnell, born 9 Jun 1975. James was employed for 25 years with Bell Atlantic Telephone Co. in the northern Virginia/Washington DC area. In 1993 he transferred to Telcordia Technologies (formerly Bellcore) located in Lisle, IL, a western suburbs of Chicago. His family lived in Naperville, IL, until May 2000, at which time he and his wife relocated to Clarksville, TN. He continues to work for Telcordia Technologies as an Education Sales Support Account Director for the Southeast and Mid-Atlantic Regions. He and his wife are members of the Hilldale Baptist Church in Clarksville.

THOMAS L. DIXON JR., E-4, born 19 Apr 1937, son of Loyd and Belvie Ricks Dixon, was drafted into the Army on 2 May 1960. He had his basic training at Fort Benning, GA and advanced training at Fort Hood, TX.

In September 1960 he was shipped to Wildflicker, Germany and served 18 months with Co. B, 3rd Armd. Rifle Bn., 50th Inf. Div. and drove a M-59 personnel carrier. He was discharged at Fort Hamilton,

NY, 30 Apr 1962, then served four years in the Reserves at Hopkinsville, KY. Medals include the Good Conduct Medal.

He married Juanice Woods 15 Jun 1963 and their children and in-laws are Terry and Sherry Dixon, Mitch and Wendy Finley, Shane and Leah Dixon, all of Trigg County. Grandchildren and step-grandchildren are Allison and Jinna Dixon, Allie Finley, Gracie Dixon, Kyle and Shaundra Finley, Kurt and Ryan Moore.

Thomas retired in June 2000 from TVA-LBL after 23 years. They live in Cadiz, KY, and attend Canton Baptist Church.

JOHN P. FOURQUREAN, Captain, graduated from Western Kentucky University ROTC program in January 1963 and received commission in U.S. Army as a second lieutenant. Received designation as Distinguished Military Graduate in the program and was member of the Scabbard and Blade Honorary Military Society, Cadet Company Commander in the ROTC Battalion.

Stationed at Fort Benning, GA and attended U.S. Army Infantry School before assignment to the 2nd Bn., 54th Inf., 4th Armd. Div., Bamberg, Germany. In January 1965 he received promotion to first lieutenant. While serving with the 4th Armd. Div. he was assigned to several different commands and received several honored recognition's.

In June 1965 he returned to civilian status but joined the Army Reserve 100th Div. and assigned to Co. D, 1st Bn., 398th Regt., 2nd Bde. (BCT) in Hardinsburg, KY. In 1967 he was assigned as commander of the company and promoted to the rank of captain in January 1969. While in the 100th Div., he completed numerous Department of Army Training Courses, including the Branch Officer Advanced Course. Due to increased responsibilities and time restraints in both Reserve and civilian duties, he asked to be discharged in June 1972.

John married Mary Ann Newman of Owensboro on 26 Aug 1961. They have three children: Elizabeth (Liz) Fourqurean Hobgood, John Perry Fourqurean Jr., and John David Fourqurean, They have four grandchildren: John David Jr. and Ella Katherine Fourqurean and Ann Michael and Natalie Diane Hobgood.

John currently resides at 138 Coyote Ridge Road, Cadiz, KY, where he is currently retired from University of Kentucky Coop. Extension Service and is working part-time at Southern States and is also a part-time farmer with his two sons.

WALTER EARL FREEMAN, Sergeant E-5, born 10 Sep 1942, Trigg County, KY. Attended and graduated Trigg County HS in Cadiz, KY, May 1960. He joined the Army 8 Jun 1960, took basic training at Fort Knox, KY and Airborne School at Fort Campbell, KY.

Assigned to A Co., 801st Maint. Bn., 101st Abn. Div. at Fort Campbell. He participated in 20 jumps from various aircraft with one malfunction on 18 Dec 1962. Attained the rank of corporal and received

the Mechanic Badge w/Driver and Mechanic Bars, Expert Rifleman, Airborne Wings, Unit Citation and Good Conduct Medal.

He joined the Illinois Army National Guard 5 Sep 1986, served as armorer and supply clerk and was discharged 15 May 1989 with the rank sergeant E-5.

As a civilian he drove a truck for Brandon Trucking, Hopkinsville; worked for Caterpillar Tractor Co., Peoria, IL; attended welding classes at Illinois Central than taught there for two semesters; attended Midwest Barber College for master license and Liberty Beauty College for teacher's certificate of cosmetology.

Attended Richland Southern Baptist Church since 1964, elected deacon in 1974 and served as chairman until 2001. Retired from Caterpillar in August 1994. He lives in Washington, IL but plans to move back to Kentucky.

Married 14 Apr 1963 to Rosemary Dunn. They have three children: Jeffrey, Kyna and Jonathan and four grandchildren: Kammi and Derek Bishop and Jacob and Savannah Freeman.

RAYMOND EARL FULLER, born 12 Dec 1935 in Trigg County to Raymond E and Louise Vanzant Fuller. He married Louise Carr 15 Dec 1956 and has two sons, Raymond Keith and John Kenneth.

After graduating from Trigg County HS he went to Chicago, IL along with several others from Trigg County to find work in construction. He received his draft papers to report for active duty 2 Jun 1958. He and Billy Carr were inducted at Fort Knox, KY. Billy completed basic training at Fort Knox with Raymond going to Fort Riley, KS. After eight weeks basic and eight weeks advanced training, he was sent home for a few days, then shipped out to Europe. He was in the 28th Inf. Div. and stationed in Munich, Germany. There he drove a duce and half and was in the field much of the time.

After a month or so his wife joined him at Munich and it was there that their son Keith was born. Russia was causing trouble at this time and an alert would mean Raymond to report to Camp and his family was to move out on a designated route. Bags and survival items were packed at all times in case of trouble with Russia. Things smoothed out and his tour of duty was fulfilled with no major problems. He was discharged 15 May 1960.

Upon returning home he and his family returned to Chicago to do drywall work and remained there until 1962. At this time they returned to Trigg County where Raymond continued to do drywall work. He has retired now and is enjoying his five grandchildren: Carson, Zachary, Rachel, Jonathan and Nathan Fuller at his home on the South Road.

JAMES MONROE GARDNER JR., PO2, born 4 Feb 1936 in Cadiz, KY, son of James Monroe Sr. and Allie Atwood Gardner. He served in USN from 1956-1960. He did his training in Bainbridge, MD.

After Boot Camp he went aboard his ship MSO USS *Direct* in Panama City, FL, then returned to home port of Charleston, SC. After duty in Charleston, he was ordered to Engine School at Great Lakes Naval Base in Great Lakes, IL. After graduating he went back to Charleston, SC to the Ship USS *Sagassity*. He spent the rest of his tour aboard the *Sagassity* with two trips to the Mediterranean with operation out of Spain, Italy, Sicily, Greece, France, Beirut, Lebanon.

Returned to Charleston for discharge on 20 Jun 1960 as engineman 2nd class petty officer. He received a Good Conduct Medal.

He married Virginia Boyd Gardner in 1960 and has two sons, James Gant Gardner, Stacy Todd Gardner, and two grandsons, James Matthew Gardner and Christian Cole Gardner.

Worked for Ford Motor Co. and farmed. Retired since March 1999. He lives in Cadiz, KY. His hobbies are hunting and collecting.

ROGER L. HATFIELD, 1st Lieutenant, born to G.S. "Sam" Hatfield and Marie H. DeGarmo on 23 May 1940 in Zanesville, OH. He is a 1958 graduate of Philo HS, Philo, OH and graduated from Ohio University in Athens, OH in 1962 with a bachelor of fine arts.

He entered into the US Army in 1962 in Zaneville, OH, and upon completion of basic training at Fort Knox, KY, he was assigned to Fort Benning, GA where he completed his airborne qualification.

He attended Officer Candidate School at Fort Benning, GA, was commissioned a 2nd lieutenant and assigned to Fort Ord, CA where he was the executive officer of Co. C, 2nd Bn., 4th Bde.

In 1965 Lt. Hatfield was in a serious car accident and medically discharged with 100% disability. He has been residing on Grigsby Lane in Cadiz since 1989 and is an active member of the Cadiz Lions Club and Masonic Lodge #283, Duncan Falls, OH. Hobbies are working in the yard, shopping and working crossword puzzles. *Submitted by Bill Mize.*

LESLIE LAYTON HERNDON, born 7 Apr 1935 in Cadiz, KY, enlisted in the USAF in April 1957. He left for Lackland AFB on 7 Apr 1957 to complete his basic training. He had to take a bus to Louisville in order to catch a flight to Texas. It was his first time to ever fly.

After basic training was completed, he was stationed in Hampton, VA at Langley Field. Then, it was on to Okinawa, Japan. He was stationed at Kadina AFB for approximately six months. After his stay in Okinawa, he was transferred to Korea.

He returned to the States two months early due to the death of his father, Nicodemus Herndon, in November 1959. He was then sent to Stewart AFB in Nashville to complete the rest of his enlistment. He received an honorable discharge on 22 Jan 1960.

Layton married Bettie Adams, of Cadiz, on 2 Jul 1960. They have two children: Leslie Franklin Herndon (b. 31 Oct 1963) and Joan Denise Herndon Terrell (b. 12 Dec 1969). They have one grandchild, Leighton Alexandra "Lexie" Terrell (b. 18 Sep 1998).

Layton retired from Johnson Controls, Inc. in February 1996. He worked there for 30 years and was a supervisor there for most of those years. Today, Layton enjoys farming part-time and watching Lexie, the "apple of his eye," part-time.

JAMES D. HOWELL, EN2, born 20 Aug 1934, Stewart County, TN. He joined the military service 24 Apr 1954 and was discharged as EN2 on 28 Feb 1958. Memorable experience was crossing the Arctic Circle.

Married Carolyn Robertson 22 May 1959 and they live in Cadiz, KY. They have three children: Sherry Larson, Joy Guess and Scott; also, six grandchildren: Taryn, Megan, Austin, Logan, Joe and Erin. James is still working. His hobbie is Bluegrass music; he sings and plays stringed instruments.

THOMAS L. HOWELL, Specialist 4, born 31 May 1942 in Detroit, MI. He enlisted in the Army 2 Nov 1961 at Louisville, KY and was discharged 10 Aug 1964 with the rank SP4. Memorable was his year of service in Germany.

He is a graduate of Austin Peay State University, Clarksville, TN and worked as an auditor at Fort Campbell, KY from 1971 to present.

Married Barbara Taylor 2 Sep 1966 and they live in Clarksville, TN. Children are son Stacy and daughter Melissa Patterson and grandchild is Caden Patterson. He is a Kentucky Wildcat fan and enjoys hobby farming and Bluegrass music.

WALLACE EDWARD HYDE, SP4-E4, born 20 Dec 1933 in Lyon County, KY. He was drafted into the Army, 20 Sep 1956. After eight weeks of basic training at Fort Carson CO he qualified for Rifle Drill and Sharpshooter.

He was sent to Fort Ord, CA as a company clerk and appointed PVT E-2 on 20 Jan 1957, where he remained until his release from active duty on 19 Sep 1958. He received the Good Conduct Metal. For two years he was in Active Duty Reserve and two years Stand By Reserve. His promotion to SP4 (E-4) was on 21 Aug 1958. His final discharge was on 19 Sep 1962.

Married Martha Adams on 4 Jul 1959 and they live in Cadiz, KY. They have three children: Debra Hyde Hardy, Teresa and Wayne Hyde, and five grandchildren: Amanda, Rachel, Daniel, Sarah, Rebekah Hardy.

JOHN KENNEDY, E-4, born 24 Jan 1938, in Cadiz, KY, not far from where he now lives. He graduated from Trigg County HS in 1956 and was drafted in the Army on 30 Nov 1960. He took his basic training and second eight weeks at Fort Jackson, SC. He was trained as a light vehicle driver.

He left there and went to Fort Eustis, VA, in the 63rd Trans. Co. Light Truck and spent his time going from Canada to Florida. He spent two summers at the United States Military Academy, West Point, NY, in training cadets how to drive; 1st Army, 1st Bn., 1st Training Regiment.

General Westmoreland was superintendent at West Point his last summer. The Bay of Pigs incident and the Cuban Crisis happened while he was in the Army.

Discharged 30 Nov 1962 and spent two years in the Reserves and two years Inactive Reserves. He received the Good Conduct Medal and Expert M-1 Carbine.

He is a farmer and a member of Wallonia Baptist Church where he is a deacon there, being ordained in 1978.

CARL G. LANCASTER, SGM, born 21 May 1940 in Cadiz, KY. He joined the USAF 5 Oct 1959 in Louisville, KY with assignments at Yokota AFB, Japan; Kunsan AFB, Korea; Custer AFS, Battle Creek, MI; USAR, 4th BN 20th FA, Lansing, MI, command sergeant major 334th Medical Group, Grand Rapids, MI, sergeant major.

SGM Lancaster was discharged 23 Nov 1993 from the USAR with 34 years total service. His awards include the Legion of Merit, Meritorious Service Medal, ARCOM w/2 OLCs, ARCAM w/5 OLCs, National Defense Service Medal (2), AFRM (2), AFLSA, AAM, Good Conduct (2), SAEMR, SOG-7, ASR and OSR.

Carl retired 20 Jun 2000 from Federal Civil Service with the USAR. He married Joy L. Morton 25 Jul 1964 and they live in Comstock Park, MI. They have two children, Stephanie Lavoie and Steven, and four grandchildren: Aubrey, Addison, Julia and Avery Lavoie.

VAN TAYLOR LANE, SP5, born 16 Apr 1936 on the family farm near Golden Pond, KY in Trigg County. From birth until 1955, Van lived on the family farm and loved every minute he spent there. After graduating from Trigg County HS in 1955, he moved to East Alton, IL and went to work for Laclede Steel as a maintenance electrician. On 19 Oct 1957, he married Helen Johnson from McClure, IL. Helen worked as a secretary for the Madison County Illinois Probation Office.

In October 1959, Van was drafted into the Army and sent to Fort Sills, OK for his basic training. On 23 Mar 1959, he left for Germany on the USS *Darby*. Van was stationed in Stuttgart, Germany and served in Btry. "C" Howitzer Battalion, 36th Arty. Div. His duty in Germany was to read and set charts for artillery guns.

Since Van's service was during peace time, his wife Helen, was allowed to go to Germany and they had an apartment on base. While serving in Germany, Van purchased a car, and he and Helen toured Europe. His wife returned home in 1960. However, peace time conflicts extended Van's time in Germany. He was honorably discharged in February 1961.

On his shipboard return, he was searching name tags of other soldiers and found two that he knew, Joe Holland, also from Trigg County, and Gerald Malloy from Lyon County.

Seeing his wife and his parents, John and Cora Lane, were first on his list of things to do. He was also very interested in returning to Kentucky to pick up his 1957 Chevrolet. His father had kept the car in topnotch condition, and as a welcome home present, his parents fitted the 57 Chevy with brand-new tires.

Van was often quoted as saying he received a good education "down on the farm." Instead of returning to the farm, Van returned to East Alton and to Laclede Steel where his job was waiting. He worked at Laclede Steel until his death. Van Lane passed away 22 Nov 1982. Helen Lane passed away 3 Sep 1997. Both are buried in Woodland Hills Cemetery, East Alton, IL.

They are survived by one daughter, Dana Lane Witt, who is married to Paul Witt and they have two children, Taylor Lane Witt and Jonathan Paul Witt.

Van Lane served his country during a time in history when the situation in Europe was still volatile. He was given a citation which stated that along with honorably serving his country, his exemplary conduct, his work ethics and his unselfish attitude towards his fellow servicemen allowed Battery "C" Howitzer Battalion 36th Arty. Div. to become one of the most qualified and best recognized battalions stationed in Germany.

ERNEST R. LAWRENCE, SFC, born 22 Sep 1938 in Trigg County to Clarence and Jettie Bleidt Lawrence. He enlisted in the Army Reserves on 31 Oct 1960 in Hopkinsville, KY. After six months of active duty at Fort Knox, KY, he returned home to continue in a farming operation with his father and brother, James Robert. (He also has a sister Freida Hennenber of Evansville, IN.)

In September 1961 the 100th Div., of which he was a member, was activated and he reported to Fort Chaffee, AR for duty. After one year of active duty during the Berlin Crisis, the 100th was deactivated and he returned home. He continued serving in the Reserves for 21 years of active duty. He retired in 1985 as SFC Dining Facility Manager.

Ernest married Clara Gentry 7 May 1966 and they are the parents of one daughter, Clara Elizabeth Hyde, a registered nurse and an instructor in nursing in the Trigg County School system. The Lawrences are the grandparents of Mason and Reagan Hyde.

Ernest and Clara are active members of the Cadiz Baptist Church and Thomas Bridges Assoc. Ernest has served as a director of board of the Bank of Cadiz for about 30 years, holds membership in various agriculture organizations, 32nd degree Mason, American Legion and Cadiz Masonic Lodge. Ernest and his brother continue in the farming operation know as Lawrence Bros. Farms and he is a tobacconist. The Lawrence family resides in Cadiz.

CHARLES L. LITCHFIELD, born 17 Aug 1933 in Cadiz, KY, the son of Layton and Woodrow Faulkner Litchfield. He entered the Army in September 1956 and did all of his military time in the States. The majority of his career was spent in the state of Georgia. He was discharged from the Army in 1958.

Charles retired from the Civil Service after employment with both Corp of Engineers and Fort Campbell, KY. Charles resides in Cadiz, KY and enjoys hunting.

HARRISON MARTIN JR., SP4, born 18 Nov 1929 and was drafted in the Army on 18 Apr 1957, from the Local Board in Indianapolis, IN. He entered basic training at Fort Knox, KY and was transferred to Fort Riley, KS, where he was a parts supply specialist (1957-59). He re-enlisted there in 1959, and transferred to Fort Sheridan, IL where he worked in Ordinance Supply for nine months. His next duty station was Fort Dix, NJ, where he was processed for overseas duty.

He boarded the USS *Geiger* with other troops and landed in Mien Hein, Germany, where he served from January 1960 to April 1962 with the 7th Army Ordinance Depot.

He returned to the States on the USS *Darby*. He was Honorably Discharged on 24 Apr 1962 in Brooklyn, NY. He returned shortly thereafter to his home and family in Cadiz, KY, where he still resides.

Mr. Martin returned to civilian employment. He later became employed at Averitt Lumber Co., Cadiz, until he became disabled and terminated employment on 26 Sep 1989. He is a native of Cadiz, and the son of the late Benjamin Harrison Martin and Helen Froman Martin. He is the youngest of four siblings, and has one surviving sister, Lillie V. Groves of Indianapolis, IN. Mr. Martin married Bertha Venus Kirby on 17 Apr 1948, and they are the parents of six children: Harrison III, Tony, Price (veteran), Helena, Henry Sr. (veteran) and George Sr. They have 17 grandchildren and 12 great-grandchildren. Four grandsons are veterans, and three are currently on active duty.

Mr. Martin is a lifelong member of Bloomfield Missionary Baptist Church, Cadiz, where he serves on the Deacon Board and as asst. superintendent of the Sunday School.

His hobbies are fishing, gardening and spending time with his family and friends.

HAROLD D. MEREDITH, 2nd Lieutenant, born 13 Jul 1943 in Stewart County, TN. He joined the Army in August 1960. After two months of basic training at Fort Knox, KY, he was sent to Fort Meade, MD for advanced training in field communications. At Fort Meade he served with the 69th Signal Battalion, Field Radio Group and took part in division size training exercises at Fort Lee, VA, Eglin AFB, FL. and Camp Pickett, VA.

In July 1961 he was transferred to the 133rd Signal Company, 9th LOG Command, Okinawa, Japan. Here he served in support of all forces in the Far East Command. Then in January 1962 he was sent TDY to serve with the Military Assistance, Advisory Group in Laos. Here he helped provide communications for Air America and train Laotian troops.

The last seven months of his three-year tour of duty he was stationed at a missile site in Texas. The unit was the 517th Arty. The missile site provided air defense for Dyess AFB, TX.

He was discharged from the active Army in August 1963. Then he was a member of the Kentucky National Guard and served with an armor unit in Hopkinsville, KY until 1968. While serving with the Kentucky National Guard he received a commission as a 2nd lieutenant.

He presently works at Pennyrile Rural Electric at its Cadiz, KY office. He is married to the former Helen Kay Fowler of Gracey, KY. They have one son Tim, two grandchildren, Cheyenne and Tuesday. Tim is serving with the rank of major in the Army and is presently stationed at Fort Stewart, GA.

OWEN F. MITCHELL, son of Woodrow Litchfield Mitchell. He enlisted in the USN 22 Jul 1959 and took his boot camp at Great Lakes, IL. Stationed at Pensacola, FL for one year, then transferred aboard USS *Des Moines* for mid cruise.

Transferred to USS *Long Beach* when it was commissioned at Boston, MA, for another mid cruise. It was the nation's first nuclear powered surface ship and commissioned 9 Sep 1961. In 1962 the ship was sent to Cuban crisis.

Latter part of 1962 he transferred to USS *Galveston*, sailed through Panama Canal to West Coast and spent rest of enlistment at Long Beach,

CA. Discharged 21 May 1963 and stayed in Reserves until 21 Jul 1965. He visited New Foundland, Africa, Italy, France, Germany, Spain, Sicily, Pontarico, Virgin Islands, Panama and Mexico.

Married 25 Oct 1963 to Ella Marie Choate and they live at 288 Cyote Ridge, Cadiz, KY. They have two children, Margie Ann and Larry Wayne. Owen is retired from TVA. His hobbies are hunting and gardening.

WILLIAM "BILL" MIZE JR., Lieutenant Colonel, born 3 Sep 1940 to William and Mary "Mae" Mize. He graduated from Trigg County High in 1958 and from Western Kentucky University in 1962. Upon graduation he was commissioned a 2nd lieutenant, Infantry, and entered the Army at Ft Benning, GA. His initial assignment in December 1962 was executive officer and later executive officer commander, HHC 11th Transportation Terminal Command, Bremerhaven, Germany. In April 1966 Bill was promoted to captain and branch transferred to the Quartermaster Corps.

He was then assigned to Eighth Army's ASCOM Depot, Bupyong, Korea. In 1968 he returned to Germany with the Seventh Army Support Command where he served as Commander, HHC, 7th SUPCOM. In March 1969 he was transferred to Boeblingen, Germany as Operations Officer, Material Management Center, VII Corps Support Command.

Promoted to major in July 1969 and transferred to Vietnam in 1970, he served briefly with the 1st Logistical Command. In 1971 he was transferred to HQ, US Army Pacific, Fort Shafter, Hawaii as a staff officer in the office of the DCSLOG. In 1975 he was assigned to the 2nd Inf. Div. in Korea where he commanded the 2nd Div Material Management Center.

He returned to the States for assignment with the 101st Abn. Div. as Security, Plans Operations (S2/3) officer, Division Support Command. He was promoted to lieutenant colonel in 1978 and elected to return to Korea in 1980 for a joint assignment with HQ, US Military Assistance Command. In 1981, he was assigned to Washington DC, but with duties at Fort Campbell, KY as the AMC Logistic Assistance Officer (LAO). Returning to Korea in 1985, he served as C-4 Plans & Operations Officer, HQ, Combined (ROK/US) Field Army. In 1986, he returned to Fort Campbell and remained until retirement in August 1990.

Bill is a graduate of the Infantry Officers' Basic Course, Quartermaster Officers' Advance Course, Command & General Staff College and the Industrial College of the Armed Forces.

His awards and decorations include the Legion of Merit, Bronze Star w/OLC, Meritorious Service Medal w/2 OLCs, Joint Service Commendation Medal and Army Commendation Medal w/3 OLCs.

Bill is married to Cynthia Hatfield and they reside on their farm on Grigsby Lane where they raise cattle and Arabian horses. They have one daughter, Deborah Mize Schal, in Germany; son Sam Gallogly, Cadiz; and grandchildren: Timothy, Laura, Christopher, Ryan and Peyton. Both Cyndi and Bill are active members of Bethel United Methodist Church.

Note: Bill is a great- grandson of Joshua Mize who appears elsewhere in this book.

DALTON NOEL, E-4, born 1 May 1935. He joined the Army in 1958 at Fort Knox, KY and took his basic training at Fort Hood, TX. He was assigned to 2nd Armd. Div.

Went from Fort Hood to New York on troop train and boarded the USS *Randal* for Germany. Elvis Presley was also on the ship. He was a clerk typist and pitched fast pitch softball. He was discharged in November 1959.

Dalton married Peggy in 1957 and they have two children, Michael (born in Frankfurt, Germany) and Angela, and one grandson, Mike. Dalton was a drywall hanger for 42 years, retiring in 1998. He lives with his wife in Murray, KY. Dalton enjoys playing golf and all sports.

JAMES DAVID PARRENT, E-4, born 5 Jun 1939 in Oxford, MS. He joined the army in July 1957 and after six months of school in field radio repair at Fort Gordon, GA, he was transferred to U.S. Army Signal Service Co. in Orleans, France.

He spent the remainder of his service time in Orleans and was discharged 8 Jul 1960. He was promoted to E-4 on 17 Feb 1959.

James married Corrine Boren of Hopkinsville on 6 Apr 1968. They had one son, James Michael (b. 31 Aug 1970), who was born at Caldwell County War memorial Hospital. Corrine passed away during the 1970s and James in 1983.

ALLEN M. "BUDDY" PERRY, born 14 Sep 1939, Dyer County, TN. Joined the service in July 1960 at Memphis, TN with assignments at Fort Jackson, SC; Fort Gordon, GA; Fort Bragg, NC. He served with the 82nd MP Det, 82nd Abn. Div. He was discharged in July 1963 and received the Good Conduct Medal.

After discharge he was a teacher, coach and athletic director. He retired from the Trigg County Board of Education in June 1994. He married Linda Hinch 26 Dec 1965 and they live at 116 Deepwood Drive, Cadiz, KY. They are parents of two children, Patrick Allen and Jon Thomas. His hobbies are golfing, fishing, wood working and traveling.

DONNIE E. POGUE, E-5, born 27 May 1943 in the Cumberland area of Trigg County, Golden Pond, KY. Attended elementary school at Golden Pond and graduated from Trigg County HS in May 1961. Donnie volunteered for the Army on 10 Jan 1962, completing basic training at Fort Knox, KY, as a private E-1. After serving in numerous enlisted assignments, Donnie completed his Army military career achieving the grade of E-5 in October 1965 with an honorable discharge, service-connected disability.

Donnie began his civil service career in May 1966 with Department of the Army, Fort Campbell, KY. Donnie worked in numerous Personnel, Operations, Logistics, and Comptroller positions including the Director of Resource Management. Donnie, while eligible for retirement in May 1998, continues to serve in a senior management capacity at Fort Campbell.

Donnie has worked on various local committees and boards, to include Cerulean United Methodist Church, currently holding the office of trustee and finance chairman; past member and chairman of the board of the Trigg County Board of Education; founding member, past president, and current member of the Executive Board of the Trigg County Education Foundation; member of the local Cerulean Kentucky Masonic Lodge, and is a 32 degree member of the Scottish Rite Temple, Louisville, KY; past member of Association of United States Army and the American Society of Military Comptrollers.

Donnie has spent nearly 40 years of his adult life with the Army; first as a soldier followed by a career in Civil Service. His focus is on supporting the soldier, who has volunteered to serve and in many cases given their life to ensure that we can live in a free country and to the soldier's family who continually make sacrifices. Donnie believes that we must have a strong national defense, He believes Fort Campbell is a key element of a strong national defense and that surrounding communities in both states must continue their support of upgrading and in some cases rebuilding of the infrastructure, much of which was built in the

1940s. As a country boy, Donnie thanks the Army and Fort Campbell for allowing him to serve and hopefully helped his fellow man along life's way. But above all, he thanks his creator for what talents and opportunities he has been given and to his wife, Linda of 39 years, for her support. Donnie and Linda reside at Cerulean, KY, and have two daughters, Sunne and Angela.

JOHN W. RANDOLPH, Captain, born 30 Dec 1936, son of Milus and Lucy Guthrie Randolph. He graduated Army ROTC, Murray State College in May 1959 and commissioned as a Reserve Commissioned Officer, 2nd lieutenant, 31 Jul 1959.

Active duty status, November 1959 to June 1960. He completed Infantry Officers Basic Training Course at Fort Benning, GA, February 1960. Assigned to Fort Knox, KY to provide basic training to trainees. Discharged from active duty in June 1960 and completed eight years of military obligation as a member of the Active Reserves.

BILLY R. REDD, AMS-2 (E-5), born 6 Aug 1937 in Donaldson Creek. He enlisted in the USN 21 Jun 1956 and went to boot camp at Bainbridge, MD. Attended Aviation Prop School at NAS, Norman, OK and Aviation Mechanics School, NAS, Memphis, TN.

Assigned to Airborne Early Warning Squadron Eleven at NAS, Patuxent River, MD in May 1957. Deployed to NAS, Argentia Newfoundland in July 1957. Squadron mission in Argentia was to fly radar surveillance across the Atlantic to the island of Azores and back, providing information on foreign naval vessels.

Returned to the States in June 1960 and was discharged at the Washington Naval Station in DC on 15 Jun 1960. Billy worked in civil service at Fort Campbell, KY until retirement in May 1987. From 1987 to 2000 he was in building and remodeling business and is presently a building inspector.

He married Cathorine Rives 21 Dec 1966 and they live in Hopkinsville, KY and plan to move soon to 259 Fairway Trace, Cadiz, KY.

RONALD E. ROBINSON, born 22 May 1934 in Ross County, OH. He was drafted in June 1956 and assigned to Fort Chaffee, AR, D Btry., 3rd Bn., 1st Regt. for basic training in Supply and Logistics.

He was sent to Fort Dix, NJ for assignment to Germany at the time when the U.S. was bringing the Hungary Refugees into this country. He was assigned to B Btry. 78th Field Artillery, 2nd Armd. Div. in Wackerheim, Germany which consisted of one 105mm Arty. Bn. and the last AA Bn. of the Occupation of Germany. As acting supply sergeant he was involved in several alerts and chasing the Russians back across the borders – packing everything up and moving out was a regular exercise.

When the order came for the whole 2nd Armd. Div. to go back to Fort Hood, TX, it was quite an experience to prepare and move every bolt and nut to large tank retrievers from one country to another. The move of the troops across the Atlantic on the troop ship *U.S. Gen. Patch* for eight days in the dead of winter was an experience not to be forgotten. At Fort Hood they trained new recruits.

He left active service in August 1958 and returned to Ohio where he was employed by Mead Papers for 42 years before retiring in Trigg County in 1993. He and his wife Ruth have two children, Christie and Jeff.

MALCOLM RAY SONS, SP4, born 15 Mar 1935, in Cadiz, KY, the son of Lonnie and Eleanor Noel Sons. He enlisted 19 Aug 1957, at Louisville, KY and received his basic training at Fort Knox, KY (8 weeks), then to Fort Riley, KS (22 months). Served with 1st Div. 121st Signal Bn. S4 Clerk, three months in California at Camp Roberts, the largest land, sea, air exercise at that time.

Discharged on 18 Aug 1959 with rank of specialist 4th class. Malcolm received Letter of Commendation from Battalion Commander upon his discharge.

Malcolm married Nancy Broadbent Sons of Cerulean, KY on 1 Aug 1954. They have two children, Jerry Ray Sons of Hopkinsville, KY and Sharon Ann Sons Butts of Cadiz, KY. Grandchildren are Samantha Anne and Jeremy Dale Butts.

Malcolm retired from the U.S. Postal Service in December 1995 after 32 plus years. He now enjoys working on small engines at his home and most of all he enjoys spending time with his grandchildren. Malcolm and Nancy reside at 7771 Cerulean Road, Cerulean, KY. They are members of Cerulean Baptist Church where Malcolm has served as Sunday school teacher, Sunday school superintendent and a deacon of his church.

BOBBY DELANE SUMNER, born 16 Dec 1938, the son of Jesse and Eunice Sumner. Delane enlisted in the Army 28 Jun 1958 during peace time and was stationed at Fort Benning, GA. He enlisted hoping to be able to travel and see more of the world but he never received that opportunity. He was discharged 18 May 1961.

He was employed with TVA after returning home. His job at that time was relocating graves to prepare for the waters of what is now Lake Barkley. At the time of his death on 2 May 1968 he was a salesman for the Coca-Cola Bottling Company in Hopkinsville where he made his home. He is buried in the Peyton Thomas Cemetery in Trigg County.

Delane was a 5th generation descendant of James Thomas Sr. who fought in the Revolutionary War and settled a large portion of the Donaldson Creek Community where Delane grew up.

He married Sue Carol Wallace 24 Nov 1962 and they were parents of three children: Terry Delane, Kevin Thomas and Jason Carol.

JAMES DOUGLAS SUMNER, SP5, born 20 Dec 1939 in Trigg County, KY. He joined the Army 26 Sep 1962 and after basic training in Fort Jackson, SC, he went to Fort Devens, MA for nine months training for Army Security Agency.

After completion of training he was assigned to Camp Zama, Japan for 40 days, then spent 10 months at Camp Casey, Korea. He returned to the States and was assigned as an instructor at ASA School, Fort Devens, MA until his discharge 25 Sep 1965.

After his discharge he worked in management in the dairy industry for 30 years. He started in Hopkinsville, KY, transferred to Atlanta, GA for 13 years then to Wisconsin until retirement.

He married Margery Jean Doom 29 Dec 1962 and they live in Trigg County, KY. They have a daughter Iva Lisa and son James Thomas.

BILL H. SUMNER, PFC, born 10 Feb 1940 in Cadiz, KY. A graduate Trigg County HS in the Class of 1958. Bill was drafted into the Army 6 Oct 1959. After two months training at Fort Jackson, SC in Co. B, Ninth Battalion, Second Training Regiment he was transferred to Fort Sam Houston, TX receiving two months medical training there.

On 20 Feb 1960 he returned to Fort Campbell, KY where he worked in medical supply at the U.S. Army Hospital for two years. He received a Letter of Commendation for commendable and outstanding service during the period 12 Jan 1960 through 5 Feb 1962. Bill was to have been discharged 7 Oct 1961, but the Berlin Crisis caused him to be extended 120 days. On 5 Feb 1962 he received an honorable discharge with PFC rank.

Bill's civilian career after discharge from the military includes being employed with the Christian County Soil Conservation Service, Hopkinsville, KY for two years, Thomas Industries, Hopkinsville, KY for 16 years prior to buying and operating his own business as a retail grocery in March 1980 and still operating the same business under the name of Sumner's South Road Market on 139 South in Trigg County near his residence.

Bill married Brenda Shemwell from the Caledonia-Pee Dee Community in Trigg County, KY on 7 Dec 1963. They have two children, Tamara Fourqurean and John Sumner. They have no grandchildren. Bill and Brenda attend East Cadiz Baptist Church in Cadiz, KY.

WILLIAM H. "BILL" SUMNER, Fire Control Tech 3/c, born 5 Jul 1938 at Cadiz, KY. He enlisted in the service at Hopkinsville, KY and was sworn in at Louisville 8 Aug 1956. Boot camp and school was at Bainbridge, MD.

He went aboard the USS *Newport News* (CA-148) in October 1957 and transferred off in June 1960. He was discharged 28 Jul 1960.

For the past 38 years he worked in Chicago, IL in the floor covering business and retired 31 Dec 2000. William and Barbara Thurman were married 1 Mar 1964 and they live in Markham, IL. They have three children: Bryan, Marsha Kmet and William Jr., and six grandchildren: Megan and Adam Sumner, Tim and Matthew Kmet, John and Michael Cowkle.

WILLIAM BARTLEY TAYLOR, SM3, born 21 Dec 1942 in Christian County, KY, the son of Bartley and Helen Dean Calhoun Taylor. He enlisted in the USN immediately after graduating from Trigg County HS in 1960. He was sworn in on 24 Jun 1960 at the Armed Forces Receiving Center in Louisville, KY.

He went through basic training at Great Lakes Naval Training Center at Great Lakes, IL. He went to Newport Naval Training Center at Newport, RI for Signal-Man "A" School. Upon completion of this training, he was assigned to the USS *Willis A. Lee* (DL-4). While he served on that ship, they made one Spring Board cruise to the Caribbean.

He was transferred to the USS *Blandy* (DD-943) in January 1962. While serving on the USS *Blandy*, they were involved in the Cuban Blockade. The USS *Blandy* was the first ship on sight at the time when the submarine USS *Thresher* went down with all hands in the North Atlantic. During his time on board the USS *Blandy*, they made two Mediterranean Cruises, one Far East cruise and two other cruises in the Caribbean. The primary duty of the Task Force the Blandy was assigned, was anti-submarine defense.

He was discharged 23 Dec 1963. His rank at the time of his discharge was signalman 3/c.

William returned to Trigg County for a short period of time. He left to attend school at Campbellsville College. He later earned two degrees from Southeastern Baptist Theological Seminary, including a Doctor of Ministries. William is now a United Methodist Minister serving in the Kentucky Annual Conference.

He is married to the former Paula E. Jones and they have five children: William Bartley Jr., John Wilford Dossett, Renee' LeAnnette, Tammy Dean and Catherine Danielle. William Jr. and Catherine Danielle both died tragic deaths. William and Paula have three grandsons and five granddaughters.

WILLIAM CURTIS TAYLOR, born 11 Apr 1935, son of Calvin and Belvie Taylor (deceased). He enlisted in the service 19 Oct 1957 and after basic training at Fort Knox, KY, was sent to Fort Leonard Wood, MO.

In June 1958 he was sent to Badherdsfield, Germany. Discharged 19 Oct 1959. During the Berlin Crisis he was called to Fort Chaffee, AR, while in the USAR.

After the service he worked in Murray, KY. He married Sue Travis and they have four children: Connie, Carol, Celia and Chris, and several grandchildren. William passed away in Georgia in 1998. *Submitted by Mary Dell Thomas.*

ANDREW, BRUCE & CHARLES THOMAS, triplet sons of Hubert and Vada Thomas, were born 7 Aug 1937 in Detroit, MI, but were reared in Trigg County, KY. After graduating from Trigg County HS they enlisted in the Army 18 Feb 1959.

After armor training at Fort Knox, they were assigned to a unit at Fairbanks, AK. Since there were no other triplet brothers serving in the Army at that time, the triplets were exceptionally recognized and according to them, they took advantage of the situation. Bruce and Charles spent their time in the Army together and also played football for the Alaska Base team, while Charles chose to play in the Army Band. The brothers were discharged in February 1961.

After the service, Andrew and Charles continued to live in Trigg County. Andrew was employed by Pennyrile Rural Electric Co. for over 30 years until his retirement. He married Carol Bridges 8 Aug 1961 and they have three children: Debbie, Andrea and Steven. Grandchildren are Josh, Tanner, Dustin, Chase, Kelvin, Stephnie and Mathew. Andrew and Carol reside 5014 Canton Road, Cadiz, KY.

Charles was discharged 9 Feb 1961 and awarded the Good Conduct Medal. He continued to follow in his father's footsteps in auto repair. Charles' first marriage was to Martha Ann Myers in May 1958; she died in September 1962, no children. His second marriage was to Ellen McKinney on 23 Apr 1965. Their children are Mitzi Thomas Jones and Nick Charles Thomas (b. 13 Nov 1967, d. 13 May 1994) and grandchildren are Maegan Lynn and Morgan Lane Jones.

Charles was the first fire chief of the East Golden Pond Volunteer Fire Dept. and held the position 15 years. Charles, Ellen and family lived five miles from Cadiz for 31 years. He died with cancer 13 May 1996 and is buried in the Lucian Thomas Family Cemetery in Trigg County, a cemetery he and his brothers developed.

Bruce retired as president/CEO of Hopkinsville Federal Bank. After serving 38 years, he also continued to serve in the Kentucky Army National Guard for 35 years, having commanded an armor battalion unit. He retired with rank of lieutenant colonel. He was a graduate of Murray State University. His medals include the Army Commendation Medal, Army Meritorious Medal and Good Conduct Medal.

Bruce married Joyce 12 Jun 1960. Their children are Russell Bruce, Krista Haymes and Kelly Wesley. They have eight grandchildren. Bruce and Joyce reside at 32 Harton Place, Hopkinsville, KY. *Submitted by Andrew, Bruce and Ellen Thomas.*

BILLY "BUTCH" THOMAS, SP4, born 6 Nov 1939, son of Oscar and Willie Adams Thomas. He joined the service in February 1959 with assignments in Louisville, KY, Fort Benning, GA; Fort Campbell, KY, and 16 months in Germany.

He served with 937th Combat Inge. Group, 511th Engr., Co. PB. Discharged from the Reserve 24 Feb 1965. His awards include the Good Conduct Medal, Marksman Badge, Expert Badge and Sharpshooter Badge.

Married Polly Herndon in 1959 and they have two children, Patricia and Michael, and three grandchildren: Amanda, Logan and Haley. Billy is retired from Civil Service and resides in Trigg County, KY.

CHARLES B. "DONALD" THOMAS, SP4, born 4 Oct 1934 in Trigg County, son of Oscar and Willie Adams Thomas. He joined the service 18 Apr 1957 with assignments in Louisville, KY; Fort Meade, MD; Fort Knox, KY and 18 months in France. He was a heavy vehicle driver.

He was discharged 19 Apr 1959 and stayed in the Reserves until 17 Apr 1963. His awards include the Good Conduct and Sharp Shooter.

Married Donna Ellis (deceased) and they had three children: Kenith (deceased), Danny and Pam, and one grandchild. In the early 1980s he retired from Libby Ford and Glass in Toledo, OH. He lived in Trigg County, died in 1986 and was buried on Donaldson Creek.

LARRY THOMAS, born 13 Nov 1942 in Trigg County. He entered the Army in November 1959 and after basic training at Fort Knox, KY, he served three years with the 45th Artillery Brigade (Air Defense Artillery) at a missile site outside Chicago, IL.

He was discharged in November 1962 and is now a self-employed house framer. He has one son, Jason Thomas.

JAMES W. THOMAS, Sergeant (E-5), born 26 Mar 1940 in Trigg County. He joined the service 25 Feb 1959 in Louisville, KY and took his basic training at Fort Benning, GA.

Other assignments at Bamberg, Germany and Fort Campbell, KY. He was discharged 11 Apr 1962 and received the Good Conduct Badge.

Married Connie 17 Jan 1976 and they have four children: James, Mellissa, Stephanie and Casey, and four grandchildren: Heather, Justin, Eddie and Elizbeth. James is still working as a carpenter and cabinet maker and lives at 365 Donaldson Creek Road, Cadiz, KY.

WILLIAM H. "BILLY" TURNER, SP4, born 24 Mar 1938 in Cerulean, KY. He was drafted into the Army on 12 Sep 1961, during the

Berlin Crisis. After the completion of basic training at Fort Gordon, GA, he reported to Fort Stewart, GA where he was assigned to Co. "C," 169th Engr. Bn., (Construction). The primary duties of the battalion were to clean up contaminated areas and build roads and bridges for military activity.

While he never served in actual combat, his battalion was placed on alert during the Cuban Crisis. All personal belongings were either placed in storage or shipped home and military belongings were packed awaiting the order to move out; however, the Russian ships retreated before the final order had to be issued.

Specialist 4th Class Turner was honorably discharged on 11 Sep 1963, following the completion of a two year tour of duty. He returned to his home in Cerulean, KY where he rejoined his father, William J. Turner, in their farming operation.

He and the former Grace Martin of Lyon County were married on 7 Nov 1964. They have two children, Leslie T. Patterson, Cadiz, KY and Kendall W. Turner, Cerulean, KY, and three grandchildren: Shane, Sloane and Shaye Patterson, Cadiz, KY.

Billy is an active member of Cerulean Baptist Church where he has held various positions of leadership including deacon, Sunday school teacher and discipleship training leader. He is a member of Cerulean Springs Masonic Lodge #875, Cerulean, KY.

He currently resides in his hometown of Cerulean, where he continues to be actively engaged in farming with his son, Kendall.

CLYDE ROGER VINSON, Lieutenant Commander, after graduation from Trigg County HS in 1957, Roger spent one year at the University of Kentucky, then received a competitive Congressional appointment to the U.S. Naval Academy at Annapolis, MD. (His was the first Congressional appointment of any Trigg County High graduate to a Service Academy.) He was sworn in as a midshipman on 1 Jul 1958 and graduated four years later on 6 Jun 1962, with a BS degree in engineering.

He was than commissioned as an ensign in the USN and began flight training in July 1962 at Pensacola, FL. He did well enough in flight training to graduate first in his class from pre-flight (and to set a new record for the fastest time ever on the physical training obstacle course at NAS Pensacola) and be selected as student of the month for his flying skills. He was joined in the flight program by William Madison "Buddy" Thomas, his cousin and Trigg County High classmate, who had attended Vanderbilt on a football scholarship. Buddy had gone through ROTC at Vanderbilt and was commissioned as a second lieutenant in the USMC. Roger and Buddy completed their basic carrier qualifications on the same day in Pensacola—6 Jun 1963.

Roger finished advanced flight training in Corpus Christi, TX, and was designated a naval aviator in October 1963. After further training in navigation, nuclear weapons delivery, antisubmarine warfare, and with

the Replacement Air Group (VP-30), he reported to VP-5 at NAS Jacksonville, FL, in May 1964. His squadron deployed on numerous occasions to locations in the Atlantic and Mediterranean, flying the SP2E and then transitioning to the P3A. Roger became a crew holding plane commander in both aircraft, one of only two first-tour pilots in the squadron to do so.

At the end of his three-year sea tour in VP-5, Roger had completed his five years of obligated service, and he submitted his letter of resignation. However, the Vietnam War was in full swing, and all Naval Academy "regular" officers were ordered to spend an extra year on active duty.

Roger spent that year, 1967-68, as a flight instructor in VT-2 at NAS Whiting Field, Milton, FL. He left active duty in April 1968 in order to attend law school at Vanderbilt. While in law school he continued to fly in the Naval Reserves at NAS Memphis from 1968-71.

Roger returned to Pensacola in 1971 to practice law, and has served there as U.S. District Judge since 1983. Although his law practice prevented him from continuing to fly, he did eventually retire from the Navy Reserves as a lieutenant commander.

DONALD EUGENE WILLIAMS, SP E-5, born 20 May 1937 in Trigg County. He joined the Army 9 Dec 1959 at Louisville, KY and was stationed at Fort Campbell, KY with the 101st Airborne as a cook.

Discharged 7 Dec 1962. His awards include the Good Conduct, Parachutist Badge and Sharpshooter Badge.

Donald retired from TVA LBL Golden Pond, KY in 1994 and now builds furniture in his work shop. He married Carolyn Bridges 6 Jun 1964 and they live at 88 Beechy Fork Road, Cadiz, KY. They have one son Donald Scott Williams, grandchild Kalesha Williams and step-granddaughter Chasity Beth Graves.

CHAPPELL R. WILSON, Colonel, born in Trigg County, KY and graduated from Trigg County HS. He attended the University of Kentucky, graduating in 1960 with a degree in

economics. As a Distinguished Military Graduate in ROTC, he was commissioned a second lieutenant in Infantry, U.S. Army.

He reported for active duty and training at Fort Benning, GA in October 1960 at the U.S. Army Infantry Center. There he completed Infantry Officer Basic Course, Airborne School, and Ranger School where he was selected as the Honor Graduate.

His next duty station was Fort Jackson, SC where he was a training officer, instructor, and commander of an Infantry Company until October 1962. After leaving Fort Jackson, SC, he attended the Special Warfare School at Fort Bragg, NC and earned his Green Beret as Special Forces qualified with a skill identifier "3" added to his MOS. He attended the Infantry Officer Advanced Course at Fort Benning, GA, followed by Jumpmaster School at Fort Campbell, KY, and qualified as a airborne jumpmaster on C-130 aircraft.

Additional training included Command and General Staff College; National Defense Security Management Course, Fort McNair, Washington, D.C.; Armor Pre-Command Course, Fort Knox, KY; Air Assault School, Fort Campbell, KY; and Army War College, Carlisle Barracks, PA.

He has served as an Infantry Company Commander, Special Forces A Team Commander, various staff assignments at brigade and division level. He also commanded a battalion and a brigade in the Army Reserves while serving 28 years of active and reserve duty.

He retired from the Army Reserves in June 1990 with rank of colonel after commanding the 2nd Bde. of the 100th Div.

He is authorized to wear the Expert Infantry Badge, Senior Parachutist Badge, Ranger Tab, Special Forces Tab and the Air Assault Badge. Among his awards and decorations are the Army Commendation Medal, Meritorious Service Medal w/2 OLCs and the Legion of Merit.

Between active duty service and Army Reserve assignments, he attended the University of Kentucky School of Law where he earned his JD degree. He was in the private law practice in Cadiz, KY before serving 21 years as district judge. His wife, Jane Ellen Wilson, is a teacher at Trigg County HS and they live on Melwood Drive, Cadiz, KY. He is the son of Ray H. Wilson and Charlotte Cunningham Wilson, also of Cadiz, KY.

DONALD K. WOOD, SP4, born 28 Apr 1934 in Clinton County, KY and moved to Trigg County at the age of 2. He graduated from Trigg County HS in 1952 and Murray State in 1958. He left Trigg County to enter the Army 27 Feb 1958. After basic training and eight weeks of On-The-Job Training at Fort Hood, TX, he left in September 1958 by troop train to Brooklyn Army Terminal in New York to be shipped to Germany on the USS *Randall.*

He was assigned to Headquarters Co., lst Medium Tank Battalion (Patton) 32nd Armor, 3rd Armd. Div. (Spearhead), General George Patton's Old Army. The division was a part of the Seventh US Army in Europe and was the vanguard of the American Army as defender of the Fulda Gap, the historic invasion route into Western Europe. This vital assignment earned the Spearhead Division the title—Post of Honor in NATO.

Another duty of the division during some of the "hottest" days of the Cold War was to make sure that the Berlin Corridor remained open. Practice "alerts," coming about every three weeks, helped maintain a high state of readiness. Each "alert" was taken seriously and could have turned out to be the real thing. The 32nd Armor was located NE of Frankfort, Germany. Wood's job was to prepare a monthly payroll for two line companies (200 men). He also was player-coach for the battalion basketball team.

His older brother Eugene served in Korea during the Korean War and his younger brother Hugh was also in the Army.

He was discharged from service at Fort Dix, NJ 25 Feb 1960 with rank of SP4. He married Melinda Edwards in June 1963. Their children are Melissa, Jeffrey and Blake. Their grandsons are Taylor and Trevor Bradley. He retired from teaching at Fairfield high after 33 years where he also coached basketball, football, and tennis. Although retired from teaching, he still coaches the high school tennis team and is in his 38th season at Fairfield, IL. He likes to camp, fish, garden, do woodworking, blacksmithing and biking. He has biked across five states and adds one new state each year.

Wood says, "We who served, during the Cold War period would like to believe that had it been required of us, we too would have responded with the same duty and devotion that others did in those other times of greater peril."

Vietnam War

DAVID RONALD ADAMS, Sergeant E-4, born 4 Feb 1947 in Cadiz, Trigg County, KY. He entered the USAF 24 Jan 1967 at Louisville, KY. His MOS was SEC POL SPECL (dog handler).

Sgt. Adams was honorably discharged 16 Jan 1971 at Travis AFB, Fairfield, CA. His awards include the National Defense Service Medal, AF Good Conduct and SAEMR.

ROBERT A. ADAMS, better known as Bobby during school years, and later as Bob, was born in Cadiz on 12 Jun 1950. He graduated from Trigg County HS in 1968, and he attended Hopkinsville Community College. In December 1973 he joined the USAF. After basic training at Lackland AFB, TX and training at Lowery AFB, CO, he received orders for Myrtle Beach AFB, SC where he served from June 1974 until July 1981.

From July 1981 until July 1985, Bob was stationed at Sembach AFB, Germany. Upon leaving in July 1985 he received orders back to Myrtle Beach AFB, SC where he remained until the base closed in March 1993. In 1989 he spent six months at a remote location in Egypt, and in 1992 was sent to Saudi Arabia for seven months in support of Operation Desert Storm. After Myrtle Beach AFB closed in 1993, he received orders to Griffiss AFB, NY. In 1995 Griffiss AFB closed but Bob remained at Griffiss until December 1997 acting as an Air Force advisor to the New York Air National Guard.

In December 1997 he retired from active duty. His awards include six Air Force Commendation Medals, one Meritorious Service Medal and the Presidential Unit Citation Medal.

Bob married the former Laurette "Laurie" George from Hopkinsville, KY on 7 Nov 1970. He and Laurie have two children: daughter Jennifer, (b. 16 Sep 1974) and son Marc Ryan (b. 16 Apr 1979). Bob now works for the Central Association for the Blind as Director of Operations for Base Supply Stores.

FRANK T. ALDERSON, Master Sergeant, born 16 Oct 1932 at Paces, VA. He enlisted in the Army 20 Mar 1952 and received his basic and AIT at Indiantown Gap, PA. After basic he went to Fort Benning, GA for airborne training, graduating in September 1952.

His first duty assignment was at Fort Campbell, KY with the 11th Abn. Div. Other assignments included Fort Gordon, Korea, Fort Jackson, Alaska, Fort Knox and two tours in Vietnam, 1967-68 and 1969-70, one with 25th Inf. Div. and the other as advisor with the Vietnamese ARVN.

MSgt. Alderson retired from the military 31 May 1972. His awards include the Bronze Star w/V, Meritorious Service Medal, ACM, Army Good Conduct Medal w/loops, Korean Service Medal, Vietnam Service Medal, RVN Commendation Medal, Combat Infantry Badge and MP Wings.

Memorable experiences include Airborne School, Drill Sergeant School as instructor and combat in Vietnam.

After discharge he worked for a company in Cincinnati, OH for 16 years. In 1986 he and is wife Nina moved to Kentucky and he worked for the state of Kentucky 13 years before retiring again.

Frank and Nina married on 12 Sep 1953 and live in Cadiz, KY. They have three children: Terry, Frank Jr. and Kathy. Grandchildren are Terry, Derrial, Kelly, Andrew and Heidi.

BURTON R. ALDRIDGE JR., born 8 Mar 1949, son of Burton R. and Eldora Aldridge. He entered the USAF 25 Jun 1969 and had basic training at San Antonio, TX, June-August 1969; Technical School for jet engine mechanic training, Chanute AFB, IL, August 1969 to December 1969.

From December 1969 to February 1973 he served with the 26th Field Maint. Squad at Ramstein AFB, Germany. He continued schooling on GE J79-15 and GE J79-15 jet engines and worked as maintenance inspector. Transferred to jet engine test cell and installed and ran GE J79-15, GE J79-17, J57 Pratt-Whitney and J33 jet engines.

From February 1973 to April 1973 at Forbes AFB, Topeka, KS, he attended heating and air conditioning school. He was discharged 13 Apr 1973.

KENNETH LEE ALEXANDER, born 18 May 1949 at Futrell Clinic in Cadiz, KY. He joined the USAF in November 1968 and after basic and AIT training at San Antonio, TX, he was assigned to Blytheville, AR and remained there until November 1970. His next assignment was Suwon, Korea and Okinawa, Japan.

Kenneth returned home in December 1971 and on 1 Jan 1972 he married is high school sweetheart, Beverly Redick, at the Cadiz United Methodist Church.

He left for his next assignment 21 Jan 1972 in Minot, ND. Beverly flew to join him in February. They remained in Minot until November 1972. Kenneth served in the AF Reserves until November 1974.

The Alexanders reside in Trigg County. They have two sons, Barry Lee and Kenneth Brandon, and a granddaughter Victoria Leigh Alexander. Kenneth has worked for Bell South for 28 years and plans to retire in 2003. They are members of the Bethesda United Methodist Church.

JERRY WAYNE ALLEN, born 2 Oct 1948 in Cadiz, KY. He was drafted into the Army on 13 Jan 1969 and was in Co. B, 4th Bn., 1st Tng. Bde. and completed basic combat training as prescribed by ATP21-114 at Fort Campbell, KY on 14 Mar 1969. From boot camp he traveled to Army QM School at Fort Lee, VA and completed the unit and organization supply specialist and armorer course on 7 May 1969.

While at Fort Lee, VA, he tried to volunteer for Vietnam and enlist in the airborne unit, but was put on hold for 30 days waiting for orders. When his orders were sent he was sent to Atlanta Army Depot, Forest Park, GA for on-the-job training in depot operations for a total of 480 hours, June-September 1969.

Next assignment was overseas duty in Vietnam. He was stationed at Cam Ranh Bay as PFC, 14 months later as buck sergeant, than supply sergeant than platoon sergeant. His awards include the National Defense Service Medal, Expert M-16 Rifle, Vietnam Service Medal, RVN Commendation Medal and two O/S Bars. Vietnam service was from 15 Oct 1969 to 10 October 1970. He was discharged 12 Jan 1975 with rank of sergeant E-5.

Shortly after returning home, he enlisted in the 100th Div. Reserves, transferred to stand-by reserve and finally released with honorable discharge on 14 Aug 1980. He is very proud to be a Vietnam veteran.

He married Shirley Shaffer 5 Sep 1972 and they have one daughter Jeanna Sevy and two granddaughters, Mical and Taylor Sevy. They all live in Owensboro, KY. Jerry owns his own business of painting and wallcovering.

ROBERT L. ALLEN, born 24 Feb 1943 in Trigg County, KY, the son of the late John Taylor and Mary Askew Allen. He was drafted into the Army on 15 Mar 1965 and entered basic training at Fort Gordon, GA. He then went on to Fort Knox, KY for his advanced training in Supply and later to Fort Lee, VA for weapons repair training.

In September of 1965, he was stationed in Germany where he was company armorer of Co. B 2nd Bn., 4th Armd. Div. He was discharged 29 Feb 1967.

Robert married Linda V. Burgess of Cerulean, KY and they now live in Cadiz, KY. They have three children: Dion, Nathan, and Crystal, and three grandchildren: Melisa, Dalin, and Johnathan.

Robert has been employed with the U.S. Postal Service in Cadiz, KY since 1974. He enjoys spending time with his family and also going coon and deer hunting.

DENNIS C. BENTLEY, Staff Sergeant, born 21 Dec 1956 in Cadiz, KY. He enlisted 28 May 1974 in the USAF at Louisville, KY, the day after the Trigg County HS baccalaureate service. The Vietnam War was winding down.

He joined to learn electronics and to see the world. Upon completing seven months of electronics and telecommunications training, he was asked to stay at Sheppard AFB, Wichita Falls, TX for a three year assignment as an instructor of electronics. He took the opportunity of this assignment to complete a bachelor's degree from Wayland Baptist College. He was awarded rating of Master Instructor in 1976. He cross-trained into weather equipment repair, and was subsequently assigned to the airfield weather station at Fort Leonard Wood, MO. Dennis and his partner, the only members of their unit, were designated as Operating Location A, 1974th Communications Group, headquartered in Scott AFB, IL. For two years they maintained and repaired weather equipment in support of the base's Army helicopter and small plane missions as well as the airfield's civilian airport role. They were occasionally called in to run their loud 4WD Scout up and down the runway to chase the deer from the path of approaching planes.

After two years, he volunteered, and was as a drill instructor at Chanute AFB, IL, but those orders were cancelled to a three year billet as a communications equipment technician for the 2114th Communications Squadron, Misawa AB, Japan. Located in the northeast coast of Japan, hundreds of miles from the sprawling Tokyo area, it was a cold, wet, windy, though beautiful area, with a climate similar to that of Maine. The facility was a secure electronic information gathering complex with its ears pointed toward the sea of Japan and the Soviet port of Vladivostok.

While there, he did tour in South Korea, to learn the basics of maintaining IBM cardpunch equipment. After three cold, cold war years, watching from afar as the civilian world was steering away from traditional electronic technologies and toward computers, he decided in 1983, it was time to take his training and experience and jump into civilian clothes and this new technology.

Dennis and his wife Angela married in June 1992; they have four children: Matthew, Leslye, Andrew and Adam and one grandchild, Ashton. Dennis is network manager, Litton Interconnect Technologies, Springfield, MO, and lives outside of Willard, MO with his family.

STEPHEN R. BENTLEY, Staff Sergeant, born 21 Nov 1950 in Cadiz, KY, the son of Sammie and Hilda Bentley of Cadiz. He enlisted into the USAF on 2 May 1972.

After basic training in San Antonio, TX, and Radiology Technology training in Wichita Falls, TX, he was assigned to Homestead AFB, FL. During this period he saw the results of what war and conflict can do to the individual serviceman.

On a more humorous note, he recalls being summoned into the Homestead Hospital on a Sunday to do X-rays on two victims involved in an earlier fight. This was not an unusual occurrence except that it was no-

ticed that there had been transportation provided directly to the hospital parking lot by a helicopter, Upon entering the building. Steve was confronted by two blue-suited, non-military men, who immediately informed Steve of the crisis. President Richard Nixon's two dogs had gotten into a fight with each other at their home on Key Biscayne and had sustained possible injuries, including hip injuries. A high-ranking veterinarian, not appreciating calls on a Sunday morning, was also called to the hospital, Steve's lack of experience x-raying canines did not seem to bother the men with large funny bulges under their coats. As required by military procedure. Steve required the men to provide social security numbers on the military individual along with their rank. Thus, the film LDDS were imprinted with the names "Vickie and Pasha Nixon, dependent of Commander-in-Chief."

At the end of the Vietnam War Steve transferred to the Tennessee Air National Guard and received an honorable discharge with the rank of staff sergeant in 1977. While in the National Guard, he received his bachelor and master's degree from Western Kentucky University. He lived in Nashville for 14 years and directed his own staffing company. In 1989 he moved to Louisville, KY and married Donna in 1993. Steve has two children, Stephen and Christy. He completed his Ph.D. in psychology in July 2000 and currently works for Seven Counties Services as a Family Preservation Therapist.

JIMMY FLOYD BOREN, PFC, the son of Herbert Floyd and Mildred Louise Oliver Boren, was born 8 Dec 1946 in Hickman County, TN. The family later moved to Trigg County when Jimmy was a small boy. He enlisted in the Army on 17 Dec 1963. His basic training was held at Fort Benning, GA. He was assigned to Co. A, 1st. BN, 5th Cav., 1st Cav. Div.

He commenced his tour of duty in Vietnam on 16 Aug 1965. While there his company was attached to the 2nd Bn., 7th Cav. At X-RAY, one of the landing zones where the Battle of the Ia Drang Valley was fought. Jimmy was killed on 17 November.

Specialist Four Jack P. Smith, a supply clerk with Co. C, described the battle this way: "There were over 100 North Vietnamese snipers tied in the trees above us, so we learned later, way above us in the top branches. The firing kept increasing. We crouched and ran to the right toward what we thought was the landing zone. All of a sudden, all the snipers opened up with automatic weapons. There were PAVN (Peoples Army of North Vietnam) with machineguns hidden behind every anthill. The noise was deafening. Then the men started dropping. It was unbelievable. I knelt there staring as at least 20 men dropped within a few seconds." This account was written in the book entitled *"We Were Soldiers Once....And Young."* This book will be made into a movie and released in December 2001.

Jimmy joined the Army to as he put it, "to make something of himself," and I am sure he died a brave soldier. This was accomplished before he reached his 18th. birthday. He was laid to rest in the Boren Cemetery in Trigg County on 9 December, the day after his 19th birthday. Jimmy has one brother, Bobby Boren, who lives in Trigg County. He and his wife, Brenda have two children, Stacy and Jay. "Rest in Peace" Jimmy. *Above information submitted by S. Faris and Lois Rundle.*

DANNY GREEN BOZARTH, Staff Sergeant, born 9 Feb 1947 in Louisville, KY, while his parents, Charles and Sylvia Bozarth, were living in Grayson County. He joined the USAF on 25 Jul 1968, in Louisville, KY.

Danny attended basic training and Security Police School at Lackland AFB, in San Antonio, TX. From November 1968 to May 1969, he was stationed at Columbus AFB, MS, with the 4140 Squadron of the

Strategic Air Command (SAC). He returned to Lackland to attend Security Police Supervisors School and Security Police Combat School in May 1969.

On 17 Jul 1969, Danny left San Francisco, CA, for Vietnam. He served in the 377th Combat Security Police Squadron at Tan Son Nhut, AFB, Vietnam. He was a Combat Security Policemen, assigned to the Joint Defense Operations Center, Base Central Security Control Center and the Base Command Post during this tour of duty.

Upon return to the States on 16 Jul 1970, Danny was stationed at Whiteman AFB, near Kansas City, MO with the 351st Security Police Squadron where he worked in ICBM Missile Security. He later was assigned to the Security Police Training Flight where he taught various Military Police courses. He was also a member of the Base Color Guard.

His decorations included the National Defense Security Medal, AF Good Conduct Medal, AF Commendation Medal and the Expert Marksman Medal. Danny attained the rank of staff sergeant (E5) and received his discharge on 24 Jul 1972 at Whiteman AFB, MO.

Danny was married to Joyce Sanders on 16 Jun 1967. His hobbies include music, golf, and technology. He is currently the executive director of the Pennyrile Area Development, where he has been employed since 1976.

CHARLES KENNETH BRIDGES, Captain, born 6 Apr 1944 in Cadiz, KY, the son of Peyton Thomas and Ida Light Bridges. He has three siblings: Alfred W. Bridges, Keidell Bridges and Juanita Bridges Stephens. He graduated from Trigg County HS in 1963 and from Murray State University in 1967 with a BS in accounting.

He entered military service in October 1968 with a direct commission as a second lieutenant in the Army as a member of the Medical Service Corps, a branch of the Army responsible for the administrative services for the military medical branches. He initially trained at the US Army Medical Field Service School at Fort Sam Houston, in San Antonio, TX from October 1968 through December 1968.

He was subsequently assigned as the assistant registrar at the US Army Hospital, at Fort Campbell, KY from December 1968 through September 1970. In September 1970, he was promoted to captain and assigned to serve in the Republic of South Vietnam.

Captain Bridges served in the Vietnam War from September 1970 through September 1971. He was assigned as the registrar of the 95th Evacuation Hospital in Da Nang, South Vietnam. The 95th Evac was a semi-mobile army surgical hospital (MASH) unit located on the coast of the South China Sea. His main responsibilities included the maintenance of medical records for military patients, operation of the admissions and disposition office and the arrangement of air evacuation of injured patients out of the war zone. Captain Bridges was the recipient of the Army Commendation Medal and the Bronze Star Medal for service in the Republic of South Vietnam.

He was honorably discharged from the service in September 1971 and returned to civilian life. He moved to Nashville, TN and is married to the former Pamela Rowe. They have two daughters, Katherine Peyton Dee and Elizabeth Haley Bridges and one grandchild, Sarah Bridges Dee. Charles Kenneth is a certified public accountant and has worked for 30 years with the state of Tennessee, Division of State Audit, where he supervises a staff of approximately 200 auditors who audit all state departments, agencies, hospitals and colleges and universities in Tennessee. He considers his three years of military service a very rewarding experience and is proud to have been able to serve his country.

CLYDE TAYLOR BRIDGES JR., Specialist 4, born 26 Oct 1944 in Cadiz, KY and was drafted in the Army 15 Nov 1965. Stationed at Fort Knox, KY with duty as truck driver. Discharged 15 Nov 1967 and received awards for Good Conduct and Sharp Shooter.

Married Charlotte Lacy 6 Jun 1970 and they live in Hopkinsville, KY. They have two children, Angela and Jeffery, and daughter-in-law Valery (Milton) Bridges.

PAUL RAYMOND BROWN, served in the Army during the Vietnam War from March 1965 to March 1967. He received his basic training at Fort Jackson, SC, and attended Military Police School at Fort Gordon, GA. Having trained to be combat ready for Vietnam, his Military Police Company was sent to Tong Du Chon, Korea. There he served in the 7th Military Police Company, 7th Inf. Div. as a military policeman and supply clerk for the company.

After serving in Korea for 13 months, he was assigned to Fort Ritchie, MD, as a military policeman. He received a Good Conduct Metal, Expert Marksmanship Badge and an Honorable Discharge in March 1967.

He is currently a resident of Trigg County. He was born in Oak Grove, KY, on 17 Oct 1941 and graduated from South Christian High School in 1959.

He is married to Mava Cunningham Brown of Trigg County who is a Speech-Language Pathologist with Christian County Schools. They have one son, William Timothy Brown, a sixth grade student at Trigg County Middle School. Paul is the son of Emma L. Brown and the late Cordell H. Brown of Gracey, KY.

DANIEL G. BRUZEWSKI, born 24 Sep 1934 in Bay City, MI. He enlisted in the US Army 16 Jan 1953 at Fort Custer, MI. After Basic and advanced infantry training with the 31st Inf. Div., Camp Atterbury, IN, he was assigned to Selfridge AFB, MI, to help build missile and anti aircraft defense sites in the Detroit, MI area.

From Selfridge AFB, he was assigned to the 66th Ambulance Train Co., Nurnberg , Germany. Their mission was to transport military patients by rail throughout France and Germany.

Daniel's specialty was in the administrative and personnel field. He held positions as personnel specialist at Fort Leonard Wood, MO; administrative supervisor at Fort Sheridan, IL and Nurnberg, Germany; chief, Staff Message Center in Phnom Penh, Cambodia; student transportation coordinator at Fort Benjamin Harrison, IN; non-commissioned officer in charge of the Initial Receiving Point, US Army Training Center, Fort Campbell, KY; senior administrative inspector, Office of the Inspector

General, Fort Campbell and administrative supervisor and chief clerk in the Office of the Chief of Staff, Fort Campbell.

Daniel served in Vietnam during four counter offenses including the tet offense in 1969. He was the non-commissioned officer in charge of the Army Aviation Division, Army Concept Team in Vietnam. He conducted door gunner training for all unit personnel, and also served as door gunner for the Chief of the Army Aviation Division, logging over 100 hours flight time over hostile territory. His medals include the Bronze Star Medal, Air Medal, Army Commendation Medal w/OLC, National Defense Service Medal w/OLC, Vietnam Service Medal w/4 stars, Vietnam Campaign Medal w/device, Good Conduct Medal (5th awd), Meritorious Unit Commendation w/OLC. Daniel retired on 31 Jan 1973 with 20 years of service.

After his retirement from the US Army, he entered the insurance field retiring as general agent. Daniel returned to Fort Campbell, KY in 1982 as a civil service employee and retired as Chief of the Military Post Office in October 1993.

Daniel and his wife, Maria, built a home on Lake Barkley and have lived there since October 1995. They have two sons.

JERRY MARSHALL BURNAM, Corporal, born 27 Jan 1945 in Trigg County. He joined the USMC 8 Oct 1968, trained at San Diego, CA and Camp Pendleton, VA. He served as rifle instructor in 1969 then sent to Vietnam in 1970 where he was a MP with HQ&HQ Bn. 1st Marine Div.

He was discharged in 1970 and received the National Defense Service Medal, Vietnam Service Medal w/star and Vietnam Campaign Medal w/device.

Jerry went to work on the river for Ingram Barge Co. until retirement 1 Feb 2001 due to health problems. He married Bonnie Ruth Marquess in 1971 and has two children, Regina Burnam and Elish Riffee and two grandchildren, McKayla Calendao and Mathew Riffee. He lives in Cadiz, KY, where his mother, Lillie Gentry, resides.

WILLIS N. BURNAM, born 15 Sep 1943 in Cadiz, KY, the son of Sam and Eunice Burnam. He was drafted into the US Army in January 1964. After basic training at Fort Polk, LA and AIT at Fort Bragg, NC, he was transferred to Vietnam with the 68th Ord. Bn. where he completed his tour of duty. He was discharged in January 1966.

He married the former Linda Adams of Cadiz on 5 Jun 1965. They have three daughters: Kelly Mitchell (b. 17 Sep 1967), Kim Humphries (b. 24 Jul 1969) and Kristen Roberts (b. 21 May 1977). They also have seven wonderful grandchildren: Amanda, Lauren, and Thomas Broadbent; Stephen and Lydia Humphries; and Alex Keys and Emily Roberts. He now works at Fort Campbell, KY as quality control manager with J & J Maintenance Co. He and Linda reside on Streetland Dr. in Cadiz, KY.

DON G. BUSH, Colonel, born 30 Sep 1941 in Trigg County, was commissioned a second lieutenant in the USAF on 10 Feb 1964 at the University of Kentucky. He retired from the Air Force in February 1990 with the rank of colonel.

During his career, Col. Bush held numerous positions in the fields of procurement and contract administration. He served as assistant for Industrial Matters in the Office of the Air Force Assistant Secretary (Acquisition) at the Pentagon. Also while assigned to the Pentagon, he was Deputy Director, Air Force Contracting and Manufacturing Policy. Much of his career was spent at Wright Patterson AFB, OH. In one of those assignments, he negotiated and managed the contract for the purchase of the gun system, ammunition and related systems for the A-10 aircraft in its early stages of development. He also served as Chief of Production at the Defense Contract Administration center in Milwaukee, WI. Other assignments took

him to Bangkok, Thailand, Sacramento, CA, Mobile and Montgomery, AL, and Norfolk, VA.

His awards included the Bronze Star Medal, Legion of Merit, Meritorious Service Medal, Joint Service Commendation Medal, Air Force Commendation Medal and others.

He holds a BS degree from University of Kentucky and a MS from the Air Force Institute of Technology. He also attended Air War College, Armed Forces Staff College and Squadron Officer School.

Following his Air Force retirement, he served as assistant administrator for Procurement at NASA HQ in Washington, DC.

He and his wife, Janice, now reside in Hopkinsville, KY. They have one son, Stephan Bush, of Cincinnati, OH.

RAY BROWNING BUSH, born 31 Jul 1946 in Cadiz, KY. He joined the service 26 Apr 1968 at Atlanta, GA. Assignments include Seebees, Port Havana, CA; Da Nang, Vietnam; and VP-30 School Command, Patuxent River, MD

Ray was released to reserve duty 26 May 1972. His awards include the National Defense Medal, Navy Unit Medal, Vietnam Service Medal, Navy Achievement Medal, Vietnam Campaign Medal and Meritorious Unit Medal.

He works for the US General Accounting Office and lives in Decatur, GA. He married Jane McDonald 2 Oct 1971 and they have two children, Kevin Browning Bush and Angela M. McDonald Bush.

RONALD J. CAIN, Sergeant E-6, born 21 Dec 1943, son of Carl and Evangeline Cain. He graduated from Trigg County HS in 1961 and entered the USAF 4 Dec 1963. Basic training was at Lackland AFB, TX and aircraft maintenance training at Amarillo, TX.

His first permanent station was at Moody AFB, GA where he met Christine Pewitt, and they were married in September 1964.

In 1968 he went to Cam Rahn Bay, Vietnam. Everyone told him he was going to the safest base in Nam, but as his luck would have it, the base was hit the first night he arrived there. Other assignments were at Udorn, Thailand; Teague, Korea; and Eglin AFB, FL.

Accomplishments include being assigned the task of establishing the original deployment package for all F-15 aircraft and to make the first deployment of F-15 aircraft to Germany in 1980 successful

In 1981 at Teague, Korea he was assigned as flight chief and was in a methane gas explosion and sustained burns to 75% of his body. He was returned to Fort Sam Houston, TX and three months later to Eglin AFB for recovery. This led to 100% disability discharge in October 1982.

Sgt. Cain and his family returned to Cadiz in 1983 to live. They attend Canton Baptist Church. They have two children, Brett D. Cain and Cyndi Broyles, and four grandchildren: Alexander and Ashley Cain and Peyton and Morgan Broyles.

BARRY NOEL CALHOUN, E-5, born 21 Sep 1947 in Cadiz, KY, son of Bill and Mag Calhoun. He was drafted into the Army on 5 Oct 1966. After three months of basic training at Fort Campbell, KY, he was sent to Aberdeen, MD for 13 weeks of advanced training. In April 1967, he reported to Fort Bragg, NC to the 3rd Army 18th Corp Combat Abn. Bn.

There were very few men in the unit because it was a new airborne battalion, and they asked for volunteers to go to airborne training at Fort Benning, GA. In July of 1967, he went to Jump School at Fort Benning and returned four weeks later to Fort Bragg with his Airborne Wings.

Barry stayed at Fort Bragg until April 1968 when he received orders to report to the 173rd Abn. Div. in South Vietnam. While on leave before going to Vietnam, he married Deborah Hickman from Spring City, TN on 5 Apr 1968. He spent 13 months in Bong Song, Vietnam with the 173rd.

In May of 1969 he flew into Seattle, WA and was discharged from Active Duty as an E-5, having received the Army Commendation Medal and the Bronze Star.

After his discharge, he returned to his wife and parents. A short time later, he and his wife moved to Michigan where they still reside. They have three grown children and one grandson. Barry has been a sheet metal worker for the past 32 years.

JERRY LLOYD "BUD" CANNON, Specialist 5, born 10 Jun 1943 at home in Trigg County, KY to Lacy Lloyd and Mary Dell Guier Cannon. He enlisted into the Army on 6 Apr 1965 in Louisville, KY, sent to basic training at Fort Jackson, SC and Electronic School at Fort Devens, MA.

He was shipped to Germany to aid in Vietnam and was part of the Army Security Agency (ASA), working on maintaining all electronic equipment of the compound. By November 1967, he reached the rank of Specialist 5.

Returned to Fort Devens, MA in October 1968 and was honorably discharged 4 Apr 1969.

Bud married Bonnie Carolyn Faughn Gibbs on 12 Sep 1992 and they reside in Cadiz and are owners of Cadiz Heating and Air Conditioning.

LUTHER CLIFFORD CARNEYHAN, E-4, born 29 Dec 1947 and was drafted into the US Army on 13 Dec 1967. He completed his basic training at Fort Campbell, KY. Upon entering the service in February 1968, he served as a cook in Fort Mammoth, NJ until December 1968. After being stationed in New Jersey, he was assigned to the Vietnam War until his discharge in December 1969.

He returned home, with the rank of E-4, to his wife Mary "Carol" Hampton Carneyhan. They had married on 11 Feb 1967. He worked at a clothing factory in Hopkinsville, KY for a short time, then employed as a technician at Outwood State Hospital and School near Dawson Springs. He died 13 Nov 1973 of electrocution, at the age of 25.

Luther and his wife had two children, Gwendolyn Carneyhan Goodwin and William "Clifford" Carneyhan. Gwendolyn has two children, Cody Alexander and Mary Alexandra. Cliff has three children: William, Megan and Trevor. *Submitted by Amy Carneyhan.*

WILLIAM DAVID CARTER, SP4, born 22 May 1946 in Shelby County, KY to Kenneth Everett and Dorothy (James) Carter. He entered the US Army Security Agency 10 Nov 1964. David went to Fort Jackson, SC for basic training and to Fort Gordon, GA, to be trained as a 72B20 Communications Center Specialist.

His first duty station was 8th US Army Security Agency Field Station (8th Radio Research Unit) Phu Bai, South Vietnam, May 1965-June 1966. Next duty station was at 5th US Army Security Agency Field Station (83 Radio Research Unit), Mekhala Station, Bangkok, Thailand, July 1966-January 1968.

When he left Thailand David was assigned to the US Army Security Agency Vint Hill Farms Station, Warrenton, VA, January 1968-May 1968 and to US Army 82nd Abn., Fort Bragg, NC, May 1968 until his honorable discharge as a SP4 on 3 Sep 1968.

While David was in Vietnam, he worked as a security control clerk. In Bangkok he worked at a variety of jobs including security control clerk, supply clerk, and in the motor pool/generator shop as mechanic and truck driver.

Awards include the Armed Forces Expeditionary Medal, National Defense Service Medal, Vietnam Service Medal, the Vietnam Campaign Medal and Good Conduct Medal.

David attended Murray State University under the GI Bill and received a BS degree in business administration with area in accounting. He is presently employed by AgriVISIONS of Cadiz.

David married Donna Jane Creamer on 5 Jun 1969. They have two children, Robin Maureen (md. Ralph L. Stevens) and Russell David (md. Jesse Harrison). Grandchildren are Aaron and Brooklyn Stevens with two more expected in 2001.

David continues to work in accounting and with computers. He enjoys gardening, woodworking and watercolor painting. David and Donna currently reside on Floyd Sumner Road in Trigg County.

EDDIE EARL CHEWNING, Senior Master Sergeant (E-8), born 28 Mar 1949, the son of Lloyd Jackson and Missoula McKinney Chewning, both parents being from southern Trigg County. Eddie was born in Osaka, Japan while his father was serving there in the US Army. At the outbreak of hostilities in Korea in 1950, he and his mother were transported to the States where they resided with his maternal grandmother, Maude A. McKinney, on her farm in southern Trigg County. His parents purchased her farm in 1962.

Eddie joined the USAF in October 1969. After completion of basic training at Lackland AFB, TX and Technical School at Sheppard AFB, TX, he was assigned to Langley AFB, VA, as an aerial cargo delivery specialist. After spending one year at Langley AFB, he was transferred to Da Nang Air Base, RVN.

Returning to the States in February 1972, he was assigned to Malmstrom AFB, MT, as the non-commissioned officer in charge of the missile supply section. In June 1975, he and his family relocated to Richards-Gebaur AFB, MO, where he was retrained into the Life Support career field, remaining there until October 1975.

From November 1975 to June 1992, he had successive assignments as the Wing Life Support Superintendent at Bitburg AB, Germany; Holloman AFB, NM; K.I. Sawyer AFB, MI; Homestead AFB, FL; Keflavik AB, Iceland; and Malmstrom AFB, MT. In June 1992, he was assigned to HQ, Air Mobility Command, Scott AFB, IL, as the command's Life Support Superintendent.

He retired as an senior master sergeant (E-8) in November 1995, ending his 26-year USAF career.

Currently, Eddie works for the civil service as an inventory management specialist, managing flight control items for the Air Force's C-5 Galaxy cargo aircraft. His family maintains their land in southern Trigg County. His wife of 31 years is the former Elizabeth Ann Watson of Louisville, KY. They have two children, a son Brian who is in the USAF, and daughter Keli Lynn, a sophomore at Southwestern Illinois College in Belleville, IL.

HOWARD WESLEY COOK JR., CPO (E-7), born 13 Nov 1942 in Murphysboro, IL. He enlisted in the USN in St. Louis, MO on 6 Jun 1961. After completing basic training at Great Lakes Naval Station, IL, and Class A Yeoman School at Bainbridge, MD, he was assigned to the Navy Radio Station at Sabana Seca, Puerto Rico from November 1961 to October 1964. From November 1964 to December 1967, Petty Officer Cook was stationed at the Registered Publication Issuing Office, Charleston, SC. From January 1968 to November 1968 Cook was assigned to the Supplementary Radio Department aboard the USS *Little Rock* (CLG4) which served as the flag ship for the Commander, Sixth Fleet, and was home ported in Gaeta, Italy.

Upon returning to the States, Howard was assigned to the Signals Exploitation Division (OP-944) located in the Pentagon from December 1968 to February 1972 where he served as the administrative aide to the director. In March 1972 he was transferred to the Navy Radio Receiving Facility, Northwest, VA where he served as the education officer until

August 1975. During his tour at Northwest, VA, Howard earned an associate degree through the University of New York. From September 1975 to September 1978 he served as the administrative officer to the Special US Liaison Office, US Consulate, Melbourne, Australia. Duties included weekly briefings to the US Consulate General.

From October 1978 to August 1981 Howard served as an Armed Forces Courier stationed in San Diego, CA as station chief, delivering classified information throughout the southwest. From August 1981 until his transfer to the fleet reserve in November 1984 he was assigned to NAS Jacksonville, FL where he again served as an Armed Forces Courier, delivering classified material between stations located on the east coast, plus delivering material throughout the Southeast, the Bahamas and Turk Islands. Awards include a Joint Service Commendation.

The Cook's have resided in Trigg County since his retirement from the Navy. Since retiring, Howard has received a bachelor's degree at Murray State University, worked for Pennyroyal Mental Health Center as a case manager and therapist, and as a Family Services Clinician for the Cabinet for Families and Children. Though retired, Howard works part time at the Cadiz Baptist Church.

He and Virginia have been married since 1961 and have four children: Eric, Gina, Michelle and Adrian, and eight grandchildren: Jason, Christopher, Justin, Derrick, Christine, Candance, Amanda and Erin. His hobbies are geneology and exotic birds - breeds Cockatoos.

PHILIP S. CONNER, SP5 (E-5), born 18 Oct 1945, in the Oak Grove Community of Trigg County. He graduated from Trigg County HS in 1964, where he served as president of the Student Body during his senior year. He attended Murray State University and later Memphis State University where he received a BA degree in 1973.

Philip was drafted into the U Army on 27 Mar 1970, during the Vietnam War and received his basic training at Fort Bragg, NC. Following basic training, he was assigned to the 1st Administration Co., 1st Inf. Div. at Fort Riley, KS. He remained there until his discharge with the rank of Specialist 5th Class (E-5) in November, 1971. He was awarded the Army Commendation Medal for Meritorious Service.

On 4 Dec 1966, at Oak Grove Baptist Church in Trigg County, he married the former Jane Wyman of Sikeston, MO. She also attended Murray State University and graduated from Memphis State University. They have one daughter, Carole Lynne Conner, a graduate of Central Methodist College in Fayette, MO, and resides in Collierville, TN.

Philip is a member of the Longstreet United Methodist Church where he has been a Sunday school teacher; Chairman of the Board of Trustees; Chairman of the Committee on Finance; and for seven years, Chairman of the Administrative Board. He is a member of the Thomas-Bridges Association and Trigg County Post 74 of the American Legion.

In April 1966, Philip was a member of the original broadcast team for WKDZ Radio in Trigg County. He later moved to Memphis, TN, where his broadcast career spanned more than 20 years. A realtor since 1976, he is co-owner of Conner & Shirley, Realtors.

Philip and Jane now reside in Germantown, TN.

RICKY FAY COSSEY, SP4, born 2 Aug 1947 in Trigg County, son of Andrew Elvis and Earnestine (Snyder) Cossey Jones. He served with How. Btry. 1st Sq. 11th ACR and was killed in battle in Vietnam on 18 Dec 1968.

THOMAS "TOMMY" ELMER CREAMER, born on 17 Oct 1946 to Grover Douglas "Bubby" and Ell Maurine Cunningham Creamer. His birth marked the onslaught of the baby boomer generation. He was

born nine months and three days after his parents wedding date, and nine months and five days after Bubby returned from a 3-1/2 year combat duty in the Pacific arena of WWII.

Tommy was among the last class of elementary students to enter Lower Donaldson School. Two years after he started there, one-room schools in Trigg County were consolidated and students were bused to the old elementary school in Cadiz. The family moved to Lyon County in December 1958, and Tommy graduated from Lyon County HS in 1964.

Tommy was drafted into the Army and inducted on 18 May 1966. He made the first trip of his life to Louisville, KY to enter military service. After boot camp at Fort Knox, KY, Tommy completed 12 weeks of infantry radio mechanic training in Fort Benning, GA. He was cited as an M-14 rifle expert. Tommy pulled a one year and 26 day tour of duty in Korea rather than Vietnam, much to the relief of his family.

Tommy was honorably discharged on 17 May 1968 from Fort Stewart, GA. He was transferred to inactive duty in the Army Reserve until 17 May 1972. He married Marilyn Kay Kirby of Trigg County on 26 Jun 1970. They have two children, Thomas Grant and Kimberly Jo. Tommy and Kay have lived in Carmel, IN for the last 20 years. He is active both in his church and as a Gideon. He works in the accounting department at Fort Harrison, IN.

BUCKNER CRUMP JR., PFC, son of Buckner Sr. and Thelma (Wilson) Crump. A native of Cadiz, KY, he graduated from Trigg County HS in 1963. Drafted in 1966 he elected to serve in the USMC.

Basic and advanced infantry training was completed at Parris Island, SC, followed by duty in Vietnam. He died 7 Jun 1967 in the vicinity of Thua Thien, RVN as the result of injuries sustained from a hostile mine while on convoy. He is buried in Crown Hill Cemetery.

His medals include the Purple Heart, Vietnam Service Medal, RVN Campaign Medal, RVN Gallantry Cross, Unit Citation and National Defense Service Medal. *Submitted by Jane Ruffin.*

BILL CUNNINGHAM, Captain, born 15 Oct 1944 in Eddyville, KY, son of Almon and Estelle Cunningham, lived at Old Lock E in Trigg County with his three sisters shortly before they moved to Eddyville, KY. His grandparents and other ancestors are from the Rockcastle area of Trigg County.

Bill was drafted into the Army in 1969, but enlisted in the Judge Advocate General's Corps where he served for four years, being stationed in Germany, Vietnam and Korea.

While in Germany, Bill was assigned to the V Corps Headquarters at the historic I.G. Farben Building in Frankfurt, Germany. In Vietnam he served with various military units to include USAR V at Long Bien and Saigon and with the 17th Cbt. Avn. Gp. at Camp Holloway at Pleiku.

He was stationed in Vietnam at the time of the cease fire in 1973. Capt. Cunningham was assigned to the Four Power Joint Military Commission (JMC) which negotiated with the North Vietnamese and Viet Cong over POW exchanges and cease fire violations.

Bill left Vietnam 31 Mar 1973. He was on the last plane load of combat troops to leave Vietnam. (Not to be confused with the military unit attached to the US Embassy until evacuated from Saigon when it fell to the Communists in 1975.)

After serving in Vietnam, Bill was attached to the 38th Air Defense Arty. Bde. at Osan AFB, Korea. After discharge from the military in September 1974, Bill married Paula Trull of Charlotte, NC. They have five sons: John, Alec, Josh, Luke and Joe.

From 1974-76, Bill served as Eddyville City Attorney and Public Defender for inmates at the Kentucky State Penitentiary. In 1976, he was elected as Commonwealth Attorney for the 56th Judicial Circuit consisting of Caldwell, Livingston, Lyon and Trigg counties. In 1991, he was elected to Circuit Judge of the 56th Judicial Circuit, a position which he currently holds.

Bill has also authored several books to include *Flames in the Wind, On Bended Knees, The Night Rider Story, Castle, A Story of A Kentucky Prison,* and *Children of Promise.* He also authored the article *Goodbye Vietnam* published in the *VFW Magazine* in 1981. Bill and his wife live in Kuttawa, KY.

STEVIE D. CUNNINGHAM,

STEVIE D. CUNNINGHAM, Staff Sergeant, born 12 Jan 1952 in Trigg County. He enlisted in the Army 24 Jan 1974 at Nashville, TN with assignments at Fort Knox, KY; Fort Sam Houston, TX, Fort Campbell, KY, 2/503rd Inf.; KYNG, 1/123rd Armor, Hopkinsville, KY; Vietnam and Desert Storm.

SSgt. Cunningham retired 19 Apr 2002 from KYNG, Frankfort, KY. His awards include Army Achievement Medal, Good Conduct (4), Army Reserve Components Achievement Medal, National Defense w/star, Armed Forces Reserve Medal (2), NCOPDR (3), Army Service Ribbon, Air Assault Badge, Kentucky Merit Ribbon (2), Kentucky Commendation Ribbon (2), Kentucky State Active Duty Ribbon (4), Kentucky Service Ribbon (4), Army Commendation and Expert Medical Badge. Stevie served a total of 26 years.

Stevie and Cindy married in September 1975 and have three children: Benji, Mindy and Tiffany. They live in Cadiz, KY. His hobbies are car shows and NASCAR collection.

LAYTON DARNALL, born 1 Jul 1951 in Cadiz, KY, son of Irvin C. and Geneva Carr Darnall. He served in the USN from 1970-74. He now lives in Winamac, IN.

STEVEN CARR DARNALL, Lieutenant Colonel, born 14 Sep 1954, in Cadiz, KY. He was commissioned second lieutenant on 8 May 1976. After attending the Infantry Officers Basic Course and Airborne School, he was assigned to the 2nd Bn. 34th Inf., 24th Inf. Div., Fort Stewart, GA. During a three-year assignment, he served as a rifle platoon leader, support platoon leader, and company executive officer and completed training in the Army's Jungle Operations School (Panama) and Amphibious Warfare School, Little Creek, VA.

He returned to Fort Benning, GA for the Infantry Officers Advanced Course (and promotion to captain) prior to a three-year assignment to the 3rd Bn., 28th Inf., 8th Inf. Div., Wiesbaden, Germany. He served as the Battalion's Supply Officer and as Commander, A Co.

Upon return to the States, he was assigned as an instructor at the Ordnance Missile and Munitions School, Redstone Arsenal, AL. While

assigned there, he met and married Deborah Felker.

In March 1987, he was assigned to the Combined Arms Center, Fort Leavenworth, KS to a newly formed organization tasked to build Combat Training Centers for the Army. By 1989, three new Combat Training Centers were established to go along with the National Training Center at Fort Irwin, CA. These Centers were credited with training the Army of Desert Storm.

In 1990, he was assigned to the Multinational Force and Observers, Sinai, Egypt, with duty as liaison officer, Cairo.

He returned to the States in 1991, and rejoined his family at Fort Campbell, KY. Twice, he served as an assistant division operations officer, and as executive officer of the 1st Bn., 327th Inf. Regt., 101st Abn. Div. (Air Assault). He also deployed to Mogadishu, Somalia, from June to November 1993. During this tour of duty, he was exposed to combat and was promoted to lieutenant colonel.

In 1994, he reported back to Fort Leavenworth as an Instructor in the Army's Command and General Staff College. Over three years, he was an instructor to over 185 captains and was the Combined Arms & Services Staff School (CAS3) Instructor of the Year.

In 1997, he was assigned as an advisor to the 10th Bn. (CAS3), 100th Tng. Div. (Institutional Training) in Lexington, KY.

Steve retired on 1 Aug 2000, following 24 years of service. He and his wife Debbie have three children: Bradley, Lindsey and Jonathan. They live Lexington, KY.

THOMAS DAVIS, Colonel, born 6 Jul 1950 in Hopkinsville, KY. His military career began in September 1965 when his parents, Carey and Marian Davis enrolled him in Castle Height Military Academy in Lebanon, TN. Thus began his 32 years wearing a uniform of some type. His senior year at Heights he was offered a nomination to West Point, NY and entered in July 1968 with the Class of 1972.

His class spent four years preparing for Vietnam. But with the peace agreement right after graduation, they found themselves instead leading an Army that was dispirited and troubled. It quickly became apparent that their job was to restore and refresh a great American institution that had served the republic loyally since 1775, and had carried the heaviest burdens of an unpopular war.

He served in Germany throughout the mid-70s, earned a master's degree at Harvard, joined the West Point faculty, had a tense tour in Korea, then went to the Pentagon for his first tour working on the budget.

His high point occurred in 1990 when he took a 700-man artillery battalion into Operation Desert Storm. Having spent his early years with his parents there, going to Arabia was somewhat like returning home. His brother Tim had been born in Dhahran in 1957, but the major thrill was the performance of the Army in the ground war. Re-organized, re-trained and re-equipped after Vietnam, in a short 100 hours our troops made the fourth largest army in the world into the second largest army in Iraq!

He retired as a colonel in 1997 and now works in northern Virginia. But throughout those 25 years of active service, whenever someone asked where he was from, the answer was Cadiz, KY.

Marion and Nancy married 22 Jul 1972 and have two children, Nathan and Nicholaus. They live in Fairfax Station, VA, where he writes and lectures on defense budget and management.

ROBERT LYNN DAVIS, Master Sergeant, born 19 Dec 1939 in Convoy, OH. He joined the USAF on 17 Mar 1958 in Ohio.

Assignments were at Amarillo, TX; Itazuke, Japan; Wright Patterson AFB, OH; Shemya AFB, AK; Holloman, NM; Clark AFB, Philippines; Tan Son Nhut, Vietnam; McConnell AFB, KS; Hickam, HI; George AFB, CA; Korat, Thailand; Eglin AFB, FL.

Robert married Michael Lynnette Davis on 18 Jul 1961. They live on Kings Chapel Road and is still working at White Hydraulics in Hopkinsville, KY. They have three children: Robert Jr., Sandra and Nolan, and two grandchildren, Ethan and Seth. His hobbies are fishing, gardening and genealogy,

KENNETH LEE DIETRICH, Sergeant Major, born 19 Aug 1946 in Chicago, IL. Kenneth married Kathy in 1965 and by 1968 they owned and operated a very successful candy store in their hometown of Fox Lake, IL. Ken received his draft notice in April 1968, closed the store and left for basic training at Fort Leonard Wood, MO on 26 Jun 1968. Kenneth was made a cook and served for eight months in Maryland, then was given orders to leave for Korea on 15 Jun 1969. Kenneth was stationed on the DMZ with the 6/37th Field Artillery, Camp Casey.

Kenneth finished his tour and came home 15 Jun 1970. He and Kathy started the business again, adding an ice cream parlor and expanding to a second store. At the end of 1973 they decided to sell the business and try something else. Kenneth and Kathy joined the Army together and on 25 Feb 1974 they both headed to basic training. They were promised their first assignment together at Fort Hood, TX. As it worked out, they received joint assignments for the next 20 years.

Kenneth was a Food Service Specialist, Dining Facility Manager and finally a Food Service NCO. While in the service he completed his Associates degree in food management. He attended the Sergeants Major Academy and was promoted to sergeant major in January 1990. He was assigned to Fort Hood, TX; Miesau Army Depot, Germany; Fort Rucker, AL; 1st AD, Furth, Germany; Readiness Group, Aurora, CO; Sergeants Major Academy, Fort Bliss, TX; 543rd ASG Bremerhaven, Germany; 7th Inf. Div. (Light), Fort Ord, CA.

Kenneth was the Dining Facility Manager for the 123rd Maint. BN in Furth, Germany. Each year the Philip A. Connelly award is presented to the best dining facility in the Army. For three years Kenneth and his cooks competed for this award, each year scoring higher and higher. Winning best in Division, best in United States Army Europe and finally best in the Army in July 1984. Kenneth was sent to the Culinary Arts Institute in New York for two weeks and to Las Vegas for a week to attend the award ceremony. It was an unforgettable experience.

Kenneth retired on 31 Mar 1992 at Fort Ord, CA. He came to Trigg County in 1993 to build a home while Kathy finished her last tour. He started a canvas shop when he couldn't find anyone to make a boat cover and currently owns Skippers Boatique and Cadiz Canvas Shop on Hwy 68/80.

LAURA LYNN P'POOL DIETRICH, PFC, born 4 Jun 1943 in Trigg County, KY. She joined the service 27 Sep 1963 in Denver, CO. Basic training was at Fort McClellan, AL, followed by Fort Gordon, GA Signal Corps; Fort Richie and Fort Meade, MD as coder and decoder for NSA.

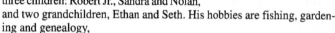

Memorable was working underground in man-made cavern at Fort Richie; working for the NSA at Fort Meade during Vietnam; meeting her Navy husband, Emory Eugene Dietrich, from the north (they were complete opposites) then losing him in an auto accident the same year; and working as nursing assistant at Fort Campbell, KY as a civilian.

Pfc. Dietrich was discharged 11 Jun 1965 and lives in Cynthiana, KY, where she is a community volunteer worker.

Laura has two children, Wallace Dietrich and Lynn Lee D. Felton, and three grandchildren: Sadee Rowe Dietrich, David A. Boone and Parker A. Felton.

HUGH EARLY DUNN, E-4, born 12 Jun 1947 in Trigg County, KY, son of Thomas Aaron Sr. and Eliza Pearl Thomas Dunn. He joined the service 19 Oct 1966 and served in Germany as heavy truck driver.

Hugh was discharged 28 Oct 1968. He lives in Cadiz, KY and is a self-employed logger. Hugh and Teresa married on 4 Jan 1980 and have two children, Christopher Aaron and Constance Amanda.

W. DALE EZELL, Staff Sergeant (E-6), born 22 Dec 1946 in Cadiz, KY. He was drafted into the Army and began training 12 Jul 1966 at Fort Benning, GA. After 16 weeks he was stationed in Munich, Germany with the 24th Inf. Div.

On 3 Jul 1967 he began a tour of duty in the RVN with the 3/34th Inf., 9th Inf. Div. "Mobile Riverine Force" based in the Me Kong Delta. During the 12 months served in country, he was directly involved in several operations to include the Tet Offensive that was initiated by the North Viet Cong 18 Apr 1968.

Returned to the States and discharged at Oakland, CA 3 Jul 1968 with the rank staff sergeant. His awards include the Vietnam Service Medal, Vietnam Campaign Medal, National Defense Medal, Combat Infantry Badge and Bronze Star Medal w/V.

In 1972 he joined the Active Army Reserve 100th Tng. Div. based in Louisville, KY with training stations at Fort Campbell and Fort Knox, KY. During a 25 year career with the 100th Div. his duty positions include tank commander of the M1A1 battle tank; drill sergeant for basic training; Co. training NCO and Co. 1st Sergeant.

He retired 14 Nov 1997 with 27 years combined military service. He now resides at 12 Jackson Terrace, Cadiz, KY with his wife Mildred. Married 33 years, they have two children, Eric Ezell and Emily Meyer, and two granddaughters Paige and Caroline Ezell. He says "I'm proud of this country and thankful for the freedom we all enjoy."

JERRY D. FARIS, MSG (E-8), born 26 Jan 1944 in Kennett, MO. He went into the US Army in May 1965 with basic training at Fort Leonard Wood, MO. He was drafted into the Army, but discovered he enjoyed the travel and challenges of military life. He served two 3-year tours in Germany and one year in Vietnam. His job descriptions were field artillery, aircraft maintenance and ground surveillance radar.

MSgt. Faris retired in 1985 at Fort Hood, TX. His awards include the Army Service Ribbon, Good Conduct (4), Over-

seas Service Ribbon (2), National Defense Service Medal, Vietnam Service Medal w/2 stars, Vietnam Cross of Gallantry w/Palm, Vietnam Campaign Medal, Overseas Service Bars (2), Meritorious Service Medal, NCO Professional Development Ribbon and Army Commendation Medal w/ OLC.

He married Sue Allen on 25 Jul 1968 and they live in Cadiz, KY. He delivers gas for Fortner Gas Co. His hobbies are golf and watching any sporting events.

BERYL FENTRESS, YN3/c, born 4 Jul 1944 in Louisville, KY. He joined the USNR in 1962 at Louisville, KY. Beryl graduated Louisville Male High, University of Louisville and worked for Kroger Co. before going on active duty in 1963.

Assignments included Bainbridge, MD and Moffett NAS, CA. He worked as yeoman (office clerk) for Commander, Fleet Air Wings, Pacific and did filing and typing correspondence for Admirals Staff. He also kept up with Navy Regs., distributed confidential and secret material to officers in his unit and drove for the admiral. Everything was fairly routine, behind the scenes type of work for P3A squadrons, but he did meet his wife while serving in California, and that was worth it all.

After his active duty stint was over, he worked in the postal service for 10 years and three years as mail clerk at Fort Knox. He entered the ministry in 1976.

Married Karen Marie Overton on 22 May 1965 and they live in Cadiz, KY. They have three children: Amy, Sean and Megan, and also two grandchildren (third on the way), Miles O'Connor and Logan Fentress. He enjoys reading, fishing, stamp and coin collecting, travel and working out.

PAUL CLINTON FINLEY, SPE-5, born 14 Feb 1950 in Cadiz, KY. He was drafted 26 Dec 1969 and entered active service 19 Jan 1970, Nashville, TN. After completing basic training at Fort Campbell, KY, he was transferred to Fort Ord, CA from April-September 1970.

Because of peace talks there was a hold put on deployment of soldiers to Vietnam, so he was sent to Oakland for two weeks than to Treasure Island for one week. When peace talks failed, he was shipped out with 5,000 other troops from Travis AFB to Long Bien near Siagon.

He was placed in the 20th Engrs., shipped to Can To in the Mekong Delta, transferred to Bien Tuy where he was attached to the 67th Engr. Co. The company was shipped to Vungtau on the coast of the Red China Sea where he remained until Christmas 1970. In January 1971 the 67th was shipped to Bien Tuy North (near Cambodia) and in September 1971 to Vin Long where he finished his tour of duty.

Left Vietnam 10 Oct 1971, landed in Oakland, CA and was discharged 12 Oct 1971.

He was relieved from terminal service 1 Jan 1976. His decorations include the National Defense Service Medal, Vietnam Service Medal, Vietnam Campaign Medal and Good Conduct.

Paul married Janice Paulette Hall on 25 Mar 1970 and they live in Cadiz, KY. They have two children, Kendell Lynn (md. Sandy Marie Freeman) and Lanny Everett. Paul worked for Boyd's Auto Parts and Repair, Kauffman and Broad Mobile Home Mfg. and US Tobacco Mfg., 1980 to present.

HERBERT R. FOLLIS, Corporal, born 20 Mar 1947 in Carrolton, IL. He enlisted in 1966 at Mt. Sterling, IL; trained at Camp Pendleton, CA; attended CBR School, Schofield Barracks, HI.

He spent 13 months, 1967-68, in Vietnam. The first three at Con Thien, four at FSB The Rockpile, four at FSB Camp Calu, and two spent in supply, civil affairs and MP.

Cpl. Follis received an honorable discharge 14 Apr 1969. His awards include National Defense Service Medal, Good Conduct Medal (2), Presidential Unit Citation, Vietnam Service Medal w/cluster, Vietnam Campaign Medal w/device, three Purple Hearts (one with device) and Marksman Rifle Badge.

Herbert married Laura J. Henninger 19 Oct 1968 and they have two children, Shelley Bunch and Bradford Follis, and three grandchildren: Katie and Magon Bunch and Lauren Follis. They reside in Cadiz, KY.

Civilian jobs include 29 years for US Army Corps of Engineers, Peoria Lock and Dam, Peoria, IL; Derrick boat operator; welder; president of Local 584 of the National Federation of Federal Employees; instructor for American Red Cross in CPR and firs aid. He enjoys building bird houses and fishing.

JAKE FOSTER, born to Joseph and Gertie Edwards Foster on 23 Mar 1934 in Duplin County, NC. He entered the Army Reserves in January 1951 and the US Army on 23 Oct 1953. He served two tours in Vietnam, 1965-66 and 1968-69. He received an honorable discharge from the US Armed Forces upon his retirement on 30 Jun 1975.

He continued his education at Coastal Carolina Community College in Jacksonville, NC and graduated with honors in 1978. He served as the maintenance supervisor for the Kentucky Parks System at both Greenbo Lake and Lake Barkley.

During his years in service the official records show that he received the following awards: National Defense Service Medal w/OLC, Sharpshooter Badge w/Pistol and Rifle Bars, Army Commendation Medal w/OLC, Good Conduct Medal (3), Vietnam Service Medal w/2 Bronze and one Silver Service Star, RVN Gallantry Cross w/Palm Unit Citation Badge, RVN Campaign Ribbon w/Device (1960), five Overseas Service Bars, Driver and Mechanics Badge with "W" Bar, Bronze Star Medal, and the Meritorious Service Medal. This official statement was issued on 4 Apr 1985 following his death on 24 Feb 1985.

Upon his death, President Ronald Reagan sent a Certificate of Honor in his memory "by a grateful nation in recognition of devoted and selfless consecration to the service of the USA in the Armed Forces of the United States."

He was married on 1 Jun 1961 to Mary Louise Sholar. Their children are Kenneth Anthony Foster (b. 19 Aug 1965), Jacqueline Foster Kennedy (b. 31 Jan 1970) and Catherine Michelle Foster (b. 16 Aug 1981). One grandchild has been born since his death, Heather Michelle Kennedy (b. 24 Feb 1994) to Jacqueline and Barron Kennedy.

LONNIE HAY FOWLER, born 22 May 1939 in Cadiz, KY, the youngest of nine children of Alice Thomas and Joe Fowler. He enlisted in the US Army on 29 Apr 1957. His basic training was at the 34th Field Artillery at Fort Carson CO. First assigned to Fort Leonard Wood, MO for training.

In September 1957, he was sent to Okinawa, where he stayed until 31 Mar 1960. Returning to the United States he was sent back to 643rd Eng. Co. at Fort Leonard Wood, MO, remaining there until 1962.

He spent 10 months in France with the 543rd Pipeline Co. Returning to the States to Ft. Leonard Wood until 1963. At this time he was assigned to Camp McDermott in Nhatrang, Vietnam for his first of two tours of the Vietnam War from 1965 until 1966.

He returned to the States and assigned to Fort Riley, KS, where he stayed until 1967, when he received transfer to the 593rd Sup and Service at Fort Wainwright, AK. He was then assigned to his second tour in Vietnam at Chu Lai from July 1965-70.

Returning to the States, he was assigned to Co. A, 3rd Supt. Bn., 1st Cav. Div. at Fort Hood, TX until 1972. He was then assigned to Schofield Barracks, HI from 1972-75.

Returning from Hawaii, he was sent to 426th Sup and Serv Bn., 101st Abn. Div. at Fort Campbell, KY, remaining there until retirement on 31 July 1977. After retirement he worked at Fort Campbell as a civil service employee until he retired 31 May 1999.

Having traveled the world, Lonnie and his wife Linda are now living in Biloxi, MS where Linda works in the military hospital. Lonnie and Linda have one son Lonnie (b. 15 Mar 1968). Lonnie had another son Russell (b. 6 Jun 1962, d. 8 Jun 1999) by another marriage.

BOBBY H. FREEMAN, Colonel, born 7 Feb 1935, Cadiz, KY. Schools attended include Army War College, Command and General Staff College, Army Installation Management, Field Artillery Officer Advanced Course, Fixed Wing Instructor Flight Examiner, OV-1 Instructor Pilot, Army Flight Training Courses, Special Warfare Counter Insurgency, Air Assault Course. He has BS degree, Murray State University, Murray, KY; MS, Florida Institute of Technology; Graduate School of Banking of the South, LSU.

Major Assignments: Garrison Commander, Fort Campbell, KY; Defense Attaché, US Embassy, Kathmandu, Nepal; Chief, Plans Division, Office Deputy Chief of Staff for Personnel, Washington, DC; Congressional Affairs Officer, Office Deputy Chief of Staff for Personnel, Washington, DC; Chief, Aviation Management, US Army Personnel Center, Alexandria, VA; Commander, 13th Avn. Bn., III Corps, Fort Hood, TX; Operations Officer, Project MASSTER, Fort Hood, TX; Commander, 117th Assault Helicopter Co., Long Binh, Vietnam; Commander, Aviation Detachment, USMA, West Point, NY; Flight Leader, 73rd Avn. Co., Vung Tau, Vietnam; Company Commander, 82nd Avn. Bn., Fort Bragg, NC; Commander, 8th Army Aerial Surveillance Detachment, Seoul, Korea; S-4, 101st Avn. Bn., Fort Campbell, KY.

Awards include Legion of Merit, Distinguished Flying Cross, Defense Meritorious Service Medal, Bronze Star Medal (2), Air Medal (16), Army Commendation Medal, Vietnam Cross of Gallantry w/palm, Vietnam Soldiers Medal 1st Class, Master Army Aviator Badge and Air Assault Badge, Army Staff Identification Badge. Col. Freeman retired 1 June 2000, Fort Campbell, KY.

Accomplishments: In 1965 he designed a system to refuel UH-1 Helicopters from OV-1 Mohawk fuel tanks at remote airfields in South Korea; designed a system and developed plans for the world-wide deployment of OV-1 Mohawk airplanes from Fort Hood, TX by one of his subordinate units; was instrumental in persuading the Vice Chief of Staff to designate aviation as Specialty 15 under the Officer Personnel Management System; started the first astronaut selection process for the Army when he learned that NASA Space Shuttle Program did not include candidates from the US Army.

He married Clarissa Jackson and they live in Hopkinsville, KY. They have three children: Gil Roberts, William and Robert, and three grandchildren: Clytie Roberts, Richard and Sarah Freeman.

Currently he is vice president, Bank of America Military Bank, part-time faculty, University of Kentucky, self-employed aircraft appraiser, farm and ranch owner and investor. He is active in numerous military, civic and professional organizations.

EWING FREEMAN, SP4, born 10 Apr 1944, fourth child of S.T. and Ora Armstrong Freeman. He was born and raised in the New Hope Community of Trigg County. He was drafted into the US Army on 21 Sep 1965 and did his basic training at Fort Gordon, GA. After basic training he was assigned to HQ&HQ Co. at Fort Gordon.

In July 1966 he was assigned to duty in Vietnam with Co. B, 228th Avn. Bn., 1st Cav. Div. (Air Assault). He served there for one year. His duty was keeping maintenance records on the Chinook Helicopters.

He received the Vietnam Service Medal, Vietnam Campaign Medal, National Defense Service Medal and Sharpshooter (Rifle M-14). He was honorably discharged on 24 Jul 1967 at the rank of SP4.

He married Bonnie Fowler on 4 Dec 1965. They still reside in the New Hope Community at 1310 New Hope Road. They have two sons, Dr. David Freeman and Dr. Todd Freeman, and two granddaughters, Kloe and Kelsee Freeman.

Since discharge from the Army, he has been self-employed as a plumbing and electrical contractor in Trigg County. He is also a part-time farmer and enjoys traveling in his spare time.

JESSE LOUIS FRYE SR., SP5, born 24 May 1949 in Louisville, KY and was drafted into the Army in April 1969 after graduating from Trigg County in May 1967 and becoming married to his Trigg County native fiancée, Connie Jo Oliver, on 28 Dec 1967. Their first son, Jesse Jr., was born 26 Sep 1968 also in Louisville where Frye was working at the GE factory when he received his draft notice.

He was sent to Fort Campbell, KY for basic training, then to Fort Sam Houston, TX for training to become a lab technician. He was never sent to Vietnam, although he witnessed its horrors while stationed at William Beaumont Army Hospital in El Paso, TX in the form of diseases and other medical atrocities. His job as a lab technician required that he assist in the study for remedies and cures for medical conditions that faced our overseas troops. He also was responsible for drawing blood from the local troops and the troops at Lackland AFB and preparing it for shipment to Vietnam and other places where our troops needed it. While he was stationed in El Paso his second son, Marcus, was born 4 Jun 1970. Jesse was honorably discharged 21 Dec 1971 as a Specialist 5.

Afterward, he moved his family to Hopkinsville, KY and began working at Jennie Stuart Hospital as a lab technician. He worked in Hopkinsville until 1978 when he went to Murray State University to obtain his bachelor's and master's degrees. He majored in agriculture.

He moved his family to Trigg County in 1981 when he began teaching agriculture, history and biology at Trigg County HS. He taught there until 1987 when he began teaching at Christian Fellowship High School near Benton, KY where he taught for two years, although he continued to reside in Trigg County.

Jesse surrendered to the ministry in 1982 and was ordained as a Southern Baptist preacher. He pastored Canton Baptist Church from 1983-85 and then pastored Victory Fellowship in Cadiz until 1989. He then obtained his nursing home director's license and pursued that career until he retired due to medical necessity in 1992.

He past away after a long illness in the Veteran's Hospital in Nashville, TN 13 Aug 1996. He is buried in Trigg Memory Acres. His sons and their families, which include Jesse Sr.'s four granddaughters: Hayla, Kanisha, Marcanah and Maylee, all reside in Trigg County.

TIM FUTRELL, Lieutenant Colonel, born 12 Oct 1948 at the Futrell Clinic in Cadiz, KY, the son of the late Ray and Jewel Thomas Futrell.

During his senior year at the University of Kentucky, Futrell joined the Kentucky National Guard on 24 Feb 1970. While in law school in Massachusetts, Futrell became a cadet at the Massachusetts Military Academy. He received an officer's commission in infantry at the Academy in June 1973. In 1975, he transferred to the Judge Advocate General Corps (JAG).

As an enlisted man, Futrell was activated to guard various National Guard armories in Massachusetts during periods of student unrest when several armories were burned. As a Reserve officer, Futrell served various stints at the Pentagon in Washington, D.C. where he provided legal advice as a member of JAG finance and trial teams. His final assignment was a staff judge advocate of the 332nd Medical Brigade, Nashville, TN, where he provided assistance in preparing the brigade for deployment in the Persian Gulf War.

Futrell retired as a lieutenant colonel in 1990 after serving 20 years and one day in the National Guard and USAR. He currently resides in Cadiz and Boston, MA.

BILLY JOE GARLAND, SP5 (T) Sergeant, born 23 Jun 1945 in Clinton, KY and moved to Trigg County soon after he was born. He enlisted into the US Army in 15 Oct 1965. Training consisted of two months regular basic military training, two months of AIT at Fort Jackson, SC, Field and Morse Code Radio Communications.

On 15 Apr 1966, PFC Garland was shipped overseas to 4th Bn., 57th Hawk Missile Battery at Bad Windchein, Germany. The Missile site was on top of one of the tallest mountains in Germany. Promoted to SP4 (E-4) in 1967, worked with supply clerk, mess hall, commo unit, and watched a lot of radar tracking, prepared for GI inspections.

In 1968, SSgt. Bastin took him to Ansbach to face the board to test for sergeant. The Board was made up of captains, majors, colonels and one presiding general. That was a very trying and nervous ordeal, but he passed.

In June 1968 he received orders to go to Vietnam. After a 30 day home leave, he left Nashville to Oakland, CA to Bein Hoa Airbase, Vietnam, bused by armored bus to HHC 79th Engr. and Transport Group at Long Bein Ammo Plantation. In 1968 the Viet Cong mounted an all-out attack to get the ammo stocks at Long Bein, fighting all day and all night until dawn, finally the Cobra Helicopters with their rockets broke the ranks of the VC and gave US the victory.

After four years of military life SP5 (T) Sgt. Garland received an honorable discharge in June 1969. He received the National Defense Medal, Vietnam Campaign Medal, Vietnam Service Medal and Good Conduct Medal.

Billy worked at several jobs until 19 May 1972 when he started at Ebonite Int'l, Hopkinsville, KY, and he continues to work there.

On 23 Oct 1972 he married Virginia Ann Morris and they have two children, Andrea Susan and Andrew Russell. They resides on Will Jackson Road.

JACK F. GIBBS, born 10 Feb 1941 at Owensboro, Daviess County, KY. He enlisted in the Marine Reserves in 1959 while in high school with basic training at Parris Island, SC.

February 1962 - Active Duty Air Force Tech School at Chanute AFB, IL; Pease AFB, NH October 1962- April 1964; Clark AFB, Philippine Islands April 1964-February 1966; air evacuated to Scott AFB. He was honorably discharged in April 1966

Married Joyce A. Midkiff on 1 Sep 1962 and they live in Cadiz, KY. They have three children: Bryan Keith Gibbs, Kecia Marie Gibbs

Whittaker, Kerry Allen Gibbs, and three grandchildren: Ashley Danielle Whittaker, Kelsey Elizabeth and Jenny Lee Gibbs. Jack and Joyce own Cadiz Antiques Mall, 34 Main Street, Cadiz.

DONALD C. GLADIS, Major, born 2 Jun 1934 in Cleveland, OH and commissioned a second lieutenant at Kent State University AFROTC on 20 Jul 1956. He entered active duty in February 1957 and was assigned navigator training at Harlingen AFB, TX. Upon receiving his wings, he traveled to Keesler AFB, MS for training as electronics warfare officer, graduating in November 1958.

Assigned to Bergstrom AFB, TX as a ground training officer and also flying duties in the B-52 as an EW. He flew numerous 25 hours airborne alert missions.

In March 1961 he received orders for B-58 training at Carswell AFB, TX, in the world's first supersonic bomber. He flew his first supersonic mission at twice the speed of sound on 21 Jun 1961. Upon completion of training, he traveled to 305th BW Bunker Hill AFB, IN as a B-58 defensive systems operator.

Received a regular commission as a 1st lieutenant in April 1962 and the following September promoted to captain. He met Mary Melloh in 1963 and they married 3 Apr 1965.

He acquired 1675 hours of flying time in the B-58 Hustler and was awarded the National Defense, Combat Readiness Medal w/2 OLCs and AF Commendation Medal for the period 1961-70, when the B-58 was retired from SAC's inventory.

Next assignment with 524th BS, Wurtsmith AFB, MI as a B-52 EWO; transferred in November 1970 to the 34th BS, Wright Patterson AFB, OH as B-52 EWO. Promoted to major in 1971, assigned a crew 13 Jun 1972 and made a six month TDY to join the war in Vietnam. He flew 62 Linebacker combat missions in Southeast Asia. He returned from Vietnam in October 1972 and was awarded the Air Medal w/3 OLCs, AF Commendation Medal w/OLC and the Vietnam Service Medal.

He was suspended from flying in November 1972 because of degenerative disc disease, then became a target materials control officer for the unit. He stayed in the job until March 1974, then attended Senior Director School and re-assignment to ADC and a two year tour in Australia. He served as senior director and SQ Chief Standardization and Training, 1974-76, when he had a heart attack and was medivaced back to the States and subsequently medically retired 24 Aug 1976.

Other decorations included the AF Outstanding Unit Award, Small Arms Expert Ribbon, Senior Navigator Wings, Missileman Badge and over 4000 total hours of flying time.

In November 1976 the family returned to their home in Brookville, OH where he got a job as a Disabled Veterans Rep at the Ohio Bureau of Employment Service.

After 22 years on the job he retired again and moved to Cadiz, KY in 2000 where they presently reside in Blue Springs Estates. Donald and Mary have four children: Jean, Elizabeth, Michael and Joseph, and one grandson.

PAUL RAY GODWIN, Sergeant, born 18 Feb 1952, in Pensacola, FL. He enlisted in the Army 14 Feb 1972, completed basic training at Fort Ord, CA, and was transferred to Fort Benning, GA, for special forces airborne training. He was then assigned to the 503rd Inf. Div. at Fort Campbell, KY, where he completed advanced infantry training in jungle tactics in preparation for Vietnam.

Paul re-enlisted with the rank of sergeant E-5, and was assigned to the Combat Support Company 503rd Inf. Abn. unit at Fort Campbell and served in this elite unit from June 1973 through February 1975. It was during this time he married Vicki DeName from Cadiz, KY.

In February 1975, Sgt. Godwin was transferred to Aschaffenburg, Germany, where he served with the 1st Bn., 4th Inf. Combat Support Co. A few months later, Vicki joined Paul in Germany for a three-year tour of duty. In October 1976, their daughter Shea Ann was born at the 97th General Hospital, Frankfurt, Germany. During Sgt. Godwin's tour of duty in Germany he served as Range Control NCOIC and NEO NCO, Arms Room NCO and squad leader in an anti-tank platoon.

In February 1978, he returned with his family to Fort Campbell, KY, serving in the 503rd Air Assault. Sgt. Godwin was honorably discharged in December 1978. His awards include the National Defense Service Medal, Parachute Badge, Good Conduct Medal, Expert Badge M-16 Rifle, Expert Infantry Badge, TOW Missile Teacher Qualification and the Army Commendation Medal.

Paul is a member of the Cadiz United Methodist Church where he has been a Sunday school teacher for 21 years. He is presently employed as a mail carrier with the US Post Office in Hopkinsville, KY.

BILLY DON GRANT, E-4, born 15 Oct 1957 in Hopkinsville, KY. He joined the USAF in October 1975 in Christian County. His assignments were basic training at Lackland AFB, TX, where he was an honor graduate; Lowry AFB, CO and Whiteman AFB, MO as a precision measuring equipment specialist.

He was discharged from the USAF in 1979 as E-4, and remained in the USAFR until 1984. He received the Good Conduct Medal.

Married Pamelia Lee Moore 19 Mar 1976 and they live in Cadiz, KY. They have three children: Shelly Malea, Aaron Christopher and Jamie Elizabeth, and one grandchild, Malea Jordon Lewis. Billy is a chiropractor. He is a Gideon and his family are members of Cadiz Baptist Church. He enjoys hunting, fishing, riding motorcycles, snow and water skiing.

JIMMY DOUGLAS GRANT, volunteered for service in the US Army National Guard on 8 Sep 1971. After basic training at Fort Knox, KY, he served seven years in the 123rd Armor Div. of the Kentucky National Guard at the Hopkinsville Armory. While in the National Guard his duties were cook and truck driver. His summer camps were spent at Fort Hood, TX.

Jimmy married Donna Marie Taylor on 15 Dec 1972 in Hopkinsville, KY. They have two children, Dana Grant Patterson and Crystal Grant. They reside in Christian County. Jimmy enjoys lots of hobbies, but his favorite is belonging to the Sons of the Confederate Veterans (Mose Gresham), and

he and his wife belong to the re-enactment group of Cobb's Battery. They travel to battle sites and re-enactments in the surrounding states. He loves genealogy and researching his family history.

RAY GRASTY, E-4, born 28 Jul 1942 in Cadiz, KY. He enlisted in October 1962 at Cadiz, KY with boot camp at San Diego, Avionics School at Memphis, TN followed by North Island, San Diego.

He was discharged as E-4 in October 1966 and received the Good Conduct Medal. Memorable was being a member of the Navy Drill Team and the many detachments to Hawaii, Puerto Rico and Japan.

Ray and Linda married 6 Jun 1969 and live in Cadiz, KY. They have one child, Darla Grasty Doss and two grandchildren, Devan and Derak Doss. Ray is still working in real estate development and sales.

JOE H. GRAHAM, Staff Sergeant, born 1 Jan 1943 in Chicago, IL. He joined the USAF in February 1966 at Louisville, KY. Assignment include Chanute AFB, IL; Da Nang AFB, RVN; Minot AFB, ND; Tet Offensive, Vietnam.

He remembers well the rocket attacks the VC made against the airbase at Da Nang, and especially the heavy attacks during Tet February 1968. SSgt. Graham was discharged in May 1970. He received the AF Commendation Medal.

He married Sylvia on 29 Jul 1971 and they live in Gainesville, VA. He is executive director of the National Rifle Association. Joe and Sylvia have four children: Marilyn, William Mary and Luke. Photography, hunting and golf are his hobbies.

WILLIE RAY GRANT, Corporal, born 26 Aug 1946 in Cadiz, KY. He was drafted into the USMC in July 1968 and went to basic training at Camp Pendleton, CA, 1st Amphibious.

Ray was soon shipped to Vietnam where he spent 11 months. He received a Good Conduct Medal and a Campaign Ribbon. Cpl. Grant was discharged in 1974.

Ray married Brenda Kelley of Princeton on 21 Dec 1969. They have three children: Kevin Ray, Kelley Marie, Amy Nicole and one grandson, Brice Whittington. They divorced in 1994.

Ray moved to Madisonville and works at G.E. Aircraft Engines Factory. He enjoys fishing and being a grandfather.

DANIEL RYAN GRAY, born 13 Jun 1946 in Trigg County. He enlisted in service 3 May 1966 at Great Lakes, IL and served in the Seebees at Gulfport, MS.

He was in lockdown for Vietnam due to go in four days when his father had a heart attack and he was discharged 31 Jul 1967. He received the Good Conduct Medal. Daniel was the only child out of 10 over 18 years of age and had to take over running the family farm until his father recovered. Daniel's father served in WWII and he also had to come home to keep the family farm going when Daniel's grandfather took ill.

Daniel married Sue Pho on 18 Dec 1976 and they have one child, Ben. He works in TVA maintenance. Fishing and hunting are his hobbies.

C. RAY HALL, Sergeant, born in Cadiz on 17 Dec 1946, son Noble Hall, a farmer, and Edna Adams Hall, a homemaker. (As a child, she won $10 in gold in a spelling bee.). He was named for uncles: Charles Adams, an Army private captured during the Battle of Bulge, and Billy Ray Adams, a Marine. C. Ray graduated second in the class of 1965 from Trigg County HS. He was president of the student council, but is better remembered for painting the wildcat in the center of the gym floor.

On 18 Nov 1965, he entered the USAF in Louisville and was a payroll clerk at Scott AFB, IL before leaving for Vietnam. He was at Cam Ranh Bay, a safe place - Officers lived in air-conditioned trailers and a beer cost a dime, the same as a Coke."

Another Vietnam memory: At the Bob Hope Christmas show, the Green Berets arrived. They were booed - mainly by other soldiers. Not all the people who questioned the Vietnam War were back home. Many were in Vietnam in uniform.

C. Ray was discharged as a sergeant 26 May 1969. By then, he had accumulated three stripes, five medals, and one injury: a broken ankle, playing basketball.

Using the GI Bill, he studied journalism at Oregon State University and the universities of Tennessee and Kentucky. He has been a writer and editor at *Inside Kentucky Sports* magazine, the *Lexington Herald-Leader,* and *AutoWeek* magazine. He joined the *Louisville Courier-Journal* in 1981. While on the *Courier's* Sunday magazine staff, he won the top national writing awards for the Gannett chain of newspapers in 1988 and 1990.

About that time, he was grand marshal of the Ham Festival parade, riding in a convertible piloted by Buddy Sivills, his childhood friend.

JOHN FRANCIS HALL, Lieutenant Colonel, born 29 Jun 1945. Enlisted in the Army June 1962 and completed infantry training at Fort Gordon, GA. During airborne training at Fort Benning M-1 rifles were loaded on the plane and he was told his next jump would be in Havana, Cuba.

After Cuban missile crisis ended he was assigned to B/I/327th Inf. 101st Abn. Div. Later he transferred to Honor Guard and security guard and served on classified missions all over the US and overseas.

He met his wife, Paula Andree Oakley, in Golden Pond. They were married at South Chapel, Fort Campbell, on 17 Apr 1965. They lived in Golden Pond until his enlistment ended.

John attended Murray State University under the GI Bill. In 1979 he received a Direct Commission as a 1st lieutenant in the Kentucky National Guard. He served in the 198th MP BN and commanded the 614th MP Co. in Murray. He was promoted to captain in 1984.

He transferred to the Army Reserves, 100th Div. He served on active duty during Desert Shield and Desert Storm on Fort Knox where he was promoted to major in 1991. He served as deputy inspector general for the 100th Div. for five years.

He transferred to the 85th Div. and served as Brigade Operations Officer. He was promoted to lieutenant colonel in 1998. He served as the inspector general of the 85th Div. until his retirement in December 2001. John received numerous awards and medals during a military career that spanned 39 years. He says, "My uncle and namesake, Pfc. Francis Race, was killed in WWII. He paid the price and gave his life for freedom is not free."

John was active in the Cadiz Lions Club and the Trigg County Historical Society. He attends Saint Stephens Catholic Church and serves as usher and writes for the ST Jerome Journal. John retired from the Kentucky State Police in October 1988. He works for the Kentucky Revenue Cabinet.

His wife, Paula, entered Civil Service in 1966 and she retired in 1997 as Chief of Admin Services of the Fort Campbell Army Hospital. They have one child, John Andrew, and three grandchildren: Andrea, Heather and John Andrew II. They reside five miles west of Cadiz in their Civil War era home.

JAMES E. HALLIDAY, Sergeant, born 21 Feb 1943 at Trenton, KY, the son of Earl and Louise (Standard) Halliday. In 1944 the family moved to Trigg County, KY, where he graduated from high school in 1961. He enrolled in Murray State College and received his BS degree in agriculture in 1965.

He joined the Army 14 Mar 1966 and some of the locations of his stations were Germany, Korea, Okinawa and Brussels, Belgium at SHAPE HQ in Secret Service assignments. He was a drill sergeant while stationed at Fort Benning, GA. His last base assignment was Fort Meade, MD.

Some of his awards are the National Defense Service Medal, Joint Service Commendation Medal, Vietnam Service Medal, Drill Sergeant ID Badge, Meritorious Unit Commendation, Meritorious Service (2nd OLC), Armed Forces Expeditionary Medal, Army Commendation Medal, NCOPD Ribbon, Overseas Service Ribbon, Army Service Ribbon, Expert Rifle M-16, Army Good Conduct (6).

After retiring in 1988, he lived in Pembroke, KY until 1993 when he moved to Trigg County, KY and had a log home built on land he purchased previous to his retirement. He lived in the basement while working on the upstairs rooms as he could.

He was never married and died suddenly on 12 May 2000. He was buried at Trigg Memory Acres with full military rites. He is survived by a sister and brother-in-law, Sara and Gene Moore of Cadiz. *Submitted by his sister Sara.* His hobbies were flowers, gardening, raising sweet potatoes and wild turkey hunting.

JERRY TAYLOR HART, Captain, born 12 Jun 1941 in Louisville when his father was earning his master's degree at Southern Baptist Theological Seminary. Jerry would see events such as the Vietnam War shape the time frame for his life. He earned his bachelor's degree at Union University in Jackson, TN, received his M.D. degree at the University of Tennessee Medical School in Memphis, completed his Internship at Methodist Hospital there, and then was sent to Okinawa as a commissioned Air Force officer in 1969.

Captain Hart lived with his wife and two young daughters, Susan and Amy, in a local civilian neighborhood for 22 months until base housing became available. Every military branch was represented on that strategic island, and everyone except the Marines could have their families. There were approximately 15,000 American school children living there in 1969, and school teachers for them were hired through the Department of Defense. (Dr. Hart's wife taught middle school and high school English the entire time.) Captain Hart was physician then to the entire family, which included people flying dangerous missions to Vietnam from Okinawa, such as those who flew the "Jolly Green Giant" helicopters, F-102 fighter planes, and C-130 cargo planes. Those missions were approximately 24 years after the significant Battle of Okinawa fought during the last months of WWII.

Before the 3-1/2 year tour of duty was completed, Capt. Hart was promoted to major and awarded the AF Commendation Medal for Meritorious Service. The honor was signed in 1972 by Lt. Gen. Gordon M. Graham, USAF, Commander.

With an Honorable Discharge on 18 Jul 1972 and his military duty completed, Major Hart became a resident in Obstetrics and Gynecology at the Medical Center of Central Georgia. That year his family grew to include a son, Taylor. Dr. Hart was chief resident his third year of residency. By the summer of 1975, Dr. Hart returned to his native state, Kentucky.

Dr. Hart has already delivered over 6,000 babies. He has practiced OB-GYN in Hopkinsville for over 26 years. This year he became a partner in OB-GYN Associates.

Finding a beautiful, peaceful location, Dr. Hart and his wife moved to Cadiz last year. The rural, scenic drive to his medical practice each day is enjoyable as a time for reflection. Significant among those thoughts is the pride he, as a war veteran, has in having served his country. Those years enabled him to gain insight that would help in all areas of his life.

This biographical data was presented by Barbara, his wife of 39 years. Hopefully, it will be meaningful to our grandchildren and great-grandchildren one day.

SIDNEY WAYNE HART, Lance Corporal, born 4 Jun 1948 in Cobb County. He enlisted in the USMC 27 Aug 1966 and served as a rifleman in Vietnam. He was assigned to Co. E, 2nd Bn. 27th Marines, 1st Mar. Div.

Cpl. Hart was discharged 30 Jun 1972. He received the Purple Heart, Vietnam Medal, Vietnam Campaign Medal w/device, Good Conduct Medal and National Defense Medal.

He married Laverne Coronado and they have two children, Kevin and Brett, and four step-grandchildren. The Harts live in Munro, LA.

JACK TURNER HENDRICKS, Senior Master Sergeant, born 9 Aug 1940 in Cadiz, KY. He enlisted in the USAF 15 Nov 1960, Madisonville, KY. After nine weeks basic training at Lackland AFB, TX, he was assigned to the 363rd Tactical Ftr. Wing, Shaw AFB, SC, where he remained until May 1966. He was then assigned to the 8th Tactical Ftr. Wing, Royal Thai AFB, Ubon, Thailand.

Returning to the US in May 1967, he was assigned to the 33rd Tactical Ftr. Wing, 560th CES, Eglin AFB, FL as an instructor. After a short stay at Eglin he was off to the 366th Tactical Ftr. Wing, Da Nang, RVN. A year later he was assigned to the 351st Strategic Missile Wing, 509th Missile Sqdn., Whiteman AFB, MO. A member of the Minuteman Missile Wing he held many positions—facility manager, instructor, inspector and was a member of the launch crew.

In 1979 he was assigned to the 8th Tactical Ftr. Wing, Tague AB, Korea; completing this tour with the 497th Ftr. Sqdn., he was assigned to SAC with the 97th BW at Blytheville AFB, AR. In 1992 he received a special assignment to Cairo, Egypt and the Middle East.

Returning to the States in 1983 he was assigned to the 375th Aerial Medical Airlift Wing at Scott AFB, IL. He returned to the Missile arena and in 1984 he was assigned to the 385th Ground Launch Cruise Missile Wing (NATO) at Florence AFB Belgium.

Returning to the States in 1985 he was assigned to the 23rd Tactical Air Training Wing at England AFB, LA. At England he served as the superintendent/firs sergeant of the 23rd Security Police Squadron from July 1985 until he retired 1 Sep 1987. He served 26 years, nine months and 16 days in the USAF. He retired with the rank of SMS.

Medals include AF Training Ribbon, Small Arms Expert Marksman Ribbon, MSM w/2 OLCs, AFCM w/4 OLCs, AFAM, AF GCM w/7 OLCs, NCO Professional Military Education Ribbon w/2 clusters, NDSM, OSR w/5 OLCs, VSM w/5 devices, RVN Cross of Gallantry w/palm, RVNCM, AFEM, PUC w/3 OLCs, AFOUA w/4 OLCs, Humanitarian Ribbon, Air Crew Wing Senior Missileman Badge w/star and Police Functional Badge.

He married Barbara Jean Bagby on 27 May 1961 and they have two children, Jeffrey and Beverley, and two grandchildren, Cail Knight and Aubry Michele Hendricks. He retired 1 Sep 1987 and lives in Hopkinsville, KY.

ROBERT "BOB" MICHAEL HERNDON, born 3 Feb 1947 in Cadiz, KY. His dad was born in the Canton area of Trigg County and his mother was born in Lafayette, Christian County and raised in Trigg County. Bob, like his dad, selected the USN, but his brother and nephew are US Army veterans. He can trace his roots back to the Sons of the American Revolution on his mother's side and the Sons of the American Revolution through the Herndon side as well. Bob enlisted in the USN 6 Jun 1967 in Paducah, KY and did basic training at Great Lakes, IL. He attended Basic Electricity School, Great Lakes, IL; Advanced Undersea Weapons School, Key West, FL; Nuclear Weapons School and US Naval Submarine School, New London, CT.

Bob served aboard the USN fast attack submarines, USS *Harder* (SS-568) and USS *Trigger* (SS-564) with most of his operations to the north Atlantic. This was during the cold war and Bob spent most of his time underwater chasing "enemy ships" and not being detected. In 1969 there was a lot of activity in the North Atlantic and the USS *Harder*, as well as all submarines, were constantly on patrol along our coast lines and north east to the North Atlantic. In 1969 he spent only 120 days on dry land and the rest of the time at sea. The last few months of his enlistment he was assigned to Subron Squadron 18, aboard the USS *Crayfish* (TWR-682) a torpedo retriever. Bob was third in command, officer of the deck, chief torpedoman and supply petty officer. The *Crayfish* was used to retrieve exercise torpedoes fired by submarines and to retrieve items fired from Fleet Ballistic Missile submarines.

Released from active duty 6 Jun 1971 at US Naval Weapons Station, North Charleston, SC, he returned to Murray, KY and graduated from Murray State University. He married a Graves County girl with roots in Trigg County (Futrells), Jen Elizabeth Brady on 12 Aug 1972 in Mayfield, KY. Bob and Jen have two sons, Christopher Michael and Joshua Brady. Bob has been in sales for over 20 years and is presently a senior industrial sales engineer for Fisher-Rosemount, Chanhassen, MN. His hobbies include SCUBA diving, sailing, restoring old cars, and genealogy. Bob, wife Jen and sons are currently living in Newburgh, IN.

MICHAEL T. "MIKE" HITE, born 25 Apr 1946, son of Clyde and Ola Hite, Cadiz, KY. He enlisted in the Army in August 1964, had basic training at Fort Knox, KY and AIT at Fort Jackson, SC.

He served in Baumholder, Germany from January 1965 to June 1966 and from July 1966 to January 1967 at Fort Riley, KS. He was discharged in August 1967 with the rank specialist E-5.

Mike drove for staff officers the entire three years in Germany and the last eight months in Thailand. He drove in and around Bangkok for officers and occasionally diplomats from Washington DC.

He was entered in a wide scale driving speed and proficiency competition in Thailand in 1967 with dozens of drivers from SE Asia. He set a speed record in the Drivers Rodeo Competition with the Army 151 (Jeep) and shattered the record by 1/3 time. He was welcomed by a special ceremony and plaque for first place in the competition—definitely his finest day in the military.

DONNIE HOLLAND, Captain, born 14 Aug 1949 in Murray, KY. He entered Murray State in the fall of 1967 in the ROTC program, and in 1969 signed up for the Advanced Corps. College campuses were ablaze with protests.

He attended a six week Advanced Corps Training Camp in the mountains of Pennsylvania the summer of 1970. The training that summer centered on Vietnam and there were mock Vietnam villages for practice. He took the first flight of his life in a "Huey" chopper practicing air assault missions with his "buddy" George James from Mayfield at his side. The Parrots Beak Invasion of Cambodia occurred while they were in camp. Back at school protests heated up. The ROTC buildings were burned to the ground at Western, and at UK and many other colleges across the country.

Murray's ROTC building, Wrather Hall, was assaulted, but not burned. However, the WWII display tank in front of the building was burned and destroyed.

Dr. Sparks, president of MSU, organized a campus wide meeting the spring of 1970 for *Moratorium Day*. He felt an organized event might prevent further trouble on campus. Donnie was invited to speak along with many others. There were antiwar activists, hippies, war supporters, preachers, Vietnam vets, professors, and even a Hell's Angel gave talks that day, along with him. He talked about his concern for the troops on the ground in Vietnam and the effect all this was having on them. He had several friends already KIA, and the guys returning alive were generally demoralized.

He graduated and received his "Gold Bars" the summer of 1971. He trained at Fort Campbell, KY, and Fort Gordon, GA. In early 1972, President Nixon started the pull out, combat for Americans ended January 1973.

His class at Fort Gordon learned they would not go to Vietnam. They were the first of the last. It was a shock! They had been trained for so long on every conceivable method of toasting yellow men, but it was also a great relief.

The Army was in chaos, as it rapidly downsized, RIFF's were issued in masse. He had a few months left at Fort Gordon to finish his basic obligation. In early August 1972, he was discharged as lieutenant and in 1978 from the Reserves as captain. Awards include the National Defense Medal, Expert Rifleman Badge and Advanced Corps Ribbon.

Returned to Cadiz, and shortly resumed his job at Hoover. Soon, everyone was home except for his friends, Ricky, Jimmie, Jerry Ray and Buckner. Stop and see them on the plaque at the courthouse. Tell them thanks and that they did a good and brave job.

Donnie and Shelia married in February 1971 and have two children, Darla and John. They live in Cadiz, KY.

HAROLD CURTIS "CURT" HOLMES, born 28 Aug 1944 in Jacksonville, FL. After living in Florida, the family returned to Atlanta, GA, and Curt graduated from College Park HS in 1962. He was working for Eastern Airlines when he joined the Army on 13 May 1966, and 10 months later he was commissioned 2nd lieutenant at Fort Sill, OK. His first duty station was Fort Hood, TX, where he served with the 1st Armd. Div.

In January 1968 he was sent to Vietnam. While in Vietnam he served in the 1st Inf. Div. and the 23rd Arty. Group as forward observer and later executive officer of the Firing Battery. He arrived back in the States in January 1969. He resumed his pursuit of a college education and graduated from Georgia State University in 1973 with a business degree. He first married in 1969. This marriage lasted only four years and produced a daughter who lives and teaches school in Nashville, TN. On 26 Jan 1974 he married a Trigg County girl, Susan Upton, and in April 1975 Jason Holmes was born. The family moved back to Trigg County in December 1979.

Curt works in Mayfield, KY for Mid America Machine as general manager. He and his family are members of Maple Grove Baptist Church where he is song leader and Sunday School Superintendent. He is a member of the VFW Post in Hopkinsville and the American Legion Post 74 in Cadiz. You can usually see Curt carrying the flag in the Christmas and Ham Festival Parades.

JAMES E. HUGHES, Sergeant E-5, born 5 Mar 1948 in Cadiz, KY, a son of Luther Bertram Hughes and Edna Thomas Hughes. He was drafted into the Army on 11 Mar 1968.

He received basic training at Fort Campbell, KY and AIT at Ft. Dix, NJ, then assigned to the 3rd Inf. of The Old Guard, Fort Lesley J. McNair, VA, where he continued to train and learn The Old Guard ceremonial procedures.

The Old Guard is an elite group who not only guard the "Tomb of the Unknown Soldier" but also participate in ceremonial services. While in this group James marched in the parade on 20 Jan 1969 commemorating the Inauguration of the 37th President of the United States, Richard M. Nixon. James participated in arrival ceremonies at both the White House and the Pentagon in Washington DC.

He received certificates for his participation in the burial ceremonies of Former President Dwight D. Eisenhower and Senator Everett Dirksen. One of the most solemn duties of The Old Guard was conducting military funerals in Arlington National Cemetery. The Old Guard assisted in approximately 1,000 funerals each year.

Upon his Honorable Discharge on 10 Mar 1970, James was awarded a Certificate of Achievement for his exceptionally meritorious service as a member of Co. A, 1st Bn. (Reinf), 3rd Inf. (The Old Guard). The award read in part "Sergeant Hughes proved himself an able and proficient soldier and non-commissioned officer. His performance was marked by the highest standards of leadership and devotion to his duty. He was a great credit to his company through his pride in his work, willingness to assume responsibility, and knowledge of his job as platoon sergeant. Sergeant Hughes' approach to training, standards as a non-commissioned officer, and grasp of the principle of prior planning have been a great credit to himself, Co. A, The Old Guard, and The US Army.

When James was drafted into the Army in 1968 he was employed by Economy Cee Bee Food Store in Cadiz. When he returned to Cadiz in

March 1970, he resumed his position at the grocery store and is now store manager.

He married Amelia Jo Shemwell 20 Apr 1973 and they have one son, James Luke Hughes (b. 7 May 1979), and they currently reside in Bumpus Mills, TN. James enjoys auctions, flea markets and collecting antiques.

BOBBY JOE HYDE, born 28 Jul 1949 in Lyon County, KY. He moved to Trigg County in 1950 and has lived in Trigg County the rest of his life.

He was drafted in the Army on 10 Sep 1968, trained at Fort Campbell for two months, then went to Fort Eustis, VA to Aviation School.

Sent to Vietnam 20 Feb 1969 and served in the 1st Inf. Div., 1st Avn. Bn. While in Vietnam he received the National Defense Service Medal, Vietnam Campaign Medal, Army Commendation Medal and Vietnam Service Medal.

He received an Honorable Discharge 20 Apr 1970 and returned to Trigg County. He went back to work at Hoover Universal, which is now Johnson Control, where he works as a maintenance-electrician.

He married Kathy Littlejohn from Caldwell County on 5 Sep 1970 and has two children, Tammy and Brian. Today he resides in Trigg County on Highway 139 North where he has a farm and raises cattle. He belongs to the Caldwell Blue Spring Baptist Church.

FOSTER W. JENKINS, Major, born 20 Apr 1939 in Northumberland, NY. He joined the Army 15 Jan 1958 and was stationed at Fort Campbell, KY in the 101st Abn., 1958-61.

Foster was assigned to National Security Agency at Fort Meade, MD. He went to OCS in 1966 at Fort Sill, OK, remaining there until 1968 when he went to Vietnam. He was injured three times and medivaced back to the States in June 1969.

He returned to Cadiz to recuperate with his wife and children, then assigned to the Officers Career Course, Fort Sill, OK. From 1970-73 he was stationed in Baumholder, Germany and from 1974-78 at Fort Benning, GA. While there he had several commands and was officer in charge of the National Infantry Museum until retirement in June 1978.

Maj. Jenkins awards include the National Defense Service Medal, Bronze Star w/V and OLC, Vietnam Service Medal w/4 stars, Vietnam Campaign Medal w/60 Device, two Overseas Bars, Parachutist Badge, Purple Heart w/2 OLCs, two Good Conduct Medals, Armed Forces Reserve Medal and Meritorious Service Medal.

He married Barbara Wadlington 25 Jun 1960 at Liberty Point Baptist Church. They have lived in Cadiz, KY since 1978 and have three daughters: Pamela, Kathy and Teresa, and four grandchildren: Steven, Christina, Kathleen and Pauline. Foster retired from the Cadiz Post Office 20 Apr 2001. His hobbies are golfing, hunting and gardening.

FRANKLIN DELANO JOHNSON, born 16 Sep 1935 in Jenkins, KY. He was drafted into the Army 21 Jun 1960. After basic training and 10 weeks medical training at Fort Sam Houston, TX, he was assigned to the 36th Med. Bn. in Hanau, Germany. Franklin returned to Germany in 1964 and again in 1972 for two additional tours respectively in Hoechst and Frankfurt, Germany.

He also served two tours in Vietnam. His first tour was with the 4th Inf. Div. in the Central Highlands in Pleiku, Vietnam where he ran a battalion aid station. His first tour was from 1968-69.

Franklin states that his most interesting duties included treating the Montanard (called "mountain yards") villagers that had diseases most American doctors had not seen for almost a 100 years. An excellent example was in applying water buffalo manure to severe lacerations and wrapped with a dirty rag. On Wednesday's he would assist the battalion surgeon in treating the leper colony located between the military base

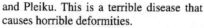

and Pleiku. This is a terrible disease that causes horrible deformities.

From 1969-70, Johnson served his second tour in Vietnam and was assigned as a medical advisor in the delta region just off the South China Sea, where all the villages were extremely isolated. The nearest contact with US military was six hours away, (radio contact was available).

Military Advisor Teams consisted of five military personnel and an interpreter, with each member having a specific area of expertise in which they were responsible for training the local forces (actually the villagers). The medical advisor was responsible for all aspects of medical training to include the Vietnamese medic and the villagers living in the outpost.

Retired 31 Jan 1985 at Fort Campbell, KY. Awards include the Combat Medic Badge, Bronze Star, National Defense, VN Service Medal w/ 4 stars, ARCOM and several others.

He married Kathleen Johnson 26 Nov 1974 and they have six children: Vicki, Franklin Jr., Jason, Sheena, Athena and Roseleen, and one grandchild, Bryce Dillon. Franklin is a medical assistant in civil service at Fort Campbell, KY and lives in Cadiz, KY.

CHARLES W. JONES, BUC, born 25 Sep 1954. He attended Golden Pond School for three years. On 12 Jul 1963 they moved from their home in the Pleasant Hill area Between the Rivers to a farm where his mother still resides. He graduated from Trigg County HS in May 1972.

He enlisted in the USN 20 Apr 1973 and after completing boot camp at Great Lakes, IL, was stationed at Port Hueneme, CA, where he attended Builder A School. He was then stationed at Gulfport, MS with the USN Seabees in NMCB133.

His first tour of overseas duty was at Camp Shields, Okinawa for two months. He went with a detail of 18 men to an AF base in Misawa, Japan where they installed an arresting gear on the runway for pilots to practice landing on an aircraft carrier.

Returned to Gulfport, MS for six months; to Guantanamo Bay, Cuba, where they built a bowling alley and handball courts; back to Gulfport for Builder C School, learning to build bridges, piers and docks; then in January 1976 to Fort Drum, NY for cold weather training.

His next tour of duty was to Diego Garcia, an island in the Indian Ocean. This island was used as a supply base for the B-52 bombers during Desert Storm. It is located 500 miles south of India and seven degrees below the Equator. They completed a new chow hall (that the group before them had started) and started a new three story barracks.

He was released from active duty on 19 Mar 1977 and on 31 Oct 1986 enlisted in the Naval Reserves. Some of the places he has been to include Pensacola, FL; New Orleans, LA; Bessemer and Huntsville, AL; Camp Lejeune, NC; Malaysia, Korea; Italy; Germany; Haiti; Sigonella, Sicily and Roosevelt Roads, Puerto Rico.

On 1 Dec 1990 he returned to active duty during Operation Desert Storm where they supported the First Marine Div. in Saudi Arabia and Kuwait. He was released from active duty on 18 May 1991.

In 1994 he was selected as the Naval Reserve Sailor of the year for the Nashville, TN, Reserve Center. He presently holds the rank of BUC (builder chief petty officer).

He does maintenance work for TVA at Kentucky Dam and does other construction projects in his spare time. He attends Blue Spring Baptist Church and lives on a small farm in the Bethesda Community where he raises registered black Angus cattle.

RONALD EDWIN KELLER,

RONALD EDWIN KELLER, SP4, born 6 Jul 1945 in Trigg County, the son of the late J.E. Keller and Loraine Owen Keller. He entered the Army 17 Jan 1966 at Nashville, TN and went to Fort Benning, GA for his basic training then to Fort Belvoir, VA for active training.

Assigned to the 5th Maint. Bn. USAREUR AUG RDY GP APO 09189 in Pirmasens, Germany for 18 months. His active duty was completed 14 Dec 1967 when he transferred to USAR CON GP (ANL TNG) USAAC, St. Louis, MO with the terminal date of reserve obligation to 16 Jan 1972. He received the National Defense Service Medal.

In civilian life Ronald is a part-time farmer and works as an associate at American National Rubber. He married Carolyn Jones 26 Sep 1980 and they reside in Cadiz, KY. They have one son, Michael Edwin. Ronald enjoys singing, church work and gospel music.

JAMES RAGON "ROD" KENNEDY, born in Trigg County in 1941. He served on active duty in the Army, 1963-65, as a medic. His basic training was at Fort Polk, LA where he was assigned to Co. L, 2nd Tng. Regt. (BCT) and AIT School at Fort Sam Houston in San Antonio, TX where he graduated and earned his MOS as an Army Medic.

After training he was reassigned to Fort Knox, KY with duty at Ireland Army Hospital. On several occasions, he was sent with crews for medical evacuation of sick and injured soldiers at many destinations throughout the world, including Vietnam.

From high school graduation in 1961 until entering the Army, Rod was employed in auto service station work. When he returned to civilian life, he resumed his employment in service station work for "Toppy" Edwards, then Earl Carr, then went into business for himself, first at the station by the local hospital, and finally to the one in East Cadiz. He remained in service station work until a disabling stroke in 1994 forced him to close his business permanently.

After Rod was treated for the initial effects of the stroke, he became a resident at Trigg Manor Rest Home. He now entertains his fellow residents at the Manor from time to time by singing spiritual hymns, and he joins in singing when attending church at Hurricane Baptist where he is a member.

All of his life he has been a friendly and caring person and loves to laugh and joke with his friends. His many friends cover a wide spectrum of people: blacks, whites, rich and poor. A person cannot be too poor or too down on life's misfortunes to be his friend. He often did work on credit, receiving only a promise to pay.

When Rod was forced to close his service station, he had thousands of dollars "on the books" from credit he had extended to his fellow man due to the kindness of his heart. He really has practiced the Christian rule of being the Good Samaritan to countless numbers of people over the years.

Rod has one son Jamie Reid Kennedy (b. 1974) and he and his wife Kelly are big into rodeo bull riding events. Jamie and Kelly made Rod very proud by making him a grandfather of Koy Reid Kennedy (b. 2000). *Submitted by Rod's loving brother, Ken Kennedy.*

KENNETH H. KENNEDY, Lieutenant Colonel, born during WWII in 1943 in Trigg County, KY, he has been a part of the US Army since the fall of 1962. He began as an officer cadet, 1962-1967, active duty 1967-75, then served in the Kentucky Army National Guard until his retirement in 1995 in the rank of lieutenant colonel. An Army board is now considering him for promotion to the rank of colonel.

Kenneth earned his commission as a second lieutenant in 1967 at Indiantown Gap Military Reservation, PA. Upon completion of advanced ROTC from Murray State University, being in the top 1/3rd of his ROTC graduating class, he was designated a Distinguished Military Graduate and as such was granted a Regular Army Commission.

He was then selected as one of 40 officers from 1600 applicants nationwide to be in the Army Excess Leave Program which allowed him to attend the University of Kentucky College of Law for preparation as a member of the Judge Advocate General's Corps—the Legal Branch).

After graduating Law School in 1970, he attended and graduated from the Basic JAGC course for Army Lawyers at the Army JAGC School, located on the grounds of the University of Virginia Law School in Charlottesville, VA. He completed the JAGC Advanced Legal Course then later the General Staff Course.

After completing his civilian and military basic legal education, he was assigned to duty at Fort Campbell, KY as an army lawyer in the Staff Judge Advocate's Office. He served in that capacity from 1970-75 when he resigned his commission when invited by Kentucky Governor Julian Carroll to join his personal staff in Frankfort, KY.

During his assignment at Fort Campbell, he served in the 101st Abn. (Air Assault) Division JAGC Office holding virtually every army lawyer position included at the Division Headquarters level including legal assistance officer, trial counsel (military prosecutor), defense counsel, then chief defense counsel, consumer judge advocate, plus running the post Claims Office, a separate office with a separate staff. He was then selected as the first Military Magistrate under the newly instituted Military Magistrate Program. When he completed his duty at Fort Campbell he was one of the few from that JAGC Office to receive the Army Commendation Medal.

While at Fort Campbell, he was granted permission to teach Aviation Law as an adjunct professor for Embry-Riddle Aeronautical University.

When he moved to Frankfort in 1975, he immediately joined the personal staff of the commanding general as senior legal officer in the JAGC section of the KYARNG HQ and served as the head Army JAGC

He moved in the fall of 1976 back to Cadiz to open his private law practice and continued to commute back to Frankfort to the KYARNG HQ. He was able to continue his military service in the NG even after being elected as County Attorney for Trigg County in 1981.

Kenneth is proud of other family members who have served their country. They include brothers Lucian Kennedy, USA, WWII in Occupied Korea, 1945-1947; Carroll "Mack" Kennedy, USMC, 1951-52; Robert L. Kennedy, pres. of TCHS Class of 1951, USMC, 1951-66, including the Korean War and a tour of duty in Vietnam, then eight years in KYARNG during 1980s and James R. "Rod" Kennedy, USA, medic, Fort Knox, 1963-65. Nephews: Warren Fred Kennedy, USARNG; Clayton Timothy Kennedy, USMC, four years active duty, then balance of career as Armor Officer in KYARNG; Marc Anthony Terrell, USARNG, during 1980s-90s with duty during Desert Storm War in 1990. First Cousins: Albert Mitchell Kennedy, of TCHS, USN, at least four years, including 1951 and John Lewis Kennedy, TCHS Class of 1956, USA, two years, December 1960-1962.

Kenneth thanks and praises his Heavenly Father for bringing himself and all family service members home alive and well.

During Constitution Day Celebration in Trigg County on 17 Sep 1991, Kenneth was honored when asked by the local DAR to deliver a patriotic speech to the local citizens. Kenneth summarized his love of country and passion for serving his nation by concluding his speech to the courthouse yard crowd with these words, words paraphrased from a familiar English song being sung all over England during WWII:

"There will always be an America
And America Shall be Free
If America means as much to you
As America means to me."

MILLARD KING JR., Corporal, born 28 Jun 1945 in Trigg County, KY. He was drafted into the USMC 16 Nov 1965 in Trigg County and had boot camp at Parris Island, SC; infantry training at Camp Geiger, NC, then stationed at Camp Lejeune, NC for a few months.

Received orders for Vietnam and landed at Da Nang in September 1966 as replacement troops. He reported to 7th Engrs., 3rd Mar. Div. who served as support for 3rd Bn., 7th Marines and 2nd Bn. 1st Marines in that area.

In early 1967 he was transferred to Chu Lai to the 1st Mar. Div., 9th Engrs. They supported different infantry units of the 1st Mar. Div., kept roads cleared of mines and participated in various operations, 1966-67.

Cpl. King was discharged 31 Oct 1967 at El Toro, CA. His awards include the National Defense, Vietnam Service Medal w/star and Vietnam Campaign Medal w/device.

He returned to his home on Rock Castle Road and in 1968 returned to work for John Woodruff Construction, TVA LBL. When on these jobs he was in the Operating Engineers Local #181. For the past 20 years he is owner/operator of King Construction.

He met Lavern Dycus in early spring and they were married 21 Jul 1968. They have three sons: Christopher, Matthew and James, and live in Princeton, KY. Millard is the son of Millard King Sr. and Georgia King.

JAMES SAMUEL LANCASTER JR., Sergeant E-5, born 20 Oct 1944 in Trigg County, KY, son of James Samuel Lancaster Sr. and Louise Light Lancaster. He graduated from Trigg County HS in 1963 and entered the Army on 10 Sep 1967. Basic training was at Fort Benning, GA and AIT at Fort Polk, LA.

In 1968 he was sent to Vietnam and fought with the 1st Air Cav. Div. After his tour of duty in Nam, he was sent to Fort Carson, CO and honorably discharged 26 Jul 1969 as sergeant E-5.

He returned to Trigg County and graduated from Murray State University. In 1977 he was employed by the city of Cadiz as the city clerk and still in that position.

Jim is single. He comes from a large family of brothers and sisters with several nieces and nephews. Jim enjoys walking, reading, tennis and golfing.

WILLIAM MONROE LANCASTER, E-4, born 6 Feb 1950 in Trigg County, KY, son of James Samuel Lancaster Sr. and Louise Light Lancaster. He graduated from Trigg County HS in 1969 and enlisted in the Army in April 1973. Basic training was at Fort Jackson, SC and AIT at Red Stone Arsenal, Huntsville, AL.

Monroe was a Hercules Nike Missile Launcher repairman and voted outstanding student of his missile repair class at Huntsville. He was stationed in Neubrooke, Germany for his final tour of duty and honorably discharged in April 1975.

Monroe returned to Trigg County where he graduated from Western Kentucky University with a BA in business administration in 1976. Since 1977 he has been employed as purchasing manager with the W.E. Stephens Co. in Nashville, TN.

He married Brenda Sholar in 1975 and they reside in Clarksville, TN. Monroe has a step-son, Chris Wallis, and two grandchildren, Blake and Brooke Wallis.

JAMES MARION "JIM" LARKINS JR., the only son of James Marion Larkins and Ann (Alexander) Larkins, was born at the Futrell Clinic in Cadiz, KY, on 25 Feb 1944. During WWII, when Jim was 9 months old, his father was killed in action in France.

Jim attended the University of Louisville on a Navy scholarship and graduated in May 1966 with a degree in mathematics and a minor in physics, and commissioned as ensign. On 5 Jun 1966, he entered Flight School in Pensacola, FL, and became carrier qualified in March 1967 aboard the USS *Lexington*. After completing multi-engine training in Corpus Christi, TX, Jim received his Pilot Wings on 25 Aug 1967. In October 1967, the Navy ordered Jim to Patrol Squadron 31 (VP-31) in San Diego, CA, for replacement air training (RAG) in the P-2V aircraft. He then joined VP-42, which was deployed to Sangley Point, Philippines; flew 130 hours of Market-time patrols off the coast of Vietnam.

In September 1968, the squadron returned to VP-42's home base at Whidbey Island, WA.

Just prior to VP-42's next deployment, the squadron was decommissioned, and Jim received orders to Corpus Christi, TX, as a multi-engine flight instructor. After seven months, he received orders to the Naval Postgraduate School in Monterey, CA.

In March 1973, Jim received a MS degree in Operations Research, was sent to Moffett Field, CA, for RAG training in the P-3 aircraft, then deployment in Naha, Okinawa, for six months before returning to VP-4's home base at Barbers Point, HI.

During the next deployment to Cubi Point, Philippines, in 1975, Vietnam fell. The following month, the Cambodians seized the cargo ship *Mayaquez*. Jim's crew located the ship off the coast of Cambodia and remained on top until other US forces arrived.

In 1976, he moved to Norfolk, VA, and Fleet Composite Squadron Six (VC-6) as the Operations Officer. After three years, he returned to VP-4, by way of the RAG. During this tour of duty, Jim was assigned as the Officer in Charge of detachments in Diego Garcia, Indian Ocean and Adak, AK.

His final tour of duty in the Navy was with the Strategic Targeting Center at Offutt AFB, Bellevue, NE.

In June 1986, Jim retired with 20 years and over 4400 pilot hours. He now lives in Pensacola, FL, and works for the city of Pensacola.

On 21 Oct 1967, he married Ruth Ann Knight. They have two children, James Marion Larkins III and Suzanne Marie.

WILLIAM GORDON LAWRENCE, Captain, born 23 Jan 1940 in Trigg County, KY. He was commissioned a 2nd lieutenant after graduating from Western Kentucky University in 1962. On 23 Jun 1963 he reported to Fort Benning, GA to complete the Infantry Officer Basic Course.

He was assigned to the 2nd Bn. 36th Inf., 3rd Armd. Div., Kirchgoens, Germany, where he served as a platoon leader, communications officer, adjutant, and company executive officer during his 32 months there. During this time the 3rd Armd. Div. held 30 day summer and winter training exercises each year. Normally there was two to three feet of snow on the ground during the winter exercises.

In 1965 he was assigned to I Corps' Military Assistance Command, Da Nang, Vietnam as advisor for the training of Regional and Popular Forces Troops. He was senior advisor of a team which included an Australian warrant officer, US Army and Marine sergeant.

Lawrence was released from active duty 15 Aug 1967. His final discharge was 29 Aug 1974 as a captain. He earned the Expert Infantryman Badge, National Defense Service Medal, Vietnam Campaign Medal, and the Vietnam Service Medal.

William married Carolyn Turner of Cerulean, KY on 19 Aug 1961. They have three children: William G. Jr., Mark Stanley, and Steven David. They have been blessed with 10 grandchildren, William G. III, Derrick, Amanda, Jaye Lyn, Tyler, Andrew, Cassidy, David, Kelsey and Alexander.

His most memorable experience was leaving his wife, who was expecting their third child in six weeks, and two small sons for duty in Vietnam.

Upon release from active duty William returned to Cadiz where he sold insurance for a year, was employed By Trigg County Farmers Bank for 23-1/2 years before returning to the insurance business. He and his wife Carolyn, a retired teacher, reside on Highway 272 in Trigg County. They are active members of the Bethel United Methodist Church. Their favorite activities are spending time with their grandchildren.

KENNETH L. LUNTE, Corporal, born 5 Jul 1948 in St. Louis, MO. He was drafted into the US Army but volunteered for the USMC in 1969. After 13 weeks of boot camp in San Diego, CA at MCRD, he was sent to Vietnam in the areas of Quang Tri Providence with Hotel Co., 2nd Bn, 3rd Mar. Div.

This area consisted of Dong Ha Mountain, The Rockpile and Mutter's Ridge. All of which were free fire zones and your enemy was the hardcore NVA (Northern Vietnamese Army).

When the 2nd Bn. 3rd Mar. Div. was pulled out to go to Okinawa, because of lack of time in country, he was sent to Echo Co., 2nd Mar. Div. to complete his tour. This area was in Quang Nam Providence in the Da Nang area.

The 1st Mar. Div. was at Marble Mountain. He served the areas of Liberty Bridge, Go No Island and Leper Ville where they dealt with the "invisible enemy" of the Viet Cong and their booby traps.

In 1971, he returned to San Diego to serve as a brig guard in the military police with the B&S Battalion, completing his active career at the rank of corporal.

He remained in the USMC Reserves until 1977 participating in various training, one taking him to Norway for cold weather training.

After returning home to St. Louis, he resumed his job with Hussmann Refrigeration. He also met and married a Trigg County girl, Alice Hall, who was living there. They married in 1972 and moved to Kentucky in 1978 due to a job change. Ken and Alice have two sons, Ben and Zac, and one granddaughter, Hailee.

HENRY ELLIS MARTIN SR., Lieutenant, born 6 Dec 1955 in Cadiz, KY, son of Harrison Martin Jr. (veteran) and Bertha Venus Kirby Martin. He has five siblings: Harrison III, Tony, Price (veteran), Helena M. Radford and George. He is the grandson of the late Benjamin Harrison Martin and Helen Froman Martin, and the late George Kirby and Marjorie Irvin, all of Cadiz. Henry graduated from Trigg County HS in 1973. He was a member of the Beta Club, DECA (officer), and a member of both the 1971 and 1972 TCHS Class A State Championship Football teams.

In April 1973, he enlisted in the USNR in Hopkinsville, KY and reported for active duty on 18 Jun 1973. He entered Recruit Training at NTC, Orlando, FL from June-August 1973 and Machinist Mate Class A School, NTC, Great Lakes, IL from August-November 1973.

He served in following commands: USS *Yosemite* (AD-19); Naval Nuclear Power School, Bainbridge, MD; Naval Station Philadelphia, PA; USS *John F. Kennedy* (CV-67); Naval Air Technical Training Center, Millington, TN; USS *Okinawa* (LPH-3), promoted to chief petty office; USS *America* (CV-66); USS *Jouett* (CG-29), received commission as limited duty officer; Naval Amphibious Base, Coronado CA; USS *Juneau* (LPD-10), served as the chief engineer; COMNAVSURFLANT Staff Norfolk, VA; supervisor of Shipbuilding and Repair, Pascagoula, MS; USS *George Washington* (CVN-73).

Memorable experience: 1978-Mediterranean Ocean: as engine room supervisor aboard the *Kennedy* when it collided with the USS *Belknap*, he kept fires lit in boilers and the only engine available for maneuvering on line. He assisted the other three engine rooms and auxiliary spaces to restore equipment.

Henry Martin participated in Desert Storm and Somalia Peacekeeping Mission. His awards include five Navy Commendation medals, Navy Achievement Medal, Presidential Unit Commendation, two Navy Unit Commendations, two Meritorious Unit Commendations, three Battle E ribbons, three Good Conduct medals, two National Defense Service medals, two Armed Forces Expedition medals, two Southwest Asia Service medals, five Sea Service Deployment ribbons, Kuwait Liberation Medal (Kingdom of Saudi Arabia), Kuwait Liberation Medal (Kuwait) and Outstanding Volunteer Service Medal.

He married Sheila Marie Cuffee of Chesapeake, VA on 3 Jun 1978. They have three sons: Shawn, Henry Jr. and Justin. (Shawn and Henry Jr. are serving in the military); one granddaughter, Hailey Marie. Henry is a lifelong member of Bloomfield Missionary Baptist Church, Cadiz, KY.

Lt. Martin retired from the USN on 1 Feb 1999. He is employed with Air Products and Chemicals Inc., Calvert City, KY.

PRICE EDWARD MARTIN, E-3, born 20 Mar 1952, in Indianapolis, IN, the son of Harrison Martin Jr. and Bertha Venus Kirby Martin. They later moved back to Cadiz, KY where he attended Dunbar Elementary, McUpton Elementary, Trigg County Junior High, and graduated in 1970 from Trigg County HS, Cadiz, KY. He attended and graduated from Nashville Technical College.

He joined the USN 4 Mar 1971, where he enlisted at AFEES, Louisville, KY. He entered basic recruit training at the Naval Recruit Training Center, Great Lakes, IL and attended Signalman A School.

He transferred to the USS *Kitty Hawk* (CV-63), San Diego, CA, where he served two tours in Vietnam. He was awarded the National Defense Service Medal, Vietnam Service Medal w/Bronze Star, Vietnam Campaign Medal w/device (1960), and the Navy Unit Commendation. He was discharged 30 Aug 1973 at the rank of E-3.

He married Suszie Mae Baker on 5 Aug 1978. They have one son, Mozell Dewayne Martin (veteran), and two grandchildren, Jerel M. Williams and Chon Devon Martin.

Price and his wife reside in Nashville, TN. He is currently a truck driver and his hobbies include hunting and fishing.

MORRIS HAYWOOD MCCORMICK JR., Corporal, born 9 Jun 1949 in Cadiz, KY, and graduated 1967 from Trigg County HS. Morris enlisted into the USMC in August 1968. After boot camp at Marine Corp Recruit Depot in San Diego, CA, he went on to AIT at Camp Pendleton, CA in January 1969.

Morris was assigned to the 5th Shore Party Battalion, 5th Mar. Div. at Camp Pendleton, CA until August 1969 when he underwent jungle warfare training for duty in the Republic of South Vietnam.

Upon arrival in Vietnam, Morris was assigned to the 3rd Marine Amphibious Force based in Camp Horn, Da Nang. While serving with the 3rd Mar. Amphibious Force, Morris's platoon was awarded the Vietnamese Cross of Gallantry for defending a neighboring orphanage from mortar rounds and fire, which destroyed over half of the orphanage, during a Viet Cong attack on Camp Horn

Upon discharge from the Marine Corps, Morris had attained the rank of corporal. Morris married a Trigg County girl, Sharon Fay Rascoe, in February 1972. They have one son Jamey and daughter-in-law Stephanie. Morris has worked since February 1972 for Johnson Controls. Morris and Sharon resides in Etowah, TN.

DAN SIDNEY MCCRAW, Master Sergeant E-7, born 28 Mar 1947, the son of the late Dan and Hazel McCraw of Trigg County. He joined the USAF on 2 Aug 1965 and served as an aircraft crew chief until 1972. He was required to fly with his aircraft. He served a six month tour in Vietnam from 1965-1972.

After Vietnam he continued to serve until his retirement in 1986 at which time he retired at the rank of master sergeant, E-7. While in the Air Force he accumulated over 1800 combat flying hours and received many decorations that included the Airman's Medal for heroism, Meritorious Service Medal, Commendation Medal and numerous other Vietnam and Air Force medals.

He met and married Billie Joan Boyd of Columbus, MS in 1966. They have four children: Dan Jr., Robin, Richard and Christopher, and five grandchildren: Tom, Nora, Ethan, Keri and Meaghan. Their three sons joined the military, each in different branches. Their daughter stayed in Trigg County and attended Murray State University from 1993-97. She married Paul Hart of Cadiz.

Dan Jr. *(see page 270 for his information).*

Richard joined the Navy in 1992, and served onboard the USS *Savannah* and the USS *Caron*. Richard was a signalman 3rd class and is presently working at a maximum security prison in Illinois.

Christopher joined the Marines in 1993. He went to boot camp in Parris Island, SC, and was stationed at Kaneohe Bay Marine Corps Base, HI. After his tour he went to college and became an electronic engineer in computers.

After retirement Dan Sidney McCraw moved back to Trigg County where he is presently living and working. He has a repair service known as Sids Repairs. In April 2001 the Joint Chief of Staffs presented Billie and Sid with two special coins for their contribution to their country by covering all branches of the armed forces.

JAMES R. MERRICK, E-5, born in Cadiz, Trigg County, KY. He joined the service 17 Aug 1965 with assignments at Fort Jackson for basic training, Redstone, Huntsville, AL and Vietnam.

He was discharged 17 Aug, 1967. Awards include the Sharpshooter, Vietnam Medal, Master Driver and honorable discharge.

James and Janice married 26 Sep 1970 and live in Cadiz, KY. They have two children, Christy Olson and Beverly Curling. James is still working.

LEROY D. MERRICK, SP4, born 15 Apr 1946 in Trigg County, KY. He was drafted by the US Army and entered service 13 Dec 1965 at Nashville, TN. After 10 weeks basic training at Fort Benning, GA, he was assigned to US Army Defense School at Fort Bliss, TX, where he trained as a fire distribution system specialist in NIKE missiles.

In May 1966 he was reassigned to the 53rd Arty. Group (Air Defense) at Belleville AF Station attached to Scott AFB, IL, where he became an electronics repair parts specialist.

Discharged from active duty 12 Dec 1967 as specialist 4/c. He qualified as Expert with M-14 rifle, Sharpshooter with M-30 carbine and received the Good Conduct Medal, National Defense Medal and USA Air Defense Certificate of Achievement.

Leroy is now manager of Cadiz Door Co., a wholesale distributor of building products which he started in 1977. He also raises black Angus cattle on the family farm in north Trigg County.

He married the former Carolyn Henderson on 30 Jan 1970. They have one child, Andrea, a student at Western Kentucky University. Leroy's hobbies and past time are working.

WILLIAM RYAN MERRICK, SPEC-E4, born 15 Sep 1939 in Trigg County, KY, the son of Morris and Barbara Merrick. He was drafted into the US Army 2 Jan 1962 and received his basic training at Fort Knox, KY.

Ryan was assigned to the HQ Co. 1st Bde. 5th Inf. Div. at Fort Carson, CO as a mechanic. He spent many cold, snowy days in Colorado. He received an Honorable Discharge on 31 Dec 1967 as a Spec E-4. He spent a total of one year 11 months and three days active service and the remainder in the US Army Reserves.

After his discharge, Ryan went to work for Kentucky Stone Co. (now Rogers Group), at Canton, KY. In 1968 he married Elizabeth Fuller and they have four children: Barbara Ann, Donnie Ryan, Bonnie Grace and Rebecca. Their grandchildren are Kendra Nicole, Derrick Bryan, Evallene and Perry.

Ryan and Elizabeth reside in the Montgomery Community where Ryan loves to garden and do yard work.

JERRY G. MITCHELL, SP4, born 29 Jul 1943 in the Blackhawk Community of Trigg County, the son of Clint and Aline Mitchell. On 14 Apr 1965, he was drafted into the Army at Nashville, TN. Basic training was taken at Fort Gordon, GA and then transferred to Fort Belvoir, VA. After two weeks there, he found himself on a cargo plane bound for South Vietnam.

On arrival in Saigon, they were put in stationary tents. He laid beside the concrete pad the entire night while the Viet Cong shot at them and they couldn't shoot back! They had rifles, but no ammunition as they had just arrived.

While in South Vietnam, he was with the 87th Engr. Bn. stationed at Cam Rahn Bay. Their battalion built the air strip at Cam Rahn Bay, roads and other sites along the Indian Ocean, while the 101st Abn. Div. guarded them. When the Monsoon Season hit, torrential rains came and they often spent the nights holding their tents down so they wouldn't blow away. The hottest day he spent while there was 134° in the shade.

During Christmas 1965, Bob Hope came to Cam Rahn Bay to entertain the troops. Other stars with him were Anita Bryant and Joey Heatherton.

While he was in Vietnam, he often cut hair and had the privilege of cutting Gen. William Westmoreland's hair, who was the general over the Vietnam War.

He spent a total of 11 months and 29 days in Vietnam. The rest of his tour was spent at Fort Campbell, KY. He was discharged 13 Apr 1967 as a Specialist 4. He received the Sharpshooter Badge (Rifle M-14), Vietnam Service Medal, National Defense Service Medal, and two Overseas Service Bars.

After his departure from the Army, he continued to work at Fort Campbell in Civil Service for 18 months. He married and had two children, Tommy and Leslie, and first grandchild is expected in July 2001. He formed Mitchell Builders in 1970 and moved back to Trigg County from Caldwell County in 1990. He married Penny H. Mitchell and has two step-daughters, Tara and Tasha. He is currently farming and does occasional construction jobs.

Jerry attends Liberty Point Baptist Church and has taken several mission trips to Africa and the Philippines. He is also a lifetime member of VFW Post 5595 in Princeton, KY.

He had a lot of good experiences while in the military, but wouldn't want to do it again. He learned one thing while overseas, America is not appreciated by her citizens as she should be. We take to much for granted, especially our freedom.

HAROLD D. MIZE, SP5, born 13 Oct 1947 in Winchester, KY, the oldest child of Harold H. and Mary Holmes Mize. The family moved to Beaver Dam, KY and Denny started Beaver Dam Grade School. In 1953 the family moved to Cadiz, KY and Denny graduated from Trigg County HS in 1965.

He attended Western Kentucky State College until 1968 when he enlisted in the USAR in March and entered active duty 6 Aug 1968. Basic and AIT were at Fort Dix, NJ.

He then returned to his reserve unit, Co. D, 3rd Bn. 399th Regt., 2nd Bde., 100th Div. (TNG), where he was promoted to SP5 and served his last two years as company clerk. Denny was honorably discharged 28 Feb 1974. Denny is employed by White Hydraulics in Hopkinsville, KY and resides in Cerulean Springs, KY.

JAMES LEWIS MIZE, Sergeant E-5, born 9 Aug 1949 at Beaver Dam, KY. He was inducted into the US Army 17 Mar 1969 at Nashville, TN and shipped to Fort Campbell, KY for basic training with Co. C, 3rd Bn., 1st Bde. USATC. He was appointed assistant squad leader for the two months.

After basic he was assigned to G-4, Weapons and Equipment Pool as assistant unit armorer. He served there until re-assigned to VII Corps Support Command in Boeblingen, Germany, December 1969 to March 1971.

Returned to Fort Dix, NJ and was discharged in March 1971. His awards include the Good Conduct and M-14 Expert.

In civilian life he is a truck driver for Carbide Graphite Group Inc. in Calvert City, KY. He lives in Cadiz, KY. He enjoys riding motorcycles.

SANDRA MYERS, a native of Eugene, OR, she entered the Women's Army Corps (WAC) in 1974 and retired in September 1994. She completed basic training at Fort Jackson, SC and her first assignment was 1st Personnel Command, Schewetzingen, Germany.

During a 20 year career she served in many administrative assignments including: HQ, 1st Personnel Command, Schwetzingen, Germany, HQ 7th MEDCOM Heidelberg, Germany, HQ IX Corps, Camp Zama Japan, Headquarters, 8th Personnel Command, Seoul, Korea, HQ, Department of the Army, Washington DC, Walter Reed Army Medical Center, Washington DC, HQ Department of the Army Health Services Branch, and Sergeants Major Branch Alexandria, VA; and assignment to Fort Bragg, NC.

A highlight of her career at Fort Benjamin Harrison, IN, was to serve as non-commissioned officer in charge of the 1990, HQ Department of the Army Promotion Board for Sergeants First Class.

She attended primary Non-Commissioned Officer Academy, Senior Personnel Administration Specialist Course, Personnel Company Administration Course (PAC), Personnel Reporting and Casualty Accounting, Staff and Faculty Middle Manages Course, Personnel and Logistic Course and the Advanced Non-Commission Officer Course.

She met her husband, a Vietnam veteran, at Fort Bragg, NC and they were married in 1978. He lost his life in an aviation accident in 1989. With five years until her own retirement, she accepted assignment to Fort Benjamin Harrison, IN, where she was responsible for helping develop an automated war time casualty reporting system.

Career highlights include: Redeployment Officer for Europe in 1976, serving on Sergeants Major of the Army Team at HQ, Department of the Army; manager/advisor for over 1300 senior level (E9) non-commissioned officers; assignment advisor to the Sergeant Major of the Army preparing nominative packets for selection of Richard Kidd as Sergeant Major of the Army; preparing selection packets for General Colin Powell prior to his assuming command of V Corps Germany.

Awards include Meritorious Service Medal, 4th OLC, Army Commendation Medal 4th OLC, Army Achievement Medal 2nd OLC, Good Conduct Medal 6th Award, National Defense Medal 3rd Award, NCO Professional Development Ribbon w/#3, Army Service Ribbon, Overseas Service Ribbon w/#3, The Horatio Gates Award, and the Major General Alexander Macomb Award.

Moving to Trigg County after retirement, she worked as an inventory clerk at Fourshee Lumber; staff reporter at *Cadiz Record*, 1996-1999; part-time DJ job at local radio station, WKDZ; and in late August 1999, she responded to an advertisement in the *Kentucky New Era* "Trigg County Correspondent wanted." She enjoys the rich histories and present-day lives of Trigg Countians as she explores and writes their stories.

She maintains membership in the Trigg County Historical Preservation Society, American Legion Post 74, VFW 7890, Cadiz Art Center, hosting a weekly radio program, *"The Veterans Voice"* and authors a veterans issue's column *"The Veterans View."*

DAVID NEIGHBORGALL, SP4, born in Columbus, OH on 27 Nov 1950 and moved to Trigg County with his family in 1968. After graduation from Trigg County HS in 1970, he was employed at Smith & Proffitt Tool and Die in Hopkinsville, KY. He received his draft notice for the US Army in the summer of 1970 and reported for eight weeks of basic training at Fort Campbell, KY in August.

After completing AIT in Fort Lee, VA, David was assigned to Kaiserslauten, Germany, where he worked as a machinist. While in Germany, David learned of President Richard Nixon's proposal of giving a six-month reduction of service to soldiers who were stationed in South Vietnam. David and friend Nick Fazzolari decided to volunteer for Vietnam duty and take advantage of the chance to get home six months early. Both men were sent to South Vietnam in September 1971 and most of David's time was spent at an Army base in Vung Tao, located on the South-China Sea, where he was assigned to the 330th TRANS CO. For a short time in February 1972 he was in a unit in Saigon. Some of his free time in Vietnam was spent in a shop cutting and polishing jade and agate for jewelry. His best memories are of surfing in the South China Sea and buying whole fresh pineapples from Vietnamese vendors on the beach.

After serving six months in the Republic of South Vietnam, David was indeed given a six-month drop from his tour of duty. He arrived in San Diego, CA in March 1972, and was honorably discharged with a rank of SPEC 4. David's parents, Wes and Frankie Neighborgall, sisters Rhonda and Ruthie, and friend Sarah Cunningham met him at the airport in Nashville, TN.

One year later, David and Sarah were married. They still reside in Trigg County where David is plant manager of Stone Plastics, INC. He is an active member of Bethel United Methodist Church. His free time is spent golfing, fishing, hunting, and collecting pre-historic Indian artifacts. David still maintains contact with his Army buddy, Nick Fazzolari who resides in Portland, OR.

JERRY LAYNE "MICKEY" NOEL, born 18 Feb 1954 in Cadiz, KY, son of Douglas C. and Addie Grant Noel. He enlisted in the Army 7 Aug 1972. After completing basic training at Fort Jackson, SC, he was sent to Fort Campbell, KY with a possibility of being sent to Vietnam.

The later part of 1973 was the most memorable moment of his military career. His commander informed them there was a good possibility that they wouldn't be sent to Vietnam since they were starting to pull troops out.

In May 1974, he was transferred to Heidelberg, Germany and served with Co. B, 95th, MP Bn. He spent the last 14 months of his military career in Germany. On 7 Aug 1975, he was honorable discharged and returned to his home in Cadiz, KY. He married Sherry Roberts on 23 Jun 1994 and they live in Gracey, KY. He is employed by Kentucky Farm Bureau Insurance Co. as an automobile damage appraiser. He has one son, Dusty Layne Noel, from a previous marriage.

PERRY R. NOEL, E-5, born 18 Dec 1949 in Christian County. During the 1960s a lot of changes were going on in our country. Probably the most life changing was the Vietnam War. He knew people were being killed there, but was not at all reluctant to serve after being drafted in May 1969.

His first stop after induction in Nashville, TN, was Fort Campbell, KY, where he spent two months in basic training. Then for the first time in his life, he boarded a plane for Fort Sill, OK where he completed AIT. His training was on self-propeller Howitzer (Artillery).

The orders he received for Vietnam about two weeks before completing AIT were changed to Germany a day or two before leaving. He was assigned to C Btry. 2/14 Arty. in Nurnberg, Germany and served there 18 months.

Discharged with the rank E-5 in May 1971 and returned to Trigg County. He married Alice on 17 Nov 1979 and they have three children: Brenna, Evan and Molly. They now reside in Bowling Green, KY.

He hurts for his brothers that died in Vietnam and the ones that are carrying physical and emotional scars from that era. They were all willing to serve and more was required and given by some than others. He is proud of our country and proud to have served. God Bless America.

TOMMY G. NOEL, SP4, born 11 Aug, 1949 in Cadiz, KY. He joined the service 15 Apr 1969 at Cadiz, KY and was inducted at Nashville, TN. After basic training at Fort Campbell, KY, he was assigned in July 1969 to Fort Benning, GA, Co. A, 197th Support Bn., 197th Inf. Bde. (clerk-typist) Orders Clerk for brigade.

Reassigned in February 1970 to 549th Light Equipment Maintenance Co., 79th Maint. Bn., 1st Log. Cmd., RVN as shop reports clerk and unit clerk. Released from active duty at Oakland, CA and served several years in active reserve.

Discharged 27 Dec 1970 as SP4. Awards include National Defense Service Medal, Vietnam Campaign Medal, Vietnam Service Medal, Bronze Star (Meritorious Service).

Memorable was leaving for the service with Larry Shelton, Roy Radford and Jesse Frye; running into Paul Finley (of Cadiz) while he was picking up supplies at supply yard; and the first rocket attack when they arrived at his unit in Vietnam.

As a civilian he was a laborer at Barkley Lake State Park and a civilian employee at Fort Campbell (prior to being drafted and to where he returned after service). While working at Fort Campbell, he worked in the reception station (for trainees), S-1, 1st Tng. Bde., US Army Hospital (MEDDAC) and Military Pay and Accounting.

He married Deborah Baldwin on 21 Jun 1988 and they live in Hopkinsville, KY. After retiring in 1992, Tommy and his wife mowed yards for a year. Tommy also worked for a temporary service and worked several seasons at U.S. Tobacco. He is now involved in internet sales and flea marketing.

DONNIE G. OLIVER, born 20 Aug 1949, in Lamasco, KY, son of James "Moody" Oliver and Floy Mae Banister Oliver. He went into the Army on 6 Mar 1967 at the age of 17 on a volunteer basis and served with the 92nd Engrs. and 20th Engr. Bde.

He was stationed at Fort Greely, AK then sent to Vietnam. He participated in TET Counter Offensive, Vietnam Counter Offensive Phase IV, Vietnam Counter Offensive Phase V and 9th Campaign. Donnie served two tours in Vietnam and his main job was building runways, bridges and roads.

Discharged 11 Oct 1969 and from the Reserves on 5 Mar 1973. Awards include the National Defense Service Medal, Vietnam Service Medal and Vietnam Campaign Medal.

He married Sandra Hinson on 29 Mar 1972 and they have two children: 1) Angel, who is married to Nacy Harper and have four children: Chassidy, Darren, Jamie and Megan. 2) James, who is married to Sherry Underhill and have two children, Kaitlyn and Amanda.

Donnie passed away 10 Oct 1998 and is buried in the Little Family Cemetery off Nicky Lane, Cadiz, KY. He was a very loving and caring person, and always willing to help other in a time of need. *Submitted by his daughter Angel Harper.*

SANDRA R. "SANDY" THOMAS OLSON, Sergeant (E-4), born 13 Sep 1953 in Cadiz, KY, daughter of R.C. Thomas, (USAF, retired and now deceased) and Margie (Adams) Thomas. She served in the USAF 30 Mar 1972-10 Sep 1974.

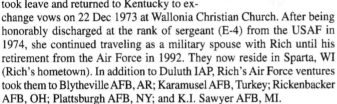

Assignments: basic training at Lackland AFB, TX; 11 weeks of technical training in the disbursement accounting field at Sheppard AFB, TX; assigned to 4787 Air Base Group, Duluth IAP, MN, where she worked in the accounting and finance office.

While stationed at Duluth, she met and married Sgt. Richard A. Olson. They both took leave and returned to Kentucky to exchange vows on 22 Dec 1973 at Wallonia Christian Church. After being honorably discharged at the rank of sergeant (E-4) from the USAF in 1974, she continued traveling as a military spouse with Rich until his retirement from the Air Force in 1992. They now reside in Sparta, WI (Rich's hometown). In addition to Duluth IAP, Rich's Air Force ventures took them to Blytheville AFB, AR; Karamusel AFB, Turkey; Rickenbacker AFB, OH; Plattsburgh AFB, NY; and K.I. Sawyer AFB, MI.

Sandra began working for the Department of the Air Force as a federal service employee at K.I. Sawyer in 1988. Currently, she works for the Department of Army, Fort McCoy, WI as a federal service employee in the Civilian Personnel Office.

She travels to Cadiz to visit her family usually once or twice a year and has attended the past three Ham Festivals. Although, her actual time residing in Cadiz is limited, due to the fact that she spent most of her life living at Air Force bases, as her father and husband were both Air Force career men, she did attend the 8th grade and a few weeks of the 9th grade at Trigg County. She made many friends and has very fond memories of Cadiz that year.

Their children are Heather Olson of La Crosse, WI and Andrew Olson of Sparta, WI.

RICHARD J. PAUZÉ, Master Sergeant, entered the Air Force in January 1958 and went to Air Craft Mechanics School at Amarillo, TX. In June 1961 he went to Flight Engineers School at Chanute Field Illinois and stayed on active duty for the Berlin Crisis until 31 Aug 1962.

He joined the New York Air National Guard September 1962 and was called to active duty for the Cuban Missile Crisis and the Civil War in Santo Domingo. Called to active duty for Vietnam and received Vietnam Service Medal w/3 Battle Stars, Expeditionary Forces and National Defense Service Medals, Air Force Commendation Medal, Air Force Combat Readiness Medal and Senior Air Crew Member Wings.

In 1971 The Air National Guard received C-130A aircraft and were designated the 109th Tactical Airlift Group. In September 1971 they served to put down the prison riots at Attica, New York and received the NY State Service in aid of Civil Authorities Medal.

In 1975 the 109th underwent another change to C-130D which had skis for Artic operation and re-supply of the DEW Line (Distant early warning Radar sites) in Greenland. In 1979 these same airplanes were used to fly in food and snow removal equipment to Buffalo NY after they received a 34 inch snowfall.

He was awarded the US Armed Forces for Humanitarian Service Medal and the New York State Conspicuous Service Medal. Retired in 1988 with 30 years service and was awarded the Air Reserve Forces Ex-

emplary Behavior Efficiency Fidelity Medal, Armed Forces Reserve Medal and 30 year Faithful Service Medal.

Richard and Jane married 10 Jan 1959 and they have two children, Jeannine and Theresa, and five grandchildren: Andrew, Daniel, Monica, Eric and Aimee. Richard retired in 1988 from Federal Civil Service and Air National Guard and again in 2000 from the Trigg County School system. They live in Trigg County, Canton, KY, where he helps veterans and their families.

LYNDELL RAY PAYTON, SP4, born 18 Sep 1947 in Greenville, KY. He entered the service 24 Jan 1968 with basic training at Fort Campbell, KY; Artillery School, Fort Sill, OK; Fort Riley, KS. He was discharged 23 Jan 1970.

On the GI Bill he attended 4.5 years of college at HCC and WKU, majoring in history, minor in folk studies, 16 hours on MA degree in historic preservation, two internships, one undergraduate, one graduate at "Homeplace 1850 LBL."

Lyndell married Kathy Skillion 8 Jul 1989 and they live in Cadiz, KY. He retired from TVA in 2000.

CHARLES DANIEL P'POOL, Tech Sergeant (E-5), born 14 Dec 1946 in Cadiz, KY. He graduated from high school at Fort Stockton, TX in 1965 and was working in the oil fields when he decided to enlist in the Army at Abilene, TX. He was sent to Fort Polk, LA for basic training and AIT; lineman and communication training at Fort Gordon, GA.

He volunteered for Vietnam, arrived there 10 May 1966 and assigned to the 1st Inf. Div., 121st Sig. Bn. at Phu Loi. Six months later he transferred to a forward observer unit as a radio operator and spotter, dividing his time between Quan Loi, An Loc and Loc Ninh.

Charles participated in Operations Junction City, Attleboro and several others. He managed to survive the Tet Offenses of 1967 and 1968.

One of his scariest memories is crash-landing in a Chinook helicopter in the middle of a rice paddy. They had lost power to both rotors and fell like a rock several hundred feet, then the blades started freewheeling and slowed them down enough that when they hit the water it wasn't harder than a normal landing. Another time he hitched a ride on a chopper that was carrying a farmer and his goat. Charles had all his worldly possessions in a large duffle bag and they tied the goat to it and took off. Soon as they cleared the populated area, the door-gunner test fired his machine gun. The gun-shy goat went out the open door, duffle bag and all. Charles lost everything, then had to give $5.00 to the farmer for his share of replacing the goat.

TSgt. P'Pool left Vietnam during his 4th tour, after being slightly wounded for the fifth time. He received an early discharge 10 Jul 1968. His awards include the National Defense Service Medal, Vietnam Campaign Medal, Vietnam Service Medal, Meritorious Unit Citation and Expert Marksmanship.

He married Vicky Mitchell on 30 May 1970 and they have two children, Kim Henley and Mike, and three grandchildren: Ty Henley; Zachary and Alexandra P'Poole. Charles is employed by Bell South Telephone and lives in Cadiz, KY. He is looking forward to retiring soon. Charles enjoys fishing, hunting and traveling.

TOMMY RAY P'POOL, Sergeant (E-5), born 13 Nov 1947 in Trigg County, KY. He joined the service 12 Aug 1968 in Trigg County. Assignments include basic training at Fort Campbell, KY and AIT at Fort Bliss, TX. He was sent to Vietnam where he was a mail clerk and participated in the Vietnam Conflict, January 1969-January 1970.

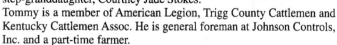

Sgt. P'Pool was discharged 11 Aug 1970. His awards include the Army Commendation Medal, Good Conduct Medal and Vietnam Campaign Ribbon.

Tommy married Sylvia Stroube on 18 Jan 1970 and they live in Cadiz. They have three children: Jason, Jodie and Juli, and one step-granddaughter, Courtney Jade Stokes.

Tommy is a member of American Legion, Trigg County Cattlemen and Kentucky Cattlemen Assoc. He is general foreman at Johnson Controls, Inc. and a part-time farmer.

PAUL LEROY PROFFITT, born 21 May 1941 at Linton, KY, the son of Roy H. and Lena Proffitt. He enlisted in the Army on 9 Oct 1963 at Louisville, KY.

After basic combat training at Fort Knox, KY, he was assigned to a Nike Hercules ballistic missile site near Pacific, MO. He also served with the air defense missile systems in Alaska, Korea and Fort Bliss, TX. He served as a radar, computer operator and section chief.

In May 1971 he was selected to attend the US Army Recruiter and Career Counselor School at Fort Harrison, IN. Upon completion he was assigned to Hot Springs, AR to the Army's recruiting efforts. Later he was assigned as recruiting station commander in Joplin and Monett, MO.

After 10-1/2 years with the US Army Recruiting Command, he was able to attend the Senior Personnel Sergeant Course at Fort Harrison, then assigned to a missile unit in Aschaffenburg, West Germany as a personnel administration center supervisor.

Returned to the States and assigned to US Army Intelligence and Security Command in Arlington, VA as the Manpower Requirements and Force Development NCO. He retired from that unit on 1 Jul 1986 and returned to Cadiz, KY.

His decorations include the MSM w/OLC, Army Commendation, Army Achievement w/OLC, Good Conduct, Expeditionary Forces, National Defense and the Gold Recruiting Badge with Sapphire Star.

He married the former Kathleen Klein on 9 Oct 1967 and they have two children, Amy Collins of Benton, KY, and Jeffrey of Cadiz, KY. Grandchildren are Ally Lynn and Dalton Collins and Tyler Proffitt.

LINZIE PROFFITT, Master Sergeant E-8, born 17 Jan 1939 in Cadiz, KY, son of Roy and Lena Proffitt. He enlisted in the military in October 1958 and took his basic training at Fort Benning, GA and AIT at Fort Jackson, SC. After this he was sent to Germany for 15 months.

Upon his return to the United States he married Carolyn Oliver in July 1960. Then went to Fort Belvoir, VA for training and from there to Aberdeen Proving Grounds, MD for advanced classes. Linzie and Carolyn made their first home in Fort Hood, TX. The next move was to France where they spent the next four years and nine months.

Their first child Lisa was born in Kentucky and the next two, Robert and Sherri, were born in France. The family spent their last month in France living in a hotel due to the fact that All-American troops were leaving France for the final time.

Upon returning to the United States Linzie was reassigned to a company in Fort Bragg, NC that was being formed to go to Vietnam, he was in Fort Bragg about nine months before leaving for Vietnam. After spending a year in Vietnam he returned and the family moved to Fort Knox, KY. The family spent two years at Fort Knox before Linzie again received orders to return to Vietnam. This time he spent 10 months before returning for a second time to Fort Knox. Again the family spent two years before they were sent to Germany. The family spent three years in Germany.

As they were preparing to return for a tour of duty in Kansas, word was received of the terminal illness of Mrs. Proffitt's father. Upon arriving in the United States Linzie was allowed to be assigned to Fort Campbell, KY. At this time the family purchased a home in Cadiz in anticipation of retiring. The family was able to remain in Cadiz for the next 18 months before retiring in October 1978. Linzie received many honors and medals for his 20 years of service.

Linzie recently retired again after over 20 years with the Trigg County School System. He hopes to now enjoy his four grandchildren: Ashley and George Elliott and Andrea and Matthew Kennedy. Linzie still works on a part-time basis as a sub-bus driver for the school system.

ROY EDWARD RADFORD, E-4, Born 14 Oct 1949 in Cerulean, KY. He graduated from Trigg County HS in 1968 and received as associates degree in business management from Hopkinsville Community College in 1979.

He was drafted into the Army 14 Apr 1969 and served basic training at Fort Campbell, KY; Radio School at Fort Huachuca, AZ; Teletype School at Fort Gordon, GA. He was in the Vietnam War from November 1969 to November 1970 as E-4. He joined the USAR in October 1973 and retired from the Reserves 100th Div., Hopkinsville, KY in May 1996.

His awards include the National Defense Service Medal, Vietnam Service Medal, Vietnam Campaign Medal, Overseas Ribbon, Good Conduct w/OLC, Army Commendation Medal (4), Army Achievement Medal w/OLC, Meritorious Service Award, NCODP-3 Drill Sergeant Badge, Armed Forces Reserve Ribbon on Hour Glass Marksmanship Badge, and numerous certificates of achievement and training.

Memorable/Accomplishments: surviving a year in Vietnam without being wounded or captured; being stationed not far from where Tommy Noel (also of Cadiz) was stationed; meeting several friends from Christian and Trigg counties in Vietnam; time spent at Fort Knox, KY, instructing young soldiers in the 19K MOS (Tankers).

Roy and Taffye married 12 Mar 1988. He has two children: Carla and Rhoda; three step-sons: Jared, Travis and John; and three grandchildren: Devorious, Keiona and Chasity Radford. Roy is a truck driver for United Van Lines and resides in Hopkinsville, KY. He is a 32nd degree Mason, a Shriner, Kentucky Colonel and social club president. Fishing is his hobby.

GORDON ROBERTS, Commander, US Naval Aviator, 1956-81, born 24 Aug 1934, son of Gordon and Mary Lee Roberts of Columbus, Hickman County, KY. He graduated from Clinton Central High in 1952 and Murray State in 1956.

His awards include Naval Aviation Gold Pilots Wings, Meritorious Service Medal, Navy Commendation Medal w/Gold Star in lieu of second award, Meritorious Unit Commendation Medal w/2 Bronze Stars, Vietnam Service Medal w/4 Bronze Stars, Armed Forces Expeditionary Medal w/Bronze Star, Vietnam Gallantry Cross w/ Palm, Vietnam Campaign Medal and National Defense Service Medal.

He completed 5700 flight hours in jets, props, and helos at 11 different permanent duty stations. Cdr. Roberts resides in Cadiz, KY.

JERRY ROBERTS, Lieutenant, born 2 Mar 1941 near Cerulean, KY, and served in the Army from June 1964 until his death in Vietnam on 5 Jul 1966. He was a helicopter pilot assigned to the 502nd Avn. Bn. On the day of his death, this was the account received from military authorities:

"Lt. Roberts was copilot of a UH1-D helicopter, the lead craft in a flight of 35, which was airlifting troops into combat. Just as his aircraft was touching down, the helicopter was hit by enemy ground fire, immobilizing it. Lt. Roberts led the crew members to the safety of a nearby ditch. After discovering that two of his crew members had been wounded during the move to the ditch, Roberts returned to them and was carrying them to safety when he was mortally wounded by small arms fire."

Roberts was a 1959 graduate of Sinking Fork HS and a 1963 graduate of Murray State College with majors in chemistry and math. He taught one year at Koffman Jr. High School before entering the Army. Teaching and farming were his plans upon completing his military duty.

Roberts wed the former Rita Ezell of La Fayette, KY on 14 Jul 1963. Two children were born from this marriage: Maranita (b. 7 Apr 1965) and Jerry Vance (b. 14 Jun 1966).

Numerous awards for heroism were presented posthumously at Fort Campbell to his widow and children. Those medals were the Purple Heart, Silver Star, Bronze Star and Air Medal w/18 OLCs. He also received the Vietnam Campaign Medal from the South Vietnamese government.

He made the Supreme Sacrifice in the service of his country for the cause of freedom. Greater love has no one than this, that a man lay down his life for his friends.

All gave some and some gave all. At the end of suffering, of mystery, God awaits us...

Today there are two grandchildren, Zachary Thomas and Anna Grace Roberts with one more Roberts on the way. Life goes on, the blessings continue and through it all love remains. *Submitted by Rita Lawrence*

BILLY ROYCE ROBERTSON, Sergeant First Class, born 21 Mar 1939 in Cadiz, KY, son of Haydon and Willie Sanders Robertson. He joined the Army 8 Sep 1958. Stations include Fort Knox, KY, basic training, AIT; Germany, September 1959 to August 1962; Columbus, OH, August 1962-April 1964; Fort Eustis, VA, April 1964-July 1965; Vietnam, July 1965-July 1966; Fort Campbell July 1966-February 1968; Germany, February 1968-March 1969; Korea April 1969-May 1970; Fort Carson, CO, May 1970-June 1971; Korea June 1971-June 1973; Germany June 1973-January 1976; Fort Leonard Wood, MO, January 1976-October 1978.

Retired 1 Oct 1978 with the rank sergeant first class. His awards include the National Defense Service Medal, Good Conduct (4th awd.) Armed Forces Expeditionary Medal, RVN Combat Medal, RVN Service Medal, Unit Citation, RVN Campaign Medal, Vietnam Service Medal w/ Bronze Star and Commendation Ribbon.

He has one son Kevin Craig and one grandson Kevin Whaylen Robertson. Billy is a truck driver and lives in Dawson Springs, KY.

JOE E. ROGERS, Sergeant, born 14 Jul 1947 in Trigg County, KY. He joined the service 15 Oct 1969 at Nashville, TN. Assignments include basic training at Fort Campbell, KY; Communications at Fort Leonard Wood, MO; airborne training, Fort Benning, GA; 8th Inf. 509th Abn. Mainz, Germany.

Accomplishments/Memorable: completion of airborne training, participating in Dawn Patrol 70, a joint airborne exercise with Italian forces held in Italy in June 1970.

Sgt. Rogers was discharged 15 Sep 1971. His awards include Leadership Award, Fort Campbell, KY and Letter of Commendation, Fort Leonard Wood, MO.

He works for Bell South, raises cattle on his farm in south Trigg County, does church work and community work. Married Patricia 11 Apr 1970 and they have two children, Amy and Brian and one grandchild, Dupree Joseph Rogers.

HENRY LEE RUSSEL SR., SSG E-6, born 3 Dec 1945 in Gracey, KY. He joined the service 1 Sep 1966 at Nashville, TN and went to basic training at Fort Campbell, KY and AIT at Fort Leonard Wood, MO.

He served with 588th Engineering Unit at Thanin, Vietnam in 1967. Memorable was Operation Mahattan—cleared 468 acres of jungle for Route 90 for military traffic; and Junction City—cleared 150 acres of jungle to construct a 700 man Special Forces camp and airfield.

Discharged 31 Aug 1969 as SP5(T) E-5. He stayed in reserves for 15 years, 1974 to 1989 (disabled), and attained rank SSG E-6. His awards include the Expert Rifle Badge, Army Commendation Medal w/OLC, Meritorious Unit Citation and Vietnam Campaign Medal.

As a civilian he was a highway construction worker and helped build I-24 from Illinois to Kentucky Lake and worked at TVA. His hobbies are working on cars and lawns.

Married Peggy Jean 27 Dec 1971 and they live in Gracey, KY, where he drives a truck and does farm work. They have three children: Melissa, Henry Jr. and Dominque and one grandchild, Jacorie Jerome Summers.

JAMES STEVEN RUTLAND, Captain, born 1 Mar 1952 in Hopkinsville, KY. Commissioned a second lieutenant in the US Army, Infantry in 1974 after completion of ROTC training and graduation from Murray State University. Assigned to the Infantry Officer Basic Course, Fort Benning, GA in November 1974, and after completion, reassigned to Initial Entry Rotary Wing flight training at Fort Rucker, AL in April 1975.

Upon completion of flight training in February 1976 he was assigned to the 118th Avn. Co., Schofield Barracks, Hawaii until March 1979. Duties with the ll8th included Aviation Section and Platoon Leader of an UH-1 Air Assault Unit. Promoted to the rank of captain in 1979 and separated from the US Army in March of that year.

Entered service with the US Coast Guard in June 1979, after receiving an appointment as a Direct Commission Aviator. Assigned to USCG Air Station,, Los Angeles, CA as a search and rescue pilot in the HH-52 helicopter. While serving at Los Angeles, he participated in a number of open sea rescue missions. One mission involving the rescue of survivors clinging to a capsized vessel at night was made into a documentary for the television program *"That's Incredible,"* in which he appeared.

Separated from the USCG in 1982 and accepted employment as an instrument instructor pilot with Aviation Contractor at Fort Rucker, AL. In 1984 he entered US Civil Service as a flight instructor of Combat Skills for the US Army at Fort Rucker, AL until present. In 1988, he earned his master's degree in aeronautical science from Embry Riddle Aeronautical University. Continued to serve in the Reserve Component as an instructor pilot in the UH-1 and pilot in the UH-60 aircraft until 1996.

During his career, he accumulated over 12,000 flight hours performing the duties of military aviation.

GERALD WAYNE RYE, Sergeant E-5, born 26 Dec 1947 in Hopkinsville, KY. His father was Van Layton Rye, Class of 43, Trigg County HS, and his grandmother was Edmonia Rye McCain of Cadiz. Gerald lived with his grandmother in Cadiz for several years as a child. After his father's discharge from the USN, but before Gerald's birth, his father worked for the Army in Civil Service at Fort Campbell, KY. They moved to Clarksville, TN in 1952 and to Atlanta, GS in 1959 when his father was promoted to a position at Fort McPherson, GA. Gerald was inducted into the service in Atlanta, GA.

He entered the Army 20 Feb 1966, was assigned to basic training at Fort Benning, GA; traveled to El Paso, TX and finished AIT at Fort Bliss in surface to air missiles. He was stationed in Regensburg, West Germany for 31 months as a HAWK fire control crewman.

His awards include the National Defense Service Medal, Good Conduct Medal Rifle and Missile Badge. Memorable was being stationed 50 km from Czech Border when Russia invaded Prague; and being the youngest NCO in Battalion at 19 years of age.

After his discharge in 1969 he became a police officer with the city of East Point, GA where he had attended high school. He met Doris Thomas while on patrol with the police department, and they were married 7

Mar 1970. They have one daughter, Tracy Deanne Rye (b. 18 Jul 1971). She has an undergraduate and masters degree from Georgia Institute of Technology (Georgia Tech) and is presently employed by the school.

Gerald has been with Delta Airlines in Atlanta since June 1974 serving in several capacities in Airport Customer Service. This job has allowed him to meet numerous celebrities passing through the busiest airport in the world.

Jerry, Doris Ann and Tracy currently reside in Douglasville, GA. Doris Ann and Tracy enjoying flying to many of the destinations which Delta serves and Jerry attends as many Atlanta Braves games as possible. At the age of 43, he was a Batboy for the Braves for two games when the Braves played the Philadelphia Phillies in Philadelphia. Other than his marriage and the birth of their daughter, it was the most exciting two days of his life.

DR. JACK ELVIS SANDERS, born 7 Aug 1941 in Cadiz, KY, on the "gully," the son of Eura "Mutt" Sanders and Elaine Baker Sanders. He graduated from Trigg County High School in 1959, Western KY University in 1963, and the University of Kentucky with a dental degree in 1967.

Sanders received U.S. Army basic training at Fort Bragg, NC. On 1 Jul 1967, he went to Fort Sam Houston, TX for Medical Field Service training. He spent two years at Fort Clayton in the Panama Canal Zone in the U.S. Army Southern Command. His son, Steven Brent Sanders, was born in Balboa, Panama Canal Zone. He was discharged at Fort Jackson, Charleston, SC in July 1969.

Dr. Jack is married to Jackie Laverne Mays Sanders. He has four children: Kelly Haugh, Steve Sanders, Kendra Redd and Ashley Hunter; one stepdaughter, Belinda Barnes; four grandchildren: Erica Anderson, Emily Anderson, Caroline Redd, Elizabeth Redd; four step-grandchildren: Allison Haugh, Rachel Haugh, Dustin Henderson and Austin Barnes.

Dr. Jack Sanders has practiced dentistry in Cadiz, KY for 32 years.

DALTON EARL SHOLAR, First Sergeant, born 9 Dec 1944, in Trigg County, KY to Noble and Katherine Sowell Sholar. He enlisted with the USAR 3 Aug 1965 at Hopkinsville, KY and served with the 3rd Bn., 399th AR Regt., 2nd Bde., 100th Div. Hopkinsville, KY.

He served as drill sergeant and tank commander and retired in 1995 as First Sergeant. Awards include the Meritorious Service Medal, Army Achievement Medal w/4 OLCs, Army Commendation Medal w/2 OLCs, Drill Sergeant Identification Badge, Armed Forces Ribbon, Army Service Ribbon and Defense Service Medal. In 1987 his unit was awarded "Best Small Unit" award.

He married Brenda Thomas Sholar 24  Aug 1968 and they have two children, Christopher Scott Sholar and Matthew Ted Sholar. They have one grandchild, Thomas Carter Sholar. Dalton has a brother Wendell Sholar and a sister Mary Agnes Sholar Moore.

He attends Locust Grove Baptist Church where he serves as Sunday School Director. He enjoys NASCAR racing and playing golf. He is employed with Southern States Cooperative in Hopkinsville as a field sales associate.

WILLIAM H. SKINNER, PFC, born 17 Dec 1943 in Cadiz, KY. He joined the service 13 Apr 1964 in Nashville, TN. Assignments include basic training at Fort Polk, LA; 1st Inf. Div. Fort Riley, KS, Tank School; Fort Irwin, CA; truck driver and artillery loader.

In Vietnam they supported the 101st Abn. Div., 173rd Abn. Div. on Search and Destroy Missions, 155th Artillery support. Memorable was hauling ammo and seeing his buddy's truck getting blown up. Pfc. Skinner was discharged 10 Apr 1966.

On 14 Jun 1976 he married Jinnie and they have one son Tony W. and one grandchild, Tony R. They live in Hopkinsville, KY, and he is a truck driver for Ebonite International in Hopkinsville.

JAMES "JIM" FRANCIS SMITH SR., Master Sergeant, born 27 Aug 1945 in Christian County, KY. He entered the Army 9 Nov 1966, and was stationed at Fort Campbell, KY for basic training. He later transferred to Fort Leonard Wood, MO and then to Fort Riley, KS.

On 10 Jul 1967, he boarded the USNS *Barret* for Vietnam, where he served the next year at Da Nang, Quang Tri, and Dong Hoi as a water supply chemist with the 111th Engineers of the 1st Logistical Command.

On 10 Jul 1968, Jim returned to Fort Leonard Wood as an instructor of the Water Supply Academy. Released from active duty 9 Aug 1969, he entered the USAR, 100th Div.

Jim retired with 30 years service as master sergeant, brigade chief supply sergeant, 2nd Brigade, 100th Div. He is holder of two Meritorious Service Medals and two Army Commendation Medals.

Jim married Peggy Lancaster 16 May 1965. They have three children: Vanessa Lea (b. 8 Jul 1966, d. 8 Jul 1966); James Francis Jr. "Frankie" (b. 12 Jan 1968, d. 1 Jun 1999); and Marc Lowe (b. 21 Jul 1970). They reside at 4355 Hopkinsville Road.

Jim is retired from the Hopkinsville Police Department and Smith's Wood Products, and is currently a realtor and auctioneer.

RICHARD E. STEVENSON, Colonel, is a native of Cadiz. He was born there on 6 Sep 1942, grew up in Cadiz and Madisonville, and graduated from Trigg County HS in 1960. He participated in Air Force ROTC at the University of Kentucky and was commissioned a second lieutenant upon graduation in May 1964.

His early career was in the Strategic Air Command, serving in B-52 wings at Eglin AFB, FL and Griffiss AFB, NY. He was selected to be the SAC spokesman for operations in Vietnam, meeting daily with the international press corps in Saigon in 1969-70.

Next he moved to SAC HQ where he directed the Commander's Distinguished Visitors program as Chief of Special Events. In 1973 he moved to the Pentagon. He was the advance man for the Secretary of the Air Force during this tour. He also worked with authors on stories about the Air Force.

His next assignment was at Mississippi State University as an instructor and Commandant of Cadets in the Air Force ROTC program. He returned to SAC HQ in 1980 as Chief of the Community Relations program.

He then served as chief of the operations division for the Commander in Chief Pacific Public Affairs Office in Hawaii. He was deputy press advance for President Ronald Reagan's visit to Hawaii, worked with the media on coverage of U.S. troops in the Pacific, and spokesman for several POW/MIA recovery missions.

While at CINCPAC, he was selected for promotion to colonel and Adm. William Crowe, future Chairman of the Joint Chiefs of Staff, conducted the promotion ceremony.

Col. Stevenson was selected as commander and editor-in-chief of the *Pacific Stars and Stripes*. From Tokyo he directed a retail and wholesale book store operation in addition to publishing a daily newspaper serving American GIs throughout the Pacific.

His last assignment was as Chief of Command Liaison and Public Affairs for the Army and Air Force Exchange Service's Pacific Headquarters in Hawaii.

Following retirement in 1991, he and his wife, the former Carolyn McAtee of Trigg County, settled in Hopkinsville. Both of their sons are serving in the military. William is a Navy lieutenant commander, and Michael is an intelligence officer in the Air Force.

Col. Stevenson has served as first vice president, legislative chair and president of the Fort Campbell Chapter of The Retired Officers Association. He presently serves as President of the Kentucky Council of TROA Chapters.

JAMES STROUD, PO1/c, born Dec. 11, 1950, the second son of Lamon Dana and June (Lacy) Stroud of Clinton, KY. He served in the USN February 1970-January 1980. James received his basic military training at Great Lakes, IL. Afterwards he was assigned to Lakehurst NTC, Lakehurst, NJ for technical training as an areographer's mate in the fields of meteorology and oceanography. For the next 10 years James worked as a "weatherman" in the Aviation Branch of the USN.

Between 1970-1980, James only spent six weeks "at sea," mainly conducting oceanographic research. His other duty assignments included Whiting Field NAS, FL (1970-72): Diego Garcia, British Indian Ocean Territory (1972-73); Pearl Harbor, HI (1973-76); and, Norfolk NAS, VA (1977-80). James attained the rank of first class petty officer before leaving the service. He was a Vietnam War Era veteran.

Shortly after joining the Navy, James married Sue (Lucas) Gale of Fulgham, KY. They have five children: Holly, Laurie, Andrew, Phillip, and Adam. Laurie and Phillip also served in the USN during the 1990s. Laurie was stationed stateside and Phillip was stationed aboard the nuclear-powered aircraft carrier, *Theodore Roosevelt,* in the Mediterranean Sea/ Persian Gulf areas during the Balkan Conflict.

James enjoyed his time in the Navy "seeing the world" (The Atlantic, Pacific, and Indian Oceans, Thailand, Japan, Vietnam, Hong Kong, Mauritius Island, plus three years in "Paradise"). What more could you ask? As the advertisement says, "Go Navy."

CARL RAY SUMNER, Sergeant E-5, born 27 Jun 1949 in Cadiz, KY. Enlisted into the Army on 10 Jun 1968 at Nashville, TN. After four months of training he volunteered to go to Vietnam. He reported to Fort Lewis, WA on his way to Vietnam.

On 10 Nov 1968 he arrived in Cam Ranh Bay, South Vietnam and ran into a lifetime friend of his, Ronald Burcham. After about eight days he was sent to the Americal Division at Chu Lai farther north.

At Chu Lai, he was assigned to Alpa Co., 3rd Bde., First Inf., 11th Light Inf. Bde. at Duc Pho. His company was a long range reconnaissance patrol company and he spent a couple of days there before going out to his company in the mountains.

It was to become an everyday war, if not fighting the enemy they would be battling the heat, rain, mosquitoes, booby traps and harassment from the enemy. Also, if we got any sleep it would only be for about three hours at the most a night. They would go on two man listening patrols for the enemy at night also. They would spend 60 days in the fields and jungles doing this before going in for a three day rest.

The most memorable experience was on 15 Aug 1969 when he attacked a machine gun nest that had them pinned down. Using his hand grenades he destroyed the nest so his comrades could get into safer fighting positions. He made and lost a lot of friends over there for nothing.

In November 1969 he returned and finished his tour at Fort Carson, CO where he was discharged in June 1970 at the rank of sergeant E-5. His awards include the national Defense Service Medal, Vietnam Service Medal w/3 Bronze Service Stars, Vietnam Campaign Medal w/60 device and Bronze Star Medal w/v device and OLC and the Combat Infantryman Badge.

He retired from the Federal Government at Fort Campbell, KY, Civil Service on 3 Nov 2000.

In December 1979 he met Janice Dunn whom he married in 1985. They have one daughter Juanita. They all live in Cadiz, KY.

DAVID SUMNER, PO3/c, born 6 May 1946 in Cadiz, KY. He enlisted in the USN 30 Sep 1965 and after three months of boot camp at the USNTC, San Diego, CA he received orders to the USS *Reeves* (DLG-24) in Long Beach, CA.

The *Reeves* departed Long Beach on 26 May 1966 for a two year tour with the US 7th Fleet. The ship, a unit of Destroyer Squadron Nine, was homeported in Yokosuka, Japan and operated in the Gulf of Tonkin as an anti-air warfare picket and search and rescue unit during the Vietnam War. The *Reeves* achieved the reputation of being an outstanding Search and Rescue Unit among both Navy and Air Force Aviators. The ship effected the actual rescue of seven downed airmen and through professional air control and air navigation services, prevented the need to rescue many others.

David returned to the States in August 1968 and was honorably discharged 8 Jul 1969. His awards include the National Defense Service Medal, Navy Commendation Ribbon, Vietnam Service Medal and Vietnam Campaign Medal.

In 1970 he entered the Boilermaker Apprenticeship Program with TVA. During the construction of the Cumberland Steam Plant, he was transferred to Johnsonville Steam Plant to complete the program. He resided in Tennessee for 15 years, retired from TVA in November 1994 and now lives in Cadiz, KY.

David married Sharon Wynn on 26 Sep 1970. They have one daughter, Ashley Paige. His hobbies are crappie fishing and geneology.

GARY SUMNER, graduated from Trigg County HS in May 1965, moved to Alton, IL in July 1965 and went to work at Alton Boxboard Company in September 1965. He received his draft notice in April 1966, and was sent to Nashville, TN, to take his physical. After passing the physical, he was told that within 21 days, if he did not choose another branch of service, he would be drafted into the Army. James Ray Owens and I had talked to his dad about the Navy, since Mr. Owens was a Navy veteran. They then decided to go into the Navy on the buddy plan. Dan Gray and Larry Watkins, also from Trigg County, went in the Navy at the same time as did Dickie Harper from Hopkinsville. They were all flown to Louisville for induction, then on to O'Hare in Chicago. They were then transported to Great Lake's Naval Training Command Center.

He lost track of James during basic training, but Larry, Dickie, Dan and himself, graduated together. Larry's parents picked them up after graduation and took them back to Trigg County.

After two weeks leave he reported to the NAS, Jacksonville, FL, where he spent two years at the Air Operations Dept. Upon completion of duty at NavAirJax, he received 30 days leave and reported to the aircraft carrier, USS *Franklin D. Roosevelt* (CVA-42) at Norfolk, VA. Upon completion of her stay at Norfolk, they spent two weeks off the VA Capes for air qualifications, then proceeded to Mayport, FL, her homeport. They operated in the South Atlantic before heading for Guantanamo Bay, Cuba for two months. After that, they operated out of the Caribbean Sea.

They visited Cuba, Haiti, the Virgin Islands, Puerto Rico, and other points of interest throughout the Caribbean. They returned to Mayport, FL, before Thanksgiving of 1969.

President Nixon authorized an early reduction of authorized strength and Gary was discharged on 31 Dec 1969. He received an honorable discharge on 2 May 1972.

While Gary was in the Navy, he met and married Jean Saunders of Amherst, VA, where they currently reside. They have three daughters: Shannon Taylor of Beaufort, SC, Jennifer Sumner of Amherst, VA, and Lisa Baldock of Madison Heights, VA, and grandchildren: Jared Sumner, Hillary Taylor, Michael Taylor, Courtney Baldock and Kathryn Baldock.

JERRY LYNN SUMNER, born 10 Feb 1945, son of Jesse and Eunice Sumner. Jerry enlisted in the USN 29 Sep 1965 and served aboard the guided missile frigate USS *Reeves* during the Vietnam Conflict.

He was called home in July 1967 due to the death of his brother. On his return back to the ship he was hospitalized in Osaka, Japan where he received a visit from the Rev. Billy Graham. He never returned to his ship. He was issued a medical discharge 12 Dec 1967.

He married Linda Yates 11 Oct 1969. Jerry worked for TVA and at the time of his death on 18 May 1977, he was employed with Union Carbide Atomic Plant in Paducah, KY. He and his wife made their home in Kuttawa, KY. He is buried in the Kuttawa Cemetery in Lyon County.

He was a 5th generation descendant from James Thomas Sr. who fought in the Revolutionary War and settled a large portion of the Donaldson Creek Community in Trigg County where Jerry grew up.

CHARLES R. TACKETT, CWO4, born 14 Apr 1944 in Sharon, TN and enlisted in the Army on 11 Dec 1962. He retired from the Army on 1 Feb 1990 at Fort McPherson, GA. He progressed through the enlisted ranks from private to staff sergeant then accepted a commission to second lieutenant followed by promotions through the commissioned ranks to major. He retired from active duty with the rank of Chief Warrant Officer 4.

Tackett's overseas assignments included a combat tour in the Republic of Vietnam, where he flew helicopters in support of US and South Vietnamese forces. Other overseas assignments, on the front lines of the Cold War, included three tours in Korea and one in Berlin, Germany, the walled city, known at that time as the Island of Freedom in a Sea of Communism.

Stateside assignments of note included Fort Knox, KY, where he met and married his wife Mary Jean Tyler, who was a civil service employee, and where several years later their only child Charles R. Junior was born. Also notable was his years at Fort Campbell, during which the Tackett family bought a house and settled in Trigg County, after becoming infatuated with the area and all it had to offer.

During his final tour in Korea, Charles was notified that his home in Trigg County had burned to the ground, but, thankfully, his family had escaped unharmed. Consequently the Tackett family was uprooted and moved to Atlanta, GA for his final years of service. His many years of service garnered him numerous awards including the Legion of Merit, two awards of the Distinguished Flying Cross, Bronze Star, Meritorious Service Medal, 22 awards of the Air Medal, multiple Army Commendation Medals, Army Achievement Medal, Good Conduct Medal, Humanitarian Service Medal plus too many campaign and service medals to list. He was also appointed a Kentucky Colonel by then Governor Julian Carroll.

Following retirement, he entered the civilian workforce by flying for an airline in Atlanta until health reasons forced him to retire his wings again. The Tackett family decided it was time to return to Kentucky so they packed their three cats and a dog into a motor home and returned to their empty lot in Trigg County and commenced to rebuild their house. They now live a quiet life surrounded by the natural beauty and abundant wildlife that Trigg County has to offer.

HOWARD WAYNE TAYLOR, Sergeant, born 2 Dec 1947 in Cadiz, KY. He joined the USAF on 1 Feb 1967 at Lexington, KY, and after six months of training at Lackland AFB, in San Antonio, TX, he was assigned to Detachment 30 Logistics at Ankara, Turkey. He performed law enforcement duties and was sent on TDY assignment to top secret nuclear weapons sites.

Returned to the States in January 1989 and was stationed at Wright Patterson AFB in Dayton, OH where he was assigned to the SAC Nuclear Weapons site.

He was discharged 1 Feb 1971 as a sergeant. Some of his more memorable experiences include meeting his future wife, Marlene Schnell, at Wright-Patterson AFB; and providing security in Turkey for Cyrus Vance, Robert MacNamoa and the Harlem Globetrotters.

After discharge he graduated from Murray State University on the GI Bill and later attained his master's degree from the University of Louisville. He worked in health care for 23 years retiring as the chief executive officer of Western State Hospital in March 1997. Since retirement he has been involved with the Fort Campbell, KY, Domestic Violence Program. His hobbies are hunting and golfing.

Howard and Marlene married 16 Oct 1970 and have two children, Jeremy and Brad.

MARLENE SCHNELL TAYLOR, 1st Lieutenant, born 25 Jun 1946 in Estherville, IA. After becoming an RN in 1967, she worked at the hospital she was born in before entering the USAF as a 2nd lieutenant on 13 Apr 1968. She was assigned to Sheppard AFB, TX to attend officer's orientation and from there to Wright-Patterson AFB, OH.

At WPAFB she served as a medical surgical nurse taking care of many of the injured from Vietnam. During her tour she was promoted to first lieutenant and received the National Defense Service Medal and the AF Outstanding Unit Award. She also met her future husband, Wayne Taylor, while he was in the USAF and stationed at WPAFB.

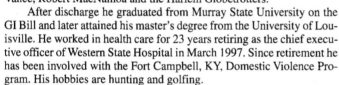

Marlene received an honorable discharge on 13 Apr 1970 and returned to her home in Iowa where she worked in a nursing home until her job in Stockton, CA was to start. She never made it to California because she had continued to correspond with Wayne, quit her nursing home job and was back out in Ohio before the Air Force had time to ship her household goods home. She worked at Dayton Tire & Rubber as an industrial nurse until they had a factory lay-off, then entered civil service with the VA in Dayton.

Wayne and Marlene were married 16 Oct 1970 and Marlene transferred to the VA in Indianapolis until Wayne got out of the Air Force. He wanted to go back to school so they moved to Kentucky and he enrolled at Murray State and Marlene worked at Trigg County Hospital until they decided to move closer to school. Both she and her husband attended MSU and Marlene worked night at Murray Calloway County Hospital in Coronary Care.

When Marlene got a job at Fort Campbell, KY, Hospital, they bought

a farm and moved back to Cadiz, KY. She returned to MSU to complete her bachelor of science in nursing while working in the Intensive Care Unit at Fort Campbell. After several years she became evening/night supervisor of Blanchfield Army Community Hospital and later head nurse of the surgical ward. With downsizing in 1996, she transferred to her present position as one of two occupational health nurses for the Fort Campbell post.

Marlene and Wayne reside three miles south of Cadiz and enjoy golf and travel. Both their sons, Jeremy and Brad, are attending college.

DORIS R. TERRELL, born 28 Dec 1947 in Cadiz, KY. He was drafted 13 Dec 1967 in Cadiz and took basic training at Fort Campbell, KY, followed by Fort Leonard Wood, MO, March to August 1968.

He was sent to Pleiku, Vietnam for a year, August 1968 to August 1969 and participated in the Vietnam Conflict.

Discharged 15 Aug 1969. His awards include the Vietnam Service Medal, Expert Rifle Badge, Army Commendation and Good Conduct.

Married Opal Christine on 26 Nov 1967 and they have three children: Tony Fowler, Melissa and Kevin, and three grandchildren: Brandi Lancaster, Derrick and Samantha Fowler.

Doris is a postal worker and plumbing contractor.

JAMES LESTER TERRELL, E-5, born 13 Feb 1948 in Lyon County, KY. He was drafted to serve in the US Army 18 Nov 1968. James received his basic training at Fort Campbell, KY then transferred to Fort Lewis, WA for advanced infantry training. Fort Benning, GA, was where he attended Ranger School, NCO School and Jump School, earning the rank of E-5.

James was assigned to the 173rd Abn. Inf. Div., B Co., 2nd Bn. in Vietnam. He received the Purple Heart along with several others medals while serving in Vietnam.

He received his honorable discharge 26 Oct 1970 and returned to work at Hoover Universal in Cadiz for the next 16 years. He is currently employed by the US Postal Service as a rural mail carrier in Cerulean, KY.

James married Judy Boren 15 Jun 1968 and they have four children: Kevin, Amy Carneyhan, Charles and LeNell, and five grandchildren: Andrew Mitchell and Jacob Cullen Terrell; Wm. Blake, Megan Caroline and Trevor James Carneyhan.

EDDIE LEON THOMAS, E-5, born 10 Dec 1947 in Trigg County, KY, son of Oscar and Willie Adams Thomas. He was drafted 12 Dec 1967 at Trigg County with assignments at Fort Campbell, KY and Vietnam.

Discharged as private first class 13 Aug 1968 and returned to Oakland, CA. Sent to Vietnam in 1969. Discharged in 1971 as E-5 and stayed in the Reserve until 11 Dec 1973. His awards include the National Defense Service Medal, Vietnam Service Medal, Vietnam Campaign Medal and Bronze Star.

He resides in Donaldson Creek, Trigg County, KY and works where he was employed before draft, Johnson Control. He has two children, Kathy and Dona, and one grandchild, Taylor.

MALCOLM RAY THOMAS, born 24 Dec 1949 at Futrell Clinic in Cadiz, KY. He was drafted into the Army 17 Jun 1969 and sent to Fort Campbell, KY for basic training, then to Fort Polk, LA for his AIT training.

On 17 Nov 1969 he was sent to Vietnam and assigned to the 196th Inf. Bde. Americal Div. He returned home from Vietnam on 31 Oct 1970.

In December 1970, he was assigned to Fort Carson, CO, where he stayed until his discharge 16 Jun 1971. He received a Bronze Star Medal, Combat Infantry Medal, Army Commendation Medal, National Defense Service Medal and the Vietnam Campaign Service Medal w/2 Bronze Service Stars.

Malcolm Ray was married on 26 Jul 1974 to Laura Redick. They reside in Trigg Country on Redick Pond Road and are members of Bethesda United Methodist Church.

Malcolm Ray has worked for BellSouth for 19 years.

PATRICK VICK THOMAS, Lieutenant Colonel, born 28 Jul 1938 in Gracey, KY. Assignments: July 1961-October 1963, 3rd Arty. Gp., Norfolk, VA, Operations Officer; October 1963-April 1966, 559th Arty. Gp., Vicenza, Italy, detachment commander and assistant S-1; April 1966-October 1967, 1st Tng. Bde., Fort Benning, GA, Company Commander and Brigade S-1; October 1967-July 1968, Artillery Advanced Course at Fort Sill, OK and Fort Bliss, TX; July 1968-July 1969, 1st Inf. Div. Arty., S-1, and 1st Logistic Group, Manpower Management; July 1975-August 1976 (White Sands Missile Range, installation veterinarian; August 1976-August 1979, veterinary meat inspection for DOD, Dallas/Fort Worth, TX; July 1980-April 1981, Fort Gordon, GA, installation veterinarian; April 1981-July 1984, installation veterinarian for Fort McClellan, AL; and July 1984-May 1987, Defense Personnel Support Center, Philadelphia, PA, Chief of the Meat/Dairy Procurement Branch.

Lt. Col. Thomas was discharged from the US Army Veterinary Corps on 1 May 1987. His awards include the Bronze Star w/OLC, Defense Meritorious Service Medal, Meritorious Service Medal and others.

It was memorable to begin a military career as an artillery officer for eight plus years and to complete his career as a veterinarian in the Army Veterinary Corps with a master's degree. Also memorable was seeing the world, working with many unforgettable people, having a variety of assignments with different responsibilities, and serving his country in two capacities.

As a civilian he was a veterinarian in the meat industry as a consultant with a major Australian agri-business for three years; director of Quality Assurance with a major meat company for two years; and a regional meat inspection veterinarian in Texas since 1992.

He married Judith Nan Thomas in February 2000. He has four children: Derrick, Dana, Emily and Andrew; and five grandchildren: Erin, Kevin, Christopher, Colin and Keith Thomas. Patrick and Judith live in Arlington, TX.

PETE THOMAS JR., born 7 Oct 1943 in Cadiz, KY. He was drafted into the Army 10 May 1965 and reported for basic training at Fort Jack-

son, SC. After completing basic, he was sent to Fort Sam Houston, TX for AIT as a medical corpsman.

Pete was stationed at Schofield Barracks, HI, home of the 25th Inf. Div. In January 1966, the 25th was deployed to the Republic of South Vietnam.

Serving one year in the war effort, Pete received the National Defense Service Medal, Vietnam Service Medal, Army Commendation Medal w/V Device, three Bronze Stars, Combat Medical Badge and Purple Heart. Returning to the States he completed his duty at Fort Gordon, GA.

Pete married Doris Jones in 1967. They have two children, Reginald and Denise Thomas.

ROBERT CLYDE "R.C." THOMAS, Tech Sergeant, born 30 Sep 1933 in Caldwell County, KY, and married Margie Adams, a Trigg County native, on 22 Dec 1951. He registered with the Local Board in Trigg County on 19 Jan 1953 and entered the USAF on 1 Apr 1953.

He took basic at Sampson AFB, NY and air frame repair tech schooling at Amarillo, TX. He was stationed at Turner AFB, GA; Tachikawa AFB in Japan; Ardmore AFB, OK; Druex AFB in France; Sewart AFB, TN; Vietnam; Grissom AFB, IN; and Anderson AFB in Guam.

His family joined him in Georgia, Oklahoma, France, Tennessee, Indiana and Guam. He was a TDY man standing for temporary duty when stationed in Tennessee and Indiana. This means he would come home pack his bag, and fly off to another country in a few hours. Sometimes R.C. would be gone for three months, other times he didn't know when he would come home to see his family. He worked on many different aircraft.

R.C. earned the AF Commendation Medal while serving at Cam Rahn Bay, Vietnam. Other medals include the AF Outstanding Unit Award w/Bronze OLC, National Defense Service Medal w/Bronze Star, Korean Service Medal, Armed Forces Expeditionary Medal, AF Longevity Service Medal w/2 Bronze OLCs, Vietnam Service Medal w/Bronze Star, RVN Service Medal, Small Arms Expert Marksmanship, UN Service Medal and the AF Good Conduct Medal w/Silver Oak Leaf (earned this medal three times).

R.C. supervised 170 men at Anderson AFB in Guam, 1971-73, and traveled to 26 different foreign countries. TSgt. Thomas retired from the Air Force 1 Jul 1973, with 20+ years.

After retirement R.C. and Margie moved back to Cadiz. His civilian jobs included park ranger, aircraft transit alert, construction foreman, instructor for Lockheed Aircraft in Jeddah, Saudi Arabia and 14 years quality control foreman at Johnson Controls in Cadiz. He retired in 1995.

R.C. and Margie have three children: Sandra, Robert and Katharine; six grandchildren; and one step great-grandchild. R.C. passed away on 25 Mar 2000.

HERMAN TINSLEY, Sergeant, born 19 Apr 1944 in Cadiz, KY. He enlisted into the Army during the height of the Vietnam era and served as a machine gunner in a special 1st Cav. Abn., Air Mobile Unit.

He was decorated seven times and finished his tour of duty as a drill sergeant in Fort Bragg, NC. Sgt. Tinsley was discharged 28 Nov 1971.

Herman is a general contractor and a minister/missionary to South Africa – building a Vocational Training and Bible Insti-

tute in Johannesburg, South Africa. He is the president of Faith Missions International.

He married Patrice 4 Jan 1997 and they live in West Govina, CA. He has two sons by a previous marriage, Terry and Michael, and two grandchildren, Tiffany and Michael Jr.

DOUGLAS EARL WADE, Lieutenant Colonel, born 15 Nov 1938 in Trigg County, KY. He was commissioned into the Army as 2nd lieutenant in February 1962 through Murray State University ROTC Program.

He met his wife Glinda and MSU and they married in March 1962. In April she remained in Louisville to finish nursing school while he went to Fort Sam Houston, TX for training.

His first assignment was Fort Hood, TX where there was another first, a son Martin Douglas (b. 16 Nov 1962). He was sent to Orleans, France, 34th Gen. Hospital serving 2-1/2 years of a three year tour. Gen. Charles DeGaul no longer wanted American troops in France so the remaining tour was served in Germany where his second son, Jeffrey Vernon (b. 5 Mar 1967).

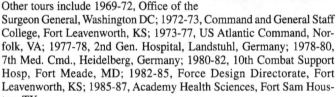

He settled his family in San Antonio, TX, 1967-68, before leaving for duty in Long Binh, Vietnam, 68th Med. Group. Other tours include 1969-72, Office of the Surgeon General, Washington DC; 1972-73, Command and General Staff College, Fort Leavenworth, KS; 1973-77, US Atlantic Command, Norfolk, VA; 1977-78, 2nd Gen. Hospital, Landstuhl, Germany; 1978-80, 7th Med. Cmd., Heidelberg, Germany; 1980-82, 10th Combat Support Hosp, Fort Meade, MD; 1982-85, Force Design Directorate, Fort Leavenworth, KS; 1985-87, Academy Health Sciences, Fort Sam Houston, TX.

In the course of his career, he received many awards, including the Bronze Star, Legion of Merit, Meritorious Service, Vietnam Gallantry Cross, Army Commendation and others.

He retired in August 1987 after which he lived and worked in Virginia Beach, VA and Fairfax, VA. During this period two granddaughters, Morgan (b. 4 Feb 1993) and her sister Raleigh (b. 14 Mar 1996) were born to Martin and Whitney. A grandson is due in June 2001 to be born to Jeffrey and Trudy.

In 1992 Douglas and Glinda moved back to Trigg County, living there two years before moving to Clarksville, TN. Douglas passed away 23 May 1999 and is buried in Blue Springs Cemetery, Caldwell County, KY.

DONALD EDWIN WEBSTER, Sergeant E-5, born 9 Jul 1941 in Friendship, TN. He joined the National Guard in 1965, Dyersburg, TN and was discharged in 1971 with the rank of sergeant E-5.

He married Julia Wilson 8 May 1976. Don met his Julia when she was a nurse in Jackson, TN. Don was a banker at Bank of Friendship for 33 years and retired in October 1999. Julia, an RN, is the daughter of Ray and Charlotte Wilson of Cadiz, KY. They have four children: Robin Salyers, Brad Webster, Kara Peters and Bart Webster, and six grandchildren: Ashley Salyers, Kara Salyers, Mason Peters, Alec Peters, Savannah Webster and Virginia Webster.

After Don's retirement they moved back to Cadiz, KY, where he is now manager of Arrowhead Golf Club in Cadiz. Don's hobbies are golfing, fishing and gardening.

EDMOND WELFORD JR., E-4, born 13 Jun 1950. He joined the service 13 May 1970 and served in Vietnam. Other stations included New Mexico, Germany, Copenhagen, Paris, France and El Paso, TX. He received the Purple Heart.

He lives with his wife Annie in Cadiz, KY and is a disabled vet. Edmond retired in 1999 from TVA, public safety and energy conservation.

HAROLD WILSON, SP5, born 30 Jun 1946 in Henderson, KY. He moved to Trigg County in 1948 where his parents, Plomer Wilson Sr. and Nellie Crisp Wilson, were born and raised. He was drafted on 15 Aug 1967 and sworn into the Army in Nashville, TN. Later the same day he was flown to Fort Benning, GA, where he took eight weeks of basic training. After basic he was transferred to Fort Dix, NJ with four more weeks of advanced training, then transferred to Fort Hamilton, NY for more training.

He was allowed two weeks of leave before he was to report to Pirmasens, Germany, where he was assigned to HHC 59th Ord. Gp. While in Germany he was assigned to assist the chaplain. This company had several units across Germany, which they visited on a regular schedule. While in Germany he had the opportunity to travel extensively. He traveled to England, France, Italy, Austria and Scotland. One of the most interesting places he visited was Berlin where he was allowed to go through Checkpoint Charlie into East Berlin. He will always remember how much difference there was between West and East Berlin.

Harold was released from active duty in Fort Dix, NJ on 23 Jul 1969 with the rank specialist 5.

He married a Trigg County girl, Beverly Simmons, daughter of Earl and Geneva Simmons of Christian County. Over the years Harold worked with the US Post Office where he retired 30 Jun 2001. The Wilsons have two children, Lesli (md. to Kevin Hatley) and Kevin (graduated from college in 2001). They attend the Cadiz Christian Church where Harold serves as Elder.

TOMMY RAY WINN, Sergeant E-5, enlisted in the USMC in February 1968 and went to boot camp at MCRD, San Diego, CA. He was assigned to Special Forces Marine Corps, C Force Recon Co., 1st Force Recon Bn., 1st Mar. Div., I Corps AMA South Vietnam making numerous patrols in controlled enemy areas.

Tommy completed two tours in Vietnam, was wounded and discharged in February 1974. His awards include the Purple Heart and Navy Commendation Medal w/Combat V.

He lives with his wife Linda in Cadiz, KY.

Post Vietnam War

RA___H H LIVESAY · JOHN A __
V __TER H ANDERSON · AN __
___FIELD · ___ __N D GRETHEN · TONY __
___CH Jr __HAEL J McGOLDRICK · J__
___URTON · ___RRENCE A TEAS · TOMMIE __
___YNE H ROWLAND · GEO__
___NNY A BOLIN · THOMAS __
___LLIAM T MAIN · LEE A ADA__
___ATCH___ ___RRELL Z MAGRUDER · A D __
___HN ABBOTT · FAMOUS L L __
___GE J SKAPINSKY · GRO__
___LES R GURTLER · MICH__
___NORRIS · DANIEL __
___MON · MIGUEL C __
___BOTT · JAMES E C __
___SAACS · GERALD B K __
___TERWILLIGER · WILL__
___HALL · HENRY PA __
___TERSON ___ KENNE__
___Jr ___ARL STAN__
___ WILLIA

268

LAURA LAVERN BAKER, PO1, born 29 Jan 1962 in Cadiz, KY. She enlisted into the USN Reserves Delayed Entry Program on 29 Jun 1987. In January 1988 she left for eight weeks of basic training in Orlando, FL and 4-1/2 weeks of Yeoman "A" School in Meridian, MS. She returned home in mid-April 1988 and was attached to the NCSO unit at Naval Reserve Center in Nashville, TN.

In August 1989 she transferred to the Army Reserves where she spent the next 11 years. She was attached to Co. B, 1st Bn., 398th Regt., 100th Div., training as a personnel administrative specialist. Seeking something a bit more challenging, in 1995 she went to Drill Sergeant School and in February 1996 was promoted to staff sergeant and graduated from Drill Sergeant School on 28 Jun 1996. "Being a drill sergeant is a job in which I am proudest of having accomplished, it is the most challenging and rewarding job, I think the military has to offer."

Other schools attended: Basic Non-Commissioned Officers Course Phases I and II, Personnel Administrative Specialists Phases I & II, & Primary Leadership Development Course.

She participated in three Boeslager Competitions, in 1992, 1993 and 1994 winning in 1994. She was selected the top female candidate in Western Kentucky to participate on the Boeslager team. Soldiers had to be in top physical condition to be selected to participate.

Awards and decorations include the Army Commendation Medal, Army Achievement Medal w/3 OLCs, Letters of Commendation for repeatedly scoring the maximum on the Physical Readiness Test, and the Physical Fitness Excellence Patch.

Even though her Army Career has been successful, to travel she transferred back into the Navy Reserves. She is presently attached to the ABFC unit at Naval Reserve Center in Nashville, TN. Her present rank is petty officer first class and her job is yeoman. She has traveled to Rota, Spain, and this year 2001 she will go to LCT School in Pensacola, FL.

She plans to finish her military career in the Navy and retire after completing 20 years of service.

She enjoys traveling, shopping, running, reading, biking, and fishing. She resides at home on the South Road in Cadiz, KY with her mother Terry Jane Baker, and is employed in Human Resources at Brazeway in Hopkinsville, KY. LaVern is a member of Pleasant Hill Baptist Church.

PATRICK ROYCE CURTIS, born 28 Feb 1964 in Hammond, IN to Mr. and Mrs. Gayle Hopson Curtis. He has two brothers, Phillip and Gregory, and two sisters, Rickki Lynn and Sammatha. He graduated in June 1982 from Michigan City HS. He moved to Trigg County, KY in 1983 to live with his grandparents Mr. and Mrs. Frank Curtis.

In 1983 he entered the US Army National Guard and was assigned to the Tank Division. He received his discharge in 1988.

He and Marie Watts Mills were married in November 1988. He is employed with Crisp Furniture in Cadiz, KY and currently resides in Trigg County. He enjoys golfing, fishing and ballgames.

JOHN T. DAVIS, Captain, born 2 Feb 1957 in Dhahran Saudi Arabia. He joined the Army in 1979 at Nashville, TN and served with 1/41 FA in Schwabish-Gmund, Germany, 1980-83.

Capt. Davis was discharged in 1983. He received the Army Achievement Medal and is a Cold War Veteran.

He married Laurie in 1983 and they have one son Anthony Chastine Davis. They live in Greenville, SC. John has been an engineer with Rockwell International since 1983 and still working.

JESSE LOUIS FRYE JR., Sergeant, born 26 Sep 1968 in Louisville, KY. He joined the Army 7 Jan 1987 and was stationed at Fort Dix, NJ for basic training, then moved to Fort Gordon, GA for advanced individual training as a radio operator.

After training he received orders for Germany where he was stationed at Bremerhaven, in northern Germany, with 581st Signal Co. While there he obtained the rank of Specialist 4. He stayed in Germany until his ETS on 7 Jan 1989.

After returning home he joined the Kentucky National Guard and has served with B Co. 1/123rd Armd. Bn. in Hopkinsville, with 20th Special Forces Group in Louisville, and is now with 2/123rd Armd. Bn., 35th ID as a senior command sergeant.

Frye was promoted to sergeant E-5 in July 1997. During his time of service he has received numerous awards including two Army Achievement Medals, two Kentucky Meritorious Service ribbons, and Kentucky Service Ribbon.

Jesse married Samantha Cunningham on 9 Aug 1997 and they have a daughter, Maylee McKenzie (b. 14 Aug 1998). Jesse is employed at Johnson Controls Inc. and has worked there since 1992.

MARCUS DEREC FRYE, Sergeant, born 4 Jun 1970 in El Paso, TX as an Army brat. He joined the Army on 22 Sep 1988, four months after graduating from Trigg County HS. After four months of basic training and advanced individual training on Lance Missiles at Fort Sill, OK, he was sent to Germany and assigned to 84th USAFAD, a nuclear warhead detachment close to Stuttgart.

Before leaving for Germany he married his high school sweetheart, Merilee Gipson, on 23 Dec 1988. While in Germany he obtained the rank of corporal and received the Army Commendation Medal. Marcus participated in the denuclearization of Europe before being sent back to the States in April 1992 for retraining as an aircraft electrician at Fort Eustis, VA, followed by orders for Fort Campbell, KY.

They moved back to their childhood home of Cadiz and built a house on the South Road where they still reside. Marcus was assigned to H Co.

159th AVN Brigade of the 101st. He stayed with that unit long enough to move to the 160th Special Operation Aviation Regiment (Airborne), also at Fort Campbell. While there he was promoted to sergeant and earned his jump wings with 10 jumps to his credit. He also attended SERE school, trained in seven countries and numerous states. He was a member of the task force that went to Haiti.

He left the service in 1996 and continues to work with the 160th in the employment of Lockheed Martin as an avionics and electrical systems instructor. He had eight years of service.

Marcus, Merilee and their three daughters: Hayla, Kanisha and Marcanah attend New Hope Baptist Church where he has served as the youth minister since September 1996.

CHRIS ERIC GARLAND, SP4, born 10 Dec 1966 in Hammond, IN to Harry and Bobbie Garland. He has a twin brother Craig Kent and two older brothers, Harry Jr. and Scott. His parents moved the family to Trigg County in 1969 and he graduated from Trig County HS in May 1985.

Two weeks after he graduated, Chris entered the Army for three years. He completed three months of basic training at Fort Jackson, SC and in September 1985 was stationed at Fort Stewart, GA where he was assigned to the 24h Signal Corp, receiving training as a multi-channel communication operator.

He received the Expert Marksman Award, earned his first Oak Leaf Cluster and was awarded the Army Achievement Medal. In 1987 his unit was sent to Karlshrue, Germany where he served for 18 months. On 24 May 1988 he received an honorable discharge with a rank of specialist 4th class.

In September 1988 he enrolled at Western Kentucky University, Bowling Green, KY and on 9 May 1992 he received a BS degree in finance. He took a managerial position with Walmart and transferred to Tulsa, OK in May 1995. He attended the Southern Nazerene University in Tulsa and on 12 May 2001 he graduated with honors and received a MBA degree. During that time he was introduced to Ms. Marsha Young, a paralegal working for a large law firm in Tulsa and a native of Oklahoma. On 7 Apr 2001 they were married in Eureka Springs, AR.

He currently resides in Broken Arrow, Ok with his wife Marsha and 6-year-old stepdaughter Arial. Chris enjoys working in his yard, golfing, tennis and fun with his family.

DAN MCCRAW JR., E-7, born 6 Apr 1967, Columbus, MS. He joined the Army in 23 Feb 1988, at Nashville, TN and has remained on active duty till the present day.

His tours were at Fort Campbell, KY where he became an Army Ranger and obtained the rank of E-7 in less than 10 years. Dan Jr. is presently stationed at the Pentagon in Washington DC.

He married Dawn on 8 May 1996 and they have three children: Ethan, Keri Anna and Meaghan. They reside in Fort Belvoir, VA and enjoy boating.

TERRY LYNN PARKER, Sergeant E-4, born in Trigg County on 18 Aug 1960, the son of Lucy and Joe Lacy Lancaster and the late Thomas L. Parker Jr. Terry graduated from Trigg County HS in 1978.

He enlisted in the USAF 25 Sep 1978 in Trigg County. He took his basic training at Lackland AFB in Texas. Terry remained there 14 weeks longer at the Police Academy, than transferred to Whiteman AFB, MO with the 351st Security Squadron. Terry served there as a law enforcement specialist. While in the Air Force he received a BA degree in business. Sgt. Parker was honorably discharged 24 Nov 1982.

Terry is married to Lisa Weaver and they have one child, Hannah. Terry also has two children by a previous marriage, Angela Farlee and Thomas Brandon Parker; and two step-children, Heather and Kirley Weaver. There is one grandchild, McKayla Farlee.

Terry has 13 years in public relations with Domino's Pizza Corp. He is now employed with P.J. Food's Corp. in Public Relations for the last five years. Terry resides in Louisville, KY.

ERIC DAMON SMITH, Major, born 6 Dec 1965 in Cadiz, KY. He attended Auburn University on an Air Force ROTC scholarship in aerospace engineering. He was commissioned in the USAF on 28 Aug 1987 after graduation.

During his time on active duty, Maj. Smith served as an astronomical strategic systems analyst at the National Air Intelligence Center (NAIC) at Wright-Patterson AFB where he analyzed scientific intelligence data to determine performance characteristics of foreign aerodynamic, ballistic, and space systems. He was the project manager and primary analyst/author of several scientific and technical analysis studies. He chaired national-level working groups that analyzed technical threats to strategic/space assets. He also produced nationally-validated battle employment scenarios that formed the baseline for the Air Force's computerized strategic and tactical war games. As this was during the end of the Cold War, he was able to observe the fall of the Soviet Union from the inside. He also served as a contract monitor and as the executive officer for the Threat Directorate.

Later, he moved to Wright Laboratory's Manufacturing Technology Directorate, where he served as Developmental Project Engineer. He attended Squadron Officer School at Maxwell AFB, AL in 1994. In 1995, Smith separated from active duty at the rank of captain and transferred to the Air Force Reserves.

As a Reservist for the Aeronautical System Center, Eric supported the Special Operational Forces (SOF) and Gunship System Program Offices. Since December 1996, he has supported the 88 Communications Group (88 CG) where he has provided web development consulting and training for WPAFB organizations. Smith led the effort to test and implement live and on-demand streaming multimedia on WPAFB web servers.

As a civilian, Smith is a Web Developer/Programmer and has been the Webmaster for the B-2 Stealth Bomber System Program Office since 1996. He has produced interactive/dynamic web sites and automated web solutions for several companies, including GE and NCR. He is recognized nationally in his field as the founder and leader of the Dayton Perl Mongers, a user group for the Perl programming language.

He married Audrey P. Schreiber on 23 May 1992. They currently have two children, Cole Damon (b. 25 Sep. 1999) and Sabrina Marie (b. 15 Dec. 2000).

ROBERT JOSEPH "SONNY" THOMAS, GMG-2, born 12 Jun 1956 at Sewart AFB, TN. He enlisted into the Navy on 13 Feb 1984 out of Hopkinsville, KY. After basic training at Great Lakes, IL, he was assigned to the Seabees. His next assignment was with the FF 1047 USS *Voge* where he functioned as a gunners mate.

His next duty station was at NAS, Mayport, FL. Thomas then was attached to the USS Coast Guard in peace keeping missions at the Panama Canal.

Thomas was discharged on 14 Feb 1988 with rank of GMG-2. He had been awarded the Meritorious Unit Commendation, National Defense Service Medal, Sea Service Deployment Ribbon x 2, US Coast Guard Operational Distinguished Service Medal and Good Conduct Medal. He also was a Weapon Specialist.

Thomas was the USS *Voge* physical instructor and the captain of the USS Voge Flag Football team. His most memorable experience was when his ship passed through the Panama Canal.

Thomas enjoys all sports. He loves to fish and the great outdoors. He is divorced and has one daughter, Nicole Leigh Thomas. His current occupation is concrete supervisor and he resides in Apex, NC.

WAYNE LEE THOMAS, Major, born 8 Jan 1962 at DOW AFB, Bangor ME. He enlisted into the Army on 18 Aug 1986 out of Hopkinsville, KY. After basic training at Fort Leonard Wood, MO he completed OCS and was commissioned on 20 Feb 1987.

Thomas started his career as platoon leader and executive officer with the 3rd Armd. Div. in Buedingen, Germany. He met his wife, USAF Capt. Karen S. Lucas at Rhein Main and they were married on 27 May 1989.

After serving as company commander at Fort Knox, KY, Thomas was sent to Fort Leavenworth, KS were he functioned as observer/controller. His next assignment was Fort Lewis, WA. At Fort Lewis he held the position of brigade adjutant. Thomas moved on to Fort Leonard Wood, MO where he was a Brigade S3.

Thomas is currently stationed at Fort Leavenworth where he is attending the Command and General Staff College. He holds the rank of active duty major.

He has been awarded three Meritorious Service Medals, three Army Commendation Medals, Army Achievement Medal and the National Defense Service Medal.

Thomas enjoys playing golf and has been the golf club champion at Ft. Leonard Wood and competed twice in the All-Army Golf Championship. He loves all sports and likes to fish and hunt.

At this writing, Thomas, his wife Karen and their three children: Kirk Preston, Rachael Lee and Cliff Nicolas, are looking forward to go-

ing to Rheindahlen, Germany this summer where Thomas will be serving with the Allied Command Europe Rapid Reaction Corps.

THOMAS WAYNE TYLER, Gunny Sergeant, born 8 Aug 1963 in Cadiz, KY, son of Thomas Clarence and Loradell Calhoun Tyler. He attended Trigg County schools until volunteering for service in the USMC in 1981.

After training at Marine Corps Depot Parris Island, SC, he proceeded to Fort Sill, OK for training as a Field Artillery Fire Direction Controlman and promoted to PFC.

He was assigned to Camp Lejeune, NC as a field artillery surveyor, promoted to lance corporal, returned to Fort Sill and promoted to corporal. After completing cold weather training in Minnesota, he boarded the USS *Spiegel Grove* and sailed to Norway and earned the Artic Service Ribbon. Cpl. Tyler reported to Okinawa, served as fire direction controlman, battalion survey chief, and platoon sergeant for Operations Platoon. The next four years, he participated in exercises in Korea, Philippines and Japan. In the Philippines, he was promoted to sergeant.

In Okinawa, he met Shirley and they married on 10 Jun 1988. He returned to Camp Lejeune and served with 10th Marines Regimental Survey until leaving the Corps in 1988.

After discharge he returned to Hopkinsville and was employed in Eddyville as a corrections officer. Civilian life not to his liking, he returned to the Corps as assistant battalion operations chief and operations platoon sergeant in Okinawa. Returning to Fort Sill he was reassigned as battery operations chief and headquarters platoon sergeant. In 1993 he was promoted to staff sergeant and reassigned as the operations platoon sergeant, regimental survey chief, regimental meteorological chief, regimental radar chief, and the regimental target processing chief. SSgt. Tyler was awarded the Honorable Order of Saint Barbara, presented annually to the Marine who excelled in the field.

SSgt. Tyler reported to MCRD Parris Island, SC as a student of Drill Instructor School where he suffered a severe kneecap injury preventing him from completion. He returned to Camp Lejeune and was reassigned platoon sergeant and battery operations chief. SSgt. Tyler left Lejeune and reported to Kaneohe Bay, Hawaii where he served as battery operations chief, battalion survey chief, battery gunnery sergeant and battalion operations chief. He was promoted to gunnery sergeant in 1998. After Hawaii, GySgt Tyler returned to Okinawa, currently serving as the regimental survey chief for 12th Marines Regiment.

GySgt and Mrs. Tyler have been blessed with two beautiful children, a daughter Nikita Cole Yoshi Tyler born on Okinawa and one son Zachary Kaishu Tyler.

Gulf War

ROBERT DION ALLEN, Corporal, born 1 Apr 1968 in Hopkinsville, KY and graduated Trigg County HS, Class of 1986. Enlisted in the USMC in 1986. Five weeks prior to shipping to boot camp in Paris Island, he married Paula Hutchens of Cadiz, KY, also a 1986 graduate of Trigg County HS.

After three months boot camp training at Paris Island, SC, he was stationed at Camp Johnson, NC for supply administration school. After completing the school at Camp Johnson in April 1987, he was assigned to Supply Company, 2nd Supply Battalion, Camp Lejeune, NC.

While there, Allen won several Marine of the Month awards and Marine of the Quarter awards for his battalion. He was awarded the Navy Achievement Medal for providing support for other Marine units deployed in the Persian Gulf. Allen achieved the rank of corporal before leaving Lejeune.

Allen spent the last year of his four years with the Marines stationed on Okinawa, Japan from July 1989 to July 1990. He was honorably discharged in July 1990 and returned to Cadiz, KY. He and Paula now live in Henderson, KY, where he works in the finance industry and they are rearing their three children.

TONY R. BAKER, Sergeant First Class, born 14 Feb 1968 in Trigg County, KY. He is a graduate from Trigg County High, Class of 1986 and a member of the Trigg County 1985 Fifth District basketball champions. He was elected to the all district team as a member of the football team, and earned The Courier-Journal All-State Football Honorable Mention in 1985 as a Defensive end.

After graduation, Baker entered the military on 8 Jul 1986. He completed training at Fort Sill, OK on 16 Oct 1986. After graduating, he was stationed in Gissen, Germany. While serving as cannoner #1 and #2, assistant gunner and unit supply clerk and armor, he earned numerous awards and letters of achievements.

In May 1988, Baker was promoted to Specialist/E-4. He was assigned to Fort Polk, LA. He was sent to the Sergeant/E-5 promotion board because of leadership potential.

Specialist Baker was assigned to Turkey on 16 Jul 1991, and was promoted to corporal while in Turkey. He served as a special weapons missile handler. After serving seven months in Turkey he was reassigned to Fort Sill, OK.

Cpl. Baker was promoted to sergeant in September 1992 and in November 1993 to staff sergeant. On 30 Oct 1995, SSgt. Baker was assigned to Charlie Battery 3rd Bn. 18th FA, Fort Sill, OK. SSgt. Baker served as a section then as a drill sergeant in August 1996.

After completing Drill Sergeant course at Fort Leonard Wood, MO. SSgt. Baker was assigned to Bravo Battery 1st Bn. 79th FA, Fort Sill, OK. As a drill instructor, he trained over 3,000 civilians to become soldiers of the US Army. He has been praised by numerous persons for

making positive influences on their kids lives. SSgt. Baker was reassigned to Fort Campbell, KY on 5 Nov 2000. On 1 Mar 2001, SSgt. Baker was promoted to sergeant first class.

SFC Baker's awards include he Army Services Ribbon, Overseas Service Ribbon (2nd award), National Defense Service Medal (1st award), SW Asia Service Medal w/2 Bronze Stars, Noncommissioned Officer Professional Development Ribbon (3rd award), Joint Meritorious Unit Award, humanitarian Service Medal (1st award), Drivers Mechanics Badge (both wheel and track), Coast Guard Meritorious Unit Commendation Award (1st award), Drill Sergeant Identification Badge, Good Conduct Medal (4th award), Army Achievement Medal (5th award), Army Commendation Medal (4th award), Meritorious Service Medal (1st award), Noncommissioned Officer of the Month (May 1995), Drill Sergeant of the Cycle (October 1999), Slingmaster Course, Air Assault Badge, Heavy PZ Course, The Honorable Order of Saint Barbara Award and the prestigious Sergeant Audie Murphy award.

SFC Baker is currently the chief of firing battery for Bravo Battery 1st Bn. 320th Field Artillery on Fort Campbell, KY. SFC Baker is the youngest son of Ernest and Lillian Baker of Cerulean, KY. He is married to Linda Wadlington Baker. They have two sons, Tony Jr. and Ivan Baker. They currently reside in Gracey and are active members of the Cave Springs Baptist Church.

TRACEY L. BAKER, Sergeant, entered the US Army on 28 Aug 1985 at Nashville, TN. He trained as a motor transport operator and graduated from basic and advanced individual training at Fort Leonard Wood, MO.

Sgt. Baker has served in the following duty positions and organizations: wheeled vehicle operator in 4-66 Armor Bn., 3rd Inf. Div., Aschaffenburg, Germany; commander's driver 509th Personnel Service Co. 2nd Inf. Div., Camp Casey, Korea; team leader 48th Forward Support Battalion, 2nd Armd. Div., Fort Hood, TX; Squad leader 541st Transportation Co. 101st Abn. Div., Fort Campbell, KY; section sergeant 1-9 Inf. 2nd Inf. Div., Camp Hovey, Korea; and assistant truckmaster 710th Main Support Bn. 10th Mtn. Div., Fort Drum, NY.

His awards and decorations include the Army Achievement Medal (4th OLC), Army Achievement Medal (9th OLC), Good Conduct Medal (5th OLC), National Defense Ribbon, Joint Service Accommodation Medal, Humanitarian Service Medal, NCO Professional Development Ribbon (with numeral 2), Army Service Ribbon, Overseas Ribbon (with numeral 4), and the North Atlantic Treaty Organization Ribbon, as well as numerous other decorations to include the Air Assault Badge, Driver's Badge, Manchu Belt Buckle and the Weapon Qualification Badge (Expert).

Sgt. Baker resides at Fort Drum with his wife Alice and their 4-year-old daughter, Januari.

Sgt. Baker is currently assigned as the assistant truckmaster of the 710th Main Support Bn., 10th Mtn. Div. (Light Infantry), Fort Drum, NY.

ANTHONY LEE BROADBENT, Staff Sergeant (E-6), born 8 Mar 1965 in Hopkinsville, KY, son of Bobby and Sylvia Broadbent of Cadiz, KY. He enlisted in the USMC 5 May 1984 in Hopkinsville, KY with the MOS of Intelligence Specialist.

Participated in the Gulf War, 19 Aug 1990 to 17 Apr 1991. Served as Intelligence Chief of Marine Air Support Squadron One. Primary duties included briefing pilots on pre-planned targets for daily bombing missions, daily intelligence briefs to commanding officer and his staff, and de-brief pilots upon returning from bombing mission.

Military awards include the Combat Action Ribbon, Southwest Asia Service Ribbon, Kuwait Liberation Medal, National Defense Medal, Sea Service Deployment, Overseas Service, Good Conduct (four awards), Navy Achievement (two awards), Navy Commendation, Meritorious Unit Citation and Naval Unit Citation.

Married in San Diego, CA to Deanna M. Broadbent and they have six children: Amanda, Lauren, Thomas, Preston, Brenton and Carolyn. They live in San Diego, CA where he is major accounts manager for Waste Management.

Most memorable experiences include meeting President Bush and Senator Dole during the Gulf War, and being at the birth of his six children.

JASON MATTHEW CRISP, 2nd Lieutenant, born 24 Dec 1970 in Cadiz, KY and entered the US Army Reserve in 1989. His basic training was at Fort Dix, NJ. One year later, he transferred to the Kentucky National Guard as a member of the 614th MP Co. located in Murray, KY and attended the MP School in Fort McClellan, AL.

In 1991 he and other volunteers from the unit deployed to Saudi Arabia in support of Operation Desert Storm. Crisp recalls his most rewarding and exciting duty in Desert Storm as being a personal guard for Maj. Gen. Patrick J. Kelly in Kuwait. He spent eight months in southwest Asia and returned to the 614th MP Co. Shortly after his return, he attended the Primary Leadership Development Course at Fort Jackson, SC in 1993.

In 1994 he was deployed to Panama to assist in security of the bases near the Panama Canal. In 1996 he entered the Army full time as a Multiple Launch Rocket System crewmember at Fort Sill, OK. His first assignment was B Btry., 6/37th FA in Camp Stanley, South Korea from July 1996 to July 1997.

Next assignment was with HQ Btry. 1/21st FA at Fort Hood, TX from August 1997 to July 1999. After Fort Hood, he volunteered to attend the Army Recruiter School in Fort Jackson, SC and was assigned to the Tampa Recruiting Bn. with duty in Naples, FL. While on recruiting duty, he was selected for Officer Candidate School at Fort Benning, GA.

During his time as an enlisted service member, Jason attained the rank of staff sergeant. After completing OCS he was assigned to the Ordnance Corps and attended the Officer Basic Course at Aberdeen Proving Ground, MD.

2nd Lt. Crisp and his wife Loretta have been married for seven years and currently reside in El Paso, TX with their daughter Skyler. He is currently attending the University of Texas to complete a bachelor's degree in health science with a follow on assignment to Fort Bliss, TX.

His awards include three Army Commendation Medals, three Army Achievement Medals, Good Conduct Medal, Kuwait Liberation Medal, National Defense Service Medal, Army Reserve Component Achievement Medal, Overseas Service Ribbon, Kentucky Commendation ribbon and Soldier of the Year in 1992 for the 614th MP Co.

KATHY ESTELLE (LAYTON) DIETRICH, Master Sergeant, born 13 May 1946 in Chicago, IL. She joined the Women's Army Corps in January 1974. The Vietnam War was ending and so was the draft. Kathy and her husband Kenneth had been married eight years and had just closed their business and were looking for employment. Kenneth had been drafted in 1967 and served two years and decided he would sign up again. They joined under the buddy system and were guaranteed their first assignment together. For the next 20 years they were assigned together.

In May 1975 the Women's Army Corps was dissolved and Kathy joined the regular Army. She was issued an M-16, combat boots, a gas mask, helmet and fatigues The Army was changing. Women were being given more job opportunities and more combat type training with the men. All women companies, platoons and barracks were being replaced with integrated units of men and women.

Kathy was a Card Punch Operator and then a computer programmer and finally a Data Processing NCO assigned to the Signal Corps. While in the service she completed her BS degree in sociology and computer science.

Kathy was assigned to Fort Hood, TX; Miesau Army Depot, Germany; Fort Rucker, AL; 1st AD, Furth, Germany; US Army Element, US Space Command, Peterson AFB, Colorado Springs; Signal Corps, Bremerhaven, Germany; 7th Inf. Div. (Light) Fort Ord, CA; U.S, Army War College, Carlisle, PA.

During Desert Storm Kathy was stationed in the port town of Bremerhaven, Germany. The post was used as a staging area for all equipment and troops leaving Europe. Everyone was on 12 hour, 7 days-a-week shifts. Soldiers would drive equipment in from all over Germany and then get on buses to return to their units. Kathy worked weekends in the dining facility making sack lunches for the soldiers to eat on the bus.

Kathy retired in February 1994 as a master sergeant and received the Legion of Merit as her highest award.

Kathy and Ken decided to retire in the Lakes area of Western Kentucky close to Fort Campbell. They started looking for land five years before retiring and finally bought two nice lake lots in the Blue Springs area of Trigg County. Ken had retired two years before Kathy because of his prior service and he started building their house in August 1993 while Kathy finished her last assignment at the Army War College.

Kenneth owns and operates Skippers Boatique on HWY 68/80 and Kathy has worked for Integra Bank since 1996.

MICHAEL JAY FELTON, Staff Sergeant, born 7 Sep 1954 in Pasco, WA. He joined the Washington Army National Guard 29 Dec 1971. After basic and advanced training at Fort Jackson, SC, he joined the Regular Army and was sent to Fort Sam Houston, TX to train as a combat medic, a job he would do the entire 20 years he was on active duty.

During his 20 years of service, Felton spent 15 years with the 101st Abn. Div., two tours in Europe and 7-1/2 months in Saudi Arabia and Iraq. He spent two years with the 1st Bn., 26th Inf., 1st Inf. Div. (FWD) and three years with the 3rd Armd. Div.

His most memorable experience was the deployment to Saudi Arabia with the 101st Abn. Div. in September 1990. The pressure to train every soldier in the command to start IVs, how to treat the biological threats and to treat battle wounds gave Felton and his medical team a great challenge.

SSgt. Felton retired in June 1992. His awards include the Bronze Star, Meritorious Service Medal, Army Commendation Medal, Army Achievement Medal (5 awds.), Good Conduct (6 awds.), National Defense (2 awds.) Overseas Ribbon (2 devices), NCO Professional Development Ribbon (3 devices), SW Asia Ribbon w/3 Bronze Stars, Kuwait Liberation Medal, Expert Field Medical Badge, Expert Jungle Badge and the Air Assault Wings.

After retiring he attended Hopkinsville Community College, where he completed two associate degrees programs, then attended Austin Peay State University where he graduated with a bachelor's degree in public administration in December 1999.

Felton is currently a special education teacher at Christian County HS. In addition to teaching he is an assistant coach for the Colonel's baseball, soccer and basketball teams.

He married Janice Marie Tyler of Cadiz, KY on 27 Dec 1988 and they have three daughters: Virginia, Amanda and Cally. They reside in Cadiz.

CRAIG KENT GARLAND,

CRAIG KENT GARLAND, MM1/c, born on 10 Dec 1966 in Hammond, IN, son of Harry and Bobbie Garland. He has a twin brother Chris Eric and two older brothers, Harry and Scott. In 1969 the family moved to Trigg County where Craig attended all grades in the Trigg County Schools, graduating an honor student in May 1985.

In May 1986 he enlisted in the USN and entered the Naval Nuclear Propulsion Program. After completing Nuclear Power School in Orlando, FL, and prototype training at Nuclear Power Training Unit, Ballston Spa, NY, he qualified as a nuclear mechanical operator and was assigned as an instructor for student training at the training unit. During his two-year rotation he received numerous citations for outstanding performance of duties, including the title "Master Training Specialist" and the Navy Good Conduct Medal.

In 1991 Craig was promoted to machinist mate first class while aboard the USS *Atlanta* (SSN 712) a nuclear powered submarine. He was awarded the Distinguished Silver Dolphins while serving as a submariner. One of his most memorable times was when they crossed the Atlantic, submerged for 63 days before surfacing near Toulon, France. He received an honorable discharge in December 1992 at Norfolk, VA.

Craig married Lenora Mignogna in November 1993 in her hometown, Greensburg, PA. They resided in Bowie, MD, while Lenora continued working in Washington, DC, and Craig attended the University of Maryland from January 1994 to May 1997. He graduated with honors and received a BS degree in engineering.

He is presently employed with Newport News Shipbuilding and Drydock Co. as a design engineer on the CVNX aircraft carrier. He currently resides in Newport News, VA with his wife Lenora, who operates her own personal chef service, and with his 2-year old son Craig Kent Jr. He enjoys golfing, boating and having fun with his family.

HARRY WALLACE GARLAND JR., Chief Petty Officer, born on 2 Apr 1957 to Harry "Hank" and Bobbie Garland in Hammond, IN. The family moved to Trigg County in 1969.

Seaman Recruit Garland enlisted in the Navy on 2 Jan 1981 and went to boot camp at Recruit Training Center Great Lakes, IL. Finishing recruit training in the upper 10% of his company, he was selected for follow on training at Naval Technical Training Center, Meridian, MS.

Seaman Recruit Garland served in a variety of ships including the USS *Forrestal* (CV-59), USS *Saratoga* (CV-60), USS *La Salle* (AGF-3), USS *Philippine Sea* (CG-58) and USS *Yorktown* (CG-48).

While onboard *Saratoga* he participated in the operation to apprehend the terrorists that hijacked the Achille Lauro cruise liner and murdered a civilian passenger. He also participated in Freedom of Navigation operations in the Gulf of Sidra off Libya. Follow on assignments sent him to the Adriatic Sea during the disintegration of the country of Yugoslavia, the Persian Gulf during Operation Desert Storm and the Caribbean Sea conducting drug interdiction.

Major shore commands included Naval Reserve Personnel Center, New Orleans, LA and Navy Recruiting District Montgomery, AL. He was promoted to the rank of chief petty officer in May 1990.

CPO Garland is authorized to wear the Navy Commendation Medal (2 awds.), Navy Achievement Medal (4 awds.), Navy Good Conduct Medal (5 awds.), the Navy Expeditionary Medal and the Armed Forces Expeditionary Medal and numerous other personal awards and unit decorations. He qualified as both an enlisted surface warfare specialist and enlisted aviation warfare specialist. Chief Garland retired from the Navy 11 May 2001.

He currently resides in Montgomery, AL with his wife Robin and daughter Melissa.

C. SAM GALLOGLY, E-4, born 11 Nov 1969 in Durant, MS, son of Tim Gallogly and Cyndi Hatfield Mize. He is a 1988 graduate of Trigg County HS and enlisted in the US Army on 12 Jul 1988.

After basic and advanced training in field artillery at Fort Sill, OK, he was assigned as a cannon crewmember with the VII Corps, B2/77FA, in Augsburg, Germany in November 1988. In October 1990, he was assigned to 101st Abn. Div., Fort Campbell, KY, where he completed Air Assault School.

He deployed to the Persian Gulf in December 1990 with 1/320 FA, A Btry, 101st Abn. and participated in Desert Shield and Desert Storm.

He was honorably separated from the Army with the rank of E-4 in December 1991. His most memorable experience while in the Army was 16 Jan 1991, the day Desert Storm commenced.

Medals awarded were the Army Achievement Medals (3), Army Commendation Medal, Good Conduct Medal, Army Service Ribbon, Kuwaiti Liberation Medal, Saudi Arabian Defense Medal, National Defense Service Medal, Southwest Asia Service Medal.

Sam has been employed as an arc welder with Johnson Controls, Cadiz, since 1995. He is a member of the VFW #1913. Sam is married to Rita Allen and they have three children: Chris, Ryan and Peyton. Sam's hobbies are golfing, hunting, fishing and 4-wheeling.

DEBRA (CRUMP) JONES, Staff Sergeant (E-6), a native of Cadiz, KY, she entered the US Army 9 Mar 1989 as an optometry technician and was stationed at Fort Stewart, GA.

Upon honorable discharge from active duty Army 21 Sep 1991, Debra joined the US Army Reserves in December 1991. She currently remains in the Reserves, serving as an administrative assistant for the 100th Div., Owensboro, KY. *Submitted by her mother Jane Retta Crump Ruffin and stepfather Lonnie Ruffin.*

JAMES LYNN "JIMMY" JONES, born 24 Aug 1953 in Hammond, IN, son of Lawrence and Katherine Lynn Jones. He lived in Hammond until 1970 when his family moved to the Rock Castle area of Trigg County where he lived until his senior year of high school, when he decided to join the Air Force.

He left Cadiz and went to Lackland AFB in San Antonio for basic training and from there to Wichita Falls, TX for his technical training. Upon finishing that he went to Colorado Springs to finish his high school education as he only needed one credit.

He spent over half of his 20 years in the military years in Alaska where he loved to hunt and fish. He left Alaska in 1990 for the last time and was sent to Eglin AFB, Fort Walton Beach, FL. While there he served in Desert Shield/Desert Storm.

He retired from Eglin AFB in June 1993 with the rank of tech sergeant. He received several medals and ribbons for good conduct, Outstanding Unit Award, National Defense Service, Short Tour and Long Tour, Longevity Service and Small Arms Expert.

While James was in basic training, he became good friends with Jimmy Bennett from Oklahoma City, OK, who had a little sister named Rebecca. Jimmy took James home to meet her and they instantly hit it off. After James graduated from St. Mary's in Colorado Springs, he was sent to Little Rock AFB.

He and Rebecca married and eventually became the parents of two daughters, Jenifer Lynn Jones Morgan and Kristina Ann Jones Conterez. There are two grandchildren. Rebecca and James divorced in 1980.

Upon his retirement he went to Denver, CO for a year then came back to Trigg County. He met a Trigg County home girl, Barbara Bland Boren and they married 16 Jun 1995. He loves to hunt, fish and restore his 55 Chevy pickup when he has time off from his job for Data Monitoring at Fort Campbell, KY as an airplane tech.

James and all three of his brothers served in one capacity or another in the military. One brother also retired from the Air Force.

STACEY V. LADD, Sergeant (E-5), born in Trigg County, KY and enlisted in the service 24 Nov 1987 at Hopkinsville, KY. Stationed at Fort Bliss, TX and participated in Desert Storm/Shield.

Sgt. Ladd was discharged 24 Nov 1996. Awards include the Army Commendation Medal, two Bronze Stars, Southeast Asia Medal and Good Conduct Medal.

He lives in Trigg County, KY and has three children: Stacy, Britteny and AJa.

MOZELLE DEWAYNE MARTIN, E-3, born 10 Sep 1972 in Hopkinsville, KY. He enlisted in the USN in Nashville, TN in August 1991. Basic training was at the Naval Recruit Training Center, Great Lakes, IL. After basic training, he was transferred to the USS *Saratoga*, Jacksonville, FL, where he was assigned to Aviation Administration (AZ).

While attached to the USS *Saratoga*, he was deployed on a Mediterranean Cruise. He was deployed and in the Adriatic Sea during the Persian Gulf War. The crew of the USS *Saratoga* assisted in the care of injured servicemen during this war.

Martin received the National Defense Service Medal. He received an Honorable Discharge at the rank of E-3, in August 1993.

He attended McCissick Elementary, McCann Elementary, and Joelton Middle Schools in Nashville, TN. He also attended Trigg County HS, Cadiz, KY and graduated in 1991 from Whites Creek HS in Nashville, TN. He attended Nashville Technical College.

His parents are Price E. and Suszie M. Baker Martin, natives of Cadiz, KY. His father, maternal and paternal grandfathers were veterans and natives of Trigg County. He has two sons, Jerel M. Williams and Chon D. Martin. He resides in Nashville, TN where he is in the music business.

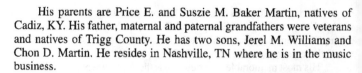

CATHY L. RADFORD, E-4, born 20 Oct 1967 in Trigg County. Enlisted in February 1986 at San Antonio, TX and was stationed at Fort Sumter AFB, SC.

Radford was discharged in January 1990. Awards include the AFTR Training Ribbon Achievement Medals and AF Good Conduct Medal.

Civilian employment as secretary, True Belief Academy and UPS Postal Service. Resides in Indianapolis, IN and has two children, Phillip and Diamond.

PERRY M. RADFORD, Staff Sergeant, born 1 Oct 1960 and enlisted in the US Army in June 1981. After basic training at Fort Jackson, SC, he attended Army Quartermaster School at Fort Lee, VA.

During his service he served two years in Korea along the DMZ with the 1/9 Inf. Bn. and the 506th Inf. Bn. From 1984-1990 he served with 326th Engr. Bn. in Karlshure, Germany.

In May 1990 he returned to the States and was assigned close to home at Fort Campbell, KY; but less than three months later after being assigned to the 2/44 Air Defense Bn. of the 101st AAST. Div. he was deployed to Saudi Arabia for Operations Desert Shield/Storm.

After returning to Fort Campbell for less than a year, he received orders for Korea. After completing this tour and returning to Fort Campbell, he decided to take advantage of the new early retirement program in June 1995 with the rank of staff sergeant.

Awards include Air Assault Badge, Army Commendation (4), Army Achievement (4), Southwest Asia Service Medal w/3 Bronze Stars, Kuwait Liberation Medal and Overseas Ribbon (5).

Married Christine on 21 Aug 1987 and they live in Cadiz, KY.

DAVID LEE SUMNER, born 23 Feb 1968 in Hopkinsville, KY, son of Jesse Calvin Sumner and Margaret Ann Hughes Sumner of Cadiz, KY. He has one sibling, Pamela Ann Sumner Freeman of Cadiz. He and his family are members of Mount Pleasant Baptist Church in Trigg County, KY.

Graduating from Trigg County HS with the Class of 1986, he attended one year at the University of Kentucky Community College in Hopkinsville, KY before entering the USN on 23 Sep 1987.

After receiving his boot camp training and attending eight weeks of Radioman "A" School in San Diego, CA, he was stationed aboard the now decommissioned USS *Joseph Hewes* (FF-1078) home ported at that time in Charleston, SC. This was his first of many more duty stations to follow including: Naval Telecommunications Center, Mayport, FL; Naval Mobile Construction Battalion Center, Gulfport, MS; Naval Telecommunications Center, Brunswick, ME; Naval Station Ingleside, Ingleside, TX and currently being stationed onboard the USS *George Washington* (CVN-73) homported in Norfolk, VA.

His achievements include three Navy Achievement Medals, Three Good Conduct Medals, two Battle "E" Ribbons, Joint Meritorious Medal, National Defense Medal and the Armed Forces Expeditionary Medal, several letters of appreciation from various groups and organizations (naval and civilian) as well as numerous college accreditations.

He never thought as a small-town boy growing up in Kentucky that he would have seen so much of the world in his 13 years as a US sailor. Through tours of duty he has seen many countries such as Spain, France, Italy, Pakistan, Israel, Greece, Croatia, Diego Garcia, Singapore, Japan, Puerto Rico, Bahamas, Cuba, Tinisa, Panama, St. Martin, US Virgin Islands and Bonair. He crossed the Equator on 4 Jul 1989.

He met Martha of Vine Grove, KY in Charleston SC, where they married and had three daughters: Leah Noelle Sumner, a student at Trigg County Middle School, Brittany Nicole and Morgan Lee Sumner, both students at Trigg County Elementary.

With God's grace he plans on retiring from the USN, taking with him the appreciation for the many opportunities and achievements that have been afforded as he transitioned from that small boy in Kentucky to the man he is today, forging memories that last a lifetime.

JOHN W. TAYLOR, Captain, born 12 Apr 1957, son of Elizabeth Carr Taylor and the late Wallace Taylor of Cadiz. He received a direct-commission into the US Army, in December 1986 and was assigned to the 489th Civil Affairs Company in Knoxville, TN.

2nd Lt. Taylor initially served with the 489th Civil Affairs Company as a broadcast officer and public affairs officer. Taylor's civilian education helped to prepare him for his initial military appointment. Before his direct-commission, Taylor received a BS in Radio-TV from Murray State University, an MA in speech from Western Kentucky University, and a Ph.D. in mass communication from Ohio University. Taylor's military education helped to hone his communication skills.

While at Fort Benjamin Harrison, Taylor completed the Adjutant General Officer Basic Course (1987) and the Defense Information School's Public Affairs Officer Course (1988). His military education continued at the John F. Kennedy Special Warfare Center and School at Fort Bragg, NC where he completed the Civil Affairs Officer Advanced Course Phase I (1988), Civil Affairs Officer Advanced Course Phase II (1990), and the Psychological Operations Officer Course (1992).

When the 489th CA Company became a battalion and was attached to the 101st Abn. Div. (AASLT), 1st Lt. Taylor became the assistant S-3. He served in exercise "Internal Look" in preparation for operation Desert Shield-Desert Storm. During Desert Storm, he was assigned to a direct support special operations team with the 1st Brigade of the 101st Abn. Div. (AASLT). After Desert Storm, Capt. Taylor served as the 489th CA Battalion's S-1.

Taylor completed his service to the 489th in 1994 prior to becoming a Fulbright Scholar to the Republic of Malta. As a Fulbright scholar Dr. Taylor taught at the Universita Ta' Malta and interned in the public affairs office of the US Embassy in Malta. Dr. Taylor currently works as a faculty member in the Department of Communication at Eastern Kentucky University where he uses his military experiences and education when teaching "Propaganda and the Media" and "International Media."

He is married to Dr. Renee Littlejohn Taylor formerly of Cadiz, and they have a daughter Tara and a son Trevor. They reside in Richmond, KY.

MARC ANTHONY TERRELL, E-4, born 25 Nov 1968 in Cadiz, KY, enlisted in the Kentucky Army National Guard with the 614th Military Police Unit on 17 Aug 1987. His basic training and advanced individual training took place at Fort McClellan, AL from 7 Jan-11 May 1988. Upon completion, he returned to Murray State University to continue his education.

After two years of service with the KYARNG, he transferred to the 1174th Transportation Unit in Dresden, TN. At the beginning of Operation Desert Shield (later to be called Operation Desert Storm), the transportation unit was activated for active duty service. Marc was transferred to the 269th MP Unit in Dyersburg, TN due to the fact that he had not completed his training as an 88M (truck driver).

One month later, the 269th received orders activating them for service. After an initial stay at Fort Campbell, Marc was sent to Saudi Arabia to assist in the incarceration, guarding and repatriation of Iraqi soldiers. After 13 weeks in the desert, the unit was chosen to act as customs agents to ensure the safe return home of American soldiers and to retrieve any illegal contraband that may try to make its way home. The 269th MP unit returned to Fort Campbell 2 Jun 1991.

One memory that comes to his mind is the first night they took prisoners into their compound. Having grown up in Cadiz, he had never been exposed to starvation and the use of children to fight in war. Some 3,500 prisoners came to their compound, many with no shoes, tattered clothing, and a fear that the Americans where there to kill all of them. A young boy, about 13, came by Marc crying with MRE packages on his feet. The interpreter told them that the boy was asking them not to shoot him. As bad as a person seems to think it gets at times, there are ALWAYS people who have it worse.

One of the many things that stand out in Marc's mind from his service was the welcome that they received when they came home. "Although he had done nothing to warrant a hero's welcome, the people here had nothing but good to say."

After receiving a BS in agriculture from Murray State, Marc married Joan Herndon, also from Cadiz, on 13 Jun 1992. Today, they have one child, Leighton Alexandra "Lexie" (b. 1998), and reside in Cadiz. He is finishing his master's degree from Murray State and has accepted a position with a risk management firm in Owensboro, KY. They are members of Calvary Missionary Baptist Church where he teaches Sunday school and Joan is pianist.

Marc ended his military service on 17 Aug 1995, after serving out his enlistment and receiving an honorable discharge from the TNARNG.

SCOTT PAXTON THOMAS, born 13 Oct 1970 in Akron, OH, son of Randy Thomas and Janet Lewis Hiner. His grandparents are Earl and Mary Ann (Sumner) Thomas, Trigg County, KY. His parents moved to Trigg County in 1972. Shortly after, they moved to Christian County and lived about five years then moved to Clarksville, TN.

After graduating from Clarksville HS, he enlisted in the Army Airborne Infantry. He took his basic training at Fort Benning, GA, then was assigned to Fort Bragg, NC. He soon was on tour of duty for six months in the Sinai Desert. He returned to Fort Bragg for a few months and the Desert Storm War began, and he was sent to Saudia Arabia. After the war ended, he returned to Fort Bragg and was soon discharged.

He now lives in Richmond, KY, working and going to college at Eastern.

J. MARK THOMPSON, Captain, born 9 Oct 1962, at Murray, KY, son of Brent D. and Dorothy S. Thompson, Cadiz, KY, Following completion of schooling in Trigg County schools, Mark enrolled at Murray State University in 1980 and was awarded a US Army ROTC scholarship. In 1984, he graduated summa cum laude from Murray as the outstanding male graduate in music with a bachelor of music degree and was commissioned second lieutenant in the US Army as a Distinguished Military Graduate.

Mark entered active duty in 1984 and was assigned to Fort Bliss, TX and the Air Defense Artillery Officers School. Upon completion, he was assigned to the 1st Inf. Div., Fort Riley, KS. He participated in "Operation Reforger" in western Europe.

During his Fort Riley assignment, Mark earned the degree of master of science in systems management from the University of Southern California. Following promotion 1st lieutenant and completion of his active duty obligation, Mark enrolled in the Graduate School of the University of Iowa from which he earned the master of music degree and the master of fine arts degree prior to earning the doctor of musical arts degree in 1991.

Mark was promoted to the rank of captain in the US Army Reserve prior to completing his military service.

He is married to the former Ami Scroggins, Springfield, MO and has three children: Katherine, Rebecca and Stephen Brent, and two stepdaughters, Whitney and Ashley.

Following eight years as professor of music at Stephen F. Austin University, Nacogdoches, TX, he has served as professor of music at Northwestern State University, Natchitoches, LA, since July 2000.

An accomplished bass trombonist, Mark has performed with major symphony orchestras in Chicago, IL; Houston and San Antonio, TX, and Jalapa, Mexico, in addition to several regional orchestras.

Of his Army service record Mark said: "In addition to the profound sense of satisfaction of serving my country, the Army afforded me the opportunity to mature and to establish and work toward goals that will serve me in a positive manner throughout my life. I am proud to be US Army Veteran."

GINGER WALLACE, Major, born 19 Feb 1968 and is the daughter of Jim and Penny Lester Wallace. She graduated with honors from Trigg County HS in 1986. After high school, she received an appointment to the USAF Academy, Colorado Springs, CO. While at the academy, she was a member of the basketball team being selected captain of the team her final year. Ginger graduated from the Air Force Academy with the Class of 1990.

Upon graduation, she was commissioned a 2nd lieutenant in the Air Force. Her first active military assignment was as current operations officer with the 314th Airlift Wing, Little Rock AFB, AR (November 1992-January 1995). While there, she scheduled, coordinated and monitored over 250 missions weekly for two C-130 formal schools and two operational squadrons. During this assignment, Ginger served in Operation Restore Hope, Mogadishu, Somalia (November 1993-January 1994).

In January 1995 Wallace was transferred to HQ Air Combat Command, Langley, AFB, VA where she served as airlift mission director. There she was responsible for the day-to-day management of over 400 C-130 aircraft, balancing aircrew training with real-world airlift mission requirements. From June 1996 through January 1997 she served as Chief of Airlift Mission Director Section.

In September 1997 she left Langley AFB to attend Intelligence Operations Course and Combat Targeting Course at Goodfellow AFB, TX. Leaving as a Distinguished Graduate in August 1998 Capt. Wallace was assigned to HQ USAF in Europe, Ramstein, AB, Germany. Ginger was promoted to major in June 2001 and is currently assistant operations officer, 32nd Air Intelligence Squadron, Ramstein AB. While at Ramstein, she served in Operation Allied Force, Italy (April-June 1999).

DUNCAN EDWARD WIGGINS, Specialist, born 1 Jul 1969 in Carmichael, CA and reared in Marysville, CA. Attended Lindhurst HS and was a member of the Jr. Air Force Reserved Officer Training Corps (ROTC) all four years.

Joined California Army National Guard in November 1986 as a combat engineer and was a member of the 132nd Engineer Battalion in Yuba City, CA. Attended basic and MOS training at Fort Leonard Wood, MO with "B" Co. 589th Engineer Training Battalion from July to November of 1987.

Joined the US Army and was stationed at Fort Campbell, KY, a member of "A" Co. 326th Engr. Bn. 101st Abn. Div. "Air Assault. He was involved in combat engineer operations during Desert Shield and Desert Storm in Saudi Arabia and Iraq.

Was honorably discharged 1 Jan 1992 at the rank of specialist. He received the Army Commendation Award for service during Desert Shield and the Southwest Asia Service Medal w/2 stars, National Defense Service Medal, Air Assault Badge, Good Conduct Medal, Combat Lifesaver and Jungle Expert.

In January 1992 he became a police officer for the city of Guthrie, KY and in May 1994 for the city of Cadiz, KY, where he still proudly serves.

Married Kimberly Diann Wiggins 22 Jul 1989 and they have one child, Jessica Ann Wiggins.

A very memorable experience was during the trip home from Desert Storm. They were all talking about how they wished they had finished the job by taking Saddam Hussein out of power. When they got to JFK Airport an unbelievable amount of supporters treated them like they were real heroes and took real good care of their needs. The next feeling he had was guilt because of the stories he had heard about the Vietnam Veterans being treated so badly upon their return from a war that was also called "unfinished."

Another thing he remembers about returning was the smell of the rich Kentucky soil in the air after being in the desert for so long.

RICHARD N. WOOD, FC3, born 20 Nov 1958 in the Trigg County Hospital, son of M.W. and Eleanor Alexander Wood. His father passed away 28 Jun 1993 and is buried in Siloam Cemetery. He enlisted in the service 28 May 1986 at Nashville, TN and served six years in the USN. His rating was firecontrolman (FC3) and he was responsible for operating and maintaining shipboard missile and gun control systems.

He went to boot camp in San Diego, CA and upon graduation attended Combat System schools in both Great Lakes, IL and Mare Island, CA. After receiving training on the AN/SPG 51-C Missile Firecontrol System he was stationed on the USS *Cochrane* (DDG-21) in Yokosuka, Japan for two years.

His next assignment was training on the Phalanx Close in Weapons System (CIWS) in Great Lakes, IL. At the completion of training he was transferred to the USS *Merrill* (DD-976) in San Diego, CA. His primary job was as a phalanx technician, and he also cross trained on the NATO Seasparrow Missile System.

While serving onboard the USS *Merrill* he participated in Operation Desert Storm. The *Merrill* was a Spruance class destroyer which provided air cover for the multi-national minesweeping effort to clear Kuwait waters of Iraqi mines.

One of his most memorable experiences happened on the way to the Persian Gulf. After laying dormant for more than 600 years, Mt. Pinatubo in the Philippines erupted. In what has been described as one of the largest peacetime evacuations in history, Operation Fiery Vigil came to life. Over 16,000 military and civilian personnel were forced to flee Clark AFB. The *Merrill* and the rest of Battlegroup Foxtrot evacuated over 4,000 people to a safe area on the island of Cebu.

Awards/Medals include the Joint Meritorious Unit Award (Fiery Vigil), Navy Unit Commendation (Desert Storm), Good Conduct Medal, National Defense Service Medal, Southwest Asia Service Medal w/Bronze Star, and Sea Service Deployment Ribbon w/Bronze Star.

After leaving the Navy in 1992 he attended Murray State University and received a BS degree in electrical engineering. He currently lives in Lexington Kentucky.

Post Gulf War

STANLEY DALE CALHOUN, Corporal (E-4), born 30 Apr 1976. After graduating from high school, he enlisted in the Marine Corps. On 28 Jun 1994, he went to boot camp for 13 weeks. After completion, he furthered his training at the school of infantry.

In December 1994 he was assigned to Fox Co, 1st PLT, 2nd BN, 6th Marines at Camp Lejeune, NC. In August 1995 he and his unit went on a six-month deployment to the Mediterranean. Three of the six months were spent off the coast of Bosnia during the beginning stages of the conflict that would last for years to come. Calhoun and his unit were relieved of their duty there and returned to the States in February 1996.

In October 1996, after two and a half years in the infantry, Calhoun took indoctrination with 16 other infantrymen and was one of only three accepted into the Scout Sniper Platoon, 2nd BN, 6th Marines.

In December 1997, Calhoun and his unit were deployed for another six months to Okinawa, Japan, with five weeks training in Korea.

After returning to the States in July 1998, Calhoun received his Honorable Discharge as Corporal (NCO). During his tour, he also received Meritorious Mast, Certificate of Commendation, National Defense Service Medal, Sea Service Deployment Ribbon w/star, Armed Forces Service Medal, North Atlantic Treaty Organization Medal and Good Conduct Medal.

Today, at age 24, Stanley Dale Calhoun works at Fort Campbell, KY, as a Dyncorp employee, with the Environmental Division, for proper disposal of hazardous wastes. He currently resides in Kentucky and has one son, Tristan Patrick (b. 5 Aug 1997).

NATHAN RANDOLPH "NATE" DAVIS, Lieutenant, born 12 Jan 1974 in Frankfurt, Germany to Lt. M. Thomas Davis and Nancy Keeling Davis. He is the grandson of Marian Rye Davis of Columbia, SC and the late Carey T. "Sonny" Davis and Col. (Ret.) and Mrs. William O. Keeling, now of Franklin, TN.

The roots of Nathan Randolph Davis go deep in the history of Trigg County, KY. Some of his ancestral families are Randolph, Rye, Garnett, Crews, Gaines, Davis, Thomas, Bridges, Sumner, Lancaster, Goode and Tart.

He attended schools near the posts of his military assignments. He was graduated from Hanau American HS in Hanau, Germany, on 5 Jun 1992. He was co-captain of the football team. In the fall of 1992 Nate entered the College of William and Mary in Williamsburg, VA on the ROTC program. He graduated 12 May 1996, where he was commissioned a 2nd lieutenant.

He served with the US Army at various posts. In late 1998 he found himself in Kuwait, the "hot" spot in the world at that time.

When his dad was attending the Marine War College in Quantico, VA, neighbors were Marine Col. Anthony Zini and his family. In December 1998 then Marine Gen. Anthony C. Zinni was the US Commander-in-Chief of the Central Command, the Middle East region command position held by Schwarzkopt in Desert Storm. He looked up his former neighbor, Nathan Davis, who had been deployed to Kuwait. The accompanying photo of General Zinni and Lt. Davis was taken in Kuwait on 9 Dec 1998, just before the attack on Iraq known as Operation Desert Fox. Lt. Davis was a rocket artillery platoon leader at the time and participated in this 4-day operation.

After his discharge from the Army, Nathan has served as an on line sports writer for USA Today. *Submitted by his great-aunt, Joyce Davis Banister.*

STACY LYNN EZELL, born 23 Nov 1969, daughter of Jim and Portia Aldridge Ezell. Entered the US Army on 30 Jul 1992.

Assignments: July 1992 to October 1992, Bravo Co., 1st Bn., 34th Inf. Regt., Fort Jackson, SC; October 1992 to December 1992, Headquarters Company, US Army Chaplain Center & School, Fort Monmouth, NJ, Chaplain Assistant Training Course, squad leader; December 1993 to December 1994, 4th QM Detachment (Airborne), Camp Hialeah, Pusan, ROK, NCOIC of the Main Post Chapel; January 1994 to July 1996, HQ Co., 306th MI BN, fort Huachuca, AZ, squad leader, NCOIC of the Main Post Chapel and Family Life Center, Non-Appropriated Chaplain's Fund Clerk Course.

Stacy was discharged 30 Jul 1996. Decorations include National Defense Service Medal, Army Service Ribbon, Sharpshooter M1-6 Rifle Badge, Certificate of Achievement, Army Achievement Medal, Overseas Service Ribbon, Post "Super Soldier" Award for July 1994, Letter of Commendation from the Sergeant Major of the Army, Army Good Conduct Medal and Army Commendation Medal.

WILLIAM BURTON EZELL, born 11 Apr 1980, son of Jim and Portia A. Ezell. Entered Marine Corps 25 May 1998.

Assignments: May-August 1998, Marine Corps Recruit Depot, Parris Island, SC; August-October 1998, Camp Geiger, NC, School of Infantry, Infantry Training Battalion; October-November 1998, NSGA, Chesapeake, VA, Security Forces School (2nd in class); November 1998 to June 1999, 8th and I Marine Corps Barracks, Washington, DC, Guard Detachment, Corporal of the Guard; June 1999 to May 2002, 8th and I Marine Corps Barracks, Washington, DC, Bravo Co. Body Bearers Section, Fire Team and Squad Leader, Saluting Battery Gun Captain, Strength Coach.

Awards/Certificates include Company High Shooter, Honor Graduate, Platoon Guide and Letter of Commendation.

DELORIS ANN GRANT, Senior Airman (E-4), born in Caldwell County, KY, daughter of Patricia and Esper T. Crump III of Cadiz, KY. She is a 1997 graduate of Trigg County HS and enlisted in the Air Force 1 Apr 1998.

She graduated from basic military training at Lackland AFB, San Antonio, TX, where she received special training in human relations and earned credits toward an associate's degree through the Community College of the Air Force.

Airman 1/c Grant was a member of the 49th Transportation Squadron. Her assignment was to 8 Trans., Kusan AFB, Korea and duty was maintenance control and analysis specialist.

Awards and medals won were Basic Training, ACC Medal, Outstanding Unit Award, Good Behavior and Holloman Hero.

Most memorable experience was her time at Holloman (one year, four months). While on-the-job training, she also volunteered for squadron functions and community charities. She was an active member of the Dorm Council and Airman Advisory Council.

Maj. Edward Kramer, 49th Trans. Sqdn. described her as a "go-getter" who continuously strives to increase her job knowledge.

In civilian activity, Airman Grant is a member of the Kusan Base Gospel Choir/OSAN; treasurer for the Unit Advisor Council, Self Aid and Buddy Care Inst. She is a member of Bloomfield Baptist Church and plans to continue her education to get a degree in pre-medical and dental. *Submitted by her parents, Patricia and Esper T. Crump III.*

SCOTT ALLEN HILL, Sergeant, born 30 Sep 1975 in Pittsburgh, PA. Joined PA National Guard on 29 Mar 1993; served with the 229th FA in New Castle, PA; and served in National Guard for about two years.

Joined Active Army 7 Apr 1995, stationed at Fort Campbell, KY and served with HSB Btry. 2/320th FA. During this time Scott completed Air Assault School.

In October 1995, Scott deployed as a rifleman with C 1/327 Inf. to Haiti during the United Nations mission Operation Uphold Democracy. During this mission Scott patrolled the capital of Port-Au-Prince, and guarded the Haitian presidential palace. There Scott remembered the 1995 Christmas in which Haitian orphans were invited to the palace and they were all given Santa hats and shirts with the picture of President Aristide on them.

Returned to the States in March 1996 and met soon-to-be wife, Christy Guinn, of Cadiz. One of the proudest moments of his career was getting pinned his sergeant stripes. Scott remained at Fort Campbell until July 2000 when he decided it was his time to get out.

Awards include Army Commendation Medal, two Army Achievement Medals, National Defense Service Medal, Armed Forces Service Medal, Good Conduct Medal, United Nations Medal, Army Service Ribbon, Professional Development Ribbon and Joint Meritorious Unit Award (earned in Haiti). His job title was 13 Foxtrot Artillery Forward Observer.

Today Scott is a member of Buffalo Lick Baptist Church, and is a full-time college student majoring in geology and chemistry. He has two daughters, Codie Marie and Gracie Jane.

CHRISTOPHER LEE MCCRAW, Lance Corporal, born 17 Aug 1975, Pulaski, AR. He enlisted in the USMC 7 Dec 1993 at Hopkinsville, KY with MOS of machine gunner and was stationed in Hawaii.

Discharged 15 Aug 1996 as lance corporal. Civilian activity: attending college and working at Office Depot. He is a computer tech and lives in Murray, KY.

RICHARD WILLIAM MCCRAW, E-4, born 2 Apr 1973 in Trigg County and joined the USN in April 1992 at Hopkinsville, KY.

Assignments: signalman 3/c at Norfolk, VA; sea duty in USS *Savanna* and USS *Caron*.

He is a guard at the maximum security prison and lives in Cadiz, KY.

AEAN TRAVIS T. MITCHELL, Aviation Electrician, born 1 Dec 1980. He joined the USN in July 1999 at Great Lakes, IL with six month tour on the *Abraham Lincoln*. Married Leah Caroline Crisp 25 Feb 2000 and they reside in San Diego, CA.

TINA MARIE (BEORN) POWELL, born 16 Oct 1977, daughter of Rusty Beorn and granddaughter of George and Dot Beorn. Tina joined the Navy after graduating from Trigg County HS. She left Nashville, TN, 7 Jul 1997 with several other inductees for Great Lakes, IL, where she did her boot camp.

Left 27 Sep 1997 for San Diego, CA and assigned to the PCU Bridge ship. They were housed on a barge while the ship being built. The ship was commissioned (USS *Bridge*) 31 Mar 1998 and they were all moved onto the ship. She met a young sailor on the ship, Nicholas Powell, and they were married a short time later.

In July 1998 the USS *Bridge* was sent north and ported at Bremerton, WA. A short time later she discovered she was pregnant which meant no ship duty. She was assigned to shore duty at the Naval Station, Bremerton Security until 25 Jun 1999.

Daughter Jamie Cheyenne was born 14 Jul 1999. Tina Marie, Nick and Jamie still reside in Washington. Nick is still assigned to the USS *Bridge*.

SIMON J. RADFORD, born 7 Jan 1978, Christian County, KY. He joined the USN 23 Aug 1996 and was discharged in November 1998, partial medical, AN.

Assignments: USS *Nassau* CHA-4, FPO AE 09557-1615, NAS Norfolk, Norfolk, VA. He teamed up with the Marines while rescuing refugees from Albania and Republic of Congo (formerly Ziare).

Married 9 Feb 2002 and has one son, Savior. Simon works as an assemblyman and lives in Cadiz, KY.

MATTHEW RYAN SKINNER, E-4, born 23 Feb 1973 in Murray, KY. He joined the service 23 Mar 1992 in Nashville, TN. He had two weeks of basic training and 19 weeks of Interor-Communications A School.

In November 1992 he was assigned to the USS *Abraham Lincoln* (CVN-72) and stationed in Almeda, CA. Also, six months deployment to the Persian Gulf in 1993 and 1995.

Matthew was discharged 22 Mar 1996. His awards include Good Conduct, Battle E Ribbon, Kuwait Liberation Medal, National Defense Medal, Armed Forces Expeditionary Medal, Sea Service Deployment Ribbon w/Bronze Star, SW Asia Service Medal w/Bronze Stars.

He married Antionette Seminario on 8 Mar 1996 and they have one child, Sabastion Nickolas. They live in Cadiz, KY. Matthew is working at Dana Inc. in Hopkinsville, KY. Hunting and fishing are his hobbies.

JOSEPH LEE THOMAS, PO2/c, born 7 Jan 1977 in Cadiz, KY. He graduated from Trigg County HS in May 1995, and joined the USN in June 1996. Upon completion of boot camp, his first tour was a two-year stint at the USN Ceremonial Guard in Washington, DC.

Airman Thomas performed in many ceremonies throughout the District at such landmarks as the White House, Pentagon, Tomb of the Unknown Soldier and Arlington National Cemetery. One notable ceremony he participated in was the inauguration of President Clinton. Another was at a White House State dinner. On Memorial Day, Thomas carried the Navy colors at the Tomb of the Unknown Soldiers as the

wreath was placed at the Tomb by President Clinton. But, probably the most memorable was his participation in the disinterment of the "unknown soldier" in the spring of 1998 when Thomas carried the Navy colors at this historical event.

In June 1998, Airman Thomas was transferred from Washington, DC to Pensacola, FL to complete six months of training at Naval Technical Training Center, Corry Station. Upon graduation, Thomas accepted orders to Oahu, Hawaii to serve at Naval Security Group Activity Kunia as a cryptologic technician-collection. This tour of duty on Oahu is scheduled to end in March 2002 for Petty Officer Second Class Thomas, at which time he plans to re-enlist for further service to his country.

Thomas is the son of Darce and Betty Thomas, Trigg County, and Margaret Hooks Thomas, Hopkinsville. He is the grandson of Alton and Stella Thomas and Leland and Monie Hooks. He is a member of Oak Grove Baptist Church, Trigg County.

Bethesda United Methodist Church

We Salute and Praise All Veterans

555 Princeton Road
Cadiz, Kentucky

Cadiz Baptist Church

Since 1844

Serving God and Country

Thank You Veterans For Your Service

Cadiz Christian Church

Honoring Our Veterans

We remember those who served with honor and courage, and remember those who gave their lives to defend our freedom. May we never take for granted the important contribution these brave men and women have made to this great nation.

(Disciples of Christ)
25 Main Street   Cadiz, KY
270-552-8402

Sunday School at 10:00 a.m.
Worship at 11:00 a.m.

Cadiz United Methodist Church

Even before Trigg County was formed in 1820, a Methodist class met in the Young Community on Bird's Creek. The organizer was John Butcher. A log house of worship was built as early as 1819 and used until the 1830's. Noted Circuit Rider Peter Cartright was presiding elder over the area that included what is presently Trigg County from 1811 to 1816.

In addition to the Young's the Wallis family was among the worshippers. After the formation of Trigg County in 182, a group conducted worship services in the little log courthouse. In 1837 a house of worship was built on West Main Street.

In 1870 a brick structure was erected on West Main Street to serve as a growing congregation. In 1884 the membership was 180. The Kentucky Conference met in Cadiz in 1878 and 1891. The brick structure was remodeled in the period of 1906-10, in 1935-36 and again in 1945.

In February 1957 the official board elected to purchase the Shelby P. Street home and lot on East Main Street across from the Trigg County High School. A building crusade held in May and June of 1957 secured $77,000 in cash and pledges. Ground breaking ceremonies were held on June 1, 1958, with construction beginning the next day.

The first service in the new sanctuary was held March 8, 1959. Stained glass memorial windows were added in the late 1980's.

The Cadiz church has changed its name three times since its formation from Methodist Episcopal Church to Methodist Episcopal Church in 1846 to the Methodist Church in 1968.

The present pastor is Rev. Beryl Fentress who was appointed in June 2000.

Dyers Chapel United Methodist Church

Dyers Chapel United Methodist Church was organized in a schoolhouse on McCalister farm. During the years 1872-1875 a church was built on land given by John J. Dyers on the Maple Grove and Linton Roads. This land is now owned by Mr. Edward Rogers, who is a member of the church.

Charter members were:

Mr. and Mrs. Battoe, John J. Dyers, Edwin Guier, Mr. and Mrs. Nathan Guier, Martha Mitchell Guier, Bettie Lawerence, Susan McCalister, Mary McCalister, and William McCalister

Dyers Chapel Methodist Episcopal Church was established in 1877 with a membership of about fifty.

Church records indicate that Dyers Chapel was a member of the Canton charge, the Princeton district and the Louisville Conference. Church minutes of 1907 list Dyers Chapel as a member of the Hopkinsville district. In November 1911 the church burned and the land where the church was sitting was traded to...

The church was later known as Dyers Chapel Methodist Episcopal Church, South. In the 1960's when the Methodist Episcopal church reunited with the United Brethren Church, Dyers Chapel became a United Methodist Church. In 1996 the church became a member of the Madionsville district and the Kentucky Conference of the United Methodist Church.

Since the beginning to the present date many people have passed through the doors to worship and to fellowship. Moving among these people was Charles Rogers. He became a minister at the age 18 and later studied at Kentucky Wesleyan College in 1953 and Southern Baptist Seminary in 1964. He is the only minister to come out of Dyers Chapel Church.

Since June of 1995 Dyers Chapel has held a homecoming service in which the Daughters of the American Revolution has helped us to honor our flag and the men and women who have served our nation, that we might enjoy our freedom.

Our present pastor, James a. Shuck, has been with us since 1988.

Hurricane Baptist Church

Established April 12, 1845

The United Baptist Church of Christ at Hurricane Meeting House, Trigg County, was constituted April 12, 1845, on six members, and with Bro. J.L. Baker, John F. White, John Cunningham, and Brother Gardener composing the presbytery. Five more members were added at a meeting in July of that year.

Names of those enrolled: Thomas Wadlington, Freusey Wadlington, Elisey Wadlington, Meedis Bolin, Reuben Harris and Sarah Holley. The next 5 names were added before the Association met in July of that year were: Elizabeth Brewer, Cecelia Mitchell, Nancy Ann Cunninghan, Miles Osbome, and Alexander Cunningham. It is interesting to note that there were 4 men and 7 women who constituted the early church.

The church was governed by 18 rules of decorum having a scriptural base and were accepted by the body at the time of its organization, The first pastor was Brother J.F. White, Cadiz, KY, and the first clerk was Thomas Waddington and treasurer was G.B. Grasty. They met a few years in the school building when it was located across the creek not far from the present church site of 1854. The original building stood at the intersection of 274 and 276 about 2 miles west of the present site. Prior to 1865, there were 27 colored members and the church only having 100 members. The church roster of Hurricane has contained the names of many God-fearing men and women who have wielded a wonderful influence for good in their day and generation. Because of Barkley Lake, the location was moved up Highway 276 and opened for worship in March 1965. A new pastors home was built in the early 1970's on this property. Additional acres were purchased on the hills above the present property to be developed for a church cemetery.

Old records reveal that church business was conducted very strictly, as the supervision of the moral and religious life

At one time, a sexton being dismissed for not properly executing his duties. A sexton was paid $5.00 for one year in one account. Many places there they would find a member being on trial for excessive use of an intoxicating drink, and once it was noted that one had been dismissed for using language unbecoming to a Christian. (The above information was prepared by Mrs. Hurley Gray and printed in the 1945 Associational minutes on the centennial. Since that time, many changes have been made.

Former pastors who have served are: J.F. White, J.U. Spurlin, W.L. Rowland, Calvin Mecham, J.W. Morehead, G.A. Patterson, J.W. Oliver, J.L. Perryman, J.H. Spurlin, S. Sumner, J.T. Cunningham, D.E. Bently, O.J. Cole, Charlie Gregston, L.L. Spurlin, E.N. Cunningham, B.F. Hyde, Owen Williams, G.H. Marshall, J.D. Woodson, L.B. Hooks, Luther Sanders, J.D. Woodson, Z. Cannon, Henry Rowland, Garnett Moss, L.L. Terrell, Keidel Thonas, Jackie Geurin, Harold Lassiter, James Beavers, Bonnell Key, Robert Herring, Randal Finley, Wade Cunningham, Duane Holland, Hicks Sheldon, T.A. Thacker, R.G. Shelton, John F. Johnson, Wallis D. Gray, Gary Pate, Norman Ellis, Dale Ford, John Ahart.

The Hurricane Baptist Church still has the mission spirit and vision of its founding fathers. There have been members in the Hurricane Baptist Church who have been active in the armed services. We are honored at Hurricane Baptist Church to be a part of this very important Veterans' book.

Hurricane Baptist, 1946

Hurricane Baptist, 1956

Mt. Pleasant Baptist Church

Mt. Pleasant Baptist Church was the third church organized in what is now Trigg County, Kentucky. Nearing its 200th anniversary it is Trigg County's second oldest surviving congregation. The church was organized in February 1807 near the site of Jefferson and Jones' Mill, south east of Cadiz on Little River. In April 1807, the church became a charter member of the Red River Baptist Association. In 1813, Mt. Pleasant

1900 - 1972

became a charter member of the Little River Baptist Association then withdrew in 1951.

Sometime prior to 1820 the church moved near the present site of Woodruff's Bridge on Highway 274. The church moved again when Mrs. Sention Mitchell donated land on Blue Spring Creek in 1846 on which the church built a new log building. In 1973, one hundred and twenty seven years and 3 buildings later, the congregation moved into a new brick structure a few yards from the original Mitchell land. This location is on highway 1489 near Lake Barkley St. Park.

Mt. Pleasant has been instrumental in organizing at least 12 other churches. Presently it offers monthly financial support to 41 missionaries. The membership of Mt Pleasant is 221 and while many old family names still populate the roll there are many new families who have become members. The present pastor is Richard Sexton.

Organized 30 years after the American Revolution, and located in an area settled by war

1972 - Present

land grants, it is reasonable to expect many original members of Mt. Pleasant to be Revolutionary War veterans. A fire destroyed the early records of the church and it is not possible to know exactly how many members have served in the US Armed Forces. It is believed that members of Mt. Pleasant have served in every American war. We are proud to salute all service men and women who have fought to insure our freedom.

Mount Zion United Methodist Church

The history of Mount Zion United Methodist Church dates back to the year 1830 when a small group organized at the residence of Robert Hawkins, about two miles from Wallonia.

On Saturday, September 8, 1830 an Arbor meeting was started on Mr. Irvin Brandon's crossroads farm with Elijah Sutton acting as leader. These meetings went on until Sunday October 3, 1830 when twenty four men and ten women organized a Methodist Class. This class consisted of Irvin Brandon, Zachariah Butts., Eli Ladd, Atwell Kennedy, Joseph Kennedy, Elijah Capon, John Audobon. Mr. and Mrs. Robert Adams, John L. Brandon, Smith Brandon. Lawson Brandon, Charles Brandon. Mr. and Mrs. Daniel Cameron, John Cameron, Mr. and Mrs. Jesse Adams, Issac Husk, Mr. and Mrs. Peter Wade, Robert Hawkins, Mr. and Mrs. Julius Houston, Abijah Sutton, O. B. Gardner, W. J. Bingham, Mr. and Mrs. Ki Watkins, John Wilson, Mrs. Polly Brandon, Miss Catherine Brandon, Miss Mary Irvin Brandon, and Miss Alm Wade.

On October 3, 1831 the group decided to build a permanent structure of logs. The building was started on November 1, 1831 and dedicated January 22, 1832. Bishop George, Walking Preacher of the Kentucky Conference preached the sermon reading from the "Big Bible' of Irvin Brandon this scripture: Psalms 48 "…the joy of the whole earth is Mt. Zion". The Bible stand was a huge limestone rock hewn out by a faithful slave belonging to Mr. Irvin Brandon. Some of the those early "friends" worshipped in the Mt.. Zion Church.

This building was used until September 1847 when a new building was started. The second building was dedicated on March 26, 1848. The old log church was used as a grist mill, grinding meal for the neighborhood for many years.

At first this church was a part of the Little River Circuit, then became a part of the Circuit of Wallonia. Later it became a part of the North Cadiz Circuit as it is today.

In August 1890, it was decided that once again a new church building was called for and on March 9, 1891, a contract was signed to start on the building. This building was erected a cost of $1,150.00 and was dedicated on June 28, 1891.

As new generations came along some wanted another building and so the fourth building was to be erected. Lloyd Burgess, Claude Burgess, Horner Rennison, Howard Barefield, Howard Rubarts, and most of the men of the church started on a new building in the summer of 1941. This church building was made of rocks from the Cerulean Rock Quarry. The rock church was dedicated on the fifth Sunday of October 1943 and the people read from the same Bible that had been used at the previous dedications and had been owned by Irvin Brandon.

Some of the early preachers who ministered to this church were: Sowell Campbell, Elijah Sutton, Robert Turner, James Bristow, Abraham Long, Abraham Quick, William Randolph, Thomas Randolph, P.L. Hardeson, Richard Love, L. Peters, J.W. Bingham, R.E. Edwards, and J.C. McDaniel.

The membership of this church has from the very beginning been made up of the most cultured and refined people of the county and the same condition exists even to the present day.

Except for the years 1861-1865 when Federal soldiers occupied the building it has been in continuous service for God.

This fourth church, still stands and its members continue to hold scared those things that have made Mt. Zion's history a noble one.

Oak Grove Baptist Church

In 1874 the residents of the Oak Grove community began planning to organize a Baptist church in the community. Those plans were realized when Oak Grove Baptist Church was organized on August 27, 1875. The 37 charter members of the church came from the Donaldson Creek Baptist Church. The church building was constructed on land donated by Stanley Thomas and Humphrey Lawrence in early 1875. The church met in its new building on the day of charter. The furniture in the building was constructed by the men of the community.

In addition to the first building, the church has had two other houses of worship. The church voted in its April 1904 business meeting to construct a new building. That building was completed in the fall of 1904 and was completely paid for in 1905. The 1904 building was built on the same foundation as the original building.

Ground was broken for the current building on September 17, 1972. Aubrey Lancaster, the church's oldest deacon, turned the first shovel of dirt for the new building. The final service in the 1904 building was the August 19, 1973, Sunday School. That day's morning worship service was the first service in the new building. The 1904 building was pushed away and burned on September 1.

The church built its parsonage in 1959; a family room and garage was added in 1979. The church began construction of its educational building in 1963; the building was completed in 1964. A picnic pavilion was constructed in 1999.

Oak Grove has had 13 pastors during its history. The first pastor, E.C. Faulkner, was called in October 1875. Bro. John T. Cunningham served as pastor for more than 52 years. The current pastor is Dr. Mike Jones.

The church has had several organizations to provide Christian training for its members. Sunday school began in Macrh 1,889.

Discipleship Training began in 1937 as the Baptist Young People's Union, BYPU. Since that time it has undergone several name changes including Baptist Training Union, Training Union and Church Training.

Women on Missions began as Women's Missionary Union in 1941. Brotherhood, the men's mission group, began on June 30, 1955.

Kids for Christ began as Kid's Time in January 1984. Vacation Bible School began in 1946.

Oak Grove Baptist Church has gone beyond learning about missions. The church became part of the Little River Baptist Association in 1876. Mission trips to Ansonia, Ohio, were sponsored by the church in 1984 and 1985. More recently the church has sent members on international mission trips to Brazil and Russia. Members have participated in state missions with trips to Jonathan Creek, Campbellsville and Oneida.

Oak Grove Baptist Church broadcast services on WKDZ from 1966 to 1986. The church went online in 2000 with its own website-www.oakgrovebaptistchurch.com.

OUR ACTIVE MILITARY

Bruce Bendler, Lisa Bendler, Jim Hardy, Paul Howard, Karen Johnson, Brian Kyler, Owen Kyler, William Purkes, Joey Thomas

OUR VETERANS

William Glenn Armstrong, William Bridges, Clifton Boyd, Carl T. Bridges, Gilbert Bridges, David Chesnut, Raybon Crump, Hale Crump, Mack Cunningham, Carrie Sholar Ealy, Samuel Evans, Dell Freeman, Jr., Tony Freeman, Tommy Gentry, Johnny Harris, T. H. Herndon, Gaylon Lancaster, Dale Light, Denny Light, Chris McCraw, Ricky McCraw, Jason Oakley, Joe Oakley, Chuck Owens, Edward Pridgen, James D. Sumner, Andrew Thomas, James W. Thomas, Tom Vinson, Felix Wadlington, Frank Wallen, Howard Wallen, Tommy Winn, Harlon Wynn

Rockcastle United Methodist Church

"Ye shall know The Truth, and The Truth shall set you free" Romans 6:18

This church had its beginnings in June 1979, in the basement of David and Betty Buck's home. With guidance of Rev. Roger Newell, who at that time was minister of Cadiz North Circuit of the Louisville Annual Conference of the Methodist of the Hopkinsville District, who was Dr. Bennett F. Hulse, Jr. and the church location committee purchased the old Rockcastle Shore's Real Estate office. The two story duplex was converted to a parsonage in the upper level and a temporary sanctuary in the lower level.

In May 1980, District Superintendent, Dr. Hulse, chaired the Charter Charge Conference. After a breif period of worship, rev. Newel opened the doors of the church for membership. At this time 20 people joined the church.

This was the first new church to be founded in the Hopkinsville District in 16 years. It was the second new church to be founded in the Louisville Annual Conference in the last 20 years.

To this date the church has had three full time ministers. They were Rev. Kenneth Spurrier (1980-1982), Rev. Bill Evans (1982-1990), and Rev. James Shuck (1990-present).

In 1990 the church moved to a building at 9023 Rockcastle Road. As we grew we realized we needed more space, so in 2001 we kicked off a big building fund to build a new church. The existing building will change to meeting rooms since our youth group has grown almost every Sunday, thanks to our youth minister Bradley Shuck and all the great workers.

In the 21 years many veterans have passed through our church doors. To the best of our knowledge those are: David and Betty Buck, Allen Clark, Ray McGuire, Ray Pugh, Louis Smith, Fred Mohr, Jim Hobbs, Frederick Nab, Lou Meachum, Buddy Cook, Buck Rowan, Bill Brown, Leonard Sizemore, Bill Worman, Allen Hallet, Howard Erasmus, John Holcomb, Jack Dibolise, George Calvert, Carl Swanberg, Frank Moore, Basil Wust, Bob Jellison, John Asmusser, Elmer Coil, Jim Clark, Henry Kohlhaas, Julius Kazmierzak, Jerry Harper, and William Hartmann.

Siloam United Methodist Church

"Where the Spirit of the Lord is, there is Liberty." 2 Co. 3:17

Siloam United Methodist Church is located six miles northwest of Cadiz and can be described as "a little white church on a great big hill."

The first meeting of the people was held in a log cabin a short distance from the present church in 1878. After the meeting it was decided to erect a church and the deed was given December 2, 1878. The church was placed on the Wallonia work with the parsonage at Wallonia. Brother Pingham was the first Pastor. Later Siloam was changed to Cadiz Circuit with the parsonage at Canton. The parsonage at Canton was sold and one bought in Cadiz.

The first trustees were W.T. Stone, Charles Morris, P. H. Cain, John J. Alexander and J.M. Shepherd. The church was dedicated June 7, 1879. Siloam has sent out four preachers, J.J. Alexander, T.V. Joiner, A.D. Litchfield, and James C. Bush. The trustees for 2001 are Denise Alexander, Arnold Gibson, Roy Alexander, Lou Cain, Junior Adams, Lola Lane, and William Michael Lane.

In 1965 Siloam and Dyers Chapel formed a charge and Rockcastle was added in 1990. A fellowship hall was added in 1999. The present pastor is Rev. James A. Shuck.

Members and friends of Siloam United Methodist Church who served in the military are: William Cain, Clifton Cain, Patrick Henry Cain, William A. Bush, Jimmie Adams, Charles E. Gray, William Alexander, Jackie Alexander, Clifton Alexander, Douglas Wallace, Lattie Vanzant, Raymond Fuller, Clarence Cunningham, James Alexander, Robert Alexander, Charles Alexander, Len Baith, Don Gary Bush, Frank S. Lane, Larwence C. Fowler, Kenneth Alexander, Malcolm Ray Thomas, Larry Wayne Russell, and Arnold Gibson.

Wallonia Christian Church

Wallonia, Kentucky
established in 1849

Salutes its

Veterans

from the Civil War to the present

Save-On Drugs

"We're Keeping America Healthy!"

Save-On Drugs, located beside the Trigg County hospital, moved to its present location in 1986, by Rick Clement owner and pharmacist. Rick is a native of Trigg County. Before 1986, his father Joe B. Clement had the business as Clement Pharmacy on Main Street in downtown Cadiz since 1953. Joe Clement came to Cadiz from Marion, Ky at the request of the Drs. John and Elias Futrell and set up his shop adjacent to their practice. Rick's brother, Bob, is also a pharmacist and occasionally works in the business. Rick's wife, Karen, also works in the business. The Clement family and all the employees at Save-On Drugs salute our veterans and thank them for what they have done for our country.

James Thomas Chapter
Daughters of the American Revolution

Cadiz, Kentucky

To Our Veterans

The Daughters of the American Revolution wish to thank you for the sacrifices you made that we might enjoy freedom. The freedom we have today was gained only through the dedication, loyalty and sacrifice of all our veterans who fought for this great nation.

The James Thomas Chapter of the National Society of the Daughters of the American Revolution was organized in Cadiz, Kentucky, on April 15, 1972 with thirty-two members. The organizing Regent was Mrs. John Alexander (Louise) Thomas, assisted by Mrs. Rumsey H. (Virginia) Alexander, Regent and Vice Regent.

The organizing members were Mrs. James Adams, Mrs. Rumsey H. Alexander, Mrs. Thomas W. Baker, Mrs. Herman Boyd, Mrs. Gilbert N. Bridges, Mrs. John T. Bridges, Mrs. Smith D. Broadbent, Jr., Mrs. Thomas Call, Mrs. L. Lee Cameron, Mrs. Meredith Christian. Mrs. O.J. Cunningham, Mrs. W. J. Daniel, Mrs. C. C. Dawson, Mrs. M. S. Dix, Mrs. Clyde Finley, Mrs. Thomas H. Gentry, Mrs. Ira Humphries, Mrs. T. Lacy Jones, Mrs. Ernest Lawrence, Mrs. Maurine T. Mabry, Mrs. R.E. Malone, Mrs. Claud Meador, Mrs. Edward Rogers, Mrs. Bernice Sivills, Mrs. W.C. Skinner, Mrs. J.O. Sumner, Mrs. Boyd Thomas, Mrs. John A. Thomas, Mrs. Douglas H. Thomas, Mrs. Carey T. Vinson, Mrs. Roy V. Witty and Mrs. C.M. Wright.

As a large percent of the organizing members were descendants of James Thomas, who was a Revolutionary War soldier in North Carolina, the Chapter was named in his honor.

Other ancestral lines were Absalom Humphries, Peter Loux, and William McClure.

The Chapter has participated in State and National Honor Roll level programs, receiving top honors on the State level.

The Chapter has been honored to have two State officers. Mrs. Henry (Mauree) Morris, State Chaplain, 1992-1995; Mrs. Rumsey (Virginia) Alexander, State Recording Secretary, 1995-1998; one State chairman, appointed during two different terms - Mrs. Ernest (Clara) Lawrence, Press Chairman First District, 1995-1998; and State Resolutions Chairman, 2001-2004.

American Legion
Cadiz-Trigg County Post 74

"Still Serving America"

Curt Holmes, ADJ
Tommy P'Pool, Commander
Richard Pauze, Service Officer

David Adams	Decator Adams	Elbert Adams
Waldon Adams	Jessie Adams	Walter Adams
Robert Allen	Robert Ayers	Sam Baldwin
Lemuel Banister	Bascom Booth	William Braucht
Clifton Bridges	Denzil Bridges	Bill Calhoun
Hollis Carr	Paul Case	Boyd Champion
Philip Conner	Kent Conners	Henry Crocetti
Alvin Crump	Jimmy Cunningham	George Dall
James Dethridge	John T. Edwards	George Fennell
William Flood	Herb Follis	Robert E. Fowler
Bill Francis	Robert E. Francis	Paul Gardner
Thomas Gentry	William Golladay	Charles Gray
F.J. Hanberry	Donald Holton	Perry Hopkins
W.J. Hopson	Winthrop Hopson	Bob Hudson
Jim Joiner	Thom Jones	Bill Kearney
James Kennedy	Henry Kohlhaas	Ernest Lawrence
Willard Lester	Raymond Lofton	Chet Maxfield
Henry McBride	Gene Moore	Sandra Myers
Robert Niles	Tommy Noel	James Noland
James Oliver	Richard Pauze	Carey Pearcy
Gary Poirier	Bob Rose	William Shoemaker
Mark Seitzinger	David Shore	Gene Stephens
Charles Tackett	Marlene Taylor	Lew Wallace
Tom White	W.C. White	Fred Wilbar
Carlton Wilkins	Willliam Williams	Paul Davis
Norris C. hooks	James W. Stubblefiled	George Starks

Veterans of Foreign Wars
Of the United States

Cadiz/Trigg County
VFW Post 7890

"Lest We Forget Our Heroes"

"In peace prepare for war, in war prepare for peace. The art of war is of vital importance to the state, it is a matter of life and death, a road either to safety or to ruin. Hence under no circumstances can it be neglected."

The Art of War, Suntzlu

Real Country WKDZ-FM 106.5

Proudly presents…

- 8 Times more power
- New 500 foot tower
- State-of-the-Art digital technology
- KDZ Country Club Weekdays 6-8:30 a.m.
- Expanded local and regional news coverage at
  6 a.m., 7 a.m., 12 p.m. and 5 p.m.
- Improved local and regional weather coverage
- Play-by-play of all Trigg County Wildcats games
- Still your favorite old and new country music
- Veteran's news featuring Sandra Myers
  Wednesday's at 7:25 a.m.

Bank of Cadiz

P.O. Box 2020   Cadiz, KY 42211
Phone - 270-522-6066

In 1970, Bank of Cadiz & Trust Company graciously opened its doors to those who live and/or work in western Kentucky based on the premise of providing the very best service in community banking.

More than 30 years later, its Board of Directors, officers, and employees strive daily to ensure that in an ever-changing financial world, this fundamental philosophy remains the focal point.

A major reason that Bank of Cadiz and Trust Company is able to maintain its stronghold in the community lies in the fact that it is the only locally owned and operated bank in Trigg County.

Whether utilizing the main office, located downtown on 79 Main Street, or the elegant new branch office, strategically constructed on Lakota Drive next door to the United States Post Office, customers continually appreciate the advantages of banking with the full-service institution where "people come first."

Goodwin Funeral Home

fourshee
Building Supply

East Main Street   **Cadiz, KY**

Since 1953

We proudly salute our veterans
who have so bravely defended
the freedom we enjoy.

We are eternally thankful
to those who gave their lives to
ensure the continuation
of the ideals of this great democracy.

In Appreciation of all Trigg County
Veterans for their Unselfish
Service to Our Country

Trigg County Judge/Executive
Berlin Moore, Jr.

Cadiz Rotary Club

THE FOUR WAY TEST

Of the things we think,
say or do

First,
Is it the Truth?

Second,
Is it Fair to all concerned?

Third,
Will it Build Goodwill
and Better Friendships?

Fourth,
Will it be Beneficial to all
concerned?

Lawrence Bros. Farms
&
Lawrence Bros.
Tobacco Whse., Inc

Ernest R. Lawrence
&
James R. Lawrence

Proudly Salute
Trigg County
Veterans

 The

E. E. "MUTT" SANDERS
Family

Salutes Their

VETERANS
Eura "Mutt" Sanders
U.S. Army
World War II

Jack E. Sanders
U.S. Army

Danny G. Bozarth
U.S. Air Force
Vietnam War

National Association
of
Retired Federal Employees

Trigg County Chapter 1730
Cadiz, Kentucky

Meetings held the second Wednesday
of the month, 10:30 a.m.

For more information, contact:
Hollis Carr   522-3388
or
Bill Williams   522-6365

Pennyrile Electric

Proud Sponsor of the Trigg County, Kentucky Veteran's History Book.

Pictured above (left to right):

William (Pippy) Tyler
>   US Army National Guard - Aug. 1965 to Aug. 1971
>   Highest Rank - Sergeant (E-5)

Harold Meredith
>   US Army Signal Corps - Aug. 1960 - Aug. 1963
>   US Army National Guard - June 1965 to June 1968
>   Highest Rank - Sergeant (E-5)

Carrol Thomas
>   US Army - Nov. 1959 - Nov. 1962
>   Highest Rank - Specialist 4 (E-4)

Jerry Tyler
>   US Army National Guard - April 1964 to Feb. 1970
>   Highest Rank - Specialist 5 (E-5)

Trigg County Veterans -- We salute you!

The Thomas - Bridges Association is proud to salute the veterans of Trigg County who have so gallantly defended our country in times of war and maintained vigilance in times of peace.

Since 1774, members of our families have heeded the call to fight tyranny and oppression. Time and again through the years, it has been necessary to defend ourselves. In so doing, some of you have made the the supreme sacrifice so those rights might be preserved. Again -- we salute you, with deep gratitude and heartfelt thanks.

The Thomas-Bridges Association

Index

Editor's Note: This index includes only the last names of those individuals listed in the publication.

Printed in the USA
CPSIA information can be obtained
at www.ICGtesting.com
LVHW082024131023
761043LV00008B/697